D1385680

gem
Collins
Spanish
Dictionary

HarperCollins Publishers
Westerhill Road
Bishopbriggs
Glasgow
G64 2QT

Ninth Edition/Novena Edición 2012

10 9 8 7 6 5 4 3

© William Collins Sons & Co. Ltd
1982, 1989
© HarperCollins Publishers 1993,
1998, 2001, 2004, 2006, 2009, 2012

ISBN 978-0-00-743791-7

Collins® and Collins Gem® are
registered trademarks of
HarperCollins Publishers Limited

www.collins.co.uk

A catalogue record for this book is
available from the British Library

Random House Mondadori, S.A.,
Travessera de Gràcia 47-49,
08021 Barcelona

www.diccionarioscollins.com

ISBN 978-84-253-4796-2

Typeset by Aptara in India

Printed and bound in Italy by LEGO
SpA, Lavis (Trento)

Acknowledgements
We would like to thank those
authors and publishers who kindly
gave permission for copyright
material to be used in the Collins
Corpus. We would also like to
thank Times Newspapers Ltd for
providing valuable data.

PROJECT MANAGEMENT/
DIRECCIÓN EDITORIAL
Gaëlle Amiot-Cadey
Ruth O'Donovan
Teresa Álvarez García

CONTRIBUTORS/
COLABORADORES
Cordelia Lilly
Genevieve Gerrard
José Martín Galera
Wendy Lee
José María Ruiz Vaca
Malihé Sanatian

EDITORIAL COORDINATION/
COORDINACIÓN EDITORIAL
Susie Beattie
Lucy Cooper
Kerry Ferguson
Susanne Reichert

PUBLISHING DIRECTOR/
DIRECTORA DE PUBLICACIONES
Elaine Higgleton

ÍNDICE		CONTENTS	

INTRODUCCIÓN

Estamos muy satisfechos de que hayas decidido comprar este diccionario y esperamos que lo disfrutes y que te sirva de gran ayuda ya sea en el colegio, en el trabajo, en tus vacaciones o en casa.

Esta introducción pretende darte algunas indicaciones para ayudarte a sacar el mayor provecho de este diccionario; no sólo de su extenso vocabulario, sino de toda la información que te proporciona cada entrada. Esta te ayudará a leer y comprender – y también a comunicarte y a expresarte – en inglés moderno. Este diccionario comienza con una lista de abreviaturas utilizadas en el texto y con una ilustración de los sonidos representados por los símbolos fonéticos.

EL MANEJO DE TU DICCIONARIO

La amplia información que te ofrece este diccionario aparece presentada en distintas tipografías, con caracteres de diversos tamaños y con distintos símbolos, abreviaturas y paréntesis. Los apartados siguientes explican las reglas y símbolos utilizados.

ENTRADAS

Las palabras que consultas en el diccionario – las entradas – aparecen ordenadas alfabéticamente y en color para una identificación más rápida. La palabra que aparece en la parte superior de cada página es la primera entrada (si aparece en la página izquierda) y la última entrada (si aparece en la página derecha) de la página en cuestión. La información sobre el uso o la forma de determinadas entradas aparece entre paréntesis, detrás de la transcripción fonética, y generalmente en forma abreviada y en cursiva

(p. ej.: (fam), (Com)). En algunos casos se ha considerado oportuno agrupar palabras de una misma familia (**nación, nacionalismo; accept, acceptance**) bajo una misma entrada que aparece en color.

Las expresiones de uso corriente en las que aparece una entrada se dan en negrita (p. ej.: **hurry:** [...] **to be in a ~**).

SÍMBOLOS FONÉTICOS

La transcripción fonética de cada entrada inglesa (que indica su pronunciación) aparece entre corchetes, inmediatamente después de la entrada (p. ej. **knife** [naif]). En las páginas xv-xviii encontrarás una lista de los símbolos fonéticos utilizados en este diccionario.

TRADUCCIONES

Las traducciones de las entradas aparecen en caracteres normales, y en los casos en los que existen significados o usos diferentes, éstos aparecen separados mediante un punto y coma. A menudo encontrarás también otras palabras en cursiva y entre paréntesis antes de las traducciones. Estas sugieren contextos en los que la entrada podría aparecer (p. ej.: **alto** (*persona*) o (*sonido*)) o proporcionan sinónimos (p. ej.: **mismo** (*semejante*)).

PALABRAS CLAVE

Particular relevancia reciben ciertas palabras inglesas y españolas que han sido consideradas palabras 'clave' en cada lengua. Estas pueden, por ejemplo, ser de utilización muy corriente o tener distintos usos (**de, haber; get, that**). La combinación de triángulos y números te permitirá distinguir las diferentes categorías gramaticales y los diferentes significados. Las indicaciones en cursiva y entre paréntesis proporcionan además importante información adicional.

FALSOS AMIGOS

Las palabras que se prestan a confusión al traducir han sido identificadas. En tales entradas existen unas notas que te ayudaran a evitar errores.

INFORMACIÓN GRAMATICAL

Las categorías gramaticales aparecen en forma abreviada y en cursiva después de la transcripción fonética de cada entrada (*vt*, *adv*, *conj*). También se indican la forma femenina y los plurales irregulares de los sustantivos del inglés (**child, -ren**).

INTRODUCTION

We are delighted that you have decided to buy this Spanish dictionary and hope you will enjoy and benefit from using it at school, at home, on holiday or at work.

This introduction gives you a few tips on how to get the most out of your dictionary – not simply from its comprehensive wordlist but also from the information provided in each entry. This will help you to read and understand modern Spanish, as well as communicate and express yourself in the language. This dictionary begins by listing the abbreviations used in the text and illustrating the sounds shown by the phonetic symbols.

USING YOUR DICTIONARY

A wealth of information is presented in the dictionary, using various typefaces, sizes of type, symbols, abbreviations and brackets. The various conventions and symbols used are explained in the following sections.

HEADWORDS

The words you look up in a dictionary – 'headwords' – are listed alphabetically. They are printed in **colour** for rapid identification. The headwords appearing at the top of each page indicate the first (if it appears on a left-hand page) and last word (if it appears on a right-hand page) dealt with on the page in question.

Information about the usage or form of certain headwords is given in brackets after the phonetic spelling. This usually appears in abbreviated form and in italics (e.g. *(fam)*, *(Com)*).

Where appropriate, words related to headwords are grouped in the same entry (**nación, nacionalismo; accept, acceptance**) and are also in colour. Common expressions in which the headword appears are shown in a different bold roman type (e.g. **cola:** [...] **hacer ~**).

PHONETIC SPELLINGS

The phonetic spelling of each headword (indicating its pronunciation) is given in square brackets immediately after the headword (e.g. **cohete** [ko'ete]). A list of these symbols is given on pages xv–xviii.

TRANSLATIONS

Headword translations are given in ordinary type and, where more than one meaning or usage exists, these are separated by a semi-colon. You will often find other words in italics in brackets before the translations. These offer suggested contexts in which the headword might appear (e.g. **fare** (*on trains, buses*)) or provide synonyms (e.g. **litter** (*rubbish*) o (*young animals*)). The gender of the Spanish translation also appears in italics immediately following the key element of the translation, except where this is a regular masculine singular noun ending in 'o', or a regular feminine noun ending in 'a'.

KEY WORDS

Special status is given to certain Spanish and English words which are considered as 'key' words in each language. They may, for example, occur very frequently or have several types of usage (e.g. **de, haber; get, that**). A combination of triangles and numbers helps you to distinguish different

parts of speech and different meanings. Further helpful
information is provided in brackets and italics.

FALSE FRIENDS

Words which can be easily confused have been identified
in the dictionary. Notes at such entries will help you to
avoid these common translation pitfalls.

GRAMMATICAL INFORMATION

Parts of speech are given in abbreviated form in italics
after the phonetic spellings of headwords (e.g. *vt, adv, conj*).
Genders of Spanish nouns are indicated as follows: *nm* for
a masculine and *nf* for a feminine noun. Feminine and
irregular plural forms of nouns are also shown (**irlandés,
esa; luz** (*pl* **luces**)).

ABBREVIATURAS

abreviatura	*ab(b)r*	abbreviation
adjetivo, locución adjetiva	*adj*	adjective, adjectival phrase
administración	*Admin*	administration
adverbio, locución adverbial	*adv*	adverb, adverbial phrase
agricultura	*Agr*	agriculture
anatomía	*Anat*	anatomy
Argentina	*Arg*	Argentina
arquitectura	*Arq, Arch*	architecture
Australia	*Aust*	Australia
el automóvil	*Aut(o)*	the motor car and motoring
aviación, viajes aéreos	*Aviac, Aviat*	flying, air travel
biología	*Bio(l)*	biology
botánica, flores	*Bot*	botany
inglés británico	*BRIT*	British English
Centroamérica	*CAM*	Central America
química	*Chem*	chemistry
comercio, finanzas, banca	*Com(m)*	commerce, finance, banking
informática	*Comput*	computing
conjunción	*conj*	conjunction
construcción	*Constr*	building
compuesto	*cpd*	compound element
Cono Sur	*CS*	Southern Cone
cocina	*Culin*	cookery
economía	*Econ*	economics
eletricidad, electrónica	*Elec*	electricity, electronics
enseñanza, sistema escolar y universitario	*Escol*	schooling, schools and universities
España	*ESP*	Spain
especialmente	*esp*	especially
exclamación, interjección	*excl*	exclamation, interjection
femenino	*f*	feminine
lengua familiar (! vulgar)	*fam(!)*	colloquial usage (! particularly offensive)
ferrocarril	*Ferro*	railways
uso figurado	*fig*	figurative use
fotografía	*Foto*	photography
(verbo inglés) del cual la partícula es inseparable	*fus*	(phrasal verb) where the particle is inseparable
generalmente	*gen*	generally
geografía, geología	*Geo*	geography, geology

ABBREVIATIONS

ABREVIATURAS		ABBREVIATIONS
geometría	*Geom*	geometry
historia	*Hist*	history
uso familiar	*inf(!)*	colloquial usage
(! vulgar)		(! particularly offensive)
infinitivo	*infin*	infinitive
informática	*Inform*	computing
invariable	*inv*	invariable
irregular	*irreg*	irregular
lo jurídico	*Jur, Law*	law
América Latina	*LAm*	Latin America
gramática, lingüística	*Ling*	grammar, linguistics
masculino	*m*	masculine
matemáticas	*Mat(h)*	mathematics
masculino/femenino	*m/f*	masculine/feminine
medicina	*Med*	medicine
México	*MÉX, MEX*	Mexico
lo militar, ejército	*Mil*	military matters
música	*Mús, Mus*	music
substantivo, nombre	*n*	noun
navegación, náutica	*Náut, Naut*	sailing, navigation
sustantivo numérico	*num*	numeral noun
Nueva Zelanda	*NZ*	New Zealand
complemento	*obj*	(grammatical) object
	o.s.	oneself
peyorativo	*pey, pej*	derogatory, pejorative
fotografía	*Phot*	photography
fisiología	*Physiol*	physiology
plural	*pl*	plural
política	*Pol*	politics
participio de pasado	*pp*	past participle
preposición	*prep*	preposition
pronombre	*pron*	pronoun
psicología, psiquiatría	*Psico, Psych*	psychology, psychiatry
tiempo pasado	*pt*	past tense
química	*Quím*	chemistry
ferrocarril	*Rail*	railways
religión	*Rel*	religion
Río de la Plata	*RPL*	River Plate
	sb	somebody
Cono Sur	*SC*	Southern Cone
enseñanza, sistema escolar	*Scol*	schooling, schools
y universitario		and universities
singular	*sg*	singular

ABREVIATURAS

		ABBREVIATIONS
España	*sp*	Spain
	sth	something
sujeto	*su(b)j*	(grammatical) subject
subjuntivo	*subjun*	subjunctive
tauromaquia	*Taur*	bullfighting
también	*tb*	also
técnica, tecnología	*Tec(h)*	technical term, technology
telecomunicaciones	*Telec, Tel*	telecommunications
imprenta, tipografía	*Tip, Typ*	typography, printing
televisión	*TV*	television
universidad	*Univ*	university
inglés norteamericano	*us*	American English
verbo	*vb*	verb
verbo intransitivo	*vi*	intransitive verb
verbo pronominal	*vr*	reflexive verb
verbo transitivo	*vt*	transitive verb
zoología	*Zool*	zoology
marca registrada	®	registered trademark
indica un equivalente cultural	≈	introduces a cultural equivalent

SPANISH PRONUNCIATION

VOWELS

a	[a]	pata	not as long as *a* in *far*. When followed by a consonant in the same syllable (i.e. in a closed syllable), as in *amante*, the *a* is short, as in *bat*
e	[e]	me	like *e* in *they*. In a closed syllable, as in *gente*, the *e* is short as in *pet*
i	[i]	pino	as in *mean* or *machine*
o	[o]	lo	as in *local*. In a closed syllable, as in *control*, the *o* is short as in *cot*
u	[u]	lunes	as in *rule*. It is silent after *q*, and in *gue*, *gui*, unless marked *güe*, *güi* e.g. *antigüedad*, when it is pronounced like *w* in *wolf*

SEMIVOWELS

i, y	[j]	bien	pronounced like *y* in *yes*
		hielo	
		yunta	
u	[w]	huevo	unstressed *u* between consonant and vowel is pronounced like *w* in *well*. See notes on *u* above.
		fuento	
		antigüedad	

DIPHTHONGS

ai, ay	[ai]	baile	as *i* in *ride*
au	[au]	auto	as *ou* in *shout*
ei, ey	[ei]	buey	as *ey* in *grey*
eu	[eu]	deuda	both elements pronounced independently [e] + [u]
oi, oy	[oi]	hoy	as *oy* in *toy*

CONSONANTS

b	[b, β]	boda	see notes on *v* below
		bomba	
		labor	
c	[k]	caja	*c* before *a*, *o*, *u* is pronounced as in *cat*
ce, ci	[θe, θi]	cero	*c* before *e* or *i* is pronounced as in *thin*
		cielo	
ch	[tʃ]	chiste	*ch* is pronounced as *ch* in *chair*
d	[d, ð]	danés	at the beginning of a phrase or after *l* or *n*, *d* is pronounced as in English. In any other position it is pronounced like *th* in *the*
		ciudad	

g	[g, ɣ]	gafas paga	*g* before *a*, *o* or *u* is pronounced as in *gap*, if at the beginning of a phrase or after *n*. In other positions the sound is softened
ge, gi	[xe, xi]	gente girar	*g* before *e* or *i* is pronounced similar to *ch* in Scottish *loch*
h		haber	*h* is always silent in Spanish
j	[x]	jugar	*j* is pronounced similar to *ch* in Scottish *loch*
ll	[ʎ]	talle	*ll* is pronounced like the *y* in *yet* or the *lli* in *million*
ñ	[ʃ]	niño	*ñ* is pronounced like the *ni* in *onion*
q	[k]	que	*q* is pronounced as *k* in *king*
r, rr	[r, rr]	quitar garra	*r* is always pronounced in Spanish, unlike the silent *r* in *dancer*. *rr* is trilled, like a Scottish *r*
s	[s]	quizás isla	*s* is usually pronounced as in *pass*, but before *b*, *d*, *g*, *l*, *m* or *n* it is pronounced as in *rose*
v	[b, β]	vía	*v* is pronounced something like *b*. At the beginning of a phrase or after *m* or *n* it is pronounced as *b* in *boy*. In any other position the sound is softened
z	[θ]	tenaz	*z* is pronounced as *th* in *thin*

f, *k*, *l*, *m*, *n*, *p*, *t* and *x* are pronounced as in English.

STRESS

The rules of stress in Spanish are as follows:

(a) when a word ends in a vowel or in *n* or *s*, the second last syllable is stressed:
pat*a*ta, pat*a*tas; c*o*me, c*o*men
(b) when a word ends in a consonant other than *n* or *s*, the stress falls on the last syllable:
par*e*d, habl*a*r
(c) when the rules set out in (a) and (b) are not applied, an acute accent appears over the stressed vowel:
com*ú*n, geograf*í*a, ingl*é*s

In the phonetic transcription, the symbol [¹] precedes the syllable on which the stress falls.

LA PRONUNCIACIÓN INGLESA

VOCALES

	Ejemplo inglés	Explicación
[ɑː]	father	Entre *a* de *padre* y *o* de *noche*
[ʌ]	but, come	*a* muy breve
[æ]	man, cat	Con los labios en la posición de *e* en *pena* y luego se pronuncia el sonido *a* parecido a la *a* de *carro*
[ə]	father, ago	Vocal neutra parecida a una *e* u *o* casi muda
[əː]	bird, heard	Entre *a* abierta y *o* cerrada, sonido alargado
[ɛ]	get, bed	Como en *perro*
[ɪ]	it, big	Más breve que en *sí*
[iː]	tea, see	Como en *fino*
[ɔ]	hot, wash	Como en *torre*
[ɔː]	saw, all	Como en *por*
[u]	put, book	Sonido breve, más cerrado que *burro*
[uː]	too, you	Sonido largo, como en *uno*

DIPTONGOS

	Ejemplo inglés	Explicación
[aɪ]	fly, high	Como en *fraile*
[au]	how, house	Como en *pausa*
[ɛə]	there, bear	Casi como en *vea*, pero el sonido *a* se mezcla con el indistinto [ə]
[eɪ]	day, obey	*e* cerrada seguida por una *i* débil
[ɪə]	here, hear	Como en *manía*, mezclándose el sonido *a* con el indistinto [ə]
[əu]	go, note	[ə] seguido por una breve *u*
[ɔɪ]	boy, oil	Como en *voy*
[uə]	poor, sure	*u* bastante larga más el sonido indistinto [ə]

CONSONANTES

	Ejemplo inglés	Explicación
[b]	big, lobby	Como en tumban
[d]	mended	Como en conde, andar
[g]	go, get, big	Como en grande, gol
[dʒ]	gin, judge	Como en la ll andaluza y en Generalitat (catalán)
[ŋ]	sing	Como en vínculo
[h]	house, he	Como la jota hispanoamericana
[j]	young, yes	Como en ya
[k]	come, mock	Como en caña, Escocia
[r]	red, tread	Se pronuncia con la punta de la lengua hacia atrás y sin hacerla vibrar
[s]	sand, yes	Como en casa, sesión
[z]	rose, zebra	Como en desde, mismo
[ʃ]	she, machine	Como en chambre (francés), roxo (portugués)
[tʃ]	chin, rich	Como en chocolate
[v]	valley	Como f, pero se retiran los dientes superiores vibrándolos contra el labio inferior
[w]	water, which	Como la u de huevo, puede
[ʒ]	vision	Como en journal (francés)
[θ]	think, myth	Como en receta, zapato
[ð]	this, the	Como en hablado, verdad

f, l, m, n, p, t y x iguales que en español.

El signo [°] indica que la r final escrita apenas se pronuncia en inglés británico cuando la palabra siguiente empieza con vocal.
El signo [¹] indica la sílaba acentuada.

SPANISH VERB TABLES

1 Gerund 2 Imperative 3 Present 4 Preterite 5 Future 6 Present subjunctive
7 Imperfect subjunctive 8 Past participle 9 Imperfect

Etc indicates that the irregular root is used for all persons of the tense,
e.g. oír: **6** oiga, oigas, oigamos, oigáis, oigan

1a HABLAR 1 hablando 2 habla,
hablad 3 hablo, hablas, habla,
hablamos, habláis, hablan
4 hablé, hablaste, habló,
hablamos, hablasteis, hablaron
5 hablaré, hablarás, hablará,
hablaremos, hablaréis, hablarán
6 hable, hables, hable, hablemos,
habléis, hablen 7 hablara,
hablaras, hablara, habláramos,
hablarais, hablaran 8 hablado
9 hablaba, hablabas, hablaba,
hablábamos, hablabais,
hablaban
1b cambiar 2 cambia 3 cambio *etc*
6 cambie *etc*
1c enviar 2 envía 3 envío, envías,
envía, envíen 6 envíe, envíes,
envíe, envíen
1d evacuar 2 evacua 3 evacuo *etc*
6 evacue *etc*
1e situar 2 sitúa 3 sitúo, sitúas,
sitúa, sitúen 6 sitúe, sitúes, sitúe,
sitúen
1f cruzar 4 crucé 6 cruce *etc*
1g picar 4 piqué 6 pique *etc*
1h pagar 4 pagué 6 pague *etc*
1i averiguar 4 averigüé
6 averigüe *etc*
1j cerrar 2 cierra 3 cierro, cierras,
cierra, cierran 6 cierre, cierres,
cierre, cierren
1k errar 2 yerra 3 yerro, yerras,
yerra, yerran 6 yerre, yerres,
yerre, yerren
1l contar 2 cuenta 3 cuento,
cuentas, cuenta, cuentan
6 cuente, cuentes, cuente,
cuenten

1m degollar 2 degüella 3 degüello,
degüellas, degüella, degüellan
6 degüelle, degüelles, degüelle,
degüellen
1n jugar 2 juega 3 juego, juegas,
juega, jueguen 6 juegue, juegues,
juegue, jueguen
10 ESTAR 2 está 3 estoy, estás,
está, están 4 estuve, estuviste,
estuvo, estuvimos, estuvisteis,
estuvieron 6 esté, estés, esté,
estén 7 estuviera *etc*
1p andar 4 anduve *etc*
7 anduviera *etc*
1q dar 3 doy 4 di, diste, dio, dimos,
disteis, dieron 7 diera *etc*
2a COMER 1 comiendo 2 come,
comed 3 como, comes, come,
comemos, coméis, comen
4 comí, comiste, comió,
comimos, comisteis, comieron
5 comeré, comerás, comerá,
comeremos, comeréis, comerán
6 coma, comas, coma,
comamos, comáis, coman
7 comiera, comieras, comiera,
comiéramos, comierais,
comieran 8 comido 9 comía,
comías, comía, comíamos,
comíais, comían
2b vencer 3 venzo 6 venza *etc*
2c coger 3 cojo 6 coja *etc*
2d parecer 3 parezco 6 parezca *etc*
2e leer 1 leyendo 4 leyó, leyeron
7 leyera *etc*
2f tañer 1 tañendo 4 tañó, tañeron
2g perder 2 pierde 3 pierdo,
pierdes, pierde, pierden 6 pierda,
pierdas, pierda, pierdan

2h mover 2 mueve **3** muevo, mueves, mueve, mueven **6** mueva, mueves, mueva, muevan

2i oler 2 huele, hueles, huele, huelen **6** huela, huelas, huela, huelan

2j HABER 3 he, has, ha, hemos, han **4** hube, hubiste, hubo, hubimos, hubisteis, hubieron **5** habré *etc* **6** haya *etc* **7** hubiera *etc*

2k tener 2 ten **3** tengo, tienes, tiene, tienen **4** tuve, tuviste, tuvo, tuvimos, tuvisteis, tuvieron **5** tendré *etc* **6** tenga *etc* **7** tuviera *etc*

2l caber 3 quepo **4** cupe, cupiste, cupo, cupimos, cupisteis, cupieron **5** cabré *etc* **6** quepa *etc* **7** cupiera *etc*

2m saber 3 sé **4** supe, supiste, supo, supimos, supisteis, supieron **5** sabré *etc* **6** sepa *etc* **7** supiera *etc*

2n caer 1 cayendo **3** caigo **4** cayó, cayeron **6** caiga *etc* **7** cayera *etc*

2o traer 1 trayendo **3** traigo **4** traje, trajiste, trajo, trajimos, trajisteis, trajeron **6** traiga *etc* **7** trajera *etc*

2p valer 2 vale **3** valgo **5** valdré *etc* **6** valga *etc*

2q poner 2 pon **3** pongo **4** puse, pusiste, puso, pusimos, pusisteis, pusieron **5** pondré *etc* **6** ponga *etc* **7** pusiera *etc*

2r hacer 2 haz **3** hago **4** hice, hiciste, hizo, hicimos, hicisteis, hicieron **5** haré *etc* **6** haga *etc* **7** hiciera *etc* **8** hecho

2s poder 1 pudiendo **2** puede **3** puedo, puedes, puede, pueden **4** pude, pudiste, pudo, pudimos, pudisteis, pudieron **5** podré *etc* **6** pueda, puedas, pueda, puedan **7** pudiera *etc*

2t querer 2 quiere **3** quiero, quieres, quiere, quieren **4** quise, quisiste, quiso, quisimos, quisisteis, quisieron **5** querré *etc* **6** quiera, quieras, quiera, quieran **7** quisiera *etc*

2u ver 3 veo **6** vea *etc* **8** visto **9** veía *etc*

2v SER 2 sé **3** soy, eres, es, somos, sois, son **4** fui, fuiste, fue, fuimos, fuisteis, fueron **6** sea *etc* **7** fuera *etc* **9** era, eras, era, éramos, erais, eran

2w placer 3 plazco **6** plazca *etc*

2x yacer 3 yace or yaz **3** yazco or yazgo **6** yazca or yazga or yazga *etc*

2y roer 1 royendo **3** roo or roigo **4** royó, royeron, **6** roa or roiga *etc* **7** royera *etc*

3a VIVIR 1 viviendo **2** vive, vivid **3** vivo, vives, vive, vivimos, vivís, viven **4** viví, viviste, vivió, vivimos, vivisteis, vivieron **5** viviré, vivirás, vivirá, viviremos, viviréis, vivirán **6** viva, vivas, viva, vivamos, viváis, vivan **7** viviera, vivieras, viviera, viviéramos, vivierais, vivieran **8** vivido **9** vivía, vivías, vivía, vivíamos, vivíais, vivían

3b esparcir 3 esparzo **6** esparza *etc*

3c dirigir 3 dirijo **6** dirija *etc*

3d distinguir 3 distingo **6** distinga *etc*

3e delinquir 3 delinco **6** delinca *etc*

3f lucir 3 luzco **6** luzca *etc*

3g instruir 1 instruyendo **2** instruye **3** instruyo, instruyes, instruye, instruyen **4** instruyó, instruyeron **6** instruya *etc* **7** instruyera *etc*

3h gruñir 1 gruñendo **4** gruñó, gruñeron

3i sentir 1 sintiendo **2** siente **3** siento, sientes, siente, sienten **4** sintió, sintieron **6** sienta, sientas, sienta, sintamos, sintáis, sientan **7** sintiera *etc*

3j dormir 1 durmiendo 2 duerme 3 duermo, duermes, duerme, duermen 4 durmió, durmieron 6 duerma, duermas, duerma, durmamos, durmáis, duerman 7 durmiera *etc*

3k pedir 1 pidiendo 2 pide 3 pido, pides, pide, piden 4 pidió, pidieron 6 pida *etc* 7 pidiera *etc*

3l reír 2 ríe 3 río, ríes, ríe, ríen 4 rei, rieron 6 ría, rías, ría, riamos, riáis, rían 7 riera *etc*

3m erguir 1 irguiendo 2 yergue 3 yergo, yergues, yergue, yerguen 4 irguió, irguieron 7 irguiera *etc*

3n reducir 3 reduzco 5 reduje *etc* 6 reduzca *etc* 7 redujera *etc*

3o decir 2 di 3 digo 4 dije, dijiste, dijo, dijimos, dijisteis, dijeron 5 diré *etc* 6 diga *etc* 7 dijera *etc* 8 dicho

3p oír 1 oyendo 2 oye 3 oigo, oyes, oye, oyen 4 oyó, oyeron 6 oiga *etc* 7 oyera *etc*

3q salir 2 sal 3 salgo 5 saldré *etc* 6 salga *etc*

3r venir 2 ven 3 vengo, vienes, viene, vienen 4 vine, viniste, vino, vinimos, vinisteis, vinieron 5 vendré *etc* 6 venga *etc* 7 viniera *etc*

3s ir 1 yendo 2 ve 3 voy, vas, va, vamos, vais, van 4 fui, fuiste, fue, fuimos, fuisteis, fueron 6 vaya, vayas, vaya, vayamos, vayáis, vayan 7 fuera *etc* 9 iba, ibas, iba, íbamos, ibais, iban

VERBOS IRREGULARES EN INGLÉS

PRESENTE	PASADO	PARTICIPIO	PRESENTE	PASADO	PARTICIPIO
arise	arose	arisen	dream	dreamed,	dreamed,
awake	awoke	awoken		dreamt	dreamt
be (am, is,	was, were	been	drink	drank	drunk
are; being)			drive	drove	driven
bear	bore	born(e)	dwell	dwelt	dwelt
beat	beat	beaten	eat	ate	eaten
become	became	become	fall	fell	fallen
begin	began	begun	feed	fed	fed
bend	bent	bent	feel	felt	felt
bet	bet,	bet,	fight	fought	fought
	betted	betted	find	found	found
bid (at auction,	bid	bid	flee	fled	fled
cards)			fling	flung	flung
bid (say)	bade	bidden	fly	flew	flown
bind	bound	bound	forbid	forbad(e)	forbidden
bite	bit	bitten	forecast	forecast	forecast
bleed	bled	bled	forget	forgot	forgotten
blow	blew	blown	forgive	forgave	forgiven
break	broke	broken	forsake	forsook	forsaken
breed	bred	bred	freeze	froze	frozen
bring	brought	brought	get	got	got,
build	built	built			(us) gotten
burn	burnt,	burnt,	give	gave	given
	burned	burned	go (goes)	went	gone
burst	burst	burst	grind	ground	ground
buy	bought	bought	grow	grew	grown
can	could	(been able)	hang	hung	hung
cast	cast	cast	hang (suspend)	hung	hung
catch	caught	caught	(execute)		
choose	chose	chosen	have	had	had
cling	clung	clung	hear	heard	heard
come	came	come	hide	hid	hidden
cost (be	cost	cost	hit	hit	hit
valued at)			hold	held	held
cost (work	costed	costed	hurt	hurt	hurt
out price of)			keep	kept	kept
creep	crept	crept	kneel	knelt,	knelt,
cut	cut	cut		kneeled	kneeled
deal	dealt	dealt	know	knew	known
dig	dug	dug	lay	laid	laid
do (does)	did	done	lead	led	led
draw	drew	drawn	lean	leant,	leant,

PRESENTE	PASADO	PARTICIPIO	PRESENTE	PASADO	PARTICIPIO
	leaned	leaned	shine	shone	shone
leap	leapt, leaped	leapt, leaped	shoot	shot	shot
learn	learnt, learned	learnt, learned	show	showed	shown
			shrink	shrank	shrunk
leave	left	left	shut	shut	shut
lend	lent	lent	sing	sang	sung
let	let	let	sink	sank	sunk
lie (lying)	lay	lain	sit	sat	sat
light	lit, lighted	lit, lighted	slay	slew	slain
lose	lost	lost	sleep	slept	slept
make	made	made	slide	slid	slid
may	might	–	sling	slung	slung
mean	meant	meant	slit	slit	slit
meet	met	met	smell	smelt, smelled	smelt, smelled
mistake	mistook	mistaken	sow	sowed	sown, sowed
mow	mowed	mown, mowed			
must	(had to)	(had to)	speak	spoke	spoken
pay	paid	paid	speed	sped, speeded	sped, speeded
put	put	put	spell	spelt, spelled	spelt, spelled
quit	quit, quitted	quit, quitted	spend	spent	spent
read	read	read	spill	spilt, spilled	spilt, spilled
rid	rid	rid	spin	spun	spun
ride	rode	ridden	spit	spat	spat
ring	rang	rung	spoil	spoiled, spoilt	spoiled, spoilt
rise	rose	risen	spread	spread	spread
run	ran	run	spring	sprang	sprung
saw	sawed	sawed, sawn	stand	stood	stood
say	said	said	steal	stole	stolen
see	saw	seen	stick	stuck	stuck
seek	sought	sought	sting	stung	stung
sell	sold	sold	stink	stank	stunk
send	sent	sent	stride	strode	stridden
set	set	set	strike	struck	struck
sew	sewed	sewn	strive	strove	striven
shake	shook	shaken	swear	swore	sworn
shear	sheared	shorn, sheared	sweep	swept	swept
shed	shed	shed	swell	swelled	swollen, swelled

PRESENTE	PASADO	PARTICIPIO	PRESENTE	PASADO	PARTICIPIO
swim	swam	swum	wear	wore	worn
swing	swung	swung	weave (on loom)	wove	woven
take	took	taken			
teach	taught	taught	weave (wind)	weaved	weaved
tear	tore	torn	wed	wedded,	wedded,
tell	told	told		wed	wed
think	thought	thought	weep	wept	wept
throw	threw	thrown	win	won	won
thrust	thrust	thrust	wind	wound	wound
tread	trod	trodden	wring	wrung	wrung
wake	woke,	woken,	write	wrote	written
	waked	waked			

a

PALABRA CLAVE

a [a] *prep* **1** (*dirección*) to; **fueron a Madrid/Grecia** they went to Madrid/ Greece; **me voy a casa** I'm going home

2 (*distancia*): **está a 15 km de aquí** it's 15 km from here

3 (*posición*): **estar a la mesa** to be at table; **al lado de** next to, beside; *V tb* **puerta**

4 (*tiempo*): **a las 10/a medianoche** at 10/midnight; **a la mañana siguiente** the following morning; **a los pocos días** after a few days; **estamos a 9 de julio** it's the 9th of July; **a los 24 años** at the age of 24; **al año/a la semana** a year/week later

5 (*manera*): **a la francesa** the French way; **a caballo** on horseback; **a oscuras** in the dark

6 (*medio, instrumento*): **a lápiz** in pencil; **a mano** by hand; **cocina a gas** gas stove

7 (*razón*): **a dos euros el kilo** at two euros a kilo; **a más de 50 km por hora** at more than 50 km per hour

8 (*dativo*): **se lo di a él** I gave it to him; **se lo compré a él** I bought it from him

9 (*complemento directo*): **vi al policía** I saw the policeman

10 (*tras ciertos verbos*): **voy a verle** I'm going to see him; **empezó a trabajar** he started working *o* to work

11 (+ *infin*): **al verle, le reconocí inmediatamente** when I saw him I recognized him at once; **el camino a recorrer** the distance we *etc* have to travel; **¡a callar!** keep quiet!; **¡a comer!** let's eat!

abad, esa [a'βað, 'ðesa] *nm/f* abbot/ abbess; **abadía** *nf* abbey

abajo [a'βaxo] *adv* (*situación*) (down) below, underneath; (*en edificio*) downstairs; (*dirección*) down, downwards; **el piso de ~** the downstairs flat; **la parte de ~** the lower part; **¡~ el gobierno!** down with the government!; **cuesta/río ~** downhill/downstream; **de arriba ~** from top to bottom; **más ~** lower *o* further down

abalanzarse [aβalan'θarse] */1f; vr:* **~ sobre** *o* **contra** to throw o.s. at

abanderado, -a [aβande'raðo, a] *nm/f* (*portaestandarte*) standard bearer; (*de un movimiento*) champion, leader; (*LAM: linier*) linesman, assistant referee

abandonado, -a [aβando'naðo, a] *adj* derelict; (*desatendido*) abandoned; (*desierto*) deserted; (*descuidado*) neglected

abandonar [aβando'nar] */1a/ vt* to leave; (*persona*) to abandon, desert; (*cosa*) to abandon, leave behind; (*descuidar*) to neglect; (*renunciar a*) to give up; (*Inform*) to quit; **abandonarse**

vr: ~se a to abandon o.s. to;
abandono nm (acto) desertion,
abandonment; (estado) abandon,
neglect; (renuncia) withdrawal,
retirement; **ganar por abandono** to
win by default

abanico [aβa'niko] nm fan; (Naut)
derrick

abarcar [aβar'kar] /1g/ vt to include,
embrace; (LAM) to monopolize

abarrotado, -a [aβarro'taðo, a]
adj packed

abarrotar [aβarro'tar] /1a/ vt (local,
estadio, teatro) to fill, pack

abarrote [aβa'rrote] nm packing;
abarrotes nmpl (LAM) groceries;
tienda de ~s (LAM) grocery store

abarrotero, -a [aβarro'tero, a] nm/f
(LAM) grocer

abastecer [aβaste'θer] /2d/
vt: **~ (de)** to supply (with);
abastecimiento nm supply

abasto [a'βasto] nm supply; **no dar ~
a algo** not to be able to cope with sth

abatible [aβa'tiβle] adj: **asiento ~**
tip-up seat; (Auto) reclining seat

abatido, -a [aβa'tiðo, a] adj dejected,
downcast

abatir [aβa'tir] /3a/ vt (muro) to
demolish; (pájaro) to shoot o bring
down; (fig) to depress

abdicar [aβði'kar] /1g/ vi to abdicate

abdomen [aβ'ðomen] nm abdomen

abdominal [aβðomi'nal] nm: **~es**
abdominals; (Deporte: tb: **ejercicios
~es**) sit-ups

abecedario [aβeθe'ðarjo] nm
alphabet

abedul [aβe'ðul] nm birch

abeja [a'βexa] nf bee

abejorro [aβe'xorro] nm bumblebee

abertura [aβer'tura] nf = **apertura**

abeto [a'βeto] nm fir

abierto, -a [a'βjerto, a] pp de **abrir**
▷ adj open

abismal [aβis'mal] adj (fig) vast,
enormous

abismo [a'βismo] nm abyss

ablandar [aβlan'dar] /1a/ vt to soften
▷ **ablandarse** vr to get softer

abocado, -a [aβo'kaðo, a] adj:
verse ~ al desastre to be heading
for disaster

abochornar [aβotʃor'nar] /1a/ vt to
embarrass; **abochornarse** vr to get
flustered; (Bot) to wilt; **~se** de to get
embarrassed about

abofetear [aβofete'ar] /1a/ vt to slap
(in the face)

abogado, -a [aβo'ɣaðo, a] nm/f
lawyer; (notario) solicitor; (en tribunal)
barrister, advocate, attorney (US);
~ defensor defence lawyer (BRIT),
defense attorney (US)

abogar [aβo'ɣar] /1h/ vi: **~ por** to
plead for; (fig) to advocate

abolir [aβo'lir] vt to abolish; (cancelar)
to cancel

abolladura [aβoʎa'ðura] nf dent

abollar [aβo'ʎar] /1a/ vt to dent

abombarse [aβom'barse] /1a/ (LAM)
vr to go bad

abominable [aβomi'naβle] adj
abominable

abonado, -a [aβo'naðo, a] adj (deuda)
paid(-up) ▷ nm/f subscriber

abonar [aβo'nar] /1a/ vt (deuda) to
settle; (terreno) to fertilize; (idea) to
endorse; **abonarse** vr to subscribe;
abono nm payment; fertilizer;
subscription

abordar [aβor'ðar] /1a/ vt (barco) to
board; (asunto) to broach

aborigen [aβo'rixen] nmf aborigine

aborrecer [aβorre'θer] /2d/ vt to
hate, loathe

abortar [aβor'tar] /1a/ vi (malparir) to
have a miscarriage; (deliberadamente)
to have an abortion; **aborto** nm
miscarriage; abortion

abovedado, -a [aβoβe'ðaðo, a] adj
vaulted, domed

abrasar [aβra'sar] /1a/ vt to burn
(up); (Agr) to dry up, parch

abrazar [aβra'θar] /1f/ vt to embrace,
hug

abrazo [aˈβraθo] nm embrace; hug; **un ~** (en carta) with best wishes

abrebotellas [aβreβoˈteʎas] nm inv bottle opener

abrecartas [aβreˈkartas] nm inv letter opener

abrelatas [aβreˈlatas] nm inv tin (BRIT) o can (US) opener

abreviatura [aβreβjaˈtura] nf abbreviation

abridor [aβriˈðor] nm bottle opener; (de latas) tin (BRIT) o can (US) opener

abrigador, a [aβriɣaˈðor, a] adj (LAM) warm

abrigar [aβriˈɣar] /1h/ vt (proteger) to shelter; (ropa) to keep warm; (fig) to cherish

abrigo [aˈβriɣo] nm (prenda) coat, overcoat; (lugar protegido, o) shelter

abril [aˈβril] nm April; V tb julio

abrillantador [aβriʎantaˈðor] nm polish

abrillantar [aβriʎanˈtar] /1a/ vt (pulir) to polish

abrir [aˈβrir] /3a/ vt to open (up) ▷ vi to open; **abrirse** vr to open up; (extenderse) to open out; (cielo) to clear; **~se paso** to find o force a way through

abrochar [aβroˈtʃar] /1a/ vt (con botones) to button (up); (zapato, con broche) to do up

abrupto, -a [aˈβrupto, a] adj abrupt; (empinado) steep

absoluto, -a [aβsoˈluto, a] adj absolute; **en ~** adv not at all

absolver [aβsolˈβer] /2h/ vt to absolve; (Jur) to pardon; (: acusado) to acquit

absorbente [aβsorˈβente] adj absorbent; (interesante) absorbing

absorber [aβsorˈβer] /2a/ vt to absorb; (embeber) to soak up

absorción [aβsorˈθjon] nf absorption; (Com) takeover

abstemio, -a [aβsˈtemjo, a] adj teetotal

abstención [aβstenˈθjon] nf abstention

abstenerse [aβsteˈnerse] /2k/ vr: **~ (de)** to abstain o refrain (from)

abstinencia [aβstiˈnenθja] nf abstinence; (ayuno) fasting

abstracto, -a [aβsˈtrakto, a] adj abstract

abstraer [aβstraˈer] /2o/ vt to abstract; **abstraerse** vr to be o become absorbed

abstraído, -a [aβstraˈiðo, a] adj absent-minded

absuelto [aβˈswelto] pp de absolver

absurdo, -a [aβˈsurðo, a] adj absurd

abuchear [aβutʃeˈar] /1a/ vt to boo

abuela [aˈβwela] nf grandmother

abuelo [aˈβwelo] nm grandfather; **abuelos** nmpl grandparents

abultado, -a [aβulˈtaðo, a] adj bulky

abultar [aβulˈtar] /1a/ vi to be bulky

abundancia [aβunˈdanθja] nf: **una ~ de** plenty of; **abundante** adj abundant, plentiful

abundar [aβunˈdar] /1a/ vi to abound, be plentiful

aburrido, -a [aβuˈrriðo, a] adj (hastiado) bored; (que aburre) boring; **aburrimiento** nm boredom, tedium

aburrir [aβuˈrrir] /3a/ vt to bore; **aburrirse** vr to be bored, get bored

abusado, -a [aβuˈsaðo, a] adj (LAM fam: astuto) sharp, cunning ▷ excl: **¡~!** (inv) look out!, careful!

abusar [aβuˈsar] /1a/ vi to go too far; **~ de** to abuse

abusivo, -a [aβuˈsiβo, a] adj (precio) exorbitant

abuso [aˈβuso] nm abuse

acá [aˈka] adv (lugar) here

acabado, -a [akaˈβaðo, a] adj finished, complete; (perfecto) perfect; (agotado) worn out; (fig) masterly ▷ nm finish

acabar [akaˈβar] /1a/ vt (llevar a su fin) to finish, complete; (consumir) to use up; (rematar) to finish off ▷ vi to finish, end; **acabarse** vr to finish, stop; (terminarse) to be over; (agotarse) to run out; **~ con** to put an end to;

~ de llegar to have just arrived; **~ haciendo o por hacer algo** to end up (by) doing sth; **¡se acabó!** *(basta!)* that's enough!; *(se terminó)* it's all over!
acabose [aka'βose] *nm*: **esto es el ~** this is the last straw
academia [aka'ðemja] *nf* academy; **~ de idiomas** language school; *V tb* **colegio**; **académico, -a** *adj* academic
acalorado, -a [akalo'raðo, a] *adj (discusión)* heated
acampar [akam'par] */1a/ vi* to camp
acantilado [akanti'laðo] *nm* cliff
acaparar [akapa'rar] */1a/ vt* to monopolize; *(acumular)* to hoard
acariciar [akari'θjar] */1b/ vt* to caress; *(esperanza)* to cherish
acarrear [akarre'ar] */1a/ vt* to transport; *(fig)* to cause, result in
acaso [a'kaso] *adv* perhaps, maybe; **(por) si ~** (just) in case
acatar [aka'tar] */1a/ vt* to respect; *(ley)* to obey, observe
acatarrarse [akata'rrarse] */1a/ vr* to catch a cold
acceder [akθe'ðer] */2a/ vi* to accede, agree; **~ a** *(petición etc)* to agree to; *(tener acceso a)* to have access to; *(Inform)* to access
accesible [akθe'siβle] *adj* accessible
acceso [ak'θeso] *nm* access, entry; *(camino)* access road; *(Med)* attack, fit
accesorio, -a [akθe'sorjo, a] *adj* accessory ▷ *nm* accessory
accidentado, -a [akθiðen'taðo, a] *adj* uneven; *(montañoso)* hilly; *(azaroso)* eventful ▷ *nm/f* accident victim
accidental [akθiðen'tal] *adj* accidental
accidente [akθi'ðente] *nm* accident; **accidentes** *nmpl (de terreno)* unevenness *sg*; **~ laboral o de trabajo/de tráfico** industrial/road o traffic accident
acción [ak'θjon] *nf* action; *(acto)* action, act; *(Com)* share; *(Jur)* action, lawsuit; **accionar** */1a/ vt* to work, operate; *(ejecutar)* to activate

accionista [akθjo'nista] *nmf* shareholder
acebo [a'θeβo] *nm* holly; *(árbol)* holly tree
acechar [aθe'tʃar] */1a/ vt* to spy on; *(aguardar)* to lie in wait for; **acecho** *nm*: **estar al acecho (de)** to lie in wait (for)
aceite [a'θeite] *nm* oil; **~ de girasol/oliva** olive/sunflower oil; **aceitera** *nf* oilcan; **aceitoso, -a** *adj* oily
aceituna [aθei'tuna] *nf* olive; **~ rellena** stuffed olive
acelerador [aθelera'ðor] *nm* accelerator
acelerar [aθele'rar] */1a/ vt* to accelerate
acelga [a'θelya] *nf* chard, beet
acento [a'θento] *nm* accent; *(acentuación)* stress
acentuar [aθen'twar] */1e/ vt* to accent; to stress; *(fig)* to accentuate
acepción [aθep'θjon] *nf* meaning
aceptable [aθep'taβle] *adj* acceptable
aceptación [aθepta'θjon] *nf* acceptance; *(aprobación)* approval
aceptar [aθep'tar] */1a/ vt* to accept; *(aprobar)* to approve; **~ hacer algo** to agree to do sth
acequia [a'θekja] *nf* irrigation ditch
acera [a'θera] *nf* pavement (BRIT), sidewalk (US)
acerca [a'θerka]: **~ de** *prep* about, concerning
acercar [aθer'kar] */1g/ vt* to move nearer o move closer; **acercarse** *vr* to approach, come near
acero [a'θero] *nm* steel
acérrimo, -a [a'θerrimo, a] *adj (partidario)* staunch; *(enemigo)* bitter
acertado, -a [aθer'taðo, a] *adj* correct; *(apropiado)* apt; *(sensato)* sensible
acertar [aθer'tar] */1j/ vt (blanco)* to hit; *(solución)* to get right; *(adivinar)* to guess ▷ *vi* to get it right, be right; **~ a** to manage to; **~ con** to happen o hit on

acertijo [aθer'tixo] nm riddle, puzzle

achacar [atʃa'kar] /1g/ vt to attribute

achacoso, -a [atʃa'koso, a] adj sickly

achicar [atʃi'kar] /1g/ vt to reduce; (Naut) to bale out

achicharrar [atʃitʃa'rrar] /1a/ vt to scorch, burn

achichincle [atʃi'tʃinkle] nmf (LAM fam) minion

achicoria [atʃi'korja] nf chicory

achuras [a'tʃuras] nf (LAM Culin) offal

acicate [aθi'kate] nm spur

acidez [aθi'deθ] nf acidity

ácido, -a ['aθiðo, a] adj sour, acid
▷ nm acid

acierto etc [a'θjerto] vb V **acertar**
▷ nm success; (buen paso) wise move; (solución) solution; (habilidad) skill, ability

acitronar [aθitro'nar] /1a/ (LAM) vt (fam) to brown

aclamar [akla'mar] /1a/ vt to acclaim; (aplaudir) to applaud

aclaración [aklara'θjon] nf clarification, explanation

aclarar [akla'rar] /1a/ vt to clarify, explain; (ropa) to rinse ▷ vi to clear up; **aclararse** vr (explicarse) to understand; **~se la garganta** to clear one's throat

aclimatación [aklimata'θjon] nf acclimatization

aclimatar [aklima'tar] /1a/ vt to acclimatize; **aclimatarse** vr to become or get acclimatized

acné [ak'ne] nm acne

acobardar [akoβar'ðar] /1a/ vt to daunt, intimidate

acogedor, a [akoxe'ðor, a] adj welcoming; (hospitalario) hospitable

acoger [ako'xer] /2c/ vt to welcome; (abrigar) to shelter

acogida [ako'xiða] nf reception; refuge

acomedido, -a [akome'ðiðo, a] (LAM) adj helpful, obliging

acometer [akome'ter] /2a/ vt to attack; (emprender) to undertake; **acometida** nf attack, assault

acomodado, -a [akomo'ðaðo, a] adj (persona) well-to-do

acomodador, a [akomoða'ðor, a] nm/f usher(ette)

acomodar [akomo'ðar] /1a/ vt to adjust; (alojar) to accommodate; **acomodarse** vr to conform; (instalarse) to install o.s.; (adaptarse) to adapt o.s.; **~se (a)** to adapt (to)

acompañar [akompa'ɲar] /1a/ vt to accompany; (documentos) to enclose

acondicionar [akondiθjo'nar] /1a/ vt to get ready, prepare; (pelo) to condition

aconsejar [akonse'xar] /1a/ vt to advise, counsel; **~ a algn hacer o que haga algo** to advise sb to do sth

acontecer [akonte'θer] /2d/ vi to happen, occur; **acontecimiento** nm event

acopio [a'kopjo] nm store, stock

acoplar [ako'plar] /1a/ vt to fit; (Elec) to connect; (vagones) to couple

acorazado, -a [akora'θaðo, a] adj armour-plated, armoured ▷ nm battleship

acordar [akor'ðar] /1l/ vt (resolver) to agree, resolve; (recordar) to remind; **acordarse** vr to agree; **~ hacer algo** to agree to do sth; **~se (de algo)** to remember (sth); **acorde** adj (Mus) harmonious ▷ nm chord; **acorde con** (medidas etc) in keeping with

acordeón [akorðe'on] nm accordion

acordonado, -a [akorðo'naðo, a] adj (calle) cordoned-off

acorralar [akorra'lar] /1a/ vt to round up, corral

acortar [akor'tar] /1a/ vt to shorten; (duración) to cut short; (cantidad) to reduce; **acortarse** vr to become shorter

acosar [ako'sar] /1a/ vt to pursue relentlessly; (fig) to hound, pester; **acoso** nm harassment; **acoso escolar** bullying; **acoso sexual** sexual harassment

acostar [akos'tar] /1l/ vt (en cama) to put to bed; (en suelo) to lay down;

acostarse vr to go to bed; to lie down; **~se con algn** to sleep with sb

acostumbrado, -a [akostum'braðo, a] adj usual; **estar ~ a (hacer) algo** to be used to (doing) sth

acostumbrar [akostum'brar] /1a/ vt: **~ a algn a algo** to get sb used to sth ▷ vi: **~ (a hacer algo)** to be in the habit (of doing sth); **acostumbrarse** vr: **~se a algo** to get used to

acotación [akota'θjon] nf marginal note; (Geo) elevation mark; (de límite) boundary mark; (Teat) stage direction

acotamiento [akota'mjento] (LAM) nm hard shoulder (BRIT), berm (US)

acre ['akre] adj (olor) acrid; (fig) biting ▷ nm acre

acreditar [akreði'tar] /1a/ vt (garantizar) to vouch for, guarantee; (autorizar) to authorize; (dar prueba de) to prove; (Com: abonar) to credit; (embajador) to accredit

acreedor, a [akree'ðor, a] nm/f creditor

acribillar [akriβi'ʎar] /1a/ vt: **~ a balazos** to riddle with bullets

acróbata [a'kroβata] nmf acrobat

acta ['akta] nf certificate; (de comisión) minutes pl, record; **~ de nacimiento/ de matrimonio** birth/marriage certificate; **~ notarial** affidavit

actitud [akti'tuð] nf attitude; (postura) posture

activar [akti'βar] /1a/ vt to activate; (acelerar) to speed up

actividad [aktiβi'ðað] nf activity

activo, -a [ak'tiβo, a] adj active; (vivo) lively ▷ nm (Com) assets pl

acto ['akto] nm act, action; (ceremonia) ceremony; (Teat) act; **en el ~** immediately

actor [ak'tor] nm actor; (Jur) plaintiff ▷ adj: **parte ~a** prosecution

actriz [ak'triθ] nf actress

actuación [aktwa'θjon] nf action; (comportamiento) conduct, behaviour;

(Jur) proceedings pl; (desempeño) performance

actual [ak'twal] adj present(-day), current; **actualidad** nf present; **en la actualidad** at present; (hoy día) nowadays; **actualizar** /1f/ vt to update, modernize; **actualmente** adv at present; (hoy día) nowadays

> No confundir actual con la palabra inglesa actual.
> No confundir actualmente con la palabra inglesa actually.

actuar [ak'twar] /1e/ vi (obrar) to work, operate; (actor) to act, perform ▷ vt to work, operate; **~ de** to act as

acuarela [akwa'rela] nf watercolour

acuario [a'kwarjo] nm aquarium; **A~** (Astro) Aquarius

acuático, -a [a'kwatiko, a] adj aquatic

acudir [aku'ðir] /3a/ vi to attend, turn up; (ir) to go; **~ a** to turn to; **~ en ayuda de** to go to the aid of; **~ a una cita** to keep an appointment

acuerdo [a'kwerðo] vb V **acordar** ▷ nm agreement; **¡de ~!** agreed!; **de ~ con** (persona) in agreement with; (acción, documento) in accordance with; **estar de ~** (persona) to agree

acumular [akumu'lar] /1a/ vt to accumulate, collect

acuñar [aku'ɲar] /1a/ vt (moneda) to mint; (frase) to coin

acupuntura [akupun'tura] nf acupuncture

acurrucarse [akurru'karse] /1g/ vr to crouch; (ovillarse) to curl up

acusación [akusa'θjon] nf accusation

acusar [aku'sar] /1a/ vt to accuse; (revelar) to reveal; (denunciar) to denounce

acuse [a'kuse] nm: **~ de recibo** acknowledgement of receipt

acústico, -a [a'kustiko, a] adj acoustic ▷ nf acoustics pl

adaptación [aðapta'θjon] nf adaptation

adaptador [aðapta'ðor] nm (Elec) adapter; **~ universal** universal adapter

adaptar [aðap'tar] /1a/ vt to adapt; (acomodar) to fit

adecuado, -a [aðe'kwaðo, a] adj (apto) suitable; (oportuno) appropriate

a. de J.C. abr (=antes de Jesucristo) B.C.

adelantado, -a [aðelan'taðo, a] adj advanced; (reloj) fast; **pagar por ~** to pay in advance

adelantamiento [aðelanta'mjento] nm (Auto) overtaking

adelantar [aðelan'tar] /1a/ vt to move forward; (avanzar) to advance; (acelerar) to speed up; (Auto) to overtake ▷ vi (ir delante) to go ahead; (progresar) to improve; **adelantarse** vr to move forward

adelante [aðe'lante] adv forward(s), ahead ▷ excl come in!; **de hoy en ~** from now on; **más ~** later on; (más allá) further on

adelanto [aðe'lanto] nm advance; (mejora) improvement; (progreso) progress

adelgazar [aðelɣa'θar] /1f/ vt to thin (down) ▷ vi to get thin; (con régimen) to slim down, lose weight

ademán [aðe'man] nm gesture; **ademanes** nmpl manners

además [aðe'mas] adv besides; (por otra parte) moreover; (también) also; **~ de** besides, in addition to

adentrarse [aðen'trarse] /1a/ vr: **~ en** to go into, get inside; (penetrar) to penetrate (into)

adentro [a'ðentro] adv inside, in; **mar ~ out** at sea; **tierra ~** inland

adepto, -a [a'ðepto, a] nm/f supporter

aderezar [aðere'θar] /1f/ vt (ensalada) to dress; (comida) to season; **aderezo** nm dressing; seasoning

adeudar [aðeu'ðar] /1a/ vt to owe

adherirse [aðe'rirse] /3i/ vr: **~ a** to adhere to; (partido) to join

adhesión [aðe'sjon] nf adhesion; (fig) adherence

adicción [aðik'θjon] nf addiction

adición [aði'θjon] nf addition

adicto, -a [a'ðikto, a] adj: **~ a** addicted to; (dedicado) devoted to ▷ nm/f supporter, follower; (toxicómano etc) addict

adiestrar [aðjes'trar] /1a/ vt to train, teach; (conducir) to guide, lead

adinerado, -a [aðine'raðo, a] adj wealthy

adiós [a'ðjos] excl (para despedirse) goodbye!, cheerio!; (al pasar) hello!

aditivo [aði'tiβo] nm additive

adivinanza [aðiβi'nanθa] nf riddle

adivinar [aðiβi'nar] /1a/ vt to prophesy; (conjeturar) to guess; **adivino, -a** nm/f fortune-teller

adj abr (=adjunto) encl

adjetivo [aðxe'tiβo] nm adjective

adjudicar [aðxuði'kar] /1g/ vt to award; **adjudicarse** vr: **~se algo** to appropriate sth

adjuntar [aðxun'tar] /1a/ vt to attach, enclose; **adjunto, -a** adj attached, enclosed ▷ nm/f assistant

administración [aðministra'θjon] nf administration; (dirección) management; **administrador, a** nm/f administrator; manager(ess)

administrar [aðminis'trar] /1a/ vt to administer; **administrativo, -a** adj administrative

admirable [aðmi'raβle] adj admirable

admiración [aðmira'θjon] nf admiration; (asombro) wonder; (Ling) exclamation mark

admirar [aðmi'rar] /1a/ vt to admire; (extrañar) to surprise

admisible [aðmi'siβle] adj admissible

admisión [aðmi'sjon] nf admission; (reconocimiento) acceptance

admitir [aðmi'tir] /3a/ vt to admit; (aceptar) to accept

adobar [aðo'βar] /1a/ vt (cocinar) to season

adobe [a'ðoβe] *nm* adobe, sun-dried brick

adolecer [aðole'θer] /2d/ *vi*: ~ **de** to suffer from

adolescente [aðoles'θente] *nmf* adolescent, teenager

adonde *conj* (to) where

adónde [a'ðonde] *adv* = **dónde**

adopción [aðop'θjon] *nf* adoption

adoptar [aðop'tar] /1a/ *vt* to adopt

adoptivo, -a [aðop'tiβo, a] *adj* (*padres*) adoptive; (*hijo*) adopted

adoquín [aðo'kin] *nm* paving stone

adorar [aðo'rar] /1a/ *vt* to adore

adornar [aðor'nar] /1a/ *vt* to adorn

adorno [a'ðorno] *nm* (*objeto*) ornament; (*decoración*) decoration

adosado, -a [aðo'saðo, a] *adj* (*casa*) semidetached

adosar [aðo'sar] /1a/ (*LAM*) *vt* (*adjuntar*) to attach, enclose (*with a letter*)

adquiera *etc vb V* **adquirir**

adquirir [aðki'rir] /3i/ *vt* to acquire, obtain

adquisición [aðkisi'θjon] *nf* acquisition

adrede [a'ðreðe] *adv* on purpose

ADSL *nm abr* ADSL

aduana [a'ðwana] *nf* customs *pl*

aduanero, -a [aðwa'nero, a] *adj* customs *cpd* ▷ *nm/f* customs officer

adueñarse [aðwe'narse] /1a/ *vr*: ~ **de** to take possession of

adular [aðu'lar] /1a/ *vt* to flatter

adulterar [aðulte'rar] /1a/ *vt* to adulterate

adulterio [aðul'terjo] *nm* adultery

adúltero, -a [a'ðultero, a] *adj* adulterous ▷ *nm/f* adulterer/adulteress

adulto, -a [a'ðulto, a] *adj*, *nm/f* adult

adverbio [að'βerβjo] *nm* adverb

adversario, -a [aðβer'sarjo, a] *nm/f* adversary

adversidad [aðβersi'ðað] *nf* adversity; (*contratiempo*) setback

adverso, -a [að'βerso, a] *adj* adverse

advertencia [aðβer'tenθja] *nf* warning; (*prefacio*) preface, foreword

advertir [aðβer'tir] /3i/ *vt* to notice; (*avisar*): ~ **a algn de** to warn sb about o of

Adviento [að'βjento] *nm* Advent

advierta *etc vb V* **advertir**

aéreo, -a [a'ereo, a] *adj* aerial

aerobic [ae'roβik] *nm*, (*LAM*) **aerobics** [ae'roβiks] *nmpl* aerobics *sg*

aerodeslizador [aeroðesliθa'ðor] *nm* hovercraft

aeromozo, -a [aero'moθo, a] *nm/f* (*LAM*) air steward(ess)

aeronáutica [aero'nautika] *nf* aeronautics *sg*

aeronave [aero'naβe] *nm* spaceship

aeroplano [aero'plano] *nm* aeroplane

aeropuerto [aero'pwerto] *nm* airport

aerosol [aero'sol] *nm* aerosol

afamado, -a [afa'maðo, a] *adj* famous

afán [a'fan] *nm* hard work; (*deseo*) desire

afanador, a [afana'ðor, a] (*LAM*) *nm/f* (*de limpieza*) cleaner

afanar [afa'nar] /1a/ *vt* to harass; (*fam*) to pinch; **afanarse** *vr*: ~**se por** to strive to

afear [afe'ar] /1a/ *vt* to disfigure

afección [afek'θjon] *nf* (*Med*) disease

afectado, -a [afek'taðo, a] *adj* affected

afectar [afek'tar] /1a/ *vt* to affect

afectísimo, -a [afek'tisimo, a] *adj* affectionate; **suyo** ~ yours truly

afectivo, -a [afek'tiβo, a] *adj* (*problema etc*) emotional

afecto [a'fekto] *nm* affection; **tenerle** ~ **a algn** to be fond of sb

afectuoso, -a [afek'twoso, a] *adj* affectionate

afeitar [afei'tar] /1a/ *vt* to shave; **afeitarse** *vr* to shave

afeminado, -a [afemi'naðo, a] *adj* effeminate

Afganistán [afɣanisˈtan] *nm* Afghanistan

afianzar [afjanˈθar] /1f/ *vt* to strengthen, secure; **afianzarse** *vr* to become established

afiche [aˈfitʃe] *nm* (LAM) poster

afición [afiˈθjon] *nf*: **~ a** a fondness o liking for; **la ~** the fans *pl*; **pinto por ~** I paint as a hobby; **aficionado, -a** *adj* keen, enthusiastic; (*no profesional*) amateur ▷ *nm/f* enthusiast, fan; amateur; **ser aficionado a algo** to be very keen on o fond of sth

aficionar [afiθjoˈnar] /1a/ *vt*: **~ a algn a algo** to make sb like sth; **aficionarse** *vr*: **~se a algo** to grow fond of sth

afilado, -a [afiˈlaðo, a] *adj* sharp

afilar [afiˈlar] /1a/ *vt* to sharpen

afiliarse [afiˈljarse] /1b/ *vr* to affiliate

afín [aˈfin] *adj* (*parecido*) similar; (*conexo*) related

afinar [afiˈnar] /1a/ *vt* (Tec) to refine; (Mus) to tune ▷ *vi* (*tocar*) to play in tune; (*cantar*) to sing in tune

afincarse [afinˈkarse] /1g/ *vr* to settle

afinidad [afiniˈðað] *nf* affinity; (*parentesco*) relationship; **por ~** by marriage

afirmación [afirmaˈθjon] *nf* affirmation

afirmar [afirˈmar] /1a/ *vt* to affirm, state; **afirmativo, -a** *adj* affirmative

afligir [afliˈxir] /3c/ *vt* to afflict; (*apenar*) to distress

aflojar [afloˈxar] /1a/ *vt* to slacken; (*desatar*) to loosen, undo; (*relajar*) to relax ▷ *vi* to drop; (*bajar*) to go down; **aflojarse** *vr* to relax

afluente [afluˈente] *adj* flowing ▷ *nm* (Geo) tributary

afmo., -a. *abr* (= *afectísimo/a suyo/a*) Yours

afónico, -a [aˈfoniko, a] *adj*: **estar ~** to have a sore throat; to have lost one's voice

aforo [aˈforo] *nm* (*de teatro etc*) capacity

afortunado, -a [afortuˈnaðo, a] *adj* fortunate, lucky

África [ˈafrika] *nf* Africa; **~ del Sur** South Africa; **africano, -a** *adj*, *nm/f* African

afrontar [afronˈtar] /1a/ *vt* to confront; (*poner cara a cara*) to bring face to face

afrutado, -a [afruˈtaðo, a] *adj* fruity

after [ˈafter] *nm*, **afterhours** [ˈafterauars] *nm inv* after-hours club

afuera [aˈfwera] *adv* out, outside; **afueras** *nfpl* outskirts

agachar [aɣaˈtʃar] /1a/ *vt* to bend, bow; **agacharse** *vr* to stoop, bend

agalla [aˈɣaʎa] *nf* (Zool) gill; **tener ~s** (*fam*) to have guts

agarradera [aɣarraˈðera] *nf* (LAM), **agarradero** [aɣarraˈðero] *nm* handle

agarrado, -a [aɣaˈrraðo, a] *adj* mean, stingy

agarrar [aɣaˈrrar] /1a/ *vt* to grasp, grab; (LAM: *tomar*) to take, catch; (*recoger*) to pick up ▷ *vi* (*planta*) to take root; **agarrarse** *vr* to hold on (tightly)

agencia [aˈxenθja] *nf* agency; **~ de créditos/publicidad/viajes** credit/advertising/travel agency; **~ inmobiliaria** estate agent's (office) (BRIT), real estate office (US)

agenciar [axenˈθjar] /1b/ *vt* to bring about; **agenciarse** *vr* to look after o.s.; **~se algo** to get hold of sth

agenda [aˈxenda] *nf* diary; **~ electrónica** PDA

> No confundir *agenda* con la palabra inglesa *agenda*.

agente [aˈxente] *nm/f* agent; (*tb*: **~ de policía**) policeman/policewoman; **~ de seguros** insurance broker; **~ de tránsito** (LAM) traffic cop; **~ inmobiliario** estate agent (BRIT), realtor (US)

ágil [ˈaxil] *adj* agile, nimble; **agilidad** *nf* agility, nimbleness

agilizar [axiliˈθar] /1f/ *vt* (*trámites*) to speed up

agiotista [axjo'tista] (*LAM*) *nmf*
(*usurero*) usurer
agitación [axita'θjon] *nf* (*de mano
etc*) shaking, waving; (*de líquido etc*)
stirring; agitation
agitado, -a [axi'taðo, a] *adj* hectic;
(*viaje*) bumpy
agitar [axi'tar] /1a/ *vt* to wave, shake;
(*líquido*) to stir; (*fig*) to stir up, excite;
agitarse *vr* to get excited; (*inquietarse*)
to get worried o upset
aglomeración [aɣlomera'θjon] *nf*:
~ **de tráfico/gente** traffic jam/mass
of people
agnóstico, -a [aɣ'nostiko, a] *adj,
nm/f* agnostic
agobiar [aɣo'βjar] /1b/ *vt* to weigh
down; (*oprimir*) to oppress; (*cargar*)
to burden
agolparse [aɣol'parse] /1a/ *vr* to
crowd together
agonía [aɣo'nia] *nf* death throes *pl*;
(*fig*) agony, anguish
agonizante [aɣoni'θante] *adj* dying
agonizar [aɣoni'θar] /1f/ *vi* to be
dying
agosto [a'ɣosto] *nm* August
agotado, -a [aɣo'taðo, a] *adj*
(*persona*) exhausted; (*acabado*)
finished; (*Com*) sold out; (: *libros*) out of
print; **agotador, a** *adj* exhausting
agotamiento [aɣota'mjento] *nm*
exhaustion
agotar [aɣo'tar] /1a/ *vt* to exhaust;
(*consumir*) to drain; (*recursos*) to use up,
deplete; **agotarse** *vr* to be exhausted,
(*acabarse*) to run out; (*libro*) to go
out of print
agraciado, -a [aɣra'θjaðo, a] *adj*
(*atractivo*) attractive; (*en sorteo etc*)
lucky
agradable [aɣra'ðaβle] *adj* pleasant,
nice
agradar [aɣra'ðar] /1a/ *vt, vi* to
please; **él me agrada** I like him
agradecer [aɣraðe'θer] /2d/ *vt*
to thank; (*favor etc*) to be grateful
for; **agradecido, -a** *adj* grateful;

¡muy agradecido! thanks a lot!;
agradecimiento *nm* thanks *pl*;
gratitude
agradezca *etc* [aɣra'ðeθka] *vb* V
agradecer
agrado [a'ɣraðo] *nm*: **ser de tu** *etc* ~
to be to your *etc* liking
agrandar [aɣran'dar] /1a/ *vt*
to enlarge; (*fig*) to exaggerate;
agrandarse *vr* to get bigger
agrario, -a [a'ɣrarjo, a] *adj* agrarian,
land *cpd*; (*política*) agricultural,
farming *cpd*
agravante [aɣra'βante] *adj*
aggravating ▷ *nm o f*: **con el** o **la** ~
de que ... with the further difficulty
that ...
agravar [aɣra'βar] /1a/ *vt* (*pesar sobre*)
to make heavier; (*irritar*) to aggravate;
agravarse *vr* to worsen, get worse
agraviar [aɣra'βjar] /1b/ *vt* to offend;
(*ser injusto con*) to wrong
agredir [aɣre'ðir] /3a/ *vt* to attack
agregado [aɣre'ɣaðo] *nm* aggregate;
(*persona*) attaché; **A- ~** teacher (*who is
not head of department*)
agregar [aɣre'ɣar] /1h/ *vt* to gather;
(*añadir*) to add; (*persona*) to appoint
agresión [aɣre'sjon] *nf* aggression
agresivo, -a [aɣre'siβo, a] *adj*
aggressive
agriar [a'ɣrjar] /1t/ *vt* (to turn) sour
agrícola [a'ɣrikola] *adj* farming *cpd*,
agricultural
agricultor, a [aɣrikul'tor, a] *nm/f*
farmer
agricultura [aɣrikul'tura] *nf*
agriculture, farming
agridulce [aɣri'ðulθe] *adj*
bittersweet; (*Culin*) sweet and sour
agrietarse [aɣrje'tarse] /1a/ *vr* to
crack; (*la piel*) to chap
agrio, -a [a'ɣrjo, a] *adj* bitter
agrupación [aɣrupa'θjon] *nf* group;
(*acto*) grouping
agrupar [aɣru'par] /1a/ *vt* to group
agua [a'ɣwa] *nf* water; (*Naut*)
wake; (*Arq*) slope of a roof:

aguas *nfpl* (Med) water *sg*, urine *sg*; (Naut) waters; **~s abajo/ arriba** downstream/upstream; **~ bendita/destilada/potable** holy/distilled/drinking water; **~ caliente** hot water; **~ corriente** running water; **~ de colonia** eau de cologne; **~ mineral (con/sin gas)** (fizzy/non-fizzy) mineral water; **~ oxigenada** hydrogen peroxide; **~s jurisdiccionales** territorial waters

aguacate [aɣwaˈkate] *nm* avocado (pear)

aguacero [aɣwaˈθero] *nm* (heavy) shower, downpour

aguado, -a [aˈɣwaðo, a] *adj* watery, watered down

aguafiestas [aɣwaˈfjestas] *nm inv, nf inv* spoilsport

aguamiel [aɣwaˈmjel] (LAM) *nf* fermented maguey o agave juice

aguanieve [aɣwaˈnjeβe] *nf* sleet

aguantar [aɣwanˈtar] /1a/ *vt* to bear, put up with; (sostener) to hold up ▷ *vi* to last; **aguantarse** *vr* to restrain o.s.; **aguante** *nm* (paciencia) patience; (resistencia) endurance

aguar [aˈɣwar] /1i/ *vt* to water down

aguardar [aɣwarˈðar] /1a/ *vt* to wait for

aguardiente [aɣwarˈðjente] *nm* brandy, liquor

aguarrás [aɣwaˈrras] *nm* turpentine

aguaviva [aɣwaˈβiβa] (RPL) *nf* jellyfish

agudeza [aɣuˈðeθa] *nf* sharpness; (ingenio) wit

agudo, -a [aˈɣuðo, a] *adj* sharp; (voz) high-pitched, piercing; (dolor, enfermedad) acute

agüero [aˈɣwero] *nm*: **buen/mal ~** good/bad omen

aguijón [aɣiˈxon] *nm* sting; (fig) spur

águila [ˈaɣila] *nf* eagle; (fig) genius

aguileño, -a [aɣiˈleɲo, a] *adj* (nariz) aquiline; (rostro) sharp-featured

aguinaldo [aɣiˈnaldo] *nm* Christmas box

aguja [aˈɣuxa] *nf* needle; (de reloj) hand; (Arq) spire; (Tec) firing-pin; **agujas** *nfpl* (Zool) ribs; (Ferro) points

agujerear [aɣuxereˈar] /1a/ *vt* to make holes in

agujero [aɣuˈxero] *nm* hole

agujetas [aɣuˈxetas] *nfpl* stitch *sg*; (rigidez) stiffness *sg*

ahí [aˈi] *adv* there; (allá) over there; **de ~ que** so that, with the result that; **~ llega** here he comes; **por ~** that way; **200 o por ~** 200 or so

ahijado, -a [aiˈxaðo, a] *nm/f* godson/ daughter

ahogar [aoˈɣar] /1h/ *vt* to drown; (asfixiar) to suffocate, smother; (fuego) to put out; **ahogarse** *vr* (en agua) to drown; (por asfixia) to suffocate

ahogo [aˈoɣo] *nm* breathlessness; (económico) financial difficulty

ahondar [aonˈdar] /1a/ *vt* to deepen, make deeper; (fig) to study thoroughly ▷ *vi*: **~ en** to study thoroughly

ahora [aˈora] *adv* now; (hace poco) a moment ago, just now; (dentro de poco) in a moment; **~ mismo** right now; **~ voy** I'm coming; **~ bien** now then; **por ~** for the present

ahorcar [aorˈkar] /1g/ *vt* to hang

ahorita [aoˈrita] *adv* (esp LAM fam: en este momento) right now; (: hace poco) just now; (dentro de poco) in a minute

ahorrar [aoˈrrar] /1a/ *vt* (dinero) to save; (esfuerzos) to save, avoid; **ahorro** *nm* (acto) saving; **ahorros** *nmpl* (dinero) savings

ahuecar [aweˈkar] /1g/ *vt* to hollow (out); (voz) to deepen; **ahuecarse** *vr* to give o.s. airs

ahumar [auˈmar] /1a/ *vt* to smoke, cure; (llenar de humo) to fill with smoke ▷ *vi* to smoke; **ahumarse** *vr* to fill with smoke

ahuyentar [aujenˈtar] /1a/ *vt* to drive off, frighten off; (fig) to dispel

aire [ˈaire] *nm* air; (viento) wind; (corriente) draught; (Mus) tune; **al ~ libre** in the open air; **~ aclimatizado**

o **acondicionado** air conditioning;
airear /1a/ vt to air; **airearse** vr to get
some fresh air; **airoso, -a** adj windy;
draughty; (fig) graceful

aislado, -a [ais'laðo, a] adj isolated;
(incomunicado) cut off; (Elec) insulated

aislar [ais'lar] /1a/ vt to isolate; (Elec)
to insulate

ajardinado, -a [axarði'naðo, a] adj
landscaped

ajedrez [axe'ðreθ] nm chess

ajeno, -a [a'xeno, a] adj (que pertenece
a otro) somebody else's; ~ a foreign to

ajetreado, -a [axetre'aðo, a] adj busy

ajetreo [axe'treo] nm bustle

ají [a'xi] nm chil(l)i, red pepper; (salsa)
chil(l)i sauce

ajillo [a'xiʎo] nm: **gambas al ~** garlic
prawns

ajo [‘axo] nm garlic

ajuar [a'xwar] nm household
furnishings pl; (de novia) trousseau; (de
niño) layette

ajustado, -a [axus'taðo, a] adj
(tornillo) tight; (cálculo) right; (ropa)
tight(-fitting); (resultado) close

ajustar [axus'tar] /1a/ vt (adaptar) to
adjust; (encajar) to fit; (Tec) to engage;
(Tip) to make up; (apretar) to tighten;
(concertar) to agree (on); (reconciliar) to
reconcile; (cuenta, deudas) to settle ▷ vi
to fit; **ajustarse** vr: **~se a** (precio etc)
to be in keeping with, fit in with; **~ las
cuentas a algn** to get even with sb

ajuste [a'xuste] nm adjustment;
(Costura) fitting; (acuerdo)
compromise; (de cuenta) settlement

al [al] = **a + el**; V **a**

ala [‘ala] nf wing; (de sombrero)
brim; (futbolista) winger; **~ delta**
hang-glider

alabanza [ala'βanθa] nf praise

alabar [ala'βar] /1a/ vt to praise

alacena [ala'θena] nf cupboard
(BRIT), closet (US)

alacrán [ala'kran] nm scorpion

alambrada [alam'braða] nm wire
fence; (red) wire netting

alambre [a'lambre] nm wire; **~ de
púas** barbed wire

alameda [ala'meða] nf (plantío)
poplar grove; (lugar de paseo) avenue,
boulevard

álamo [‘alamo] nm poplar

alarde [a'larðe] nm show, display;
hacer ~ de to boast of

alargador [alarɣa'ðor] nm extension
cable o lead

alargar [alar'ɣar] /1h/ vt to lengthen,
extend; (paso) to hasten; (brazo)
to stretch out; (cuerda) to pay out;
(conversación) to spin out; **alargarse** vr
to get longer

alarma [a'larma] nf alarm; **~ de
incendios** fire alarm; **alarmante** adj
alarming; **alarmar** /1a/ vt to alarm;
alarmarse vr to get alarmed

alba [‘alβa] nf dawn

albahaca [al'βaka] nf (Bot) basil

Albania [al'βanja] nf Albania

albañil [alβa'ɲil] nm bricklayer;
(cantero) mason

albarán [alβa'ran] nm (Com) delivery
note, invoice

albaricoque [alβari'koke] nm apricot

albedrío [alβe'ðrio] nm: **libre ~** free will

alberca [al'βerka] nf reservoir; (ʌM)
swimming pool

albergar [alβer'ɣar] /1h/ vt to shelter

albergue [al'βerɣe] vb V **albergar**
▷ nm shelter, refuge; **~ juvenil** youth
hostel

albóndiga [al'βondiɣa] nf meatball

albornoz [alβor'noθ] nm (de los
drabes) burnous; (para el baño) bathrobe

alborotar [alβoro'tar] /1a/ vi to
make a row ▷ vt to agitate, stir up;
alborotarse vr to get excited; (mar) to
get rough; **alboroto** nm row, uproar

álbum [‘alβum] (pl **álbums** o
álbumes) nm album; **~ de recortes**
scrapbook

albur [al'βur] (ʌM) nm (juego de
palabras) pun; (doble sentido) double
entendre

alcachofa [alka'tʃofa] nf (globe) artichoke

alcalde, -esa [al'kalde, alkal'desa] nm/f mayor(ess)

alcaldía [alkal'dia] nf mayoralty; (lugar) mayor's office

alcance [al'kanθe] vb V **alcanzar** ▷ nm (Mil, Radio) range; (fig) scope; (Com) adverse balance; **estar al/ fuera del ~ de algn** to be within/ beyond sb's reach

alcancía [alkan'θia] (LAm) nf (para ahorrar) money box; (para colectas) collection box

alcantarilla [alkanta'riʎa] nf (de aguas cloacales) sewer; (en la calle) gutter

alcanzar [alkan'θar] /1f/ vt (algo: con la mano, el pie) to reach; (alguien: en el camino etc) to catch up (with); (autobús) to catch; (bala) to hit, strike ▷ vi (ser suficiente) to be enough; **~ a hacer** to manage to do

alcaparra [alka'parra] nf (Bot) caper

alcayata [alka'jata] nf hook

alcázar [al'kaθar] nm fortress; (Naut) quarter-deck

alcoba [al'koβa] nf bedroom

alcohol [al'kol] nm alcohol; **~ metílico** methylated spirits pl (BRIT), wood alcohol (US); **alcohólico, -a** adj, nm/f alcoholic; **alcoholímetro** nm Breathalyser®, drunkometer (US); **alcoholismo** nm alcoholism

alcornoque [alkor'noke] nm cork tree; (fam) idiot

aldea [al'dea] nf village; **aldeano, -a** adj village cpd ▷ nm/f villager

aleación [alea'θjon] nf alloy

aleatorio, -a [alea'torjo, a] adj random

aleccionar [alekθjo'nar] /1a/ vt to instruct; (adiestrar) to train

alegar [ale'ɣar] /1h/ vt (dificultad etc) to plead; (Jur) to allege ▷ vi (LAm) to argue

alegoría [aleɣo'ria] nf allegory

alegrar [ale'ɣrar] /1a/ vt (causar alegría) to cheer (up); (fuego) to poke;

(fiesta) to liven up; **alegrarse** vr (fam) to get merry o tight; **~se de** to be glad about

alegre [a'leɣre] nf happy, cheerful; (fam) merry, tight; (chiste) risqué, blue; **alegría** nf happiness; merriment

alejar [ale'xar] /1a/ vt to move away, remove; (fig) to estrange; **alejarse** vr to move away

alemán, -ana [ale'man, ana] adj, nm/f German ▷ nm (lengua) German

Alemania [ale'manja] nf Germany

alentador, a [alenta'ðor, a] adj encouraging

alentar [alen'tar] /1j/ vt to encourage

alergia [a'lerxja] nf allergy

alero [a'lero] nm (de tejado) eaves pl; (Auto) mudguard

alerta [a'lerta] adj inv, nm alert

aleta [a'leta] nf (de pez) fin; (de ave) wing; (de foca, Deporte) flipper; (de coche) mudguard

aletear [alete'ar] /1a/ vi to flutter

alevín [ale'βin] nm fry, young fish

alevosía [aleβo'sia] nf treachery

alfabeto [alfa'βeto] nm alphabet

alfalfa [al'falfa] nf alfalfa, lucerne

alfarería [alfare'ria] nf pottery; (tienda) pottery shop; **alfarero, -a** nm/f potter

alféizar [al'feiθar] nm window-sill

alférez [al'fereθ] nm (Mil) second lieutenant; (Naut) ensign

alfil [al'fil] nm (Ajedrez) bishop

alfiler [alfi'ler] nm pin; (broche) clip

alfombra [al'fombra] nf carpet; (más pequeña) rug; **alfombrilla** nf rug, mat; (Inform) mouse mat o pad

alforja [al'forxa] nf saddlebag

algas ['alɣas] nfpl seaweed sg

álgebra ['alxeβra] nf algebra

algo ['alɣo] pron something; (en frases interrogativas) anything ▷ adv somewhat, rather; **¿~ más?** anything else?; (en tienda) is that all?; **por ~ será** there must be some reason for it

algodón [alɣo'ðon] nm cotton; (planta) cotton plant; **~ de azúcar**

candy floss (BRIT), cotton candy (US); ~ **hidrófilo** cotton wool (BRIT), absorbent cotton (US)

alguien ['alɣjen] pron someone, somebody; (en frases interrogativas) anyone, anybody

alguno, -a [al'ɣuno, a] adj some; (después de n) **no tiene talento ~** he has no talent, he doesn't have any talent ⊳ pron (alguien) someone, somebody; **algún que otro libro** some book or other; **algún día iré** I'll go one o some day; **sin interés ~** without the slightest interest; **~ que otro** an occasional one; **~s piensan** some (people) think

alhaja [a'laxa] nf jewel; (tesoro) precious object, treasure

alhelí [ale'li] nm wallflower, stock

aliado, -a [a'ljaðo, a] adj allied

alianza [a'ljanθa] nf alliance; (anillo) wedding ring

aliar [a'ljar] /1c/ vt to ally; **aliarse** vr to form an alliance

alias ['aljas] adv alias

alicatado [alika'taðo] (ESP) nm tiling

alicate [ali'kate] nm, **alicates** [ali'kates] nmpl pliers pl

aliciente [ali'θjente] nm incentive; (atracción) attraction

alienación [aljena'θjon] nf alienation

aliento [a'ljento] nm breath; (respiración) breathing; **sin ~** breathless

aligerar [alixe'rar] /1a/ vt to lighten; (reducir) to shorten; (aliviar) to alleviate; (mitigar) to ease; (paso) to quicken

alijo [a'lixo] nm (Naut: descarga) unloading

alimaña [ali'maɲa] nf pest

alimentación [alimenta'θjon] nf (comida) food; (acción) feeding; (tienda) grocer's (shop)

alimentar [alimen'tar] /1a/ vt to feed; (nutrir) to nourish; **alimentarse** vr: **~se (de)** to feed on

alimenticio, -a [alimen'tiθjo, a] adj food cpd; (nutritivo) nourishing, nutritious

alimento [ali'mento] nm food; (nutrición) nourishment

alineación [alinea'θjon] nf alignment; (Deporte) line-up

alinear [aline'ar] /1a/ vt to align; (Deporte) to select, pick; **alinearse** vr

aliñar [ali'ɲar] /1a/ vt (Culin) to dress; **aliño** nm (Culin) dressing

alioli [ali'oli] nm garlic mayonnaise

alisar [ali'sar] /1a/ vt to smooth

alistar [alis'tar] /1a/ vt to recruit; **alistarse** vr to enlist; (inscribirse) to enrol

aliviar [ali'βjar] /1b/ vt (carga) to lighten; (persona) to relieve; (dolor) to relieve, alleviate

alivio [a'liβjo] nm alleviation, relief

aljibe [al'xiβe] nm cistern

allá [a'ʎa] adv (lugar) there; (por ahí) over there; (tiempo) then; **~ abajo** down there; **más ~** further on; **más ~ de** beyond; **¡~ tú!** that's your problem!

allanamiento [aʎana'mjento] nm (LAM Policía) raid, search; **~ de morada** breaking and entering

allanar [aʎa'nar] /1a/ vt to flatten, level (out); (igualar) to smooth (out); (fig) to subdue; (Jur) to burgle, break into

allegado, -a [aʎe'ɣaðo, a] adj near, close ⊳ nm/f relation

allí [a'ʎi] adv there; **~ mismo** right there; **por ~** over there; (por ese camino) that way

alma ['alma] nf soul; (persona) person

almacén [alma'θen] nm (depósito) warehouse, store; (Mil) magazine; (LAM) grocer's shop, food store, grocery store (US); (grandes) **almacenes** nmpl department store sg; **almacenaje** nm storage

almacenar [almaθe'nar] /1a/ vt to store, put in storage; (proveerse) to stock up with

almanaque [alma'nake] nm almanac

almeja [al'mexa] nf clam

almendra [al'mendra] nf almond;
almendro nm almond tree

almíbar [al'miβar] nm syrup

almidón [almi'ðon] nm starch

almirante [almi'rante] nm admiral

almohada [almo'aða] nf pillow;
(funda) pillowcase; **almohadilla** nf
cushion; (Tec) pad; (LAm) pincushion

almohadón [almoa'ðon] nm large
pillow

almorranas [almo'rranas] nfpl piles,
haemorrhoids (BRIT), hemorrhoids
(US)

almorzar [almor'θar] /1f, 1l/ vt: ~
una tortilla to have an omelette for
lunch ▷ vi to (have) lunch

almuerzo [al'mwerθo] vb V
almorzar ▷ nm lunch

alocado, -a [alo'kaðo, a] adj crazy

alojamiento [aloxa'mjento] nm
lodging(s) (pl); (viviendas) housing

alojar [alo'xar] /1a/ vt to lodge;
alojarse vr: ~**se en** to stay at; (bala)
to lodge in

alondra [a'londra] nf lark, skylark

alpargata [alpar'yata] nf rope-soled
shoe, espadrille

Alpes ['alpes] nmpl: **los** ~ the Alps

alpinismo [alpi'nismo] nm
mountaineering, climbing; **alpinista**
nmf mountaineer, climber

alpiste [al'piste] nm birdseed

alquilar [alki'lar] /1a/ vt (propietario,
inmuebles) to let, rent (out); (coche) to
hire (out); (TV) to rent (out); (alquilador,
inmuebles, TV) to rent; (coche) to hire;
"se alquila casa" "house to let (BRIT)
o for rent (US)"

alquiler [alki'ler] nm renting; letting;
hiring; (arriendo) rent; hire charge; **de
~** for hire; **de automóviles** car hire

alquimia [al'kimja] nf alchemy

alquitrán [alki'tran] nm tar

alrededor [alreðe'ðor] adv
around, about; **alrededores** nmpl
surroundings; **~ de** around, about;
mirar a su ~ to look (round) about one

alta ['alta] nf (certificate of) discharge

altar [al'tar] nm altar

altavoz [alta'βoθ] nm loudspeaker;
(amplificador) amplifier

alteración [altera'θjon] nf
alteration; (alboroto) disturbance

alterar [alte'rar] /1a/ vt to alter;
to disturb; **alterarse** vr (persona) to
get upset

altercado [alter'kaðo] nm argument

alternar [alter'nar] /1a/ vt to
alternate ▷ vi to alternate; (turnar)
to take turns; **alternarse** vr to alternate;
(turnar) to take turns; **~ con** to mix
with; **alternativo, -a** adj alternative;
(alterno) alternating ▷ nf alternative;
(elección) choice; **alterno, -a** adj
alternate; (Elec) alternating

Alteza [al'teθa] nf (tratamiento)
Highness

altibajos [alti'βaxos] nmpl ups and
downs

altiplanicie [altipla'niθje] nf,
altiplano [alti'plano] nm high
plateau

altisonante [altiso'nante] adj high-
flown, high-sounding

altitud [alti'tuð] nf height; (Aviat,
Geo) altitude

altivo, -a [al'tiβo, a] adj haughty,
arrogant

alto, -a ['alto, a] adj high; (persona)
tall; (sonido) high, sharp; (noble) high,
lofty ▷ nm halt; (Mus) alto; (Geo)
hill ▷ adv (estar) high; (hablar) loud,
loudly ▷ excl halt!; **la pared tiene dos
metros de ~** the wall is two metres
high; **en alta mar** on the high seas;
en voz alta in a loud voice; **las altas
horas de la noche** the small (BRIT)
o wee (US) hours; **en lo ~ de** at the
top of; **pasar por ~** to overlook;
altoparlante nm (LAm) loudspeaker

altura [al'tura] nf height; (Naut)
depth; (Geo) latitude; **la pared tiene
1.80 de ~** the wall is 1 metre 80 (cm)
high; **a estas ~s** at this stage; **a esta
~ del año** at this time of the year

alubia [a'luβja] nf bean; (judía verde) French bean; (judía blanca) cannellini bean

alucinación [aluθina'θjon] nf hallucination

alucinar [aluθi'nar] /1a/ vi to hallucinate ▷ vt to deceive; (fascinar) to fascinate

alud [a'luð] nm avalanche; (fig) flood

aludir [alu'ðir] /3a/ vi: ~ **a** to allude to; **darse por aludido** to take the hint

alumbrado [alum'braðo] nm lighting

alumbrar [alum'brar] /1a/ vt to light (up) ▷ vi (Med) to give birth

aluminio [alu'minjo] nm aluminium (BRIT), aluminum (US)

alumno, -a [a'lumno, a] nm/f pupil, student

alusión [alu'sjon] nf allusion

alusivo, -a [alu'siβo, a] adj allusive

aluvión [alu'βjon] nm (Geo) alluvium; (fig) flood

alverja [al'βerxa] nf (LAM) pea

alza ['alθa] nf rise; (Mil) sight

alzamiento [alθa'mjento] nm (rebelión) rising

alzar [al'θar] /1f/ vt to lift (up); (precio, muro) to raise; (cuello de abrigo) to turn up; (Agr) to gather; (Tip) to gather; **alzarse** to get up, rise; (rebelarse) to revolt; (Com) to go fraudulently bankrupt; (Jur) to appeal

ama ['ama] nf lady of the house; (dueña) owner; (institutriz) governess; (madre adoptiva) foster mother; ~ **de casa** housewife; ~ **de llaves** housekeeper

amabilidad [amaβili'ðað] nf kindness; (simpatía) niceness; **amable** adj kind; nice; **es usted muy amable** that's very kind of you

amaestrado, -a [amaes'traðo, a] adj (en circo etc) performing

amaestrar [amaes'trar] /1a/ vt to train

amago [a'maɣo] nm threat; (gesto) threatening gesture; (Med) symptom

amainar [amai'nar] /1a/ vi (viento) to die down

amamantar [amaman'tar] /1a/ vt to suckle, nurse

amanecer [amane'θer] /2d/ vi to dawn ▷ nm dawn; ~ **afiebrado** to wake up with a fever

amanerado, -a [amane'raðo, a] adj affected

amante [a'mante] adj: ~ **de** fond of ▷ nmf lover

amapola [ama'pola] nf poppy

amar [a'mar] /1a/ vt to love

amargado, -a [amar'ɣaðo, a] adj bitter

amargar [amar'ɣar] /1h/ vt to make bitter; (fig) to embitter; **amargarse** vr to become embittered

amargo, -a [a'marɣo, a] adj bitter

amarillento, -a [amari'ʎento, a] adj yellowish; (tez) sallow

amarillo, -a [ama'riʎo, a] adj, nm yellow

amarra [a'marra] nf (Naut) mooring line; **amarras** nfpl: **soltar ~s** (Naut) to set sail

amarrado, -a [ama'rraðo, a] (LAM) adj (fam) mean, stingy

amarrar [ama'rrar] /1a/ vt to moor; (sujetar) to tie up

amasar [ama'sar] /1a/ vt (masa) to knead; (mezclar) to mix, prepare; (confeccionar) to concoct

amateur [ama'tur] nmf amateur

amazona [ama'θona] nf horsewoman; **Amazonas** nm: **el (río) Amazonas** the Amazon

ámbar ['ambar] nm amber

ambición [ambi'θjon] nf ambition; **ambicionar** /1a/ vt to aspire to; **ambicioso, -a** adj ambitious

ambidextro, -a [ambi'ðekstro, a] adj ambidextrous

ambientación [ambjenta'θjon] nf (Cine, Lit etc) setting; (Radio etc) sound effects pl

ambiente [am'bjente] nm atmosphere; (medio) environment

ambigüedad [ambiɣweˈðað]
nf ambiguity; **ambiguo, -a** adj
ambiguous

ámbito [ˈambito] nm (campo) field;
(fig) scope

ambos, -as [ˈambos, as] adj pl, pron
pl both

ambulancia [ambuˈlanθja] nf
ambulance

ambulante [ambuˈlante] adj
travelling, itinerant

ambulatorio [ambulaˈtorjo] nm
state health-service clinic

amén [aˈmen] excl amen; **~ de** besides

amenaza [ameˈnaθa] nf threat;
amenazar /nf/ vt to threaten ▷ vi:
amenazar con hacer to threaten
to do

ameno, -a [aˈmeno, a] adj pleasant

América [aˈmerika] nf America; **~ del
Norte/del Sur** North/South America;
~ Central/Latina Central/Latin
America; **americano, -a** adj, nm/f
American; Latin o South American

ametralladora [ametraʎaˈðora] nf
machine gun

amigable [amiˈɣaβle] adj friendly

amígdala [aˈmiɣðala] nf tonsil;
amigdalitis nf tonsillitis

amigo, -a [aˈmiɣo, a] adj friendly
▷ nm/f friend; (amante) lover; **ser ~ de**
to like, be fond of

aminorar [aminoˈrar] /1a/ vt to
diminish; (reducir) to reduce; **~ la
marcha** to slow down

amistad [amisˈtað] nf friendship;
amistades nfpl (amigos) friends;
amistoso, -a adj friendly

amnesia [amˈnesja] nf amnesia

amnistía [amnisˈtia] nf amnesty

amo [ˈamo] nm owner; (jefe) boss

amoldar [amolˈdar] /1a/ vt to mould;
(adaptar) to adapt

amonestación [amonestaˈθjon]
nf warning; **amonestaciones** nfpl
marriage banns

amonestar [amonesˈtar] /1a/ vt to
warn; (Rel) to publish the banns of

amontonar [amontoˈnar] /1a/ vt to
collect, pile up; **amontonarse** vr to
crowd together; (acumularse) to pile up

amor [aˈmor] nm love; (amante) lover;
hacer el ~ to make love; **~ propio**
self-respect

amoratado, -a [amoraˈtaðo, a]
adj purple

amordazar [amorðaˈθar] /1f/ vt to
muzzle; (fig) to gag

amorfo, -a [aˈmorfo, a] adj
amorphous, shapeless

amoroso, -a [amoˈroso, a] adj
affectionate, loving

amortiguador [amortiɣwaˈðor]
nm shock absorber; (parachoques)
bumper; **amortiguadores** nmpl (Auto)
suspension sg

amortiguar [amortiˈɣwar] /1i/ vt
to deaden; (ruido) to muffle; (color)
to soften

amotinar [amotiˈnar] /1a/ vt to stir
up, incite (to riot); **amotinarse** vr
to mutiny

amparar [ampaˈrar] /1a/ vt to
protect; **ampararse** vr to seek
protection; (de la lluvia etc) to shelter;
amparo nm help, protection; **al
amparo de** under the protection of

amperio [amˈperjo] nm ampère, amp

ampliación [ampljaˈθjon] nf
enlargement; (extensión) extension

ampliar [amˈpljar] /1c/ vt to enlarge;
to extend

amplificador [amplifikaˈðor] nm
amplifier

amplificar [amplifiˈkar] /1g/ vt
to amplify

amplio, -a [ˈampljo, a] adj
spacious; (falda etc) full; (extenso)
extensive; (ancho) wide; **amplitud** nf
spaciousness; extent; (fig) amplitude

ampolla [amˈpoʎa] nf blister; (Med)
ampoule

amputar [ampuˈtar] /1a/ vt to cut
off, amputate

amueblar [amweˈβlar] /1a/ vt to furnish

anales [aˈnales] nmpl annals

analfabetismo [analfaβeˈtismo] nm illiteracy; **analfabeto, -a** adj, nm/f illiterate

analgésico [analˈxesiko] nm painkiller, analgesic

análisis [aˈnalisis] nm inv analysis

analista [anaˈlista] nmf (gen) analyst

analizar [analiˈθar] /1f/ vt to analyse

analógico, -a [anaˈloxiko, a] adj (Inform) analog; (reloj) analogue (BRIT), analog (US)

análogo, -a [aˈnaloɣo, a] adj analogous, similar

ananá [anaˈna] nm pineapple

anarquía [anarˈkia] nf anarchy; **anarquista** nmf anarchist

anatomía [anatoˈmia] nf anatomy

anca [ˈanka] nf rump, haunch; **ancas** nfpl (fam) behind sg

ancho, -a [ˈantʃo, a] adj wide; (falda) full; (fig) liberal ⊳ nm width; (Ferro) gauge; **le viene muy ~ el cargo** (fig) the job is too much for him; **ponerse ~** to get conceited; **quedarse tan ~** to go on as if nothing had happened; **estar a sus anchas** to be at one's ease

anchoa [anˈtʃoa] nf anchovy

anchura [anˈtʃura] nf width; (amplitud) wideness

anciano, -a [anˈθjano, a] adj old, aged ⊳ nm/f old man/woman ⊳ nm elder

ancla [ˈankla] nf anchor

Andalucía [andaluˈθia] nf Andalusia; **andaluz, -a** adj, nm/f Andalusian

andamiaje [andaˈmjaxe], **andamio** [anˈdamjo] nm scaffold(ing)

andar [anˈdar] /1p/ vt to go, cover, travel ⊳ vi to go, walk, travel; (funcionar) to go, work; (estar) to be ⊳ nm walk, gait, pace; **andarse** vr (irse) to go away or off; **~ a pie/a caballo/en bicicleta** to go on foot/on horseback/by bicycle; **¡anda!**

(sorpresa) go on!; **anda en** o **por los 40** he's about 40; **~ haciendo algo** to be doing sth

andén [anˈden] nm (Ferro) platform; (Naut) quayside; (LAM: acera) pavement (BRIT), sidewalk (US)

Andes [ˈandes] nmpl: **los ~** the Andes

andinismo [andiˈnismo] nm (LAM) mountaineering, climbing

Andorra [anˈdorra] nf Andorra

andrajoso, -a [andraˈxoso, a] adj ragged

anduve [anˈduβe] vb V **andar**

anécdota [aˈnekðota] nf anecdote, story

anegar [aneˈɣar] /1h/ vt to flood; (ahogar) to drown

anemia [aˈnemja] nf anaemia

anestesia [anesˈtesja] nf anaesthetic; **~ general/local** general/local anaesthetic

anexar [anekˈsar] /1a/ vt to annex; (documento) to attach; **anexión** [anekˈsjon] nf annexation; **anexo, -a** adj attached ⊳ nm annexe

anfibio, -a [anˈfiβjo, a] adj amphibious ⊳ nm amphibian

anfiteatro [anfiteˈatro] nm amphitheatre; (Teat) dress circle

anfitrión, -ona [anfiˈtrjon, ona] nm/f host/hostess

ánfora [ˈanfora] nf (cántaro) amphora; (LAM Pol) ballot box

ángel [ˈanxel] nm angel; **~ de la guarda** guardian angel

angina [anˈxina] nf (Med) inflammation of the throat; **~ de pecho** angina; **tener ~s** to have tonsillitis, have a sore throat

anglicano, -a [angliˈkano, a] adj, nm/f Anglican

anglosajón, -ona [anglosaˈxon, ˈxona] adj Anglo-Saxon

anguila [anˈɡila] nf eel

angula [anˈɡula] nf elver, baby eel

ángulo [ˈanɡulo] nm angle; (esquina) corner; (curva) bend

angustia [anˈɡustja] nf anguish

anhelar [ane'lar] /1a/ vt to be eager for; (desear) to long for, desire ▷ vi to pant, gasp; **anhelo** nm eagerness; desire

anidar [ani'ðar] /1a/ vi to nest

anillo [a'niʎo] nm ring; **~ de boda** wedding ring; **~ de compromiso** engagement ring

animación [anima'θjon] nf liveliness; (vitalidad) life; (actividad) bustle

animado, -a [ani'maðo, a] adj lively; (vivaz) animated; **animador, a** nm/f (TV) host(ess), compère ▷ nf (Deporte) cheerleader

animal [ani'mal] adj animal; (fig) stupid ▷ nm animal; (fig) food; (bestia) brute

animar [ani'mar] /1a/ vt (Bio) to animate, give life to; (fig) to liven up, brighten up, cheer up; (estimular) to stimulate; **animarse** vr to cheer up, feel encouraged; (decidirse) to make up one's mind

ánimo ['animo] nm (alma) soul; (mente) mind; (valentía) courage ▷ excl cheer up!

animoso, -a [ani'moso, a] adj brave; (vivo) lively

aniquilar [aniki'lar] /1a/ vt to annihilate, destroy

anís [a'nis] nm aniseed; (licor) anisette

aniversario [aniβer'sarjo] nm anniversary

anoche [a'notʃe] adv last night; **antes de ~** the night before last

anochecer [anotʃe'θer] /2d/ vi to get dark ▷ nm nightfall, dark; **al ~** at nightfall

anodino, -a [ano'ðino, a] adj dull, anodyne

anomalía [anoma'lia] nf anomaly

anonadado, -a [anona'ðaðo, a] adj: **estar ~** to be stunned

anonimato [anoni'mato] nm anonymity

anónimo, -a [a'nonimo, a] adj anonymous; (Com) limited ▷ nm

(carta) anonymous letter; (: maliciosa) poison-pen letter

anormal [anor'mal] adj abnormal

anotación [anota'θjon] nf note; annotation

anotar [ano'tar] /1a/ vt to note down; (comentar) to annotate

ansia ['ansja] nf anxiety; (añoranza) yearning; **ansiar** /1b/ vt to long for

ansiedad [ansje'ðað] nf anxiety

ansioso, -a [an'sjoso, a] adj anxious; (anhelante) eager; **~ de o por algo** greedy for sth

antaño [an'taɲo] adv in years gone by, long ago

Antártico [an'tartiko] nm: **el (océano) ~** the Antarctic (Ocean)

ante ['ante] prep before, in the presence of; (encarado con) faced with ▷ nm (piel) suede; **~ todo** above all

anteanoche [antea'notʃe] adv the night before last

anteayer [antea'jer] adv the day before yesterday

antebrazo [ante'βraθo] nm forearm

antecedente [anteθe'ðente] adj previous ▷ nm antecedent; **antecedentes** nmpl (profesionales) background sg; **~s penales** criminal record

anteceder [anteθe'ðer] /2a/ vt to precede, go before

antecesor, a [anteθe'sor, a] nm/f predecessor

antelación [antela'θjon] nf: **con ~** in advance

antemano [ante'mano]: **de ~** adv beforehand, in advance

antena [an'tena] nf antenna; (de televisión etc) aerial; **~ parabólica** satellite dish

antenoche [ante'notʃe] adv (LAM) the night before last

anteojo [ante'oxo] nm eyeglass; **anteojos** nmpl (esp LAM) glasses, spectacles

antepasados [antepa'saðos] nmpl ancestors

anteponer [antepo'ner] /2q/ vt to place in front; (fig) to prefer

anterior [ante'rjor] adj preceding, previous; **anterioridad** nf: **con anterioridad** a prior to, before

antes ['antes] adv (con anterioridad) before ▷ prep: ~ **de** before ▷ conj: ~ **(de) que** before; ~ **bien** (but) rather; **dos días** ~ two days before o previously; **no quiso venir** ~ she didn't want to come any earlier; **tomo el avión** ~ **que el barco** I take the plane rather than the boat; ~ **de** o **que nada** (en el tiempo) first of all; ~ **que yo** before me; **lo** ~ **posible** as soon as possible; **cuanto** ~ **mejor** the sooner the better

antibalas [anti'βalas] adj inv: **chaleco** ~ bulletproof jacket

antibiótico [anti'βjotiko] nm antibiotic

anticaspa [anti'kaspa] adj inv anti-dandruff cpd

anticipación [antiθipa'θjon] nf anticipation; **con 10 minutos de** ~ 10 minutes early

anticipado, -a [antiθi'paðo, a] adj (in) advance; **por** ~ in advance

anticipar [antiθi'par] /1a/ vt to anticipate; (adelantar) to bring forward; (Com) to advance; **anticiparse** vr: ~**se a su época** to be ahead of one's time

anticipo [anti'θipo] nm (Com) advance

anticonceptivo, -a [antikonθep'tiβo, a] adj, nm contraceptive

anticongelante [antikonxe'lante] nm antifreeze

anticuado, -a [anti'kwaðo, a] adj out-of-date, old-fashioned; (desusado) obsolete

anticuario [anti'kwarjo] nm antique dealer

anticuerpo [anti'kwerpo] nm (Med) antibody

antidepresivo [antiðepre'siβo] nm antidepressant

antidoping [anti'ðopin] adj inv: **control** ~ drugs test

antídoto [an'tiðoto] nm antidote

antiestético, -a [anties'tetiko, a] adj unsightly

antifaz [anti'faθ] nm mask; (velo) veil

antiglobalización [antiɣloβaliθa'θjon] nf anti-globalization; **antiglobalizador, a** adj anti-globalization cpd

antiguamente [antiɣwa'mente] adv formerly; (hace mucho tiempo) long ago

antigüedad [antiɣwe'ðað] nf antiquity; (artículo) antique; (rango) seniority

antiguo, -a [an'tiɣwo, a] adj old, ancient; (que fue) former

Antillas [an'tiʎas] nfpl: **las** ~ the West Indies

antílope [an'tilope] nm antelope

antinatural [antinatu'ral] adj unnatural

antipatía [antipa'tia] nf antipathy, dislike; **antipático, -a** adj disagreeable, unpleasant

antirrobo [anti'rroβo] adj inv (alarma etc) anti-theft

antisemita [antise'mita] adj anti-Semitic ▷ nmf anti-Semite

antiséptico, -a [anti'septiko, a] adj antiseptic ▷ nm antiseptic

antisistema [antisis'tema] adj inv anticapitalist

antivirus [anti'birus] nm inv (Inform) antivirus program

antojarse [anto'xarse] /1a/ vr (desear): **se me antoja comprarlo** I have a mind to buy it; (pensar): **se me antoja que ...** I have a feeling that ...

antojo [an'toxo] nm caprice, whim; (rosa) birthmark; (lunar) mole

antología [antolo'xia] nf anthology

antorcha [an'tortʃa] nf torch

antro ['antro] nm cavern

antropología [antropolo'xia] nf anthropology

anual [a'nwal] adj annual

anuario [a'nwarjo] nm yearbook

anublado, -a adj overcast

anulación [anula'θjon] nf (de un matrimonio) annulment; (cancelación) cancellation

anular [anu'lar] /1a/ vt (contrato) to annul, cancel; (suscripción) to cancel; (ley) to repeal ▷ nm ring finger

anunciar [anun'θjar] /1b/ vt to announce; (proclamar) to proclaim; (Com) to advertise

anuncio [a'nunθjo] nm announcement; (señal) sign; (Com) advertisement; (cartel) poster

anzuelo [an'θwelo] nm hook; (para pescar) fish hook

añadidura [anaði'ðura] nf addition, extra; **por ~** besides, in addition

añadir [aɲa'ðir] /3a/ vt to add

añejo, -a [a'ɲexo, a] adj old; (vino) mature

añicos [a'ɲikos] nmpl: **hacer ~** to smash, shatter

año [ˈaɲo] nm year; **¡Feliz A~ Nuevo!** Happy New Year!; **tener 15 ~s** to be 15 (years old); **los ~s 80** the eighties; **~ bisiesto/escolar/fiscal/sabático** leap/school/tax/sabbatical year; **el ~ que viene** next year

añoranza [aɲo'ranθa] nf nostalgia; (anhelo) longing

apa ['apa] excl (LAM) goodness me!, good gracious!

apabullar [apaβuˈʎar] /1a/ vt to crush

apacible [apa'θiβle] adj gentle, mild

apaciguar [apaθi'ɣwar] /1i/ vt to pacify, calm (down)

apadrinar [apaðri'nar] /1a/ vt to sponsor, support; (Rel: niño) to be godfather to

apagado, -a [apa'ɣaðo, a] adj (volcán) extinct; (color) dull; (voz) quiet; (sonido) muted, muffled; (persona: apático) listless; **estar ~** (fuego, luz) to be out; (radio, TV etc) to be off

apagar [apa'ɣar] /1h/ vt to put out; (sonido) to silence, muffle; (sed) to quench; (Elec, Radio, TV) to turn off; (Inform) to toggle off

apagón [apa'ɣon] nm blackout, power cut

apalabrar [apala'βrar] /1a/ vt to agree to; (obrero) to engage

apalear [apale'ar] /1a/ vt to beat, thrash

apantallar [apanta'ʎar] /1a/ vt (LAM) to impress

apañar [apa'ɲar] /1a/ vt to pick up; (asir) to take hold of, grasp; (reparar) to mend, patch up; **apañarse** vr to manage, get along

apapachar [apapa'tʃar] /1a/ vt (LAM fam) to cuddle, hug

aparador [apara'ðor] nm sideboard; (LAM: escaparate) shop window

aparato [apa'rato] nm apparatus; (máquina) machine; (doméstico) appliance; (boato) ostentation; **al ~** (Telec) speaking; **~ digestivo** digestive system; **aparatoso, -a** adj showy, ostentatious

aparcamiento [aparka'mjento] nm car park (BRIT), parking lot (US)

aparcar [apar'kar] /1g/ vt, vi to park

aparear [apare'ar] /1a/ vt (objetos) to pair, match; (animales) to mate; **aparearse** vr to form a pair; to mate

aparecer [apare'θer] /2d/ vi to appear; **aparecerse** vr to appear

aparejador, a [aparexa'ðor, a] nm/f (Arq) quantity surveyor

aparejo [apa'rexo] nm harness; (Naut) rigging; (de poleas) block and tackle

aparentar [aparen'tar] /1a/ vt (edad) to look like; (fingir): **~ tristeza** to pretend to be sad

aparente [apa'rente] adj apparent; (adecuado) suitable

aparezca etc vb V **aparecer**

aparición [apari'θjon] nf appearance; (de libro) publication; (de fantasma) apparition

apariencia [apa'rjenθja] nf (outward) appearance; **en ~** outwardly, seemingly

apartado, -a [apar'taðo, a] adj separate; (lejano) remote ▷ nm (tipográfico) paragraph; **~ de correos** (ESP), **~ postal** (BRIT) post office box

apartamento [aparta'mento] nm apartment, flat (BRIT)

apartar [apar'tar] /1a/ vt to separate; (quitar) to remove; **apartarse** vr to separate, part; (irse) to move away; (mantenerse aparte) to keep away

aparte [a'parte] adv (separadamente) separately; (además) besides ▷ nm aside; (tipográfico) new paragraph

aparthotel [aparto'tel] nm serviced apartments

apasionado, -a [apasjo'naðo, a] adj passionate

apasionar [apasjo'nar] /1a/ vt to excite; **apasionarse** vr to get excited; **le apasiona el fútbol** she's crazy about football

apatía [apa'tia] nf apathy

apático, -a [a'patiko, a] adj apathetic

Apdo. nm abr (= Apartado (de Correos)) P.O. Box

apeadero [apea'ðero] nm halt, stopping place

apearse [ape'arse] /1a/ vr (jinete) to dismount; (bajarse) to get down o out; (de coche) to get out

apechugar [apetʃu'ɣar] /1h/ vi: **~ con algo** to face up to sth

apegarse [ape'ɣarse] /1h/ vr: **~ a** to become attached to; **apego** nm attachment, devotion

apelar [ape'lar] /1a/ vi to appeal; **~ a** (fig) to resort to

apellidar [apeʎi'ðar] /1a/ vt to call, name; **apellidarse** vr: **se apellida Pérez** her (sur)name's Pérez

apellido [ape'ʎiðo] nm surname

apenar [ape'nar] /1a/ vt to grieve, trouble; (LAM: avergonzar) to embarrass; **apenarse** vr to grieve; (LAM: avergonzarse) to be embarrassed

apenas [a'penas] adv scarcely, hardly ▷ conj as soon as, no sooner

apéndice [a'pendiθe] nm appendix; **apendicitis** nf appendicitis

aperitivo [aperi'tiβo] nm (bebida) aperitif; (comida) appetizer

apertura [aper'tura] /1a/ vt to infect ▷ vi: **~ (a)** to stink (of)

apestar [apes'tar] /2d/ vt: **¿te apetece una tortilla?** do you fancy an omelette?; **apetecible** adj desirable; (comida) appetizing

apetito [ape'tito] nm appetite; **apetitoso, -a** adj appetizing; (fig) tempting

apiadarse [apja'ðarse] /1a/ vr: **~ de** to take pity on

ápice ['apiθe] nm whit, iota

apilar [api'lar] /1a/ vt to pile o heap up

apiñar [api'nar] /1a/ vt to crowd; **apiñarse** vr to crowd o press together

apio ['apjo] nm celery

apisonadora [apisona'ðora] nf steamroller

aplacar [apla'kar] /1g/ vt to placate

aplastante [aplas'tante] adj overwhelming; (lógica) compelling

aplastar [aplas'tar] /1a/ vt to squash (flat); (fig) to crush

aplaudir [aplau'ðir] /3a/ vt to applaud

aplauso [a'plauso] nm applause; (fig) approval, acclaim

aplazamiento [aplaθa'mjento] nm postponement

aplazar [apla'θar] /1f/ vt to postpone, defer

aplicación [aplika'θjon] nf application; (para móvil, internet) app; (esfuerzo) effort

aplicado, -a [apli'kaðo, a] adj diligent, hard-working

aplicar [apli'kar] /1g/ vt (ejecutar) to apply; **aplicarse** vr to apply o.s.

aplique etc [a'plike] vb V **aplicar** ▷ nm wall light o lamp

aplomo [a'plomo] *nm* aplomb, self-assurance

apodar [apo'ðar] /1a/ *vt* to nickname

apoderado [apoðe'raðo] *nm* agent, representative

apoderar [apoðe'rar] /1a/ *vt* to authorize; **apoderarse**: **~se de** to take possession of

apodo [a'poðo] *nm* nickname

apogeo [apo'xeo] *nm* peak, summit

apoquinar [apoki'nar] /1a/ *vt* (*fam*) to cough up, fork out

aporrear [aporre'ar] /1a/ *vt* to beat (up)

aportar [apor'tar] /1a/ *vt* to contribute ▷ *vi* to reach port; **aportarse** *vr* (*LAM: llegar*) to arrive, come

aposta [a'posta] *adv* deliberately, on purpose

apostar [apos'tar] /1a, 1l/ *vt* to bet, stake; (*tropas etc*) to station, post ▷ *vi* to bet

apóstol [a'postol] *nm* apostle

apóstrofo [a'postrofo] *nm* apostrophe

apoyar [apo'jar] /1a/ *vt* to lean, rest; (*fig*) to support, back; **apoyarse** *vr*: **~se en** to lean on; **apoyo** *nm* support, backing

apreciable [apre'θjaβle] *adj* considerable; (*fig*) esteemed

apreciar [apre'θjar] /1b/ *vt* to evaluate, assess; (*Com*) to appreciate, value; (*persona*) to respect; (*tamaño*) to gauge, assess; (*detalles*) to notice

aprecio [a'preθjo] *nm* valuation, estimate; (*fig*) appreciation

aprehender [apreen'der] /2a/ *vt* to apprehend, detain

apremio [a'premjo] *nm* urgency

aprender [apren'der] /2a/ *vt*, *vi* to learn; **aprenderse** *vr*: **~se algo de memoria** to learn sth (off) by heart

aprendiz, a [apren'diθ, a] *nm/f* apprentice; (*principiante*) learner; **aprendizaje** *nm* apprenticeship

aprensión [apren'sjon] *nm* apprehension, fear; **aprensivo, -a** *adj* apprehensive

apresar [apre'sar] /1a/ *vt* to seize; (*capturar*) to capture

apresurado, -a [apresu'raðo, a] *adj* hurried, hasty

apresurar [apresu'rar] /1a/ *vt* to hurry, accelerate; **apresurarse** *vr* to hurry, make haste

apretado, -a [apre'taðo, a] *adj* tight; (*escritura*) cramped

apretar [apre'tar] /1j/ *vt* to squeeze; (*Tec*) to tighten; (*presionar*) to press together, pack ▷ *vi* to be too tight

apretón [apre'ton] *nm* squeeze; **~ de manos** handshake

aprieto [a'prjeto] *nm* squeeze; (*dificultad*) difficulty; **estar en un ~** to be in a fix

aprisa [a'prisa] *adv* quickly, hurriedly

aprisionar [aprisjo'nar] /1a/ *vt* to imprison

aprobación [aproβa'θjon] *nf* approval

aprobar [apro'βar] /1l/ *vt* to approve (of); (*examen, materia*) to pass ▷ *vi* to pass

apropiado, -a [apro'pjaðo, a] *adj* appropriate, suitable

apropiarse [apro'pjarse] /1b/ *vr*: **~ de** to appropriate

aprovechado, -a [aproβe'tʃaðo, a] *adj* industrious, hardworking; (*económico*) thrifty; (*pey*) unscrupulous

aprovechar [aproβe'tʃar] /1a/ *vt* to use; (*explotar*) to exploit; (*experiencia*) to profit from; (*oferta, oportunidad*) to take advantage of ▷ *vi* to progress, improve; **aprovecharse** *vr*: **~se de** to make use of; (*pey*) to take advantage of; **¡que aproveche!** enjoy your meal!

aproximación [aproksima'θjon] *nf* approximation; (*de lotería*) consolation prize

aproximadamente [aproksimaða'mente] *adv* approximately

aproximar [aproksi'mar] /1a/ vt to bring nearer, approach; **aproximarse** vr to come near, approach

apruebe etc vb V **aprobar**

aptitud [apti'tuð] nf aptitude

apto, -a ['apto, a] adj: **~ (para)** suitable (for)

apuesto, -a [a'pwesto, a] adj neat, elegant ▷ nf bet, wager

apuntar [apun'tar] /1a/ vt (con arma) to aim at; (con dedo) to point at o to; (anotar) to note (down); (Teat) to prompt; **apuntarse** vr (Deporte: tanto, victoria) to score; (Escol) to enrol

No confundir apuntar con la palabra inglesa appoint.

apunte [a'punte] nm note

apuñalar [apuɲa'lar] /1a/ vt to stab

apurado, -a [apu'raðo, a] adj needy; (difícil) difficult; (peligroso) dangerous; (LAM: con prisa) hurried, rushed

apurar [apu'rar] /1a/ vt (agotar) to drain; (recursos) to use up; (molestar) to annoy; **apurarse** vr (preocuparse) to worry; (esp LAM: darse prisa) to hurry

apuro [a'puro] nm (aprieto) fix, jam; (escasez) want, hardship; (vergüenza) embarrassment; (LAM: prisa) haste, urgency

aquejado, -a [ake'xaðo, a] adj: **~ de** (Med) afflicted by

aquel, aquella, aquellos, -as [a'kel, a'keʎa, a'keʎos, -as] adj that, those pl ▷ pron that (one), those (ones) pl

aquél, aquélla, aquéllos, -as [a'kel, a'keʎa, a'keʎos, -as] pron that (one), those (ones) pl

aquello [a'keʎo] pron that, that business

aquí [a'ki] adv (lugar) here; (tiempo) now; **~ arriba** up here; **~ mismo** right here; **~ yace** here lies; **de ~ a siete días** a week from now

ara ['ara] nf: **en ~s de** for the sake of

árabe ['araβe] adj Arab ▷ nmf Arab ▷ nm (Ling) Arabic

Arabia [a'raβja] nf Arabia; **~ Saudí** o **Saudita** Saudi Arabia

arado [a'raðo] nm plough

Aragón [ara'ɣon] nm Aragon; **aragonés, -esa** adj, nm/f Aragonese

arancel [aran'θel] nm tariff, duty

arandela [aran'dela] nf (Tec) washer

araña [a'raɲa] nf (Zool) spider; (lámpara) chandelier

arañar [ara'ɲar] /1a/ vt to scratch

arañazo [ara'ɲaθo] nm scratch

arbitrar [arβi'trar] /1a/ vt to arbitrate in; (Deporte) to referee ▷ vi to arbitrate

arbitrario, -a [arβi'trarjo, a] adj arbitrary

árbitro ['arβitro] nm arbitrator; (Deporte) referee; (Tenis) umpire

árbol ['arβol] nm (Bot) tree; (Naut) mast; (Tec) axle, shaft; **~ de Navidad** Christmas tree

arboleda [arβo'leða] nf grove, plantation

arbusto [ar'βusto] nm bush, shrub

arca ['arka] nf chest, box

arcada [ar'kaða] nf arcade; (de puente) arch, span; **arcadas** nfpl (náuseas) retching sg

arcaico, -a [ar'kaiko, a] adj archaic

arce ['arθe] nm maple tree

arcén [ar'θen] nm (de autopista) hard shoulder; (de carretera) verge

archipiélago [artʃi'pjelaɣo] nm archipelago

archivador [artʃiβa'ðor] nm filing cabinet

archivar [artʃi'βar] /1a/ vt to file (away); **archivo** nm archive(s) (pl); (Inform) file; **archivo adjunto** (Inform) attachment; **archivo de seguridad** (Inform) backup file

arcilla [ar'θiʎa] nf clay

arco ['arko] nm arch; (Mat) arc; (Mil, Mus) bow; **~ iris** rainbow

arder [ar'ðer] /2a/ vi to burn; **estar que arde** (persona) to fume

ardid [ar'ðið] nm ploy, trick

ardiente [ar'ðjente] adj ardent

ardilla [ar'ðiʎa] nf squirrel

ardor [ar'ðor] nm (calor) heat; (fig) ardour; **~ de estómago** heartburn

arduo, -a [ˈarðwo, a] *adj* arduous

área [ˈarea] *nf* area; (*Deporte*) penalty area

arena [aˈrena] *nf* sand; (*de una lucha*) arena; **arenal** *nm* (*terreno arenoso*) sandy area

arenisca [areˈniska] *nf* sandstone; (*cascajo*) grit

arenoso, -a [areˈnoso, a] *adj* sandy

arenque [aˈrenke] *nm* herring

arete [aˈrete] *nm* (*LAM*) earring

Argel [arˈxel] *n* Algiers

Argelia [arˈxelja] *nf* Algeria; **argelino, -a** *adj, nm/f* Algerian

Argentina [arxenˈtina] *nf*: **(la) ~** Argentina

argentino, -a [arxenˈtino, a] *adj* Argentinian; (*de plata*) silvery ▷ *nm/f* Argentinian

argolla [arˈɣoʎa] *nf* (*large*) ring

argot [arˈɣo] *nm* slang

argucia [arˈɣuθja] *nf* subtlety, sophistry

argumentar [arɣumenˈtar] /1a/ *vt, vi* to argue

argumento [arɣuˈmento] *nm* argument; (*razonamiento*) reasoning; (*de novela etc*) plot; (*Cine, TV*) storyline

aria [ˈarja] *nf* aria

aridez [ariˈðeθ] *nf* aridity, dryness

árido, -a [ˈariðo, a] *adj* arid, dry

Aries [ˈarjes] *nm* Aries

arisco, -a [aˈrisko, a] *adj* surly; (*insociable*) unsociable

aristócrata [arisˈtokrata] *nmf* aristocrat

arma [ˈarma] *nf* arm; **armas** *nfpl* arms; **~ blanca** blade, knife; **~ de doble filo** double-edged sword; **~ de fuego** firearm; **~s de destrucción masiva** weapons of mass destruction

armada [arˈmaða] *nf* armada; (*flota*) fleet

armadillo [armaˈðiʎo] *nm* armadillo

armado, -a [arˈmaðo, a] *adj* armed; (*Tec*) reinforced

armadura [armaˈðura] *nf* (*Mil*) armour; (*Tec*) framework; (*Zool*) skeleton; (*Física*) armature

armamento [armaˈmento] *nm* armament; (*Naut*) fitting-out

armar [arˈmar] /1a/ *vt* (*soldado*) to arm; (*máquina*) to assemble; (*navío*) to fit out; **~la, ~ un lío** to start a row, kick up a fuss

armario [arˈmarjo] *nm* wardrobe; (*de cocina, baño*) cupboard; **~ empotrado** built-in cupboard

armatoste [armaˈtoste] *nm* (*mueble*) monstrosity; (*máquina*) contraption

armazón [armaˈθon] *nm o f* body, chassis; (*de mueble etc*) frame; (*Arq*) skeleton

armiño [arˈmiɲo] *nm* stoat; (*piel*) ermine

armisticio [armisˈtiθjo] *nm* armistice

armonía [armoˈnia] *nf* harmony

armónica [arˈmonika] *nf* harmonica

armonizar [armoniˈθar] /1f/ *vt* to harmonize; (*diferencias*) to reconcile

aro [ˈaro] *nm* ring; (*tejo*) quoit; (*LAM: pendiente*) earring

aroma [aˈroma] *nm* aroma; **aromaterapia** *nf* aromatherapy; **aromático, -a** *adj* aromatic

arpa [ˈarpa] *nf* harp

arpía [arˈpia] *nf* shrew

arpón [arˈpon] *nm* harpoon

arqueología [arkeoloˈxia] *nf* archaeology; **arqueólogo, -a** *nm/f* archaeologist

arquetipo [arkeˈtipo] *nm* archetype

arquitecto [arkiˈtekto] *nm/f* architect; **arquitectura** *nf* architecture

arrabal [arraˈβal] *nm* suburb; (*LAM*) slum; **arrabales** *nmpl* (*afueras*) outskirts

arraigar [arraiˈɣar] /1h/ *vi* to take root

arrancar [arranˈkar] /1g/ *vt* (*sacar*) to extract, pull out; (*arrebatar*) to snatch (away); (*Inform*) to boot; (*fig*) to extract ▷ *vi* (*Auto, máquina*) to start; (*ponerse en marcha*) to get going; **~ de** to stem from

arranque *etc* [aˈrranke] *vb V* **arrancar** ▷ *nm* sudden start; (*Auto*) start; (*fig*) fit, outburst

arrasar [arra'sar] /1a/ vt (aplanar) to level, flatten; (destruir) to demolish

arrastrar [arras'trar] /1a/ vt to drag (along); (fig) to drag down, degrade; (agua, viento) to carry away ▷ vi to drag, trail on the ground; **arrastrarse** vr to crawl; (fig) to grovel; **llevar algo arrastrado** to drag sth along

arrear [arre'ar] /1a/ vt to drive on, urge on ▷ vi to hurry along

arrebatar [arreβa'tar] /1a/ vt to snatch (away), seize; (fig) to captivate

arrebato [arre'βato] nm fit of rage, fury; (éxtasis) rapture

arrecife [arre'θife] nm reef

arreglado, -a [arre'ɣlaðo, a] adj (ordenado) neat, orderly; (moderado) moderate, reasonable

arreglar [arre'ɣlar] /1a/ vt (poner orden) to tidy up; (algo roto) to fix, repair; (problema) to solve; **arreglarse** vr to reach an understanding; **arreglárselas** (fam) to get by, manage

arreglo [arre'ɣlo] nm settlement; (orden) order; (acuerdo) agreement; (Mus) arrangement, setting

arremangar [arreman'gar] /1h/ vt to roll up, turn up; **arremangarse** vr to roll up one's sleeves

arremeter [arreme'ter] /2a/ vi: ~ **contra algn** to attack sb

arrendamiento [arrenda'mjento] nm letting; (el alquilar) hiring; (contrato) lease; (alquiler) rent; **arrendar** /1j/ vt to let; to lease; to rent; **arrendatario, -a** nm/f tenant

arreos [a'rreos] nmpl (de caballo) harness sg, trappings

arrepentimiento [arrepenti'mjento] nm regret, repentance

arrepentirse [arrepen'tirse] /3i/ vr to repent; ~ **de (haber hecho) algo** to regret (doing) sth

arresto [a'rresto] nm arrest; (Mil) detention; (audacia) boldness, daring; ~ **domiciliario** house arrest

arriar [a'rrjar] /1c/ vt (velas) to haul down; (bandera) to lower, strike; (un cable) to pay out

PALABRA CLAVE

arriba [a'rriβa] adv 1 (posición) above; **desde arriba** from above; **arriba del todo** at the very top, right on top; **Juan está arriba** Juan is upstairs; **lo arriba mencionado** the aforementioned

2 (dirección): **calle arriba** up the street

3: **de arriba abajo** from top to bottom; **mirar a algn de arriba abajo** to look sb up and down

4: **para arriba: de 50 euros para arriba** from 50 euros up(wards)

▷ adj: **de arriba: el piso de arriba** the upstairs flat (BRIT) o apartment; **la parte de arriba** the top o upper part

▷ prep: **arriba de** (LAM: por encima de) above; **arriba de 200 dólares** more than 200 dollars

▷ excl: **¡arriba!** up!; **¡manos arriba!** hands up!; **¡arriba España!** long live Spain!

arribar [arri'βar] /1a/ vi to put into port; (llegar) to arrive

arriendo etc [a'rrjendo] vb V **arrendar** ▷ nm = **arrendamiento**

arriesgado, -a [arrjes'ɣaðo, a] adj (peligroso) risky; (audaz) bold, daring

arriesgar [arrjes'ɣar] /1h/ vt to risk; (poner en peligro) to endanger; **arriesgarse** vr to take a risk

arrimar [arri'mar] /1a/ vt (acercar) to bring close; (poner de lado) to set aside; **arrimarse** vr to come close o closer; ~**se a** to lean on

arrinconar [arrinko'nar] /1a/ vt (colocar) to put in a corner; (enemigo) to corner; (fig) to put on one side; (abandonar) to push aside

arroba [a'rroβa] nf (en dirección electrónica) at sign, @

arrodillarse [arroði'ʎarse] /1a/ vr to kneel (down)

arrogante [arro'ɣante] adj arrogant

arrojar [arro'xar] /1a/ vt to throw, hurl; (humo) to emit, give out; (Com) to yield, produce; **arrojarse** vr to throw o hurl o.s.

arrojo [a'rroxo] nm daring

arrollador, a [arroʎa'ðor, a] adj overwhelming

arrollar [arro'ʎar] /1a/ vt (Auto) to run over; (Deporte) to crush

arropar [arro'par] /1a/ vt to cover (up), wrap up; **arroparse** vr to wrap o.s. up

arroyo [a'rrojo] nm stream; (de la calle) gutter

arroz [a'rroθ] nm rice; **~ con leche** rice pudding

arruga [a'rruɣa] nf (de cara) wrinkle; (de vestido) crease; **arrugar** /1h/ vt to wrinkle; to crease; **arrugarse** vr to get creased

arruinar [arrwi'nar] /1a/ vt to ruin, wreck; **arruinarse** vr to be ruined

arsenal [arse'nal] nm naval dockyard; (Mil) arsenal

arte ['arte] nm (gen m en sg, f en pl) art; (maña) skill, guile; **artes** nfpl arts; **Bellas A~s** Fine Art sg

artefacto [arte'fakto] nm appliance

arteria [ar'terja] nf artery

artesanía [artesa'nia] nf craftsmanship; (artículos) handicrafts pl; **artesano, a** nm/f artisan, craftsman/woman

ártico, -a ['artiko, a] adj Arctic ▷ nm: **el (océano) Á~** the Arctic (Ocean)

articulación [artikula'θjon] nf articulation; (Med, Tec) joint

artículo [ar'tikulo] nm article; (cosa) thing, article; **artículos** nmpl goods; **~s de escritorio** stationery

artífice [ar'tifiθe] nmf (fig) architect

artificial [artifi'θjal] adj artificial

artillería [artiʎe'ria] nf artillery

artilugio [arti'luxjo] nm gadget

artimaña [arti'maɲa] nf trap, snare; (astucia) cunning

artista [ar'tista] nmf (pintor) artist, painter; (Teat) artist, artiste; **~ de cine** film actor/actress; **artístico, -a** adj artistic

artritis [ar'tritis] nf arthritis

arveja [ar'βexa] nf (LAM) pea

arzobispo [arθo'βispo] nm archbishop

as [as] nm ace

asa ['asa] nf handle; (fig) lever

asado [a'saðo] nm roast (meat); (LAM: barbacoa) barbecue

○ **ASADO**
○
○ Traditional Latin American
○ barbecues, especially in the River
○ Plate area, are celebrated in the
○ open air around a large grill which is
○ used to grill mainly beef and various
○ kinds of spicy pork sausage. They
○ are usually very common during
○ the summer and can go on for
○ several days.

asador [asa'ðor] nm spit

asadura, asaduras [asa'ðura(s)] nf, nfpl entrails or offal, offal sg

asalariado, a [asala'rjaðo, a] adj paid, salaried ▷ nm/f wage earner

asaltar [asal'tar] /1a/ vt to attack, assault; (fig) to assail; **asalto** nm attack, assault; (Deporte) round

asamblea [asam'blea] nf assembly; (reunión) meeting

asar [a'sar] /1a/ vt to roast

ascendencia [asθen'denθja] nf ancestry; (LAM: influencia) ascendancy; **de ~ francesa** of French origin

ascender [asθen'der] /2g/ vi (subir) to ascend, rise; (ser promovido) to gain promotion ▷ vt to promote; **~ a** to amount to; **ascendiente** nm influence ▷ nmf ancestor

ascensión [asθen'sjon] nf ascent; **la A~** the Ascension

ascenso [as'θenso] nm ascent; (promoción) promotion

ascensor [asθen'sor] nm lift (BRIT), elevator (US)

asco ['asko] nm: **el ajo me da ~** I hate o loathe garlic; **estar hecho un ~** to be filthy; **¡qué ~!** how revolting o disgusting!

ascua ['askwa] nf ember

aseado, -a [ase'aðo, a] adj clean; (arreglado) tidy; (pulcro) smart

asear [ase'ar] /1a/ vt (lavar) to wash; (ordenar) to tidy (up)

asediar [ase'ðjar] /1b/ vt (Mil) to besiege, lay siege to; (fig) to chase, pester; **asedio** nm siege; (Com) run

asegurado, a [aseɣura'ðo, a] adj insured

asegurador, -a [aseɣura'ðor, a] nm/f insurer

asegurar [aseɣu'rar] /1a/ vt (consolidar) to secure, fasten; (dar garantía de) to guarantee; (preservar) to safeguard; (afirmar, dar por cierto) to assure, affirm; (tranquilizar) to reassure; (hacer un seguro) to insure; **asegurarse** vr to assure o.s., make sure

asemejarse [aseme'xarse] /1a/ vr to be alike; **~ a** to be like, resemble

asentado, -a [asen'taðo, a] adj established, settled

asentar [asen'tar] /1j/ vt (sentar) to seat, sit down; (poner) to place, establish; (alisar) to level, smooth down o out; (anotar) to note down ▷ vi to be suitable, suit

asentir [asen'tir] /3i/ vi to assent, agree; **~ con la cabeza** to nod (one's head)

aseo [a'seo] nm cleanliness; **aseos** nmpl toilet sg (BRIT), cloakroom sg (BRIT), restroom sg (US)

aséptico, -a [a'septiko, a] adj germ-free, free from infection

asequible [ase'kiβle] adj (precio) reasonable; (meta) attainable; (persona) approachable

asesinar [asesi'nar] /1a/ vt to murder; (Pol) to assassinate; **asesinato** nm murder; assassination

asesino, -a [ase'sino, a] nm/f murderer, killer; (Pol) assassin

asesor, a [ase'sor, a] nm/f adviser, consultant; **asesorar** /1a/ vt (Jur) to advise, give legal advice to; (Com) to act as consultant to; **asesorarse** vr: **asesorarse con** o **de** to take advice from, consult; **asesoría** nf (cargo) consultancy; (oficina) consultant's office

asestar [ases'tar] /1a/ vt (golpe) to deal

asfalto [as'falto] nm asphalt

asfixia [as'fiksja] nf asphyxia, suffocation; **asfixiar** /1b/ vt to asphyxiate, suffocate; **asfixiarse** vr to be asphyxiated, suffocate

así [a'si] adv (de esta manera) in this way, like this, thus; (aunque) although; (tan pronto como) as soon as; **~ que** so; **~ como** as well as; **~ y todo** even so; **¿no es ~?** isn't it?, didn't you? etc; **~ de grande** this big

Asia ['asja] nf Asia; **asiático, -a** adj, nm/f Asian, Asiatic

asiduo, -a [a'siðwo, a] adj assiduous; (frecuente) frequent ▷ nm/f regular (customer)

asiento [a'sjento] nm (mueble) seat, chair; (de coche, en tribunal etc) seat; (localidad) seat, place; (fundamento) site; **~ delantero/trasero** front/back seat

asignación [asiɣna'θjon] nf (atribución) assignment; (reparto) allocation; (sueldo) salary; (Com) allowance; **~ (semanal)** (weekly) pocket money

asignar [asiɣ'nar] /1a/ vt to assign, allocate

asignatura [asiɣna'tura] nf subject; (curso) course

asilo [a'silo] nm (refugio) asylum, refuge; (establecimiento) home, institution; **~ político** political asylum

asimilar [asimi'lar] /1a/ vt to assimilate

asimismo [asiˈmismo] *adv* in the same way, likewise

asistencia [asisˈtenθja] *nf* audience; (Med) attendance; (ayuda) assistance; **~ en carretera** roadside assistance; **asistente, -a** *nm/f* assistant; **los asistentes** those present; **asistente social** social worker

asistido, -a [asisˈtiðo, a] *adj*: **~ por ordenador** computer-assisted

asistir [asisˈtir] /3a/ *vt* to assist, help ▷ *vi*: **~ a** to attend, be present at

asma [ˈasma] *nf* asthma

asno [ˈasno] *nm* donkey; (fig) ass

asociación [asoθjaˈθjon] *nf* association; (Com) partnership; **asociado, -a** *adj* associate ▷ *nm/f* associate; (Com) partner

asociar [asoˈθjar] /1b/ *vt* to associate

asomar [asoˈmar] /1a/ *vt* to show, stick out ▷ *vi* to appear; **asomarse** *vr* to appear, show up; **~ la cabeza por la ventana** to put one's head out of the window

asombrar [asomˈbrar] /1a/ *vt* to amaze, astonish; **asombrarse** *vr*: **~se (de)** (sorprenderse) to be amazed (at); (asustarse) to be frightened (at); **asombro** *nm* amazement, astonishment; (susto) fright; **asombroso, -a** *adj* amazing

asomo [aˈsomo] *nm* hint, sign

aspa [ˈaspa] *nf* (cruz) cross; (de molino) sail; **en ~** X-shaped

aspaviento [aspaˈβjento] *nm* exaggerated display of feeling; (fam) fuss

aspecto [asˈpekto] *nm* (apariencia) look, appearance; (fig) aspect

áspero, -a [ˈaspero, a] *adj* (al tacto) rough; (al gusto) sharp, sour; (voz) harsh

aspersión [asperˈsjon] *nf* sprinkling

aspiración [aspiraˈθjon] *nf* breath, inhalation; (Mus) short pause; **aspiraciones** *nfpl* (ambiciones) aspirations

aspirador [aspiraˈðor] *nm* = **aspiradora**

aspiradora [aspiraˈðora] *nf* vacuum cleaner, Hoover®

aspirante [aspiˈrante] *nmf* (candidato) candidate; (Deporte) contender

aspirar [aspiˈrar] /1a/ *vt* to breathe in ▷ *vi*: **~ a** to aspire to

aspirina [aspiˈrina] *nf* aspirin

asqueroso, -a [askeˈroso, a] *adj* disgusting, sickening

asta [ˈasta] *nf* lance; (arpón) spear; (mango) shaft, handle; (Zool) horn; **a media ~** at half mast

asterisco [asteˈrisko] *nm* asterisk

astilla [asˈtiʎa] *nf* splinter; (pedacito) chip; **astillas** *nfpl* (leña) firewood *sg*

astillero [astiˈʎero] *nm* shipyard

astro [ˈastro] *nm* star

astrología [astroloˈxia] *nf* astrology; **astrólogo, -a** *nm/f* astrologer

astronauta [astroˈnauta] *nmf* astronaut

astronomía [astronoˈmia] *nf* astronomy

astucia [asˈtuθja] *nf* astuteness; (destreza) clever trick

asturiano, -a [astuˈrjano, a] *adj, nm/f* Asturian

astuto, -a [asˈtuto, a] *adj* astute; (taimado) cunning

asumir [asuˈmir] /3a/ *vt* to assume

asunción [asunˈθjon] *nf* assumption; (Rel): **A~** Assumption

asunto [aˈsunto] *nm* (tema) matter, subject; (negocio) business

asustar [asusˈtar] /1a/ *vt* to frighten; **asustarse** *vr* to be/become frightened

atacar [ataˈkar] /1g/ *vt* to attack

atadura [ataˈðura] *nf* bond, tie

atajar [ataˈxar] /1a/ *vt* (enfermedad, mal) to stop ▷ *vi* (persona) to take a short cut

atajo [aˈtaxo] *nm* short cut

atañer [ataˈɲer] *vi*: **~ a** to concern

ataque *etc* [aˈtake] *vb* V **atacar**; attack; **~ cardíaco** heart attack

atar [aˈtar] /1a/ *vt* to tie, tie u

atarantado, -a [ataran'taðo, a] *adj* (*LAM: aturdido*) dazed

atardecer [atarðe'θer] /2d/ *vi* to get dark ▷ *nm* evening; (*crepúsculo*) dusk

atareado, -a [atare'aðo, a] *adj* busy

atascar [atas'kar] /1g/ *vt* to clog up; (*obstruir*) to jam; (*fig*) to hinder; **atascarse** *vr* to stall; (*cañería*) to get blocked up; **atasco** *nm* obstruction; (*Auto*) traffic jam

ataúd [ata'uð] *nm* coffin

ataviar [ata'βjar] /1c/ *vt* to deck, array

atemorizar [atemori'θar] /1f/ *vt* to frighten, scare

Atenas [a'tenas] *nf* Athens

atención [aten'θjon] *nf* attention; (*bondad*) kindness ▷ *excl* (be) careful!, look out! **en ~ a esto** in view of this

atender [aten'der] /2g/ *vt* to attend to, look after; (*Telec*) to answer ▷ *vi* to pay attention

atenerse [ate'nerse] /2k/ *vr*: **~ a** to abide by, adhere to

atentado [aten'taðo] *nm* crime, illegal act; (*asalto*) assault; (*tb*: **~ terrorista**) terrorist attack; **~ contra la vida de algn** attempt on sb's life; **~ suicida** suicide bombing

atentamente [atenta'mente] *adv*: **Le saluda ~** Yours faithfully

atentar [aten'tar] /1a/ *vi*: **~ a o contra** to commit an outrage against

atento, -a [a'tento, a] *adj* attentive, observant; (*cortés*) polite, thoughtful; **estar ~ a** (*explicación*) to pay attention to

atenuar [ate'nwar] /1e/ *vt* (*disminuir*) to lessen, minimize

ateo, -a [a'teo, a] *adj* atheistic ▷ *nm/f* atheist

aterrador, a [aterra'ðor, a] *adj* frightening

aterrizaje [aterri'θaxe] *nm* landing; **~ forzoso** emergency o forced landing

aterrizar [aterri'θar] /1f/ *vi* to land

aterrorizar [aterrori'θar] /1f/ *vt* to terrify

atesorar [ateso'rar] /1a/ *vt* to hoard

atestar [ates'tar] /1a, 1j/ *vt* to pack, stuff; (*Jur*) to attest, testify to

atestiguar [atesti'ɣwar] /1i/ *vt* to testify to, bear witness to

atiborrar [atiβo'rrar] /1a/ *vt* to fill, stuff; **atiborrarse** *vr* to stuff o.s.

ático [a'tiko] *nm* (*desván*) attic; **~ de lujo** penthouse flat

atinado, -a [ati'naðo, a] *adj* correct; (*sensato*) wise, sensible

atinar [ati'nar] /1a/ *vi* (*acertar*) to be right; **~ al blanco** to hit the target; (*fig*) to be right

atizar [ati'θar] /1f/ *vt* to poke; (*horno etc*) to stoke; (*fig*) to stir up, rouse

atlántico, -a [at'lantiko, a] *adj* Atlantic ▷ *nm*: **el (océano) A~** the Atlantic (Ocean)

atlas ['atlas] *nm inv* atlas

atleta [at'leta] *nmf* athlete; **atlético, -a** *adj* athletic; **atletismo** *nm* athletics *sg*

atmósfera [at'mosfera] *nf* atmosphere

atolladero [atoʎa'ðero] *nm*: **estar en un ~** to be in a jam

atómico, -a [a'tomiko, a] *adj* atomic

átomo ['atomo] *nm* atom

atónito, -a [a'tonito, a] *adj* astonished, amazed

atontado, -a [aton'taðo, a] *adj* stunned; (*bobo*) silly, daft

atormentar [atormen'tar] /1a/ *vt* to torture; (*molestar*) to torment; (*acosar*) to plague, harass

atornillar [atorni'ʎar] /1a/ *vt* to screw on o down

atosigar [atosi'ɣar] /1h/ *vt* to harass, pester

atracador, a [atraka'ðor, a] *nm/f* robber

atracar [atra'kar] /1g/ *vt* (*Naut*) to moor; (*robar*) to hold up, rob ▷ *vi* to moor; **atracarse** *vr*: **~se (de)** to stuff o.s. (with)

atracción [atrak'θjon] *nf* attraction

atraco [a'trako] *nm* holdup, robbery

atracón [atra'kon] *nm*: **darse** o **pegarse un ~ (de)** *(fam)* to stuff o.s. (with)

atractivo, -a [atrak'tiβo, a] *adj* attractive ▷ *nm* appeal

atraer [atra'er] /2o/ *vt* to attract

atragantarse [atraɣan'tarse] /1a/ *vr*: **~ (con algo)** to choke (on sth); **se me ha atragantado el chico ese/el inglés** I can't stand that boy/English

atrancar [atran'kar] /1g/ *vt (con tranca, barra)* to bar, bolt

atrapar [atra'par] /1a/ *vt* to trap; *(resfriado etc)* to catch

atrás [a'tras] *adv (movimiento)* back(wards); *(lugar)* behind; *(tiempo)* previously; **ir hacia ~** to go back(wards); to go to the rear; **estar ~** to be behind o at the back

atrasado, -a [atra'saðo, a] *adj* slow; *(pago)* overdue, late; *(país)* backward

atrasar [atra'sar] /1a/ *vi* to be slow; **atrasarse** *vr* to stay behind o; *(tren)* to be o run late; *(llegar tarde)* to be late; **atraso** *nm* slowness; lateness, delay; *(de país)* backwardness; **atrasos** *nmpl (Com)* arrears

atravesar [atraβe'sar] /1j/ *vt (cruzar)* to cross (over); *(traspasar)* to pierce; *(período)* to go through; *(poner al través)* to lay o put across; **atravesarse** *vr* to come in between; *(intervenir)* to interfere

atraviese etc [atra'βjese] *vb* V **atravesar**

atreverse [atre'βerse] /2a/ *vr* to dare; *(insolentarse)* to be insolent; **atrevido, -a** *adj* daring; insolent; **atrevimiento** *nm* daring; insolence

atribución [atriβu'θjon] *nf* attribution; **atribuciones** *nfpl (Pol)* powers, functions; *(Admin)* responsibilities

atribuir [atriβu'ir] /3g/ *vt* to attribute; *(funciones)* to confer

atributo [atri'βuto] *nm* attribute

atril [a'tril] *nm (para libro)* lectern; *(Mus)* music stand

atropellar [atrope'ʎar] /1a/ *vt (derribar)* to knock over o down; *(empujar)* to push (aside); *(Auto)* to run over o down; *(agraviar)* to insult; **atropello** *nm (Auto)* accident; *(empujón)* push; *(agravio)* wrong; *(atrocidad)* outrage

atroz [a'troθ] *adj* atrocious, awful

A.T.S. *nm abr, nf abr* (= *Ayudante Técnico Sanitario*) nurse

atuendo [a'twendo] *nm* attire

atún [a'tun] *nm* tuna, tunny

aturdir [atur'ðir] /3a/ *vt* to stun; *(ruido)* to deafen; *(fig)* to dumbfound, bewilder

audacia [au'ðaθja] *nf* boldness, audacity; **audaz** *adj* bold, audacious

audición [auði'θjon] *nf* hearing; *(Teat)* audition

audiencia [au'ðjenθja] *nf* audience; *(Jur)* high court

audífono [au'ðifono] *nm (para sordos)* hearing aid

auditor [auði'tor] *nm (Jur)* judge advocate; *(Com)* auditor

auditorio [auði'torjo] *nm* audience; *(sala)* auditorium

auge ['auxe] *nm* boom; *(clímax)* climax

augurar [auɣu'rar] /1a/ *vt* to predict; *(presagiar)* to portend

augurio [au'ɣurjo] *nm* omen

aula ['aula] *nf* classroom; *(en universidad etc)* lecture room

aullar [au'ʎar] /1a/ *vi* to howl, yell

aullido [au'ʎiðo] *nm* howl, yell

aumentar [aumen'tar] /1a/ *vt* to increase; *(precios)* to put up; *(producción)* to step up; *(con microscopio, anteojos)* to magnify ▷ *vi* to increase, be on the increase; **aumento** *nm* increase; rise

aun [a'un] *adv* even; **~ así** even so; **~ más** even o yet more

aún [a'un] *adv* still, yet; **~ está aquí** he's still here; **~ no lo sabemos** we don't know yet; **¿no ha venido ~?** hasn't she come yet?

aunque [a'unke] *conj* though, although, even though

aúpa [a'upa] *excl* come on!

auricular [auriku'lar] nm (Telec) earpiece; **auriculares** nmpl (cascos) headphones

aurora [au'rora] nf dawn

ausencia [au'senθja] nf absence

ausentarse [ausen'tarse] /1a/ vr to go away; (por poco tiempo) to go out

ausente [au'sente] adj absent

austero, -a [aus'tero, a] adj austere

austral [aus'tral] adj southern ▷ nm monetary unit of Argentina (1985-1991)

Australia [aus'tralja] nf Australia; **australiano, -a** adj, nm/f Australian

Austria ['austrja] nf Austria

austríaco, -a, austríaco, -a [aus'triako, a] adj Austrian ▷ nm/f Austrian

auténtico, -a [au'tentiko, a] adj authentic

auto ['auto] nm (Jur) edict, decree; (: orden) writ; **autos** nmpl (Jur) proceedings; (: acta) court record sg

autoadhesivo, -a [autoaðe'siβo, a] adj self-adhesive; (sobre) self-sealing

autobiografía [autoβjoɣra'fia] nf autobiography

autobomba [auto'bomba] nm (RPL) fire engine

autobronceador, a [autoβronθea'ðor, a] adj (self-)tanning

autobús [auto'βus] nm bus; **~ de línea** long-distance coach

autocar [auto'kar] nm coach (BRIT), (passenger) bus (US); **~ de línea** intercity coach or bus

autóctono, -a [au'toktono, a] adj native, indigenous

autodefensa [autoðe'fensa] nf self-defence

autodidacta [autoði'ðakta] adj self-taught

autoescuela [autoes'kwela] nf (ESP) driving school

autógrafo [au'toɣrafo] nm autograph

autómata [au'tomata] nm automaton

automático, -a [auto'matiko, a] adj automatic ▷ nm press stud

automóvil [auto'moβil] nm (motor) car (BRIT), automobile (US); **automovilismo** nm (actividad) motoring; (Deporte) motor racing; **automovilista** nmf motorist, driver

autonomía [autono'mia] nf autonomy; **autónomo, -a,** (ESP) **autonómico** adj autonomous

autopista [auto'pista] nf motorway (BRIT), freeway (US); **~ de cuota** (LAM) o **peaje** (ESP) toll (BRIT) o turnpike (US) road

autopsia [au'topsja] nf post-mortem, autopsy

autor, a [au'tor, a] nm/f author

autoridad [autori'ðað] nf authority; **autoritario, -a** adj authoritarian

autorización [autoriθa'θjon] nf authorization; **autorizado, -a** adj authorized; (aprobado) approved

autorizar [autori'θar] /1f/ vt to authorize; to approve

autoservicio [autoser'βiβjo] nm (tienda) self-service shop o store; (restaurante) self-service restaurant

autostop [auto'stop] nm hitch-hiking; **hacer ~** to hitch-hike; **autostopista** nmf hitch-hiker

autovía [auto'βia] nf ≈ dual carriageway (BRIT), ≈ divided highway (US)

auxiliar [auksi'ljar] /1b/ vt to help ▷ nmf assistant; **auxilio** nm assistance, help; **primeros auxilios** first aid sg

Av abr (= Avenida) Av(e)

aval [a'βal] nm guarantee; (persona) guarantor

avalancha [aβa'lantʃa] nf avalanche

avance [a'βanθe] nm advance; (pago) advance payment; (Cine) trailer

avanzar [aβan'θar] /1f/ vt, vi to advance

avaricia [aβa'riθja] nf avarice, greed; **avaricioso, -a** adj avaricious, greedy

avaro, -a [a'βaro, a] adj miserly, mean ▷ nm/f miser

Avda abr (= Avenida) Av(e)

AVE ['aβe] *nm abr* (= *Alta Velocidad Española*) = bullet train

ave ['aβe] *nf* bird; **- de rapiña** bird of prey

avecinarse [aβeθi'narse] /1a/ *vr* (*tormenta, fig*) be on the way

avellana [aβe'ʎana] *nf* hazelnut; **avellano** *nm* hazel tree

avemaría [aβema'ria] *nm* Hail Mary, Ave Maria

avena [a'βena] *nf* oats *pl*

avenida [aβe'niða] *nf* (*calle*) avenue

aventajar [aβenta'xar] /1a/ *vt* (*sobrepasar*) to surpass, outstrip

aventón [aβen'ton] *nm* push; **pedir -** to hitch a lift, hitch a ride (us)

aventura [aβen'tura] *nf* adventure; **aventurero, -a** *adj* adventurous

avergonzar [aβeryon'θar] /1f, 1l/ *vt* to shame; (*desconcertar*) to embarrass; **avergonzarse** *vr* to be ashamed; to be embarrassed

avería [aβe'ria] *nf* (*Tec*) breakdown, fault

averiado, -a [aβe'rjaðo, a] *adj* broken-down; **"-"** "out of order"

averiar [aβe'rjar] /1c/ *vt* to break; **averiarse** *vr* to break down

averiguar [aβeri'ɣwar] /1i/ *vt* to investigate; (*descubrir*) to find out, ascertain

avestruz [aβes'truθ] *nm* ostrich

aviación [aβja'θjon] *nf* aviation; (*fuerzas aéreas*) air force

aviador, a [aβja'ðor, a] *nm/f* aviator, airman/woman

ávido, -a ['aβiðo, a] *adj* avid, eager

avinagrado, -a [aβina'ɣraðo, a] *adj* sour, acid

avión [a'βjon] *nm* aeroplane; (*ave*) martin; **- de reacción** jet (plane)

avioneta [aβjo'neta] *nf* light aircraft

avisar [aβi'sar] /1a/ *vt* (*advertir*) to warn, notify; (*informar*) to tell; (*aconsejar*) to advise, counsel; **aviso** *nm* warning; (*noticia*) notice

avispa [a'βispa] *nf* wasp

avispado, -a [aβis'paðo, a] *adj* sharp, clever

avivar [aβi'βar] /1a/ *vt* to strengthen, intensify

axila [ak'sila] *nf* armpit

ay [ai] *excl* (*dolor*) ow!, ouch!; (*aflicción*) oh!, oh dear!; **¡ay de mí!** poor me!

ayer [a'jer] *adv, nm* yesterday; **antes de -** the day before yesterday; **- por la tarde** yesterday afternoon/evening; **- mismo** only yesterday

ayote [a'jote] *nm* (LAM) pumpkin

ayuda [a'juða] *nf* help, assistance ▷ *nm* page; **ayudante, -a** *nm/f* assistant, helper; (*Escol*) assistant; (*Mil*) adjutant

ayudar [aju'ðar] /1a/ *vt* to help, assist

ayunar [aju'nar] /1a/ *vi* to fast; **ayunas**: *nfpl*: **estar en ayunas** to be fasting; **ayuno** *nm* fast; fasting

ayuntamiento [ajunta'mjento] *nm* (*consejo*) town/city council; (*edificio*) town/city hall

azafata [aθa'fata] *nf* air hostess (BRIT) ▷ stewardess

azafrán [aθa'fran] *nm* saffron

azahar [aθa'ar] *nm* orange/lemon blossom

azar [a'θar] *nm* (*casualidad*) chance, fate; (*desgracia*) misfortune, accident; **por -** by chance; **al -** at random

Azores [a'θores] *nfpl*: **las (Islas) -** the Azores

azotar [aθo'tar] /1a/ *vt* to whip, beat; (*pegar*) to spank; **azote** *nm* (*látigo*) whip; (*latigazo*) lash, stroke; (*en las nalgas*) spank; (*calamidad*) calamity

azotea [aθo'tea] *nf* (flat) roof

azteca [aθ'teka] *adj, nmf* Aztec

azúcar [a'θukar] *nm* sugar; **azucarado, -a** *adj* sugary, sweet

azucarero, -a [aθuka'rero, a] *adj* sugar *cpd* ▷ *nm* sugar bowl

azucena [aθu'θena] *nf* white lily

azufre [a'θufre] *nm* sulphur

azul [a'θul] *adj, nm* blue; **- celeste/marino** sky/navy blue

azulejo [aθu'lexo] *nm* tile

azuzar [aθu'θar] /1f/ *vt* to incite, egg on

b

B.A. abr (= Buenos Aires) B.A.

baba ['baβa] nf spittle, saliva; **babear** /1a/ vi to drool, slaver

babero [ba'βero] nm bib

babor [ba'βor] nm port (side)

babosada [baβo'saða] nf: **decir ~s** (LAM fam) to talk rubbish; **baboso, -a** adj (LAM) silly

baca ['baka] nf (Auto) luggage o roof rack

bacalao [baka'lao] nm cod(fish)

bache ['batʃe] nm pothole, rut; (fig) bad patch

bachillerato [batʃiʎe'rato] nm two-year advanced secondary school course

bacinica [baθi'nika] nf potty

bacteria [bak'terja] nf bacterium, germ

Bahama [ba'ama]: **las (islas) ~, las ~s** nfpl the Bahamas

bahía [ba'ia] nf bay

bailar [bai'lar] /1a/ vt, vi to dance; **bailarín, -ina** nm/f dancer; (de *ballet*) ballet dancer; **baile** nm dance; (*formal*) ball

baja ['baxa] nf drop, fall; (Mil) casualty; **dar de ~** (*soldado*) to discharge; (*empleado*) to dismiss

bajada [ba'xaða] nf descent; (*camino*) slope; (*de aguas*) ebb

bajar [ba'xar] /1a/ vi to go o come down; (*temperatura, precios*) to drop, fall ▷ vt (*cabeza*) to bow; (*escalera*) to go o come down; (*precio, voz*) to lower; (*llevar abajo*) to take down; **bajarse** vr (*de vehículo*) to get out; (*de autobús*) to get off; **~ de** (*coche*) to get out of; (*autobús*) to get off; **~se algo de internet** to download sth from the internet

bajío [ba'xio] nm (LAM) lowlands pl

bajo, -a ['baxo, a] adj (*mueble, número, precio*) low; (*piso*) ground cpd; (*de estatura*) small, short; (*color*) pale; (*sonido*) faint, soft, low; (*voz, tono*) deep; (*metal*) base; (*humilde*) low, humble ▷ adv (*hablar*) softly, quietly; (*volar*) low ▷ prep under, below, underneath ▷ nm (Mus) bass; **~ la lluvia** in the rain

bajón [ba'xon] nm fall, drop

bakalao [baka'lao] nm (Mus) rave music

bala ['bala] nf bullet

balacear [balaθe'ar] /1a/ vt (LAM, CAM) to shoot

balance [ba'lanθe] nm (Com) balance; (: *libro*) balance sheet; (: *cuenta general*) stocktaking

balancear [balanθe'ar] /1a/ vt to balance ▷ vi to swing (to and fro); (*vacilar*) to hesitate; **balancearse** vr to swing (to and fro); (*vacilar*) to hesitate

balanza [ba'lanθa] nf scales pl, balance; **~ comercial** balance of trade; **~ de pagos/de poder(es)** balance of payments/of power

balaustrada [balaus'traða] nf balustrade; (*pasamanos*) banister

balazo [ba'laθo] nm (*tiro*) shot; (*herida*) bullet wound

balbucear [balβuθe'ar] /1a/ *vi, vt* to stammer, stutter

balcón [bal'kon] *nm* balcony

balde ['balde] *nm* bucket, pail; **de ~** (for) free, for nothing; **en ~** in vain

baldosa [bal'dosa] *nf (azulejo)* floor tile; *(grande)* flagstone; **baldosín** *nm* tile

Baleares [bale'ares] *nfpl*: **las (Islas) ~** the Balearic Islands

balero [ba'lero] *nm (LAM: juguete)* cup-and-ball toy

baliza [ba'liθa] *nf (Aviat)* beacon; *(Naut)* buoy

ballena [ba'ʎena] *nf* whale

ballet *(pl* **ballets**) [ba'le] *nm* ballet

balneario, -a [balne'arjo, a] *adj* ▷ *nm* spa; *(LAM: en la costa)* seaside resort

balón [ba'lon] *nm* ball

baloncesto [balon'θesto] *nm* basketball

balonmano [balon'mano] *nm* handball

balonred [balon'reð] *nm* netball

balsa ['balsa] *nf* raft; *(Bot)* balsa wood

bálsamo ['balsamo] *nm* balsam, balm

baluarte [ba'lwarte] *nm* bastion, bulwark

bambú [bam'bu] *nm* bamboo

banana [ba'nana] *nf (LAM)* banana; **banano** *nm (LAM)* banana tree; *(fruta)* banana

banca ['banka] *nf (Com)* banking

bancario, -a [ban'karjo, a] *adj* banking *cpd*, bank *cpd*

bancarrota [banka'rrota] *nf* bankruptcy; **declararse** *o* **hacer ~** to go bankrupt

banco ['banko] *nm* bench; *(Escol)* desk; *(Com)* bank; *(Geo)* stratum; **~ de crédito/de ahorros** credit/savings bank; **~ de arena** sandbank; **~ de datos** *(Inform)* data bank

banda ['banda] *nf* band; *(pandilla)* gang; *(Naut)* side, edge; **la B~ Oriental** Uruguay; **~ sonora** soundtrack

bandada [ban'daða] *nf (de pájaros)* flock; *(de peces)* shoal

bandazo [ban'daθo] *nm*: **dar ~s** to veer from side to side

bandeja [ban'dexa] *nf* tray; **~ de entrada/salida** in-tray/out-tray

bandera [ban'dera] *nf* flag

banderilla [bande'riʎa] *nf* banderilla

bandido [ban'diðo] *nm* bandit

bando ['bando] *nm (edicto)* edict, proclamation; *(facción)* faction; **los ~s** *(Rel)* the banns

bandolera [bando'lera] *nf*: **llevar en ~** to wear across one's chest

banquero [ban'kero] *nm* banker

banqueta [ban'keta] *nf* stool; *(LAM: acera)* pavement *(BRIT)*, sidewalk *(US)*

banquete [ban'kete] *nm* banquet; *(para convidados)* formal dinner; **~ de boda** wedding reception

banquillo [ban'kiʎo] *nm (Jur)* dock, prisoner's bench; *(banco)* bench; *(para los pies)* footstool

banquina [ban'kina] *nf (RPL)* hard shoulder *(BRIT)*, berm *(US)*

bañadera [baɲa'ðera] *nf (LAM)* bath(tub)

bañador [baɲa'ðor] *nm* swimming costume *(BRIT)*, bathing suit *(US)*

bañar [ba'ɲar] /1a/ *vt* to bath, bathe; *(objeto)* to dip; *(de barniz)* to coat; **bañarse** *vr (en el mar)* to bathe, swim; *(en la bañera)* to have a bath

bañera [ba'ɲera] *nf (ESP)* bath(tub)

bañero, -a [ba'ɲero, a] *nm/f* lifeguard

bañista [ba'ɲista] *nmf* bather

baño ['baɲo] *nm (en bañera)* bath; *(en río, mar)* dip, swim; *(cuarto)* bathroom; *(bañera)* bath(tub); *(capa)* coating; **darse** *o* **tomar un ~** *(en bañera)* to have *o* take a bath; *(en mar, piscina)* to have a swim; **~ María** bain-marie

bar [bar] *nm* bar

barahúnda [bara'unda] *nf* uproar, hubbub

baraja [ba'raxa] *nf* pack (of cards); **barajar** /1a/ *vt (naipes)* to shuffle; *(fig)* to jumble up

baranda [ba'randa], **barandilla** [baran'diʎa] nf rail, railing

barata [ba'rata] nf (LAM) (bargain) sale

baratillo [bara'tiʎo] nm (tienda) junk shop; (subasta) bargain sale; (conjunto de cosas) second-hand goods pl

barato, -a [ba'rato, a] adj cheap ▷ adv cheap, cheaply

barba ['barβa] nf (mentón) chin; (pelo) beard

barbacoa [barβa'koa] nf (parrilla) barbecue; (carne) barbecued meat

barbaridad [barβari'ðað] nf barbarity; (acto) barbarism; (atrocidad) outrage; **una ~ de** (fam) loads of; **¡qué ~!** (fam) how awful!

barbarie [bar'βarje] nm barbarism; (crueldad) barbarity

bárbaro, -a ['barβaro, a] adj barbarous, cruel; (grosero) rough, uncouth ▷ nm/f barbarian ▷ adv: **lo pasamos ~** (fam) we had a great time; **¡qué ~!** (fam) how marvellous!; **un éxito ~** (fam) a terrific success; **es un tipo ~** (fam) he's a great bloke

barbero [bar'βero] nm barber, hairdresser

barbilla [bar'βiʎa] nf chin, tip of the chin

barbudo, -a [bar'βuðo, a] adj bearded

barca ['barka] nf (small) boat; **barcaza** nf barge

Barcelona [barθe'lona] nf Barcelona

barco ['barko] nm boat; (buque) ship; **~ de carga** cargo boat; **~ de vela** sailing ship

barda ['barða] nf (LAM: de madera) fence

baremo [ba'remo] nm scale

barítono [ba'ritono] nm baritone

barman ['barman] nm barman

barniz [bar'niθ] nm varnish; (en la loza) glaze; (fig) veneer; **barnizar** /1f/ vt to varnish; (loza) to glaze

barómetro [ba'rometro] nm barometer

barquillo [bar'kiʎo] nm cone, cornet

barra ['barra] nf bar, rod; (de un bar, café) bar; (Pan) French loaf; (palanca)

---

lever; **~ de carmín** o **de labios** lipstick; **~ libre** free bar

barraca [ba'rraka] nf hut, cabin

barranco [ba'rranko] nm ravine; (fig) difficulty

barrena [ba'rrena] nf drill

barrer [ba'rrer] /2a/ vt to sweep; (quitar) to sweep away

barrera [ba'rrera] nf barrier

barriada [ba'rrjaða] nf quarter, district

barricada [barri'kaða] nf barricade

barrida [ba'rriða] nm sweep, sweeping

barriga [ba'rriɣa] nf belly; (panza) paunch; **barrigón, -ona, barrigudo, -a** adj potbellied

barril [ba'rril] nm barrel, cask

barrio ['barrjo] nm (vecindad) area, neighborhood (US); (en las afueras) suburb; **~ chino** red-light district

barro ['barro] nm (lodo) mud; (objetos) earthenware; (Med) pimple

barroco, -a [ba'rroko, a] adj, nm Baroque

barrote [ba'rrote] nm (de ventana etc) bar

bartola [bar'tola] nf: **tirarse a la ~** to take it easy, be lazy

bártulos ['bartulos] nmpl things, belongings

barullo [ba'ruʎo] nm row, uproar

basar [ba'sar] /1a/ vt to base; **basarse** vr: **~ en** to be based on

báscula ['baskula] nf (platform) scales pl

base ['base] nf base; **a ~ de** on the basis of; (mediante) by means of; **~ de datos** database

básico, -a ['basiko, a] adj basic

basílica [ba'silika] nf basilica

básquetbol ['basketbol] nm (LAM) basketball

PALABRA CLAVE

bastante [bas'tante] adj **1** (suficiente) enough; **bastante dinero** enough o sufficient money; **bastantes libros** enough books

2 (valor intensivo): **bastante gente** quite a lot of people; **tener bastante calor** to be rather hot

▸ adv: **bastante bueno/malo** quite good/rather bad; **bastante rico** pretty rich; **(lo) bastante inteligente (como) para hacer algo** clever enough o sufficiently clever to do sth

bastar [bas'tar] /1a/ vi to be enough o sufficient; **bastarse** vr to be self-sufficient; **~ para** to be enough to; **¡basta!** (that's enough)!

bastardo, -a [bas'tarðo, a] adj, nm/f bastard

bastidor [basti'ðor] nm frame; (de coche) chassis; (Teat) wing; **entre ~es** behind the scenes

basto, -a ['basto, a] adj coarse, rough ▸ nmpl: **~s** (Naipes) one of the suits in the Spanish card deck

bastón [bas'ton] nm stick, staff; (para pasear) walking stick

bastoncillo [baston'θiʎo] nm cotton bud

basura [ba'sura] nf rubbish, refuse (BRIT), garbage (US) ▸ adj: **comida/televisión** junk food/TV

basurero [basu'rero] nm (hombre) dustman (BRIT), garbage collector o man (US); (lugar) rubbish dump; (cubo) (rubbish) bin (BRIT), trash can (US)

bata ['bata] nf (gen) dressing gown; (cubretodo) smock, overall; (Med, Tec etc) lab(oratory) coat

batalla [ba'taʎa] nf battle; **de ~** for everyday use; **~ campal** pitched battle

batallón [bata'ʎon] nm battalion

batata [ba'tata] nf sweet potato

batería [bate'ria] nf battery; (Mus) drums pl; **~ de cocina** kitchen utensils pl

batido, -a [ba'tiðo, a] adj (camino) beaten, well-trodden ▸ nm (Culin) batter; **~ (de leche)** milk shake

batidora [bati'ðora] nf beater, mixer; **~ eléctrica** food mixer, blender

batir [ba'tir] /3a/ vt to beat, strike; (vencer) to beat, defeat; (revolver) to beat, mix; **batirse** vr to fight; **~ palmas** to clap, applaud

batuta [ba'tuta] nf baton; **llevar la ~** (fig) to be the boss

baúl [ba'ul] nm trunk; (LAM Auto) boot (BRIT), trunk (US)

bautismo [bau'tismo] nm baptism, christening

bautizar [bauti'θar] /1f/ vt to baptize, christen; (fam: diluir) to water down; **bautizo** nm baptism, christening

bayeta [ba'jeta] nf floor cloth

baza ['baθa] nf trick; **meter ~** to butt in

bazar [ba'θar] nm bazaar

bazofia [ba'θofja] nf trash

be [be] nf name of the letter B; **be chica/grande** (LAM) V/B; **be larga** (LAM) B

beato, -a [be'ato, a] adj blessed; (piadoso) pious

bebé [be'βe] (pl **bebés**) nm baby

bebedero [beβe'ðero] nm (para animales) drinking trough

bebedor, a [beβe'ðor, a] adj hard-drinking

beber [be'βer] /2a/ vt, vi to drink

bebido, -a [be'βiðo, a] adj drunk ▸ nf drink

beca ['beka] nf grant, scholarship; **becario, -a** [be'karjo, a] nm/f scholarship holder, grant holder; (en prácticas laborales) intern

bedel [be'ðel] nm porter, janitor; (Univ) porter

béisbol ['beisβol] nm baseball

Belén [be'len] nm Bethlehem; **belén** (de Navidad) nativity scene, crib

belga ['belɣa] adj, nmf Belgian

Bélgica ['belxika] nf Belgium

bélico, -a ['beliko, a] adj (actitud) warlike

belleza [be'ʎeθa] nf beauty

bello, -a ['beʎo, a] adj beautiful, lovely; **Bellas Artes** Fine Art sg

bellota [be'ʎota] nf acorn

bemol [be'mol] nm (Mus) flat; **esto tiene ~es** (fam) this is a tough one

bencina [ben'sina] nf (LAM: gasolina) petrol (BRIT), gas (US)

bendecir [bende'θir] /3o/ vt to bless

bendición [bendi'θjon] nf blessing

bendito, -a [ben'dito, a] pp de **bendecir** ▷ adj holy; (afortunado) lucky; (feliz) happy; (sencillo) simple ▷ nm/f simple soul

beneficencia [benefi'θenθja] nf charity

beneficiario, -a [benefi'θjarjo, a] nm/f beneficiary

beneficio [bene'fiθjo] nm (bien) benefit, advantage; (Com) profit, gain; **a ~ de** for the benefit of; **beneficioso, -a** adj beneficial

benéfico, -a [be'nefiko, a] adj charitable

beneplácito [bene'plaθito] nm approval, consent

benévolo, -a [be'neβolo, a] adj benevolent, kind

benigno, -a [be'niɣno, a] adj kind; (suave) mild; (Med: tumor) benign, non-malignant

berberecho [berβe'retʃo] nm cockle

berenjena [beren'xena] nf aubergine (BRIT), eggplant (US)

Berlín [ber'lin] nm Berlin

berlinesa [berli'nesa] nf (LAM) doughnut, donut (US)

bermudas [ber'muðas] nfpl Bermuda shorts

berrido [be'rriðo] nm bellow(ing)

berrinche [be'rrintʃe] nm (fam) temper, tantrum

berro ['berro] nm watercress

berza ['berθa] nf cabbage

besamel [besa'mel] nf (Culin) white sauce, bechamel sauce

besar [be'sar] /1a/ vt to kiss; (fig: tocar) to graze; **besarse** vr to kiss (one another); **beso** nm kiss

bestia ['bestja] nf beast, animal; (fig) idiot; **~ de carga** beast of burden;

bestial adj bestial; (fam) terrific;
bestialidad nf bestiality; (fam) stupidity

besugo [be'suɣo] nm sea bream; (fam) idiot

besuquear [besuke'ar] /1a/ vt to cover with kisses; **besuquearse** vr to kiss and cuddle

betabel [beta'bel] nm (LAM) beetroot (BRIT), beet (US)

betún [be'tun] nm shoe polish; (Química) bitumen

biberón [biβe'ron] nm feeding bottle

Biblia ['biβlja] nf Bible

bibliografía [biβljoɣra'fia] nf bibliography

biblioteca [biβljo'teka] nf library; (estantes) bookshelves pl; **~ de consulta** reference library; **bibliotecario, -a** nm/f librarian

bicarbonato [bikarβo'nato] nm bicarbonate

bicho ['bitʃo] nm (animal) small animal; (sabandija) bug, insect; (Taur) bull

bici ['biθi] nf (fam) bike

bicicleta [biθi'kleta] nf bicycle, cycle; **ir en ~** to cycle

bidé [bi'ðe] nm bidet

bidón [bi'ðon] nm (grande) drum; (pequeño) can

PALABRA CLAVE

bien [bjen] nm 1 (bienestar) good; **te lo digo por tu bien** I'm telling you for your own good; **el bien y el mal** good and evil

2 (posesión): **bienes** goods; **bienes de consumo/equipo** consumer/capital goods; **bienes inmuebles** o **raíces/ bienes muebles** real estate sg/ personal property sg

▷ adv 1 (de manera satisfactoria, correcta etc) well; **trabaja/come bien** she works/eats well; **contestó bien** she answered correctly; **me siento bien** I feel fine; **no me siento bien** I don't feel very well; **se está bien aquí** it's nice here

2: **hiciste bien en llamarme** you were right to call me

3 (valor intensivo) very; **un cuarto bien caliente** a nice warm room; **bien se ve que ...** it's quite clear that ...

4: **estar bien: estoy muy bien aquí** I feel very happy here; **está bien que vengan** it's all right for them to come; **¡está bien!** all right then, I'll do it

5 (de buena gana): **yo bien que iría pero ...** I'd gladly go but ...

▷ excl: **¡bien!** (aprobación) OK!; **¡muy bien!** well done!

▷ adj inv: **gente bien** posh people

▷ conj **1**: **bien ... bien: bien en coche bien en tren** either by car or by train

2: **no bien** (esp LAM): **no bien llegue te llamaré** as soon as I arrive I'll call you

3: **si bien** even though; V tb **más**

bienal [bje'nal] adj biennial

bienestar [bjenes'tar] nm well-being

bienvenido, -a [bjembe'niðo, a] excl welcome! ▷ nf welcome; **dar la bienvenida a algn** to welcome sb

bife ['bife] nm (LAM) steak

bifurcación [bifurka'θjon] nf fork

bígamo, -a ['biɣamo, a] adj bigamous ▷ nm/f bigamist

bigote [bi'ɣote] nm moustache; **bigotudo, -a** adj with a big moustache

bikini [bi'kini] nm bikini; (Culin) toasted cheese and ham sandwich

bilingüe [bi'lingwe] adj bilingual

billar [bi'ʎar] nm billiards sg; **billares** nmpl (lugar) billiard hall; (galería de atracciones) amusement arcade; **~ americano** pool

billete [bi'ʎete] nm banknote; (de banco) banknote (BRIT), bill (US); (carta) note; **~ de ida o sencillo** single (BRIT) o one-way (US) ticket; **~ de ida y vuelta** return (BRIT) o round-trip (US) ticket; **~ electrónico** e-ticket; **sacar (un) ~**

to get a ticket; **un ~ de cinco libras** a five-pound note

billetera [biʎe'tera] nf wallet

billón [bi'ʎon] nm billion

bimensual [bimen'swal] adj twice monthly

bingo ['bingo] nm bingo

biocarburante [biokarβu'rante], **biocombustible** [biokomβus'tiβle] nm biofuel

biodegradable [bioðeɣra'ðaβle] adj biodegradable

biografía [bjoɣra'fia] nf biography

biología [biolo'xia] nf biology; **biológico, -a** adj biological; (cultivo, producto) organic; **biólogo, -a** nm/f biologist

biombo ['bjombo] nm (folding) screen

bioterrorismo [bioterro'rismo] nm bioterrorism

biquini [bi'kini] nm = **bikini**

birlar [bir'lar] /1a/ vt (fam) to pinch

Birmania [bir'manja] nf Burma

birome [bi'rome] nf (LAM) ballpoint (pen)

birria ['birrja] nf (fam): **ser una ~** (película, libro) to be rubbish

bis [bis] excl encore!

bisabuelo, -a [bisa'βwelo, a] nm/f great-grandfather/mother

bisagra [bi'saɣra] nf hinge

bisiesto [bi'sjesto] adj: **año ~** leap year

bisnieto, -a [bis'njeto, a] nm/f great-grandson/daughter

bisonte [bi'sonte] nm bison

bistec [bis'tek], **bisté** [bis'te] nm steak

bisturí [bistu'ri] nm scalpel

bisutería [bisute'ria] nf imitation o costume jewellery

bit [bit] nm (Inform) bit

bizco, -a ['biθko, a] adj cross-eyed

bizcocho [biθ'kotʃo] nm (Culin) sponge cake

blanco, -a ['blanko, a] adj white ▷ nm/f white man/woman; white ▷ nm (color) white; (en texto) blank;

(Mil, fig) target; **en ~** blank; **noche en ~** sleepless night; **estar sin blanca** to be broke

blandir [blan'dir] *vt* to brandish

blando, -a ['blando, a] *adj* soft; *(tierno)* tender, gentle; *(carácter)* mild; *(fam)* cowardly

blanqueador [blankea'ðor] *nm* (LAM) bleach

blanquear [blanke'ar] /1a/ *vt* to whiten; *(fachada)* to whitewash; *(paño)* to bleach; *(dinero)* to launder ▷ *vi* to turn white

blanquillo [blan'kiʎo] *nm* (LAM, CAM) egg

blasfemar [blasfe'mar] /1a/ *vi* to blaspheme; *(fig)* to curse

bledo ['bleðo] *nm*: **(no) me importa un ~** I couldn't care less

blindado, -a [blin'daðo, a] *adj* (Mil) armour-plated; *(antibalas)* bulletproof; **coche a** (LAM) **carro ~** armoured car

bloc [blok] *(pl* **blocs)** *nm* writing pad

blof [blof] *nm* (LAM) bluff; **blofear** /1a/ *vi* (LAM) to bluff

blog [bloɣ] *(pl* **blogs)** *nm* blog

bloguero, -a [blo'ɣero, a] *nm/f* blogger

bloque ['bloke] *nm* block; *(Pol)* bloc

bloquear [bloke'ar] /1a/ *vt* to blockade; **bloqueo** *nm* blockade; *(Com)* freezing, blocking; **bloqueo mental** mental block

blusa ['blusa] *nf* blouse

boa ['boa] *nf* boa

bobada [bo'βaða] *nf* foolish action *(o* statement); **decir ~s** to talk nonsense

bobina [bo'βina] *nf* (Tec) bobbin; *(Foto)* spool; *(Elec)* coil

bobo, -a ['boβo, a] *adj* (tonto) daft, silly; *(cándido)* naive ▷ *nm/f* fool, idiot ▷ *nm* (Teat) clown, funny man

boca ['boka] *nf* mouth; *(de crustáceo)* pincer; *(de cañón)* muzzle; *(entrada)* mouth, entrance; **bocas** *nfpl* (de río) mouth *sg*; **~ abajo/arriba** face down/up; **se me hace la ~ agua** my mouth is watering; **~ de incendios** hydrant; **~ del estómago** pit of the stomach;

~ de metro tube *(BRIT) o* subway *(US)* entrance

bocacalle [boka'kaʎe] *nf* side street; **la primera ~** the first turning *o* street

bocadillo [boka'ðiʎo] *nm* sandwich

bocado [bo'kaðo] *nm* mouthful, bite; *(de caballo)* bridle

bocajarro [boka'xarro]: **a ~** *adv* (Mil) at point-blank range

bocanada [boka'naða] *nf* (de vino) mouthful, swallow; *(de aire)* gust, puff

bocata [bo'kata] *nm* (fam) sandwich

bocazas [bo'kaθas] *nm inv, nf inv* (fam) bigmouth

boceto [bo'θeto] *nm* sketch, outline

bochorno [bo'tʃorno] *nm* (vergüenza) embarrassment; *(color)*: **hace ~** it's very muggy

bocina [bo'θina] *nf* (Mus) trumpet; *(Auto)* horn; *(para hablar)* megaphone

boda ['boða] *nf* (tb: **~s)** wedding, marriage; *(fiesta)* wedding reception; **~s de plata/de oro** silver/golden wedding *sg*

bodega [bo'ðeɣa] *nf* (de vino) (wine) cellar; *(depósito)* storeroom; *(de barco)* hold

bodegón [boðe'ɣon] *nm* (Arte) still life

bofetada [bofe'taða] *nf* slap (in the face)

boga ['boɣa] *nf*: **en ~** in vogue

Bogotá [boɣo'ta] *n* Bogota

bohemio, -a [bo'emjo, a] *adj, nm/f* Bohemian

bohío [bo'io] *nm* (LAM) shack, hut

boicot [boi'ko(t)] *(pl* **boicots)** *nm* boycott; **boicotear** /1a/ *vt* to boycott

bóiler ['boiler] *nm* (LAM) boiler

boina ['boina] *nf* beret

bola ['bola] *nf* ball; *(canica)* marble; *(Naipes)* (grand) slam; *(betún)* shoe polish; *(mentira)* tale, story; **bolas** *nfpl* (LAM) balls; **~ de billar** billiard ball; **~ de nieve** snowball

boleadoras [bolea'ðoras] *nfpl* bolas *sg*

bolear [bole'ar] /1a/ *vt* (LAM: zapatos) to polish, shine

bolera [bo'lera] nf skittle o bowling alley

bolero, -a [bo'lero, a] nm bolero ▷ nm/f (LAM: limpiabotas) shoeshine boy/girl

boleta [bo'leta] nf (LAM: permiso) pass, permit; (de rifa) ticket; (recibo) receipt; (para votar) ballot; ~ **de calificaciones** report card

boletería [bole'teria] nf (LAM) ticket office

boletín [bole'tin] nm bulletin; (periódico) journal, review; ~ **de noticias** news bulletin

boleto [bo'leto] nm (esp LAM) ticket; ~ **de apuestas** betting slip; ~ **de ida y vuelta** (LAM) round-trip ticket; ~ **electrónico** (LAM) e-ticket; ~ **redondo** (LAM) round-trip ticket

boli [boli] nm Biro®

bolígrafo [bo'liɣrafo] nm ball-point pen, Biro®

bolilla [bo'lika] nf (LAM) topic

bolillo [bo'liʎo] nm (LAM) (bread) roll

bolita [bo'lita] nf (LAM) marble

bolívar [bo'liβar] nm monetary unit of Venezuela

Bolivia [bo'liβja] nf Bolivia; **boliviano, -a** adj, nm/f Bolivian

bollería [boʎe'ria] nf cakes pl and pastries pl

bollo [boʎo] nm (de pan) roll; (chichón) bump, lump; (abolladura) dent

bolo [bolo] nm skittle; (píldora) (large) pill; **(juego de) ~s** skittles sg

bolsa [bolsa] nf (saco) bag; (LAM) pocket; (de mujer) handbag; (Anat) cavity, sac; (Com) stock exchange; (Minería) pocket; ~ **de agua caliente** hot water bottle; ~ **de aire** air pocket; ~ **de dormir** sleeping bag; ~ **de papel** paper bag; ~ **de plástico** plastic (o carrier) bag; ~ **de la compra** shopping bag

bolsillo [bol'siʎo] nm pocket; (cartera) purse; **de ~** pocket

bolso [bolso] nm (bolsa) bag; (de mujer) handbag

bomba [bomba] nf (Mil) bomb; (Tec) pump ▷ adj (fam): **noticia** ~ bombshell ▷ adv (fam): **pasarlo** ~ to have a great time; ~ **atómica/de humo/de retardo** atomic/smoke/time bomb

bombacha [bom'batʃa] nf (LAM) panties pl

bombardear [bombarde'ar] /1a/ vt to bombard; (Mil) to bomb; **bombardeo** nm bombardment; bombing

bombazo [bom'baθo] nm (LAM: explosión) explosion; (fam: noticia) bombshell; (éxito) smash hit

bombear [bombe'ar] /1a/ vt (agua) to pump (out o up)

bombero [bom'bero] nm fireman

bombilla [bom'biʎa] (ESP), **bombita** [bom'bita] (LAM) nf (light) bulb

bombo [bombo] nm (Mus) bass drum; (Tec) drum

bombón [bom'bon] nm chocolate; (LAM: de caramelo) marshmallow

bombona [bom'bona] nf: ~ **de butano** gas cylinder

bonachón, -ona [bona'tʃon, ona] adj good-natured

bonanza [bo'nanθa] nf (Naut) fair weather; (fig) bonanza; (Minería) rich pocket o vein

bondad [bon'dad] nf goodness, kindness; **tenga la** ~ **de** (please) be good enough to

bonito, -a [bo'nito, a] adj pretty; (agradable) nice ▷ nm (atún) tuna (fish)

bono [bono] nm voucher; (Finanzas) bond

bonobús [bono'βus] nm (ESP) bus pass

Bono Loto, bonoloto [bono'loto] nm o f (ESP) state-run weekly lottery; V tb **lotería**

boquerón [boke'ron] nm (pez) (kind of) anchovy; (agujero) large hole

boquete [bo'kete] nm gap, hole

boquiabierto, -a [bokia'βjerto, a] adj open-mouthed (in astonishment); **quedarse** ~ to be amazed o flabbergasted

boquilla [bo'kiʎa] nf (de riego) nozzle; (de cigarro) cigarette holder; (Mus) mouthpiece

borbotón [borβo'ton] nm: **salir a borbotones** to gush out

borda ['borða] nf (Naut) gunwale, rail; **echar o tirar algo por la ~** to throw sth overboard

bordado [bor'ðaðo] nm embroidery

bordar [bor'ðar] /1a/ vt to embroider

borde ['borðe] nm edge, border; (de camino etc) side; (en la costura) hem; **al ~ de** (fig) on the verge o brink of ▷ adj: **ser ~** (ESP fam) to be rude; **bordear** /1a/ vt to border

bordillo [bor'ðiʎo] nm kerb (BRIT), curb (US)

bordo ['borðo] nm (Naut) side; **a ~** on board

borlote [bor'lote] nm (LAM) row, uproar

borra ['borra] nf fluff

borrachera [borra'tʃera] nf (ebriedad) drunkenness; (orgía) spree, binge

borracho, -a [bo'rratʃo, a] adj drunk ▷ nm/f (que bebe mucho) drunkard, drunk; (temporalmente) drunk, drunk man/woman

borrador [borra'ðor] nm (escritura) first draft, rough sketch; (goma) rubber (BRIT), eraser

borrar [bo'rrar] /1a/ vt to erase, rub out

borrasca [bo'rraska] nf storm

borrego, -a [bo'rreɣo, a] nm/f (oveja) sheep; (fig) simpleton ▷ nm (LAM fam) false rumour

borrico, -a [bo'rriko, a] nm donkey; (fig) stupid man ▷ nf she-donkey; (fig) stupid woman

borrón [bo'rron] nm (mancha) stain

borroso, -a [bo'rroso, a] adj vague, unclear; (escritura) illegible

bosque ['boske] nm wood; (grande) forest

bostezar [boste'θar] /1f/ vi to yawn; **bostezo** nm yawn

bota ['bota] nf (calzado) boot; (de vino) leather wine bottle; **~s de agua o goma** Wellingtons

botánico, -a [bo'taniko, a] adj botanical ▷ nm/f botanist

botar [bo'tar] /1a/ vt to throw, hurl; (Naut) to launch; (esp LAM fam) to throw out ▷ vi to bounce

bote ['bote] nm (salto) bounce; (golpe) thrust; (vasija) tin, can; (embarcación) boat; (LAM pey: cárcel) jail; **de ~ en ~** packed, jammed full; **~ salvavidas** lifeboat; **~ de la basura** (LAM) dustbin (BRIT), trash can (US)

botella [bo'teʎa] nf bottle; **botellín** nm small bottle; **botellón** nm (ESP fam) outdoor drinking session (involving groups of young people)

botijo [bo'tixo] nm (earthenware) jug

botín [bo'tin] nm (calzado) half boot; (polaina) spat; (Mil) booty

botiquín [boti'kin] nm (armario) medicine chest; (portátil) first-aid kit

botón [bo'ton] nm button; (Bot) bud; **botones** nm inv bellboy, bellhop (US)

bóveda ['boβeða] nf (Arq) vault

boxeador [boksea'ðor] nm boxer

boxeo [bok'seo] nm boxing

boya ['boja] nf (Naut) buoy; (flotador) float

boyante [bo'jante] adj prosperous

bozal [bo'θal] nm (de caballo) halter; (de perro) muzzle

braga ['braɣa] nf (de bebé) nappy, diaper (US); **bragas** nfpl (de mujer) panties

bragueta [bra'ɣeta] nf fly (BRIT), flies pl (BRIT), zipper (US)

braille [breil] nm braille

brasa ['brasa] nf live o hot coal

brasero [bra'sero] nm brazier

brasier [bra'sjer] nm (LAM) bra

Brasil [bra'sil] nm: **(el) ~** Brazil; **brasileño, -a** adj, nm/f Brazilian

brassier [bra'sjer] nm (LAM) V **brasier**

bravo, -a [' braβo, a] adj (valiente) brave; (feroz) ferocious; (salvaje) wild; (mar etc) rough, stormy ▷ excl bravo!; **bravura** nf bravery; ferocity

braza ['braθa] nf fathom; **nadar a la ~** to swim (the) breast-stroke

brazalete [braθa'lete] nm (pulsera) bracelet; (banda) armband

brazo ['braθo] nm arm; (Zool) foreleg; (Bot) limb, branch; **cogidos** etc **del ~** arm in arm

brebaje [bre'βaxe] nm potion

brecha ['bretʃa] nf (hoyo, vacío) gap, opening; (Mil, fig) breach

brega ['breɣa] nf (lucha) struggle; (trabajo) hard work

breva ['breβa] nf (Bot) early fig

breve ['breβe] adj short, brief; **en ~** (pronto) shortly ▷ nf (Mus) breve; **brevedad** nf brevity, shortness

bribón, -ona [bri'βon, ona] adj idle, lazy ▷ nm/f (pícaro) rascal, rogue

bricolaje [briko'laxe] nm do-it-yourself, DIY

brida ['briða] nf bridle, rein; (Tec) clamp

bridge [britʃ] nm bridge

brigada [bri'ɣaða] nf (unidad) brigade; (trabajadores) squad, gang ▷ nm = sergeant major

brillante [bri'ʎante] adj brilliant ▷ nm diamond

brillar [bri'ʎar] /1a/ vi to shine; (joyas) to sparkle

brillo ['briʎo] nm shine; (brillantez) brilliance; (fig) splendour; **sacar ~ a** to polish

brincar [brin'kar] /1g/ vi to skip about, hop about, jump about

brinco ['brinko] nm jump, leap

brindar [brin'dar] /1a/ vi: **~ a o por** to drink (a toast) to ▷ vt to offer, present

brindis ['brindis] nm inv toast

brío ['brio] nm spirit, dash

brisa ['brisa] nf breeze

británico, -a [bri'taniko, a] adj British ▷ nm/f Briton, British person

brizna ['briθna] nf (de hierba) blade; (de tabaco) leaf

broca ['broka] nf (Tec) drill bit

brocha ['brotʃa] nf (large) paintbrush; **~ de afeitar** shaving brush

broche ['brotʃe] nm brooch

broma ['broma] nf joke; **en ~** in fun, as a joke; **~ pesada** practical joke; **bromear** /1a/ vi to joke

bromista [bro'mista] adj fond of joking ▷ nmf joker, wag

bronca ['bronka] nf row; **echar una ~ a algn** to tell sb off

bronce ['bronθe] nm bronze; **bronceado, -a** adj bronze cpd; (por el sol) tanned ▷ nm (sun)tan; (Tec) bronzing

bronceador [bronθea'ðor] nm suntan lotion

broncearse [bronθe'arse] /1a/ vr to get a suntan

bronquios ['bronkjos] nmpl bronchial tubes

bronquitis [bron'kitis] nf inv bronchitis

brotar [bro'tar] /1a/ vi (Bot) to sprout; (aguas) to gush (forth); (Med) to break out

brote ['brote] nm (Bot) shoot; (Med, fig) outbreak

bruces ['bruθes]: **de ~** adv, **caer** o **dar de ~** to fall headlong, fall flat

bruja ['bruxa] nf witch; **brujería** nf witchcraft

brujo ['bruxo] nm wizard, magician

brújula ['bruxula] nf compass

bruma ['bruma] nf mist

brusco, -a ['brusko, a] adj (súbito) sudden; (áspero) brusque

Bruselas [bru'selas] nf Brussels

brutal [bru'tal] adj brutal; **brutalidad** nf brutality

bruto, -a ['bruto, a] adj (idiota) stupid; (bestial) brutish; (peso) gross; **en ~** raw, unworked

Bs.As. abr = **Buenos Aires**

bucal [bu'kal] adj oral; **por vía ~** orally

bucear [buθe'ar] /1a/ vi to dive ▷ vt to explore; **buceo** nm diving

bucle ['bukle] nm curl

budismo [bu'ðismo] nm Buddhism

buen [bwen] adj V **bueno**

buenamente [bwena'mente] adv (fácilmente) easily; (voluntariamente) willingly

buenaventura [bwena'βen'tura] *nf* (suerte) good luck; (adivinación) fortune

buenmozo [bwen'moθo] *adj* (LAM) handsome

PALABRA CLAVE

bueno, -a, antes de nm *sg* **buen** ['bweno, a] *adj* 1 (excelente etc) good; **es un libro bueno, es un buen libro** it's a good book; **hace bueno, hace buen tiempo** the weather is fine, it is fine; **el bueno de Paco** good old Paco; **fue muy bueno conmigo** he was very nice o kind to me

2 (apropiado): **ser bueno para** to be good for; **creo que vamos por buen camino** I think we're on the right track

3 (irónico): **le di un buen rapapolvo** I gave him a good o real ticking off; **¡buen conductor estás hecho!** some driver o a fine driver you are!; **¡estaría bueno que …!** I a fine thing it would be if …!

4 (atractivo, sabroso): **está bueno este bizcocho** this sponge is delicious; **Julio está muy bueno** (fam) Julio's gorgeous

5 (saludos): **¡buen día!** (LAM), **¡buenos días!** (good) morning!; **¡buenas tardes!** (good) afternoon!; (más tarde) good evening!; **¡buenas noches!** good night!

6 (otras locuciones): **estar de buenas** to be in a good mood; **por las buenas o por las malas** by hook or by crook; **de buenas a primeras** all of a sudden

► *excl*: **¡bueno!** all right!; **bueno, ¿y qué?** well, so what?

Buenos Aires ['bweno'saires] *nm* Buenos Aires

buey [bwei] *nm* ox

búfalo ['bufalo] *nm* buffalo

bufanda [bu'fanda] *nf* scarf

bufete [bu'fete] *nm* (despacho de abogado) lawyer's office

bufón [bu'fon] *nm* clown

buhardilla [buar'ðiʎa] *nf* attic

búho ['buo] *nm* owl; (fig) hermit, recluse

buitre ['bwitre] *nm* vulture

bujía [bu'xia] *nf* (vela) candle; (Elec) candle (power); (Auto) spark plug

bula ['bula] *nf* (papal) bull

bulbo ['bulβo] *nm* (Bot) bulb

bulevar [bule'βar] *nm* boulevard

Bulgaria [bul'yarja] *nf* Bulgaria; **búlgaro, -a** *adj, nm/f* Bulgarian

bulla ['buʎa] *nf* (ruido) uproar; (de gente) crowd

bullicio [bu'ʎiθjo] *nm* (ruido) uproar; (movimiento) bustle

bulto ['bulto] *nm* (paquete) package; (fardo) bundle; (tamaño) size, bulkiness; (Med) swelling, lump; (silueta) vague shape

buñuelo [bu'nwelo] *nm* ≈ doughnut, ≈ donut (US); (fruta de sartén) fritter

buque ['buke] *nm* ship, vessel; **~ de guerra** warship

burbuja [bur'βuxa] *nf* bubble

burdel [bur'ðel] *nm* brothel

burgués, -esa [bur'ɣes, esa] *adj* middle-class, bourgeois; **burguesía** *nf* middle class, bourgeoisie

burla ['burla] *nf* (mofa) gibe; (broma) joke; (engaño) trick; **burlar** /1a/ *vt* (engañar) to deceive ▷ *vi* to joke; **burlarse** *vr* to joke; **burlarse de** to make fun of

burlón, -ona [bur'lon, ona] *adj* mocking

buró [bu'ro] *nm* bureau

burocracia [buro'kraθja] *nf* bureaucracy

burrada [bu'rraða] *nf*: **decir ~s** to talk nonsense; **hacer ~s** to act stupid; **una ~** (ESP: mucho) a (hell of a) lot

burro, -a ['burro, a] *nm/f* (Zool) donkey; (fig) ass, idiot

bursátil [bur'satil] *adj* stock-exchange *cpd*

bus [bus] *nm* bus

busca ['buska] *nf* search, hunt ▷ *nm* bleeper; **en ~ de** in search of

buscador [buska'ðor] nm (Internet) search engine

buscar [bus'kar] /1g/ vt to look for; (Inform) to search ▷ vi to look, search, seek; **se busca secretaria** secretary wanted

busque etc ['buske] vb V **buscar**

búsqueda ['buskeða] nf = **busca**

busto ['busto] nm (Anat, Arte) bust

butaca [bu'taka] nf armchair; (de cine, teatro) stall, seat

butano [bu'tano] nm butane (gas)

buzo ['buθo] nm diver

buzón [bu'θon] nm (gen) letter box; (en la calle) pillar box (BRIT)

C

cabal [ka'βal] adj (exacto) exact; (correcto) right, proper; (acabado) finished, complete; **cabales** nmpl: **estar en sus ~es** to be in one's right mind

cabalgar [kaβal'ɣar] /1h/ vt to ride, vi to ride

cabalgata [kaβal'ɣata] nf procession

caballa [ka'βaʎa] nf mackerel

caballería [kaβaʎe'ria] nf mount; (Mil) cavalry

caballero [kaβa'ʎero] nm gentleman; (de la orden de caballería) knight; (trato directo) sir

caballete [kaβa'ʎete] nm (Arte) easel; (Tec) trestle

caballito [kaβa'ʎito] nm (caballo pequeño) small horse, pony; **caballitos** nmpl merry-go-round sg

caballo [ka'βaʎo] nm horse; (Ajedrez) knight; (Naipes) = queen; **ir en ~** to ride; **~ de carreras** racehorse; **~ de vapor** o **de fuerza** horsepower

cabaña [ka'βaɲa] nf (casita) hut, cabin

cabecear [kaβeθe'ar] /1a/ vt, vi to nod

cabecera [kaβe'θera] nf head; (Imprenta) headline

cabecilla [kaβe'θiʎa] nm ringleader

cabellera [kaβe'ʎera] nf (head of) hair; (de cometa) tail

cabello [ka'βeʎo] nm (tb: **-s**) hair sg; **- de ángel** confectionery and pastry filling made of pumpkin and syrup

caber [ka'βer] /2j/ vi (entrar) to fit, go; **caben tres más** there's room for three more

cabestrillo [kaβes'triʎo] nm sling

cabeza [ka'βeθa] nf head; (Pol) chief, leader; **- de ajo** bulb of garlic; **- de familia** head of the household; **- rapada** skinhead; **cabezada** nf (golpe) butt; **dar una cabezada** to nod (off); **cabezón, -ona** adj with a big head; (vino) heady; (obstinado) pig-headed

cabida [ka'βiða] nf space

cabina [ka'βina] nf (de avión) cockpit; (de camión) cab; **- telefónica** (tele)phone box (BRIT) o booth

cabizbajo, -a [kaβiθ'βaxo, a] adj crestfallen, dejected

cable ['kaβle] nm cable

cabo ['kaβo] nm (de objeto) end, extremity; (Mil) corporal; (Naut) rope, cable; (Geo) cape; **al - de tres días** after three days; **llevar a -** to carry out

cabra ['kaβra] nf goat

cabré etc [ka'βre] vb V **caber**

cabrear [kaβre'ar] /1a/ vt to annoy; **cabrearse** vr (enfadarse) to fly off the handle

cabrito [ka'βrito] nm kid

cabrón [ka'βron] nm cuckold; (fam!) bastard (!)

caca ['kaka] nf pooh

cacahuete [kaka'wete] nm (ESP) peanut

cacao [ka'kao] nm cocoa; (Bot) cacao

cacarear [kakare'ar] /1a/ vi (persona) to boast; (gallo) to crow

cacarizo, -a [kaka'riθo, a] adj (LAM) pockmarked

cacería [kaθe'ria] nf hunt

cacerola [kaθe'rola] nf pan, saucepan

cachalote [katʃa'lote] nm sperm whale

cacharro [ka'tʃarro] nm (cerámica) piece of pottery; **cacharros** nmpl pots and pans

cachear [katʃe'ar] /1a/ vt to search, frisk

cachemir [katʃe'mir] nm cashmere

cachetada [katʃe'taða] nf (LAM fam: bofetada) slap

cachete [ka'tʃete] nm (Anat) cheek; (bofetada) slap (in the face)

cachivache [katʃi'βatʃe] nm piece of junk; **cachivaches** nmpl junk sg

cacho ['katʃo] nm (small) bit; (LAM: cuerno) horn

cachondeo [katʃon'deo] nm (ESP fam) farce, joke

cachondo, -a [ka'tʃondo, a] adj (Zool) on heat; (caliente) randy, sexy; (gracioso) funny

cachorro, -a [ka'tʃorro, a] nm/f (de perro) pup, puppy; (de león) cub

cachucha [ka'tʃutʃa] (MÉX fam) nf cap

cacique [ka'θike] nm chief, local ruler; (Pol) local party boss

cacto ['kakto] nm, **cactus** ['kaktus] nm inv cactus

cada ['kaða] adj inv each; (antes de número) every; **- día** each day, every day; **- dos días** every other day; **- uno/a** each one, every one; **- vez más/menos** more and more/less and less; **- vez que** ... whenever, every time (that) ...; **uno de - diez** one out of every ten

cadáver [ka'ðaβer] nm (dead) body, corpse

cadena [ka'ðena] nf chain; (TV) channel; **trabajo en -** assembly line work; **- montañosa** mountain range; **- perpetua** (Jur) life imprisonment; **- de caracteres** (Inform) character string

cadera [ka'ðera] nf hip

cadete [ka'ðete] nm cadet

caducar [kaðu'kar] /1g/ vi to expire; **caduco, -a** adj (idea etc) outdated, outmoded; **de hoja caduca** deciduous

caer [ka'er] /2n/ vi to fall; **caerse** vr to fall (down); **dejar ~** to drop; **su cumpleaños cae en viernes** her birthday falls on a Friday

café [ka'fe] (pl **cafés**) nm (bebida, planta) coffee; (lugar) café ▷ adj (color) brown; **~ con leche** white coffee; **~ solo, ~ negro** (LAM) (small) black coffee

cafetera [kafe'tera] nf V **cafetero**

cafetería [kafete'ria] nf cafe

cafetero, -a [kafe'tero, a] adj coffee cpd ▷ nf coffee pot; **ser muy ~** to be a coffee addict

cagar [ka'ɣar] /1h/ (fam!) vt to bungle, mess up ▷ vi to have a shit (!)

caído, -a [ka'iðo, a] adj fallen ▷ nf fall; (declive) slope; (disminución) fall, drop

caiga etc ['kaiɣa] vb V **caer**

caimán [kai'man] nm alligator

caja ['kaxa] nf box; (para reloj) case; (de ascensor) shaft; (Com) cash box; (donde se hacen los pagos) cashdesk; (en supermercado) checkout, till; **~ de ahorros** savings bank; **~ de cambios** gearbox; **~ de fusibles** fuse box; **~ fuerte** o **de caudales** safe, strongbox

cajero, -a [ka'xero, a] nm/f cashier ▷ nm: **~ automático** cash dispenser

cajetilla [kaxe'tiʎa] nf (de cigarrillos) packet

cajón [ka'xon] nm big box; (de mueble) drawer

cajuela [kax'wela] nf (MÉX: Auto) boot (BRIT), trunk (US)

cal [kal] nf lime

cala ['kala] nf (Geo) cove, inlet; (de barco) hold

calabacín [kalaβa'θin] nm (Bot) baby marrow; (: más pequeño) courgette (BRIT), zucchini (US)

calabacita [kalaβa'θita] (LAM) nf courgette (BRIT), zucchini (US)

calabaza [kala'βaθa] nf (Bot) pumpkin

calabozo [kala'βoθo] nm (cárcel) prison; (celda) cell

calado, -a [ka'laðo, a] adj (prenda) lace cpd ▷ nm (Naut) draught ▷ nf (de cigarrillo) puff; **estar ~ (hasta los huesos)** to be soaked (to the skin)

calamar [kala'mar] nm squid

calambre [ka'lambre] nm (Elec) shock

calar [ka'lar] /1a/ vt to soak, drench; (penetrar) to pierce, penetrate; (comprender) to see through; (vela, red) to lower; **calarse** vr (Auto) to stall; **~se las gafas** to stick one's glasses on

calavera [kala'βera] nf skull

calcar [kal'kar] /1g/ vt (reproducir) to trace; (imitar) to copy

calcetín [kalθe'tin] nm sock

calcio ['kalθjo] nm calcium

calcomanía [kalkoma'nia] nf transfer

calculador, a [kalkula'ðor, a] adj calculating ▷ nf calculator

calcular [kalku'lar] /1a/ vt (Mat) to calculate, compute; **~ que...** to reckon that...

cálculo ['kalkulo] nm calculation

caldera [kal'dera] nf boiler

calderilla [kalde'riʎa] nf (moneda) small change

caldo ['kaldo] nm stock; (consomé) consommé

calefacción [kalefak'θjon] nf heating; **~ central** central heating

calefón [kale'fon] nm (RPL) boiler

calendario [kalen'darjo] nm calendar

calentador [kalenta'ðor] nm heater

calentamiento [kalenta'mjento] nm (Deporte) warm-up; **~ global** global warming

calentar [kalen'tar] /1j/ vt to heat (up); **calentarse** vr to heat up, warm up; (fig: discusión etc) to get heated

calentón, -ona [kalen'ton, ona] (RPL fam) adj (sexualmente) horny, randy (BRIT)

calentura [kalen'tura] nf (Med) fever, (high) temperature

calesita [kale'sita] nf (LAM) merry-go-round, carousel

calibre [ka'liβre] nm (de cañón) calibre, bore; (diámetro) diameter; (fig) calibre

calidad [kali'ðað] nf quality; **de ~** quality cpd; **en ~ de** in the capacity of

cálido, -a [ka'liðo, a] adj hot; (fig) warm

caliente [ka'ljente] vb V **calentar** ▷ adj hot; (fig) fiery; (disputa) heated; (fam: cachondo) randy

calificación [kalifika'θjon] nf qualification; (de alumno) grade, mark

calificado, -a [kalifi'kaðo, a] adj (LAM: competente) qualified; (obrero) skilled

calificar [kalifi'kar] /1g/ vt to qualify; (alumno) to grade, mark; **~ de** to describe as

calima [ka'lima] nf (cerca del mar) mist

cáliz ['kaliθ] nm chalice

caliza [ka'liθa] nf limestone

callado, -a [ka'ʎaðo, a] adj quiet

callar [ka'ʎar] /1a/ vt (asunto delicado) to keep quiet about, say nothing about; (persona, oposición) to silence ▷ vi to keep quiet, be silent; (dejar de hablar) to stop talking; **callarse** vr to keep quiet, be silent; **¡calla!** be quiet!

calle ['kaʎe] nf street; (Deporte) lane; **~ arriba/abajo** up/down the street; **~ de sentido único** one-way street; **~ mayor** (ESP) high (BRIT) o main (US) street; **~ peatonal** pedestrianized o pedestrian street; **~ principal** (LAM) high (BRIT) o main (US) street; **poner a algn (de patitas) en la ~** to kick sb out; **callejear** /1a/ vi to wander (about) the streets; **callejero, -a** adj street cpd ▷ nm street map; **callejón** nm alley, passage; **callejón sin salida** cul-de-sac; **callejuela** nf side-street, alley

callista [ka'ʎista] nmf chiropodist

callo ['kaʎo] nm callus; (en el pie) corn; **callos** nmpl (Culin) tripe sg

calma ['kalma] nf calm

calmante [kal'mante] nm sedative, tranquilizer

calmar [kal'mar] /1a/ vt to calm, calm down; **calmarse** vr (tempestad) to abate; (mente etc) to become calm

calor [ka'lor] nm heat; (calor agradable) warmth; **tener ~** to be o feel hot

caloría [kalo'ria] nf calorie

calumnia [ka'lumnja] nf slander

caluroso, -a [kalu'roso, a] adj hot; (sin exceso) warm; (fig) enthusiastic

calva ['kalβa] nf bald patch; (en bosque) clearing

calvario [kal'βarjo] nm stations pl of the cross

calvicie [kal'βiθje] nf baldness

calvo, -a ['kalβo, a] adj bald; (terreno) bare, barren; (tejido) threadbare

calza [kalθa] nf wedge, chock

calzado, -a [kal'θaðo, a] adj shod ▷ nm footwear ▷ nf roadway, highway

calzador [kalθa'ðor] nm shoehorn

calzar [kal'θar] /1f/ vt (zapatos etc) to wear; (un mueble) to put a wedge under; **calzarse** vr: **~se los zapatos** to put on one's shoes; **¿qué (número) calza?** what size do you take?

calzón [kal'θon] nm (tb: **calzones**) shorts pl; (LAM: de hombre) pants pl; (: de mujer) panties pl

calzoncillos [kalθon'θiʎos] nmpl underpants

cama ['kama] nf bed; **~ individual/ de matrimonio** single/double bed; **hacer la ~** to make the bed

camaleón [kamale'on] nm chameleon

cámara ['kamara] nf chamber; (habitación) room; (sala) hall; (Cine) cine camera; (fotográfica) camera; **~ de aire** inner tube; **~ de comercio** chamber of commerce; **~ digital** digital camera; **~ de gas** gas chamber; **~ frigorífica** cold-storage room

camarada [kama'raða] nm comrade, companion

camarero, -a [kama'rero, a] nm waiter ▷ nf (en restaurante) waitress; (en casa, hotel) maid

camarógrafo, -a [kama'roɣrafo, a] nm/f (LAM) cameraman/camerawoman

camarón [kama'ron] nm shrimp

camarote [kama'rote] nm cabin

cambiable [kam'bjaβle] adj (variable) changeable, variable; (intercambiable) interchangeable

cambiante [kam'bjante] adj variable

cambiar [kam'bjar] /1b/ vt to change; (trocar) to exchange ▷ vi to change; **cambiarse** vr (mudarse) to move; (de ropa) to change; **~ de idea u opinión** to change one's mind; **~se de ropa** to change (one's clothes)

cambio ['kambjo] nm change; (trueque) exchange; (Com) rate of exchange; (oficina) bureau de change; (dinero menudo) small change; **a ~ de** in return o exchange for; **en ~** on the other hand; (en lugar de eso) instead; **~ climático** climate change; **~ de divisas** (Com) foreign exchange; **~ de velocidades** gear lever

camelar [kame'lar] /1a/ vt (persuadir) to sweet-talk

camello [ka'meʎo] nm camel; (fam: traficante) pusher

camerino [kame'rino] nm dressing room

camilla [ka'miʎa] nf (Med) stretcher

caminar [kami'nar] /1a/ vi (marchar) to walk, go ▷ vt (recorrer) to cover, travel

caminata [kami'nata] nf long walk; (por el campo) hike

camino [ka'mino] nm way, road; (sendero) track; **a medio ~** halfway (there); **en el ~** on the way, en route; **~ de** on the way to; **~ particular** private road; **C~ de Santiago** Way of St James; see note **"Camino de Santiago"**

camión [ka'mjon] nm lorry, truck (US); (LAM: autobús) bus; **~ cisterna** tanker; **~ de la basura** dustcart, refuse lorry; **~ de mudanzas** removal (BRIT) o moving (US) van; **camionero** nm lorry o truck (US) driver, trucker (esp US); **camioneta** [kamjo'neta] nf van, small truck; **camionista** nmf (LAM) lorry o truck driver

camisa [ka'misa] nf shirt; (Bot) skin; **~ de fuerza** straitjacket

camiseta [kami'seta] nf tee-shirt; (ropa interior) vest; (de deportista) top

camisón [kami'son] nm nightdress, nightgown

camorra [ka'morra] nf: **buscar ~** to look for trouble

camote [ka'mote] nm (LAM) sweet potato; (bulbo) tuber, bulb; (fam: enamoramiento) crush

campamento [kampa'mento] nm camp

campana [kam'pana] nf bell; **campanada** nf peal; **campanario** nm belfry

campanilla [kampa'niʎa] nf small bell

campaña [kam'paɲa] nf (Mil, Pol) campaign; **~ electoral** election campaign

campechano, -a [kampe'tʃano, a] adj (franco) open

campeón, -ona [kampe'on, ona] nm/f champion; **campeonato** nm championship

cámper ['kamper] nm o f (LAM) caravan (BRIT), trailer (US)

campera [kam'pera] nf (RPL) anorak

campesino, -a [kampe'sino, a] adj country cpd, rural; (gente) peasant cpd ▷ nm/f countryman/woman; (agricultor) farmer

campestre [kam'pestre] adj country cpd, rural

camping ['kampin] nm camping; (lugar) campsite; **ir de** o **hacer ~** to go camping

campista [kam'pista] nmf camper

campo ['kampo] nm (fuera de la ciudad) country, countryside; (Agr, Elec, Inform) field; (de fútbol) pitch; (de golf) course; (Mil) camp; **~ de batalla** battlefield; **~ de minas** minefield; **~ petrolífero** oilfield; **~ visual** field of vision; **~ de concentración/ de internación/de trabajo** concentration/internment/labour camp; **~ de deportes** sports ground, playing field

camuflaje [kamu'flaxe] nm camouflage

cana ['kana] nf V **cano**

Canadá [kana'ða] nm Canada; **canadiense** adj, nmf Canadian ▷ nf fur-lined jacket

canal [ka'nal] nm canal; (Geo) channel, strait; (de televisión) channel; (de tejado) gutter; **C~ de la Mancha** English Channel; **C~ de Panamá** Panama Canal

canaleta [kana'leta] nf (LAM: de tejado) gutter

canalizar [kanali'θar] /1f/ vt to channel

canalla [ka'naʎa] nf rabble, mob ▷ nm swine

canapé [kana'pe] (pl **canapés**) nm sofa, settee; (Culin) canapé

Canarias [ka'narjas] nfpl: **las (Islas) ~** the Canaries

canario, -a [ka'narjo, a] adj of o from the Canary Isles ▷ nm/f native o inhabitant of the Canary Isles ▷ nm (Zool) canary

canasta [ka'nasta] nf (round) basket

canasto [ka'nasto] nm large basket

cancela [kan'θela] nf (wrought-iron) gate

cancelación [kanθela'θjon] nf cancellation

cancelar [kanθe'lar] /1a/ vt to cancel; (una deuda) to write off

cáncer ['kanθer] nm (Med) cancer; **C~** (Astro) Cancer

cancha ['kantʃa] nf (de baloncesto, tenis etc) court; (LAM: de fútbol etc) pitch; **~ de tenis** (LAM) tennis court

canciller [kanθi'ʎer] nm chancellor

canción [kan'θjon] nf song; **~ de cuna** lullaby

candado [kan'daðo] nm padlock

candente [kan'dente] adj red-hot; (tema) burning

candidato, -a [kandi'ðato, a] nm/f candidate

cándido, -a ['kandiðo, a] adj simple; naive

⬛ No confundir cándido con la palabra inglesa candid.

candil [kan'dil] nm oil lamp; **candilejas** nfpl (Teat) footlights

canela [ka'nela] nf cinnamon

canelones [kane'lones] nmpl cannelloni

cangrejo [kan'grexo] nm crab

canguro [kan'guro] nm kangaroo; **hacer de ~** to baby-sit

caníbal [ka'niβal] adj, nmf cannibal

canica [ka'nika] nf marble

canijo, -a [ka'nixo, a] adj frail, sickly

canilla [ka'niʎa] nf (LAM) tap (BRIT), faucet (US)

canjear [kanxe'ar] /1a/ vt to exchange

cano, -a ['kano, a] adj grey-haired, white-haired ▷ nf (tb: **canas**) white o grey hair; **tener canas** to be going grey

canoa [ka'noa] nf canoe

canon ['kanon] nm canon; (pensión) rent; (Com) tax

canonizar [kanoni'θar] /1f/ vt to canonize

canoso, -a [ka'noso, a] adj grey-haired

cansado, -a [kan'saðo, a] adj tired, weary; (tedioso) tedious, boring

cansancio [kan'sanθjo] nm tiredness, fatigue

cansar [kan'sar] /1a/ vt (fatigar) to tire, tire out; (aburrir) to bore; (fastidiar) to bother; **cansarse** vr to tire, get tired; (aburrirse) to get bored

cantábrico, -a [kan'taβriko, a] adj Cantabrian

cantante [kan'tante] adj singing ▷ nmf singer

cantar [kan'tar] /1a/ vt to sing ▷ vi to sing; (insecto) to chirp ▷ nm (acción) singing; (canción) song; (poema) poem

cántaro ['kantaro] nm pitcher, jug; **llover a ~s** to rain cats and dogs

cante ['kante] nm Andalusian folk song; **~ jondo** flamenco singing

cantera [kan'tera] nf quarry

cantero [kan'tero] nm (AM: arriate) border

cantidad [kanti'ðað] nf quantity, amount; **~ de** lots of

cantimplora [kantim'plora] nf water bottle, canteen

cantina [kan'tina] nf canteen; (de estación) buffet; (esp LAM) bar

cantinero, -a [kanti'nero, a] nm/f (LAM) barman/barmaid, bartender (US)

canto ['kanto] nm singing; (canción) song; (borde) edge, rim; (de un cuchillo) back; **~ rodado** boulder

cantor, a [kan'tor, a] nm/f singer

canturrear [kanturre'ar] /1a/ vi to sing softly

canuto [ka'nuto] nm (tubo) small tube; (fam: porro) joint

caña ['kaɲa] nf (Bot: tallo) stem, stalk; (: carrizo) reed; (de cerveza) glass of beer; (Anat) shinbone; **~ de azúcar** sugar cane; **~ de pescar** fishing rod

cañada [ka'naða] nf (entre dos montañas) gully, ravine; (camino) cattle track

cáñamo ['kaɲamo] nm hemp

cañería [kaɲe'ria] nf (tubo) pipe

caño ['kaɲo] nm (tubo) tube, pipe; (de aguas servidas) sewer; (Mus) pipe; (de fuente) jet

cañón [ka'ɲon] nm (Mil) cannon; (de fusil) barrel; (Geo) canyon, gorge

caoba [ka'oβa] nf mahogany

caos ['kaos] nm chaos

capa ['kapa] nf cloak, cape; (Geo) layer, stratum; **~ de ozono** ozone layer

capacidad [kapaθi'ðað] nf (medida) capacity; (aptitud) capacity, ability

capacitar [kapaθi'tar] /1a/ vt: **~ algn para algo** to qualify sb for sth; **capacitarse** vr: **~se para algo** to qualify for sth

caparazón [kapara'θon] nm shell

capataz [kapa'taθ] nm foreman

capaz [ka'paθ] adj able, capable; (amplio) capacious, roomy

capellán [kape'ʎan] nm chaplain; (sacerdote) priest

capicúa [kapi'kua] adj inv (número, fecha) reversible

capilla [ka'piʎa] nf chapel

capital [kapi'tal] adj capital ▷ nm (Com) capital ▷ nf (de nación) capital (city); **~ social** equity o share capital

capitalismo [kapita'lismo] nm capitalism; **capitalista** adj, nmf capitalist

capitán [kapi'tan] nm captain

capítulo [ka'pitulo] nm chapter

capó [ka'po] nm (Auto) bonnet (BRIT), hood (US)

capón [ka'pon] nm (gallo) capon

capota [ka'pota] nf (de mujer) bonnet; (Auto) hood (BRIT), top (US)

capote [ka'pote] nm (abrigo: de militar) greatcoat; (: de torero) cloak

capricho [ka'pritʃo] nm whim, caprice; **caprichoso, -a** adj capricious

Capricornio [kapri'kornjo] nm
Capricorn

cápsula ['kapsula] nf capsule

captar [kap'tar] /1a/ vt (comprender)
to understand; (Radio) to pick up;
(atención, apoyo) to attract

captura [kap'tura] nf capture; (Jur)
arrest; **capturar** /1a/ vt to capture; (Jur)
(Jur) to arrest

capucha [ka'putʃa] nf hood, cowl

capuchón [kapu'tʃon] nm (ESP: de
bolígrafo) cap

capullo [ka'puʎo] nm (Zool) cocoon;
(Bot) bud; (fam!) idiot

caqui ['kaki] nm khaki

cara ['kara] nf (Anat, de moneda) face;
(de disco) side; (fig) boldness ▷ prep: ~ a
facing; **de ~ a** opposite, facing; **dar la
~** to face the consequences; **¿~ o cruz?**
heads or tails?; **¡qué ~ más dura!**
what a nerve

Caracas [ka'rakas] nf Caracas

caracol [kara'kol] nm (Zool) snail;
(concha) (sea)shell

carácter (pl **caracteres**) [ka'rakter,
karak'teres] nm character; **tener
buen/mal** ~ to be good-natured/bad
tempered

característico, -a [karakte'ristiko,
a] adj characteristic ▷ nf characteristic

caracterizar [karakteri'θar] /1f/ vt
to characterize, typify

caradura [kara'ðura] nmf: **es un** ~
he's got a nerve

carajillo [kara'xiʎo] nm black coffee
with brandy

carajo [ka'raxo] nm (fam!): **¡~!** shit! (!)

caramba [ka'ramba] excl good
gracious!

caramelo [kara'melo] nm (dulce)
sweet; (azúcar fundido) caramel

caravana [kara'βana] nf caravan;
(fig) group; (de coches) tailback

carbón [kar'βon] nm coal; **papel** ~
carbon paper

carbono [kar'βono] nm carbon

carburador [karβura'ðor] nm
carburettor

carburante [karβu'rante] nm fuel

carcajada [karka'xaða] nf (loud)
laugh, guffaw

cárcel [ka'rθel] nf prison, jail; (Tec)
clamp

carcoma [kar'koma] nf woodworm

cardar [kar'ðar] /1a/ vt (Tec) to card,
comb; (pelo) to backcomb

cardenal [karðe'nal] nm (Rel)
cardinal; (Med) bruise

cardiaco, -a [kar'ðjako, a],
cardíaco, a [kar'ðjako, a] adj
cardiac; (ataque) heart cpd

cardinal [karði'nal] adj cardinal

cardo ['karðo] nm thistle

carecer [kare'θer] /2d/ vi: **~ de** to
lack, be in need of

carencia [ka'renθja] nf lack; (escasez)
shortage; (Med) deficiency

careta [ka'reta] nf mask

carga ['karɣa] nf (peso, Elec) load; (de
barco) cargo, freight; (Mil) charge;
(obligación, responsabilidad) duty,
obligation

cargado, -a [kar'ɣaðo, a] adj loaded;
(Elec) live; (café, té) strong; (cielo)
overcast

cargamento [karɣa'mento] nm
(acción) loading; (mercancías) load,
cargo

cargar [kar'ɣar] /1h/ vt (barco, arma)
to load; (Elec) to charge; (Com: algo
en cuenta) to charge, debit; (Mil) to
charge; (Inform) to load ▷ vi (Auto) to
load (up); **~ con** to pick up, carry away;
(peso: fig) to shoulder, bear; **cargarse**
vr (fam: estropear) to break; (: matar)
to bump off

cargo ['karɣo] nm (puesto) post, office;
(responsabilidad) duty, obligation; (Jur)
charge; **hacerse ~ de** to take charge
of o responsibility for

carguero [kar'ɣero] nm freighter,
cargo boat; (avión) freight plane

Caribe [ka'riβe] nm: **el ~** the
Caribbean; **del ~** Caribbean;
caribeño, -a adj Caribbean

caricatura [karika'tura] nf caricature

caricia [ka'riθja] nf caress
caridad [kari'ðað] nf charity
caries ['karjes] nf inv tooth decay
cariño [ka'riɲo] nm affection, love; (caricia) caress; (en carta) love …; **tener ~ a** to be fond of; **cariñoso, -a** adj affectionate
carisma [ka'risma] nm charisma
caritativo, -a [karita'tiβo, a] adj charitable
cariz [ka'riθ] nm: **tener o tomar buen/mal ~** to look good/bad
carmín [kar'min] nm (tb: **~ de labios**) lipstick
carnal [kar'nal] adj carnal; **primo ~** first cousin
carnaval [karna'βal] nm carnival

○ **CARNAVAL**
○
○ The 3 days before *miércoles de ceniza*
○ (Ash Wednesday), when fasting
○ traditionally starts, are the time for
○ *carnaval*, an exuberant celebration
○ which dates back to pre-Christian
○ times. Although in decline during
○ the Franco years, the *carnaval* has
○ grown in popularity recently in
○ Spain, Cádiz and Tenerife being
○ particularly well-known for their
○ celebrations. *El martes de carnaval*
○ (Shrove Tuesday) is the biggest day,
○ with colourful street parades, fancy
○ dress, fireworks and a general party
○ atmosphere.

carne ['karne] nf flesh; (Culin) meat; **se me pone la ~ de gallina sólo verlo** I get the creeps just seeing it; **~ de cerdo/de cordero/de ternera/de vaca** pork/lamb/veal/beef; **~ molida** (LAM), **~ picada** (ESP) mince (BRIT), ground meat (US); **~ de gallina** (fig) gooseflesh
carné [kar'ne] (pl **carnés**) (ESP) nm: **~ de conducir** driving licence (BRIT), driver's license (US); **~ de identidad** identity card; **~ de socio** membership card

carnero [kar'nero] nm sheep, ram; (carne) mutton
carnet [kar'ne] (pl **carnets**) nm (ESP) = **carné**
carnicería [karniθe'ria] nf butcher's (shop); (fig: matanza) carnage, slaughter
carnicero, -a [karni'θero, a] adj carnivorous ▷ nm/f (tb fig) butcher ▷ nm carnivore
carnívoro, -a [kar'niβoro, a] adj carnivorous
caro, -a ['karo, a] adj dear; (Com) dear, expensive ▷ adv dear, dearly
carpa ['karpa] nf (pez) carp; (de circo) big top; (LAM: de camping) tent
carpeta [kar'peta] nf folder, file
carpintería [karpinte'ria] nf carpentry, joinery; **carpintero** nm carpenter
carraspear [karraspe'ar] /1a/ vi to clear one's throat
carraspera [karras'pera] nf hoarseness
carrera [ka'rrera] nf (acción) run(ning); (espacio recorrido) run; (certamen) race; (trayecto) course; (profesión) career; **a la ~** at (full) speed; **~ de obstáculos** (Deporte) steeplechase
carrete [ka'rrete] nm reel, spool; (Tec) coil
carretera [karre'tera] nf (main) road, highway; **~ nacional** ≈ A road (BRIT), ≈ state highway (US); **~ de circunvalación** ring road
carretilla [karre'tiʎa] nf trolley; (Agr) (wheel)barrow
carril [ka'rril] nm furrow; (de autopista) lane; (Ferro) rail
carril bici [karil'βiθi] nm cycle lane, bikeway (US)
carrito [ka'rrito] nm trolley
carro ['karro] nm cart, wagon; (Mil) tank; (LAM: coche) car; **~ patrulla** (LAM), **~ patrulla** (BRIT) patrol o panda (BRIT) car
carrocería [karroθe'ria] nf bodywork no pl (BRIT)

carroña [ka'rɾoɲa] *nf* carrion *no pl*

carroza [ka'rɾoθa] *nf* (*vehículo*) coach

carrusel [karru'sel] *nm* merry-go-round, roundabout (BRIT)

carta ['karta] *nf* letter; (*Culin*) menu; (*naipe*) card; (*mapa*) map; (*Jur*) document; **~ certificada/urgente** registered/special delivery letter

cartabón [karta'βon] *nm* set square

cartearse [karte'arse] /1a/ *vr* to correspond

cartel [kar'tel] *nm* (*anuncio*) poster, placard; (*Escol*) wall chart; (*Com*) cartel; **cartelera** *nf* hoarding, billboard; (*en periódico etc*) entertainments guide; **"en cartelera"** "showing"

cartera [kar'tera] *nf* (*de bolsillo*) wallet; (*de colegial, cobrador*) satchel; (*de señora*) handbag (BRIT), purse (US); (*para documentos*) briefcase; (*Com*) portfolio; **ocupa la ~ de Agricultura** he is Minister of Agriculture

carterista [karte'rista] *nmf* pickpocket

cartero [kar'tero] *nm* postman

cartilla [kar'tiʎa] *nf* primer, first reading book; **~ de ahorros** savings book

cartón [kar'ton] *nm* cardboard; **~ piedra** papier-mâché

cartucho [kar'tutʃo] *nm* (*Mil*) cartridge

cartulina [kartu'lina] *nf* card

casa ['kasa] *nf* house; (*hogar*) home; (*Com*) firm, company; **~ consistorial** town hall; **~ de huéspedes** boarding house; **~ de socorro** first aid post; **~ independiente** detached house; **~ rodante** (cs) caravan (BRIT), trailer (US); **en ~** at home

casado, -a [ka'saðo, a] *adj* married ▷ *nm/f* married man/woman

casar [ka'sar] /1a/ *vt* to marry; (*Jur*) to quash, annul; **casarse** *vr* to marry, get married

cascabel [kaska'βel] *nm* (small) bell

cascada [kas'kaða] *nf* waterfall

cascanueces [kaska'nweθes] *nm inv* (a pair of) nutcrackers, nutcracker *sg*

cascar [kas'kar] /1g/ *vt* to split; (*nuez*) to crack; **cascarse** *vr* to crack, split, break (open)

cáscara ['kaskara] *nf* (*de huevo, fruta seca*) shell; (*de fruta*) skin; (*de limón*) peel

casco ['kasko] *nm* (*de bombero, soldado*) helmet; (*Naut: de barco*) hull; (*Zool: de caballo*) hoof; (*botella*) empty bottle; (*de ciudad*) **el ~ antiguo** the old part; **el ~ urbano** the town centre; **los ~s azules** the UN peace-keeping force, the blue helmets

cascote [kas'kote] *nm* piece of rubble; **cascotes** *nmpl* rubble *sg*

caserío [kase'rio] *nm* hamlet, group of houses; (*casa*) farmhouse

casero, -a [ka'sero, a] *adj* (*pan etc*) home-made; (*persona*): **ser muy ~** to be home-loving ▷ *nm/f* (*propietario*) landlord/lady; **"comida casera"** "home cooking"

caseta [ka'seta] *nf* hut; (*para bañista*) cubicle; (*de feria*) stall

casete [ka'sete] *nm o f* cassette

casi ['kasi] *adv* almost; **~ nunca** hardly ever, almost never; **~ nada** next to nothing; **~ te caes** you almost o nearly fell

casilla [ka'siʎa] *nf* (*casita*) hut, cabin; (*para cartas*) pigeonhole; (*Ajedrez*) square; **C~ postal** o **de Correo(s)** (LAM) P.O. Box; **casillero** *nm* (*para cartas*) pigeonholes *pl*

casino [ka'sino] *nm* club; (*de juego*) casino

caso ['kaso] *nm* case; **en ~ de ...** in case of ...; **el ~ es que** the fact is that; **en ese ~** in that case; **en todo ~** in any case; **hacer ~ a** to pay attention to; **hacer o venir al ~** to be relevant

caspa ['kaspa] *nf* dandruff

cassette [ka'set] *nm o f* = **casete**

castaña [kas'taɲa] *nf* V **castaño**

castaño, -a [kas'taɲo, a] *adj*
chestnut(-coloured), brown ▷ *nm*
chestnut tree ▷ *nf* beaver

castañuelas [kasta'ɲwelas] *nfpl*
castanets

castellano, -a [kaste'ʎano, a] *adj*
Castilian ▷ *nm/f* Castilian ▷ *nm* (Ling)
Castilian, Spanish

castigar [kasti'ɣar] /1h/ *vt* to punish;
(*Deporte*) to penalize; **castigo** *nm*
punishment; (*Deporte*) penalty

Castilla [kas'tiʎa] *nf* Castile

castillo [kas'tiʎo] *nm* castle

castizo, -a [kas'tiθo, a] *adj* (Ling) pure

casto, -a ['kasto, a] *adj* chaste, pure

castor [kas'tor] *nm* beaver

castrar [kas'trar] /1a/ *vt* to castrate

casual [ka'swal] *adj* chance,
accidental; **casualidad** *nf*
chance, accident; (*combinación de
circunstancias*) coincidence; **da la
casualidad de que ...** it (just) so
happens that ...; **¡qué casualidad!**
what a coincidence!

> No confundir *casual* con la palabra
> inglesa *casual*.

cataclismo [kata'klismo] *nm*
cataclysm

catador [kata'ðor] *nm* taster

catalán, -ana [kata'lan, ana] *adj,
nm/f* Catalan ▷ *nm* (Ling) Catalan

catalizador [kataliθa'ðor] *nm*
catalyst; (*Auto*) catalytic converter

catalogar [katalo'ɣar] /1h/ *vt* to
catalogue; **~ (de)** (*fig*) to classify as

catálogo [ka'taloɣo] *nm* catalogue

Cataluña [kata'luɲa] *nf* Catalonia

catar [ka'tar] /1a/ *vt* to taste, sample

catarata [kata'rata] *nf* (Geo) (water)
fall; (*Med*) cataract

catarro [ka'tarro] *nm* catarrh;
(*constipado*) cold

catástrofe [ka'tastrofe] *nf*
catastrophe

catear [kate'ar] /1a/ *vt* (fam: *examen,
alumno*) to fail

cátedra ['kateðra] *nf* (Univ) chair,
professorship

catedral [kate'ðral] *nf* cathedral

catedrático, -a [kate'ðratiko, a]
nm/f professor

categoría [kateɣo'ria] *nf* category;
(*rango*) rank, standing; (*calidad*)
quality; **de ~** (hotel) top-class

cateto [ka'teto, a] *nm/f* yokel

catolicismo [katoli'θismo] *nm*
Catholicism

católico, -a [ka'toliko, a] *adj, nm/f*
Catholic

catorce [ka'torθe] *num* fourteen

cauce ['kauθe] *nm* (de río) riverbed;
(*fig*) channel

caucho ['kauʧo] *nm* rubber

caudal [kau'ðal] *nm* (de río) volume,
flow; (*fortuna*) wealth; (*abundancia*)
abundance

caudillo [kau'ðiʎo] *nm* leader, chief

causa ['kausa] *nf* cause; (*razón*)
reason; (*Jur*) lawsuit, case; **a o por ~
de** because of; **causar** /1a/ *vt* to cause

cautela [kau'tela] *nf* caution,
cautiousness; **cauteloso, -a** *adj*
cautious, wary

cautivar [kauti'βar] /1a/ *vt* to
capture; (*fig*) to captivate

cautiverio [kauti'βerjo] *nm*,
cautividad [kautiβi'ðað] *nf*
captivity

cautivo, -a [kau'tiβo, a] *adj, nm/f*
captive

cauto, -a ['kauto, a] *adj* cautious,
careful

cava ['kaβa] *nm* champagne-type wine

cavar [ka'βar] /1a/ *vt* to dig

caverna [ka'βerna] *nf* cave, cavern

cavidad [kaβi'ðað] *nf* cavity

cavilar [kaβi'lar] /1a/ *vt* to ponder

cayendo *etc* [ka'jendo] *vb* V **caer**

caza ['kaθa] *nf* (*acción: gen*) hunting;
(: *con fusil*) shooting; (*una caza*) hunt,
chase; (*animales*) game ▷ *nm* (Aviat)
fighter; **ir de ~** to go hunting; **~
mayor** game hunting; **cazador, a**
nm/f hunter/huntress ▷ *nf* jacket;
cazar /1f/ *vt* to hunt; (*perseguir*) to
chase; (*prender*) to catch

cazo ['kaθo] *nm* saucepan

cazuela [ka'θwela] *nf (vasija)* pan; *(guisado)* casserole

CD *nm abr (= compact disc)* CD

CD-ROM [θeðe'rom] *nm abr* CD-ROM

CE *nm abr (= Consejo de Europa)* Council of Europe

cebada [θe'βaða] *nf* barley

cebar [θe'βar] /1a/ *vt (animal)* to fatten (up); *(anzuelo)* to bait; *(Mil, Tec)* to prime

cebo ['θeβo] *nm (para animales)* feed, food; *(para peces, fig)* bait; *(de arma)* charge

cebolla [θe'βoʎa] *nf* onion; **cebolleta** *nf* spring onion

cebra ['θeβra] *nf* zebra

cecear [θeθe'ar] /1a/ *vi* to lisp

ceder [θe'ðer] /2a/ *vt* to hand over; *(renunciar a)* to give up, part with ▷ *vi (renunciar)* to give in, yield; *(disminuir)* to diminish, decline; *(romperse)* to give way

cederom [θeðe'rom] *nm* CD-ROM

cedro ['θeðro] *nm* cedar

cédula ['θeðula] *nf* certificate, document; **~ de identidad** (LAM) identity card; **~ electoral** (LAM) ballot

cegar [θe'ɣar] /1h, 1j/ *vt* to blind; *(tubería etc)* to block up, stop up ▷ *vi* to go blind; **cegarse** *vr:* **~se (de)** to be blinded (by)

ceguera [θe'ɣera] *nf* blindness

ceja ['θexa] *nf* eyebrow

cejar [θe'xar] /1a/ *vi (fig)* to back down

celador, a [θela'ðor, a] *nm/f (de edificio)* watchman; *(de museo etc)* attendant

celda ['θelda] *nf* cell

celebración [θeleβra'θjon] *nf* celebration

celebrar [θele'βrar] /1a/ *vt* to celebrate; *(alabar)* to praise ▷ *vi* to be glad; **celebrarse** *vr* to occur, take place

célebre ['θeleβre] *adj* famous

celebridad [θeleβri'ðað] *nf* fame; *(persona)* celebrity

celeste [θe'leste] *adj* sky-blue

celestial [θeles'tjal] *adj* celestial, heavenly

celo[1] ['θelo] *nm* zeal; *(Rel)* fervour; **celos** *nmpl* jealousy *sg;* **dar ~s a algn** to make sb jealous; **tener ~s de algn** to be jealous of sb; **en ~** *(animales)* on heat

celo[2]® ['θelo] *nm* Sellotape®

celofán [θelo'fan] *nm* Cellophane®

celoso, -a [θe'loso, a] *adj* jealous; *(trabajador)* zealous

celta ['θelta] *adj* Celtic ▷ *nmf* Celt

célula ['θelula] *nf* cell

celulitis [θelu'litis] *nf* cellulite

cementerio [θemen'terjo] *nm* cemetery, graveyard

cemento [θe'mento] *nm* cement; *(hormigón)* concrete; *(LAM: cola)* glue

cena ['θena] *nf* evening meal, dinner; **cenar** /1a/ *vt* to have for dinner ▷ *vi* to have dinner

cenicero [θeni'θero] *nm* ashtray

ceniza [θe'niθa] *nf* ash, ashes *pl*

censo ['θenso] *nm* census; **~ electoral** electoral roll

censura [θen'sura] *nf (Pol)* censorship; **censurar** /1a/ *vt (idea)* to censure; *(cortar: película)* to censor

centella [θen'teʎa] *nf* spark

centenar [θente'nar] *nm* hundred

centenario, -a [θente'narjo, a] *adj* hundred-year-old ▷ *nm* centenary; **ser ~** to be one hundred years old

centeno [θen'teno] *nm* rye

centésimo, -a [θen'tesimo, a] *adj* hundredth

centígrado [θen'tiɣraðo] *adj* centigrade

centímetro [θen'timetro] *nm* centimetre (BRIT), centimeter (US)

céntimo ['θentimo] *nm* cent

centinela [θenti'nela] *nm* sentry, guard

centollo, -a [θen'toʎo, a] *nm/f* large *(o* spider*)* crab

central [θen'tral] *adj* central ▷ *nf* head office; *(Tec)* plant; *(Telec)* exchange; **~ eléctrica** power station; **~ nuclear** nuclear power station; **~ telefónica** telephone exchange

centralita [θentra'lita] nf switchboard

centralizar [θentrali'θar] /1f/ vt to centralize

centrar [θen'trar] /1a/ vt to centre

céntrico, -a ['θentriko, a] adj central

centrifugar [θentrifu'yar] /1h/ vt to spin-dry

centro ['θentro] nm centre; **~ comercial** shopping centre; **~ de atención al cliente** call centre; **~ de salud** health centre; **~ escolar** school; **~ juvenil** youth club; **~ social** community centre; **~ turístico** (lugar muy visitado) tourist centre; **~ urbano** urban area, city

centroamericano, -a [θentroameri'kano, a] adj, nm/f Central American

ceñido, -a [θe'niðo, a] adj tight

ceñir [θe'nir] vt (rodear) to encircle, surround; (ajustar) to fit (tightly)

ceño ['θeno] nm frown, scowl; **fruncir el ~** to frown, knit one's brow

cepillar [θepi'ʎar] /1a/ vt to brush; (madera) to plane (down)

cepillo [θe'piʎo] nm brush; (para madera) plane; **~ de dientes** toothbrush

cera ['θera] nf wax

cerámica [θe'ramika] nf pottery; (arte) ceramics sg

cerca ['θerka] nf fence ▷ adv near, nearby, close ▷ prep: **~ de** near, close to

cercanía [θerka'nia] nf closeness; **cercanías** nfpl outskirts, suburbs

cercano, -a [θer'kano, a] adj close, near

cercar [θer'kar] /1g/ vt to fence in; (rodear) to surround

cerco ['θerko] nm (Agr) enclosure; (LAM) fence; (Mil) siege

cerdo ['θerðo] nm pig; **carne de ~** pork

cereal [θere'al] nm cereal; **cereales** nmpl cereals, grain sg

cerebro [θe'reβro] nm brain; (fig) brains pl

ceremonia [θere'monja] nf ceremony; **ceremonioso, -a** adj ceremonious

cereza [θe'reθa] nf cherry

cerilla [θe'riʎa] nf, **cerillo** [se'riʎo] nm (LAM) match

cero ['θero] nm nothing, zero

cerquillo [θer'kiʎo] nm (LAM) fringe (BRIT), bangs pl (US)

cerrado, -a [θe'rraðo, a] adj closed, shut; (con llave) locked; (tiempo) cloudy, overcast; (curva) sharp; (acento) thick, broad

cerradura [θerra'ðura] nf (acción) closing; (mecanismo) lock

cerrajero, -a [θerra'xero, a] nm/f locksmith

cerrar [θe'rrar] /1j/ vt to close, shut; (paso, carretera) to close; (grifo) to turn off; (trato, cuenta, negocio) to close ▷ vi to close, shut; (la noche) to come down; **cerrarse** vr to close, shut; **~ con llave** to lock; **~ un trato** to strike a bargain

cerro ['θerro] nm hill

cerrojo [θe'rroxo] nm (herramienta) bolt; (de puerta) latch

certamen [θer'tamen] nm competition, contest

certero, -a [θer'tero, a] adj accurate

certeza [θer'teθa] nf certainty

certidumbre [θerti'ðumbre] nf = **certeza**

certificado, -a [θertifi'kaðo, a] adj certified; (Correos) registered ▷ nm certificate; **~ médico** medical certificate

certificar [θertifi'kar] /1g/ vt (asegurar, atestar) to certify

cervatillo [θerβa'tiʎo] nm fawn

cervecería [θerβeθe'ria] nf (fábrica) brewery; (taberna) public house, pub

cerveza [θer'βeθa] nf beer

cesar [θe'sar] /1a/ vi to cease, stop
▷ vt to remove from office

cesárea [θe'sarea] nf Caesarean (section)

cese ['θese] nm (de trabajo) dismissal; (de pago) suspension

césped ['θespeð] nm grass, lawn

cesta ['θesta] nf basket

cesto ['θesto] nm (large) basket, hamper

cfr abr (= confróntese, compárese) cf

chabacano, -a [tʃaβa'kano, a] adj vulgar, coarse

chabola [tʃa'βola] nf shack; **barriada** or **barrio de ~s** shanty town

chacal [tʃa'kal] nm jackal

chacha ['tʃatʃa] nf (fam) maid

cháchara ['tʃatʃara] nf chatter; **estar de ~** to chatter away

chacra ['tʃakra] nf (LAM) smallholding

chafa ['tʃafa] adj (LAM fam) useless, dud

chafar [tʃa'far] /1a/ vt (aplastar) to crush; (arruinar) to ruin

chal [tʃal] nm shawl

chalado, -a [tʃa'laðo, a] adj (fam) crazy

chalé [tʃa'le] (pl **chalés**) nm = **chalet**

chaleco [tʃa'leko] nm waistcoat, vest (US); **~ salvavidas** life jacket; **~ de seguridad**, **~ reflectante** (Auto) high-visibility vest

chalet [tʃa'let] (pl **chalets**) nm [tʃa'le, tʃa'les] nm villa, ~ detached house

chamaco, -a [tʃa'mako, a] nm/f (LAM) kid

champán [tʃam'pan] nm champagne

champiñón [tʃampi'ɲon] nm mushroom

champú [tʃam'pu] (pl **champús** o **champúes**) nm shampoo

chamuscar [tʃamus'kar] /1g/ vt to scorch, singe

chance ['tʃanθe] nm o f (LAM) chance, opportunity

chancho, -a [tʃantʃo, a] nm/f (LAM) pig

chanchullo [tʃan'tʃuʎo] nm (fam) fiddle

chandal [tʃan'dal] nm tracksuit

chantaje [tʃan'taxe] nm blackmail

chapa ['tʃapa] nf (de metal) plate, sheet; (de madera) board, panel; (LAM Auto) number (BRIT) o license (US) plate; **chapado, -a** adj: **chapado en oro** gold-plated

chaparrón [tʃapa'rron] nm downpour, cloudburst

chaperón [tʃape'ron] nm (LAM): **hacer de ~** to play gooseberry; **chaperona** nf (LAM): **hacer de chaperona** to play gooseberry

chapulín [tʃapu'lin] nm (LAM) grasshopper

chapurrar [tʃapurr'ar] /1a/, **chapurrear** [tʃapurre'ar] /1a/ vt (idioma) to speak badly

chapuza [tʃa'puθa] nf botched job

chapuzón [tʃapu'θon] nm: **darse un ~** to go for a dip

chaqueta [tʃa'keta] nf jacket

chaquetón nm (three-quarter-length) coat

charca ['tʃarka] nf pond, pool

charco ['tʃarko] nm pool, puddle

charcutería [tʃarkute'ria] nf (tienda) shop selling chiefly pork meat products; (productos) cooked pork meats pl

charla ['tʃarla] nf talk, chat; (conferencia) lecture; **charlar** /1a/ vi to talk, chat; **charlatán, -ana** nm/f chatterbox; (estafador) trickster

charol¹ [tʃa'rol] nm varnish; (cuero) patent leather

charol² [tʃa'rol] nm, **charola** [tʃa'rola] nf (LAM) tray

charro ['tʃarro] nm (vaquero) typical Mexican

chasco ['tʃasko] nm (desengaño) disappointment

chasis ['tʃasis] nm inv chassis

chasquido [tʃas'kiðo] nm (de lengua) click; (de látigo) crack

chat [tʃat] nm (Internet) chat room

chatarra [tʃa'tarra] nf scrap (metal)

chatear [tʃate'ar] /1a/ vi (Internet) to chat

chato, -a ['tʃato, a] adj flat; (nariz) snub

chaucha ['tʃautʃa] (LAM) nf runner (BRIT) o pole (US) bean

chaval, -a [tʃa'βal, a] nm/f kid (fam), lad/lass

chavo, -a ['tʃaβo, a] nm/f (LAM fam) guy/girl

checar [tʃe'kar] /1g/ vt (LAM): **~ tarjeta** (al entrar) to clock in o on; (al salir) to clock off o out

checo, -a ['tʃeko, a] adj, nm/f Czech ▷ nm (Ling) Czech

checo(e)slovaco, -a [tʃeko(e)slo'βako, a] adj, nm/f Czech, Czechoslovak

Checo(e)slovaquia [tʃeko(e)slo'βakja] nf Czechoslovakia

cheque ['tʃeke] nm cheque (BRIT), check (US); **cobrar un ~** to cash a cheque; **~ abierto/en blanco/cruzado** open/blank/crossed cheque; **~ al portador** cheque payable to bearer; **~ de viajero** traveller's cheque

chequeo [tʃe'keo] nm (Med) check-up; (Auto) service

chequera [tʃe'kera] nf (LAM) chequebook (BRIT), checkbook (US)

chévere ['tʃeβere] adj (LAM) great

chícharo ['tʃitʃaro] nm pea

chichón [tʃi'tʃon] nm bump, lump

chicle ['tʃikle] nm chewing gum

chico, -a ['tʃiko, a] adj small, little ▷ nm/f child; (muchacho) boy; (muchacha) girl

chiflado, -a [tʃi'flaðo, a] adj crazy

chiflar [tʃi'flar] /1a/ vt to hiss, boo ▷ vi (esp LAM) to whistle

chilango, -a [tʃi'lango, a] adj (LAM) of o from Mexico City

Chile ['tʃile] nm Chile

chile ['tʃile] nm chilli pepper

chileno, -a adj, nm/f Chilean

chillar [tʃi'ʎar] /1a/ vi (persona) to yell, scream; (animal salvaje) to howl; (cerdo) to squeal

chillido [tʃi'ʎiðo] nm (de persona) yell, scream; (de animal) howl

chimenea [tʃime'nea] nf chimney; (hogar) fireplace

China ['tʃina] nf: **(la) ~** China

chinche ['tʃintʃe] nf bug; (Tec) drawing pin (BRIT), thumbtack (US) ▷ nmf nuisance, pest

chincheta [tʃin'tʃeta] nf drawing pin (BRIT), thumbtack (US)

chingado, -a [tʃin'gaðo, a] adj (esp LAM fam!) lousy; **hijo de la chingada** bastard (!)

chino, -a ['tʃino, a] adj, nm/f Chinese ▷ nm (Ling) Chinese

chipirón [tʃipi'ron] nm squid

Chipre ['tʃipre] nf Cyprus; **chipriota** adj Cypriot ▷ nmf Cypriot

chiquillo, -a [tʃi'kiʎo, a] nm/f kid (fam)

chirimoya [tʃiri'moja] nf custard apple

chiringuito [tʃirin'gito] nm small open-air bar

chiripa [tʃi'ripa] nf fluke

chirriar [tʃi'rrjar] /1b/ vi to creak, squeak

chirrido [tʃi'rriðo] nm creak(ing), squeak(ing)

chisme ['tʃisme] nm (habladurías) piece of gossip; (fam: objeto) thingummyjig

chismoso, -a [tʃis'moso, a] adj gossiping ▷ nm/f gossip

chispa ['tʃispa] nf spark; (fig) sparkle; (ingenio) wit; (fam) drunkenness

chispear [tʃispe'ar] /1a/ vi (lloviznar) to drizzle

chiste ['tʃiste] nm joke, funny story

chistoso, -a [tʃis'toso, a] adj funny, amusing

chivo, -a ['tʃiβo, a] nm/f (billy-/nanny-) goat; **~ expiatorio** scapegoat

chocante [tʃo'kante] adj startling; (extraño) odd; (ofensivo) shocking

chocar [tʃo'kar] /1g/ vi (coches etc) to collide, crash ▷ vt to shock; (sorprender) to startle; **~ con** to collide with; (fig) to run into, run up against; **¡chócala!** (fam) put it there!

chochear [tʃotʃe'ar] /1a/ vi to dodder, be senile

chocho, -a ['tʃotʃo, a] adj doddering, senile; (fig) soft, doting

choclo ['tʃoklo] (ʌм) nm (grano) sweetcorn; (mazorca) corn on the cob

chocolate [tʃoko'late] adj chocolate ▷ nm chocolate; **chocolatina** nf chocolate

chófer ['tʃofer] nm driver

chollo ['tʃoʎo] nm (fam) bargain, snip

choque ['tʃoke] vb V **chocar** ▷ nm (impacto) impact; (golpe) jolt; (Auto) crash; (fig) conflict; **~ frontal** head-on collision

chorizo [tʃo'riθo] nm hard pork sausage (type of salami)

chorrada [tʃo'rraða] nf (fam): **¡es una ~!** that's crap! (!); **decir ~s** to talk crap (!)

chorrear [tʃorre'ar] /1a/ vi to gush (out), spout (out); (gotear) to drip, trickle

chorro ['tʃorro] nm jet; (fig) stream

choza ['tʃoθa] nf hut, shack

chubasco [tʃu'βasko] nm squall

chubasquero [tʃuβas'kero] nm cagoule, raincoat

chuche ['tʃutʃe] nf (fam) sweetie (BRIT fam), candy (US)

chuchería [tʃutʃe'ria] nf trinket

chuleta [tʃu'leta] nf chop, cutlet

chulo, -a ['tʃulo, a] adj (encantador) charming; (fam: estupendo) great, fantastic ▷ nm (tb: **~ de putas**) pimp

chupaleta [tʃupa'leta] nf (ʌм) lollipop

chupar [tʃu'par] /1a/ vt to suck; (absorber) to absorb; **chuparse** vr to grow thin

chupete [tʃu'pete] nm dummy (BRIT), pacifier (US)

chupetín [tʃupe'tin] nf (ʌм) lollipop

chupito [tʃu'pito] nm (fam) shot

chupón [tʃu'pon] nm (piruleta) lollipop; (ʌм: chupete) dummy (BRIT), pacifier (US)

churrería [tʃurre'ria] nf stall or shop which sells "churros"

churro ['tʃurro] nm (type of) fritter

chusma ['tʃusma] nf rabble, mob

chutar [tʃu'tar] /1a/ vi to shoot (at goal)

Cía abr (= compañía) Co.

cianuro [θja'nuro] nm cyanide

ciberacoso [θiβera'koso] nm cyberbullying

ciberataque [θiβera'take] nm cyber attack

cibercafé [θiβerka'fe] nm cybercafé

cibernauta [θiβer'nauta] nmf cybernaut

ciberterrorista [θiβerterro'rista] nmf cyberterrorist

cicatriz [θika'triθ] nf scar

cicatrizar [θikatri'θar] /1f/ vt to heal; **cicatrizarse** vr to heal (up), form a scar

ciclismo [θi'klismo] nm cycling

ciclista [θi'klista] adj cycle cpd ▷ nmf cyclist

ciclo ['θiklo] nm cycle

ciclón [θi'klon] nm cyclone

cicloturismo [θiklotu'rismo] nm touring by bicycle

ciego, -a ['θjeɣo, a] adj blind ▷ nm/f blind man/woman

cielo ['θjelo] nm sky; (Rel) heaven; **¡~s!** good heavens!

ciempiés [θjem'pjes] nm inv centipede

cien [θjen] num V **ciento**

ciencia [θjen'θja] nf science; **ciencias** nfpl science sg; **ciencia-ficción** nf science fiction

científico, -a [θjen'tifiko, a] adj scientific ▷ nm/f scientist

ciento ['θjento] num hundred; **pagar al 10 por ~** to pay at 10 per cent

cierre ['θjerre] vb V **cerrar** ▷ nm closing, shutting; (con llave) locking; **~ de cremallera** zip (fastener)

cierro etc vb V **cerrar**

cierto, -a ['θjerto, a] adj sure, certain; (un tal) a certain; (correcto) right, correct; **~ hombre** a certain man; **ciertas personas** certain o some people; **sí, es ~** yes, that's correct; **por ~** by the way

ciervo [ˈθjerβo] nm deer; (macho) stag

cifra [ˈθifra] nf number; (secreta) code; **cifrar** /1a/ vt to code, write in code

cigala [θiˈɣala] nf Norway lobster

cigarra [θiˈɣarra] nf cicada

cigarrillo [θiɣaˈrriʎo] nm cigarette

cigarro [θiˈɣarro] nm cigarette; (puro) cigar

cigüeña [θiˈɣweɲa] nf stork

cilíndrico, -a [θiˈlindriko, a] adj cylindrical

cilindro [θiˈlindro] nm cylinder

cima [ˈθima] nf (de montaña) top, peak; (de árbol) top; (fig) height

cimentar [θimenˈtar] /1j/ vt to lay the foundations of; (fig: fundar) to found

cimiento [θiˈmjento] nm foundation

cincel [θinˈθel] nm chisel

cinco [ˈθinko] num five

cincuenta [θinˈkwenta] num fifty

cine [ˈθine] nm cinema; **cinematográfico, -a** [θine-] adj cine-, film cpd

cínico, -a [ˈθiniko, a] adj cynical ▷ nm/f cynic

cinismo [θiˈnismo] nm cynicism

cinta [ˈθinta] nf band, strip; (de tela) ribbon; (película) reel; (de máquina de escribir) ribbon; (magnetofónica) tape; **~ adhesiva** sticky tape; **~ aislante** insulating tape; **~ de vídeo** videotape; **~ métrica** tape measure

cintura [θinˈtura] nf waist

cinturón [θintuˈron] nm belt; **~ de seguridad** safety belt

ciprés [θiˈpres] nm cypress (tree)

circo [ˈθirko] nm circus

circuito [θirˈkwito] nm circuit

circulación [θirkulaˈθjon] nf circulation; (Auto) traffic

circular [θirkuˈlar] /1a/ adj, nf circular ▷ vt to circulate ▷ vi (Auto) to drive;

"circule por la derecha" "keep (to the) right"

círculo [ˈθirkulo] nm circle; **~ vicioso** vicious circle

circunferencia [θirkunfeˈrenθja] nf circumference

circunstancia [θirkunsˈtanθja] nf circumstance

cirio [ˈθirjo] nm (wax) candle

ciruela [θiˈrwela] nf plum; **~ pasa** prune

cirugía [θiruˈxia] nf surgery; **~ estética** o **plástica** plastic surgery

cirujano [θiruˈxano] nm surgeon

cisne [ˈθisne] nm swan

cisterna [θisˈterna] nf cistern, tank

cita [ˈθita] nf appointment, meeting; (de novios) date; (referencia) quotation

citación [θitaˈθjon] nf (Jur) summons sg

citar [θiˈtar] /1a/ vt to make an appointment with; (Jur) to summons; (un autor, texto) to quote; **citarse** vr: **se ~on en el cine** they arranged to meet at the cinema

cítrico, -a [ˈθitriko, a] adj citric ▷ nm: **~s** citrus fruits

ciudad [θjuˈðað] nf town; (capital de país etc) city; **ciudadano, -a** nm/f citizen

cívico, -a [ˈθiβiko, a] adj civic

civil [θiˈβil] adj civil ▷ nm (guardia) policeman; **civilización** nf civilization; **civilizar** /1f/ vt to civilize

cizaña [θiˈθaɲa] nf (fig) discord

cl abr (= centilitro) cl.

clamor [klaˈmor] nm clamour, protest

clandestino, -a [klandesˈtino, a] adj clandestine; (Pol) underground

clara [ˈklara] nf (de huevo) egg white

claraboya [klaraˈβoja] nf skylight

clarear [klareˈar] /1a/ vi (el día) to dawn; (el cielo) to clear up, brighten up; **clarearse** vr to be transparent

claridad [klariˈðað] nf (del día) brightness; (de estilo) clarity

clarificar [klarifiˈkar] /1g/ vt to clarify

clarinete [klari'nete] *nm* clarinet

claro, -a ['klaro, a] *adj* clear; (*luminoso*) bright; (*color*) light; (*evidente*) clear, evident; (*poco espeso*) thin ▷ *nm* (*en bosque*) clearing ▷ *adv* clearly ▷ *excl*: **¡~ que sí!** of course!; **¡~ que no!** of course not!

clase ['klase] *nf* class; **~ alta/media/obrera** upper/middle/working class; **dar ~s** to teach; **~s particulares** private lessons o tuition *sg*

clásico, -a ['klasiko, a] *adj* classical

clasificación [klasifika'θjon] *nf* classification; (*Deporte*) league (table)

clasificar [klasifi'kar] /1g/ *vt* to classify

claustro ['klaustro] *nm* cloister

cláusula ['klausula] *nf* clause

clausura [klau'sura] *nf* closing, closure

clavar [kla'βar] /1a/ *vt* (*clavo*) to hammer in; (*cuchillo*) to stick, thrust

clave ['klaβe] *nf* key; (*Mus*) clef; **~ de acceso** password; **~ lada** (*LAM*) dialling (*BRIT*) o area (*US*) code

clavel [kla'βel] *nm* carnation

clavícula [kla'βikula] *nf* collar bone

clavija [kla'βixa] *nf* peg, pin; (*Elec*) plug

clavo ['klaβo] *nm* (*de metal*) nail; (*Bot*) clove

claxon ['klakson] (*pl* **claxons**) *nm* horn

clérigo ['kleriɣo] *nm* priest

clero ['klero] *nm* clergy

clicar [kli'kar] /1a/ *vi* (*Inform*) to click; **clica en el icono** click on the icon; **~ dos veces** to double-click

cliché [kli'tʃe] *nm* cliché; (*Foto*) negative

cliente, -a ['kljente, a] *nm/f* client, customer; **clientela** *nf* clientele, customers *pl*

clima ['klima] *nm* climate; **climatizado, -a** *adj* air-conditioned

clímax ['klimaks] *nm inv* climax

clínico, -a ['kliniko, a] *adj* clinical ▷ *nf* clinic; (*particular*) private hospital

clip [klip] (*pl* **clips**) *nm* paper clip

clítoris ['klitoris] *nm inv* clitoris

cloaca [klo'aka] *nf* sewer, drain

clonar [klo'nar] /1a/ *vt* to clone

cloro ['kloro] *nm* chlorine

club [kluβ] (*pl* **clubs** o **clubes**) *nm* club; **~ nocturno** night club

cm *abr* (= *centímetro*) cm

coágulo [ko'aɣulo] *nm* clot

coalición [koali'θjon] *nf* coalition

coartada [koar'taða] *nf* alibi

coartar [koar'tar] /1a/ *vt* to limit, restrict

coba [ko'βa] *nf*: **dar ~ a algn** (*adular*) to suck up to sb

cobarde *adj* cowardly ▷ *nmf* coward; **cobardía** *nf* cowardice

cobaya [ko'βaja] *nf* guinea pig

cobertizo [koβer'tiθo] *nm* shelter

cobertura [koβer'tura] *nf* cover; (*Com*) coverage; **~ de dividendo** (*Com*) dividend cover; **no tengo ~** (*Telec*) I can't get a signal

cobija [ko'βixa] *nf* (*LAM*) blanket; **cobijar** /1a/ *vt* (*cubrir*) to cover; (*abrigar*) to shelter; **cobijo** *nm* shelter

cobra ['koβra] *nf* cobra

cobrador, -a [koβra'ðor, a] *nm/f* (*de autobús*) conductor/conductress; (*de impuestos, gas*) collector

cobrar [ko'βrar] /1a/ *vt* (*cheque*) to cash; (*sueldo*) to collect, draw; (*objeto*) to recover; (*precio*) to charge; (*deuda*) to collect ▷ *vi* to be paid; **cóbrese al entregar** cash on delivery (COD) (*BRIT*), collect on delivery (COD) (*US*); **¿me cobra, por favor?** (*en tienda*) how much do I owe you?; (*en restaurante*) can I have the bill, please?

cobre ['koβre] *nm* copper; **cobres** *nmpl* (*Mus*) brass instruments

cobro ['koβro] *nm* (*de cheque*) cashing; **presentar al ~** to cash

cocaína [koka'ina] *nf* cocaine

cocción [kok'θjon] *nf* (*Culin*) cooking; (*el hervir*) boiling

cocer [ko'θer] /2b, 2h/ *vt, vi* to cook; (*en agua*) to boil; (*en horno*) to bake

coche ['kotʃe] nm (Auto) car, automobile (US); (de tren, de caballos) coach, carriage; (para niños) pram (BRIT), baby carriage (US); **ir en ~** to drive; **~ de bomberos** fire engine; **~ (-comedor)** (Ferro) (dining) car; **~ de carreras** racing car; **~-escuela** learner car; **~ fúnebre** hearse; **coche-cama** nm (Ferro) sleeping car, sleeper

cochera [ko'tʃera] nf garage; (de autobuses, trenes) depot

coche-restaurante ['kotʃerestau'rante] (pl **coches-restaurante**) nm (Ferro) dining-car, diner

cochinillo [kotʃi'niʎo] nm suckling pig

cochino, -a [ko'tʃino, a] adj filthy, dirty ▷ nm/f pig

cocido [ko'θiðo] nm stew

cocina [ko'θina] nf kitchen; (aparato) cooker, stove; (actividad) cookery; **~ eléctrica** electric cooker; **~ de gas** gas cooker; **cocinar** /1a/ vt, vi to cook

cocinero, -a [koθi'nero, a] nm/f cook

coco ['koko] nm coconut

cocodrilo [koko'ðrilo] nm crocodile

cocotero [koko'tero] nm coconut palm

cóctel ['koktel] nm cocktail; **~ Molotov** Molotov cocktail, petrol bomb

codazo [ko'ðaθo] nm: **dar un ~ a algn** to nudge sb

codicia [ko'ðiθja] nf greed; **codiciar** /1b/ vt to covet

código ['koðiɣo] nm code; **~ de barras** bar code; **~ de (la) circulación** highway code; **~ de la zona** (LAM) dialling (BRIT) o area (US) code; **~ postal** postcode

codillo [ko'ðiʎo] nm (Zool) knee; (Tec) elbow (joint)

codo ['koðo] nm (Anat, de tubo) elbow; (Zool) knee

codorniz [koðor'niθ] nf quail

coexistir [koeksis'tir] /3a/ vi to coexist

cofradía [kofra'ðia] nf brotherhood, fraternity

cofre ['kofre] nm (de joyas) box; (de dinero) chest

coger [ko'xer] /2c/ vt (ESP) to take (hold of); (: objeto caído) to pick up; (: frutas) to pick, harvest; (: resfriado, ladrón, pelota) to catch ▷ vi: **~ por el buen camino** to take the right road; **cogerse** vr (el dedo) to catch; **~se a algo** to get hold of sth

cogollo [ko'ɣoʎo] nm (de lechuga) heart

cogote [ko'ɣote] nm back o nape of the neck

cohabitar [koaβi'tar] /1a/ vi to live together, cohabit

coherente [koe'rente] adj coherent

cohesión [koe'sjon] nm cohesion

cohete [ko'ete] nm rocket

cohibido, -a [koi'βiðo, a] adj (Psico) inhibited; (tímido) shy

coincidencia [koinθi'ðenθja] nf coincidence

coincidir [koinθi'ðir] /3a/ vi (en idea) to coincide, agree; (en lugar) to coincide

coito ['koito] nm intercourse, coitus

coja etc vb V **coger**

cojear [koxe'ar] /1a/ vi (persona) to limp, hobble; (mueble) to wobble, rock

cojera [ko'xera] nf limp

cojín [ko'xin] nm cushion

cojo, -a ['koxo, a] vb V **coger** ▷ adj (que no puede andar) lame, crippled; (mueble) wobbly ▷ nm/f lame person, cripple

cojón [ko'xon] nm (fam!): **¡cojones!** shit! (!); **cojonudo, -a** adj (fam) great, fantastic

col [kol] nf cabbage; **~es de Bruselas** Brussels sprouts

cola ['kola] nf tail; (de gente) queue; (lugar) end, last place; (para pegar) glue, gum; **hacer ~** to queue (up)

colaborador, a [kolaβora'ðor, a] nm/f collaborator

colaborar [kolaβo'rar] /1a/ vi to collaborate

colado, -a [ko'laðo, a] *adj (metal)*
cast ▷ *nf*: **hacer la colada** to do the
washing

colador [kola'ðor] *nm (de té)* strainer;
(para verduras etc) colander

colapso [ko'lapso] *nm* collapse

colar [ko'lar] /1l/ *vt (líquido)* to strain
off; *(metal)* to cast ▷ *vi* to ooze, seep
(through); **colarse** *vr* to jump the
queue; **~se en** to get into without
paying; *(en una fiesta)* to gatecrash

colcha ['koltʃa] *nf* bedspread

colchón [kol'tʃon] *nm* mattress; **~
inflable** air bed, inflatable mattress

colchoneta [koltʃo'neta] *nf (en
gimnasio)* mat; **~ hinchable** air bed,
inflatable mattress

colección [kolek'θjon] *nf* collection;
coleccionar /1a/ *vt* to collect;
coleccionista *nmf* collector

colecta [ko'lekta] *nf* collection

colectivo, -a [kolek'tiβo, a] *adj*
collective, joint ▷ *nm (LAM: autobús)*
(small) bus

colega [ko'leɣa] *nmf* colleague; (ESP:
amigo) mate

colegial, a [kole'xjal, a] *nm/f*
schoolboy/girl

colegio [ko'lexjo] *nm* college; *(escuela)*
school; *(de abogados etc)* association;
~ electoral polling station; **~ mayor**
(ESP) hall of residence; *see note*
"colegio"

○ **COLEGIO**

● A *colegio* is often a private primary
● or secondary school. In the state
● system it means a primary school
● although these are also called
● *escuela*. State secondary schools
● are called *institutos*. Extracurricular
● subjects, such as computing or
● foreign languages, are offered in
● private schools called *academias*.

cólera ['kolera] *nf (ira)* anger ▷ *nm*
(Med) cholera

colesterol [koleste'rol] *nm*
cholesterol

coleta [ko'leta] *nf* pigtail

colgante [kol'ɣante] *adj* hanging
▷ *nm (joya)* pendant

colgar [kol'ɣar] /1h, 1l/ *vt* to hang
(up); *(ropa)* to hang out ▷ *vi* to hang;
(teléfono) to hang up

cólico ['koliko] *nm* colic

coliflor [koli'flor] *nf* cauliflower

colilla [ko'liʎa] *nf* cigarette end, butt

colina [ko'lina] *nf* hill

colisión *nf* collision; **~ frontal** head-
on crash

collar [ko'ʎar] *nm* necklace; *(de
perro)* collar

colmar [kol'mar] /1a/ *vt* to fill to the
brim; *(fig)* to fulfil, realize

colmena [kol'mena] *nf* beehive

colmillo [kol'miʎo] *nm (diente)* eye
tooth; *(de elefante)* tusk; *(de perro)* fang

colmo ['kolmo] *nm*: **¡eso es ya el ~!**
that's beyond a joke!

colocación [koloka'θjon] *nf (acto)*
placing; *(empleo)* job, position

colocar [kolo'kar] /1g/ *vt* to place,
put, position; *(poner en empleo)* to find
a job for; **~ dinero** to invest money;
colocarse *vr (conseguir trabajo)* to
find a job

Colombia [ko'lombja] *nf* Colombia;
colombiano, -a *adj, nm/f* Colombian

colonia [ko'lonja] *nf* colony; *(de
casas)* housing estate; *(agua de
colonia)* cologne; **~ proletaria** (LAM)
shantytown

colonización [koloniθa'θjon] *nf*
colonization; **colonizador, a** *adj*
colonizing ▷ *nm/f* colonist, settler

colonizar [koloni'θar] /1f/ *vt* to
colonize

coloquio [ko'lokjo] *nm* conversation;
(congreso) conference

color [ko'lor] *nm* colour

colorado, -a [kolo'raðo, a] *adj (rojo)*
red; *(LAM: chiste)* rude

colorante [kolo'rante] *nm* colouring
(matter)

colorear [kolore'ar] /1a/ vt to colour
colorete [kolo'rete] nm blusher
colorido [kolo'riðo] nm colour(ing)
columna [ko'lumna] nf column;
(pilar) pillar; (apoyo) support; **~
vertebral** spine, spinal column; (fig)
backbone
columpiar [kolum'pjar] /1b/ vt to
swing; **columpiarse** vr to swing;
columpio nm swing
coma ['koma] nf comma ▷ nm (Med)
coma
comadre [ko'maðre] nf (madrina)
godmother; (chismosa) gossip;
comadrona nf midwife
comal [ko'mal] nm (LAM) griddle
comandante [koman'dante] nm
commandant
comarca [ko'marka] nf region
comba ['komba] nf (cuerda) skipping
rope; **saltar a la ~** to skip
combate [kom'bate] nm fight
combatir [komba'tir] /3a/ vt to
fight, combat
combinación [kombina'θjon] nf
combination; (Química) compound;
(prenda) slip
combinar [kombi'nar] /1a/ vt to
combine
combustible [kombus'tiβle]
nm fuel
comedia [ko'meðja] nf comedy;
(Teat) play, drama; **comediante** nmf
(comic) actor/actress
comedido, -a [kome'ðiðo, a] adj
moderate
comedor [kome'ðor] nm (habitación)
dining room; (cantina) canteen
comensal [komen'sal] nmf fellow
guest/diner
comentar [komen'tar] /1a/ vt
to comment on; **comentario** nm
comment, remark; (Lit) commentary;
comentarios nmpl gossip sg;
comentarista nmf commentator
comenzar [komen'θar] /1f, 1j/ vt,
vi to begin, start; **~ a hacer algo** to
begin o start doing o to do sth

comer [ko'mer] /2a/ vt to eat; (Damas,
Ajedrez) to take, capture ▷ vi to eat;
(almorzar) to have lunch; **comerse**
vr to eat up
comercial [komer'θjal] adj
commercial; (relativo al negocio)
business cpd; **comercializar** /1f/
vt (producto) to market; (pey) to
commercialize
comerciante [komer'θjante] nmf
trader, merchant
comerciar [komer'θjar] /1b/ vi to
trade, do business
comercio [ko'merθjo] nm commerce,
trade; (tienda) shop, store; (negocio)
business; (grandes empresas)
big business; (fig) dealings pl; **~
electrónico** e-commerce; **~ exterior**
foreign trade
comestible [komes'tiβle] adj
eatable, edible ▷ nm: **~s** food sg,
foodstuffs
cometa [ko'meta] nm comet ▷ nf kite
cometer [kome'ter] /2a/ vt to
commit
cometido [kome'tiðo] nm task,
assignment
cómic ['komik] (pl **cómics**) nm comic
comicios [ko'miθjos] nmpl elections
cómico, -a ['komiko, a] adj comic(al)
▷ nm/f comedian
comida [ko'miða] nf (alimento)
food; (almuerzo, cena) meal; (de
mediodía) lunch; **~ basura** junk food;
~ chatarra (LAM) junk food
comidilla [komi'ðiʎa] nf: **ser la ~
del barrio o pueblo** to be the talk of
the town
comienzo [ko'mjenθo] vb V
comenzar ▷ nm beginning, start
comillas [ko'miʎas] nfpl quotation
marks
comilón, -ona [komi'lon, ona] adj
greedy ▷ nf (fam) blow-out
comino [ko'mino] nm cumin (seed); **no
me importa un ~** I don't give a damn!
comisaría [komisa'ria] nf police
station; (Mil) commissariat

comisario [komi'sarjo] *nm (Mil etc)* commissary; *(Pol)* commissar

comisión [komi'sjon] *nf* commission

comité [komi'te] *(pl* **comités)** *nm* committee

comitiva [komi'tiβa] *nf* retinue

como ['komo] *adv* as; *(tal como)* like; *(aproximadamente)* about, approximately ▷ *conj (ya que, puesto que)* as, since; **¡~ no!** of course!; **~ no lo haga hoy** unless he does it today; **~ si** as if; **es tan alto ~ ancho** it is as high as it is wide

cómo ['komo] *adv* how?, why? ▷ *excl* what?, I beg your pardon? ▷ *nm:* **el ~ y el porqué** the whys and wherefores

cómoda ['komoða] *nf* chest of drawers

comodidad [komoði'ðað] *nf* comfort

comodín [komo'ðin] *nm* joker

cómodo, -a ['komoðo, a] *adj* comfortable; *(práctico, de fácil uso)* convenient

compact [kom'pakt] *(pl* **compacts)** *nm (tb:* **~ disc)** compact disk

compacto, -a [kom'pakto, a] *adj* compact

compadecer [kompaðe'θer] /2d/ *vt* to pity, be sorry for; **compadecerse** *vr:* **~se de** to pity, be sorry for

compadre [kom'paðre] *nm (padrino)* godfather; *(amigo)* friend, pal

compañero, -a [kompa'ɲero, a] *nm/f* companion; *(novio)* boyfriend/ girlfriend; **~ de clase** classmate

compañía [kompa'ɲia] *nf* company; **hacer ~ a algn** to keep sb company

comparación [kompara'θjon] *nf* comparison; **en ~ con** in comparison with

comparar [kompa'rar] /1a/ *vt* to compare

comparecer [kompare'θer] /2d/ *vi* to appear (in court)

comparsa [kom'parsa] *nmf* extra

compartim(i)ento [komparti'm(i)ento] *nm (Ferro)* compartment

compartir [kompar'tir] /3a/ *vt* to share; *(dinero, comida etc)* to divide (up), share (out)

compás [kom'pas] *nm (Mus)* beat, rhythm; *(Mat)* compasses *pl;* *(Naut etc)* compass

compasión [kompa'sjon] *nf* compassion, pity

compasivo, -a [kompa'siβo, a] *adj* compassionate

compatible [kompa'tiβle] *adj* compatible

compatriota [kompa'trjota] *nmf* compatriot, fellow countryman/ woman

compenetrarse [kompene'trarse] /1a/ *vr* to be in tune

compensación [kompensa'θjon] *nf* compensation

compensar [kompen'sar] /1a/ *vt* to compensate

competencia [kompe'tenθja] *nf* *(incumbencia)* domain, field; *(Jur, habilidad)* competence; *(rivalidad)* competition

competente [kompe'tente] *adj* competent

competición [kompeti'θjon] *nf* competition

competir [kompe'tir] /3k/ *vi* to compete

compinche [kom'pintʃe] *nmf (ᴌᴀм fam)* mate, buddy *(us)*

complacer [kompla'θer] /2w/ *vt* to please; **complacerse** *vr* to be pleased

complaciente [kompla'θjente] *adj* kind, obliging, helpful

complejo, -a [kom'plexo, a] *adj,* *nm* complex

complementario, -a [komplemen'tarjo, a] *adj* complementary

completar [komple'tar] /1a/ *vt* to complete

completo, -a [kom'pleto, a] *adj* complete; *(perfecto)* perfect; *(lleno)* full ▷ *nm* full complement

complicado, -a [kompli'kaðo, a]
adj complicated; **estar ~ en** to be
mixed up in

cómplice ['kompliθe] nmf
accomplice

complot [kom'plo(t)] (pl **complots**)
nm plot

componer [kompo'ner] /2q/ vt
(Mus, Lit, Imprenta) to compose; (algo
roto) to mend, repair; (arreglar) to
arrange; **componerse** vr: **~se de** to
consist of

comportamiento
[komporta'mjento] nm behaviour,
conduct

comportarse [kompor'tarse] /1a/
vr to behave

composición [komposi'θjon] nf
composition

compositor, a [komposi'tor, a] nm/f
composer

compostura [kompos'tura] nf
(actitud) composure

compra ['kompra] nf purchase;
hacer la ~/ir de ~s to do the/go
shopping; **comprador, a** nm/f buyer,
purchaser; **comprar** /1a/ vt to buy,
purchase

comprender [kompren'der] /2a/ vt
to understand; (incluir) to comprise,
include

comprensión [kompren'sjon] nf
understanding; **comprensivo, -a** adj
(actitud) understanding

compresa [kom'presa] nf (higiénica)
sanitary towel (BRIT) o napkin (US)

comprimido, -a [kompri'miðo, a]
adj compressed ▷ nm (Med) pill, tablet

comprimir /3a/ vt to compress;
(Inform) to compress, zip

comprobante [kompro'βante] nm
proof; (Com) voucher; **~ de compra**
proof of purchase

comprobar [kompro'βar] /1l/ vt
to check; (probar) to prove; (Tec) to
check, test

comprometer [komprome'ter]
/2a/ vt to compromise; (exponer)

to endanger; **comprometerse** vr
(involucrarse) to get involved

compromiso [kompro'miso] nm
(obligación) obligation; (cometido)
commitment; (convenio) agreement;
(dificultad) awkward situation

compuesto, -a [kom'pwesto, a] adj:
~ de composed of, made up of ▷ nm
compound

computador [komputa'ðor] nm,
computadora [komputa'ðora]
nf computer; **~ central** mainframe
computer; **~ personal** personal
computer

cómputo ['komputo] nm calculation

comulgar [komul'ɣar] /1h/ vi to
receive communion

común [ko'mun] adj common ▷ nm:
el ~ the community

comunicación [komunika'θjon] nf
communication; (informe) report

comunicado [komuni'kaðo] nm
announcement; **~ de prensa** press
release

comunicar [komuni'kar] /1g/ vt to
communicate ▷ vi to communicate;
comunicarse vr to communicate;
está comunicando (Telec) the
line's engaged (BRIT) o busy (US);
comunicativo, -a adj communicative

comunidad [komuni'ðað] nf
community; **~ autónoma** (ESP)
autonomous region; **~ de vecinos**
residents' association; **C~ Económica
Europea (CEE)** European Economic
Community (EEC)

comunión [komu'njon] nf
communion

comunismo [komu'nismo] nm
communism; **comunista** adj, nmf
communist

PALABRA CLAVE

con [kon] prep **1** (medio, compañía,
modo) with; **comer con cuchara** to
eat with a spoon; **pasear con algn** to
go for a walk with sb

2 (*a pesar de*): **con todo, merece nuestros respetos** all the same o even so, he deserves our respect

3 (*para con*): **es muy bueno para con los niños** he's very good with (the) children

4 (+ *infin*): **con llegar tan tarde se quedó sin comer** by arriving o because he arrived so late he missed out on eating

▶ *conj*: **con que: será suficiente con que le escribas** it will be enough if you write to her

concebir [konθe'βir] /3k/ *vt* to conceive ▷ *vi* to conceive

conceder [konθe'ðer] /2a/ *vt* to concede

concejal, a [konθe'xal, a] *nm/f* town councillor

concentración [konθentra'θjon] *nf* concentration

concentrar [konθen'trar] /1a/ *vt* to concentrate; **concentrarse** *vr* to concentrate

concepto [kon'θepto] *nm* concept

concernir [konθer'nir] *vi* to concern; **en lo que concierne a ...** with regard to ...; **en lo que a mí concierne** as far as I'm concerned

concertar [konθer'tar] /1j/ *vt* (*entrevista*) to arrange; (*precio*) to agree ▷ *vi* to harmonize, be in tune

concesión [konθe'sjon] *nf* concession

concesionario, -a [konθesjo'narjo, a] *nm/f* (*Com*) (licensed) dealer, agent

concha ['kontʃa] *nf* shell

conciencia [kon'θjenθja] *nf* conscience; **tener/tomar ~ de** to be/ become aware of; **tener la ~ limpia** o **tranquila** to have a clear conscience

concienciar [konθjen'θjar] /1b/ *vt* to make aware; **concienciarse** *vr* to become aware

concienzudo, -a [konθjen'θuðo, a] *adj* conscientious

concierto [kon'θjerto] *vb* V **concertar** ▷ *nm* concert; (*obra*) concerto

conciliar [konθi'ljar] /1b/ *vt* to reconcile; **~ el sueño** to get to sleep

concilio [kon'θiljo] *nm* council

conciso, -a [kon'θiso, a] *adj* concise

concluir [konklu'ir] /3g/ *vt* to conclude ▷ **concluirse** *vr* to conclude

conclusión [konklu'sjon] *nf* conclusion

concordar [konkor'ðar] /1l/ *vt* to reconcile ▷ *vi* to agree, tally

concordia [kon'korðja] *nf* harmony

concretar [konkre'tar] /1a/ *vt* to make concrete, make more specific; **concretarse** *vr* to become more definite

concreto, -a [kon'kreto, a] *adj, nm* (*AM*) concrete; **en ~** (*en resumen*) to sum up; (*específicamente*) specifically; **no hay nada en ~** there's nothing definite

concurrido, -a [konku'rriðo, a] *adj* (*calle*) busy; (*local, reunión*) crowded

concursante [konkur'sante] *nm* competitor

concurso [kon'kurso] *nm* (*de público*) crowd; (*Escol, Deporte, competición*) competition; (*ayuda*) help, cooperation

condal [kon'dal] *adj*: **la ciudad ~** Barcelona

conde ['konde] *nm* count

condecoración [kondekora'θjon] *nf* (*Mil*) medal

condena [kon'dena] *nf* sentence; **condenación** *nf* condemnation; (*Rel*) damnation; **condenar** /1a/ *vt* to condemn; (*Jur*) to convict; **condenarse** *vr* (*Rel*) to be damned

condesa [kon'desa] *nf* countess

condición [kondi'θjon] *nf* condition; **a ~ de que ...** on condition that ...; **condicional** *adj* conditional

condimento [kondi'mento] *nm* seasoning

condominio [kondo'minjo] nm
condominium

condón [kon'don] nm condom

conducir [kondu'θir] /3n/ vt to take,
convey; (Auto) to drive ▷ vi to drive;
(fig) to lead; **conducirse** vr to behave

conducta [kon'dukta] nf conduct,
behaviour

conducto [kon'dukto] nm pipe, tube;
(fig) channel

conductor, a [konduk'tor, a]
adj leading, guiding ▷ nm (Física)
conductor; (de vehículo) driver

conduje etc [kon'duxe] vb V **conducir**

conduzco etc vb V **conducir**

conectado, -a [konek'taðo, a] adj
(Inform) on-line

conectar [konek'tar] /1a/ vt to
connect (up); (enchufar) plug in

conejillo [kone'xiλo] nm: **~ de Indias**
guinea pig

conejo [ko'nexo] nm rabbit

conexión [konek'sjon] nf connection

confección [konfek'θjon] nf
preparation; (industria) clothing
industry

confeccionar [konfekθjo'nar] /1a/
vt to make (up)

conferencia [konfe'renθja] nf
conference; (lección) lecture; (Telec)
call; **~ de prensa** press conference

conferir [konfe'rir] /3i/ vt to award

confesar [konfe'sar] /1j/ vt to
confess, admit

confesión [konfe'sjon] nf confession

confesionario [konfesjo'narjo] nm
confessional

confeti [kon'feti] nm confetti

confiado, -a [kon'fjaðo, a] adj
(crédulo) trusting; (seguro) confident

confianza [kon'fjanθa] nf trust;
(aliento, confidencia) confidence;
(familiaridad) intimacy, familiarity

confiar [kon'fjar] /1c/ vt to entrust
▷ vi to trust; **~ en algn** to trust sb;
~ en que ... to hope that ...

confidencial [konfiðen'θjal] adj
confidential

confidente [konfi'ðente] nmf
confidant/confidante; (policial)
informer

configurar [konfiɣu'rar] /1a/ vt to
shape, form

confín [kon'fin] nm limit; **confines**
nmpl confines, limits

confirmar [konfir'mar] /1a/ vt to
confirm

confiscar [konfis'kar] /1g/ vt to
confiscate

confite [kon'fite] nm sweet (BRIT),
candy (US); **confitería** nf (tienda)
confectioner's (shop)

confitura [konfi'tura] nf jam

conflictivo, -a [konflik'tiβo, a] adj
(asunto, propuesta) controversial; (país,
situación) troubled

conflicto [kon'flikto] nm conflict;
(fig) clash

confluir [konflu'ir] /3g/ vi (ríos etc) to
meet; (gente) to gather

conformar [konfor'mar] /1a/ vt
to shape, fashion ▷ vi to agree;
conformarse vr to conform;
(resignarse) to resign o.s.; **-se con
algo** to be happy with sth

conforme [kon'forme] adj
(correspondiente): **- con** in line with; (de
acuerdo) agreed ▷ adv as ▷ excl agreed!
▷ prep: **- a** in accordance with; **estar
~s (con algo)** to be in an agreement
(with sth); **quedarse - (con algo)** to
be satisfied (with sth)

confortable [konfor'taβle] adj
comfortable

confortar [konfor'tar] /1a/ vt to
comfort

confrontar [konfron'tar] /1a/ vt to
confront; (dos personas) to bring face
to face; (cotejar) to compare

confundir [konfun'dir] /3a/ vt
(equivocar) to mistake, confuse;
(turbar) to confuse; **confundirse**
vr (turbarse) to get confused;
(equivocarse) to make a mistake;
(mezclarse) to mix

confusión [konfu'sjon] nf confusion

confuso, -a [kon'fuso, a] *adj* confused

congelado, -a [konxe'laðo, a] *adj* frozen ▷ *nmpl*: **-s** frozen food *sg o* foods; **congelador** *nm* freezer, deep freeze

congelar [konxe'lar] /1a/ *vt* to freeze; **congelarse** *vr* (*sangre, grasa*) to congeal

congeniar [konxe'njar] /1b/ *vi* to get on (BRIT) *o* along (US) (well)

congestión [konxes'tjon] *nf* congestion

congestionar [konxestjo'nar] /1a/ *vt* to congest

congraciarse [kongra'θjarse] /1b/ *vr* to ingratiate o.s.

congratular [kongratu'lar] /1a/ *vt* to congratulate

congregar [kongre'ɣar] /1h/ *vt* to gather together; **congregarse** *vr* to gather together

congresista [kongre'sista] *nmf* delegate, congressman/woman

congreso [kon'greso] *nm* congress

conjetura [konxe'tura] *nf* guess; **conjeturar** /1a/ *vt* to guess

conjugar [konxu'ɣar] /1h/ *vt* to combine, fit together; (*Ling*) to conjugate

conjunción [konxun'θjon] *nf* conjunction

conjunto, -a [kon'xunto, a] *adj* joint, united ▷ *nm* whole; (*Mus*) band; **en ~** as a whole

conmemoración [konmemora'θjon] *nf* commemoration

conmemorar [konmemo'rar] /1a/ *vt* to commemorate

conmigo [kon'miɣo] *pron* with me

conmoción [konmo'θjon] *nf* shock; (*fig*) upheaval; **~ cerebral** (*Med*) concussion

conmovedor, a [konmoβe'ðor, a] *adj* touching, moving; (*emocionante*) exciting

conmover [konmo'βer] /2h/ *vt* to shake, disturb; (*fig*) to move

conmutador [konmuta'ðor] *nm* switch; (LAM: *Telec*) switchboard; (: *central*) telephone exchange

cono ['kono] *nm* cone; **C~ Sur** Southern Cone

conocedor, a [konoθe'ðor, a] *adj* expert, knowledgeable ▷ *nm* expert

conocer [kono'θer] /2d/ *vt* to know; (*por primera vez*) to meet, get to know; (*entender*) to know about; (*reconocer*) to recognize; **conocerse** *vr* (*una persona*) to know o.s.; (*dos personas*) to (get to) know each other; **~ a algn de vista** to know sb by sight

conocido, -a [kono'θiðo, a] *adj* (well-)known ▷ *nm/f* acquaintance

conocimiento [konoθi'mjento] *nm* knowledge; (*Med*) consciousness; **conocimientos** *nmpl* (*saber*) knowledge *sg*

conozco *etc* [ko'noθko] *vb* V **conocer**

conque ['konke] *conj* and so, so then

conquista [kon'kista] *nf* conquest; **conquistador, a** *adj* conquering ▷ *nm* conqueror; **conquistar** /1a/ *vt* to conquer

consagrar [konsa'ɣrar] /1a/ *vt* (*Rel*) to consecrate; (*fig*) to devote

consciente [kons'θjente] *adj* conscious

consecución [konseku'θjon] *nf* acquisition; (*de fin*) attainment

consecuencia [konse'kwenθja] *nf* consequence, outcome; (*firmeza*) consistency

consecuente [konse'kwente] *adj* consistent

consecutivo, -a [konseku'tiβo, a] *adj* consecutive

conseguir [konse'ɣir] /3d, 3k/ *vt* to get, obtain; (*sus fines*) to attain

consejero, -a [konse'xero, a] *nm/f* adviser, consultant; (*Pol*) minister (*in a regional government*)

consejo [kon'sexo] *nm* advice; (*Pol*) council; (*Com*) board; **~ de administración** board of directors;

~ de guerra court-martial; **~ de ministros** cabinet meeting
consenso [kon'senso] nm consensus
consentimiento [konsenti'mjento] nm consent
consentir [konsen'tir] /3i/ vt (permitir, tolerar) to consent to; (mimar) to pamper, spoil; (aguantar) to put up with ▷ vi to agree, consent; **~ que algn haga algo** to allow sb to do sth
conserje [kon'serxe] nm caretaker; (portero) porter
conserva [kon'serβa] nf: **en ~** (alimentos) tinned (BRIT), canned; **conservas** nfpl (tb: **~s alimenticias**) tinned (BRIT) o canned foods
conservación [konserβa'θjon] nf conservation; (de alimentos, vida) preservation
conservador, a [konserβa'ðor, a] adj (Pol) conservative ▷ nm/f conservative
conservante [konser'βante] nm preservative
conservar [konser'βar] /1a/ vt to conserve, keep; (alimentos, vida) to preserve; **conservarse** vr to survive
conservatorio [konserβa'torjo] nm (Mus) conservatoire, conservatory
considerable [konsiðe'raβle] adj considerable
consideración [konsiðera'θjon] nf consideration; (estimación) respect
considerado, -a [konsiðe'raðo, a] adj (atento) considerate; (respetado) respected
considerar [konsiðe'rar] /1a/ vt to consider
consigna [kon'siɣna] nf (orden) order, instruction; (para equipajes) left-luggage office (BRIT), checkroom (US)
consigo [kon'siɣo] vb V **conseguir** ▷ pron (m) with him; (f) with her; (usted) with you; (reflexivo) with o.s.
consiguiendo etc [konsi'ɣjendo] vb V **conseguir**

consiguiente [konsi'ɣjente] adj consequent; **por ~** and so, therefore, consequently
consistente [konsis'tente] adj consistent; (sólido, firme, válido) sound
consistir [konsis'tir] /3a/ vi: **~ en** (componerse de) to consist of
consola [kon'sola] nf (mueble) console table; **~ de juegos** games console
consolación [konsola'θjon] nf consolation
consolar [konso'lar] /1l/ vt to console
consolidar [konsoli'ðar] /1a/ vt to consolidate
consomé [konso'me] (pl **consomés**) nm consommé, clear soup
consonante [konso'nante] adj consonant, harmonious ▷ nf consonant
consorcio [kon'sorθjo] nm consortium
conspiración [konspira'θjon] nf conspiracy
conspirar [konspi'rar] /1a/ vi to conspire
constancia [kons'tanθja] nf constancy; **dejar ~ de algo** to put sth on record
constante [kons'tante] adj, nf constant
constar [kons'tar] /1a/ vi (evidenciarse) to be clear o evident; **~ de** to consist of
constipado, -a [konsti'paðo, a] adj: **estar ~** to have a cold ▷ nm cold
⬛ No confundir constipado con la palabra inglesa constipated.
constitución [konstitu'θjon] nf constitution
constituir [konstitu'ir] /3g/ vt (formar, componer) to constitute, make up; (fundar, erigir, ordenar) to constitute, establish
construcción [konstruk'θjon] nf construction, building
constructor, a [konstruk'tor, a] nm/f builder

construir [konstru'ir] /3g/ vt to build, construct

construyendo etc [konstru'jendo] vb V **construir**

consuelo [kon'swelo] nm consolation, solace

cónsul ['konsul] nm consul; **consulado** nm consulate

consulta [kon'sulta] nf consultation; **horas de ~** (Med) surgery hours; **consultar** /1a/ vt to consult; **consultar algo con algn** to discuss sth with sb; **consultorio** nm (Med) surgery

consumición [konsumi'θjon] nf consumption; (bebida) drink; (comida) food; **~ mínima** cover charge

consumidor, a [konsumi'ðor, a] nm/f consumer

consumir [konsu'mir] /3a/ vt to consume; **consumirse** vr to be consumed; (persona) to waste away

consumismo [konsu'mismo] nm consumerism

consumo [kon'sumo] nm consumption

contabilidad [kontaβili'ðað] nf accounting, book-keeping; (profesión) accountancy; **contable** nmf accountant

contactar [kontak'tar] /1a/ vi: **~ con algn** to contact sb

contacto [kon'takto] nm contact; (Auto) ignition; **estar en ~ con** to be in touch with

contado, -a [kon'taðo, a] adj: **~s** (escasos) numbered, scarce, few ▷ nm: **pagar al ~** to pay (in) cash

contador [konta'ðor] nm (aparato) meter; (LAM: contable) accountant

contagiar [konta'xjar] /1b/ vt (enfermedad) to pass on, transmit; (persona) to infect; **contagiarse** vr to become infected

contagio [kon'taxjo] nm infection; **contagioso, -a** adj infectious; (fig) catching

contaminación [kontamina'θjon] nf contamination; (del ambiente etc) pollution

contaminar [kontami'nar] /1a/ vt to contaminate; (aire, agua) to pollute

contante [kon'tante] adj: **dinero ~ (y sonante)** hard cash

contar [kon'tar] /1l/ vt (páginas, dinero) to count; (anécdota etc) to tell ▷ vi to count; **~ con** to rely on, count on

contemplar [kontem'plar] /1a/ vt to contemplate; (mirar) to look at

contemporáneo, -a [kontempo'raneo, a] adj, nm/f contemporary

contenedor [kontene'ðor] nm container

contener [konte'ner] /2k/ vt to contain, hold; (risa etc) to hold back, contain; **contenerse** vr to control o restrain o.s.

contenido, -a [konte'niðo, a] adj (moderado) restrained; (risa etc) suppressed ▷ nm contents pl, content

contentar [konten'tar] /1a/ vt (satisfacer) to satisfy; (complacer) to please; **contentarse** vr to be satisfied

contento, -a [kon'tento, a] adj (alegre) pleased; (feliz) happy

contestación [kontesta'θjon] nf answer, reply

contestador [kontesta'ðor] nm: **~ automático** answering machine

contestar [kontes'tar] /1a/ vt to answer (back), reply; (Jur) to corroborate, confirm

No confundir **contestar** con la palabra inglesa contest.

contexto [kon'teksto] nm context

contigo [kon'tiyo] pron with you

contiguo, -a [kon'tiywo, a] adj adjacent, adjoining

continente [konti'nente] adj, nm continent

continuación [kontinwa'θjon] nf continuation; **a ~** then, next

continuar [konti'nwar] /1e/ vt to continue, go on with ▷ vi to continue, go on; **~ hablando** to continue talking o to talk

continuidad [kontinwi'ðað] nf continuity

continuo, -a [kon'tinwo, a] adj (sin interrupción) continuous; (acción perseverante) continual

contorno [kon'torno] nm outline; (Geo) contour; **contornos** nmpl neighbourhood sg, surrounding area sg

contra ['kontra] prep against ▷ adv against ▷ nm con ▷ nf: **la C-(nicaragüense)** the Contras pl

contraataque [kontraa'take] nm counterattack

contrabajo [kontra'βaxo] nm double bass

contrabandista [kontraβan'dista] nmf smuggler

contrabando [kontra'βando] nm (acción) smuggling; (mercancías) contraband

contracción [kontrak'θjon] nf contraction

contracorriente [kontrako'rrjente] nf cross-current

contradecir [kontraðe'θir] /3o/ vt to contradict

contradicción [kontraðik'θjon] nf contradiction

contradictorio, -a [kontraðik'torjo, a] adj contradictory

contraer [kontra'er] /2o/ vt to contract; (limitar) to restrict; **contraerse** vr to contract; (limitarse) to limit o.s.

contraluz [kontra'luθ] nm o f view against the light

contrapartida [kontrapar'tiða] nf: **como ~ (de)** in return (for)

contrapelo [kontra'pelo]: **a ~** adv the wrong way

contrapeso [kontra'peso] nm counterweight

contraportada [kontrapor'taða] nf (de revista) back cover

contraproducente [kontraproðu'θente] adj counterproductive

contrario, -a [kon'trarjo, a] adj contrary; (persona) opposed; (sentido, lado) opposite ▷ nm/f enemy, adversary; (Deporte) opponent; **al ~, por el ~** on the contrary; **de lo ~** otherwise

contrarreloj [kontrarre'lo(x)] nf (tb: **prueba ~**) time trial

contrarrestar [kontrarres'tar] /1a/ vt to counteract

contrasentido [kontrasen'tiðo] nm contradiction

contraseña [kontra'seɲa] nf (frase) password

contrastar [kontras'tar] /1a/ vt to verify ▷ vi to contrast

contraste [kon'traste] nm contrast

contratar [kontra'tar] /1a/ vt (firmar un acuerdo para) to contract for; (empleados, obreros) to hire, engage

contratiempo [kontra'tjempo] nm setback

contratista [kontra'tista] nmf contractor

contrato [kon'trato] nm contract

contraventana [kontraβen'tana] nf shutter

contribución [kontriβu'θjon] nf (municipal etc) tax; (ayuda) contribution

contribuir [kontriβu'ir] /3g/ vt, vi to contribute; (Com) to pay (in taxes)

contribuyente [kontriβu'jente] nmf (Com) taxpayer; (que ayuda) contributor

contrincante [kontrin'kante] nm opponent

control [kon'trol] nm control; (inspección) inspection, check; **~ de pasaportes** passport inspection; **controlador, a** nm/f controller; **controlador aéreo** air-traffic controller; **controlar** /1a/ vt to control; to inspect, check

contundente [kontun'dente] adj
(argumento) convincing; **instrumento**
~ blunt instrument

contusión [kontu'sjon] nf bruise

convalecencia [kombale'θenθja] nf
convalescence

convalecer [kombale'θer] /2d/ vi to
convalesce, get better

convalidar [kombali'ðar] /1a/ vt
(título) to recognize

convencer [komben'θer] /2b/ vt to
convince; (persuadir) to persuade

convención [komben'θjon] nf
convention

conveniente [komben'njente] adj
suitable; (útil) useful

convenio [kom'benjo] nm
agreement, treaty

convenir [kombe'nir] /3r/ vi (estar de
acuerdo) to agree; (ser conveniente) to
suit, be suitable

> No confundir convenir con la
> palabra inglesa convene.

convento [kom'bento] nm
monastery; (de monjas) convent

convenza etc [kom'benθa] vb V
convencer

converger [komber'xer] /2c/,
convergir [komber'xir] /3c/ vi to
converge

conversación [kombersa'θjon] nf
conversation

conversar [komber'sar] /1a/ vi to
talk, converse

conversión [komber'sjon] nf
conversion

convertir [komber'tir] /3i/ vt to convert

convidar [kombi'ðar] /1a/ vt to
invite; ~ **a algn a una cerveza** to
buy sb a beer

convincente [kombin'θente] adj
convincing

convite [kom'bite] nm invitation;
(banquete) banquet

convivencia [kombi'βenθja] nf
coexistence, living together

convivir [kombi'βir] /3a/ vi to live
together

convocar [kombo'kar] /1g/ vt to
summon, call (together)

convocatoria [komboka'torja]
nf summons sg; (anuncio) notice of
meeting

cónyuge ['konyuxe] nmf spouse

coñac ['koɲa(k)] (pl **coñacs**) nm
cognac, brandy

coño ['koɲo] (fam!) excl (enfado) shit (!);
(sorpresa) bloody hell (!)

cool [kul] adj (fam) cool

cooperación [koopera'θjon] nf
cooperation

cooperar [koope'rar] /1a/ vi to
cooperate

coordinar [koorði'nar] /1a/ vt to
coordinate

copa ['kopa] nf cup; (vaso) glass; (de
árbol) top; (de sombrero) crown; **copas**
nfpl (Naipes) one of the suits in the
Spanish card deck; **(tomar una)** ~ (to
have a) drink

copia ['kopja] nf copy; (Inform): ~ **de
respaldo** o **de seguridad** backup
copy; **copiar** /1b/ vt to copy

copla ['kopla] nf verse; (canción)
(popular) song

copo ['kopo] nm: ~**s de maíz**
cornflakes; ~ **de nieve** snowflake

coqueta [ko'keta] adj flirtatious,
coquettish; **coquetear** /1a/ vi to flirt

coraje [ko'raxe] nm courage; (ánimo)
spirit; (ira) anger

coral [ko'ral] adj choral ▷ nf choir ▷ nm
(Zool) coral

coraza [ko'raθa] nf (armadura)
armour; (blindaje) armour-plating

corazón [kora'θon] nm heart

corazonada [koraθo'naða] nf
impulse; (presentimiento) hunch

corbata [kor'βata] nf tie

corchete [kor'tʃete] nm catch, clasp

corcho ['kortʃo] nm cork; (Pesca) float

cordel [kor'ðel] nm cord, line

cordero [kor'ðero] nm lamb

cordial [kor'ðjal] adj cordial

cordillera [korði'ʎera] nf range (of
mountains)

Córdoba [ˈkorðoβa] nf Cordova

cordón [korˈðon] nm (cuerda) cord, string; (de zapatos) lace; (Mil etc) cordon; **~ umbilical** umbilical cord

cordura [korˈðura] nf: **con ~** (obrar, hablar) sensibly

corneta [korˈneta] nf bugle

cornisa [korˈnisa] nf cornice

coro [ˈkoro] nm chorus; (conjunto de cantores) choir

corona [koˈrona] nf crown; (de flores) garland

coronel [koroˈnel] nm colonel

coronilla [koroˈniʎa] nf (Anat) crown (of the head)

corporal [korpoˈral] adj corporal, bodily

corpulento, -a [korpuˈlento, a] adj (persona) heavily-built

corral [koˈrral] nm farmyard

correa [koˈrrea] nf strap; (cinturón) belt; (de perro) lead, leash; **~ del ventilador** (Auto) fan belt

corrección [korrekˈθjon] nf correction; (reprensión) rebuke; **correccional** nm reformatory

correcto, -a [koˈrrekto, a] adj correct; (persona) well-mannered

corredizo, -a [korreˈðiθo, a] adj (puerta etc) sliding

corredor, a [korreˈðor, a] nm/f (Deporte) runner ▷ nm (pasillo) corridor; (balcón corrido) gallery; (Com) agent, broker

corregir [korreˈxir] /3c, 3k/ vt (error) to correct; **corregirse** vr to reform

correo [koˈrreo] nm post, mail; (persona) courier; **Correos** nmpl Post Office sg; **~ aéreo** airmail; **~ basura** (por Internet) spam; **~ electrónico** email, electronic mail; **~ web** webmail

correr [koˈrrer] /2a/ vt to run; (cortinas) to draw; (cerrojo) to shoot ▷ vi to run; (líquido) to run, flow; (colores) to run, slide, move; **correrse** vr (colores) to run

correspondencia [korrespon'denθja] nf correspondence; (Ferro) connection

corresponder [korrespon'der] /2a/ vi to correspond; (convenir) to be suitable; (pertenecer) to belong; (tocar) to concern; **corresponderse** vr (por escrito) to correspond; (amarse) to love one another

correspondiente [korrespon'djente] adj corresponding

corresponsal [korrespon'sal] nmf (newspaper) correspondent

corrido, -a [koˈrriðo, a] adj (avergonzado) abashed ▷ nf (de toros) bullfight; **un kilo ~** a good kilo

corriente [koˈrrjente] adj (agua) running; (dinero, cuenta etc) current; (común) ordinary, normal ▷ nf current ▷ nm current month; **~ eléctrica** electric current; **estar al ~ de** to be informed about

corrija etc [koˈrrixa] vb V **corregir**

corro [ˈkorro] nm ring, circle (of people)

corromper [korrom'per] /2a/ vt (madera) to rot; (fig) to corrupt

corrosivo, -a [korro'siβo, a] adj corrosive

corrupción [korrup'θjon] nf rot, decay; (fig) corruption

corsé [kor'se] nm corset

cortacésped [korta'θespeð] nm lawn mower

cortado, -a [kor'taðo, a] adj (con cuchillo) cut; (leche) sour; (desconcertado) embarrassed; (tímido) shy ▷ nm coffee with a little milk

cortafuegos [korta'fweɣos] nm inv (en el bosque) firebreak, fire lane (us); (Internet) firewall

cortalápices [korta'lapiθes] nm inv (pencil) sharpener

cortar [kor'tar] /1a/ vt to cut; (suministro) to cut off; (un pasaje) to cut out ▷ vi to cut; **cortarse** vr (turbarse) to become embarrassed; (leche) to turn, curdle; **~se el pelo** to have one's hair cut

cortauñas [korta'uɲas] nm inv nail clippers pl

corte ['korte] nm cut, cutting; (de tela) piece, length ▷ nf(real) court; ~ y confección dressmaking; ~ de corriente o luz power cut; las C~s the Spanish Parliament sg

cortejo [kor'texo] nm entourage; ~ fúnebre funeral procession

cortés [kor'tes] adj courteous, polite

cortesía [korte'sia] nf courtesy

corteza [kor'teθa] nf(de árbol) bark; (de pan) crust

cortijo [kor'tixo] nm (ESP) farm, farmhouse

cortina [kor'tina] nf curtain

corto, -a ['korto, a] adj (breve) short; (tímido) bashful; ~ de luces not very bright; ~ de vista short-sighted; estar ~ de fondos to be short of funds; cortocircuito nm short-circuit; cortometraje nm (Cine) short

cosa ['kosa] nf thing; ~ de about; son es ~ mía that's my business

coscorrón [kosko'rron] nm bump on the head

cosecha [ko'setʃa] nf(Agr) harvest; (de vino) vintage; cosechar /1a/ vt to harvest, gather (in)

coser [ko'ser] /2a/ vt to sew

cosmético, -a [kos'metiko, a] adj, nm cosmetic

cosquillas [kos'kiʎas] nfpl: hacer ~ to tickle; tener ~ to be ticklish

costa ['kosta] nf(Geo) coast; C~ Brava Costa Brava; C~ Cantábrica Cantabrian Coast; C~ del Sol Costa del Sol; a toda ~ at any price

costado [kos'taðo] nm side

costanera [kosta'nera] nf(LAM) promenade, sea front

costar [kos'tar] /1l/ vt (valer) to cost; me cuesta hablarle I find it hard to talk to him

Costa Rica ['kosta 'rika] nf Costa Rica; costarricense adj, nmf Costa Rican

coste ['koste] nm V costo

costear [koste'ar] /1a/ vt to pay for

costero [kos'tero, a] adj coastal

costilla [kos'tiʎa] nf rib; (Culin) cutlet

costo ['kosto] nm cost, price; ~ de la vida cost of living; costoso, -a adj costly, expensive

costra ['kostra] nf(corteza) crust; (Med) scab

costumbre [kos'tumbre] nf custom, habit; como de ~ as usual

costura [kos'tura] nf sewing, needlework; (zurcido) seam

costurera [kostu'rera] nf dressmaker

costurero [kostu'rero] nm sewing box o case

cotidiano, -a [koti'ðjano, a] adj daily, day to day

cotilla [ko'tiʎa] nf gossip; cotillear /1a/ vi to gossip; cotilleo nm gossip(ing)

cotizar [koti'θar] /1f/ vt (Com) to quote, price; cotizarse vr: ~se a to sell at, fetch; (Bolsa) to stand at, be quoted at

coto ['koto] nm (terreno cercado) enclosure; (de caza) reserve

cotorra [ko'torra] nf parrot

coyote [ko'jote] nm coyote, prairie wolf

coz [koθ] nf kick

crack [krak] nm (droga) crack

cráneo ['kraneo] nm skull, cranium

cráter ['krater] nm crater

crayón [kra'jon] nm (LAM: lápiz) (coloured) pencil; (cera) crayon

creación [krea'θjon] nf creation

creador, a [krea'ðor, a] adj creative ▷ nm/f creator

crear [kre'ar] /1a/ vt to create, make

creativo, -a [krea'tiβo, a] adj creative

crecer [kre'θer] /2d/ vi to grow; (precio) to rise

creces ['kreθes]: con ~ adv amply, fully

crecido, -a [kre'θiðo, a] adj (persona, planta) full-grown; (cantidad) large

crecimiento [kreθi'mjento] nm growth; (aumento) increase

credencial [kreðen'θjal] nf (LAM: tarjeta) card; credenciales *nfpl* credentials; **~ de socio** (*LAM*) membership card

crédito [ˈkreðito] *nm* credit

credo [ˈkreðo] *nm* creed

creencia [kreˈenθja] *nf* belief

creer [kreˈer] /2e/ *vt, vi* to think, believe; **creerse** *vr* to believe o.s. (to be); **~ en** to believe in; **creo que sí/ no** I think/don't think so; **¡ya lo creo!** I should think so!

creído, -a [kreˈiðo, a] *adj* (*engreído*) conceited

crema [ˈkrema] *nf* cream; **~ batida** (*LAM*) whipped cream; **~ pastelera** (*confectioner's*) custard

cremallera [kremaˈʎera] *nf* zip (fastener) (*BRIT*), zipper (*US*)

crepe [ˈkrepe] *nf* (*LAM*) pancake

cresta [ˈkresta] *nf* (*Geo, Zool*) crest

creyendo *etc* [kreˈjendo] *vb* V **creer**

creyente [kreˈjente] *nmf* believer

creyó *etc* [kreˈjo] *vb* V **creer**

crezco *etc* [ˈkreθko] *vb* V **crecer**

cría [ˈkria] *vb* V **criar** ▷ *nf* (*de animales*) rearing, breeding; (*animal*) young; V *tb* **crío**

criadero [kriaˈðero] *nm* (*Zool*) breeding place

criado, -a [kriˈaðo, a] *nm* servant ▷ *nf* servant, maid

criador [kriaˈðor] *nm* (*ESP*) breeder

crianza [kriˈanθa] *nf* rearing, breeding; (*fig*) breeding

criar [kriˈar] /1c/ *vt* (*educar*) to bring up; (*producir*) to grow, produce; (*animales*) to breed

criatura [kriaˈtura] *nf* creature; (*niño*) baby, (small) child

cribar [kriˈβar] /1a/ *vt* to sieve

crimen [ˈkrimen] *nm* crime

criminal [krimiˈnal] *adj, nmf* criminal

crin [krin] *nf* (*tb*: **-es**) mane

crío, -a [ˈkrio, a] *nm/f* (*fam: chico*) kid

crisis [ˈkrisis] *nf inv* crisis; **~ nerviosa** nervous breakdown

crisma [ˈkrisma] *nm inv* (*ESP*) Christmas card

cristal [krisˈtal] *nm* crystal; (*de ventana*) glass, pane; (*lente*) lens; **cristalino, -a** *adj* crystalline; (*fig*) clear ▷ *nm* lens of the eye

cristianismo [kristjaˈnismo] *nm* Christianity

cristiano, -a [krisˈtjano, a] *adj, nm/f* Christian

Cristo [ˈkristo] *nm* Christ; (*crucifijo*) crucifix

criterio [kriˈterjo] *nm* criterion; (*juicio*) judgement

crítico, -a [ˈkritiko, a] *adj* critical ▷ *nm* critic ▷ *nf* criticism

Croacia [kroˈaθja] *nf* Croatia

croissan, croissant [krwaˈsan] *nm* croissant

cromo [ˈkromo] *nm* chrome

crónico, -a [ˈkroniko, a] *adj* chronic ▷ *nf* chronicle, account

cronómetro [kroˈnometro] *nm* stopwatch

croqueta [kroˈketa] *nf* croquette, rissole

cruce [ˈkruθe] *vb* V **cruzar** ▷ *nm* (*para peatones*) crossing; (*de carreteras*) crossroads

crucero [kruˈθero] *nm* (*viaje*) cruise

crucificar [kruθifiˈkar] /1g/ *vt* to crucify

crucifijo [kruθiˈfixo] *nm* crucifix

crucigrama [kruθiˈɣrama] *nm* crossword (puzzle)

cruda [ˈkruða] *nf* (*LAM fam*) hangover

crudo, -a [ˈkruðo, a] *adj* raw; (*no maduro*) unripe; (*petróleo*) crude; (*rudo, cruel*) cruel ▷ *nm* crude (oil)

cruel [krwel] *adj* cruel; **crueldad** *nf* cruelty

crujiente [kruˈxjente] *adj* (*galleta etc*) crunchy

crujir [kruˈxir] /3a/ *vi* (*madera etc*) to creak; (*dedos*) to crack; (*dientes*) to grind; (*nieve, arena*) to crunch

cruz [kruθ] *nf* cross; (*de moneda*) tails *sg*; **~ gamada** swastika; **C~ Roja** Red Cross

cruzado, -a [kru'θaðo, a] *adj* crossed
▷ *nm* crusader ▷ *nf* crusade

cruzar [kru'θar] /1f/ *vt* to cross;
cruzarse *vr* (*líneas etc*) to cross;
(*personas*) to pass each other

cuaderno [kwa'ðerno] *nm* notebook;
(*de escuela*) exercise book; (*Naut*)
logbook

cuadra [kwaðra] *nf* (*caballeriza*)
stable; (ʌм) (city) block

cuadrado, -a [kwa'ðraðo, a] *adj*
square ▷ *nm* (*Mat*) square

cuadrar [kwa'ðrar] /1a/ *vt* to square
▷ *vi*: **~ con** to square with, tally with;
cuadrarse *vr* (*soldado*) to stand to
attention

cuadrilátero [kwaðri'latero]
nm (*Deporte*) boxing ring; (*Mat*)
quadrilateral

cuadrilla [kwa'ðriʎa] *nf* party, group

cuadro [kwaðro] *nm* square; (*Arte*)
painting; (*Teat*) scene; (*diagrama*)
chart; (*Deporte, Med*) team; **tela a
~s** checked (ʙʀɪт) o chequered (ʊs)
material

cuajar [kwa'xar] /1a/ *vt* (*leche*) to
curdle; (*sangre*) to congeal; (*Culin*)
to set; **cuajarse** *vr* to curdle; to congeal;
(*llenarse*) to fill up

cuajo [kwaxo] *nm*: **de ~** (*arrancar*) by
the roots; (*cortar*) completely

cual [kwal] *adv* like, as ▷ *pron*: **el ~** *etc*
which; (*persona, sujeto*) who; (*persona,
objeto*) whom ▷ *adj* such as; **cada ~**
each one; **tal ~** just as it is

cuál [kwal] *pron interrogativo* which
(one)

cualesquier [kwales'kjer],
cualesquiera [kwales'kjera] *adj pl*,
pron pl de **cualquier**

cualidad [kwali'ðað] *nf* quality

cualquier [kwal'kjer], **cualquiera**
[kwal'kjera] *adj any* ▷ *pron* anybody;
~ día/libro any day/book; **un coche
~a servirá** any car will do; **no es un
hombre ~** he isn't just anybody; **eso
~a lo sabe hacer** anybody can do
that; **es un ~** he's a nobody

cuando ['kwando] *adv* when; (*aún
si*) if, even if ▷ *conj* (*puesto que*) since
▷ *prep*: **yo ... niño ...** when I was a
child o as a child I ...; **~ no sea así**
even if it is not so; **~ más** at (the)
most; **~ menos** at least; **~ no** if not,
otherwise; **de ~ en ~** from time
to time

cuándo ['kwando] *adv* when; **¿desde
~?** since when?

cuantía [kwan'tia] *nf* (*importe: de
pérdidas, deuda, daños*) extent

PALABRA CLAVE

cuanto, -a ['kwanto, a] *adj* 1 (*todo*):
tiene todo cuanto desea he's got
everything he wants; **le daremos
cuantos ejemplares necesite** we'll
give him as many copies as o all the
copies he needs; **cuantos hombres
la ven** all the men who see her
2: **unos cuantos: había unos
cuantos periodistas** there were
(quite) a few journalists
3 (+*más*): **cuanto más vino bebas
peor te sentirás** the more wine you
drink the worse you'll feel
▷ *pron*: **tiene cuanto desea** he has
everything he wants; **tome cuanto/
cuantos quiera** take as much/many
as you want
▷ *adv*: **en cuanto: en cuanto
profesor** as a teacher; **en cuanto a
mí** as for me; *V tb* **antes**
▷ *conj* 1: **cuanto más gana menos
gasta** the more he earns the less he
spends; **cuanto más joven se es
más se es confiado** the younger you
are the more trusting you are
2: **en cuanto: en cuanto llegue/
llegué** as soon as I arrive/arrived

cuánto, -a ['kwanto, a] *adj*
(*exclamación*) what a lot of;
(*interrogativo: sg*) how much?
(*: pl*) how many? ▷ *pron, adv* how;
(*interrogativo: sg*) how much? (*: pl*)

how many?; **¡cuánta gente!** what a lot of people!; **¿~ cuesta?** how much does it cost?; **¿a ~s estamos?** what's the date?

cuarenta [kwa'renta] num forty

cuarentena [kwaren'tena] nf quarantine

cuaresma [kwa'resma] nf Lent

cuarta ['kwarta] nf V **cuarto**

cuartel [kwar'tel] nm (Mil) barracks pl; **~ de bomberos** (LAM) fire station; **~ general** headquarters pl

cuarteto [kwar'teto] nm quartet

cuarto, -a ['kwarto, a] adj fourth ▷ nm (Mat) quarter, fourth; (habitación) room ▷ nf (Mat) quarter, fourth; (palmo) span; **~ de baño** bathroom; **~ de estar** living room; **~ de hora** quarter (of an) hour; **~ de kilo** quarter kilo; **~s de final** quarter finals

cuatro ['kwatro] num four

Cuba ['kuβa] nf Cuba

cuba ['kuβa] nf cask, barrel

cubalibre [kuβa'liβɾe] nm (white) rum and coke®

cubano, -a [ku'βano, a] adj, nm/f Cuban

cubata [ku'βata] nm = **cubalibre**

cubeta [ku'βeta] nf (balde) bucket, tub

cúbico, -a ['kuβiko, a] adj cubic

cubierto, -a [ku'βjerto, a] pp de **cubrir** ▷ adj covered ▷ nm cover; (en la mesa) place ▷ nf cover, covering; (neumático) tyre; (Naut) deck; **cubiertos** nmpl cutlery sg; **a ~** under cover

cubilete [kuβi'lete] nm (en juegos) cup

cubito [ku'βito] nm: **~ de hielo** ice cube

cubo ['kuβo] nm cube; (balde) bucket, tub; (Tec) drum; **~ de (la) basura** dustbin (BRIT), trash can (US)

cubrir [ku'βɾir] /3a/ vt to cover; **cubrirse** vr (cielo) to become overcast

cucaracha [kuka'ratʃa] nf cockroach

cuchara [ku'tʃara] nf spoon; (Tec) scoop; **cucharada** nf spoonful; **cucharadita** nf teaspoonful

cucharilla [kutʃa'riʎa] nf teaspoon

cucharón [kutʃa'ron] nm ladle

cuchilla [ku'tʃiʎa] nf (large) knife; (de arma blanca) blade; **~ de afeitar** razor blade

cuchillo [ku'tʃiʎo] nm knife

cuchitril [kutʃi'tril] nm hovel

cuclillas [ku'kliʎas] nfpl: **en ~** squatting

cuco, -a ['kuko, a] adj pretty; (astuto) sharp ▷ nm cuckoo

cucurucho [kuku'rutʃo] nm cornet

cueca ['kweka] nf Chilean national dance

cuello ['kweʎo] nm (Anat) neck; (de vestido, camisa) collar

cuenca ['kwenka] nf (Anat) eye socket; (Geo) bowl, deep valley

cuenco ['kwenko] nm (earthenware) bowl

cuenta ['kwenta] vb V **contar** ▷ nf (cálculo) count, counting; (en café, restaurante) bill (BRIT), check (US); (Com) account; (de collar) bead; **a fin de ~s** in the end; **caer en la ~** to catch on; **darse ~ de** to realize; **tener en ~** to bear in mind; **echar ~s** to take stock; **~ atrás** countdown; **~ corriente/de ahorros/a plazo (fijo)** current/savings/deposit account; **~ de correo** (Internet) email account; **cuentakilómetros** nm inv ≈ milometer, clock; (velocímetro) speedometer

cuento ['kwento] vb V **contar** ▷ nm story; **~ chino** tall story; **~ de hadas** fairy tale ▷ story

cuerda ['kwerδa] nf rope; (hilo) string; (de reloj) spring; (~s) **floja** tightrope; **~s vocales** vocal cords; **dar ~ a un reloj** to wind up a clock

cuerdo, -a ['kwerδo, a] adj sane; (prudente) wise, sensible

cuerno ['kwerno] nm horn

cuero ['kwero] nm leather; **en ~s** stark naked; **~ cabelludo** scalp

cuerpo ['kwerpo] nm body

cuervo ['kwerβo] nm crow

cuesta ['kwesta] vb V **costar** ⊳ nf slope; (en camino etc) hill; **~ arriba/abajo** uphill/downhill; **a ~s** on one's back

cueste etc vb V **costar**

cuestión [kwes'tjon] nf matter, question, issue

cuete ['kwete] adj (LAM fam) drunk ⊳ nm (cohete) rocket; (fam: embriaguez) drunkenness; (Culin) steak

cueva ['kweβa] nf cave

cuidado [kwi'ðaðo] nm care, carefulness; (preocupación) care, worry ⊳ excl carefull, look out!; **eso me tiene sin ~** I'm not worried about that

cuidadoso, -a [kwiða'ðoso, a] adj careful; (preocupado) anxious

cuidar [kwi'ðar] /1a/ vt (Med) to care for; (ocuparse de) to take care of, look after ⊳ vi: **~ de** to take care of, look after; **cuidarse** vr to look after o.s.; **~se de hacer algo** to take care to do sth

culata [ku'lata] nf (de fusil) butt

culebra [ku'leβra] nf snake

culebrón [kule'βron] nm (fam) soap (opera)

culo ['kulo] nm bottom, backside; (de vaso) bottom

culpa ['kulpa] nf fault; (Jur) guilt; **por ~ de** because of; **echar la ~ a algn** to blame sb for sth; **tener la ~ (de)** to be to blame (for); **culpable** adj guilty ⊳ nmf culprit; **culpar** /1a/ vt to blame; (acusar) to accuse

cultivar [kulti'βar] /1a/ vt to cultivate

cultivo [kul'tiβo] nm (acto) cultivation; (plantas) crop

culto, -a ['kulto, a] adj (que tiene cultura) cultured, educated ⊳ nm (homenaje) worship; (religión) cult

cultura [kul'tura] nf culture

culturismo [kultu'rismo] nm body-building

cumbia ['kumbja] nf popular Colombian dance

cumbre ['kumbre] nf summit, top

cumpleaños [kumple'aɲos] nm inv birthday

cumplido, -a [kum'pliðo, a] adj (abundante) plentiful; (cortés) courteous ⊳ nm compliment; **visita de ~** courtesy call

cumplidor, a [kumpli'ðor, a] adj reliable

cumplimiento [kumpli'mjento] nm (de un deber) fulfilment; (acabamiento) completion

cumplir [kum'plir] /3a/ vt (orden) to carry out, obey; (promesa) to carry out, fulfil; (condena) to serve; **cumplirse** vr (plazo) to expire; **hoy cumple dieciocho años** he is eighteen today; **~ con** (deber) to carry out, fulfil

cuna ['kuna] nf cradle, cot

cundir [kun'dir] /3a/ vi (noticia, rumor, pánico) to spread; (rendir) to go a long way

cuneta [ku'neta] nf ditch

cuña ['kuɲa] nf wedge

cuñado, -a [ku'ɲaðo, a] nm/f brother-/sister-in-law

cuota ['kwota] nf (parte proporcional) share; (cotización) fee, dues pl

cupe etc ['kupe] vb V **caber**

cupiera etc [ku'pjera] vb V **caber**

cupo etc ['kupo] vb V **caber** ⊳ nm quota

cupón [ku'pon] nm coupon

cúpula ['kupula] nf dome

cura ['kura] nf (curación) cure; (método curativo) treatment ⊳ nm priest

curación [kura'θjon] nf cure; (acción) curing

curandero, -a [kuran'dero, a] nm/f healer; (pey) quack

curar [ku'rar] /1a/ vt (Med: herida) to treat, dress; (: enfermo) to cure; (Culin) to cure, salt; (cuero) to tan ⊳ **curarse** vr to get well, recover

curiosear [kurjose'ar] /1a/ vt to glance at, look over ⊳ vi to look round, wander round; (explorar) to poke about

curiosidad [kurjosi'ðað] nf curiosity

curioso, -a [ku'rjoso, a] *adj* curious
▷ *nm/f* bystander, onlooker
curita [ku'rita] *nf* (LAM) sticking plaster
currante [ku'rrante] *nmf* (fam) worker
currar [ku'rrar] /1a/ *vi* to work
currículo [ku'rrikulo], **currículum** [ku'rrikulum] *nm* curriculum vitae
cursi ['kursi] *adj* (fam) affected
cursillo [kur'siʎo] *nm* short course
cursiva [kur'siβa] *nf* italics *pl*
curso ['kurso] *nm* course; **en ~** (año) current; (proceso) going on, under way
cursor [kur'sor] *nm* (Inform) cursor
curul [ku'rul] *nm* (LAM: escaño) seat
custodia [kus'toðja] *nf* (cuidado) safekeeping; (Jur) custody
cutis ['kutis] *nm inv* skin, complexion
cutre ['kutre] *adj* (fam: lugar) grotty
cuyo, -a ['kujo, a] *pron* (de quien) whose; (de que) whose, of which; **en ~ caso** in which case
C.V. *abr* (= caballos de vapor) H.P.

D. *abr* (= Don) Esq
dado, -a ['daðo, a] *pp de* **dar** ▷ *nm* die; **dados** *nmpl* dice; **~ que** given that
daltónico, -a [dal'toniko, a] *adj* colour-blind
dama ['dama] *nf* (gen) lady; (Ajedrez) queen; **damas** *nfpl* draughts; **~ de honor** bridesmaid
damasco [da'masko] *nm* (LAM) apricot
danés, -esa [da'nes, esa] *adj* Danish
▷ *nm/f* Dane
dañar [da'ɲar] /1a/ *vt* (objeto) to damage; (persona) to hurt; **dañarse** *vr* (objeto) to get damaged
dañino, -a [da'ɲino, a] *adj* harmful
daño ['daɲo] *nm* (a un objeto) damage; (a una persona) harm, injury; **~s y perjuicios** (Jur) damages; **hacer ~ a** to damage; (persona) to hurt, injure; **hacerse ~** to hurt o.s.
dañoso, -a [da'ɲoso, a] *adj* harmful

PALABRA CLAVE

dar [dar] /1q/ vt 1 (gen) to give; (obra de teatro) to put on; (film) to show; (fiesta) to have; **dar algo a algn** to give sth to sb o sth to sb; **dar de beber a algn** to give sb a drink; **dar de comer** to feed
2 (producir: intereses) to yield; (: fruta) to produce
3 (locuciones + n): **da gusto escucharle** it's a pleasure to listen to him; V tb **paseo**
4 (+ n: = perífrasis de verbo): **me da asco** it sickens me
5 (considerar): **dar algo por descontado/entendido** to take sth for granted/as read; **dar algo por concluido** to consider sth finished
6 (hora): **el reloj dio las seis** the clock struck six (o'clock)
7: **me da lo mismo** it's all the same to me; V tb **igual; más**
▶ vi 1: **dar a** (habitación) to overlook, look on to; (: accionar: botón etc) to press, hit
2: **dar con**: dimos con él dos horas más tarde we came across him two hours later; **al final di con la solución** I eventually came up with the answer
3: **dar en** (blanco, suelo) to hit; **el sol me da en la cara** the sun is shining (right) in my face
4: **dar de sí** (zapatos etc) to stretch, give
▶**darse** vr 1: **darse un baño** to have a bath; **darse un golpe** to hit o.s.
2: **darse por vencido** to give up
3 (ocurrir): **se han dado muchos casos** there have been a lot of cases
4: **darse a: se ha dado a la bebida** he's taken to drinking
5: **se me dan bien/mal las ciencias** I'm good/bad at science
6: **dárselas de: se las da de experto** he fancies himself o poses as an expert

dardo ['darðo] nm dart

dátil ['datil] nm date
dato ['dato] nm fact, piece of information; **~s personales** personal details

dcha. abr (= derecha) r
d. de C. abr (= después de Cristo) A.D.
= Anno Domini

PALABRA CLAVE

de [de] prep (de + el = del) 1 (posesión, pertenencia) of; **la casa de Isabel/mis padres** Isabel's/my parents' house; **es de ellos/ella** it's theirs/hers
2 (origen, distancia, con números) from; **soy de Gijón** I'm from Gijón; **de 8 a 20** from 8 to 20; **salir del cine** to go out of o leave the cinema; **de 2 en 2** by 2, 2 at a time
3 (valor descriptivo): **una copa de vino** a glass of wine; **la mesa de la cocina** the kitchen table; **un billete de 50 euros** a 50-euro note; **un niño de tres años** a three-year-old (child); **una máquina de coser** a sewing machine; **ir vestido de gris** to be dressed in grey; **la niña del vestido azul** the girl in the blue dress; **trabaja de profesora** she works as a teacher; **de lado** sideways; **de atrás/delante** rear/front
4 (hora, tiempo): **a las 8 de la mañana** at 8 o'clock in the morning; **de día/noche** by day/night; **de hoy en ocho días** a week from now; **de niño era gordo** as a child he was fat
5 (comparaciones): **más/menos de cien personas** more/less than a hundred people; **el más caro de la tienda** the most expensive in the shop; **menos/más de lo pensado** less/more than expected
6 (causa): **del calor** from the heat
7 (tema) about; **clases de inglés** English classes; **¿sabes algo de él?** do you know anything about him?; **un libro de física** a physics book
8 (adj + de + infin): **fácil de entender** easy to understand

9 (oraciones pasivas): **fue respetado de todos** he was loved by all
10 (condicional + infin) if; **de ser posible** if possible; **de no terminarlo hoy** if I etc don't finish it today

dé [de] vb V **dar**

debajo [de'βaxo] adv underneath; **~ de** below, under; **por ~ de** beneath

debate [de'βate] nm debate; **debatir** /3a/ vt to debate

deber [de'βer] /2a/ nm duty ▷ vt to owe ▷ vi: **debe (de)** it must, it should; **deberse** vr: **~se a** to be owing o due to; **deberes** nmpl (Escol) homework sg; **debo hacerlo** I must do it; **debe de ir** he should go

debido, -a [de'βiðo, a] adj proper, due; **~ a** due to, because of

débil ['deβil] adj weak; (luz) dim; **debilidad** nf weakness; dimness

debilitar [deβili'tar] /1a/ vt to weaken; **debilitarse** vr to grow weak

débito ['deβito] nm debit; **~ bancario** (LAM) direct debit (BRIT) o billing (US)

debutar [deβu'tar] /1a/ vi to make one's debut

década ['dekaða] nf decade

decadencia [deka'ðenθja] nf (estado) decadence; (proceso) decline, decay

decaído, -a [deka'iðo, a] adj: **estar ~** (persona) to be down

decano, -a [de'kano, a] nm/f (Univ etc) dean

decena [de'θena] nf: **una ~** ten (or so)

decente [de'θente] adj decent

decepción [deθep'θjon] nf disappointment

> No confundir decepción con la palabra inglesa deception.

decepcionar [deθepθjo'nar] /1a/ vt to disappoint

decidir [deθi'ðir] /3a/ vt to decide ▷ vi to decide; **decidirse** vr: **~se a** to make up one's mind to

décimo, -a ['deθimo, a] num tenth ▷ nf tenth

decir [de'θir] /3o/ vt to say; (contar) to tell; (hablar) to speak ▷ nm saying; **decirse** vr: **se dice** it is said; **~ para o entre sí** to say to o.s.; **querer ~** to mean; **es ~** that is to say; **¡dígame!** (en tienda etc) can I help you?; (Telec) hello?

decisión [deθi'sjon] nf decision; (firmeza) decisiveness

decisivo, -a [deθi'siβo, a] adj decisive

declaración [deklara'θjon] nf (manifestación) statement; (de amor) declaration; **~ de ingresos o de la renta** income tax return

declarar [dekla'rar] /1a/ vt to declare ▷ vi to declare; (Jur) to testify; **declararse** vr to propose

decoración [dekora'θjon] nf decoration

decorado [deko'raðo] nm (Cine, Teat) scenery, set

decorar [deko'rar] /1a/ vt to decorate; **decorativo, -a** adj ornamental, decorative

decreto [de'kreto] nm decree

dedal [de'ðal] nm thimble

dedicación [deðika'θjon] nf dedication

dedicar [deði'kar] /1g/ vt (libro) to dedicate; (tiempo, dinero) to devote; (palabras: decir, consagrar) to dedicate, devote; **dedicatoria** nf (de libro) dedication

dedo ['deðo] nm finger; **~ (del pie)** toe; **~ pulgar** thumb; **~ índice** index finger; **~ mayor o cordial** middle finger; **~ anular** ring finger; **~ meñique** little finger

deducción [deðuk'θjon] nf deduction

deducir [deðu'θir] /3n/ vt (concluir) to deduce, infer; (Com) to deduct

defecto [de'fekto] nm defect, flaw; **defectuoso, -a** adj defective, faulty

defender [defen'der] /2g/ vt to defend; **defenderse** vr: **me defiendo en inglés** (fig) I can get by in English

defensa [de'fensa] *nf* defence ▷ *nm*
(*Deporte*) defender, back; **defensivo,
-a** *adj* defensive ▷ *nf*: **a la defensiva**
on the defensive

defensor, -a [defen'sor, a] *adj*
defending ▷ *nm/f* (*abogado defensor*)
defending counsel; (*protector*)
protector

deficiencia [defi'θjenθja] *nf*
deficiency

deficiente [defi'θjente] *adj*
(*defectuoso*) defective; **~ en** lacking o
deficient in ▷ *nm*: **ser un ~ mental**
to be mentally handicapped

déficit ['defiθit] (*pl* **déficits**) *nm*
deficit

definición [defini'θjon] *nf* definition

definir [defi'nir] /3a/ *vt* (*determinar*)
to determine, establish; (*decidir*) to
define; (*aclarar*) to clarify; **definitivo,
-a** *adj* definitive; **en definitiva**
definitively; (*en resumen*) in short

deformación [deforma'θjon] *nf*
(*alteración*) deformation; (*Radio etc*)
distortion

deformar [defor'mar] /1a/ *vt* (*gen*)
to deform; **deformarse** *vr* to become
deformed; **deforme** *adj* (*informe*)
deformed; (*feo*) ugly; (*mal hecho*)
misshapen

defraudar [defrau'ðar] /1a/ *vt*
(*decepcionar*) to disappoint; (*estafar*)
to defraud

defunción [defun'θjon] *nf* death,
demise

degenerar [dexene'rar] /1a/ *vi* to
degenerate

degollar /1m/ *vt* to cut s.o.'s throat

degradar [deɣra'ðar] /1a/ *vt* to
debase, degrade; **degradarse** *vr* to
demean o.s.

degustación [deɣusta'θjon] *nf*
sampling, tasting

dejar [de'xar] /1a/ *vt* to leave;
(*permitir*) to allow, let; (*abandonar*)
to abandon, forsake; (*beneficios*) to
produce, yield ▷ *vi*: **~ de** (*parar*) to
stop; (*no hacer*) to fail to; **dejarse:**

~ a un lado to leave o set aside;
~ entrar/salir to let in/out; **~ pasar**
to let through

del [del] = **de + el**; *ver* **de**

delantal [delan'tal] *nm* apron

delante [de'lante] *adv* in front;
(*enfrente*) opposite; (*adelante*) ahead
▷ *prep*: **~ de** in front of, before

delantero, -a [delan'tero, a] *adj*
front; (*patas de animal*) fore ▷ *nm*
(*Deporte*) forward, striker

delatar [dela'tar] /1a/ *vt* to inform
on o against, betray; **delator, -a** *nm/f*
informer

delegación [deleɣa'θjon] *nf* (*acción:
delegados*) delegation; (*Com: oficina*)
district office, branch; **~ de policía**
(ᴌᴀᴍ) police station

delegado, -a [dele'ɣaðo, a] *nm/f*
delegate; (*Com*) agent

delegar [dele'ɣar] /1h/ *vt* to delegate

deletrear [deletre'ar] /1a/ *vt* to
spell (out)

delfín [del'fin] *nm* dolphin

delgado, -a [del'ɣaðo, a] *adj* thin;
(*persona*) slim, thin; (*tela etc*) light,
delicate

deliberar [deliβe'rar] /1a/ *vt* to
debate, discuss

delicadeza [delika'ðeθa] *nf* delicacy;
(*refinamiento, sutileza*) refinement

delicado, -a [deli'kaðo, a] *adj*
delicate; (*sensible*) sensitive; (*sensible*)
touchy

delicia [de'liθja] *nf* delight

delicioso, -a [deli'θjoso, a] *adj*
(*gracioso*) delightful; (*exquisito*)
delicious

delimitar [delimi'tar] /1a/ *vt* (*función,
responsabilidades*) to define

delincuencia [delin'kwenθja] *nf*:
~ juvenil juvenile delinquency;
delincuente *nmf* delinquent;
(*criminal*) criminal

delineante [deline'ante] *nmf* (*m*)
draughtsman/draughtswoman; (*us*)
draftsman/draftswoman

delirante [deli'rante] *adj* delirious

delirar [deli'rar] /1a/ *vi* to be delirious, rave

delirio [de'lirjo] *nm* (*Med*) delirium; (*palabras insensatas*) ravings *pl*

delito [de'lito] *nm* (*gen*) crime; (*infracción*) offence

delta ['delta] *nm* delta

demacrado, -a [dema'kraðo, a] *adj*: **estar ~** to look pale and drawn, be wasted away

demanda [de'manda] *nf* (*pedido*, *Com*) demand; (*petición*) request; (*Jur*) action, lawsuit; **demandar** /1a/ *vt* (*gen*) to demand; (*Jur*) to sue, file a lawsuit against

demás [de'mas] *adj*: **los ~ niños** the other children, the remaining children ▷ *pron*: **los/las ~** the others, the rest (of them); **lo ~** the rest (of it)

demasía [dema'sia] *nf* (*exceso*) excess, surplus; **comer en ~** to eat to excess

demasiado, -a [dema'sjaðo, a] *adj*: **~ vino** too much wine ▷ *adv* (*antes de adj*, *adv*) too; **~s libros** too many books; **¡es ~!** it's too much!; **~ despacio** too slowly; **~s** too many

demencia [de'menθja] *nf* (*locura*) madness

democracia [demo'kraθja] *nf* democracy

demócrata [de'mokrata] *nmf* democrat; **democrático, -a** *adj* democratic

demoler [demo'ler] /2h/ *vt* to demolish; **demolición** *nf* demolition

demonio [de'monjo] *nm* devil, demon; **¡~s!** hell!, damn!; **¿cómo ~s?** how the hell?

demora [de'mora] *nf* delay

demos ['demos] *vb V* **dar**

demostración [demostra'θjon] *nf* demonstration; (*de cariño*, *fuerza*) show; (*de cólera*, *gimnasia*) display

demostrar [demos'trar] /1l/ *vt* (*probar*) to prove; (*mostrar*) to show; (*manifestar*) to demonstrate

den [den] *vb V* **dar**

denegar [dene'ɣar] /1h, 1j/ *vt* (*rechazar*) to refuse; (*Jur*) to reject

denominación [denomina'θjon] *nf* (*acto*) naming

● **DENOMINACIÓN**

● The *denominación de origen*, often
● abbreviated to *D.O.*, is a prestigious
● product classification given to
● designated regions by the awarding
● body, the *Consejo Regulador de la*
● *Denominación de Origen*, when their
● produce meets the required quality
● and production standards. It is
● often associated with *manchego*
● cheeses and many of the wines
● from the Rioja and Ribera de Duero
● regions.

densidad [densi'ðað] *nf* density; (*fig*) thickness

denso, -a ['denso, a] *adj* (*apretado*) solid; (*espeso*, *pastoso*) thick, dense; (*fig*) heavy

dentadura [denta'ðura] *nf* (*set of*) teeth *pl*; **~ postiza** false teeth *pl*

dentera [den'tera] *nf* (*grima*): **dar ~ a algn** to set sb's teeth on edge

dentífrico, -a [den'tifriko, a] *adj* dental ▷ *nm* toothpaste

dentista [den'tista] *nmf* dentist

dentro ['dentro] *adv* inside ▷ *prep*: **~ de** in, inside, within; **por ~** (on the) inside; **mirar por ~** to look inside; **~ de tres meses** within three months

denuncia [de'nunθja] *nf* (*delación*) denunciation; (*acusación*) accusation; (*de accidente*) report; **denunciar** /1b/ *vt* to report; (*delatar*) to inform on o against

departamento [departa'mento] *nm* (*sección*) department, section; (*LAM: piso*) flat (*BRIT*), apartment (*US*)

depender [depen'der] /2a/ *vi*: **~ de** to depend on; **depende** it (all) depends

dependienta [depen'djenta] *nf* saleswoman, shop assistant

dependiente [depen'djente] adj dependent ▷ nm salesman, shop assistant

depilar [depi'lar] /1a/ vt (con cera) to wax; (cejas) to pluck

deportar [depor'tar] /1a/ vt to deport

deporte [de'porte] nm sport; **hacer ~** to play sports; **deportista** adj sports cpd ▷ nmf sportsman/woman; **deportivo, -a** adj sports cpd ▷ nm sports car

depositar [deposi'tar] /1a/ vt (dinero) to deposit; (mercaderías) to put away, store; **depositarse** vr to settle

depósito [de'posito] nm (gen) deposit; (de mercaderías) warehouse, store; (de agua, gasolina etc) tank; **~ de cadáveres** mortuary

depredador, a [depreða'ðor, a] adj predatory ▷ nm predator

depresión [depre'sjon] nf depression; **~ nerviosa** nervous breakdown

deprimido, -a [depri'miðo, a] adj depressed

deprimir [depri'mir] /3a/ vt to depress; **deprimirse** vr (persona) to become depressed

deprisa [de'prisa] adv quickly, hurriedly

depurar [depu'rar] /1a/ vt to purify; (purgar) to purge

derecha [de'retʃa] nf V **derecho**

derecho, -a [de'retʃo, a] adj right, right-hand ▷ nm (privilegio) right; (lado) right(-hand) side; (leyes) law ▷ nf right(-hand) side; (Pol) right ▷ adv straight, directly; **derechos** nmpl (impuestos) taxes; (de autor) royalties; **la(s) derecha(s)** (Pol) the Right; **tener ~ a** to have a right to; **a la derecha** on the right; (dirección) to the right

deriva [de'riβa] nf: **ir o estar a la ~** to drift, be adrift

derivado [deri'βaðo] nm (Industria, Química) by-product

derivar [deri'βar] /1a/ vt to derive; (desviar) to direct ▷ vi to derive, be derived; (Naut) to drift; **derivarse** vr to derive, be derived

derramamiento [derrama'mjento] nm (dispersión) spilling; **~ de sangre** bloodshed

derramar [derra'mar] /1a/ vt to spill; (verter) to pour out; (esparcir) to scatter; **derramarse** vr to pour out

derrame [de'rrame] nm (de líquido) spilling; (de sangre) shedding; (de tubo etc) overflow; (pérdida) leakage; **~ cerebral** brain haemorrhage

derredor [derre'ðor] adv: **al o en ~ de** around, about

derretir [derre'tir] /3k/ vt (gen) to melt; (nieve) to thaw; **derretirse** vr to melt

derribar [derri'βar] /1a/ vt to knock down; (construcción) to demolish; (persona, político) to bring down

derrocar [derro'kar] /1g/ vt (gobierno) to bring down, overthrow

derrochar [derro'tʃar] /1a/ vt to squander; **derroche** nm (despilfarro) waste, squandering

derrota [de'rrota] nf (Naut) course; (Mil) defeat, rout; **derrotar** /1a/ vt (gen) to defeat; **derrotero** nm (rumbo) course

derrumbar [derrum'bar] /1a/ vt to knock down; **derrumbarse** vr to collapse

des [des] vb V **dar**

desabrochar [desaβro'tʃar] /1a/ vt (botones, broches) to undo, unfasten; **desabrocharse** vr (ropa etc) to come undone

desacato [desa'kato] nm (falta de respeto) disrespect; (Jur) contempt

desacertado, -a [desaθer'taðo, a] adj (equivocado) mistaken; (inoportuno) unwise

desacierto [desa'θjerto] nm mistake, error

desaconsejar [desakonse'xar] /1a/ vt: ~ **algo a algn** to advise sb against sth

desacreditar [desakreδi'tar] /1a/ vt (*desprestigiar*) to discredit, bring into disrepute; (*denigrar*) to run down

desacuerdo [desa'kwerδo] nm disagreement, discord

desafiar [desa'fjar] /1c/ vt (*retar*) to challenge; (*enfrentarse a*) to defy

desafilado, -a [desafi'laδo, a] adj blunt

desafinado, -a [desafi'naδo, a] adj: **estar ~** to be out of tune

desafinar [desafi'nar] /1a/ vi to be out of tune; **desafinarse** vr to go out of tune

desafío [desa'fio] nm (*reto*) challenge; (*combate*) duel; (*resistencia*) defiance

desafortunado, -a [desafortu'naδo, a] adj (*desgraciado*) unfortunate, unlucky

desagradable [desaɣra'δaβle] adj (*fastidioso, enojoso*) unpleasant; (*irritante*) disagreeable

desagradar [desaɣra'δar] /1a/ vi (*disgustar*) to displease; (*molestar*) to bother

desagradecido, -a [desaɣraδe'θiδo, a] adj ungrateful

desagrado [desa'ɣraδo] nm (*disgusto*) displeasure; (*contrariedad*) dissatisfaction

desagüe [de'saɣwe] nm (*de un líquido*) drainage; (*cañería*) drainpipe; (*salida*) outlet, drain

desahogar [desao'ɣar] /1h/ vt (*aliviar*) to ease, relieve; (*ira*) to vent; **desahogarse** vr (*distenderse*) to relax; (*desfogarse*) to let off steam (*fam*)

desahogo [desa'oɣo] nm (*alivio*) relief; (*comodidad*) comfort, ease

desahuciar [desau'θjar] /1b/ vt (*enfermo*) to give up hope for; (*inquilino*) to evict

desairar [desai'rar] /1a/ vt (*menospreciar*) to slight, snub

desalentador, -a [desalenta'δor, a] adj discouraging

desaliño [desa'liɲo] nm slovenliness

desalmado, -a [desal'maδo, a] adj (*cruel*) cruel, heartless

desalojar [desalo'xar] /1a/ vt (*expulsar, echar*) to eject; (*abandonar*) to move out of ⊳ vi to move out

desamor [desa'mor] nm (*frialdad*) indifference; (*odio*) dislike

desamparado, -a [desampa'raδo, a] adj (*persona*) helpless; (*lugar: expuesto*) exposed; (: *desierto*) deserted

desangrar [desan'grar] /1a/ vt to bleed; (*fig: persona*) to bleed dry; **desangrarse** vr to lose a lot of blood

desanimado, -a [desani'maδo, a] adj (*persona*) downhearted; (*espectáculo, fiesta*) dull

desanimar [desani'mar] /1a/ vt (*desalentar*) to discourage; (*deprimir*) to depress; **desanimarse** vr to lose heart

desapacible [desapa'θiβle] adj unpleasant

desaparecer [desapare'θer] /2d/ vi to disappear; (*el sol, la luz*) to vanish; **desaparecido, -a** adj missing; **desaparición** nf disappearance; (*de especie etc*) extinction

desapercibido, -a [desaperθi'βiδo, a] adj (*desprevenido*) unprepared; **pasar ~** to go unnoticed

desaprensivo, -a [desapren'siβo, a] adj unscrupulous

desaprobar [desapro'βar] /1l/ vt (*reprobar*) to disapprove of; (*condenar*) to condemn; (*no consentir*) to reject

desaprovechado, -a [desaproβe'tʃaδo, a] adj (*oportunidad, tiempo*) wasted; (*estudiante*) slack

desaprovechar [desaproβe'tʃar] /1a/ vt to waste

desarmador [desarma'δor] nm (LAM) screwdriver

desarmar [desar'mar] /1a/ vt (*Mil, fig*) to disarm; (*Tec*) to take apart, dismantle; **desarme** nm disarmament

desarraigar [desarraiˈɣar] /1h/ vt to uproot; **desarraigo** nm uprooting

desarreglar [desarreˈɣlar] /1a/ vt (desordenar) to disarrange; (trastocar) to upset, disturb

desarrollar [desarroˈʎar] /1a/ vt (gen) to develop; **desarrollarse** vr to develop; (ocurrir) to take place; (film) to develop; **desarrollo** nm development

desarticular [desartikuˈlar] /1a/ vt (huesos) to dislocate; (objeto) to take apart; (grupo terrorista etc) to break up

desasosegar [desasoseˈɣar] /1h, 1j/ vt (inquietar) to disturb, make uneasy

desasosiego etc [desasoˈsjeɣo] vb V **desasosegar** ⊳ nm (intranquilidad) uneasiness, restlessness; (ansiedad) anxiety

desastre [deˈsastre] nm disaster; **desastroso, -a** adj disastrous

desatar [desaˈtar] /1a/ vt (nudo) to untie; (paquete) to undo; (separar) to detach; **desatarse** vr (zapatos) to come untied; (tormenta) to break

desatascar [desatasˈkar] /1g/ vt (cañería) to unblock, clear

desatender [desatenˈder] /2g/ vt (no prestar atención a) to disregard; (abandonar) to neglect

desatino [desaˈtino] nm (idiotez) foolishness, folly; (error) blunder

desatornillar [desatorniˈʎar] /1a/ vt to unscrew

desatrancar [desatranˈkar] /1g/ vt (puerta) to unbolt; (cañería) to unblock

desautorizado, -a [desautoriˈθaðo, a] adj unauthorized

desautorizar [desautoriˈθar] /1f/ vt (oficial) to deprive of authority; (informe) to deny

desayunar [desajuˈnar] /1a/ vi to have breakfast ⊳ vt to have for breakfast; **desayuno** nm breakfast

desazón [desaˈθon] nf anxiety

desbarajuste [desβaraˈxuste] nm confusion, disorder

desbaratar [desβaraˈtar] /1a/ vt (deshacer, destruir) to ruin

desbloquear [desβloˈkear] /1a/ vt (negociaciones, tráfico) to get going again; (Com: cuenta) to unfreeze

desbordar [desβorˈðar] /1a/ vt (sobrepasar) to go beyond; (exceder) to exceed ⊳ **desbordarse** vr (líquido, río) to overflow; (entusiasmo) to erupt

descabellado, -a [deskaβeˈʎaðo, a] adj (disparatado) wild, crazy

descafeinado, -a [deskafeiˈnaðo, a] adj decaffeinated ⊳ nm decaffeinated coffee

descalabro [deskaˈlaβro] nm blow; (desgracia) misfortune

descalificar [deskalifiˈkar] /1g/ vt to disqualify; (desacreditar) to discredit

descalzar [deskalˈθar] /1f/ vt (zapato) to take off; **descalzo, -a** adj barefoot(ed)

descambiar [deskamˈbjar] /1b/ vt to exchange

descaminado, -a [deskamiˈnaðo, a] adj (equivocado) on the wrong road; (fig) misguided

descampado [deskamˈpaðo] nm open space

descansado, -a [deskanˈsaðo, a] adj (gen) rested; (que tranquiliza) restful

descansar [deskanˈsar] /1a/ vt (gen) to rest ⊳ vi to rest, have a rest; (echarse) to lie down

descansillo [deskanˈsiʎo] nm (de escalera) landing

descanso [desˈkanso] nm (reposo) rest; (alivio) relief; (pausa) break; (Deporte) interval, half time

descapotable [deskapoˈtaβle] nm (tb: **coche ~**) convertible

descarado, -a [deskaˈraðo, a] adj shameless; (insolente) cheeky

descarga [desˈkarɣa] nf (Arq, Elec, Mil) discharge; (Naut) unloading; (Inform) download; **descargable** adj downloadable; **descargar** /1h/ vt to unload; (golpe) to let fly; **descargarse** vr to unburden o.s.; **descargarse algo de Internet** to download sth from the internet

descaro [des'karo] nm nerve

descarriar [deska'rrjar] /1c/ vt (descaminar) to misdirect; (fig) to lead astray; **descarriarse** vr (perderse) to lose one's way; (separarse) to stray; (pervertirse) to err, go astray

descarrilamiento [deskarrila'mjento] nm (de tren) derailment

descarrilar [deskarri'lar] /1a/ vi to be derailed

descartar [deskar'tar] /1a/ vt (rechazar) to reject; (eliminar) to rule out; **descartarse** vr (Naipes) to discard; **~se de** to shirk

descendencia [desθen'denθja] nf (origen) origin, descent; (hijos) offspring

descender [desθen'der] /2g/ vt (bajar: escalera) to go down ▷ vi to descend; (temperatura, nivel) to fall, drop; **~ de** to be descended from

descendiente [desθen'djente] nmf descendant

descenso [des'θenso] nm descent; (de temperatura) drop

descifrar [desθi'frar] /1a/ vt to decipher; (mensaje) to decode

descolgar [deskol'γar] /1h, 1l/ vt (bajar) to take down; (teléfono) to pick up; **descolgarse** vr to let o.s. down

descolorido, -a [deskolo'riðo, a] adj faded; (pálido) pale

descompasado, -a [deskompa'saðo, a] adj (sin proporción) out of all proportion; (excesivo) excessive

descomponer [deskompo'ner] /2q/ vt (desordenar) to disarrange, disturb; (Tec) to put out of order; **descomponerse** vr (corromperse) to rot, decompose; (Tec) to break down

descomposición [deskomposi'θjon] nf (de un objeto) breakdown; (de fruta etc) decomposition; **~ de vientre** (Med) stomach upset, diarrhoea, diarrhea (us)

descompostura [deskompos'tura] nf breakdown, fault; (LAM: diarrea) diarrhoea, diarrhea (us)

descompuesto, -a [deskom'pwesto, a] adj (corrompido) decomposed; (roto) broken (down)

desconcertado, -a [deskonθer'taðo, a] adj disconcerted, bewildered

desconcertar [deskonθer'tar] /1j/ vt (confundir) to baffle; (incomodar) to upset, put out; **desconcertarse** vr (turbarse) to be upset

desconchado, -a [deskon'tʃaðo, a] adj (pintura) peeling

desconcierto etc [deskon'θjerto] vb V **desconcertar** ▷ nm (gen) disorder; (desorientación) uncertainty; (inquietud) uneasiness

desconectar [deskonek'tar] /1a/ vt to disconnect

desconfianza [deskon'fjanθa] nf distrust

desconfiar [deskon'fjar] /1c/ vi to be distrustful; **~ de** to mistrust, suspect

descongelar [deskonxe'lar] /1a/ vt to defrost; (Com, Pol) to unfreeze

descongestionar [deskonxestjo'nar] /1a/ vt (cabeza, tráfico) to clear

desconocer [deskono'θer] /2d/ vt (ignorar) not to know, to be ignorant of

desconocido, -a [deskono'θiðo, a] adj unknown ▷ nm/f stranger

desconocimiento [deskonoθi'mjento] nm (falta de conocimientos) ignorance

desconsiderado, -a [deskonsiðe'raðo, a] adj inconsiderate; (insensible) thoughtless

desconsuelo [deskon'swelo] nm (tristeza) distress; (desesperación) despair

descontado, -a [deskon'taðo, a] adj: **dar por ~ (que)** to take it for granted (that)

descontar [deskon'tar] /1l/ vt (deducir) to take away, deduct; (rebajar) to discount

descontento, -a [deskon'tento, a]
adj dissatisfied ▷ *nm* dissatisfaction,
discontent

descorchar [deskor'tʃar] /1a/ *vt*
to uncork

descorrer [desko'rrer] /2a/ *vt*
(*cortina, cerrojo*) to draw back

descortés [deskor'tes] *adj* (*mal
educado*) discourteous; (*grosero*) rude

descoser [desko'ser] /2a/ *vt* to
unstitch; **descoserse** *vr* to come apart
(at the seams)

descosido, -a [desko'siðo, a] *adj*
(*costura*) unstitched

descreído, -a [deskre'iðo, a] *adj*
(*incrédulo*) incredulous; (*falto de fe*)
unbelieving

descremado, -a [deskre'maðo, a]
adj skimmed

describir [deskri'βir] /3a/ *vt* to
describe; **descripción** *nf* description

descrito [des'krito] *pp de* **describir**

descuartizar [deskwarti'θar] /1f/ *vt* (
animal) to carve up, cut up

descubierto, -a [desku'βjerto, a] *pp
de* **descubrir** ▷ *adj* uncovered; bare;
(*persona*) bare-headed ▷ *nm* (*bancario*)
overdraft; **al** ~ in the open

descubrimiento [deskuβri'mjento]
nm (*hallazgo*) discovery; (*revelación*)
revelation

descubrir [desku'βrir] /3a/ *vt* to
discover, find; (*inaugurar*) to unveil;
(*vislumbrar*) to detect; (*revelar*) to
reveal, show; (*quitar la tapa de*) to
uncover; **descubrirse** *vr* to reveal o.s.;
(*quitarse sombrero*) to take off one's
hat; (*confesar*) to confess

descuento [des'kwento] *vb* V
descontar ▷ *nm* discount

descuidado, -a [deskwi'ðaðo, a] *adj*
(*sin cuidado*) careless; (*desordenado*)
untidy; (*olvidadizo*) forgetful; (*dejado*)
neglected; (*desprevenido*) unprepared

descuidar [deskwi'ðar] /1a/ *vt*
(*dejar*) to neglect; (*olvidar*) to overlook
▷ **descuidarse** *vr* (*distraerse*) to be
careless; (*estar desaliñado*) to let o.s.

go; (*desprevenirse*) to drop one's guard;
¡descuida! don't worry!; **descuido**
nm (*dejadez*) carelessness; (*olvido*)
negligence

PALABRA CLAVE

desde ['desðe] *prep* **1** (*lugar*) from;
**desde Burgos hasta mi casa hay 30
km** it's 30 km from Burgos to my house
2 (*posición*): **hablaba desde el balcón**
she was speaking from the balcony
3 (*tiempo*, + *adv, n*): **desde ahora** from
now on; **desde entonces/la boda**
since then/the wedding; **desde niño**
since I *etc* was a child; **desde tres
años atrás** since three years ago
4 (*tiempo*, + *vb*) since; for; **nos
conocemos desde 1988/desde
hace 20 años** we've known each
other since 1988/for 20 years; **no
le veo desde 2005/desde hace 5
años** I haven't seen him since 2005/
for 5 years
5 (*gama*): **desde los más lujosos
hasta los más económicos** from the
most luxurious to the most reasonably
priced
6: **desde luego (que no)** of course
(not)
▷ *conj*: **desde que**: **desde que
recuerdo** for as long as I can
remember; **desde que llegó no
ha salido** he hasn't been out since
he arrived

desdén [des'ðen] *nm* scorn

desdeñar [desðe'ɲar] /1a/ *vt*
(*despreciar*) to scorn

desdicha [des'ðitʃa] *nf* (*desgracia*)
misfortune; (*infelicidad*) unhappiness;
desdichado, -a *adj* (*sin suerte*)
unlucky; (*infeliz*) unhappy

desear [dese'ar] /1a/ *vt* to want,
desire, wish for

desechar [dese'tʃar] /1a/ *vt* (*basura*)
to throw out o away; (*ideas*) to reject,
discard

desecho [de'setʃo] *nm* (*desprecio*) contempt; **desechos** *nmpl* rubbish *sg*, waste *sg*

desembalar [desemba'lar] /1a/ *vt* to unpack

desembarazar [desembara'θar] /1f/ *vt* (*desocupar*) to clear; (*desenredar*) to free; **desembarazarse** *vr*: **~se de** to free o.s. of, get rid of

desembarcar [desembar'kar] /1g/ *vt* (*mercancías etc*) to unload ▷ *vi* to disembark

desembocadura [desemboka'ðura] *nf* (*de río*) mouth; (*de calle*) opening

desembocar [desembo'kar] /1g/ *vi*: **~ en** to flow into; (*fig*) to result in

desembolso [desem'bolso] *nm* payment

desembrollar [desembro'ʎar] /1a/ *vt* (*madeja*) to unravel; (*asunto, malentendido*) to sort out

desemejanza [deseme'xanθa] *nf* dissimilarity

desempaquetar [desempake'tar] /1a/ *vt* (*regalo*) to unwrap; (*mercancía*) to unpack

desempate [desem'pate] *nm* (*Fútbol*) replay, play-off; (*Tenis*) tie-break(er)

desempeñar [desempe'ɲar] /1a/ *vt* (*cargo*) to hold; (*deber, función*) to perform; (*lo empeñado*) to redeem; **~ un papel** (*fig*) to play a role

desempleado, -a [desemple'aðo, a] *nm/f* unemployed person; **desempleo** *nm* unemployment

desencadenar [desenkaðe'nar] /1a/ *vt* to unchain; (*ira*) to unleash; **desencadenarse** *vr* to break loose; (*tormenta*) to burst; (*guerra*) to break out

desencajar [desenka'xar] /1a/ *vt* (*mandíbula*) to dislocate; (*mecanismo, pieza*) to disconnect, disengage

desencanto [desen'kanto] *nm* disillusionment

desenchufar [desentʃu'far] /1a/ *vt* to unplug

desenfadado, -a [desenfa'ðaðo, a] *adj* (*desenvuelto*) uninhibited; (*descarado*) forward; **desenfado** *nm* (*libertad*) freedom; (*comportamiento*) free and easy manner; (*descaro*) forwardness

desenfocado, -a [desenfo'kaðo, a] *adj* (*Foto*) out of focus

desenfreno [desen'freno] *nm* wildness; (*falta de control*) lack of self-control

desenganchar [desengan'tʃar] /1a/ *vt* (*gen*) to unhook; (*Ferro*) to uncouple

desengañar [desenga'ɲar] /1a/ *vt* to disillusion; **desengañarse** *vr* to become disillusioned; **desengaño** *nm* disillusionment; (*decepción*) disappointment

desenlace *etc* [desen'laθe] *nm* outcome

desenmascarar [desenmaska'rar] /1a/ *vt* to unmask

desenredar [desenre'ðar] /1a/ *vt* (*pelo*) to untangle; (*problema*) to sort out

desenroscar [desenros'kar] /1g/ *vt* to unscrew

desentenderse [desenten'derse] /2g/ *vr*: **~ de** to pretend not to know about; (*apartarse*) to have nothing to do with

desenterrar [desente'rrar] /1j/ *vt* to exhume; (*tesoro, fig*) to unearth, dig up

desentonar [desento'nar] /1a/ *vi* (*Mus*) to sing (o play) out of tune; (*color*) to clash

desentrañar [desentra'ɲar] /1a/ *vt* (*misterio*) to unravel

desenvoltura [desembol'tura] *nf* ease

desenvolver [desembol'βer] /2h/ *vt* (*paquete*) to unwrap; (*fig*) to develop; **desenvolverse** *vr* (*desarrollarse*) to unfold, develop; (*arreglárselas*) to cope

deseo [de'seo] *nm* desire, wish; **deseoso, -a** *adj*: **estar deseoso de hacer** to be anxious to do

desequilibrado, -a [desekili'βraðo, a] *adj* unbalanced

desertar [deser'tar] /1a/ vi to desert

desértico, -a [de'sertiko, a] adj desert cpd

desesperación [desespera'θjon] nf desperation, despair; (irritación) fury

desesperar [desespe'rar] /1a/ vt to drive to despair; (exasperar) to drive to distraction ▷ vi: **~ de** to despair of; **desesperarse** vr to despair, lose hope

desestabilizar [desestaβili'θar] /1f/ vt to destabilize

desestimar [desesti'mar] /1a/ vt (menospreciar) to have a low opinion of; (rechazar) to reject

desfachatez [desfatʃa'teθ] nf (insolencia) impudence; (descaro) rudeness

desfalco [des'falko] nm embezzlement

desfallecer [desfaʎe'θer] /2d/ vi (perder las fuerzas) to become weak; (desvanecerse) to faint

desfasado, -a [desfa'saðo, a] adj (anticuado) old-fashioned; **desfase** nm (diferencia) gap

desfavorable [desfaβo'raβle] adj unfavourable

desfigurar [desfiɣu'rar] /1a/ vt (cara) to disfigure; (cuerpo) to deform

desfiladero [desfila'ðero] nm gorge

desfilar [desfi'lar] /1a/ vi to parade; **desfile** nm procession; **desfile de modelos** fashion show

desgana [des'ɣana] nf (falta de apetito) loss of appetite; (renuencia) unwillingness; **desganado, -a** adj: **estar desganado** (sin apetito) to have no appetite; (sin entusiasmo) to have lost interest

desgarrar [desɣa'rrar] /1a/ vt to tear (up); (fig) to shatter; **desgarro** nm (en tela) tear; (aflicción) grief

desgastar [desɣas'tar] /1a/ vt (deteriorar) to wear away o down; (estropear) to spoil; **desgastarse** vr to get worn out; **desgaste** nm wear (and tear)

desglosar [desɣlo'sar] /1a/ vt to detach; (factura) to break down

desgracia [des'ɣraθja] nf misfortune; (accidente) accident; (vergüenza) disgrace; (contratiempo) setback; **por ~** unfortunately; **desgraciado, -a** adj (sin suerte) unlucky, unfortunate; (miserable) wretched; (infeliz) miserable

desgravar [desɣra'βar] /1a/ vt (producto) to reduce the tax o duty on

desguace [des'ɣwaθe] nm (lugar) scrapyard

deshabitado, -a [desaβi'taðo, a] adj uninhabited

deshacer [desa'θer] /2r/ vt (casa) to break up; (Tec) to take apart; (enemigo) to defeat; (diluir) to melt; (contrato) to break; (intriga) to solve; **deshacerse** vr (disolverse) to melt; (despedazarse) to come apart o undone; **~ de** to get rid of; **~se en lágrimas** to burst into tears

deshecho, -a [de'setʃo, a] adj undone; (roto) smashed; (persona) weak; **estoy ~** I'm shattered

desheredar [desere'ðar] /1a/ vt to disinherit

deshidratar [desiðra'tar] /1a/ vt to dehydrate

deshielo [des'jelo] nm thaw

deshonesto, -a [deso'nesto, a] adj indecent

deshonra [de'sonra] nf (deshonor) dishonour; (vergüenza) shame

deshora [de'sora]: **a ~** adv at the wrong time

deshuesadero [deswesa'ðero] nm (ʌм) junkyard

deshuesar [deswe'sar] /1a/ vt (carne) to bone; (fruta) to stone

desierto, -a [de'sjerto, a] adj (casa, calle, negocio) deserted ▷ nm desert

designar [desiɣ'nar] /1a/ vt (nombrar) to designate; (indicar) to fix

desigual [desi'ɣwal] adj (lucha) unequal; (terreno) uneven

desilusión [desilu'sjon] nf disillusionment; (decepción) disappointment; **desilusionar** /1a/ vt to disillusion; (decepcionar) to disappoint; **desilusionarse** vr to become disillusioned

desinfectar [desinfek'tar] /1a/ vt to disinfect

desinflar [desin'flar] /1a/ vt to deflate

desintegración [desinteɣra'θjon] nf disintegration

desinterés [desinte'res] nm (desgana) lack of interest; (altruismo) unselfishness

desintoxicar [desintoksi'kar] /1g/ vt to detoxify; **desintoxicarse** vr (drogadicto) to undergo detoxification

desistir [desis'tir] /3a/ vi (renunciar) to stop, desist

desleal [desle'al] adj (infiel) disloyal; (Com: competencia) unfair; **deslealtad** nf disloyalty

desligar [desli'ɣar] /1h/ vt (desatar) to untie, undo; (separar) to separate; **desligarse** vr (de un compromiso) to extricate o.s.

desliz [des'liθ] nm (fig) lapse; **deslizar** /1f/ vt to slip, slide

deslumbrar [deslum'brar] /1a/ vt to dazzle

desmadrarse [desma'ðrarse] /1a/ vr (fam: descontrolarse) to run wild; (: divertirse) to let one's hair down; **desmadre** nm (fam: desorganización) chaos; (: jaleo) commotion

desmán [des'man] nm (exceso) outrage; (abuso de poder) abuse

desmantelar [desmante'lar] /1a/ vt (deshacer) to dismantle; (casa) to strip

desmaquillador [desmakiʎa'ðor] nm make-up remover

desmayar [desma'jar] /1a/ vi to lose heart; **desmayarse** vr (Med) to faint; **desmayo** nm (Med: acto) faint; (: estado) unconsciousness

desmemoriado, -a [desmemo'rjaðo, a] adj forgetful

desmentir [desmen'tir] /3i/ vt (contradecir) to contradict; (refutar) to deny

desmenuzar [desmenu'θar] /1f/ vt (deshacer) to crumble; (carne) to chop; (examinar) to examine closely

desmesurado, -a [desmesu'raðo, a] adj disproportionate

desmontable [desmon'taβle] adj (que se quita) detachable; (que se puede plegar etc) collapsible, folding

desmontar [desmon'tar] /1a/ vt (deshacer) to dismantle; (tierra) to level ▷ vi to dismount

desmoralizar [desmorali'θar] /1f/ vt to demoralize

desmoronar [desmoro'nar] /1a/ vt to wear away, erode; **desmoronarse** vr (edificio, dique) to collapse; (economía) to decline

desnatado, -a [desna'taðo, a] adj skimmed

desnivel [desni'βel] nm (de terreno) unevenness

desnudar [desnu'ðar] /1a/ vt (desvestir) to undress; (despojar) to strip; **desnudarse** vr (desvestirse) to get undressed; **desnudo, -a** adj naked ▷ nm nude; **desnudo de** devoid o bereft of

desnutrición [desnutri'θjon] nf malnutrition; **desnutrido, -a** adj undernourished

desobedecer [desoβeðe'θer] /2d/ vt, vi to disobey; **desobediencia** nf disobedience

desocupado, -a [desoku'paðo, a] adj at leisure; (desempleado) unemployed; (deshabitado) empty, vacant

desodorante [desoðo'rante] nm deodorant

desolación [desola'θjon] nf (de lugar) desolation; (fig) grief

desolar [deso'lar] /1a/ vt to ruin, lay waste

desorbitado, -a [desorβi'taðo, a] adj (excesivo: ambición) boundless; (: deseos) excessive; (: precio) exorbitant

desorden [de'sorðen] nm confusion; (político) disorder

desorganización
[desorɣaniθa'θjon] *nf (de persona)*
disorganization; *(en empresa, oficina)*
disorder, chaos

desorientar [desorjen'tar]
/1a/ vt *(extraviar)* to mislead;
(confundir, desconcertar) to confuse;
desorientarse vr *(perderse)* to lose
one's way

despabilado, -a [despaβi'laðo,
a] *adj (despierto)* wide-awake; *(fig)*
alert, sharp

despachar [despa'tʃar] /1a/ vt
(negocio) to do, complete; *(enviar)* to
send, dispatch; *(vender)* to sell, deal
in; *(billete)* to issue; *(mandar ir)* to
send away

despacho [des'patʃo] *nm (oficina)*
office; *(de paquetes)* dispatch; *(venta)*
sale (of goods); *(comunicación)*
message; **~ de billetes** o *(LAM)*
boletos booking office

despacio [des'paθjo] *adv* slowly

desparpajo [despar'paxo] *nm* self-
confidence; *(pey)* nerve

desparramar [desparra'mar]
/1a/ vt *(esparcir)* to scatter; *(líquido)*
to spill

despecho [des'petʃo] *nm* spite

despectivo, -a [despek'tiβo, a]
adj (despreciativo) derogatory; *(Ling)*
pejorative

despedida [despe'ðiða] *nf (adiós)*
farewell; *(de obrero)* sacking

despedir [despe'ðir] /3k/ vt *(visita)*
to see off, show out; *(empleado)*
to dismiss; *(inquilino)* to evict;
(objeto) to hurl; *(olor etc)* to give out
o off; **despedirse** vr: **~se de** to say
goodbye to

despegar [despe'ɣar] /1h/ vt to
unstick o vi *(avión)* to take off;
despegarse vr to come loose, come
unstuck; **despego** *nm* detachment

despegue etc [des'peɣe] vb V
despegar ▷ *nm* takeoff

despeinado, -a [despei'naðo, a] *adj*
dishevelled, unkempt

despejado, -a [despe'xaðo, a] *adj*
(lugar) clear, free; *(cielo)* clear; *(persona)*
wide-awake, bright

despejar [despe'xar] /1a/ vt *(gen)*
to clear; *(misterio)* to clarify, clear up
▷ vi *(el tiempo)* to clear; **despejarse** vr
(tiempo, cielo) to clear (up); *(misterio)* to
become clearer; *(cabeza)* to clear

despensa [des'pensa] *nf* larder

despeñar [despe'nar] /1a/ vt *(arrojar)*
to fling down; **despeñarse** vr to fling
o.s. down; *(coche)* to tumble over

desperdicio [desper'ðiθjo]
nm (despilfarro) squandering;
desperdicios *nmpl (basura)* rubbish *sg*,
garbage *sg (US)*; *(residuos)* waste *sg*

desperezarse [despere'θarse] /1f/
vr to stretch

desperfecto [desper'fekto] *nm*
(deterioro) slight damage; *(defecto)*
flaw, imperfection

despertador [desperta'ðor] *nm*
alarm clock

despertar [desper'tar] /1j/ vt
(persona) to wake up; *(recuerdos)* to
revive; *(sentimiento)* to arouse ▷ vi to
awaken, wake up; **despertarse** vr to
awaken, wake up

despido etc [des'piðo] vb V **despedir**
▷ *nm* dismissal, sacking

despierto, -a [des'pjerto, a] *pp de*
despertar ▷ *adj* awake; *(fig)* sharp,
alert

despilfarro [despil'farro] *nm*
(derroche) squandering; *(lujo
desmedido)* extravagance

despistar [despis'tar] /1a/ vt to
throw off the track o scent; *(fig)* to
mislead, confuse; **despistarse** vr to
take the wrong road; *(fig)* to become
confused

despiste [des'piste] *nm* absent-
mindedness; **un ~** a mistake o slip

desplazamiento
[desplaθa'mjento] *nm* displacement

desplazar [despla'θar] /1f/ vt to
move; *(Física, Naut, Tec)* to displace;
(fig) to oust; *(Inform)* to scroll;

desplazarse vr (persona, vehículo) to travel

desplegar [desple'ɣar] /1h, 1j/ vt (tela, papel) to unfold, open out; (bandera) to unfurl

despliegue etc [des'pljeɣe] vb V **desplegar** ▷ nm display

desplomarse [desplo'marse] /1a/ vr (edificio, gobierno, persona) to collapse

desplumar [desplu'mar] /1a/ vt (ave) to pluck; (fam: estafar) to fleece

despoblado, -a [despo'βlaðo, a] adj (sin habitantes) uninhabited

despojar [despo'xar] /1a/ vt (a alguien: de sus bienes) to divest of, deprive of; (casa) to strip, leave bare; (de su cargo) to strip of

despojo [des'poxo] nm (acto) plundering; (objetos) plunder, loot; **despojos** nmpl (de ave, res) offal sg

desposado, -a [despo'saðo, a] adj, nm/f newly-wed

despreciar [despre'θjar] /1b/ vt (desdeñar) to despise, scorn; (afrentar) to slight; **desprecio** nm scorn, contempt; slight

desprender [despren'der] /2a/ vt (desatar) to unfasten; (olor) to give off; **desprenderse** vr (botón: caerse) to fall off; (broche) to come unfastened; (olor, perfume) to be given off; **~se de algo que ...** to draw from sth that ...

desprendimiento [desprendi'mjento] nm (gen) loosening; (generosidad) disinterestedness; (de tierra, rocas) landslide; **~ de retina** detachment of the retina

despreocupado, -a [despreoku'paðo, a] adj (sin preocupación) unworried; nonchalant; (negligente) careless

despreocuparse [despreoku'parse] /1a/ vr to be carefree, not to worry; **~ de** to have no interest in

desprestigiar [despresti'xjar] /1b/ vt (criticar) to run down; (desacreditar) to discredit

desprevenido, -a [despreβe'niðo, a] adj (no preparado) unprepared, unready

desproporcionado, -a [desproporθjo'naðo, a] adj disproportionate, out of proportion

desprovisto, -a [despro'βisto, a] adj: **~ de** devoid of

después [des'pwes] adv afterwards, later; (próximo paso) next; **poco ~** soon after; **un año ~** a year later; **~ se debatió el tema** next the matter was discussed; **~ de comer** after lunch; **~ de corregido el texto** after the text had been corrected; **~ de todo** after all

desquiciado, -a [deski'θjaðo, a] adj deranged

destacar [desta'kar] /1g/ vt to emphasize, point up; (Mil) to detach, detail ▷ vi (resaltarse) to stand out; (persona) to be outstanding o exceptional; **destacarse** vr to stand out; (persona) to be outstanding o exceptional

destajo [des'taxo] nm: **trabajar a ~** to do piecework

destapar [desta'par] /1a/ vt (botella) to open; (cacerola) to take the lid off; (descubrir) to uncover; **destaparse** vr (revelarse) to reveal one's true character

destartalado, -a [destarta'laðo, a] adj (desordenado) untidy; (ruinoso) tumbledown

destello [des'teʎo] nm (de estrella) twinkle; (de faro) signal light

destemplado, -a [destem'plaðo, a] adj (Mus) out of tune; (voz) harsh; (Med) out of sorts; (Meteorología) unpleasant, nasty

desteñir [deste'ɲir] vt, vi to fade; **desteñirse** vr to fade; **esta tela no destiñe** this fabric will not run

desternillarse [desterni'ʎarse] /1a/ vr: **~ de risa** to split one's sides laughing

desterrar [deste'rrar] /1j/ vt (exilar) to exile; (fig) to banish, dismiss

destiempo [des'tjempo]: **a** ~ adv at
the wrong time

destierro etc [des'tjerro] vb V
desterrar ▷ nm exile

destilar [desti'lar] /1a/ vt to distil;
destilería nf distillery

destinar [desti'nar] /1a/ vt
(funcionario) to appoint, assign;
(fondos) to set aside

destinatario, -a [destina'tarjo, a]
nm/f addressee

destino [des'tino] nm (suerte) destiny;
(de viajero) destination; **con ~ a
Londres** (avión, barco) (bound) for
London; (carta) to London

destituir [destitu'ir] /3g/ vt to
dismiss

destornillador [destorniʎa'ðor] nm
screwdriver

destornillar [destorni'ʎar] /1a/ vt
(tornillo) to unscrew; **destornillarse**
vr to unscrew

destreza [des'treθa] nf (habilidad)
skill; (maña) dexterity

destrozar [destro'θar] /1f/ vt (romper)
to smash, break (up); (estropear) to
ruin; (nervios) to shatter

destrozo [des'troθo] nm (acción)
destruction; (desastre) smashing;
destrozos nmpl (pedazos) pieces;
(daños) havoc sg

destrucción [destruk'θjon] nf
destruction

destruir [destru'ir] /3g/ vt to destroy

desuso [de'suso] nm disuse; **caer en
~** to fall into disuse, become obsolete

desvalijar [desβali'xar] /1a/ vt
(persona) to rob; (casa, tienda) to
burgle; (coche) to break into

desván [des'βan] nm attic

desvanecer [desβane'θer] /2d/ vt
(disipar) to dispel; (borrar) to blur;
desvanecerse vr (humo etc) to vanish,
disappear; (duda) to be dispelled;
(color) to fade; (recuerdo, sonido) to fade
away; (Med) to pass out

desvariar [desβa'rjar] /1c/ vi
(enfermo) to be delirious

desvelar [desβe'lar] /1a/ vt to keep
awake; **desvelarse** vr (no poder dormir)
to stay awake; (vigilar) to be vigilant
o watchful

desventaja [desβen'taxa] nf
disadvantage

desvergonzado, -a
[desβerɣon'θaðo, a] adj shameless

desvestir [desβes'tir] /3k/ vt to
undress; **desvestirse** vr to undress

desviación [desβja'θjon] nf
deviation; (Auto) diversion, detour

desviar [desβi'ar] /1c/ vt to turn
aside; (río) to alter the course
of; (navío) to divert, re-route;
(conversación) to sidetrack; **desviarse**
vr (apartarse del camino) to turn aside;
(: barco) to go off course

desvío [des'βio] vb V **desviar** ▷ nm
(desviación) detour, diversion; (fig)
indifference

desvivirse [desβi'βirse] /3a/ vr:
~ por to long for, crave for; **~ por
los amigos** to do anything for one's
friends

detallar [deta'ʎar] /1a/ vt to detail

detalle [de'taʎe] nm detail; (fig)
gesture, token; **al ~** in detail; (Com)
retail cpd

detallista [deta'ʎista] nmf retailer

detective [detek'tiβe] nmf
detective; **~ privado** private
detective

detención [deten'θjon] nf (arresto)
arrest; (prisión) detention

detener [dete'ner] /2k/ vt (gen)
to stop; (Jur) to arrest; (objeto) to
keep; **detenerse** vr to stop; **~se en**
(demorarse) to delay over, linger over

detenidamente [deteniða'mente]
adv (minuciosamente) carefully;
(extensamente) at great length

detenido, -a [dete'niðo, a] adj
(arrestado) under arrest ▷ nm/f person
under arrest, prisoner

detenimiento [deteni'mjento] nm:
con ~ thoroughly; (observar, considerar)
carefully

detergente [deter'xente] nm
detergent
deteriorar [deterjo'rar] /1a/ vt
to spoil, damage; **deteriorarse**
vr to deteriorate; **deterioro** nm
deterioration
determinación [determina'θjon]
nf (empeño) determination; (decisión)
decision; **determinado, -a** adj
(preciso) certain
determinar [determi'nar] /1a/
vt (plazo) to fix; (precio) to settle;
determinarse vr to decide
detestar [detes'tar] /1a/ vt to detest
detractor, a [detrak'tor, a] nm/f
detractor
detrás [de'tras] adv (tb: **por ~**) behind;
(atrás) at the back ▷ prep: **~ de** behind
detrimento [detri'mento] nm: **en ~
de** to the detriment of
deuda [de'uða] nf debt; **~ exterior/
pública** foreign/national debt
devaluación [deβalwa'θjon] nf
devaluation
devastar [deβas'tar] /1a/ vt (destruir)
to devastate
deveras [de'βeras] nf inv (ʟᴀᴍ): **un
amigo de (a) ~** a true o real friend
devoción [deβo'θjon] nf devotion
devolución [deβolu'θjon] nf
(reenvío) return, sending back;
(reembolso) repayment; (Jur)
devolution
devolver [deβol'βer] /2h/ vt to
return; (lo extraviado, prestado) to give
back; (carta al correo) to send back;
(Com) to repay, refund; (fam: vomitar)
to throw up ▷ vi (fam) to be sick
devorar [deβo'rar] /1a/ vt to devour
devoto, -a [de'βoto, a] adj devout
▷ nm/f admirer
devuelto [de'βwelto], **devuelva** etc
[de'βwelβa] vb V **devolver**
di [di] vb V **dar; decir**
día ['dia] nm day; **~ libre** day off; **D~
de Reyes** Epiphany (6 January); **D~
de la Independencia** Independence
Day; **¿qué ~ es?** what's the date?;

estar/poner al ~ to be/keep up to
date; **el ~ de hoy/de mañana** today/
tomorrow; **al ~ siguiente** on the
following day; **vivir al ~** to live from
hand to mouth; **de ~** by day; **en pleno
~** in full daylight
diabetes [dja'betes] nf diabetes sg
diablo ['djaβlo] nm devil; **diablura**
nf prank
diadema [dja'ðema] nf tiara
diafragma [dja'fraɣma] nm
diaphragm
diagonal [djaɣo'nal] adj diagonal
diagrama [dja'ɣrama] nm diagram
dial [dial] nm dial
dialecto [dja'lekto] nm dialect
dialogar [djalo'ɣar] /1h/ vi: **~ con**
(Pol) to hold talks with
diálogo ['djaloɣo] nm dialogue
diamante [dja'mante] nm diamond
diana ['djana] nf (Mil) reveille; (de
blanco) centre, bull's-eye
diapositiva [djaposi'tiβa] nf (Foto)
slide, transparency
diario, -a ['djarjo, a] adj daily ▷ nm
newspaper; **a ~** daily; **de o para ~**
everyday
diarrea [dja'rrea] nf diarrhoea
dibujar [diβu'xar] /1a/ vt to draw,
sketch; **dibujo** nm drawing; **dibujos
animados** cartoons
diccionario [dikθjo'narjo] nm
dictionary
dice etc vb V **decir**
dicho, -a ['ditʃo, a] pp de **decir** ▷ adj
(susodicho) aforementioned ▷ nm
saying
dichoso, -a [di'tʃoso, a] adj happy
diciembre [di'θjembre] nm
December
dictado [dik'taðo] nm dictation
dictador [dikta'ðor] nm dictator;
dictadura nf dictatorship
dictar [dik'tar] /1a/ vt (carta) to
dictate; (Jur: sentencia) to pass;
(decreto) to issue; (ʟᴀᴍ: clase) to give
didáctico, -a [di'ðaktiko, a] adj
educational

diecinueve [djeθinu'eβe] num
nineteen

dieciocho [djeθi'otʃo] num eighteen

dieciséis [djeθi'seis] num sixteen

diecisiete [djeθi'sjete] num
seventeen

diente ['djente] nm (Anat, Tec) tooth;
(Zool) fang; (: de elefante) tusk; (de
ajo) clove

diera etc ['djera] vb V **dar**

diesel ['disel] adj: **motor ~** diesel
engine

diestro, -a ['djestro, a] adj (derecho)
right; (hábil) skilful

dieta ['djeta] nf diet; **estar a ~** to be
on a diet

diez [djeθ] num ten

diferencia [dife'renθja] nf difference;
a ~ de unlike; **diferenciar** /1b/ vt to
differentiate between ▷ vi to differ;
diferenciarse vr to differ, be different;
(distinguirse) to distinguish o.s.

diferente [dife'rente] adj different

diferido [dife'riðo] nm: **en ~** (TV etc)
recorded

difícil [di'fiθil] adj difficult

dificultad [difikul'taθ] nf difficulty;
(problema) trouble

dificultar [difikul'tar] /1a/ vt
(complicar) to complicate, make
difficult; (estorbar) to obstruct

difundir [difun'dir] /3a/ vt (calor,
luz) to diffuse; (Radio) to broadcast;
difundirse vr to spread (out); **~ una
noticia** to spread a piece of news

difunto, -a [di'funto, a] adj dead,
deceased ▷ nm/f deceased (person)

difusión [difu'sjon] nf (de programa)
broadcasting

diga etc ['diɣa] vb V **decir**

digerir [dixe'rir] /3i/ vt to digest; (fig)
to absorb; **digestión** nf digestion;
digestivo, -a adj digestive

digital [dixi'tal] adj digital

dignarse [diɣ'narse] /1a/ vr to
deign to

dignidad [diɣni'ðaθ] nf dignity

digno, -a ['diɣno, a] adj worthy

digo etc vb V **decir**

dije etc vb V **decir**

dilatar [dila'tar] /1a/ vt to dilate;
(prolongar) to prolong

dilema [di'lema] nm dilemma

diluir [dilu'ir] /3g/ vt to dilute

diluvio [di'luβjo] nm deluge, flood

dimensión [dimen'sjon] nf
dimension

diminuto, -a [dimi'nuto, a] adj tiny,
diminutive

dimitir [dimi'tir] /3a/ vi to resign

dimos ['dimos] vb V **dar**

Dinamarca [dina'marka] nf
Denmark

dinámico, -a [di'namiko, a] adj
dynamic

dinamita [dina'mita] nf dynamite

dinamo [di'namo], (ᴌᴀᴍ) **dínamo**
['dinamo] nf dynamo

dineral [dine'ral] nm fortune

dinero [di'nero] nm money; **~
efectivo o metálico** cash; **~ suelto**
(loose) change

dio [djo] vb V **dar**

dios [djos] nm god; **D~** God; **¡D~ mío!**
(oh) my God!; **¡por D~!** for God's sake!;
diosa nf goddess

diploma [di'ploma] nm diploma

diplomacia [diplo'maθja] nf
diplomacy; (fig) tact

diplomado, -a [diplo'maðo, a] adj
qualified

diplomático, -a [diplo'matiko, a]
adj diplomatic ▷ nm/f diplomat

diputación [diputa'θjon] nf (tb: ~
provincial) ≈ county council

diputado, -a [dipu'taðo, a]
nm/f delegate; (Pol) ≈ member of
parliament (ʙʀɪᴛ) ≈ representative
(us)

dique ['dike] nm dyke

diré etc [di're] vb V **decir**

dirección [direk'θjon] nf direction;
(señas) address; (Auto) steering;
(gerencia) management; (Pol)
leadership; **"~ única"** "one-way
street"; **"~ prohibida"** "no entry"

direccional [direkθjo'nal] *nf* (LAM Auto) indicator

directa [di'rekta] *nf* (Auto) top gear

directivo, -a [direk'tiβo, a] *adj* (junta) managing ▷ *nf* (tb: **junta directiva**) board of directors

directo, -a [di'rekto, a] *adj* direct; (TV) live; **transmitir en ~** to broadcast live

director, a [direk'tor, a] *adj* leading ▷ *nm/f* director; (Escol) head (teacher) (BRIT), principal (US); (gerente) manager/manageress; (Prensa) editor; **~ de cine** film director; **~ general** general manager

directorio [direk'torjo] *nm* (LAM: telefónico) phone book

dirigente [diri'xente] *nmf* (Pol) leader

dirigir [diri'xir] /3c/ *vt* to direct; (carta) to address; (obra de teatro, film) to direct; (Mus) to conduct; (comercio) to manage; **dirigirse** *vr*: **~se a** to go towards, make one's way towards; (hablar con) to speak to

dirija etc [di'rixa] *vb V* **dirigir**

disciplina [disθi'plina] *nf* discipline

discípulo, -a [dis'θipulo, a] *nm/f* disciple

Discman® ['diskman] *nm* Discman®

disco ['disko] *nm* disc (BRIT), disk (US); (Deporte) discus; (Telec) dial; (Auto: semáforo) light; (Mus) record; **~ compacto** compact disc; **~ de larga duración** long-playing record (LP); **~ flexible** o **floppy** floppy disk; **~ de freno** brake disc; **~ rígido** hard disk

disconforme [diskon'forme] *adj* differing; **estar ~ (con)** to be in disagreement (with)

discordia [dis'korðja] *nf* discord

discoteca [disko'teka] *nf* disco(theque)

discreción [diskre'θjon] *nf* discretion; (reserva) prudence; **comer a ~** to eat as much as one wishes

discreto, -a [dis'kreto, a] *adj* discreet

discriminación [diskrimina'θjon] *nf* discrimination

disculpa [dis'kulpa] *nf* excuse; (pedir perdón) apology; **pedir ~s a/por** to apologize to/for; **disculpar** /1a/ *vt* to excuse, pardon; **disculparse** *vr* to excuse o.s.; to apologize

discurso [dis'kurso] *nm* speech

discusión [disku'sjon] *nf* (diálogo) discussion; (riña) argument

discutir [disku'tir] /3a/ *vt* (debatir) to discuss; (pelear) to argue about; (contradecir) to argue against ▷ *vi* to discuss; (disputar) to argue

disecar [dise'kar] /1g/ *vt* (para conservar: animal) to stuff; (: planta) to dry

diseñar [dise'ɲar] /1a/ *vt, vi* to design

diseño [di'seɲo] *nm* design

disfraz [dis'fraθ] *nm* (máscara) disguise; (excusa) pretext; **disfrazar** /1f/ *vt* to disguise; **disfrazarse** *vr*: **disfrazarse de** to disguise o.s. as

disfrutar [disfru'tar] /1a/ *vt* to enjoy ▷ *vi* to enjoy o.s.; **~ de** to enjoy, possess

disgustar [disɣus'tar] /1a/ *vt* (no gustar) to displease; (contrariar, enojar) to annoy; to upset; **disgustarse** *vr* to get upset; (dos personas) to fall out

> No confundir **disgustar** con la palabra inglesa **disgust**.

disgusto [dis'ɣusto] *nm* (contrariedad) annoyance; (tristeza) grief; (riña) quarrel

disimular [disimu'lar] /1a/ *vt* (ocultar) to hide, conceal ▷ *vi* to dissemble

diskette [dis'ket] *nm* (Inform) diskette, floppy disk

dislocar [dislo'kar] /1g/ *vt* to dislocate; **dislocarse** *vr* (articulación) to sprain, dislocate

disminución [disminu'θjon] *nf* decrease, reduction

disminuido, -a [disminu'iðo, a] *nm/f*: **~ mental/físico** mentally/physically-handicapped person

disminuir [disminu'ir] /3g/ *vt* to decrease, diminish

disolver [disol'βer] /2h/ vt (gen) to dissolve; **disolverse** vr to dissolve; (Com) to go into liquidation

dispar [dis'par] adj different

disparar [dispa'rar] /1a/ vt, vi to shoot, fire

disparate [dispa'rate] nm (tontería) foolish remark; (error) blunder; **decir ~s** to talk nonsense

disparo [dis'paro] nm shot

dispersar [disper'sar] /1a/ vt to disperse; **dispersarse** vr to scatter

disponer [dispo'ner] /2q/ vt (arreglar) to arrange; (ordenar) to put in order; (preparar) to prepare, get ready ▷ vi: **~ de** to have, own; **disponerse** vr: **~se para** to prepare to, prepare for

disponible [dispo'niβle] adj available

disposición [disposi'θjon] nf arrangement, disposition; (voluntad) willingness; (Inform) layout; **a su ~ at** your service

dispositivo [disposi'tiβo] nm device, mechanism

dispuesto, -a [dis'pwesto, a] pp de **disponer** ▷ adj (arreglado) arranged; (preparado) disposed

disputar [dispu'tar] /1a/ vt (carrera) to compete in

disquete [dis'kete] nm (Inform) diskette, floppy disk

distancia [dis'tanθja] nf distance; **distanciar** /1b/ vt to space out; **distanciarse** vr to become estranged; **distante** adj distant

diste ['diste], **disteis** ['disteis] vb V **dar**

distinción [distin'θjon] nf distinction; (elegancia) elegance; (honor) honour

distinguido, -a [distin'giðo, a] adj distinguished

distinguir [distin'gir] /3d/ vt to distinguish; (escoger) to single out; **distinguirse** vr to be distinguished

distintivo [distin'tiβo] nm badge; (fig) characteristic

distinto, -a [dis'tinto, a] adj different; (claro) clear

distracción [distrak'θjon] nf distraction; (pasatiempo) hobby, pastime; (olvido) absent-mindedness, distraction

distraer [distra'er] /2o/ vt (atención) to distract; (divertir) to amuse; (fondos) to embezzle; **distraerse** vr (entretenerse) to amuse o.s.; (perder la concentración) to allow one's attention to wander

distraído, -a [distra'iðo, a] adj (gen) absent-minded; (entretenido) amusing

distribuidor, a [distriβui'ðor, a] nm/f distributor; (Com) dealer, agent

distribuir [distriβu'ir] /3g/ vt to distribute

distrito [dis'trito] nm (sector, territorio) region; (barrio) district; **~ postal** postal district; **D~ Federal** (LAM) Federal District

disturbio [dis'turβjo] nm disturbance; (desorden) riot

disuadir [diswa'ðir] /3a/ vt to dissuade

disuelto [di'swelto] pp de **disolver**

DIU nm abr (= dispositivo intrauterino) IUD

diurno, -a ['djurno, a] adj day cpd

divagar [diβa'ɣar] /1h/ vi (desviarse) to digress

diván [di'βan] nm divan

diversidad [diβersi'ðað] nf diversity, variety

diversión [diβer'sjon] nf (gen) entertainment; (actividad) hobby, pastime

diverso, -a [di'βerso, a] adj diverse ▷ nm: **~s** (Com) sundries; **~s libros** several books

divertido, -a [diβer'tiðo, a] adj (chiste) amusing; (fiesta etc) enjoyable

divertir [diβer'tir] /3i/ vt (entretener, recrear) to amuse; **divertirse** vr (pasarlo bien) to have a good time; (distraerse) to amuse o.s.

dividendo [diβi'ðendo] nm (Com: often pl) dividend, dividends

dividir [diβi'ðir] /3a/ vt (gen) to divide; (distribuir) to distribute, share out

divierta etc [di'βjerta] vb V **divertir**

divino, -a [di'βino, a] adj divine

divirtiendo etc [diβir'tjendo] vb V **divertir**

divisa [di'βisa] nf (emblema) emblem, badge; **divisas** nfpl foreign exchange sg

divisar [diβi'sar] /1a/ vt to make out, distinguish

división [diβi'sjon] nf division; (de partido) split; (de país) partition

divorciar [diβor'θjar] /1b/ vt to divorce; **divorciarse** vr to get divorced; **divorcio** nm divorce

divulgar [diβul'ɣar] /1h/ vt (desparramar) to spread; (hacer circular) to divulge

DNI nm abr (ESP) = **Documento Nacional de Identidad** see note

- **DNI**
-
- The Documento Nacional de Identidad
- is a Spanish ID card which must be
- carried at all times and produced on
- request for the police. It contains
- the holder's photo, fingerprints and
- personal details. It is also known as
- the DNI or carnet de identidad.

Dña. abr (= Doña) Mrs

do [do] nm (Mus) C

dobladillo [doβla'ðiʎo] nm (de vestido) hem; (de pantalón: vuelta) turn-up (BRIT), cuff (US)

doblar [do'βlar] /1a/ vt to double; (papel) to fold; (caño) to bend; (la esquina) to turn, go round; (film) to dub ▷ vi to turn; (campana) to toll; **doblarse** vr (plegarse) to fold (up), crease; (encorvarse) to bend; **~ a la derecha/izquierda** to turn right/left

doble ['doβle] adj double; (de dos aspectos) dual; (fig) two-faced ▷ nm double ▷ nmf (Teat) double, stand-in;

dobles nmpl (Deporte) doubles sg; **con ~ sentido** with a double meaning

doce ['doθe] num twelve; **docena** nf dozen

docente [do'θente] adj: **personal ~** teaching staff; **centro ~** educational institution

dócil ['doθil] adj (pasivo) docile; (obediente) obedient

doctor, a [dok'tor, a] nm/f doctor

doctorado [dokto'raðo] nm doctorate

doctrina [dok'trina] nf doctrine, teaching

documentación [dokumenta'θjon] nf documentation; (de identidad etc) papers pl

documental [dokumen'tal] adj, nm documentary

documento [doku'mento] nm (certificado) document; **~ adjunto** (Inform) attachment; **D~ Nacional de Identidad** national identity card; V **DNI**

dólar ['dolar] nm dollar

doler [do'ler] /2h/ vt, vi to hurt; (fig) to grieve; **dolerse** vr (de su situación) to grieve, feel sorry; (de las desgracias ajenas) to sympathize; **me duele el brazo** my arm hurts

dolor [do'lor] nm pain; (fig) grief, sorrow; **~ de cabeza** headache; **~ de estómago** stomach ache

domar [do'mar] /1a/ vt to tame

domesticar [domesti'kar] /1g/ vt to tame

doméstico, -a [do'mestiko, a] adj (vida, servicio) home; (tareas) household; (animal) tame, pet

domicilio [domi'θiljo] nm home; **~ particular** private residence; **servicio a ~** delivery service; **sin ~ fijo** of no fixed abode

dominante [domi'nante] adj dominant; (persona) domineering

dominar [domi'nar] /1a/ vt to dominate; (idiomas) to be fluent in ▷ vi to dominate, prevail

domingo [do'miŋgo] nm Sunday;
D~ de Ramos Palm Sunday; **D~ de
Resurrección** Easter Sunday
dominio [do'minjo] nm (tierras)
domain; (autoridad) power, authority;
(de las pasiones) grip, hold; (de idioma)
command
don [don] nm (talento) gift; **D~ Juan
Gómez** Mr Juan Gómez, Juan Gómez
Esq. (BRIT); see note "don"

DON

Don or doña is a term used before
someone's first name – eg Don
Diego, Doña Inés – when showing
respect or being polite to someone
of a superior social standing or to
an older person. It is becoming
somewhat rare, but it does however
continue to be used with names and
surnames in official documents and
in correspondence: eg Sr. D. Pedro
Rodríguez Hernández, Sra. Dña Inés
Rodríguez Hernández.

dona ['dona] nf (LAM) doughnut,
donut (US)
donar [do'nar] /1a/ vt to donate
donativo [dona'tißo] nm donation
donde ['donde] adv where ⊳ prep: **el
coche está allí ~ el farol** the car is
over there by where o where the
lamppost is; **en ~** where, in which
dónde ['donde] adv interrogativo
where?; **¿a ~ vas?** where are you going
(to)?; **¿de ~ vienes?** where have you
been?; **¿por ~?** where?, whereabouts?
dondequiera [donde'kjera] adv
anywhere ⊳ conj: **~ que** wherever;
por ~ everywhere, all over the place
donut® [do'nut] nm (ESP) doughnut,
donut (US)
doña ['dona] nf: **~ Alicia** Alicia; **D~
Carmen Gómez** Mrs Carmen Gómez;
V tb **don**
dorado, -a [do'raðo, a] adj (color)
golden; (Tec) gilt

dormir [dor'mir] /3j/ vt: **~ la siesta**
to have an afternoon nap ⊳ vi to sleep;
dormirse vr to fall asleep
dormitorio [dormi'torjo] nm
bedroom
dorsal [dor'sal] nm (Deporte) number
dorso ['dorso] nm (de mano) back; (de
hoja) other side
dos [dos] num two
dosis ['dosis] nf inv dose, dosage
dotado, -a [do'taðo, a] adj gifted; **~
de** endowed with
dotar [do'tar] /1a/ vt to endow; **dote**
nf dowry; **dotes** nfpl (talentos) gifts
doy [doj] vb V **dar**
drama ['drama] nm drama;
dramaturgo, -a nm/f dramatist,
playwright
drástico, -a ['drastiko, a] adj drastic
drenaje [dre'naxe] nm drainage
droga ['droɣa] nf drug; **drogadicto, -a**
nm/f drug addict
drogar [dro'ɣar] /1h/ vt to drug;
drogarse vr to take drugs
droguería [droɣe'ria] nf = hardware
shop (BRIT) o store (US)
ducha ['dutʃa] nf (de baño) shower; (Med)
douche
ducharse [du'tʃarse] /1a/ vr to take
a shower
duda ['duða] nf doubt; **no cabe ~**
there is no doubt about it; **dudar** /1a/
vt to doubt ⊳ vi to doubt; **dudoso,
-a** adj (incierto) hesitant; (sospechoso)
doubtful
duela etc vb V **doler**
duelo ['dwelo] vb V **doler** ⊳ nm
(combate) duel; (luto) mourning
duende ['dwende] nm imp, goblin
dueño, -a ['dweɲo, a] nm/f
(propietario) owner; (de pensión,
taberna) landlord/lady; (empresario)
employer
duerma etc vb V **dormir**
dulce ['dulθe] adj sweet ⊳ adv gently,
softly ⊳ nm sweet
dulcería [dulθe'ria] nf (LAM)
confectioner's (shop)

dulzura [dul'θura] nf sweetness; (ternura) gentleness

dúo ['duo] nm duet

duplicar [dupli'kar] /1g/ vt (hacer el doble de) to duplicate

duque ['duke] nm duke; **duquesa** nf duchess

durable [du'raβle] adj durable

duración [dura'θjon] nf (de película, disco etc) length; (de pila etc) life; (curso: de acontecimientos etc) duration

duradero, -a [dura'δero, a] adj (tela) hard-wearing; (fe, paz) lasting

durante [du'rante] adv during

durar [du'rar] /1a/ vi to last; (recuerdo) to remain

durazno [du'rasno] nm (LAM: fruta) peach; (: árbol) peach tree

durex ['dureks] nm (LAM: tira adhesiva) Sellotape® (BRIT), Scotch tape® (US)

dureza [du'reθa] nf (cualidad) hardness

duro, -a ['duro, a] adj hard; (carácter) tough ▷ adv hard ▷ nm (moneda) five peseta coin

DVD nm abr (= disco de vídeo digital) DVD

E abr (= este) E

e [e] conj and

ébano ['eβano] nm ebony

ebrio, -a ['eβrjo, a] adj drunk

ebullición [eβuʎi'θjon] nf boiling

echar [e'tʃar] /1a/ vt to throw; (agua, vino) to pour (out); (empleado: despedir) to fire, sack; (hojas) to sprout; (cartas) to post; (humo) to emit, give out ▷ vi: ~ a correr to start running o to run, break into a run; ~ a llorar to burst into tears; echarse vr to lie down; ~ llave a to lock (up); ~ abajo (gobierno) to overthrow; (edificio) to demolish; ~ mano a to lay hands on; ~ una mano a algn (ayudar) to give sb a hand; ~ de menos to miss; ~ una mirada to give a look; ~ sangre to bleed; ~se atrás to back out

eclesiástico, -a [ekle'sjastiko, a] adj ecclesiastical

eco ['eko] nm echo; **tener ~** to catch on

ecología [ekolo'xia] nf ecology;
ecológico, -a adj (producto,
método) environmentally-friendly;
(agricultura) organic; **ecologista** adj
environmental, conservation cpd
▷ nmf environmentalist

economía [ekono'mia] nf (sistema)
economy; (carrera) economics

económico, -a [eko'nomiko, a] adj
(barato) cheap, economical; (persona)
thrifty; (Com: año etc) financial;
(: situación) economic

economista [ekono'mista] nmf
economist

Ecuador [ekwa'ðor] nm Ecuador

ecuador [ekwa'ðor] nm equator

ecuatoriano, -a [ekwato'rjano, a]
adj, nm/f Ecuador(i)an

ecuestre [e'kwestre] adj equestrian

edad [e'ðað] nf age; **¿qué ~ tienes?**
how old are you?; **tiene ocho años
de ~** he is eight (years old); **ser de ~
mediana/avanzada** to be middle-
aged/getting on; **la E~ Media** the
Middle Ages

edición [eði'θjon] nf (acto)
publication; (ejemplar) edition

edificar [eðifi'kar] /1g/ vt to build

edificio [eði'fiθjo] nm building; (fig)
edifice, structure

Edimburgo [eðim'burɣo] nm
Edinburgh

editar [eði'tar] /1a/ vt (publicar) to
publish; (preparar textos) to edit

editor, a [eði'tor, a] nm/f (que
publica) publisher; (redactor) editor
▷ adj: **casa ~a** a publishing company;
editorial adj editorial ▷ nm leading
article, editorial; (tb: **casa editorial**)
publisher

edredón [eðre'ðon] nm; duvet

educación [eðuka'θjon] nf
education; (crianza) upbringing;
(modales) (good) manners pl

educado, -a [eðu'kaðo, a] adj well-
mannered; **mal ~** ill-mannered

educar [eðu'kar] /1g/ vt to educate;
(criar) to bring up; (voz) to train

efectivamente [efektiβa'mente]
adv (como respuesta) exactly, precisely;
(verdaderamente) really; (de hecho)
in fact

efectivo, -a [efek'tiβo, a] adj
effective; (real) actual, real ▷ nm:
pagar en ~ to pay (in) cash; **hacer ~
un cheque** to cash a cheque

efecto [e'fekto] nm effect, result;
efectos nmpl (personales) effects;
(bienes) goods; (Com) assets;
~ invernadero greenhouse effect;
~s especiales special effects; **~s
secundarios** side effects; **~s sonoros**
sound effects; **en ~** in fact; (respuesta)
exactly, indeed

efectuar [efek'twar] /1e/ vt to carry
out; (viaje) to make

eficacia [efi'kaθja] nf (de persona)
efficiency; (de medicamento etc)
effectiveness

eficaz [efi'kaθ] adj (persona) efficient;
(acción) effective

eficiente [efi'θjente] adj efficient

egipcio, -a [e'xipθjo, a] adj, nm/f
Egyptian

Egipto [e'xipto] nm Egypt

egoísmo [eɣo'ismo] nm egoism

egoísta [eɣo'ista] adj egoistical,
selfish ▷ nmf egoist

Eire ['eire] nm Eire

ej. abr (= ejemplo) eg

eje ['exe] nm (Geo, Mat) axis; (de rueda)
axle; (de máquina) shaft, spindle

ejecución [exeku'θjon] nf execution;
(cumplimiento) fulfilment; (actuación)
performance; (Jur: embargo de deudor)
attachment

ejecutar [exeku'tar] /1a/ vt to
execute, carry out; (matar) to execute;
(cumplir) to fulfil; (Mus) to perform;
(Jur: embargar) to attach, distrain

ejecutivo, -a [exeku'tiβo, a] adj
executive; **el (poder) ~** the executive
(power)

ejemplar [exem'plar] adj exemplary
▷ nm example; (Zool) specimen; (de
libro) copy; (de periódico) number, issue

ejemplo [e'xemplo] *nm* example; **por ~** for example

ejercer [exer'θer] /2b/ *vt* to exercise; *(influencia)* to exert; *(un oficio)* to practise ▷ *vi*: **~ de** to practise as

ejercicio [exer'θiθjo] *nm* exercise; *(período)* tenure; **~ comercial** business year; **hacer ~** to take exercise

ejército [e'xerθito] *nm* army; **E~ del Aire/de Tierra** Air Force/Army; **entrar en el ~** to join the army, join up

ejote [e'xote] *nm (AM)* green bean

PALABRA CLAVE

el [el] *(fem* **la***, neutro* **lo***, pl* **los, las)** *artículo definido* **1** the; **el libro/la mesa/los estudiantes/las flores** the book/table/students/flowers
2 *(con n abstracto o propio, no se traduce)*: **el amor/la juventud** love/youth
3 *(posesión, se traduce a menudo por adj posesivo)*: **romperse el brazo** to break one's arm; **levantó la mano** he put his hand up; **se puso el sombrero** she put her hat on
4 *(valor descriptivo)*: **tener la boca grande/los ojos azules** to have a big mouth/blue eyes
5 *(con días)* on; **me iré el viernes** I'll leave on Friday; **los domingos suelo ir a nadar** on Sundays I generally go swimming
6 *(lo + adj)*: **lo difícil/caro** what is difficult/expensive; *(cuán)*: **no se da cuenta de lo pesado que es** he doesn't realize how boring he is
▷ *pron demostrativo* **1**: **mi libro y el de usted** my book and yours; **las de Pepe son mejores** Pepe's are better; **no la(s) blanca(s) sino la(s) gris(es)** not the white one(s) but the grey one(s)
2: **lo de ayer**: **lo de ayer** what happened yesterday; **lo de las facturas** that business about the invoices
▷ *pron relativo* **1**: **el que** *etc* *(indef)*: **el (los) que quiera(n) que se vaya(n)** anyone who wants to can leave; **llévese el/la que más le guste** take the one you like best; *(def)*: **el que compré ayer** the one I bought yesterday; **los que se van** those who leave
2: **lo que pienso yo/más me gusta** what I think/like most
▷ *conj*: **el que**: **el que lo diga** the fact that he says so; **el que sea tan vago me molesta** his being so lazy bothers me
▷ *excl*: **¡el susto que me diste!** what a fright you gave me!
▷ *pron personal* **1** *(persona: m)* him; *(: f)* her; *(: pl)* them; **lo/las veo** I can see him/them
2 *(animal, cosa: sg)* it; *(: pl)* them; **lo (o la) veo** I can see it; **los (o las) veo** I can see them
3: **lo** *(como sustituto de frase)*: **no lo sabía** I didn't know; **ya lo entiendo** I understand now

él [el] *pron (persona)* he; *(cosa)* it; *(después de prep: persona)* him; *(: cosa)* it; **mis libros y los de él** my books and his

elaborar [elaβo'rar] /1a/ *vt (producto)* to make, manufacture; *(preparar)* to prepare; *(madera, metal etc)* to work; *(proyecto etc)* to work on o out

elástico, -a [e'lastiko, a] *adj* elastic; *(flexible)* flexible ▷ *nm* elastic; *(gomita)* elastic band

elección [elek'θjon] *nf* election; *(selección)* choice, selection; **elecciones generales** general election *sg*

electorado [elekto'raðo] *nm* electorate, voters *pl*

electricidad [elektriθi'ðað] *nf* electricity

electricista [elektri'θista] *nmf* electrician

eléctrico, -a [e'lektriko, a] *adj* electric

electro... [elektro] *pref* electro...;
electrocardiograma *nm*
electrocardiogram; **electrocutar**
/1a/ *vt* to electrocute; **electrodo**
nm electrode; **electrodomésticos**
nmpl (electrical) household
appliances

electrónico, -a [elek'troniko, a] *adj*
electronic ▷ *nf* electronics *sg*

electrotren [elektro'tren] *nm*
express electric train

elefante [ele'fante] *nm* elephant

elegancia [ele'yanθja] *nf* elegance,
grace; (estilo) stylishness

elegante [ele'yante] *adj* elegant,
graceful; (estiloso) stylish,
fashionable

elegir [ele'xir] /3c, 3k/ *vt* (escoger)
to choose, select; (optar) to opt for;
(presidente) to elect

elemental [elemen'tal] *adj* (claro,
obvio) elementary; (fundamental)
elemental, fundamental

elemento [ele'mento] *nm* element;
(fig) ingredient; **elementos** *nmpl*
elements, rudiments

elepé [ele'pe] *nm* LP

elevación [eleβa'θjon] *nf* elevation;
(acto) raising, lifting; (de precios) rise;
(Geo etc) height, altitude

elevado, -a [ele'βaðo, a] *pp de* elevar
▷ *adj* high

elevar [ele'βar] /1a/ *vt* to raise, lift
(up); (precio) to put up; **elevarse** *vr*
(edificio) to rise; (precios) to go up

eligiendo etc [eli'xjenðo], **elija** etc
[e'lixa] *vb V* **elegir**

eliminar [elimi'nar] /1a/ *vt* to
eliminate, remove

eliminatoria [elimina'torja] *nf*
heat, (preliminary) round)

elite [e'lite], **élite** ['elite] *nf* elite

ella [e'ʎa] *pron* (persona) she; (cosa) it;
(después de prep: persona) her; (: cosa)
it; **de ~** hers

ellas ['eʎas] *pron V* **ellos**

ello ['eʎo] *pron neutro* it; **es por ~
que ...** that's why ...

ellos, -as ['eʎos, as] *pron personal pl*
they; (después de prep) them; **de ~** theirs

elogiar [elo'xjar] /1b/ *vt* to praise;
elogio *nm* praise

elote [e'lote] *nm* (ʌm) corn on the cob

eludir [elu'ðir] /3a/ *vt* to avoid

email ['imeil] *nm* email m; (dirección)
email address; **mandar un ~ a algn**
to email sb, send sb an email

embajada [emba'xaða] *nf* embassy

embajador, a [embaxa'ðor, a] *nm/f*
ambassador/ambassadress

embalar [emba'lar] /1a/ *vt* to parcel,
wrap (up); **embalarse** *vr* to go too fast

embalse [em'balse] *nm* (presa) dam;
(lago) reservoir

embarazada [embara'θaða] *adj f*
pregnant ▷ *nf* pregnant woman

  ▨ No confundir *embarazada* con la
  palabra inglesa *embarrassed*.

embarazo [emba'raθo] *nm* (de mujer)
pregnancy; (impedimento) obstacle,
obstruction; (timidez) embarrassment;
embarazoso, -a *adj* awkward;
(violento) embarrassing

embarcación [embarka'θjon] *nf*
(barco) boat, craft; (acto) embarkation

embarcadero [embarka'ðero] *nm*
pier, landing stage

embarcar [embar'kar] /1g/ *vt*
(cargamento) to ship, stow; (persona)
to embark, put on board; **embarcarse** *vr*
to embark, go on board

embargar [embar'ɣar] /1h/ *vt* (Jur) to
seize, impound

embargo [em'barɣo] *nm* (Jur) seizure;
(Com etc) embargo

embargue etc [em'barɣe] *vb V*
embargar

embarque etc [em'barke] *vb V*
embarcar ▷ *nm* shipment, loading

embellecer [embeʎe'θer] /2d/ *vt* to
embellish, beautify

embestida [embes'tiða] *nf* attack,
onslaught; (carga) charge

embestir [embes'tir] /3k/ *vt* to
attack, assault; to charge, attack ▷ *vi*
to attack

emblema [em'blema] nm emblem

embobado, -a [embo'βaðo, a] adj (atontado) stunned, bewildered

embolia [em'bolja] nf (Med) clot, embolism

émbolo ['embolo] nm (Auto) piston

emborrachar [emborra't∫ar] /1a/ vt to make drunk, intoxicate; **emborracharse** vr to get drunk

emboscada [embos'kaða] nf ambush

embotar [embo'tar] /1a/ vt to blunt, dull

embotellamiento [emboteʎa'mjento] nm (Auto) traffic jam

embotellar [embote'ʎar] /1a/ vt to bottle

embrague [em'braɣe] nm (tb: **pedal de ~**) clutch

embrión [em'brjon] nm embryo

embrollo [em'broʎo] nm (enredo) muddle, confusion; (aprieto) fix, jam

embrujado, -a [embru'xaðo, a] adj bewitched; **casa embrujada** haunted house

embrutecer [embrute'θer] /2d/ vt (atontar) to stupefy

embudo [em'buðo] nm funnel

embuste [em'buste] nm (mentira) lie; **embustero, -a** adj lying, deceitful ▷ nm/f (mentiroso) liar

embutido [embu'tiðo] nm (Culin) sausage; (Tec) inlay

emergencia [emer'xenθja] nf emergency; (surgimiento) emergence

emerger [emer'xer] /2c/ vi to emerge, appear

emigración [emiɣra'θjon] nf emigration; (de pájaros) migration

emigrar [emi'ɣrar] /1a/ vi (personas) to emigrate; (pájaros) to migrate

eminente [emi'nente] adj eminent, distinguished; (elevado) high

emisión [emi'sjon] nf (acto) emission; (Com etc) issue; (Radio, TV: acto) broadcasting; (: programa) broadcast, programme, program (us)

emisor, a [emi'sor, a] nm transmitter ▷ nf radio o broadcasting station

emitir [emi'tir] /3a/ vt (olor etc) to emit, give off; (moneda etc) to issue; (opinión) to express; (Radio) to broadcast

emoción [emo'θjon] nf emotion; (excitación) excitement; (sentimiento) feeling

emocionante [emoθjo'nante] adj (excitante) exciting, thrilling

emocionar [emoθjo'nar] /1a/ vt (excitar) to excite, thrill; (conmover) to move, touch; (impresionar) to impress

emoticón [emoti'kon], **emoticono** [emoti'kono] nm smiley

emotivo, -a [emo'tiβo, a] adj emotional

empacho [em'pat∫o] nm (Med) indigestion; (fig) embarrassment

empalagoso, -a [empala'ɣoso, a] adj cloying; (fig) tiresome

empalmar [empal'mar] /1a/ vt to join, connect ▷ vi (dos caminos) to meet, join; **empalme** nm joint, connection; (de vías) junction; (de trenes) connection

empanada [empa'naða] nf pie, pasty

empañarse [empa'narse] /1a/ vr (nublarse) to get misty, steam up

empapar [empa'par] /1a/ vt (mojar) to soak, saturate; (absorber) to soak up, absorb; **empaparse** vr: **~se de** to soak up

empapelar [empape'lar] /1a/ vt (paredes) to paper

empaquetar [empake'tar] /1a/ vt to pack, parcel up

empastar [empas'tar] /1a/ vt (embadurnar) to paste; (diente) to fill

empaste [em'paste] nm (de diente) filling

empatar [empa'tar] /1a/ vt to draw, tie; **~on a dos** they drew two-all; **empate** nm draw, tie

empecé [empe'θe] vb V **empezar**

empedernido, -a [empeðer'niðo, a] adj hard, heartless; (fijado) inveterate; **un fumador ~** a heavy smoker

empeine [em'peine] nm (de pie, zapato) instep

empeñado, -a [empe'ɲaðo, a] adj (persona) determined; (objeto) pawned

empeñar [empe'ɲar] /1a/ vt (objeto) to pawn, pledge; (persona) to compel; **empeñarse** vr (endeudarse) to get into debt; **~se en hacer** to be set on doing, be determined to do

empeño [em'peɲo] nm (determinación) determination; **casa de ~s** pawnshop

empeorar [empeo'rar] /1a/ vt to make worse, worsen ⊳ vi to get worse, deteriorate

empezar [empe'θar] /1f, 1j/ vt, vi to begin, start

empiece etc [em'pjeθe] vb V **empezar**

empiezo etc [em'pjeθo] vb V **empezar**

emplasto [em'plasto] nm (Med) plaster

emplazar [empla'θar] /1f/ vt (ubicar) to site, place, locate; (Jur) to summons; (convocar) to summon

empleado, -a [emple'aðo, a] nm/f (gen) employee; (de banco etc) clerk

emplear [emple'ar] /1a/ vt (usar) to use, employ; (dar trabajo a) to employ; **emplearse** vr (conseguir trabajo) to be employed; (ocuparse) to occupy o.s.

empleo [em'pleo] nm (puesto) job; (puestos: colectivamente) employment; (uso) use, employment

empollar [empo'ʎar] /1a/ vt (fam) to swot (up); **empollón, -ona** nm/f (fam) swot

emporio [em'porjo] nm (LAM: gran almacén) department store

empotrado, -a [empo'traðo, a] adj (armario etc) built-in

emprender [empren'der] /2a/ vt (empezar) to begin, embark on; (acometer) to tackle, take on

empresa [em'presa] nf enterprise; (Com) firm, company; **empresariales** nfpl business studies; **empresario, -a** nm/f (Com) businessman/woman

empujar [empu'xar] /1a/ vt to push, shove

empujón [empu'xon] nm push, shove

empuñar [empu'ɲar] /1a/ vt (asir) to grasp, take (firm) hold of

PALABRA CLAVE

en [en] prep **1** (posición) in; (: sobre) on; **está en el cajón** it's in the drawer; **en Argentina/La Paz** in Argentina/La Paz; **en el colegio/la oficina** at school/the office; **está en el suelo/quinto piso** on the floor/the fifth floor

2 (dirección) into; **entró en el aula** she went into the classroom; **meter algo en el bolso** to put sth into one's bag

3 (tiempo) in; on; **en 1605/3 semanas/invierno** in 1605/3 weeks/winter; **en (el mes de) enero** in (the month of) January; **en aquella ocasión/época** on that occasion/at that time

4 (precio) for; **lo vendió en 20 dólares** he sold it for 20 dollars

5 (diferencia) by; **reducir/aumentar en una tercera parte/un 20 por ciento** to reduce/increase by a third/20 per cent

6 (manera, forma): **en avión/autobús** by plane/bus; **escrito en inglés** written in English

7 (después de vb que indica gastar etc) on; **han cobrado demasiado en dietas** they've charged too much to expenses; **se le va la mitad del sueldo en comida** half his salary goes on food

8 (tema, ocupación): **experto en la materia** expert on the subject; **trabaja en la construcción** he works in the building industry

9 (adj + en + infin): **lento en reaccionar** slow to react

enagua(s) [ena'ɣwa(s)] nf (pl) (esp LAM) petticoat sg, underskirt sg

enajenación [enaxena'θjon] *nf*: **~mental** mental derangement

enamorado, -a [enamo'raðo, a] *adj* in love ▷ *nm/f* lover; **estar ~ (de)** to be in love (with)

enamorar [enamo'rar] /1a/ *vt* to win the love of; **enamorarse** *vr*: **~se (de)** to fall in love (with)

enano, -a [e'nano, a] *adj* tiny ▷ *nm/f* dwarf

encabezamiento [enkaβeθa'mjento] *nm* (*de carta*) heading; (*de periódico*) headline

encabezar [enkaβe'θar] /1f/ *vt* (*movimiento, revolución*) to lead, head; (*lista*) to head; (*carta*) to put a heading to

encadenar [enkaðe'nar] /1a/ *vt* to chain (together); (*poner grilletes a*) to shackle

encajar [enka'xar] /1a/ *vt* (*ajustar*): **~ en** to fit (into) ▷ *vi* to fit (well); (*fig: corresponder a*) to match

encaje [en'kaxe] *nm* (*labor*) lace

encallar [enka'ʎar] /1a/ *vi* (*Naut*) to run aground

encaminar [enkami'nar] /1a/ *vt* to direct, send

encantado, -a [enkan'taðo, a] *adj* (*hechizado*) bewitched; (*muy contento*) delighted; **¡~!** how do you do!, pleased to meet you

encantador, -a [enkanta'ðor, a] *adj* charming, lovely ▷ *nm/f* magician, enchanter/enchantress

encantar [enkan'tar] /1a/ *vt* to charm, delight; (*hechizar*) to bewitch, cast a spell on; **me encanta eso** I love that; **encanto** *nm* (*magia*) spell, charm; (*fig*) charm, delight

encarcelar [enkarθe'lar] /1a/ *vt* to imprison, jail

encarecer [enkare'θer] /2d/ *vt* to put up the price of ▷ **encarecerse** *vr* to get dearer

encargado, -a [enkar'ɣaðo, a] *adj* in charge ▷ *nm/f* agent, representative; (*responsable*) person in charge

encargar [enkar'ɣar] /1h/ *vt* to entrust; (*recomendar*) to urge, recommend; **encargarse** *vr*: **~se de** to look after, take charge of; **~ algo a algn** to put sb in charge of sth

encargo [en'karɣo] *nm* (*pedido*) assignment, job; (*responsabilidad*) responsibility; (*Com*) order

encariñarse [enkari'ɲarse] /1a/ *vr*: **~ con** to grow fond of, get attached to

encarnación [enkarna'θjon] *nf* incarnation, embodiment

encarrilar [enkarri'lar] /1a/ *vt* (*tren*) to put back on the rails; (*fig*) to correct, put on the right track

encasillar [enkasi'ʎar] /1a/ *vt* (*Teat*) to typecast; (*pey*) to pigeonhole

encendedor [enθende'ðor] *nm* lighter

encender [enθen'der] /2g/ *vt* (*con fuego*) to light; (*luz, radio*) to put on, switch on; (*avivar: pasiones etc*) to inflame; **encenderse** *vr* to catch fire; (*excitarse*) to get excited; (*de cólera*) to flare up; (*el rostro*) to blush

encendido, -a [enθen'diðo, a] *adj* alight; (*aparato*) (switched) on ▷ *nm* (*Auto*) ignition

encerado, -a [enθe'raðo, a] *adj* (*suelo*) waxed ▷ *nm* (*Escol*) blackboard

encerrar [enθe'rrar] /1j/ *vt* (*confinar*) to shut in u up; (*comprender, incluir*) to include, contain; **encerrarse** *vr* to shut o.s. up in

encharcado, -a [entʃar'kaðo, a] *adj* (*terreno*) flooded

encharcar [entʃar'kar] /1g/ *vt* to swamp, flood; **encharcarse** *vr* to become flooded

enchufado, -a [entʃu'faðo, a] *nm/f* (*fam*) well-connected person

enchufar [entʃu'far] /1a/ *vt* (*Elec*) to plug in; (*Tec*) to connect, fit together; **enchufe** *nm* (*Elec: clavija*) plug; (*: toma*) socket; (*de dos tubos*) joint, connection; (*fam: influencia*) contact, connection; (*: puesto*) cushy job

encía [en'θia] *nf* gum

encienda etc [en'θjenda] vb V
encender

encierro etc [en'θjerro] vb V
encerrar ▷ nm shutting in o up;
(calabozo) prison

encima [en'θima] adv (sobre) above,
over; (además) besides; **~ de** (en) on,
on top of; (sobre) above, over; (además
de) besides, on top of; **por ~ de** over;
¿llevas dinero ~? have you (got) any
money on you?; **se me vino ~** it took
me by surprise

encina [en'θina] nf (holm) oak

encinta [en'θinta] adj f pregnant

enclenque [en'klenke] adj weak,
sickly

encoger [enko'xer] /2c/ vt (gen) to
shrink, contract; **encogerse** vr to
shrink, contract; (fig) to cringe; **~se de
hombros** to shrug one's shoulders

encomendar [enkomen'dar]
/1j/ vt to entrust, commend;
encomendarse vr: **~se a** to put one's
trust in

encomienda etc [enko'mjenda]
vb V **encomendar** ▷ nf (encargo)
charge, commission; (elogio) tribute;
(LAM) parcel, package; **~ postal** (LAM:
servicio) parcel post

encontrar [enkon'trar] /1l/ vt (hallar)
to find; (inesperadamente) to meet, run
into; **encontrarse** vr to meet (each
other); (situarse) to be (situated); **~se
con** to meet; **~se bien (de salud)**
to feel well

encrucijada [enkruθi'xaða] nf
crossroads sg

encuadernación
[enkwaðerna'θjon] nf binding

encuadrar [enkwa'ðrar] /1a/ vt
(retrato) to frame; (ajustar) to fit,
insert; (encerrar) to contain

encubrir [enku'βrir] /3a/ vt (ocultar)
to hide, conceal; (criminal) to harbour,
shelter

encuentro [en'kwentro] vb V
encontrar ▷ nm (de personas)
meeting; (Auto etc) collision, crash;

(Deporte) match, game; (Mil)
encounter

encuerado, -a [enkwe'raðo, a] adj
(LAM) nude, naked

encuesta [en'kwesta] nf inquiry,
investigation; (sondeo) public opinion
poll

encumbrar [enkum'brar] /1a/ vt
(persona) to exalt

endeble [en'deβle] adj (argumento,
excusa, persona) weak

endemoniado, -a [endemo'njaðo,
a] adj possessed (of the devil);
(travieso) devilish

enderezar [endere'θar] /1f/ vt
(poner derecho) to straighten (out);
(: verticalmente) to set upright; (fig) to
straighten o sort out; (dirigir) to direct;
enderezarse vr (persona sentada) to
sit up straight

endeudarse [endeu'ðarse] /1a/ vr to
get into debt

endiablado, -a [endja'βlaðo, a]
adj devilish, diabolical; (humorístico)
mischievous

endilgar [endil'ɣar] /1h/ vt (fam):
~ algo a algn to lumber sb with sth

endiñar [endi'nar] /1a/ vt: **~ algo a
algn** to land sth on sb

endosar [endo'sar] /1a/ vt (cheque etc)
to endorse

endulzar [endul'θar] /1f/ vt to
sweeten; (suavizar) to soften

endurecer [endure'θer] /2d/ vt to
harden; **endurecerse** vr to harden,
grow hard

enema [e'nema] nm (Med) enema

enemigo, -a [ene'miɣo, a] adj
enemy, hostile ▷ nm/f enemy

enemistad [enemis'tað] nf enmity

enemistar [enemis'tar] /1a/ vt
to make enemies of, cause a rift
between; **enemistarse** vr to become
enemies; (amigos) to fall out

energía [ener'xia] nf (vigor)
energy, drive; (empuje) push; (Tec,
Elec) energy, power; **~ atómica/
eléctrica/eólica** atomic/electric/

enérgico, -a [e'nerxiko, a] adj (gen) energetic; (voz, modales) forceful

energúmeno, -a [ener'yumeno, a] nm/f madman/woman

enero [e'nero] nm January

enfadado, -a [enfa'ðaðo, a] adj angry, annoyed

enfadar [enfa'ðar] /1a/ vt to anger, annoy; **enfadarse** vr to get angry o annoyed

enfado [en'faðo] nm (enojo) anger, annoyance; (disgusto) trouble, bother

énfasis ['enfasis] nm emphasis, stress

enfático, -a [en'fatiko, a] adj emphatic

enfermar [enfer'mar] /1a/ vt to make ill ▷ vi to fall ill, be taken ill

enfermedad [enferme'ðað] nf illness; ~ **venérea** venereal disease

enfermera [enfer'mera] nf V **enfermero**

enfermería [enferme'ria] nf infirmary; (de colegio etc) sick bay

enfermero, -a [enfer'mero, a] nm (male) nurse ▷ nf nurse

enfermizo, -a [enfer'miθo, a] adj (persona) sickly, unhealthy; (fig) unhealthy

enfermo, -a [en'fermo, a] adj ill, sick ▷ nm/f invalid, sick person; (en hospital) patient; **caer** o **ponerse** ~ to fall ill

enfocar [enfo'kar] /1g/ vt (foto etc) to focus; (problema etc) to consider, look at

enfoque etc [en'foke] vb V **enfocar** ▷ nm focus

enfrentar [enfren'tar] /1a/ vt (peligro) to face (up to), confront; (oponer) to bring face to face; **enfrentarse** vr (dos personas) to face o confront each other; (Deporte: dos equipos) to meet; ~**se a** o **con** to face up to, confront

enfrente [en'frente] adv opposite; ~ **de** opposite, facing; **la casa de** ~ the house opposite, the house across the street

enfriamiento [enfria'mjento] nm chilling, refrigeration; (Med) cold, chill

enfriar [enfri'ar] /1c/ vt (alimentos) to cool, chill; (algo caliente) to cool down; **enfriarse** vr to cool down; (Med) to catch a chill; (amistad) to cool

enfurecer [enfure'θer] /2d/ vt to enrage, madden; **enfurecerse** vr to become furious, fly into a rage; (mar) to get rough

enganchar [engan'tʃar] /1a/ vt to hook; (dos vagones) to hitch up; (Tec) to couple, connect; (Mil) to recruit; **engancharse** vr (Mil) to enlist, join up

enganche [en'gantʃe] nm hook; (Tec) coupling, connection; (acto) hooking (up); (Mil) recruitment, enlistment; (LAM: depósito) deposit

engañar [enga'ɲar] /1a/ vt to deceive; (estafar) to cheat, swindle; **engañarse** vr (equivocarse) to be wrong; (asimismo) to deceive o kid o.s.

engaño [en'gaɲo] nm deceit; (estafa) trick, swindle; (error) mistake, misunderstanding; (ilusión) delusion; **engañoso, -a** adj (tramposo) crooked; (mentiroso) dishonest, deceitful; (aspecto) deceptive; (consejo) misleading

engatusar [engatu'sar] /1a/ vt (fam) to coax

engendro [en'xendro] nm (Bio) foetus; (fig) monstrosity

englobar [englo'βar] /1a/ vt to include, comprise

engordar [engor'ðar] /1a/ vt to fatten ▷ vi to get fat, put on weight

engorroso, -a [engo'rroso, a] adj bothersome, trying

engranaje [engra'naxe] nm (Auto) gear

engrasar [engra'sar] /1a/ vt (Tec: poner grasa) to grease; (: lubricar) to lubricate, oil; (manchar) to make greasy

engreído, -a [eŋˈgreiðo, a] adj vain, conceited

enhebrar [eneˈβrar] /1a/ vt to thread

enhorabuena [enoraˈβwena] excl: **¡~!** congratulations! ▷ nf: **dar la ~ a** to congratulate

enigma [eˈniɣma] nm enigma; (problema) puzzle; (misterio) mystery

enjambre [enˈxambre] nm swarm

enjaular [enxauˈlar] /1a/ vt to (put in a cage); (fam) to jail, lock up

enjuagar [enxwaˈɣar] /1h/ vt (ropa) to rinse (out)

enjuague etc [enˈxwaɣe] vb V **enjuagar** ▷ nm (Med) mouthwash; (de ropa) rinse, rinsing

enjugar [enxuˈɣar] /1h/ vt to wipe (off); (lágrimas) to dry; (déficit) to wipe out

enlace [enˈlaθe] nm link, connection; (relación) relationship; (tb: **~ matrimonial**) marriage; (de trenes) connection; **~ sindical** shop steward

enlatado, -a [enlaˈtaðo, a] adj (alimentos, productos) tinned, canned

enlazar [enlaˈθar] /1f/ vt (unir con lazos) to bind together; (atar) to tie; (conectar) to link, connect; (LAm) to lasso

enloquecer [enlokeˈθer] /2d/ vt to drive mad ▷ vi to go mad

enmarañar [enmaraˈɲar] /1a/ vt (enredar) to tangle up, entangle; (complicar) to complicate; (confundir) to confuse

enmarcar [enmarˈkar] /1g/ vt (cuadro) to frame

enmascarar [enmaskaˈrar] /1a/ vt to mask; **enmascararse** vr to put on a mask

enmendar [enmenˈdar] /1j/ vt to emend, correct; (constitución etc) to amend; (comportamiento) to reform; **enmendarse** vr to reform, mend one's ways; **enmienda** nf correction; amendment; reform

enmudecer [enmuðeˈθer] /2d/ vi (perder el habla) to fall silent; (guardar silencio) to remain silent

ennoblecer [ennoβleˈθer] /2d/ vt to ennoble

enojado, -a [enoˈxaðo, a] adj (LAm) angry

enojar [enoˈxar] /1a/ vt (encolerizar) to anger; (disgustar) to annoy, upset; **enojarse** vr to get angry; to get annoyed

enojo [eˈnoxo] nm (cólera) anger; (irritación) annoyance

enorme [eˈnorme] adj enormous, huge; (fig) monstrous

enredadera [enreðaˈðera] nf (Bot) creeper, climbing plant

enredar [enreˈðar] /1a/ vt (cables, hilos etc) to tangle (up), entangle; (situación) to complicate, confuse; (meter cizaña) to sow discord among o between; (implicar) to embroil, implicate; **enredarse** vr to get entangled, get tangled (up); (situación) to get complicated; (persona) to get embroiled; (LAm fam) to meddle

enredo [enˈreðo] nm (maraña) tangle; (confusión) mix-up, confusion; (intriga) intrigue

enriquecer [enrikeˈθer] /2d/ vt to make rich; (fig) to enrich; **enriquecerse** vr to get rich

enrojecer [enroxeˈθer] /2d/ vt to redden ▷ vi (persona) to blush; **enrojecerse** vr to blush

enrollar [enroˈʎar] /1a/ vt to roll (up), wind (up)

ensalada [ensaˈlaða] nf salad

ensaladilla [ensalaˈðiʎa] nf (tb: **~ rusa**) ≈ Russian salad

ensanchar [ensanˈtʃar] /1a/ vt (hacer más ancho) to widen; (agrandar) to enlarge, expand; (Costura) to let out; **ensancharse** vr to get wider, expand

ensayar [ensaˈjar] /1a/ vt to test, try (out); (Teat) to rehearse

ensayo [enˈsajo] nm test, trial; (Química) experiment; (Teat) rehearsal; (Deporte) try; (Escol, Lit) essay

enseguida [enseˈɣuiða] adv at once, right away

ensenada [ense'naða] *nf* inlet, cove
enseñanza [ense'ɲanθa] *nf* (educación) education; (acción) teaching; (doctrina) teaching, doctrine; **~ primaria/secundaria/superior** primary/secondary/higher education
enseñar [ense'ɲar] /1a/ *vt* (educar) to teach; (mostrar, señalar) to show
enseres [en'seres] *nmpl* belongings
ensuciar [ensu'θjar] /1b/ *vt* (manchar) to dirty, soil; (fig) to defile; **ensuciarse** *vr* to get dirty; (niño) to dirty one's nappy
entablar [enta'βlar] /1a/ *vt* (recubrir) to board (up); (Ajedrez, Damas) to set up; (conversación) to strike up; (Jur) to file ▷ *vi* to draw
ente ['ente] *nm* (organización) body, organization; (fam: persona) odd character
entender [enten'der] /2g/ *vt* (comprender) to understand; (darse cuenta) to realize ▷ *vi* to understand; (creer) to think, believe ▷ **a mi ~** in my opinion; **entenderse** *vr* (comprenderse) to be understood; (ponerse de acuerdo) to agree, reach an agreement; **~ de** to know all about; **~ algo de** to know a little about; **~ en** to deal with, have to do with; **~se mal** to get on badly
entendido, -a [enten'diðo, a] *adj* (comprendido) understood; (hábil) skilled; (inteligente) knowledgeable ▷ *nm/f* (experto) expert ▷ *excl* agreed!; **entendimiento** *nm* (comprensión) understanding; (inteligencia) mind, intellect; (juicio) judgement
enterado, -a [ente'raðo, a] *adj* well-informed; **estar ~ de** to know about, be aware of
enteramente [entera'mente] *adv* entirely, completely
enterar [ente'rar] /1a/ *vt* (informar) to inform, tell; **enterarse** *vr* to find out, get to know
enterito [ente'rito] *nm* (ʟᴀᴍ) boiler suit (ʙʀɪᴛ), overalls (ᴜs)

entero, -a [en'tero, a] *adj* (total) whole, entire; (fig: recto) resolute ▷ *nm* (Com: punto) point
enterrar [ente'rrar] /1j/ *vt* to bury
entidad [enti'ðað] *nf* (empresa) firm, company; (organismo) body; (sociedad) society; (Filosofía) entity
entienda etc [en'tjenda] *vb V* **entender**
entierro [en'tjerro] *nm* (acción) burial; (funeral) funeral
entonación [entona'θjon] *nf* (Ling) intonation
entonar [ento'nar] /1a/ *vt* (canción) to intone; (colores) to tone; (Med) to tone up ▷ *vi* to be in tune
entonces [en'tonθes] *adv* then, at that time; **desde ~** since then; **en aquel ~** at that time; **(pues) ~** and so
entornar [entor'nar] /1a/ *vt* (puerta, ventana) to half close, leave ajar; (los ojos) to screw up
entorno [en'torno] *nm* setting, environment; **~ de redes** (Inform) network environment
entorpecer [entorpe'θer] /2d/ *vt* (entendimiento) to dull; (impedir) to obstruct, hamper; (: tránsito) to slow down, delay
entrado, -a [en'traðo, a] *adj*: **~ en años** elderly; **(una vez) ~ el verano** in the summer(time), when summer comes ▷ *nf* (acción) entry, access; (sitio) entrance, way in; (Com) receipts *pl*, takings *pl*; (Culin) entrée; (Deporte) innings *sg*; (Teat) house, audience; (para el cine etc) ticket; (Inform) input; **entradas y salidas** (Com) income and expenditure; **entrada de aire** (Tec) air intake o inlet; **de entrada** from the outset
entramparse [entram'parse] /1a/ *vr* to get into debt
entrante [en'trante] *adj* next, coming; **entrantes** *nmpl* starters; **mes/año ~** next month/year
entraña [en'traɲa] *nf* (fig: centro) heart, core; (raíz) root; **entrañas**

nfpl (Anat) entrails; (fig) heart sg;
entrañable adj (amigo) dear;
(recuerdo) fond; **entrañar** /1a/ vt
to entail

entrar [en'trar] /1a/ vt (introducir) to
bring in; (Inform) to input ▷ vi (meterse)
to go o come in, enter; (comenzar):
~ **diciendo** to begin by saying; **me
entró sed/sueño** I started to feel
thirsty/sleepy; **no me entra** I can't
get the hang of it

entre ['entre] prep (dos) between; (en
medio de) among(st)

entreabrir [entrea'βrir] /3a/ vt to
half-open, open halfway

entrecejo [entre'θexo] nm: **fruncir
el ~** to frown

entredicho [entre'ðitʃo] nm (Jur)
injunction; **poner en ~** to cast doubt
on; **estar en ~** to be in doubt

entrega [en'treɣa] nf (de mercancías)
delivery; (de novela etc) instalment;
entregar /1h/ vt (dar) to hand (over),
deliver; **entregarse** vr (rendirse)
to surrender, give in, submit;
entregarse a (dedicarse) to devote
o.s. to

entremeses [entre'meses] nmpl
hors d'œuvres

entremeter [entreme'ter] /2a/ vt
to insert, put in; **entremeterse** vr to
meddle, interfere; **entremetido, -a**
adj meddling, interfering

entremezclar [entremeθ'klar] /1a/
vt to intermingle; **entremezclarse** vr
to intermingle

entrenador, a [entrena'ðor, a] nm/f
trainer, coach

entrenar [entre'nar] /1a/ vt (Deporte)
to train ▷ **entrenarse** vr to train

entrepierna [entre'pjerna] nf crotch

entresuelo [entre'swelo] nm
mezzanine

entretanto [entre'tanto] adv
meanwhile, meantime

entretecho [entre'tetʃo] nm (ᴄᴀᴍ) attic

entretejer [entrete'xer] /2a/ vt to
interweave

entretener [entrete'ner] /2k/ vt
(divertir) to entertain, amuse; (detener)
to hold up, delay; **entretenerse** vr
(divertirse) to amuse o.s.; (retrasarse)
to delay, linger; **entretenido,
-a** adj entertaining, amusing;
entretenimiento nm entertainment,
amusement

entrever [entre'βer] /2u/ vt to
glimpse, catch a glimpse of

entrevista [entre'βista] nf interview;
entrevistar /1a/ vt to interview;
entrevistarse vr: **entrevistarse con**
to have an interview with

entristecer [entriste'θer] /2d/ vt
to sadden, grieve; **entristecerse** vr
to grow sad

entrometerse [entrome'terse] /2a/
vr: **~ (en)** to interfere (in o with)

entumecer [entume'θer] /2d/ vt to
numb, benumb; **entumecerse** vr (por
el frío) to go o become numb

enturbiar [entur'βjar] /1b/ vt (el
agua) to make cloudy; (fig) to confuse;
enturbiarse vr (oscurecerse) to become
cloudy; (fig) to get confused, become
obscure

entusiasmar [entusjas'mar] /1a/ vt
to excite, fill with enthusiasm; (gustar
mucho) to delight; **entusiasmarse**
vr: **~se con o por** to get enthusiastic o
excited about

entusiasmo [entu'sjasmo] nm
enthusiasm; (excitación) excitement

entusiasta [entu'sjasta] adj
enthusiastic ▷ nmf enthusiast

enumerar [enume'rar] /1a/ vt to
enumerate

envainar [embai'nar] /1a/ vt to
sheathe

envalentonar [embalento'nar]
/1a/ vt to give courage to;
envalentonarse vr (pey: jactarse) to
boast, brag

envasar [emba'sar] /1a/ vt
(empaquetar) to pack, wrap; (enfrascar)
to bottle; (enlatar) to can; (embolsar)
to pocket

envase [em'base] nm packing, wrapping; bottling; canning; (recipiente) container; (paquete) package; (botella) bottle; (lata) tin (BRIT), can

envejecer [embexe'θer] /2d/ vt to make old, age ▷ vi (volverse viejo) to grow old; (parecer viejo) to age

envenenar [embene'nar] /1a/ vt to poison; (fig) to embitter

envergadura [emberɣa'ðura] nf (fig) scope

enviar [em'bjar] /1c/ vt to send; **~ un mensaje a algn** (por móvil) to text sb, send sb a text message

enviciar [embi'θjar] /1b/ vt (trabajo etc) to be addictive; **enviciarse** vr: **~se (con o en)** to get addicted (to)

envidia [em'biðja] nf envy; **tener ~ a** to envy, be jealous of; **envidiar** /1b/ vt to envy

envío [em'bio] nm (acción) sending; (de mercancías) consignment; (de dinero) remittance

enviudar [embju'ðar] /1d/ vi to be widowed

envoltorio [embol'torjo] nm package

envoltura [embol'tura] nf (cobertura) cover; (embalaje) wrapper, wrapping

envolver [embol'βer] /2h/ vt to wrap (up); (cubrir) to cover; (enemigo) to surround; (implicar) to involve, implicate

envuelto [em'bwelto] vb V **envolver**

enyesar [enje'sar] /1a/ vt (pared) to plaster; (Med) to put in plaster

enzarzarse [enθar'θarse] /1f/ vr: **~ en algo** to get mixed up in sth; (disputa) to get involved in sth

épico, -a [ˈepiko, a] adj epic ▷ nf epic (poetry)

epidemia [epiˈðemja] nf epidemic

epilepsia [epiˈlepsja] nf epilepsy

episodio [epiˈsoðjo] nm episode

época [ˈepoka] nf period, time; (Historia) age, epoch; **hacer ~** to be epoch-making

equilibrar [ekiliˈβrar] /1a/ vt to balance; **equilibrio** nm balance, equilibrium; **mantener/perder el equilibrio** to keep/lose one's balance; **equilibrista** nmf (funámbulo) tightrope walker; (acróbata) acrobat

equipaje [ekiˈpaxe] nm luggage (BRIT), baggage (US); (avíos) equipment, kit; **~ de mano** hand luggage; **hacer el ~** to pack

equipar [ekiˈpar] /1a/ vt (proveer) to equip

equiparar [ekipaˈrar] /1a/ vt (comparar): **~ con** to compare with; **equipararse** vr: **~se con** to be on a level with

equipo [eˈkipo] nm (conjunto de cosas) equipment; (Deporte) team; (de obreros) shift; **~ de música** music centre

equis [ˈekis] nf (the letter) X

equitación [ekitaˈθjon] nf (acto) riding

equivalente [ekiβaˈlente] adj, nm equivalent

equivaler [ekiβaˈler] /2p/ vi: **~ a** to be equivalent o equal to

equivocación [ekiβokaˈθjon] nf mistake, error

equivocado, -a [ekiβoˈkaðo, a] adj wrong, mistaken

equivocarse [ekiβoˈkarse] /1g/ vr to be wrong, make a mistake; **~ de camino** to take the wrong road

era [ˈera] vb V **ser** ▷ nf era, age

erais [ˈerais], **éramos** [ˈeramos], **eran** [ˈeran] vb V **ser**

eras [ˈeras], **eres** [ˈeres] vb V **ser**

erección [erekˈθjon] nf erection

lift; (poner derecho) to straighten

erigir [eriˈxir] /3c/ vt to erect, build; **erigirse vr**: **~ en** to set o.s. up as

erizo [eˈriθo] nm hedgehog; **~ de mar** sea urchin

ermita [erˈmita] nf hermitage; **ermitaño, -a** nm/f hermit

erosión [eroˈsjon] nf erosion

erosionar [erosjoˈnar] /1a/ vt to erode

erótico, -a [e'rotiko, a] *adj* erotic;
erotismo *nm* eroticism

errante [e'rrante] *adj* wandering,
errant

errar *vt*: **~ el camino** to take the
wrong road; **~ el tiro** to miss

erróneo, -a [e'rroneo, a] *adj*
(*equivocado*) wrong, mistaken

error [e'rror] *nm* error, mistake;
(*Inform*) bug; **~ de imprenta** misprint

eructar [eruk'tar] /1a/ *vt* to belch,
burp

erudito, -a [eru'ðito, a] *adj* erudite,
learned

erupción [erup'θjon] *nf* eruption;
(*Med*) rash

es [es] *vb* V **ser**

esa ['esa], **esas** ['esas] *adj*
demostrativo, pron V **ese**

ésa ['esa], **ésas** *pron* V **ése**

esbelto, -a [es'βelto, a] *adj* slim,
slender

esbozo [es'βoθo] *nm* sketch, outline

escabeche [eskaβu'ʎirse] /3a/ *vr*
aceitunas etc) pickle; **en ~** pickled

escabullirse [eskaβu'ʎirse] /3a/ *vr*
to slip away; (*largarse*) to clear out

escafandra [eska'fandra] *nf* (*buzo*)
diving suit; (*escafandra espacial*)
spacesuit

escala [es'kala] *nf* (*proporción*,
Mus) scale; (*de mano*) ladder; (*Aviat*)
stopover; **hacer ~ en** (*gen*) to stop off
at o call in at; (*Aviat*) to stop over at

escalafón [eskala'fon] *nm* (*escala de
salarios*) salary scale, wage scale

escalar [eska'lar] /1a/ *vt* to climb,
scale

escalera [eska'lera] *nf* stairs *pl*,
staircase; (*escala*) ladder; (*Naipes*) run;
~ mecánica escalator; **~ de caracol**
spiral staircase; **~ de incendios** fire
escape

escalfar [eskal'far] /1a/ *vt* (*huevos*)
to poach

escalinata [eskali'nata] *nf* staircase

escalofriante [eskalo'frjante] *adj*
chilling

escalofrío [eskalo'frio] *nm* (*Med*)
chill; **escalofríos** *nmpl* (*fig*) shivers

escalón [eska'lon] *nm* step, stair; (*de
escalera*) rung

escalope [eska'lope] *nm* (*Culin*)
escalope

escama [es'kama] *nf* (*de pez, serpiente*)
scale; (*de jabón*) flake; (*fig*) resentment

escampar [eskam'par] /1a/ *vb
impersonal* to stop raining

escandalizar [eskandali'θar] /1f/ *vt*
to scandalize, shock; **escandalizarse**
vr to be shocked; (*ofenderse*) to be
offended

escándalo [es'kandalo] *nm* scandal;
(*alboroto, tumulto*) row, uproar;
escandaloso, -a *adj* scandalous,
shocking

escandinavo, -a [eskandi'naβo, a]
adj, nm/f Scandinavian

escanear [eskane'ar] /1a/ *vt* to scan

escaño [es'kaɲo] *nm* bench; (*Pol*) seat

escapar [eska'par] /1a/ *vi* (*gen*) to
escape, run away; (*Deporte*) to break
away; **escaparse** *vr* to escape, get
away; (*agua, gas, noticias*) to leak (out)

escaparate [eskapa'rate] *nm* shop
window; **ir de ~s** to go window
shopping

escape [es'kape] *nm* (*de agua, gas*)
leak; (*de motor*) exhaust

escarabajo [eskara'βaxo] *nm* beetle

escaramuza [eskara'muθa] *nf*
skirmish

escarbar [eskar'βar] /1a/ *vt* (*gallina*)
to scratch

escarceos [eskar'θeos] *nmpl*: **en sus
~ con la política** in his occasional
forays into politics; **~ amorosos**
love affairs

escarcha [es'kartʃa] *nf* frost;
escarchado, -a *adj* (*Culin: fruta*)
crystallized

escarlatina [eskarla'tina] *nf* scarlet
fever

escarmentar [eskarmen'tar] /1j/
vt to punish severely ▷ *vi* to learn
one's lesson

escarmiento *etc* [eskar'mjento] *vb* V **escarmentar** ▷ *nm (ejemplo)* lesson; *(castigo)* punishment

escarola [eska'rola] *nf* endive

escarpado, -a [eskar'paðo, a] *adj (pendiente)* sheer, steep; *(rocas)* craggy

escasear [eskase'ar] /1a/ *vi* to be scarce

escasez [eska'seθ] *nf (falta)* shortage, scarcity; *(pobreza)* poverty

escaso, -a [es'kaso, a] *adj (poco)* scarce; *(raro)* rare; *(ralo)* thin, sparse; *(limitado)* limited

escatimar [eskati'mar] /1a/ *vt* to skimp (on), be sparing with

escayola [eska'jola] *nf* plaster

escena [es'θena] *nf* scene; **escenario** *nm (Teat)* stage; *(Cine)* set; *(fig)* scene; **escenografía** *nf* set o stage design

 ▣ No confundir *escenario* con la palabra inglesa *scenery*.

escéptico, -a [es'θeptiko, a] *adj* sceptical ▷ *nm/f* sceptic

esclarecer [esklare'θer] /2d/ *vt (misterio, problema)* to shed light on

esclavitud [esklaβi'tuð] *nf* slavery

esclavizar [esklaβi'θar] /1f/ *vt* to enslave

esclavo, -a [es'klaβo, a] *nm/f* slave

escoba [es'koβa] *nf* broom; **escobilla** *nf* brush

escocer [esko'θer] /2b, 2h/ *vi* to burn, sting; **escocerse** *vr* to chafe, get chafed

escocés, -esa [esko'θes, esa] *adj* Scottish ▷ *nm/f* Scotsman/woman, Scot

Escocia [es'koθja] *nf* Scotland

escoger [esko'xer] /2c/ *vt* to choose, pick, select; **escogido, -a** *adj* chosen, selected

escolar [esko'lar] *adj* school *cpd* ▷ *nmf* schoolboy/girl, pupil

escollo [es'koλo] *nm (fig)* pitfall

escolta [es'kolta] *nf* escort; **escoltar** /1a/ *vt* to escort

escombros [es'kombros] *nmpl (basura)* rubbish *sg; (restos)* debris *sg*

esconder [eskon'der] /2a/ *vt* to hide, conceal; **esconderse** *vr* to hide; **escondidas** *nfpl:* **a escondidas** secretly; **escondite** *nm* hiding place; *(juego)* hide-and-seek; **escondrijo** *nm* hiding place, hideout

escopeta [esko'peta] *nf* shotgun

escoria [es'korja] *nf (desecho mineral)* slag; *(fig)* scum, dregs *pl*

Escorpio [es'korpjo] *nm* Scorpio

escorpión [eskor'pjon] *nm* scorpion

escotado, -a [esko'taðo, a] *adj* low-cut

escote [es'kote] *nm (de vestido)* low neck; **pagar a ~** to share the expenses

escotilla [esko'tiʎa] *nf (Naut)* hatchway

escozor [esko'θor] *nm (dolor)* sting(ing)

escribible [eskri'βiβle] *adj* writable

escribir [eskri'βir] /3a/ *vt, vi* to write; **~ a máquina** to type; **¿cómo se escribe?** how do you spell it?

escrito, -a [es'krito, a] *pp de* **escribir** ▷ *nm (documento)* document; *(manuscrito)* text, manuscript; **por ~** in writing

escritor, a [eskri'tor, a] *nm/f* writer

escritorio [eskri'torjo] *nm* desk

escritura [eskri'tura] *nf (acción)* writing; *(caligrafía)* (hand)writing; *(Jur: documento)* deed

escrúpulo [es'krupulo] *nm* scruple; *(minuciosidad)* scrupulousness; **escrupuloso, -a** *adj* scrupulous

escrutinio [eskru'tinjo] *nm (examen atento)* scrutiny; *(Pol: recuento de votos)* count(ing)

escuadra [es'kwaðra] *nf (Mil etc)* squad; *(Naut)* squadron; *(de coches etc)* fleet; **escuadrilla** *nf (de aviones)* squadron; *(ʌм: de obreros)* gang

escuadrón [eskwa'ðron] *nm* squadron

escuálido, -a [es'kwaliðo, a] *adj* skinny, scraggy; *(sucio)* squalid

escuchar [esku'tʃar] /1a/ *vt* to listen to ▷ *vi* to listen

escudo [es'kuðo] nm shield
escuela [es'kwela] nf school; **~ de artes y oficios** (ESP) ≈ technical college; **~ de choferes** (LAM) driving school; **~ de manejo** (LAM) driving school
escueto, -a [es'kweto, a] adj plain; (estilo) simple
escuincle [es'kwinkle] nm (LAM fam) kid
esculpir [eskul'pir] /3a/ vt to sculpt; (grabar) to engrave; (tallar) to carve; **escultor, a** nm/f sculptor; **escultura** nf sculpture
escupidera [eskupi'ðera] nf spittoon
escupir [esku'pir] /3a/ vt to spit out ▷ vi to spit
▶**escurreplatos** [eskurre'platos] nm inv plate rack
escurridero [eskurri'ðero] nm (LAM) draining board (BRIT), drainboard (US)
escurridizo, -a [eskurri'ðiθo, a] adj slippery
escurridor [eskurri'ðor] nm colander
escurrir [esku'rrir] /3a/ vt (ropa) to wring out; (verduras, platos) to drain ▷ vi (los líquidos) to drip; **escurrirse** vr (secarse) to drain; (resbalarse) to slip, slide; (escaparse) to slip away
ese ['ese], **esa** ['esa], **esos** ['esos], **esas** ['esas] adj demostrativo that sg, those pl ▷ pron that (one) sg, those (ones) pl
ése ['ese], **ésa** ['esa], **ésos** ['esos], **ésas** ['esas] pron that (one) sg, those (ones) pl; **~ ... éste ...** the former ... the latter ...; **¡no me vengas con ésas!** don't give me any more of that nonsense!
esencia [e'senθja] nf essence; **esencial** adj essential
esfera [es'fera] nf sphere; (de reloj) face; **esférico, -a** adj spherical
esforzarse [esfor'θarse] /1f, 1l/ vr to exert o.s., make an effort
esfuerzo [es'fwerθo] vb V **esforzarse** ▷ nm effort

esfumarse [esfu'marse] /1a/ vr (apoyo, esperanzas) to fade away
esgrima [es'ɣrima] nf fencing
esguince [es'ɣinθe] nm (Med) sprain
eslabón [esla'βon] nm link
slip [ez'lip] nm pants pl (BRIT), briefs pl
eslovaco, -a [eslo'βako, a] adj, nm/f Slovak, Slovakian ▷ nm (Ling) Slovak, Slovakian
Eslovaquia [eslo'βakja] nf Slovakia
esmalte [es'malte] nm enamel; **~ de uñas** nail varnish o polish
esmeralda [esme'ralda] nf emerald
esmerarse [esme'rarse] /1a/ vr (aplicarse) to take great pains, exercise great care; (afanarse) to work hard
esmero [es'mero] nm (great) care
esnob [es'nob] adj inv (persona) snobbish ▷ nmf snob
eso ['eso] pron that, that thing o matter; **~ de su coche** that business about his car; **~ de ir al cine** all that about going to the cinema; **a ~ de las cinco** at about five o'clock; **en ~** thereupon, at that point; **~ es** that's it; **¡~ sí que es vida!** now this is really living!; **por ~ te lo dije** that's why I told you; **y ~ que llovía** in spite of the fact it was raining
esos ['esos] adj demostrativo V **ese**
ésos ['esos] pron V **ése**
espacial [espa'θjal] adj (del espacio) space cpd
espaciar [espa'θjar] /1b/ vt to space (out)
espacio [es'paθjo] nm space; (Mus) interval; (Radio, TV) programme, program (us); **el ~** space; **~ aéreo/ exterior** air/outer space; **espacioso, -a** adj spacious, roomy
espada [es'paða] nf sword; **espadas** nfpl (Naipes) one of the suits in the Spanish card deck
espaguetis [espa'ɣetis] nmpl spaghetti sg
espalda [es'palda] nf (gen) back; **~s** nf pl (hombros) shoulders; **a ~s de algn**

behind sb's back; **estar de ~s** to have one's back turned; **tenderse de ~s** to lie (down) on one's back; **volver la ~ a algn** to cold-shoulder sb

espantajo [espan'taxo] nm, **espantapájaros** [espanta'paxaros] nm inv scarecrow

espantar [espan'tar] /1a/ vt (asustar) to frighten, scare; (ahuyentar) to frighten off; (asombrar) to horrify, appal; **espantarse** vr to get frightened o scared; to be appalled

espanto [es'panto] nm (susto) fright; (terror) terror; (asombro) astonishment; **espantoso, -a** adj frightening, terrifying; (ruido) dreadful

España [es'paɲa] nf Spain; **español, a** adj Spanish ▷ nm/f Spaniard ▷ nm (Ling) Spanish

esparadrapo [espara'ðrapo] nm surgical tape

esparcir [espar'θir] /3b/ vt to spread; (derramar) to scatter; **esparcirse** vr to spread (out); to scatter; (divertirse) to enjoy o.s.

espárrago [es'parraɣo] nm asparagus

esparto [es'parto] nm esparto (grass)

espasmo [es'pasmo] nm spasm

espátula [es'patula] nf spatula

especia [es'peθja] nf spice

especial [espe'θjal] adj special; **especialidad** nf speciality, specialty (us)

especie [es'peθje] nf (Bio) species; (clase) kind, sort; **pagar en ~** to pay in kind

especificar [espeθifi'kar] /1g/ vt to specify; **específico, -a** adj specific

espécimen [es'peθimen] (pl **especímenes**) nm specimen

espectáculo [espek'takulo] nm (gen) spectacle; (Teat etc) show

espectador, a [espekta'ðor, a] nm/f spectator

especular [espeku'lar] /1a/ vt, vi to speculate

espejismo [espe'xismo] nm mirage

espejo [es'pexo] nm mirror; **~ retrovisor** rear-view mirror

espeluznante [espeluθ'nante] adj horrifying, hair-raising

espera [es'pera] nf (pausa, intervalo) wait; (Jur: plazo) respite; **en ~ de** waiting for; (con expectativa) expecting

esperanza [espe'ranθa] nf (confianza) hope; (expectativa) expectation; **hay pocas ~s de que venga** there is little prospect of his coming; **~ de vida** life expectancy

esperar [espe'rar] /1a/ vt (aguardar) to wait for; (tener expectativa de) to expect; (desear) to hope for ▷ vi to wait; to expect; to hope; **hacer ~ a algn** to keep sb waiting; **~ un bebé** to be expecting (a baby)

esperma [es'perma] nf sperm

espeso, -a [es'peso, a] adj thick; **espesor** nm thickness

espía [es'pia] nmf spy; **espiar** /1c/ vt (observar) to spy on

espiga [es'piɣa] nf (Bot: de trigo etc) ear

espigón [espi'ɣon] nm (Bot) ear; (Naut) breakwater

espina [es'pina] nf thorn; (de pez) bone; **~ dorsal** (Anat) spine

espinaca [espi'naka] nf spinach

espinazo [espi'naθo] nm spine, backbone

espinilla [espi'niʎa] nf (Anat: tibia) shin(bone); (: en la piel) blackhead

espinoso, -a [espi'noso, a] adj (planta) thorny, prickly; (asunto) difficult

espionaje [espjo'naxe] nm spying, espionage

espiral [espi'ral] adj, nf spiral

espirar [espi'rar] /1a/ vt to breathe out, exhale

espiritista [espiri'tista] adj, nmf spiritualist

espíritu [es'piritu] nm spirit; **E-Santo** Holy Ghost; **espiritual** adj spiritual

espléndido, -a [es'plendiðo, a] adj (magnífico) magnificent, splendid; (generoso) generous

esplendor [esplen'dor] nm splendour

espolvorear [espolβore'ar] /1a/ vt to dust, sprinkle

esponja [es'ponxa] nf sponge; (fig) sponger; **esponjoso, -a** adj spongy

espontaneidad [espontanei'ðað] nf spontaneity; **espontáneo, -a** adj spontaneous

esposa [es'posa] nf V **esposo**; **esposar** /1a/ vt to handcuff

esposo, -a [es'poso, a] nm husband ▷ nf wife; **esposas** nfpl handcuffs

espray [es'prai] nm spray

espuela [es'pwela] nf spur

espuma [es'puma] nf foam; (de cerveza) froth, head; (de jabón) lather; ~ **de afeitar** shaving foam; **espumadera** nf skimmer; **espumoso, -a** adj frothy, foamy; (vino) sparkling

esqueleto [eske'leto] nm skeleton

esquema [es'kema] nm (diagrama) diagram; (dibujo) plan; (Filosofía) schema

esquí [es'ki] (pl **esquís**) nm (objeto) ski; (deporte) skiing; ~ **acuático** water-skiing; **esquiar** /1c/ vi to ski

esquilar [eski'lar] /1a/ vt to shear

esquimal [eski'mal] adj, nmf Eskimo

esquina [es'kina] nf corner; **esquinazo** nm: **dar esquinazo a algn** to give sb the slip

esquirol [eski'rol] nm (ESP) strikebreaker, blackleg

esquivar [eski'βar] /1a/ vt to avoid

esta [esta] adj demostrativo, pron V **este**[1]

está [es'ta] vb V **estar**

ésta [esta] pron V **éste**

estabilidad [estaβili'ðað] nf stability; **estable** adj stable

establecer [estaβle'θer] /2d/ vt to establish; **establecerse** vr to establish o.s.; (echar raíces) to settle (down); **establecimiento** nm establishment

establo [es'taβlo] nm (Agr) stall; (para vacas) cowshed; (para caballos) stable; (esp LAM) barn

estaca [es'taka] nf stake, post; (de tienda de campaña) peg

estacada [esta'kaða] nf (cerca) fence, fencing; (palenque) stockade

estación [esta'θjon] nf station; (del año) season; ~ **de autobuses/ferrocarril** bus/railway station; ~ **balnearia (de turistas)** seaside resort; ~ **de servicio** service station

estacionamiento [estaθjona'mjento] nm (Auto) parking; (Mil) stationing

estacionar [estaθjo'nar] /1a/ vt (Auto) to park; (Mil) to station

estada [es'taða], **estadía** [esta'ðia] nf (LAM) stay

estadio [es'taðjo] nm (fase) stage, phase; (Deporte) stadium

estadista [esta'ðista] nm (Pol) statesman; (Estadística) statistician

estadística [esta'ðistika] nf figure, statistic; (ciencia) statistics sg

estado [es'taðo] nm (Pol: condición) state; ~ **civil** marital status; ~ **de ánimo** state of mind; ~ **de cuenta(s)** bank statement; ~ **mayor** staff; **E-s Unidos (EE.UU.)** United States (of America) (USA); **estar en ~ (de buena esperanza)** to be pregnant

estadounidense [estaðouni'ðense] adj United States cpd, American ▷ nmf American

estafa [es'tafa] nf swindle, trick; **estafar** /1a/ vt to swindle, defraud

estáis vb V **estar**

estallar [esta'ʎar] /1a/ vi to burst; (bomba) to explode, go off; (epidemia, guerra, rebelión) to break out; ~ **en llanto** to burst into tears; **estallido** nm explosion; (fig) outbreak

estampa [es'tampa] nf print, engraving; **estampado, -a** adj printed ▷ nm (dibujo) print; (impresión) printing; **estampar** /1a/ vt (imprimir) to print; (marcar) to stamp; (metal) to engrave; (poner sello en) to stamp; (fig) to stamp, imprint

estampida [estam'piða] nf
stampede

estampido [estam'piðo] nm bang,
report

estampilla [estam'piʎa] nf (LAM)
(postage) stamp

están [es'tan] vb V **estar**

estancado, -a [estan'kaðo, a] adj
stagnant

estancar [estan'kar] /1g/ vt (aguas)
to hold up, hold back; (Com) to
monopolize; (fig) to block, hold up;
estancarse vr to stagnate

estancia [es'tanθja] nf (permanencia)
stay; (sala) room; (LAM) farm, ranch;
estanciero nm (LAM) farmer, rancher

estanco, -a [es'tanko, a] adj
watertight ▷ nm tobacconist's (shop)

○ **ESTANCO**

● Cigarettes, tobacco, postage
● stamps and official forms are all sold
● under state monopoly and usually
● through a shop called an *estanco*.
● Tobacco products are also sold in
● *quioscos* and bars but are generally
● more expensive. The number of
● *estanco* licences is regulated by
● the state.

estándar [es'tandar] adj, nm
standard

estandarte [estan'darte] nm banner,
standard

estanque [es'tanke] nm (lago) pool,
pond; (Agr) reservoir

estanquero, -a [estan'kero, a] nm/f
tobacconist

estante [es'tante] nm (armario) rack,
stand; (biblioteca) bookcase; (anaquel)
shelf; **estantería** nf shelving,
shelves pl

⊙ **PALABRA CLAVE**

estar [es'tar] /1o/ vi **1** (posición) to be;
está en la plaza it's in the square;

¿está Juan? is Juan in?; **estamos a 30
km de Junín** we're 30 km from Junín

2 (+ adj o adv: estado) to be; **estar
enfermo** to be ill; **está muy elegante**
he's looking very smart; **¿cómo
estás?** how are you keeping?

3 (+ gerundio) to be; **estoy leyendo**
I'm reading

4 (uso pasivo): **está condenado a
muerte** he's been condemned to
death; **está envasado en ...** it's
packed in ...

5: **estar a: ¿a cuántos estamos?**
what's the date today?; **estamos a 9
de mayo** it's the 9th of May

6 (locuciones): **¿estamos?** (¿de
acuerdo?) okay?; (¿listo?) ready?

7: **estar con: está con gripe** he's
got (the) flu

8: **estar de: estar de vacaciones/
viaje** to be on holiday/away on a
trip; **está de camarero** he's working
as a waiter

9: **estar para: está para salir**
he's about to leave; **no estoy para
bromas** I'm not in the mood for jokes

10: **estar por** (propuesta etc) to be in
favour of; (persona etc) to support, side
with; **está por limpiar** it still has to
be cleaned

11: **estar sin: estar sin dinero** to have
no money; **está sin terminar** it isn't
finished yet

▷ **estarse** vr: **se estuvo en la cama
toda la tarde** he stayed in bed all
afternoon

estas ['estas] adj demostrativo, pron
V **este¹**

éstas ['estas] pron V **éste**

estatal [esta'tal] adj state cpd

estático, -a [es'tatiko, a] adj static

estatua [es'tatwa] nf statue

estatura [esta'tura] nf stature,
height

este¹ ['este] nm east

este² ['este], **esta** ['esta], **estos**
['estos], **estas** ['estas] adj

demostrativo this *sg*, these *pl* ▷ *pron* this (one) *sg*, these (ones) *pl*

esté [es'te] *vb* V **estar**

éste ['este], **ésta** ['esta], **éstos** ['estos], **éstas** ['estas] *pron* this (one) *sg*, these (ones) *pl*; **éste … ~ …** the former … the latter …

estén [es'ten] *vb* V **estar**

estepa [es'tepa] *nf* (Geo) steppe

estera [es'tera] *nf* matting

estéreo [es'tereo] *adj inv, nm* stereo; **estereotipo** *nm* stereotype

estéril [es'teril] *adj* sterile, barren; (*fig*) vain, futile; **esterilizar** /1f/ *vt* to sterilize

esterlina [ester'lina] *adj*: **libra ~** pound sterling

estés [es'tes] *vb* V **estar**

estético, -a [es'tetiko, a] *adj* aesthetic ▷ *nf* aesthetics *sg*

estiércol [es'tjerkol] *nm* dung, manure

estigma [es'tiɣma] *nm* stigma

estilo [es'tilo] *nm* style; (*Tec*) stylus; (*Natación*) stroke; **algo por el ~** something along those lines

estima [es'tima] *nf* esteem, respect

estimación [estima'θjon] *nf* (*evaluación*) estimation; (*aprecio, afecto*) esteem, regard

estimulante [estimu'lante] *adj* stimulating ▷ *nm* stimulant

estimular [estimu'lar] /1a/ *vt* to stimulate; (*excitar*) to excite

estímulo [es'timulo] *nm* stimulus; (*ánimo*) encouragement

estirar [esti'rar] /1a/ *vt* to stretch; (*dinero, suma etc*) to stretch out; **estirarse** *vr* to stretch

estirón [esti'ron] *nm* pull, tug; (*crecimiento*) spurt, sudden growth; **dar un ~** (*niño*) to shoot up

estirpe [es'tirpe] *nf* stock, lineage

estival [esti'βal] *adj* summer *cpd*

esto ['esto] *pron* this, this thing *o* matter; **~ de la boda** this business about the wedding

Estocolmo [esto'kolmo] *nm* Stockholm

estofado [esto'faðo] *nm* stew

estómago [es'tomaɣo] *nm* stomach; **tener ~** to be thick-skinned

estorbar [estor'βar] /1a/ *vt* to hinder, obstruct; (*fig*) to bother, disturb ▷ *vi* to be in the way; **estorbo** *nm* (*molestia*) bother, nuisance; (*obstáculo*) hindrance, obstacle

estornudar [estornu'ðar] /1a/ *vi* to sneeze

estos ['estos] *adj demostrativo* V **este¹**

éstos ['estos] *pron* V **éste**

estoy [es'toi] *vb* V **estar**

estrado [es'traðo] *nm* platform

estrafalario, -a [estrafa'larjo, a] *adj* odd, eccentric

estrago [es'traɣo] *nm* ruin, destruction; **hacer ~s en** to wreak havoc among

estragón [estra'ɣon] *nm* tarragon

estrambótico, -a [estram'botiko, a] *adj* odd, eccentric; (*peinado, ropa*) outlandish

estrangular [estraŋgu'lar] /1a/ *vt* (*persona*) to strangle; (*Med*) to strangulate

estratagema [estrata'xema] *nf* (Mil) stratagem; (*astucia*) cunning

estrategia [estra'texja] *nf* strategy; **estratégico, -a** *adj* strategic

estrato [es'trato] *nm* stratum, layer

estrechar [estre'tʃar] /1a/ *vt* (*reducir*) to narrow; (*vestido*) to take in; (*persona*) to hug, embrace; **estrecharse** *vr* (*reducirse*) to grow narrow; (2 *personas*) to embrace; **~ la mano** to shake hands

estrechez [estre'tʃeθ] *nf* narrowness; (*de ropa*) tightness; **estrecheces** *nfpl* financial difficulties

estrecho, -a [es'tretʃo, a] *adj* narrow; (*apretado*) tight; (*íntimo*) close,

intimate; (*miserable*) mean ▷ *nm* strait;
~ de miras narrow-minded

estrella [es'treʎa] *nf* star; **~ fugaz**
shooting star; **~ de mar** starfish

estrellar [estre'ʎar] /1a/ *vt* (*hacer
añicos*) to smash (to pieces); (*huevos*) to
fry; **estrellarse** *vr* to smash; (*chocarse*)
to crash; (*fracasar*) to fail

estremecer [estreme'θer] /2d/ *vt*
to shake; **estremecerse** *vr* to shake,
tremble

estrenar [estre'nar] /1a/ *vt* (*vestido*)
to wear for the first time; (*casa*) to
move into; (*película, obra de teatro*) to
première; **estrenarse** *vr* (*persona*) to
make one's début; **estreno** *nm* (*Cine
etc*) première

estreñido, -a [estre'ɲiðo, a] *adj*
constipated

estreñimiento [estreɲi'mjento] *nm*
constipation

estrepitoso, -a [estrepi'toso, a] *adj*
noisy; (*fiesta*) rowdy

estrés [es'tres] *nm* stress

estría [es'tria] *nf* groove

estribar [estri'βar] /1a/ *vi*: **~ en** to
rest on

estribillo [estri'βiʎo] *nm* (*Lit*) refrain;
(*Mus*) chorus

estribo [es'triβo] *nm* (*de jinete*)
stirrup; (*de coche, tren*) step; (*de puente*)
support; (*Geo*) spur; **perder los ~s** to
fly off the handle

estribor [estri'βor] *nm* (*Naut*)
starboard

estricto, -a [es'trikto, a] *adj* (*riguroso*)
strict; (*severo*) severe

estridente [estri'ðente] *adj* (*color*)
loud; (*voz*) raucous

estropajo [estro'paxo] *nm* scourer

estropear [estrope'ar] /1a/ *vt* to
spoil; (*dañar*) to damage; **estropearse**
vr (*objeto*) to get damaged; (*la piel etc*)
to be ruined

estructura [estruk'tura] *nf* structure

estrujar [estru'xar] /1a/ *vt* (*apretar*)
to squeeze; (*aplastar*) to crush; (*fig*) to
drain, bleed

estuario [es'twarjo] *nm* estuary

estuche [es'tutʃe] *nm* box, case

estudiante [estu'ðjante] *nmf*
student; **estudiantil** *adj inv* student
cpd

estudiar [estu'ðjar] /1b/ *vt* to study

estudio [es'tuðjo] *nm* study; (*Cine,
Arte, Radio*) studio; **estudios** *nmpl*
studies; (*erudición*) learning *sg*;
estudioso, -a *adj* studious

estufa [es'tufa] *nf* heater, fire

estupefaciente [estupefa'θjente]
nm narcotic

estupefacto, -a [estupe'fakto, a]
adj speechless, thunderstruck

estupendo, -a [estu'pendo, a] *adj*
wonderful, terrific; (*fam*) great; **¡~!**
that's great!, fantastic!

estupidez [estupi'ðeθ] *nf* (*torpeza*)
stupidity; (*acto*) stupid thing (to do)

estúpido, -a [es'tupiðo, a] *adj*
stupid, silly

estuve *etc* [es'tuβe] *vb* V **estar**

ETA ['eta] *nf abr* (*Pol*: = *Euskadi Ta
Askatasuna*) ETA

etapa [e'tapa] *nf* (*de viaje*) stage;
(*Deporte*) (*parada*) stopping place;
(*fig*) stage, phase

etarra [e'tarra] *nmf* member of ETA

etc. *abr* (= *etcétera*) etc

etcétera [et'θetera] *adv* etcetera

eternidad [eterni'ðað] *nf* eternity;
eterno, -a *adj* eternal, everlasting;
(*despectivo*) never-ending

ético, -a ['etiko, a] *adj* ethical ▷ *nf*
ethics

etiqueta [eti'keta] *nf* (*modales*)
etiquette; (*rótulo*) label, tag

Eucaristía [eukaris'tia] *nf* Eucharist

euforia [eu'forja] *nf* euphoria

euro ['euro] *nm* (*moneda*) euro

eurodiputado, -a [euroðipu'taðo,
a] *nm/f* Euro MP, MEP

Europa [eu'ropa] *nf* Europe; **europeo,
-a** *adj, nm/f* European

Euskadi [eus'kaði] *nm* the Basque
Provinces *pl*

euskera [eus'kera] *nm* (*Ling*) Basque

evacuación [eβakwa'θjon] nf evacuation

evacuar [eβa'kwar] /1d/ vt to evacuate

evadir [eβa'ðir] /3a/ vt to evade, avoid; **evadirse** vr to escape

evaluar [eβa'lwar] /1e/ vt to evaluate

evangelio [eβan'xeljo] nm gospel

evaporar [eβapo'rar] /1a/ vt to evaporate; **evaporarse** vr to vanish

evasión [eβa'sjon] nf escape, flight; (fig) evasion; **~ de capitales** flight of capital

evasivo, -a [eβa'siβo, a] adj evasive ▷ nf (pretexto) excuse; **contestar con evasivas** to avoid giving a straight answer

evento [e'βento] nm event

eventual [eβen'twal] adj possible, conditional (upon circumstances); (cambio) change; (trabajador) casual, temporary

▍ No confundir eventual con la palabra inglesa eventual.

evidencia [eβi'ðenθja] nf evidence, proof

evidente [eβi'ðente] adj obvious, clear, evident

evitar [eβi'tar] /1a/ vt (evadir) to avoid; (impedir) to prevent; **~ hacer algo** to avoid doing sth

evocar [eβo'kar] /1g/ vt to evoke, call forth

evolución [eβolu'θjon] nf (desarrollo) evolution, development; (cambio) change; (Mil) manoeuvre; **evolucionar** /1a/ vi to evolve; (Mil, Aviat) to manoeuvre

ex [eks] adj ex-; **el ex ministro** the former minister, the ex-minister

exactitud [eksakti'tuð] nf exactness; (precisión) accuracy; (puntualidad) punctuality; **exacto, -a** (puntualidad) accurate; punctual; **¡exacto!** exactly!

exageración [eksaxera'θjon] nf exaggeration

exagerar [eksaxe'rar] /1a/ vt to exaggerate

exaltar [eksal'tar] /1a/ vt to exalt, glorify; **exaltarse** vr (excitarse) to get excited o worked up

examen [ek'samen] nm examination; **~ de conducir** driving test; **~ de ingreso** entrance examination

examinar [eksami'nar] /1a/ vt to examine; **examinarse** vr to be examined, take an examination

excavadora [ekskaβa'ðora] nf digger

excavar [ekska'βar] /1a/ vt to excavate

excedencia [eksθe'ðenθja] nf (Mil) leave; **estar en ~** to be on leave; **pedir o solicitar la ~** to ask for leave

excedente [eksθe'ðente] adj, nm excess, surplus

exceder [eksθe'ðer] /2a/ vt to exceed, surpass; **excederse** vr (extralimitarse) to go too far

excelencia [eksθe'lenθja] nf excellence; **E~** Excellency; **excelente** adj excellent

excéntrico, -a [eks'θentriko, a] adj, nm/f eccentric

excepción [eksθep'θjon] nf exception; **a ~ de** with the exception of, except for; **excepcional** adj exceptional

excepto [eks'θepto] adv excepting, except (for)

exceptuar [eksθep'twar] /1e/ vt to except, exclude

excesivo, -a [eksθe'siβo, a] adj excessive

exceso [eks'θeso] nm excess; (Com) surplus; **~ de equipaje/peso** excess luggage/weight; **~ de velocidad** speeding

excitado, -a [eksθi'taðo, a] adj excited; (emociones) aroused

excitar [eksθi'tar] /1a/ vt to excite; (incitar) to urge; **excitarse** vr to get excited

exclamación [eksklama'θjon] nf exclamation

exclamar [ekskla'mar] /1a/ vi to exclaim

excluir [eksklu'ir] /3g/ vt to exclude; (dejar fuera) to shut out; (solución) to reject

exclusiva [eksklu'siβa] nf V **exclusivo**

exclusivo, -a [eksklu'siβo, a] adj exclusive ▷ nf (Prensa) exclusive, scoop; (Com) sole right o agency; **derecho ~** sole o exclusive right

Excmo. abr (= Excelentísimo) courtesy title

excomulgar [eskomul'ɣar] /1h/ vt (Rel) to excommunicate

excomunión [eskomu'njon] nf excommunication

excursión [ekskur'sjon] nf excursion, outing; **excursionista** nmf (turista) sightseer

excusa [eks'kusa] nf excuse; (disculpa) apology; **excusar** /1a/ vt to excuse

exhaustivo, -a [eksaus'tiβo, a] adj (análisis) thorough; (estudio) exhaustive

exhausto, -a [ek'sausto, a] adj exhausted

exhibición [eksiβi'θjon] nf exhibition; (demostración) display, show

exhibir [eksi'βir] /3a/ vt to exhibit; to display, show

exigencia [eksi'xenθja] nf demand, requirement; **exigente** adj demanding

exigir [eksi'xir] /3c/ vt (gen) to demand, require; **~ el pago** to demand payment

exiliado, -a [eksi'ljaðo, a] adj exiled ▷ nm/f exile

exilio [ek'siljo] nm exile

eximir [eksi'mir] /3a/ vt to exempt

existencia [eksis'tenθja] nf existence; **existencias** nfpl stock sg

existir [eksis'tir] /3a/ vi to exist, be

éxito [ˈeksito] nm (triunfo) success; (Mus, Teat) hit; **tener ~** to be successful

No confundir **éxito** con la palabra inglesa exit.

exorbitante [eksorβi'tante] adj (precio) exorbitant; (cantidad) excessive

exótico, -a [ek'sotiko, a] adj exotic

expandir [ekspan'dir] /3a/ vt to expand

expansión [ekspan'sjon] nf expansion

expansivo, -a [ekspan'siβo, a] adj: **onda expansiva** shock wave

expatriarse [ekspa'trjarse] /1b/ vr to emigrate; (Pol) to go into exile

expectativa [ekspekta'tiβa] nf (espera) expectation; (perspectiva) prospect

expedición [ekspeði'θjon] nf (excursión) expedition

expediente [ekspe'ðjente] nm expedient; (Jur: procedimiento) action, proceedings pl; (: papeles) dossier, file, record

expedir [ekspe'ðir] /3k/ vt (despachar) to send, forward; (pasaporte) to issue

expensas [eks'pensas] nfpl: **a ~ de** at the expense of

experiencia [ekspe'rjenθja] nf experience

experimentado, -a [eksperimen'taðo, a] adj experienced

experimentar [eksperimen'tar] /1a/ vt (en laboratorio) to experiment with; (probar) to test, try out; (notar, observar) to experience; (deterioro, pérdida) to suffer; **experimento** nm experiment

experto, -a [eks'perto, a] adj expert ▷ nm/f expert

expirar [ekspi'rar] /1a/ vi to expire

explanada [ekspla'naða] nf (paseo) esplanade

explayarse [ekspla'jarse] /1a/ vr (en discurso) to speak at length; **~ con algn** to confide in sb

explicación [eksplika'θjon] nf explanation

explicar [ekspli'kar] /1g/ vt to explain; **explicarse** vr to explain (o.s.)

explícito, -a [eks'pliθito, a] *adj* explicit

explique *etc* [eks'plike] *vb* V **explicar**

explorador, a [eksplora'ðor, a] *nm/f (pionero)* explorer; *(Mil)* scout ▷ *nm (Med)* probe; *(radar)* radar scanner

explorar [eksplo'rar] /1a/ *vt* to explore; *(Med)* to probe; *(radar)* to scan

explosión [eksplo'sjon] *nf* explosion; **explosivo, -a** *adj* explosive

explotación [eksplota'θjon] *nf* exploitation; *(de planta etc)* running

explotar [eksplo'tar] /1a/ *vt* to exploit; *(planta)* to run, operate ▷ *vi* to explode

exponer [ekspo'ner] /2q/ *vt* to expose; *(cuadro)* to display; *(vida)* to risk; *(idea)* to explain; **exponerse** *vr:* **~se a (hacer) algo** to run the risk of (doing) sth

exportación [eksporta'θjon] *nf (acción)* export; *(mercancías)* exports *pl*

exportar [ekspor'tar] /1a/ *vt* to export

exposición [eksposi'θjon] *nf (gen)* exposure; *(de arte)* show, exhibition; *(explicación)* explanation; *(narración)* account, statement

expresamente [ekspresa'mente] *adv (decir)* clearly; *(concretamente)* expressly

expresar [ekspre'sar] /1a/ *vt* to express; **expresión** *nf* expression

expresivo, -a [ekspre'siβo, a] *adj* expressive; *(cariñoso)* affectionate

expreso, -a [eks'preso, a] *adj (explícito)* express; *(claro)* specific, clear; *(tren)* fast

express [eks'pres] *adv* (LAM): **enviar algo ~** to send sth special delivery

exprimidor [eksprimi'ðor] *nm* (lemon) squeezer

exprimir [ekspri'mir] /3a/ *vt (fruta)* to squeeze; *(zumo)* to squeeze out

expuesto, -a [eks'pwesto, a] *pp de* **exponer** ▷ *adj* exposed; *(cuadro etc)* on show, on display

expulsar [ekspul'sar] /1a/ *vt (echar)* to eject, throw out; *(alumno)* to expel; *(despedir)* to sack, fire; *(Deporte)* to send off; **expulsión** *nf* expulsion; sending-off

exquisito, -a [ekski'sito, a] *adj* exquisite; *(comida)* delicious

éxtasis ['ekstasis] *nm* ecstasy

extender [eksten'der] /2g/ *vt* to extend; *(los brazos)* to stretch out; hold out; *(mapa, tela)* to spread (out), open (out); *(mantequilla)* to spread; *(certificado)* to issue; *(cheque, recibo)* to make out; *(documento)* to draw up; **extenderse** *vr* to extend; *(persona: en el suelo)* to stretch out; *(costumbre, epidemia)* to spread; **extendido, -a** *adj (abierto)* spread out, open; *(brazos)* outstretched; *(costumbre etc)* widespread

extensión [eksten'sjon] *nf (de terreno, mar)* expanse, stretch; *(de tiempo)* length, duration; *(Telec)* extension; **en toda la ~ de la palabra** in every sense of the word

extenso, -a [eks'tenso, a] *adj* extensive

exterior [ekste'rjor] *adj (de fuera)* external; *(afuera)* outside, exterior; *(apariencia)* outward; *(deuda, relaciones)* foreign ▷ *nm* exterior, outside; *(aspecto)* outward appearance; *(Deporte)* wing(er); *(países extranjeros)* abroad; **al ~** outwardly, on the outside

exterminar [ekstermi'nar] /1a/ *vt* to exterminate

externo, -a [eks'terno, a] *adj (exterior)* external, outside; *(superficial)* outward ▷ *nm/f* day pupil

extinguir [ekstin'gir] /3d/ *vt (fuego)* to extinguish, put out; *(raza, población)* to wipe out; **extinguirse** *vr (fuego)* to go out; *(Bio)* to die out, become extinct

extintor [ekstin'tor] *nm* (fire) extinguisher

extirpar [ekstir'par] /1a/ *vt (Med)* to remove (surgically)

extra ['ekstra] *adj inv (tiempo)* extra; *(vino)* vintage; *(chocolate)* good-quality ▷ *nmf* extra ▷ *nm* extra; *(bono)* bonus

extracción [ekstrak'θjon] *nf* extraction; *(en lotería)* draw

extracto [eks'trakto] *nm* extract

extradición [ekstraði'θjon] *nf* extradition

extraer [ekstra'er] /2o/ *vt* to extract, take out

extraescolar [ekstraesko'lar] *adj*: **actividad ~** extracurricular activity

extranjero, -a [ekstran'xero, a] *adj* foreign ▷ *nm/f* foreigner ▷ *nm* foreign countries *pl*; **en el ~** abroad

> No confundir *extranjero* con la palabra inglesa *stranger*.

extrañar [ekstra'ɲar] /1a/ *vt (sorprender)* to find strange o odd; *(echar de menos)* to miss; **extrañarse** *vr (sorprenderse)* to be amazed, be surprised; **me extraña** I'm surprised

extraño, -a [eks'traɲo, a] *adj (extranjero)* foreign; *(raro, sorprendente)* strange, odd

extraordinario, -a [ekstraorði'narjo, a] *adj* extraordinary; *(edición, número)* special ▷ *nm (de periódico)* special edition; **horas extraordinarias** overtime *sg*

extrarradio [ekstra'rraðjo] *nm* suburbs *pl*

extravagante [ekstraβa'ɣante] *adj (excéntrico)* eccentric; *(estrafalario)* outlandish

extraviado, -a [ekstra'βjaðo, a] *adj* lost, missing

extraviar [ekstra'βjar] /1c/ *vt* to mislead, misdirect; *(perder)* to lose, misplace; **extraviarse** *vr* to lose one's way, get lost

extremar [ekstre'mar] /1a/ *vt* to carry to extremes

extremaunción [ekstremaun'θjon] *nf* extreme unction

extremidad [ekstremi'ðað] *nf (punta)* extremity; **extremidades** *nfpl (Anat)* extremities

extremo, -a [eks'tremo, a] *adj* extreme; *(último)* last ▷ *nm* end; *(situación)* extreme; **en último ~** as a last resort

extrovertido, -a [ekstroβer'tiðo, a] *adj* ▷ *nm/f* extrovert

exuberante [eksuβe'rante] *adj* exuberant; *(fig)* luxuriant, lush

eyacular [ejaku'lar] /1a/ *vt, vi* to ejaculate

f

fa [fa] *nm* (*Mus*) F

fabada [fa'βaða] *nf* bean and sausage stew

fábrica ['faβrika] *nf* factory; **marca de ~** trademark; **precio de ~** factory price

> No confundir *fábrica* con la palabra inglesa *fabric*.

fabricación [faβrika'θjon] *nf* (*manufactura*) manufacture; (*producción*) production; **de ~ casera** home-made; **~ en serie** mass production

fabricante [faβri'kante] *nmf* manufacturer

fabricar [faβri'kar] /1g/ *vt* (*manufacturar*) to manufacture, make; (*construir*) to build; (*cuento*) to fabricate, devise

fábula ['faβula] *nf* (*cuento*) fable; (*chisme*) rumour; (*mentira*) fib

fabuloso, -a [faβu'loso, a] *adj* fabulous, fantastic

facción [fak'θjon] *nf* (*Pol*) faction; **facciones** *nfpl* (*del rostro*) features

faceta [fa'θeta] *nf* facet

facha ['fatʃa] (*fam*) *nf* (*aspecto*) look; (*cara*) face

fachada [fa'tʃaða] *nf* (*Arq*) façade, front

fácil ['faθil] *adj* (*simple*) easy; (*probable*) likely

facilidad [faθili'ðað] *nf* (*capacidad*) ease; (*sencillez*) simplicity; (*de palabra*) fluency; **facilidades** *nfpl* facilities; **"~es de pago"** "credit facilities"

facilitar [faθili'tar] /1a/ *vt* (*hacer fácil*) to make easy; (*proporcionar*) to provide

factor [fak'tor] *nm* factor

factura [fak'tura] *nf* (*cuenta*) bill; **facturación** *nf*: **facturación de equipajes** luggage check-in; **facturar** /1a/ *vt* (*Com*) to invoice, charge for; (*Aviat*) to check in

facultad [fakul'tað] *nf* (*aptitud, Escol etc*) faculty; (*poder*) power

faena [fa'ena] *nf* (*trabajo*) work; (*quehacer*) task, job

faisán [fai'san] *nm* pheasant

faja ['faxa] *nf* (*para la cintura*) sash; (*de mujer*) corset; (*de tierra*) strip

fajo ['faxo] *nm* (*de papeles*) bundle; (*de billetes*) wad

falda ['falda] *nf* (*prenda de vestir*) skirt; **~ pantalón** culottes *pl*, split skirt

falla ['faʎa] *nf* (*defecto*) fault, flaw; **~ humana** (*Am*) human error

fallar [fa'ʎar] /1a/ *vt* (*Jur*) to pronounce sentence on; (*Naipes*) to trump ▷ *vi* (*memoria*) to fail; (*plan*) to go wrong; (*motor*) to miss; **~ a algn** to let sb down

Fallas ['faʎas] *nfpl* see note **"Fallas"**

○ **FALLAS**

○
○ In the week of the 19th of March
○ (the feast of St Joseph, San José),
○ Valencia honours its patron
○ saint with a spectacular *fiesta*
○ called *las Fallas*. The *Fallas* are

- huge sculptures, made of wood,
- cardboard, paper and cloth,
- depicting famous politicians and
- other targets for ridicule, which are
- set alight and burned by the *falleros*,
- members of the competing local
- groups who have just spent months
- preparing them.

fallecer [faʎe'θer] /2d/ vi to pass away, die; **fallecimiento** nm decease, demise

fallido, -a [fa'ʎiðo, a] adj frustrated, unsuccessful

fallo ['faʎo] nm (Jur) verdict, ruling; (fracaso) failure; ~ **cardíaco** heart failure; ~ **humano** (ESP) human error

falsificar [falsifi'kar] /1g/ vt (firma etc) to forge; (moneda) to counterfeit

falso, -a ['falso, a] adj false; (moneda etc) fake; **en ~** falsely

falta ['falta] nf (defecto) fault, flaw; (privación) lack, want; (ausencia) absence; (carencia) shortage; (equivocación) mistake; (Deporte) foul; **echar en ~** to miss; **hacer ~** **hacer algo** to be necessary to do sth; **me hace ~ una pluma** I need a pen; ~ **de educación** bad manners pl; ~ **de ortografía** spelling mistake

faltar [fal'tar] /1a/ vi (escasear) to be lacking, be wanting; (ausentarse) to be absent, be missing; **faltan dos horas para llegar** there are two hours to go till arrival; ~ **(al respeto) a algn** to be disrespectful to sb; **¡no faltaba más!** (no hay de qué) don't mention it!

fama ['fama] nf (renombre) fame; (reputación) reputation

familia [fa'milja] nf family; ~ **numerosa** large family; ~ **política** in-laws pl

familiar [fami'ljar] adj (relativo a la familia) family cpd; (conocido, informal) familiar ▷ nmf relative, relation

famoso, -a [fa'moso, a] adj famous ▷ nm/f celebrity

fan [fan] (pl **fans**) nm fan

fanático, -a [fa'natiko, a] adj fanatical ▷ nm/f fanatic; (Cine, Deporte etc) fan

fanfarrón, -ona [fanfa'rron, ona] adj boastful

fango ['fango] nm mud

fantasía [fanta'sia] nf fantasy, imagination; **joyas de ~** imitation jewellery sg

fantasma [fan'tasma] nm (espectro) ghost, apparition; (presumido) show-off

fantástico, -a [fan'tastiko, a] adj fantastic

farmacéutico, -a [farma'θeutiko, a] adj pharmaceutical ▷ nm/f chemist (BRIT), pharmacist

farmacia [far'maθja] nf chemist's (shop) (BRIT), pharmacy; ~ **de guardia** all-night chemist

fármaco [farmako] nm drug

faro ['faro] nm (Naut: torre) lighthouse; (Auto) headlamp; ~**s antiniebla** fog lamps; ~**s delanteros/traseros** headlights/rear lights

farol [fa'rol] nm lantern, lamp

farola [fa'rola] nf street lamp (BRIT) o light (US)

farra ['farra] nf (LAM fam) party; **ir de ~** to go on a binge

farsa ['farsa] nf farce

farsante [far'sante] nmf fraud, fake

fascículo [fas'θikulo] nm part, instalment (BRIT), installment (US)

fascinar [fasθi'nar] /1a/ vt to fascinate

fascismo [fas'θismo] nm fascism; **fascista** adj, nmf fascist

fase ['fase] nf phase

fashion ['faʃon] adj (fam) trendy

fastidiar [fasti'ðjar] /1b/ vt (disgustar) to annoy, bother; (estropear) to spoil; **fastidiarse** vr: **¡que se fastidie!** (fam) he'll just have to put up with it!

fastidio [fas'tiðjo] nm (disgusto) annoyance; **fastidioso, -a** adj (molesto) annoying

fatal [fa'tal] adj (gen) fatal; (desgraciado) ill-fated; (fam: malo, pésimo) awful; **fatalidad** nf (destino) fate; (mala suerte) misfortune

fatiga [fa'tiɣa] nf (cansancio) fatigue, weariness

fatigar [fati'ɣar] /1h/ vt to tire, weary

fatigoso, -a [fati'ɣoso, a] adj (que cansa) tiring

fauna [fauna] nf fauna

favor [fa'βor] nm favour (BRIT), favor (US); **haga el - de ...** would you be so good as to ..., kindly ...; **por ~** please; **a ~ de** in favo(u)r of; **favorable** adj favourable (BRIT), favorable (US)

favorecer [faβore'θer] /2d/ vt to favour (BRIT), favor (US); (vestido etc) to become, flatter; **este peinado le favorece** this hairstyle suits him

favorito, -a [faβo'rito, a] adj, nm/f favourite (BRIT), favorite (US)

fax [faks] nm inv fax; **mandar por ~** to fax

fe [fe] nf (Rel) faith; (documento) certificate; **actuar con buena/mala fe** to act in good/bad faith

febrero [fe'βrero] nm February

fecha ['fetʃa] nf date; **~ límite** o **tope** closing o last date; **~ de caducidad** (de alimentos) sell-by date; (de contrato) expiry date; **con ~ adelantada** postdated; **en ~ próxima** soon; **hasta la ~ to** date, so far

fecundo, -a [fe'kundo, a] adj (fértil) fertile; (fig) prolific; (productivo) productive

federación [feðera'θjon] nf federation

felicidad [feliθi'ðað] nf happiness; **felicidades** nfpl best wishes, congratulations; (en cumpleaños) happy birthday

felicitación [feliθita'θjon] nf (tarjeta) greetings card

felicitar [feliθi'tar] /1a/ vt to congratulate

feliz [fe'liθ] adj happy

felpudo [fel'puðo] nm doormat

femenino, -a [feme'nino, a] adj ▷ nm feminine

feminista [femi'nista] adj, nmf feminist

fenomenal [fenome'nal] adj phenomenal

fenómeno [fe'nomeno] nm phenomenon; (fig) freak, accident ▷ excl great!, marvellous!

feo, -a ['feo, a] adj (gen) ugly; (desagradable) bad, nasty

féretro ['feretro] nm (ataúd) coffin; (sarcófago) bier

feria ['ferja] nf (gen) fair; (descanso) holiday, rest day; (LAM: cambio) small change; (LAM: mercado) village market

feriado, -a [fe'rjaðo, a] (LAM) nm (public) holiday

fermentar [fermen'tar] /1a/ vi to ferment

feroz [fe'roθ] adj (cruel) cruel; (salvaje) fierce

férreo, -a ['ferreo, a] adj iron cpd

ferretería [ferrete'ria] nf (tienda) ironmonger's (shop) (BRIT), hardware store; **ferretero** nm ironmonger

ferrocarril [ferroka'rril] nm railway

ferroviario, -a [ferrovja'rjo, a] adj rail cpd

ferry ['ferri] (pl **ferrys** o **ferries**) nm ferry

fértil ['fertil] adj (productivo) fertile; (rico) rich; **fertilidad** nf (gen) fertility; (productividad) fruitfulness

fervor [fer'βor] nm fervour (BRIT), fervor (US)

festejar [feste'xar] /1a/ vt (celebrar) to celebrate

festejo [fes'texo] nm celebration; **festejos** nmpl (fiestas) festivals

festín [fes'tin] nm feast, banquet

festival [festi'βal] nm festival

festividad [festiβi'ðað] nf festivity

festivo, -a [fes'tiβo, a] adj (de fiesta) festive; (Cine, Lit) humorous; **día ~** holiday

feto ['feto] nm foetus

fiable [fi'aβle] adj (persona) trustworthy; (máquina) reliable

fiambre ['fjambre] nm (Culin) cold meat (BRIT), cold cut (US)

fiambrera [fjam'brera] nf = lunch box

fianza ['fjanθa] nf surety; (Jur): **libertad bajo ~** release on bail

fiar [fi'ar] /1c/ vt (salir garante de) to guarantee; (vender a crédito) to sell on credit; (secreto) to confide ▷ vi: **~ (de)** to trust (in); **fiarse** vr: **~se de** to trust (in), rely on; **~se de algn** to rely on sb

fibra ['fiβra] nf fibre (BRIT), fiber (US); **~ óptica** (Inform) optical fibre (BRIT) o fiber (US)

ficción [fik'θjon] nf fiction

ficha ['fitʃa] nf (Telec) token; (en juegos) counter, marker; (tarjeta) (index) card; **fichaje** nm signing-up; **fichar** /1a/ vt (archivar) to file, index; (Deporte) to sign (up); **estar fichado** to have a record; **fichero** nm box file; (Inform) file

ficticio, -a [fik'tiθjo, a] adj (imaginario) fictitious; (falso) fabricated

fidelidad [fiðeli'ðað] nf (lealtad) fidelity, loyalty; **alta ~** high fidelity, hi-fi

fideos [fi'ðeos] nmpl noodles

fiebre ['fjeβre] nf (Med) fever; (fig) fever, excitement; **tener ~** to have a temperature; **~ aftosa** foot-and-mouth disease

fiel [fjel] adj (leal) faithful, loyal; (fiable) reliable; (exacto) accurate; **los fieles** nmpl the faithful

fieltro ['fjeltro] nm felt

fiera ['fjera] nf V **fiero**

fiero, -a ['fjero, a] adj (cruel) cruel; (feroz) fierce; (duro) harsh ▷ nf (animal feroz) wild animal o beast; (fig) dragon

fierro ['fjerro] nm (LAM) iron

fiesta ['fjesta] nf party; (de pueblo) festival; **(día de) ~** (public) holiday; **~ mayor** annual festival; **~ patria** (LAM) independence day

○ **FIESTA**

● *Fiestas* can be official public holidays
● (such as the *Día de la Constitución*), or

● special holidays for each *comunidad*
● *autónoma*, many of which are
● religious feast days. All over Spain
● there are also special local *fiestas* for
● a patron saint or the Virgin Mary.
● These often last several days and
● can include religious processions,
● carnival parades, bullfights,
● dancing and feasts of typical local
● produce.

figura [fi'ɣura] nf (gen) figure; (forma, imagen) shape, form; (Naipes) face card

figurar [fiɣu'rar] /1a/ vt (representar) to represent; (fingir) to feign ▷ vi to figure; **figurarse** vr (imaginarse) to imagine; (suponer) to suppose

fijador [fixa'ðor] nm (Foto etc) fixative; (de pelo) gel

fijar [fi'xar] /1a/ vt (gen) to fix; (estampilla) to affix, stick (on); **fijarse** vr: **~se en** to notice

fijo, -a ['fixo, a] adj (gen) fixed; (firme) firm; (permanente) permanent ▷ adv: **mirar ~** to stare; **teléfono ~** landline

fila ['fila] nf row; (Mil) rank; **~ india** single file; **ponerse en ~** to line up, get into line

filatelia [fila'telja] nf philately, stamp collecting

filete [fi'lete] nm (de carne) fillet steak; (pescado) fillet

filiación [filja'θjon] nf (Pol etc) affiliation

filial [fi'ljal] adj filial ▷ nf subsidiary

Filipinas [fili'pinas] nfpl: **las (Islas) ~** the Philippines; **filipino, -a** adj, nm/f Philippine

filmar [fil'mar] /1a/ vt to film, shoot

filo ['filo] nm (gen) edge; **sacar ~ a** to sharpen; **al ~ del medio día** at about midday; **de doble ~** double-edged

filología [filolo'xia] nf philology; **~ inglesa** (Univ) English Studies

filón [fi'lon] nm (Minería) vein, lode; (fig) gold mine

filosofía [filoso'fia] nf philosophy

filósofo, -a nm/f philosopher

filtrar [fil'trar] /1a/ vt, vi to filter, strain; **filtrarse** vr to filter; **filtro** nm (Tec, utensilio) filter

fin [fin] nm (end; (objetivo) aim, purpose; **al ~ y al cabo** when all's said and done; **a ~ de** in order to; **por ~** finally; **en ~** in short; **~ de semana** weekend

final [fi'nal] adj final ▷ nm end, conclusion ▷ nf final; **al ~** in the end; **a ~es de** at the end of the; **finalidad** nf (propósito) purpose, aim; **finalista** nmf finalist; **finalizar** /1f/ vt to end, finish ▷ vi to end, come to an end; (Inform) to log out or off

financiar [finan'θjar] /1b/ vt to finance; **financiero, -a** adj financial ▷ nm/f financier

finca ['finka] nf (casa de recreo) house in the country; (ESP: bien inmueble) property, land; (LAM: granja) farm

finde ['finde] nm abr (fam: = fin de semana) weekend

fingir [fin'xir] /3c/ vt (simular) to simulate, feign ▷ vi (aparentar) to pretend

finlandés, -esa [finlan'des, esa] adj Finnish ▷ nm/f Finn ▷ nm (Ling) Finnish

Finlandia [fin'landja] nf Finland

fino, -a ['fino, a] adj fine; (delgado) slender; (de buenas maneras) polite, refined; (jerez) fino, dry

firma ['firma] nf signature; (Com) firm, company

firmamento [firma'mento] nm firmament

firmar [fir'mar] /1a/ vt to sign

firme ['firme] adj firm; (estable) stable; (sólido) solid; (constante) steady; (resoluto) resolute ▷ nm road (surface); **firmeza** nf firmness; (constancia) steadiness; (solidez) solidity

fiscal [fis'kal] adj fiscal ▷ nm (Jur) public prosecutor; **año ~** tax o fiscal year

fisgar [fis'ɣar] /1h/ vt to poke about in, pry, spy

físico, -a ['fisiko, a] adj physical ▷ nm physique ▷ nm/f physicist ▷ nf physics sg

fisura [fi'sura] nf crack; (Med) fracture

flácido, -a ['flakθiðo, a] adj flabby

flaco, -a ['flako, a] adj (muy delgado) skinny, thin; (débil) weak, feeble

flagrante [fla'ɣrante] adj flagrant

flama ['flama] nf (LAM) flame; **flamable** adj (LAM) flammable

flamante [fla'mante] adj (fam) brilliant; (: nuevo) brand-new

flamenco, -a [fla'menko, a] adj (de Flandes) Flemish; (baile, música) flamenco ▷ nm (baile, música) flamenco; (Zool) flamingo

flamingo [fla'mingo] nm (LAM) flamingo

flan [flan] nm creme caramel

No confundir *flan* con la palabra inglesa *flan*.

flash [flaʃ o flas] (pl **flashes**) nm (Foto) flash

flauta ['flauta] (Mus) nf flute

flecha ['fletʃa] nf arrow

flechazo [fle'tʃaθo] nm: **fue un ~** it was love at first sight

fleco ['fleko] nm fringe

flema ['flema] nm phlegm

flequillo [fle'kiʎo] nm (de pelo) fringe

flexible [flek'siβle] adj flexible

flexión [flek'sjon] nf press-up

flexo ['flekso] nm adjustable table lamp

flirtear [flirte'ar] /1a/ vi to flirt

flojera [flo'xera] nf (LAM): **me da ~** I can't be bothered

flojo, -a ['floxo, a] adj (gen) loose; (sin fuerzas) limp; (débil) weak

flor [flor] nf flower; **a ~ de** on the surface of; **flora** nf flora; **florecer** /2d/ vi (Bot) to flower, bloom; (fig) to flourish; **florería** nf (LAM) florist's (shop); **florero** nm vase; **floristería** nf florist's (shop)

flota ['flota] nf fleet

flotador [flota'ðor] nm (gen) float; (para nadar) rubber ring

flotar [flo'tar] /1a/ vi to float; **flote**
nm: **a flote** afloat; **salir a flote** (fig) to
get back on one's feet
fluidez [flui'ðeθ] nf fluidity; (fig)
fluency
fluido, -a [ˈflwiðo, a] adj ▷ nm fluid
fluir [flu'ir] /3g/ vi to flow
flujo [ˈfluxo] nm flow; ~ **y re~** ebb
and flow
flúor [ˈfluor] nm fluoride
fluorescente [flwores'θente]
adj fluorescent ▷ nm (tb: **tubo ~**)
fluorescent tube
fluvial [fluβi'al] adj (navegación,
cuenca) fluvial, river cpd
fobia [ˈfoβja] nf phobia; ~ **a las
alturas** fear of heights
foca [ˈfoka] nf seal
foco [ˈfoko] nm focus; (Elec) floodlight;
(Teat) spotlight; (ᴌᴀᴍ) (light) bulb
fofo, -a [ˈfofo, a] adj soft, spongy;
(músculo) flabby
fogata [fo'ɣata] nf bonfire
fogón [fo'ɣon] nm (de cocina) ring,
burner
folio [ˈfoljo] nm (hoja) sheet (of
paper), page
follaje [fo'ʎaxe] nm foliage
folleto [fo'ʎeto] nm pamphlet
follón [fo'ʎon] nm (fam: lío) mess;
(: conmoción) fuss; **armar un ~** to kick
up a fuss
fomentar [fomen'tar] /1a/ vt (Med)
to foment
fonda [ˈfonda] nf ≈ boarding house
fondo [ˈfondo] nm (de caja etc)
bottom; (de coche, sala) back; (Arte
etc) background; (reserva) fund;
fondos nmpl (Com) funds, resources;
una investigación a ~ a thorough
investigation; **en el ~** at bottom,
deep down
fonobuzón [fonoβu'θon] nm
voice mail
fontanería [fontane'ria] nf
plumbing; **fontanero** nm plumber
footing [ˈfutin] nm jogging; **hacer
~** to jog

forastero, -a [foras'tero, a] nm/f
stranger
forcejear [forθexe'ar] /1a/ vi (luchar)
to struggle
forense [fo'rense] nmf pathologist
forma [ˈforma] nf (figura) form,
shape; (Med) fitness; (método) way,
means; **estar en ~** to be fit; **las ~s** the
conventions; **de ~ que ...** so that ...;
de todas ~s in any case
formación [forma'θjon] nf (gen)
formation; (enseñanza) training; ~
profesional vocational training
formal [for'mal] adj (gen) formal; (fig:
persona) serious; (: de fiar) reliable;
formalidad nf formality; seriousness;
formalizar /1f/ vt (Jur) to formalize;
(situación) to put in order, regularize;
formalizarse vr (situación) to be put in
order, be regularized
formar [for'mar] /1a/ vt (componer)
to form, shape; (constituir) to make
up, constitute; (Escol) to train,
educate; **formarse** vr (Escol) to be
trained (o educated); (cobrar forma)
to form, take form; (desarrollarse)
to develop
formatear [formate'ar] /1a/ vt to
format
formato [for'mato] nm format; **sin ~**
unformatted
formidable [formi'ðaβle] adj
(temible) formidable; (asombroso)
tremendous
fórmula [ˈformula] nf formula
formulario [formu'larjo] nm form
fornido, -a [for'niðo, a] adj well-built
foro [ˈforo] nm forum
forrar [fo'rrar] /1a/ vt (abrigo) to line;
(libro) to cover; **forro** nm (de cuaderno)
cover; (costura) lining; (de sillón)
upholstery; **forro polar** fleece
fortalecer [fortale'θer] /2d/ vt to
strengthen
fortaleza [forta'leθa] nf (Mil)
fortress, stronghold; (fuerza) strength;
(determinación) resolution
fortuito, -a [for'twito, a] adj
accidental

fortuna [for'tuna] nf (suerte) fortune, (good) luck; (riqueza) fortune, wealth

forzar [for'θar] /1f, 1l/ vt (puerta) to force (open); (compeler) to compel

forzoso, -a [for'θoso, a] adj necessary

fosa ['fosa] nf (sepultura) grave; (en tierra) pit; **~s nasales** nostrils

fósforo ['fosforo] nm (Química) phosphorus; (cerilla) match

fósil ['fosil] nm fossil

foso ['foso] nm ditch; (Teat) pit

foto ['foto] nf photo, snap(shot); **sacar una ~** to take a photo o picture; **~ (de) carné** passport(-size) photo

fotocopia [foto'kopja] nf photocopy; **fotocopiadora** nf photocopier; **fotocopiar** /1b/ vt to photocopy

fotografía [fotoyra'fia] nf (arte) photography; (una fotografía) photograph; **fotografiar** /1c/ vt to photograph

fotógrafo, -a [fo'toyrafo, a] nm/f photographer

fotomatón [fotoma'ton] nm photo booth

FP nf abr (ESP) = **Formación Profesional**

fracasar [fraka'sar] /1a/ vi (gen) to fail

fracaso [fra'kaso] nm failure

fracción [frak'θjon] nf fraction

fractura [frak'tura] nf fracture, break

fragancia [fra'yanθja] nf (olor) fragrance, perfume

frágil ['fraxil] adj (débil) fragile; (Com) breakable

fragmento [fray'mento] nm fragment

fraile ['fraile] nm (Rel) friar; (: monje) monk

frambuesa [fram'bwesa] nf raspberry

francés, -esa [fran'θes, esa] adj French ▷ nm/f Frenchman/woman ▷ nm (Ling) French

Francia ['franθja] nf France

franco, -a [fran'ko, a] adj (cándido) frank, open; (Com: exento) free ▷ nm (moneda) franc

francotirador, a [frankotira'ðor, a] nm/f sniper

franela [fra'nela] nf flannel

franja ['franxa] nf fringe

franquear [franke'ar] /1a/ vt (camino) to clear; (carta, paquete) to frank, stamp; (obstáculo) to overcome

franqueo [fran'keo] nm postage

franqueza [fran'keθa] nf frankness

frasco ['frasko] nm bottle, flask

frase ['frase] nf sentence; **~ hecha** set phrase; (pey) stock phrase

fraterno, -a [fra'terno, a] adj brotherly, fraternal

fraude ['frauðe] nm (cualidad) dishonesty; (acto) fraud

frazada [fra'saða] nf (AM) blanket

frecuencia [fre'kwenθja] nf frequency; **con ~** frequently, often

frecuentar [frekwen'tar] /1a/ vt to frequent

frecuente [fre'kwente] adj frequent

fregadero [freya'ðero] nm (kitchen) sink

fregar [fre'yar] /1h, 1j/ vt (frotar) to scrub; (platos) to wash (up); (AM fam: fastidiar) to annoy; (: malograr) to screw up

freír [fre'ir] /3l/ vt to fry

frenar [fre'nar] /1a/ vt to brake; (fig) to check

frenazo [fre'naθo] nm: **dar un ~** to brake sharply

frenesí [frene'si] nm frenzy

freno ['freno] nm (Tec, Auto) brake; (de cabalgadura) bit; (fig) check; **~ de mano** handbrake

frente ['frente] nm (Arq, Mil, Pol) front; (de objeto) front part ▷ nf forehead, brow; **~ a** in front of; (en situación opuesta a) opposite; **chocar de ~** to crash head-on; **hacer ~ a** to face up to

fresa ['fresa] nf (ESP) strawberry

fresco, -a ['fresko, a] adj (nuevo) fresh; (frío) cool; (fam: descarado) cheeky ▷ nm (aire) fresh air; (Arte) fresco; (AM: bebida) fruit juice o drink ▷ nm/f (fam): **ser un(a) ~/a** to have a nerve; **tomar**

el ~ to get some fresh air; **frescura** nf freshness; (descaro) cheek, nerve

frialdad [frjal'dað] nf (gen) coldness; (indiferencia) indifference

frigidez [frixi'ðeθ] nf frigidity

frigo ['friyo] nm fridge

frigorífico [friyo'rifiko] nm refrigerator

frijol [fri'xol] nm kidney bean

frío, -a ['frio, a] vb V **freír** ⊳ adj cold; (indiferente) indifferent ⊳ nm cold(ness); indifference; **hace ~** it's cold; **tener ~** to be cold

frito, -a ['frito, a] adj fried; **fritos** nmpl fried food; **me trae ~ man**o I'm sick and tired of that man

frívolo, -a ['friβolo, a] adj frivolous

frontal [fron'tal] adj frontal ⊳ nm: **choque ~** head-on collision

frontera [fron'tera] nf frontier; **fronterizo, -a** adj frontier cpd; (contiguo) bordering

frontón [fron'ton] nm (Deporte: cancha) pelota court; (: juego) pelota

frotar [fro'tar] /1a/ vt to rub; **frotarse** vr: **~se las manos** to rub one's hands

fructífero, -a [fruk'tifero, a] adj fruitful

fruncir [frun'θir] /3b/ vt to pucker; (Costura) to gather; **~ el ceño** to knit one's brow

frustrar [frus'trar] /1a/ vt to frustrate

fruta ['fruta] nf fruit; **frutería** nf fruit shop; **frutero, -a** adj fruit cpd ⊳ nm/f fruiterer ⊳ nm fruit dish o bowl

frutilla [fru'tiʎa] nf (ᴄᴀᴍ) strawberry

fruto ['fruto] nm fruit; (fig: resultado) result; (: beneficio) benefit; **~s secos** nuts and dried fruit

fucsia ['fuksja] nf fuchsia

fue [fwe] vb V **ser**; **ir**

fuego ['fweyo] nm (gen) fire; **~ amigo** friendly fire; **~s artificiales** o **de artificio** fireworks; **a ~ lento** on a low flame o gas; **¿tienes ~?** have you (got) a light?

fuente ['fwente] nf fountain; (manantial, fig) spring; (origen) source; (plato) large dish

fuera ['fwera] vb V **ser**; **ir** ⊳ adv out(side); (en otra parte) away; (excepto, salvo) except, save ⊳ prep: **~ de** outside; (fig) besides; **~ de sí** beside o.s.; **por ~** (on the) outside

fuera-borda ['fwera'βorða] nm inv (barco) speedboat

fuerte ['fwerte] adj strong; (golpe) hard; (ruido) loud; (comida) rich; (lluvia) heavy; (dolor) intense ⊳ adv strongly; hard; loud; **ser ~ en** to be good at

fuerza ['fwerθa] vb V **forzar** ⊳ nf (fortaleza) strength; (Tec, Elec) power; (coacción) force; (Mil: tb: **~s**) forces pl; **~s armadas (FF.AA.)** armed forces; **~s aéreas** air force sg; **a ~ de** by (dint of); **cobrar ~s** to recover one's strength; **tener ~s para** to have the strength to; **a la ~** forcibly, by force; **por ~** of necessity; **~ de voluntad** willpower

fuga ['fuya] nf (huida) flight, escape; (de gas etc) leak

fugarse [fu'yarse] /1h/ vr to flee, escape

fugaz [fu'yaθ] adj fleeting

fugitivo, -a [fuxi'tiβo, a] adj fugitive ⊳ nm/f fugitive

fui etc [fwi] vb V **ser**; **ir**

fulano, -a [fu'lano, a] nm/f so-and-so, what's-his-name

fulminante [fulmi'nante] adj (fig: mirada) withering; (Med) sudden, serious; (fam) terrific, tremendous; (éxito, golpe) sudden; **ataque ~** stroke

fumador, a [fuma'ðor, a] nm/f smoker

fumar [fu'mar] /1a/ vt, vi to smoke; **~ en pipa** to smoke a pipe

función [fun'θjon] nf function; (de puesto) duties pl; (Teat etc) show; **entrar en funciones** to take up one's duties

funcionar [funθjo'nar] /1a/ vi (gen) to function; (máquina) to work; **"no funciona"** "out of order"

funcionario, -a [funθjo'narjo, a] nm/f civil servant

funda ['funda] nf (gen) cover; (de almohada) pillowcase

fundación [funda'θjon] nf
foundation

fundamental [fundamen'tal] adj
fundamental, basic

fundamento [funda'mento] nm
(base) foundation

fundar [fun'dar] /1a/ vt to found;
fundarse vr: **~se en** to be founded on

fundición [fundi'θjon] nf (acción)
smelting; (fábrica) foundry

fundir [fun'dir] /3a/ vt (gen) to fuse;
(metal) to smelt, melt down; (nieve etc)
to melt; (Com) to merge; (estatua) to
cast; **fundirse** vr (colores etc) to merge,
blend; (unirse) to fuse together; (Elec:
fusible, lámpara etc) to blow; (nieve
etc) to melt

fúnebre ['funeβre] adj funeral cpd,
funeral

funeral [fune'ral] nm funeral;
funeraria nf undertaker's (BRIT),
mortician's (US)

funicular [funiku'lar] nm (tren)
funicular; (teleférico) cable car

furgón [fur'ɣon] nm wagon;
furgoneta nf (Auto, Com) (transit) van
(BRIT), pickup (truck) (US)

furia ['furja] nf (ira) fury; (violencia)
violence; **furioso, -a** adj (iracundo)
furious; (violento) violent

furtivo, -a [fur'tiβo, a] adj furtive
▷ nm poacher

fusible [fu'siβle] nm fuse

fusil [fu'sil] nm rifle; **fusilar** /1a/ vt
to shoot

fusión [fu'sjon] nf (gen) melting;
(unión) fusion; (Com) merger,
amalgamation

fútbol ['futβol] nm football (BRIT),
soccer (US); **~ americano** American
football (BRIT), football (US); **~ sala**
indoor football (BRIT) o soccer (US);
futbolín nm table football; **futbolista**
nmf footballer

futuro, -a [fu'turo, a] adj future
▷ nm future

g

gabardina [gaβar'ðina] nf
gabardine; (prenda) raincoat

gabinete [gaβi'nete] nm (Pol)
cabinet; (estudio) study; (de abogados
etc) office

gachas ['gatʃas] nfpl porridge sg

gafas ['gafas] nfpl glasses; **~ de sol**
sunglasses

gafe ['gafe] nm (fam) jinx

gaita ['gaita] nf bagpipes pl

gajes ['gaxes] nmpl: **los ~ del oficio**
occupational hazards

gajo ['gaxo] nm (de naranja) segment

gala ['gala] nf full dress; **galas** nfpl
finery sg; **estar de ~** to be in one's best
clothes; **hacer ~ de** to display

galápago [ga'lapaɣo] nm (Zool)
turtle, sea/freshwater turtle (US)

galardón [galar'ðon] nm award,
prize

galaxia [ga'laksja] nf galaxy

galera [ga'lera] nf (nave) galley; (carro)
wagon; (Tip) galley

galería [gale'ria] nf (gen) gallery; (balcón) veranda(h); (de casa) corridor; **~ comercial** shopping mall

Gales ['gales] nm: **(el País de) ~** Wales; **galés, -esa** adj Welsh ▷ nm/f Welshman/woman ▷ nm (Ling) Welsh

galgo, -a ['galɣo, a] nm/f greyhound

gallego, -a [ga'ʎeɣo, a] adj ▷ nm/f Galician

galleta [ga'ʎeta] nf biscuit (BRIT), cookie (US)

gallina [ga'ʎina] nf hen ▷ nm (fam) chicken; **gallinero** nm henhouse; (Teat) top gallery

gallo ['gaʎo] nm cock, rooster

galopar [galo'par] /1a/ vi to gallop

gama ['gama] nf (fig) range

gamba ['gamba] nf prawn (BRIT), shrimp (US)

gamberro, -a [gam'berro, a] nm/f hooligan, lout

gamuza [ga'muθa] nf chamois

gana ['gana] nf (deseo) desire, wish; (apetito) appetite; (voluntad) will; (añoranza) longing; **de buena ~** willingly; **de mala ~** reluctantly; **me da ~s de** I feel like, I want to; **tener ~s de** to feel like; **no me da la (real) ~** I (really) don't feel like it

ganadería [ganaðe'ria] nf (ganado) livestock; (ganado vacuno) cattle pl; (cría, comercio) cattle raising

ganadero, -a [gana'ðero, a] nm/f (hacendado) rancher

ganado [ga'naðo] nm livestock; **~ caballar/cabrío** horses pl/goats pl; **~ porcino/vacuno** pigs pl/cattle pl

ganador, -a [gana'ðor, a] adj winning ▷ nm/f winner

ganancia [ga'nanθja] nf (lo ganado) gain; (aumento) increase; (beneficio) profit; **ganancias** nfpl (ingresos) earnings; (beneficios) profit sg, winnings

ganar [ga'nar] /1a/ vt (obtener) to get, obtain; (sacar ventaja) to gain; (Com) to earn; (Deporte, premio) to win; (derrotar) to beat; (alcanzar) to reach

▷ vi (Deporte) to win; **ganarse** vr: **~se la vida** to earn one's living

ganchillo [gan'tʃiʎo] nm crochet

gancho ['gantʃo] nm (gen) hook; (colgador) hanger

gandul, -a [gan'dul, a] adj, nm/f good-for-nothing, layabout

ganga ['ganga] nf bargain

gangrena [gan'grena] nf gangrene

ganso, -a ['ganso, a] nm/f (Zool) gander/goose; (fam) idiot

ganzúa [gan'θua] nf skeleton key

garabato [gara'βato] nm (escritura) scrawl, scribble

garaje [ga'raxe] nm garage; **garajista** nmf mechanic

garantía [garan'tia] nf guarantee

garantizar [garanti'θar] /1f/ vt to guarantee

garbanzo [gar'βanθo] nm chickpea

garfio ['garfjo] nm grappling iron

garganta [gar'ɣanta] nf (interna) throat; (externa, de botella) neck; **gargantilla** nf necklace

gárgara ['garɣara] nf gargling; **hacer ~s** to gargle

gargarear [garɣare'ar] /1a/ vi (LAM) to gargle

garita [ga'rita] nf cabin, hut; (Mil) sentry box

garra ['garra] nf (de gato, Tec) claw; (de ave) talon; (fam) hand, paw

garrafa [ga'rrafa] nf carafe, decanter

garrapata [garra'pata] nf tick

gas [gas] nm gas; **~es lacrimógenos** tear gas sg

gasa ['gasa] nf gauze

gaseoso, -a [gase'oso, a] adj gassy, fizzy ▷ nf lemonade, pop (fam)

gasoil [ga'soil], **gasóleo** [ga'soleo] nm diesel (oil)

gasolina [gaso'lina] nf petrol, gas(oline) (US); **gasolinera** nf petrol (BRIT) o gas (US) station

gastado, -a [gas'taðo, a] adj (dinero) spent; (ropa) worn out; (usado: frase etc) trite

gastar [gas'tar] /1a/ vt (dinero, tiempo) to spend; (consumir) to use (up); (desperdiciar) to waste; (llevar) to wear; **gastarse** vr to wear out; (estropearse) to waste; **~ en** to spend on; **~ bromas** to crack jokes; **¿qué número gastas?** what size (shoe) do you take?

gasto ['gasto] nm (desembolso) expenditure, spending; (consumo, uso) use; **gastos** nmpl (desembolsos) expenses; (cargos) charges, costs

gastronomía [gastrono'mia] nf gastronomy

gatear [gate'ar] /1a/ vi (andar a gatas) to go on all fours

gatillo [ga'tiʎo] nm (de arma de fuego) trigger; (de dentista) forceps

gato ['gato] nm cat; (Tec) jack; **andar a gatas** to go on all fours

gaucho, -a ['gautʃo, a] nm/f gaucho

gaviota [ga'βjota] nf seagull

gay [ge] adj, nm gay, homosexual

gazpacho [gaθ'patʃo] nm gazpacho

gel [xel] nm gel; **~ de baño/ducha** bath/shower gel

gelatina [xela'tina] nf jelly; (polvos etc) gelatine

gema ['xema] nf gem

gemelo, -a [xe'melo, a] adj, nm/f twin; **gemelos** nmpl (de camisa) cufflinks; **~s de campo** field glasses, binoculars

gemido [xe'miðo] nm (quejido) moan, groan; (lamento) howl

Géminis ['xeminis] nm Gemini

gemir [xe'mir] /3k/ vi (quejarse) to moan, groan; (viento) to howl

generación [xenera'θjon] nf generation

general [xene'ral] adj general ▷ nm general; **por lo o en ~** in general; **Generalitat** nf regional government of Catalonia; **generalizar** /1f/ vt to generalize; **generalizarse** vr to become generalized, spread

generar [xene'rar] /1a/ vt to generate

género ['xenero] nm (clase) kind, sort; (tipo) type; (Bio) genus; (Ling)

gender; (Com) material; **~ humano** human race

generosidad [xenerosi'ðað] nf generosity; **generoso, -a** adj generous

genial [xe'njal] adj inspired; (idea) brilliant; (estupendo) wonderful

genio ['xenjo] nm (carácter) nature, disposition; (humor) temper; (facultad creadora) genius; **de mal ~** bad-tempered

genital [xeni'tal] adj genital ▷ nm: **~es** genitals

gente ['xente] nf (personas) people pl; (parientes) relatives pl

gentil [xen'til] adj (elegante) graceful; (encantador) charming

▌ No confundir gentil con la palabra inglesa gentle.

genuino, -a [xe'nwino, a] adj genuine

geografía [xeoɣra'fia] nf geography

geología [xeolo'xia] nf geology

geometría [xeome'tria] nf geometry

gerente [xe'rente] nmf (supervisor) manager; (jefe) director

geriatría [xerja'tria] nf (Med) geriatrics sg

germen ['xermen] nm germ

gesticulación [xestikula'θjon] nf (ademán) gesticulation; (mueca) grimace

gesticular [xestiku'lar] /1a/ vi (con ademanes) to gesticulate; (con muecas) to make faces

gestión [xes'tjon] nf management; (diligencia, acción) negotiation

gesto ['xesto] nm (mueca) grimace; (ademán) gesture

Gibraltar [xiβral'tar] nm Gibraltar; **gibraltareño, -a** adj of o from Gibraltar, Gibraltarian ▷ nm/f Gibraltarian

gigante [xi'yante] adj, nmf giant; **gigantesco, -a** adj gigantic

gilipollas [xili'poʎas] (fam) adj inv daft ▷ nmf berk (BRIT), jerk (esp US)

gimnasia [xim'nasja] nf gymnastics pl; **gimnasio** nm gym(nasium); **gimnasta** nmf gymnast; **gimnástica** nf gymnastics sg

ginebra [xi'neβra] nf gin

ginecólogo, -a [xine'koloɣo, a] nm/f gyn(a)ecologist

gira ['xira] nf tour, trip

girar [xi'rar] /1a/ vt (dar la vuelta) to turn (around); (: rápidamente) to spin; (Com: giro postal) to draw; (comerciar: letra de cambio) to issue ▷ vi to turn (round); (rápido) to spin

girasol [xira'sol] nm sunflower

giratorio, -a [xira'torjo, a] adj revolving

giro ['xiro] nm (movimiento) turn, revolution; (Ling) expression; (Com) draft; **~ bancario** bank draft; **~ postal** money order

gis [xis] nm (LAM) chalk

gitano, -a [xi'tano, a] adj, nm/f gypsy

glacial [gla'θjal] adj icy, freezing

glaciar [gla'θjar] nm glacier

glándula ['glandula] nf gland

global [glo'βal] adj global; **globalización** nf globalization

globo ['gloβo] nm (esfera) globe, sphere; (aeróstato, juguete) balloon

glóbulo ['gloβulo] nm globule; (Anat) corpuscle

gloria ['glorja] nf glory

glorieta [glo'rjeta] nf (de jardín) bower, arbour, arbor (us); (Auto) roundabout (BRIT), traffic circle (US)

glorioso, -a [glo'rjoso, a] adj glorious

glotón, -ona [glo'ton, ona] adj gluttonous, greedy ▷ nm/f glutton

glucosa [glu'kosa] nf glucose

gobernador, -a [goβerna'ðor, a] adj governing ▷ nm/f governor; **gobernante** nf governing

gobernar [goβer'nar] /1j/ vt (dirigir) to guide, direct; (Pol) to rule, govern ▷ vi to govern; (Naut) to steer

gobierno [go'βjerno] vb V **gobernar** ▷ nm (Pol) government; (dirección) guidance, direction; (Naut) steering

goce etc ['goθe] vb V **gozar** ▷ nm enjoyment

gol [gol] nm goal

golf [golf] nm golf

golfo, -a ['golfo, a] nm/f (pilluelo) street urchin; (vagabundo) tramp; (gorrón) loafer; (gamberro) lout ▷ nf (Geo) gulf ▷ nf (fam: prostituta) slut, whore

golondrina [golon'drina] nf swallow

golosina [golo'sina] nf (dulce) sweet; **goloso, -a** adj sweet-toothed

golpe ['golpe] nm blow; (de puño) punch; (de mano) smack; (de remo) stroke; (fig: choque) clash; **no dar ~** to be bone idle; **de un ~** with one blow; **de ~** suddenly; **~ (de estado)** coup (d'état); **golpear** /1a/ vt, vi to strike, knock; (asestar) to beat; (de puño) to punch; (golpetear) to tap

goma ['goma] nf (caucho) rubber; (elástico) elastic; (tira) rubber o elastic (BRIT) band; **~ (de borrar)** eraser, rubber (BRIT); **~ espuma** foam rubber

gomina [go'mina] nf hair gel

gomita [go'mita] nf rubber o elastic (BRIT) band

gordo, -a ['gorðo, a] adj (gen) fat; (fam) enormous; **el (premio) ~** (en lotería) first prize

gorila [go'rila] nm gorilla

gorra ['gorra] nf cap; (de niño) bonnet; (militar) bearskin; **andar** o **ir** o **vivir de ~** to sponge; **entrar de ~** (fam) to gatecrash

gorrión [go'rrjon] nm sparrow

gorro ['gorro] nm cap; (de niño, mujer) bonnet

gorrón, -ona [go'rron, ona] nm/f scrounger; **gorronear** /1a/ vi (fam) to sponge, scrounge

gota ['gota] nf (de agua) drop; (de sudor) bead; (Med) gout; **gotear** /1a/ vi to drip; (lloviznar) to drizzle; **gotera** nf leak

gozar [go'θar] /1f/ vi to enjoy o.s.; **~ de** (disfrutar) to enjoy; (poseer) to possess

GPS nm abr (= global positioning system) GPS

gr abr (= gramo(s)) g

grabación [graβa'θjon] nf recording

grabado [gra'βaðo] nm print, engraving

grabador, -a [graβa'ðor, a] nm/f engraver ▷ nf tape-recorder; **~a de CD/DVD** CD/DVD writer

grabar [gra'βar] /1a/ vt to engrave; (discos, cintas) to record

gracia ['graθja] nf (encanto) grace, gracefulness; (humor) humour, wit; **¡muchas ~s!** thanks very much!; **~s a** thanks to; **tener ~** (chiste etc) to be funny; **no me hace ~** I am not too keen; **dar las ~s a algn por algo** to thank sb for sth; **gracioso, -a** adj (garboso) graceful; (chistoso) funny; (cómico) comical ▷ nm/f (Teat) comic character

grada ['graða] nf (de escalera) step; (de anfiteatro) tier, row; **gradas** nfpl (de estadio) terraces

grado ['graðo] nm degree; (de aceite, vino) grade; (grada) step; (Mil) rank; **de buen ~** willingly; **~ centí-/Fahrenheit** degree centigrade/Fahrenheit

graduación [graðwa'θjon] nf (del alcohol) proof, strength; (Escol) graduation; (Mil) rank

gradual [gra'ðwal] adj gradual

graduar [gra'ðwar] /1e/ vt (gen) to graduate; (Mil) to commission; **graduarse** vr to graduate; **~se la vista** to have one's eyes tested

gráfico, -a ['grafiko, a] adj graphic ▷ nm diagram ▷ nf graph; **gráficos** nmpl (tb Inform) graphics

grajo ['graxo] nm rook

gramático, -a [gra'matiko, a] nm/f (persona) grammarian ▷ nf grammar

gramo ['gramo] nm gramme (BRIT), gram (US)

gran [gran] adj V **grande**

grana ['grana] nf (color) scarlet

granada [gra'naða] nf pomegranate; (Mil) grenade

granate [gra'nate] adj inv maroon

Gran Bretaña [grambre'taɲa] nf Great Britain

grande ['grande] (antes de nmsg) adj (de tamaño) big, large; (alto) tall; (espacioso) great; (impresionante) grand ▷ nm grandee

granel [gra'nel] nm: **a ~** (Com) in bulk

granero [gra'nero] nm granary, barn

granito [gra'nito] nm (Agr) small grain; (roca) granite

granizado [grani'θaðo] nm iced drink

granizar [grani'θar] /1f/ vi to hail; **granizo** nm hail

granja ['granxa] nf (gen) farm; **granjero, -a** nm/f farmer

grano ['grano] nm grain; (semilla) seed; (Med) pimple, spot; **~ de café** coffee bean

granuja [gra'nuxa] nm rogue; (golfillo) urchin

grapa ['grapa] nf staple; (Tec) clamp; **grapadora** nf stapler

grasa ['grasa] nf V **graso**; **grasiento, -a** adj greasy; (de aceite) oily; **graso, -a** adj fatty; (aceitoso) greasy ▷ nf grease; (de cocina) fat, lard; (sebo) suet; (mugre) filth

gratinar [grati'nar] /1a/ vt to cook au gratin

gratis ['gratis] adv free

grato, -a ['grato, a] adj (agradable) pleasant, agreeable

gratuito, -a [gra'twito, a] adj (gratis) free; (sin razón) gratuitous

grave ['graβe] adj heavy; (fig, Med) grave, serious; **gravedad** nf gravity

Grecia ['greθja] nf Greece

gremio ['gremjo] nm trade, industry

griego, -a ['grjeɣo, a] adj ▷ nm/f Greek

grieta ['grjeta] nf crack

grifo ['grifo] nm tap (BRIT), faucet (US)

grillo ['griʎo] nm (Zool) cricket

gripa ['gripa] nf (ʌм) (ᴜм) flu, influenza

gripe ['gripe] nf flu, influenza; **~ A** swine flu; **~ aviar** bird flu

gris [gris] adj grey

gritar [gri'tar] /1a/ vt, vi to shout, yell; **grito** nm shout, yell; (de horror) scream

grosella [gro'seʎa] nf (red)currant

grosero, -a [gro'sero, a] adj (poco cortés) rude, bad-mannered; (ordinario) vulgar, crude

grosor [gro'sor] nm thickness

grúa ['grua] nf (Tec) crane; (de petróleo) derrick

grueso, -a ['grweso, a] adj thick; (persona) stout ▷ nm bulk; **el ~ de** the bulk of

grulla ['gruʎa] nf crane

grumo ['grumo] nm clot, lump

gruñido [gru'niðo] nm grunt; (fig) grumble

gruñir [gru'nir] /3h/ vi (animal) to grunt, growl; (fam) to grumble

grupo ['grupo] nm group; (Tec) unit, set; **~ de presión** pressure group

gruta ['gruta] nf grotto

guacho, -a ['gwatʃo, a] nm/f (LAM) homeless child

guajolote [gwaxo'lote] nm (LAM) turkey

guante ['gwante] nm glove; **~s de goma** rubber gloves; **guantera** nf glove compartment

guapo, -a ['gwapo, a] adj good-looking; attractive; (elegante) smart

guarda ['gwarða] nmf (persona) warden, keeper ▷ nf (acto) guarding; (custodia) custody; **~ jurado** (armed) security guard; **guardabarros** nm inv mudguard (BRIT), fender (US); **guardabosques** nm inv gamekeeper; **guardacostas** nm inv coastguard vessel ▷ nmf guardian, protector; **guardaespaldas** nm inv, nf inv bodyguard; **guardameta** nm goalkeeper; **guardar** /1a/ vt (gen) to keep; (vigilar) to guard, watch over; (dinero: ahorrar) to save; **guardarse** vr (preservarse) to protect o.s.; **guardarse de algo** (evitar) to avoid sth; **guardar cama** to stay in bed; **guardarropa** nm (armario) wardrobe; (en establecimiento público) cloakroom

guardería [gwarðe'ria] nf nursery

guardia ['gwarðja] nf (Mil) guard; (cuidado) care, custody ▷ nmf guard; (policía) policeman/woman; **estar de ~** to be on guard; **montar ~** to mount guard; **la G~ Civil** the Civil Guard

guardián, -ana [gwar'ðjan, ana] nm/f (gen) guardian, keeper

guarida [gwa'riða] nf (de animal) den, lair; (refugio) refuge

guarnición [gwarni'θjon] nf (de vestimenta) trimming; (de piedra) mount; (Culin) garnish; (arneses) harness; (Mil) garrison

guarro, -a ['gwarro, a] nm/f pig

guasa ['gwasa] nf joke; **guasón, -ona** adj (bromista) joking ▷ nm/f wit; joker

Guatemala [gwate'mala] nf Guatemala

guay [gwai] adj (fam) super, great

güero, -a ['gwero, a] adj (LAM) blond(e)

guerra ['gerra] nf war; **~ civil/fría** civil/cold war; **dar ~** to be a nuisance; **guerrero, -a** adj fighting; (carácter) warlike ▷ nm/f warrior

guerrilla [ge'rriʎa] nf guerrilla warfare; (tropas) guerrilla band o group

guía ['gia] vb V **guiar** ▷ nmf (persona) guide ▷ nf (de libro) guidebook; **~ telefónica** telephone directory; **~ del turista/del viajero** tourist/traveller's guide

guiar [gi'ar] /1c/ vt to guide, direct; (Auto) to steer; **guiarse** vr: **~se por** to be guided by

guinda ['ginda] nf morello cherry

guindilla [gin'diʎa] nf chil(l)i pepper

guiñar [gi'nar] /1a/ vi to wink

guión [gi'on] nm (Ling) hyphen, dash; (Cine) script; **guionista** nmf scriptwriter

guiri ['giri] nmf (fam, pey) foreigner

guirnalda [gir'nalda] nf garland

guisado [gi'saðo] nm stew

guisante [gi'sante] nm pea

guisar [gi'sar] /1a/ vt, vi to cook; **guiso** nm cooked dish

guitarra [gi'tarra] *nf* guitar

gula ['gula] *nf* gluttony, greed

gusano [gu'sano] *nm* worm; (*lombriz*) earthworm

gustar [gus'tar] /1a/ *vt* to taste, sample ▷ *vi* to please, be pleasing; **~ de algo** to like o enjoy sth; **me gustan las uvas** I like grapes; **le gusta nadar** she likes o enjoys swimming

gusto ['gusto] *nm* (*sentido*, *sabor*) taste; (*placer*) pleasure; **tiene un ~ amargo** it has a bitter taste; **tener buen ~** to have good taste; **sentirse a ~** to feel at ease; **¡mucho** o **tanto ~ (en conocerle)!** how do you do?, pleased to meet you; **el ~ es mío** the pleasure is mine; **tomar ~ a** to take a liking to; **con ~** willingly, gladly

ha [a] *vb* V **haber**

haba ['aβa] *nf* bean

Habana [a'βana] *nf*: **la ~** Havana

habano [a'βano] *nm* Havana cigar

habéis *vb* V **haber**

 PALABRA CLAVE

haber [a'βer] /2j/ *vb auxiliar* **1** (*tiempos compuestos*) to have; **había comido** I have/had eaten; **antes/después de haberlo visto** before seeing/after seeing o having seen it

2: **¡haberlo dicho antes!** you should have said so before!

3: **haber de: he de hacerlo** I must do it; **ha de llegar mañana** it should arrive tomorrow

▷ *vb impersonal* **1** (*existencia*: *sg*) there is; (: *pl*) there are; **hay un hermano/dos hermanos** there is one brother/there are two brothers; **¿cuánto hay de aquí a Sucre?** how far is it from here to Sucre?

2 (*obligación*): **hay que hacer algo** something must be done; **hay que apuntarlo para acordarse** you have to write it down to remember

3: **¡hay que ver!** well I never!

4: **¡no hay de qué!**, (*LAM*) **¡no hay por qué!** don't mention it!, not at all!

5: **¿qué hay?** (*¿qué pasa?*) what's up?, what's the matter?; (*¿qué tal?*) how's it going?

▸ **haberse** *vb impersonal*: **habérselas con algn** to have it out with sb

▸ *vt*: **he aquí unas sugerencias** here are some suggestions

▸ *nm* (*en cuenta*) credit side

▸ **haberes** *nmpl* assets; **¿cuánto tengo en el haber?** how much do I have in my account?; **tiene varias novelas en su haber** he has several novels to his credit

habichuela [aβiˈtʃwela] *nf* kidney bean

hábil [ˈaβil] *adj* (*listo*) clever, smart; (*capaz*) fit, capable; (*experto*) expert; **día ~** working day; **habilidad** *nf* skill, ability

habitación [aβitaˈθjon] *nf* (*cuarto*) room; (*Bio: morada*) habitat; **~ sencilla o individual** single room; **~ doble o de matrimonio** double room

habitante [aβiˈtante] *nmf* inhabitant

habitar [aβiˈtar] /1a/ *vt* (*residir en*) to inhabit; (*ocupar*) to occupy ▸ *vi* to live

hábito [ˈaβito] *nm* habit

habitual [aβiˈtwal] *adj* habitual

habituar [aβiˈtwar] /1e/ *vt* to accustom; **habituarse** *vr*: **~se a** to get used to

habla [ˈaβla] *nf* (*capacidad de hablar*) speech; (*idioma*) language; (*dialecto*) dialect; **perder el ~** to become speechless; **de ~ francesa** French-speaking; **estar al ~** to be in contact; (*Telec*) to be on the line; **¡González al ~!** (*Telec*) Gonzalez speaking!

hablador, a [aβlaˈðor, a] *adj* talkative ▸ *nm/f* chatterbox

habladuría [aβlaðuˈria] *nf* rumour; **habladurías** *nfpl* gossip *sg*

hablante [aˈβlante] *adj* speaking ▸ *nmf* speaker

hablar [aˈβlar] /1a/ *vt* to speak, talk ▸ *vi* to speak; **hablarse** *vr* to speak to each other; **~ con** to speak to; **de eso ni ~** no way, that's out of the question; **~ de** to speak of o about; **"se habla inglés"** "English spoken here"

habré *etc* [aˈβre] *vb* V **haber**

hacendado, -a [aθenˈdaðo, a] *nm/f* (*LAM*) rancher, farmer

hacendoso, -a [aθenˈdoso, a] *adj* industrious

PALABRA CLAVE

hacer [aˈθer] /2r/ *vt* **1** (*fabricar, producir, conseguir*) to make; **hacer una película/un ruido** to make a film/noise; **el guisado lo hice yo** I made o cooked the stew

2 (*ejecutar: trabajo etc*) to do; **hacer la colada** to do the washing; **hacer la comida** to do the cooking; **¿qué haces?** what are you doing?; **hacer el malo** o **el papel del malo** (*Teat*) to play the villain

3 (*estudios, algunos deportes*) to do; **hacer español/económicas** to do o study Spanish/economics; **hacer yoga/gimnasia** to do yoga/go to the gym

4 (*transformar, incidir en*): **esto lo hará más difícil** this will make it more difficult; **salirte hará sentir mejor** going out will make you feel better

5 (*cálculo*): **2 y 2 hacen 4** 2 and 2 make 4; **éste hace 100** this one makes 100

6 (+ *sub*): **esto hará que ganemos** this will make us win; **harás que no quiera venir** you'll stop him wanting to come

7 (*como sustituto de vb*) to do; **él bebió y yo hice lo mismo** he drank and I did likewise

8: **no hace más que criticar** all he does is criticize
▶ vb semi-auxiliar (+ infin: directo): **les hice venir** I made o had them come; **hacer trabajar a los demás** to get others to work
▶ vi **1**: **haz como que no lo sabes** act as if you don't know
2 (ser apropiado): **si os hace** if it's alright with you
3: **hacer de: hacer de Otelo** to play Othello
▶ vb impersonal **1**: **hace calor/frío** it's hot/cold; V tb **bueno; sol; tiempo**
2 (tiempo): **hace tres años** three years ago; **hace un mes que voy/no voy** I've been going/I haven't been for a month
3: **¿cómo has hecho para llegar tan rápido?** how did you manage to get here so quickly?
▶ **hacerse** vr **1** (volverse): to become; **se hicieron amigos** they became friends
2 (acostumbrarse): **hacerse a** to get used to
3: **se hace con huevos y leche** it's made out of eggs and milk; **eso no se hace** that's not done
4 (obtener): **hacerse de** o **con algo** to get hold of sth
5 (fingirse): **hacerse el sordo/sueco** to turn a deaf ear/pretend not to notice

hacha ['atʃa] nf axe; (antorcha) torch

hachís [a'tʃis] nm hashish

hacia ['aθja] prep (en dirección de) towards; (cerca de) near; (actitud) towards; **~ adelante/atrás** forwards/backwards; **~ arriba/abajo** up(wards)/down(wards); **~ mediodía** about noon

hacienda [a'θjenda] nf (propiedad) property; (finca) farm; (ʌʌ) ranch; **~ pública** public finance; **(Ministerio de) H~** Exchequer (ʙʀɪ⊤), Treasury Department (us)

hada ['aða] nf fairy

haga etc ['aɣa] vb V **hacer**

Haití [ai'ti] nm Haiti

halagar [ala'ɣar] /1h/ vt to flatter

halago [a'laɣo] nm flattery

halcón [al'kon] nm falcon, hawk

hallar [a'ʎar] /1a/ vt (gen) to find; (descubrir) to discover; (toparse con) to run into; **hallarse** vr to be (situated)

halterofilia [altero'filja] nf weightlifting

hamaca [a'maka] nf hammock

hambre ['ambre] nf hunger; (carencia) famine; (fig) longing; **tener ~** I'm hungry; **¡me muero de ~!** I'm starving!; **hambriento, -a** adj hungry, starving

hamburguesa [ambur'ɣesa] nf hamburger; **hamburguesería** nf burger bar

hámster ['xamster] nm hamster

han [an] vb V **haber**

harapo [a'rapo] nm rag

haré etc [a're] vb V **hacer**

harina [a'rina] nf flour; **~ de maíz** cornflour (ʙʀɪ⊤), cornstarch (us); **~ de trigo** wheat flour

hartar [ar'tar] /1a/ vt to satiate, glut; (fig) to tire, sicken; **hartarse** vr (de comida) to fill o.s., gorge o.s.; (cansarse): **~se de** to get fed up with; **harto, -a** adj (lleno) full; (cansado) fed up ▷ adv (bastante) enough; (muy) very; **estar harto de** to be fed up with

has [as] vb V **haber**

hasta ['asta] adv even ▷ prep (alcanzando a) as far as, up/down to; (de tiempo: a tal hora) till, until; (: antes de) before ▷ conj: **~ que** until; **~ luego** o **ahora/el sábado** see you soon/on Saturday; **~ pronto** see you soon

hay [ai] vb V **haber**

Haya ['aja] nf: **la ~** The Hague

haya etc ['aja] vb V **haber** ▷ nf beech tree

haz [aθ] vb V **hacer** ▷ nm (de luz) beam

hazaña [a'θaɲa] nf feat, exploit

hazmerreír [aθmerre'ir] nm inv laughing stock

he [e] vb V **haber**

hebilla [e'βiʎa] nf buckle, clasp

hebra ['eβra] nf thread; (Bot: fibra) fibre, grain

hebreo, -a [e'βreo, a] adj, nm/f Hebrew ▷ nm (Ling) Hebrew

hechizar [etʃi'θar] /1f/ vt to cast a spell on, bewitch

hechizo [e'tʃiθo] nm witchcraft, magic; (acto de magia) spell, charm

hecho, -a ['etʃo, a] pp de **hacer** ▷ adj (carne) done; (Costura) ready-to-wear ▷ nm deed, act; (dato) fact; (cuestión) matter; (suceso) event ▷ excl agreed!, done!; **¡bien ~!** well done!; **de ~** in fact, as a matter of fact; **el ~ es que ...** the fact is that ...

hechura [e'tʃura] nf (forma) form, shape; (de persona) build

hectárea [ek'tarea] nf hectare

helada [e'laða] nf frost

heladera [ela'ðera] nf (LAM: refrigerador) refrigerator

helado, -a [e'laðo, a] adj frozen; (glacial) icy; (fig) chilly, cold ▷ nm ice-cream

helar [e'lar] /1j/ vt to freeze, ice (up); (dejar atónito) to amaze ▷ vi to freeze; **helarse** vr to freeze

helecho [e'letʃo] nm fern

hélice ['eliθe] nf (Tec) propeller

helicóptero [eli'koptero] nm helicopter

hembra ['embra] nf (Bot, Zool) female; (mujer) woman; (Tec) nut

hemorragia [emo'rraxja] nf haemorrhage (BRIT), hemorrhage (US)

hemorroides [emo'rroiðes] nfpl haemorrhoids (BRIT), hemorrhoids (US)

hemos ['emos] vb V **haber**

heno ['eno] nm hay

heredar [ere'ðar] /1a/ vt to inherit; **heredero, -a** nm/f heir(ess)

hereje [e'rexe] nm/f heretic

herencia [e'renθja] nf inheritance

herido, -a [e'riðo, a] adj injured, wounded ▷ nm/f casualty ▷ nf wound, injury

herir [e'rir] /3i/ vt to wound, injure; (fig) to offend

hermanación [ermana'θjon] nf (de ciudades) twinning

hermanado, -a [erma'naðo, a] adj (ciudad) twinned

hermanastro, -a [erma'nastro, a] nm/f stepbrother/sister

hermandad [erman'dað] nf brotherhood

hermano, -a [er'mano, a] nm brother ▷ nf sister; **~ gemelo** twin brother; **~ político** brother-in-law; **hermana política** sister-in-law

hermético, -a [er'metiko, a] adj hermetic; (fig) watertight

hermoso, -a [er'moso, a] adj beautiful, lovely; (estupendo) splendid; (guapo) handsome; **hermosura** nf beauty

hernia ['ernja] nf hernia; **~ discal** slipped disc

héroe ['eroe] nm hero

heroína [ero'ina] nf (mujer) heroine; (droga) heroin

herradura [erra'ðura] nf horseshoe

herramienta [erra'mjenta] nf tool

herrero [e'rrero] nm blacksmith

hervidero [erβi'ðero] nm (fig) swarm; (Pol etc) hotbed

hervir [er'βir] /3i/ vi to boil; (burbujear) to bubble; **~ a fuego lento** to simmer; **hervor** nm boiling; (fig) ardour, fervour

heterosexual [eterosek'swal] adj heterosexual

hice etc ['iθe] vb V **hacer**

hidratante [iðra'tante] adj: **crema ~** moisturizing cream, moisturizer; **hidratar** /1a/ vt to moisturize; **hidrato** nm hydrate; **hidrato de carbono** carbohydrate

hidráulico, -a [i'ðrauliko, a] adj hydraulic

hidro... [iðro] *pref* hydro..., water-...;
hidrodeslizador *nm* hovercraft;
hidroeléctrico, -a *adj* hydroelectric;
hidrógeno *nm* hydrogen

hiedra ['jeðra] *nf* ivy

hiel [jel] *nf* gall, bile; (*fig*) bitterness

hielo ['jelo] *vb* V **helar** ▷ *nm* (*gen*) ice;
(*escarcha*) frost; (*fig*) coldness, reserve

hiena ['jena] *nf* hyena

hierba ['jerβa] *nf* (*pasto*) grass; (*Culin, Med: planta*) herb; **mala ~** weed; (*fig*)
evil influence; **hierbabuena** *nf* mint

hierro ['jerro] *nm* (*metal*) iron; (*objeto*)
iron object

hígado ['iɣaðo] *nm* liver

higiene [i'xjene] *nf* hygiene;
higiénico, -a *adj* hygienic

higo ['iɣo] *nm* fig; **~ seco** dried fig;
higuera *nf* fig tree

hijastro, -a [i'xastro, a] *nm/f*
stepson/daughter

hijo, -a ['ixo, a] *nm/f* son/daughter,
child; (*uso vocativo*) dear; **hijos** *nmpl*
children, sons and daughters; **~/hija
político/a** son-/daughter-in-law; **~
adoptivo** adopted child; **~ de papá/
mamá** daddy's/mummy's boy; **~ de
puta** (*fam!*) bastard (*!*), son of a bitch
(*!*); **~ único** only child

hilera [i'lera] *nf* row, file

hilo ['ilo] *nm* thread; (*Bot*) fibre; (*de
metal*) wire; (*de agua*) trickle, thin
stream

hilvanar [ilβa'nar] /1a/ *vt* (*Costura*)
to tack (*BRIT*), baste (*US*); (*fig*) to do
hurriedly

himno ['imno] *nm* hymn; **~ nacional**
national anthem

hincapié [inka'pje] *nm*: **hacer ~ en**
to emphasize

hincar [in'kar] /1g/ *vt* to drive (in),
thrust (in)

hincha ['intʃa] *nmf* (*fam*) fan

hinchado, -a [in'tʃaðo, a] *adj* (*gen*)
swollen; (*persona*) pompous

hinchar [in'tʃar] /1a/ *vt* (*gen*) to swell;
(*inflar*) to blow up, inflate; (*fig*) to
exaggerate; **hincharse** (*inflarse*) to

swell up; (*fam: llenarse*) to stuff o.s.;
hinchazón *nf* (*Med*) swelling; (*altivez*)
arrogance

hinojo [i'noxo] *nm* fennel

hipermercado [ipermer'kaðo] *nm*
hypermarket, superstore

hípico, -a ['ipiko, a] *adj* horse *cpd*

hipnotismo [ipno'tismo] *nm*
hypnotism; **hipnotizar** /1f/ *vt* to
hypnotize

hipo ['ipo] *nm* hiccups *pl*

hipocresía [ipokre'sia] *nf* hypocrisy;
hipócrita *adj* hypocritical ▷ *nmf*
hypocrite

hipódromo [i'poðromo] *nm*
racetrack

hipopótamo [ipo'potamo] *nm*
hippopotamus

hipoteca [ipo'teka] *nf* mortgage

hipótesis [i'potesis] *nf inv* hypothesis

hispánico, -a [is'paniko, a] *adj*
Hispanic

hispano, -a [is'pano, a] *adj* Hispanic,
Spanish, Hispano- ▷ *nm/f* Spaniard;
Hispanoamérica *nf* Spanish o Latin
America; **hispanoamericano, -a** *adj,
nm/f* Spanish o Latin American

histeria [is'terja] *nf* hysteria

historia [is'torja] *nf* history; (*cuento*)
story, tale; **historias** *nfpl* (*chismes*)
gossip *sg*; **dejarse de ~s** to come to
the point; **pasar a la ~** to go down
in history; **historiador, a** *nm/f*
historian; historical *nm* (*profesional*)
curriculum vitae, C.V.; (*Med*) case
history; **histórico, -a** *adj* historical;
(*fig*) historic

historieta [isto'rjeta] *nf* tale,
anecdote; (*de dibujos*) comic strip

hito ['ito] *nm* (*fig*) landmark

hizo ['iθo] *vb* V **hacer**

hocico [o'θiko] *nm* snout

hockey ['xoki] *nm* hockey; **~ sobre
hielo** ice hockey

hogar [o'ɣar] *nm* fireplace, hearth;
(*casa*) home; (*vida familiar*) home life;
hogareño, -a *adj* home *cpd*; (*persona*)
home-loving

hoguera [o'ɣera] nf (gen) bonfire
hoja ['oxa] nf (gen) leaf; (de flor) petal; (de papel) sheet; (página) page; **~ de afeitar** razor blade; **~ de cálculo electrónica** spreadsheet; **~ informativa** leaflet, handout; **~ de solicitud** application form
hojalata [oxa'lata] nf tin(plate)
hojaldre [o'xaldre] nm (Culin) puff pastry
hojear [oxe'ar] /1a/ vt to leaf through, turn the pages of
hojuela [o'xwela] nf flake
hola ['ola] excl hello!
Holanda [o'landa] nf Holland; **holandés, -esa** adj Dutch ▷ nm/f Dutchman/woman ▷ nm (Ling) Dutch
holgado, -a [ol'ɣaðo, a] adj loose, baggy; (rico) well-to-do
holgar [ol'ɣar] /1h, 1l/ vi (descansar) to rest; (sobrar) to be superfluous
holgazán, -ana [olɣa'θan, ana] adj idle, lazy ▷ nm/f loafer
hollín [o'ʎin] nm soot
hombre ['ombre] nm man; (raza humana): **el ~** man(kind) ▷ excl (para énfasis) man, old chap; **¡sí ~!** (claro) of course!; **~ de negocios** businessman; **~-rana** frogman; **~ de bien** o **pro** honest man
hombrera [om'brera] nf shoulder strap
hombro ['ombro] nm shoulder
homenaje [ome'naxe] nm (gen) homage; (tributo) tribute
homicida [omi'θiða] adj homicidal ▷ nmf murderer; **homicidio** nm murder, homicide
homologar [omolo'ɣar] /1h/ vt (Com) to standardize
homólogo, -a [o'moloɣo, a] nm/f counterpart, opposite number
homosexual [omosek'swal] adj, nmf homosexual
honda ['onda] nf (cs) catapult
hondo, -a ['ondo, a] adj deep; **lo ~** the depth(s) (pl), the bottom;

hondonada nf hollow, depression; (cañón) ravine
Honduras [on'duras] nf Honduras
hondureño, -a [ondu'reno, a] adj, nm/f Honduran
honestidad [onesti'ðað] nf purity, chastity; (decencia) decency; **honesto, -a** adj chaste; decent, honest; (justo) just
hongo ['ongo] nm (Bot: gen) fungus; (: comestible) mushroom; (: venenoso) toadstool
honor [o'nor] nm (gen) honour (BRIT), honor (US); **en ~ a la verdad** to be fair; **honorable** adj honourable (BRIT), honorable (US)
honorario, -a [ono'rarjo, a] adj honorary ▷ nm: **~s** fees
honra ['onra] nf (gen) honour (BRIT), honor (US); (renombre) good name; **honradez** nf honesty; (de persona) integrity; **honrado, -a** adj honest, upright; **honrar** /1a/ vt to honour
hora ['ora] nf hour; (tiempo) time; **¿qué ~ es?** what time is it?; **¿a qué ~?** at what time?; **media ~** half an hour; **a la ~ de recreo** o **de comer** at lunchtime/at playtime; **a primera ~** first thing (in the morning); **a última ~** at the last moment; **a altas ~s** in the small hours; **¡a buena ~!** about time, too!; **pedir ~** to make an appointment; **dar la ~** to strike the hour; **~s de oficina/de trabajo** office/working hours; **~s de visita** visiting times; **~s extras** o **extraordinarias** overtime sg; **~s pico** (LAM) rush o peak hours; **~s punta** rush hours
horario, -a [o'rarjo, a] adj hourly, hour cpd ▷ nm timetable; **~ comercial** business hours
horca ['orka] nf gallows sg
horcajadas [orka'xaðas]: **a ~** adv astride
horchata [or'tʃata] nf cold drink made from tiger nuts and water, tiger nut milk

h

horizontal [oriθon'tal] *adj* horizontal

horizonte [ori'θonte] *nm* horizon

horma ['orma] *nf* mould

hormiga [or'miɣa] *nf* ant; **hormigas** *nfpl* (Med) pins and needles

hormigón [ormi'ɣon] *nm* concrete; **~ armado/pretensado** reinforced/ prestressed concrete; **hormigonera** *nf* cement mixer

hormigueo [ormi'ɣeo] *nm* (comezón) itch

hormona [or'mona] *nf* hormone

hornillo [or'niʎo] *nm* (cocina) portable stove; **~ de gas** gas ring

horno ['orno] *nm* (Culin) oven; (Tec) furnace; **alto ~** blast furnace

horóscopo [o'roskopo] *nm* horoscope

horquilla [or'kiʎa] *nf* hairpin; (Agr) pitchfork

horrendo, -a [o'rrendo, a] *adj* horrendous, frightful

horrible [o'rriβle] *adj* horrible, dreadful

horripilante [orripi'lante] *adj* hair-raising, horrifying

horror [o'rror] *nm* horror, dread; (atrocidad) atrocity; **¡qué ~!** (fam) how awful!; **horrorizar** /1f/ *vt* to horrify, frighten; **horrorizarse** *vr* to be horrified; **horroroso, -a** *adj* horrifying, ghastly

hortaliza [orta'liθa] *nf* vegetable

hortelano, -a [orte'lano, a] *nm/f* (market) gardener

hortera [or'tera] *adj* (fam) tacky

hospedar [ospe'ðar] /1a/ *vt* to put up; **hospedarse** *vr*: **~se (con/en)** to stay o lodge (with/at)

hospital [ospi'tal] *nm* hospital

hospitalario, -a [ospita'larjo, a] *adj* (acogedor) hospitable; **hospitalidad** *nf* hospitality

hostal [os'tal] *nm* small hotel

hostelería [ostele'ria] *nf* hotel business o trade

hostia ['ostja] *nf* (Rel) host, consecrated wafer; (fam: golpe)

whack, punch ▷ *excl*: **¡~(s)!** (fam!) damn!

hostil [os'til] *adj* hostile

hotdog [ot'doɣ] *nm* (ʌm) hot dog

hotel [o'tel] *nm* hotel; *see note* **"hotel"**; **hotelero, -a** *adj* hotel *cpd* ▷ *nm/f* hotelier

● **HOTEL**

● In Spain you can choose from
● the following categories of
● accommodation, in descending
● order of quality and price: hotel
● (from 5 stars to 1), hostal, pensión,
● casa de huéspedes, fonda. Quality
● can vary widely even within these
● categories. The State also runs
● luxury hotels called paradores,
● which are usually sited in places
● of particular historical interest
● and are often historic buildings
● themselves.

hoy [oi] *adv* (este día) today; (en la actualidad) now(adays) ▷ *nm* present time; **~ (en) día** now(adays)

hoyo ['oʝo] *nm* hole, pit

hoz [oθ] *nf* sickle

hube *etc* ['uβe] *vb* V **haber**

hucha ['utʃa] *nf* money box

hueco, -a ['weko, a] *adj* (vacío) hollow, empty; (resonante) booming ▷ *nm* hollow, cavity

huelga ['welɣa] *vb* V **holgar** ▷ *nf* strike; **declararse en ~** to go on strike, come out on strike; **~ general** general strike; **~ de hambre** hunger strike

huelguista [wel'ɣista] *nmf* striker

huella ['weʎa] *nf* (acto de pisar, pisada) tread(ing); (marca del paso) footprint, footstep; (: de animal, máquina) track; **~ de carbono** carbon footprint; **~ dactilar o digital** fingerprint

huelo *etc* *vb* V **oler**

huérfano, -a ['werfano, a] *adj* orphan(ed) ▷ *nm/f* orphan

huerta ['werta] nf market garden (BRIT): truck farm (US); (de Murcia, Valencia) irrigated region

huerto ['werto] nm kitchen garden; (de árboles frutales) orchard

hueso ['weso] nm (Anat) bone; (de fruta) stone

huésped, a ['wespeð, a] nm/f guest

huevas ['weβas] nfpl roe sg

huevera [we'βera] nf eggcup

huevo ['weβo] nm egg; ~ **duro/ escalfado/estrellado** o **frito/ pasado por agua** hard-boiled/ poached/fried/soft-boiled egg; ~**s revueltos** scrambled eggs; ~ **tibio** (LAM) soft-boiled egg

huida [u'iða] nf escape, flight

huir [u'ir] /3g/ vt (escapar) to flee, escape; (evadir) to avoid

hule ['ule] nm oilskin; (esp LAM) rubber

hulera [u'lera] nf (LAM) catapult

humanidad [umani'ðað] nf (género humano) man(kind); (cualidad) humanity

humanitario, -a [umani'tarjo, a] adj humanitarian

humano, -a [u'mano, a] adj (gen) human; (humanitario) humane ▷ nm human; **ser** ~ human being

humareda [uma'reða] nf cloud of smoke

humedad [ume'ðað] nf (del clima) humidity; (de pared etc) dampness; **a prueba de** ~ damp-proof;

humedecer /2d/ vt to moisten, wet; **humedecerse** vr to get wet

húmedo, -a [u'meðo, a] adj (mojado) damp, wet; (tiempo etc) humid

humilde [u'milde] adj humble, modest

humillación [umiʎa'θjon] nf humiliation; **humillante** adj humiliating

humillar [umi'ʎar] /1a/ vt to humiliate

humo ['umo] nm (de fuego) smoke; (gas nocivo) fumes pl; (vapor) steam, vapour; **humos** nmpl (fig) conceit sg

humor [u'mor] nm (disposición) mood, temper; (lo que divierte) humour; **de buen/mal** ~ in a good/bad mood;

humorista nmf comic; **humorístico, -a** adj funny, humorous

hundimiento [undi'mjento] nm (gen) sinking; (colapso) collapse

hundir [un'dir] /3a/ vt to sink; (edificio, plan) to ruin, destroy; **hundirse** vr to sink, collapse

húngaro, -a [ungaro, a] adj, nm/f Hungarian

Hungría [un'gria] nf Hungary

huracán [ura'kan] nm hurricane

huraño, -a [u'raɲo, a] adj (antisocial) unsociable

hurgar [ur'ɣar] /1h/ vt to poke, jab; (remover) to stir (up); **hurgarse** vr: ~**se (las narices)** to pick one's nose

hurón [u'ron] nm (Zool) ferret

hurtadillas [urta'ðiʎas]: **a** ~ adv stealthily, on the sly

hurtar [ur'tar] /1a/ vt to steal; **hurto** nm theft, stealing

husmear [usme'ar] /1a/ vt (oler) to sniff out, scent; (fam) to pry into

huyo etc vb V **huir**

h

i

iba *etc* ['iβa] *vb* V **ir**

ibérico, -a [i'βeriko, a] *adj* Iberian

iberoamericano, -a [iβeroameri'kano, a] *adj, nm/f* Latin American

Ibiza [i'βiθa] *nf* Ibiza

iceberg [iθe'ber] *nm* iceberg

icono [i'kono] *nm* icon

ida ['iða] *nf* going, departure; **~ y vuelta** round trip, return

idea [i'ðea] *nf* idea; **no tengo la menor ~** I haven't a clue

ideal [iðe'al] *adj, nm* ideal; **idealista** *nmf* idealist; **idealizar** /1f/ *vt* to idealize

ídem ['iðem] *pron* ditto

idéntico, -a [i'ðentiko, a] *adj* identical

identidad [iðenti'ðað] *nf* identity

identificación [iðentifika'θjon] *nf* identification

identificar [iðentifi'kar] /1g/ *vt* to identify; **identificarse** *vr*: **~se con** to identify with

ideología [iðeolo'xia] *nf* ideology

idilio [i'ðiljo] *nm* love affair

idioma [i'ðjoma] *nm* language

> No confundir *idioma* con la palabra inglesa *idiom*.

idiota [i'ðjota] *adj* idiotic ⊳ *nmf* idiot

ídolo ['iðolo] *nm* (tb *fig*) idol

idóneo, -a [i'ðoneo, a] *adj* suitable

iglesia [i'ɣlesja] *nf* church

ignorante [iɣno'rante] *adj* ignorant, uninformed ⊳ *nmf* ignoramus

ignorar [iɣno'rar] /1a/ *vt* not to know, be ignorant of; (*no hacer caso a*) to ignore

igual [i'ɣwal] *adj* equal; (*similar*) like, similar; (*mismo*) (the) same; (*constante*) constant; (*temperatura*) even ⊳ *nmf, conj* equal; **al ~ que** *prep* like, just like; **~ que** the same as; **me da o es ~** I don't care; **son ~es** they're the same

iguaiar [iɣwa'lar] /1a/ *vt* (*gen*) to equalize, make equal; (*terreno*) to make even; (*allanar, nivelar*) to level (off); **igualarse** *vr* (*platos de balanza*) to balance out

igualdad [iɣwal'dað] *nf* equality; (*similaridad*) sameness; (*uniformidad*) uniformity

igualmente [iɣwal'mente] *adv* equally; (*también*) also, likewise ⊳ *excl* the same to you!

ilegal [ile'ɣal] *adj* illegal

ilegítimo, -a [ile'xitimo, a] *adj* illegitimate

ileso, -a [i'leso, a] *adj* unhurt

ilimitado, -a [ilimi'taðo, a] *adj* unlimited

iluminación [ilumina'θjon] *nf* illumination; (*alumbrado*) lighting

iluminar [ilumi'nar] /1a/ *vt* to illuminate, light (up); (*fig*) to enlighten

ilusión [ilu'sjon] *nf* illusion; (*quimera*) delusion; (*esperanza*) hope; **hacerse ilusiones** to build up one's hopes; **ilusionado, -a** *adj* excited; **ilusionar** /1a/ *vi*: **le ilusiona ir de vacaciones** he's looking forward to going on holiday; **ilusionarse** vr (entusiasmarse) to get excited

iluso, -a [i'luso, a] adj easily deceived ▷ nm/f dreamer

ilustración [ilustra'θjon] nf illustration; (saber) learning, erudition; **la I~** the Enlightenment; **ilustrado, -a** adj illustrated; learned

ilustrar [ilus'trar] /1a/ vt to illustrate; (instruir) to instruct; (explicar) to explain, make clear

ilustre [i'lustre] adj famous, illustrious

imagen [i'maxen] nf (gen) image; (dibujo) picture

imaginación [imaxina'θjon] nf imagination

imaginar [imaxi'nar] /1a/ vt (gen) to imagine; (idear) to think up; (suponer) to suppose; **imaginarse** vr to imagine; **imaginario, -a** adj imaginary; **imaginativo, -a** adj imaginative

imán [i'man] nm magnet

imbécil [im'beθil] nm/f imbecile, idiot

imitación [imita'θjon] nf imitation; **a ~ de** in imitation of

imitar [imi'tar] /1a/ vt to imitate; (parodiar, remedar) to mimic, ape

impaciente [impa'θjente] adj impatient; (nervioso) anxious

impacto [im'pakto] nm impact

impar [im'par] adj odd

imparcial [impar'θjal] adj impartial, fair

impecable [impe'kaβle] adj impeccable

impedimento [impeði'mento] nm impediment, obstacle

impedir [impe'ðir] /3k/ vt (obstruir) to impede, obstruct; (estorbar) to prevent; **~ a algn hacer** o **que algn haga algo** to prevent sb (from) doing sth

imperativo, -a [impera'tiβo, a] adj (urgente, Ling) imperative

imperdible [imper'ðiβle] nm safety pin

imperdonable [imperðo'naβle] adj unforgivable, inexcusable

imperfecto, -a [imper'fekto, a] adj imperfect

imperio [im'perjo] nm empire; (autoridad) rule, authority; (fig) pride, haughtiness

impermeable [imperme'aβle] adj waterproof ▷ nm raincoat, mac (BRIT)

impersonal [imperso'nal] adj impersonal

impertinente [imperti'nente] adj impertinent

ímpetu ['impetu] nm (impulso) impetus, impulse; (impetuosidad) impetuosity; (violencia) violence

implantar [implan'tar] /1a/ vt (costumbre) to introduce

implemento [imple'mento] nm (LAM) tool, implement

implicar [impli'kar] /1g/ vt to involve; (entrañar) to imply

implícito, -a [im'pliθito, a] adj (tácito) implicit; (sobreentendido) implied

imponente [impo'nente] adj (impresionante) impressive, imposing; (solemne) grand

imponer [impo'ner] /2q/ vt (gen) to impose; (exigir) to exact; **imponerse** vr to assert o.s.; (prevalecer) to prevail; **imponible** adj (Com) taxable

impopular [impopu'lar] adj unpopular

importación [importa'θjon] nf (acto) importing; (mercancías) imports pl

importancia [impor'tanθja] nf importance; (valor) value, significance; (extensión) size, magnitude; **no tiene ~** it's nothing; **importante** adj important; valuable, significant

importar [impor'tar] /1a/ vt (del extranjero) to import; (costar) to amount to ▷ vi to be important, matter; **me importa un rábano** o **un bledo** I couldn't care less; **¿le**

importa que fume? do you mind if I smoke?; **no importa** it doesn't matter

importe [im'porte] *nm* (*cantidad*) amount; (*valor*) value

imposible [impo'siβle] *adj* impossible; (*insoportable*) unbearable, intolerable

imposición [imposi'θjon] *nf* imposition; (*Com*) tax; (*inversión*) deposit

impostor, a [impos'tor, a] *nm/f* impostor

impotencia [impo'tenθja] *nf* impotence; **impotente** *adj* impotent

impreciso, -a [impre'θiso, a] *adj* imprecise, vague

impregnar [impreɣ'nar] /1a/ *vt* to impregnate; **impregnarse** *vr* to become impregnated

imprenta [im'prenta] *nf* (*acto*) printing; (*aparato*) press; (*casa*) printer's; (*letra*) print

imprescindible [impresθin'diβle] *adj* essential, vital

impresión [impre'sjon] *nf* impression; (*Imprenta*) printing; (*edición*) edition; (*Foto*) print; (*marca*) imprint; **~ digital** fingerprint

impresionante [impresjo'nante] *adj* impressive; (*tremendo*) tremendous; (*maravilloso*) great, marvellous

impresionar [impresjo'nar] /1a/ *vt* (*conmover*) to move; (*afectar*) to impress, strike; (*película fotográfica*) to expose; **impresionarse** *vr* to be impressed; (*conmoverse*) to be moved

impreso, -a [im'preso, a] *pp de* **imprimir** ▷ *adj* printed; **impresos** *nmpl* printed matter *sg*; **impresora** *nf* printer

imprevisto, -a [impre'βisto, a] *adj* unforeseen; (*inesperado*) unexpected

imprimir [impri'mir] /3a/ *vt* to stamp; (*textos*) to print; (*Inform*) to output, print out

improbable [impro'βaβle] *adj* improbable; (*inverosímil*) unlikely

impropio, -a [im'propjo, a] *adj* improper

improvisado, -a [improβi'saðo, a] *adj* improvised

improvisar [improβi'sar] /1a/ *vt* to improvise

improviso [impro'βiso] *adv*: **de ~** unexpectedly, suddenly

imprudencia [impru'ðenθja] *nf* imprudence; (*indiscreción*) indiscretion; (*descuido*) carelessness; **imprudente** *adj* unwise, imprudent; (*indiscreto*) indiscreet

impuesto, -a [im'pwesto, a] *adj* imposed ▷ *nm* tax; **~ de venta** sales tax; **~ sobre el valor añadido (IVA)** value added tax (VAT)

impulsar [impul'sar] /1a/ *vt* to drive; (*promover*) to promote, stimulate

impulsivo, -a [impul'siβo, a] *adj* impulsive; **impulso** *nm* impulse; (*fuerza, empuje*) thrust, drive; (*fig*: *sentimiento*) urge, impulse

impureza [impu'reθa] *nf* impurity; **impuro, -a** *adj* impure

inaccesible [inakθe'siβle] *adj* inaccessible

inaceptable [inaθep'taβle] *adj* unacceptable

inactivo, -a [inak'tiβo, a] *adj* inactive

inadecuado, -a [inaðe'kwaðo, a] *adj* (*insuficiente*) inadequate; (*inapto*) unsuitable

inadvertido, -a [inaðβer'tiðo, a] *adj* (*no visto*) unnoticed

inaguantable [inaɣwan'taβle] *adj* unbearable

inalámbrico, -a [ina'lambriko, a] *adj* cordless, wireless

inanimado, -a [inani'maðo, a] *adj* inanimate

inaudito, -a [inau'ðito, a] *adj* unheard-of

inauguración [inauɣura'θjon] *nf* inauguration; (*de exposición*) opening

inaugurar [inauɣu'rar] /1a/ *vt* to inaugurate; (*exposición*) to open

inca ['inka] *nmf* Inca

incalculable [inkalku'laβle] *adj* incalculable

incandescente [inkandes'θente] *adj* incandescent

incansable [inkan'saβle] *adj* tireless, untiring

incapacidad [inkapaθi'ðað] *nf* incapacity; (*incompetencia*) incompetence; **~ física/mental** physical/mental disability

incapacitar [inkapaθi'tar] /1a/ *vt* (*inhabilitar*) to incapacitate, handicap; (*descalificar*) to disqualify

incapaz [inka'paθ] *adj* incapable

incautarse [inkau'tarse] /1a/ *vr*: **~ de** to seize, confiscate

incauto, -a [in'kauto, a] *adj* (*imprudente*) incautious, unwary

incendiar [inθen'djar] /1b/ *vt* to set fire to; (*fig*) to inflame; **incendiarse** *vr* to catch fire; **incendiario, -a** *adj* incendiary

incendio [in'θendjo] *nm* fire

incentivo [inθen'tiβo] *nm* incentive

incertidumbre [inθerti'ðumbre] *nf* (*inseguridad*) uncertainty; (*duda*) doubt

incesante [inθe'sante] *adj* incessant

incesto [in'θesto] *nm* incest

incidencia [inθi'ðenθja] *nf* (*Mat*) incidence

incidente [inθi'ðente] *nm* incident

incidir [inθi'ðir] /3a/ *vi*: **~ en** (*influir*) to influence; (*afectar*) to affect

incienso [in'θjenso] *nm* incense

incierto, -a [in'θjerto, a] *adj* uncertain

incineración [inθinera'θjon] *nf* incineration; (*de cadáveres*) cremation

incinerar [inθine'rar] /1a/ *vt* to burn; (*cadáveres*) to cremate

incisión [inθi'sjon] *nf* incision

incisivo, -a [inθi'siβo, a] *adj* sharp, cutting; (*fig*) incisive

incitar [inθi'tar] /1a/ *vt* to incite, rouse

inclemencia [inkle'menθja] *nf* (*severidad*) harshness, severity; (*del tiempo*) inclemency

inclinación [inklina'θjon] *nf* (*gen*) inclination; (*de tierras*) slope, incline; (*de cabeza*) nod, bow; (*fig*) leaning, bent

inclinar [inkli'nar] /1a/ *vt* to incline; (*cabeza*) to nod, bow; **inclinarse** *vr* to lean, slope; to bow; (*encorvarse*) to stoop; **~se a** (*parecerse*) to take after, resemble; **~se ante** to bow down to; **me inclino a pensar que ...** I'm inclined to think that ...

incluir [inklu'ir] /3g/ *vt* to include; (*incorporar*) to incorporate; (*meter*) to enclose

inclusive [inklu'siβe] *adv* inclusive ▷ *prep* including

incluso, -a [in'kluso, a] *adv* even

incógnita [in'koɣnita] *nf* (*Mat*) unknown quantity

incógnito [in'koɣnito] *nm*: **de ~** incognito

incoherente [inkoe'rente] *adj* incoherent

incoloro, -a [inko'loro, a] *adj* colourless

incomodar [inkomo'ðar] /1a/ *vt* to inconvenience; (*molestar*) to bother, trouble; (*fastidiar*) to annoy

incomodidad [inkomoði'ðað] *nf* inconvenience; (*fastidio, enojo*) annoyance; (*de vivienda*) discomfort

incómodo, -a [in'komoðo, a] *adj* (*inconfortable*) uncomfortable; (*molesto*) annoying; (*inconveniente*) inconvenient

incomparable [inkompa'raβle] *adj* incomparable

incompatible [inkompa'tiβle] *adj* incompatible

incompetente [inkompe'tente] *adj* incompetent

incompleto, -a [inkom'pleto, a] *adj* incomplete, unfinished

incomprensible [inkompren'siβle] *adj* incomprehensible

incomunicado, -a [inkomuni'kaðo, a] *adj* (*aislado*) cut off, isolated; (*confinado*) in solitary confinement

incondicional [inkondiθjo'nal] *adj* unconditional; *(apoyo)* wholehearted; *(partidario)* staunch

inconfundible [inkonfun'diβle] *adj* unmistakable

incongruente [inkon'grwente] *adj* incongruous

inconsciente [inkons'θjente] *adj* unconscious; thoughtless

inconsecuente [inkonse'kwente] *adj* inconsistent

inconstante [inkons'tante] *adj* inconstant

incontable [inkon'taβle] *adj* countless, innumerable

inconveniencia [inkombe'njenθja] *nf* unsuitability, inappropriateness; *(falta de cortesía)* impoliteness; **inconveniente** *adj* unsuitable; impolite ▷ *nm* obstacle; *(desventaja)* disadvantage; **el inconveniente es que ...** the trouble is that ...

incordiar [inkor'ðjar] /1b/ *vt (fam)* to hassle

incorporar [inkorpo'rar] /1a/ *vt* to incorporate; **incorporarse** *vr* to sit up; **~se** to join

incorrecto, -a [inko'rrekto, a] *adj* incorrect, wrong; *(comportamiento)* bad-mannered

incorregible [inkorre'xiβle] *adj* incorrigible

incrédulo, -a [in'kreðulo, a] *adj* incredulous, unbelieving; sceptical

increíble [inkre'iβle] *adj* incredible

incremento [inkre'mento] *nm* increment; *(aumento)* rise, increase

increpar [inkre'par] /1a/ *vt* to reprimand

incruento, -a [in'krwento, a] *adj* bloodless

incrustar [inkrus'tar] /1a/ *vt* to incrust; *(piedras: en joya)* to inlay

incubar [inku'βar] /1a/ *vt* to incubate

inculcar [inkul'kar] /1g/ *vt* to inculcate

inculto, -a [in'kulto, a] *adj (persona)* uneducated; *(grosero)* uncouth ▷ *nm/f* ignoramus

incumplimiento [inkumpli'mjento] *nm* non-fulfilment; **~ de contrato** breach of contract

incurrir [inku'rrir] /3a/ *vi*: **~ en** to incur; *(crimen)* to commit

indagar [inda'ɣar] /1h/ *vt* to investigate; to search; *(averiguar)* to ascertain

indecente [inde'θente] *adj* indecent, improper; *(lascivo)* obscene

indeciso, -a [inde'θiso, a] *adj (por decidir)* undecided; *(vacilante)* hesitant

indefenso, -a [inde'fenso, a] *adj* defenceless

indefinido, -a [indefi'niðo, a] *adj* indefinite; *(vago)* vague, undefined

indemne [in'demne] *adj (objeto)* undamaged; *(persona)* unharmed, unhurt

indemnizar [indemni'θar] /1f/ *vt* to indemnify; *(compensar)* to compensate

independencia [indepen'denθja] *nf* independence

independiente [indepen'djente] *adj (libre)* independent; *(autónomo)* self-sufficient

indeterminado, -a [indetermi'naðo, a] *adj* indefinite; *(desconocido)* indeterminate

India ['indja] *nf*: **la ~** India

indicación [indika'θjon] *nf* indication; *(señal)* sign; *(sugerencia)* suggestion, hint

indicado, -a [indi'kaðo, a] *adj (momento, método)* right; *(tratamiento)* appropriate; *(solución)* likely

indicador [indika'ðor] *nm* indicator; *(Tec)* gauge, meter

indicar [indi'kar] /1g/ *vt (mostrar)* to indicate, show; *(termómetro etc)* to read, register; *(señalar)* to point to

índice ['indiθe] *nm* index; *(catálogo)* catalogue; *(Anat)* index finger, forefinger; **~ de materias** table of contents

indicio [in'diθjo] *nm* indication, sign; *(en pesquisa etc)* clue

indiferencia [indife'renθja] nf
indifference; (apatía) apathy;
indiferente adj indifferent

indígena [in'dixena] adj indigenous,
native ▷ nmf native

indigestión [indixes'tjon] nf
indigestion

indigesto, -a [indi'xesto, a] adj
indigestible; (fig) turgid

indignación [indiɣna'θjon] nf
indignation

indignar [indiɣ'nar] /1a/ vt to anger,
make indignant; **indignarse** vr: **~se
por** to get indignant about

indigno, -a [in'diɣno, a] adj
(despreciable) low, contemptible;
(inmerecido) unworthy

indio, -a [in'djo, a] adj, nm/f Indian

indirecto, -a [indi'rekto, a] adj
indirect ▷ nf insinuation, innuendo;
(sugerencia) hint

indiscreción [indiskre'θjon] nf
(imprudencia) indiscretion; (irreflexión)
tactlessness; (acto) gaffe, faux pas

indiscreto, -a [indis'kreto, a] adj
indiscreet

indiscutible [indisku'tiβle] adj
indisputable, unquestionable

indispensable [indispen'saβle] adj
indispensable, essential

indispuesto, -a [indis'pwesto, a]
adj (enfermo) unwell, indisposed

indistinto, -a [indis'tinto, a] adj
indistinct; (vago) vague

individual [indiβi'ðwal] adj
individual; (habitación) single ▷ nm
(Deporte) singles sg

individuo, -a [indi'βiðwo, a] adj
▷ nm individual

índole ['indole] nf (naturaleza) nature;
(clase) sort, kind

inducir [indu'θir] /3n/ vt to induce;
(inferir) to infer; (persuadir) to persuade

indudable [indu'ðaβle] adj
undoubted; (incuestionable)
unquestionable

indultar [indul'tar] /1a/ vt (perdonar)
to pardon, reprieve; (librar de pago)

to exempt; **indulto** nm pardon;
exemption

industria [in'dustrja] nf industry;
(habilidad) skill; **industrial** adj
industrial ▷ nm industrialist

inédito, -a [i'neðito, a] adj (libro)
unpublished; (nuevo) new

ineficaz [inefi'kaθ] adj (inútil)
ineffective; (ineficiente) inefficient

ineludible [inelu'ðiβle] adj
inescapable, unavoidable

ineptitud [inepti'tuð] nf ineptitude,
incompetence; **inepto, -a** adj inept,
incompetent

inequívoco, -a [ine'kiβoko, a]
adj unequivocal; (inconfundible)
unmistakable

inercia [i'nerθja] nf inertia; (pasividad)
passivity

inerte [i'nerte] adj inert; (inmóvil)
motionless

inesperado, -a [inespe'raðo, a] adj
unexpected, unforeseen

inestable [ines'taβle] adj unstable

inevitable [ineβi'taβle] adj
inevitable

inexacto, -a [inek'sakto, a] adj
inaccurate; (falso) untrue

inexperto, -a [ineks'perto, a] adj
(novato) inexperienced

infalible [infa'liβle] adj infallible;
(plan) foolproof

infame [in'fame] adj infamous;
infamia nf infamy; (deshonra)
disgrace

infancia [in'fanθja] nf infancy,
childhood

infantería [infante'ria] nf infantry

infantil [infan'til] adj child's,
children's; (pueril, aniñado) infantile;
(cándido) childlike

infarto [in'farto] nm (tb: **~ de
miocardio**) heart attack; **~ cerebral**
stroke

infatigable [infati'ɣaβle] adj tireless,
untiring

infección [infek'θjon] nf infection;
infeccioso, -a adj infectious

infectar [infek'tar] /1a/ vt to infect;
infectarse vr

infeliz [infe'liθ] adj unhappy,
wretched ▷ nmf wretch

inferior [infe'rjor] adj inferior;
(situación) lower ▷ nmf inferior,
subordinate

inferir [infe'rir] /3i/ vt (deducir) to
infer, deduce; (causar) to cause

infidelidad [infiδeli'δaδ] nf
infidelity, unfaithfulness

infiel [in'fjel] adj unfaithful, disloyal;
(falso) inaccurate ▷ nmf infidel,
unbeliever

infierno [in'fjerno] nm hell

ínfimo, -a ['infimo, a] adj (vil) vile,
mean; (más bajo) lowest

infinidad [infini'δaδ] nf infinity;
(abundancia) great quantity

infinito, -a [infi'nito, a] adj ▷ nm
infinite

inflación [infla'θjon] nf (hinchazón)
swelling; (monetaria) inflation; (fig)
conceit

inflamable [infla'maβle] adj
flammable

inflamar [infla'mar] /1a/ vt (Med, fig)
to inflame; **inflamarse** vr to catch fire;
to become inflamed

inflar [in'flar] /1a/ vt (hinchar) to
inflate, blow up; (fig) to exaggerate;
inflarse vr to swell (up); (fig) to get
conceited

inflexible [inflek'siβle] adj inflexible;
(fig) unbending

influencia [influ'enθja] nf influence

influir [influ'ir] /3g/ vt to influence

influjo [in'fluxo] nm influence

influya etc vb V **influir**

influyente [influ'jente] adj
influential

información [informa'θjon] nf
information; (noticias) news sg; (Jur)
inquiry; **I~** (oficina) information desk;
(Telec) Directory Enquiries (BRIT),
Directory Assistance (US); (mostrador)
Information Desk

informal [infor'mal] adj informal

informar [infor'mar] /1a/ vt (gen) to
inform; (revelar) to reveal, make known
▷ vi (Jur) to plead; (denunciar) to inform;
(dar cuenta de) to report on; **informarse**
vr to find out; **~se de** to inquire into

informática [infor'matika] nf V
informático

informático, -a [infor'matiko,
a] adj computer cpd ▷ nf (Tec)
information technology; computing;
(Escol) computer science o studies

informe [in'forme] adj shapeless
▷ nm report

infracción [infrak'θjon] nf
infraction, infringement

infravalorar [infraβalo'rar]
/1a/ vt to undervalue; (Finanzas) to
underestimate

infringir [infrin'xir] /3c/ vt to
infringe, contravene

infundado, -a [infun'daδo, a] adj
groundless, unfounded

infundir [infun'dir] /3a/ vt to
infuse, instil

infusión [infu'sjon] nf infusion; **~ de
manzanilla** camomile tea

ingeniería [inxenje'ria] nf
engineering; **~ genética** genetic
engineering; **ingeniero, -a** nm/f
engineer; **ingeniero de caminos**
civil engineer

ingenio [in'xenjo] nm (talento) talent;
(agudeza) wit; (habilidad) ingenuity,
inventiveness; **~ azucarero** sugar
refinery; **ingenioso, -a** adj ingenious,
clever; (divertido) witty

ingenuo, -a [in'xenwo, a] adj
ingenuous

ingerir [inxe'rir] /3i/ vt to ingest;
(tragar) to swallow; (consumir) to
consume

Inglaterra [ingla'terra] nf England

ingle ['ingle] nf groin

inglés, -esa [in'gles, esa] adj English
▷ nm/f Englishman/woman ▷ nm
(Ling) English

ingrato, -a [in'grato, a] adj
ungrateful

ingrediente [ingre'ðjente] *nm* ingredient

ingresar [ingre'sar] /1a/ *vt* (*dinero*) to deposit ▷ *vi* to come o go in; **~ en el hospital** to go into hospital

ingreso [in'greso] *nm* (*entrada*) entry; (: *en hospital etc*) admission; **ingresos** *nmpl* (*dinero*) income *sg*; (: *Com*) takings *pl*

inhabitable [inaβi'taβle] *adj* uninhabitable

inhalar [ina'lar] /1a/ *vt* to inhale

inhibir [ini'βir] /3a/ *vt* to inhibit

inhóspito, -a [i'nospito, a] *adj* (*región, paisaje*) inhospitable

inhumano, -a [inu'mano, a] *adj* inhuman

inicial [ini'θjal] *adj, nf* initial

iniciar [ini'θjar] /1b/ *vt* (*persona*) to initiate; (*empezar*) to begin, commence; (*conversación*) to start up

iniciativa [iniθja'tiβa] *nf* initiative; **~ privada** private enterprise

ininterrumpido, -a [ininterrum'piðo, a] *adj* uninterrupted

injertar [inxer'tar] /1a/ *vt* to graft; **injerto** *nm* graft

injuria [in'xurja] *nf* (*agravio, ofensa*) offence; (*insulto*) insult

No confundir *injuria* con la palabra inglesa *injury*.

injusticia [inxus'tiθja] *nf* injustice

injusto, -a [in'xusto, a] *adj* unjust, unfair

inmadurez [inmaðu'reθ] *nf* immaturity

inmediaciones [inmeðja'θjones] *nfpl* neighbourhood *sg*, environs

inmediato, -a [inme'ðjato, a] *adj* immediate; (*contiguo*) adjoining; (*rápido*) prompt; (*próximo*) neighbouring, next; **de ~** immediately

inmejorable [inmexo'raβle] *adj* unsurpassable; (*precio*) unbeatable

inmenso, -a [in'menso, a] *adj* immense, huge

inmigración [inmiɣra'θjon] *nf* immigration

inmolar [inmo'lar] /1a/ *vt* to immolate, sacrifice

inmoral [inmo'ral] *adj* immoral

inmortal [inmor'tal] *adj* immortal; **inmortalizar** /1f/ *vt* to immortalize

inmóvil [in'moβil] *adj* immobile

inmueble [in'mweβle] *adj*: **bienes ~s** real estate *sg*, landed property *sg* ▷ *nm* property

inmundo, -a [in'mundo, a] *adj* filthy

inmune [in'mune] *adj*: **~ (a)** (*Med*) immune (to)

inmunidad [inmuni'ðað] *nf* immunity

inmutarse [inmu'tarse] /1a/ *vr* to turn pale; **no se inmutó** he didn't turn a hair; **siguió sin ~** he carried on unperturbed

innato, -a [in'nato, a] *adj* innate

innecesario, -a [inneθe'sarjo, a] *adj* unnecessary

innovación [innoβa'θjon] *nf* innovation

innovar [inno'βar] /1a/ *vt* to introduce

inocencia [ino'θenθja] *nf* innocence

inocentada [inoθen'taða] *nf* practical joke

inocente [ino'θente] *adj* (*ingenuo*) naive, innocent; (*no culpable*) innocent; (*sin malicia*) harmless ▷ *nmf* simpleton; **día de los (Santos) I~s** ≈ April Fools' Day

DÍA DE LOS INOCENTES

The 28th December, *el día de los (Santos) Inocentes*, is when the Church commemorates the story of Herod's slaughter of the innocent children of Judea in the time of Christ. On this day Spaniards play *inocentadas* (practical jokes) on each other, much like our April Fools' Day pranks, eg typically sticking a *monigote* (cut-out paper figure) on

● someone's back, or broadcasting
● unlikely news stories.

inodoro [ino'ðoro] *nm* toilet (BRIT),
lavatory (BRIT), washroom (US)
inofensivo, -a [inofen'siβo, a] *adj*
inoffensive
inolvidable [inolβi'ðaβle] *adj*
unforgettable
inoportuno, -a [inopor'tuno, a] *adj*
untimely; *(molesto)* inconvenient
inoxidable [inoksi'ðaβle] *adj:* **acero**
~ stainless steel
inquietar [inkje'tar] /1a/ *vt* to
worry, trouble; **inquietarse** *vr* to
worry, get upset; **inquieto, -a** *adj*
anxious, worried; **inquietud** *nf*
anxiety, worry
inquilino, -a [inki'lino, a] *nm/f*
tenant
insaciable [insa'θjaβle] *adj*
insatiable
inscribir [inskri'βir] /3a/ *vt* to
inscribe; *(en lista)* to put; *(en censo)*
to register
inscripción [inskrip'θjon] *nf*
inscription; *(Escol etc)* enrolment; *(en
censo)* registration
insecticida [insekti'θiða] *nm*
insecticide
insecto [in'sekto] *nm* insect
inseguridad [inseɣuri'ðað] *nf*
insecurity; ~ **ciudadana** lack of safety
in the streets
inseguro, -a [inse'ɣuro, a] *adj*
insecure; *(inconstante)* unsteady;
(incierto) uncertain
insensato, -a [insen'sato, a] *adj*
foolish, stupid
insensible [insen'siβle] *adj*
(gen) insensitive; *(movimiento)*
imperceptible; *(sin sensación)* numb
insertar [inser'tar] /1a/ *vt* to insert
inservible [inser'βiβle] *adj* useless
insignia [in'siɣnja] *nf (señal distintiva)*
badge; *(estandarte)* flag
insignificante [insiɣnifi'kante] *adj*
insignificant

insinuar [insi'nwar] /1e/ *vt* to
insinuate, imply
insípido, -a [in'sipiðo, a] *adj* insipid
insistir [insis'tir] /3a/ *vi* to insist; ~
en algo to insist on sth; *(enfatizar)* to
stress sth
insolación [insola'θjon] *nf (Med)*
sunstroke
insolente [inso'lente] *adj* insolent
insólito, -a [in'solito, a] *adj* unusual
insoluble [inso'luβle] *adj* insoluble
insomnio [in'somnjo] *nm* insomnia
insonorizado, -a [insonori'θaðo, a]
adj (cuarto etc) soundproof
insoportable [insopor'taβle] *adj*
unbearable
inspección [inspek'θjon] *nf*
inspection, check; **inspeccionar** /1a/
vt (examinar) to inspect, examine;
(controlar) to check
inspector, a [inspek'tor, a] *nm/f*
inspector
inspiración [inspira'θjon] *nf*
inspiration
inspirar [inspi'rar] /1a/ *vt* to inspire;
(Med) to inhale; **inspirarse** *vr:* ~**se en**
to be inspired by
instalación [instala'θjon] *nf (equipo)*
fittings *pl*, equipment; ~ **eléctrica**
wiring
instalar [insta'lar] /1a/ *vt (establecer)*
to install; *(erguir)* to set up, erect;
instalarse *vr* to establish o.s.; *(en una
vivienda)* to move into
instancia [ins'tanθja] *nf (ruego)*
request; *(Jur)* petition; **en última** ~ as
a last resort
instantáneo, -a [instan'taneo,
a] *adj* instantaneous; **café** ~ instant
coffee
instante [ins'tante] *nm* instant,
moment; **al** ~ right now
instar [ins'tar] /1a/ *vt* to press, urge
instaurar [instau'rar] /1a/ *vt*
(costumbre) to establish; *(normas,
sistema)* to bring in, introduce;
(gobierno) to install
instigar [insti'ɣar] /1h/ *vt* to instigate

instinto [ins'tinto] nm instinct; **por ~** instinctively
institución [institu'θjon] nf institution, establishment
instituir [institu'ir] /3g/ vt to establish; (fundar) to found; **instituto** nm (gen) institute; **Instituto Nacional de Enseñanza** (ESP) ≈ (state) secondary (BRIT) o high (US) school
institutriz [institu'triθ] nf governess
instrucción [instruk'θjon] nf instruction
instructor [instruk'tor] nm instructor
instruir [instru'ir] /3g/ vt (gen) to instruct; (enseñar) to teach, educate
instrumento [instru'mento] nm instrument; (herramienta) tool, implement
insubordinarse [insuβorði'narse] /1a/ vr to rebel
insuficiente [insufi'θjente] adj (gen) insufficient; (Escol: nota) unsatisfactory
insular [insu'lar] adj insular
insultar [insul'tar] /1a/ vt to insult; **insulto** nm insult
insuperable [insupe'raβle] adj (excelente) unsurpassable; (problema etc) insurmountable
insurrección [insurrek'θjon] nf insurrection, rebellion
intachable [inta'tʃaβle] adj irreproachable
intacto, -a [in'takto, a] adj intact
integral [inte'γral] adj integral; (completo) complete; **pan ~** wholemeal bread
integrar [inte'γrar] /1a/ vt to make up, compose; (Mat, fig) to integrate
integridad [inteγri'ðað] nf wholeness; (carácter) integrity; **íntegro, -a** adj whole, entire; (honrado) honest
intelectual [intelek'twal] adj, nmf intellectual

inteligencia [inteli'xenθja] nf intelligence; (ingenio) ability; **inteligente** adj intelligent
intemperie [intem'perje] nf: **a la ~** outdoors, out in the open, exposed to the elements
intención [inten'θjon] nf intention, purpose; **con segundas intenciones** maliciously; **con ~** deliberately
intencionado, -a [intenθjo'naðo, a] adj deliberate; **mal ~** ill-disposed, hostile
intensidad [intensi'ðað] nf (gen) intensity; (Elec, Tec) strength; **llover con ~** to rain hard
intenso, -a [in'tenso, a] adj intense; (sentimiento) profound, deep
intentar [inten'tar] /1a/ vt (tratar) to try, attempt; **intento** nm attempt
interactivo, -a [interak'tiβo, a] adj interactive
intercalar [interka'lar] /1a/ vt to insert
intercambio [inter'kambjo] nm exchange; swap
interceder [interθe'ðer] /2a/ vi to intercede
interceptar [interθep'tar] /1a/ vt to intercept
interés [inte'res] nm interest; (parte) share, part; (pey) self-interest; **intereses creados** vested interests
interesado, -a [intere'saðo, a] adj interested; (prejuiciado) prejudiced; (pey) mercenary, self-seeking
interesante [intere'sante] adj interesting
interesar [intere'sar] /1a/ vt to interest, be of interest to ▷ vi to interest, be of interest; **interesarse** vr: **~se en** o **por** to take an interest in
interferir [interfe'rir] /3i/ vt to interfere with; (Telec) to jam ▷ vi to interfere
interfono [inter'fono] nm intercom, entry phone
interino, -a [inte'rino, a] adj temporary ▷ nm/f temporary holder

of a post; (Med) locum; (Escol) supply teacher

interior [inte'rjor] adj inner, inside; (Com) domestic, internal ▷ nm interior, inside; (fig) soul, mind; **Ministerio del I~** ≈ Home Office (BRIT), ≈ Department of the Interior (US)

interjección [interxek'θjon] nf interjection

interlocutor, a [interloku'tor, a] nm/f speaker

intermedio, -a [inter'meðjo, a] adj intermediate ▷ nm interval

interminable [intermi'naβle] adj endless

intermitente [intermi'tente] adj intermittent ▷ nm (Auto) indicator

internacional [internaθjo'nal] adj international

internado [inter'naðo] nm boarding school

internar [inter'nar] /1a/ vt to intern; (en un manicomio) to commit; **internarse** vr (penetrar) to penetrate

internauta [inter'nauta] nmf web surfer, internet user

Internet [inter'net] nm o f internet, Internet

interno, -a [in'terno, a] adj internal, interior; (Pol etc) domestic ▷ nm/f (alumno) boarder

interponer [interpo'ner] /2q/ vt to interpose, put in; **interponerse** vr to intervene

interpretación [interpreta'θjon] nf interpretation

interpretar [interpre'tar] /1a/ vt to interpret; (Teat, Mus) to perform, play; **intérprete** nmf (Ling) interpreter, translator; (Mus, Teat) performer, artist(e)

interrogación [interroγa'θjon] nf interrogation; (Ling: tb: **signo de ~**) question mark

interrogar [interro'γar] /1h/ vt to interrogate, question

interrumpir [interrum'pir] /3a/ vt to interrupt

interrupción [interrup'θjon] nf interruption

interruptor [interrup'tor] nm (Elec) switch

intersección [intersek'θjon] nf intersection

interurbano, -a [interur'βano, a] adj (Telec) long-distance

intervalo [inter'βalo] nm interval; (descanso) break

intervenir [interβe'nir] /3r/ vt (controlar) to control, supervise; (Med) to operate on ▷ vi (participar) to take part, participate; (mediar) to intervene

interventor, a [interβen'tor, a] nm/f inspector; (Com) auditor

intestino [intes'tino] nm intestine

intimar [inti'mar] /1a/ vi to become friendly

intimidad [intimi'ðað] nf intimacy; (familiaridad) familiarity; (vida privada) private life; (Jur) privacy

íntimo, -a [in'timo, a] adj intimate

intolerable [intole'raβle] adj intolerable, unbearable

intoxicación [intoksika'θjon] nf poisoning; **~ alimenticia** food poisoning

intranet [intra'net] nf intranet

intranquilo, -a [intran'kilo, a] adj worried

intransitable [intransi'taβle] adj impassable

intrépido, -a [in'trepiðo, a] adj intrepid

intriga [in'triγa] nf intrigue; (plan) plot; **intrigar** /1h/ vt, vi to intrigue

intrínseco, -a [in'trinseko, a] adj intrinsic

introducción [introðuk'θjon] nf introduction

introducir [introðu'θir] /3n/ vt (gen) to introduce; (moneda) to insert; (Inform) to input, enter

intromisión [intromi'sjon] nf interference, meddling

introvertido, -a [introβer'tiðo, a] adj, nm/f introvert

intruso, -a [in'truso, a] *adj* intrusive
▷ *nm/f* intruder
intuición [intwi'θjon] *nf* intuition
inundación [inunda'θjon] *nf*
flood(ing); **inundar** /1a/ *vt* to flood;
(*fig*) to swamp, inundate
insitado, -a [insi'taðo, a] *adj*
unusual
inútil [i'nutil] *adj* useless; (*esfuerzo*)
vain, fruitless
inutilizar [inutili'θar] /1f/ *vt* to make
unusable
invadir [imba'ðir] /3a/ *vt* to invade
inválido, -a [im'baliðo, a] *adj* invalid
▷ *nm/f* invalid
invasión [imba'sjon] *nf* invasion
invasor, a [imba'sor, a] *adj* invading
▷ *nm/f* invader
invención [imben'θjon] *nf* invention
inventar [imben'tar] /1a/ *vt* to invent
inventario [imben'tarjo] *nm*
inventory
invento [im'bento] *nm* invention
inventor, a [imben'tor, a] *nm/f*
inventor
invernadero [imberna'ðero] *nm*
greenhouse
inverosímil [imbero'simil] *adj*
implausible
inversión [imber'sjon] *nf* (*Com*)
investment
inverso, a [im'berso, a] *adj* inverse,
opposite; **en el orden** = in reverse
order; **a la inversa** inversely, the
other way round
inversor, -a [imber'sor, a] *nm/f*
(*Com*) investor
invertir [imber'tir] /3i/ *vt* (*Com*) to
invest; (*volcar*) to turn upside down;
(*tiempo etc*) to spend
investigación [imbestiγa'θjon]
nf investigation; (*Univ*) research; ~
y desarrollo (*Com*) research and
development (R & D)
investigar [imbesti'γar] /1h/ *vt* to
investigate; (*estudiar*) to do research
into
invierno [im'bjerno] *nm* winter

invisible [imbi'siβle] *adj* invisible
invitación [imbita'θjon] *nf*
invitation
invitado, -a [imbi'taðo, a] *nm/f*
guest
invitar [imbi'tar] /1a/ *vt* to invite;
(*incitar*) to entice; ~ **a algo** to pay
for sth
invocar [imbo'kar] /1g/ *vt* to invoke,
call on
involucrar [imbolu'krar] /1a/ *vt*:
~ **a algn en algo** to involve sb in sth;
involucrarse *vr* to get involved
involuntario, -a [imbolun'tarjo,
a] *adj* involuntary; (*ofensa etc*)
unintentional
inyección [injek'θjon] *nf* injection
inyectar [injek'tar] /1a/ *vt* to inject
iPod® ['ipoð] (*pl* **iPods**) *nm* iPod®

PALABRA CLAVE

ir [ir] /3s/ *vi* **1** to go; **ir caminando** to
walk; **fui en tren** I went o travelled by
train; **¡(ahora) voy!** (I'm just) coming!
2: **ir (a) por: ir (a) por el médico** to
fetch the doctor
3 (*progresar: persona, cosa*) to go; **el
trabajo va muy bien** work is going
very well; **¿cómo te va?** how are
things going?; **me va muy bien** I'm
getting on very well; **le fue fatal** it
went awfully badly for him
4 (*funcionar*): **el coche no va muy
bien** the car isn't running very well
5: **te va estupendamente ese color**
that colour suits you fantastically well
6 (*aspecto*): **iba muy bien vestido** he
was very well dressed
7 (*locuciones*): **¿vino? — ¡que va!** did
he come? — of course not!; **vamos,
no llores** come on, don't cry; **¡vaya
coche!** (*admiración*) what a car!, that's
some car!
8: **no vaya a ser: tienes que correr,
no vaya a ser que pierdas el tren**
you'll have to run so as not to miss
the train

9: no me *etc* **va ni me viene** *etc* don't care

▶ *vb auxiliar* **1: ira: voy/iba a hacerlo hoy** I am/was going to do it today **2** (+ *gerundio*): **iba anocheciendo** it was getting dark; **todo se me iba aclarando** everything was gradually becoming clearer to me **3** (+ *pp* = *pasivo*): **van vendidos 300 ejemplares** 300 copies have been sold so far

▶ **irse** *vr* **1: ¿por dónde se va al zoológico?** which is the way to the zoo? **2** (*marcharse*) to leave; **ya se habrán ido** they must already have left *o* gone

ira ['ira] *nf* anger, rage

Irak [i'rak] *nm* Iraq; **irakí,** *nmf* Iraqui

Irán [i'ran] *nm* Iran; **iraní** *adj, nmf* Iranian

Iraq [i'rak] *nm* = **Irak**

iris ['iris] *nm inv* (*arco iris*) rainbow; (*Anat*) iris

Irlanda [ir'landa] *nf* Ireland; **~ del Norte** Northern Ireland; **irlandés, -esa** *adj* Irish ▷ *nm/f* Irishman/ woman; **los irlandeses** the Irish

ironía [iro'nia] *nf* irony; **irónico, -a** *adj* ironic(al)

IRPF *nm abr* (*ESP*) = **impuesto sobre la renta de las personas físicas**

irreal [irre'al] *adj* unreal

irregular [irreɣu'lar] *adj* irregular; (*situación*) abnormal

irremediable [irreme'ðjaβle] *adj* irremediable; (*vicio*) incurable

irreparable [irrepa'raβle] *adj* (*daños*) irreparable; (*pérdida*) irrecoverable

irrespetuoso, -a [irrespe'twoso, a] *adj* disrespectful

irresponsable [irrespon'saβle] *adj* irresponsible

irreversible [irreβer'siβle] *adj* irreversible

irrigar [irri'ɣar] /1h/ *vt* to irrigate

irrisorio, -a [irri'sorjo, a] *adj* derisory, ridiculous

irritar [irri'tar] /1a/ *vt* to irritate, annoy

irrupción [irrup'θjon] *nf* irruption; (*invasión*) invasion

isla ['isla] *nf* island

Islam [is'lam] *nm* Islam; **islámico, -a** *adj* Islamic

islandés, -esa [islan'des, esa] *adj* Icelandic ▷ *nm/f* Icelander

Islandia [is'landja] *nf* Iceland

isleño, -a [is'leɲo, a] *adj* island *cpd* ▷ *nm/f* islander

Israel [isra'el] *nm* Israel; **israelí** *adj, nmf* Israeli

istmo ['istmo] *nm* isthmus

Italia [i'talja] *nf* Italy; **italiano, -a** *adj, nm/f* Italian

itinerario [itine'rarjo] *nm* itinerary, route

ITV *nf abr* (= *Inspección Técnica de Vehículos*) ≈ MOT (test)

IVA ['iβa] *nm abr* (= *Impuesto sobre el Valor Añadido*) VAT

izar [i'θar] /1f/ *vt* to hoist

izdo., izq.⁰ *abr* (= *izquierdo*) L, l

izquierda [iθ'kjerða] *nf* V **izquierdo**

izquierdo, -a [iθ'kjerðo, a] *adj* left ▷ *nf* left; (*Pol*) left (*wing*); **a la izquierda** on the left; (*torcer etc*) (to the) left

J

jabalí [xaβaˈli] nm wild boar
jabalina [xaβaˈlina] nf javelin
jabón [xaˈβon] nm soap
jaca [ˈxaka] nf pony
jacal [xaˈkal] nm (LAM) shack
jacinto [xaˈθinto] nm hyacinth
jactarse [xakˈtarse] /1a/ vr: ~ **de** to boast o brag (about o of)
jadear [xaðeˈar] /1a/ vi to pant, gasp for breath
jaguar [xaˈɣwar] nm jaguar
jaiba [ˈxaiβa] nf (LAM) crab
jalar [xaˈlar] /1a/ vt (LAM) to pull
jalea [xaˈlea] nf jelly
jaleo [xaˈleo] nm racket, uproar; **armar un ~** to kick up a racket
jalón [xaˈlon] nm (LAM) tug
jamás [xaˈmas] adv never
jamón [xaˈmon] nm ham; ~ **(de) York** boiled ham; ~ **dulce/serrano** boiled/cured ham
Japón [xaˈpon] nm: Japan; **japonés, -esa** adj, nm/f Japanese ▷ nm (Ling) Japanese

jaque [ˈxake] nm: ~ **mate** checkmate
jaqueca [xaˈkeka] nf (very bad) headache, migraine
jarabe [xaˈraβe] nm syrup
jardín [xarˈðin] nm garden; ~ **de (la) infancia** (ESP) o **de niños** (LAM) o **infantil** nursery school; **jardinaje** nm gardening; **jardinería** nf gardening; **jardinero, -a** nm/f gardener
jarra [ˈxarra] nf jar; (jarro) jug
jarro [ˈxarro] nm jug
jarrón [xaˈrron] nm vase
jaula [ˈxaula] nf cage
jauría [xauˈria] nf pack of hounds
jazmín [xaθˈmin] nm jasmine
J. C. abr = **Jesucristo**
jeans [jins, dʒins] nmpl (LAM) jeans, denims; **unos ~** a pair of jeans
jefatura [xefaˈtura] nf: ~ **de policía** police headquarters sg
jefe, -a [ˈxefe, a] nm/f (gen) chief, head; (patrón) boss; ~ **de cocina** chef; ~ **de estación** stationmaster; ~ **de estado** head of state; ~ **de estudios** (Escol) director of studies; ~ **de gobierno** head of government
jengibre [xenˈxiβre] nm ginger
jeque [ˈxeke] nm sheik(h)
jerárquico, -a [xeˈrarkiko, a] adj hierarchic(al)
jerez [xeˈreθ] nm sherry
jerga [ˈxerɣa] nf jargon
jeringa [xeˈrinɡa] nf syringe; (LAM) annoyance, bother; **jeringuilla** nf syringe
jeroglífico [xeroˈɣlifiko] nm hieroglyphic
jersey [xerˈsei] nm (pl **jerseys**) nm jersey, pullover, jumper
Jerusalén [xerusaˈlen] n Jerusalem
Jesucristo [xesuˈkristo] nm Jesus Christ
jesuita [xeˈswita] adj, nm Jesuit
Jesús [xeˈsus] nm Jesus; **¡~!** good heavens!; (al estornudar) bless you!
jinete, -a [xiˈnete, a] nm/f horseman/ woman
jipijapa [xipiˈxapa] nm (LAM) straw hat

jirafa [xi'rafa] *nf* giraffe

jirón [xi'ron] *nm* rag, shred

jitomate [xito'mate] *nm* (ᴸᴀᴍ) tomato

joder [xo'ðer] /2a/ (fam!) *vt* to fuck (!)

jogging ['joɣin] *nm* (ᴸᴀᴍ) tracksuit (ʙʀɪᴛ), sweat suit (ᴜs)

jornada [xor'naða] *nf* (viaje de un día) day's journey; (camino o viaje entero) journey; (día de trabajo) working day

jornal [xor'nal] *nm* (day's) wage; **jornalero, -a** *nm/f* (day) labourer

joroba [xo'roβa] *nf* hump; **jorobado, -a** *adj* hunchbacked ▷ *nm/f* hunchback

jota ['xota] *nf* letter J; (danza) Aragonese dance; **no saber ni ~** to have no idea

joven ['xoβen] *adj* young ▷ *nm* young man, youth ▷ *nf* young woman, girl

jovial [xo'βjal] *adj* cheerful, jovial

joya ['xoja] *nf* jewel, gem; (fig: persona) gem; **~s de fantasía** imitation jewellery sg; **joyería** (joyas) jewellery; (tienda) jeweller's (shop); **joyero** (persona) jeweller; (caja) jewel case

Juan [xwan] *nm:* **Noche de San ~** V **noche**

juanete [xwa'nete] *nm* (del pie) bunion

jubilación [xuβila'θjon] *nf* (retiro) retirement

jubilado, -a [xuβi'laðo, a] *adj* retired ▷ *nm/f* pensioner (ʙʀɪᴛ), senior citizen (ᴜs)

jubilar [xuβi'lar] /1a/ *vt* to pension off, retire; (fam) to discard; **jubilarse** *vr* to retire

júbilo ['xuβilo] *nm* joy, rejoicing; **jubiloso, -a** *adj* jubilant

judía [xu'ðia] *nf* V **judío**

judicial [xuði'θjal] *adj* judicial

judío, -a [xu'ðio, a] *adj* Jewish ▷ *nm* Jew ▷ *nf* Jewess; (Culin) bean; **judía blanca** haricot bean; **judía verde** French o string bean

judo ['juðo] *nm* judo

juego ['xweɣo] *vb* V **jugar** ▷ *nm* (gen) play; (pasatiempo, partido) game; (en casino) gambling; (conjunto) set; **~ de**

mesa board game; **~ de palabras** pun, play on words; **J~s Olímpicos** Olympic Games; **fuera de ~** (Deporte: persona) offside; (: pelota) out of play

juerga ['xwerɣa] *nf* binge; (fiesta) party; **ir de ~** to go out on a binge

jueves ['xweβes] *nm inv* Thursday

juez [xweθ] *nmf* judge; **~ de instrucción** examining magistrate; **~ de línea** linesman; **~ de salida** starter

jugada [xu'ɣaða] *nf* play; **buena ~** good move o shot o stroke etc

jugador, a [xuɣa'ðor, a] *nm/f* player; (en casino) gambler

jugar [xu'ɣar] /1h, 1n/ *vt* to play; (en casino) to gamble; (apostar) to bet; **~ al fútbol** to play football

juglar [xu'ɣlar] *nm* minstrel

jugo ['xuɣo] *nm* (Bot) juice; (fig) essence, substance; **~ de naranja** (esp ᴸᴀᴍ) orange juice; **jugoso, -a** *adj* juicy; (fig) substantial, important

juguete [xu'ɣete] *nm* toy; **juguetear** /1a/ *vi* to play; **juguetería** *nf* toyshop

juguetón, -ona [xuɣe'ton, ona] *adj* playful

juicio ['xwiθjo] *nm* judgement; (sana razón) sanity, reason; (opinión) opinion

julio ['xuljo] *nm* July

jumper ['dʒumper] *nm* (ᴸᴀᴍ) pinafore dress (ʙʀɪᴛ), jumper (ᴜs)

junco ['xunko] *nm* rush, reed

jungla ['xungla] *nf* jungle

junio ['xunjo] *nm* June

junta ['xunta] *nf* V **junto**

juntar [xun'tar] /1a/ *vt* to join, unite; (maquinaria) to assemble, put together; (dinero) to collect; **juntarse** *vr* to join, meet; (reunirse: personas) to meet, assemble; (arrimarse) to approach, draw closer; **~se con algn** to join sb

junto, -a ['xunto, a] *adj* joined; (unido) united; (anexo) near, close; (contiguo, próximo) next, adjacent ▷ *nf* (asamblea) meeting, assembly; (comité, consejo) board, council, committee; (articulación) joint ▷ *adv:* **todo ~** all at

once ▷ *prep*: **~ a** near (to), next to; **~s** together; **~ con** (together) with
jurado [xu'raðo] *nm* (*Jur: individuo*) juror; (: *grupo*) jury; (*de concurso: grupo*) panel (of judges); (: *individuo*) member of a panel
juramento [xura'mento] *nm* oath; (*maldición*) oath, curse; **prestar ~** to take the oath; **tomar ~ a** to swear in, administer the oath to
jurar [xu'rar] /1a/ *vt, vi* to swear; **~ en falso** to commit perjury; **jurárselas a algn** to have it in for sb
jurídico, -a [xu'riðiko, a] *adj* legal
jurisdicción [xurisðik'θjon] *nf* (*poder, autoridad*) jurisdiction; (*territorio*) district
justamente [xusta'mente] *adv* justly, fairly; (*precisamente*) just, exactly
justicia [xus'tiθja] *nf* justice; (*equidad*) fairness, justice
justificación [xustifika'θjon] *nf* justification; **justificar** /1g/ *vt* to justify
justo, -a ['xusto, a] *adj* (*equitativo*) just, fair, right; (*preciso*) exact, correct; (*ajustado*) tight ▷ *adv* (*precisamente*) exactly, precisely; (*apenas a tiempo*) just in time
juvenil [xuβe'nil] *adj* youthful
juventud [xuβen'tuð] *nf* (*adolescencia*) youth; (*jóvenes*) young people *pl*
juzgado [xuθ'γaðo] *nm* tribunal; (*Jur*) court
juzgar [xuθ'γar] /1h/ *vt* to judge; **a ~ por ...** to judge by ..., judging by ...

kárate ['karate], **karate** [ka'rate] *nm* karate
Kg, kg *abr* (= *kilogramo(s)*) K, kg
kilo ['kilo] *nm* kilo; **kilogramo** *nm* kilogramme (BRIT), kilogram (US); **kilometraje** *nm* distance in kilometres, ≈ mileage; **kilómetro** *nm* kilometre (BRIT), kilometer (US); **kilovatio** *nm* kilowatt
kiosco ['kjosko] *nm* = **quiosco**
kleenex® [kli'neks] *nm* paper handkerchief, tissue
km *abr* (= *kilómetro(s)*) km
Kosovo [koso'βo] *nm* Kosovo
kv *abr* (= *kilovatio*) kw

l abr (= litro(s)) l

la [la] artículo definido fsg the ▷ pron her; (en relación a usted) you; (en relación a una cosa) it ▷ nm (Mus) A; **está en la cárcel** he's in jail; **la del sombrero rojo** the woman/girl/one in the red hat

laberinto [laβe'rinto] nm labyrinth

labio ['laβjo] nm lip

labor [la'βor] nf labour; (Agr) farm work; (tarea) job, task; (Costura) needlework; **~es domésticas o del hogar** household chores; **laborable** adj (Agr) workable; **día laborable** working day; **laboral** adj (accidente, conflictividad) industrial; (jornada) working

laboratorio [laβora'torjo] nm laboratory

laborista [laβo'rista] adj: **Partido L~** Labour Party

labrador, a [laβra'ðor, a] adj farming cpd ▷ nm/f farmer

labranza [la'βranθa] nf (Agr) cultivation

labrar [la'βrar] /1a/ vt (gen) to work; (madera etc) to carve; (fig) to cause, bring about

laca ['laka] nf lacquer

lacio, -a ['laθjo, a] adj (pelo) straight

lacón [la'kon] nm shoulder of pork

lactancia [lak'tanθja] nf lactation, breast-feeding

lácteo, -a ['lakteo, a] adj: **productos ~s** dairy products

ladear [laðe'ar] /1a/ vt to tip, tilt ▷ vi to tilt; **ladearse** vr to lean

ladera [la'ðera] nf slope

lado ['laðo] nm (gen) side; (fig) protection; (Mil) flank; **al ~ de** beside; **poner de ~** to put on its side; **poner a un ~** to put aside; **por todos ~s** on all sides, all round (BRIT)

ladrar [la'ðrar] /1a/ vi to bark; **ladrido** nm bark, barking

ladrillo [la'ðriʎo] nm (gen) brick; (azulejo) tile

ladrón, -ona [la'ðron, ona] nm/f thief

lagartija [laɣar'tixa] nf (small) lizard

lagarto [la'ɣarto] nm (Zool) lizard

lago ['laɣo] nm lake

lágrima ['laɣrima] nf tear

laguna [la'ɣuna] nf (lago) lagoon; (en escrito, conocimientos) gap

lamentable [lamen'taβle] adj lamentable, regrettable; (miserable) pitiful

lamentar [lamen'tar] /1a/ vt (sentir) to regret; (deplorar) to lament; **lamentarse** vr to lament; **lo lamento mucho** I'm very sorry

lamer [la'mer] /2a/ vt to lick

lámina ['lamina] nf (plancha delgada) sheet; (para estampar, estampa) plate

lámpara ['lampara] nf lamp; **~ de alcohol/gas** spirit/gas lamp; **~ de pie** standard lamp

lana ['lana] nf wool

lancha ['lantʃa] nf launch; **~ motora** motorboat

langosta [laŋ'gosta] nf (crustáceo) lobster; (: de río) crayfish; **langostino** nm prawn

lanza ['lanθa] nf (arma) lance, spear

lanzamiento [lanθa'mjento] nm (gen) throwing; (Naut, Com) launch, launching; **~ de pesos** putting the shot

lanzar [lan'θar] /1f/ vt (gen) to throw; (Deporte: pelota) to bowl; to launch; (Jur) to evict; **lanzarse** vr to throw o.s.

lapa ['lapa] nf limpet

lapicero [lapi'θero] nm pencil; (LAM) propelling (BRIT) o mechanical (US) pencil; (: bolígrafo) ballpoint pen, Biro®

lápida ['lapiða] nf stone; **~ mortuoria** headstone

lápiz ['lapiθ] nm pencil; **~ de color** coloured pencil; **~ de labios** lipstick; **~ de ojos** eyebrow pencil

largar [lar'ɣar] /1h/ vt (soltar) to release; (aflojar) to loosen; (lanzar) to launch; (fam) to let fly; (velas) to unfurl; (LAM) to throw; **largarse** vr (fam) to beat it; **~se a** (LAM) to start to

largo, -a ['larɣo, a] adj (longitud) long; (tiempo) lengthy; (fig) generous ▷ nm length; (Mus) largo; **dos años ~s** two long years; **a lo ~ de** along; (tiempo) all through; throughout; **a la larga** in the long run; **largometraje** nm full-length o feature film

▌ No confundir largo con la palabra inglesa large.

laringe [la'rinxe] nf larynx; **laringitis** nf laryngitis

las [las] artículo definido fpl the ▷ pron them; **~ que cantan** the ones/ women/girls who sing

lasaña [la'saɲa] nf lasagne, lasagna

láser ['laser] nm laser

lástima ['lastima] nf (pena) pity; **dar ~** to be pitiful; **es una ~ que** it's a pity that; **¡qué ~!** what a pity!; **estar hecho una ~** to be a sorry sight

lastimar [lasti'mar] /1a/ vt (herir) to wound; (ofender) to offend; **lastimarse** vr to hurt o.s.

lata ['lata] nf (metal) tin; (envase) tin, (envase) tin, tinned; **dar (la) ~** to be a nuisance

latente [la'tente] adj latent

lateral [late'ral] adj side, lateral ▷ nm (Teat) wings pl

latido [la'tiðo] nm (del corazón) beat

latifundio [lati'fundjo] nm large estate

latigazo [lati'ɣaθo] nm (golpe) lash; (sonido) crack

látigo ['latiɣo] nm whip

latín [la'tin] nm Latin

latino, -a [la'tino, a] adj Latin; **latinoamericano, -a** adj, nm/f Latin American

latir [la'tir] /3a/ vi (corazón, pulso) to beat

latitud [lati'tuð] nf (Geo) latitude

latón [la'ton] nm brass

laurel [lau'rel] nm (Bot) laurel; (Culin) bay

lava ['laβa] nf lava

lavabo [la'βaβo] nm (jofaina) washbasin; (retrete) toilet (BRIT), washroom (US)

lavado [la'βaðo] nm washing; (de ropa) laundry; (Arte) wash; **~ de cerebro** brainwashing; **~ en seco** dry-cleaning

lavadora [laβa'ðora] nf washing machine

lavanda [la'βanda] nf lavender

lavandería [laβande'ria] nf laundry; **~ automática** launderette

lavaplatos [laβa'platos] nm inv dishwasher

lavar [la'βar] /1a/ vt to wash; (borrar) to wipe away; **lavarse** vr to wash o.s.; **~se las manos** to wash one's hands; **~se los dientes** to brush one's teeth; **~ y marcar** (pelo) to shampoo and set; **~ en seco** to dry-clean; **~ los platos** to wash the dishes

lavarropas [laβa'rropas] nm inv (RPL) washing machine

lavavajillas [laβaβa'xiʎas] nm inv dishwasher

laxante [lak'sante] nm laxative

lazarillo [laθa'riʎo] nm: **perro de ~** guide dog

lazo ['laθo] nm knot; (lazada) bow; (para animales) lasso; (trampa) snare; (vínculo) tie

le [le] pron (directo) him (o her); (: en relación a usted) you; (indirecto) to him (o her o it); (: a usted) to you

leal [le'al] adj loyal; **lealtad** nf loyalty

lección [lek'θjon] nf lesson

leche ['letʃe] nf milk; **tener mala ~** (fam) to be a nasty piece of work; **~ condensada/en polvo** condensed/ powdered milk; **~ desnatada** skimmed milk

lechería [letʃe'ria] nf dairy

lecho ['letʃo] nm (cama, de río) bed; (Geo) layer

lechón [le'tʃon] nm sucking (BRIT) o suckling (US) pig

lechoso, a [le'tʃoso, a] adj milky

lechuga [le'tʃuɣa] nf lettuce

lechuza [le'tʃuθa] nf (barn) owl

lector, a [lek'tor, a] nm/f reader ▷ nm: **~ de discos compactos** CD player

lectura [lek'tura] nf reading

leer [le'er] /2e/ vt to read

legado [le'ɣaðo] nm (don) bequest; (herencia) legacy; (enviado) legate

legajo [le'ɣaxo] nm file

legal [le'ɣal] adj legal; (persona) trustworthy; **legalizar** /1f/ vt to legalize; (documento) to authenticate

legaña [le'ɣaɲa] nf sleep (in eyes)

legión [le'xjon] nf legion; **legionario, -a** adj legionary ▷ nm legionnaire

legislación [lexisla'θjon] nf legislation

legislar [lexis'lar] /1a/ vt to legislate; **legislatura** [lexisla'tura] nf (Pol) period of office

legítimo, -a [le'xitimo, a] adj (genuino) authentic; (legal) legitimate

legua ['leɣwa] nf league

legumbres [le'ɣumbres] nfpl pulses

leído, -a [le'iðo, a] adj well-read

lejanía [lexa'nia] nf distance; **lejano, -a** adj far-off; (en el tiempo) distant; (fig) remote

lejía [le'xia] nf bleach

lejos [le'xos] adv far, far away; **a lo ~** in the distance; **de o desde ~** from a distance; **~ de** far from

lema ['lema] nm motto; (Pol) slogan

lencería [lenθe'ria] nf linen, drapery

lengua ['lengwa] nf tongue; (Ling) language; **morderse la ~** to hold one's tongue

lenguado [len'gwaðo] nm sole

lenguaje [len'gwaxe] nm language; **~ de programación** programming language

lengüeta [len'gweta] nf (Anat) epiglottis; (de zapatos) tongue; (Mus) reed

lente ['lente] nm o f lens; (lupa) magnifying glass; **lentes** nmpl glasses; **~s bifocales/de sol** (LAM) bifocals/ sunglasses; **~s de contacto** contact lenses

lenteja [len'texa] nf lentil; **lentejuela** nf sequin

lentilla [len'tiʎa] nf contact lens

lentitud [lenti'tuð] nf slowness; **con ~** slowly

lento, -a ['lento, a] adj slow

leña ['leɲa] nf firewood; **leñador, a** nm/f woodcutter

leño ['leɲo] nm (trozo de árbol) log; (madera) timber; (fig) blockhead

Leo ['leo] nm Leo

león [le'on] nm lion; **~ marino** sea lion

leopardo [leo'parðo] nm leopard

leotardos [leo'tarðos] nmpl tights

lepra ['lepra] nf leprosy; **leproso, -a** nm/f leper

les [les] pron (directo) them; (: en relación a ustedes) you; (indirecto) to them; (: a ustedes) to you

lesbiana [les'βjana] adj, nf lesbian

lesión [le'sjon] nf wound, lesion; (Deporte) injury; **lesionado, -a** adj injured ▷ nm/f injured person

letal [le'tal] adj lethal

letanía [leta'nia] nf litany
letra ['letra] nf letter; (escritura)
handwriting; (Mus) lyrics pl; **~ de
cambio** bill of exchange; **~ de
imprenta** print; **letrado, -a** adj
learned ▷ nm/f lawyer; **letrero**
(cartel) sign; (etiqueta) label
letrina [le'trina] nf latrine
leucemia [leu'θemja] nf leukaemia
levadura [leβa'ðura] nf yeast; **~ de
cerveza** brewer's yeast
levantar [leβan'tar] /1a/ vt (gen)
to raise; (del suelo) to pick up; (hacia
arriba) to lift (up); (plan) to make, draw
up; (mesa) to clear; (campamento)
to strike; (fig) to cheer up, hearten;
levantarse vr to get up; (enderezarse)
to straighten up; (rebelarse) to rebel; **~
el ánimo** to cheer up
levante [le'βante] nm east; **el L-**
region of Spain extending from Castellón
to Murcia
levar [le'βar] /1a/ vt, vi: **~ (anclas)** to
weigh anchor
leve ['leβe] adj light; (fig) trivial
levita [le'βita] nf frock coat
léxico ['leksiko] nm vocabulary
ley [lei] nf (gen) law; (metal) standard
leyenda [le'jenda] nf legend
leyó etc vb V **leer**
liar [li'ar] /1c/ vt to tie (up); (unir) to
bind; (envolver) to wrap (up); (enredar)
to confuse; (cigarrillo) to roll; **liarse** vr
(fam) to get involved; **~se a palos** to
get involved in a fight
Líbano ['liβano] nm: **el ~** the Lebanon
libélula [li'βelula] nf dragonfly
liberación [liβera'θjon] nf liberation;
(de la cárcel) release
liberal [liβe'ral] adj, nmf liberal
liberar [liβe'rar] /1a/ vt to liberate
libertad [liβer'tað] nf liberty,
freedom; **~ de asociación/de culto/
de prensa/de comercio/de palabra**
freedom of association/of worship/
of the press/of trade/of speech; **~
condicional** probation; **~ bajo
palabra** parole; **~ bajo fianza** bail

libertar [liβer'tar] /1a/ vt (preso) to
set free; (de una obligación) to release;
(eximir) to exempt
libertino, -a [liβer'tino, a] adj
permissive ▷ nm/f permissive person
libra ['liβra] nf pound; **L-** (Astro) Libra;
~ esterlina pound sterling
libramiento [liβra'mjento] (ʌм) nm
ring road (BRIT), beltway (US)
librar [li'βrar] /1a/ vt (de peligro) to
save; (batalla) to wage, fight; (de
impuestos) to exempt; (cheque) to make
out; (Jur) to exempt; **librarse** vr: **~se
de** to escape form, free o.s. from
libre ['liβre] adj free; (lugar)
unoccupied; (asiento) vacant; (de
deudas) free of debts; **~ de impuestos**
free of tax; **tiro ~** free kick; **los 100
metros ~** the 100 metres freestyle
(race); **al aire ~** in the open air
librería [liβre'ria] nf (tienda)
bookshop; **librero, -a** nm/f bookseller
⚠ No confundir librería con la
palabra inglesa library.
libreta [li'βreta] nf notebook
libro ['liβro] nm book; **~ de bolsillo**
paperback; **~ electrónico** e-book; **~
de texto** textbook
Lic. abr = **Licenciado, a**
licencia [li'θenθja] nf (gen) licence;
(permiso) permission; **~ por
enfermedad/con goce de sueldo**
sick/paid leave; **~ de armas/de
caza** gun/game licence; **licenciado,
-a** adj licensed ▷ nm/f graduate;
licenciar /1b/ vt (empleado) to
dismiss; (permitir) to permit, allow;
(soldado) to discharge; (estudiante) to
confer a degree upon; **licenciarse** vr:
licenciarse en derecho to graduate
in law
licenciatura [liθenθja'tura] nf
(título) degree; (estudios) degree course
lícito, -a ['liθito, a] adj (legal)
lawful; (justo) fair, just; (permisible)
permissible
licor [li'kor] nm spirits pl (BRIT), liquor
(US); (con hierbas etc) liqueur

licuadora [likwa'ðora] *nf* blender

líder ['liðer] *nm* leader; **liderazgo,** **liderato** *nm* leadership

lidia ['liðja] *nf* bullfighting; *(una lidia)* bullfight; **toros de ~** fighting bulls; **lidiar** /1b/ *vt, vi* to fight

liebre ['ljeβre] *nf* hare

lienzo ['ljenθo] *nm* linen; *(Arte)* canvas; *(Arq)* wall

liga ['liɣa] *nf (de medias)* garter, suspender; *(confederación)* league; *(LAM: gomita)* rubber band

ligadura [liɣa'ðura] *nf* bond, tie; *(Med, Mus)* ligature

ligamento [liɣa'mento] *nm* ligament

ligar [li'ɣar] /1h/ *vt (atar)* to tie; *(unir)* to join; *(Med)* to bind up; *(Mus)* to slur ▷ *vi* to mix, blend; **ligarse** *vr* to commit o.s.; **(él) liga mucho** *(fam)* he pulls a lot of women

ligero, -a [li'xero, a] *adj (de peso)* light; *(tela)* thin; *(rápido)* swift, quick; *(ágil)* agile, nimble; *(de importancia)* slight; *(de carácter)* flippant, superficial ▷ *adv:* **a la ligera** superficially

liguero [li'ɣero] *nm* suspender (BRIT) o garter (US) belt

lija ['lixa] *nf (Zool)* dogfish; **(papel de)** **~** sandpaper

lila ['lila] *nf* lilac

lima ['lima] *nf* file; *(Bot)* lime; **~ de** **uñas** nail file; **limar** /1a/ *vt* to file

limitación [limita'θjon] *nf* limitation, limit

limitar [limi'tar] /1a/ *vt* to limit; *(reducir)* to reduce, cut down ▷ *vi:* **~** **con** to border on; **limitarse** *vr:* **~se a** to limit o confine o.s. to

límite ['limite] *nm (gen)* limit; *(fin)* end; *(frontera)* border; **~ de velocidad** speed limit

limítrofe [li'mitrofe] *adj* neighbouring

limón [li'mon] *nm* lemon ▷ *adj:* **amarillo ~** lemon-yellow; **limonada** *nf* lemonade

limosna [li'mosna] *nf* alms *pl*; **pedir ~** to beg; **vivir de ~** to live on charity

limpiador, a [limpja'ðor, a] *adj* cleaning, cleansing ▷ *nm/f* cleaner ▷ *nm (LAM)* = **limpiaparabrisas**

limpiaparabrisas [limpjapara'βrisas] *nm inv* windscreen (BRIT) o windshield (US) wiper

limpiar [lim'pjar] /1b/ *vt* to clean; *(con trapo)* to wipe; *(quitar)* to wipe away; *(zapatos)* to shine, polish; *(Inform)* to debug; *(fig)* to clean up

limpieza [lim'pjeθa] *nf (estado)* cleanliness; *(acto)* cleaning; (: *de* *las calles)* cleansing; (: *de zapatos)* polishing; *(habilidad)* skill; *(fig:* *Policía)* clean-up; *(pureza)* purity; *(Mil):* **operación de ~** mopping-up operation; **~ en seco** dry cleaning

limpio, -a ['limpjo, a] *adj* clean; *(moralmente)* pure; *(Com)* clear, net; *(fam)* honest ▷ *adv:* **jugar ~** to play fair; **pasar a ~** to make a fair copy

lince ['linθe] *nm* lynx

linchar [lin'tʃar] /1a/ *vt* to lynch

lindar [lin'dar] /1a/ *vi* to adjoin; **~ con** to border on

lindo, -a ['lindo, a] *adj* pretty, lovely ▷ *adv:* **canta muy ~** *(LAM)* he sings beautifully; **se divertían de lo ~** they enjoyed themselves enormously

línea ['linea] *nf* line; *(Inform):* **en ~** on line; **~ aérea** airline; **~ de meta** goal line; *(de carrera)* finishing line; **~** **discontinua** *(Auto)* broken line; **~** **recta** straight line

lingote [lin'gote] *nm* ingot

lingüista [lin'gwista] *nmf* linguist; **lingüística** *nf* linguistics *sg*

lino ['lino] *nm* linen; *(Bot)* flax

linterna [lin'terna] *nf:* torch (BRIT), flashlight (US)

lío ['lio] *nm* bundle; *(desorden)* muddle, mess; *(fam: follón)* fuss; **armar un ~** to make a fuss

liquen ['liken] *nm* lichen

liquidación [likiða'θjon] *nf* liquidation; **venta de ~** clearance sale

liquidar [liki'ðar] /1a/ vt (Com) to liquidate; (deudas) to pay off; (empresa) to wind up

líquido, -a ['likiðo, a] adj liquid; (ganancia) net ▷ nm liquid; ~ **imponible** net taxable income

lira ['lira] nf (Mus) lyre; (moneda) lira

lírico, -a ['liriko, a] adj lyrical

lirio ['lirjo] nm (Bot) iris

lirón [li'ron] nm (Zool) dormouse; (fig) sleepyhead

Lisboa [lis'βoa] nf Lisbon

lisiar [li'sjar] /1b/ vt to maim

liso, -a ['liso, a] adj (terreno) flat; (cabello) straight; (superficie) even; (tela) plain

lista ['lista] nf list; (en escuela) school register; (de libros) catalogue; (tb: ~ **de platos**) menu; (tb: ~ **de precios**) price list; **pasar** ~ to call the roll; ~ **de espera** waiting list; **tela a ~s** striped material

listo, -a ['listo, a] adj (perspicaz) smart, clever; (preparado) ready

listón [lis'ton] nm (de madera, metal) strip

litera [li'tera] nf (en barco, tren) berth; (en dormitorio) bunk, bunk bed

literal [lite'ral] adj literal

literario, -a [lite'rarjo, a] adj literary

literato, -a [lite'rato, a] adj literary ▷ nm/f writer

literatura [litera'tura] nf literature

litigio [li'tixjo] nm (Jur) lawsuit; (fig): **en ~ con** in dispute with

litografía [litoɣra'fia] nf lithography; (una litografía) lithograph

litoral [lito'ral] adj coastal ▷ nm coast, seaboard

litro ['litro] nm litre, liter (us)

lívido, -a ['liβiðo, a] adj livid

llaga ['ʎaɣa] nf wound

llama ['ʎama] nf flame; (Zool) llama

llamada [ʎa'maða] nf call; ~ **a cobro revertido** reverse-charge call; ~ **al orden** call to order; ~ **de atención** warning; ~ **metropolitana**, ~ **local** local call; ~ **por cobrar** (ʌм) reverse-charge call

llamamiento [ʎama'mjento] nm call

llamar [ʎa'mar] /1a/ vt to call; (atención) to attract ▷ vi (por teléfono) to phone; (a la puerta) to knock (o ring); (por señas) to beckon; **llamarse** vr to be called, be named; **¿cómo se llama usted?** what's your name?

llamativo, -a [ʎama'tiβo, a] adj showy; (color) loud

llano, -a ['ʎano, a] adj (superficie) flat; (persona) straightforward; (estilo) clear ▷ nm plain, flat ground

llanta ['ʎanta] nf (wheel) rim; (ʌм: neumático) tyre; (: cámara) (inner) tube; ~ **de repuesto** (ʌм) spare tyre

llanto ['ʎanto] nm weeping

llanura [ʎa'nura] nf plain

llave ['ʎaβe] nf key; (de gas, agua) tap (ввiт), faucet (us); (Mecánica) spanner; (de la luz) switch; (Mus) key; ~ **inglesa** monkey wrench; ~ **maestra** master key; ~ **de contacto**, ~ **de encendido** (ʌм Auto) ignition key; ~ **de paso** stopcock; **echar** ~ **a** to lock up; **llavero** nm keyring

llegada [ʎe'ɣaða] nf arrival

llegar [ʎe'ɣar] /1h/ vi to arrive; (bastar) to be enough; **llegarse** vr: ~**se a** to approach; ~ **a** (alcanzar) to reach; to manage to, succeed in; ~ **a saber** to find out; ~ **a las manos de** to come into the hands of

llenar [ʎe'nar] /1a/ vt to fill; (superficie) to cover; (formulario) to fill in o out; (fig) to heap

lleno, -a ['ʎeno, a] adj full, filled; (repleto) full up ▷ nm (Teat) full house; **dar de ~ contra un muro** to hit a wall head-on

llevadero, -a [ʎeβa'ðero, a] adj bearable, tolerable

llevar [ʎe'βar] /1a/ vt to take; (ropa) to wear; (cargar) to carry; (quitar) to take away; (en coche) to drive; (transportar) to transport; (traer: dinero) to carry; (conducir) to lead; (Mat) to carry ▷ vi (suj: camino etc): ~ **a** to lead to;

llevarse vt to carry off, take away; **llevamos dos días aquí** we have been here for two days; **él me lleva dos años** he's two years older than me; **~ los libros** (Com) to keep the books; **~se bien** to get on well (together)

llorar [ʎo'ɾaɾ] /1a/ vt to cry ▷ vi to cry, weep; **~ de risa** to cry with laughter

llorón, -ona [ʎo'ɾon, ona] adj tearful ▷ nm/f cry-baby

lloroso, -a [ʎo'ɾoso, a] adj (gen) weeping, tearful; (triste) sad, sorrowful

llover etc [ʎo'βeɾ] vb V **llover**

llovizna [ʎo'βiθna] nf drizzle; **lloviznar** /1a/ vi to drizzle

llueve etc [ˈʎweβe] vb V **llover**

lluvia [ˈʎuβja] nf rain; **~ radioactiva** radioactive fallout; **lluvioso, -a** adj rainy

lo [lo] artículo definido neutro; **lo bueno** the good ▷ pron (en relación a una persona) him; (en relación a una cosa) it; **lo que** what, that which; **lo que sea** whatever; V tb **el**

loable [lo'aβle] adj praiseworthy

lobo [ˈloβo] nm wolf; **~ de mar** (fig) sea dog

lóbulo [ˈloβulo] nm lobe

local [lo'kal] adj local ▷ nm place, site; (oficinas) premises pl; **localidad** (de barrio) locality; (lugar) location; (Teat) seat, ticket; **localizar** /1f/ vt (ubicar) to locate, find; (restringir) to localize; (situar) to place

loción [lo'θjon] nf lotion

loco, -a [ˈloko, a] adj mad ▷ nm/f lunatic, madman/woman; **estar~ con o por algo/por algn** to be mad about sth/sb

locomotora [lokomo'toɾa] nf engine, locomotive

locuaz [lo'kwaθ] adj loquacious

locución [loku'θjon] nf expression

locura [lo'kuɾa] nf madness; (acto) crazy act

locutor, a [loku'toɾ, a] nm/f (Radio) announcer; (comentarista) commentator; (TV) newsreader

locutorio [loku'toɾjo] nm (Telec) telephone box o booth

lodo [ˈloðo] nm mud

lógico, -a [ˈloxiko, a] adj logical ▷ nf logic

login [ˈloxin] nm login

logotipo [loɣo'tipo] nm logo

logrado, -a [lo'ɣɾaðo, a] adj (interpretación, reproducción) polished, excellent

lograr [lo'ɣɾaɾ] /1a/ vt (obtener) to get, obtain; (conseguir) to achieve; **~ hacer** to manage to do; **~ que algn venga** to manage to get sb to come

logro [ˈloɣɾo] nm achievement, success

lóker [ˈlokeɾ] nm (ʌм) locker

loma [ˈloma] nf hillock, low ridge

lombriz [lom'bɾiθ] nf (earth)worm

lomo [ˈlomo] nm (de animal) back; (Culin: de cerdo) pork loin; (: de vaca) rib steak; (de libro) spine

lona [ˈlona] nf canvas

loncha [ˈlontʃa] nf = **lonja**

lonchería [lontʃe'ɾia] nf (ʌм) snack bar, diner (ʊs)

Londres [ˈlondɾes] nm London

longaniza [longa'niθa] nf pork sausage

longitud [lonxi'tuð] nf length; (Geo) longitude; **tener tres metros de ~** to be three metres long; **~ de onda** wavelength

lonja [ˈlonxa] nf slice; (de tocino) rasher; **~ de pescado** fish market

loro [ˈloɾo] nm parrot

los [los] artículo definido mpl the ▷ pron them; (en relación a ustedes) you; **mis libros y ~ tuyos** my books and yours

losa [ˈlosa] nf stone

lote [ˈlote] nm portion; (Com) lot

lotería [lote'ɾia] nf lottery; (juego) lotto

● **LOTERÍA**

●
● Millions of euros are spent every
● year on loterías, lotteries. There

- is the weekly *Lotería Nacional*
- which is very popular especially at
- Christmas. Other weekly lotteries
- are the *Bono Loto* and the (*Lotería*)
- *Primitiva*. One of the most famous
- lotteries is run by the wealthy and
- influential society for the blind, *la
- ONCE*, and the form is called *el cupón
- de la ONCE* or *el cupón de los ciegos*.

loza ['loθa] *nf* crockery

lubina [lu'βina] *nf* sea bass

lubricante [luβri'kante] *nm*
lubricant

lubricar [luβri'kar] /1g/ *vt* to
lubricate

lucha ['lutʃa] *nf* fight, struggle;
~ de clases class struggle; **~ libre**
wrestling; **luchar** /1a/ *vi* to fight

lúcido, -a [lu'θiðo, a] *adj* (*persona*)
lucid; (*mente*) logical; (*idea*) crystal-clear

luciérnaga [lu'θjernaɣa] *nf* glow-
worm

lucir [lu'θir] /3f/ *vt* to illuminate, light
(up); (*ostentar*) to show off ▷ *vi* (*brillar*)
to shine; **lucirse** *vr* (*irónico*) to make
a fool of o.s.

lucro ['lukro] *nm* profit, gain

lúdico, -a ['luðiko, a] *adj* playful;
(*actividad*) recreational

luego ['lweɣo] *adv* (*después*) next; (*más
tarde*) later, afterwards

lugar [lu'ɣar] *nm* place; (*sitio*) spot;
en ~ de instead of; **en primer ~** in the
first place, firstly; **dar ~ a** to give rise
to; **hacer ~** to make room; **fuera de
~** out of place; **sin ~ a dudas** without
doubt, undoubtedly; **tener ~** to take
place; **~ común** commonplace; **yo en
su ~** if I were him

lúgubre ['luɣuβre] *adj* mournful

lujo ['luxo] *nm* luxury; (*fig*) profusion,
abundance; **de ~** luxury *cpd*, de luxe;
lujoso, -a *adj* luxurious

lujuria [lu'xurja] *nf* lust

lumbre ['lumbre] *nf* (*luz*) light; (*fuego*)
fire; **¿tienes ~?** (*para cigarro*) have you
got a light?

luminoso, -a [lumi'noso, a] *adj*
luminous, shining

luna ['luna] *nf* moon; (*de un espejo*)
glass; (*de gafas*) lens; (*fig*) crescent;
**~ creciente/llena/menguante/
nueva** crescent/full/waning/new
moon; **~ de miel** honeymoon; **estar
en la ~** to have one's head in the clouds

lunar [lu'nar] *adj* lunar ▷ *nm* (*Anat*)
mole; **tela a ~es** spotted material

lunes ['lunes] *nm inv* Monday

lupa ['lupa] *nf* magnifying glass

lustre ['lustre] *nm* polish; (*fig*) lustre;
dar ~ a to polish

luto ['luto] *nm* mourning; **llevar el o
vestirse de ~** to be in mourning

Luxemburgo [luksem'burɣo] *nm*
Luxembourg

luz [luθ] (*pl* **luces**) *nf* light; **dar a ~ un
niño** to give birth to a child; **sacar
a la ~** to bring to light; **dar la ~** to
switch on the light; **encender** (*ESP*) *o*
prender (*LAM*)/**apagar la ~** to switch
the light on/off; **tener pocas luces**
to be dim o stupid; **~ roja/verde** red/
green light; **~ de freno** brake light;
luces de tráfico traffic lights; **traje
de luces** bullfighter's costume

m *abr* (= **metro(s)**) m; (= **minuto(s)**) min., m

macana [ma'kana] *nf* (*LAM: porra*) club

macarrones [maka'rrones] *nmpl* macaroni *sg*

macedonia [maθe'ðonja] *nf*: **~ de frutas** fruit salad

maceta [ma'θeta] *nf* (*de flores*) pot of flowers; (*para plantas*) flowerpot

machacar [matʃa'kar] /1g/ *vt* to crush, pound ▷ *vi* (*insistir*) to go on, keep on

machete [ma'tʃete] *nm* machete, (large) knife

machetear [matʃete'ar] /1a/ *vt* (*LAM*) to swot (*BRIT*), grind away (*US*)

machismo [ma'tʃismo] *nm* male chauvinism; **machista** *adj, nm* sexist

macho ['matʃo] *adj* male; (*fig*) virile ▷ *nm* male; (*fig*) he-man

macizo, -a [ma'θiθo, a] *adj* (*grande*) massive; (*fuerte, sólido*) solid ▷ *nm* mass, chunk

madeja [ma'ðexa] *nf* (*de lana*) skein, hank; (*de pelo*) mass, mop

madera [ma'ðera] *nf* wood; (*fig*) nature, character; **una ~** a piece of wood

madrastra [ma'ðrastra] *nf* stepmother

madre ['maðre] *adj* mother *cpd* ▷ *nf* mother; (*de vino etc*) dregs *pl*; **~ adoptiva/política/soltera** foster mother/mother-in-law/unmarried mother

Madrid [ma'ðrið] *n* Madrid

madriguera [maðri'ɣera] *nf* burrow

madrileño, -a [maðri'leɲo, a] *adj* of o from Madrid ▷ *nm/f* native o inhabitant of Madrid

madrina [ma'ðrina] *nf* godmother; (*Arq*) prop, shore; (*Tec*) brace; **~ de boda** bridesmaid

madrugada [maðru'ɣaða] *nf* early morning; (*alba*) dawn, daybreak

madrugador, a [maðruɣa'ðor, a] *adj* early-rising

madrugar [maðru'ɣar] /1h/ *vi* to get up early; (*fig*) to get ahead

madurar [maðu'rar] /1a/ *vt, vi* (*fruta*) to ripen; (*fig*) to mature; **madurez** *nf* ripeness; (*fig*) maturity; **maduro, -a** *adj* ripe; (*fig*) mature

maestra [ma'estra] *nf* V **maestro**

maestría [maes'tria] *nf* mastery; (*habilidad*) skill, expertise

maestro, -a [ma'estro, a] *adj* masterly; (*principal*) main ▷ *nm/f* master/mistress; (*profesor*) teacher ▷ *nm* (*autoridad*) authority; (*Mus*) maestro; (*experto*) master; **~ albañil** master mason

magdalena [maɣða'lena] *nf* fairy cake

magia ['maxja] *nf* magic; **mágico, -a** *adj* magic(al) ▷ *nm/f* magician

magisterio [maxis'terjo] *nm* (*enseñanza*) teaching; (*profesión*) teaching profession; (*maestros*) teachers *pl*

magistrado [maxis'traðo] *nm* magistrate

magistral [maxis'tral] *adj* magisterial; (fig) masterly

magnate [maɣ'nate] *nm* magnate, tycoon

magnético, -a [maɣ'netiko, a] *adj* magnetic

magnetofón [maɣneto'fon], **magnetófono** [maɣ'netofono] *nm* tape recorder

magnífico, -a [maɣ'nifiko, a] *adj* splendid, magnificent

magnitud [maɣni'tuð] *nf* magnitude

mago, -a ['maɣo, a] *nm/f* magician; **los Reyes M~s** the Three Wise Men

magro, -a ['maɣro, a] *adj* (carne) lean

mahonesa [mao'nesa] *nf* mayonnaise

maître ['metre] *nm* head waiter

maíz [ma'iθ] *nm* maize (BRIT), corn (US); sweet corn

majestad [maxes'tað] *nf* majesty

majo, -a ['maxo, a] *adj* nice; (guapo) attractive, good-looking; (elegante) smart

mal [mal] *adv* badly; (equivocadamente) wrongly ▷ *adj* = **malo** ▷ *nm* evil; (desgracia) misfortune; (daño) harm, damage; (Med) illness; **ir de ~ en peor** to go from bad to worse; **~ que bien** rightly or wrongly

malabarista [malaβa'rista] *nmf* juggler

malaria [ma'larja] *nf* malaria

malcriado, -a [mal'krjaðo, a] *adj* spoiled

maldad [mal'dað] *nf* evil, wickedness

maldecir [malde'θir] /3o/ *vt* to curse

maldición [maldi'θjon] *nf* curse

maldito, -a [mal'dito, a] *adj* (condenado) damned; (perverso) wicked; **¡~ sea!** damn it!

malecón [male'kon] *nm* pier, jetty; (LAM: paseo) sea front, promenade

maleducado, -a [maleðu'kaðo, a] *adj* bad-mannered, rude

malentendido [malenten'diðo] *nm* misunderstanding

malestar [males'tar] *nm* (gen) discomfort; (fig: inquietud) uneasiness; (Pol) unrest

maleta [ma'leta] *nf* case, suitcase; (Auto) boot (BRIT), trunk (US); **hacer la ~** to pack; **maletero** *nm* (Auto) boot (BRIT), trunk (US); **maletín** *nm* small case, bag

maleza [ma'leθa] *nf* (malas hierbas) weeds *pl*; (arbustos) thicket

malgastar [malɣas'tar] /1a/ *vt* (tiempo, dinero) to waste; (salud) to ruin

malhechor, a [male'tʃor, a] *nm/f* delinquent

malhumorado, -a [malumo'raðo, a] *adj* bad-tempered

malicia [ma'liθja] *nf* (maldad) wickedness; (astucia) slyness, guile; (mala intención) malice, spite; (carácter travieso) mischievousness

maligno, -a [ma'liɣno, a] *adj* evil; (malévolo) malicious; (Med) malignant

malla ['maʎa] *nf* mesh; (de baño) swimsuit; (de ballet, gimnasia) leotard; **~ de alambre** wire mesh; **mallas** *nfpl* tights; **~ de alambre** wire mesh

Mallorca [ma'ʎorka] *nf* Majorca

malo, -a ['malo, a] *adj* bad; false ▷ *nm/f* villain; **estar ~** to be ill

malograr [malo'ɣrar] /1a/ *vt* to spoil; (plan) to upset; (ocasión) to waste

malparado, -a [malpa'raðo, a] *adj*: **salir ~** to come off badly

malpensado, -a [malpen'saðo, a] *adj* nasty

malteada [malte'aða] *nf* (LAM) milk shake

maltratar [maltra'tar] /1a/ *vt* to ill-treat, mistreat

malvado, -a [mal'βaðo, a] *adj* evil, villainous

Malvinas [mal'βinas] *nfpl*: **Islas ~** Falkland Islands

mama ['mama] *nf* (de animal) teat; (de mujer) breast

mamá [ma'ma] *nf* (fam) mum, mummy

mamar [ma'mar] /1a/ vt to suck
▷ vi to suck

mamarracho [mama'rratʃo] nm
sight, mess

mameluco [mame'luko] (ʌм) nm
dungarees pl (ʙʀɪт), overalls pl (us)

mamífero [ma'mifero] nm mammal

mampara [mam'para] nf (entre
habitaciones) partition; (biombo) screen

mampostería [mamposte'ria] nf
masonry

manada [ma'naða] nf (Zool) herd; (: de
leones) pride; (: de lobos) pack

manantial [manan'tjal] nm spring

mancha ['mantʃa] nf stain, mark; (de
vegetación) patch; **manchar** /1a/ vt to
stain, mark; (ensuciar) to soil, dirty

manchego, -a [man'tʃeɣo, a] adj of o
from La Mancha

manco, -a ['manko, a] adj (de un
brazo) one-armed; (de una mano) one-
handed; (fig) defective, faulty

mandado [man'daðo] nm errand

mandamiento [manda'mjento]
nm (orden) order, command; (Rel)
commandment

mandar [man'dar] /1a/ vt (ordenar)
to order; (dirigir) to lead, command;
(enviar) to send; (pedir) to order, ask for
▷ vi to be in charge; (pey) to be bossy;
¿mande? pardon?, excuse me? (us); ~
hacer un traje to have a suit made

mandarina [manda'rina] nf (fruta)
tangerine, mandarin (orange)

mandato [man'dato] nm (orden)
order; (Pol: período) term of office;
(: territorio) mandate

mandíbula [man'diβula] nf jaw

mandil [man'dil] nm apron

mando ['mando] nm (Mil) command;
(de país) rule; (el primer lugar) lead;
(Pol) term of office; (Tec) control; ~
a la izquierda left-hand drive; ~ **a
distancia** remote control

mandón, -ona [man'don, ona] adj
bossy, domineering

manejar [mane'xar] /1a/ vt to
manage; (máquina) to work, operate;

(caballo etc) to handle; (casa) to
run, manage; (ʌм Auto) to drive;
manejarse vr (comportarse) to act,
behave; (arreglárselas) to manage;
manejo nm (de bicicleta) handling;
(de negocio) management, running;
(Auto) driving; (facilidad de trato) ease,
confidence; **manejos** nmpl intrigues

manera [ma'nera] nf way, manner,
fashion; **maneras** nfpl (modales)
manners; **su ~ de ser** the way he
is; (aire) his manner; **de ninguna ~**
no way, by no means; **de otra ~**
otherwise; **de todas ~s** at any rate;
no hay ~ de persuadirle there's no
way of convincing him

manga ['manga] nf (de camisa) sleeve;
(de riego) hose

mango ['mango] nm handle; (Bot)
mango

manguera [man'gera] nf hose

maní [ma'ni] nm peanut

manía [ma'nia] nf (Med) mania; (fig:
moda) rage, craze; (disgusto) dislike;
(malicia) spite; **coger ~ a algn** to
take a dislike to sb; **tener ~ a algn** to
dislike sb; **maníaco, -a** adj maniac(al)
▷ nm/f maniac

maniático, -a [ma'njatiko, a] adj
maniac(al) ▷ nm/f maniac

manicomio [mani'komjo] nm
mental hospital (ʙʀɪт), insane
asylum (us)

manifestación [manifesta'θjon] nf
(declaración) statement, declaration;
(demostración) show, display; (Pol)
demonstration; (concentración) mass
meeting

manifestar [manifes'tar] /1j/ vt to
show, manifest; (declarar) to state,
declare; **manifiesto, -a** adj clear,
manifest ▷ nm manifesto

manillar [mani'ʎar] nm
handlebars pl

maniobra [ma'njoβra] nf
manoeuvre; **maniobras** nfpl
manoeuvres; **maniobrar** /1a/ vt to
manoeuvre

manipulación [manipula'θjon] *nf* manipulation

manipular [manipu'lar] /1a/ *vt* to manipulate; (*manejar*) to handle

maniquí [mani'ki] *nmf* model ▷ *nm* dummy

manivela [mani'βela] *nf* crank

manjar [man'xar] *nm* (tasty) dish

mano ['mano] *nf* hand; (*Zool*) foot, paw; (*de pintura*) coat; (*serie*) lot, series; **a ~** by hand; **a ~ derecha/izquierda** on (o to) the right(-hand side)/left(-hand side); **robo a ~ armada** armed robbery; **de primera ~** (at) first hand; **de segunda ~** (at) second hand; **estrechar la ~ algn** to shake sb's hand; **~ de obra** labour, manpower

manojo [ma'noxo] *nm* handful, bunch; **~ de llaves** bunch of keys

manopla [ma'nopla] *nf* (*paño*) flannel; **manoplas** *nfpl* mittens

manosear [manose'ar] /1a/ *vt* (*tocar*) to handle, touch; (*desordenar*) to mess up, rumple; (*insistir en*) to overwork; (*acariciar*) to caress, fondle

manos libres *adj inv* (*teléfono, dispositivo*) hands-free ▷ *nm inv* hands-free kit

manotazo [mano'taθo] *nm* slap, smack

mansalva [man'salβa]: **a ~** *adv* indiscriminately

mansión [man'sjon] *nf* mansion

manso, -a ['manso, a] *adj* gentle, mild; (*animal*) tame

manta ['manta] *nf* blanket

manteca [man'teka] *nf* fat; (*LAM*) butter; **~ de cerdo** lard

mantecado [mante'kaðo] *nm* (*ESP*: *dulce navideño*) Christmas sweet made from flour, almonds and lard; (*helado*) ice cream

mantel [man'tel] *nm* tablecloth

mantendré *etc* [manten'dre] *vb V* **mantener**

mantener [mante'ner] /2k/ *vt* to support, maintain; (*alimentar*) to

sustain; (*conservar*) to keep; (*Tec*) to maintain, service; **mantenerse** *vr* (*seguir de pie*) to be still standing; (*no ceder*) to hold one's ground; (*subsistir*) to subsist, survive o.s., keep going; **mantenimiento** *nm* maintenance; sustenance; (*sustento*) support

mantequilla [mante'kiʎa] *nf* butter

mantilla [man'tiʎa] *nf* mantilla; **mantillas** *nfpl* baby clothes

manto ['manto] *nm* (*capa*) cloak; (*de ceremonia*) robe, gown

mantuve *etc* [man'tuβe] *vb V* **mantener**

manual [ma'nwal] *adj* manual ▷ *nm* manual, handbook

manuscrito, -a [manus'krito, a] *adj* handwritten ▷ *nm* manuscript

manutención [manuten'θjon] *nf* maintenance; (*sustento*) support

manzana [man'θana] *nf* apple; (*Arq*) block

manzanilla [manθa'niʎa] *nf* (*planta*) camomile; (*infusión*) camomile tea

manzano [man'θano] *nm* apple tree

maña ['maɲa] *nf* (*destreza*) skill; (*pey*) guile; (*ardid*) trick

mañana [ma'ɲana] *adv* tomorrow ▷ *nm* future ▷ *nf* morning; **de o por la ~** in the morning; **¡hasta ~!** see you tomorrow!; **~ por la ~** tomorrow morning

mapa ['mapa] *nm* map

maple ['maple] *nm* (*LAM*) maple

maqueta [ma'keta] *nf* (*scale*) model

maquillador, a [makiʎa'ðor, a] *nm/f* (*Teat etc*) make-up artist ▷ *nf* (*LAM Com*) bonded assembly plant

maquillaje [maki'ʎaxe] *nm* make-up; (*acto*) making up

maquillar [maki'ʎar] /1a/ *vt* to make up; **maquillarse** *vr* to put on (some) make-up

máquina ['makina] *nf* machine; (*de tren*) locomotive, engine; (*Foto*) camera; (*fig*) machinery; **escrito a ~** typewritten; **~ de afeitar** electric razor; **~ de coser** sewing machine; **~ de escribir** typewriter; **~ fotográfica** camera

maquinaria [maki'narja] nf (*máquinas*) machinery; (*mecanismo*) mechanism, works pl

maquinilla [maki'niʎa] nf: **~ de afeitar** razor

maquinista [maki'nista] nmf (*Ferro*) engine driver (BRIT), engineer (US); (*Tec*) operator; (*Naut*) engineer

mar [mar] nm sea; **~ adentro** o **afuera** out at sea; **en alta ~** on the high seas; **un ~ de** lots of; **el M~ Negro/Báltico** the Black/Baltic Sea

maraña [ma'raŋa] nf (*maleza*) thicket; (*confusión*) tangle

maravilla [mara'βiʎa] nf marvel, wonder; (*Bot*) marigold; **maravillar** /1a/ vt to astonish, amaze; **maravillarse** vr to be astonished, be amazed; **maravilloso, -a** adj wonderful, marvellous

marca ['marka] nf mark; (*sello*) stamp; (*Com*) make, brand; **de ~** excellent, outstanding; **~ de fábrica** trademark; **~ registrada** registered trademark

marcado, -a [mar'kaðo, a] adj marked, strong

marcador [marka'ðor] nm (*Deporte*) scoreboard; (: *persona*) scorer

marcapasos [marka'pasos] nm inv pacemaker

marcar [mar'kar] /1g/ vt to mark; (*número de teléfono*) to dial; (*gol*) to score; (*números*) to record, keep a tally of; (*el pelo*) to set ▸ vi (*Deporte*) to score; (*Telec*) to dial

marcha ['martʃa] nf march; (*Tec*) running, working; (*Auto*) gear; (*velocidad*) speed; (*fig*) progress; (*curso*) course; **dar ~ atrás** to reverse, put into reverse; **estar en ~** to be under way, be in motion; **poner en ~** to put into gear; **ponerse en ~** to start, get going; **marchar** /1a/ vi (*ir*) to go; (*funcionar*) to work, go; **marcharse** vr to go (away), leave

marchitar [martʃi'tar] /1a/ vt to wither, dry up; **marchitarse** vr to wither; (*fig*) to fade away; **marchito, -a** adj withered, faded; (*fig*) in decline

marciano, -a [mar'θjano, a] adj Martian

marco ['marko] nm frame; (*moneda*) mark; (*fig*) framework

marea [ma'rea] nf tide; **~ negra** oil slick

marear [mare'ar] /1a/ vt (*fig*) to annoy, upset; (*Med*): **~ a algn** to make sb feel sick; **marearse** vr (*tener náuseas*) to feel sick; (*desvanecerse*) to feel faint; (*aturdirse*) to feel dizzy; (*fam: emborracharse*) to get tipsy

maremoto [mare'moto] nm tidal wave

mareo [ma'reo] nm (*náusea*) sick feeling; (*en viaje*) travel sickness; (*aturdimiento*) dizziness; (*fam: lata*) nuisance

marfil [mar'fil] nm ivory

margarina [marɣa'rina] nf margarine

margarita [marɣa'rita] nf (*Bot*) daisy; (*en máquina impresora*) daisy wheel

margen ['marxen] nm (*borde*) edge, border; (*fig*) margin, space ▸ nf (*de río etc*) bank; **dar ~ para** to give an opportunity for; **mantenerse al ~** to keep out (of things)

marginar [marxi'nar] /1a/ vt to exclude; (*socialmente*) to marginalize, ostracize

mariachi [ma'rjatʃi] nm (*música*) mariachi music; (*grupo*) mariachi band; (*persona*) mariachi musician

● **MARIACHI**

● Mariachi music is the musical style
● most characteristic of Mexico.
● From the state of Jalisco in the 19th
● century, this music spread rapidly
● throughout the country, until each
● region had its own particular style

of the mariachi "sound". A mariachi band can be made up of several singers, up to eight violins, two trumpets, guitars, a *vihuela* (an old form of guitar), and a harp. The dance associated with this music is called the *zapateado*.

marica [ma'rika] *nm* (*fam*) sissy

maricón [mari'kon] *nm* (*fam*) queer

marido [ma'riðo] *nm* husband

marihuana [mari'wəna] *nf* marijuana, cannabis

marina [ma'rina] *nf* navy;
~ **mercante** merchant navy

marinero, -a [mari'nero, a] *adj* sea *cpd* ▷ *nm* sailor, seaman

marino, -a [ma'rino, a] *adj* sea *cpd*, marine ▷ *nm* sailor

marioneta [marjo'neta] *nf* puppet

mariposa [mari'posa] *nf* butterfly

mariquita [mari'kita] *nf* ladybird (BRIT), ladybug (US)

marisco [ma'risko] *nm* (*tb*: ~**s**) shellfish, seafood

marítimo, -a [ma'ritimo, a] *adj* sea *cpd*, maritime

mármol ['marmol] *nm* marble

marqués, -esa [mar'kes, esa] *nm/f* marquis/marchioness

marrón [ma'rron] *adj* brown

marroquí [marro'ki] *adj, nmf* Moroccan ▷ *nm* Morocco (leather)

Marruecos [ma'rrwekos] *nm* Morocco

martes ['martes] *nm inv* Tuesday; ~ **y trece** ≈ Friday 13th

● **MARTES Y TRECE**
●
● According to Spanish superstition
● Tuesday is an unlucky day, even
● more so if it falls on the 13th of the
● month.

martillo [mar'tiʎo] *nm* hammer

mártir ['martir] *nmf* martyr; **martirio** *nm* martyrdom; (*fig*) torture, torment

marxismo [mark'sismo] *nm* Marxism

marzo ['marθo] *nm* March

mas [mas] *conj* but

  PALABRA CLAVE

más [mas] *adj, adv* **1**: **más (que, de)** (*comparar*) more (than), ...+ er (than); **más grande/inteligente** bigger/ more intelligent; **trabaja más (que yo)** he works more (than me); V *tb* **cada**

2 (*superl*): **el más** the most, ...+ est; **el más grande/inteligente (de)** the biggest/most intelligent (in)

3 (*negativo*): **no tengo más dinero** I haven't got any more money; **no viene más por aquí** he doesn't come round here any more

4 (*adicional*): **no le veo más solución que ...** I see no other solution than to ...; **¿quién más?** anybody else?

5 (+ *adj, valor intensivo*): **¡qué perro más sucio!** what a filthy dog!; **¡es más tonto!** he's so stupid!

6 (*locuciones*): **más o menos** more or less; **los más** most people; **es más** furthermore; **más bien** rather; **¡qué más da!** what does it matter!; V *tb* **no**

7: **por más: por más que** lo intento no matter how much o hard I try; **por más que quisiera ayudar** much as I should like to help

8: **de más: veo que aquí estoy de más** I can see I'm not needed here; **tenemos uno de más** we've got one extra

▶ *prep*: **2 más 2 son 4** 2 and o plus 2 are 4

▶ *nm inv*: **este trabajo tiene sus más y sus menos** this job's got its good points and its bad points

masa ['masa] *nf* (*mezcla*) dough; (*volumen*) volume, mass; (*Física*) mass; **en** ~ en masse; **las** ~**s** (*Pol*) the masses

masacre [ma'sakre] *nf* massacre

masaje [ma'saxe] nm massage

máscara ['maskara] nf mask;
~ antigás gas mask; **mascarilla**
nf mask

masculino, -a [masku'lino, a] adj
masculine; (Bio) male

masía [ma'sia] nf farmhouse

masivo, -a [ma'siβo, a] adj (en
masa) mass

masoquista [maso'kista] nmf
masochist

máster ['master] nm master's degree

masticar [masti'kar] /1g/ vt to chew

mástil [mastil] nm (de navío) mast; (de
guitarra) neck

mastín [mas'tin] nm mastiff

masturbarse [mastur'βarse] /1a/ vr
to masturbate

mata ['mata] nf (arbusto) bush, shrub;
(de hierbas) tuft

matadero [mata'ðero] nm
slaughterhouse, abattoir

matador, a [mata'ðor, a] adj killing
▷ nm/f (Taur) matador, bullfighter

matamoscas [mata'moskas] nm inv
(palo) fly swat

matanza [ma'tanθa] nf slaughter

matar [ma'tar] /1a/ vt, vi to kill;
matarse vr (suicidarse) to kill o.s.,
commit suicide; (morir) to be
killed; **~ el hambre** to stave off
hunger

matasellos [mata'seʎos] nm inv
postmark

mate ['mate] adj matt ▷ nm (en ajedrez)
(check)mate; (LAm: hierba) maté;
(: vasija) gourd

matemáticas [mate'matikas] nfpl
mathematics; **matemático, -a** adj
mathematical ▷ nm/f mathematician

materia [ma'terja] nf (gen) matter;
(Tec) material; (Escol) subject; **en ~
de** on the subject of; **~ prima** raw
material; **material** adj material
▷ nm (Tec) equipment; **materialista**
adj materialist(ic); **materialmente**
adv materially; (fig)
absolutely

maternal [mater'nal] adj motherly,
maternal

maternidad [materni'ðað] nf
motherhood, maternity; **materno, -a**
adj maternal; (lengua) mother cpd

matinal [mati'nal] adj morning cpd

matiz [ma'tiθ] nm shade; **matizar**
/1f/ vt (variar) to vary; (Arte) to blend;
matizar de to tinge with

matón [ma'ton] nm bully

matorral [mato'rral] nm thicket

matrícula [ma'trikula] nf (registro)
register; (Auto) registration number;
(: placa) number plate; **~ de honor**
(Univ) top marks in a subject at university
with the right to free registration the
following year; **matricular** /1a/ vt to
register, enrol

matrimonio [matri'monjo] nm
(pareja) (married) couple; (acto)
marriage

matriz [ma'triθ] nf (Anat) womb;
(Tec) mould

matrona [ma'trona] nf (mujer de edad)
matron; (comadrona) midwife

matufia [ma'tufja] nf (LAm fam)
put-up job

maullar [mau'ʎar] /1a/ vi to mew,
miaow

maxilar [maksi'lar] nm jaw(bone)

máxima [maksima] nf V **máximo**

máximo, -a ['maksimo, a] adj
maximum; (más alto) highest; (más
grande) greatest ▷ nm maximum ▷ nf
maxim; **como ~** at most

mayo ['majo] nm May

mayonesa [majo'nesa] nf
mayonnaise

mayor [ma'jor] adj main, chief;
(adulto) elderly; (Mus) major;
(comparativo: de tamaño) bigger; (: de
edad) older; (superlativo: de tamaño)
biggest; (: de edad) oldest ▷ nm adult;
mayores nmpl (antepasados) ancestors;
al por ~ wholesale; **~ de edad** adult

mayoral [majo'ral] nm foreman

mayordomo [major'ðomo] nm
butler

mayoría [majo'ria] *nf* majority, greater part

mayorista [majo'rista] *nmf* wholesaler

mayoritario, -a [majori'tarjo, a] *adj* majority *cpd*

mayúsculo, -a [ma'juskulo, a] *adj* (*fig*) big, tremendous ▷ *nf* capital (letter)

mazapán [maθa'pan] *nm* marzipan

mazo ['maθo] *nm* (*martillo*) mallet; (*de flores*) bunch; (*Deporte*) bat

me [me] *pron* (*directo*) me; (*indirecto*) (to) me; (*reflexivo*) (to) myself; **¡dámelo!** give it to me!

mear [me'ar] /1a/ (*fam*) *vi* to pee, piss (!)

mecánica [me'kanika] *nf* V **mecánico**

mecánico, -a [me'kaniko, a] *adj* mechanical ▷ *nm/f* mechanic ▷ *nf* (*estudio*) mechanics *sg*; (*mecanismo*) mechanism

mecanismo [meka'nismo] *nm* mechanism; (*engranaje*) gear

mecanografía [mekanoɣra'fia] *nf* typewriting; **mecanógrafo, -a** *nm/f* (*copy*) typist

mecate [me'kate] *nm* (*LAM*) rope

mecedor [mese'ðor] *nm* (*LAM*), **mecedora** [meθe'ðora] *nf* rocking chair

mecer [me'θer] /2b/ *vt* (*cuna*) to rock; **mecerse** *vr* to rock; (*rama*) to sway

mecha ['metʃa] *nf* (*de vela*) wick; (*de bomba*) fuse

mechero [me'tʃero] *nm* (*cigarette*) lighter

mechón [me'tʃon] *nm* (*gen*) tuft; (*de pelo*) lock

medalla [me'ðaʎa] *nf* medal

media ['meðja] *nf* V **medio**

mediado, -a [me'ðjaðo, a] *adj* half-full; (*trabajo*) half-completed; **a -s de** in the middle of, halfway through

mediano, -a [me'ðjano, a] *adj* (*regular*) medium, average; (*mediocre*) mediocre

medianoche [meðja'notʃe] *nf* midnight

mediante [me'ðjante] *adv* by (means of), through

mediar [me'ðjar] /1b/ *vi* (*interceder*) to mediate, intervene

medicamento [meðika'mento] *nm* medicine, drug

medicina [meði'θina] *nf* medicine

médico, -a ['meðiko, a] *adj* medical ▷ *nm/f* doctor

medida [me'ðiða] *nf* measure; (*medición*) measurement; (*moderación*) moderation, prudence; **en cierta/gran –** up to a point/to a great extent; **un traje a la –** a made-to-measure suit; **– de cuello** collar size; **a – de** in proportion to; (*de acuerdo con*) in keeping with; **a – que ...** (at the same time) as ...; **medidor** [me'ðiðor] *nm* (*LAM*) meter

medio, -a ['meðjo, a] *adj* half (*a*); (*punto*) mid, middle; (*promedio*) average ▷ *adv* half- ▷ *nm* (*centro*) middle, centre; (*método*) means, way; (*ambiente*) environment ▷ *nf* stocking; (*LAM*) sock; (*promedio*) average; **medias** *nfpl* tights; **– litro** half a litre; **las tres y media** half past three; **M– Oriente** Middle East; **– de transporte** means of transport; **a – terminar** half finished; **– ambiente** environment; *V tb* **medios**; **medioambiental** *adj* environmental

mediocre [me'ðjokre] *adj* mediocre

mediodía [meðjo'ðia] *nm* midday, noon

medios ['meðjos] *nmpl* means, resources; **los – de comunicación** the media; **los – sociales** social media

medir [me'ðir] /3k/ *vt* to measure

meditar [meði'tar] /1a/ *vt* to ponder, think over, meditate on; (*planear*) to think out

mediterráneo, -a [meðite'rraneo, a] *adj* Mediterranean ▷ *nm*: **el (mar) M–** the Mediterranean (Sea)

médula ['meðula] *nf* (*Anat*) marrow; **– espinal** spinal cord

medusa [me'ðusa] *nf* (*ESP*) jellyfish

megáfono [me'γafono] *nm* megaphone

megapíxel [meγa'piksel] (*pl* **megapixels** *o* **megapíxeles**) *nm* megapixel

mejicano, -a [mexi'kano, a] *adj, nm/f* Mexican

Méjico ['mexiko] *nm* Mexico

mejilla [me'xiʎa] *nf* cheek

mejillón [mexi'ʎon] *nm* mussel

mejor [me'xor] *adj, adv* (*comparativo*) better; (*superlativo*) best; **a lo ~** probably; (*quizá*) maybe; **~ dicho** rather; **tanto ~** so much the better; **mejora** [me'xora] *nm* improvement; **mejorar** /1a/ *vt* to improve, make better ▷ *vi* to improve, get better; **mejorarse** *vr* to improve, get better

melancólico, -a [melan'koliko, a] *adj* (*triste*) sad, melancholy; (*soñador*) dreamy

melena [me'lena] *nf* (*de persona*) long hair; (*Zool*) mane

mellizo, -a [me'ʎiθo, a] *adj, nm/f* twin

melocotón [meloko'ton] *nm* (*ESP*) peach

melodía [melo'ðia] *nf* melody; tune

melodrama [melo'ðrama] *nm* melodrama; **melodramático, -a** *adj* melodramatic

melón [me'lon] *nm* melon

membrete [mem'brete] *nm* letterhead

membrillo [mem'briʎo] *nm* quince; **carne de ~** quince jelly

memoria [me'morja] *nf* (*gen*) memory; **memorias** *nfpl* (*de autor*) memoirs; **memorizar** /1f/ *vt* to memorize

menaje [me'naxe] *nm* (*tb*: **artículos de ~**) household items *pl*

mencionar [menθjo'nar] /1a/ *vt* to mention

mendigo, -a [men'diγo, a] *nm/f* beggar

menear [mene'ar] /1a/ *vt* to move; **menearse** *vr* to shake; (*balancearse*)

to sway; (*moverse*) to move; (*fig*) to get a move on

menestra [me'nestra] *nf*: **~ de verduras** vegetable stew

menopausia [meno'pausja] *nf* menopause

menor [me'nor] *adj* (*más pequeño*: *comparativo*) smaller; (: *superlativo*) smallest; (*más joven*: *comparativo*) younger; (: *superlativo*) youngest; (*Mus*) minor ▷ *nmf* (*joven*) young person, juvenile; **no tengo la ~ idea** I haven't the faintest idea; **al por ~** retail; **~ de edad** minor

Menorca [me'norka] *nf* Minorca

PALABRA CLAVE

menos [menos] *adj* **1** (*compar*): **menos (que, de)** (*cantidad*) less (than); (*número*) fewer (than); **con menos entusiasmo** with less enthusiasm; **menos gente** fewer people; *V tb* **cada**

2 (*superl*): **es el que menos culpa tiene** he is the least to blame

▶ *adv* **1** (*compar*): **menos (que, de)** less (than); **me gusta menos que el otro** I like it less than the other one

2 (*superl*): **es el menos listo (de su clase)** he's the least bright (in his class); **de todas ellas es la que menos me agrada** out of all of them she's the one I like least

3 (*locuciones*): **no quiero verle y menos visitarle** I don't want to see him let alone visit him; **tenemos siete (de) menos** we're seven short; **al/por lo menos** at (the very) least; **¡menos mal!** thank goodness!

▶ *prep* except; (*cifras*) minus; **todos menos él** everyone except (for) him; **5 menos 2** 5 minus 2; **las 7 menos 20** (*hora*) 20 to 7

▶ *conj*: **a menos que: a menos que venga mañana** unless he comes tomorrow

menospreciar [menospre'θjar] /1b/ vt to underrate, undervalue; (despreciar) to scorn, despise

mensaje [men'saxe] nm message; **enviar un ~ a algn** (por móvil) to text sb, send sb a text message; **~ de texto** text message; **~ electrónico** email; **mensajero, -a** nm/f messenger

menso, -a ['menso, a] adj (LAM fam) stupid

menstruación [menstrwa'θjon] nf menstruation

mensual [men'swal] adj monthly; **10 euros -es** 10 euros a month; **mensualidad** nf (salario) monthly salary; (Com) monthly payment o instalment

menta ['menta] nf mint

mental [men'tal] adj mental; **mentalidad** nf mentality; **mentalizar** /1f/ vt (sensibilizar) to make aware; (convencer) to convince; (preparar mentalmente) to prepare mentally; **mentalizarse** vr (concienciarse) to become aware; **mentalizarse (de)** to get used to the idea (of); **mentalizarse de que ...** (convencerse) to get it into one's head that ...

mente ['mente] nf mind

mentir [men'tir] /3i/ vi to lie; **mentira** nf (una mentira) lie; (acto) lying; (invención) fiction; **parece mentira que ...** it seems incredible that ..., I can't believe that ...; **mentiroso, -a** adj lying ▷ nm/f liar

menú [me'nu] nm menu; **~ del día** set meal; **~ turístico** tourist menu

menudo, -a [me'nuðo, a] adj (pequeño) small, tiny; (sin importancia) petty, insignificant; **¡~ negocio!** (fam) some deal!; **a ~** often, frequently

meñique [me'ɲike] nm little finger

mercadillo [merka'ðiʎo] nm (ESP) flea market

mercado [mer'kaðo] nm market; **~ de pulgas** (LAM) flea market

mercancía [merkan'θia] nf commodity; **mercancías** nfpl goods, merchandise sg

mercenario, -a [merθe'narjo, a] adj, nm mercenary

mercería [merθe'ria] nf haberdashery (BRIT), notions pl (US); (tienda) haberdasher's shop (BRIT), drapery (BRIT), notions store (US)

mercurio [mer'kurjo] nm mercury

merecer [mere'θer] /2d/ vt to deserve, merit ▷ vi to be deserving, be worthy; **merece la pena** it's worthwhile; **merecido, -a** adj (well) deserved; **llevarse su merecido** to get one's deserts

merendar [meren'dar] /1j/ vt to have for tea ▷ vi to have tea; (en el campo) to have a picnic; **merendero** nm (open-air) café

merengue [me'renge] nm meringue

meridiano [meri'ðjano] nm (Astro, Geo) meridian

merienda [me'rjenda] nf (light) tea, afternoon snack; (de campo) picnic

mérito ['merito] nm merit; (valor) worth, value

merluza [mer'luθa] nf hake

mermelada [merme'laða] nf jam

mero, -a ['mero, a] adj mere; (LAM fam) very

merodear [meroðe'ar] /1a/ vi (de noche) to prowl (about)

mes [mes] nm month

mesa ['mesa] nf table; (de trabajo) desk; (Geo) plateau; **~ electoral** officials in charge of a polling station; **~ redonda** (reunión) round table; **poner/quitar la ~** to lay/clear the table; **mesero, -a** nm/f (LAM) waiter/ waitress

meseta [me'seta] nf (Geo) tableland

mesilla [me'siʎa] nf: **~ de noche** bedside table

mesón [me'son] nm inn

mestizo, -a [mes'tiθo, a] adj mixed-race ▷ nm/f person of mixed race

meta ['meta] nf goal; (de carrera) finish

metabolismo [metaβo'lismo] *nm* metabolism

metáfora [me'tafora] *nf* metaphor

metal [me'tal] *nm* (*materia*) metal; (*Mus*) brass; **metálico, -a** *adj* metallic; (*de metal*) metal ▷ *nm* (*dinero contante*) cash

meteorología [meteorolo'xia] *nf* meteorology

meter [me'ter] /2a/ *vt* (*colocar*) to put, place; (*introducir*) to put in, insert; (*involucrar*) to involve; (*causar*) to make, cause; **meterse** *vr*: **~se en** to go into, enter; (*fig*) to interfere in, meddle in; **~se a** to start; **~se a escritor** to become a writer; **~se con algn** to provoke sb, pick a quarrel with sb

meticuloso, -a [metiku'loso, a] *adj* meticulous, thorough

metódico, -a [me'toðiko, a] *adj* methodical

método ['metoðo] *nm* method

metralleta [metra'ʎeta] *nf* sub-machine-gun

métrico, -a ['metriko, a] *adj* metric

metro ['metro] *nm* metre; (*tren*) underground (BRIT), subway (US)

metrosexual [metrosexu'al] *adj, nm* metrosexual

mexicano, -a [mexi'kano, a] *adj, nm/f* Mexican

México ['mexiko] *nm* Mexico; **Ciudad de ~** Mexico City

mezcla ['meθkla] *nf* mixture; **mezclar** /1a/ *vt* to mix (up); **mezclarse** *vr* to mix, mingle; **mezclar en** to get mixed up in, get involved in

mezquino, -a [meθ'kino, a] *adj* mean

mezquita [meθ'kita] *nf* mosque

mg *abr* (= *miligramo(s)*) mg

mí [mi] *adj posesivo* my ▷ *nm* (*Mus*) E

mí [mi] *pron me*, myself

mía ['mia] *pron* V **mío**

michelín [mitʃe'lin] *nm* (*fam*) spare tyre

microbio [mi'kroβjo] *nm* microbe

micrófono [mi'krofono] *nm* microphone

microonda [mikro'onda] *nf*, **microondas** [mikro'ondas] *nm inv* microwave; (**horno**) **~s** microwave (oven)

microscopio [mikros'kopjo] *nm* microscope

miedo ['mjeðo] *nm* fear; (*nerviosismo*) apprehension, nervousness; **tener ~ to** be afraid; **de ~** wonderful, marvellous; **hace un frío de ~** (*fam*) it's terribly cold; **miedoso, -a** *adj* fearful, timid

miel [mjel] *nf* honey

miembro ['mjembro] *nm* limb; (*socio*) member; **~ viril** penis

mientras ['mjentras] *conj* while; (*duración*) as long as ▷ *adv* meanwhile; **~ tanto** meanwhile

miércoles ['mjerkoles] *nm inv* Wednesday

mierda ['mjerða] *nf* (*fam!*) shit (!)

miga ['miya] *nf* crumb; (*fig*: *meollo*) essence; **hacer buenas ~s** (*fam*) to get on well

mil [mil] *num* thousand; **dos ~ libras** two thousand pounds

milagro [mi'layro] *nm* miracle; **milagroso, -a** *adj* miraculous

milésima [mi'lesima] *nf* (*de segundo*) thousandth

mili ['mili] *nf*: **hacer la ~** (*fam*) to do one's military service

milímetro [mi'limetro] *nm* millimetre (BRIT), millimeter (US)

militante [mili'tante] *adj* militant

militar [mili'tar] /1a/ *adj* military ▷ *nmf* soldier ▷ *vi* to serve in the army

milla ['miʎa] *nf* mile

millar [mi'ʎar] *nm* thousand

millón [mi'ʎon] *num* million; **millonario, -a** *adj, nm/f* millionaire

milusos [mi'lusos] *nm inv* (LAM) odd-job man

mimar [mi'mar] /1a/ *vt* to spoil, pamper

mimbre ['mimbre] *nm* wicker

mímica ['mimika] nf (para comunicarse) sign language; (imitación) mimicry

mimo ['mimo] nm (caricia) caress; (de niño) spoiling; (Teat) mime; (: actor) mime artist

mina ['mina] nf mine

mineral [mine'ral] adj mineral ▷ nm (Geo) mineral; (mena) ore

minero, -a [mi'nero, a] adj mining cpd ▷ nm/f miner

miniatura [minja'tura] adj inv, nf miniature

minidisco [mini'ðisko] nm diskette

minifalda [mini'falda] nf miniskirt

mínimo, -a ['minimo, a] adj ▷ nm minimum

minino, -a [mi'nino, a] nm/f (fam) puss, pussy

ministerio [minis'terjo] nm ministry (BRIT), department (US); **M~ de Asuntos Exteriores** Foreign Office (BRIT), State Department (US); **M~ de Hacienda** Treasury (BRIT), Treasury Department (US)

ministro, -a [mi'nistro, a] nm/f minister

minoría [mino'ria] nf minority

minúsculo, -a [mi'nuskulo, a] adj tiny, minute ▷ nf small letter

minusválido, -a [minus'βaliðo, a] adj (physically) handicapped o disabled ▷ nm/f disabled person

minuta [mi'nuta] nf (de comida) menu

minutero [minu'tero] nm minute hand

minuto [mi'nuto] nm minute

mío, -a ['mio, a] pron: **el ~** mine; **un amigo ~** a friend of mine; **lo ~** what is mine

miope ['mjope] adj short-sighted

mira ['mira] nf (de arma) sight(s) pl; (fig) aim, intention

mirada [mi'raða] nf look, glance; (expresión) look, expression; **clavar la ~ en** to stare at; **echar una ~ a** to glance at

mirado, -a [mi'raðo, a] adj (sensato) sensible; (considerado) considerate; **bien/mal ~** well/not well thought of; **bien ~ ...** all things considered ...

mirador [mira'ðor] nm viewpoint, vantage point

mirar [mi'rar] /1a/ vt to look at; (observar) to watch; (considerar) to consider, think over; (vigilar, cuidar) to watch, look after ▷ vi to look; (Arq) to face; **mirarse vr** (dos personas) to look at each other; **~ bien/mal** to think highly of/have a poor opinion of; **~se al espejo** to look at o.s. in the mirror

mirilla [mi'riʎa] nf spyhole, peephole

mirlo ['mirlo] nm blackbird

misa ['misa] nf mass

miserable [mise'raβle] adj (avaro) mean, stingy; (nimio) miserable, paltry; (lugar) squalid; (fam) vile, despicable ▷ nmf (malvado) rogue

miseria [mi'serja] nf (pobreza) poverty; (tacañería) meanness, stinginess; (condiciones) squalor; **una ~** a pittance

misericordia [miseri'korðja] nf (compasión) compassion, pity; (perdón) mercy

misil [mi'sil] nm missile

misión [mi'sjon] nf mission; **misionero, -a** nm/f missionary

mismo, -a [l'mismo, a] adj (semejante) same; (después de pronombre) -self; (para énfasis) very ▷ adv: **aquí/ayer/hoy ~** right here/only yesterday/this very day; **ahora ~** right now ▷ conj: **lo ~ que** just like, just as; **por lo ~** for the same reason; **el ~ traje** the same suit; **en ese ~ momento** at that very moment; **vino el ~ Ministro** the Minister himself came; **yo ~ lo vi** I saw it myself; **lo ~ the** same (thing); **da lo ~** it's all the same; **quedamos en las mismas** we're no further forward

misterio [mis'terjo] nm mystery; **misterioso, -a** adj mysterious

mitad [mi'tað] nf (medio) half; (centro) middle; **a ~ de precio** (at) half-price;

en o **a ~ del camino** halfway along the road; **cortar por la ~** to cut through the middle

mitin ['mitin] nm meeting

mito ['mito] nm myth

mixto, -a ['miksto, a] adj mixed

ml abr (= mililitro(s)) ml

mm abr (= milímetro(s)) mm

mobiliario [moβi'ljarjo] nm furniture

mochila [mo'tʃila] nf rucksack (BRIT), backpack

moco ['moko] nm mucus; **mocos** nmpl (fam) snot; **limpiarse los ~s** to blow one's nose

moda ['moða] nf fashion; (estilo) style; **de** o **a la ~** in fashion, fashionable; **pasado de ~** out of fashion

modal [mo'ðal] adj modal; **modales** nmpl manners

modelar [moðe'lar] /1a/ vt to model

modelo [mo'ðelo] adj inv ➤ nmf model

módem ['moðem] nm (Inform) modem

moderado, -a [moðe'raðo, a] adj moderate

moderar [moðe'rar] /1a/ vt to moderate; (violencia) to restrain, control; (velocidad) to reduce; **moderarse** vr to restrain o.s., control o.s.

modernizar [moðerni'θar] /1f/ vt to modernize

moderno, -a [mo'ðerno, a] adj modern; (actual) present-day

modestia [mo'ðestja] nf modesty; **modesto, -a** adj modest

modificar [moðifi'kar] /1g/ vt to modify

modisto, -a [mo'ðisto, a] nm/f (diseñador) couturier, designer; (que confecciona) dressmaker

modo ['moðo] nm way, manner; (Inform, Mus) mode; **modos** nmpl manners; **"~ de empleo"** "instructions for use"; **de ningún ~** in no way; **de todos ~s** at any rate

mofarse [mo'farse] /1a/ vr: **~ de** to mock, scoff at

mofle ['mofle] nm (LAM) silencer (BRIT), muffler (US)

mogollón [moɣo'ʎon] (fam) adv: **un ~** a hell of a lot

moho ['moo] nm mould, mildew; (en metal) rust

mojar [mo'xar] /1a/ vt to wet; (humedecer) to damp(en), moisten; (calar) to soak; **mojarse** vr to get wet

molcajete [molka'xete] (LAM) nm mortar

molde ['molde] nm mould; (de costura) pattern; (fig) model; **moldeado** nm soft perm; **moldear** /1a/ vt to mould

mole ['mole] nf mass, bulk; (edificio) pile

moler [mo'ler] /2h/ vt to grind, crush

molestar [moles'tar] /1a/ vt to bother; (fastidiar) to annoy; (incomodar) to inconvenience, put out ➤ vi to be a nuisance; **molestarse** vr to bother; (incomodarse) to go to a lot of trouble; (ofenderse) to take offence; **¿le molesta el ruido?** do you mind the noise?

> No confundir *molestar* con la palabra inglesa *molest*.

molestia [mo'lestja] nf bother, trouble; (incomodidad) inconvenience; (Med) discomfort; **es una ~** it's a nuisance; **molesto, -a** adj (que fastidia) annoying; (incómodo) inconvenient; (inquieto) uncomfortable, ill at ease; (enfadado) annoyed

molido, -a [mo'liðo, a] adj: **estar ~** (fig) to be exhausted o dead beat

molinillo [moli'niʎo] nm hand mill; **~ de carne/café** mincer/coffee grinder

molino [mo'lino] nm (edificio) mill; (máquina) grinder

momentáneo, -a [momen'taneo, a] adj momentary

momento [mo'mento] nm moment; **de ~** at the moment, for the moment

momia ['momja] nf mummy

monarca [mo'narka] nmf monarch, ruler; **monarquía** nf monarchy

monasterio [monas'terjo] nm monastery

mondar [mon'dar] /1a/ vt to peel; **mondarse** vr: **~ se de risa** (fam) to split one's sides laughing

mondongo [mon'doŋgo] nm (LAM) tripe

moneda [mo'neða] nf (tipo de dinero) currency, money; (pieza) coin; **una ~ de 50 céntimos** a 50-cent coin; **monedero** nm purse

monitor, a [moni'tor, a] nm/f instructor, coach ▷ nm (TV) set; (Inform) monitor

monja ['monxa] nf nun

monje ['monxe] nm monk

mono, -a ['mono, a] adj (bonito) lovely, pretty; (gracioso) nice, charming ▷ nm/f monkey, ape ▷ nm dungarees pl; (traje de faena) overalls pl

monopatín [monopa'tin] nm skateboard

monopolio [mono'poljo] nm monopoly; **monopolizar** /1f/ vt to monopolize

monótono, -a [mo'notono, a] adj monotonous

monstruo ['monstrwo] nm monster ▷ adj inv fantastic; **monstruoso, -a** adj monstrous

montaje [mon'taxe] nm assembly; (Teat) décor; (Cine) montage

montaña [mon'taɲa] nf (monte) mountain; (sierra) mountains pl, mountainous area; **~ rusa** roller coaster; **montañero, -a** nm/f mountaineer; **montañismo** nm mountaineering

montar [mon'tar] /1a/ vt (subir a) to mount, get on; (Tec) to assemble, put together; (negocio) to set up; (colocar) to lift on to; (Culin) to whip, beat ▷ vi to mount, get on; (sobresalir) to overlap; **~ en bicicleta** to ride a bicycle; **~ en cólera** to get angry; **~ a caballo** to ride, go horseriding

monte ['monte] nm (montaña) mountain; (bosque) woodland; (área sin cultivar) wild area, wild country; **~ de piedad** pawnshop

montón [mon'ton] nm heap, pile; **un ~ de** (fig) heaps of, lots of

monumento [monu'mento] nm monument

moño ['moɲo] nm bun

moqueta [mo'keta] nf fitted carpet

mora ['mora] nf blackberry

morado, -a [mo'raðo, a] adj purple, violet ▷ nm bruise

moral [mo'ral] adj moral ▷ nf (ética) ethics pl; (moralidad) morals pl, morality; (ánimo) morale

moraleja [mora'lexa] nf moral

morboso, -a [mor'βoso, a] adj morbid

morcilla [mor'θiλa] nf blood sausage, ≈ black pudding (BRIT)

mordaza [mor'ðaθa] nf (para la boca) gag; (Tec) clamp

morder [mor'ðer] /2h/ vt to bite; (fig: consumir) to eat away, eat into; **mordisco** nm bite

moreno, -a [mo'reno, a] adj (color) (dark) brown; (de tez) dark; (de pelo moreno) dark-haired; (negro) black

morfina [mor'fina] nf morphine

moribundo, -a [mori'βundo, a] adj dying

morir [mo'rir] /3j/ vi to die; (fuego) to die down; (luz) to go out; **morirse** vr to die; (fig) to be dying; **fue muerto a tiros/en un accidente** he was shot (dead)/was killed in an accident; **~se por algo** to be dying for sth

moro, -a ['moro, a] adj Moorish ▷ nm/f Moor

moroso, -a [mo'roso, a] nm/f (Com) bad debtor, defaulter

morro ['morro] nm (Zool) snout, nose; (Auto, Aviat) nose

morsa ['morsa] nf walrus

mortadela [morta'ðela] nf mortadella

mortal [mor'tal] adj mortal; (golpe) deadly; **mortalidad** nf mortality

mortero [mor'tero] nm mortar

mosca ['moska] *nf* fly

Moscú [mos'ku] *nm* Moscow

mosquear [moske'ar] /1a/ (*fam*) *vt* (*fastidiar*) to annoy; **mosquearse** *vr* (*enfadarse*) to get annoyed; (*ofenderse*) to take offence

mosquitero [moski'tero] *nm* mosquito net

mosquito [mos'kito] *nm* mosquito

mostaza [mos'taθa] *nf* mustard

mosto ['mosto] *nm* unfermented grape juice

mostrador [mostra'ðor] *nm* (*de tienda*) counter; (*de café*) bar

mostrar [mos'trar] /1l/ *vt* to show; (*exhibir*) to display, exhibit; (*explicar*) to explain; **mostrarse** *vr*: **~se amable** to be kind; to prove to be kind; **no se muestra muy inteligente** he doesn't seem (to be) very intelligent

mota ['mota] *nf* speck, tiny piece; (*en diseño*) dot

mote ['mote] *nm* nickname

motín [mo'tin] *nm* (*del pueblo*) revolt, rising; (*del ejército*) mutiny

motivar [moti'βar] /1a/ *vt* (*causar*) to cause, motivate; (*explicar*) to explain, justify; **motivo** *nm* motive, reason

moto ['moto] *nf*, **motocicleta** [motoθi'kleta] *nf* motorbike (BRIT), motorcycle

motociclista [motoθi'klista] *nmf* motorcyclist, biker

motoneta [moto'neta] *nf* (LAM) (*motor*) scooter

motor, a [mo'tor, a] *nm* motor, engine ▷ *nf* motorboat; **~ a chorro** *o* **de reacción/de explosión** jet engine/internal combustion engine

movedizo, -a [moβe'ðiθo, a] *adj* (*inseguro*) unsteady; (*fig*) unsettled

mover [mo'βer] /2h/ *vt* to move; (*cabeza*) to shake; (*accionar*) to drive; (*fig*) to cause, provoke; **moverse** *vr* to move; (*fig*) to get a move on

móvil ['moβil] *adj* mobile; (*pieza de máquina*) moving; (*mueble*) movable

▷ *nm* (*motivo*) motive; (*teléfono*) mobile, cellphone (US)

movimiento [moβi'mjento] *nm* movement; (*Tec*) motion; (*actividad*) activity

mozo, -a ['moθo, a] *adj* (*joven*) young ▷ *nm/f* youth, young man/girl; (*camarero*) waiter; (*camarera*) waitress

MP3 *nm* MP3; **reproductor (de) ~** MP3 player

mucama [mu'kama] *nf* (LAM) maid

muchacho, -a [mu'tʃatʃo, a] *nm/f* (*niño*) boy/girl; (*criado*) servant/ servant *o* maid

muchedumbre [mutʃe'ðumbre] *nf* crowd

PALABRA CLAVE

mucho, -a ['mutʃo, a] *adj* **1** (*cantidad*) a lot of, much; (*número*) lots of, a lot of, many; **mucho dinero** it's very hot; **muchas amigas** lots *o* a lot *o* many friends

2 (*sg: fam*): **ésta es mucha casa para él** this house is much too big for him
▶ *pron* **1**: **tengo mucho que hacer** I've got a lot to do; **muchos dicen que ...** a lot of people say that ...; *V tb* **tener**
▶ *adv* **1**: **me gusta mucho** I like it a lot *o* very much; **lo siento mucho** I'm very sorry; **come mucho** he eats a lot; **¿te vas a quedar mucho?** are you going to be staying long?

2 (*respuesta*) very; **¿estás cansado? — ¡mucho!** are you tired? — very!

3 (*locuciones*): **como mucho** at (the) most; **el mejor con mucho** by far the best; **no es rico ni mucho menos** he's far from being rich

4: **por mucho que: por mucho que le creas** however much *o* no matter how much you believe him

muda ['muða] *nf* change of clothing

mudanza [mu'ðanθa] *nf* (*de casa*) move

mudar [mu'ðar] /1a/ vt to change; (Zool) to shed ▷ vi to change; **mudarse** vr (la ropa) to change; **~se de casa** to move house

mudo, -a ['muðo, a] adj dumb; (callado) silent

mueble ['mweβle] nm piece of furniture; **muebles** nmpl furniture sg

mueca ['mweka] nf face, grimace; **hacer ~s** to make faces at

muela ['mwela] nf tooth; **~ del juicio** wisdom tooth

muelle ['mweʎe] nm spring; (Naut) wharf; (malecón) pier

muerte ['mwerte] nf death; (homicidio) murder; **dar ~ a** to kill

muerto, -a ['mwerto, a] pp de **morir** ▷ adj dead ▷ nm/f dead man/ woman; (difunto) deceased; (cadáver) corpse; **estar ~ de cansancio** to be dead tired; **Día de los M~s** (LAM) All Souls' Day

● **DÍA DE LOS MUERTOS**
●
● All Souls' Day (or "Day of the Dead")
● in Mexico coincides with All Saints'
● Day, which is celebrated in the
● Catholic countries of Latin America
● on November 1st and 2nd. All Souls'
● Day is actually a celebration which
● begins in the evening of October
● 31st and continues until November
● 2nd. It is a combination of the
● Catholic tradition of honouring
● the Christian saints and martyrs,
● and the ancient Mexican or Aztec
● traditions, in which death was
● not something sinister. For this
● reason all the dead are honoured by
● bringing offerings of food, flowers
● and candles to the cemetery.

muestra ['mwestra] nf (señal) indication, sign; (demostración) demonstration; (prueba) proof; (estadística) sample; (modelo) model, pattern; (testimonio) token

muestro etc vb V **mostrar**

muevo etc vb V **mover**

mugir [mu'xir] /3c/ vi (vaca) to moo

mugre ['muɣre] nf dirt, filth

mujer [mu'xer] nf woman; (esposa) wife; **mujeriego** nm womaniser

mula ['mula] nf mule

muleta [mu'leta] nf (para andar) crutch; (Taur) stick with red cape attached

multa ['multa] nf fine; **echar** o **poner una ~ a** to fine; **multar** /1a/ vt to fine

multicines [multi'θine] nmpl multiscreen cinema

multinacional [multinaθjo'nal] nf multinational

múltiple ['multiple] adj multiple, many pl, numerous

multiplicar [multipli'kar] /1g/ vt (Mat) to multiply; (fig) to increase; **multiplicarse** vr (Bio) to multiply; (fig) to be everywhere at once

multitud [multi'tuð] nf (muchedumbre) crowd; **~ de** lots of

mundial [mun'djal] adj world-wide, universal; (guerra, récord) world cpd

mundo ['mundo] nm world; **todo el ~** everybody; **tener ~** to be experienced, know one's way around

munición [muni'θjon] nf ammunition

municipal [muniθi'pal] adj municipal; local

municipio [muni'θipjo] nm (ayuntamiento) town council, corporation; (territorio administrativo) town, municipality

muñeca [mu'ɲeka] nf (Anat) wrist; (juguete) doll

muñeco [mu'ɲeko] nm (figura) figure; (marioneta) puppet; (fig) puppet, pawn

mural [mu'ral] adj mural, wall cpd ▷ nm mural

muralla [mu'raʎa] nf (city) walls pl

murciélago [mur'θjelaɣo] nm bat

murmullo [mur'muʎo] nm murmur(ing); (cuchicheo) whispering

murmurar [murmu'rar] /1a/ vi to murmur, whisper; (*cotillear*) to gossip

muro ['muro] nm wall

muscular [musku'lar] adj muscular

músculo ['muskulo] nm muscle

museo [mu'seo] nm museum; **~ de arte** o **de pintura** art gallery

musgo ['musɣo] nm moss

músico, -a ['musiko, a] adj musical ▷ nm/f musician ▷ nf music

muslo ['muslo] nm thigh

musulmán, -ana [musul'man, ana] nm/f Moslem

mutación [muta'θjon] nf (Bio) mutation; (*cambio*) (sudden) change

mutilar [muti'lar] /1a/ vt to mutilate; (*a una persona*) to maim

mutuo, -a ['mutwo, a] adj mutual

muy [mwi] adv very; (*demasiado*) too; **M~ Señor mío** Dear Sir; **~ de noche** very late at night; **eso es ~ de él** that's just like him

N abr (= norte) N

nabo ['naβo] nm turnip

nacer [na'θer] /2d/ vi to be born; (*huevo*) to hatch; (*vegetal*) to sprout; (*río*) to rise; **nací en Barcelona** I was born in Barcelona; **nacido, -a** adj born; **recién nacido** newborn; **nacimiento** nm birth; (*de Navidad*) Nativity; (*de río*) source

nación [na'θjon] nf nation; **nacional** adj national; **nacionalidad** nf nationality; **nacionalismo** nm nationalism

nada ['naða] pron nothing ▷ adv not at all, in no way; **no decir ~ (más)** to say nothing (else), not to say anything (else); **¡~ más!** that's all; **de ~** don't mention it

nadador, a [naða'ðor, a] nm/f swimmer

nadar [na'ðar] /1a/ vi to swim

nadie ['naðje] pron nobody, no-one; **~ habló** nobody spoke; **no había ~**

there was nobody there, there wasn't anybody there

nado ['naðo]: **a ~** *adv*: **pasar a ~** to swim across

nafta ['nafta] *nf* (LAM) petrol (BRIT), gas(oline) (US)

naipe ['naipe] *nm* (playing) card; **naipes** *nmpl* cards

nalgas ['nalɣas] *nfpl* buttocks

nalguear [nalɣe'ar] /1a/ vt (LAM, CAM) to spank

nana ['nana] *nf* lullaby

naranja [na'ranxa] *adj inv*, *nf* orange; **media ~** (*fam*) better half; **naranjada** *nf* orangeade; **naranjo** *nm* orange tree

narciso [nar'θiso] *nm* narcissus

narcótico, -a [nar'kotiko, a] *adj, nm* narcotic; **narcotizar** /1f/ vt to drug; **narcotráfico** *nm* narcotics o drug trafficking

nariz [na'riθ] *nf* nose; **~ chata-, respingona** snub/turned-up nose

narración [narra'θjon] *nf* narration

narrar [na'rrar] /1a/ vt to narrate, recount

narrativo, -a [narra'tiβo, a] *adj, nf* narrative

nata ['nata] *nf* cream (tb fig); (en leche cocida etc) skin; **~ batida** whipped cream

natación [nata'θjon] *nf* swimming

natal [na'tal] *adj*: **~ ciudad ~** home town; **natalidad** *nf* birth rate

natillas [na'tiʎas] *nfpl* (egg) custard sg

nativo, -a [na'tiβo, a] *adj, nm/f* native

natural [natu'ral] *adj* natural; (*fruta etc*) fresh > *nmf* native > *nm* disposition, temperament; **buen ~** good nature

naturaleza [natura'leθa] *nf* nature; (*género*) nature, kind; **~ muerta** still life

naturalmente [natural'mente] *adv* (*de modo natural*) in a natural way; **¡~!** of course!

naufragar [naufra'ɣar] /1h/ vi to sink; **naufragio** *nm* shipwreck

náusea ['nausea] *nf* nausea; **me da ~s** it makes me feel sick

nauseabundo, -a [nausea'βundo, a] *adj* nauseating, sickening

náutico, -a ['nautiko, a] *adj* nautical

navaja [na'βaxa] *nf* penknife; **~ (de afeitar)** razor

naval [na'βal] *adj* naval

Navarra [na'βarra] *nf* Navarre

nave ['naβe] *nf* (*barco*) ship, vessel; (*Arq*) nave; **~ espacial** spaceship; **~ industrial** factory premises *pl*

navegador [naβeɣa'ðor] *nm* (*Inform*) browser

navegante [naβe'ɣante] *nmf* navigator

navegar [naβe'ɣar] /1h/ vi (*barco*) to sail; (*avión*) to fly; **~ por Internet** to surf the Net

Navidad [naβi'ðað] *nf* Christmas; **Navidades** *nfpl* Christmas time *sg*; **¡Feliz ~!** Merry Christmas!; **navideño, -a** *adj* Christmas *cpd*

nazca etc *vb V* **nacer**

nazi [naθi] *adj*, *nmf* Nazi

NE *abr* (= nor(d)este) NE

neblina [ne'βlina] *nf* mist

necesario, -a [neθe'sarjo, a] *adj* necessary

neceser [neθe'ser] *nm* toilet bag; (*bolsa grande*) holdall

necesidad [neθesi'ðað] *nf* need; (*lo inevitable*) necessity; (*miseria*) poverty; **en caso de ~** in case of need o emergency; **hacer sus ~es** to relieve o.s.

necesitado, -a [neθesi'tado, a] *adj* needy, poor; **~ de** in need of

necesitar [neθesi'tar] /1a/ vt to need, require

necio, -a ['neθjo, a] *adj* foolish

nectarina [nekta'rina] *nf* nectarine

nefasto, -a [ne'fasto, a] *adj* ill-fated, unlucky

negación [neɣa'θjon] *nf* negation; (*rechazo*) refusal, denial

negar [ne'ɣar] /1h, 1j/ vt (*renegar, rechazar*) to refuse; (*prohibir*) to refuse,

deny; (*desmentir*) to deny; **negarse** *vr*:
~se a hacer algo to refuse to do sth

negativo, -a [neɣa'tiβo, a] *adj*, *adj*
negative ▷ *nm* negative; (*rechazo*)
refusal, denial

negligente [neɣli'xente] *adj*
negligent

negociación [neɣoθja'θjon] *nf*
negotiation

negociante [neɣo'θjante] *nmf*
businessman/woman

negociar [neɣo'θjar] /1b/ *vt*, *vi* to
negotiate; **~ en** to deal in, trade in

negocio [ne'ɣoθjo] *nm* (*Com*)
business; (*asunto*) affair, business;
(*operación comercial*) deal, transaction;
(*lugar*) place of business; **los ~s**
business *sg*; **hacer ~** to do business

negra ['neɣra] *nf* (*Mus*) crotchet;
V tb **negro**

negro, -a ['neɣro, a] *adj* black;
(*suerte*) awful ▷ *nm* black ▷ *nm/f*
black person

nene, -a ['nene, a] *nm/f* baby, small
child

neón [ne'on] *nm*: **luces/lámpara de**
~ neon lights/lamp

neoyorquino, -a [neojor'kino, a]
adj New York *cpd*

nervio ['nerβjo] *nm* nerve;
nerviosismo *nm* nervousness, nerves
pl; **nervioso, -a** *adj* nervous

neto, -a ['neto, a] *adj* net

neumático, -a [neu'matiko, a] *adj*
pneumatic ▷ *nm* (*ESP*) tyre (*BRIT*), tire
(*US*); **~ de recambio** spare tyre

neurólogo, -a [neu'roloɣo, a] *nm/f*
neurologist

neurona [neu'rona] *nf* neuron

neutral [neu'tral] *adj* neutral;
neutralizar /1f/ *vt* to neutralize;
(*contrarrestar*) to counteract

neutro, -a ['neutro, a] *adj* (*Bio*, *Ling*)
neuter

neutrón [neu'tron] *nm* neutron

nevado, -a [ne'βaðo, a] *adj* snow-
covered ▷ *nf* snowstorm; (*caída de*
nieve) snowfall

nevar [ne'βar] /1j/ *vi* to snow

nevera [ne'βera] *nf* (*ESP*) refrigerator
(*BRIT*), icebox (*US*)

nevería [neβe'ria] *nf* (*LAM*) ice-cream
parlour

nexo ['nekso] *nm* link, connection

ni [ni] *conj* nor, neither; (*tb*: **ni**
siquiera) not even; **ni que** not even
if; **ni blanco ni negro** neither white
nor black

Nicaragua [nika'raɣwa] *nf*
Nicaragua; **nicaragüense** *adj*, *nmf*
Nicaraguan

nicho ['nitʃo] *nm* niche

nicotina [niko'tina] *nf* nicotine

nido ['niðo] *nm* nest

niebla ['njeβla] *nf* fog; (*neblina*) mist

niego *etc* ['njeɣo] *vb V* **negar**

nieto, -a ['njeto, a] *nm/f* grandson/
granddaughter; **nietos** *nmpl*
grandchildren

nieve ['njeβe] *vb V* **nevar** ▷ *nf* snow;
(*LAM*) ice cream

ninfa ['ninfa] *nf* nymph

ningún [nin'ɡun] *adj V* **ninguno**

ninguno, -a [nin'ɡuno, a] *adj*
(*before nmsg*: **ningún**) no ▷ *pron*
(*nadie*) nobody; (*ni uno*) none,
not one; (*ni uno ni otro*) neither; **de**
ninguna manera by no means,
not at all

niña ['nina] *nf V* **niño**

niñera [ni'nera] *nf* nursemaid, nanny

niñez [ni'neθ] *nf* childhood; (*infancia*)
infancy

niño, -a [ni'no, a] *adj* (*joven*) young;
(*inmaduro*) immature ▷ *nm* boy, child
▷ *nf* girl, child; (*Anat*) pupil

nipón, -ona [ni'pon, ona] *adj*, *nm/f*
Japanese

níquel ['nikel] *nm* nickel

níspero ['nispero] *nm* medlar

nítido, -a [ni'tiðo, a] *adj* clear, sharp

nitrato [ni'trato] *nm* nitrate

nitrógeno [ni'troxeno] *nm* nitrogen

nivel [ni'βel] *nm* (*Geo*) level; (*norma*)
level, standard; (*altura*) height; **~ de**
aceite oil level; **~ de aire** spirit level;
~ de vida standard of living; **nivelar**

/ia/ vt to level out; (fig) to even up; (Com) to balance

no [no] adv no; (con verbo) not ▷ excl no!; **no tengo nada** I don't have anything, I have nothing; **no es el mío** it's not mine; **ahora no** not now; **¿no lo sabes?** don't you know?; **no mucho** not much; **no bien termine, lo entregaré** as soon as I finish I'll hand it over; **ayer no más** just yesterday; **¡pase no más!** come in!; **¡a que no lo sabes!** I bet you don't know!; **¡cómo no!** of course!; **la no intervención** non-intervention

noble [noβle] adj, nmf noble; **nobleza** nf nobility

noche [notʃe] nf night, night-time; (la tarde) evening; **de ~, por la ~** at night; **ayer por la ~** last night; **esta ~** tonight; **(en) toda la ~** all night; **hacer ~ en un sitio** to spend the night in a place; **se hace de ~** it's getting dark; **es de ~** it's dark; **N~ de San Juan** see note

● **NOCHE DE SAN JUAN**
●
● The *Noche de San Juan* on the 24th
● June is a *fiesta* coinciding with the
● summer solstice and which has
● taken the place of other ancient
● pagan festivals. Traditionally
● fire plays a major part in these
● festivities with celebrations and
● dancing taking place around
● bonfires in towns and villages
● across the country.

nocivo, -a [no'θiβo, a] adj harmful

noctámbulo, -a [nok'tambulo, a] nm/f sleepwalker

nocturno, -a [nok'turno, a] adj (de la noche) nocturnal, night cpd; (de la tarde) evening cpd ▷ nm nocturne

nogal [no'ɣal] nm walnut tree

nómada [nomaða] adj nomadic ▷ nmf nomad

nombrar [nom'brar] /1a/ vt to name; (mencionar) to mention; (designar) to appoint

nombre [nombre] nm name; (sustantivo) noun; **~ y apellidos** name in full; **poner ~ a** to call name; **~ común/propio** common/proper noun; **~ de pila/de soltera** Christian/maiden name

nómina [nomina] nf (Com) payroll; (hoja) payslip

nominal [nomi'nal] adj nominal

nominar [nomi'nar] /1a/ vt to nominate

nominativo, -a [nomina'tiβo, a] adj (Com): **un cheque ~ a X** a cheque made out to X

nordeste [nor'ðeste] adj north-east, north-eastern, north-easterly ▷ nm north-east

nórdico, -a [norðiko, a] adj Nordic

noreste [no'reste] adj, nm = **nordeste**

noria [norja] nf (Agr) waterwheel; (de carnaval) big (BRIT) or Ferris (US) wheel

norma [norma] nf rule

normal [nor'mal] adj (corriente) normal; (habitual) usual, natural; **normalizar** /1f/ vt to normalize; (Com, Tec) to standardize; **normalizarse** vr to return to normal; **normalmente** adv normally

normativo, -a [norma'tiβo, a] adj: **es ~ en todos los coches nuevos** it is standard in all new cars ▷ nf rules pl, regulations pl

noroeste [noro'este] adj north-west, north-western, north-westerly ▷ nm north-west

norte [norte] adj north, northern, northerly ▷ nm north; (fig) guide

norteamericano, -a [norteameri'kano, a] adj, nm/f (North) American

Noruega [no'rweɣa] nf Norway

noruego, -a [no'rweɣo, a] adj, nm/f Norwegian

nos [nos] pron (directo) us; (indirecto) (to) us; (reflexivo) (to) ourselves;

n

(recíproco) (to) each other; **~ levantamos a las siete** we get up at seven

nosotros, -as [no'sotros, as] *pron (sujeto)* we; *(después de prep)* us

nostalgia [nos'talxja] *nf* nostalgia

nota ['nota] *nf* note; *(Escol)* mark

notable [no'taβle] *adj* notable; *(Escol etc)* outstanding

notar [no'tar]/1a/ *vt* to notice, note; **notarse** *vr* to be obvious; **se nota que ...** one observes that ...

notario [no'tarjo] *nm* notary

noticia [no'tiθja] *nf (información)* piece of news; **las ~s** the news *sg*; **tener ~s de algn** to hear from sb

▌ No confundir *noticia* con la palabra inglesa *notice*.

noticiero [noti'θjero] *nm (LAM)* news bulletin

notificar [notifi'kar] /1g/ *vt* to notify, inform

notorio, -a [no'torjo, a] *adj (público)* well-known; *(evidente)* obvious

novato, -a [no'βato, a] *adj* inexperienced ▷ *nm/f* beginner, novice

novecientos, -as [noβe'θjentos, as] *num* nine hundred

novedad [noβe'ðað] *nf (calidad de nuevo)* newness; *(noticia)* piece of news; *(cambio)* change, (new) development

novel [no'βel] *adj* new; *(inexperto)* inexperienced ▷ *nm/f* beginner

novela [no'βela] *nf* novel

noveno, -a [no'βeno, a] *num* ninth

noventa [no'βenta] *num* ninety

novia ['noβja] *nf* V **novio**

noviazgo [no'βjaθyo] *nm* engagement

novicio, -a [no'βiθjo, a] *nm/f* novice

noviembre [no'βjembre] *nm* November

novillada [noβi'ʎaða] *nf (Taur)* bullfight with young bulls; *(novillos)* novice bullfighter; **novillo** *nm* young bull, bullock; **hacer novillos** *(fam)* to play truant *(BRIT)* o hooky *(US)*

novio, -a ['noβjo, a] *nm/f* boyfriend/ girlfriend; *(prometido)* fiancé/fiancée; *(recién casado)* bridegroom/bride; **los ~s** the newly-weds

nube ['nuβe] *nf* cloud

nublado, -a [nu'βlaðo, a] *adj* cloudy

nublar [nu'βlar] /1a/ *vt (oscurecer)* to darken; *(confundir)* to cloud; **nublarse** *vr* to cloud over

nuboso, -a [nu'βoso, a] *adj* cloudy

nuca ['nuka] *nf* nape of the neck

nuclear [nukle'ar] *adj* nuclear

núcleo ['nukleo] *nm (centro)* core; *(Física)* nucleus; **~ urbano** city centre

nudillo [nu'ðiʎo] *nm* knuckle

nudista [nu'dista] *adj* nudist

nudo ['nuðo] *nm* knot; *(Ferro)* junction

nuera ['nwera] *nf* daughter-in-law

nuestro, -a ['nwestro, a] *adj posesivo* our ▷ *pron* ours; **~ padre** our father; **un amigo ~** a friend of ours; **es el ~** it's ours

Nueva York [-'jork] *nf* New York

Nueva Zelanda [-θe'landa] *nf* New Zealand

nueve ['nweβe] *num* nine

nuevo, -a ['nweβo, a] *adj (gen)* new; **de ~** again

nuez [nweθ] *nf* walnut; **~ de Adán** Adam's apple; **~ moscada** nutmeg

nulo, -a ['nulo, a] *adj (inepto, torpe)* useless; *(inválido)* (null and) void; *(Deporte)* drawn, tied

núm. *abr* (= *número*) no.

numerar [nume'rar] /1a/ *vt* to number

número ['numero] *nm (gen)* number; *(tamaño: de zapato)* size; *(ejemplar: de diario)* number, issue; **sin ~** numberless, unnumbered; **~ de matrícula/de teléfono** registration/ telephone number; **~ impar/par** odd/even number; **~ romano** Roman numeral; **~ atrasado** back number

numeroso, -a [nume'roso, a] *adj* numerous

nunca ['nunka] *adv (jamás)* never; **~ lo pensé** I never thought it; **no viene ~**

he never comes; **~ más** never again;
más que ~ more than ever
nupcias ['nupθjas] *nfpl* wedding *sg*,
nuptials
nutria ['nutrja] *nf* otter
nutrición [nutri'θjon] *nf* nutrition
nutrir [nu'trir] /3a/ *vt* (*alimentar*)
to nourish; (*dar de comer*) to feed;
(*fig*) to strengthen; **nutritivo, -a** *adj*
nourishing, nutritious
nylon [ni'lon] *nm* nylon
ñango, -a ['nango, a] *adj* (*LAM*) puny
ñapa ['napa] *nf* (*LAM*) extra
ñata ['nata] *nf* (*LAM fam*) nose; V
tb **ñato**
ñato, -a ['nato, a] *adj* (*LAM*) snub-
nosed
ñoñería [none'ria] *nf* insipidness
ñoño, -a ['nono, a] *adj* (*fam: tonto*)
silly, stupid; (*soso*) insipid; (*débil:
persona*) spineless; (*ESP: película,
novela*) sentimental

O

O *abr* (= *oeste*) W
o [o] *conj* or; **o ... o** either ... or
oasis [o'asis] *nm inv* oasis
obcecarse [oβθe'karse] /1g/ *vr* to
become obsessed
obedecer [oβeðe'θer] /2d/ *vt* to obey;
obediente *adj* obedient
obertura [oβer'tura] *nf* overture
obeso, -a [o'βeso, a] *adj* obese
obispo [o'βispo] *nm* bishop
obituario [oβi'twarjo] *nm* (*LAM*)
obituary
objetar [oβxe'tar] /1a/ *vt, vi* to object
objetivo, -a [oβxe'tiβo, a] *adj* ▷ *nm*
objective
objeto [oβ'xeto] *nm* (*cosa*) object;
(*fin*) aim
objetor, a [oβxe'tor, a] *nm/f* objector
obligación [oβliɣa'θjon] *nf*
obligation; (*Com*) bond
obligar [oβli'ɣar] /1h/ *vt* to force;
obligarse *vr*: **~se a** to commit o.s.
to; **obligatorio, -a** *adj* compulsory,
obligatory

oboe [o'βoe] nm oboe

obra ['oβra] nf work; (Arq)
construction, building; (Teat) play; ~
maestra masterpiece; ~s **públicas**
public works; **por ~ de** thanks to (the
efforts of); **obrar** /1a/ vt to work;
(tener efecto) to have an effect on ▷ vi
to act, behave; (tener efecto) to have an
effect; **la carta obra en su poder** the
letter is in his/her possession

obrero, -a [o'βrero, a] adj working;
(movimiento) labour cpd ▷ nm/f (gen)
worker; (sin oficio) labourer

obsceno, -a [oβs'θeno, a] adj obscene

obscu... pref = **oscu...**

obsequiar [oβse'kjar] /1b/ vt (ofrecer)
to present; (agasajar) to make a fuss
of, lavish attention on; **obsequio**
nm (regalo) gift; (cortesía) courtesy,
attention

observación [oβserβa'θjon] nf
observation; (reflexión) remark

observador, a [oβserβa'ðor, a] nm/f
observer

observar [oβser'βar] /1a/ vt to
observe; (notar) to notice; **observarse**
vr to keep to, observe

obsesión [oβse'sjon] nf obsession;
obsesivo, -a adj obsessive

obstáculo [oβs'takulo] nm obstacle;
(impedimento) hindrance, drawback

obstante [oβs'tante]: **no ~** adv
nevertheless

obstinado, -a [oβsti'naðo, a] adj
obstinate; stubborn

obstinarse [oβsti'narse] /1a/ vr to be
obstinate; ~ **en** to persist in

obstruir [oβstru'ir] /3g/ vt to
obstruct

obtener [oβte'ner] /2k/ vt to obtain;
(ganar) to gain; (premio) to win

obturador [oβtura'ðor] nm (Foto)
shutter

obvio, -a ['oββjo, a] adj obvious

oca ['oka] nf goose; (tb: **juego de la ~**)
= snakes and ladders

ocasión [oka'sjon] nf (oportunidad)
opportunity, chance; (momento)
occasion, time; (causa) cause; **de
~** secondhand; **ocasionar** /1a/ vt
to cause

ocaso nm (fig) decline

occidente [okθi'ðente] nm west

O.C.D.E. nf abr (= Organización de
Cooperación y Desarrollo Económicos)
OECD

océano [o'θeano] nm ocean; **el ~
Índico** the Indian Ocean

ochenta [o'tʃenta] num eighty

ocho ['otʃo] num eight; **dentro de ~
días** within a week

ocio ['oθjo] nm (tiempo) leisure; (pey)
idleness

octavilla [okta'βiʎa] nf leaflet,
pamphlet

octavo, -a [ok'taβo, a] num eighth

octubre [ok'tuβre] nm October

oculista [oku'lista] nmf oculist

ocultar [okul'tar] /1a/ vt (esconder)
to hide; (callar) to conceal; **oculto, -a** adj
hidden; (fig) secret

ocupación [okupa'θjon] nf
occupation

ocupado, -a [oku'paðo, a] adj
(persona) busy; (plaza) occupied, taken;
(teléfono) engaged

ocupar /1a/ vt (gen) to occupy;
ocuparse vr: ~**se de o en** to concern
o.s. with; (cuidar) to look after

ocurrencia [oku'rrenθja] nf (idea)
bright idea

ocurrir [oku'rrir] /3a/ vi to happen;
ocurrirse vr: **se me ocurrió que ...** it
occurred to me that ...

odiar [o'ðjar] /1b/ vt to hate; **odio**
nm hate, hatred; **odioso, -a** adj (gen)
hateful; (malo) nasty

odontólogo, -a [oðon'toloɣo, a]
nm/f dentist, dental surgeon

oeste [o'este] nm west; **una película
del ~** a western

ofender [ofen'der] /2a/ vt (agraviar)
to offend; (insultar) to insult;
ofenderse vr to take offence; **ofensa**
nf offence; **ofensivo, -a** adj offensive
▷ nf offensive

oferta [o'ferta] *nf* offer; (*propuesta*) proposal; **la ~ y la demanda** supply and demand; **artículos en ~** goods on offer

oficial [ofi'θjal] *adj* official ▷ *nm* (*Mil*) officer

oficina [ofi'θina] *nf* office; **~ de correos** post office; **~ de información** information bureau; **~ de turismo** tourist office; **oficinista** *nmf* clerk

oficio [o'fiθjo] *nm* (*profesión*) profession; (*puesto*) post; (*Rel*) service; **ser del ~** to be an old hand; **tener mucho ~** to have a lot of experience; **~ de difuntos** funeral service

ofimática [ofi'matika] *nf* office automation

ofrecer [ofre'θer] /2d/ *vt* (*dar*) to offer; (*proponer*) to propose; **ofrecerse** *vr* (*persona*) to offer o.s., volunteer; (*situación*) to present itself; **¿qué se le ofrece?, ¿se le ofrece algo?** what can I do for you?, can I get you anything?

ofrecimiento [ofreθi'mjento] *nm* offer

oftalmólogo, -a [oftal'moloγo, a] *nm/f* ophthalmologist

oída [o'iða] *nf*: **de ~s** by hearsay

oído [o'iðo] *nm* (*Anat, Mus*) ear; (*sentido*) hearing

oigo *etc vb V* **oír**

oír [o'ir] /3p/ *vt* (*gen*) to hear; (*escuchar*) to listen to; **¡oiga!** excuse me!; (*Telec*) hullo?; **~ misa** to attend mass; **como quien oye llover** without paying (the slightest) attention

ojal [o'xal] *nm* buttonhole

ojalá [oxa'la] *excl* if only (it were so)!, some hope! ▷ *conj* if only...!, I would that...!; **~ que venga hoy** I hope he comes today

ojeada [oxe'aða] *nf* glance

ojera [o'xera] *nf*: **tener ~s** to have bags under one's eyes

ojo ['oxo] *nm* eye; (*de puente*) span; (*de cerradura*) keyhole ▷ *excl* careful!; **tener ~ para** to have an eye for; **~ de buey** porthole

okey ['okei] *excl* (*LAM*) O.K.

okupa [o'kupa] *nmf* (*fam*) squatter

ola ['ola] *nf* wave

olé [o'le] *excl* bravo!, olé!

oleada [ole'aða] *nf* big wave, swell; (*fig*) wave

oleaje [ole'axe] *nm* swell

óleo ['oleo] *nm* oil; **oleoducto** *nm* (oil) pipeline

oler [o'ler] /2i/ *vt* (*gen*) to smell; (*inquirir*) to pry into; (*fig: sospechar*) to sniff out ▷ *vi* to smell; **~ a** to smell of

olfatear [olfate'ar] /1a/ *vt* to smell; (*inquirir*) to pry into; **olfato** *nm* sense of smell

olimpiada [olim'piaða] *nf*: **la ~ o las ~s** the Olympics; **olímpico, -a** *adj* Olympic

oliva [o'liβa] *nf* (*aceituna*) olive; **aceite de ~** olive oil; **olivo** *nm* olive tree

olla ['oʎa] *nf* pan; (*comida*) stew; **~ a presión** pressure cooker; **~ podrida** type of Spanish stew

olmo ['olmo] *nm* elm (tree)

olor [o'lor] *nm* smell; **oloroso, -a** *adj* scented

olvidar [olβi'ðar] /1a/ *vt* to forget; (*omitir*) to omit; **olvidarse** *vr* (*fig*) to forget o.s.; **se me olvidó** I forgot

olvido [ol'βiðo] *nm* oblivion; (*despiste*) forgetfulness

ombligo [om'bliγo] *nm* navel

omelette [ome'lete] *nf* (*LAM*) omelet(te)

omisión [omi'sjon] *nf* (*abstención*) omission; (*descuido*) neglect

omiso, -a [o'miso, a] *adj*: **hacer caso ~ de** to ignore, pass over

omitir [omi'tir] /3a/ *vt* to leave o miss out, omit

omnipotente [omnipo'tente] *adj* omnipotent

omoplato [omo'plato], **omóplato** [o'moplato] *nm* shoulder-blade

OMS *nf abr* (= *Organización Mundial de la Salud*) WHO

once ['onθe] *num* eleven; **onces** *nfpl* tea break *sg*

onda ['onda] nf wave; **~ corta/larga/ media** short/long/medium wave; **ondear** /1a/ vi to wave; (tener ondas) to be wavy; (agua) to ripple

ondulación [ondula'θjon] nf undulation; **ondulado, -a** adj wavy

ONG nf abr (= organización no gubernamental) NGO

ONU ['onu] nf abr (= Organización de las Naciones Unidas) UN

opaco, -a [o'pako, a] adj opaque

opción [op'θjon] nf (gen) option; (derecho) right, option

O.P.E.P. [o'pep] nf abr (= Organización de Países Exportadores de Petróleo) OPEC

ópera ['opera] nf opera; **~ bufa** o **cómica** comic opera

operación [opera'θjon] nf (gen) operation; (Com) transaction, deal

operador, a [opera'ðor, a] nm/f operator; (Cine: proyección) projectionist; (: rodaje) cameraman

operar [ope'rar] /1a/ vt (producir) to produce, bring about; (Med) to operate on ▷ vi (Com) to operate, deal; **operarse** vr to occur; (Med) to have an operation

opereta [ope'reta] nf operetta

opinar [opi'nar] /1a/ vt to think ▷ vi to give one's opinion; **opinión** nf (creencia) belief; (criterio) opinion

opio ['opjo] nm opium

oponer [opo'ner] /2q/ vt (resistencia) to put up, offer; **oponerse** vr (objetar) to object; (estar frente a frente) to be opposed; (dos personas) to oppose each other; **~ A a B** to set A against B; **me opongo a pensar que ...** I refuse to believe o think that ...

oportunidad [oportuni'ðað] nf (ocasión) opportunity; (posibilidad) chance

oportuno, -a [opor'tuno, a] adj (en su tiempo) opportune, timely; (respuesta) suitable; **en el momento ~** at the right moment

oposición [oposi'θjon] nf opposition; **oposiciones** nfpl (Escol) public examinations

opositor, -a [oposi'tor, a] nm/f (Admin) candidate to a public examination; (adversario) opponent; **~ (a)** candidate (for)

opresión [opre'sjon] nf oppression; **opresor, a** nm/f oppressor

oprimir [opri'mir] /3a/ vt to squeeze; (fig) to oppress

optar [op'tar] /1a/ vi (elegir) to choose; **~ a** o **por** to opt for; **optativo, -a** adj optional

óptico, -a ['optiko, a] adj optic(al) ▷ nm/f optician ▷ nf (ciencia) optics sg; (tienda) optician's; (fig) viewpoint; **desde esta óptica** from this point of view

optimismo [opti'mismo] nm optimism; **optimista** nmf optimist

opuesto, -a [o'pwesto, a] adj (contrario) opposite; (antagónico) opposing

oración [ora'θjon] nf (Rel) prayer; (Ling) sentence

orador, a [ora'ðor, a] nm/f orator; (conferenciante) speaker

oral [o'ral] adj oral

orangután [orangu'tan] nm orang-utan

orar [o'rar] /1a/ vi to pray

oratoria [ora'torja] nf oratory

órbita ['orβita] nf orbit

orden ['orðen] nm (colocación) order ▷ nf (mandato) order; (Inform) command; **en ~ de prioridad** in order of priority; **el ~ del día** the agenda

ordenado, -a [orðe'naðo, a] adj (metódico) methodical; (arreglado) orderly

ordenador [orðena'ðor] nm computer; **~ central** mainframe computer

ordenar [orðe'nar] /1a/ vt (mandar) to order; (poner orden) to put in order, arrange; **ordenarse** vr (Rel) to be ordained

ordeñar [orðe'ɲar] /1a/ vt to milk

ordinario, -a [orði'narjo, a] adj (común) ordinary, usual; (vulgar) vulgar, common

orégano [o'reɣano] *nm* oregano

oreja [o'rexa] *nf* ear; (*Mecánica*) lug, flange

orfanato [orfa'nato] *nm* orphanage

orfebrería [orfeβre'ria] *nf* gold/ silver work

orgánico, -a [or'ɣaniko, a] *adj* organic

organismo [orɣa'nismo] *nm* (*Bio*) organism; (*Pol*) organization

organización [orɣaniθa'θjon] *nf* organization; **O~ de las Naciones Unidas (ONU)** United Nations Organization; **O~ del Tratado del Atlántico Norte (OTAN)** North Atlantic Treaty Organization (NATO); **organizar** /1f/ *vt* to organize

órgano ['orɣano] *nm* organ

orgasmo [or'ɣasmo] *nm* orgasm

orgía [or'xia] *nf* orgy

orgullo [or'ɣuʎo] *nm* pride; **orgulloso, -a** *adj* (*gen*) proud; (*altanero*) haughty

orientación [orjenta'θjon] *nf* (*posición*) position; (*dirección*) direction

oriental [orjen'tal] *adj* oriental; (*región etc*) eastern

orientar [orjen'tar] /1a/ *vt* (*situar*) to orientate; (*señalar*) to point; (*dirigir*) to direct; (*guiar*) to guide; **orientarse** *vr* to get one's bearings

oriente [o'rjente] *nm* east; **Cercano/ Medio/Lejano O~** Near/Middle/ Far East

origen [o'rixen] *nm* origin

original [orixi'nal] *adj* (*nuevo*) original; (*extraño*) odd, strange; **originalidad** *nf* originality

originar [orixi'nar] /1a/ *vt* to start, cause; **originarse** *vr* to originate; **originario, -a** *adj* original; **ser originario de** to originate from

orilla [o'riʎa] *nf* (*borde*) border; (*de río*) bank; (*de bosque, tela*) edge; (*de mar*) shore

orina [o'rina] *nf* urine; **orinal** *nm* (*chamber*) pot; **orinar** /1a/ *vi* to urinate; **orinarse** *vr* to wet o.s.

oro ['oro] *nm* gold; V tb **oros**

oros ['oros] *nmpl* (*Naipes*) one of the suits in the Spanish card deck

orquesta [or'kesta] *nf* orchestra; **~ de cámara/sinfónica** chamber/ symphony orchestra

orquídea [or'kiðea] *nf* orchid

ortiga [or'tiɣa] *nf* nettle

ortodoxo, -a [orto'ðokso, a] *adj* orthodox

ortografía [ortoɣra'fia] *nf* spelling

ortopedia [orto'peðja] *nf* orthop(a)edics *sg*; (*a vosotros*) **ortopédico, -a** *adj* orthop(a)edic

oruga [o'ruɣa] *nf* caterpillar

orzuelo [or'θwelo] *nm* stye

os [os] *pron* you; (*a vosotros*) (to) you

osa ['osa] *nf* (she-)bear; **O~ Mayor/ Menor** Great/Little Bear

osadía [osa'ðia] *nf* daring

osar [o'sar] /1a/ *vi* to dare

oscilación [osθila'θjon] *nf* (*movimiento*) oscillation; (*fluctuación*) fluctuation

oscilar [osθi'lar] /1a/ *vi* to oscillate; to fluctuate

oscurecer [oskure'θer] /2d/ *vt* to darken ▷ *vi* to grow dark; **oscurecerse** *vr* to grow o get dark

oscuridad [oskuri'ðað] *nf* obscurity; (*tinieblas*) darkness

oscuro, -a [os'kuro, a] *adj* dark; (*fig*) obscure; **a oscuras** in the dark

óseo, -a ['oseo, a] *adj* bone *cpd*

oso ['oso] *nm* bear; **~ de peluche** teddy bear; **~ hormiguero** anteater

ostentar [osten'tar] /1a/ *vt* (*gen*) to show; (*pey*) to flaunt, show off; (*poseer*) to have, possess

ostión [os'tjon] *nm* (LAM) = **ostra**

ostra ['ostra] *nf* oyster

OTAN ['otan] *nf abr* (= *Organización del Tratado del Atlántico Norte*) NATO

otitis [o'titis] *nf* earache

otoñal [oto'nal] *adj* autumnal

otoño [o'toɲo] *nm* autumn, fall (US)

otorgar [otor'ɣar] /1h/ *vt* (*conceder*) to concede; (*dar*) to grant

otorrinolaringólogo, -a
[otorrinolarinˈɣo loɣo, a] nm/f (Med: tb:
otorrino) ear, nose and throat specialist

PALABRA CLAVE

otro, -a [ˈotro, a] adj **1** (distinto:
sg) another; (: pl) other; **con otros
amigos** with other o different friends
2 (adicional): **tráigame otro café
(más), por favor** can I have another
coffee please; **otros 10 días más**
another 10 days
▶ pron **1**: **el otro** the other one; **de
otro** somebody o someone else's; **que
lo haga otro** let somebody o someone
else do it
2 (pl): **(los) otros** (the) others
3 (recíproco): **se odian (la) una a
(la) otra** they hate one another o
each other
4: **otro tanto: comer otro tanto** to
eat the same o as much again; **recibió
una decena de telegramas y otras
tantas llamadas** he got about ten
telegrams and as many calls

ovación [oβaˈθjon] nf ovation
oval [oˈβal], **ovalado, -a** [oβaˈlaðo,
a] adj oval; **óvalo** nm oval
ovario [oˈβarjo] nm ovary
oveja [oˈβexa] nf sheep
overol [oβeˈrol] nm (ʌм) overalls pl
ovillo [oˈβiʎo] nm (de lana) ball
OVNI [ˈoβni] nm abr (= objeto volante (o
volador) no identificado) UFO
ovulación [oβulaˈθjon] nf ovulation;
óvulo nm ovum
oxidación [oksiðaˈθjon] nf rusting
oxidar [oksiˈðar] /1a/ vt to rust;
oxidarse vr to go rusty
óxido [ˈoksiðo] nm oxide
oxigenado, -a [oksixeˈnaðo, a] adj
(Química) oxygenated; (pelo) bleached
oxígeno [okˈsixeno] nm oxygen
oyente [oˈjente] nmf listener
oyes etc vb V **oír**
ozono [oˈθono] nm ozone

p

pabellón [paβeˈʎon] nm bell tent;
(Arq) pavilion; (de hospital etc) block,
section; (bandera) flag
pacer [paˈθer] /2d/ vi to graze
paciencia [paˈθjenθja] nf patience
paciente [paˈθjente] adj, nmf patient
pacificación [paθifikaˈθjon] nf
pacification
pacífico, -a [paˈθifiko, a] adj (persona)
peaceable; (existencia) peaceful; **el
(océano) P~** the Pacific (Ocean)
pacifista [paθiˈfista] nmf pacifist
pacotilla [pakoˈtiʎa] nf: **de ~** shoddy
pactar [pakˈtar] /1a/ vt to agree to,
agree on ▷ vi to come to an agreement
pacto [ˈpakto] nm (tratado) pact;
(acuerdo) agreement
padecer [paðeˈθer] /2d/ vt (sufrir) to
suffer; (soportar) to endure, put up
with; **padecimiento** nm suffering
padrastro [paˈðrastro] nm stepfather
padre [ˈpaðre] nm father ▷ adj (fam):
un éxito ~ a tremendous success;

padres nmpl parents; **~ político** father-in-law

padrino [pa'ðrino] nm godfather; (fig) sponsor, patron; **padrinos** nmpl godparents; **~ de boda** best man

padrón [pa'ðron] nm (censo) census, roll

padrote [pa'ðrote] nm (LAM fam) pimp

paella [pa'eʎa] nf paella dish of rice with meat, shellfish etc

paga ['paɣa] nf (dinero pagado) payment; (sueldo) pay, wages pl

pagano, -a [pa'ɣano, a] adj, nm/f pagan, heathen

pagar [pa'ɣar] /1h/ vt to pay; (las compras, crimen) to pay for; (fig: favor) to repay ▷ vi to pay; **~ al contado/a plazos** to pay (in) cash/in instalments

pagaré [paɣa're] nm IOU

página ['paxina] nf page; **~ de inicio** (Inform) home page; **~ web** (Internet) web page

pago ['paɣo] nm (dinero) payment; (fig) return; **~ anticipado/a cuenta/a la entrega/en especie/inicial** advance payment/payment on account/cash on delivery/payment in kind/down payment; **en ~ de** in return for

pág(s). abr (= página(s)) p(p)

pague etc ['paɣe] vb V **pagar**

país [pa'is] nm (gen) country; (región) land; **los P~es Bajos** the Low Countries; **el P~ Vasco** the Basque Country

paisaje [pai'saxe] nm landscape; (vista) scenery

paisano, -a [pai'sano, a] adj of the same country ▷ nm/f (compatriota) fellow countryman/woman; **vestir de ~** (soldado) to be in civilian clothes; (guardia) to be in plain clothes

paja ['paxa] nf straw; (fig) trash, rubbish

pajarita [paxa'rita] nf bow tie

pájaro ['paxaro] nm bird; **~ carpintero** woodpecker

pajita [pa'xita] nf (drinking) straw

pala ['pala] nf spade; shovel; (raqueta etc) bat; (: de tenis) racquet; (Culin) slice; **~ mecánica** power shovel

palabra [pa'laβra] nf word; (facultad) (power of speech; (derecho de hablar) right to speak; **tomar la ~** to speak, take the floor

palabrota [pala'βrota] nf swearword

palacio [pa'laθjo] nm palace; (mansión) mansion, large house; **~ de justicia** courthouse; **~ municipal** town/city hall

paladar [pala'ðar] nm palate; **paladear** /1a/ vt to taste

palanca [pa'lanka] nf lever; (fig) pull, influence

palangana [palaŋ'gana] nf washbasin

palco ['palko] nm box

Palestina [pales'tina] nf Palestine; **palestino, -a** nm/f Palestinian

paleto, -a [pa'leto, a] nm/f yokel, hick (us) ▷ nf (pala) small shovel; (Arte) palette; (Deporte: de ping-pong) bat; (LAM: helado) ice lolly (BRIT), Popsicle® (us)

palidecer [paliðe'θer] /2d/ vi to turn pale; **palidez** nf paleness; **pálido, -a** adj pale

palillo [pa'liʎo] nm (para dientes) toothpick; **~s (chinos)** chopsticks

paliza [pa'liθa] nf beating, thrashing

palma ['palma] nf (Anat) palm; (árbol) palm tree; **batir o dar ~s** to clap, applaud; **palmada** nf slap; **palmadas** nfpl clapping sg, applause sg

palmar [pal'mar] /1a/ vi (tb: **~la**) to die, kick the bucket

palmear [palme'ar] /1a/ vi to clap

palmera [pal'mera] nf (Bot) palm tree

palmo ['palmo] nm (medida) span; (fig) small amount; **~ a ~** inch by inch

palo ['palo] nm stick; (poste) post, pole; (mango) handle, shaft; (golpe) blow, hit; (de golf) club; (de béisbol) bat; (Naut) mast; (Naipes) suit

paloma [pa'loma] nf dove, pigeon

P

palomitas [palo'mitas] *nfpl*
popcorn *sg*

palpar [pal'par] /1a/ *vt* to touch, feel

palpitar [palpi'tar] /1a/ *vi* to
palpitate; (*latir*) to beat

palta ['palta] *nf* (*LAM*) avocado

paludismo [palu'ðismo] *nm* malaria

pamela [pa'mela] *nf* sun hat

pampa ['pampa] *nf* (*LAM*) pampa(s),
prairie

pan [pan] *nm* bread; (*una barra*)
loaf; **~ integral** wholemeal bread;
~ rallado breadcrumbs *pl*; **~ tostado**
toast

pana ['pana] *nf* corduroy

panadería [panaðe'ria] *nf* baker's
(shop); **panadero, -a** *nm/f* baker

Panamá [pana'ma] *nm* Panama;
panameño, -a *adj* Panamanian

pancarta [pan'karta] *nf* placard,
banner

panceta [pan'θeta] *nf* bacon

pancho, -a ['pantʃo, a] *adj*: **estar
tan ~** to remain perfectly calm ▷ *nm*
(*LAM*) hot dog

pancito [pan'sito] *nm* (*LAM*) (bread)
roll

panda ['panda] *nm* panda

pandemia [pan'demja] *nf* pandemic

pandereta [pande'reta] *nf*
tambourine

pandilla [pan'diʎa] *nf* set, group; (*de
criminales*) gang; (*pey*) clique

panecillo [pane'θiʎo] *nm* (bread) roll

panel [pa'nel] *nm* panel; **~ solar**
solar panel

panfleto [pan'fleto] *nm* pamphlet

pánico ['paniko] *nm* panic

panorama [pano'rama] *nm*
panorama; (*vista*) view

panqué [pan'ke], **panqueque**
[pan'keke] *nm* (*LAM*) pancake

pantalla [pan'taʎa] *nf* (*de cine*)
screen; (*cubreluz*) lampshade

pantalón, pantalones
[panta'lon(es)] *nm(pl)* trousers *pl*,
pants *pl* (*US*); **pantalones cortos**
shorts *pl*

pantano [pan'tano] *nm* (*ciénaga*)
marsh, swamp; (*depósito: de agua*)
reservoir; (*fig*) jam, difficulty

panteón [pante'on] *nm* (*monumento*)
pantheon

pantera [pan'tera] *nf* panther

pantimedias [panti'meðjas] *nfpl*
(*LAM*) = **pantis**

pantis [pantis] *nm(pl)* tights (*BRIT*),
pantyhose (*US*)

pantomima [panto'mima] *nf*
pantomime

pantorrilla [panto'rriʎa] *nf* calf
(of the leg)

pants [pants] *nmpl* (*LAM*) tracksuit
(*BRIT*), sweat suit (*US*)

pantufla [pan'tufla] *nf* slipper

panty(s) [panti(s)] *nm(pl)* tights
(*BRIT*), pantyhose (*US*)

panza [pan'θa] *nf* belly, paunch

pañal [pa'ɲal] *nm* nappy, diaper (*US*);
(*fig*) early stages, infancy *sg*

paño [pa'ɲo] *nm* (*tela*) cloth; (*pedazo
de tela*) (piece of) cloth; (*trapo*) duster,
rag; **~s menores** underclothes

pañuelo [pa'ɲwelo] *nm* handkerchief,
hanky (*fam*); (*para la cabeza*) (head)
scarf

papa ['papa] *nf* (*LAM*: *patata*) potato
▷ *nm*: **el P~** the Pope; **~s fritas**
French fries, chips (*BRIT*); (*de bolsa*)
crisps (*BRIT*), potato chips (*US*)

papá [pa'pa] *nm* (*fam*) dad, daddy,
pop (*US*)

papada [pa'paða] *nf* double chin

papagayo [papa'yajo] *nm* parrot

papalote [papa'lote] *nm* (*LAM*) kite

papanatas [papa'natas] *nm inv* (*fam*)
simpleton

papaya [pa'paja] *nf* papaya

papear [pape'ar] /1a/ *vt*, *vi* (*fam*)
to eat

papel [pa'pel] *nm* (*hoja de papel*)
sheet of paper; (*Teat*) role; **~ de arroz/
envolver/fumar** rice/wrapping/
cigarette paper; **~ de aluminio/lija**
tinfoil/sandpaper; **~ higiénico** toilet
paper; **~ moneda** paper money;

~ pintado wallpaper; **~ secante** blotting paper

papeleo [pape'leo] *nm* red tape

papelera [pape'lera] *nf* wastepaper basket; **~ de reciclaje** (*Inform*) wastebasket

papelería [papele'ria] *nf* stationer's (shop)

papeleta [pape'leta] *nf* (*Pol*) ballot paper

paperas [pa'peras] *nfpl* mumps *sg*

papilla [pa'piʎa] *nf* (*de bebé*) baby food

paquete [pa'kete] *nm* (*caja*) packet; (*bulto*) parcel

par [par] *adj* (*igual*) like, equal; (*Mat*) even ▷ *nm* equal; (*de guantes*) pair; (*de veces*) couple; (*título*) peer; (*Golf*, *Com*) par; **abrir de ~ en ~** to open wide

para ['para] *prep* for; **no es ~ comer** it's not for eating; **decir ~ sí** to say to o.s.; **¿~ qué lo quieres?** what do you want it for?; **se casaron ~ separarse otra vez** they married only to separate again; **lo tendré ~ mañana** I'll have it for tomorrow; **ir ~ casa** to go home, head for home; **~ profesor es muy estúpido** he's very stupid for a teacher; **¿quién es usted ~ gritar así?** who are you to shout like that?; **tengo bastante ~ vivir** I have enough to live on

parabién [para'βjen] *nm* congratulations *pl*

parábola [pa'raβola] *nf* parable; (*Mat*) parabola, **parabólica** *nf* (*tb*: **antena parabólica**) satellite dish

parabrisas [para'βrisas] *nm inv* windscreen, windshield (*us*)

paracaídas [paraka'iðas] *nm inv* parachute; **paracaidista** *nmf* parachutist; (*Mil*) paratrooper

parachoques [para'tʃokes] *nm inv* bumper; shock absorber

parada [pa'raða] *nf* V **parado**

paradero [para'ðero] *nm* stopping-place; (*situación*) whereabouts

parado, -a [pa'raðo, a] *adj* (*persona*) motionless, standing still; (*fábrica*)

closed, at a standstill; (*coche*) stopped; (*LAM*: *de pie*) standing (up); (*sin empleo*) unemployed, idle ▷ *nf* stop; (*acto*) stopping; (*de industria*) shutdown, stoppage; (*lugar*) stopping-place; **parada de autobús** bus stop; **parada de taxis** taxi rank

paradoja [para'ðoxa] *nf* paradox

parador [para'ðor] *nm* (*ESP*) (luxury) hotel (*owned by the state*)

paragolpes [para'golpes] *nm inv* (*LAM* *Auto*) bumper, fender (*us*)

paraguas [pa'raɣwas] *nm inv* umbrella

Paraguay [para'ɣwai] *nm*: Paraguay; **paraguayo, -a** *adj*, *nm/f* Paraguayan

paraíso [para'iso] *nm* paradise, heaven

paraje [pa'raxe] *nm* place, spot

paralelo, -a [para'lelo, a] *adj* parallel

parálisis [pa'ralisis] *nf inv* paralysis; **paralítico, -a** *adj*, *nm/f* paralytic

paralizar [parali'θar] /1f/ *vt* to paralyse; **paralizarse** *vr* to become paralysed; (*fig*) to come to a standstill

páramo ['paramo] *nm* bleak plateau

paranoico, -a [para'noiko, a] *nm/f* paranoid

parapente [para'pente] *nm* (*deporte*) paragliding; (*aparato*) paraglider

parapléjico, -a [para'plexiko, a] *adj*, *nm/f* paraplegic

parar [pa'rar] /1a/ *vt* to stop; (*golpe*) to ward off ▷ *vi* to stop; **pararse** *vr* to stop; (*LAM*) to stand up; **ha parado de llover** it has stopped raining; **van a ~ en la comisaría** they're going to end up in the police station; **~se en** to pay attention to

pararrayos [para'rrajos] *nm inv* lightning conductor

parásito, -a [pa'rasito, a] *nm/f* parasite

parasol [para'sol] *nm* parasol, sunshade

parcela [par'θela] *nf* plot, piece of ground

parche ['partʃe] *nm* patch

parchís [par'tʃis] nm ludo

parcial [par'θjal] adj (eclipse) part-; (eclipse) partial; (juez) prejudiced, biased; (Pol) partisan

parecer [pare'θer] /2d/ nm (opinión) opinion, view; (aspecto) looks pl ▷ vi (tener apariencia) to seem, look; (asemejarse) to look like, seem like; (aparecer, llegar) to appear; **parecerse** vr to look alike, resemble each other; **según parece** evidently, apparently; **~se a** to look like, resemble; **al ~** apparently; **me parece que** I think (that), it seems to me that

parecido, -a [pare'θiðo, a] adj similar ▷ nm similarity, likeness, resemblance; **bien ~** good-looking, nice-looking

pared [pa'reð] nf wall

parejo, -a [pa'rexo, a] adj equal ▷ nf pair; (de personas) couple; (el otro: de un par) other one (of a pair); (: persona) partner

parentesco [paren'tesko] nm relationship

paréntesis [pa'rentesis] nm inv parenthesis; (en escrito) bracket

parezco etc vb V **parecer**

pariente, -a [pa'rjente, a] nm/f relative, relation

> No confundir *pariente* con la palabra inglesa *parent*.

parir [pa'rir] /3a/ vt to give birth to ▷ vi (mujer) to give birth, have a baby

París [pa'ris] nm Paris

parka ['parka] nf (ʟᴀᴍ) anorak

parking ['parkin] nm car park, parking lot (us)

parlamentar [parlamen'tar] /1a/ vi to parley

parlamentario, -a [parlamen'tarjo, a] adj parliamentary ▷ nm/f member of parliament

parlamento [parla'mento] nm parliament

parlanchín, -ina [parlan'tʃin, ina] adj indiscreet ▷ nm/f chatterbox

parlar [par'lar] /1a/ vi to chatter (away)

paro ['paro] nm (huelga) stoppage (of work), strike; (desempleo) unemployment; **~ cardíaco** cardiac arrest; **estar en ~** (ᴇsᴘ) to be unemployed; **subsidio de ~** unemployment benefit

parodia [pa'roðja] nf parody

parodiar /1b/ vt to parody

parpadear [parpaðe'ar] /1a/ vi (los ojos) to blink; (luz) to flicker

párpado [par'paðo] nm eyelid

parque ['parke] nm (lugar verde) park; (ʟᴀᴍ: munición) ammunition; **~ de atracciones/de bomberos** fairground/fire station; **~ infantil/ temático/zoológico** playground/ theme park/zoo

parqué [par'ke] nm parquet

parquímetro [par'kimetro] nm parking meter

parra ['parra] nf grapevine

párrafo ['parrafo] nm paragraph; **echar un ~** (fam) to have a chat

parranda [pa'rranda] nf (fam) spree, binge

parrilla [pa'rriʎa] nf (Culin) grill; **(carne a la ~)** grilled meat, barbecue; **parrillada** nf barbecue

párroco ['parroko] nm parish priest

parroquia [pa'rrokja] nf parish; (iglesia) parish church; (Com) clientele, customers pl; **parroquiano, -a** nf/f parishioner; client, customer

parte ['parte] nm message; (informe) report ▷ nf part; (lado, cara) side; (de reparto) share; (Jur) party; **en alguna ~ de Europa** somewhere in Europe; **en o por todas ~s** everywhere; **en gran ~** to a large extent; **la mayor ~ de los españoles** most Spaniards; **de algún tiempo a esta ~** for some time past; **de ~ de algn** on sb's behalf; **¿de ~ de quién?** (Telec) who is speaking?; **por ~ de** on the part of; **yo por mi ~** I for my part; **por una ~ ... por otra ~** on the one hand, ... on the other (hand); **dar ~ a algn** to report to sb; **tomar ~ to**

take part; **~ meteorológico** weather forecast o report

participación [partiθipa'θjon] *nf* *(acto)* participation, taking part; *(parte)* share; *(Com)* share, stock (*us*); *(de lotería)* shared prize; *(aviso)* notice, notification

participante [partiθi'pante] *nmf* participant

participar [partiθi'par] /1a/ *vt* to notify, inform ▷ *vi* to take part, participate

partícipe [par'tiθipe] *nmf* participant

particular [partiku'lar] *adj (especial)* particular, special; *(individual, personal)* private, personal ▷ *nm (punto, asunto)* particular, point; *(individuo)* individual; **tiene coche ~** he has a car of his own

partida [par'tiða] *nf (salida)* departure; *(Com)* entry, item; *(juego)* game; *(grupo, bando)* band, group; **mala ~** dirty trick; **~ de nacimiento/ matrimonio/defunción** birth/ marriage/death certificate

partidario, -a [parti'ðarjo, a] *adj* partisan ▷ *nm/f* supporter

partido [par'tiðo] *nm (Pol)* party; *(encuentro)* game, match; **sacar ~ de** to profit from, benefit from; **tomar ~** to take sides

partir [par'tir] /3a/ *vt (dividir)* to split, divide; *(compartir, distribuir)* to share (out), distribute; *(romper)* to break open, split open; *(rebanada)* to cut (off) ▷ *vi (ponerse en camino)* to set off, set out; **partirse** *vr* to crack o split o break (in two *etc*); **a ~ de** (starting) from

partitura [parti'tura] *nf* score

parto [parto] *nm* birth, delivery; *(fig)* product, creation; **estar de ~** to be in labour

parvulario [parβu'larjo] *nm* nursery school, kindergarten

pasa ['pasa] *nf* V **paso**

pasacintas [pasa'θintas] *nm (LAM)* cassette player

pasada [pa'saða] *nf* V **pasado**

pasadizo [pasa'ðiθo] *nm (pasillo)* passage, corridor; *(callejuela)* alley

pasado, -a [pa'saðo, a] *adj* past; *(malo: comida, fruta)* bad; *(muy cocido)* overdone; *(anticuado)* out of date ▷ *nm* past; **~ mañana** the day after tomorrow; **el mes ~** last month; **de pasada** in passing, incidentally; **una mala pasada** a dirty trick

pasador [pasa'ðor] *nm* bolt; *(de pelo)* slide; *(horquilla)* grip

pasaje [pa'saxe] *nm* passage; *(pago de viaje)* fare; *(los pasajeros)* passengers *pl*; *(pasillo)* passageway

pasajero, -a [pasa'xero, a] *adj* passing; *(situación, estado)* temporary; *(amor, enfermedad)* brief ▷ *nm/f* passenger

pasamanos [pasa'manos] *nm inv* (hand)rail; *(de escalera)* banister(s)

pasamontañas [pasamon'taɲas] *nm inv* balaclava (helmet)

pasaporte [pasa'porte] *nm* passport

pasar [pa'sar] /1a/ *vt (gen)* to pass; *(tiempo)* to spend; *(durezas)* to suffer, endure; *(noticia)* to give, pass on; *(película)* to show; *(río)* to cross; *(barrera)* to pass through; *(falta)* to overlook, tolerate; *(contrincante)* to surpass, do better than; *(coche)* to overtake; *(enfermedad)* to give, infect with ▷ *vi (gen)* to pass; *(terminarse)* to be over; *(ocurrir)* to happen; **pasarse** *vr (flores)* to fade; *(comida)* to go bad, go off; *(fig)* to overdo it, go too far o over the top; **~ de** to go beyond, exceed; **¡pase!** come in!; **~ por** to fetch; **~lo bien/bomba o de maravilla** to have a good/great time; **~se al enemigo** to go over to the enemy; **se me pasó** I forgot; **no se le pasa nada** he misses nothing; **ya se te ~á** you'll get over it; **¿qué pasa?** what's going on?, what's up?; **¿qué te pasa?** what's wrong?

pasarela [pasa'rela] *nf* footbridge; *(en barco)* gangway

pasatiempo [pasa'tjempo] *nm* pastime, hobby

Pascua ['paskwa] *nf*: **~ (de Resurrección)** Easter; **Pascuas** *nfpl*

Christmas time *sg*; ¡**felices ~s!** Merry Christmas!

pase ['pase] *nm* pass; (*Cine*) performance, showing

pasear [pase'ar] /1a/ *vt* to take for a walk; (*exhibir*) to parade, show off ▷ *vi* to walk, go for a walk; **pasearse** *vr* to walk, go for a walk; **~ en coche** to go for a drive; **paseo** *nm* (*distancia corta*) (short) walk, stroll; (*avenida*) avenue; **paseo marítimo** promenade; **dar un paseo** to go for a walk

pasillo [pa'siʎo] *nm* passage, corridor

pasión [pa'sjon] *nf* passion

pasivo, -a [pa'siβo, a] *adj* passive; (*inactivo*) inactive ▷ *nm* (*Com*) liabilities *pl*, debts *pl*

pasmoso, -a [pas'moso, a] *adj* amazing, astonishing

paso, -a ['paso, a] *adj* dried ▷ *nm* step; (*modo de andar*) walk; (*huella*) footprint; (*rapidez*) speed, pace, rate; (*camino accesible*) way through, passage; (*cruce*) crossing; (*pasaje*) passing, passage; (*Geo*) pass; (*estrecho*) strait ▷ *nf* raisin; **pasa de Corinto/ de Esmirna** currant/sultana; **a ese ~** (*fig*) at that rate; **estar de ~** to be passing through; **prohibido el ~** no entry; **ceda el ~** give way; **~ a nivel** (*Ferro*) level-crossing; **~ (de) cebra** (*ESP*) zebra crossing; **~ de peatones** pedestrian crossing; **~ elevado** flyover

pasota [pa'sota] *adj, nmf* (*fam*) ≈ dropout; **ser un (tipo) ~** to be a bit of a dropout; (*ser indiferente*) not to care about anything

pasta ['pasta] *nf* paste; (*Culin: masa*) dough; (: *de bizcochos etc*) pastry; (*fam*) dough; **pastas** *nfpl* (*bizcochos*) pastries, small cakes; (*espaguetis etc*) pasta *sg*; **~ dentífrica** o **dentífrico** toothpaste

pastar [pas'tar] /1a/ *vt*, *vi* to graze

pastel [pas'tel] *nm* (*dulce*) cake; (*Arte*) pastel; **~ de carne** meat pie; **pastelería** *nf* cake shop

pastilla [pas'tiʎa] *nf* (*de jabón, chocolate*) bar; (*píldora*) tablet, pill

pasto ['pasto] *nm* (*hierba*) grass; (*lugar*) pasture, field; **pastor, a** *nm/f* shepherd(ess) ▷ *nm* clergyman, pastor; **pastor alemán** Alsatian

pata ['pata] *nf* (*pierna*) leg; (*pie*) foot; (*de muebles*) leg; **~s arriba** upside down; **meter la ~** to put one's foot in it; **~ de cabra** (*Tec*) crowbar; **metedura de ~** (*fam*) gaffe; **tener buena/mala ~** to be lucky/unlucky; **patada** *nf* stamp; (*puntapié*) kick

patata [pa'tata] *nf* potato; **~s fritas** o **a la española** chips, French fries; (*de bolsa*) crisps

paté [pa'te] *nm* pâté

patente [pa'tente] *adj* obvious, evident; (*Com*) patent ▷ *nf* patent

paternal [pater'nal] *adj* fatherly, paternal; **paterno, -a** *adj* paternal

patético, -a [pa'tetiko, a] *adj* pathetic, moving

patilla [pa'tiʎa] *nf* (*de gafas*) sidepiece; **patillas** *nfpl* sideburns

patín [pa'tin] *nm* skate; (*de tobogán*) runner; **patines de ruedas** rollerskates; **patinaje** *nm* skating; **patinar** /1a/ *vi* to skate; (*resbalarse*) to skid, slip; (*fam*) to slip up, blunder

patineta [pati'neta] *nf* (*patinete*) scooter; (*LAM: monopatín*) skateboard

patinete [pati'nete] *nm* scooter

patio ['patjo] *nm* (*de casa*) patio, courtyard; **~ de recreo** playground

pato ['pato] *nm* duck; **pagar el ~** (*fam*) to take the blame, carry the can

patoso, -a [pa'toso, a] *adj* clumsy

patotero [pato'tero] *nm* (*LAM*) hooligan, lout

patraña [pa'traɲa] *nf* story, fib

patria ['patrja] *nf* native land, mother country

patrimonio [patri'monjo] *nm* inheritance; (*fig*) heritage

patriota [pa'trjota] *nmf* patriot

patrocinar [patroθi'nar] /1a/ *vt* to sponsor

patrón, -ona [pa'tron, ona] *nm/f* (*jefe*) boss, chief, master/mistress; (*propietario*) landlord/lady; (*Rel*) patron saint ▷ *nm* (*Costura*) pattern

patronato [patro'nato] *nm* sponsorship; (*acto*) patronage; (*fundación*) trust

patrulla [pa'truʎa] *nf* patrol

pausa ['pausa] *nf* pause; break

pauta ['pauta] *nf* line, guide line

pava ['paβa] *nf* (*LAM*) kettle

pavimento [paβi'mento] *nm* (*de losa*) pavement, paving

pavo ['paβo] *nm* turkey; **~ real** peacock

payaso, -a [pa'jaso, a] *nm/f* clown

payo, -a ['pajo, a] *nm/f* non-gipsy

paz [paθ] *nf* peace; (*tranquilidad*) peacefulness, tranquillity; **hacer las paces** to make peace; (*fig*) to make up; **¡déjame en ~!** leave me alone!

PC *nm* PC, personal computer

P.D. *abr* (= *posdata*) P.S.

peaje [pe'axe] *nm* toll

peatón [pea'ton] *nm* pedestrian; **peatonal** *adj* pedestrian

peca ['peka] *nf* freckle

pecado [pe'kaðo] *nm* sin; **pecador, a** *adj* sinful ▷ *nm/f* sinner

pecaminoso, -a [pekami'noso, a] *adj* sinful

pecar [pe'kar] /1g/ *vi* (*Rel*) to sin; (*fig*): **~ de generoso** to be too generous

pecera [pe'θera] *nf* fish tank; (*redonda*) goldfish bowl

pecho ['petʃo] *nm* (*Anat*) chest; (*de mujer*) breast(s *pl*); **dar el ~ a** to breast-feed; **tomar algo a ~** to take sth to heart

pechuga [pe'tʃuɣa] *nf* breast

peculiar [peku'ljar] *adj* special, peculiar; (*característico*) typical, characteristic

pedal [pe'ðal] *nm* pedal; **pedalear** /1a/ *vi* to pedal

pédalo ['peðalo] *nm* pedalo, pedal boat

pedante [pe'ðante] *adj* pedantic ▷ *nmf* pedant

pedazo [pe'ðaθo] *nm* piece, bit; **hacerse ~s** to smash, shatter

pediatra [pe'ðjatra] *nmf* paediatrician (*BRIT*), pediatrician (*US*)

pedido [pe'ðiðo] *nm* (*Com*) order; (*petición*) request

pedir [pe'ðir] /3k/ *vt* to ask for, request; (*comida, Com: mandar*) to order; (*necesitar*) to need, demand, require ▷ *vi* to ask; **me pidió que cerrara la puerta** he asked me to shut the door; **¿cuánto piden por el coche?** how much are they asking for the car?

pedo ['peðo] (*fam*) *nm* fart (!)

pega ['peɣa] *nf* snag; **poner ~s** to raise objections

pegadizo, -a [peɣa'ðiθo, a] *adj* (*canción etc*) catchy

pegajoso, -a [peɣa'xoso, a] *adj* sticky, adhesive

pegamento [peɣa'mento] *nm* gum, glue

pegar [pe'ɣar] /1h/ *vt* (*papel, sellos*) to stick (on); (*cartel*) to post, stick up; (*coser*) to sew (on); (*unir: partes*) to join, fix together; (*Inform*) to paste; (*Med*) to give, infect with; (*dar: golpe*) to give, deal ▷ *vi* (*adherirse*) to stick, adhere; (*ir juntos: colores*) to match, go together; (*golpear*) to hit; (*quemar: el sol*) to strike hot, burn; **pegarse** *vr* (*gen*) to stick; (*dos personas*) to hit each other, fight; **~ un grito** to let out a yell; **~ un salto** to jump (with fright); **~ fuego** to catch fire; **~ en** to touch; **~se un tiro** to shoot o.s.

pegatina [peɣa'tina] *nf* sticker

pegote [pe'ɣote] *nm* (*fam*) eyesore, sight

peinado [pei'naðo] *nm* hairstyle

peinar [pei'nar] /1a/ *vt* to comb sb's hair; (*con un cierto estilo*) to style; **peinarse** *vr* to comb one's hair

peine ['peine] *nm* comb; **peineta** *nf* ornamental comb

p.ej. *abr (= por ejemplo)* e.g.

Pekín [pe'kin] *n* Peking, Beijing

pelado, -a [pe'laðo, a] *adj (cabeza)* shorn; *(fruta)* peeled; *(campo, fig)* bare; *(fam: sin dinero)* broke

pelar [pe'lar] /1a/ *vt (cabeza)* to peel; *(cortar el pelo a)* to cut the hair of; *(quitar la piel: animal)* to skin; **pelarse** *vr (la piel)* to peel off; **voy a ~me** I'm going to get my hair cut

peldaño [pel'daɲo] *nm* step

pelea [pe'lea] *nf (lucha)* fight; *(discusión)* quarrel, row; **peleado, -a** *adj*: **estar peleado (con algn)** to have fallen out (with sb); **pelear** /1a/ *vi* to fight; **pelearse** *vr* to fight; *(reñir)* to fall out, quarrel

pelela [pe'lela] *nf (AM)* potty

peletería [pelete'ria] *nf* furrier's, fur shop

pelícano [pe'likano] *nm* pelican

película [pe'likula] *nf* film; *(cobertura ligera)* thin covering; *(Foto: rollo)* roll o reel of film; **~ de dibujos (animados)** cartoon film

peligro [pe'liɣro] *nm* danger; *(riesgo)* risk; **correr ~ de** to be in danger of, run the risk of; **peligroso, -a** *adj* dangerous; risky

pelirrojo, -a [peli'rroxo, a] *adj* red-haired, red-headed ▷ *nm/f* redhead

pellejo [pe'ʎexo] *nm (de animal)* skin, hide

pellizcar [peʎiθ'kar] /1g/ *vt* to pinch, nip

pelma [pelma] *nmf*, **pelmazo, -a** [pel'maθo, a] *nm/f (fam)* pain (in the neck)

pelo [pelo] *nm (cabellos)* hair; *(de barba, bigote)* whisker; *(de animal: piel)* fur, coat; *(de perro etc)* hair, coat; **venir al ~** to be exactly what one needs; **un hombre de ~ en pecho** a brave man; **por los ~s** by the skin of one's teeth; **no tener ~s en la lengua** to be outspoken, not mince words; **con ~s y señales** in minute detail; **tomar el ~ a algn** to pull sb's leg

pelota [pe'lota] *nf* ball; **en ~(s)** stark naked; **~ vasca** pelota; **hacer la ~ (a algn)** to creep (to sb)

pelotón [pelo'ton] *nm (Mil)* squad, detachment

peluca [pe'luka] *nf* wig

peluche [pe'lutʃe] *nm*: **muñeco de ~** soft toy

peludo, -a [pe'luðo, a] *adj* hairy, shaggy

peluquería [peluke'ria] *nf* hairdresser's; **peluquero, -a** *nm/f* hairdresser

pelusa [pe'lusa] *nf (Bot)* down; *(Costura)* fluff

pena ['pena] *nf (congoja)* grief, sadness; *(remordimiento)* regret; *(dificultad)* trouble; *(dolor)* pain; *(Jur)* sentence; **~ capital** capital punishment; **~ de muerte** death penalty; **merecer o valer la ~** to be worthwhile; **a duras ~s** with great difficulty; **¡qué ~!** what a shame o pity!

penal [pe'nal] *adj* penal ▷ *nm (cárcel)* prison

penalidad [penali'ðað] *nf (problema, dificultad)* trouble, hardship; *(Jur)* penalty, punishment; **penalidades** *nfpl* trouble sg, hardship sg

penalti, penalty [pe'nalti] *(pl* **penalties** o **penaltys)** *nm (Deporte)* penalty (kick)

pendiente [pen'djente] *adj* pending, unsettled ▷ *nm* earring ▷ *nf* hill, slope

pene ['pene] *nm* penis

penetrante [pene'trante] *adj (herida)* deep; *(persona, arma)* sharp; *(sonido)* penetrating, piercing; *(mirada)* searching; *(viento, ironía)* biting

penetrar [pene'trar] /1a/ *vt* to penetrate, pierce; *(entender)* to grasp ▷ *vi* to penetrate, go in; *(entrar)* to enter; *(líquido)* to soak in; *(emoción)* to pierce

penicilina [peniθi'lina] *nf* penicillin

península [pe'ninsula] *nf* peninsula; **peninsular** *adj* peninsular

penique [pe'nike] *nm* penny

penitencia [peni'tenθja] nf penance

penoso, -a [pe'noso, a] adj laborious, difficult; (*lamentable*) distressing

pensador, a [pensa'ðor, a] nm/f thinker

pensamiento [pensa'mjento] nm thought; (*mente*) mind; (*idea*) idea

pensar [pen'sar] /1j/ vt to think over, think out; (*considerar*) to think over, think out; (*proponerse*) to intend, plan; (*imaginarse*) to think up, invent ▷ vi to think; **~ en** to aim at, aspire to; **pensativo, -a** adj thoughtful, pensive

pensión [pen'sjon] nf (*casa*) guest house; (*dinero*) pension; (*cama y comida*) board and lodging; **~ completa** full board; **media ~** half board; **pensionista** nmf (*jubilado*) (old-age) pensioner; (*el que vive en una pensión*) lodger

penúltimo, -a [pe'nultimo, a] adj penultimate, second last

penumbra [pe'numbra] nf half-light

peña ['peɲa] nf (*roca*) rock; (*acantilado*) cliff, crag; (*grupo*) group, circle; (LAM: *club*) folk club

peñasco [pe'nasko] nm large rock, boulder

peñón [pe'ɲon] nm crag; **el P~** the Rock of Gibraltar

peón [pe'on] nm labourer; (LAM) farm labourer, farmhand; (*Ajedrez*) pawn

peonza [pe'onθa] nf spinning top

peor [pe'or] adj (*comparativo*) worse; (*superlativo*) worst ▷ adv worse; worst; **de mal en ~** from bad to worse

pepinillo [pepi'niʎo] nm gherkin

pepino [pe'pino] nm cucumber; **(no) me importa un ~** I don't care one bit

pepita [pe'pita] nf (Bot) pip; (*Minería*) nugget

pepito [pe'pito] nm (ESP: tb: **~ de ternera**) steak sandwich

pequeño, -a [pe'keɲo, a] adj small, little

pera ['pera] nf pear; **peral** nm pear tree

percance [per'kanθe] nm setback, misfortune

percatarse [perka'tarse] /1a/ vr: **~ de** to notice, take note of

percebe [per'θeβe] nm barnacle

percepción [perθep'θjon] nf (*vista*) perception; (*idea*) notion, idea

percha ['pertʃa] nf coat hanger; (*ganchos*) coat hooks pl; (*de ave*) perch

percibir [perθi'βir] /3a/ vt to perceive, notice; (Com) to earn, get

percusión [perku'sjon] nf percussion

perdedor, a [perðe'ðor, a] adj losing ▷ nm/f loser

perder [per'ðer] /2g/ vt to lose; (*tiempo, palabras*) to waste; (*oportunidad*) to lose, miss; (*tren*) to miss ▷ vi to lose; **perderse** vr (*extraviarse*) to get lost; (*desaparecer*) to disappear, be lost to view; (*arruinarse*) to be ruined; **echar a ~** (*comida*) to spoil, ruin; (*oportunidad*) to waste

pérdida ['perðiða] nf loss; (*de tiempo*) waste; **pérdidas** nfpl (Com) losses

perdido, -a [per'ðiðo, a] adj lost

perdiz [per'ðiθ] nf partridge

perdón [per'ðon] nm (*disculpa*) pardon, forgiveness; (*clemencia*) mercy; **¡~!** sorry!, I beg your pardon!; **perdonar** /1a/ vt to pardon, forgive; (*la vida*) to spare; (*excusar*) to exempt, excuse; **¡perdone (usted)!** sorry!, I beg your pardon!

perecedero, -a [pereθe'ðero, a] adj perishable

perecer [pere'θer] /2d/ vi to perish, die

peregrinación [pereɣrina'θjon] nf (*Rel*) pilgrimage

peregrino, -a [pere'ɣrino, a] adj (*extraño*) strange ▷ nm/f pilgrim

perejil [pere'xil] nm parsley

perenne [pe'renne] adj perennial

pereza [pe'reθa] nf laziness; **perezoso, -a** adj lazy

perfección [perfek'θjon] nf perfection; **perfeccionar** /1a/ vt to perfect; (*mejorar*) to improve; (*acabar*) to complete, finish

perfecto, -a [perˈfekto, a] *adj* perfect
▷ *nm* (Ling) perfect (tense)

perfil [perˈfil] *nm* profile; (*silueta*)
silhouette, outline; (*Tec*) (*cross*)
section; **perfiles** *nmpl* features

perforación [perforaˈθjon] *nf*
perforation; (*con taladro*) drilling

perforadora [perforaˈðora] *nf*
card-punch

perforar [perfoˈrar] /1a/ *vt* to
perforate; (*agujero*) to drill, bore;
(*papel*) to punch a hole in ▷ *vi* to
drill, bore

perfume [perˈfume] *nm* perfume,
scent

periferia [periˈferja] *nf* periphery; (*de
ciudad*) outskirts *pl*

periférico, -a [periˈferiko, a] *adj*
peripheral ▷ *nm* (*con Auto*) ring road
(*BRIT*), beltway (*US*)

perilla [peˈriʎa] *nf* (*barba*) goatee;
(*LAM: de puerta*) doorknob, door handle

perímetro [peˈrimetro] *nm*
perimeter

periódico, -a [peˈrjoðiko, a] *adj*
periodic(al) ▷ *nm* (*news*)paper

periodismo [perjoˈðismo] *nm*
journalism; **periodista** *nmf* journalist

periodo [peˈrjoðo] *nm*, **período**
[peˈrioðo] *nm* period

periquito [periˈkito] *nm* budgerigar,
budgie (*fam*)

perito, -a [peˈrito, a] *adj* (*experto*)
expert; (*diestro*) skilled, skilful ▷ *nm/f*
expert; skilled worker; (*técnico*)
technician

perjudicar [perxuðiˈkar] /1g/ *vt* (*gen*)
to damage, harm; **perjudicial** *adj*
damaging, harmful; (*en detrimento*)
detrimental; **perjuicio** *nm* damage,
harm

perjurar [perxuˈrar] /1a/ *vi* to commit
perjury

perla [ˈperla] *nf* pearl; **me viene de ~s**
it suits me fine

permanecer [permaneˈθer] /2d/ *vi*
(*quedarse*) to stay, remain; (*seguir*) to
continue to be

permanente [permaˈnente] *adj*
permanent; (*constante*) constant
▷ *nf* perm

permiso [perˈmiso] *nm* permission;
(*licencia*) permit, licence (*BRIT*),
license (*US*); **con ~** excuse me;
estar de ~ (*Mil*) to be on leave; **~ de
conducir** o **conductor** driving licence
(*BRIT*), driver's license (*US*); **~ por
enfermedad** (*LAM*) sick leave

permitir [permiˈtir] /3a/ *vt* to
permit, allow

pernera [perˈnera] *nf* trouser leg

pero [ˈpero] *conj* but; (*aún*) yet
▷ *nm* (*defecto*) flaw, defect; (*reparo*)
objection

perpendicular [perpendikuˈlar] *adj*
perpendicular

perpetuo, -a [perˈpetwo, a] *adj*
perpetual

perplejo, -a [perˈplexo, a] *adj*
perplexed, bewildered

perra [ˈperra] *nf* (*Zool*) bitch; (*fam:
dinero*) money; **estar sin una ~** to be
flat broke

perrera [peˈrrera] *nf* kennel

perrito [peˈrrito] *nm* (*tb:* **~ caliente**)
hot dog

perro [ˈperro] *nm* dog

persa [ˈpersa] *adj*, *nmf* Persian

persecución [persekuˈθjon] *nf*
pursuit, chase; (*Rel, Pol*) persecution

perseguir [perseˈyir] /3d, 3k/ *vt* to
pursue, hunt; (*cortejar*) to chase after;
(*molestar*) to pester, annoy; (*Rel, Pol*)
to persecute

persiana [perˈsjana] *nf* (Venetian)
blind

persistente [persisˈtente] *adj*
persistent

persistir [persisˈtir] /3a/ *vi* to persist

persona [perˈsona] *nf* person;
~ mayor elderly person

personaje [persoˈnaxe] *nm*
important person, celebrity; (*Teat*)
character

personal [persoˈnal] *adj* (*particular*)
personal; (*para una persona*) single,

for one person ▷ nm personnel, staff;
personalidad nf personality

personarse [perso'narse] /1a/ vr to
appear in person

personificar [personifi'kar] /1g/ vt
to personify

perspectiva [perspek'tiβa] nf
perspective; (vista, panorama) view,
panorama; (posibilidad futura) outlook,
prospect

persuadir [perswa'ðir] /3a/ vt (gen)
to persuade; (convencer) to convince;
persuadirse vr to become convinced;
persuasión nf persuasion

pertenecer [pertene'θer] /2d/ vi:
~ **a** to belong to; (fig) to concern;
perteneciente adj: **perteneciente
a** belonging to; **pertenencia** nf
ownership; **pertenencias** nfpl
possessions, property sg

pertenezca etc [perte'neθka] vb V
pertenecer

pértiga ['pertiɣa] nf: **salto de ~**
pole vault

pertinente [perti'nente] adj
relevant, pertinent; (apropiado)
appropriate; **~ a** concerning,
relevant to

perturbación [perturβa'θjon]
nf (Pol) disturbance; (Med) upset,
disturbance

Perú [pe'ru] nm Peru; **peruano, -a**
nm/f Peruvian

perversión [perβer'sjon] nf
perversion; **perverso, -a** adj perverse;
(depravado) depraved

pervertido, -a [perβer'tiðo, a] adj
perverted ▷ nm/f pervert

pervertir [perβer'tir] /3i/ vt to
pervert, corrupt

pesa ['pesa] nf weight; (Deporte) weight

pesadez [pesa'ðeθ] nf (calidad de
pesado) heaviness; (lentitud) slowness;
(aburrimiento) tediousness

pesadilla [pesa'ðiʎa] nf nightmare,
bad dream

pesado, -a [pe'saðo, a] adj heavy;
(lento) slow; (difícil, duro) tough, hard;

(aburrido) tedious, boring; (bochornoso)
sultry

pésame ['pesame] nm expression of
condolence, message of sympathy;
dar el ~ to express one's condolences

pesar [pe'sar] /1a/ vt to weigh ▷ vi to
weigh; (ser pesado) to weigh a lot, be
heavy; (fig: opinión) to carry weight
▷ nm (sentimiento) regret; (pena) grief,
sorrow; **no pesa mucho** it's not very
heavy; **a ~ de (que)** in spite of, despite

pesca ['peska] nf (acto) fishing;
(cantidad de pescado) catch; **ir de ~** to
go fishing

pescadería [peskaðe'ria] nf fish
shop, fishmonger's

pescadilla [peska'ðiʎa] nf whiting

pescado [pes'kaðo] nm fish

pescador, a [peska'ðor, a] nm/f
fisherman/woman

pescar [pes'kar] /1g/ vt (coger) to
catch; (tratar de coger) to fish for;
(conseguir: trabajo) to manage to get
▷ vi to fish, go fishing

pesebre [pe'seβre] nm manger

peseta [pe'seta] nf peseta

pesimista [pesi'mista] adj
pessimistic ▷ nmf pessimist

pésimo, -a ['pesimo, a] adj awful,
dreadful

peso ['peso] nm weight; (balanza)
scales pl; (moneda) peso; **~ bruto/
neto** gross/net weight; **~ mosca/
pesado** fly-/heavyweight; **vender a ~**
to sell by weight

pesquero, -a [pes'kero, a] adj
fishing cpd

pestaña [pes'taɲa] nf (Anat) eyelash;
(borde) rim

peste ['peste] nf plague; (mal olor)
stink, stench

pesticida [pesti'θiða] nm pesticide

pestillo [pes'tiʎo] nm bolt; (picaporte)
(door) handle

petaca [pe'taka] nf (de cigarrillos)
cigarette case; (de pipa) tobacco
pouch; (ᴌᴀᴍ: maleta) suitcase

pétalo ['petalo] nm petal

petardo [pe'tarðo] nm firework, firecracker

petición [peti'θjon] nf (pedido) request, plea; (memorial) petition; (Jur) plea

peto ['peto] nm dungarees pl, overalls pl (us)

petróleo [pe'troleo] nm oil, petroleum; **petrolero, -a** adj petroleum cpd ▷ nm (Naut) (oil) tanker

peyorativo, -a [pejora'tiβo, a] adj pejorative

pez [peθ] nm fish; **~ de colores** goldfish; **~ espada** swordfish

pezón [pe'θon] nm teat, nipple

pezuña [pe'θuɲa] nf hoof

pianista [pja'nista] nmf pianist

piano ['pjano] nm piano

piar [pjar] /1c/ vi to cheep

pibe, -a ['piβe, a] nm/f (LAM) boy/girl

picadero [pika'ðero] nm riding school

picadillo [pika'ðiʎo] nm mince, minced meat

picado, -a [pi'kaðo, a] adj pricked, punctured; (Culin) minced, chopped; (mar) choppy; (diente) bad; (tabaco) cut; (enfadado) cross

picador [pika'ðor] nm (Taur) picador; (minero) faceworker

picadura [pika'ðura] nf (pinchazo) puncture; (de abeja) sting; (de mosquito) bite; (tabaco picado) cut tobacco

picante [pi'kante] adj hot; (comentario) racy, spicy

picaporte [pika'porte] nm (tirador) handle; (pestillo) latch

picar [pi'kar] /1g/ vt (agujerear, perforar) to prick, puncture; (abeja) to sting; (mosquito, serpiente) to bite; (Culin) to mince, chop; (incitar) to incite, goad; (dañar, irritar) to annoy, bother; (quemar: lengua) to burn, sting ▷ vi (pez) to bite, take the bait; (el sol) to burn, scorch; (abeja, Med) to sting; (mosquito) to bite; **picarse** vr (agriarse) to turn sour, go off; (ofenderse) to take offence

picardía [pikar'ðia] nf villainy; (astucia) slyness, craftiness; (una picardía) dirty trick; (palabra) rude/bad word o expression

pícaro, -a ['pikaro, a] adj (malicioso) villainous; (travieso) mischievous ▷ nm (astuto) sly sort; (sinvergüenza) rascal, scoundrel

pichi ['pitʃi] nm (ESP) pinafore dress (BRIT), jumper (US)

pichón [pi'tʃon] nm young pigeon

pico ['piko] nm (de ave) beak; (punta aguda) sharp point; (Tec) pick, pickaxe; (Geo) peak, summit; **y ~** and a bit; **las seis y ~** six and a bit

picor [pi'kor] nm itch

picoso, -a [pi'koso, a] adj (LAM) (comida) hot

picudo, -a [pi'kuðo, a] adj pointed, with a point

pidió etc vb V **pedir**

pido etc vb V **pedir**

pie [pje] (pl **pies**) nm foot; (fig: motivo) motive, basis; (: fundamento) foothold; **ir a ~** to go on foot, walk; **estar de ~** to be standing (up); **ponerse de ~** to stand up; **al ~ de la letra** (citar) literally, verbatim; (copiar) exactly, word for word; **de ~s a cabeza** from head to foot; **en ~ de guerra** on a war footing; **dar ~ a** to give cause for; **hacer ~** (en el agua) to touch (the) bottom

piedad [pje'ðað] nf (lástima) pity, compassion; (clemencia) mercy; (devoción) piety, devotion

piedra ['pjeðra] nf stone; (roca) rock; (de mechero) flint; (Meteorología) hailstone; **~ preciosa** precious stone

piel [pjel] nf (Anat) skin; (Zool) skin, hide; fur; (cuero) leather; (Bot) skin, peel

pienso etc ['pjenso] vb V **pensar**

pierdo etc ['pjerðo] vb V **perder**

pierna ['pjerna] nf leg

pieza ['pjeθa] nf piece; (habitación) room; **~ de recambio o repuesto** spare (part)

pigmeo, -a [piɣ'meo, a] adj, nm/f pigmy

pijama [pi'xama] nm pyjamas pl

pila ['pila] nf (Elec) battery; (montón) heap, pile; (de fuente) sink

píldora ['pildora] nf pill; **la ~ (anticonceptiva)** the pill

pileta [pi'leta] nf (: de cocina) sink; (: piscina) swimming pool

pillar [pi'ʎar] /1a/ vt (saquear) to pillage, plunder; (fam: coger) to catch; (: agarrar) to grasp, seize; (: entender) to grasp, catch on to; **pillarse** vr: **~ se un dedo con la puerta** to catch one's finger in the door

pillo, -a ['piʎo, a] adj villainous; (astuto) sly, crafty ▷ nm/f rascal, rogue, scoundrel

piloto [pi'loto] nm pilot; (de aparato) (pilot) light; (Auto) rear light, tail light; (conductor) driver; **~ automático** automatic pilot

pimentón [pimen'ton] nm paprika

pimienta [pi'mjenta] nf pepper

pimiento [pi'mjento] nm pepper, pimiento

pin [pin] (pl **pins**) nm badge

pinacoteca [pinako'teka] nf art gallery

pinar [pi'nar] nm pinewood

pincel [pin'θel] nm paintbrush

pinchadiscos [pintʃa'diskos] nm/f inv disc jockey, DJ

pinchar [pin'tʃar] /1a/ vt (perforar) to prick, pierce; (neumático) to puncture; (incitar) to prod; (Inform) to click

pinchazo [pin'tʃaθo] nm (perforación) prick; (de llanta) puncture; (fig) prod

pincho ['pintʃo] nm savoury (snack); **~ moruno** shish kebab; **~ de tortilla** small slice of omelette

ping-pong ['pimpon] nm table tennis

pingüino [pin'gwino] nm penguin

pino ['pino] nm pine (tree)

pinta ['pinta] nf spot; (gota) spot, drop; (aspecto) appearance, look(s) pl; **pintado, -a** adj spotted; (de muchos colores) colourful; **pintas** nfpl political graffiti sg

pintalabios [pinta'laβjos] nm inv (ESP) lipstick

pintar [pin'tar] /1a/ vt to paint ▷ vi to paint; (fam) to count, be important; **pintarse** vr to put on make-up

pintor, a [pin'tor, a] nm/f painter

pintoresco, -a [pinto'resko, a] adj picturesque

pintura [pin'tura] nf painting; **~ al óleo** oil painting

pinza ['pinθa] nf (Zool) claw; (para colgar ropa) clothes peg; (Tec) pincers pl; **pinzas** nfpl (para depilar) tweezers

piña ['piɲa] nf (del fruto del pino) pine cone; (fruta) pineapple; (fig) group

piñata [pi'ɲata] nf piñata (figurine hung up at parties to be beaten with sticks until sweets or presents fall out)

piñón [pi'ɲon] nm (Bot) pine nut; (Tec) pinion

pío, -a ['pio, a] adj (devoto) pious, devout; (misericordioso) merciful

piojo ['pjoxo] nm louse

pipa ['pipa] nf (de pipe; (Bot) seed, pip; (de girasol) sunflower seed

pipí [pi'pi] nm (fam): **hacer ~** to have a wee(-wee)

pique ['pike] nm (resentimiento) pique, resentment; (rivalidad) rivalry, competition; **irse a ~** to sink; (familia) to be ruined

piqueta [pi'keta] nf pick(axe)

piquete [pi'kete] nm (Mil) squad, party; (de obreros) picket; (ʌм: de insecto) bite

pirado, -a [pi'raðo, a] adj (fam) round the bend ▷ nm/f nutter

piragua [pi'raɣwa] nf canoe; **piragüismo** nm canoeing

pirámide [pi'ramiðe] nf pyramid

pirata [pi'rata] adj, nm pirate; (tb: **~ informático**) hacker

Pirineo(s) [piri'neo(s)] nm(pl) Pyrenees pl

pirómano, -a [pi'romano, a] nm/f (Jur) arsonist

piropo [pi'ropo] nm compliment, (piece of) flattery

pirueta [pi'rweta] nf pirouette

piruleta [piru'leta] nf lollipop

pis [pis] nm (fam) pee; **hacer ~** to have a pee; (para niños) to wee-wee

pisada [pi'saða] nf (paso) footstep; (huella) footprint

pisar [pi'sar] /1a/ vt (caminar sobre) to walk on, tread on; (apretar con el pie) to press; (fig) to trample on, walk all over ▷ vi to tread, step, walk

piscina [pis'θina] nf swimming pool

Piscis [pis'θis] nm Pisces

piso ['piso] nm (suelo) floor; (ʟᴀᴍ) ground; (apartamento) flat, apartment; **primer ~** (ᴇsᴘ) first o second (us) floor; (ʟᴀᴍ) ground o first (us) floor

pisotear [pisote'ar] /1a/ vt to trample (on o underfoot)

pista ['pista] nf track, trail; (indicio) clue; **~ de aterrizaje** runway; **~ de baile** dance floor; **~ de tenis** tennis court; **~ de hielo** ice rink

pistola [pis'tola] nf pistol; (Tec) spray-gun

pistón [pis'ton] nm (Tec) piston; (Mus) key

pitar [pi'tar] /1a/ vt (hacer sonar) to blow; (rechiflar) to whistle at, boo ▷ vi to whistle; (Auto) to sound o toot one's horn; (ʟᴀᴍ) to smoke

pitillo [pi'tiʎo] nm cigarette

pito ['pito] nm whistle; (de coche) horn

pitón [pi'ton] nm (Zool) python

pitonisa [pito'nisa] nf fortune-teller

pitorreo [pito'rreo] nm joke, laugh; **estar de ~** to be in a joking mood

píxel ['piksel] nm (Inform) pixel

piyama [pi'jama] nm (ʟᴀᴍ) pyjamas pl, pajamas pl (us)

pizarra [pi'θarra] nf (piedra) slate; (encerado) blackboard; **~ blanca** whiteboard; **~ interactiva** interactive whiteboard

pizarrón [piθa'rron] nm (ʟᴀᴍ) blackboard

pizca ['piθka] nf pinch, spot; (fig) spot, speck; **ni ~** not a bit

placa ['plaka] nf plate; (distintivo) badge; **~ de matrícula** number plate

placard [pla'kar] nm (ʟᴀᴍ) built-in cupboard

placer [pla'θer] /2w/ nm pleasure ▷ vt to please; **a ~** at one's pleasure

plaga ['plaɣa] nf (Zool) pest; (Med) plague; (fig) swarm; (: abundancia) abundance

plagio ['plaxjo] nm plagiarism

plan [plan] nm (esquema, proyecto) plan; (idea, intento) idea, intention; **tener ~** (fam) to have a date; **tener un ~** to have an affair; **en ~ económico** (fam) on the cheap; **vamos un ~ de turismo** we're going as tourists; **si te pones en ese ~ ...** if that's your attitude ...

plana ['plana] nf V **plano**

plancha ['plantʃa] nf (para planchar) iron; (rótulo) plate, sheet; (Naut) gangway; **a la ~** (Culin) grilled; **planchar** /1a/ vt to iron ▷ vi to do the ironing

planear [plane'ar] /1a/ vt to plan ▷ vi to glide

planeta [pla'neta] nm planet

plano, -a ['plano, a] adj flat, level, even ▷ nm (Mat, Tec, Aviat) plane; (Foto) shot; (Arq) plan; (Geo) map; (de ciudad) map, street plan ▷ nf sheet of paper, page; (Tec) trowel; **primer ~** close-up; **en primera plana** on the front page

planta ['planta] nf (Bot, Tec) plant; (Anat) sole of the foot, foot; (piso) floor; (ʟᴀᴍ: personal) staff; **~ baja** ground floor

plantar [plan'tar] /1a/ vt (Bot) to plant; (levantar) to erect, set up; **plantarse** vr to stand firm; **~ a algn en la calle** to chuck sb out; **dejar plantado a algn** (fam) to stand sb up

plantear [plante'ar] /1a/ vt (problema) to pose; (dificultad) to raise

plantilla [plan'tiʎa] *nf (de zapato)* insole; *(personal)* personnel; **ser de ~** to be on the staff

plantón [plan'ton] *nm (Mil)* guard, sentry; *(fam)* long wait; **dar (un) ~ a algn** to stand sb up

plasta ['plasta] *nf* soft mass, lump ▷ *nmf (ESP fam)* bore ▷ *adj (ESP fam)* boring

plástico, -a ['plastiko, a] *adj* plastic ▷ *nm* plastic

Plastilina® [plasti'lina] *nf* Plasticine®

plata ['plata] *nf (metal)* silver; *(cosas hechas de plata)* silverware; *(LAM)* cash

plataforma [plata'forma] *nf* platform; **~ de lanzamiento/perforación** launch(ing) pad/drilling rig

plátano ['platano] *nm (fruta)* banana; *(árbol)* plane tree; banana tree

platea [pla'tea] *nf (Teat)* pit

plática ['platika] *nf* talk, chat; **platicar** /1g/ *vi* to talk, chat

platillo [pla'tiʎo] *nm* saucer; **platillos** *nmpl* cymbals; **~ volador o volante** flying saucer

platino [pla'tino] *nm* platinum; **platinos** *nmpl (Auto)* (contact) points

plato ['plato] *nm* plate, dish; *(parte de comida)* course; *(guiso)* dish; **primer ~** first course; **~ combinado** set main course *(served on one plate)*; **~ fuerte** main course

playa ['plaja] *nf* beach; *(costa)* seaside; **~ de estacionamiento** *(LAM)* car park

playero, -a [pla'jero, a] *adj* beach *cpd* ▷ *nf (LAM: camiseta)* T-shirt; **playeras** *nfpl* canvas shoes

plaza ['plaθa] *nf* square; *(mercado)* market(place); *(sitio)* room, space; *(en vehículo)* seat, place; *(colocación)* post, job; **~ de toros** bullring

plazo ['plaθo] *nm (lapso de tiempo)* time, period; *(fecha de vencimiento)* expiry date; *(pago parcial)* instalment; **a corto/largo ~** short-/long-term;

comprar a ~s to buy on hire purchase, pay for in instalments

plazoleta [plaθo'leta] *nf* small square

plebeyo, -a [ple'βejo, a] *adj* plebeian; *(pey)* coarse, common

plegable [ple'ɣaβle] *adj* pliable; *(silla)* folding

pleito ['pleito] *nm (Jur)* lawsuit, case; *(fig)* dispute, feud

plenitud [pleni'tuð] *nf* plenitude, fullness; *(abundancia)* abundance

pleno, -a ['pleno, a] *adj* full; *(completo)* complete ▷ *nm* plenum; **en ~ día** in broad daylight; **en ~ verano** at the height of summer; **en plena cara** full in the face

pliego ['pljeɣo] *nm (hoja)* sheet (of paper); *(carta)* sealed letter/document; **~ de condiciones** details *pl*, specifications *pl*

pliegue ['pljeɣe] *nm* fold, crease; *(de vestido)* pleat

plomería [plome'ria] *nf (LAM)* plumbing; **plomero** *nm (LAM)* plumber

plomo ['plomo] *nm (metal)* lead; *(Elec)* fuse; **sin ~** unleaded

pluma ['pluma] *nf* feather; *(para escribir)*: **~ (estilográfica)** ink pen; **~ fuente** *(LAM)* fountain pen

plumero [plu'mero] *nm (quitapolvos)* feather duster

plumón [plu'mon] *nm (de ave)* down

plural [plu'ral] *adj* plural

pluriempleo [pluriem'pleo] *nm* having more than one job

plus [plus] *nm* bonus

población [poβla'θjon] *nf* population; *(pueblo, ciudad)* town, city

poblado, -a [po'βlaðo, a] *adj* inhabited ▷ *nm (aldea)* village; *(pueblo)* (small) town; **densamente ~** densely populated

poblador, a [poβla'ðor, a] *nm/f* settler, colonist

pobre ['poβre] *adj* poor ▷ *nmf* poor person; **pobreza** *nf* poverty

pocilga [po'θilɣa] *nf* pigsty

PALABRA CLAVE

poco, -a ['poko, a] adj 1 (sg) little, not much; **poco tiempo** little o not much time; **de poco interés** of little interest, not very interesting; **poca cosa** not much

2 (pl) few, not many; **unos pocos** a few, some; **pocos niños comen lo que les conviene** few children eat what they should

▸ adv 1 little, not much; **cuesta poco** it doesn't cost much

2 (+ adj: negativo, antónimo): **poco amable/inteligente** not very nice/ intelligent

3: **por poco me caigo** I almost fell

4: **a poco de haberse casado** shortly after getting married

5: **poco a poco** little by little

▸ nm a little, a bit; **un poco triste/de dinero** a little sad/money

podar [po'ðar] /1a/ vt to prune

podcast ['poðkast] nm podcast; **podcastear** /1a/ vi to podcast

PALABRA CLAVE

poder [po'ðer] /2s/ vi 1 (capacidad) can, be able to; **no puedo hacerlo** I can't do it, I'm unable to do it

2 (permiso) can, may, be allowed to; **¿se puede?** may I (o we)?; **puedes irte ahora** you may go now; **no se puede fumar en este hospital** smoking is not allowed in this hospital

3 (posibilidad) may, might, could; **puede llegar mañana** he may o might arrive tomorrow; **pudiste haberte hecho daño** you might o could have hurt yourself; **¡podías habérmelo dicho antes!** you might have told me before!

4: **puede (ser)** perhaps; **puede que lo sepa Tomás** Tomás may o might know

5: **¡no puedo más!** I've had enough!; **es tonto a más no poder** he's as stupid as they come

6: **poder con: no puedo con este crío** this kid's too much for me

▸ nm power; **el poder** the Government; **poder adquisitivo** purchasing power; **detentar** u **ocupar** o **estar en el poder** to be in power o office; **poder judicial** judiciary

poderoso, -a [poðe'roso, a] adj powerful

podio ['poðjo] nm podium

podium ['poðjum] = **podio**

podrido, -a [po'ðriðo, a] adj rotten, bad; (fig) rotten, corrupt

podrir [po'ðrir] = **pudrir**

poema [po'ema] nm poem

poesía [poe'sia] nf poetry

poeta [po'eta] nm poet; **poético, -a** poetic(al); **poetisa** nf (woman) poet

póker ['poker] nm poker

polaco, -a [po'lako, a] adj Polish
▸ nm/f Pole

polar [po'lar] adj polar

polea [po'lea] nf pulley

polémica [po'lemika] nf polemics sg; (una polémica) controversy

polen ['polen] nm pollen

policía [poli'θia] nm policeman/ woman ▸ nf police; **policíaco, -a** adj police cpd; **novela policíaca** detective story; **policial** adj police cpd

polideportivo [poliðepor'tiβo] nm sports centre

polígono [po'liɣono] nm (Mat) polygon; **~ industrial** industrial estate

polilla [po'liʎa] nf moth

polio ['poljo] nf polio

político, -a [po'litiko, a] adj political; (discreto) tactful; (pariente) in-law
▸ nm/f politician ▸ nf politics sg; (económica, agraria) policy; **padre ~** father-in-law; **política exterior/de**

ingresos y precios foreign/prices and incomes policy

póliza [ˈpoliθa] nf certificate, voucher; (impuesto) tax o fiscal stamp; **~ de seguro(s)** insurance policy

polizón [poliˈθon] nm stowaway

pollera [poˈʎera] nf (LAM) skirt

pollo [ˈpoʎo] nm chicken

polo [ˈpolo] nm (Geo, Elec) pole; (helado) ice lolly (BRIT), Popsicle® (US); (Deporte) polo; (suéter) polo-neck; **P~ Norte/Sur** North/South Pole

Polonia [poˈlonja] nf Poland

poltrona [polˈtrona] nf easy chair

polución [poluˈθjon] nf pollution

polvera [polˈβera] nf powder compact

polvo [ˈpolβo] nm dust; (Química, Culin, Med) powder; **polvos** nmpl (maquillaje) powder sg; **en ~** powdered; **~ de talco** talcum powder; **estar hecho ~** to be worn out o exhausted

pólvora [ˈpolβora] nf gunpowder

polvoriento, -a [polβoˈrjento, a] adj (superficie) dusty; (sustancia) powdery

pomada [poˈmaða] nf cream

pomelo [poˈmelo] nm grapefruit

pómez [ˈpomeθ] nf: **piedra ~** pumice stone

pomo [ˈpomo] nm knob, handle

pompa [ˈpompa] nf (burbuja) bubble; (bomba) pump; (esplendor) pomp, splendour

pómulo [ˈpomulo] nm cheekbone

pon [pon] vb V **poner**

ponchadura [pontʃaˈdura] nf (LAM) puncture (BRIT), flat (US); **ponchar** /ˈa/ vt (LAM: llanta) to puncture

ponche [ˈpontʃe] nm punch

poncho [ˈpontʃo] nm poncho

pondré etc [ponˈdre] vb V **poner**

PALABRA CLAVE

poner [poˈner] /2q/ vt 1 to put; (colocar) to place; (telegrama) to send; (obra de teatro) to put on; (película) to

show; **ponlo más alto** turn it up; **¿qué ponen en el Excelsior?** what's on at the Excelsior?

2 (tienda) to open; (instalar: gas etc) to put in; (radio, TV) to switch o turn on

3 (suponer): **pongamos que ...** let's suppose that ...

4 (contribuir): **el gobierno ha puesto otro millón** the government has contributed another million

5 (Telec): **póngame con el Sr. López** can you put me through to Mr. López?

6: **poner de**: **le han puesto de director general** they've appointed him general manager

7 (+ adj) to make; **me estás poniendo nerviosa** you're making me nervous

8 (dar nombre): **al hijo le pusieron Diego** they called their son Diego

▶ vi (gallina) to lay

▶ **ponerse** vr (colocarse): **se puso a mi lado** he came and stood beside me; **tú ponte en esa silla** you go and sit on that chair; **ponerse en camino** to set off

2 (vestido, cosméticos) to put on; **¿por qué no te pones el vestido nuevo?** why don't you put on o wear your new dress?

3 (sol) to set

4 (+ adj) to get, become; to turn; **se puso muy serio** he got very serious; **después de lavarla la tela se puso azul** after washing it the material turned blue

5: **ponerse a**: **se puso a llorar** he started to cry; **tienes que ponerte a estudiar** you must get down to studying

pongo etc [ˈpongo] vb V **poner**

poniente [poˈnjente] nm west; (viento) west wind

pontífice [ponˈtifiθe] nm pope, pontiff

pop [pop] adj inv, nm (Mus) pop

popa [ˈpopa] nf stern; **a ~** astern, abaft; **de ~ a proa** fore and aft

popote [po'pote] *nm* (LAM) straw

popular [popu'lar] *adj* popular; (*del pueblo*) of the people; **popularidad** *nf* popularity

PALABRA CLAVE

por [por] *prep* **1** (*objetivo*) for; **luchar por la patria** to fight for one's country
2 (+ *infin*): **por no llegar tarde** so as not to arrive late; **por citar unos ejemplos** to give a few examples
3 (*causa*) out of, because of; **por escasez de fondos** through o for lack of funds
4 (*tiempo*): **por la mañana/noche** in the morning/at night; **se queda por una semana** she's staying (for) a week
5 (*lugar*): **pasar por Madrid** to pass through Madrid; **ir a Guayaquil por Quito** to go to Guayaquil via Quito; **caminar por la calle** to walk along the street; **¿hay un banco por aquí?** is there a bank near here?
6 (*cambio, precio*): **te doy uno nuevo por el que tienes** I'll give you a new one (in return) for the one you've got
7 (*valor distributivo*): **30 euros por hora/cabeza** 30 euros an o per hour/a o per head
8 (*modo, medio*) by; **por correo/avión** by post/air; **entrar por la entrada principal** to go in through the main entrance
9 (*agente*) by; **hecho por él** done by him
10: **10 por 10 son 100** 10 times 10 is 100
11 (*en lugar de*): **vino él por su jefe** he came instead of his boss
12: **por mí que revienten** as far as I'm concerned they can drop dead
13: **por qué** why; **¿por qué?** why?; **¿por qué no?** why not?

porcelana [porθe'lana] *nf* porcelain; (*china*) china

porcentaje [porθen'taxe] *nm* percentage

porción [por'θjon] *nf* (*parte*) portion, share; (*cantidad*) quantity, amount

porfiar [por'fjar] /1c/ *vi* to persist, insist; (*disputar*) to argue stubbornly

pormenor [porme'nor] *nm* detail, particular

pornografía [pornoɣra'fia] *nf* pornography

poro [poro] *nm* pore

pororó [poro'ro] *nm* (LAM) popcorn

poroso, -a [po'roso, a] *adj* porous

poroto [po'roto] *nm* (LAM) kidney bean

porque [porke] *conj* (*a causa de*) because; (*ya que*) since; (*con el fin de*) so that, in order that

porqué [por'ke] *nm* reason, cause

porquería [porke'ria] *nf* (*suciedad*) filth, dirt; (*acción*) dirty trick; (*objeto*) small thing, trifle; (*fig*) rubbish

porra ['porra] *nf* (*arma*) stick, club

porrazo [po'rraθo] *nm* (*golpe*) blow; (*caída*) bump

porro ['porro] *nm* (*fam*: *droga*) joint

porrón [po'rron] *nm* glass wine jar with a long spout

portaaviones [port(a)a'βjones] *nm inv* aircraft carrier

portada [por'taða] *nf* (*de revista*) cover

portador, a [porta'ðor, a] *nm/f* carrier, bearer; (*Com*) bearer, payee

portaequipajes [portaeki'paxes] *nm inv* boot (BRIT), trunk (US); (*baca*) luggage rack

portafolio [porta'foljo] *nm* briefcase

portal [por'tal] *nm* (*entrada*) vestibule, hall; (*pórtico*) porch, doorway; (*puerta de entrada*) main door; (*Internet*) portal; **portales** *nmpl* arcade *sg*

portamaletas [portama'letas] *nm inv* (Auto: *maletero*) boot; (: *baca*) roof rack

portamonedas [portamo'neðas] *nm inv* (LAM) purse

portar [por'tar] /1a/ *vt* to carry; **portarse** *vr* to behave, conduct o.s.

portátil [por'tatil] *adj* portable; (**ordenador**) ~ laptop (computer)

portavoz [porta'βoθ] *nmf* spokesman/woman

portazo [por'taθo] *nm*: **dar un ~** to slam the door

porte ['porte] *nm* (*Com*) transport; (*precio*) transport charges *pl*

portentoso, -a [porten'toso, a] *adj* marvellous, extraordinary

porteño, -a [por'teɲo, a] *adj* of o from Buenos Aires

portería [porte'ria] *nf* (*oficina*) porter's office; (*gol*) goal

portero, -a [por'tero, a] *nm/f* porter; (*conserje*) caretaker; (*ujier*) doorman; (*Deporte*) goalkeeper; **~ automático** (*esp*) entry phone

pórtico ['portiko] *nm* (*porche*) portico, porch; (*fig*) gateway; (*arcada*) arcade

portorriqueño, -a [portorri'keɲo, a] *adj* Puerto Rican

Portugal [portu'ɣal] *nm* Portugal; **portugués, -esa** *adj*, *nm/f* Portuguese ▷ *nm* (*Ling*) Portuguese

porvenir [porβe'nir] *nm* future

pos [pos]: **en ~ de** *prep* after, in pursuit of

posaderas [posa'ðeras] *nfpl* backside *sg*, buttocks

posar [po'sar] /1a/ *vt* (*en el suelo*) to lay down, put down; (*la mano*) to place, put gently ▷ *vi* to sit, pose; **posarse** *vr* to settle; (*pájaro*) to perch; (*avión*) to land, come down

posavasos [posa'basos] *nm inv* coaster; (*para cerveza*) beermat

posdata [pos'ðata] *nf* postscript

pose ['pose] *nf* pose

poseedor, a [posee'ðor, a] *nm/f* owner, possessor; (*de récord, puesto*) holder

poseer [pose'er] /2e/ *vt* to have, possess, own; (*ventaja*) to enjoy; (*récord, puesto*) to hold

posesivo, -a [pose'siβo, a] *adj* possessive

posgrado [pos'ɣraðo] *nm* = postgrado

posibilidad [posiβili'ðað] *nf* possibility; (*oportunidad*) chance; **posibilitar** /1a/ *vt* to make possible; (*hacer factible*) to make feasible

posible [po'siβle] *adj* possible; (*factible*) feasible; **de ser ~** if possible; **en o dentro de lo ~** as far as possible

posición [posi'θjon] *nf* position; (*rango social*) status

positivo, -a [posi'tiβo, a] *adj* positive

poso ['poso] *nm* sediment; (*heces*) dregs *pl*

posponer [pospo'ner] /2q/ *vt* (*relegar*) to put behind o below; (*aplazar*) to postpone

post [post] (*pl* **posts**) *nm* (*en sitio web*) post

posta ['posta] *nf*: **a ~** on purpose, deliberately

postal [pos'tal] *adj* postal ▷ *nf* postcard

poste ['poste] *nm* (*de telégrafos*) post, pole; (*columna*) pillar

póster ['poster] (*pl* **posters**) *nm* poster

posterior [poste'rjor] *adj* back, rear; (*siguiente*) following, subsequent; (*más tarde*) later

postgrado [post'ɣraðo] *nm*: **curso de ~** postgraduate course

postizo, -a [pos'tiθo, a] *adj* false, artificial ▷ *nm* hairpiece

postre ['postre] *nm* sweet, dessert

póstumo, -a ['postumo, a] *adj* posthumous

postura [pos'tura] *nf* (*del cuerpo*) posture, position; (*fig*) attitude, position

potable [po'taβle] *adj* drinkable; **agua ~** drinking water

potaje [po'taxe] *nm* thick vegetable soup

potencia [po'tenθja] *nf* power; **potencial** *adj*, *nm* potential

potente [po'tente] *adj* powerful

potro ['potro] *nm* (*Zool*) colt; (*Deporte*) vaulting horse

P

pozo ['poθo] nm well; (de río) deep pool; (de mina) shaft

PP nm abr = **Partido Popular**

práctica ['praktika] nf V **práctico**

practicable [prakti'kaβle] adj practicable; (camino) passable

practicante [prakti'kante] nmf (Med: ayudante de doctor) medical assistant; (: enfermero) nurse; (el que practica algo) practitioner ▷ adj practising

practicar [prakti'kar] /1g/ vt to practise; (deporte) to go in for, play; (ejecutar) to carry out, perform

práctico, -a ['praktiko, a] adj practical; (instruido: persona) skilled, expert ▷ nf practice; (método) method; (arte, capacidad) skill; **en la práctica** in practice

practique etc [prak'tike] vb V **practicar**

pradera [pra'ðera] nf meadow; (de Canadá) prairie

prado ['praðo] nm (campo) meadow, field; (pastizal) pasture

Praga ['praya] nf Prague

pragmático, -a [pray'matiko, a] adj pragmatic

precario, -a [pre'karjo, a] adj precarious

precaución [prekau'θjon] nf (medida preventiva) preventive measure, precaution; (prudencia) caution, wariness

precedente [preθe'ðente] adj preceding; (anterior) former ▷ nm precedent

preceder [preθe'ðer] /2a/ vt, vi to precede, go/come before

precepto [pre'θepto] nm precept

precinto [pre'θinto] nm (tb: ~ de **garantía**) seal

precio ['preθjo] nm price; (costo) cost; (valor) value, worth; (de viaje) fare; **~ de coste** o **de cobertura** cost price; **~ al contado** cash price; **~ al detalle** o **al por menor** retail price; **~ de salida** upset price; **~ tope** top price

preciosidad [preθjosi'ðað] nf (valor) (high) value, (great) worth; (encanto) charm; (cosa bonita) beautiful thing; **es una ~** it's lovely, it's really beautiful

precioso, -a [pre'θjoso, a] adj precious; (de mucho valor) valuable; (fam) lovely, beautiful

precipicio [preθi'piθjo] nm cliff, precipice; (fig) abyss

precipitación [preθipita'θjon] nf haste; (lluvia) rainfall

precipitado, -a [preθipi'taðo, a] adj hasty, rash; (salida) hasty, sudden

precipitar [preθipi'tar] /1a/ vt (arrojar) to hurl, throw; (apresurar) to hasten; (acelerar) to speed up, accelerate; **precipitarse** vr to throw o.s.; (apresurarse) to rush; (actuar sin pensar) to act rashly

precisamente [preθisa'mente] adv precisely; (justo) precisely, exactly

precisar [preθi'sar] /1a/ vt (necesitar) to need, require; (fijar) to determine exactly, fix; (especificar) to specify

precisión [preθi'sjon] nf (exactitud) precision

preciso, -a [pre'θiso, a] adj (exacto) precise; (necesario) necessary, essential

preconcebido, -a [prekonθe'βiðo, a] adj preconceived

precoz [pre'koθ] adj (persona) precocious; (calvicie) premature

predecir [preðe'θir] /3o/ vt to predict, forecast

predestinado, -a [preðesti'naðo, a] adj predestined

predicar [preði'kar] /1g/ vt, vi to preach

predicción [preðik'θjon] nf prediction

predilecto, -a [preði'lekto, a] adj favourite

predisposición [preðisposi'θjon] nf inclination; prejudice, bias

predominar [preðomi'nar] /1a/ vt to dominate ▷ vi to predominate;

(*prevalecer*) to prevail; **predominio** nm predominance; prevalence

preescolar [preesko'lar] *adj* preschool

prefabricado, -a [prefaβri'kaðo, a] *adj* prefabricated

prefacio [pre'faθjo] nm preface

preferencia [prefe'renθja] nf preference; **de ~** preferably, for preference

preferible [prefe'riβle] *adj* preferable

preferido, -a [prefe'riðo, a] *adj, nm/f* favourite, favorite (*us*)

preferir [prefe'rir] /3i/ vt to prefer

prefiero *etc* [pre'fjero] vb V **preferir**

prefijo [pre'fixo] nm (*Telec*) (dialling) code

pregunta [pre'ɣunta] nf question; **hacer una ~** to ask a question; **~s frecuentes** FAQs, frequently asked questions; **preguntar** /1a/ vt to ask; (*cuestionar*) to question ▷ vi to ask; **preguntarse** vr to wonder; **preguntar por algn** to ask for sb; **preguntón, -ona** *adj* inquisitive

prehistórico, -a [preis'toriko, a] *adj* prehistoric

prejuicio [pre'xwiθjo] nm prejudice; (*preconcepción*) preconception (*prejuzgar*) prejudice, bias

preludio [pre'luðjo] nm prelude

prematuro, -a [prema'turo, a] *adj* premature

premeditar [premeði'tar] /1a/ vt to premeditate

premiar [pre'mjar] /1b/ vt to reward; (*en un concurso*) to give a prize to

premio ['premjo] nm reward; prize; (*Com*) premium

prenatal [prena'tal] *adj* antenatal, prenatal

prenda ['prenda] nf (*de ropa*) garment, article of clothing; (*garantía*) pledge; **prendas** nfpl talents, gifts

prender [pren'der] /2a/ vt (*captar*) to catch, capture; (*detener*) to arrest; (*coser*) to pin, attach; (*sujetar*) to fasten

▷ vi to catch; (*arraigar*) to take root; **prenderse** vr (*encenderse*) to catch fire

prendido, -a [pren'diðo, a] *adj* (*LAM*: *luz*) on

prensa ['prensa] nf press; **la P~** the press

preñada, -a [pre'ɲaðo, a] *adj* pregnant; **~ de** pregnant with, full of

preocupación [preokupa'θjon] nf worry, concern; (*ansiedad*) anxiety

preocupado, -a [preoku'paðo, a] *adj* worried, concerned; anxious

preocupar [preoku'par] /1a/ vt to worry; **preocuparse** vr to worry; **~se de algo** (*hacerse cargo de algo*) to take care of sth

preparación [prepara'θjon] nf (*acto*) preparation; (*estado*) readiness; (*entrenamiento*) training

preparado, -a [prepa'raðo, a] *adj* (*dispuesto*) prepared; (*Culin*) ready (to serve) ▷ nm preparation

preparar [prepa'rar] /1a/ vt (*disponer*) to prepare, get ready; (*Tec*: *tratar*) to prepare, process; (*entrenar*) to teach, train; **prepararse** vr: **~se a o para hacer algo** to prepare o get ready to do sth; **preparativo, -a** *adj* preparatory, preliminary; **preparativos** nmpl preparations; **preparatoria** nf (*LAM*) sixth form college (*BRIT*), senior high school (*US*)

presa ['presa] nf (*cosa apresada*) catch; (*víctima*) victim; (*de animal*) prey; (*de agua*) dam

presagiar [presa'xjar] /1b/ vt to presage; **presagio** nm omen

prescindir [presθin'dir] /3a/ vi: **~ de** (*privarse de*) to do without, go without; (*descartar*) to dispense with

prescribir [preskri'βir] /3a/ vt to prescribe

presencia [pre'senθja] nf presence; **presenciar** /1b/ vt to be present at; (*asistir a*) to attend; (*ver*) to see, witness

presentación [presenta'θjon] nf presentation; (*introducción*) introduction

presentador, a [presenta'ðor, a] nm/f compère

presentar [presen'tar] /1a/ vt to present; (ofrecer) to offer; (mostrar) to show, display; (a una persona) to introduce; **presentarse** vr (llegar inesperadamente) to appear, turn up; (ofrecerse: como candidato) to run, stand; (aparecer) to show, appear; (solicitar empleo) to apply

presente [pre'sente] adj present ▷ nm present; **hacer ~** to state, declare; **tener ~** to remember, bear in mind

presentimiento [presenti'mjento] nm premonition, presentiment

presentir [presen'tir] /3i/ vt to have a premonition of

preservación [preserβa'θjon] nf protection, preservation

preservar [preser'βar] /1a/ vt to protect, preserve; **preservativo** nm sheath, condom

presidencia [presi'ðenθja] nf presidency; (de comité) chairmanship

presidente [presi'ðente] nmf president; (de comité) chairman/ woman

presidir [presi'ðir] /3a/ vt (dirigir) to preside at, preside over; (: comité) to take the chair at; (dominar) to dominate, rule ▷ vi to preside; to take the chair

presión [pre'sjon] nf pressure; **~ atmosférica** atmospheric o air pressure; **presionar** /1a/ vt to press; (fig) to press, put pressure on ▷ vi: **presionar para** o **por** to press for

preso, -a ['preso, a] nm/f prisoner; **tomar** o **llevar ~ a algn** to arrest sb, take sb prisoner

prestación [presta'θjon] nf service; (subsidio) benefit; **prestaciones** nfpl (Auto) performance features

prestado, -a [pres'taðo, a] adj on loan; **pedir ~** to borrow

prestamista [presta'mista] nmf moneylender

préstamo ['prestamo] nm loan; **~ hipotecario** mortgage

prestar [pres'tar] /1a/ vt to lend, loan; (atención) to pay; (ayuda) to give; (servicio) to do, render; (juramento) to take, swear; **prestarse** vr (ofrecerse) to offer o volunteer

prestigio [pres'tixjo] nm prestige; **prestigioso, -a** adj (honorable) prestigious; (famoso, renombrado) renowned, famous

presumido, -a [presu'miðo, a] adj conceited

presumir [presu'mir] /3a/ vt to presume ▷ vi (darse aires) to be conceited; **presunto, -a** adj (supuesto) supposed, presumed; (así llamado) so-called; **presuntuoso, -a** adj conceited, presumptuous

presupuesto [presu'pwesto] nm (Finanzas) budget; (estimación: de costo) estimate

pretencioso, -a [preten'θjoso, a] adj pretentious

pretender [preten'der] /2a/ vt (intentar) to try to, seek to; (reivindicar) to claim; (buscar) to seek, try for; (cortejar) to woo, court; **~ que** to expect that; **pretendiente** nmf (amante) suitor; (al trono) pretender; **pretensión** nf (aspiración) aspiration; (reivindicación) claim; (orgullo) pretension

⚠ No confundir **pretender** con la palabra inglesa pretend.

pretexto [pre'teksto] nm pretext; (excusa) excuse

prevención [preβen'θjon] nf prevention; (precaución) precaution

prevenido, -a [preβe'niðo, a] adj prepared, ready; (cauteloso) cautious

prevenir [preβe'nir] /3r/ vt (impedir) to prevent; (predisponer) to prejudice, bias; (avisar) to warn; (preparar) to prepare, get ready; **prevenirse** vr to get ready, prepare; **~se contra** to take precautions against; **preventivo, -a** adj preventive, precautionary

prever [pre'βer] /2u/ vt to foresee

previo, -a ['preβjo, a] adj (anterior) previous; (preliminar) preliminary ▷ prep: **~ acuerdo de los otros** subject to the agreement of the others

previsión [preβi'sjon] nf (perspicacia) foresight; (predicción) forecast; (prevención) foresight

previsto, -a adj anticipated, forecast

prima ['prima] nf V **primo**

primario, -a [pri'marjo, a] adj primary

primavera [prima'βera] nf (temporada) spring; (período) springtime

Primer Ministro [pri'mer-] nm Prime Minister

primero, -a [pri'mero, a] adj first; (fig) prime ▷ adv first; (más bien) sooner, rather ▷ nf (Auto) first gear; (Ferro) first class; **de primera** (fam) first-class, first-rate; **primera plana** front page

primitivo, -a [primi'tiβo, a] adj primitive; (original) original

primo, -a ['primo, a] adj (Mat) prime ▷ nm/f cousin; (fam) fool, idiot ▷ nf (Com) bonus; (de seguro) premium; **~ hermano** first cousin; **hacer el ~** to be taken for a ride

primogénito, -a [primo'xenito, a] adj first-born

primoroso, -a [primo'roso, a] adj exquisite, fine

princesa [prin'θesa] nf princess

principal [prinθi'pal] adj principal, main ▷ nm (jefe) chief, principal

príncipe ['prinθipe] nm prince

principiante [prinθi'pjante] nmf beginner

principio [prin'θipjo] nm (comienzo) beginning, start; (origen) origin; (base) rudiment, basic idea; (moral) principle; **a ~s de** at the beginning of; **desde el ~** from the first; **en un ~** at first

pringue ['pringe] nm (grasa) grease, fat, dripping

prioridad [priori'ðað] nf priority

prisa ['prisa] nf (apresuramiento) hurry, haste; (rapidez) speed; (urgencia) (sense of) urgency; **a o de ~** quickly; **correr ~** to be urgent; **darse ~** to hurry up; **estar de o tener ~** to be in a hurry

prisión [pri'sjon] nf (cárcel) prison; (período de cárcel) imprisonment;

prisionero, -a nm/f prisoner

prismáticos [pris'matikos] nmpl binoculars

privado, -a [pri'βaðo, a] adj private

privar [pri'βar] /1a/ vt to deprive;

privativo, -a adj exclusive

privilegiar [priβile'xjar] /1b/ vt to grant a privilege to; (favorecer) to favour

privilegio [priβi'lexjo] nm privilege; (concesión) concession

pro [pro] nm o f profit, advantage ▷ prep: **asociación ~ ciegos** association for the blind ▷ pref: **~ soviético/americano** pro-Soviet/-American; **en ~ de** on behalf of, for; **los ~ s y los contras** the pros and cons

proa ['proa] nf (Naut) bow, prow; **de ~** bow cpd, fore; V tb **popa**

probabilidad [proβaβili'ðað] nf probability, likelihood; (oportunidad, posibilidad) chance, prospect;

probable adj probable, likely

probador [proβa'ðor] nm (en una tienda) fitting room

probar [pro'βar] /1l/ vt (demostrar) to prove; (someter a prueba) to test, try out; (ropa) to try on; (comida) to taste ▷ vi to try; **probarse** vr: **~se un traje** to try on a suit

probeta [pro'βeta] nf test tube

problema [pro'βlema] nm problem

procedente [proθe'ðente] adj (razonable) reasonable; (conforme a derecho) proper, fitting; **~ de** coming from, originating in

proceder [proθe'ðer] /2a/ vi (avanzar) to proceed; (actuar) to act; (ser correcto) to be right (and proper), be fitting ▷ nm (comportamiento) behaviour, conduct; **~ de** to come from, originate in; **procedimiento** nm procedure; (proceso) process; (método) means, method

procesador [proθesaˈðor] nm: **~ de textos** word processor

procesar [proθeˈsar] /1a/ vt to try, put on trial; (Inform) to process

procesión [proθeˈsjon] nf procession

proceso [proˈθeso] nm process; (Jur) trial

proclamar [proklaˈmar] /1a/ vt to proclaim

procrear [prokreˈar] /1a/ vt, vi to procreate

procurador, a [prokuraˈðor, a] nm/f attorney

procurar [prokuˈrar] /1a/ vt (intentar) to try, endeavour; (conseguir) to get, obtain; (asegurar) to secure; (producir) to produce

prodigio [proˈðixjo] nm prodigy; (milagro) wonder, marvel; **prodigioso, -a** adj prodigious, marvellous

pródigo, -a [ˈproðiɣo, a] adj: **hijo ~** prodigal son

producción [proðukˈθjon] nf production; (suma de productos) output; **~ en serie** mass production

producir [proðuˈθir] /3n/ vt to produce; (generar) to cause, bring about; **producirse** vr (cambio) to come about; (hacerse) to be produced, be made; (estallar) to break out; (accidente) to take place; (problema etc) to arise

productividad [proðuktiβiˈðað] nf productivity; **productivo, -a** adj productive; (provechoso) profitable

producto [proˈðukto] nm product

productor, a [proðukˈtor, a] adj productive, producing ⊳ nm/f producer

proeza [proˈeθa] nf exploit, feat

profano, -a [proˈfano, a] adj profane ⊳ nm/f layman/woman

profecía [profeˈθia] nf prophecy

profesión [profeˈsjon] nf profession; (en formulario) occupation; **profesional** adj professional

profesor, a [profeˈsor, a] nm/f teacher; **profesorado** nm teaching profession

profeta [proˈfeta] nmf prophet

prófugo, -a [ˈprofuɣo, a] nm/f fugitive; (desertor) deserter

profundidad [profundiˈðað] nf depth; **profundizar** /1f/ (fig) vt to go into deeply ⊳ vi: **profundizar en** to go into deeply; **profundo, -a** adj deep; (misterio, pensador) profound

progenitor [proxeniˈtor] nm ancestor; **progenitores** nmpl parents

programa [proˈɣrama] nm programme; (Inform) program; **~ de estudios** curriculum, syllabus; **programación** nf (Inform) programming; **programador, a** nm/f (computer) programmer; **programar** /1a/ vt (Inform) to program

progresar [proɣreˈsar] /1a/ vi to progress, make progress; **progresista** adj, nmf progressive; **progresivo, -a** adj progressive; (gradual) gradual; (continuo) continuous; **progreso** nm progress

prohibición [proiβiˈθjon] nf prohibition, ban; **levantar la ~ de** to remove the ban on

prohibir [proiˈβir] /3a/ vt to prohibit, ban, forbid; **se prohíbe fumar** no smoking; **"prohibido el paso"** "no entry"

prójimo [ˈproximo] nm fellow man

prólogo [ˈproloɣo] nm prologue

prolongar [prolonˈɡar] /1h/ vt to extend; (en el tiempo) to prolong; (calle, tubo) to make longer, extend

promedio [proˈmeðjo] nm average; (de distancia) middle, mid-point

promesa [proˈmesa] nf promise

prometer [promeˈter] /2a/ vt to promise ⊳ vi to show promise; **prometerse** vr (dos personas) to get engaged; **prometido, -a** adj promised; engaged ⊳ nm/f fiancé/fiancée

prominente [promiˈnente] adj prominent

promoción [promo'θjon] nf
promotion

promotor [promo'tor] nm promoter;
(instigador) instigator

promover [promo'βer] /2h/ vt to
promote; (causar) to cause; (motín) to
instigate, stir up

promulgar [promul'ɣar] /1h/ vt to
promulgate; (fig) to proclaim

pronombre [pro'nombre] nm
pronoun

pronosticar [pronosti'kar] /1g/ vt to
predict, foretell, forecast; **pronóstico**
nm prediction, forecast; **pronóstico
del tiempo** weather forecast

pronto, -a ['pronto, a] adj (rápido)
prompt, quick; (preparado) ready ▷ adv
quickly, promptly; (en seguida) at once,
right away; (dentro de poco) soon;
(temprano) early ▷ nm: **de ~** suddenly;
tiene unos ~s muy malos he gets
ratty all of a sudden (fam); **por lo ~**
meanwhile, for the present

pronunciación [pronunθja'θjon] nf
pronunciation

pronunciar [pronun'θjar] /1b/ vt to
pronounce; (discurso) to make, deliver;
pronunciarse vr to revolt, rebel;
(declararse) to declare o.s.

propaganda [propa'ɣanda] nf
(política) propaganda; (comercial)
advertising

propenso, -a [pro'penso, a] adj: ~
a prone o inclined to; **ser ~ a hacer
algo** to be inclined o have a tendency
to do sth

propicio, -a [pro'piθjo, a] adj
favourable, propitious

propiedad [propje'ðað] nf property;
(posesión) possession, ownership;
~ particular private property

propietario, -a [propje'tarjo, a]
nm/f owner, proprietor

propina [pro'pina] nf tip

propio, -a ['propjo, a] adj own,
of one's own; (característico)

characteristic, typical; (conveniente)
proper; (mismo) selfsame, very; **el
~ ministro** the minister himself;
¿tienes casa propia? have you a
house of your own?

proponer [propo'ner] /2q/ vt to
propose, put forward; (problema)
to pose; **proponerse** vr to propose,
intend

proporción [propor'θjon] nf
proportion; (Mat) ratio; **proporciones**
nfpl (fig) dimensions; size sg;
proporcionado, -a adj proportionate;
(regular) medium, middling; (justo) just
right; **proporcionar** /1a/ vt (dar) to
give, supply; provide

proposición [proposi'θjon] nf
proposition; (propuesta) proposal

propósito [pro'posito] nm purpose;
(intento) aim, intention ▷ adv: **a ~**
by the way, incidentally; (a posta) on
purpose, deliberately; **a ~ de** about,
with regard to

propuesto, -a [pro'pwesto, a] pp de
proponer ▷ nf proposal

propulsar [propul'sar] /1a/ vt
to drive, propel; (fig) to promote,
encourage; **propulsión** nf propulsion;
propulsión a chorro o **por reacción**
jet propulsion

prórroga ['prorroɣa] nf extension;
(Jur) stay; (Com) deferment; (Deporte)
extra time; **prorrogar** /1h/ vt (período)
to extend; (decisión) to defer, postpone

prosa ['prosa] nf prose

proseguir [prose'ɣir] /3d, 3k/ vt to
continue, carry on ▷ vi to continue,
go on

prospecto [pros'pekto] nm
prospectus

prosperar [prospe'rar] /1a/ vi to
prosper, thrive, flourish; **prosperidad**
nf prosperity; (éxito) success;
próspero, -a adj prosperous, thriving;
(que tiene éxito) successful

prostíbulo [pros'tiβulo] nm brothel

prostitución [prostitu'θjon] nf
prostitution

p

prostituir [prosti'twir] /3g/ vt
to prostitute; **prostituirse** vr to
prostitute o.s., become a prostitute
prostituta [prosti'tuta] nf prostitute
protagonista [protaɣo'nista] nmf
protagonist
protección [protek'θjon] nf
protection
protector, a [protek'tor, a] adj
protective, protecting ▷ nm/f
protector
proteger [prote'xer] /2c/ vt to
protect; **protegido, -a** nm/f protégé/
protégée
proteína [prote'ina] nf protein
protesta [pro'testa] nf protest;
(declaración) protestation
protestante [protes'tante] adj
Protestant
protestar [protes'tar] /1a/ vt to
protest, declare ▷ vi to protest
protocolo [proto'kolo] nm protocol
prototipo [proto'tipo] nm prototype
provecho [pro'βetʃo] nm advantage,
benefit; (Finanzas) profit; **¡buen ~!**
bon appétit!; **en ~ de** to the benefit
of; **sacar ~ de** to benefit from,
profit by
provenir [proβe'nir] /3r/ vi: **~ de** to
come from
proverbio [pro'βerβjo] nm proverb
providencia [proβi'ðenθja] nf
providence
provincia [pro'βinθja] nf province
provisión [proβi'sjon] nf provision;
(abastecimiento) provision, supply;
(medida) measure, step
provisional [proβisjo'nal] adj
provisional
provocar [proβo'kar] /1g/ vt to
provoke; (alentar) to tempt, invite;
(causar) to bring about, lead to;
(promover) to promote; (estimular) to
rouse, stimulate; (LAm): **¿te provoca
un café?** would you like a coffee?;
provocativo, -a adj provocative
proxeneta [prokse'neta] nmf (de
prostitutas) pimp/procuress

próximamente [proksima'mente]
adv shortly, soon
proximidad [proksimi'ðað] nf
closeness, proximity; **próximo, -a** adj
near, close; (vecino) neighbouring; (el
que viene) next
proyectar [projek'tar] /1a/ vt
(objeto) to hurl, throw; (luz) to cast,
shed; (Cine) to screen, show; (planear)
to plan
proyectil [projek'til] nm projectile,
missile
proyecto [pro'jekto] nm plan;
(estimación de costo) detailed estimate
proyector [projek'tor] nm (Cine)
projector
prudencia [pru'ðenθja] nf (sabiduría)
wisdom; (cautela) care; **prudente** adj
sensible, wise; (cauteloso) careful
prueba ['prweβa] vb V **probar** ▷ nf
proof; (ensayo) test, trial; (saboreo)
testing, sampling; (de ropa) fitting; **a
~ on** trial; **a ~ de** proof against; **a ~ de
agua/fuego** waterproof/fireproof;
someter a ~ to put to the test
psico... [siko] pref psycho...;
psicología nf psychology;
psicológico, -a adj psychological;
psicólogo, -a nm/f psychologist;
psicópata nmf psychopath; **psicosis**
nf inv psychosis
psiquiatra [si'kjatra] nmf
psychiatrist; **psiquiátrico, -a** adj
psychiatric
PSOE [pe'soe] nm abr = **Partido
Socialista Obrero Español**
púa nf (Bot, Zool) prickle, spine; (para
guitarra) plectrum; **alambre de ~s**
barbed wire
pubertad [puβer'tað] nf puberty
publicación [puβlika'θjon] nf
publication
publicar [puβli'kar] /1g/ vt (editar)
to publish; (hacer público) to publicize;
(divulgar) to make public, divulge
publicidad [puβliθi'ðað] nf publicity;
(Com) advertising; **publicitario, -a** adj
publicity cpd; advertising cpd

público, -a ['puβliko, a] *adj* public
▷ *nm* public; (*Teat etc*) audience

puchero [pu'tʃero] *nm* (Culin: olla)
cooking pot; (: *guiso*) stew; **hacer
~s** to pout

pucho ['putʃo] (ʌᴍ fam) *nm* cigarette,
fag (BRIT)

pude *etc vb* V **poder**

pudiente [pu'ðjente] *adj* (opulento)
wealthy

pudiera *etc vb* V **poder**

pudor [pu'ðor] *nm* modesty

pudrir [pu'ðrir] /3a/ *vt* to rot;
pudrirse *vr* to rot, decay

pueblo ['pweβlo] *nm* people; (nación)
nation; (aldea) village

puedo *etc* ['pweðo] *vb* V **poder**

puente ['pwente] *nm* bridge; **~
aéreo** shuttle service; **~ colgante**
suspension bridge; **~ levadizo**
drawbridge; **hacer ~** (fam) to take a
long weekend

○ **HACER PUENTE**
○
○ When a public holiday in Spain
○ falls on a Tuesday or Thursday it is
○ common practice for employers to
○ make the Monday or Friday a holiday
○ as well and to give everyone a four-
○ day weekend. This is known as *hacer
○ puente*. When a named public holiday
○ such as the *Día de la Constitución* falls
○ on a Tuesday or Thursday, people
○ refer to the whole holiday period as
○ e.g. the *puente de la Constitución*.

puerco, -a [pu'werko, a] *adj* (sucio)
dirty, filthy; (obsceno) disgusting
▷ *nm/f* pig/sow; **~ espín** porcupine

pueril [pwe'ril] *adj* childish

puerro [pu'werro] *nm* leek

puerta ['pwerta] *nf* door; (de jardín)
gate; (portal) doorway; (fig) gateway;
(gol) goal; **a la ~** at the door; **a ~
cerrada** behind closed doors; **~
corredera/giratoria** sliding/swing o
revolving door

puerto ['pwerto] *nm* port; (paso) pass;
(fig) haven, refuge

Puerto Rico [pwerto'riko] *nm*
Puerto Rico; **puertorriqueño, -a** *adj*,
nm/f Puerto Rican

pues [pwes] *adv* (entonces) then;
(¡entonces!) well, well then; (así que)
so ▷ *conj* (porque) since; **¡~ sí!** yes!,
certainly!

puesto, -a ['pwesto, a] *pp de* **poner**
▷ *adj* dressed ▷ *nm* (lugar, posición)
place; (trabajo) post, job; (Com) stall
▷ *conj*: **~ que** since, as ▷ *nf* (apuesta)
bet, stake; **tener algo ~** to have sth
on, be wearing sth; **~ de mercado**
market stall; **~ de policía** police
station; **~ de socorro** first aid post;
puesta al día updating; **puesta en
marcha** starting; **puesta a punto**
fine tuning; **puesta del sol** sunset

púgil ['puxil] *nm* boxer

pulga ['pulɣa] *nf* flea

pulgada [pul'ɣaða] *nf* inch

pulgar [pul'ɣar] *nm* thumb

pulir [pu'lir] /3a/ *vt* to polish;
(alisar) to smooth; (fig) to polish up,
touch up

pulmón [pul'mon] *nm* lung;
pulmonía [pulmo'nia] *nf* pneumonia

pulpa ['pulpa] *nf* pulp; (de fruta) flesh,
soft part

pulpería [pulpe'ria] *nf* (ʌᴍ) small
grocery store

púlpito ['pulpito] *nm* pulpit

pulpo ['pulpo] *nm* octopus

pulque ['pulke] *nm* pulque

○ **PULQUE**
○
○ Pulque is a thick, white, alcoholic
○ drink which is very popular in
○ Mexico. In ancient times it was
○ considered sacred by the Aztecs. It
○ is produced by fermenting the juice
○ of the *maguey*, a Mexican cactus
○ similar to the agave. It can be drunk
○ by itself or mixed with fruit or
○ vegetable juice.

P

pulsación [pulsa'θjon] *nf* beat; **pulsaciones** pulse rate

pulsar [pul'sar] /1a/ *vt* (*tecla*) to touch, tap; (*Mus*) to play; (*botón*) to press, push ▷ *vi* to pulsate; (*latir*) to beat, throb

pulsera [pul'sera] *nf* bracelet

pulso ['pulso] *nm* (*Med*) pulse; (*fuerza*) strength; (*firmeza*) steadiness, steady hand

pulverizador [pulβeriθa'ðor] *nm* spray, spray gun

pulverizar [pulβeri'θar] /1f/ *vt* to pulverize; (*líquido*) to spray

puna ['puna] *nf* (ʌм) mountain sickness

punta ['punta] *nf* point, tip; (*extremidad*) end; (*fig*) touch, trace; **horas ~s** peak hours, rush hours; **sacar ~ a** to sharpen

puntada [pun'taða] *nf* (*Costura*) stitch

puntal [pun'tal] *nm* prop, support

puntapié [punta'pje] *nm* kick

puntería [punte'ria] *nf* (*de arma*) aim, aiming; (*destreza*) marksmanship

puntero, -a [pun'tero, a] *adj* leading ▷ *nm* (*señal, Inform*) pointer

puntiagudo, -a [puntja'yuðo, a] *adj* sharp, pointed

puntilla [pun'tiʎa] *nf* (*Costura*) lace edging; (**andar**) **de ~s** (to walk) on tiptoe

punto ['punto] *nm* (*gen*) point; (*señal diminuta*) spot, dot; (*lugar*) spot, place; (*momento*) point, moment; (*Costura*) stitch; **a ~** ready; **estar a ~ de** to be on the point of *o* about to; **en ~** on the dot; **hasta cierto ~** to some extent; **hacer ~** to knit; **~ de vista** point of view, viewpoint; **~ muerto** dead centre; (*Auto*) neutral (gear); **~ final** full stop; **dos ~s** colon; **~ y coma** semicolon; **~ acápite** (ʌм) full stop, new paragraph; **~ de interrogación** question mark

puntocom [punto'kom] *nf inv, adj inv* dotcom

puntuación [puntwa'θjon] *nf* punctuation; (*puntos: en examen*) mark(s) *pl*; (*Deporte*) score

puntual [pun'twal] *adj* (*a tiempo*) punctual; (*cálculo*) exact, accurate; **puntualidad** *nf* punctuality; exactness, accuracy

puntuar [pun'twar] /1e/ *vi* (*Deporte*) to score, count

punzante [pun'θante] *adj* (*dolor*) shooting, sharp; (*herramienta*) sharp

puñado [pu'ɲaðo] *nm* handful (*tb fig*)

puñal [pu'ɲal] *nm* dagger; **puñalada** *nf* stab

puñetazo [puɲe'taθo] *nm* punch

puño ['puɲo] *nm* (*Anat*) fist; (*cantidad*) fistful, handful; (*Costura*) cuff; (*de herramienta*) handle

pupila [pu'pila] *nf* pupil

pupitre [pu'pitre] *nm* desk

puré [pu're] *nm* purée; (*sopa*) (thick) soup; **~ de patatas** (ESP), **~ de papas** (ʌм) mashed potatoes

purga ['purɣa] *nf* purge; **purgante** *adj, nm* purgative

purgatorio [purɣa'torjo] *nm* purgatory

purificar [purifi'kar] /1g/ *vt* to purify; (*refinar*) to refine

puritano, -a [puri'tano, a] *adj* (*actitud*) puritanical; (*iglesia, tradición*) puritan ▷ *nm/f* puritan

puro, -a ['puro, a] *adj* pure; (*verdad*) simple, plain ▷ *nm* cigar

púrpura ['purpura] *nf* purple

pus [pus] *nm* pus

puse *etc* ['puse] *vb V* **poner**

pusiera *etc vb V* **poder**

puta ['puta] *nf* whore, prostitute

putrefacción [putrefak'θjon] *nf* rotting, putrefaction

PVP *abr* (ESP: = *Precio Venta al Público*) ≈ RRP

PYME ['pime] *nf abr* (= *Pequeña y Mediana Empresa*) SME

q

que [ke] *conj* **1** (con oración subordinada: *muchas veces no se traduce*) that; **dijo que vendría** he said (that) he would come; **espero que lo encuentres** I hope (that) you find it; V tb **el 2** (en oración independiente): **¡que entre!** send him in!; **¡que aproveche!** enjoy your meal!; **¡que se mejore tu padre!** I hope your father gets better **3** (enfático): **¿me quieres? — ¡que sí!** do you love me? — of course! **4** (consecutivo: *muchas veces no se traduce*) that; **es tan grande que no lo puedo levantar** it's so big (that) I can't lift it **5** (comparaciones) than; **yo que tú/él** if I were you/him; **más; menos 6** (valor disyuntivo): **que le guste o no** whether he likes it or not; **que venga o que no venga** whether he comes or not **7** (porque): **no puedo, que tengo que quedarme en casa** I can't, I've got to stay in ▸ *pron* **1** (cosa) that, which; (: + prep) which; **el sombrero que te compraste** the hat (that *o* which) you bought; **la cama en que dormí** the bed (that *o* which) I slept in **2** (persona: suj) that, who; (: objeto) that, whom; **el amigo que me acompañó al museo** the friend that *o* who went to the museum with me; **la chica que invité** the girl (that *o* whom) I invited

qué [ke] *adj* what?, which? ▷ *pron* what?; **¡~ divertido/asco!** how funny/revolting!; **¿~ edad tienes?** how old are you?; **¿de ~ me hablas?** what are you saying to me?; **¿~ tal?** how are you?, how are things?; **¿~ hay (de nuevo)?** what's new?

quebrado, -a [ke'βraðo, a] *adj* (roto) broken ▷ *nm/f* bankrupt ▷ *nm* (Mat) fraction

quebrantar [keβran'tar] /1a/ *vt* (infringir) to violate, transgress

quebrar [ke'βrar] /1j/ *vt* to break, smash ▷ *vi* to go bankrupt

quedar [ke'ðar] /1a/ *vi* to stay, remain; (encontrarse) to be; (restar) to remain, be left; **quedarse** *vr* to remain, stay (behind); **~ en** (acordar) to agree on/ to; **~ por hacer** to be still to be done; **~ ciego/mudo** to be left blind/dumb; **no te queda bien ese vestido** that dress doesn't suit you; **quedamos a las seis** we agreed to meet at six; **~se (con) algo** to keep sth; **~se con algn** (fam) to swindle sb; **~se en nada** to come to nothing *o* nought

quedo, -a ['keðo, a] *adj* still ▷ *adv* softly, gently

quehacer [kea'θer] *nm* task, job; **~es (domésticos)** household chores

queja ['kexa] *nf* complaint; **quejarse** /1a/ *vr* (enfermo) to moan, groan;

(protestar) to complain; **quejarse de que ...** to complain (about the fact) that ...; **quejido** *nm* moan

quemado, -a [ke'maðo, a] *adj* burnt

quemadura [kema'ðura] *nf* burn, scald

quemar [ke'mar] /1a/ *vt* to burn; *(fig: malgastar)* to burn up, squander ▷ *vi* to be burning hot; **quemarse** *vr (consumirse)* to burn (up); *(del sol)* to get sunburnt

quemarropa [kema'rropa]: **a ~** *adv* point-blank

quepo *etc* [ˈkepo] *vb* V **caber**

querella [keˈreʎa] *nf (Jur)* charge; *(disputa)* dispute

○ **PALABRA CLAVE**

querer [keˈrer] /2t/ *vt* 1 *(desear)* to want; **quiero más dinero** I want more money; **quisiera o querría un té** I'd like a tea; **sin querer** unintentionally; **quiero ayudar/que vayas** I want to help/you to go

2 *(preguntas: para pedir u ofrecer algo):* **¿quiere abrir la ventana?** could you open the window?; **¿quieres echarme una mano?** can you give me a hand?

3 *(amar)* to love; **te quiero** I love you; **no estoy enamorado, pero la quiero mucho** I'm not in love, but I'm very fond of her

querido, -a [keˈriðo, a] *adj* dear ▷ *nm/f* darling; *(amante)* lover

queso [ˈkeso] *nm* cheese; **~ rallado** grated cheese; **~ crema** (ʟᴀᴍ), **~ de untar** (ᴇsᴘ) cream cheese; **~ manchego** sheep's milk cheese made in La Mancha; **dárselas con ~ a algn** *(fam)* to take sb in

quicio [ˈkiθjo] *nm* hinge; **sacar a algn de ~** to drive sb up the wall

quiebra [ˈkjeβra] *nf* break, split; *(Com)* bankruptcy; *(Econ)* slump

quiebro *etc* [ˈkjeβro] *nm (del cuerpo)* swerve

quien [kjen] *pron relativo (suj)* who; **hay ~ piensa que** there are those who think that; **no hay ~ lo haga** no-one will do it

quién [kjen] *pron interrogativo* who; *(complemento)* whom; **¿~ es?** who's there?

quienquiera [kjenˈkjera] *(pl* **quienesquiera)** *pron* whoever

quiero *etc* **vb** V **querer**

quieto, -a [ˈkjeto, a] *adj* still; *(carácter)* placid; **quietud** *nf* stillness

⚠ No confundir *quieto* con la palabra inglesa *quiet*.

quilate [kiˈlate] *nm* carat

químico, -a [ˈkimiko, a] *adj* chemical ▷ *nm/f* chemist ▷ *nf* chemistry

quincalla [kinˈkaʎa] *nf* hardware, ironmongery (ʙʀɪᴛ)

quince [ˈkinθe] *num* fifteen; **~ días** a fortnight; **quinceañero, -a** *nm/f* teenager; **quincena** *nf* fortnight; *(pago)* fortnightly pay; **quincenal** *adj* fortnightly

quiniela [kiˈnjela] *nf* football pools *pl*; **quinielas** *nfpl* pools coupon *sg*

quinientos, -as [kiˈnjentos, as] *num* five hundred

quinto, -a [ˈkinto, a] *adj* fifth ▷ *nf* country house; *(Mil)* call-up, draft

quiosco [ˈkjosko] *nm (de música)* bandstand; *(de periódicos)* news stand *(also selling sweets, cigarettes etc)*

quirófano [kiˈrofano] *nm* operating theatre

quirúrgico, -a [kiˈrurxiko, a] *adj* surgical

quise *etc* [ˈkise] *vb* V **querer**

quisiera *etc* **vb** V **querer**

quisquilloso, -a [kiskiˈʎoso, a] *adj (susceptible)* touchy; *(meticuloso)* pernickety

quiste [ˈkiste] *nm* cyst

quitaesmalte [kitaesˈmalte] *nm* nail polish remover

quitamanchas [kitaˈmantʃas] *nm inv* stain remover

quitanieves [kita'njeβes] *nm inv* snowplough (BRIT), snowplow (US)

quitar [ki'tar] /1a/ *vt* to remove, take away; (*ropa*) to take off; (*dolor*) to relieve ▷ *vi*: **¡quita de ahí!** get away!; **quitarse** *vr* to withdraw; (*ropa*) to take off; **se quitó el sombrero** he took off his hat

Quito ['kito] *n* Quito

quizá(s) [ki'θa(s)] *adv* perhaps, maybe

rábano ['raβano] *nm* radish; **me importa un ~** I don't give a damn

rabia ['raβja] *nf* (*Med*) rabies *sg*; (*ira*) fury, rage; **rabiar** /1b/ *vi* to have rabies; to rage, be furious; **rabiar por algo** to long for sth

rabieta [ra'βjeta] *nf* tantrum, fit of temper

rabino [ra'βino] *nm* rabbi

rabioso, -a [ra'βjoso, a] *adj* rabid; (*fig*) furious

rabo ['raβo] *nm* tail

racha ['ratʃa] *nf* gust of wind; **buena/mala ~** spell of good/bad luck

racial [ra'θjal] *adj* racial, race *cpd*

racimo [ra'θimo] *nm* bunch

ración [ra'θjon] *nf* portion; **raciones** *nfpl* rations

racional [raθjo'nal] *adj* (*razonable*) reasonable; (*lógico*) rational

racionar [raθjo'nar] /1a/ *vt* to ration (out)

racismo [ra'θismo] nm racism;
racista adj, nmf racist
radar [ra'ðar] nm radar
radiador [raðja'ðor] nm radiator
radiante [ra'ðjante] adj radiant
radical [raði'kal] adj, nmf radical
radicar [raði'kar] /1g/ vi: ~ **en**
(dificultad, problema) to lie in; (solución)
to consist in
radio [ˈraðjo] nf radio; (aparato)
radio (set) ▷ nm (Mat) radius;
(Química) radium; **radioactividad**
nf radioactivity; **radioactivo, -a** adj
radioactive; **radiografía** nf X-ray;
radioterapia nf radiotherapy;
radioyente nmf listener
ráfaga [ˈrafaɣa] nf gust; (de luz) flash;
(de tiros) burst
raíz [raˈiθ] nf root; ~ **cuadrada** square
root; **a ~ de** as a result of
raja [ˈraxa] nf (de melón etc) slice;
(grieta) crack; **rajar** /1a/ vt to split;
(fam) to slash; **rajarse** vr to split, crack;
rajarse de to back out of
rajatabla [raxaˈtaβla] **a ~** adv
(estrictamente) strictly, to the letter
rallador [raʎaˈðor] nm grater
rallar [raˈʎar] /1a/ vt to grate
rama [ˈrama] nf branch; **ramaje** nm
branches pl, foliage; **ramal** nm (de
cuerda) strand; (Ferro) branch line;
(Auto) branch (road)
rambla [ˈrambla] nf (avenida)
avenue
ramo [ˈramo] nm branch; (sección)
department, section
rampa [ˈrampa] nf ramp; ~ **de acceso**
entrance ramp
rana [ˈrana] nf frog; **salto de ~**
leapfrog
ranchero [ranˈtʃero] nm (LAM)
rancher; (pequeño propietario)
smallholder
rancho [ˈrantʃo] nm (grande) ranch;
(pequeño) small farm
rancio, -a [ˈranθjo, a] adj (comestibles)
rancid; (vino) aged, mellow; (fig)
ancient

rango [ˈrango] nm rank; (prestigio)
standing
ranura [raˈnura] nf groove; (de
teléfono etc) slot
rapar [raˈpar] /1a/ vt to shave; (los
cabellos) to crop
rapaz [raˈpaθ] adj (Zool) predatory
▷ nm young boy
rape [ˈrape] nm (pez) monkfish; **al ~**
cropped
rapé [raˈpe] nm snuff
rapidez [rapiˈðeθ] nf speed, rapidity;
rápido, -a adj fast, quick ▷ adv
quickly ▷ nm (Ferro) express; **rápidos**
nmpl rapids
rapiña [raˈpiɲa] nf robbery; **ave de ~**
bird of prey
raptar [rapˈtar] /1a/ vt to kidnap;
rapto nm kidnapping; (impulso)
sudden impulse; (éxtasis) ecstasy,
rapture
raqueta [raˈketa] nf racket
raquítico, -a [raˈkitiko, a] adj
stunted; (fig) poor, inadequate
rareza [raˈreθa] nf rarity; (fig)
eccentricity
raro, -a [ˈraro, a] adj (poco común) rare;
(extraño) odd, strange; (excepcional)
remarkable
ras [ras] nm: **a ~ de** level with; **a ~ de
tierra** at ground level
rasar [raˈsar] /1a/ vt to level
rascacielos [raskaˈθjelos] nm inv
skyscraper
rascar [rasˈkar] /1g/ vt (con las uñas
etc) to scratch; (raspar) to scrape;
rascarse vr to scratch (o.s.)
rasgar [rasˈɣar] /1h/ vt to tear,
rip (up)
rasgo [ˈrasɣo] nm (con pluma) stroke;
rasgos nmpl features, characteristics;
a grandes ~s in outline, broadly
rasguño [rasˈɣuɲo] nm scratch
raso, -a [ˈraso, a] adj (liso) flat, level; (a
baja altura) very low ▷ nm satin; **cielo
~** clear sky
raspadura [raspaˈðura] nf (acto)
scrape, scraping; (marca) scratch;

raspaduras [raspa'ðuras] *nfpl* (*de papel etc*) scrapings

raspar [ras'par] /1a/ *vt* to scrape; (*arañar*) to scratch; (*limar*) to file

rastra ['rastra] *nf* (*Agr*) rake; **a ~s** by dragging; (*fig*) unwillingly

rastrear [rastre'ar] /1a/ *vt* (*seguir*) to track

rastrero, -a [ras'trero, a] *adj* (*Bot, Zool*) creeping; (*fig*) despicable, mean

rastrillo [ras'triλo] *nm* rake

rastro ['rastro] *nm* (*Agr*) rake; (*pista*) track, trail; (*huella*) trace; **el R~** the Madrid flea market

rasurado [rasu'raðo] *nm* shaving; **rasurador** *nm*, (ʟᴀᴍ) **rasuradora** [rasura'ðora] *nf* electric shaver o razor; **rasurar** /1a/ *vt* (ʟᴀᴍ) to shave; **rasurarse** *vr* to shave

rata ['rata] *nf* rat

ratear [rate'ar] /1a/ *vt* (*robar*) to steal

ratero, -a [ra'tero, a] *adj* light-fingered ▷ *nm/f* (*carterista*) pickpocket; (*ladrón*) petty thief

rato ['rato] *nm* while, short time; **a ~s** from time to time; **al poco ~** shortly after, soon afterwards; **~s libres** o **de ocio** free o leisure time *sg*; **hay para ~** there's still a long way to go

ratón [ra'ton] *nm* mouse; **ratonera** *nf* mousetrap

raudal [rau'ðal] *nm* torrent; **a ~es** in abundance

raya ['raja] *nf* line; (*marca*) scratch; (*en tela*) stripe; (*puntuación*) dash; (*de pelo*) parting; (*límite*) boundary; (*pez*) ray; **a ~s** striped; **pasarse de la ~** to overstep the mark; **tener a ~** to keep in check; **rayar** /1a/ *vt* to line; to scratch; (*subrayar*) to underline ▷ *vi*: **rayar en** o **con** to border on

rayo ['rajo] *nm* (*del sol*) ray, beam; (*de luz*) shaft; (*en una tormenta*) (*flash of*) lightning; **~s X** X-rays

raza ['raθa] *nf* race; **~ humana** human race

razón [ra'θon] *nf* reason; (*justicia*) right, justice; (*razonamiento*) reasoning; (*motivo*) reason, motive; (*Mat*) ratio; **a ~ de 10 cada día** at the rate of 10 a day; **en ~ de** with regard to; **dar ~ a algn** to agree that sb is right; **tener/no tener ~** to be right/ wrong; **~ directa/inversa** direct/ inverse proportion; **~ de ser** raison d'être; **razonable** *adj* reasonable; (*justo, moderado*) fair; **razonamiento** *nm* (*juicio*) judgement; (*argumento*) reasoning; **razonar** /1a/ *vt, vi* to reason, argue

re [re] *nm* (*Mus*) D

reacción [reak'θjon] *nf* reaction; **avión a ~** jet plane; **~ en cadena** chain reaction; **reaccionar** /1a/ *vi* to react

reacio, -a [re'aθjo, a] *adj* stubborn

reactivar [reakti'βar] /1a/ *vt* to reactivate

reactor [reak'tor] *nm* reactor

real [re'al] *adj* real; (*del rey, fig*) royal;

realidad [reali'ðað] *nf* reality; (*verdad*) truth

realista [rea'lista] *nmf* realist

realización [realiθa'θjon, a] *nf* fulfilment

realizador, -a [realiθa'ðor, a] *nm/f* film-maker; (*TV etc*) producer

realizar [reali'θar] /1f/ *vt* (*objetivo*) to achieve; (*plan*) to carry out; (*viaje*) to make, undertake; **realizarse** *vr* to come about, come true

realmente [real'mente] *adv* really, actually

realzar [real'θar] /1f/ *vt* to enhance; (*acentuar*) to highlight

reanimar [reani'mar] /1a/ *vt* to revive; (*alentar*) to encourage; **reanimarse** *vr* to revive

reanudar [reanu'ðar] /1a/ *vt* (*renovar*) to renew; (*historia, viaje*) to resume

reaparición [reapari'θjon] *nf* reappearance

rearme [re'arme] *nm* rearmament

rebaja [re'βaxa] *nf* reduction, lowering; (*Com*) discount; **rebajas** *nfpl* (*Com*) sale; **"grandes ~s"** "big

reductions", "sale"; **rebajar** /1a/ vt
(bajar) to lower; (reducir) to reduce;
(disminuir) to lessen; (humillar) to
humble

rebanada [reβa'naða] nf slice
rebañar [reβa'nar] /1a/ vt (comida) to
scrape up; (plato) to scrape clean
rebaño [re'βaɲo] nm herd; (de ovejas)
flock
rebatir [reβa'tir] /3a/ vt to refute
rebeca [re'βeka] nf cardigan
rebelarse [reβe'larse] /1a/ vr to
rebel, revolt
rebelde [re'βelde] adj rebellious;
(niño) unruly ▷ nmf rebel; **rebeldía**
nf rebelliousness; (desobediencia)
disobedience
rebelión [reβe'ljon] nf rebellion
reblandecer [reβlande'θer] /2d/ vt
to soften
rebobinar [reβoβi'nar] /1a/ vt to
rewind
rebosante [reβo'sante] adj: ~ **de** (fig)
brimming o overflowing with
rebosar [reβo'sar] /1a/ vi to overflow;
(abundar) to abound, be plentiful
rebotar [reβo'tar] /1a/ vi to bounce;
(rechazar) to repel ▷ vi (pelota) to
bounce; (bala) to ricochet; **rebote** nm
rebound; **de rebote** on the rebound
rebozado, -a [reβo'θaðo, a] adj fried
in batter o breadcrumbs o flour
rebozar [reβo'θar] /1f/ vt to wrap up;
(Culin) to fry in batter etc
rebuscado, -a [reβus'kaðo, a]
adj (amanerado) affected; (palabra)
recherché; (idea) far-fetched
rebuscar [reβus'kar] /1g/ vi (en
habitación) to search high and low
recado [re'kaðo] nm message;
(encargo) errand; **dejar/tomar un ~**
(Telec) to leave/take a message
recaer [reka'er] /2n/ vi to relapse;
~ en to fall to o on; (criminal etc) to
fall back into, relapse into; **recaída**
nf relapse
recalcar [rekal'kar] /1g/ vt (fig) to
stress, emphasize

recalentar [rekalen'tar] /1j/ vt
(comida) to warm up, reheat;
(demasiado) to overheat
recámara [re'kamara] nf (LAM)
bedroom
recambio [re'kambjo] nm spare; (de
pluma) refill
recapacitar [rekapaθi'tar] /1a/ vi
to reflect
recargado, -a [rekar'ɣaðo, a] adj
overloaded; (exagerado) over-elaborate
recargar [rekar'ɣar] /1h/ vt to
overload; (batería) to recharge; (tarjeta
de móvil) to top up; **recargo** nm
surcharge; (aumento) increase
recatado, -a [reka'taðo, a] adj
(modesto) modest, demure; (prudente)
cautious
recaudación [rekauða'θjon] nf
(acción) collection; (cantidad) takings
pl; (en deporte) gate; **recaudador, a**
nmf tax collector
recepción [reθep'θjon] nf reception;
recepcionista nmf receptionist
receptor, a [reθep'tor, a] nm/f
recipient ▷ nm (Telec) receiver
recesión [reθe'sjon] nf (Com)
recession
receta [re'θeta] nf (Culin) recipe; (Med)
prescription

No confundir receta con la palabra
inglesa receipt.

rechazar [retʃa'θar] /1f/ vt to repel;
(idea) to reject; (oferta) to turn down
rechazo [re'tʃaθo] nm (de propuesta, tb
Med: de un órgano) rejection
rechinar [retʃi'nar] /1a/ vi to creak;
(dientes) to grind
rechistar [retʃis'tar] /1a/ vi: **sin ~**
without complaint
rechoncho, -a [re'tʃontʃo, a]
(fam) thickset (BRIT), heavy-set (US)
rechupete [retʃu'pete]: **de ~** adj
(comida) delicious

recibidor [reθiβi'ðor] nm entrance hall

recibimiento [reθiβi'mjento] nm reception, welcome

recibir [reθi'βir] /3a/ vt to receive; (dar la bienvenida) to welcome ▷ vi to entertain; **recibo** nm receipt

reciclable [reθi'klaβle] adj recyclable

reciclar [reθi'klar] /1a/ vt to recycle

recién [re'θjen] adv recently, newly; **~ casado** newly-wed; **el ~ llegado** the newcomer; **el ~ nacido** the newborn child

reciente [re'θjente] adj recent; (fresco) fresh

recinto [re'θinto] nm enclosure; (área) area, place

recio, -a ['reθjo, a] adj strong, tough; (voz) loud ▷ adv hard; loud(ly)

recipiente [reθi'pjente] nm receptacle

recíproco, -a [re'θiproko, a] adj reciprocal

recital [reθi'tal] nm (Mus) recital; (Lit) reading

recitar [reθi'tar] /1a/ vt to recite

reclamación [reklama'θjon] nf claim, demand; (queja) complaint; **libro de reclamaciones** complaints book

reclamar [rekla'mar] /1a/ vt to claim, demand ▷ vi: **~ contra** to complain about; **reclamo** nm (anuncio) advertisement; (tentación) attraction

reclinar [rekli'nar] /1a/ vt to recline, lean; **reclinarse** vr to lean back

reclusión [reklu'sjon] nf (prisión) prison; (refugio) seclusion

recluta [re'kluta] nmf recruit ▷ nf recruitment; **reclutamiento** nm recruitment; **reclutar** /1a/ vt (datos) to collect; (dinero) to collect up

recobrar [reko'βrar] /1a/ vt (recuperar) to recover; (rescatar) to get back; **recobrarse** vr to recover

recodo [re'koðo] nm (de río, camino) bend

recogedor, a [rekoxe'ðor, a] nm dustpan ▷ nm/f picker, harvester

recoger [reko'xer] /2c/ vt to collect; (Agr) to harvest; (levantar) to pick up; (juntar) to gather; (pasar a buscar) to come for, get; (dar asilo) to give shelter to; (faldas) to gather up; (pelo) to put up; **recogerse** vr (retirarse) to retire; **recogido, -a** adj (lugar) quiet, secluded; (pequeño) small ▷ nf (Correos) collection; (Agr) harvest

recolección [rekolek'θjon] nf (Agr) harvesting; (colecta) collection

recomendación [rekomenda'θjon] nf (sugerencia) suggestion, recommendation; (referencia) reference

recomendar [rekomen'dar] /1j/ vt to suggest, recommend; (confiar) to entrust

recompensa [rekom'pensa] nf reward, recompense; **recompensar** /1a/ vt to reward, recompense

reconciliación [rekonθilja'θjon] nf reconciliation

reconciliar [rekonθi'ljar] /1b/ vt to reconcile; **reconciliarse** vr to become reconciled

recóndito, -a [re'kondito, a] adj (lugar) hidden, secret

reconocer [rekono'θer] /2d/ vt to recognize; (registrar) to search; (Med) to examine; **reconocido, -a** adj (agradecido) grateful; **reconocimiento** nm recognition; (registro) search; (inspección) examination; (gratitud) gratitude; (confesión) admission

reconquista [rekon'kista] nf reconquest; **la R~** the Reconquest (of Spain)

reconstituyente [rekonstitu'jente] nm tonic

reconstruir [rekonstru'ir] /3g/ vt to reconstruct

reconversión [rekomber'sjon] nf restructuring, reorganization; (tb: **~ industrial**) rationalization

recopilación [rekopila'θjon] nf (resumen) summary; (compilación) compilation; **recopilar** [/a/ vt to compile

récord ['rekorð] nm record

recordar [rekor'ðar] /1l/ vt (acordarse de) to remember; (recordar a otro) to remind ▷ vi to remember

No confundir *recordar* con la palabra inglesa *record*.

recorrer [reko'rrer] /2a/ vt (país) to cross, travel through; (distancia) to cover; (registrar) to search; (repasar) to look over; **recorrido** nm run, journey; **tren de largo recorrido** main-line o inter-city (BRIT) train

recortar [rekor'tar] /1a/ vt to cut out; **recorte** nm (acción, de prensa) cutting; (de telas, chapas) trimming; **recorte presupuestario** budget cut

recostar [rekos'tar] /1l/ vt to lean; **recostarse** vr to lie down

recoveco [reko'βeko] nm (de camino, río etc) bend; (en casa) cubbyhole

recreación [rekrea'θjon] nf recreation

recrear [rekre'ar] /1a/ vt (entretener) to entertain; (volver a crear) to recreate; **recreativo, -a** adj recreational; **recreo** nm recreation; (Escol) break, playtime

recriminar [rekrimi'nar] /1a/ vt to reproach ▷ vi to recriminate; **recriminarse** vr to reproach each other

recrudecer [rekruðe'θer] /2d/ vt, vi to worsen; **recrudecerse** vr to worsen

recta ['rekta] nf V **recto**

rectángulo, -a [rek'tangulo, a] adj rectangular ▷ nm rectangle

rectificar [rektifi'kar] /1g/ vt to rectify; (volverse recto) to straighten ▷ vi to correct o.s.

rectitud [rekti'tuð] nf straightness

recto, -a ['rekto, a] adj straight; (persona) honest, upright ▷ nm rectum ▷ nf straight line; **siga todo ~** go straight on

rector, a [rek'tor, a] adj governing

recuadro [re'kwaðro] nm box; (Tip) inset

recubrir [reku'βir] /3a/ vt: **~ (con)** (pintura, crema) to cover (with)

recuento [re'kwento] nm inventory; **hacer el ~ de** to count o reckon up

recuerdo [re'kwerðo] nm souvenir; **recuerdos** nmpl memories; **¡~s a tu madre!** give my regards to your mother!

recular [reku'lar] /1a/ vi to back down

recuperación [rekupera'θjon] nf recovery

recuperar [rekupe'rar] /1a/ vt to recover; (tiempo) to make up; **recuperarse** vr to recuperate

recurrir [reku'rrir] /3a/ vi (Jur) to appeal; **~ a** to resort to; (persona) to turn to; **recurso** nm resort; (medio) means pl, resource; (Jur) appeal; **recursos naturales** natural resources

red [reð] nf net, mesh; (Ferro, Inform) network; (trampa) trap; **la R~** (Internet) the Net; **~es sociales** social networks; (páginas web) social networking sites

redacción [reðak'θjon] nf (acción) writing; (Escol) essay, composition; (limpieza de texto) editing; (personal) editorial staff

redactar [reðak'tar] /1a/ vt to draw up, draft; (periódico) to edit

redactor, a [reðak'tor, a] nm/f editor

redada [re'ðaða] nf: **~ policial** police raid, round-up

rededor [reðe'ðor] nm: **al** o **en ~** around, round about

redoblar [reðo'βlar] /1a/ vt to redouble ▷ vi (tambor) to roll

redonda [re'ðonda] nf V **redondo**

redondear [reðonde'ar] /1a/ vt to round, round off

redondel [reðon'del] nm (círculo) circle; (Taur) bullring, arena

redondo, -a [re'ðondo, a] adj (circular) round; (completo) complete ▷ nf: **a la redonda** around, round about

reducción [reðuk'θjon] nf reduction

reducido, -a [reðu'θiðo, a] adj reduced; (limitado) limited; (pequeño) small

reducir [reðu'θir] /3n/ vt to reduce, limit; **reducirse** vr to diminish

redundancia [reðun'danθja] nf redundancy

reembolsar [re(e)mbol'sar] /1a/ vt (persona) to reimburse; (dinero) to repay, pay back; (depósito) to refund; **reembolso** nm reimbursement; refund

reemplazar [re(e)mpla'θar] /1f/ vt to replace; **reemplazo** nm replacement; **de reemplazo** (Mil) reserve

reencuentro [re(e)n'kwentro] nm reunion

reescribible [reeskri'βiβle] adj rewritable

refacción [refak'θjon] nf repair(s); **refacciones** nfpl (piezas de repuesto) spare parts

referencia [refe'renθja] nf reference; **con ~ a** with reference to

referéndum [refe'rendum] (pl **referéndums**) nm referendum

referente [refe'rente] adj: **~ a** concerning, relating to

réferi ['referi] nmf (LAM) referee

referir [refe'rir] /3i/ vt (contar) to tell, recount; (relacionar) to refer, relate; **referirse** vr: **~se a** to refer to

refilón [refi'lon]: **de ~** adv obliquely

refinado, -a [refi'naðo, a] adj refined

refinar [refi'nar] /1a/ vt to refine; **refinería** nf refinery

reflejar [refle'xar] /1a/ vt to reflect; **reflejo, -a** adj reflected; (movimiento) reflex ▷ nm reflection; (Anat) reflex

reflexión [reflek'sjon] nf reflection; **reflexionar** /1a/ vt to reflect on ▷ vi to reflect; (detenerse) to pause (to think)

reflexivo, -a [reflek'siβo, a] adj thoughtful; (Ling) reflexive

reforma [re'forma] nf reform; (Arq etc) repair; **~ agraria** agrarian reform

reformar [refor'mar] /1a/ vt to reform; (modificar) to change, alter; (Arq) to repair; **reformarse** vr to mend one's ways

reformatorio [reforma'torjo] nm reformatory

reforzar [refor'θar] /1f, 1l/ vt to strengthen; (Arq) to reinforce; (fig) to encourage

refractario, -a [refrak'tarjo, a] adj (Tec) heat-resistant

refrán [re'fran] nm proverb, saying

refregar [refre'ɣar] /1h, 1j/ vt to scrub

refrescante [refres'kante] adj refreshing, cooling

refrescar [refres'kar] /1g/ vt to refresh ▷ vi to cool down; **refrescarse** vr to get cooler; (tomar aire fresco) to go out for a breath of fresh air; (beber) to have a drink

refresco [re'fresko] nm soft drink, cool drink; **"-s"** "refreshments"

refriega etc [re'frjeɣa] nf scuffle, brawl

refrigeración [refrixera'θjon] nf refrigeration; (de casa) air-conditioning

refrigerador [refrixera'ðor] nm refrigerator, icebox (us)

refrigerar [refrixe'rar] /1a/ vt to refrigerate; (sala) to air-condition

refuerzo etc [re'fwerθo] nm reinforcement; (Tec) support

refugiado, -a [refu'xjaðo, a] nm/f refugee

refugiarse [refu'xjarse] /1b/ vr to take refuge, shelter

refugio [re'fuxjo] nm refuge; (protección) shelter

refunfuñar [refunfu'ɲar] /1a/ vi to grunt, growl; (quejarse) to grumble

regadera [reɣa'ðera] nf watering can

regadío [reɣa'ðio] nm irrigated land

regalado, -a [reɣa'laðo, a] adj comfortable, luxurious; (gratis) free, for nothing

regalar [reɣa'lar] /1a/ vt (dar) to give (as a present); (entregar) to give away; (mimar) to pamper, make a fuss of

regaliz [reɣaˈliθ] nm liquorice
regalo [reˈɣalo] nm (obsequio) gift, present; (gusto) pleasure
regañadientes [reɣaɲaˈðjentes]: **a ~** adv reluctantly
regañar [reɣaˈɲar] /1a/ vt to scold ▷ vi to grumble; **regañón, -ona** adj nagging
regar [reˈɣar] /1h, 1j/ vt to water, irrigate; (fig) to scatter, sprinkle
regatear [reɣateˈar] /1a/ vt (Com) to bargain over; (escatimar) to be mean with ▷ vi to bargain, haggle; (Deporte) to dribble; **regateo** nm bargaining, (Deporte) dribbling; (con el cuerpo) swerve, dodge
regazo [reˈɣaθo] nm lap
regenerar [rexeneˈrar] /1a/ vt to regenerate
régimen [ˈreximen] (pl **regímenes**) nm regime; (Med) diet
regimiento [rexiˈmjento] nm regiment
regio, -a [ˈrexjo, a] adj royal, regal; (fig: suntuoso) splendid; (ᴌᴀᴍ fam) great, terrific
región [reˈxjon] nf region
regir [reˈxir] /3c, 3k/ vt to govern, rule; (dirigir) to manage, run ▷ vi to apply, be in force
registrar [rexisˈtrar] /1a/ vt (buscar) to search; (en cajón) to look through; (inspeccionar) to inspect; (anotar) to register, record; (Inform) to log; **registrarse** vr to register; (ocurrir) to happen
registro [reˈxistro] nm (acto) registration; (Mus, libro) register; (inspección) inspection, search; **~ civil** registry office
regla [ˈreɣla] nf (ley) rule, regulation; (de medir) ruler, rule; (Med: período) period; **en ~** in order
reglamentación [reɣlamentaˈθjon] nf (acto) regulation; (lista) rules pl
reglamentar [reɣlamenˈtar] /1a/ vt to regulate; **reglamentario, -a** adj statutory; **reglamento** nm rules pl, regulations pl

regocijarse [reɣoθiˈxarse] /1a/ vr: **~ de o por** to rejoice at; **regocijo** nm joy, happiness
regrabadora [reɣraβaˈðora] nf rewriter; **~ de DVD** DVD rewriter
regresar [reɣreˈsar] /1a/ vi to come/go back, return; **regreso** nm return
reguero [reˈɣero] nm (de sangre) trickle; (de humo) trail
regulador [reɣulaˈðor] nm regulator; (de radio etc) knob, control
regular [reɣuˈlar] /1a/ adj regular; (normal) normal, usual; (común) ordinary; (organizado) regular, orderly; (mediano) average; (fam) not bad, so-so ▷ adv: **estar ~** to be so-so o all right ▷ vt (controlar) to control, regulate; (Tec) to adjust; **por lo ~** as a rule; **regularidad** nf regularity; **regularizar** /1f/ vt to regularize
rehabilitación [reaβilitaˈθjon] nf rehabilitation; (Arq) restoration
rehabilitar [reaβiliˈtar] /1a/ vt to rehabilitate; (Arq) to restore; (reintegrar) to reinstate
rehacer [reaˈθer] /2r/ vt (reparar) to mend, repair; (volver a hacer) to redo, repeat; **rehacerse** vr (Med) to recover
rehén [reˈen] nmf hostage
rehuir [reuˈir] /3g/ vt to avoid, shun
rehusar [reuˈsar] /1a/ vt, vi to refuse
reina [ˈreina] nf queen; **reinado** nm reign
reinar [reiˈnar] /1a/ vi to reign
reincidir [reinθiˈðir] /3a/ vi to relapse
reincorporarse [reinkorpoˈrarse] /1a/ vr: **~ a** to rejoin
reino [ˈreino] nm kingdom; **~ animal/vegetal** animal/plant kingdom; **el R~ Unido** the United Kingdom
reintegrar [reinteˈɣrar] /1a/ vt (reconstituir) to reconstruct; (persona) to reinstate; (dinero) to refund, pay back; **reintegrarse** vr: **~se a** to return to
reír [reˈir] vi to laugh; **reírse** vr to laugh; **~se de** to laugh at

reiterar [reite'rar] /1a/ vt to reiterate

reivindicación [reiβindika'θjon] nf (demanda) claim, demand; (justificación) vindication

reivindicar [reiβindi'kar] /1g/ vt to claim

reja ['rexa] nf (de ventana) grille, bars pl; (en la calle) grating

rejilla [re'xiʎa] nf grating, grille; (muebles) wickerwork; (de ventilación) vent; (de coche etc) luggage rack

rejoneador [rexonea'ðor] nm mounted bullfighter

rejuvenecer [rexuβene'θer] /2d/ vt, vi to rejuvenate

relación [rela'θjon] nf relation, relationship; (narración) report; **relaciones laborales/ públicas** labour/public relations; **con ~ a, en ~ con** in relation to; **relacionar** /1a/ vt to relate, connect; **relacionarse** vr to be connected o linked

relajación [relaxa'θjon] nf relaxation

relajar [rela'xar] /1a/ vt to relax; **relajarse** vr to relax

relamerse [rela'merse] /2a/ vr to lick one's lips

relámpago [re'lampaɣo] nm flash of lightning; **visita/huelga ~** lightning visit/strike

relatar [rela'tar] /1a/ vt to tell, relate

relativo, -a [rela'tiβo, a] adj relative; **en lo ~ a** concerning

relato [re'lato] nm (narración) story, tale

relegar [rele'ɣar] /1h/ vt to relegate

relevante [rele'βante] adj eminent, outstanding

relevar [rele'βar] /1a/ vt (sustituir) to relieve; **relevarse** vr to relay; **~ a algn de un cargo** to relieve sb of his post

relevo [re'leβo] nm relief; **carrera de ~s** relay race

relieve [re'ljeβe] nm (Arte, Tec) relief; (fig) prominence, importance; **bajo ~** bas-relief

religión [reli'xjon] nf religion; **religioso, -a** adj religious ▷ nm/f monk/nun

relinchar [relin'tʃar] /1a/ vi to neigh

reliquia [re'likja] nf relic; **~ de familia** heirloom

rellano [re'ʎano] nm (Arq) landing

rellenar [reʎe'nar] /1a/ vt (llenar) to fill up; (Culin) to stuff; (Costura) to pad; **relleno, -a** adj full up; (Culin) stuffed ▷ nm stuffing; (de tapicería) padding

reloj [re'lo(x)] nm clock; **poner el ~ (en hora)** to set one's watch o the clock; **~ (de pulsera)** (wrist)watch; **~ despertador** alarm (clock); **~ digital** digital watch; **relojero, -a** nm/f clockmaker; watchmaker

reluciente [relu'θjente] adj brilliant, shining

relucir [relu'θir] /3f/ vi to shine; (fig) to excel

remachar [rema'tʃar] /1a/ vt to rivet; (fig) to hammer home, drive home; **remache** nm rivet

remangar [reman'ɡar] /1h/ vt to roll up; **remangarse** vr to roll one's sleeves up

remanso [re'manso] nm pool

remar [re'mar] /1a/ vi to row

rematado, -a [rema'taðo, a] adj complete, utter

rematar [rema'tar] /1a/ vt to finish off; (Com) to sell off cheap ▷ vi to end, finish off; (Deporte) to shoot

remate [re'mate] nm end, finish; (punta) tip; (Deporte) shot; (Arq) top; **de o para ~** to crown it all (BRIT), to top it off

remedar [reme'ðar] /1a/ vt to imitate

remediar [reme'ðjar] /1b/ vt to remedy; (subsanar) to make good, repair; (evitar) to avoid

remedio [re'meðjo] nm remedy; (alivio) relief, help; (Jur) recourse, remedy; **poner ~ a** to correct, stop; **no tener más ~** to have no alternative; **¡qué ~!** there's no choice!; **sin ~** hopeless

remendar [remen'dar] /1j/ vt to repair; (con parche) to patch

remiendo etc [re'mjendo] nm mend; (con parche) patch; (cosido) darn

remilgado, -a [remil'yaðo, a] adj prim; (afectado) affected

remilgo [re'milyo] nm primness

remise [re'miso, a] adj slack, slow

remite [re'mite] nm (en sobre) name and address of sender; **remitente** nmf (Correos) sender; **remitir** /3a/ vt to remit, send ▷ vi to slacken; (en carta): **remite: X** sender: X

remo ['remo] nm (de barco) oar; (Deporte) rowing

remojar [remo'xar] /1a/ vt to steep, soak; (galleta etc) to dip, dunk

remojo [re'moxo] nm: **dejar la ropa en ~** to leave clothes to soak

remolacha [remo'latʃa] nf beet, beetroot (BRIT)

remolcador [remolka'ðor] nm (Naut) tug; (Auto) breakdown lorry

remolcar [remol'kar] /1g/ vt to tow

remolino [remo'lino] nm eddy; (de agua) whirlpool; (de viento) whirlwind; (de gente) crowd

remolque [re'molke] nm tow, towing; (cuerda) towrope; **llevar a ~** to tow

remontar [remon'tar] /1a/ vt to mend; **remontar** vr to soar; **~se a** (Com) to amount to; **~ el vuelo** to soar

remorder [remor'ðer] /2h/ vt to distress, disturb; **~le la conciencia a algn** to have a guilty conscience; **remordimiento** nm remorse

remoto, -a [re'moto, a] adj remote

remover [remo'βer] /2h/ vt to stir; (tierra) to turn over; (objetos) to move round

remuneración [remunera'θjon] nf remuneration

remunerar [remune'rar] /1a/ vt to remunerate; (premiar) to reward

renacer [rena'θer] /2d/ vi to be reborn; (fig) to revive; **renacimiento** nm rebirth; **el Renacimiento** the Renaissance

renacuajo [rena'kwaxo] nm (Zool) tadpole

renal [re'nal] adj renal, kidney cpd

rencilla [ren'θiʎa] nf quarrel

rencor [ren'kor] nm rancour, bitterness; **rencoroso, -a** adj spiteful

rendición [rendi'θjon] nf surrender

rendido, -a [ren'diðo, a] adj (sumiso) submissive; (agotado) worn-out, exhausted

rendija [ren'dixa] nf (hendidura) crack

rendimiento [rendi'mjento] nm (producción) output; (Tec, Com) efficiency

rendir [ren'dir] /3k/ vt (vencer) to defeat; (producir) to produce; (dar beneficio) to yield; (agotar) to exhaust ▷ vi to pay; **rendirse** vr (someterse) to surrender; (cansarse) to wear o.s. out; **~ homenaje** o **culto a** to pay homage to

renegar [rene'yar] /1h, 1j/ vi (blasfemar) to blaspheme; **~ de** (renunciar) to renounce; (quejarse) to complain about

RENFE ['renfe] nf abr = **Red Nacional de Ferrocarriles Españoles**

renglón [ren'glon] nm (línea) line; (Com) item, article; **a ~ seguido** immediately after

renombre [re'nombre] nm renown

renovación [renoβa'θjon] nf (de contrato) renewal; (Arq) renovation

renovar [reno'βar] /1l/ vt to renew; (Arq) to renovate

renta ['renta] nf (ingresos) income; (beneficio) profit; (alquiler) rent; **~ vitalicia** annuity; **rentable** adj profitable

renuncia [re'nunθja] nf resignation; **renunciar** /1b/ vt to renounce, give up ▷ vi to resign; **renunciar a** (tabaco, alcohol etc) to give up; (oferta, oportunidad) to turn down; (puesto) to resign

reñido, -a [re'niðo, a] adj (batalla) bitter, hard-fought; **estar ~ con algn** to be on bad terms with sb

reñir [re'ɲir] /3h, 3k/ vt (regañar) to scold ▷ vi (estar peleado) to quarrel, fall out; (combatir) to fight

reo ['reo] nmf culprit, offender; (Jur) accused

reojo [re'oxo]: **de ~** adv out of the corner of one's eye

reparación [repara'θjon] nf (acto) mending, repairing; (Tec) repair; (fig) amends, reparation

reparador, -a [repara'ðor, a] adj refreshing; (comida) fortifying ▷ nm repairer

reparar [repa'rar] /1a/ vt to repair; (fig) to make amends for; (observar) to observe ▷ vi: **~ en** (darse cuenta de) to notice; (poner atención en) to pay attention to

reparo [re'paro] nm (advertencia) observation; (duda) doubt; (dificultad) difficulty; **poner ~s (a)** to raise objections (to)

repartidor, a [reparti'ðor, a] nm/f distributor

repartir [repar'tir] /3a/ vt to distribute, share out; (Com, Correos) to deliver; **reparto** nm distribution; (Com, Correos) delivery; (Teat, Cine) cast; (LAM: urbanización) housing estate (BRIT), real estate development (US)

repasar [repa'sar] /1a/ vt (Escol) to revise; (Mecánica) to check, overhaul; (Costura) to mend; **repaso** nm revision; (Mecánica) overhaul, checkup; (Costura) mending

repecho [re'petʃo] nm steep incline

repelente [repe'lente] adj repellent, repulsive

repeler [repe'ler] /2a/ vt to repel

repente [re'pente] nm: **de ~** suddenly

repentino, -a [repen'tino, a] adj sudden

repercusión [reperku'sjon] nf repercussion

repercutir [reperku'tir] /3a/ vi (objeto) to rebound; (sonido) to echo;

~ en (fig) to have repercussions o effects on

repertorio [reper'torjo] nm list; (Teat) repertoire

repetición [repeti'θjon] nf repetition

repetir [repe'tir] /3k/ vt to repeat; (plato) to have a second helping of ▷ vi to repeat; (sabor) to come back; **repetirse** vr to repeat o.s.

repetitivo, -a [repeti'tiβo, a] adj repetitive, repetitious

repique [re'pike] nm pealing, ringing; **repiqueteo** nm pealing; (de tambor) drumming

repisa [re'pisa] nf ledge, shelf; **~ de chimenea** mantelpiece; **~ de ventana** windowsill

repito etc vb V **repetir**

replantear [replante'ar] /1a/ vt (cuestión pública) to readdress; **replantearse** vr: **~se algo** to reconsider sth

repleto, -a [re'pleto, a] adj replete, full up

réplica ['replika] nf answer; (Arte) replica

replicar [repli'kar] /1g/ vi to answer; (objetar) to argue, answer back

repliegue [re'pljeɣe] nm (Mil) withdrawal

repoblación [repoβla'θjon] nf repopulation; (de río) restocking; **~ forestal** reafforestation

repoblar [repo'βlar] /1l/ vt to repopulate; (con árboles) to reafforest

repollito [repo'ʎito] nm (LAM): **~s de Bruselas** (Brussels) sprouts

repollo [re'poʎo] nm cabbage

reponer [repo'ner] /2q/ vt to replace, put back; (Teat) to revive; **reponerse** vr to recover; **~ que** to reply that

reportaje [repor'taxe] nm report, article

reportero, -a [repor'tero, a] nm/f reporter

reposacabezas [reposaka'βeθas] nm inv headrest

reposar [repo'sar] /1a/ vi to rest, repose

reposición [reposi'θjon] nf replacement; (Cine) second showing

reposo [re'poso] nm rest

repostar [repos'tar] /1a/ vt to replenish; (Auto) to fill up (with petrol o gasoline)

repostería [reposte'ria] nf confectioner's (shop)

represa [re'presa] nf dam; (lago artificial) lake, pool

represalia [repre'salja] nf reprisal

representación [representa'θjon] nf representation; (Teat) performance; **representante** nmf representative; (Teat) performer

representar [represen'tar] /1a/ vt to represent; (Teat) to perform; (edad) to look; **representarse** vr to imagine; **representativo, -a** adj representative

represión [repre'sjon] nf repression

reprimenda [repri'menda] nf reprimand, rebuke

reprimir [repri'mir] /3a/ vt to repress

reprobar [repro'βar] /1l/ vt to censure, reprove

reprochar [repro'tʃar] /1a/ vt to reproach; **reproche** nm reproach

reproducción [reproduk'θjon] nf reproduction

reproducir [reprodu'θir] /3n/ vt to reproduce; **reproducirse** vr to breed; (situación) to recur

reproductor, a [reproduk'tor, a] adj reproductive ▷ nm: **= de CD** CD player

reptil [rep'til] nm reptile

república [re'puβlika] nf republic; **R~ Dominicana** Dominican Republic; **republicano, -a** adj, nm/f republican

repudiar [repu'ðjar] /1b/ vt to repudiate; (fe) to renounce

repuesto [re'pwesto] nm (pieza de recambio) spare (part); (abastecimiento) supply; **rueda de ~** spare wheel

repugnancia [repuɣ'nanθja] nf repugnance; **repugnante** adj repugnant, repulsive

repugnar [repuɣ'nar] /1a/ vt to disgust

repulsa [re'pulsa] nf rebuff

repulsión [repul'sjon] nf repulsion, aversion; **repulsivo, -a** adj repulsive

reputación [reputa'θjon] nf reputation

requerir [reke'rir] /3i/ vt (pedir) to ask, request; (exigir) to require; (llamar) to send for, summon

requesón [reke'son] nm cottage cheese

requete... [rekete] pref extremely

réquiem ['rekjem] nm requiem

requisito [reki'sito] nm requirement, requisite

res [res] nf beast, animal

resaca [re'saka] nf (en el mar) undertow, undercurrent; (fam) hangover

resaltar [resal'tar] /1a/ vi to project, stick out; (fig) to stand out

resarcir [resar'θir] /3b/ vt to compensate; **resarcirse** vr to make up for

resbaladero [resβala'ðero] nm (ᴌᴀᴍ) slide

resbaladizo, -a [resβala'ðiθo, a] adj slippery

resbalar [resβa'lar] /1a/ vi to slip, slide; (fig) to slip (up); **resbalarse** vr to slip, slide; (fig) to slip (up); **resbalón** nm (acción) slip

rescatar [reska'tar] /1a/ vt (salvar) to save, rescue; (objeto) to get back, recover; (cautivos) to ransom

rescate [res'kate] nm rescue; (de objeto) recovery; **pagar un ~** to pay a ransom

rescindir [resθin'dir] /3a/ vt rescind

rescisión [resθi'sjon] nf cancellation

resecar [rese'kar] /1g/ vt to dry off, dry thoroughly; (Med) to cut out, remove; **resecarse** vr to dry up

reseco, -a [re'seko, a] adj very dry; (fig) skinny

resentido, -a [resen'tiðo, a] adj resentful

resentimiento [resenti'mjento] nm resentment, bitterness

resentirse [resen'tirse] /3i/ vr (debilitarse: persona) to suffer; **~ de** (sufrir las consecuencias de) to feel the effects of; **~ de** o **por algo** to resent sth, be bitter about sth

reseña [re'seɲa] nf (cuenta) account; (informe) report; (Lit) review; **reseñar** /1a/ vt to describe; (Lit) to review

reserva [re'serβa] nf reserve; (reservación) reservation

reservación [reserβa'θjon] nf (LAM) reservation

reservado, -a [reser'βaðo, a] adj reserved; (retraído) cold, distant ▷ nm private room

reservar [reser'βar] /1a/ vt (guardar) to keep; (Ferro, Teat etc) to reserve, book; **reservarse** vr to save o.s.; (callar) to keep to o.s.

resfriado [res'frjaðo] nm cold; **resfriarse** /1c/ vr to cool off; (Med) to catch (a) cold

resguardar [resɣwar'ðar] /1a/ vt to protect, shield; **resguardarse** vr: **~se de** to guard against; **resguardo** nm defence; (vale) voucher; (recibo) receipt, slip

residencia [resi'ðenθja] nf residence; (Univ) hall of residence; **~ para ancianos** o **jubilados** residential home, old people's home; **residencial** adj residential

residente [resi'ðente] adj, nmf resident

residir [resi'ðir] /3a/ vi to reside, live; **~ en** to reside o lie in

residuo [re'siðwo] nm residue

resignación [resiɣna'θjon] nf resignation; **resignarse** /1a/ vr: **resignarse a** o **con** to resign o.s. to, be resigned to

resina [re'sina] nf resin

resistencia [resis'tenθja] nf (dureza) endurance, strength; (oposición, Elec) resistance; **resistente** adj strong, hardy; (Tec) resistant

resistir [resis'tir] /3a/ vt (soportar) to bear; (oponerse a) to resist, oppose; (aguantar) to put up with ▷ vi to resist; (aguantar) to last, endure; **resistirse** vr: **~se a** to refuse to, resist

resoluto, -a [reso'luto, a] adj resolute

resolver [resol'βer] /2h/ vt to resolve; (solucionar) to solve, resolve; (decidir) to decide, settle; **resolverse** vr to make up one's mind

resonar [reso'nar] /1l/ vi to ring, echo

resoplar [reso'plar] /1a/ vi to snort; **resoplido** nm heavy breathing

resorte [re'sorte] nm spring; (fig) lever

resortera [resor'tera] nf (LAM) catapult

respaldar [respal'dar] /1a/ vt to back (up), support; **respaldarse** vr to lean back; **~se con** o **en** (fig) to take one's stand on; **respaldo** nm (de sillón) back; (fig) support, backing

respectivo, -a [respek'tiβo, a] adj respective; **en lo ~ a** with regard to

respecto [res'pekto] nm: **al ~** on this matter; **con ~ a, ~ de** with regard to, in relation to

respetable [respe'taβle] adj respectable

respetar [respe'tar] /1a/ vt to respect; **respeto** nm respect; (acatamiento) deference; **respetos** nmpl respects; **respetuoso, -a** adj respectful

respingo [res'pingo] nm start, jump

respiración [respira'θjon] nf breathing; (Med) respiration; (ventilación) ventilation; **~ asistida** artificial respiration (by machine)

respirar [respi'rar] /1a/ vi to breathe; **respiratorio, -a** adj respiratory; **respiro** nm breathing; (fig: descanso) respite

resplandecer [resplande'θer] /2d/ vi to shine; **resplandeciente** adj resplendent, shining; **resplandor** nm brilliance, brightness; (del fuego) blaze

responder [respon'der] /2a/ vt
to answer ▷ vi to answer; (fig) to
respond; (pey) to answer back; **– de o
por** to answer for; **respondón, -ona**
adj cheeky

responsabilidad [responsaβili'ðað]
nf responsibility

responsabilizarse
[responsaβili'θarse] /1f/ vr to make
o.s. responsible, take charge

responsable [respon'saβle] adj
responsible

respuesta [res'pwesta] nf answer,
reply

resquebrajar [reskeβra'xar] /1a/ vt
to crack, split; **resquebrajarse** vr to
crack, split

resquicio [res'kiθjo] nm chink;
(hendidura) crack

resta ['resta] nf (Mat) remainder

restablecer [restaβle'θer] /2d/ vt to
re-establish, restore; **restablecerse**
vr to recover

restante [res'tante] adj remaining; **lo
– the** remainder

restar [res'tar] /1a/ vt (Mat) to
subtract; (fig) to take away ▷ vi to
remain, be left

restauración [restaura'θjon] nf
restoration

restaurante [restau'rante] nm
restaurant

restaurar [restau'rar] /1a/ vt to
restore

restituir [restitu'ir] /3g/ vt (devolver)
to return, give back; (rehabilitar) to
restore

resto ['resto] nm (residuo) rest,
remainder; (apuesta) stake; **restos**
nmpl remains

restorán [resto'ran] nm (LAM)
restaurant

restregar [restre'ɣar] /1h, 1j/ vt to
scrub, rub

restricción [restrik'θjon] nf
restriction

restringir [restrin'xir] /3c/ vt to
restrict, limit

resucitar [resuθi'tar] /1a/ vt, vi to
resuscitate, revive

resuelto, -a [re'swelto, a] pp de
resolver ▷ adj resolute, determined

resultado [resul'taðo] nm result;
(conclusión) outcome; **resultante** adj
resulting, resultant

resultar [resul'tar] /1a/ vi (ser) to
be; (llegar a ser) to turn out to be;
(salir bien) to turn out well; (Com) to
amount to; **– de** to stem from; **me
resulta difícil hacerlo** it's difficult for
me to do it

resumen [re'sumen] nm summary,
résumé; **en –** in short

resumir [resu'mir] /3a/ vt to sum up;
(cortar) to abridge, cut down

⬛ No confundir resumir con la
palabra inglesa resume.

resurgir [resur'xir] /3c/ vi (reaparecer)
to reappear

resurrección [resurrek'θjon] nf
resurrection

retablo [re'taβlo] nm altarpiece

retaguardia [reta'ɣwarðja] nf
rearguard

retahíla [reta'ila] nf series, string

retal [re'tal] nm remnant

retar [re'tar] /1a/ vt to challenge;
(desafiar) to defy, dare

retazo [re'taθo] nm snippet (BRIT),
fragment

retención [reten'θjon] nf (tráfico)
hold-up; **– fiscal** deduction for tax
purposes

retener [rete'ner] /2k/ vt (intereses)
to withhold

reticente [reti'θente] adj (insinuador)
insinuating; (postura) reluctant; **ser
– a hacer algo** to be reluctant o
unwilling to do sth

retina [re'tina] nf retina

retintín [retin'tin] nm jangle,
jingle; **decir algo con –** to say sth
sarcastically

retirado, -a adj (lugar) remote; (vida)
quiet; (jubilado) retired ▷ nf (Mil)
retreat; (de dinero) withdrawal; (de

embajador) recall; **batirse en retirada** to retreat

retirar [reti'rar] /1a/ vt to withdraw; (*quitar*) to remove; (*jubilar*) to retire, pension off; **retirarse** vr to retreat, withdraw; (*jubilarse*) to retire; (*acostarse*) to retire, go to bed; **retiro** nm retreat; (*jubilación*) retirement; (*pago*) pension

reto ['reto] nm dare, challenge

retocar [reto'kar] /1g/ vt (*fotografía*) to touch up, retouch

retoño [re'toɲo] nm sprout, shoot; (*fig*) offspring, child

retoque [re'toke] nm retouching

retorcer [retor'θer] /2b, 2h/ vt to twist; (*manos, lavado*) to wring; **retorcerse** vr to become twisted; (*persona*) to writhe

retorcido, -a [retor'θiðo, a] adj (tb fig) twisted

retorcijón [retorθi'xon] nm (LAM: tb: **~ de tripas**) stomach cramp

retorno [re'torno] nm return

retortijón [retorti'xon] nm: **~ de tripas** stomach cramp

retozar [reto'θar] /1f/ vi (*juguetear*) to frolic, romp; (*saltar*) to gambol

retracción [retrak'θjon] nf retraction

retraerse [retra'erse] /2o/ vr to retreat, withdraw; **retraído, -a** adj shy, retiring; **retraimiento** nm retirement; (*timidez*) shyness

retransmisión [retransmi'sjon] nf repeat (broadcast)

retransmitir [retransmi'tir] /3a/ vt (*mensaje*) to relay; (*TV etc*) to repeat, retransmit; (: *en vivo*) to broadcast live

retrasado, -a [retra'saðo, a] adj (*Med*) mentally retarded; (*país etc*) backward, underdeveloped

retrasar [retra'sar] /1a/ vt (*demorar*) to postpone, put off; (*retardar*) to slow down ▷ vi (*atrasarse*) to be late; (*reloj*) to be slow; (*producción*) to fall (off); (*quedarse atrás*) to lag behind; **retrasarse** vr to be late; to be slow; to fall (off); to lag behind

retraso [re'traso] nm (*demora*) delay; (*lentitud*) slowness; (*tardanza*) lateness; (*atraso*) backwardness; **retrasos** nmpl (*Com*) arrears; **llegar con ~** to arrive late; **~ mental** mental deficiency

retratar [retra'tar] /1a/ vt (*Arte*) to paint the portrait of; (*fotografiar*) to photograph; (*fig*) to depict, describe; **retrato** nm portrait; (*fig*) likeness; **retrato-robot** nm Identikit® picture

retrete [re'trete] nm toilet

retribuir [retriβu'ir] /3g/ vt (*recompensar*) to reward; (*pagar*) to pay

retro... [retro] pref retro...

retroceder [retroθe'ðer] /2a/ vi (*echarse atrás*) to move back(wards); (*fig*) to back down

retroceso [retro'θeso] nm backward movement; (*Med*) relapse; (*fig*) backing down

retrospectivo, -a [retrospek'tiβo, a] adj retrospective

retrovisor [retroβi'sor] nm rear-view mirror

retumbar [retum'bar] /1a/ vi to echo, resound

reuma ['reuma] nm rheumatism

reunión [reu'njon] nf (*asamblea*) meeting; (*fiesta*) party

reunir [reu'nir] /3a/ vt (*juntar*) to reunite, join (together); (*recoger*) to gather (together); (*personas*) to bring o get together; (*cualidades*) to combine; **reunirse** vr (*personas: en asamblea*) to meet, gather

revalidar [reβali'ðar] /1a/ vt (*ratificar*) to confirm, ratify

revalorizar [reβalori'θar] /1f/ vt to revalue, reassess

revancha [re'βantʃa] nf revenge

revelación [reβela'θjon] nf revelation

revelado [reβe'laðo] nm developing

revelar [reβe'lar] /1a/ vt to reveal; (*Foto*) to develop

reventa [re'βenta] nf (*de entradas*) touting

reventar [reβen'tar] /1j/ vt to burst,
explode

reventón [reβen'ton] nm (Auto)
blow-out (BRIT), flat (US)

reverencia [reβe'renθja] nf
reverence; **reverenciar** /1b/ vt to
revere

reverendo, -a [reβe'rendo, a] adj
reverend

reverente [reβe'rente] adj reverent

reversa [re'βersa] nf (LAM) (reverse)
gear

reversible [reβer'siβle] adj reversible

reverso [re'βerso] nm back, other
side; (de moneda) reverse

revertir [reβer'tir] /3i/ vi to revert

revés [re'βes] nm back, wrong side;
(fig) reverse, setback; (Deporte)
backhand; **al ~** the wrong way round;
(de arriba abajo) upside down; (ropa)
inside out; **volver algo del ~** to turn
sth round; (ropa) to turn sth inside out

revisar [reβi'sar] /1a/ vt (examinar) to
check; (texto etc) to revise; **revisión**
nf revision; **revisión salarial** wage
review

revisor, a [reβi'sor, a] nm/f inspector;
(Ferro) ticket collector

revista [re'βista] nf magazine,
review; (Teat) revue; (inspección)
inspection; **~ del corazón** magazine
featuring celebrity gossip and real-life
romance stories; **pasar ~ a** to review,
inspect

revivir [reβi'βir] /3a/ vi to revive

revolcar [reβol'kar] /1g, 1l/ vt to
knock down; **revolcarse** vr to roll
about

revoltijo [reβol'tixo] nm mess,
jumble

revoltoso, -a [reβol'toso, a] adj
(travieso) naughty, unruly

revolución [reβolu'θjon] nf
revolution; **revolucionario, -a** adj,
nm/f revolutionary

revolver [reβol'βer] /2h/ vt
(desordenar) to disturb, mess up; (mover)
to move about ▷ vi: **~ en** to go through,

rummage (about) in; **revolverse** vr:
~se contra to turn on o against

revólver [re'βolβer] nm revolver

revuelo [re'βwelo] nm fluttering; (fig)
commotion

revuelto, -a [re'βwelto, a] pp de
revolver ▷ adj (mezclado) mixed-up, in
disorder ▷ nf (motín) revolt; (agitación)
commotion

rey [rei] nm king; **Día de R~es** Twelfth
Night; **los R~es Magos** the Three
Wise Men, the Magi

reyerta [re'jerta] nf quarrel, brawl

rezagado, -a [reθa'γaðo, a] nm/f
straggler

rezar [re'θar] /1f/ vi to pray; **~ con**
(fam) to concern, have to do with; **rezo**
nm prayer

rezumar [reθu'mar] /1a/ vt to ooze

ría ['ria] nf estuary

riada [ri'aða] nf flood

ribera [ri'βera] nf (de río) bank; (: área)
riverside

ribete [ri'βete] nm (de vestido) border;
(fig) addition

ricino [ri'θino] nm: **aceite de ~**
castor oil

rico, -a ['riko, a] adj (adinerado) rich;
(lujoso) luxurious; (comida) delicious;
(niño) lovely, cute ▷ nm/f rich person

ridículo, -a [ri'ðikuleθ] nf absurdity

ridiculizar [riðikuli'θar] /1f/ vt to
ridicule

ridículo, -a [ri'ðikulo, a] adj
ridiculous; **hacer el ~** to make a fool
of o.s.; **poner a algn en ~** to make
a fool of sb

riego ['rjeɣo] nm (aspersión) watering;
(irrigación) irrigation; **~ sanguíneo**
blood flow o circulation

riel [rjel] nm rail

rienda ['rjenda] nf rein; **dar ~ suelta
a** to give free rein to

riesgo ['rjesɣo] nm risk; **correr el ~ de**
to run the risk of

rifa ['rifa] nf (lotería) raffle; **rifar** /1a/
vt to raffle

rifle ['rifle] nm rifle

rigidez [rixi'ðeθ] nf rigidity, stiffness;
(fig) strictness; **rígido, -a** adj rigid,
stiff; (moralmente) strict, inflexible

rigor [ri'ɣor] nm strictness, rigour;
(inclemencia) harshness; **de ~** de
rigueur, essential; **riguroso, -a** adj
rigorous; (Meteorología) harsh; (severo)
severe

rimar [ri'mar] /1a/ vi to rhyme

rimbombante [rimbom'bante] adj
pompous

rímel, rímmel ['rimel] nm mascara

rímmel ['rimel] nm = **rímel**

rin [rin] nm (LAM) (wheel) rim

rincón [riŋ'kon] nm corner (inside)

rinoceronte [rinoθe'ronte] nm
rhinoceros

riña ['riɲa] nf (disputa) argument;
(pelea) brawl

riñón [ri'ɲon] nm kidney

río ['rio] vb V **reír** ▷ nm river; (fig)
torrent, stream; **~ abajo/arriba**
downstream/upstream; **R~ de la
Plata** River Plate

rioja ['rioxa] nm rioja wine ▷ nf: **La
R~** La Rioja

rioplatense [riopla'tense] adj de o
from the River Plate region

riqueza [ri'keθa] nf wealth, riches pl;
(cualidad) richness

risa ['risa] nf laughter; (una risa) laugh;
¡qué ~! what a laugh!

risco ['risko] nm crag, cliff

ristra ['ristra] nf string

risueño, -a [ri'sweɲo, a] adj
(sonriente) smiling; (contento) cheerful

ritmo ['ritmo] nm rhythm; **a ~ lento**
slowly; **trabajar a ~ lento** to go slow;
~ cardíaco heart rate

rito ['rito] nm rite

ritual [ri'twal] adj, nm ritual

rival [ri'βal] adj, nmf rival; **rivalidad** nf
rivalry; **rivalizar** /1f/ vi: **rivalizar con**
to rival, vie with

rizado, -a [ri'θaðo, a] adj curly ▷ nm
curls pl

rizar [ri'θar] /1f/ vt to curl; **rizarse** vr (el
pelo) to curl; (agua) to ripple; **rizo** nm
curl; (en agua) ripple

RNE nf abr = **Radio Nacional de
España**

robar [ro'βar] /1a/ vt to rob; (objeto) to
steal; (casa etc) to break into; (Naipes)
to draw

roble [ro'βle] nm oak; **robledal** nm
oakwood

robo ['roβo] nm robbery, theft

robot adj, nm robot ▷ nm (tb: **~ de
cocina**) food processor

robustecer [roβuste'θer] /2d/ vt to
strengthen

robusto, -a [ro'βusto, a] adj robust,
strong

roca ['roka] nf rock

roce ['roθe] nm (caricia) brush; (Tec)
friction; (en la piel) graze; **tener ~ con**
to have a brush with

rociar [ro'θjar] /1c/ vt to sprinkle,
spray

rocín [ro'θin] nm nag, hack

rocío [ro'θio] nm dew

rocola [ro'kola] nf (LAM) jukebox

rocoso, -a [ro'koso, a] adj rocky

rodaballo [roða'βaʎo] nm turbot

rodaja [ro'ðaxa] nf slice

rodaje [ro'ðaxe] nm (Cine) shooting,
filming; (Auto): **en ~** running in

rodar [ro'ðar] /1l/ vt (vehículo) to wheel
(along); (escalera) to roll down; (viajar
por) to travel (over) ▷ vi to roll; (coche)
to go, run; (Cine) to shoot, film

rodear [roðe'ar] /1a/ vt to surround
▷ vi to go round; **rodearse** vr: **~se de amigos** to surround o.s. with friends

rodeo [ro'ðeo] nm (desvío) detour; (evasión) evasion; (Am) rodeo; **hablar sin ~s** to come to the point, speak plainly

rodilla [ro'ðiʎa] nf knee; **de ~s** kneeling; **ponerse de ~s** to kneel (down)

rodillo [ro'ðiʎo] nm roller; (Culin) rolling-pin

roedor, -a [roe'ðor, a] adj gnawing ▷ nm rodent

roer [ro'er] /2y/ vt (masticar) to gnaw; (corroer, fig) to corrode

rogar [ro'ɣar] /1h, 1l/ vt (pedir) to beg, ask for ▷ vi (suplicar) to beg, plead; **rogarse** vr: **se ruega no fumar** please do not smoke

rojizo, -a [ro'xiθo, a] adj reddish

rojo, -a ['roxo, a] adj red ▷ nm red; **al ~ vivo** red-hot

rol [rol] nm list, role; (papel) role

rollito [ro'ʎito] nm (tb: **~ de primavera**) spring roll

rollizo, -a [ro'ʎiθo, a] adj (objeto) cylindrical; (persona) plump

rollo ['roʎo] nm roll; (de cuerda) coil; (de madera) log; (fam) bore; **¡qué ~!** what a carry-on!

Roma ['roma] nf Rome

romance [ro'manθe] nm (amoroso) romance; (Lit) ballad

romano, -a [ro'mano, a] adj Roman ▷ nm/f Roman; **a la romana** in batter

romanticismo [romanti'θismo] nm romanticism

romántico, -a [ro'mantiko, a] adj romantic

rombo ['rombo] nm (Mat) rhombus

romería [rome'ria] nf (Rel) pilgrimage; (excursión) trip, outing

● **ROMERÍA**

● Originally a pilgrimage to a shrine
● or church to express devotion to

● Our Lady or a local Saint, the *romería*
● has also become a rural *fiesta* which
● accompanies the pilgrimage.
● People come from all over to attend,
● bringing their own food and drink,
● and spend the day in celebration.

romero, -a [ro'mero, a] nm/f pilgrim ▷ nm rosemary

romo, -a ['romo, a] adj blunt; (fig) dull

rompecabezas [rompeka'βeθas] nm inv riddle, puzzle; (juego) jigsaw (puzzle)

rompehuelgas [rompe'welɣas] nm inv (Am) strikebreaker, scab

rompeolas [rompe'olas] nm inv breakwater

romper [rom'per] /2a/ vt to break; (hacer pedazos) to smash; (papel, tela etc) to tear, rip ▷ vi (olas) to break; (sol, diente) to break through; **~ un contrato** to break a contract; **~ a** to start (suddenly) to; **~ a llorar** to burst into tears; **~ con algn** to fall out with sb

ron [ron] nm rum

roncar [ron'kar] /1g/ vi to snore

ronco, -a ['ronko, a] adj (afónico) hoarse; (áspero) raucous

ronda ['ronda] nf (de bebidas etc) round; (patrulla) patrol; **rondar** /1a/ vt to patrol ▷ vi to patrol; (fig) to prowl round

ronquido [ron'kiðo] nm snore, snoring

ronronear [ronrone'ar] /1a/ vi to purr

roña ['roɲa] nf (en veterinaria) mange; (mugre) dirt, grime; (óxido) rust

roñoso, -a [ro'ɲoso, a] adj (mugriento) filthy; (tacaño) mean

ropa ['ropa] nf clothes pl, clothing; **~ blanca** linen; **~ de cama** bed linen; **~ de color** coloureds pl; **~ interior** underwear; **~ sucia** dirty clothes pl, dirty washing; **ropaje** nm gown, robes pl

ropero [ro'pero] nm linen cupboard; (guardarropa) wardrobe

rosa ['rosa] adj inv pink ▷ nf rose

rosado, -a [ro'saðo, a] adj pink ▷ nm rosé

rosal [ro'sal] nm rosebush

rosario [ro'sarjo] nm (Rel) rosary; **rezar el ~** to say the rosary

rosca ['roska] nf (de tornillo) thread; (de humo) coil, spiral; (pan, postre) ring-shaped roll/pastry

rosetón [rose'ton] nm rosette; (Arq) rose window

rosquilla [ros'kiʎa] nf ring-shaped cake

rostro ['rostro] nm (cara) face

rotativo, -a [rota'tiβo, a] adj rotary

roto, -a ['roto, a] pp de **romper** ▷ adj broken

rotonda [ro'tonda] nf roundabout

rótula ['rotula] nf kneecap; (Tec) ball-and-socket joint

rotulador [rotula'ðor] nm felt-tip pen

rótulo ['rotulo] nm heading, title; (etiqueta) label; (letrero) sign

rotundamente [rotunda'mente] adv (negar) flatly; (responder, afirmar) emphatically; **rotundo, -a** adj round; (enfático) emphatic

rotura [ro'tura] nf (rompimiento) breaking; (Med) fracture

rozadura [roθa'ðura] nf abrasion, graze

rozar [ro'θar] /f/ vt (frotar) to rub; (arañar) to scratch; (tocar ligeramente) to shave; **rozarse** vr to rub (together); **~ con** (fam) to rub shoulders with

Rte. abr = **remite; remitente**

RTVE nf abr = **Radiotelevisión Española**

rubí [ru'βi] nm ruby; (de reloj) jewel

rubio, -a ['ruβjo, a] adj fair-haired, blond(e) ▷ nm/f blond/blonde; **tabaco ~** Virginia tobacco

rubor [ru'βor] nm (sonrojo) blush; (timidez) bashfulness; **ruborizarse** /f/ vr to blush

rúbrica ['ruβrika] nf (de la firma) flourish; **rubricar** /1g/ vt (firmar) to

sign with a flourish; (concluir) to sign and seal

rudimentario, -a [ruðimen'tarjo, a] adj rudimentary

rudo, -a ['ruðo, a] adj (sin pulir) unpolished; (grosero) coarse; (violento) violent; (sencillo) simple

rueda ['rweða] nf wheel; (círculo) ring, circle; (rodaja) slice, round; **~ de auxilio** (LAM) spare tyre; **~ delantera/trasera/de repuesto** front/back/spare wheel; **~ de prensa** press conference; **~ gigante** (LAM) big (BRIT) o Ferris (US) wheel

ruedo etc ['rweðo] vb V **rogar** ▷ nm (círculo) circle; (Taur) arena, bullring

ruego etc ['rweɣo] vb V **rogar** ▷ nm request

rugby ['ruɣβi] nm rugby

rugido [ru'xiðo] nm roar

rugir [ru'xir] /3c/ vi to roar

rugoso, -a [ru'ɣoso, a] adj (arrugado) wrinkled; (áspero) rough; (desigual) ridged

ruido ['rwiðo] nm noise; (sonido) sound; (alboroto) racket, row; (escándalo) commotion, rumpus; **ruidoso, -a** adj noisy, loud; (fig) sensational

ruin [rwin] adj contemptible, mean

ruina ['rwina] nf ruin; (hundimiento) collapse; (de persona) ruin, downfall

ruinoso, -a [rwi'noso, a] adj ruinous; (destartalado) dilapidated, tumbledown; (Com) disastrous

ruiseñor [rwise'ɲor] nm nightingale

rulero [ru'lero] nm (LAM) roller

ruleta [ru'leta] nf roulette

rulo ['rulo] nm (para el pelo) curler

Rumanía [ru'manja] nf Rumania

rumba ['rumba] nf rumba

rumbo ['rumbo] nm (ruta) route, direction; (ángulo de dirección) course, bearing; (fig) course of events; **ir con ~ a** to be heading for

rumiante [ru'mjante] nm ruminant

rumiar [ru'mjar] /1b/ vt to chew; (fig) to chew over ▷ vi to chew the cud

rumor [ru'mor] *nm* (ruido sordo) low
sound; (murmuración) murmur, buzz;
rumorearse /1a/ *vr*: **se rumorea que**
it is rumoured that
rupestre [ru'pestre] *adj* rock *cpd*
ruptura [rup'tura] *nf* rupture
rural [ru'ral] *adj* rural
Rusia ['rusja] *nf* Russia; **ruso, -a** *adj,*
nm/f Russian
rústico, -a ['rustiko, a] *adj* rustic;
(ordinario) coarse, uncouth ▷ *nm/f*
yokel
ruta ['ruta] *nf* route
rutina [ru'tina] *nf* routine

S

S *abr* (= san, santo, a) St.; (= sur) S
s. *abr* (= siglo) c.; (= siguiente) foll.
S.A. *abr* (= Sociedad Anónima) Ltd.,
Inc. (us)
sábado ['saβaðo] *nm* Saturday
sábana ['saβana] *nf* sheet
sabañón [saβa'ɲon] *nm* chilblain
saber [sa'βer] /2m/ *vt* to know; (llegar
a conocer) to find out, learn; (tener
capacidad de) to know how to ▷ *vi*: **~ a**
to taste of, taste like ▷ *nm* knowledge,
learning; **a ~** namely; **¿sabes
conducir/nadar?** can you drive/swim?;
¿sabes francés? do you o can you speak
French?; **~ de memoria** to know by
heart; **hacer ~** to inform, let know
sabiduría [saβiðu'ria] *nf*
(conocimientos) wisdom; (instrucción)
learning
sabiendas [sa'βjendas]: **a ~** *adv*
knowingly
sabio, -a ['saβjo, a] *adj* (docto)
learned; (prudente) wise, sensible

sabor [sa'βor] nm taste, flavour;
saborear/1a/ vt to taste, savour;
(fig) to relish

sabotaje [saβo'taxe] nm sabotage

sabré etc [sa'βre] vb V **saber**

sabroso, -a [sa'βroso, a] adj tasty;
(fig: fam) racy, salty

sacacorchos [saka'kortʃos] nm inv
corkscrew

sacapuntas [saka'puntas] nm inv
pencil sharpener

sacar [sa'kar] /1g/ vt to take out;
(fig: extraer) to get (out); (picar) to
remove, get out; (hacer salir) to bring
out; (conclusión) to draw; (novela etc)
to publish, bring out; (ropa) to take
off; (obra) to make; (premio) to receive;
(entradas) to get; (Tenis) to serve; **~
adelante** (niño) to bring up; (negocio)
to carry on, go on with; **~ una
bailar** to get sb up to dance; **~ una
foto** to take a photo; **~ la lengua** to
stick out one's tongue; **~ buenas/
malas notas** to get good/bad marks

sacarina [saka'rina] nf saccharin(e)

sacerdote [saθer'ðote] nm priest

saciar [sa'θjar] /1b/ vt to satisfy;
saciarse vr (de comida) to get full up

saco [sako] nm bag; (grande) sack;
(contenido) bagful; (am: chaqueta)
jacket; **~ de dormir** sleeping bag

sacramento [sakra'mento] nm
sacrament

sacrificar [sakrifi'kar] /1g/ vt to
sacrifice; **sacrificio** nm sacrifice

sacristía [sakris'tia] nf sacristy

sacudida [saku'ðiða] nf (agitación)
shake, shaking; (sacudimiento) jolt,
bump; **~ eléctrica** electric shock

sacudir [saku'ðir] /3a/ vt to shake;
(golpear) to hit

Sagitario [saxi'tarjo] nm Sagittarius

sagrado, -a [sa'ɣraðo, a] adj sacred,
holy

Sáhara ['saara] nm: **el ~ the** Sahara
(desert)

sal [sal] vb V **salir** ▷ nf salt; **~es de
baño** bath salts

sala ['sala] nf large room; (tb: **~ de
estar**) living room; (Teat) house,
auditorium; (de hospital) ward; **~ de
espera** waiting room; **~ de estar**
living room

salado, -a [sa'laðo, a] adj salty;
(fig) witty, amusing; **agua salada**
salt water

salar [sa'lar] /1a/ vt to salt, add salt to

salariado, -a adj (empleado) salaried

salario [sa'larjo] nm wage, pay

salchicha [sal'tʃitʃa] nf (pork)
sausage; **salchichón** nm (salami-
type) sausage

saldo ['saldo] nm (pago) settlement;
(de una cuenta) balance; (lo restante)
remnant(s) (pl), remainder; (de móvil)
credit; **saldos** nmpl (en tienda) sale

saldré etc V **saldre** [sal'dre] nm

salero [sa'lero] nm salt cellar

salgo etc vb V **salir**

salida [sa'liða] nf (puerta etc) exit, way
out; (acto) leaving, going out; (de tren,
Aviat) departure; (Com, Tec) output,
production; (fig) way out; (Com)
opening; (Geo, válvula) outlet; (de gas)
leak; **calle sin ~** cul-de-sac; **~ de
baño** (lam) bathrobe; **~ de incendios**
fire escape

○ PALABRA CLAVE

salir [sa'lir] /3q/ vi **1** to leave; **Juan ha
salido** Juan has gone out; **salió de la
cocina** he came out of the kitchen
2 (disco, libro) to come out; **anoche
salió en la tele** she appeared on was
on TV last night; **salió en todos los
periódicos** it was in all the papers
3 (resultar): **la muchacha nos salió
muy trabajadora** the girl turned out
to be a very hard worker; **la comida
te ha salido exquisita** the food was
delicious; **sale muy caro** it's very
expensive
4: **salir adelante: no sé como haré
para salir adelante** I don't know
how I'll get by

▸ **salirse** vr (líquido) to spill; (animal) to escape

saliva [sa'liβa] nf saliva

salmo ['salmo] nm psalm

salmón [sal'mon] nm salmon

salmonete [salmo'nete] nm red mullet

salón [sa'lon] nm (de casa) living-room, lounge; (muebles) lounge suite; **~ de belleza** beauty parlour; **~ de baile** dance hall; **~ de actos/sesiones** assembly hall

salpicadera [salpika'ðera] nf (LAM) mudguard (BRIT), fender (US)

salpicadero [salpika'ðero] nm (Auto) dashboard

salpicar [salpi'kar] /1g/ vt (rociar) to sprinkle, spatter; (esparcir) to scatter

salpicón [salpi'kon] nm (tb: **~ de marisco**) seafood salad

salsa ['salsa] nf sauce; (con carne asada) gravy; (fig) spice

saltamontes [salta'montes] nm inv grasshopper

saltar [sal'tar] /1a/ vt to jump (over), leap (over); (dejar de lado) to skip, miss out ▷ vi to jump, leap; (pelota) to bounce; (al aire) to fly up; (quebrarse) to break; (al agua) to dive; (fig) to explode, blow up

salto ['salto] nm jump, leap; (al agua) dive; **~ de agua** waterfall; **~ de altura** high jump

salud [sa'luð] nf health; **¡(a su) ~!** cheers!, good health!; **saludable** adj (de buena salud) healthy; (provechoso) good, beneficial

saludar [salu'ðar] /1a/ vt to greet; (Mil) to salute; **saludo** nm greeting; **saludos** (en carta) best wishes, regards

salvación [salβa'θjon] nf salvation; (rescate) rescue

salvado [sal'βaðo] nm bran

salvaje [sal'βaxe] adj wild; (tribu) savage

salvamanteles [salβaman'teles] nm inv table mat

salvamento [salβa'mento] nm rescue

salvapantallas [salβapan'taλas] nm inv screensaver

salvar [sal'βar] /1a/ vt (rescatar) to save, rescue; (resolver) to overcome, resolve; (cubrir distancias) to travel; (hacer excepción) to except, exclude; (un barco) to salvage

salvavidas [salβa'βiðas] adj inv: **bote/chaleco/cinturón ~** lifeboat/lifejacket/lifebelt

salvo, -a ['salβo, a] adj safe ▷ prep except (for), save; **a ~** out of danger; **~ que** unless

san [san] n saint; **~ Juan** St. John

sanar [sa'nar] /1a/ vt (herida) to heal; (persona) to cure ▷ vi (persona) to get well, recover; (herida) to heal

sanatorio [sana'torjo] nm sanatorium

sanción [san'θjon] nf sanction

sancochado, -a [sanko'tʃaðo, a] adj (LAM Culin) underdone, rare

sandalia [san'dalja] nf sandal

sandía [san'dia] nf watermelon

sándwich ['sandwitʃ] (pl **sándwichs** o **sandwiches**) nm sandwich

Sanfermines [sanfer'mines] nmpl festivities in celebration of San Fermín

sangrar [san'grar] /1a/ vt, vi to bleed; **sangre** nf blood

sangría [san'gria] nf sangria (sweetened drink of red wine with fruit)

sangriento, -a [san'grjento, a] adj bloody

sanguíneo, -a [san'gineo, a] adj blood cpd

sanidad [sani'ðað] nf: **~ pública** public health (department)

San Isidro [sani'siðro] nm patron saint of Madrid

- **SAN ISIDRO**
-
- San Isidro is the patron saint of
- Madrid, giving his name to
- the week-long festivities which
- take place around the 15th May.
- Originally an 18th-century trade
- fair, the San Isidro celebrations
- now include music, dance, a
- famous romería, theatre and
- bullfighting.

sanitario, -a [sani'tarjo, a] adj health cpd; **sanitarios** nmpl toilets (BRIT), restroom sg (US)

sano, -a ['sano, a] adj healthy; (sin daños) sound; (comida) wholesome; (entero) whole, intact; **~ y salvo** safe and sound

⚠ No confundir sano con la palabra inglesa sane.

Santiago [san'tjaɣo] nm: **~ (de Chile)** Santiago

santiamén [santja'men] nm: **en un ~** in no time at all

santidad [santi'ðað] nf holiness, sanctity

santiguarse [santi'ɣwarse] /1i/ vr to make the sign of the cross

santo, -a ['santo, a] adj holy; (fig) wonderful, miraculous ▷ nm/f saint ▷ nm saint's day; **~ y seña** password

santuario [san'twarjo] nm sanctuary, shrine

sapo ['sapo] nm toad

saque ['sake] nm (Tenis) service, serve; (Fútbol) throw-in; **~ de esquina** corner (kick)

saquear [sake'ar] /1a/ vt (Mil) to sack; (robar) to loot, plunder; (fig) to ransack

sarampión [saram'pjon] nm measles sg

sarcástico, -a [sar'kastiko, a] adj sarcastic

sardina [sar'ðina] nf sardine

sargento [sar'xento] nm sergeant

sarmiento [sar'mjento] nm vine shoot

sarna ['sarna] nf itch; (Med) scabies

sarpullido [sarpu'ʎiðo] nm (Med) rash

sarro ['sarro] nm (en dientes) tartar, plaque

sartén [sar'ten] nf frying pan

sastre ['sastre] nm tailor; **sastrería** nf (arte) tailoring; (tienda) tailor's (shop)

Satanás [sata'nas] nm Satan

satélite [sa'telite] nm satellite

sátira ['satira] nf satire

satisfacción [satisfak'θjon] nf satisfaction

satisfacer [satisfa'θer] /2r/ vt to satisfy; (gastos) to meet; (pérdida) to make good; **satisfacerse** vr to satisfy o.s., be satisfied; (vengarse) to take revenge; **satisfecho, -a** adj satisfied; (contento) content(ed), happy; (tb: **satisfecho de sí mismo**) self-satisfied, smug

saturar [satu'rar] /1a/ vt to saturate; **saturarse** vr (mercado, aeropuerto) to reach saturation point

sauce ['sauθe] nm willow; **~ llorón** weeping willow

sauna ['sauna] nf sauna

savia ['saβja] nf sap

saxofón [sakso'fon] nm saxophone

sazonar [saθo'nar] /1a/ vt to ripen; (Culin) to flavour, season

scooter [e'skuter] nf (ESP) scooter

Scotch® [skotʃ] nm (LAM) Sellotape® (BRIT), Scotch tape® (US)

SE abr (= sudeste) SE

PALABRA CLAVE

se [se] *pron* 1 (*reflexivo: sg: m*) himself;
(: *f*) herself; (: *pl*) themselves; (: *cosa*)
itself; (: *de Vd*) yourself; (: *de Vds*)
yourselves; **se está preparando** she's
getting (herself) ready
2 (*como complemento indirecto*) to him;
to her; to them; to it; to you; **se lo**
dije ayer (*a Vd*) I told you yesterday;
se compró un sombrero he bought
himself a hat; **se rompió la pierna** he
broke his leg
3 (*uso recíproco*) each other, one
another; **se miraron (el uno al**
otro) they looked at each other *o* one
another
4 (*en oraciones pasivas*): **se han**
vendido muchos libros a lot of books
have been sold
5 (*impers*): **se dice que** people say
that, it is said that; **allí se come muy**
bien the food there is very good, you
can eat very well there

sé [se] *vb V* **saber**; **ser**
sea *etc* [ˈsea] *vb V* **ser**
sebo [ˈseβo] *nm* fat, grease
secador, **-a** [sekaˈðor] *nm*: **~ para el**
pelo hairdryer
secadora [sekaˈðora] *nf* tumble dryer
secar [seˈkar] /1g/ *vt* to dry; **secarse**
vr to dry (off); (*río, planta*) to dry up
sección [sekˈθjon] *nf* section
seco, **-a** [ˈseko, a] *adj* dry; (*carácter*)
cold; (*respuesta*) sharp, curt; **decir**
algo a secas to say sth curtly; **parar**
en ~ to stop dead
secretaría [sekretaˈria] *nf*
secretariat
secretario, **-a** [sekreˈtarjo, a] *nm/f*
secretary
secreto, **-a** [seˈkreto, a] *adj* secret;
(*persona*) secretive ▷ *nm* secret;
(*calidad*) secrecy
secta [ˈsekta] *nf* sect
sector [sekˈtor] *nm* sector (*tb Inform*)
secuela [seˈkwela] *nf* consequence

secuencia [seˈkwenθja] *nf*
sequence
secuestrar [sekwesˈtrar] /1a/ *vt* to
kidnap; (*bienes*) to seize, confiscate;
secuestro *nm* kidnapping; seizure,
confiscation
secundario, **-a** [sekunˈdarjo, a] *adj*
secondary
sed [seð] *nf* thirst; **tener ~** to be thirsty
seda [ˈseða] *nf* silk
sedal [seˈðal] *nm* fishing line
sedán [seˈðan] *nm* (*LAM*) saloon (*BRIT*);
sedan (*US*)
sedante [seˈðante] *nm* sedative
sede [ˈseðe] *nf* (*de gobierno*) seat; (*de*
compañía) headquarters *pl*; **Santa**
S~ Holy See
sedentario, **-a** [seðenˈtarjo, a] *adj*
sedentary
sediento, **-a** [seˈðjento, a] *adj* thirsty
sedimento [seðiˈmento] *nm*
sediment
seducción [seðukˈθjon] *nf* seduction
seducir [seðuˈθir] /3n/ *vt* to seduce;
(*cautivar*) to charm, fascinate; (*atraer*)
to attract; **seductor,** **a** *adj* seductive;
charming, fascinating; attractive
▷ *nm/f* seducer
segar [seˈɣar] /1h, 1j/ *vt* (*mies*) to reap,
cut; (*hierba*) to mow, cut
seglar [seˈɣlar] *adj* secular, lay
seguido, **-a** [seˈɣiðo, a] *adj* (*continuo*)
continuous, unbroken; (*recto*) straight
▷ *adv* (*directo*) straight (on); (*después*)
after; (*LAM: a menudo*) often ▷ *nf*: **en**
seguida at once, right away; **cinco**
días ~s five days running, five days
in a row
seguidor, **-a** [seɣiˈðor, a] *nm/f*
follower
seguir [seˈɣir] /3d, 3k/ *vt* to follow;
(*venir después*) to follow on, come after;
(*proseguir*) to continue; (*perseguir*)
to chase, pursue ▷ *vi* (*gen*) to follow;
(*continuar*) to continue, carry *o* go
on; **seguirse** *vr* to follow; **sigo sin**
comprender I still don't understand;
sigue lloviendo it's still raining

según [se'ɣun] prep according to ▷ adv: **~ (y conforme)** it all depends ▷ conj as

segundo, -a [se'ɣundo, a] adj second ▷ nm second ▷ nf second meaning; **segunda (clase)** second class; **segunda (marcha)** (Auto) second (gear); **de segunda mano** second hand

seguramente [seɣura'mente] adv surely; **(con certeza)** for sure, with certainty

seguridad [seɣuri'ðað] nf safety; **(del estado, de casa etc)** security; **(certidumbre)** certainty; **(confianza)** confidence; **(estabilidad)** stability; **~ social** social security

seguro, -a [se'ɣuro, a] adj (cierto) sure, certain; **(fiel)** trustworthy; **(libre de peligro)** safe; **(bien defendido, firme)** secure ▷ adv for sure, certainly ▷ nm (Com) insurance; **~ contra terceros/a todo riesgo** third party/comprehensive insurance; **~s sociales** social security sg

seis [seis] num six

seísmo [se'ismo] nm tremor, earthquake

selección [selek'θjon] nf selection; **seleccionar** /1a/ vt to pick, choose, select

selectividad [selektiβi'ðað] nf (Univ) entrance examination

selecto, -a [se'lekto, a] adj select, choice; **(escogido)** selected

sellar [se'ʎar] /1a/ vt (documento oficial) to seal; **(pasaporte, visado)** to stamp

sello ['seʎo] nm stamp; **(precinto)** seal

selva ['selβa] nf (bosque) forest, woods pl; **(jungla)** jungle

semáforo [se'maforo] nm (Auto) traffic lights pl; **(Ferro)** signal

semana [se'mana] nf week; **S~ Santa** Holy Week; **entre ~** during the week; see note **"Semana Santa"**; **semanal** adj weekly; **semanario** nm weekly (magazine)

○ **SEMANA SANTA**
○
○ Semana Santa is a holiday in Spain.
○ All regions have the Viernes Santo, Good
○ Friday, Sábado Santo, Holy Saturday,
○ and Domingo de Resurrección, Easter
○ Sunday. Other holidays at this time
○ vary according to each region.
○ There are spectacular procesiones all
○ over the country, with members of
○ cofradías (brotherhoods) dressing
○ in hooded robes and parading their
○ pasos (religious floats or sculptures)
○ through the streets. Seville has the
○ most renowned celebrations, on
○ account of the religious fervour
○ shown by the locals.

sembrar [sem'brar] /1j/ vt to sow; **(objetos)** to sprinkle, scatter about; **(noticias etc)** to spread

semejante [seme'xante] adj (parecido) similar; **~s alike**, similar ▷ nm fellow man, fellow creature; **nunca hizo cosa ~** he never did such a thing; **semejanza** nf similarity, resemblance

semejar [seme'xar] /1a/ vi to seem like, resemble; **semejarse** vr to look alike, be similar

semen ['semen] nm semen

semestral [semes'tral] adj half-yearly, bi-annual

semicírculo [semi'θirkulo] nm semicircle

semidesnatado, -a [semiðesna'taðo, a] adj semi-skimmed

semifinal [semifi'nal] nf semifinal

semilla [se'miʎa] nf seed

seminario [semi'narjo] nm (Rel) seminary; **(Escol)** seminar

sémola ['semola] nf semolina

senado [se'naðo] nm senate; **senador, a** nm/f senator

sencillez [senθi'ʎeθ] nf simplicity; **(de persona)** naturalness; **sencillo, -a** adj simple; **(carácter)** natural, unaffected

senda ['senda] nf path, track

senderismo [sende'rismo] nm hiking

sendero [sen'dero] nm path, track

sendos, -as ['sendos, as] adj pl: **les dio ~ golpes** he hit both of them

senil [se'nil] adj senile

seno ['seno] nm (Anat) bosom, bust; (fig) bosom; **senos** nmpl breasts

sensación [sensa'θjon] nf sensation; (sentido) sense; (sentimiento) feeling; **sensacional** adj sensational

sensato, -a [sen'sato, a] adj sensible

sensible [sen'sible] adj sensitive; (apreciable) perceptible, appreciable; (pérdida) considerable; **sensiblero, a** adj sentimental

> No confundir **sensible** con la palabra inglesa **sensible**.

sensitivo, -a [sensi'tiβo, a] adj sense cpd

sensorial [senso'rjal] adj sensory

sensual [sen'swal] adj sensual

sentado, -a [sen'taðo, a] adj (establecido) settled ▷ nf sitting; (Pol) sit-in; **dar por ~** to take for granted, assume; **estar ~** to sit, be sitting (down)

sentar [sen'tar] /1j/ vt to sit, seat; (fig) to establish ▷ vi (vestido) to suit; (alimento): **~ bien/mal a** to agree/disagree with; **sentarse** vr (persona) to sit, sit down; (los depósitos) to settle

sentencia [sen'tenθja] nf (máxima) maxim, saying; (Jur) sentence; **sentenciar** /1b/ vt to sentence

sentido, -a [sen'tiðo, a] adj (pérdida) regrettable; (carácter) sensitive ▷ nm sense; (sentimiento) feeling; (significado) sense, meaning; (dirección) direction; **mi más ~ pésame** my deepest sympathy; **~ del humor** sense of humour; **~ común** common sense; **tener ~** to make sense; **~ único** one-way (street)

sentimental [sentimen'tal] adj sentimental; **vida ~** love life

sentimiento [senti'mjento] nm feeling

sentir [sen'tir] /3i/ vt to feel; (percibir) to perceive, sense; (lamentar) to regret, be sorry for ▷ vi to feel; (lamentarse) to feel sorry ▷ nm opinion, judgement; **sentirse** vr: **lo siento** I'm sorry; **~se mejor/mal** to feel better/ill

seña ['seɲa] nf sign; (Mil) password; **señas** nfpl address sg; **~s personales** personal description sg

señal [se'ɲal] nf sign; (síntoma) symptom; (Ferro, Telec) signal; (marca) mark; (Com) deposit; **en ~ de** as a token of, as a sign of; **señalar** /1a/ vt to mark; (indicar) to point out, indicate

señor, a [se'ɲor, a] nm (hombre) man; (caballero) gentleman; (dueño) owner, master; (trato: antes de nombre propio) Mr; (: hablando directamente) sir ▷ nf (dama) lady; (trato: antes de nombre propio) Mrs; (: hablando directamente) madam; (esposa) wife; **Muy ~ mío** Dear Sir; **Nuestra S~a** Our Lady

señorita [seɲo'rita] nf Miss; (mujer joven) young lady

señorito [seɲo'rito] nm young gentleman; (pey) toff

sepa etc ['sepa] vb V **saber**

separación [separa'θjon] nf separation; (división) division; (distancia) gap

separar [sepa'rar] /1a/ vt to separate; (dividir) to divide; **separarse** vr (parte) to come away; (partes) to come apart; (persona) to leave, go away; (matrimonio) to separate; **separatismo** nm separatism

sepia ['sepja] nf cuttlefish

septentrional [septentrjo'nal] adj northern

septiembre [sep'tjembre] nm September

séptimo, -a ['septimo, a] adj, nm seventh

sepulcral [sepul'kral] adj (fig) gloomy, dismal; (silencio, atmósfera) deadly; **sepulcro** nm tomb, grave

sepultar [sepul'tar] /1a/ vt to bury; **sepultura** nf (acto) burial; (tumba) grave, tomb

sequía [se'kia] nf drought

séquito ['sekito] nm (de rey etc) retinue; (Pol) followers pl

PALABRA CLAVE

ser [ser] /2v/ vi **1** (descripción, identidad) to be; **es médica/muy alta** she's a doctor/very tall; **su familia es de Cuzco** his family is from Cuzco; **soy Ana** I'm Ana; (por teléfono) it's Ana

2 (propiedad): **es de Joaquín** it's Joaquín's, it belongs to Joaquín

3 (horas, fechas, números): **es la una** it's one o'clock; **son las seis y media** it's half-past six; **el 1 de junio** it's the first of June; **somos/son seis** there are six of us/them

4 (suceso): **¿qué ha sido eso?** what was that?; **la fiesta es en mi casa** the party's at my house

5 (en oraciones pasivas): **ha sido descubierto** it's already been discovered

6: **es de esperar que ...** it is to be hoped o I etc hope that ...

7 (locuciones con subjun): **o sea** that is to say; **sea él sea su hermana** either him or his sister

8: **a o de no ser por él ...** but for him ...

9: **a no ser que: a no ser que tenga uno ya** unless he's got one already

▶ nm being; **ser humano** human being

sereno, -a [se'reno, a] adj (persona) calm, unruffled; (tiempo) fine, settled; (ambiente) calm, peaceful ▶ nm night watchman

serial [se'rjal] nm serial

serie ['serje] nf series; (cadena) sequence, succession; **fuera de ~** out of order; (fig) special, out of the ordinary; **fabricación en ~** mass production

seriedad [serje'ðað] nf seriousness; (formalidad) reliability

serigrafía [seriɣra'fia] nf silk screen printing

serio, -a ['serjo, a] adj serious; reliable, dependable; grave, serious; **en ~** seriously

sermón [ser'mon] nm (Rel) sermon

seropositivo, -a [seroposi'tiβo, a] adj HIV-positive

serpentear [serpente'ar] /1a/ vi to wriggle; (camino, río) to wind, snake

serpentina [serpen'tina] nf streamer

serpiente [ser'pjente] nf snake; **~ de cascabel** rattlesnake

serranía [serra'nia] nf mountainous area

serrar [se'rrar] /1j/ vt to saw

serrín [se'rrin] nm sawdust

serrucho [se'rrutʃo] nm handsaw

service ['serβis] nm (LAm Auto) service

servicio [ser'βiθjo] nm service; (LAm Auto) service; **servicios** nmpl toilet(s); **~ incluido** service charge included; **~ militar** military service

servidumbre [serβi'ðumbre] nf (sujeción) servitude; (criados) servants pl, staff

servil [ser'βil] adj servile

servilleta [serβi'ʎeta] nf serviette, napkin

servir [ser'βir] /3k/ vt to serve ▶ vi to serve; (tener utilidad) to be of use, be useful; **servirse** vr to serve o help o.s.; **~se de algo** to make use of sth, use sth; **sírvase pasar** please come in

sesenta [se'senta] num sixty

sesión nf (Pol) session, sitting; (Cine) showing

seso ['seso] nm brain; **sesudo, -a** adj sensible, wise

seta ['seta] nf mushroom; **~ venenosa** toadstool

setecientos, -as [sete'θjentos, as] num seven hundred

setenta [se'tenta] num seventy

severo, -a [se'βero, a] adj severe

Sevilla [se'βiλa] *nf* Seville; **sevillano, -a** *adj* of o from Seville ▷ *nm/f* native o inhabitant of Seville

sexo ['sekso] *nm* sex

sexto, -a ['seksto, a] *num* sixth

sexual [sek'swal] *adj* sexual; **vida ~** sex life

si [si] *conj* if; whether ▷ *nm* (*Mus*) B; **me pregunto si ...** I wonder if o whether ...

sí [si] *adv* yes ▷ *nm* consent ▷ *pron* (*uso impersonal*) oneself; (*sg: m*) himself; (*: f*) herself; (*: de cosa*) itself; (*: de usted*) yourself; (*pl*) themselves; (*: de ustedes*) yourselves; (*: recíproco*) each other; **él no quiere pero yo sí** he doesn't want to but I do; **ella sí vendrá** she will certainly come, she is sure to come; **claro que sí** of course; **creo que sí** I think so

siamés, -esa [sja'mes, esa] *adj*, *nm/f* Siamese

SIDA ['siða] *nm abr* (= *síndrome de inmunodeficiencia adquirida*) AIDS

siderúrgico, -a [siðe'rurxico, a] *adj* iron and steel *cpd*

sidra ['siðra] *nf* cider

siembra ['sjembra] *nf* sowing

siempre ['sjempre] *adv* always; (*todo el tiempo*) all the time ▷ *conj*: **~ que ...** (+ *indic*) whenever ...; (+ *subjun*) provided that ...; **como ~** as usual; **para ~** forever

sien [sjen] *nf* temple

siento *etc* [sjento] *vb* V **sentar; sentir**

sierra ['sjerra] *nf* (*Tec*) saw; (*Geo*) mountain range

siervo, -a ['sjerβo, a] *nm/f* slave

siesta ['sjesta] *nf* siesta, nap; **dormir la o echarse una siesta o tomar una ~** to have an afternoon nap o a doze

siete ['sjete] *num* seven

sifón [si'fon] *nm* syphon

sigla ['siɣla] *nf* abbreviation

siglo ['siɣlo] *nm* century; (*fig*) age

significado [siɣnifi'kaðo] *nm* (*de palabra etc*) meaning

significar [siɣnifi'kar] /1g/ *vt* to mean, signify; (*notificar*) to make known, express

significativo, -a [siɣnifika'tiβo, a] *adj* significant

signo ['siɣno] *nm* sign; **~ de admiración o exclamación** exclamation mark; **~ de interrogación** question mark

sigo *etc* *vb* V **seguir**

siguiente [si'ɣjente] *adj* following; (*próximo*) next

siguió *etc* *vb* V **seguir**

sílaba ['silaβa] *nf* syllable

silbar [sil'βar] /1a/ *vt*, *vi* to whistle

silbato [sil'βato] *nm* whistle; **silbido** *nm* whistle, whistling

silenciador [silenθja'ðor] *nm* silencer

silenciar [silen'θjar] /1b/ *vt* (*persona*) to silence; (*escándalo*) to hush up; **silencio** *nm* silence, quiet; **silencioso, -a** *adj* silent, quiet

silla ['siλa] *nf* (*asiento*) chair; (*tb*: **~ de montar**) saddle; **~ de ruedas** wheelchair

sillón [si'λon] *nm* armchair, easy chair

silueta [si'lweta] *nf* silhouette; (*de edificio*) outline; (*figura*) figure

silvestre [sil'βestre] *adj* wild

simbólico, -a [sim'boliko, a] *adj* symbolic(al)

simbolizar [simboli'θar] /1f/ *vt* to symbolize

símbolo ['simbolo] *nm* symbol

similar [simi'lar] *adj* similar

simio ['simjo] *nm* ape

simpatía [simpa'tia] *nf* liking; (*afecto*) affection; (*amabilidad*) kindness; **simpático, -a** *adj* nice, pleasant; (*bondadoso*) kind

▮ No confundir *simpático* con la palabra inglesa *sympathetic*.

simpatizante [simpati'θante] *nmf* sympathizer

simpatizar [simpati'θar] /1f/ *vi*: **~ con** to get on well with

simple ['simple] *adj* simple; (*elemental*) simple, easy; (*mero*) mere; (*puro*) pure, sheer ▷ *nmf* simpleton; **simpleza** *nf* simpleness; (*necedad*) silly thing; **simplificar** /1g/ *vt* to simplify

simposio [sim'posjo] *nm* symposium

simular [simu'lar] /1a/ *vt* to simulate

simultáneo, -a [simul'taneo, a] *adj* simultaneous

sin [sin] *prep* without ▷ *conj*: **~ que** (+ *subjun*) without; **la ropa está ~ lavar** the clothes are unwashed; **~ embargo** however

sinagoga [sina'yoya] *nf* synagogue

sinceridad [sinθeri'ðað] *nf* sincerity; **sincero, -a** *adj* sincere

sincronizar [sinkroni'θar] /1f/ *vt* to synchronize

sindical [sindi'kal] *adj* union *cpd*, trade-union *cpd*; **sindicalista** *adj* ▷ *nmf* trade unionist

sindicato [sindi'kato] *nm* (*de trabajadores*) trade(s) o labor (*US*) union; (*de negociantes*) syndicate

síndrome ['sindrome] *nm* syndrome; **~ de abstinencia** withdrawal symptoms; **~ de la clase turista** economy-class syndrome

sinfín [sin'fin] *nm*: **un ~ de** a great many, no end of

sinfonía [sinfo'nia] *nf* symphony

singular [singu'lar] *adj* singular; (*fig*) outstanding, exceptional; (*pey*) peculiar, odd

siniestro, -a [si'njestro, a] *adj* sinister ▷ *nm* (*accidente*) accident

sinnúmero [sin'numero] *nm* = **sinfín**

sino ['sino] *nm* fate, destiny ▷ *conj* (*pero*) but; (*salvo*) except, save

sinónimo, -a [si'nonimo, a] *adj* synonymous ▷ *nm* synonym

síntesis ['sintesis] *nf inv* synthesis; **sintético, -a** *adj* synthetic

sintió *vb V* **sentir**

síntoma ['sintoma] *nm* symptom

sintonía [sinto'nia] *nf* (*Radio*) tuning; **sintonizar** /1f/ *vt* (*Radio*) to tune (in) to

sinvergüenza [simber'ɣwenθa] *nmf* rogue, scoundrel; **¡es un ~!** he's got a nerve!

siquiera [si'kjera] *conj* even if, even though ▷ *adv* at least; **ni ~** not even

Siria ['sirja] *nf* Syria

sirviente, -a [sir'βjente, a] *nm/f* servant

sirvo *etc vb V* **servir**

sistema [sis'tema] *nm* system; (*método*) method; **sistemático, -a** *adj* systematic

sitiar [si'tjar] /1b/ *vt* to besiege, lay siege to

sitio ['sitjo] *nm* (*lugar*) place; (*espacio*) room, space; (*Mil*) siege; **~ de taxis** (*LAM: parada*) taxi stand o rank (*BRIT*); **~ web** website

situación [sitwa'θjon] *nf* situation, position; (*estatus*) position, standing

situado, -a [si'twaðo, a] *adj* situated, placed

situar [si'twar] /1e/ *vt* to place, put; (*edificio*) to locate, situate

slip [es'lip] *nm* pants *pl*, briefs *pl*

smoking [(e)'smokin] (*pl* **smokings**) *nm* dinner jacket (*BRIT*), tuxedo (*US*)

> No confundir *smoking* con la palabra inglesa *smoking*.

SMS *nm* (*mensaje*) text (message), SMS (message)

snob [es'nob] = **esnob**

SO *abr* (= *suroeste*) SW

sobaco [so'βako] *nm* armpit

sobar [so'βar] /1a/ vt (ropa) to rumple; (comida) to play around with

soberanía [soβera'nia] nf sovereignty; **soberano, -a** adj sovereign; (fig) supreme ▷ nm/f sovereign

soberbio, -a [so'βerβjo, a] adj (orgulloso) proud; (altivo) arrogant; (fig) magnificent, superb ▷ nf pride; haughtiness, arrogance; magnificence

sobornar [soβor'nar] /1a/ vt to bribe; **soborno** nm bribe

sobra ['soβra] nf excess, surplus; **sobras** nfpl left-overs, scraps; **de ~** surplus, extra; **tengo de ~** I've more than enough; **sobrado, -a** adj (más que suficiente) more than enough; (superfluo) excessive; **sobrante** adj remaining, extra ▷ nm surplus, remainder; **sobrar** /1a/ vt to exceed, surpass ▷ vi (tener de más) to be more than enough; (quedar) to remain, be left (over)

sobrasada [soβra'saða] nf ≈ sausage spread

sobre ['soβre] prep (gen) on; (encima) on (top of); (por encima de, arriba de) over, above; (más que) more than; (además) in addition to, besides; (alrededor de) about ▷ nm envelope; **~ todo** above all

sobrecama [soβre'kama] nf bedspread

sobrecargar [soβrekar'ɣar] /1h/ vt (camión) to overload; (Com) to surcharge

sobredosis [soβre'ðosis] nf inv overdose

sobreentender [soβreenten'der] /2g/ vt to deduce, infer; **sobreentenderse** vr: **se sobreentiende que ...** it is implied that ...

sobrehumano, -a [soβreu'mano, a] adj superhuman

sobrellevar [soβreʎe'βar] /1a/ vt to bear, endure

sobremesa [soβre'mesa] nf: **durante la ~** after dinner

sobrenatural [soβrenatu'ral] adj supernatural

sobrenombre [soβre'nombre] nm nickname

sobrepasar [soβrepa'sar] /1a/ vt to exceed, surpass

sobreponer [soβrepo'ner] /2q/ vt (poner encima) to put on top; (añadir) to add; **sobreponerse** vr: **~se a** to overcome

sobresaliente [soβresa'ljente] adj outstanding, excellent

sobresalir [soβresa'lir] /3q/ vi to project, jut out; (fig) to stand out, excel

sobresaltar [soβresal'tar] /1a/ vt (asustar) to scare, frighten; (sobrecoger) to startle; **sobresalto** nm (movimiento) start; (susto) scare; (turbación) sudden shock

sobretodo [soβre'toðo] nm overcoat

sobrevenir [soβreβe'nir] /3r/ vi (ocurrir) to happen (unexpectedly); (resultar) to follow, ensue

sobrevivir [soβreβi'βir] /3a/ vi to survive

sobrevolar [soβreβo'lar] /1l/ vt to fly over

sobriedad [soβrje'ðað] nf sobriety, soberness; (moderación) moderation, restraint

sobrino, -a [so'βrino, a] nm/f nephew/niece

sobrio, -a ['soβrjo, a] adj sober; (moderado) moderate, restrained

socarrón, -ona [soka'rron, ona] adj (sarcástico) sarcastic, ironic(al)

socavón [soka'βon] nm (en la calle) hole

sociable [so'θjaβle] adj (persona) sociable, friendly; (animal) social

social [so'θjal] adj social; (Com) company cpd

socialdemócrata [soθjalde'mokrata] nmf social democrat

socialista [soθja'lista] adj, nmf socialist

socializar [soθjali'θar] /1f/ vt to socialize

sociedad [soθje'ðað] nf society; (Com) company; **~ anónima (S.A.)** limited company (Ltd) (BRIT), incorporated company (Inc) (US); **~ de consumo** consumer society

socio, -a ['soθjo, a] nm/f (miembro) member; (Com) partner

sociología [soθjolo'xia] nf sociology; **sociólogo, -a** nm/f sociologist

socorrer [soko'rrer] /2a/ vt to help; **socorrista** nmf first aider; (en piscina, playa) lifeguard; **socorro** nm (ayuda) help, aid; (Mil) relief; **¡socorro!** help!

soda ['soða] nf (sosa) soda; (bebida) soda (water)

sofá [so'fa] nm sofa, settee; **sofá-cama** nm studio couch, sofa bed

sofocar [sofo'kar] /1g/ vt to suffocate; (apagar) to smother, put out; **sofocarse** vr to suffocate; (fig) to blush, feel embarrassed; **sofoco** nm suffocation; (azoro) embarrassment

sofreír [sofre'ir] /3l/ vt to fry lightly

soft ['sof], **software** ['sofwer] nm (Inform) software

soga ['soɣa] nf rope

sois [sois] vb V **ser**

soja ['soxa] nf soya

sol [sol] nm sun; (luz) sunshine, sunlight; (Mus) G; **hace ~** it is sunny

solamente [sola'mente] adv only, just

solapa [so'lapa] nf (de chaqueta) lapel; (de libro) jacket

solapado, -a [sola'paðo, a] adj (intenciones) underhand; (gestos, movimientos) sly

solar [so'lar] adj solar, sun cpd ▷ nm (terreno) plot (of ground)

soldado [sol'daðo] nm soldier; **~ raso** private

soldador [solda'ðor] nm soldering iron; (persona) welder

soldar [sol'dar] /1l/ vt to solder, weld

soleado, -a [sole'aðo, a] adj sunny

soledad [sole'ðað] nf solitude; (estado infeliz) loneliness

solemne [so'lemne] adj solemn

soler [so'ler] vi to be in the habit of, be accustomed to; **suele salir a las ocho** she usually goes out at 8 o'clock

solfeo [sol'feo] nm sol-fa, singing of scales

solicitar [soliθi'tar] /1a/ vt (permiso) to ask for, seek; (puesto) to apply for; (votos) to canvass for; (atención) to attract

solícito, -a [so'liθito, a] adj (diligente) diligent; (cuidadoso) careful; **solicitud** nf (calidad) great care; (petición) request; (a un puesto) application

solidaridad [soliðari'ðað] nf solidarity; **solidario, -a** adj (participación) joint, common; (compromiso) mutually binding

sólido, -a ['soliðo, a] adj solid

soliloquio [soli'lokjo] nm soliloquy

solista [so'lista] nmf soloist

solitario, -a [soli'tarjo, a] adj (persona) lonely, solitary; (lugar) lonely, desolate ▷ nm/f (recluso) recluse; (en la sociedad) loner ▷ nm solitaire

sollozar [soʎo'θar] /1f/ vi to sob; **sollozo** nm sob

solo¹, -a ['solo, a] adj (único) single, sole; (sin compañía) alone; (solitario) lonely; **hay una sola dificultad** there is just one difficulty; **a solas** alone, by o.s.

solo², sólo ['solo] adv only, just

solomillo [solo'miʎo] nm sirloin

soltar [sol'tar] /1l/ vt (dejar ir) to let go of; (desprender) to unfasten, loosen; (librar) to release, set free; (risa etc) to let out

soltero, -a [sol'tero, a] adj single, unmarried ▷ nm bachelor ▷ nf single woman; **solterón** nm confirmed bachelor

soltera [solte'rona] nf spinster

soltura [sol'tura] nf looseness, slackness; (de los miembros) agility,

s

ease of movement; (en el hablar) fluency, ease

soluble [so'luβle] adj (Química) soluble; (problema) solvable; ~ **en agua** soluble in water

solución [solu'θjon] nf solution; **solucionar** /1a/ vt (problema) to solve; (asunto) to settle, resolve

solventar [solβen'tar] /1a/ vt (pagar) to settle, pay; (resolver) to resolve; **solvente** adj solvent

sombra ['sombra] nf shadow; (como protección) shade; **sombras** nfpl darkness sg, shadows; **tener buena/ mala** ~ to be lucky/unlucky

sombrero [som'brero] nm hat

sombrilla [som'briʎa] nf parasol, sunshade

sombrío, -a [som'brio, a] adj (oscuro) dark; (fig) sombre, sad; (persona) gloomy

someter [some'ter] /2a/ vt (país) to conquer; (persona) to subject to one's will; (informe) to present, submit; **someterse** vr to give in, yield, submit; ~ **a** to subject to

somier [so'mjer] (pl **somiers**) nm spring mattress

somnífero [som'nifero] nm sleeping pill o tablet

somos ['somos] vb V **ser**

son [son] vb V **ser** ▷ nm See

sonaja [so'naxa] nf (LAM) = **sonajero**

sonajero [sona'xero] nm (baby's) rattle

sonámbulismo [sonambu'lismo] nm sleepwalking; **sonámbulo, -a** nm/f sleepwalker

sonar [so'nar] /1l/ vt to sound ▷ vi to sound; (hacer ruido) to make a noise; (Ling) to be sounded, be pronounced; (ser conocido) to sound familiar; (campana) to ring; (reloj) to strike, chime; **sonarse** vr: ~**se (la nariz)** to blow one's nose; **me suena ese nombre** that name rings a bell

sonda ['sonda] nf (Naut) sounding; (Tec) bore, drill; (Med) probe

sondear [sonde'ar] /1a/ vt to sound; to bore (into), drill; to probe, sound; (fig) to sound out; **sondeo** nm sounding; boring, drilling; (encuesta) poll, enquiry

sonido [so'niðo] nm sound

sonoro, -a [so'noro, a] adj sonorous; (resonante) loud, resonant

sonreír [sonre'ir] /3l/ vi to smile; **sonriente** adj smiling; **sonrisa** nf smile

sonrojar [sonro'xar] /1a/ vt: ~ **a algn** to make sb blush; **sonrojarse** vr: ~**se (de)** to blush (at)

sonrojo nm blush

soñador, a [soɲa'ðor, a] nm/f dreamer

soñar [so'ɲar] /1l/ vt, vi to dream; ~ **con** to dream about o of

soñoliento, -a [soɲo'ljento, a] adj sleepy, drowsy

sopa ['sopa] nf soup

soplar [so'plar] /1a/ vt (polvo) to blow away, blow off; (inflar) to blow up; (vela) to blow out ▷ vi to blow; **soplo** nm blow, puff; (de viento) puff, gust

soplón, -ona [so'plon, ona] nm/f (fam: chismoso) telltale; (: de policía) informer, grass

soporífero, -a [sopo'rifero, a] adj sleep-inducing ▷ nm sleeping pill

soportable [sopor'taβle] adj bearable

soportar [sopor'tar] /1a/ vt to bear, carry; (fig) to bear, put up with; **soporte** nm support; (fig) pillar, support

> No confundir soportar con la palabra inglesa support.

soprano [so'prano] nf soprano

sorber [sor'βer] /2a/ vt (chupar) to sip; (inhalar) to sniff, inhale; (absorber) to soak up, absorb

sorbete [sor'βete] nm iced fruit drink

sorbo [sor'βo] nm (trago) gulp, swallow; (chupada) sip

sordera [sor'ðera] nf deafness

sórdido, -a [ˈsorðiðo, a] *adj* dirty, squalid

sordo, -a [ˈsorðo, a] *adj* (*persona*) deaf ▷ *nm/f* deaf person; **sordomudo, -a** *adj* deaf and dumb

sorna [ˈsorna] *nf* sarcastic tone

soroche [soˈrotʃe] *nm* (LAM) mountain sickness

sorprendente [sorprenˈdente] *adj* surprising

sorprender [sorprenˈder] /2a/ *vt* to surprise; **sorpresa** *nf* surprise

sortear [sorteˈar] /1a/ *vt* to draw lots for; (*rifar*) to raffle; (*dificultad*) to dodge, avoid; **sorteo** *nm* (*en lotería*) draw; (*rifa*) raffle

sortija [sorˈtixa] *nf* ring; (*rizo*) ringlet, curl

sosegado, -a [soseˈɣaðo, a] *adj* quiet, calm

sosiego [soˈsjeɣo] *nm* quiet(ness), calm(ness)

soso, -a [ˈsoso, a] *adj* (Culin) tasteless; (*fig*) dull, uninteresting

sospecha [sosˈpetʃa] *nf* suspicion; **sospechar** /1a/ *vt* to suspect; **sospechoso, -a** *adj* suspicious; (*testimonio, opinión*) suspect ▷ *nm/f* suspect

sostén [sosˈten] *nm* (*apoyo*) support; (*sujetador*) bra; (*alimentación*) sustenance, food

sostener [sosteˈner] /2k/ *vt* to support; (*mantener*) to keep up, maintain; (*alimentar*) to sustain, keep going; **sostenerse** *vr* to support o.s.; (*seguir*) to continue, remain; **sostenido, -a** *adj* continuous, sustained; (*prolongado*) prolonged

sotana [soˈtana] *nf* (Rel) cassock

sótano [ˈsotano] *nm* basement

soy [soi] *vb V* **ser**

soya [ˈsoja] *nf* (LAM) soya (bean)

Sr. *abr* (= Señor) Mr

Sra. *abr* (= Señora) Mrs

Sras. *abr* (= Señoras) Mrs

Sres. *abr* (= Señores) Messrs

Srta. *abr* = **señorita**

Sta. *abr* (= Santa) St

Sto. *abr* (= Santo) St

su [su] *pron* (*de él*) his; (*de ella*) her; (*de una cosa*) its; (*de ellos, ellas*) their; (*de usted, ustedes*) your

suave [ˈswaβe] *adj* gentle; (*superficie*) smooth; (*trabajo*) easy; (*música, voz*) soft, sweet; **suavidad** *nf* gentleness; (*de superficie*) smoothness; (*de música*) softness, sweetness; **suavizante** *nm* (*de ropa*) softener; (*del pelo*) conditioner; **suavizar** /1f/ *vt* to soften; (*quitar la aspereza*) to smooth (out)

subasta [suˈβasta] *nf* auction; **subastar** /1a/ *vt* to auction (off)

subcampeón, -ona [suβkampeˈon, ona] *nm/f* runner-up

subconsciente [suβkonsˈθjente] *adj* subconscious

subdesarrollado, -a [suβðesarroˈλaðo, a] *adj* underdeveloped

subdesarrollo [suβðesaˈrroλo] *nm* underdevelopment

subdirector, -a [suβðirekˈtor, a] *nm/f* assistant o deputy manager

súbdito, -a [ˈsuβðito, a] *nm/f* subject

subestimar [suβestiˈmar] /1a/ *vt* to underestimate, underrate

subir [suˈβir] /3a/ *vt* (*objeto*) to raise, lift up; (*cuesta, calle*) to go up; (*colina, montaña*) to climb; (*precio*) to raise, put up ▷ *vi* to go/come up; (*a un coche*) to get in; (*a un autobús, tren*) to get on; (*precio*) to rise, go up; (*río, marea*) to rise; **subirse** *vr* to get up, climb

súbito, -a [ˈsuβito, a] *adj* (*repentino*) sudden; (*imprevisto*) unexpected

subjetivo, -a [suβxeˈtiβo, a] *adj* subjective

sublevar [suβleˈβar] /1a/ *vt* to rouse to revolt; **sublevarse** *vr* to revolt, rise

sublime [suˈβlime] *adj* sublime

submarinismo [suβmariˈnismo] *nm* scuba diving

submarino, -a [suβmaˈrino, a] *adj* underwater ▷ *nm* submarine

s

subnormal [suβnor'mal] *adj* subnormal ▷ *nmf* subnormal person

subordinado, -a [suβorði'naðo, a] *adj, nm/f* subordinate

subrayar [suβra'jar] /1a/ *vt* to underline

subsanar [suβsa'nar] /1a/ *vt* (*reparar*) to rectify

subsidio [suβ'siðjo] *nm* (*ayuda*) aid, financial help; (*subvención*) subsidy, grant; (*de enfermedad, paro etc*) benefit, allowance

subsistencia [suβsis'tenθja] *nf* subsistence

subsistir [suβsis'tir] /3a/ *vi* to subsist; (*sobrevivir*) to survive, endure

subte [suβte] *nm* (RPL) underground (BRIT), subway (US)

subterráneo, -a [suβte'rraneo, a] *adj* underground, subterranean ▷ *nm* underpass, underground passage

subtitulado, -a [suβtitu'laðo, a] *adj* subtitled

subtítulo [suβ'titulo] *nm* subtitle

suburbio [su'βurβjo] *nm* (*barrio*) slum quarter

subvención [suββen'θjon] *nf* subsidy, grant; **subvencionar** /1a/ *vt* to subsidize

sucedáneo, -a [suθe'ðaneo, a] *adj* substitute ▷ *nm* substitute (food)

suceder [suθe'ðer] /2a/ *vi* to happen; (*seguir*) to succeed, follow; **lo que sucede es que ...** the fact is that ...; **sucesión** /nf succession; (*serie*) sequence, series

sucesivamente [suθesiβa'mente] *adv*: **y así** ~ and so on

sucesivo, -a [suθe'siβo, a] *adj* successive, following; **en lo** ~ in future, from now on

suceso [su'θeso] *nm* (*hecho*) event, happening; (*incidente*) incident

> No confundir *suceso* con la palabra inglesa *success*.

suciedad [suθje'ðað] *nf* (*estado*) dirtiness; (*mugre*) dirt, filth

sucio, -a ['suθjo, a] *adj* dirty

suculento, -a [suku'lento, a] *adj* succulent

sucumbir [sukum'bir] /3a/ *vi* to succumb

sucursal [sukur'sal] *nf* branch (office)

sudadera [suða'ðera] *nf* sweatshirt

Sudáfrica [su'ðafrika] *nf* South Africa

Sudamérica [suða'merika] *nf* South America; **sudamericano, -a** *adj, nm/f* South American

sudar [su'ðar] /1a/ *vt, vi* to sweat

sudeste [su'ðeste] *nm* south-east

sudoeste [suðo'este] *nm* south-west

sudoku [su'ðoku] *nm* sudoku

sudor [su'ðor] *nm* sweat; **sudoroso, -a** *adj* sweaty, sweating

Suecia ['sweθja] *nf* Sweden; **sueco, -a** *adj* Swedish ▷ *nm/f* Swede

suegro [a'sweyro, a] *nm/f* father-/mother-in-law

suela ['swela] *nf* sole

sueldo ['sweldo] *nm* pay, wage(s) (pl)

suelo ['swelo] *vb* V **soler** ▷ *nm* (*tierra*) ground; (*de casa*) floor

suelto, -a ['swelto, a] *adj* loose; (*libre*) free; (*separado*) detached; (*ágil*) quick, agile ▷ *nm* (*loose*) change, small change

sueñito [swe'ɲito] *nm* (LAM) nap

sueño ['sweɲo] *vb* V **soñar** ▷ *nm* sleep; (*somnolencia*) sleepiness, drowsiness; (*lo soñado, fig*) dream; **tener** ~ to be sleepy

suero ['swero] *nm* (Med) serum; (*de leche*) whey

suerte ['swerte] *nf* (*fortuna*) luck; (*azar*) chance; (*destino*) fate, destiny; (*género*) sort, kind; **tener** ~ to be lucky

suéter ['sweter] *nm* sweater

suficiente [sufi'θjente] *adj* enough, sufficient ▷ *nm* (Escol) pass

sufragio [su'fraxjo] *nm* (*voto*) vote; (*derecho de voto*) suffrage

sufrido, -a [su'friðo, a] *adj* (*de carácter fuerte*) tough; (*paciente*) long-suffering, patient

sufrimiento [sufri'mjento] *nm* suffering

sufrir [su'frir] /3a/ vt (padecer) to suffer; (soportar) to bear, put up with; (apoyar) to hold up, support ▷ vi to suffer

sugerencia [suxe'renθja] nf suggestion

sugerir [suxe'rir] /3i/ vt to suggest; (sutilmente) to hint

sugestión [suxes'tjon] nf suggestion; (influjo) hint; **sugestionar** /1a/ vt to influence

sugestivo, -a [suxes'tiβo, a] adj stimulating; (fascinante) fascinating

suicida [sui'θiða] adj suicidal ▷ nmf suicidal person; (muerto) suicide, person who has committed suicide; **suicidarse** /1a/ vr to commit suicide, kill o.s.; **suicidio** nm suicide

Suiza ['swiθa] nf Switzerland; **suizo, -a** adj, nm/f Swiss

sujeción [suxe'θjon] nf subjection

sujetador [suxeta'ðor] nm (prenda femenina) bra

sujetar [suxe'tar] /1a/ vt (fijar) to fasten; (detener) to hold down; **sujetarse** vr to subject o.s.; **sujeto, -a** adj fastened, secure ▷ nm subject; (individuo) individual; **sujeto a** subject to

suma ['suma] nf (cantidad) total, sum; (de dinero) sum; (acto) adding (up), addition; **en -** in short

sumamente [suma'mente] adv extremely, exceedingly

sumar [su'mar] /1a/ vt to add (up) ▷ vi to add up

sumergir [sumer'xir] /3c/ vt to submerge; (hundir) to sink

suministrar [suminis'trar] /1a/ vt to supply, provide; **suministro** nm supply; (acto) supplying, providing

sumir [su'mir] /3a/ vt to sink, submerge; (fig) to plunge

sumiso, -a [su'miso, a] adj submissive, docile

sumo, -a ['sumo, a] adj great, extreme; (mayor) highest, supreme

suntuoso, -a [sun'twoso, a] adj sumptuous, magnificent

supe etc ['supe] vb V **saber**

súper ['super] adj (fam) super, great ▷ nf (gasolina) four-star (petrol)

super... [super] pref super..., over...

superar [supe'tar] /1a/ vt (sobreponerse a) to overcome; (rebasar) to surpass, do better than; (pasar) to go beyond; **superarse** vr to excel o.s.

superbueno, a [super'bweno, a] adj great, fantastic

superficial [superfi'θjal] adj superficial; (medida) surface cpd

superficie [super'fiθje] nf surface; (área) area

superfluo, -a [su'perflwo, a] adj superfluous

superior [supe'rjor] adj (piso, clase) upper; (temperatura, número, nivel) higher; (mejor: calidad, producto) superior, better ▷ nmf superior; **superioridad** nf superiority

supermercado [supermer'kaðo] nm supermarket

superponer [superpo'ner] /2q/ vt to superimpose

superstición [supersti'θjon] nf superstition; **supersticioso, -a** adj superstitious

supervisar [superβi'sar] /1a/ vt to supervise

supervivencia [superβi'βenθja] nf survival

superviviente [superβi'βjente] adj surviving

supiera etc vb V **saber**

suplantar [suplan'tar] /1a/ vt to supplant

suplementario, -a [suplemen'tarjo, a] adj supplementary

suplemento [suple'mento] nm supplement

suplente [su'plente] adj substitute ▷ nmf substitute

supletorio, -a [suple'torjo, a] adj supplementary ▷ nm supplement; **teléfono -** extension

súplica ['suplika] nf request; (Jur) petition

suplicar [supli'kar] /1g/ vt (cosa) to beg (for), plead for; (persona) to beg, plead with

suplicio [su'pliθjo] nm torture

suplir [su'plir] /3a/ vt (compensar) to make good, make up for; (reemplazar) to replace, substitute ▷ vi: **~ a** to take the place of, substitute for

supo etc ['supo] vb V **saber**

suponer [supo'ner] /2q/ vt to suppose; **suposición** nf supposition

suprimir [supri'mir] /3a/ vt to suppress; (derecho, costumbre) to abolish; (palabra etc) to delete; (restricción) to cancel, lift

supuesto, -a [su'pwesto, a] pp de **suponer** ▷ adj (hipotético) supposed ▷ nm assumption, hypothesis ▷ conj: **~ que** since; **por ~** of course

sur [sur] nm south

suramericano, -a [surameri'kano, a] adj South American ▷ nm/f South American

surcar [sur'kar] /1g/ vt to plough; **surco** nm (en metal, disco) groove; (Agr) furrow

surfear [surfe'ar] /1a/ vt: **~ el Internet** to surf the internet

surgir [sur'xir] /3c/ vi to arise, emerge; (dificultad) to come up, crop up

suroeste [suro'este] nm south-west

surtido, -a [sur'tiðo, a] adj mixed, assorted ▷ nm (selección) selection, assortment; (abastecimiento) supply, stock; **surtidor** nm: **surtidor de gasolina** petrol o (us) gas (us) pump

surtir [sur'tir] /3a/ vt to supply, provide ▷ vi to spout, spurt

susceptible [susθep'tiβle] adj susceptible; (sensible) sensitive; **~ de** capable of

suscitar [susθi'tar] /1a/ vt to cause, provoke; (interés, sospechas) to arouse

suscribir [suskri'βir] /3a/ vt (firmar) to sign; (respaldar) to subscribe to,

endorse; **suscribirse** vr to subscribe; **suscripción** nf subscription

susodicho, -a [suso'ditʃo, a] adj above-mentioned

suspender [suspen'der] /2a/ vt (objeto) to hang (up), suspend; (trabajo) to stop, suspend; (Escol) to fail; (interrumpir) to adjourn; (atrasar) to postpone

suspense [sus'pense] nm suspense; **película/novela de ~** thriller

suspensión [suspen'sjon] nf suspension; (fig) stoppage, suspension

suspenso, -a [sus'penso, a] adj hanging, suspended; (Escol) failed ▷ nm (Escol) fail(ure); **quedar** o **estar en ~** to be pending; **película** o **novela de ~** (LAM) thriller

suspicaz [suspi'kaθ] adj suspicious, distrustful

suspirar [suspi'rar] /1a/ vi to sigh; **suspiro** nm sigh

sustancia [sus'tanθja] nf substance

sustento [sus'tento] nm support; (alimento) sustenance, food

sustituir [sustitu'ir] /3g/ vt to substitute, replace; **sustituto, -a** nm/f substitute, replacement

susto ['susto] nm fright, scare

sustraer [sustra'er] /2p/ vt to remove, take away; (Mat) to subtract

susurrar [susu'rrar] /1a/ vi to whisper; **susurro** nm whisper

sutil [su'til] adj (aroma) subtle; (tenue) thin; (inteligencia) sharp

suyo, -a ['sujo, a] adj (con artículo o después del verbo ser: de él) his; (: de ella) hers; (: de ellos, ellas) theirs; (: de usted, ustedes) yours; **un amigo ~** a friend of his (o hers o theirs o yours)

t

Tabacalera [taβaka'lera] *nf* former Spanish state tobacco monopoly

tabaco [ta'βako] *nm* tobacco; (*fam*) cigarettes *pl*

tabaquería [tabake'ria] *nf* tobacconist's (BRIT), cigar store (US)

taberna [ta'βerna] *nf* bar

tabique [ta'βike] *nm* partition

tabla ['taβla] *nf* (*de madera*) plank; (*estante*) shelf; (*de vestido*) pleat; (*Arte*) panel; **tablas** *nfpl:* **estar** *o* **quedar en ~s** to draw; **tablado** *nm* (*plataforma*) platform; (*Teat*) stage

tablao [ta'βlao] *nm* (*tb:* **~ flamenco**) flamenco show

tablero [ta'βlero] *nm* (*de madera*) plank, board; (*de ajedrez, damas*) board; (*Auto*) dashboard; **~ de mandos** (LAM Auto) dashboard

tableta [ta'βleta] *nf* (*Med*) tablet; (*de chocolate*) bar

tablón [ta'βlon] *nm* (*de suelo*) plank; (*de techo*) beam; (*de anuncios*) notice board

tabú [ta'βu] *nm* taboo

taburete [taβu'rete] *nm* stool

tacaño, -a [ta'kaɲo, a] *adj* mean

tacha ['tatʃa] *nf* flaw; (*Tec*) stud; **tachar** /1a/ *vt* (*borrar*) to cross out; **tachar de** to accuse of

tacho ['tatʃo] *nm* (LAM) bucket; **~ de la basura** rubbish bin (BRIT), trash can (US)

taco ['tako] *nm* (*Billar*) cue; (*libro de billetes*) book; (*LAM*) (*tarugo*) peg; (*palabrota*) swear word

tacón [ta'kon] *nm* heel; **de ~ alto** high-heeled

táctico, -a ['taktiko, a] *adj* tactical ▷ *nf* tactics *pl*

tacto ['takto] *nm* touch; (*fig*) tact

tajada [ta'xaða] *nf* slice

tajante [ta'xante] *adj* sharp

tajo ['taxo] *nm* (*corte*) cut; (*Geo*) cleft

tal [tal] *adj* such ▷ *pron* (*persona*) someone, such a one; (*cosa*) something, such a thing; **~ como** such as; **~ para cual** two of a kind ▷ *adv:* **~ como** (*igual*) just as; **~ cual** (*como es*) just as it is; **¿qué ~?** how are things?; **¿qué ~ te gusta?** how do you like it? ▷ *conj:* **con ~ (de) que** provided that

taladrar [tala'ðrar] /1a/ *vt* to drill; **taladro** *nm* drill

talante [ta'lante] *nm* (*humor*) mood; (*voluntad*) will, willingness

talar [ta'lar] /1a/ *vt* to fell, cut down; (*fig*) to devastate

talco ['talko] *nm* (*polvos*) talcum powder

talento [ta'lento] *nm* talent; (*capacidad*) ability

Talgo ['talgo] *nm abr* (= *tren articulado ligero Goicoechea Oriol*) high-speed train

talismán [talis'man] *nm* talisman

talla ['taʎa] *nf* (*estatura, fig, Med*) height, stature; (*de ropa*) size; (*palo*) measuring rod; (*Arte*) carving

tallar [ta'ʎar] /1a/ *vt* (*grabar*) to engrave; (*medir*) to measure

tallarín [taʎa'rin] *nm* noodle

talle ['taʎe] *nm* (*Anat*) waist; (*fig*) appearance

taller [ta'ʎer] nm (Tec) workshop; (de artista) studio

tallo ['taʎo] nm (de planta) stem; (de hierba) blade; (brote) shoot

talón [ta'lon] nm heel; (Com) counterfoil; (cheque) cheque (BRIT), check (US)

talonario [talo'narjo] nm (de cheques) chequebook (BRIT), checkbook (US); (de recibos) receipt book

tamaño, -a [ta'maɲo, a] adj (tan grande) such a big; (tan pequeño) such a small ▷ nm size; **de ~ natural** full-size

tamarindo [tama'rindo] nm tamarind

tambalearse [tambale'arse] /1a/ vr (persona) to stagger; (vehículo) to sway

también [tam'bjen] adv (igualmente) also, too, as well; (además) besides

tambor [tam'bor] nm drum; (Anat) eardrum; **~ del freno** brake drum

Támesis ['tamesis] nm Thames

tamizar [tami'θar] /1f/ vt to sieve

tampoco [tam'poko] adv nor, neither; **yo ~ lo compré** I didn't buy it either

tampón [tam'pon] nm tampon

tan [tan] adv so; **~ es así que** so much so that

tanda ['tanda] nf (gen) series; (turno) shift

tangente [tan'xente] nf tangent

tangerina [tanxe'rina] nf (LAM) tangerine

tangible [tan'xiβle] adj tangible

tanque ['tanke] nm tank; (Auto, Naut) tanker

tantear [tante'ar] /1a/ vt (calcular) to reckon (up); (medir) to take the measure of; (probar) to test, try out; (tomar la medida: persona) to take the measurements of; (considerar) to weigh up; (persona: opinión) to sound out ▷ vi (Deporte) to score; **tanteo** nm (cálculo aproximado) (rough) calculation; (prueba) test, trial; (Deporte) scoring

○ **PALABRA CLAVE**

tanto, -a ['tanto, a] adj (cantidad) so much, as much; **tantos** so many, as many; **20 y tantos** 20-odd ▷ adv (cantidad) so much, as much; (tiempo) so long, as long; **tanto tú como yo** both you and I; **tanto como eso** as much as that; **tanto más ... cuanto que** it's all the more ... because; **tanto mejor/peor** so much the better/the worse; **tanto si viene como si va** whether he comes or whether he goes; **tanto es así que** so much so that; **por tanto, por lo tanto** therefore
▷ conj: **en tanto que** while; **hasta tanto (que)** until such time as
▷ nm 1 (suma) certain amount; (proporción) so much; **un tanto perezoso** somewhat lazy
2 (punto) point; (: gol) goal
3 (locuciones): **al tanto** up to date; **al tanto de que** because of the fact that
▷ pron: **cada uno paga tanto** each one pays so much; **a tantos de agosto** on such and such a day in August; **entre tanto** meanwhile

tapa ['tapa] nf (de caja, olla) lid; (de botella) top; (de libro) cover; (de comida) snack

tapadera [tapa'ðera] nf lid, cover

tapar [ta'par] /1a/ vt (cubrir) to cover; (envolver) to wrap o cover up; (la vista) to obstruct; (persona, falta) to conceal; (LAM) to fill; **taparse** vr to wrap o. s. up

taparrabo [tapa'rraβo] nm loincloth

tapete [ta'pete] nm table cover

tapia ['tapja] nf (garden) wall

tapicería [tapiθe'ria] nf tapestry; (para muebles) upholstery; (tienda) upholsterer's (shop)

tapiz [ta'piθ] nm (alfombra) carpet; (tela tejida) tapestry; **tapizar** /1f/ vt (muebles) to upholster

tapón [ta'pon] nm (de botella) top; (Tec) plug; **~ de rosca o de tuerca** screw-top

taquigrafía [takiɣra'fia] nf
shorthand; **taquígrafo, -a** nm/f
shorthand writer, stenographer (us)

taquilla [ta'kiʎa] nf (de estación
etc) booking office; (suma recogida)
takings pl

tarántula [ta'rantula] nf tarantula

tararear [tarare'ar] /1a/ vi to hum

tardar [tar'ðar] /1a/ vi (tomar tiempo)
to take a long time; (llegar tarde)
to be late; (demorar) to delay; **¿tarda
mucho el tren?** does the train take
long?; **a más ~** at the (very) latest; **no
tardes en venir** come soon

tarde ['tarðe] adv late ▷ nf (de día)
afternoon; (de noche) evening; **de ~
en ~** from time to time; **¡buenas ~s!**
good afternoon!; (noche) good evening!;
a o por la ~ in the afternoon; in the evening

tardío, -a [tar'ðio, a] adj (retrasado)
late; (lento) slow (to arrive)

tarea [ta'rea] nf task; **tareas** nfpl (Escol)
homework sg; **~ de ocasión** chore

tarifa [ta'rifa] nf (lista de precios) price
list; (Com) tariff

tarima [ta'rima] nf (plataforma)
platform

tarjeta [tar'xeta] nf card; **~ postal/
de crédito/de Navidad** postcard/
credit card/Christmas card; **~ de
embarque** boarding pass; **~ de
memoria** memory card; **~ prepago**
top-up card; **~ SIM card**

tarro ['taro] nm jar, pot

tarta ['tarta] nf (pastel) cake; (torta) tart

tartamudear [tartamuðe'ar] /1a/ vi
to stutter, stammer; **tartamudo, -a**
adj stammering ▷ nm/f stammerer

tártaro, -a ['tartaro, a] adj: **salsa
tártara** tartar(e) sauce

tasa ['tasa] nf (precio) (fixed) price,
rate; (valoración) valuation; (medida,
norma) measure, standard; **~
de cambio** exchange rate; **~s
de aeropuerto** airport tax; **~s
universitarias** university fees; **tasar**
/1a/ vt (arreglar el precio) to fix a price
for; (valorar) to value, assess

tasca ['taska] nf (fam) pub

tatarabuelo, -a [tatara'βwelo,
a] nm/f great-great-grandfather/
mother

tatuaje [ta'twaxe] nm (dibujo) tattoo;
(acto) tattooing

tatuar [ta'twar] /1d/ vt to tattoo

taurino, -a [tau'rino, a] adj
bullfighting cpd

Tauro ['tauro] nm Taurus

tauromaquia [tauro'makja] nf (art
of) bullfighting

taxi ['taksi] nm taxi; **taxista** nmf
taxi driver

taza ['taθa] nf cup; (de retrete) bowl;
~ para café coffee cup; **~ de café** cup
of coffee; **tazón** nm mug, large cup;
(escudilla) basin

te [te] pron (complemento de objeto)
you; (complemento indirecto) (to) you;
(reflexivo) (to) yourself; **¿te duele
mucho el brazo?** does your arm hurt
a lot?; **te equivocas** you're wrong;
¡cálmate! calm yourself!

té [te] nm tea

teatral [tea'tral] adj theatre cpd; (fig)
theatrical

teatro [te'atro] nm theatre; (Lit) plays
pl, drama

tebeo [te'βeo] nm children's comic

techo ['tetʃo] nm (externo) roof;
(interno) ceiling

tecla ['tekla] nf (Inform, Mus, Tip) key;
teclado nm keyboard (tb Inform);
teclear /1a/ vi to strum; (fam) to drum
▷ vt (Inform) to key (in)

técnico, -a ['tekniko, a] adj technical
▷ nm/f technician; (experto) expert ▷ nf
(procedimientos) technique; (tecnología)
technology

tecnología [teknolo'xia] nf
technology; **tecnológico, -a** adj
technological

tecolote [teko'lote] nm (ʌм) owl

tedioso, -a [te'ðjoso, a] adj boring;
tedious

teja ['texa] nf tile; (Bot) lime (tree);
tejado nm (tiled) roof

tejano, -a [te'xano, a] *adj, nm/f* Texan
▷ *nmpl:* **~s** (*vaqueros*) jeans

tejemaneje [texema'nexe] *nm* (*lío*)
fuss; (*intriga*) intrigue

tejer [te'xer] /2a/ *vt* to weave; (*LAM*)
to knit; (*fig*) to fabricate; **tejido** *nm*
fabric; (*estofa, tela*) (knitted) material;
(*telaraña*) web; (*Anat*) tissue

tel. *abr* (= *teléfono*) tel.

tela ['tela] *nf* (*material*) material; (*de
fruta, en líquido*) skin; **~ de araña**
cobweb, spider's web; **telar** *nm*
(*máquina*) loom

telaraña [tela'raɲa] *nf* cobweb

tele ['tele] *nf* (*fam*) TV

tele... [tele] *pref* tele...; **telebasura**
nf trash TV; **telecomunicación** *nf*
telecommunication; **telediario** *nm*
television news; **teledirigido, -a** *adj*
remote-controlled

teleférico [tele'feriko] *nm* (*de esquí*)
ski-lift

telefonear [telefone'ar] /1a/ *vi* to
telephone

telefónico, -a [tele'foniko, a] *adj*
telephone *cpd*

telefonillo [telefo'niʎo] *nm* (*de
puerta*) intercom

telefonista [telefo'nista] *nmf*
telephonist

teléfono [te'lefono] *nm* (tele)phone;
~ móvil mobile phone; **está
hablando por ~** he's on the phone;
llamar a algn por ~ to ring sb (up) o
phone sb (up); **~ celular** (*LAM*) mobile
phone; **~ con cámara** camera phone;
~ inalámbrico cordless phone

telégrafo [te'leɣrafo] *nm* telegraph

telegrama [tele'ɣrama] *nm* telegram

tele...: telenovela *nf* soap (opera);
teleobjetivo *nm* telephoto lens;
telepatía *nf* telepathy; **telepático,
-a** *adj* telepathic; **telerrealidad** *nf*
reality TV; **telescopio** *nm* telescope;
telesilla *nm* chairlift; **telespectador,
a** *nm/f* viewer; **telesquí** *nm* ski-lift;
teletarjeta *nf* phonecard; **teletipo**
nm teletype(writer); **teletrabajador,**

a *nm/f* teleworker; **teletrabajo**
nm teleworking; **televentas** *nfpl*
telesales

televidente [teleβi'ðente] *nmf*
viewer

televisar [teleβi'sar] /1a/ *vt* to televise

televisión [teleβi'sjon] *nf* television;
~ digital digital television

televisor [teleβi'sor] *nm* television
set

télex ['teleks] *nm* telex

telón [te'lon] *nm* curtain; **~ de
acero** (*Pol*) iron curtain; **~ de fondo**
backcloth, background

tema ['tema] *nm* (*asunto*) subject,
topic; (*Mus*) theme; **temático, -a** *adj*
thematic

temblar [tem'blar] /1j/ *vi* to shake,
tremble; (*de frío*) to shiver; **temblor**
nm trembling; (*de tierra*) earthquake;
tembloroso, -a *adj* trembling

temer [te'mer] /2a/ *vt* to fear ▷ *vi*
to be afraid; **temo que Juan llegue
tarde** I am afraid Juan may be late

temible [te'miβle] *adj* fearsome

temor [te'mor] *nm* (*miedo*) fear; (*duda*)
suspicion

témpano ['tempano] *nm:* **~ de hielo**
ice floe

temperamento [tempera'mento]
nm temperament

temperatura [tempera'tura] *nf*
temperature

tempestad [tempes'tað] *nf* storm

templado, -a [tem'plaðo, a] *adj*
(*agua*) lukewarm; (*clima*) mild;
(*Mus*) well-tuned; **templanza** *nf*
moderation

templar [tem'plar] /1a/ *vt* (*moderar*)
to moderate; (*furia*) to restrain;
(*calor*) to reduce; (*afinar*) to tune (up);
(*acero*) to temper; (*tuerca*) to tighten
up; **temple** *nm* (*ajuste*) tempering;
(*afinación*) tuning; (*pintura*) tempera

templo ['templo] *nm* (*iglesia*) church;
(*pagano etc*) temple

temporada [tempo'raða] *nf* time,
period; (*estación, social*) season

temporal [tempoˈral] *adj (no permanente)* temporary ▸ *nf* storm

temprano, -a [temˈprano, a] *adj* early ▸ *adv* early; *(demasiado pronto)* too soon, too early

ten [ten] *vb V* **tener**

tenaces [teˈnaθes] *adj pl V* **tenaz**

tenaz [teˈnaθ] *adj (material)* tough; *(persona)* tenacious; *(terco)* stubborn

tenaza(s) [teˈnaθa(s)] *nf, nfpl (Med)* forceps; *(Tec)* pliers; *(Zool)* pincers

tendedero [tendeˈðero] *nm (para ropa)* drying-place; *(cuerda)* clothes line

tendencia [tenˈdenθja] *nf* tendency; **tener ~ a** to tend o have a tendency to

tender [tenˈder] /2g/ *vt (extender)* to spread out; *(ropa)* to hang out; *(vía férrea, cable)* to lay; *(cuerda)* to stretch ▸ *vi* to tend; **tenderse** *vr* to lie down; **~ la cama/la mesa** (ᴌᴀᴍ) to make the bed/lay the table

tenderete [tendeˈrete] *nm (puesto)* stall; *(exposición)* display of goods

tendero, -a [tenˈdero, a] *nm/f* shopkeeper

tendón [tenˈdon] *nm* tendon

tendré *etc* [tenˈdre] *vb V* **tener**

tenebroso, -a [teneˈβroso, a] *adj (oscuro)* dark; *(fig)* gloomy

tenedor [teneˈðor] *nm (Culin)* fork

tenencia [teˈnenθja] *nf (de casa)* tenancy; *(de oficio)* tenure; *(de propiedad)* possession

PALABRA CLAVE

tener [teˈner] /2k/ *vt* **1** *(poseer, gen)* to have; (: *en la mano*) to hold; **¿tienes un boli?** have you got a pen?; **va a tener un niño** she's going to have a baby; **¡ten o tengan!, ¡aquí tienes o tiene!** here you are!

2 *(edad, medidas)* to be; **tiene siete años** she's seven (years old); **tiene 15 cm de largo** it's 15 cm long

3 *(sentimientos, sensaciones)*: **tener sed/hambre/frío/calor** to be

thirsty/hungry/cold/hot; **tener razón** to be right

4 *(considerar)*: **lo tengo por brillante** I consider him to be brilliant; **tener en mucho a algn** to think very highly of sb

5 (+ *pp*): **tengo terminada ya la mitad del trabajo** I've done half the work already

6: **tener que hacer algo** to have to do sth; **tengo que acabar este trabajo hoy** I have to finish this job today

7: **¿qué tienes, estás enfermo?** what's the matter with you, are you ill?

▸ **tenerse** *vr* **1**: **tenerse en pie** to stand up

2: **tenerse por** to think o.s.

tengo *etc* ['tengo] *vb V* **tener**

tenia ['tenja] *nf* tapeworm

teniente [teˈnjente] *nm* lieutenant; *(ayudante)* deputy

tenis ['tenis] *nm* tennis; **~ de mesa** table tennis; **tenista** *nmf* tennis player

tenor [teˈnor] *nm (sentido)* meaning; *(Mus)* tenor; **a ~ de** on the lines of

tensar [tenˈsar] /1a/ *vt* to tauten; *(arco)* to draw

tensión [tenˈsjon] *nf* tension; *(Tec)* stress; **~ arterial** blood pressure; **tener la ~ alta** to have high blood pressure

tenso, -a ['tenso, a] *adj* tense

tentación [tentaˈθjon] *nf* temptation

tentáculo [tenˈtakulo] *nm* tentacle

tentador, a [tentaˈðor, a] *adj* tempting

tentar [tenˈtar] /1j/ *vt (seducir)* to tempt; *(atraer)* to attract

tentempié [tentemˈpje] *nm* snack

tenue ['tenwe] *adj (delgado)* thin, slender; *(neblina)* light; *(lazo, vínculo)* slight

teñir [teˈɲir] *vt* to dye; *(fig)* to tinge; **teñirse** *vr* to dye; **~se el pelo** to dye one's hair

teología [teoloˈxia] *nf* theology

t

teoría [teoˈria] nf theory; **en ~** in theory; **teórico, -a** adj theoretic(al) ▷ nm/f theoretician, theorist; **teorizar** /1f/ vi to theorize

terapéutico, -a [teraˈpeutiko, a] adj therapeutic(al)

terapia [teˈrapja] nf therapy

tercer [terˈθer] adj V **tercero**

tercermundista [terθermunˈdista] adj Third World cpd

tercero, -a [terˈθero, a] adj third ▷ nm (Jur) third party

terceto [terˈθeto] nm trio

terciar [terˈθjar] /1b/ vi (participar) to take part; (hacer de árbitro) to mediate; **terciario, -a** adj tertiary

tercio [ˈterθjo] nm third

terciopelo [terθjoˈpelo] nm velvet

terco, -a [ˈterko, a] adj obstinate

tergal® [terˈɣal] nf Terylene®, Dacron® (us)

tergiversar [terxiβerˈsar] /1a/ vt to distort

termal [terˈmal] adj thermal

termas [ˈtermas] nfpl hot springs

térmico, -a [ˈtermiko, a] adj thermal

terminal [termiˈnal] adj terminal ▷ nm, nf terminal

terminante [termiˈnante] adj (final) final, definitive; (tajante) categorical; **terminantemente** adv: **terminantemente prohibido** strictly forbidden

terminar [termiˈnar] /1a/ vt (completar) to complete, finish; (concluir) to end ▷ vi (llegar a su fin) to end; (parar) to stop; (acabar) to finish; **terminarse** vr to come to an end; **~ por hacer algo** to end up (by) doing sth

término [ˈtermino] nm end, conclusion; (parada) terminus; (límite) boundary; **en último ~** (a fin de cuentas) in the last analysis; (como último recurso) as a last resort; **~ medio** average; (fig) middle way

termo® [ˈtermo] nm Thermos® (flask)

termómetro [terˈmometro] nm thermometer

termostato [termosˈtato] nm thermostat

ternero, -a [terˈnero, a] nm/f (animal) calf ▷ nf (carne) veal, beef

ternura [terˈnura] nf (trato) tenderness; (palabra) endearment; (cariño) fondness

terrado [teˈraðo] nm terrace

terraplén [terraˈplen] nm embankment

terrateniente [terrateˈnjente] nm landowner

terraza [teˈraθa] nf (balcón) balcony; (techo) flat roof; (Agr) terrace

terremoto [terreˈmoto] nm earthquake

terrenal [terreˈnal] adj earthly

terreno [teˈrreno] nm (tierra) land; (parcela) plot; (suelo) soil; (fig) field; **un ~ a piece of land**

terrestre [teˈrrestre] adj terrestrial; (ruta) land cpd

terrible [teˈrriβle] adj terrible; awful

territorio [terriˈtorjo] nm territory

terrón [teˈrron] nm (de azúcar) lump; (de tierra) clod, lump

terror [teˈrror] nm terror; **terrorífico, -a** adj terrifying; **terrorista** adj, nmf terrorist; **terrorista suicida** suicide bomber

terso, -a [ˈterso, a] adj (liso) smooth; (pulido) polished

tertulia [terˈtulja] nf (reunión informal) social gathering; (grupo) group, circle

tesis [ˈtesis] nf inv thesis

tesón [teˈson] nm (firmeza) firmness; (tenacidad) tenacity

tesorero, -a [tesoˈrero, a] nm/f treasurer

tesoro [teˈsoro] nm treasure; (Com, Pol) treasury

testamento [testaˈmento] nm will

testarudo, -a [testaˈruðo, a] adj stubborn

testículo [tesˈtikulo] nm testicle

testificar [testifi'kar] /1g/ vt to testify; (fig) to attest ▷ vi to give evidence

testigo [tes'tiɣo] nmf witness; **~ de cargo/descargo** witness for the prosecution/defence; **~ ocular** eye witness

testimonio [testi'monjo] nm testimony

teta ['teta] nf (de biberón) teat; (Anat: fam) breast

tétanos ['tetanos] nm tetanus

tetera [te'tera] nf teapot

tétrico, -a ['tetriko, a] adj gloomy, dismal

textear [tekste'ar] /1a/ vt (LAM) to text

textil [teks'til] adj textile

texto ['teksto] nm text; **textual** adj textual

textura [teks'tura] nf (de tejido) texture

tez [teθ] nf (cutis) complexion

ti [ti] pron you; (reflexivo) yourself

tía ['tia] nf (pariente) aunt; (fam: mujer) girl

tibio, -a ['tiβjo, a] adj lukewarm

tiburón [tiβu'ron] nm shark

tic [tik] nm (ruido) click; (de reloj) tick; **~ nervioso** nervous tic

tictac [tik'tak] nm (de reloj) tick tock

tiempo ['tjempo] nm time; (época, período) age, period; (Meteorología) weather; (Ling) tense; (de juego) half; **a ~** in time; **a un o al mismo ~** at the same time; **al poco ~** very soon (after); **se quedó poco ~** he didn't stay very long; **hace poco** = not long ago; **mucho ~** a long time; **de ~ en ~** from time to time; **hacer buen/ mal ~** the weather is fine/bad; **estar a ~** to be in time; **hace ~** some time ago; **hacer ~** to while away the time; **motor de 2 ~s** two-stroke engine; **primer ~** first half

tienda ['tjenda] nf (Tip) shop; store; **~ de campaña** tent; **~ de comestibles** grocer's (shop) (BRIT), grocery (store) (US)

tiene etc ['tjene] vb V **tener**

tienta ['tjenta] vb V **tentar** ▷ nf: **andar a ~s** to grope one's way along

tiento etc ['tjento] vb V **tentar** ▷ nm (tacto) touch; (precaución) wariness

tierno, -a ['tjerno, a] adj (blando, dulce) tender; (fresco) fresh

tierra ['tjerra] nf earth; (suelo) soil; (mundo) world; (país) country, land; **~ adentro** inland

tieso, -a ['tjeso, a] adj (rígido) rigid; (duro) stiff; (fam: orgulloso) conceited

tiesto ['tjesto] nm flowerpot

tifón [ti'fon] nm typhoon

tifus ['tifus] nm typhus

tigre ['tiɣre] nm tiger

tijera [ti'xera] nf (una tijera) (pair of) scissors pl; (Zool) claw; **tijeras** nfpl scissors; (para plantas) shears

tila ['tila] nf lime flower tea

tildar [til'dar] /1a/ vt: **~ de** to brand as

tilde ['tilde] nf (Tip) tilde

tilín [ti'lin] nm tinkle

timar [ti'mar] /1a/ vt (estafar) to swindle

timbal [tim'bal] nm small drum

timbre ['timbre] nm (sello) stamp; (campanilla) bell; (tono) timbre; (Com) stamp duty

timidez [timi'ðeθ] nf shyness; **tímido, -a** adj shy

timo ['timo] nm swindle

timón [ti'mon] nm helm, rudder; **timonel** nm helmsman

tímpano ['timpano] nm (Anat) eardrum; (Mus) small drum

tina ['tina] nf tub; (baño) bath(tub); **tinaja** nf large earthen jar

tinieblas [ti'njeβlas] nfpl darkness sg; (sombras) shadows

tino ['tino] nm (habilidad) skill; (juicio) insight

tinta ['tinta] nf ink; (Tec) dye; (Arte) colour

tinte ['tinte] nm dye

tintero [tin'tero] nm inkwell

tinto ['tinto] nm red wine

tintorería [tintore'ria] nf dry cleaner's

tío ['tio] nm (pariente) uncle; (fam: hombre) bloke, guy (us)

tiovivo [tio'βiβo] nm merry-go-round

típico, -a ['tipiko, a] adj typical

tipo ['tipo] nm (clase) type, kind; (hombre) fellow; (Anat) build; (: de mujer) figure; (Imprenta) type; ~ **bancario/de descuento** bank/ discount rate; ~ **de interés** interest rate; ~ **de cambio** exchange rate

tipografía [tipoɣra'fia] nf printing

tiquet ['tiket] (pl **tíquets**) nm ticket; (en tienda) cash slip

tiquismiquis [tikis'mikis] nm fussy person ▷ nmpl (querellas) squabbling sg; (escrúpulos) silly scruples

tira ['tira] nf strip; (fig) abundance ▷ nm: ~ **y afloja** give and take

tirabuzón [tiraβu'θon] nm (rizo) curl

tirachinas [tira'tʃinas] nm inv catapult

tirado, -a [ti'raðo, a] adj (barato) dirt-cheap; (fam: fácil) very easy ▷ nf (acto) cast, throw; (serie) series; (Tip) printing, edition; **de una tirada** at one go; **está** ~ (fam) it's a cinch

tirador [tira'ðor] nm (mango) handle

tirano, -a [ti'rano, a] adj tyrannical ▷ nm/f tyrant

tirante [ti'rante] adj (cuerda) tight, taut; (relaciones) strained ▷ nf (Arq) brace; (Tec) stay; **tirantes** nmpl braces, suspenders (us); **tirantez** nf tightness; (fig) tension

tirar [ti'rar] /1a/ vt to throw; (volcar) to upset; (derribar) to knock down o over; (bomba) to drop; (desechar) to throw out o away; (disipar) to squander; (imprimir) to print ▷ vi (disparar) to shoot; (dar un tirón) to pull; (fam: andar) to go; (tender a) to tend to; (Deporte) to shoot; **tirarse** vr to throw o.s.; ~ **abajo** to bring down, destroy; **tira más a su padre** he takes more after his father; **tira** [fig] to manage

tirita [ti'rita] nf (sticking) plaster, Band-Aid® (us)

tiritar [tiri'tar] /1a/ vi to shiver

tiro ['tiro] nm (lanzamiento) throw; (disparo) shot; (Deporte) shot; (Tenis, Golf) drive; (alcance) range; ~ **al blanco** target practice; **caballo de** ~ cart-horse

tirón [ti'ron] nm (sacudida) pull, tug; **de un** ~ in one go

tiroteo [tiro'teo] nm exchange of shots, shooting

tisis ['tisis] nf consumption, tuberculosis

títere ['titere] nm puppet

titubear [tituβe'ar] /1a/ vi to stagger; (tartamudear) to stammer; (vacilar) to hesitate; **titubeo** nm staggering; stammering; hesitation

titulado, -a [titu'laðo, a] adj (libro) entitled; (persona) titled

titular [titu'lar] /1a/ adj titular ▷ nmf holder ▷ nm headline ▷ vt to title; **titularse** vr to be entitled; **título** nm title; (de diario) headline; (certificado) professional qualification; (universitario) university degree; **a título de** in the capacity of

tiza ['tiθa] nf chalk

toalla [to'aʎa] nf towel

tobillo [to'βiʎo] nm ankle

tobogán [toβo'ɣan] nm (montaña rusa) roller-coaster; (resbaladilla) chute, slide

tocadiscos [toka'ðiskos] nm inv record player

tocado, -a [to'kaðo, a] adj (fam) touched ▷ nm headdress

tocador [toka'ðor] nm (mueble) dressing table; (cuarto) boudoir; (fam) ladies' room

tocar [to'kar] /1g/ vt to touch; (Mus) to play; (campana) to ring; (referirse a) to allude to ▷ vi (a la puerta) to knock (on o at the door); (ser el turno) to fall to, be the turn of; (ser hora) to be due; **tocarse** vr (cubrirse la cabeza) to cover one's head; (tener contacto) to touch (each other); **por lo que a mí me toca** as far as I am concerned; **te toca a ti** it's your turn

tocayo, -a [to'kajo, a] *nm/f* namesake

tocino [to'θino] *nm* bacon

todavía [toða'βia] *adv (aun)* even; *(aún)* still, yet; **~ más** yet o still more; **~ no** not yet

PALABRA CLAVE

todo, -a [ˈtoðo, a] *adj 1 (sg)* all; **toda la carne** all the meat; **toda la noche** all night, the whole night; **todo el libro** the whole book; **toda una botella** a whole bottle; **todo lo contrario** quite the opposite; **está toda sucia** she's all dirty; **por todo el país** throughout the whole country
2 *(pl)* all; every; **todos los libros** all the books; **todas las noches** every night; **todos los que quieran salir** all those who want to leave
▶ *pron 1* everything, all; **todos** everyone, everybody; **lo sabemos todo** we know everything; **todos querían más tiempo** everybody o everyone wanted more time; **nos marchamos todos** all of us left
2 *(con preposición)*: **con todo él me sigue gustando** even so I still like him; **no me agrada del todo** I don't entirely like it
▶ *adv* all; **vaya todo seguido** keep straight on o ahead
▶ *nm*: **como un todo** as a whole

todopoderoso, -a [toðopoðe'roso, a] *adj* all-powerful; *(Rel)* almighty

todoterreno [toðote'rreno] *nm* four-wheel drive, SUV *(esp us)*

toga [ˈtoɣa] *nf* toga; *(Escol)* gown

Tokio [ˈtokjo] *n* Tokyo

toldo [ˈtoldo] *nm (para el sol)* sunshade; *(en tienda)* marquee

tolerancia [tole'ranθja] *nf* tolerance; **tolerante** *adj (tol.)*; *(sociedad)* liberal; *(fig)* open-minded

tolerar [tole'rar] /1a/ *vt* to tolerate; *(resistir)* to endure

toma [ˈtoma] *nf (gen)* taking; *(Med)* dose; *(Elec: tb:* **~ de corriente**) socket; **~ de tierra** *(Aviat)* landing; **tomacorriente** *nm (LAM)* socket

tomar [toˈmar] /1a/ *vt* to take; *(aspecto)* to take on; *(beber)* to drink ▶ *vi* to take; *(LAM)* to drink; **tomarse** *vr* to take; **~se por** to consider o.s. to be; **¡toma!** here you are!; **~ a bien/a mal** to take well/badly; **~ en serio** to take seriously; **~ el pelo a algn** to pull sb's leg; **~la con algn** to pick a quarrel with sb; **~ el sol** to sunbathe

tomate [toˈmate] *nm* tomato

tomillo [toˈmiʎo] *nm* thyme

tomo [ˈtomo] *nm (libro)* volume

ton [ton] *abr* = **tonelada** ▶ *nm*: **sin ~ ni son** without rhyme or reason

tonalidad [tonali'ðað] *nf* tone

tonel [toˈnel] *nm* barrel

tonelada [toneˈlaða] *nf* ton; **tonelaje** *nm* tonnage

tónico, -a [ˈtoniko, a] *adj* tonic ▶ *nm (Med)* tonic ▶ *nf (Mus)* tonic; *(fig)* keynote

tono [ˈtono] *nm* tone; **fuera de ~** inappropriate; **~ de llamada** ringtone

tontería [tonteˈria] *nf (estupidez)* foolishness; *(una tontería)* silly thing; **tonterías** *nfpl* rubbish *sg*, nonsense *sg*

tonto, -a [ˈtonto, a] *adj* stupid; *(ridículo)* silly ▶ *nm/f* fool

topar [toˈpar] /1a/ *vi*: **~ contra** o **en** to run into; **~ con** to run up against

tope [ˈtope] *adj* maximum ▶ *nm (fin)* end; *(límite)* limit; *(Ferro)* buffer; *(Auto)* bumper; **al ~** end to end

tópico, -a [ˈtopiko, a] *adj* topical ▶ *nm* platitude

topo [ˈtopo] *nm (Zool)* mole; *(fig)* blunderer

toque *etc* [ˈtoke] *vb V* **tocar** ▶ *nm* touch; *(Mus)* beat; *(de campana)* chime, ring; **dar un ~ a** to test; **~ de queda** curfew

toqué *etc* *vb V* **tocar**

toquetear [tokete'ar] /1a/ *vt* to finger

toquilla [to'kiʎa] nf (pañuelo) headscarf; (chal) shawl

tórax ['toraks] nm inv thorax

torbellino [torβe'ʎino] nm whirlwind; (fig) whirl

torcedura [torθe'ðura] nf twist; (Med) sprain

torcer [tor'θer] /2b, 2h/ vt to twist; (la esquina) to turn; (Med) to sprain ▷ vi (desviar) to turn off; **torcerse** vr (doblar) to bend; (desviarse) to go astray; (fracasar) to go wrong; **torcido, -a** adj twisted; (fig) crooked ▷ nm curl

tordo, -a ['torðo, a] adj dappled ▷ nm thrush

torear [tore'ar] /1a/ vt (fig: evadir) to dodge; (jugar con) to tease ▷ vi to fight bulls; **toreo** nm bullfighting; **torero, -a** nm/f bullfighter

tormenta [tor'menta] nf storm; (fig: confusión) turmoil

tormento [tor'mento] nm torture; (fig) anguish

tornar [tor'nar] /1a/ vt (devolver) to return, give back; (transformar) to transform ▷ vi to go back

tornasolado, -a [tornaso'laðo, a] adj (brillante) iridescent; (reluciente) shimmering

torneo [tor'neo] nm tournament

tornillo [tor'niʎo] nm screw

torniquete [torni'kete] nm (Med) tourniquet

torno ['torno] nm (Tec) winch; (tambor) drum; **en ~ (a)** round, about

toro ['toro] nm bull; (fam) he-man; **los ~s** bullfighting sg

toronja [to'ronxa] nf grapefruit

torpe ['torpe] adj (poco hábil) clumsy, awkward; (necio) dim; (lento) slow

torpedo [tor'peðo] nm torpedo

torpeza [tor'peθa] nf (falta de agilidad) clumsiness; (lentitud) slowness; (error) mistake

torre ['torre] nf tower; (de petróleo) derrick

torrefacto, -a [torre'fakto, a] adj roasted

torrente [to'rrente] nm torrent

torrija [to'rrixa] nf fried bread; **~s** French toast sg

torsión [tor'sjon] nf twisting

torso ['torso] nm torso

torta ['torta] nf cake; (fam) slap

tortícolis [tor'tikolis] nm inv stiff neck

tortilla [tor'tiʎa] nf omelette; (ʟᴀᴍ) maize pancake; **~ francesa/española** plain/potato omelette

tórtola ['tortola] nf turtledove

tortuga [tor'tuɣa] nf tortoise

tortuoso, -a [tor'twoso, a] adj winding

tortura [tor'tura] nf torture; **torturar** /1a/ vt to torture

tos [tos] nf inv cough; **~ ferina** whooping cough

toser [to'ser] /2a/ vi to cough

tostado, -a adj toasted; (por el sol) dark brown; (piel) tanned ▷ nf piece of toast; **tostadas** nfpl toast sg

tostador [tosta'ðor] nm, **tostadora** [tosta'ðora] nf toaster

tostar [tos'tar] /1l/ vt to toast; (café) to roast; (al sol) to tan; **tostarse** vr to get brown

total [to'tal] adj total ▷ adv in short; (al fin y al cabo) when all is said and done ▷ nm total; **en ~** in all; **~ que** to cut a long story short

totalidad [totali'ðað] nf whole

totalitario, -a [totali'tarjo, a] adj totalitarian

tóxico, -a ['toksiko, a] adj toxic ▷ nm poison; **toxicómano, -a** nm/f drug addict

toxina [to'ksina] nf toxin

tozudo, -a [to'θuðo, a] adj obstinate

trabajador, a [traβaxa'ðor, a] nm/f worker ▷ adj hard-working; **~ autónomo** o **por cuenta propia** self-employed person

trabajar [traβa'xar] /1a/ vt to work; (arar) to till; (empeñarse en) to work at; (convencer) to persuade ▷ vi to work; (esforzarse) to strive; **trabajo** nm work;

(tarea) task; *(Pol)* labour; *(fig)* effort;
tomarse el trabajo de to take the
trouble to: **trabajo por turno/a
destajo** shift work/piecework;
trabajo en equipo teamwork;
trabajos forzados hard labour sg

trabalenguas [traβa'leŋgwas] nm
inv tongue twister

tracción [trak'θjon] nf traction;
~ delantera/trasera front-wheel/
rear-wheel drive

tractor [trak'tor] nm tractor

tradición [traði'θjon] nf tradition;
tradicional adj traditional

traducción [traðuk'θjon] nf
translation

traducir [traðu'θir]/3n/ vt to
translate; **traductor, a** nm/f translator

traer [tra'er]/2o/ vt to bring; *(llevar)* to
carry; *(ropa)* to wear; *(incluir)* to carry;
(fig) to cause; **traerse** vr: **~se algo** to
be up to sth

traficar [trafi'kar]/1g/ vi to trade

tráfico ['trafiko] nm *(Com)* trade;
(Auto) traffic

tragaluz [traɣa'luθ] nm skylight

tragamonedas [traɣamo'neðas] nm
inv, **tragaperras** [traɣa'perras] nm
inv slot machine

tragar [tra'ɣar]/1h/ vt to swallow;
(devorar) to devour, bolt down;
tragarse vr to swallow

tragedia [tra'xeðja] nf tragedy;
trágico, -a adj tragic

trago ['traɣo] nm *(de líquido)* drink;
(comido de golpe) gulp; *(fam: de bebida)*
swig; *(desgracia)* blow; **echar un ~** to
have a drink

traición [trai'θjon] nf treachery; *(Jur)*
treason; *(una traición)* act of treachery;
traicionar /1a/ vt to betray

traidor, a [trai'ðor, a] adj treacherous
▷ nm/f traitor

traigo etc ['traiɣo] vb V **traer**

traje ['traxe] vb V **traer** ▷ nm dress;
(de hombre) suit; *(traje típico)* costume;
~ de baño swimsuit; **~ de luces**
bullfighter's costume

trajera etc [tra'xera] vb V **traer**

trajín [tra'xin] nm *(fam: movimiento)*
bustle; **trajinar** /1a/ vi *(moverse)* to
bustle about

trama ['trama] nf *(intriga)* plot; *(de
tejido)* weft; **tramar** /1a/ vt to plot;
(Tec) to weave

tramitar [trami'tar] /1a/ vt *(asunto)*
to transact; *(negociar)* to negotiate

trámite ['tramite] nm *(paso)*
step; *(Jur)* transaction; **trámites**
nmpl *(burocracia)* procedures; *(Jur)*
proceedings

tramo ['tramo] nm *(de tierra)* plot; *(de
escalera)* flight; *(de vía)* section

trampa ['trampa] nf trap; *(en el suelo)*
trapdoor; *(engaño)* trick; *(fam)* fiddle;
trampear /1a/ vt, vi to cheat

trampolín nm trampoline; *(de piscina
etc)* diving board

tramposo, -a [tram'poso, a] adj
crooked, cheating ▷ nm/f crook,
cheat

tranca ['traŋka] nf *(palo)* stick; *(de
puerta, ventana)* bar; **trancar** /1g/
vt to bar

trance ['tranθe] nm *(momento difícil)*
difficult moment; *(estado de hipnosis)*
trance

tranquilidad [trankili'ðað] nf
(calma) calmness, stillness; *(paz)*
peacefulness

tranquilizar [trankili'θar] /1f/ vt
(calmar) to calm (down); *(asegurar)* to
reassure; **tranquilizarse** vr to calm
down; **tranquilo, -a** adj *(calmado)*
calm; *(apacible)* peaceful; *(mar)* calm;
(mente) untroubled

transacción [transak'θjon] nf
transaction

transbordador [transβorða'ðor]
nm ferry

transbordo [trans'βorðo] nm
transfer; **hacer ~** to change (trains)

transcurrir [transku'rrir] /3a/ vi
(tiempo) to pass; *(hecho)* to turn out

transcurso [trans'kurso] nm: **~ del
tiempo** lapse (of time)

transeúnte [transe'unte] *nmf* passer-by

transferencia [transfe'renθja] *nf* transference; (Com) transfer

transferir [transfe'rir] /3i/ *vt* to transfer

transformación [transforma'θjon] *nf* transformation

transformador [transforma'ðor] *nm* transformer

transformar [transfor'mar] /1a/ *vt* to transform; (convertir) to convert

transfusión [transfu'sjon] *nf* (tb: ~ **de sangre**) (blood) transfusion

transgénico, -a [trans'xeniko, a] *adj* genetically modified

transición [transi'θjon] *nf* transition

transigir [transi'xir] /3c/ *vi* to compromise; (ceder) to make concessions

transitar [transi'tar] /1a/ *vi* to go (from place to place); **tránsito** *nm* transit; (Auto) traffic; **transitorio, -a** *adj* transitory

transmisión [transmi'sjon] *nf* (Radio, TV) transmission; (transferencia) transfer; ~ **en directo/exterior** live/outside broadcast

transmitir [transmi'tir] /3a/ *vt* to transmit; (Radio, TV) to broadcast

transparencia [transpa'renθja] *nf* transparency; (claridad) clearness, clarity; (foto) slide

transparentar [transparen'tar] /1a/ *vt* to reveal ▷ *vi* to be transparent; **transparente** *adj* transparent; (aire) clear

transpirar [transpi'rar] /1a/ *vi* to perspire

transportar [transpor'tar] /1a/ *vt* to transport; (llevar) to carry; **transporte** *nm* transport; (Com) haulage

transversal [transβer'sal] *adj* transverse, cross

tranvía [tram'bia] *nm* tram

trapeador [trapea'ðor] *nm* (ʌᴍ) mop; **trapear** /1a/ *vt* (ʌᴍ) to mop

trapecio [tra'peθjo] *nm* trapeze; **trapecista** *nmf* trapeze artist

trapero, -a [tra'pero, a] *nm/f* ragman

trapicheos [trapi'tʃeos] *nmpl* (fam) schemes, fiddles

trapo ['trapo] *nm* (tela) rag; (de cocina) cloth

tráquea ['trakea] *nf* windpipe

traqueteo [trake'teo] *nm* rattling

tras [tras] *prep* (detrás) behind; (después) after

trasatlántico [trasat'lantiko] *nm* (barco) (cabin) cruiser

trascendencia [trasθen'denθja] *nf* (importancia) importance; (en filosofía) transcendence

trascendental [trasθenden'tal] *adj* important; transcendental

trasero, -a [tra'sero, a] *adj* back, rear ▷ *nm* (Anat) bottom

trasfondo [tras'fondo] *nm* background

trasgredir [trasɣre'ðir] /3a/ *vt* to contravene

trashumante [trasu'mante] *adj* migrating

trasladar [trasla'ðar] /1a/ *vt* to move; (persona) to transfer; (postergar) to postpone; (copiar) to copy; **trasladarse** *vr* (mudarse) to move; **traslado** *nm* move; (mudanza) move, removal

traslucir [traslu'θir] /3f/ *vt* to show

trasluz [tras'luθ] *nm* reflected light; **al ~** against o up to the light

trasnochador, a *nm/f* (fig) night owl

trasnochar [trasno'tʃar] /1a/ *vi* (acostarse tarde) to stay up late

traspapelar [traspape'lar] /1a/ *vt* (documento, carta) to mislay, misplace

traspasar [traspa'sar] /1a/ *vt* (bala) to pierce, go through; (propiedad) to sell, transfer; (calle) to cross over; (límites) to go beyond; (ley) to break; **traspaso** *nm* (venta) transfer, sale

traspié [tras'pje] *nm* (tropezón) trip; (fig) blunder

trasplantar [trasplan'tar] /1a/ *vt* to transplant

traste ['traste] nm (Mus) fret; **dar al ~ con algo** to ruin sth

trastero [tras'tero] nm lumber room

trastienda [tras'tjenda] nf back room (of shop)

trasto ['trasto] nm (pey: cosa) piece of junk; (: persona) dead loss

trastornado, -a [trastor'naðo, a] adj (loco) mad; crazy

trastornar [trastor'nar] /1a/ vt (fig: ideas) to confuse; (: nervios) to shatter; (: persona) to drive crazy; **trastornarse** vr (volverse loco) to go mad o crazy; **trastorno** nm (acto) overturning; (confusión) confusion

tratable [tra'taβle] adj friendly

tratado [tra'taðo] nm (Pol) treaty; (Com) agreement

tratamiento [trata'mjento] nm treatment; **~ de textos** (Inform) word processing

tratar [tra'tar] /1a/ vt (ocuparse de) to treat; (manejar, Tec) to handle; (Med) to treat; (dirigirse a: persona) to address ▷ vi: **~ de** (hablar sobre) to deal with, be about; (intentar) to try to; **tratarse** vr to treat each other; **~ con** (Com) to trade in; (negociar con) to negotiate with; (tener tratos con) to have dealings with; **¿de qué se trata?** what's it about?; **trato** nm dealings pl; (relaciones) relationship; (comportamiento) manner; (Com, Jur) agreement

trauma ['trauma] nm trauma

través [tra'βes] nm (contratiempo) reverse; **al ~** across, crossways; **a ~ de** across; (sobre) over; (por) through

travesaño [traβe'saɲo] nm (Arq) crossbeam; (Deporte) crossbar

travesía [traβe'sia] nf (calle) cross-street; (Naut) crossing

travesura [traβe'sura] nf (broma) prank; (ingenio) wit

travieso, -a [tra'βjeso, a] adj (niño) naughty

trayecto [tra'jekto] nm (ruta) road, way; (viaje) journey; (tramo) stretch; **trayectoria** nf trajectory; (fig) path

traza ['traθa] nf (aspecto) looks pl; (señal) sign; **trazado, -a** adj: **bien trazado** shapely, well-formed ▷ nm (Arq) plan, design; (fig) outline

trazar [tra'θar] /1f/ vt (Arq) to plan; (Arte) to sketch; (fig) to trace; (plan) to draw up; **trazo** nm (línea) line; (bosquejo) sketch

trébol ['treβol] nm (Bot) clover

trece ['treθe] num thirteen

trecho ['tretʃo] nm (distancia) distance; (de tiempo) while

tregua ['treɣwa] nf (Mil) truce; (fig) lull, respite

treinta ['treinta] num thirty

tremendo, -a [tre'mendo, a] adj (terrible) terrible; (imponente: cosa) imposing; (fam: fabuloso) tremendous

tren [tren] nm train; **~ de aterrizaje** undercarriage; **~ de cercanías** suburban train

trenca ['trenka] nf duffel coat

trenza ['trenθa] nf (de pelo) plait

trepar [tre'par] /1a/ vt, vi to climb

tres [tres] num three

tresillo [tre'siʎo] nm three-piece suite; (Mus) triplet

treta ['treta] nf trick

triángulo [tri'angulo] nm triangle

tribu ['triβu] nf tribe

tribuna [tri'βuna] nf (plataforma) platform; (Deporte) stand

tribunal [triβu'nal] nm (en juicio) court; (comisión, fig) tribunal; **~ popular** jury

tributo [tri'βuto] nm (Com) tax

trigal [tri'ɣal] nm wheat field

trigo ['triɣo] nm wheat

trigueño, -a [tri'ɣeɲo, a] adj (pelo) corn-coloured

trillar [tri'ʎar] /1a/ vt (Agr) to thresh

trimestral [trimes'tral] adj quarterly; (Escol) termly

trimestre [tri'mestre] nm (Escol) term

trinar [tri'nar] /1a/ vi (ave) to sing; (rabiar) to fume, be angry

trinchar [trin'tʃar] /1a/ vt to carve

trinchera [trin'tʃera] nf (fosa) trench

trineo [tri'neo] nm sledge

trinidad [trini'ðað] nf trio; (Rel): la **T~** the Trinity

tripa ['tripa] nf (Anat) intestine; (fam) belly; **tripas** nfpl insides

triple ['triple] adj triple

triplicado [tripli'kaðo, a] adj: **por~** in triplicate

tripulación [tripula'θjon] nf crew

tripulante [tripu'lante] nmf crewman/woman

tripular [tripu'lar] /1a/ vt (barco) to man; (Auto) to drive

triquiñuela [triki'ɲwela] nf trick

tris [tris] nm crack

triste ['triste] adj sad; (lamentable) sorry, miserable; **tristeza** nf (aflicción) sadness; (melancolía) melancholy

triturar [tritu'rar] /1a/ vt (moler) to grind; (mascar) to chew

triunfar [triun'far] /1a/ vi (tener éxito) to triumph; (ganar) to win; **triunfo** nm triumph

trivial [tri'βjal] adj trivial

triza ['triθa] nf: **hacer algo ~s** to smash sth to bits; (papel) to tear sth to shreds

trocear [troθe'ar] /1a/ vt to cut up

trocha ['trotʃa] nf short cut

trofeo [tro'feo] nm (premio) trophy

tromba ['tromba] nf: **~ de agua** downpour

trombón [trom'bon] nm trombone

trombosis [trom'bosis] nf inv thrombosis

trompa ['trompa] nf horn; (trompo) humming top; (hocico) snout; **cogerse una ~** (fam) to get tight

trompazo [trom'paθo] nm (choque) bump, bang; (puñetazo) punch

trompeta [trom'peta] nf trumpet; (clarín) bugle

trompicón [trompi'kon]: a **trompicones** adv in fits and starts

trompo ['trompo] nm spinning top

trompón [trom'pon] nm bump

tronar [tro'nar] /1l/ vt (LAM) to shoot; (: examen) to flunk ▷ vi to thunder; (fig) to rage

tronchar [tron'tʃar] /1a/ vt (árbol) to chop down; (fig: vida) to cut short; (esperanza) to shatter; (persona) to tire out; **troncharse** vr to fall down

tronco ['tronko] nm (de árbol, Anat) trunk

trono ['trono] nm throne

tropa ['tropa] nf (Mil) troop; (soldados) soldiers pl

tropezar [trope'θar] /1f, 1j/ vi to trip, stumble; (fig) to slip up; **~ con** to run into; (topar con) to bump into; **tropezón** nm trip; (fig) blunder

tropical [tropi'kal] adj tropical

trópico ['tropiko] nm tropic

tropiezo etc [tro'pjeθo] vb V **tropezar** ▷ nm (error) slip, blunder; (desgracia) misfortune; (obstáculo) snag

trotamundos [trota'mundos] nm inv globetrotter

trotar [tro'tar] /1a/ vi to trot; **trote** nm trot; (fam) travelling; **de mucho trote** hard-wearing

trozar [tro'θar] /1f/ vt (LAM) to cut up, cut into pieces

trozo ['troθo] nm bit, piece

trucha ['trutʃa] nf trout

truco ['truko] nm (habilidad) knack; (engaño) trick

trueno ['trweno] nm thunder; (estampido) bang

trueque ['trweke] nm exchange; (Com) barter

trufa ['trufa] nf (Bot) truffle

truhán, -ana ['truˈan, ana] nm/f rogue

truncar [trun'kar] /1g/ vt (cortar) to truncate; (la vida etc) to cut short; (el desarrollo) to stunt

tu [tu] adj your

tú [tu] pron you

tubérculo [tu'βerkulo] nm (Bot) tuber

tuberculosis [tuβerku'losis] nf inv tuberculosis

tubería [tuβe'ria] nf pipes pl; (conducto) pipeline

tubo ['tuβo] nm tube, pipe; **~ de ensayo** test-tube; **~ de escape** exhaust (pipe)

tuerca ['twerka] nf nut
tuerto, -a ['twerto, a] adj blind in one eye ▷ nm/f one-eyed person
tuerza etc ['twerθa] vb V **torcer**
tuétano ['twetano] nm marrow; (Bot) pith
tufo ['tufo] nm (pey) stench
tuitear [tuite'ar] vt, vi to tweet
tul [tul] nm tulle
tulipán [tuli'pan] nm tulip
tullido, -a [tu'ʎiðo, a] adj crippled
tumba ['tumba] nf (sepultura) tomb
tumbar [tum'bar] /1a/ vt to knock down; **tumbarse** vr (echarse) to lie down; (extenderse) to stretch out
tumbo ['tumbo] nm: **dar ~s** to stagger
tumbona [tum'bona] nf (butaca) easy chair; (de playa) deckchair (BRIT), beach chair (US)
tumor [tu'mor] nm tumour
tumulto [tu'multo] nm turmoil
tuna ['tuna] nf (Mus) student music group; V tb **tuno**

◦ **TUNA**
◦
◦ A tuna is made up of university
◦ students, or quite often former
◦ students, who dress up in costumes
◦ from the Edad de Oro, the Spanish
◦ Golden Age. These musical troupes
◦ go through the town playing their
◦ guitars, lutes and tambourines
◦ and serenade the young ladies
◦ in the halls of residence, or
◦ make impromptu appearances
◦ at weddings or parties singing
◦ traditional Spanish songs for a
◦ few coins.

tunante [tu'nante] nm rogue
túnel ['tunel] nm tunnel
Túnez ['tuneθ] nm Tunis
tuning ['tunin] nm (Auto) car styling, modding (fam)
tuno, -a ['tuno, a] nm/f (fam) rogue ▷ nm (Mus) member of a "tuna"; V **tuna**

tupido, -a [tu'piðo, a] adj (denso) dense; (tela) close-woven
turbante [tur'ßante] nm turban
turbar [tur'ßar] /1a/ vt (molestar) to disturb; (incomodar) to upset
turbina [tur'ßina] nf turbine
turbio, -a [tur'ßjo, a] adj cloudy; (tema) confused
turbulencia [turßu'lenθja] nf turbulence; (fig) restlessness; **turbulento, -a** adj turbulent; (fig: intranquilo) restless; (ruidoso) noisy
turco, -a ['turko, a] adj Turkish ▷ nm/f Turk
turismo [tu'rismo] nm tourism; (coche) saloon car; **turista** nmf tourist; **turístico, -a** adj tourist cpd
turnarse [tur'narse] /1a/ vr to take (it in) turns; **turno** nm (de trabajo) shift; (Deporte etc) turn
turquesa [tur'kesa] nf turquoise
Turquía [tur'kia] nf Turkey
turrón [tu'rron] nm (dulce) nougat
tutear [tute'ar] /1a/ vt to address as familiar "tú"; **tutearse** vr to be on familiar terms
tutela [tu'tela] nf (legal) guardianship; **tutelar** /1a/ adj tutelary ▷ vt to protect
tutor, a [tu'tor, a] nm/f (legal) guardian; (Escol) tutor
tuve etc ['tuße] vb V **tener**
tuviera etc vb V **tener**
tuyo, -a ['tujo, a] adj yours, of yours ▷ pron yours; **un amigo ~** a friend of yours; **los ~s** (fam) your relations, your family
TV nf abr (= televisión) TV
TVE nf abr = **Televisión Española**
tweet [twit] (pl **tweets**) nm (en Twitter) tweet

u [u] *conj* or

ubicar [uβi'kar] /1g/ *vt* to place, situate; (*encontrar*) to find; **ubicarse** *vr* to be situated, be located

ubre ['uβre] *nf* udder

UCI *sigla f* (= *Unidad de Cuidados Intensivos*) ICU

Ud(s) *abr* = **usted**

UE *nf abr* (= *Unión Europea*) EU

ufanarse [ufa'narse] /1a/ *vr* to boast; **ufano, -a** *adj* (*arrogante*) arrogant; (*presumido*) conceited

UGT *nf abr* V **Unión General de Trabajadores (UGT)**

úlcera ['ulθera] *nf* ulcer

ulterior [ulte'rjor] *adj* (*más allá*) farther, further; (*subsecuente, siguiente*) subsequent

últimamente ['ultimamente] *adv* (*recientemente*) lately, recently

ultimar [ulti'mar] /1a/ *vt* to finish; (*finalizar*) to finalize; (*LAM: matar*) to kill

ultimátum [ulti'matum] *nm* ultimatum

último, -a ['ultimo, a] *adj* last; (*más reciente*) latest, most recent; (*más bajo*) bottom; (*más alto*) top; **en las últimas** on one's last legs; **por ~** finally

ultra ['ultra] *adj* ultra ▷ *nmf* extreme right-winger

ultraje [ul'traxe] *nm* outrage; insult

ultramar [ultra'mar] *nm*: **de** o **en ~** abroad, overseas

ultranza [ul'tranθa]: **a ~** *adv* (*a toda costa*) at all costs; (*completo*) outright

umbral [um'bral] *nm* (*gen*) threshold

PALABRA CLAVE

un, -una [un, 'una] *artículo indefinido*
1 a; (*antes de vocal*) an; **una mujer/naranja** a woman/an orange
2: unos/unas: hay unos regalos para ti there are some presents for you; **hay unas cervezas en la nevera** there are some beers in the fridge; V *tb* **uno**

unánime [u'nanime] *adj* unanimous; **unanimidad** *nf* unanimity

undécimo, -a [un'deθimo, a] *adj* eleventh

ungir [un'xir] /3c/ *vt* to anoint

ungüento [un'gwento] *nm* ointment

único, -a ['uniko, a] *adj* only; sole; (*sin par*) unique

unidad [uni'ðað] *nf* unity; (*Tec*) unit

unido, -a [u'niðo, a] *adj* joined, linked; (*fig*) united

unificar [unifi'kar] /1g/ *vt* to unite, unify

uniformar [unifor'mar] /1a/ *vt* to make uniform; (*persona*) to put into uniform

uniforme [uni'forme] *adj* uniform, equal; (*superficie*) even ▷ *nm* uniform

unilateral [unilate'ral] *adj* unilateral

unión [u'njon] *nf* union; (*acto*) uniting, joining; (*calidad*) unity; (*Tec*) joint; **U~ General de Trabajadores (UGT)** (*ESP*) Socialist Union Confederation; **U~ Europea** European Union

unir [u'nir] /3a/ *vt* (*juntar*) to join, unite; (*atar*) to tie, fasten; (*combinar*) to combine; **unirse** vr to join together, unite; (empresas) to merge

unísono [u'nisono] nm: **al ~** in unison

universal [uniβer'sal] adj universal; (mundial) world cpd

universidad [uniβersi'ðað] nf university

universitario, -a [uniβersi'tarjo, a] adj university cpd ▷ nm/f (profesor) lecturer; (estudiante) (university) student; (graduado) graduate

universo [uni'βerso] nm universe

○ PALABRA CLAVE

uno, -a ['uno, a] adj one; **unos pocos** a few; **unos cien** about a hundred
▶ pron 1 one; **quiero uno solo** I only want one; **uno de ellos** one of them
2 (alguien) somebody, someone; **conozco a uno que se te parece** I know somebody o someone who looks like you; **unos querían quedarse** some (people) wanted to stay
3 (impersonal) one; **uno mismo** oneself
4: **unos ... otros ...** some ... others
▶ nf one; **es la una** it's one o'clock
▶ num (number) one; V tb **un**

---

untar [un'tar] /1a/ vt (mantequilla) to spread; (engrasar) to grease, oil

uña ['uɲa] nf (Anat) nail; (garra) claw; (casco) hoof; (arrancaclavos) claw

uranio [u'ranjo] nm uranium

urbanización [urβaniθa'θjon] nf (colonia, barrio) estate, housing scheme

urbanizar [urβani'θar] /1f/ vt (zona) to develop, urbanize

urbano, -a [ur'βano, a] adj (de ciudad) urban; (cortés) courteous, polite

urbe ['urβe] nf large city

urdir [ur'ðir] /3a/ vt to warp; (fig) to plot, contrive

urgencia [ur'xenθja] nf urgency; (prisa) haste, rush; (emergencia) emergency; **servicios de ~** emergency services; **"U~s"** "Casualty"; **urgente** adj urgent

urgir [ur'xir] /3c/ vi to be urgent; **me urge** I'm in a hurry for

urinario, -a [uri'narjo, a] adj urinary
▷ nm urinal

urna ['urna] nf urn; (Pol) ballot box

urraca [u'rraka] nf magpie

URSS nf abr (Historia: = Unión de Repúblicas Socialistas Soviéticas) USSR

Uruguay [uru'ɣwai] nm: **El ~** Uruguay; **uruguayo, -a** adj, nm/f Uruguayan

usado, -a [u'saðo, a] adj used; (de segunda mano) secondhand

usar [u'sar] /1a/ vt to use; (ropa) to wear; (tener costumbre) to be in the habit of; **usarse** vr to be used; **uso** nm use; (Mecánica etc) wear; (costumbre) usage, custom; (moda) fashion; **al uso** in keeping with custom; **al uso de** in the style of; **de uso externo** (Med) for external use

usted [us'teð] pron you sg; **~es** you pl

usual [u'swal] adj usual

usuario, -a [u'swarjo, a] nm/f user

usura [u'sura] nf usury; **usurero, -a** nm/f usurer

usurpar [usur'par] /1a/ vt to usurp

utensilio [uten'siljo] nm tool; (Culin) utensil

útero ['utero] nm uterus, womb

útil ['util] adj useful ▷ nm tool; **utilidad** nf usefulness; (Com) profit; **utilizar** /1f/ vt to use, utilize

utopía [uto'pia] nf Utopia; **utópico, -a** adj Utopian

uva ['uβa] nf grape

◇ UVA

● In Spain las uvas play a big part on New Years' Eve (Nochevieja), when on the stroke of midnight people from every part of Spain, at home, in restaurants or in the plaza mayor eat a grape for each stroke of the clock – especially the one at Puerta del Sol in Madrid. It is said to bring luck for the following year.

u

V

va [ba] *vb* V **ir**

vaca [ˈbaka] *nf* (*animal*) cow; (*carne*) beef

vacaciones [bakaˈθjones] *nfpl* holiday(s)

vacante [baˈkante] *adj* vacant, empty ▷ *nf* vacancy

vaciar [baˈθjar] /1c/ *vt* to empty (out); (*ahuecar*) to hollow out; (*moldear*) to cast; **vaciarse** *vr* to empty

vacilar [baθiˈlar] /1a/ *vi* to be unsteady; to falter; (*desecupado*) to hesitate, waver; (*memoria*) to fail

vacío, -a [baˈθio, a] *adj* empty; (*puesto*) vacant; (*desecupado*) idle; (*vano*) vain ▷ *nm* emptiness; (*Física*) vacuum; (*un vacío*) space

vacuna [baˈkuna] *nf* vaccine;

vacunar /1a/ *vt* to vaccinate

vacuno, -a [baˈkuno, a] *adj* bovine; **ganado ~** cattle

vadear [baðeˈar] /1a/ *vt* (*río*) to ford; **vado** *nm* ford; **"vado permanente"** "keep clear"

vagabundo, -a [baɣaˈβundo, a] *adj* wandering ▷ *nm/f* tramp

vagancia [baˈɣanθja] *nf* (*pereza*) idleness, laziness; (*vagabundeo*) vagrancy

vagar [baˈɣar] /1h/ *vi* to wander; (*no hacer nada*) to idle

vagina [baˈxina] *nf* vagina

vago, -a [ˈbaɣo, a] *adj* vague; (*perezoso*) lazy ▷ *nm/f* (*vagabundo*) tramp; (*perezoso*) lazybones *sg*, idler

vagón [baˈɣon] *nm* (*de pasajeros*) carriage; (*de mercancías*) wagon

vaho [ˈbao] *nm* (*vapor*) vapour, steam; (*respiración*) breath

vaina [ˈbaina] *nf* sheath

vainilla [baiˈniʎa] *nf* vanilla

vais [bais] *vb* V **ir**

vaivén [baiˈβen] *nm* to-and-fro movement; (*de tránsito*) coming and going; **vaivenes** *nmpl* (*fig*) ups and downs

vajilla [baˈxiʎa] *nf* crockery, dishes *pl*; (*una vajilla*) service

valdré *etc vb* V **valer**

vale [ˈbale] *nm* voucher; (*recibo*) receipt; (*pagaré*) IOU

valedero, -a [baleˈðero, a] *adj* valid

valenciano, -a [balenˈθjano, a] *adj* Valencian

valentía [balenˈtia] *nf* courage, bravery

valer [baˈler] /2p/ *vt* to be worth; (*Mat*) to equal; (*costar*) to cost ▷ *vi* (*ser útil*) to be useful; (*ser válido*) to be valid; **valerse** *vr* to take care of o.s.; **~ la pena** to be worthwhile; **¿vale?** O.K.?; **más vale que nos vayamos** we'd better go; **~se de** to make use of, take advantage of; **¡eso a mí no me vale!** (*Am fam: no importar*) I couldn't care less about that

valeroso, -a [baleˈroso, a] *adj* brave, valiant

valgo *etc* [ˈbalɣo] *vb* V **valer**

valía [baˈlia] *nf* worth

validar [baliˈðar] /1a/ *vt* to validate; **validez** *nf* validity; **válido, -a** *adj* valid

valiente [ba'ljente] *adj* brave, valiant
▷ *nmf* brave man/woman

valija [ba'lixa] *nf* (ʟᴀᴍ) case, suitcase;
~ diplomática diplomatic bag

valioso, -a [ba'ljoso, a] *adj* valuable

valla [ˈbaʎa] *nf* fence; (*Deporte*) hurdle;
~ publicitaria hoarding (*esp* BRIT),
billboard (*esp* US); **vallar** /1a/ *vt* to
fence in

valle [ˈbaʎe] *nm* valley

valor [baˈlor] *nm* value, worth; (*precio*)
price; (*valentía*) valour, courage;
(*importancia*) importance; *V tb*
valores; **valorar** /1a/ *vt* to value;
valores *nmpl* (*Com*) securities

vals [bals] *nm* waltz

válvula [ˈbalβula] *nf* valve

vamos [ˈbamos] *vb V* **ir**

vampiro, -iresa [bamˈpiro, iˈresa]
nm/f vampire

van [ban] *vb V* **ir**

vanguardia [banˈgwardja] *nf*
vanguard; (*Arte*) avant-garde

vanidad [baniˈðað] *nf* vanity;
vanidoso, -a *adj* vain, conceited

vano, -a [ˈbano, a] *adj* vain

vapor [baˈpor] *nm* vapour; (*vaho*)
steam; **al ~** (*Culin*) steamed; **~ de
agua** water vapour; **vaporizador** *nm*
spray; **vaporizar** /1f/ *vt* to vaporize;
vaporoso, -a *adj* vaporous

vaquero, -a [baˈkero, a] *adj* cattle *cpd*
▷ *nm* cowboy; **vaqueros** *nmpl* jeans

vaquilla [baˈkiʎa] *nf* heifer

vara [ˈbara] *nf* stick; (*Tec*) rod

variable [baˈrjaβle] *adj, nf* variable
(*tb Inform*)

variación [barjaˈθjon] *nf* variation

variar [baˈrjar] /1c/ *vt* to vary;
(*modificar*) to modify; (*cambiar de
posición*) to switch around ▷ *vi* to vary

varicela [bariˈθela] *nf* chicken pox

varices [baˈriθes] *nfpl* varicose veins

variedad [barjeˈðað] *nf* variety

varilla [baˈriʎa] *nf* stick; (*Bot*) twig;
(*Tec*) rod; (*de rueda*) spoke

vario, -a [ˈbarjo, a] *adj* varied; **~s**
various, several

varita [baˈrita] *nf*: **~ mágica** magic
wand

varón [baˈron] *nm* male, man; **varonil**
adj manly

Varsovia [barˈsoβja] *nf* Warsaw

vas [bas] *vb V* **ir**

vasco, -a [ˈbasko, a], **vascongado,
-a** [baskonˈgaðo, a] *adj, nm/f* Basque

vaselina [baseˈlina] *nf* Vaseline®

vasija [baˈsixa] *nf* (earthenware)
vessel

vaso [ˈbaso] *nm* glass, tumbler; (*Anat*)
vessel

> No confundir *vaso* con la palabra
> inglesa *vase*.

vástago [ˈbastaɣo] *nm* (*Bot*) shoot;
(*Tec*) rod; (*fig*) offspring

vasto, -a [ˈbasto, a] *adj* vast, huge

Vaticano [batiˈkano] *nm*: **el ~** the
Vatican

vatio [ˈbatjo] *nm* (*Elec*) watt

vaya *etc V* [ˈbaja] *vb V* **ir**

Vd *abr* = **usted**

Vds *abr* = **ustedes**; *V* **usted**

ve [be] *vb V* **ir**; **ver**

vecindad [beθinˈdað] *nf*,
vecindario [beθinˈdarjo] *nm*
neighbourhood; (*habitantes*)
residents *pl*

vecino, -a [beˈθino, a] *adj*
neighbouring ▷ *nm/f* neighbour;
(*residente*) resident

veda [ˈbeða] *nf* prohibition; **vedar** /1a/
vt (*prohibir*) to ban, prohibit; (*impedir*)
to stop, prevent

vegetación [bexetaˈθjon] *nf*
vegetation

vegetal [bexeˈtal] *adj, nm* vegetable

vegetariano, -a [bexetaˈrjano, a]
adj, nm/f vegetarian

vehículo [beˈikulo] *nm* vehicle;
(*Med*) carrier

veía *etc V* **ver**

veinte [ˈbeinte] *num* twenty

vejar [beˈxar] /1a/ *vt* (*irritar*) to annoy,
vex; (*humillar*) to humiliate

vejez [beˈxeθ] *nf* old age

vejiga [beˈxiɣa] *nf* (*Anat*) bladder

vela ['bela] nf (de cera) candle; (Naut) sail; (insomnio) sleeplessness; (vigilia) vigil; (Mil) sentry duty; **estar a dos ~s** (fam) to be skint

velado, -a [be'laðo, a] adj veiled; (sonido) muffled; (Foto) blurred ▷ nf soirée

velar [be'lar] /1a/ vt (vigilar) to keep watch over ▷ vi to stay awake; **~ por** to watch over, look after

velatorio [bela'torjo] nm (funeral) wake

velero [be'lero] nm (Naut) sailing ship; (Aviat) glider

veleta [be'leta] nf weather vane

veliz [be'lis] nm (AM) suitcase

vello ['beʎo] nm down, fuzz

velo ['belo] nm veil

velocidad [beloθi'ðað] nf speed; (Tec) rate; (Mecánica, Auto) gear

velocímetro [belo'θimetro] nm speedometer

velorio [be'lorjo] nm (AM) (funeral) wake

veloz [be'loθ] adj fast

ven [ben] vb V **venir**

vena ['bena] nf vein

venado [be'naðo] nm deer

vencedor, a [benθe'ðor, a] adj victorious ▷ nm/f victor, winner

vencer [ben'θer] /2b/ vt (dominar) to defeat, beat; (derrotar) to vanquish; (superar, controlar) to overcome, master ▷ vi (triunfar) to win (through), triumph; (plazo) to expire; **vencido, -a** adj (derrotado) defeated, beaten; (Com) due ▷ adv: **pagar vencido** to pay in arrears

venda ['benda] nf bandage; **vendaje** nm bandage, dressing; **vendar** /1a/ vt to bandage; **vendar los ojos a** to blindfold

vendaval [benda'βal] nm (viento) gale

vendedor, a [bende'ðor, a] nm/f seller

vender [ben'der] /2a/ vt to sell; **venderse** vr (estar a la venta) to be on sale; **~ al contado/al por mayor/**

al por menor/a plazos to sell for cash/wholesale/retail/on credit; **"se vende"** "for sale"

vendimia [ben'dimja] nf grape harvest

vendré etc [ben'dre] vb V **venir**

veneno [be'neno] nm poison; (de serpiente) venom; **venenoso, -a** adj poisonous; venomous

venerable [bene'raβle] adj venerable; **venerar** /1a/ vt (respetar) to revere; (reconocer) to venerate; (adorar) to worship

venéreo, -a [be'nereo, a] adj: **enfermedad venérea** venereal disease

venezolano, -a [beneθo'lano, a] adj Venezuelan

Venezuela [bene'θwela] nf Venezuela

venganza [ben'ganθa] nf vengeance, revenge; **vengar** /1h/ vt to avenge; **vengarse** vr to take revenge; **vengativo, -a** adj (persona) vindictive

vengo etc vb V **venir**

venia ['benja] nf (perdón) pardon; (permiso) consent

venial [be'njal] adj venial

venida [be'niða] nf (llegada) arrival; (regreso) return

venidero, -a [beni'ðero, a] adj coming, future

venir [be'nir] /3r/ vi to come; (llegar) to arrive; (ocurrir) to happen; **venirse** vr: **~se abajo** to collapse; **~ bien** to be suitable; **~ mal** to be unsuitable o inconvenient; **el año que viene** next year

venta ['benta] nf (Com) sale; **~ a plazos** hire purchase; **"en ~"** "for sale"; **~ al contado/al por mayor/al por menor** o **al detalle** cash sale/wholesale/retail; **~ a domicilio** door-to-door selling; **estar de** o **en ~** to be (up) for sale o on the market

ventaja [ben'taxa] nf advantage; **ventajoso, -a** adj advantageous

ventana [ben'tana] nf window; **ventanilla** nf (de taquilla) window

ventilación [bentila'θjon] nf
ventilation; (corriente) draught
ventilador [bentila'ðor] nm fan
ventilar [benti'lar] /1a/ vt to
ventilate; (poner a secar) to put out to
dry; (fig) to air, discuss
ventisca [ben'tiska] nf blizzard
ventrílocuo, -a [ben'trilokwo, a]
nm/f ventriloquist
ventura [ben'tura] nf (felicidad)
happiness; (buena suerte) luck; (destino)
fortune; **a la (buena)** - at random;
venturoso, -a adj happy; (afortunado)
lucky, fortunate
veo etc vb V **ver**
ver [ber] /2u/ vt, vi to see; (mirar) to
look at, watch; (investigar) to look
into; (entender) to see, understand;
verse vr (encontrarse) to meet; (dejarse
ver) to be seen; (hallarse: en un apuro)
to find o.s., be; **a ver** let's see; **no tener
nada que ~ con** to have nothing to do
with; **a mi modo de ~** as I see it; **ya
veremos** we'll see
vera ['bera] nf edge, verge; (de río) bank
veraneante [berane'ante] nmf
holidaymaker, (summer) vacationer
(us)
veranear [berane'ar] /1a/ vi to
spend the summer; **veraneo** nm
summer holiday; **veraniego, -a** adj
summer cpd
verano [be'rano] nm summer
veras ['beras] nfpl: **de** - really, truly
verbal [ber'βal] adj verbal
verbena [ber'βena] nf street party;
(baile) open-air dance
verbo ['berβo] nm verb
verdad [ber'ðað] nf truth; (fiabilidad)
reliability; **de** - real, proper; **a decir
~, no quiero** to tell (you) the truth,
I don't want to; **verdadero, -a** adj
(veraz) true, truthful; (fiable) reliable;
(fig) real
verde ['berðe] adj green; (chiste etc)
blue, dirty ▷ nm green; **viejo** ~ dirty
old man; **verdear** /1a/ vi to turn
green; **verdor** nm greenness

verdugo [ber'ðuɣo] nm executioner
verdulero, -a [berðu'lero, a] nm/f
greengrocer
verdura [ber'ðura] nf greenness;
verduras nfpl (Culin) greens
vereda [be'reða] nf path; (LAm)
pavement, sidewalk (us)
veredicto [bere'ðikto] nm verdict
vergonzoso, -a [berɣon'θoso, a] adj
shameful; (tímido) timid, bashful
vergüenza [ber'ɣwenθa] nf shame,
sense of shame; (timidez) bashfulness;
(pudor) modesty; **me da ~ decírselo**
I feel too shy o it embarrasses me to
tell him
verídico, -a [be'riðiko, a] adj true,
truthful
verificar [berifi'kar] /1g/ vt to
check; (corroborar) to verify (tb
Inform); (llevar a cabo) to carry out;
verificarse vr (profecía etc) to come
o prove true
verja ['berxa] nf (cancela) iron gate;
(cerca) railing(s); (rejado) grating
vermut [ber'mu] (pl **vermuts**) nm
vermouth
verosímil [bero'simil] adj likely,
probable; (relato) credible
verruga [be'rruɣa] nf wart
versátil [ber'satil] adj versatile
versión [ber'sjon] nf version
verso ['berso] nm verse; **un** ~ a line
of poetry
vértebra ['berteβra] nf vertebra
verter [ber'ter] /2g/ vt (vaciar) to
empty, pour (out); (sin querer) to spill;
(basura) to dump ▷ vi to flow
vertical [berti'kal] adj vertical
vértice ['bertiθe] nm vertex, apex
vertidos [ber'tiðos] nmpl waste sg
vertiente [ber'tjente] nf slope;
(fig) aspect
vértigo ['bertiɣo] nm vertigo; (mareo)
dizziness
vesícula [be'sikula] nf blister
vespino® [bes'pino] nm o f ≈ moped
vestíbulo [bes'tiβulo] nm hall; (de
teatro) foyer

v

vestido [bes'tiðo] *nm* (*ropa*) clothes *pl*, clothing; (*de mujer*) dress, frock

vestidor [besti'ðor] *nm* (LAM *Deporte*) changing (BRIT) *o* locker (US) room

vestimenta [besti'menta] *nf* clothing

vestir [bes'tir] /3k/ *vt* (*poner: ropa*) to put on; (*llevar: ropa*) to wear; (*pagar: la ropa*) to clothe; (*sastre*) to make clothes for ▷ *vi* to dress; (*verse bien*) to look good; **vestirse** *vr* to get dressed, dress o.s.; **estar vestido de** to be dressed o clad in; (*como disfraz*) to be dressed as

vestuario [bes'twarjo] *nm* clothes *pl*, wardrobe; (*Teat: para actores*) dressing room; (*Deporte*) changing room

vetar [be'tar] /1a/ *vt* to veto

veterano, -a [bete'rano, a] *adj, nm/f* veteran

veterinario, -a [beteri'narjo, a] *nm/f* vet(erinary surgeon) ▷ *nf* veterinary science

veto ['beto] *nm* veto

vez [beθ] *nf* time; (*turno*) turn; **a la ~ que** at the same time as; **a su ~** in its turn; **una ~** once; **dos veces** twice; **de una ~** in one go; **de una ~ para siempre** once and for all; **en ~ de** instead of; **a veces** sometimes; **otra ~** again; **una y otra ~** repeatedly; **de ~ en cuando** from time to time; **7 veces 9** 7 times 9; **hacer las veces de** to stand in for; **tal ~** perhaps

vía ['bia] *nf* track, route; (*Ferro*) line; (*fig*) way; (*Anat*) passage, tube ▷ *prep* via, by way of; **por ~ judicial** by legal means; **en ~s de** in the process of; **~ aérea** airway; **V~ Láctea** Milky Way; **~ pública** public highway *o* thoroughfare

viable ['bjaβle] *adj* (*plan etc*) feasible

viaducto [bja'ðukto] *nm* viaduct

viajante [bja'xante] *nm* commercial traveller

viajar [bja'xar] /1a/ *vi* to travel; **viaje** *nm* journey; (*gira*) tour; (*Naut*) voyage; **estar de viaje** to be on a journey

viaje de ida y vuelta round trip; **viaje de novios** honeymoon; **viajero, -a** *adj* travelling (BRIT), traveling (US); (*Zool*) migratory ▷ *nm/f* (*quien viaja*) traveller; (*pasajero*) passenger

víbora ['biβora] *nf* viper; (LAM: *venenoso*) poisonous snake

vibración [biβra'θjon] *nf* vibration

vibrar [bi'βrar] /1a/ *vt* to vibrate ▷ *vi* to vibrate

vicepresidente [biθepresi'ðente] *nmf* vice president

viceversa [biθe'βersa] *adv* vice versa

vicio ['biθjo] *nm* vice; (*mala costumbre*) bad habit; **vicioso, -a** *adj* (*muy malo*) vicious; (*corrompido*) depraved ▷ *nm/f* depraved person

víctima ['biktima] *nf* victim

victoria [bik'torja] *nf* victory; **victorioso, -a** *adj* victorious

vid [bið] *nf* vine

vida ['biða] *nf* life; (*duración*) lifetime; **de por ~** for life; **en la/mi ~** never; **estar con ~** to be still alive; **ganarse la ~** to earn one's living

vídeo ['bideo] *nm* video; **película de ~** videofilm; **videocámara** *nf* camcorder; **videoclub** *nm* video club; **videojuego** *nm* video game; **videollamada** *nf* video call; **videoteléfono** *nf* videophone

vidrio ['biðrjo] *nm* glass

vieira ['bjeira] *nf* scallop

viejo, -a ['bjexo, a] *adj* old ▷ *nm/f* old man/woman; **hacerse** *o* **ponerse ~** to grow *o* get old

Viena ['bjena] *nf* Vienna

viene *etc* ['bjene] *vb* V **venir**

vienés, -esa [bje'nes, esa] *adj* Viennese

viento ['bjento] *nm* wind; **hacer ~** to be windy

vientre ['bjentre] *nm* belly; (*matriz*) womb

viernes ['bjernes] *nm inv* Friday; **V~ Santo** Good Friday

Vietnam [bjet'nam] *nm*: Vietnam; **vietnamita** *adj* Vietnamese

viga ['biɣa] *nf* beam, rafter; *(de metal)* girder

vigencia [bi'xenθja] *nf* validity; **estar/entrar en ~** to be in/come into effect o force; **vigente** *adj* valid, in force; *(imperante)* prevailing

vigésimo, -a [bi'xesimo, a] *num* twentieth

vigía [bi'xia] *nm* look-out

vigilancia [bixi'lanθja] *nf*: **tener a algn bajo ~** to keep watch on sb

vigilar [bixi'lar] /1a/ *vt* to watch over ▷ *vi* to be vigilant; *(hacer guardia)* to keep watch; **~ por** to take care of

vigilia [vi'xilja] *nf* wakefulness; *(Rel)* vigil; *(: ayuno)* fast

vigor [bi'ɣor] *nm* vigour, vitality; **en ~** in force; **entrar/poner en ~** to come/put into effect; **vigoroso, -a** *adj* vigorous

VIH *nm abr* (= *virus de inmunodeficiencia humana*) HIV; **~ negativo/positivo** HIV-negative/-positive

vil [bil] *adj* vile, low

villa ['biʎa] *nf* (*casa*) villa; (*pueblo*) small town; (*municipalidad*) municipality

villancico [biʎan'θiko] *nm* (Christmas) carol

vilo ['bilo]: **en ~** *adv* in the air, suspended; *(fig)* on tenterhooks, in suspense

vinagre [bi'naɣre] *nm* vinegar

vinagreta [bina'ɣreta] *nf* vinaigrette, French dressing

vinculación [binkula'θjon] *nf* (*lazo*) link, bond; (*acción*) linking

vincular [binku'lar] /1a/ *vt* to link, bind; **vínculo** *nm* link, bond

vine *etc* *vb* V **venir**

vinicultor, -a [binikul'tor, a] *nm/f* wine grower

vinicultura [binikul'tura] *nf* wine growing

viniera *etc* *vb* V **venir**

vino ['bino] *vb* V **venir** ▷ *nm* wine; **~ de solera/seco/tinto** vintage/ dry/red wine

viña ['biɲa] *nf*, **viñedo** [bi'ɲeðo] *nm* vineyard

viola ['bjola] *nf* viola

violación [bjola'θjon] *nf* violation; **~ (sexual)** rape

violar [bjo'lar] /1a/ *vt* to violate; (*cometer estupro*) to rape

violencia [bjo'lenθja] *nf* (*fuerza*) violence, force; (*embarazo*) embarrassment; (*acto injusto*) unjust act; **violentar** /1a/ *vt* to force; (*casa*) to break into; (*agredir*) to assault; (*violar*) to violate; **violento, -a** *adj* violent; (*furioso*) furious; (*situación*) embarrassing; (*acto*) forced, unnatural

violeta [bjo'leta] *nf* violet

violín [bjo'lin] *nm* violin

violón [bjo'lon] *nm* double bass

viral [bi'ral] *adj* viral

virar [bi'rar] /1a/ *vi* to change direction

virgen ['birxen] *adj* virgin ▷ *nmf* virgin

Virgo ['birɣo] *nm* Virgo

viril [bi'ril] *adj* virile; **virilidad** *nf* virility

virtud [bir'tuð] *nf* virtue; **en ~ de** by virtue of; **virtuoso, -a** *adj* virtuous ▷ *nm/f* virtuoso

viruela [bi'rwela] *nf* smallpox

virulento, -a [biru'lento, a] *adj* virulent

virus ['birus] *nm inv* virus

visa ['bisa] *nf* (*LAM*), **visado** [bi'saðo] *nm* (*ESP*) visa

víscera ['bisθera] *nf* internal organ; **vísceras** *nfpl* entrails

visceral [bisθe'ral] *adj* (*odio*) deep-rooted; **reacción ~** gut reaction

visera [bi'sera] *nf* visor

visibilidad [bisiβili'ðað] *nf* visibility; **visible** *adj* visible; *(fig)* obvious

visillo [bi'siʎo] *nm* lace curtain

visión [bi'sjon] *nf* (*Anat*) vision, (*eye*) sight; (*fantasía*) vision, fantasy

visita [bi'sita] *nf* call, visit; (*persona*) visitor; **visitante** *adj* visiting ▷ *nmf* visitor; **visitar** /1a/ *vt* to visit, call on

visón [bi'son] *nm* mink

visor [bi'sor] *nm* (*Foto*) viewfinder

víspera ['bispera] nf day before; **la ~ o en ~s de** on the eve of

vista ['bista] nf sight, vision; (capacidad de ver) (eye)sight; (mirada) look(s); **a primera ~** at first glance; **hacer la ~ gorda** to turn a blind eye; **volver la ~** to look back; **está a la ~ que** it's obvious that; **en ~ de** in view of; **en ~ de que** in view of the fact that; **¡hasta la ~!** so long!, see you!; **con ~s a** with a view to; **vistazo** nm glance; **dar o echar un vistazo a** to glance at

visto, -a ['bisto, a] vb V **vestir** ▷ pp de ver ▷ adj seen; (considerado) considered ▷ nm: **~ bueno** approval; **por lo ~** apparently; **está ~ que** it's clear that; **está bien/mal** it's acceptable/unacceptable; **~ que** since, considering that

vistoso, -a [bis'toso, a] adj colourful

visual [bi'swal] adj visual

vital [bi'tal] adj life cpd, living cpd; (fig) vital; (persona) lively, vivacious; **vitalicio, -a** person for life; **vitalidad** nf vitality; (de persona, negocio) energy; (de ciudad) liveliness

vitamina [bita'mina] nf vitamin

vitorear [bitore'ar] /1a/ vt to cheer, acclaim

vítrina [bi'trina] nf glass case; (en casa) display cabinet; (LAM) shop window

viudo, -a ['bjuðo, a] adj widowed ▷ nm widower ▷ nf widow

viva ['biβa] excl hurrah!; **¡~ el rey!** long live the King!

vivaracho, -a [biβa'ratʃo, a] adj jaunty, lively; (ojos) bright, twinkling

vivaz [bi'βaθ] adj lively

víveres ['biβeres] nmpl provisions

vivero [bi'βero] nm (Horticultura) nursery; (para peces) fish farm; (fig) hotbed

viveza [bi'βeθa] nf liveliness; (agudeza: mental) sharpness

vivienda [bi'βjenda] nf housing; (casa) house; (piso) flat (BRIT), apartment (US)

viviente [bi'βjente] adj living

vivir [bi'βir] /3a/ vt to live o go through ▷ vi: **~ (de)** to live (by, off, on) ▷ nm life, living

vivo, -a ['biβo, a] adj living, alive; (fig) vivid; (persona: astuto) smart, clever; **en ~** (TV etc) live

vocablo [bo'kaβlo] nm (palabra) word; (término) term

vocabulario [bokaβu'larjo] nm vocabulary

vocación [boka'θjon] nf vocation; **vocacional** nf (LAM) = technical college

vocal [bo'kal] adj vocal ▷ nf vowel; **vocalizar** /1f/ vt to vocalize

vocero [bo'θero, a] nm/f (LAM) spokesman/woman

voces ['boθes] nfpl de **voz**

vodka ['boðka] nf vodka

vol abr = **volumen**

volado [a, bo'laðo, a] adv (LAM) in a rush, hastily

volador [a, bola'ðor, a] adj flying

volandas [bo'landas]: **en ~** adv in o through the air

volante [bo'lante] adj flying ▷ nm (de máquina, coche) steering wheel; (de reloj) balance

volar [bo'lar] /1l/ vt to blow up ▷ vi to fly

volátil [bo'latil] adj volatile

volcán [bol'kan] nm volcano; **volcánico, -a** adj volcanic

volcar [bol'kar] /1g, 1l/ vt to upset, overturn; (tumbar, derribar) to knock over; (vaciar) to empty out ▷ vi to overturn; **volcarse** vr to tip over

voleibol [bolei'βol] nm volleyball

volqué [bol'ke] vb V **volcar**

voltaje [bol'taxe] nm voltage

voltear [bolte'ar] /1a/ vt to turn over; (volcar) to knock over

voltereta [bolte'reta] nf somersault

voltio [bol'tjo] nm volt

voluble [bo'luβle] adj fickle

volumen [bo'lumen] nm volume; **voluminoso, -a** adj voluminous; (enorme) massive

voluntad [bolun'taθ] *nf* will, willpower; (*deseo*) desire, wish

voluntario, -a [bolun'tarjo, a] *adj* voluntary ▷ *nm/f* volunteer

volver [bol'βer] /2h/ *vt* to turn; (*boca abajo*) to turn (over); (*voltear*) to turn round, turn upside down; (*poner del revés*) to turn inside out; (*devolver*) to return ▷ *vi* to return, go/come back; **volverse** *vr* to turn round; **~ la espalda** to turn one's back; **~ a hacer** to do again; **~ en sí** to come to o round; **~ triste** *etc* **a algn** to make sb sad *etc*; **~se loco** to go mad

vomitar [bomi'tar] /1a/ *vt*, *vi* to vomit; **vómito** *nm* vomit

voraz [bo'raθ] *adj* voracious

vos [bos] *pron* (AM) you

vosotros, -as [bo'sotros, as] *pron* you *pl*; (*reflexivo*): **entre ~** among yourselves

votación [bota'θjon] *nf* (*acto*) voting; (*voto*) vote

votar [bo'tar] /1a/ *vi* to vote; **voto** *nm* vote; (*promesa*) vow; **votos** *nmpl* (good) wishes

voy [boi] *vb* V **ir**

voz [boθ] *nf* voice; (*grito*) shout; (*chisme*) rumour; (*Ling*) word; **dar voces** to shout, yell; **en ~ baja** in a low voice; **de viva ~** verbally; **en ~ alta** aloud; **~ de mando** command

vuelco *etc* ['bwelko] *vb* V **volcar** ▷ *nm* spill, overturning

vuelo ['bwelo] *vb* V **volar** ▷ *nm* flight; (*encaje*) lace, frill; **coger al ~** to catch in flight; **~ libre** hang-gliding; **~ regular** scheduled flight

vuelque *etc* ['bwelke] *vb* V **volcar**

vuelta ['bwelta] *nf* turn; (*curva*) bend, curve; (*regreso*) return; (*revolución*) revolution; (*circuito*) lap; (*de papel, tela*) reverse; (*cambio*) change; **~ ciclista** (*Deporte*) (cycle) tour; **a la ~** (ESP) on one's return; **a la ~ de la esquina** round the corner; **a ~ de correo** by return of post; **dar ~s** to turn, revolve; (*cabeza*) to spin; **dar(se) la ~** (*volverse*)

to turn round; **dar ~s a una idea** to turn over an idea (in one's mind); **dar una ~** to go for a walk; (*en coche*) to go for a drive

vuelto ['bwelto] *pp de* **volver**

vuelvo *etc* ['bwelβo] *vb* V **volver**

vuestro, -a ['bwestro, a] *adj* your ▷ *pron*: **el ~/la vuestra/los ~s/las vuestras** yours; **un amigo ~** a friend of yours

vulgar [bul'ɣar] *adj* (*ordinario*) vulgar; (*común*) common; **vulgaridad** *nf* commonness; (*acto*) vulgarity; (*expresión*) coarse expression

vulnerable [bulne'raβle] *adj* vulnerable

vulnerar [bulne'rar] /1a/ *vt* (*Jur, Com*) to violate; (*derechos*) to violate, to interfere with; (*reputación*) to harm, damage

V

W X

walkie-talkie [walki'talki] *nm*
walkie-talkie

walkman® ['wal(k)man] *nm*
Walkman®

wáter ['bater] *nm (taza)* toilet; (LAM:
lugar) toilet (BRIT), rest room (US)

web [web] *nm o f (página)* website;
(red) (World Wide) Web; **webcam**
nf webcam; **webmaster** *nmf*
webmaster; **website** *nm* website

western ['western] (*pl* **westerns**)
nm western

whisky ['wiski] *nm* whisky

wifi ['waifai] *nm* Wi-Fi

windsurf ['winsurf] *nm* windsurfing;
hacer ~ to go windsurfing

xenofobia [seno'foβja] *nf*
xenophobia

xilófono [si'lofono] *nm* xylophone

xocoyote, -a [ksoko'jote, a] *nm/f*
(LAM) baby of the family, youngest
child

yoga ['joɣa] *nm* yoga
yogur(t) [jo'ɣur(t)] *nm* yogurt
yuca ['juka] *nf* (Bot) cassava; (alimento) cassava, manioc root
Yugoslavia [juɣos'laβja] *nf* (Historia) Yugoslavia
yugular [juɣu'lar] *adj* jugular
yunque ['junke] *nm* anvil
yuyo ['jujo] *nm* (LAM: mala hierba) weed

y [i] *conj* and; (hora): **la una y cinco** five past one
ya [ja] *adv* (gen) already; (ahora) now; (en seguida) at once; (pronto) soon ▷ *excl* all right! ▷ *conj* (ahora que) now that; **ya lo sé** I know; **¡ya está bien!** that's (quite) enough!; **¡ya voy!** coming!; **ya que** since
yacer [ja'θer] /2x/ *vi* to lie
yacimiento [jaθi'mjento] *nm* deposit; (arqueológico) site
yanqui ['janki] *adj* ▷ *nmf* Yankee
yate ['jate] *nm* yacht
yazco *etc* ['jaθko] *vb V* **yacer**
yedra ['jeðra] *nf* ivy
yegua ['jeɣwa] *nf* mare
yema ['jema] *nf* (del huevo) yolk; (Bot) leaf bud; (fig) best part; **~ del dedo** fingertip
yerno ['jerno] *nm* son-in-law
yeso ['jeso] *nm* plaster
yo [jo] *pron personal* I; **soy yo** it's me
yodo ['joðo] *nm* iodine

Z

zafar [θa'far] /1a/ vt (soltar) to untie; (superficie) to clear; **zafarse** vr (escaparse) to escape; (Tec) to slip off

zafiro [θa'firo] nm sapphire

zaga ['θaɣa] nf: **a la ~** behind, in the rear

zaguán [θa'ɣwan] nm hallway

zalamero, -a [θala'mero, a] adj flattering; (relamido) suave

zamarra [θa'marra] nf (chaqueta) sheepskin jacket

zambullirse [θambu'ʎirse] /3h/ vr to dive

zampar [θam'par] /1a/ vt to gobble

zanahoria [θana'orja] nf carrot

zancadilla [θanka'ðiʎa] nf trip

zanco ['θanko] nm stilt

zángano ['θanɡano] nm drone

zanja ['θanxa] nf ditch; **zanjar** /1a/ vt (conflicto) to resolve

zapata [θa'pata] nf (Mecánica) shoe

zapatería [θapate'ria] nf (oficio) shoemaking; (tienda) shoe-shop; (fábrica) shoe factory; **zapatero, -a** nm/f shoemaker

zapatilla [θapa'tiʎa] nf slipper; (de deporte) training shoe

zapato [θa'pato] nm shoe

zapping ['θapin] nm channel-hopping; **hacer ~** to channel-hop, flick through the channels

zar [θar] nm tsar, czar

zarandear [θarande'ar] /1a/ vt (fam) to shake vigorously

zarpa ['θarpa] nf (garra) claw

zarpar [θar'par] /1a/ vi to weigh anchor

zarza ['θarθa] nf (Bot) bramble

zarzamora [θarθa'mora] nf blackberry

zarzuela [θar'θwela] nf Spanish light opera

zigzag [θiɣ'θaɣ] adj zigzag

zinc [θink] nm zinc

zíper ['siper] nm (LAM) zip, zipper (us)

zócalo ['θokalo] nm (Arq) plinth, base; (de pared) skirting board

zoclo ['θoklo] nm (LAM) skirting board (BRIT), baseboard (us)

zodíaco [θo'ðiako] nm zodiac

zona ['θona] nf area, zone; **~ fronteriza** border area; **~ roja** (LAM) red-light district

zonzo, -a ['θonθo, a] (LAM) adj silly ▷ nm/f fool

zoo ['θoo] nm zoo

zoología [θoolo'xia] nf zoology; **zoológico, -a** adj zoological ▷ nm (tb: **parque zoológico**) zoo; **zoólogo, -a** nm/f zoologist

zoom [θum] nm zoom lens

zopilote [θopi'lote] nm (LAM) buzzard

zoquete [θo'kete] nm (fam) blockhead

zorro, -a ['θorro, a] adj crafty ▷ nm/f fox/vixen

zozobrar [θoθo'βrar] /1a/ vi (hundirse) to capsize; (fig) to fail

zueco ['θweko] nm clog

zumbar [θum'bar] /1a/ vt (golpear) to hit ▷ vi to buzz; **zumbido** nm buzzing

zumo ['θumo] nm juice

zurcir [θur'θir] /3b/ vt (coser) to darn

zurdo, -a ['θurðo, a] adj (persona) left-handed

zurrar [θu'rrar] /1a/ vt (fam) to wallop

Phrasefinder

Guía del viajero

TOPICS		TEMAS

Hello!	¡Buenos días!
Good evening!	¡Buenas tardes!
Good night!	¡Buenas noches!
Goodbye!	¡Adiós!
What's your name?	¿Cómo se llama usted?
My name is ...	Me llamo ...
This is ...	Le presento a ...
my wife.	*mi mujer.*
my husband.	*mi marido.*
my partner.	*mi pareja.*
Where are you from?	¿De dónde es usted?
I come from ...	Soy de ...
How are you?	¿Cómo está usted?
Fine, thanks.	Bien, gracias.
And you?	¿Y usted?
Do you speak English?	¿Habla usted inglés?
I don't understand Spanish.	No entiendo el español.
Thanks very much!	¡Muchas gracias!

Asking the Way | ¿Cómo ir hasta ...?

Where is the nearest ...?	¿Dónde está el/la ... más próximo(-a)?
How do I get to ...?	¿Cómo voy hasta el/la ...?
Is it far?	¿Está muy lejos?
How far is it to there?	¿Qué distancia hay hasta allí?
Is this the right way to ...?	¿Es éste el camino correcto para ir al/a la/a ...?
I'm lost.	Me he perdido.
Can you show me on the map?	¿Me lo puede señalar en el mapa?
You have to turn round.	Tiene que dar la vuelta.
Go straight on.	Siga todo recto.
Turn left/right.	Tuerza a la izquierda/ a la derecha.
Take the second street on the left/right.	Tome la segunda calle a la izquierda/a la derecha.

Car Hire | Alquiler de coches

I want to hire ...	Quisiera alquilar ...
a car.	un coche.
a moped.	una motocicleta.
a motorbike.	una moto.
How much is it for ...?	¿Cuánto cuesta por ...?
one day	un día
a week	una semana
I'd like a child seat for a ... -year-old child.	Quisiera un asiento infantil para un niño de ... años.
What do I do if I have an accident/if I break down?	¿Qué debo hacer en caso de accidente/de avería?

Breakdowns	Averías
My car has broken down.	Tengo una avería.
Where is the next garage?	¿Dónde está el taller más próximo?
The exhaust	*El escape*
The gearbox	*El cambio*
... is broken.	*... está roto.*
The brakes	*Los frenos*
The headlights	*Las luces*
The windscreen wipers	*Los limpiaparabrisas*
... are not working.	*... no funcionan.*
The battery is flat.	La batería está descargada.
The car won't start.	El motor no arranca.
The engine is overheating.	El motor se recalienta.
I have a flat tyre.	He tenido un pinchazo.
Can you repair it?	¿Puede repararlo?
When will the car be ready?	¿Cuándo estará listo el coche?

Parking	Aparcamiento
Can I park here?	¿Puedo aparcar aquí?
Do I need to buy a (car-parking) ticket?	¿Tengo que sacar un ticket de estacionamiento?
Where is the ticket machine?	¿Dónde está el expendedor de tickets de estacionamiento?
The ticket machine isn't working.	El expendedor de tickets de estacionamiento no funciona.

Petrol Station	Gasolinera
Where is the nearest petrol station?	¿Dónde está la gasolinera más próxima?
Fill it up, please.	Lleno, por favor.

30 euros' worth of ..., please.	30 euros de ...
diesel	*diesel*
(unleaded) economy petrol	*gasolina normal.*
premium unleaded	*súper.*
Pump number ... please.	Número ..., por favor.
Please check ...	Por favor, compruebe ...
the tyre pressure.	*la presión de los neumáticos.*
the oil.	*el aceite.*
the water.	*el agua.*

Accident | Accidentes

Please call ...	Por favor, llame ...
the police.	*a la policía.*
the emergency doctor.	*al médico de urgencia.*
Here are my insurance details.	Éstos son los datos de mi seguro.
Give me your insurance details, please.	Por favor, deme los datos de su seguro.
Can you be a witness for me?	¿Puede ser usted mi testigo?
You were driving too fast.	Usted conducía muy rápido.
It wasn't your right of way.	Usted no tenía preferencia.

Travelling by Car | Viajando en coche

What's the best route to ...?	¿Cuál es el mejor camino para ir a ...?
I'd like a motorway tax sticker ...	Quisiera un indicativo de pago de peaje ...
for a week.	*para una semana.*
for a year.	*para un año.*
Do you have a road map of this area?	¿Tiene un mapa de carreteras de esta zona?

Cycling | En bicicleta

Where is the cycle path to ...?	¿Dónde está el carril-bici para ir a ...?
Can I keep my bike here?	¿Puedo dejar aquí mi bicicleta?
My bike has been stolen.	Me han robado la bicicleta.
Where is the nearest bike repair shop?	¿Dónde hay por aquí un taller de bicicletas?
The brake isn't/the gears aren't working.	El freno/el cambio de marchas no funciona.
The chain is broken.	La cadena se ha roto.
I've got a flat tyre.	He tenido un pinchazo.
I need a puncture repair kit.	Necesito una caja de parches.

Train | Ferrocarril

A single to ..., please.	Un billete sencillo para ..., por favor.
I would like to travel first/second class.	Me gustaría viajar en primera/segunda clase.
Two returns to ..., please.	Dos billetes de ida y vuelta para ..., por favor.
Is there a reduction ...?	¿Hay descuento ...?
for students	*para estudiantes*
for pensioners	*para pensionistas*
for children	*para niños*
with this pass	*con este carnet*

GETTING AROUND	TRASLADOS
I'd like to reserve a seat on the train to ... please.	Una reserva para el tren que va a ..., por favor.
Non smoking/smoking, please.	No fumadores/fumadores, por favor.
I want to book a couchette/a berth to ...	Quisiera reservar una litera/coche-cama para ...
When is the next train to ...?	¿Cuándo sale el próximo tren para ...?
Is there a supplement to pay?	¿Tengo que pagar suplemento?
Do I need to change?	¿Hay que hacer transbordo?
Where do I change?	¿Dónde tengo que hacer transbordo?
Is this the train for ...?	¿Es éste el tren que va a ...?
Excuse me, that's my seat.	Perdone, éste es mi asiento.
I have a reservation.	Tengo una reserva.
Is this seat free?	¿Está libre este asiento?
Please let me know when we get to ...	¿Por favor, avíseme cuando lleguemos a ...?
Where is the buffet car?	¿Dónde está el coche restaurante?
Where is coach number ...?	¿Cuál es el vagón número ...?

Ferry | Transbordador

Ferry	Transbordador
Is there a ferry to ...?	¿Sale algún transbordador para ...?
When is the next ferry to ...?	¿Cuándo sale el próximo transbordador para ...?
How much is it for a car/camper with ... people?	¿Cuánto cuesta transportar el coche/coche caravana con ... personas?

How long does the crossing take?	¿Cuánto dura la travesía?
Where is ...?	¿Dónde está ...?
the restaurant	el restaurante
the bar	el bar
the duty-free shop	la tienda de duty-free
Where is cabin number ...?	¿Dónde está la cabina número ...?
Do you have anything for seasickness?	¿Tienen algo para el mareo?

Plane | Avión

Where is the luggage for the flight from ...?	¿Dónde está el equipaje procedente de...?
Where is ...?	¿Dónde está ...?
the taxi rank	la parada de taxis
the bus stop	la parada del bus
the information office	la oficina de información
My luggage hasn't arrived.	Mi equipaje no ha llegado.
Can you page ...?	¿Puede llamar por el altavoz a ...?
Where do I check in for the flight to ...?	¿Dónde hay que facturar para el vuelo a ...?
Which gate for the flight to ...?	¿Cuál es la puerta de embarque del vuelo para ...?
When is the latest I can check in?	¿Hasta qué hora como máximo se puede facturar?
When does boarding begin?	¿Cuándo es el embarque?
Window/aisle, please.	Ventanilla/pasillo, por favor.
I've lost my boarding pass/ my ticket.	He perdido la tarjeta de embarque/el billete.

Local Public Transport	Transporte público de cercanías
How do I get to ...?	¿Cómo se llega al/a la/hasta ...?
Where is the nearest ...?	¿Dónde está la próxima ...?
bus stop	*parada del bus*
underground station	*estación de metro*
Where is the bus station?	¿Dónde está la estación de autobuses?
A ticket to ..., please.	Un billete a ..., por favor.
Is there a reduction ...?	¿Hay descuento ...?
for students	*para estudiantes*
for pensioners	*para pensionistas*
for children	*para niños*
for the unemployed	*para desempleados*
with this card	*con este carnet*
How does the (ticket) machine work?	¿Cómo funciona la máquina (de billetes)?
Please tell me when to get off.	¿Puede decirme cuándo tengo que bajar?
What is the next stop?	¿Cuál es la próxima parada?
Can I get past, please?	¿Me deja pasar?

Taxi	Taxi
Where can I get a taxi?	¿Dónde puedo coger un taxi?
Call me a taxi, please.	¿Puede llamar a un taxi?
To the airport/station, please.	Al aeropuerto/a la estación, por favor.
To this address, please.	A esta dirección, por favor.
I'm in a hurry.	Tengo mucha prisa.
How much is it?	¿Cuánto cuesta el trayecto?
I need a receipt.	Necesito un recibo.
Keep the change.	Quédese con el cambio.
Stop here, please.	Pare aquí, por favor.

Camping | Camping

Is there a campsite here?	¿Hay un camping por aquí?
We'd like a site for ...	Quisiéramos un lugar para ...
a tent.	*una tienda de campaña.*
a caravan.	*una caravana.*
We'd like to stay one night/... nights.	Queremos quedarnos una noche/... noches.
How much is it per night?	¿Cuánto es por noche?
Where are ...?	¿Dónde están ...?
the toilets	*los lavabos*
the showers	*las duchas*
Where is ...?	¿Dónde está ...?
the site office	*la oficina de administración*
Can we camp/park here overnight?	¿Podemos acampar/aparcar aquí esta noche?

Self-Catering | Vivienda para las vacaciones

Where do we get the key for the apartment/house?	¿Dónde nos dan la llave para el piso/la casa?
Do we have to pay extra for electricity/gas?	¿Hay que pagar aparte la luz/el gas?
How does the heating work?	¿Cómo funciona la calefacción?
Whom do I contact if there are any problems?	¿Con quién debo hablar si hubiera algún problema?
We need ...	Necesitamos ...
a second key.	*otra copia de la llave.*
more sheets.	*más sábanas.*
The gas has run out.	Ya no queda gas.
There is no electricity.	No hay corriente.
Do we have to clean the apartment/the house before we leave?	¿Hay que limpiar el piso/la casa antes de marcharnos?

Hotel	Hotel
Do you have a ... for tonight?	¿Tienen una ... para esta noche?
single room	*habitación individual*
double room	*habitación doble*
with bath	con baño
with shower	con ducha
I want to stay for one night/ ... nights.	Quisiera pasar una noche/ ... noches.
I booked a room in the name of ...	Tengo reservada una habitación a nombre de ...
I'd like another room.	Quisiera otra habitación.
What time is breakfast?	¿Cuándo sirven el desayuno?
Can I have breakfast in my room?	¿Podrían traerme el desayuno a la habitación?
Where is ...?	¿Dónde está ...?
the gym	*el gimnasio*
I'd like an alarm call for tomorrow morning at ...	Por favor, despiértenme mañana a las ...
I'd like to get these things washed/cleaned.	¿Puede lavarme/limpiarme esto?
Please bring me ...	Por favor, tráigame ...
... doesn't work.	... no funciona.
Room number ...	Número de habitación ...
Are there any messages for me?	¿Hay mensajes para mí?

SHOPPING	DE COMPRAS
I'd like ...	Quisiera ...
Do you have ...?	¿Tienen ...?
Do you have this ...?	¿Lo tiene ...?
in another size	*en otra talla*
in another colour	*en otro color*
I take size ...	Mi talla es la ...
I'm a size 5½.	Calzo un cuarenta.
I'll take it.	Me lo quedo.
Do you have anything else?	¿Tienen alguna otra cosa distinta?
That's too expensive.	Es demasiado caro.
I'm just looking.	Sólo estaba mirando.
Do you take credit cards?	¿Aceptan tarjetas de crédito?

Food Shopping — Alimentos

Where is the nearest ...?	¿Dónde hay por aquí cerca ...?
supermarket	*un supermercado*
baker's	*una panadería*
butcher's	*una carnicería*
Where is the market?	¿Dónde está el mercado?
When is the market on?	¿Cuándo hay mercado?
a kilo/pound of ...	un kilo/medio kilo de ...
200 grams of ...	doscientos gramos de ...
... slices of ...	... lonchas de ...
a litre of ...	un litro de ...
a bottle/packet of ...	una botella/un paquete de ...

Post Office — Correos

Where is the nearest post office?	¿Dónde queda la oficina de Correos más cercana?
When does the post office open?	¿Cuándo abre Correos?
Where can I buy stamps?	¿Dónde puedo comprar sellos?

I'd like ... stamps for postcards/letters to Britain/the United States.
Quisiera ... sellos para postales/cartas a Gran Bretaña/Estados Unidos.

I'd like to post/send ...
Quisiera entregar ...

this letter.
esta carta.

this parcel.
este paquete.

By airmail/express mail/registered mail.
Por avión/por correo urgente/certificado.

Is there any mail for me?
¿Tengo correo?

Where is the nearest postbox?
¿Dónde hay un buzón de correos por aquí cerca?

Photos | Fotografía

A colour film/slide film, please.
Un carrete en color/un carrete para diapositivas, por favor.

My memory card is full.
Tengo la tarjeta de memoria llena.

Can I have batteries for this camera, please?
Quisiera pilas para esta cámara, por favor.

Where can I buy a digital camera?
¿Dónde puedo comprar una cámara digital?

I'd like the photos ...
Las fotos las quiero ...

matt.
en mate.

glossy.
en brillo.

ten by fifteen centimetres.
en formato de diez por quince.

Can I print my digital photos here?
¿Puedo imprimir mis fotos digitales aquí?

How much do the photos cost?
¿Cuánto cuesta el revelado?

Could you take a photo of us, please?
¿Podría sacarnos una foto?

Sightseeing | Visitas turísticas

Where is the tourist office?	¿Dónde está la oficina de turismo?
Do you have any leaflets about ...?	¿Tienen folletos sobre ...?
Are there any sightseeing tours of the town?	¿Se organizan visitas por la ciudad?
When is ... open?	¿Cuándo está abierto(-a) ...?
the museum	*el museo*
the church	*la iglesia*
the castle	*el palacio*
How much does it cost to get in?	¿Cuánto cuesta la entrada?
Are there any reductions ...?	¿Hay descuento ...?
for students	*para estudiantes*
for children	*para niños*
for pensioners	*para pensionistas*
for the unemployed	*para desempleados*
Is there a guided tour in English?	¿Hay alguna visita guiada en inglés?
Can I take photos here?	¿Puedo sacar fotos?
Can I film here?	¿Puedo filmar?

Entertainment | Ocio

What is there to do here?	¿Qué se puede hacer por aquí?
Where can we ...?	¿Dónde se puede ...?
go dancing	*bailar*
hear live music	*escuchar música en directo*
Where is there ...?	¿Dónde hay ... ?
a nice bar	*un buen bar*
a good club	*una buena discoteca*
What's on tonight ...?	¿Qué dan esta noche ...?

at the cinema	*en el cine*
at the theatre	*en el teatro*
at the opera	*en la ópera*
at the concert hall	*en la sala de conciertos*
Where can I buy tickets for ...?	¿Dónde puedo comprar entradas para ...?
the theatre	*el teatro*
the concert	*el concierto*
the opera	*la ópera*
the ballet	*el ballet*
How much is it to get in?	¿Cuánto cuesta la entrada?
I'd like a ticket/... tickets for ...	Quisiera una entrada/... entradas para ...
Are there any reductions for ...?	¿Hay descuento para ...?
children	*niños*
pensioners	*pensionistas*
students	*estudiantes*
the unemployed	*desempleados*

At the Beach — En la playa

How deep is the water?	¿Qué profundidad tiene el agua?
Is it safe to swim here?	¿Se puede nadar aquí sin peligro?
Is there a lifeguard?	¿Hay socorrista?
Where can you ...?	¿Dónde se puede ... por aquí?
go surfing	*hacer surf*
go waterskiing	*practicar esquí acuático*
go diving	*bucear*
go paragliding	*hacer parapente*

I'd like to hire ...	Quisiera alquilar ...
a deckchair.	*una tumbona.*
a sunshade.	*una sombrilla.*
a surfboard.	*una tabla de surf.*
a jet-ski.	*una moto acuática.*
a rowing boat.	*un bote de remos.*
a pedal boat.	*un patín a pedales.*

Sport | Deporte

Where can we ...?	¿Dónde se puede ...?
play tennis/golf	*jugar a tenis/golf*
go swimming	*ir a nadar*
go riding	*montar a caballo*
go fishing	*ir a pescar*
How much is it per hour?	¿Cuánto cuesta la hora?
Where can I book a court?	¿Dónde puedo reservar una pista?
Where can I hire rackets?	¿Dónde puedo alquilar raquetas de tenis?
Where can I hire a rowing boat/a pedal boat?	¿Dónde puedo alquilar un bote de remos/ un patín a pedales?
Do you need a fishing permit?	¿Se necesita un permiso de pesca?

Skiing | Esquí

Where can I hire skiing equipment?	¿Dónde puedo alquilar un equipo de esquí?
I'd like to hire ...	Quisiera alquilar ...
downhill skis.	*unos esquís (de descenso).*
cross-country skis.	*unos esquís de fondo.*
ski boots.	*unas botas de esquí.*
ski poles.	*unos bastones de esquí.*

Can you tighten my bindings, please?	¿Podría ajustarme la fijación, por favor?
Where can I buy a ski pass?	¿Dónde puedo comprar el forfait?
I'd like a ski pass ...	Quisiera un forfait ...
for a day.	*para un día.*
for five days.	*para cinco días.*
for a week.	*para una semana.*
How much is a ski pass?	¿Cuánto cuesta el forfait?
When does the first/ last chair-lift leave?	¿Cuándo sale el primer/ el último telesilla?
Do you have a map of the ski runs?	¿Tiene un mapa de las pistas?
Where are the beginners' slopes?	¿Dónde están las pistas para principiantes?
How difficult is this slope?	¿Cuál es la dificultad de esta pista?
Is there a ski school?	¿Hay una escuela de esquí?
Where is the nearest mountain rescue service post?	¿Dónde se encuentra la unidad más próxima de servicio de salvamento?
Where is the nearest mountain hut?	¿Dónde se encuentra el refugio más próximo?
What's the weather forecast?	¿Cuál es el pronóstico del tiempo?
What is the snow like?	¿Cómo es el estado de la nieve?
Is there a danger of avalanches?	¿Hay peligro de aludes?

A table for ... people, please.	Una mesa para ... personas, por favor.
The ... please.	Por favor, ...
menu	*la carta.*
wine list	*la carta de vinos.*
What do you recommend?	¿Qué me recomienda?
Do you have ...?	¿Sirven ...?
any vegetarian dishes	*platos vegetarianos*
children's portions	*raciones para niños*
Does that contain ...?	¿Tiene esto ...?
peanuts	*cacahuetes*
alcohol	*alcohol*
Can you bring (more) ... please?	Por favor, traiga (más) ...
I'll have ...	Para mí ...
The bill, please.	La cuenta, por favor.
All together, please.	Cóbrelo todo junto.
Separate bills, please.	Haga cuentas separadas, por favor.
Keep the change.	Quédese con el cambio.
I didn't order this.	Yo no he pedido esto.
The bill is wrong.	La cuenta está mal.
The food is cold/too salty.	La comida está fría/demasiado salada.

Where can I make a phone call?	¿Dónde puedo hacer una llamada por aquí cerca?
Can I pay for a call using my credit card?	¿Puedo pagar una llamada con mi tarjeta de crédito?
I'd like a twenty-five euro phone card.	Quisiera una tarjeta de teléfono de veinticinco euros.
I'd like some coins for the phone, please.	Necesito monedas para llamar por teléfono.
I'd like to make a reverse charge call.	Quisiera hacer una llamada a cobro revertido.
Hello.	Hola.
This is ...	Soy ...
Who's speaking, please?	¿Con quién hablo?
Can I speak to Mr/Ms ..., please?	¿Puedo hablar con el señor/ la señora ...?
Extension ..., please.	Por favor, póngame con el número ...
I'll phone back later.	Volveré a llamar más tarde.
Can you text me your answer?	¿Puede contestarme con mensaje de móvil?
Where can I charge my mobile (phone)?	¿Dónde puedo cargar la batería del móvil?
I need a new battery.	Necesito una batería nueva.
Where can I buy a top-up card?	¿Dónde venden tarjetas para móviles?
I can't get a network.	No hay cobertura.

Passport/Customs	Pasaporte/Aduana

Here is ...	Aquí tiene ...
my passport.	*mi pasaporte.*
my identity card.	*mi documento de identidad.*
my driving licence.	*mi permiso de conducir.*
my green card.	*mi carta verde.*
Here are my vehicle documents.	Aquí tiene la documentación de mi vehículo.
The children are on this passport.	Los niños están incluidos en este pasaporte.
Do I have to pay duty on this?	¿Tengo que declararlo?
This is ...	Esto es ...
a present.	*un regalo.*
a sample.	*una muestra.*
This is for my own personal use.	Es para consumo propio.
I'm on my way to ...	Estoy de paso para ir a ...

At the Bank	En el banco

Where can I change money?	¿Dónde puedo cambiar dinero?
Is there a bank/bureau de change here?	¿Hay por aquí un banco/ una casa de cambio?
When is the bank/bureau de change open?	¿Cuándo está abierto el banco/ abierta la casa de cambio?
I'd like ... euros.	Quisiera ... euros.
I'd like to cash these traveller's cheques/ eurocheques.	Quisiera cobrar estos cheques de viaje/eurocheques.

What's the commission?	¿Cuánto cobran de comisión?
Can I use my credit card to get cash?	¿Puedo sacar dinero en efectivo con mi tarjeta de crédito?
Where is the nearest cash machine?	¿Dónde hay por aquí un cajero automático?
The cash machine swallowed my card.	El cajero automático no me ha devuelto la tarjeta.
Can you give me some change, please.	Deme cambio en monedas, por favor.

Repairs | Reparaciones

Where can I get this repaired?	¿Dónde pueden repararme esto?
Can you repair ...?	¿Puede reparar ...?
these shoes	*estos zapatos*
this watch	*este reloj*
this jacket	*esta chaqueta*
Is it worth repairing?	¿Vale la pena repararlo?
How much will the repairs cost?	¿Cuánto cuesta la reparación?
Where can I have my shoes reheeled?	¿Dónde me pueden poner tacones nuevos?
When will it be ready?	¿Cuándo estará listo?
Can you do it straight away?	¿Puede hacerlo ahora mismo?

Emergency Services	Servicios de urgencia
Help!	¡Socorro!
Fire!	¡Fuego!
Please call ...	Por favor, llame a ...
the emergency doctor.	un médico de urgencia.
the fire brigade.	los bomberos.
the police.	la policía.
I need to make an urgent phone call.	Tengo que hacer una llamada urgente.
I need an interpreter.	Necesito un intérprete.
Where is the police station?	¿Dónde está la comisaría?
Where is the nearest hospital?	¿Dónde está el hospital más cercano?
I want to report a theft.	Quisiera denunciar un robo.
... has been stolen.	Han robado ...
There's been an accident.	Ha habido un accidente.
There are ... people injured.	Hay ... heridos.
My location is ...	Estoy en ...
I've been ...	Me han ...
robbed.	robado.
attacked.	atracado.
raped.	violado.
I'd like to phone my embassy.	Quisiera hablar con mi embajada.

Pharmacy | Farmacia

Where is the nearest pharmacy?	¿Dónde hay por aquí una farmacia?
Which pharmacy provides emergency service?	¿Qué farmacia está de guardia?
I'd like something for ...	Quisiera algo para ...
diarrhoea.	*la diarrea.*
a temperature.	*la fiebre.*
travel sickness.	*el mareo.*
a headache.	*el dolor de cabeza.*
a cold.	*el resfriado.*
I'd like ...	Quisiera ...
plasters.	*tiritas.*
a bandage.	*un vendaje.*
some paracetamol.	*paracetamol.*
I can't take ...	Soy alérgico(-a) a la ...
aspirin.	*aspirina.*
penicillin.	*penicilina.*
Is is safe to give to children?	¿Pueden tomarlo los niños?
How should I take it?	¿Cómo tengo que tomarlo?

At the Doctor's | En la consulta médica

I need a doctor.	Necesito que me atienda un médico.
Where is casualty?	¿Dónde está Urgencias?
I have a pain here.	Me duele aquí.
I feel ...	Tengo ...
hot.	*mucho calor.*
cold.	*frío.*
I feel sick.	Me siento mal.
I feel dizzy.	Tengo mareos.

HEALTH | SALUD

I'm allergic to ...	Tengo alergia a ...
I am ...	Yo ...
pregnant.	*estoy embarazada.*
diabetic.	*soy diabético(-a).*
HIV-positive.	*soy seropositivo(-a).*
I'm on this medication.	Estoy tomando este medicamento.
My blood group is ...	Mi grupo sanguíneo es ...

At the Hospital | En el hospital

Which ward is ... in?	¿En qué unidad está ...?
When are visiting hours?	¿Cuándo son las horas de visita?
I'd like to speak to ...	Quisiera hablar con ...
a doctor.	*un médico.*
a nurse.	*una enfermera.*
When will I be discharged?	¿Cuándo me van a dar de alta?

At the Dentist's | En el dentista

I need a dentist.	Tengo que ir al dentista.
This tooth hurts.	Me duele este diente.
One of my fillings has fallen out.	Se me ha caído un empaste.
I have an abscess.	Tengo un absceso.
I want/don't want an injection for the pain.	Quiero/no quiero que me ponga una inyección para calmar el dolor.
Can you repair my dentures?	¿Me puede reparar la dentadura?
I need a receipt for the insurance.	Necesito un recibo para mi seguro.

Business Travel / Viajes de negocios

Business Travel	Viajes de negocios
I'd like to arrange a meeting with ...	Quisiera concertar hora para una reunión con ...
I have an appointment with Mr/Ms ...	Tengo una cita con el señor/ la señora ...
Here is my card.	Aquí tiene mi tarjeta.
I work for ...	Trabajo para ...
How do I get to ...?	¿Cómo se llega ...?
your office	*a su despacho*
I need an interpreter.	Necesito un intérprete.
Can you copy that for me, please?	Por favor, hágame una copia de eso.
May I use ...?	¿Puedo usar ...?
your phone	*su teléfono*
your computer	*su ordenador*

Disabled Travellers / Minusválidos

Disabled Travellers	Minusválidos
Is it possible to visit ... with a wheelchair?	¿La visita a ... es posible también para personas en silla de ruedas?
Where is the wheelchair-accessible entrance?	¿Por dónde se puede entrar con la silla de ruedas?
Is your hotel accessible to wheelchairs?	¿Tiene su hotel acceso para minusválidos?
I need a room ...	Necesito una habitación ...
on the ground floor.	*en la planta baja.*
with wheelchair access.	*con acceso para minusuálidos.*
Do you have a lift for wheelchairs?	¿Tienen ascensor para minusválidos?
Do you have wheelchairs?	¿Tienen sillas de ruedas?

Where is the disabled toilet?	¿Dónde está el lavabo para minusválidos?
Can you help me get on/ off please?	¿Podría ayudarme a subir/ bajar, por favor?
A tyre has burst.	Se ha reventado un neumático.
The battery is flat.	La batería está descargada.
The wheels lock.	Las ruedas se bloquean.

Travelling with children   Viajando con niños

Are children allowed in too?	¿Pueden entrar niños?
Is there a reduction for children?	¿Hay descuento para niños?
Do you have children's portions?	¿Sirven raciones para niños?
Do you have ...?	¿Tienen ...?
a high chair	*una sillita*
a cot	*una cama infantil*
a child's seat	*un asiento infantil*
a baby's changing table	*una mesa para cambiar al bebé*
Where can I change the baby?	¿Dónde puedo cambiar al bebé?
Where can I breast-feed the baby?	¿Dónde puedo dar el pecho al niño?
Can you warm this up, please?	¿Puede calentarlo, por favor?
What is there for children to do?	¿Qué pueden hacer aquí los niños?
Is there a child-minding service?	¿Hay aquí un servicio de guardería?
My son/daughter is ill.	Mi hijo/mi hija está enfermo(-a).

bangers and mash salchichas con puré de patatas, cebolla frita y salsa hecha con jugo de carne asada

banoffee pie tarta rellena de plátano, caramelo y nata

BLT (sandwich) sándwich de bacón, lechuga, tomate y mayonesa

butternut squash variedad de calabaza de color amarillo y sabor dulce, que a menudo se sirve asada

Caesar salad ensalada César

chocolate brownie brownie: pastelito de chocolate y nueces

chowder guiso de pescado

chicken Kiev pollo a la Kiev

chicken nuggets croquetas de pollo

club sandwich sándwich caliente de tres pisos; normalmente relleno de carne, queso, lechuga, tomate y cebollas

cottage pie pastel de carne picada y verduras, cubierto con puré de patatas y queso

English breakfast desayuno inglés: huevos, bacón, salchichas, alubias cocidas, pan frito y champiñones

filo pastry masa de hojaldre

haggis plato escocés a base de hígado y corazón de cordero, avena y otros condimentos, hervidos en una bolsa formada por el estómago del animal

hash browns trocitos de patata sofritos con cebolla, que a menudo se sirven con el desayuno

hotpot estofado de carne, verdura y patatas

Irish stew estofado irlandés, a base de cordero, patatas y cebolla

monkfish rape

oatcake galleta de avellana

pavlova pastel de merengue con frutas y nata

ploughman's lunch almuerzo de pub a base de pan, queso y encurtidos

purée puré

Quorn® proteína vegetal usada como sustituto de carne

Savoy cabbage col rizada

sea bass lubina

Scotch broth sopa de carne, cebada y verduras

Scotch egg huevo duro envuelto en carne de salchicha y rebozado

spare ribs costillas de cerdo

spring roll rollito de primavera

Stilton Stilton: queso azul
  inglés

sundae sundae: helado con
  jarabe, nueces y nata

Thousand Island dressing
  salsa rosa

toad in the hole salchichas
  horneadas en una masa de
  huevos, leche y harina

Waldorf salad ensalada
  Waldorf: manzanas
  troceadas, apio, nueces
  y mayonesa

Welsh rarebit tostada
  cubierta con queso derretido
  y huevo

Yorkshire pudding buñuelo,
  a veces relleno de verduras,
  que se sirve acompañando
  al rosbif

adobo, ... en marinated

ajillo, ... al with garlic

arroz negro black rice (with squid in its own ink)

asadillo roasted sliced red peppers in olive oil and garlic

bandeja de quesos cheese platter

brasa, ... a la barbecued

buñuelos type of fritter. Savoury ones are filled with cheese, ham, mussels or prawns. Sweet ones can be filled with fruit

caldereta stew/casserole

cazuela de fideos bean, meat and noodle stew

chilindrón, ... al sauce made with pepper, tomato, fried onions and meat pork or lamb

chistorra spicy sausage from Navarra

chorizo spicy red sausage

chuletón large steak

churros fried batter sticks sprinkled with sugar, usually eaten with thick hot chocolate.

crema catalana similar to crème brûlée

cuajada cream-based dessert like junket, served with honey or sugar

dulces cakes and pastries

empanadilla pasty/small pie filled with meat or fish

empanado breadcrumbed and fried

ensalada de la casa lettuce, tomato and onion salad (may include tuna)

fritura de pescado fried assortment of fish

gazpacho traditional cold tomato soup of southern Spain. Basic ingredients are water, tomatoes, garlic, fresh bread-crumbs, salt, vinegar and olive oil

horno, ...al baked (in oven)

ibéricos traditional Spanish gourmet products; a surtido de ibéricos means assorted products such as cured ham, cheese, chorizo and salchichón

jamón serrano dark red cured ham

leche frita very thick custard dipped into an egg and breadcrumb mixture, fried and served hot

mariscada mixed shellfish

medallón thick steak (medallion)

mollejas sweetbreads

moros y cristianos rice, black beans and onions with garlic sausage

paella Paella varies from region to region but usually consists of rice, chicken, shellfish, vegetables, garlic and saffron. Paella Valenciana contains rabbit, chicken and sometimes eel

parrilla, ... a la grilled

patatas bravas fried diced potatoes mixed with a garlic, oil and vinegar dressing and flavoured with tomatoes and red chilli peppers

pepitoria de pavo/pollo turkey/chicken fricassée

pimientos morrones sweet red peppers

pote thick soup with beans and sausage which has many regional variations

puchero hotpot made from meat or fish

revuelto scrambled eggs often cooked with another ingredient

romesco sauce made traditionally with olive oil, red pepper and bread. Other ingredients are often added, such as almonds and garlic

salsa verde garlic, olive oil and parsley sauce

sofrito basic sauce made with slowly fried onions, garlic and tomato

tapas Bar snacks. A larger portion of tapas is called a ración. A pincho is a tapa on a cocktail stick.

tortilla (española) traditional potato and onion omelette, often served as a tapa

zarzuela de mariscos mixed seafood with wine and saffron

a

A [eɪ] *n (Mus)* la *m*; **A road** *n (BRIT Aut)* ≈ carretera nacional

KEYWORD

a [ə] *indef art (before vowel and silent h* **an**) **1** un(a); **a book** un libro; **an apple** una manzana; **she's a nurse** (ella) es enfermera
2 *(instead of the number "one")* un(a); **a year ago** hace un año; **a hundred/ thousand pounds** cien/mil libras
3 *(in expressing ratios, prices etc)*: **three a day/week** tres al día/a la semana; **10 km an hour** 10 km por hora; **£5 a person** £5 por persona; **30p a kilo** 30p el kilo

A2 *n (BRIT Scol) segunda parte de los "A levels" (módulos 4–6)*
AA *n abbr (BRIT: = Automobile Association)* ≈ RACE *m (SP)*; *(= Alcoholics Anonymous)* A.A.
AAA *n abbr (= American Automobile Association)* ≈ RACE *m (SP)*
aback [ə'bæk] *adv*: **to be taken ~** quedar(se) desconcertado
abandon [ə'bændən] *vt* abandonar; *(renounce)* renunciar a
abattoir ['æbətwɑːʳ] *n (BRIT)* matadero
abbey ['æbɪ] *n* abadía
abbreviation [əbriːvɪ'eɪʃən] *n (short form)* abreviatura
abdomen ['æbdəmən] *n* abdomen *m*
abduct [æb'dʌkt] *vt* raptar, secuestrar
abide [ə'baɪd] *vt*: **I can't ~ it/him** no lo/le puedo ver *or* aguantar; **abide by** *vt fus* atenerse a
ability [ə'bɪlɪtɪ] *n* habilidad *f*, capacidad *f*; *(talent)* talento
able ['eɪbl] *adj* capaz; *(skilled)* hábil; **to be ~ to do sth** poder hacer algo
abnormal [æb'nɔːməl] *adj* anormal
aboard [ə'bɔːd] *adv* a bordo ▷ *prep* a bordo de
abolish [ə'bɔlɪʃ] *vt* suprimir, abolir
abolition [æbəu'lɪʃən] *n* supresión *f*, abolición *f*
abort [ə'bɔːt] *vt* abortar; *(Comput)* interrumpir ▷ *vi (Comput)* interrumpir el programa; **abortion** *n* aborto; **to have an abortion** abortar

KEYWORD

about [ə'baut] *adv* **1** *(approximately)* más o menos, aproximadamente; **about a hundred/thousand** *etc* unos/as *or* como cien/mil *etc*; **it takes about 10 hours** se tarda unas *or* más o menos 10 horas; **at about two o'clock** sobre las dos; **I've just about finished** casi he terminado
2 *(referring to place)* por todas partes; **to leave things lying about** dejar las cosas (tiradas) por ahí; **to run about** correr por todas partes; **to walk about** pasearse, ir y venir
3: **to be about to do sth** estar a punto de hacer algo

▶ prep 1 *(relating to)* de, sobre, acerca de; **a book about London** un libro sobre or acerca de Londres; **what is it about?** ¿de qué se trata?; **we talked about it** hablamos de eso or ello; **what** or **how about doing this?** ¿qué tal si hacemos esto?
2 *(referring to place)* por; **to walk about the town** caminar por la ciudad

above [ə'bʌv] *adv* encima, por encima, arriba ▶ *prep* encima de; *(greater than: in number)* más de; *(: in rank)* superior a; **mentioned** ~ susodicho; **~ all** sobre todo

abroad [ə'brɔ:d] *adv (be)* en el extranjero; *(go)* al extranjero

abrupt [ə'brʌpt] *adj (sudden)* brusco

abscess ['æbsɪs] *n* absceso

absence ['æbsəns] *n* ausencia

absent ['æbsənt] *adj* ausente; **absent-minded** *adj* distraído

absolute ['æbsəlu:t] *adj* absoluto; **absolutely** *adv* totalmente; **oh yes, absolutely!** ¡claro or por supuesto que sí!

absorb [əb'zɔ:b] *vt* absorber; **to be ~ed in a book** estar absorto en un libro; **absorbent** *adj* absorbente; **absorbent cotton** *n (US)* algodón *m* hidrófilo; **absorbing** *adj* absorbente

abstain [əb'steɪn] *vi*: **to ~ (from)** abstenerse de

abstract ['æbstrækt] *adj* abstracto

absurd [əb'sɜ:d] *adj* absurdo

abundance [ə'bʌndəns] *n* abundancia

abundant [ə'bʌndənt] *adj* abundante

abuse [n ə'bju:s] *n (insults)* insultos *mpl*; *(misuse)* abuso ▶ *vt* [ə'bju:z] *(ill-treat)* maltratar; *(take advantage of)* abusar de; **abusive** *adj* ofensivo

abysmal [ə'bɪzməl] *adj* pésimo; *(failure)* garrafal; *(ignorance)* supino

academic [ækə'demɪk] *adj* académico, universitario ▶ *n (pej:*

issue) puramente teórico ▶ *n* estudioso/a; *(lecturer)* profesor(a) *m/f* universitario/a; **academic year** *n (Univ)* año académico

academy [ə'kædəmɪ] *n (learned body)* academia; *(school)* instituto, colegio

accelerate [æk'seləreɪt] *vi* acelerar; **acceleration** *n* aceleración *f*; **accelerator** *n (BRIT)* acelerador *m*

accent ['æksent] *n* acento; *(fig)* énfasis *m*

accept [ək'sept] *vt* aceptar; *(concede)* admitir; **acceptable** *adj* aceptable; **acceptance** *n* aceptación *f*

access ['ækses] *n* acceso ▶ *vt*: **to have ~ to** tener acceso a; **accessible** *adj (place, person)* accesible; *(knowledge etc)* asequible

accessory [æk'sesərɪ] *n* accesorio; *(Law)*: ~ **to** cómplice de

accident ['æksɪdənt] *n* accidente *m*; *(chance)* casualidad *f*; **by ~** *(unintentionally)* sin querer; *(by coincidence)* por casualidad; **accidental** *adj* accidental, fortuito; **accidentally** *adv* sin querer; por casualidad; **Accident and Emergency Department** *n (BRIT)* Urgencias *fpl*; **accident insurance** *n* seguro contra accidentes

acclaim [ə'kleɪm] *vt* aclamar, aplaudir ▶ *n* aclamación *f*, aplausos *mpl*

accommodate [ə'kɒmədeɪt] *vt* alojar, hospedar; *(car, hotel etc)* tener cabida para; *(oblige, help)* complacer; **this car ~s four people comfortably** en este coche caben cuatro personas cómodamente

accommodation *n*, *(US)* **accommodations** *npl* [əkɒmə'deɪʃ(ə)n(z)] alojamiento

accompaniment [ə'kʌmpənɪmənt] *n* acompañamiento

accompany [ə'kʌmpənɪ] *vt* acompañar

accomplice [ə'kʌmplɪs] *n* cómplice *mf*

accomplish [əˈkʌmplɪʃ] vt (finish) concluir; **accomplishment** n (bringing about) realización f; (skill) talento

accord [əˈkɔːd] n acuerdo ▷ vt conceder; **of his own ~** espontáneamente; **accordance** n: **in accordance with** de acuerdo con; **according**: **according to** prep según; (in accordance with) conforme a; **accordingly** adv (thus) por consiguiente; (appropriately) de acuerdo con esto

account [əˈkaunt] n (Comm) cuenta; (report) informe m; **accounts** npl (Comm) cuentas fpl; **of little ~** de poca importancia; **on ~** a crédito; **to buy sth on ~** comprar algo a crédito; **on no ~** bajo ningún concepto; **on ~ of** a causa de, por motivo de; **to take into ~, take ~ of** tener en cuenta; **account for** vt fus (explain) explicar; **accountable** adj: **accountable (for)** responsable (de); **accountant** n contable mf, contador(a) m/f (LAm); **account number** n (at bank etc) número de cuenta

accumulate [əˈkjuːmjuleɪt] vt acumular ▷ vi acumularse

accuracy [ˈækjurəsɪ] n (of total) exactitud f; (of description etc) precisión f

accurate [ˈækjurɪt] adj (number) exacto; (answer) acertado; (shot) certero; **accurately** adv con precisión

accusation [ækjuˈzeɪʃən] n acusación f

accuse [əˈkjuːz] vt acusar; (blame) echar la culpa a; **to ~ sb (of sth)** acusar a algn (de algo); **accused** n acusado/a

accustomed [əˈkʌstəmd] adj: **~ to** acostumbrado a

ace [eɪs] n as m

ache [eɪk] n dolor m ▷ vi doler; **my head ~s** me duele la cabeza

achieve [əˈtʃiːv] vt (reach) alcanzar; (victory, success) lograr, conseguir;

achievement n (completion) realización f; (success) éxito

acid [ˈæsɪd] adj ácido; (bitter) agrio ▷ n (Chem, inf) ácido

acknowledge [əkˈnɒlɪdʒ] vt (letter: also: **~ receipt of**) acusar recibo de; (fact) reconocer; **acknowledgement** n acuse m de recibo

acne [ˈæknɪ] n acné m

acorn [ˈeɪkɔːn] n bellota

acoustic [əˈkuːstɪk] adj acústico

acquaintance [əˈkweɪntəns] n conocimiento; (person) conocido/a; **to make sb's ~** conocer a algn

acquire [əˈkwaɪə*] vt adquirir

acquisition [ækwɪˈzɪʃən] n adquisición f

acquit [əˈkwɪt] vt absolver, exculpar; **to ~ o.s. well** salir con éxito

acre [ˈeɪkə*] n acre m

acronym [ˈækrənɪm] n siglas fpl

across [əˈkrɒs] prep (on the other side of) al otro lado de; (crosswise) a través de ▷ adv de un lado a otro, de una parte a otra a través, al través; **to run/swim ~** atravesar corriendo/nadando; **~ from** enfrente de; **the lake is 12 km ~** el lago tiene 12 km de ancho

acrylic [əˈkrɪlɪk] adj acrílico

act [ækt] n acto, acción f; (Theat) acto; (in music-hall etc) número; (Law) decreto, ley f ▷ vi (behave) comportarse; (Theat) actuar; (pretend) fingir; (take action) tomar medidas ▷ vt (part) hacer; **to catch sb in the ~** coger a algn in fraganti or con las manos en la masa; **to ~ Hamlet** hacer el papel de Hamlet; **to ~ as** actuar or hacer de; **act up** vi (inf: person) portarse mal; **acting** adj suplente ▷ n: **to do some acting** hacer algo de teatro

action [ˈækʃən] n acción f, acto; (Mil) acción f; (Law) proceso, demanda; **out of ~** (person) fuera de combate; (thing) averiado, estropeado; **to take ~** tomar medidas; **action replay** n (TV) repetición f

activate ['æktɪveɪt] vt activar

active ['æktɪv] adj activo, enérgico; (volcano) en actividad; **actively** adv (participate) activamente; (discourage, dislike) enérgicamente

activist ['æktɪvɪst] n activista mf

activity [æk'tɪvɪtɪ] n actividad f; **activity holiday** n vacaciones con actividades organizadas

actor ['æktə'] n actor m

actress ['æktrɪs] n actriz f

actual ['æktjuəl] adj verdadero, real
Be careful not to translate actual by the Spanish word actual.

actually ['æktjuəlɪ] adv realmente, en realidad
Be careful not to translate actually by the Spanish word actualmente.

acupuncture ['ækjupʌŋktʃə'] n acupuntura

acute [ə'kju:t] adj agudo

ad [æd] n abbr = **advertisement**

adamant ['ædəmənt] adj firme, inflexible

adapt [ə'dæpt] vt adaptar ▷ vi: to ~ (to) adaptarse (a), ajustarse (a); **adapter, adaptor** n (Elec) adaptador m; (for several plugs) ladrón m

add [æd] vt añadir, agregar (esp LAM); **add up** vt (figures) sumar ▷ vi (fig): **it doesn't ~ up** no tiene sentido; **it doesn't ~ up to much** es poca cosa, no tiene gran o mucha importancia

addict ['ædɪkt] n adicto/a; (enthusiast) entusiasta mf; **addicted** [ə'dɪktɪd] adj: **to be addicted to** ser adicto a; ser aficionado a; **addiction** [ə'dɪkʃən] n (to drugs etc) adicción f; **addictive** [ə'dɪktɪv] adj que causa adicción

addition [ə'dɪʃən] n (adding up) adición f; (thing added) añadidura, añadido; **in ~** además, por añadidura; **in ~ to** además de; **additional** adj adicional

additive ['ædɪtɪv] n aditivo

address [ə'drɛs] n dirección f, señas fpl; (speech) discurso ▷ vt (letter) dirigir; (speak to) dirigirse a, dirigir la palabra

a; **to ~ o.s. to sth** (issue, problem) abordar; **address book** n agenda (de direcciones)

adequate ['ædɪkwɪt] adj (satisfactory) adecuado; (enough) suficiente

adhere [əd'hɪə'] vi: **to ~ to** adherirse a; (fig: abide by) observar

adhesive [əd'hi:zɪv] n adhesivo; **adhesive tape** n (BRIT) cinta adhesiva; (us Med) esparadrapo

adjacent [ə'dʒeɪsənt] adj: **~ to** contiguo a, inmediato a

adjective ['ædʒɛktɪv] n adjetivo

adjoining [ə'dʒɔɪnɪŋ] adj contiguo, vecino

adjourn [ə'dʒəːn] vt aplazar ▷ vi suspenderse

adjust [ə'dʒʌst] vt (change) modificar; (arrange) arreglar; (machine) ajustar ▷ vi: **to ~ (to)** adaptarse (a); **adjustable** adj ajustable; **adjustment** n adaptación f; (of prices, wages) ajuste m

administer [əd'mɪnɪstə'] vt administrar

administration [ədmɪnɪ'streɪʃən] n administración f; (government) gobierno

administrative [əd'mɪnɪstrətɪv] adj administrativo

administrator [əd'mɪnɪstreɪtə'] n administrador(a) m/f

admiral ['ædmərəl] n almirante m

admiration [ædmə'reɪʃən] n admiración f

admire [əd'maɪə'] vt admirar; **admirer** n admirador(a) m/f

admission [əd'mɪʃən] n (to exhibition, nightclub) entrada; (enrolment) ingreso; (confession) confesión f

admit [əd'mɪt] vt dejar entrar, dar entrada a; (permit) admitir; (acknowledge) reconocer; **to be ~ted to hospital** ingresar en el hospital; **admit to** vt fus confesarse culpable de; **admittance** n entrada; **admittedly** adv es cierto que

adolescent [ædəu'lɛsnt] *adj, n* adolescente *mf*

adopt [ə'dɒpt] *vt* adoptar; **adopted** *adj* adoptivo; **adoption** *n* adopción *f*

adore [ə'dɔ:ʳ] *vt* adorar

adorn [ə'dɔ:n] *vt* adornar

Adriatic [eɪdrɪ'ætɪk] *n*: **the ~ (Sea)** el (Mar) Adriático

adrift [ə'drɪft] *adv* a la deriva

ADSL *n abbr* (= *asymmetrical digital subscriber line*) ADSL *m*

adult [ˈædʌlt] *n* adulto/a ▷ *adj*: **~ education** educación *f* para adultos

adultery [ə'dʌltərɪ] *n* adulterio

advance [əd'vɑ:ns] *n* adelanto, progreso; (*money*) anticipo; (*Mil*) avance *m* ▷ *vt* avanzar, adelantar; (*money*) anticipar ▷ *vi* avanzar, adelantarse; **in ~** por adelantado; **to make ~s to sb** hacer una proposición a algn; (*amorously*) insinuarse a algn; **advanced** *adj* avanzado; (*Scol: studies*) adelantado

advantage [əd'vɑ:ntɪdʒ] *n* (*also Tennis*) ventaja; **to take ~ of** aprovecharse de

advent [ˈædvənt] *n* advenimiento; **A~** Adviento

adventure [əd'vɛntʃəʳ] *n* aventura; **adventurous** *adj* aventurero

adverb [ˈædvə:b] *n* adverbio

adversary [ˈædvəsərɪ] *n* adversario, contrario

adverse [ˈædvə:s] *adj* adverso, contrario

advert [ˈædvə:t] *n abbr* (*BRIT*) = **advertisement**

advertise [ˈædvətaɪz] *vi* (*in newspaper etc*) poner un anuncio, anunciarse; **to ~ for** buscar por medio de anuncios ▷ *vt* anunciar; **advertisement** [əd'və:tɪsmənt] *n* anuncio; **advertiser** *n* anunciante *mf*; **advertising** *n* publicidad *f*, anuncios *mpl*; (*industry*) industria publicitaria

advice [əd'vaɪs] *n* consejo, consejos *mpl*; (*notification*) aviso; **a piece of ~**

un consejo; **to take legal ~** consultar a un abogado

advisable [əd'vaɪzəbl] *adj* aconsejable, conveniente

advise [əd'vaɪz] *vt* aconsejar; **to ~ sb of sth** informar a algn de algo; **to ~ sb against sth/doing sth** desaconsejar a algn algo/ aconsejar a algn que no haga algo/ **adviser** *n* consejero/a; (*business adviser*) asesor/a *m/f*; **advisory** *adj* consultivo

advocate [ˈædvəkeɪt] *vt* abogar por ▷ *n* [ˈædvəkɪt] abogado/a; (*supporter*): **~ of** defensor(a) *m/f* de

Aegean [i:'dʒi:ən] *n*: **the ~ (Sea)** el (Mar) Egeo

aerial [ˈɛərɪəl] *n* antena ▷ *adj* aéreo

aerobics [ɛə'rəubɪks] *nsg* aerobic *m*

aeroplane [ˈɛərəpleɪn] *n* (*BRIT*) avión *m*

aerosol [ˈɛərəsɒl] *n* aerosol *m*

affair [ə'fɛəʳ] *n* asunto; (*also*: **love ~**) aventura amorosa

affect [ə'fɛkt] *vt* afectar, influir en; (*move*) conmover; **affected** *adj* afectado

affection *n* afecto, cariño; **affectionate** *adj* afectuoso, cariñoso

afflict [ə'flɪkt] *vt* afligir

affluent [ˈæfluənt] *adj* acomodado; **the ~ society** la sociedad opulenta

afford [ə'fɔ:d] *vt* (*provide*) proporcionar; **can we ~ a car?** ¿podemos permitirnos el gasto de comprar un coche?; **affordable** *adj* asequible

Afghanistan [æf'gænɪstæn] *n* Afganistán *m*

afraid [ə'freɪd] *adj*: **to be ~ of** (*person*) tener miedo a; (*thing*) tener miedo de; **to be ~ to** tener miedo de, temer; **I am ~ that** me temo que; **I'm ~ so** me temo que sí; **I'm ~ not** lo siento, pero no

Africa [ˈæfrɪkə] *n* África; **African** *adj, n* africano/a; **African-American** *adj, n* afroamericano/a

after ['ɑ:ftər] *prep (time)* después de; *(place, order)* detrás de, tras ▷ *adv* después ▷ *conj* después de (que); **what/who are you ~?** ¿qué/a quién buscas?; **~ having done/he left** después de haber hecho/después de que se marchó; **to ask ~ sb** preguntar por algn; **~ all** después de todo, al fin y al cabo; **~ you!** ¡pase usted!; **after-effects** *npl* secuelas *fpl*, efectos *mpl*; **aftermath** *n* consecuencias *fpl*, resultados *mpl*; **afternoon** *n* tarde *f*; **after-shave (lotion)** *n* aftershave *m*; **aftersun (lotion)** *n* aftersun *m inv*; **afterwards** *adv* después, más tarde

again [ə'gen] *adv* otra vez, de nuevo; **to do sth ~** volver a hacer algo; **~ and ~** una y otra vez

against [ə'genst] *prep (opposed)* en contra de; *(close to)* contra, junto a

age [eɪdʒ] *n* edad *f*; *(period)* época *f* ▷ *vi* envejecer(se) ▷ *vt* envejecer; **he is 20 years of ~** tiene 20 años; **under ~** menor de edad; **to come of ~** llegar a la mayoría de edad; **it's been ~s since I saw you** hace siglos que no te veo; **age group** *n*: **to be in the same age group** tener la misma edad; **age limit** *n* límite *m* de edad, edad *f* tope

agency ['eɪdʒənsɪ] *n* agencia *f*

agenda [ə'dʒendə] *n* orden *m* del día

▌ Be careful not to translate *agenda* by the Spanish word *agenda*.

agent ['eɪdʒənt] *n* agente *mf*; *(representative)* representante *mf*, delegado/a

aggravate ['ægrəveɪt] *vt* agravar; *(annoy)* irritar

aggression [ə'greʃən] *n* agresión *f*

aggressive [ə'gresɪv] *adj* agresivo; *(vigorous)* enérgico

agile ['ædʒaɪl] *adj* ágil

agitated ['ædʒɪteɪtɪd] *adj* agitado

AGM *n abbr* (= *annual general meeting*) junta *f* general

ago [ə'gəʊ] *adv*: **two days ~** hace dos días; **not long ~** hace poco; **how long ~?** ¿hace cuánto tiempo?

agony ['ægənɪ] *n (pain)* dolor *m* atroz; *(distress)* angustia *f*; **to be in ~** retorcerse de dolor

agree [ə'gri:] *vt (price)* acordar, quedar en ▷ *vi (statements etc)* coincidir, concordar; **to ~ (with)** *(person)* estar de acuerdo (con), ponerse de acuerdo (con); **to ~ to do** aceptar hacer; **to ~ to sth** consentir en algo; **to ~ that** *(admit)* estar de acuerdo en que; **garlic doesn't ~ with me** el ajo no me sienta bien; **agreeable** *adj* agradable; *(person)* simpático; *(willing)* de acuerdo, conforme; **agreed** *adj (time, place)* convenido; **agreement** *n* acuerdo; *(Comm)* contrato; **in agreement** de acuerdo, conforme

agricultural [ægrɪ'kʌltʃərəl] *adj* agrícola

agriculture ['ægrɪkʌltʃər] *n* agricultura *f*

ahead [ə'hed] *adv* delante; **~ of** delante de; *(fig: schedule etc)* antes de; **~ of time** antes de la hora; **go right** or **straight ~** siga adelante

aid [eɪd] *n* ayuda, auxilio ▷ *vt* ayudar, auxiliar; **in ~ of** a beneficio de

aide [eɪd] *n* ayudante *mf*

AIDS [eɪdz] *n abbr* (= *acquired immune (or immuno-)deficiency syndrome*) SIDA *m*

ailing ['eɪlɪŋ] *adj (person, economy)* enfermizo

ailment ['eɪlmənt] *n* enfermedad *f*, achaque *m*

aim [eɪm] *vt (gun)* apuntar; *(missile, remark)* dirigir; *(blow)* asestar ▷ *vi (also: take ~)* apuntar ▷ *n* puntería; *(objective)* propósito, meta; **to ~ at** *(objective)* aspirar a, pretender; **to ~ to do** tener la intención de hacer, aspirar a hacer

ain't [eɪnt] *(inf)* = **are not; aren't; isn't**

air [eər] *n* aire *m*; *(appearance)* aspecto ▷ *vt (room)* ventilar; *(clothes, bed, grievances, ideas)* airear ▷ *cpd* aéreo; **to throw sth into the ~** *(ball etc)* lanzar algo al aire; **by ~** *(travel)* en avión; **to**

be on the ~ (*Radio, TV: programme*) estarse emitiendo; (*: station*) estar en antena; **airbag** n airbag m inv; **air bed** n (BRIT) colchoneta inflable or neumática; **airborne** adj (*in the air*) en el aire; **as soon as the plane was airborne** tan pronto como el avión estuvo en el aire; **air-conditioned** adj climatizado; **air conditioning** n aire m acondicionado; **aircraft** n (*pl inv*) avión m; **airfield** n campo de aviación; **Air Force** n fuerzas aéreas fpl, aviación f; **air hostess** (BRIT) n azafata; **airing cupboard** n (BRIT) armario m para oreo; **airlift** n puente m aéreo; **airline** n línea aérea; **airliner** n avión m de pasajeros; **airmail** n: **by airmail** por avión; **airplane** n (US) avión m; **airport** n aeropuerto; **air raid** n ataque m aéreo; **airsick** adj: **to be airsick** marearse (en avión); **airspace** n espacio aéreo; **airstrip** n pista de aterrizaje; **air terminal** n terminal f; **airtight** adj hermético; **air traffic controller** n controlador/a m/f aéreo/a; **airy** adj (*room*) bien ventilado; (*manners*) desenfadado

aisle [aɪl] n (*of church*) nave f lateral; (*of theatre, plane*) pasillo; **aisle seat** n (*on plane*) asiento de pasillo

ajar [ə'dʒɑːʳ] adj entreabierto

à la carte [æːlæ'kɑːt] adv a la carta

alarm [ə'lɑːm] n alarma; (*anxiety*) inquietud f ▷ vt asustar, alarmar; **alarm call** n (*in hotel etc*) alarma; **alarm clock** n despertador m; **alarmed** adj (*person*) alarmado, asustado; (*house, car etc*) con alarma; **alarming** adj alarmante

Albania [æl'beɪnɪə] n Albania

albeit [ɔːl'biːɪt] conj aunque

album ['ælbəm] n álbum m; (L.P.) elepé m

alcohol ['ælkəhɒl] n alcohol m; **alcohol-free** adj sin alcohol; **alcoholic** adj, n alcohólico/a

alcove ['ælkəʊv] n nicho, hueco

ale [eɪl] n cerveza

alert [ə'lɜːt] adj alerta inv; (*sharp*) despierto, atento ▷ n alerta m, alarma ▷ vt poner sobre aviso; **to be on the ~** estar alerta or sobre aviso

algebra ['ældʒɪbrə] n álgebra

Algeria [æl'dʒɪərɪə] n Argelia

alias ['eɪlɪəs] adv alias, conocido por ▷ n alias m; (*of criminal*) apodo; (*of writer*) seudónimo

alibi ['ælɪbaɪ] n coartada

alien ['eɪlɪən] n (*foreigner*) extranjero/a; (*extraterrestrial*) extraterrestre m/f ▷ adj: **~ to** ajeno a; **alienate** vt enajenar, alejar

alight [ə'laɪt] adj ardiendo ▷ vi apearse, bajar

align [ə'laɪn] vt alinear

alike [ə'laɪk] adj semejantes, iguales ▷ adv igualmente, del mismo modo; **to look ~** parecerse

alive [ə'laɪv] adj vivo; (*lively*) alegre

KEYWORD

all [ɔːl] adj todo/a sg, todos/as pl; **all day** todo el día; **all night** toda la noche; **all men** todos los hombres; **all five came** vinieron los cinco; **all the books** todos los libros; **all the time/ his life** todo el tiempo/toda su vida ▷ pron 1 todo; **I ate it all, I ate all of it** me lo comí todo; **all of us went** fuimos todos; **all the boys went** fueron todos los chicos; **is that all?** ¿eso es todo?, ¿algo más?; (*in shop*) ¿algo más?, ¿alguna cosa más?

2 (*in phrases*): **above all** sobre todo; por encima de todo; **after all** después de todo; **at all: anything at all** lo que sea; **not at all** (*in answer to question*) en absoluto; (*in answer to thanks*) ¡de nada!, ¡no hay de qué!; **I'm not at all tired** no estoy nada cansado; **anything at all will do** cualquier cosa viene bien; **all in all** a fin de cuentas

▷ adv: **all alone** completamente solo/a; **it's not as hard as all that** no es tan difícil como lo pintas; **all the more/the better** tanto más/mejor; **all but** casi; **the score is two all** están empatados a dos

Allah [ælə] n Alá m

allegation [ælɪˈgeɪʃən] n alegato

alleged [əˈledʒd] adj supuesto, presunto; **allegedly** [əˈledʒɪdlɪ] adv supuestamente, según se afirma

allegiance [əˈliːdʒəns] n lealtad f

allergic [əˈlɜːdʒɪk] adj: **~ to** alérgico a

allergy [ˈælədʒɪ] n alergia

alleviate [əˈliːvɪeɪt] vt aliviar

alley [ˈælɪ] n callejuela

alliance [əˈlaɪəns] n alianza

allied [ˈælaɪd] adj aliado

alligator [ˈælɪgeɪtəʳ] n caimán m

all-in [ˈɔːlɪn] adj, adv (BRIT: charge) todo incluido

allocate [ˈæləkeɪt] vt (share out) repartir; (devote) asignar

allot [əˈlɒt] vt asignar

all-out [ˈɔːlaut] adj (effort etc) supremo

allow [əˈlau] vt permitir, dejar; (a claim) admitir; (sum to spend, time estimated) dar, conceder; (concede): **to ~ that** reconocer que; **to ~ sb to do** permitir a algn hacer; **he is ~ed to** se le permite ...; **allow for** vt fus tener en cuenta; **allowance** n subvención f, pensión f; (tax allowance) desgravación f; **to make allowances for** (person) disculpar a; (thing) tener en cuenta

all right adv bien; (as answer) ¡de acuerdo!, ¡está bien!

ally n [ˈælaɪ] aliado/a ▷ vt [əˈlaɪ]: **to ~ o.s. with** aliarse con

almighty [ɔːlˈmaɪtɪ] adj todopoderoso; (row etc) imponente

almond [ˈɑːmənd] n almendra

almost [ˈɔːlməust] adv casi; **he ~ fell** casi or por poco se cae

alone [əˈləun] adj solo ▷ adv solo; **to leave sb ~** dejar a algn en paz; **to leave sth ~** no tocar algo; **let ~ ...** y mucho menos ...

along [əˈlɒŋ] prep a lo largo de, por ▷ adv: **is he coming ~ with us?** ¿viene con nosotros?; **he was limping ~** iba cojeando; **~ with** junto con; **all ~** (all the time) desde el principio; **alongside** prep al lado de ▷ adv (Naut) de costado

aloof [əˈluːf] adj distante ▷ adv: **to stand ~** mantenerse a distancia

aloud [əˈlaud] adv en voz alta

alphabet [ˈælfəbet] n alfabeto

Alps [ælps] npl: **the ~** los Alpes

already [ɔːlˈredɪ] adv ya

alright [ˈɔːlˈraɪt] adv (BRIT) = **all right**

also [ˈɔːlsəu] adv también, además

altar [ˈɔltəʳ] n altar m

alter [ˈɔltəʳ] vt cambiar, modificar ▷ vi cambiar, modificarse; **alteration** n cambio, modificación f; **alterations** npl (Sewing) arreglos mpl

alternate adj [ɔlˈtɜːnɪt] alterno ▷ vi [ˈɔltəneɪt]: **to ~ (with)** alternar (con); **on ~ days** en días alternos

alternative [ɔlˈtɜːnətɪv] adj alternativo ▷ n alternativa; **~ medicine** medicina alternativa; **alternatively** adv: **alternatively one could ...** por otra parte se podría ...

although [ɔːlˈðəu] conj aunque

altitude [ˈæltɪtjuːd] n altura

altogether [ɔːltəˈgeðəʳ] adv completamente, del todo; (on the whole, in all) en total, en conjunto

aluminium [æljuˈmɪnɪəm], (US) **aluminum** [əˈluːmɪnəm] n aluminio

always [ˈɔːlweɪz] adv siempre

Alzheimer's [ˈæltshaɪməz] n (also: **~ disease**) (enfermedad f de) m Alzheimer

am [æm] vb see **be**

a.m. adv abbr (= ante meridiem) de la mañana

amalgamate [əˈmælgəmeɪt] vi amalgamarse ▷ vt amalgamar

amass [əˈmæs] vt amontonar, acumular

amateur ['æmətə'] n aficionado/a, amateur mf

amaze [ə'meɪz] vt asombrar, pasmar; **to be ~d (at)** asombrarse (de); **amazed** adj asombrado; **amazement** n asombro, sorpresa; **amazing** adj extraordinario; (bargain, offer) increíble

Amazon ['æməzən] n (Geo) Amazonas m

ambassador [æm'bæsədə'] n embajador(a) m/f

amber ['æmbə'] n ámbar m; **at ~** (BRIT Aut) en amarillo

ambiguous [æm'bɪɡjuəs] adj ambiguo

ambition [æm'bɪʃən] n ambición f; **ambitious** adj ambicioso

ambulance ['æmbjuləns] n ambulancia

ambush ['æmbuʃ] n emboscada ▷ vt tender una emboscada a

amen [ɑ:'mɛn] excl amén

amend [ə'mɛnd] vt enmendar; **to make ~s** dar cumplida satisfacción; **amendment** n enmienda

amenities [ə'mi:nɪtɪz] npl comodidades fpl

America [ə'mɛrɪkə] n América (del Norte); (USA) Estados m pl Unidos; **American** adj, n (norte) americano/a, estadounidense m/f; **American football** n (BRIT) fútbol m americano

amicable ['æmɪkəbl] adj amistoso, amigable

amid(st) [ə'mɪd(st)] prep entre, en medio de

ammunition [æmju'nɪʃən] n municiones fpl

amnesty ['æmnɪstɪ] n amnistía

among(st) [ə'mʌŋ(st)] prep entre, en medio de

amount [ə'maunt] n cantidad f; (of bill etc) suma, importe m ▷ vi: **to ~ to** sumar; (be same as) equivaler a, significar

amp(ère) ['æmp(ɛə')] n amperio

ample ['æmpl] adj (spacious) amplio; (abundant) abundante; **to have ~ time** tener tiempo de sobra

amplifier ['æmplɪfaɪə'] n amplificador m

amputate ['æmpjuteɪt] vt amputar

Amtrak ['æmtræk] n (US) empresa nacional de ferrocarriles de los EE.UU.

amuse [ə'mju:z] vt divertir; (distract) distraer, entretener; **amusement** n diversión f; (pastime) pasatiempo; (laughter) risa; **amusement arcade** n salón m de juegos; **amusement park** n parque m de atracciones

amusing [ə'mju:zɪŋ] adj divertido

an [æn, ən, n] indef art see **a**

anaemia [ə'ni:mɪə] n anemia

anaemic [ə'ni:mɪk] adj anémico; (fig) flojo

anaesthetic [ænɪs'θɛtɪk] n anestesia

analog(ue) ['ænələɡ] adj analógico

analogy [ə'nælədʒɪ] n analogía

analyse ['ænəlaɪz] vt (BRIT) analizar; **analysis** (pl **analyses**) n análisis m inv; **analyst** ['ænəlɪst] n (political analyst, psychoanalyst) analista mf

analyze ['ænəlaɪz] vt (US) = **analyse**

anarchy ['ænəkɪ] n anarquía, desorden m

anatomy [ə'nætəmɪ] n anatomía

ancestor ['ænsɪstə'] n antepasado

anchor ['æŋkə'] n ancla, áncora ▷ vi (also: **to drop ~**) anclar; **to weigh ~** levar anclas

anchovy ['æntʃəvɪ] n anchoa

ancient ['eɪnʃənt] adj antiguo

and [ænd] conj y; (before i, hi) e; **~ so on** etcétera; **try ~ come** procura venir; **better ~ better** cada vez mejor

Andes ['ændi:z] npl: **the ~** los Andes

Andorra [æn'dɔ:rə] n Andorra

anemia [ə'ni:mɪə] n (US) = **anaemia**

anemic [ə'ni:mɪk] adj (US) = **anaemic**

anesthetic [ænɪs'θɛtɪk] n (US) = **anaesthetic**

angel ['eɪndʒəl] n ángel m

anger ['æŋɡə'] n cólera

angina [æn'dʒaɪnə] n angina (del pecho)

angle ['æŋgl] n ángulo; **from their ~** desde su punto de vista

angler ['æŋglə'] n pescador(a) m/f (de caña)

Anglican ['æŋglɪkən] adj, n anglicano/a

angling ['æŋglɪŋ] n pesca con caña

angrily ['æŋgrɪlɪ] adv enojado, enfadado

angry ['æŋgrɪ] adj enfadado, enojado (esp LAM); **to be ~ with sb** or **at sth** estar enfadado con algn/por algo; **to get ~** enfadarse, enojarse (esp LAM)

anguish ['æŋgwɪʃ] n (physical) tormentos mpl; (mental) angustia f

animal ['ænɪml] n animal m; (pej: person) bestia

animated ['ænɪmeɪtɪd] adj animado

animation [ænɪ'meɪʃən] n animación f

aniseed ['ænɪsiːd] n anís m

ankle ['æŋkl] n tobillo m

annex n ['æneks] (BRIT: also: **annexe** building) edificio anexo ▷ vt [æ'neks] (territory) anexionar

anniversary [ænɪ'vəːsərɪ] n aniversario

announce [ə'nauns] vt anunciar; **announcement** n anuncio; (declaration) declaración f; **announcer** n (Radio) locutor(a) m/f; (TV) presentador(a) m/f

annoy [ə'nɔɪ] vt molestar, fastidiar; **don't get ~ed!** ¡no se enfade! **annoying** adj molesto, fastidioso; (person) pesado

annual ['ænjuəl] adj anual ▷ n (Bot) anual m; (book) anuario; **annually** adv anualmente, cada año

annum ['ænəm] n see **per annum**

anonymous [ə'nɔnɪməs] adj anónimo

anorak ['ænəræk] n anorak m

anorexia [ænə'reksɪə] n (Med) anorexia

anorexic [ænə'reksɪk] adj, n anoréxico/a

another [ə'nʌðə'] adj: **~ book** otro libro ▷ pron otro; see also **one**

answer ['ɑːnsə'] n respuesta, contestación f; (to problem) solución f ▷ vi contestar, responder ▷ vt (reply to) contestar a, responder a; (problem) resolver; **in ~ to your letter** contestando o en contestación a su carta; **to ~ the phone** contestar el teléfono; **to ~ the bell** or **the door** abrir la puerta; **answer back** vi replicar, ser respondón/ona; **answer for** vt fus responder de or por; **answer to** vt fus (description) corresponder a; **answerphone** n (esp BRIT) contestador m (automático)

ant [ænt] n hormiga

Antarctic [ænt'ɑːktɪk] n: **the ~** el Antártico

antelope ['æntɪləup] n antílope m

antenatal ['æntɪ'neɪtl] adj prenatal

antenna (pl **antennae**) [æn'tɛnə, -niː] n antena

anthem ['ænθəm] n: **national ~** himno nacional

anthology [æn'θɔlədʒɪ] n antología

anthrax ['ænθræks] n ántrax m

anthropology [ænθrə'pɔlədʒɪ] n antropología

anti... [æntɪ] pref anti...; **antibiotic** [æntɪbaɪ'ɔtɪk] n, adj antibiótico; **antibody** ['æntɪbɔdɪ] n anticuerpo

anticipate [æn'tɪsɪpeɪt] vt prever; (expect) esperar, contar con; (forestall) anticiparse a, adelantarse a; **anticipation** [æntɪsɪ'peɪʃən] n previsión f; esperanza; anticipación f

anticlimax [æntɪ'klaɪmæks] n decepción f

anticlockwise [æntɪ'klɔkwaɪz] adv en dirección contraria a la de las agujas del reloj

antics ['æntɪks] npl gracias fpl

anti: antidote ['æntɪdəut] n antídoto; **antifreeze** ['æntɪfriːz] n anticongelante m; **antihistamine**

[ˌæntɪˈhɪstəmiːn] n antihistamínico;
antiperspirant [ˈæntɪpəˈspɪrənt] n
antitranspirante m

antique [ænˈtiːk] n antigüedad f ▷ adj
antiguo; **antique shop** n tienda de
antigüedades

antiseptic [ˌæntɪˈsɛptɪk] adj, n
antiséptico

antisocial [ˌæntɪˈsəʊʃəl] adj antisocial

antivirus [ˌæntɪˈvaɪərəs] adj
antivirus; **~ software** antivirus m

antlers [ˈæntləz] npl cornamenta

anxiety [æŋˈzaɪətɪ] n (worry)
inquietud f; (eagerness) ansia, anhelo

anxious [ˈæŋkʃəs] adj (worried)
inquieto; (keen) deseoso; **to be ~ to do**
tener muchas ganas de hacer

KEYWORD

any [ˈɛnɪ] adj 1 (in questions etc) algún/
alguna; **have you any butter/
children?** ¿tienes mantequilla/
hijos?; **if there are any tickets left** si
quedan billetes, si queda algún billete
2 (with negative): **I haven't any
money/books** no tengo dinero/libros
3 (no matter which) cualquier; **any
excuse will do** valdrá o servirá
cualquier excusa; **choose any book
you like** escoge el libro que quieras
4 (in phrases): **in any case** de todas
formas, en cualquier caso; **any day
now** cualquier día (de estos); **at any
moment** en cualquier momento, de
un momento a otro; **at any rate** en
todo caso; **any time: come (at) any
time** ven cuando quieras; **he might
come (at) any time** podría llegar de
un momento a otro

▷ pron 1 (in questions etc): **have you
got any?** ¿tienes alguno/a?; **can any
of you sing?** ¿sabe cantar alguno de
vosotros/ustedes?
2 (with negative): **I haven't any (of
them)** no tengo ninguno
3 (no matter which one(s)): **take any of
those books (you like)** toma el libro

que quieras de ésos
▷ adv 1 (in questions etc): **do you
want any more soup/sandwiches?**
¿quieres más sopa/bocadillos?; **are
you feeling any better?** ¿te sientes
algo mejor?
2 (with negative): **I can't hear him any
more** ya no le oigo; **don't wait any
longer** no esperes más

anybody [ˈɛnɪbɒdɪ] pron cualquiera,
(in interrogative sentences) alguien; (in
negative sentences): **I don't see ~** no
veo a nadie

anyhow [ˈɛnɪhaʊ] adv de todos
modos, de todas maneras; (carelessly)
de cualquier manera; (haphazardly)
de cualquier modo; **I shall go ~** iré de
todas maneras

anyone [ˈɛnɪwʌn] pron = **anybody**

anything [ˈɛnɪθɪŋ] pron cualquier
cosa; (in interrogative sentences)
algo; (in negative sentences) nada;
(everything) todo; **~ else?** ¿algo más?;
can you see ~? ¿ves algo?; **he'll eat ~**
come de todo o lo que sea

anytime [ˈɛnɪtaɪm] adv (at any
moment) en cualquier momento, de
un momento a otro; (whenever) no
importa cuándo, cuando quiera

anyway [ˈɛnɪweɪ] adv (at any rate)
de todos modos, de todas formas;
(besides) además; **~, I couldn't come
even if I wanted to** además, no
podría venir aunque quisiera; **I shall
go ~** iré de todos modos; **why are
you phoning, ~?** ¿entonces, por qué
llamas?, ¿por qué llamas, pues?

anywhere [ˈɛnɪwɛə'] adv
dondequiera; (interrogative) en algún
sitio; (negative sense) en ningún sitio;
(everywhere) en o por todas partes; **I
don't see him ~** no le veo en ningún
sitio; **are you going ~?** ¿vas a algún
sitio?; **~ in the world** en cualquier
parte del mundo

apart [əˈpɑːt] adv aparte,
separadamente; **10 miles ~** separados

por 10 millas; **to take ~** desmontar;
~ from prep aparte de
apartment [ə'pɑːtmənt] n (US) piso,
departamento (LAM), apartamento;
(room) cuarto; **apartment block**, (US)
apartment building n bloque m de
apartamentos
apathy ['æpəθɪ] n apatía, indiferencia
ape [eɪp] n mono ▷ vt imitar, remedar
aperitif [ə'pɛrɪtiːf] n aperitivo
aperture ['æpətʃjuə'] n rendija,
resquicio; (Phot) abertura
APEX ['eɪpɛks] n abbr (Aviat: = advance
purchase excursion) tarifa f APEX
apologize [ə'pɒlədʒaɪz] vi: **to ~
(for sth to sb)** disculparse (con algn
por algo)
apology [ə'pɒlədʒɪ] n disculpa,
excusa

Be careful not to translate apology
by the Spanish word apología.

apostrophe [ə'pɒstrəfɪ] n
apóstrofo m
app n abbr (inf: Comput: = application)
aplicación f
appal [ə'pɔːl] vt horrorizar, espantar;
appalling adj espantoso; (awful)
pésimo
apparatus [æpə'reɪtəs] n (equipment)
equipo; (organization) aparato; (in
gymnasium) aparatos mpl
apparent [ə'pærənt] adj aparente;
(obvious) evidente; **apparently** adv
por lo visto, al parecer
appeal [ə'piːl] vi (Law) apelar ▷ n (Law)
apelación f; (request) llamamiento;
(plea) petición f; (charm) atractivo; **to
~ for** solicitar; **to ~ to** (thing) atraer;
it doesn't ~ to me no me atrae, no
me llama la atención; **appealing** adj
(nice) atractivo
appear [ə'pɪə'] vi aparecer,
presentarse; (Law) comparecer;
(publication) salir (a luz), publicarse;
(seem) parecer; **to ~ on TV/in
"Hamlet"** salir en la tele/hacer
un papel en "Hamlet"; **it would ~
that** parecería que; **appearance** n

aparición f; (look, aspect) apariencia,
aspecto; **to keep up appearances**
salvar las apariencias; **to all
appearances** al parecer
appendices [ə'pɛndɪsiːz] npl of
appendix
appendicitis [əpɛndɪ'saɪtɪs] n
apendicitis f
appendix (pl **appendices**)
[ə'pɛndɪks, -dɪsiːz] n apéndice m
appetite ['æpɪtaɪt] n apetito; (fig)
deseo, anhelo
appetizer ['æpɪtaɪzə'] n (drink)
aperitivo; (food) tapas fpl (SP)
applaud [ə'plɔːd] vt, vi aplaudir
applause [ə'plɔːz] n aplausos mpl
apple ['æpl] n manzana; **apple pie**
n pastel m de manzana, pay m de
manzana (LAM)
appliance [ə'plaɪəns] n aparato
applicable [ə'plɪkəbl] adj aplicable;
to be ~ to referirse a
applicant ['æplɪkənt] n candidato/a;
solicitante mf
application [æplɪ'keɪʃən] n (also
Comput) aplicación f; (for a job, a grant
etc) solicitud f; **application form** n
solicitud f
apply [ə'plaɪ] vt: **to ~ (to)** aplicar (a);
(fig) emplear (para) ▷ vi: **to ~ to** (ask)
dirigirse a; (be suitable for) ser aplicable
a; **to ~ for** (permit, grant, job) solicitar;
to ~ o.s. to aplicarse a, dedicarse a
appoint [ə'pɔɪnt] vt (to post)
nombrar

Be careful not to translate appoint
by the Spanish word apuntar.

appointment [ə'pɔɪntmənt] n
(engagement) cita; (act) nombramiento; (post) puesto; **to
make an ~ (with)** (doctor) pedir hora
(con); (friend) citarse (con)
appraisal [ə'preɪzl] n evaluación f
appreciate [ə'priːʃɪeɪt] vt apreciar,
tener en mucho; (be grateful for)
agradecer; (be aware of) comprender
▷ vi (Comm) aumentar en valor;
appreciation n apreciación f;
(gratitude) reconocimiento,

agradecimiento; (*Comm*) aumento en valor

apprehension [æprɪˈhenʃən] *n* (*fear*) aprensión *f*

apprehensive [æprɪˈhensɪv] *adj* aprensivo

apprentice [əˈprentɪs] *n* aprendiz *m*, *m/f*

approach [əˈprəutʃ] *vi* acercarse ▷ *vt* acercarse a; (*ask, apply to*) dirigirse a; (*problem*) abordar ▷ *n* acercamiento; (*access*) acceso; (*to problem etc*) enfoque *m*

appropriate [əˈprəuprɪət] *adj* apropiado, conveniente ▷ *vt* [-rɪeɪt] (*take*) apropiarse de

approval [əˈpruːvəl] *n* aprobación *f*, visto bueno; **on ~** (*Comm*) a prueba

approve [əˈpruːv] *vt* aprobar; **approve of** *vt fus* aprobar; **they don't ~ of her** (ella) no les parece bien

approximate [əˈprɒksɪmɪt] *adj* aproximado; **approximately** *adv* aproximadamente, más o menos

Apr. *abbr* (= *April*) abr

apricot [ˈeɪprɪkɒt] *n* albaricoque *m* (*SP*), damasco (*LAM*)

April [ˈeɪprəl] *n* abril *m*; **April Fools' Day** *n* ≈ día *m* de los (Santos) Inocentes

apron [ˈeɪprən] *n* delantal *m*

apt [æpt] *adj* acertado, oportuno; **~ to do** (*likely*) propenso a hacer

aquarium [əˈkweərɪəm] *n* acuario

Aquarius [əˈkweərɪəs] *n* Acuario

Arab [ˈærəb] *adj*, *n* árabe *mf*

Arabia [əˈreɪbɪə] *n* Arabia; **Arabian** *adj* árabe; **Arabic** [ˈærəbɪk] *adj* árabe, arábigo ▷ *n* árabe *m*; **Arabic numerals** numeración *f* arábiga

arbitrary [ˈɑːbɪtrərɪ] *adj* arbitrario

arbitration [ɑːbɪˈtreɪʃən] *n* arbitraje *m*

arc [ɑːk] *n* arco

arcade [ɑːˈkeɪd] *n* (*round a square*) soportales *mpl*; (*shopping arcade*) galería comercial

arch [ɑːtʃ] *n* arco; (*of foot*) puente *m* ▷ *vt* arquear

archaeology [ɑːkɪˈɒlədʒɪ] *n* arqueología

archbishop [ɑːtʃˈbɪʃəp] *n* arzobispo

archeology *etc* [ɑːkɪˈɒlədʒɪ] (*US*) *see* **archaeology** *etc*

architect [ˈɑːkɪtekt] *n* arquitecto/a; **architectural** *adj* arquitectónico; **architecture** *n* arquitectura

archive [ˈɑːkaɪv] *n* (*often pl*: *also* Comput) archivo

Arctic [ˈɑːktɪk] *adj* ártico ▷ *n*: **the ~** el Ártico

are [ɑː] *vb see* **be**

area [ˈeərɪə] *n* área; (*Math etc*) superficie *f*, (*zone*) región *f*, zona; (*of knowledge, experience*) campo; **area code** *n* (*us* Tel) prefijo

arena [əˈriːnə] *n* arena; (*of circus*) pista

aren't [ɑːnt] = **are not**

Argentina [ɑːdʒənˈtiːnə] *n* Argentina; **Argentinian** [ɑːdʒənˈtɪnɪən] *adj*, *n* argentino/a

arguably [ˈɑːɡjuəblɪ] *adv*: **it is ~ ...** es discutiblemente ...

argue [ˈɑːɡjuː] *vi* (*quarrel*) discutir; (*reason*) razonar, argumentar; **to ~ that** sostener que

argument [ˈɑːɡjumənt] *n* (*reasons*) argumento; (*quarrel*) discusión *f*

Aries [ˈeərɪz] *n* Aries *m*

arise [əˈraɪz] (*pt* **arose**, *pp* **arisen** [əˈrɪzn]) *vi* surgir, presentarse

arithmetic [əˈrɪθmətɪk] *n* aritmética

arm [ɑːm] *n* brazo ▷ *vt* armar; **~ in ~** cogidos del brazo; **armchair** *n* sillón *m*, butaca

armed [ɑːmd] *adj* armado; **armed robbery** *n* robo a mano armada

armour, (*us*) **armor** [ˈɑːmə] *n* armadura

armpit [ˈɑːmpɪt] *n* sobaco, axila

armrest [ˈɑːmrest] *n* reposabrazos *m inv*

army [ˈɑːmɪ] *n* ejército; (*fig*) multitud *f*

A road *n* (*BRIT*) ≈ carretera *f* nacional

aroma [əˈrəʊmə] n aroma m, fragancia; **aromatherapy** n aromaterapia

arose [əˈrəʊz] pt of **arise**

around [əˈraʊnd] adv alrededor; (in the area) a la redonda ▷ prep alrededor de

arouse [əˈraʊz] vt despertar; (anger) provocar

arrange [əˈreɪndʒ] vt arreglar, ordenar; (programme) organizar; **to ~ to do sth** quedar en hacer algo; **arrangement** n arreglo, (agreement) acuerdo; **arrangements** npl (preparations) preparativos mpl

array [əˈreɪ] n: **~ of** (things) serie f or colección f de; (people) conjunto de

arrears [əˈrɪəz] npl atrasos mpl; **to be in ~ with one's rent** estar retrasado en el pago del alquiler

arrest [əˈrest] vt detener; (sb's attention) llamar ▷ n detención f; **under ~** detenido

arrival [əˈraɪvl] n llegada; **new ~** recién llegado/a

arrive [əˈraɪv] vi llegar; **arrive at** vt fus (decision, solution) llegar a

arrogance [ˈærəgəns] n arrogancia, prepotencia (LAM)

arrogant [ˈærəgənt] adj arrogante

arrow [ˈærəʊ] n flecha

arse [ɑːs] n (BRIT inf!) culo, trasero

arson [ˈɑːsn] n incendio provocado

art [ɑːt] n arte m; (skill) destreza f; **art college** n escuela f de Bellas Artes

artery [ˈɑːtəri] n arteria

art gallery n pinacoteca f; (Comm) galería de arte

arthritis [ɑːˈθraɪtɪs] n artritis f

artichoke [ˈɑːtɪtʃəʊk] n alcachofa; **Jerusalem ~** aguaturma

article [ˈɑːtɪkl] n artículo

articulate [ɑːˈtɪkjʊlɪt] (speech) claro ▷ vt [ɑːˈtɪkjʊleɪt] expresar

artificial [ɑːtɪˈfɪʃəl] adj artificial

artist [ˈɑːtɪst] n artista mf; (Mus) intérprete mf; **artistic** adj artístico

art school n escuela de bellas artes

as [æz] conj **1** (referring to time: while) mientras; **as the years go by** con el paso de los años; **he came in as I was leaving** entró cuando me marchaba; **as from tomorrow** a partir de or desde mañana

2 (in comparisons): **as big as** tan grande como; **twice as big as** el doble de grande que; **as much money/many books as** tanto dinero/tantos libros como; **as soon as** en cuanto

3 (since, because) como, ya que; **as I don't speak German I can't understand him** no le entiendo ya que no hablo alemán

4 (referring to manner, way): **do as you wish** haz lo que quieras; **as she said** como dijo

5 (concerning): **as for** or **to that** por or en lo que respecta a eso

6: **as if** or **though** como si; **he looked as if he was ill** parecía como si estuviera enfermo, tenía aspecto de enfermo; see also **long**; **such**; **well**

▷ prep (in the capacity of): **he works as a barman** trabaja de barman; **as chairman of the company, he ...** como presidente de la compañía, ...; **he gave it to me as a present** me lo dio de regalo

a.s.a.p. abbr (= as soon as possible) cuanto antes

asbestos [æzˈbestəs] n asbesto, amianto

ascent [əˈsent] n subida; (slope) cuesta, pendiente f

ash [æʃ] n ceniza; (tree) fresno

ashamed [əˈʃeɪmd] adj avergonzado; **to be ~ of** avergonzarse de

ashore [əˈʃɔː] adv en tierra; (swim etc) a tierra

ashtray [ˈæʃtreɪ] n cenicero

Ash Wednesday n miércoles m de Ceniza

Asia ['eɪʃə] n Asia; **Asian** adj, n asiático/a

aside [ə'saɪd] adv a un lado ▷ n aparte m

ask [ɑːsk] vt (question) preguntar; (invite) invitar; **to ~ sb sth/to do sth** preguntar algo a algn/pedir a algn que haga algo; **to ~ (sb) a question** hacer una pregunta (a algn); **to ~ sb out to dinner** invitar a cenar a algn; **ask for** vt fus pedir; **it's just ~ing for trouble** or **for it** es buscarse problemas

asleep [ə'sliːp] adj dormido; **to fall ~** dormirse, quedarse dormido

asparagus [əs'pærəgəs] n espárragos mpl

aspect ['æspekt] n aspecto, apariencia; (direction in which a building etc faces) orientación f

aspirations [æspə'reɪʃənz] npl aspiraciones fpl; (ambition) ambición f

aspire [əs'paɪə] vi: **to ~** aspirar a, ambicionar

aspirin ['æsprɪn] n aspirina

ass [æs] n asno, burro; (inf) imbécil mf; (us inf!) culo, trasero

assassin [ə'sæsɪn] n asesino/a; **assassinate** vt asesinar

assault [ə'sɔːlt] n asalto; (Law) agresión f ▷ vt asaltar; (sexually) violar

assemble [ə'sembl] vt reunir, juntar; (Tech) montar ▷ vi reunirse, juntarse

assembly [ə'semblɪ] n reunión f, asamblea; (parliament) parlamento; (construction) montaje m

assert [ə'səːt] vt afirmar; (insist on) hacer valer; **assertion** n afirmación f

assess [ə'ses] vt valorar, calcular; (tax, damages) fijar; (for tax) gravar; **assessment** n valoración f; gravamen m

asset ['æset] n ventaja; **assets** npl (funds) activo sg, fondos mpl

assign [ə'saɪn] vt (date) fijar; (task) asignar; (resources) destinar; **assignment** n tarea

assist [ə'sɪst] vt ayudar; **assistance** n ayuda, auxilio; **assistant** n ayudante mf; (BRIT: also: **shop assistant**) dependiente/a m/f

associate [adj, n ə'səʊʃɪɪt, vt, vi ə'səʊʃɪeɪt] adj asociado ▷ n colega mf ▷ vt asociar; (ideas) relacionar ▷ vi: **to ~ with sb** tratar con algn

association [əsəʊsɪ'eɪʃən] n asociación f

assorted [ə'sɔːtɪd] adj surtido, variado

assortment [ə'sɔːtmənt] n (of shapes, colours) surtido; (of books) colección f; (of people) mezcla

assume [ə'sjuːm] vt suponer; (responsibilities etc) asumir; (attitude, name) adoptar, tomar

assumption [ə'sʌmpʃən] n suposición f, presunción f; (act) asunción f

assurance [ə'ʃuərəns] n garantía, promesa; (confidence) confianza, aplomo; (insurance) seguro

assure [ə'ʃuə] vt asegurar

asterisk ['æstərɪsk] n asterisco

asthma ['æsmə] n asma

astonish [ə'stɒnɪʃ] vt asombrar, pasmar; **astonished** adj estupefacto, pasmado; **to be astonished (at)** asombrarse (de); **astonishing** adj asombroso, pasmoso; **I find it astonishing that ...** me asombra or pasma que ...; **astonishment** n asombro, sorpresa

astound [ə'staund] vt asombrar, pasmar

astray [ə'streɪ] adv: **to go ~** extraviarse; **to lead ~** llevar por mal camino

astrology [əs'trɒlədʒɪ] n astrología

astronaut ['æstrənɔːt] n astronauta mf

astronomer [əs'trɒnəmə] n astrónomo/a

astronomical [æstrə'nɒmɪkəl] adj astronómico

astronomy [əs'trɒnəmɪ] n astronomía

astute [əsˈtjuːt] *adj* astuto
asylum [əˈsaɪləm] *n* (*refuge*) asilo;
(*hospital*) manicomio

🔵 **KEYWORD**

at [æt] *prep* **1** (*referring to position*) en;
(*direction*) a; **at the top** lo alto; **at
home/school** en casa/la escuela; **to
look at sth/sb** mirar algo/a algn
2 (*referring to time*): **at four o'clock**
a las cuatro; **at night** por la noche;
at Christmas en Navidad; **at times**
a veces
3 (*referring to rates, speed etc*): **at £1 a
kilo** a una libra el kilo; **two at a time**
de dos en dos; **at 50 km/h** a 50 km/h
4 (*referring to manner*): **at a stroke** de
un golpe; **at peace** en paz
5 (*referring to activity*): **to be at work**
estar trabajando; (*in office*) estar en el
trabajo; **to play at cowboys** jugar a
los vaqueros; **to be good at sth** ser
bueno en algo
6 (*referring to cause*): **shocked/
surprised/annoyed at sth**
asombrado/sorprendido/fastidiado
por algo; **I went at his suggestion**
fui a instancias suyas
▶ **n** (*symbol @*) arroba

ate [ɛt, eɪt] *pt of* **eat**
atheist [ˈeɪθɪɪst] *n* ateo/a
Athens [ˈæθɪnz] *n* Atenas f
athlete [ˈæθliːt] *n* atleta *mf*
athletic [æθˈlɛtɪk] *adj* atlético;
athletics *n* atletismo
Atlantic [ətˈlæntɪk] *adj* atlántico ▶ *n*:
the ~ (Ocean) el (Océano) Atlántico
atlas [ˈætləs] *n* atlas *m inv*
A.T.M. *n abbr* (= *Automated Telling
Machine*) *cajero automático*
atmosphere [ˈætməsfɪəʳ] *n*
atmósfera f; (*fig*) ambiente *m*
atom [ˈætəm] *n* átomo; **atomic**
[əˈtɒmɪk] *adj* atómico; **atom(ic)
bomb** *n* bomba atómica
A to Z® *n* (*map*) callejero

atrocity [əˈtrɒsɪtɪ] *n* atrocidad f
attach [əˈtætʃ] *vt* sujetar; (*document,
email, letter*) adjuntar; **to be ~ed to
sb/sth** (*like*) tener cariño a sb/
algo; **attachment** *n* (*tool*) accesorio;
(*Comput*) archivo o documento
adjunto; (*love*): **attachment (to)**
apego *m*
attack [əˈtæk] *vt* (*Mil*) atacar;
(*criminal*) agredir, asaltar; (*criticize*)
criticar; (*task etc*) emprender ▶ *n*
ataque *m*, asalto; (*on sb's life*)
atentado; (*fig: criticism*) crítica; **heart
~** infarto (de miocardio); **attacker** *n*
agresor/a *m/f*, asaltante *mf*
attain [əˈteɪn] *vt* (*also:* **~ to**) alcanzar;
(*achieve*) lograr, conseguir
attempt [əˈtɛmpt] *n* tentativa,
intento; (*attack*) atentado ▶ *vt*
intentar
attend *vt* asistir a; (*patient*) atender;
attend to *vt fus* (*needs, affairs etc*)
ocuparse de; (*speech etc*) prestar
atención a; (*customer*) atender a;
attendance *n* asistencia, presencia;
(*people present*) concurrencia;
attendant *n* sirviente *m/f*,
ayudante *mf* ▶ *adj* concomitante
attention [əˈtɛnʃən] *n* atención f
▶ *excl* (*Mil*) ¡firme(s)!; **for the ~ of ...**
(*Admin*) a la atención de ...
attic [ˈætɪk] *n* desván m
attitude [ˈætɪtjuːd] *n* actitud f;
(*disposition*) disposición f
attorney [əˈtɜːnɪ] *n* (*lawyer*)
abogado/a; **Attorney General** *n*
(*BRIT*) ≈ fiscal *mf* general del Estado;
(*US*) ≈ ministro/a de Justicia
attract [əˈtrækt] *vt* atraer;
(*attention*) llamar; **attraction** *n*
encanto; (*Physics*) atracción f;
(*towards sth*) atracción f; **attractive**
adj atractivo
attribute *n* [ˈætrɪbjuːt] *n* atributo
▶ *vt* [əˈtrɪbjuːt]: **to ~ sth to** atribuir
algo a
aubergine [ˈəʊbəʒiːn] *n* (*BRIT*)
berenjena; (*colour*) morado

auburn ['ɔːbən] *adj* color castaño rojizo

auction ['ɔːkʃən] *n* (*also*: **sale by ~**) subasta ▷ *vt* subastar

audible ['ɔːdɪbl] *adj* audible, que se puede oír

audience ['ɔːdɪəns] *n* público; (*Radio*) radioescuchas *mpl*; (*TV*) telespectadores *mpl*; (*interview*) audiencia

audit ['ɔːdɪt] *vt* revisar, intervenir

audition [ɔːˈdɪʃən] *n* audición *f*

auditor ['ɔːdɪtə'] *n* interventor(a) *m/f*, censor(a) *m/f* de cuentas

auditorium [ɔːdɪˈtɔːrɪəm] *n* auditorio

Aug. *abbr* (= *August*) ag

August ['ɔːɡəst] *n* agosto

aunt [ɑːnt] *n* tía; **auntie, aunty** ['ɑːntɪ] *n diminutive of* **aunt**

au pair ['əʊ'pɛə'] *n* (*also*: **~ girl**) chica *f* au pair

aura ['ɔːrə] *n* aura; (*atmosphere*) ambiente *m*

austerity [ɔːˈstɛrɪtɪ] *n* austeridad *f*

Australia [ɔːˈstreɪlɪə] *n* Australia; **Australian** *adj*, *n* australiano/a

Austria ['ɔstrɪə] *n* Austria; **Austrian** *adj*, *n* austríaco/a

authentic [ɔːˈθɛntɪk] *adj* auténtico

author ['ɔːθə'] *n* autor(a) *m/f*

authority [ɔːˈθɒrɪtɪ] *n* autoridad *f*; **the authorities** *npl* las autoridades

authorize ['ɔːθəraɪz] *vt* autorizar

auto ['ɔːtəu] *n* (*us*) coche *m*, carro (*LAM*), automóvil *m*; **autobiography** [ɔːtəbaɪˈɒɡrəfɪ] *n* autobiografía; **autograph** ['ɔːtəɡrɑːf] *n* autógrafo ▷ *vt* (*photo etc*) dedicar; **automatic** [ɔːtəˈmætɪk] *adj* automático ▷ *n* (*gun*) pistola automática; **automatically** *adv* automáticamente; **automobile** ['ɔːtəməbiːl] *n* (*us*) coche *m*, carro (*LAM*), automóvil *m*; **autonomous** [ɔːˈtɒnəməs] *adj* autónomo; **autonomy** [ɔːˈtɒnəmɪ] *n* autonomía *f*

autumn ['ɔːtəm] *n* otoño

auxiliary [ɔːɡˈzɪlɪərɪ] *adj* auxiliar

avail [əˈveɪl] *vt*: **to ~ o.s. of** aprovechar(se) de ▷ *n*: **to no ~** en vano, sin resultado

availability [əveɪlə'bɪlɪtɪ] *n* disponibilidad *f*

available [ə'veɪləbl] *adj* disponible

avalanche ['ævəlɑːnʃ] *n* alud *m*, avalancha

Ave. *abbr* (= *avenue*) Av., Avda

avenue ['ævənjuː] *n* avenida; (*fig*) camino

average ['ævərɪdʒ] *n* promedio, media ▷ *adj* (*mean*) medio; (*ordinary*) regular, corriente ▷ *vt* alcanzar un promedio de; **on ~** por término medio

avert [ə'vɜːt] *vt* prevenir; (*blow*) desviar; (*one's eyes*) apartar

avid ['ævɪd] *adj* ávido

avocado [ævə'kɑːdəu] *n* (*BRIT*: *also*: **~ pear**) aguacate *m*, palta (*LAM*)

avoid [ə'vɔɪd] *vt* evitar, eludir

await [ə'weɪt] *vt* esperar, aguardar

awake [ə'weɪk] (*pt* **awoke**, *pp* **awoken** *or* **awaked**) *adj* despierto ▷ *vt* despertar ▷ *vi* despertarse; **to be ~** estar despierto

award [ə'wɔːd] *n* premio; (*Law*) fallo, sentencia ▷ *vt* otorgar, conceder; (*Law: damages*) adjudicar

aware [ə'weə'] *adj* consciente; **to become ~ of** darse cuenta de, enterarse de; **awareness** *n* conciencia, conocimiento

away [ə'weɪ] *adv* (*place*) fuera; (*far away*) lejos; **two kilometres ~** a dos kilómetros (de distancia); **two hours ~ by car** a dos horas en coche; **the holiday was two weeks ~** faltaban dos semanas para las vacaciones; **he's ~ for a week** estará ausente una semana; **to work/pedal** ~ seguir trabajando/ pedaleando; **to fade ~** desvanecerse; (*sound*) apagarse

awe [ɔː] *n* respeto, admiración *f* respetuosa; **awesome** ['ɔːsəm] *adj* (*esp us*: *excellent*) formidable

awful ['ɔːfəl] adj terrible; **an ~ lot of** (people, cars, dogs) la mar de, muchísimos; **awfully** adv (very) terriblemente

awkward ['ɔːkwəd] adj desmañado, torpe; (shape, situation) incómodo; (question) difícil

awoke [ə'wəuk] pt of **awake**

awoken [ə'wəukən] pp of **awake**

axe, (us) **ax** [æks] n hacha ▷ vt (project etc) cortar; (jobs) reducir

axle ['æksl] n eje m, árbol m

ay(e) [aɪ] excl (yes) sí

azalea [ə'zeɪlɪə] n azalea

b

B [biː] n (Mus) si m

baby ['beɪbɪ] n bebé mf; (us inf: darling) mi amor; **baby carriage** n (us) cochecito; **baby-sit** vi hacer de canguro; **baby-sitter** n canguro mf; **baby wipe** n toallita húmeda (para bebés)

bachelor ['bætʃələ] n soltero; **B~ of Arts/Science (BA/BSc)** licenciado/a en Filosofía y Letras/Ciencias

back [bæk] n (of person) espalda; (of animal) lomo; (of hand, page) dorso; (as opposed to front) parte f de atrás; (of chair) respaldo; (of page) reverso; (Football) defensa m ▷ vt (candidate: also: ~ **up**) respaldar, apoyar; (horse: at races) apostar a; (car) dar marcha atrás a or con ▷ vi (car etc) dar marcha atrás ▷ adj (garden, room) de atrás ▷ adv (not forward) (hacia) atrás; **he's ~** (returned) ha vuelto; **~ seats/ wheels** (Aut) asientos mpl traseros, ruedas fpl traseras; **~ payments**

pagos mpl con efecto retroactivo; **~ rent** renta atrasada; **he ran ~** volvió corriendo; **throw the ball ~** (restitution) devuelve la pelota; **can I have it ~?** ¿me lo devuelve?; **he called ~** (again) volvió a llamar; **back down** vi echarse atrás; **back out** vi (of promise) volverse atrás; **back up** vt (person) apoyar, respaldar; (theory) defender; (Comput) hacer una copia de seguridad de; **backache** n dolor m de espalda; **backbencher** n (BRIT) diputado sin cargo oficial en el gobierno o la oposición; **backbone** n columna vertebral; **back door** n puerta f trasera; **backfire** vi (Aut) petardear; (plans) fallar, salir mal; **backgammon** n backgammon m; **background** n fondo; (of events) antecedentes mpl; (basic knowledge) bases fpl; (experience) conocimientos mpl, educación f; **family background** origen m, antecedentes mpl familiares; **backing** n (fig) apoyo, respaldo; (Comm) respaldo financiero; (Mus) acompañamiento; **backlog** n: **backlog of work** trabajo atrasado; **backpack** n mochila; **backpacker** n mochilero/a; **backslash** n pleca, barra inversa; **backstage** adv entre bastidores; **backstroke** n espalda; **backup** adj suplementario; (Comput: disk, file) de reserva ▷ n (support) apoyo; (also: **backup file**) copia de reserva; **backward** adj (person, country) atrasado; **backwards** adv hacia atrás; (read a list) al revés; (fall) de espaldas; **backyard** n patio trasero

bacon ['beɪkən] n tocino, beicon m

bacteria [bæk'tɪərɪə] npl bacterias fpl

bad [bæd] adj malo; (serious) grave; (meat, food) podrido, pasado; **to go ~** pasarse

badge [bædʒ] n insignia; (metal badge) chapa; (of policeman) placa

badger ['bædʒə'] n tejón m

badly ['bædlɪ] adv (work, dress etc) mal; **to reflect ~ on sb** influir negativamente en la reputación de

algn; **~ wounded** gravemente herido; **he needs it** – le hace mucha falta; **to be ~ off (for money)** andar mal de dinero

bad-mannered ['bæd'mænəd] adj mal educado

badminton ['bædmɪntən] n bádminton m

bad-tempered ['bæd'tɛmpəd] adj de mal genio or carácter; (temporarily) de mal humor

bag [bæg] n bolsa; (handbag) bolso; (satchel) mochila; (case) maleta; **~s of** (inf) un montón de

baggage ['bægɪdʒ] n equipaje m; **baggage allowance** n límite m de equipaje; **baggage (re)claim** n recogida de equipajes

baggy ['bægɪ] adj (trousers) ancho, holgado

bagpipes ['bægpaɪps] npl gaita sg

bail [beɪl] n fianza ▷ vt (prisoner: also: **~ grant ~**) poner en libertad bajo fianza; (boat: also: **~ out**) achicar; **on ~** (prisoner) bajo fianza; **to ~ sb out** pagar la fianza de algn

bait [beɪt] n cebo ▷ vt poner el cebo en

bake [beɪk] vt cocer (al horno) ▷ vi cocerse; **baked beans** npl judías fpl en salsa de tomate; **baked potato** n patata al horno; **baker** n panadero/a; **bakery** n panadería; (for cakes) pastelería; **baking** n (act) cocción f; (batch) hornada; **baking powder** n levadura (en polvo)

balance ['bæləns] n equilibrio; (Comm: sum) balance m; (remainder) resto; (scales) balanza ▷ vt equilibrar; (budget) nivelar; (account) saldar; (compensate) compensar; **~ of trade/payments** balanza de comercio/pagos; **balanced** adj (personality, diet) equilibrado; (report) objetivo; **balance sheet** n balance m

balcony ['bælkənɪ] n (open) balcón m; (closed) galería; (in theatre) anfiteatro

bald [bɔːld] adj calvo; (tyre) liso

ball [bɔːl] n (football) balón m; (for tennis, golf etc) pelota; (of wool, string) ovillo; (dance) baile m; **to play ~ (with sb)** jugar a la pelota (con algn); (fig) cooperar

ballerina [bæləˈriːnə] n bailarina

ballet [ˈbæleɪ] n ballet m; **ballet dancer** n bailarín/ina m/f (de ballet)

balloon [bəˈluːn] n globo

ballot [ˈbælət] n votación f

ballroom [ˈbɔːlrʊm] n salón m de baile

Baltic [ˈbɔːltɪk] n: **the ~ (Sea)** el (Mar) Báltico

bamboo [bæmˈbuː] n bambú m

ban [bæn] n prohibición f ▷ vt prohibir; (exclude) excluir

banana [bəˈnɑːnə] n plátano, banana (LAM)

band [bænd] n (group) banda; (strip) faja, tira; (at a dance) orquesta; (Mil) banda; (rock band) grupo

bandage [ˈbændɪdʒ] n venda, vendaje m ▷ vt vendar

Band-Aid® [ˈbændeɪd] n (US) tirita

bandit [ˈbændɪt] n bandido

bang [bæŋ] n (of gun, exhaust) estallido; (of door) portazo; (blow) golpe m ▷ vt (door) cerrar de golpe; (one's head) golpear ▷ vi estallar; see also **bangs**

Bangladesh [bæŋɡləˈdeʃ] n Bangladesh f

bangle [ˈbæŋɡl] n brazalete m, ajorca

bangs [bæŋz] npl (US) flequillo sg

banish [ˈbænɪʃ] vt desterrar

banister(s) [ˈbænɪstə(z)] n(pl) barandilla f, pasamanos m inv

banjo [ˈbændʒəʊ] n (pl **banjoes** or **banjos**) n banjo

bank [bæŋk] n (Comm) banco; (of river, lake) ribera, orilla; (of earth) terraplén m ▷ vi (Aviat) ladearse; **bank on** vt fus contar con; **bank account** n cuenta bancaria; **bank balance** n saldo; **bank card** n tarjeta bancaria; **bank charges** npl comisión fsg; **banker** n banquero; **bank holiday** n (BRIT)

día m festivo or de fiesta; ver nota **"bank holiday"**; **banking** n banca; **bank manager** n director(a) m/f (de sucursal) de banco; **banknote** n billete m de banco

● **BANK HOLIDAY**
●
● El término **bank holiday** se aplica en
● el Reino Unido a todo día festivo
● oficial en el que cierran bancos y
● comercios. Los más destacados
● coinciden con Navidad, Semana
● Santa, finales de mayo y finales
● de agosto. Al contrario que en los
● países de tradición católica, no se
● celebran las festividades dedicadas
● a los santos.

bankrupt [ˈbæŋkrʌpt] adj quebrado, insolvente; **to go ~** hacer bancarrota; **to be ~** estar en quiebra; **bankruptcy** n quiebra

bank statement n extracto de cuenta

banner [ˈbænə] n pancarta

bannister(s) [ˈbænɪstə(z)] n(pl) = **banister(s)**

banquet [ˈbæŋkwɪt] n banquete m

baptism [ˈbæptɪzəm] n bautismo; (act) bautizo

baptize [bæpˈtaɪz] vt bautizar

bar [bɑː] n barra; (on door) tranca; (of window, cage) reja; (of soap) pastilla; (of chocolate) tableta; (fig: hindrance) obstáculo; (prohibition) prohibición f; (pub) bar m; (counter) barra, mostrador m; (Mus) barra ▷ vt (road) obstruir; (person) excluir; (activity) prohibir; **behind ~s** entre rejas; **the B~** (Law) la abogacía; **~ none** sin excepción

barbaric [bɑːˈbærɪk] adj bárbaro

barbecue [ˈbɑːbɪkjuː] n barbacoa

barbed wire [ˈbɑːbd-] n alambre m de espino

barber [ˈbɑːbə] n peluquero, barbero; **barber's (shop)**, (US) **barber (shop)** n peluquería

bar code n código de barras

bare [beə^r] adj desnudo; (trees) sin hojas ▷ vt desnudar; **to ~ one's teeth** enseñar los dientes; **barefoot** adj, adv descalzo; **barely** adv apenas

bargain ['bɑ:gɪn] n pacto; (transaction) negocio; (good buy) ganga ▷ vi negociar; (haggle) regatear; **into the ~** además, por añadidura; **bargain for** vt fus (inf): **he got more than he ~ed for** le resultó peor de lo que esperaba

barge [bɑ:dʒ] n barcaza; **barge in** vi irrumpir; (in conversation) entrometerse

bark [bɑ:k] n (of tree) corteza; (of dog) ladrido ▷ vi ladrar

barley ['bɑ:lɪ] n cebada

barmaid ['bɑ:meɪd] n camarera

barman ['bɑ:mən] n camarero, barman m

barn [bɑ:n] n granero

barometer [bə'rɒmɪtə^r] n barómetro

baron ['bærən] n barón m; (fig) magnate m; **baroness** n baronesa

barracks ['bærəks] npl cuartel msg

barrage ['bærɑ:ʒ] n (Mil) cortina de fuego; (dam) presa; (of criticism etc) lluvia, aluvión m

barrel ['bærəl] n barril m; (of gun) cañón m

barren ['bærən] adj estéril

barrette [bə'ret] n (US) pasador m (LAM, SP), broche m (MEX)

barricade [bærɪ'keɪd] n barricada

barrier ['bærɪə^r] n barrera

barring ['bɑ:rɪŋ] prep excepto, salvo

barrister ['bærɪstə^r] n (BRIT) abogado/a

barrow ['bærəu] n (cart) carretilla

bartender ['bɑ:tendə^r] n (US) camarero, barman m

base [beɪs] n base f ▷ vt: **to ~ sth on** basar or fundar algo en ▷ adj bajo, infame

baseball ['beɪsbɔ:l] n béisbol m; **baseball cap** n gorra f de béisbol

basement ['beɪsmənt] n sótano

bases ['beɪsi:z] npl of **basis**

bash [bæʃ] vt (inf) golpear

basic ['beɪsɪk] adj básico; **basically** adv fundamentalmente, en el fondo; **basics** npl: **the basics** los fundamentos

basil ['bæzl] n albahaca

basin ['beɪsn] n cuenco, tazón m; (Geo) cuenca; (also: **wash~**) lavabo

basis ['beɪsɪs] n (pl **bases**) base f; **on a part-time/trial ~** a tiempo parcial/a prueba

basket ['bɑ:skɪt] n cesta, cesto; **basketball** n baloncesto

bass [beɪs] n (Mus) bajo

bastard ['bɑ:stəd] n bastardo/a; (inf!) hijo de puta (!)

bat [bæt] n (Zool) murciélago; (for ball games) palo; (BRIT: for table tennis) pala ▷ vt: **he didn't ~ an eyelid** ni pestañeó

batch [bætʃ] n lote m; (of bread) hornada

bath [bɑ:θ] n (act) baño; (bathtub) bañera, tina (esp LAM) ▷ vt bañar; **to have a ~** bañarse, darse un baño; see also **baths**

bathe [beɪð] vi bañarse ▷ vt (wound etc) lavar

bathing ['beɪðɪŋ] n baño; **bathing costume**, (US) **bathing suit** n traje m de baño

bath: **bathrobe** n albornoz m; **bathroom** n (cuarto de) baño; **baths** [bɑ:ðz] npl piscina sg; **bath towel** n toalla de baño; **bathtub** n bañera

baton ['bætən] n (Mus) batuta; (weapon) porra

batter ['bætə^r] vt maltratar; (wind, rain) azotar ▷ n batido; **battered** adj (hat, pan) estropeado

battery ['bætərɪ] n batería; (of torch) pila; **battery farming** n cría intensiva

battle ['bætl] n batalla; (fig) lucha ▷ vi luchar; **battlefield** n campo m de batalla

bay [beɪ] n (Geo) bahía; **to hold sb at ~** mantener a alguien a raya

bazaar [bəˈzɑːʳ] n bazar m
BBC n abbr (= British Broadcasting Corporation) BBC f

KEYWORD

be [biː] (pt **was, were**, pp **been**) aux vb **1** (with present participle, forming continuous tenses): **what are you doing?** ¿qué estás haciendo?, ¿qué haces?; **they're coming tomorrow** vienen mañana; **I've been waiting for you for hours** llevo horas esperándole

2 (with pp: forming passives) ser (but often replaced by active or reflexive constructions): **to be murdered** ser asesinado; **the box had been opened** habían abierto la caja; **the thief was nowhere to be seen** no se veía al ladrón por ninguna parte **3** (in tag questions): **it was fun, wasn't it?** fue divertido, ¿no? or ¿verdad?; **he's good-looking, isn't he?** es guapo, ¿no te parece?; **she's back again, is she?** entonces, ¿ha vuelto?

4 (+ to + infin): **the house is to be sold** (necessity) hay que vender la casa; (future) van a vender la casa; **he's not to open it** no tiene que abrirlo

▷ vb +complement **1** (with n or num complement): **he's a doctor** es médico; **2 and 2 are 4** 2 y 2 son 4 **2** (with adj complement, expressing permanent or inherent quality): ser (: expressing state seen as temporary or reversible) estar; **I'm English** soy inglés/esa; **she's tall/pretty** es alta/bonita; **he's young** es joven; **be careful/good/quiet** ten cuidado/pórtate bien/cállate; **I'm tired** estoy cansado/a; **it's dirty** está sucio/a **3** (of health) estar: **how are you?** ¿cómo estás?; **he's very ill** está muy enfermo; **I'm better now** ya estoy mejor

4 (of age) tener: **how old are you?** ¿cuántos años tienes?; **I'm sixteen**

(years old) tengo dieciséis años **5** (cost) costar; ser; **how much was the meal?** ¿cuánto fue or costó la comida?; **that'll be £5.75, please** son £5.75, por favor; **this shirt is £17** esta camisa cuesta £17

▷ vi **1** (exist, occur etc) existir, haber; **the best singer that ever was** el mejor cantante que existió jamás; **is there a God?** ¿hay un Dios?, ¿existe Dios?; **be that as it may** sea como sea; **so be it** así sea

2 (referring to place) estar; **I won't be here tomorrow** no estaré aquí mañana

3 (referring to movement): **where have you been?** ¿dónde has estado? ▷ impers vb **1** (referring to time): **it's 5 o'clock** son las 5; **it's the 28th of April** estamos a 28 de abril

2 (referring to distance): **it's 10 km to the village** el pueblo está a 10 km **3** (referring to the weather): **it's too hot/cold** hace demasiado calor/frío; **it's windy today** hace viento hoy **4** (emphatic): **it's me** soy yo; **it was Maria who paid the bill** fue María la que pagó la cuenta

beach [biːtʃ] n playa ▷ vt varar
beacon [ˈbiːkən] n (lighthouse) faro; (marker) guía
bead [biːd] n cuenta; (of dew, sweat) gota; **beads** npl (necklace) collar m
beak [biːk] n pico
beam [biːm] n (Arch) viga; (of light) rayo, haz m de luz ▷ vi brillar; (smile) sonreír
bean [biːn] n judía; **runner/broad ~** habichuela/haba; **coffee ~** grano de café; **bean sprouts** npl brotes mpl de soja
bear [bɛəʳ] (pt **bore**, pp **borne**) n oso ▷ vt (weight etc) llevar; (cost) pagar; (responsibility) tener; (endure) soportar, aguantar; (children) tener; (fruit) dar ▷ vi: **to ~ right/left** torcer a la derecha/izquierda

beard [bɪəd] n barba

bearer ['bɛərə'] n portador(a) m/f

bearing ['bɛərɪŋ] n porte m; (connection) relación f

beast [biːst] n bestia; (inf) bruto, salvaje m

beat [biːt] (pt **beat**, pp **beaten** ['biːtn]) n (of heart) latido; (Mus) ritmo, compás m; (of policeman) ronda ▷ vt (hit) golpear, pegar; (eggs) batir; (defeat) vencer, derrotar; (better) sobrepasar; (drum) redoblar ▷ vi (heart) latir; **off the ~en track** aislado; **to ~ it** largarse; **beat up** vt (inf: person) dar una paliza a; **beating** n paliza

beautiful ['bjuːtɪful] adj hermoso, bello; **beautifully** adv de maravilla

beauty ['bjuːtɪ] n belleza; **beauty parlour** n, (us) **beauty parlor** n salón m de belleza; **beauty salon** n salón m de belleza; **beauty spot** n (Tourism) lugar m pintoresco

beaver ['biːvə'] n castor m

became [bɪ'keɪm] pt of **become**

because [bɪ'kɔz] conj porque; **~ of** prep debido a, a causa de

beckon ['bɛkən] vt (also: **~ to**) llamar con señas

become [bɪ'kʌm] (like **come**) vi (+noun) hacerse, llegar a ser; (+adj) volverse, volverse y (of suit) favorecer, ir bien a; **to ~ fat** engordar

bed [bɛd] n cama; (of flowers) ... ...; (of sea, lake) fondo; (of river) ...; (of coal, clay) capa; **to go to ~** ... ...; **bed and breakfast** ... n; ver nota **"bed and ..."**; **bedclothes** npl ropa ... **~edding** n ropa de cama; ... (BRIT) ropa f de cama; ... ...ormitorio; **bedside** ... ...**side** a la cabecera de ... **de lamp** n lámpara de ... ...**table** n mesilla de ... ...r) n (BRIT) estudio; ... ...recama m, colcha; ... ...acostarse

● **BED AND BREAKFAST**

● Se llama *Bed and Breakfast* a la casa
● de hospedaje particular, o granja
● si es en el campo, que ofrece cama
● y desayuno a tarifas inferiores a
● las de un hotel. El servicio se suele
● anunciar con carteles colocados en
● las ventanas del establecimiento,
● en el jardín o en la carretera y en
● ellos aparece a menudo únicamente
● el símbolo "B & B".

bee [biː] n abeja

beech [biːtʃ] n haya

beef [biːf] n carne f de vaca; **roast ~** rosbif m; **beefburger** n hamburguesa

been [biːn] pp of **be**

beer [bɪə'] n cerveza; **beer garden** n (BRIT) terraza f de verano, jardín m (de un bar)

beet [biːt] n (us) remolacha

beetle ['biːtl] n escarabajo

beetroot ['biːtruːt] n (BRIT) remolacha

before [bɪ'fɔː'] prep (of time) antes de; (of space) delante de ▷ conj antes (de) que ▷ adv (time) antes; (space) delante, adelante; **~ going** antes de marcharse; **~ she goes** antes de que se vaya; **the week ~** la semana anterior; **I've never seen it ~** no lo he visto nunca; **beforehand** adv de antemano, con anticipación

beg [bɛg] vi pedir limosna ▷ vt pedir, rogar; (entreat) suplicar; **to ~ sb to do sth** rogar a algn que haga algo; see also **pardon**

began [bɪ'gæn] pt of **begin**

beggar ['bɛgə'] n mendigo/a

begin [bɪ'gɪn] (pt **began**, pp **begun**) vt, vi empezar, comenzar; **to ~ doing** or **to do sth** empezar a hacer algo; **beginner** n principiante mf; **beginning** n principio, comienzo

begun [bɪ'gʌn] pp of **begin**

behalf [bɪ'hɑːf] n: **on ~ of** en nombre de, por; (for benefit of) en beneficio de; **on my/his ~** por mí/él

behave [bɪ'heɪv] vi (person) portarse, comportarse; (well: also: **~ o.s.**) portarse bien; **behaviour**, (us) **behavior** n comportamiento, conducta

behind [bɪ'haɪnd] prep detrás de ▷ adv detrás, por detrás, atrás ▷ n trasero; **to be ~ (schedule)** ir retrasado; **~ the scenes** (fig) entre bastidores

beige [beɪʒ] adj (color) beige

Beijing [beɪ'dʒɪŋ] n Pekín m

being ['biːɪŋ] n ser m; **to come into ~** nacer, aparecer

belated [bɪ'leɪtɪd] adj atrasado, tardío

belch [beltʃ] vi eructar ▷ vt (also: **~ out**: smoke etc) arrojar

Belgian ['beldʒən] adj, n belga mf

Belgium ['beldʒəm] n Bélgica f

belief [bɪ'liːf] n opinión f; (trust, faith) fe f

believe [bɪ'liːv] vt, vi creer; **to ~ in** creer en; **believer** n partidario/a; (Rel) creyente mf, fiel mf

bell [bel] n campana f; (small) campanilla; (on door) timbre m

bellboy ['belbɔɪ], (us) **bellhop** ['belhɔp] n botones m inv

bellow ['beləʊ] vi bramar; (person) rugir

bell pepper n (esp us) pimiento, pimentón m (LAM)

belly ['belɪ] n barriga, panza; **belly button** (inf) n ombligo

belong [bɪ'lɔŋ] vi: **to ~ to** pertenecer a; (club etc) ser socio de; **this book ~s here** este libro va aquí; **belongings** npl pertenencias fpl

beloved [bɪ'lʌvɪd] adj, n querido/a

below [bɪ'ləʊ] prep bajo, debajo de; (less than) inferior a ▷ adv abajo, (por) debajo; **see ~** véase más abajo

belt [belt] n cinturón m; (Tech) correa, cinta ▷ vt (thrash) pegar con correa; **beltway** n (us Aut) carretera de circunvalación

bemused [bɪ'mjuːzd] adj perplejo

bench [bentʃ] n banco; (BRIT Pol): **the Government/Opposition ~es** (los asientos de) los miembros del Gobierno/de la Oposición; **the B~** (Law) la magistratura

bend [bend] (pt, pp bent) vt doblar ▷ vi inclinarse ▷ n (in road, river) recodo; (in pipe) codo; **bend down** vi inclinarse, doblarse; **bend over** vi inclinarse

beneath [bɪ'niːθ] prep bajo, debajo de; (unworthy of) indigno de ▷ adv abajo, (por) debajo

beneficial [benɪ'fɪʃəl] adj: **~ to** beneficioso para

benefit ['benɪfɪt] n beneficio; (allowance of money) subsidio ▷ vt beneficiar ▷ vi: **he'll ~ from it** le sacará provecho

benign [bɪ'naɪn] adj benigno; (smile) afable

bent [bent] pt, pp of **bend** ▷ n inclinación f ▷ adj: **to be ~ on** estar empeñado en

bereaved [bɪ'riːvd] n: **the ~** los allegados mpl del difunto

beret ['bereɪ] n boina

Berlin [bəː'lɪn] n Berlín m

Bermuda [bəː'mjuːdə] n las (Islas) Bermudas

berry ['berɪ] n baya

berth [bəːθ] n (bed) litera; (cabin) camarote m; (for ship) amarradero ▷ vi atracar, amarrar

beside [bɪ'saɪd] prep junto a, al lado de; **to be ~ o.s. with anger** estar fuera de sí; **that's ~ the point** eso no tiene nada que ver; **besides** adv además ▷ prep además de

best [best] adj (el/la) mejor ▷ adv (l mejor; **the ~ part of** (most) la may parte de; **at ~** en el mejor de los casos; **to make the ~ of sth** saca mejor partido de algo; **to do one** hacer todo lo posible; **to the ~ of** **knowledge** que yo sepa; **to the b my ability** como mejor puedo; **'** **before date** n fecha de consum preferente; **best man** n padri boda; **bestseller** n éxito de ve bestseller m

bet [bɛt] n apuesta ▷ vt, vi (pt, pp **bet** or **betted**): **to ~ (on)** apostar (a)

betray [bɪ'treɪ] vt traicionar; (trust) faltar a

better ['bɛtəʳ] adj mejor ▷ adv mejor ▷ vt superar ▷ n: **to get the ~ of sb** quedar por encima de algn; **you had ~ do it** más vale que lo hagas; **he thought ~ of it** cambió de parecer; **to get ~** mejorar(se)

betting ['bɛtɪŋ] n juego, apuestas fpl; **betting shop** n (BRIT) casa de apuestas

between [bɪ'twi:n] prep entre ▷ adv (time) mientras tanto; (place) en medio

beverage ['bɛvərɪdʒ] n bebida

beware [bɪ'wɛəʳ] vi: **to ~ (of)** tener cuidado (con); **"~ of the dog"** "perro peligroso"

bewildered [bɪ'wɪldəd] adj aturdido, perplejo

beyond [bɪ'jɔnd] prep más allá de; (past: understanding) fuera de; (after: date) después de, más allá de; (above) superior a ▷ adv (in space) más allá; (in time) posteriormente; **~ doubt** fuera de toda duda; **~ repair** irreparable

bias ['baɪəs] n (prejudice) prejuicio; (preference) predisposición f

bias(s)ed ['baɪəst] adj parcial

bib [bɪb] n babero

Bible ['baɪbl] n Biblia

bicarbonate of soda [baɪ'kɑ:bənɪt-] n bicarbonato sódico

biceps ['baɪsɛps] n bíceps m

bicycle ['baɪsɪkl] n bicicleta; **bicycle pump** n bomba de bicicleta

bid [bɪd] n oferta, postura; (attempt) tentativa, conato ▷ vi hacer una oferta ▷ vt (offer) ofrecer; **to ~ sb good day** dar a algn los buenos días; **bidder** n: **the highest bidder** el mejor postor

bidet ['bi:deɪ] n bidet m

big [bɪg] adj grande; (brother, sister) mayor; **bigheaded** adj engreído; **big toe** n dedo gordo (del pie)

bike [baɪk] n bici f; **bike lane** n carril m bici

bikini [bɪ'ki:nɪ] n bikini m

bilateral [baɪ'lætərl] adj bilateral

bilingual [baɪ'lɪŋgwəl] adj bilingüe

bill [bɪl] n cuenta; (invoice) factura; (Pol) proyecto de ley; (US: banknote) billete m; (of bird) pico; (Theat) programa m; **"post no ~s"** "prohibido fijar carteles"; **to fit** or **fill the ~** (fig) cumplir con los requisitos; **billboard** n valla publicitaria; **billfold** n (US) cartera

billiards ['bɪljədz] n billar m

billion ['bɪljən] n (BRIT) billón m; (US) mil millones mpl

bin [bɪn] n cubo or bote m (LAM) de la basura; (litterbin) papelera

bind [baɪnd] (pt, pp **bound**) vt atar; (book) encuadernar; (oblige) obligar ▷ n (inf: nuisance) lata

binge [bɪndʒ] n: **to go on a ~** ir de juerga

bingo ['bɪŋgəu] n bingo m

binoculars [bɪ'nɔkjuləz] npl prismáticos mpl

bio...:biochemistry [baɪə'kɛmɪstrɪ] n bioquímica; **biodegradable** [baɪəudɪ'greɪdəbl] adj biodegradable; **biofuel** ['baɪəufjuəl] n biocombustible m, biocarburante m; **biography** [baɪ'ɔgrəfɪ] n biografía; **biological** [baɪə'lɔdʒɪkəl] adj biológico; **biology** [baɪ'ɔlədʒɪ] n biología; **biometric** [baɪə'mɛtrɪk] adj biométrico

birch [bə:tʃ] n abedul m

bird [bə:d] n ave f, pájaro; (BRIT inf: girl) chica; **bird flu** n gripe aviar; **bird of prey** n ave f de presa; **bird-watching** n: **he likes to go bird-watching on Sundays** los domingos le gusta ver pájaros

Biro® ['baɪrəu] n bolígrafo

birth [bə:θ] n (Med) parto; **to give ~ to** parir, dar a luz a; (fig) dar origen a; **birth certificate** n partida de nacimiento; **birth control** n control m de natalidad; (methods) métodos mpl anticonceptivos; **birthday** n cumpleaños m inv; **birthmark** n antojo, marca de nacimiento; **birthplace** n lugar m de nacimiento

biscuit ['bɪskɪt] n (BRIT) galleta

bishop ['bɪʃəp] n obispo; (Chess) alfil m

bistro ['bi:strəʊ] n café-bar m

bit [bɪt] pt of **bite** ▷ n trozo, pedazo, pedacito; (Comput) bit m; (for horse) freno, bocado; **a ~ of** un poco de; **a ~ mad** un poco loco; **~ by ~** poco a poco

bitch [bɪtʃ] n (dog) perra; (inf!: woman) zorra (!)

bite [baɪt] vt, vi (pt **bit**, pp **bitten**) morder; (insect etc) picar ▷ n (insect) picadura; (mouthful) bocado; **to ~ one's nails** morderse las uñas; **let's have a ~ (to eat)** vamos a comer algo

bitten ['bɪtn] pp of **bite**

bitter ['bɪtə'] adj amargo; (wind, criticism) cortante, penetrante; (battle) encarnizado ▷ n (BRIT: beer) cerveza típica británica a base de lúpulos

bizarre [bɪ'zɑ:'] adj raro, extraño

black [blæk] adj negro ▷ n color m negro; (person): **B~** negro/a ▷ vt (BRIT Industry) boicotear; **to give sb a ~ eye** ponerle a algn el ojo morado; **~ coffee** café m solo; **~ and blue** adj amoratado; **black out** vi (faint) desmayarse; **blackberry** n zarzamora; **blackbird** n mirlo; **blackboard** n pizarra; **blackcurrant** n grosella negra; **black ice** n hielo invisible en la carretera; **blackmail** n chantaje m ▷ vt chantajear; **black market** n mercado negro; **blackout** n (Elec) apagón m; (TV) bloqueo informativo; (fainting) desmayo, pérdida de conocimiento; **black pepper** n pimienta f negra; **black pudding** n morcilla; **Black Sea: the Black Sea** el Mar Negro

bladder ['blædə'] n vejiga

blade [bleɪd] n hoja; **a ~ of grass** una brizna de hierba

blame [bleɪm] n culpa ▷ vt: **to ~ sb for sth** echar a algn la culpa de algo; **to be to ~ (for)** tener la culpa (de)

bland [blænd] adj (taste) soso

blank [blæŋk] adj en blanco; (look) sin expresión ▷ n blanco, espacio en blanco; (cartridge) cartucho sin bala o de fuego; **my mind is a ~** no puedo recordar nada

blanket ['blæŋkɪt] n manta, cobija (LAM); (of snow) capa; (of fog) manto

blast [blɑ:st] n (of wind) ráfaga, soplo; (of explosive) explosión f ▷ vt (blow up) volar

blatant ['bleɪtənt] adj descarado

blaze [bleɪz] n (fire) fuego; (fig) arranque m ▷ vi (fire) arder en llamas; (fig) brillar ▷ vt: **to ~ a trail** (fig) abrir (un) camino; **in a ~ of publicity** bajo los focos de la publicidad

blazer ['bleɪzə'] n chaqueta de uniforme de colegial o de socio de club

bleach [bli:tʃ] n (also: **household ~**) lejía ▷ vt blanquear; **bleachers** npl (US Sport) gradas fpl

bleak [bli:k] adj (countryside) desierto; (weather) desapacible; (smile) triste; (prospect, future) poco prometedor(a)

bled [blɛd] pt, pp of **bleed**

bleed [bli:d] (pt, pp **bled**) vi sangrar ▷ vi sangrar; **my nose is ~ing** me está sangrando la nariz

blemish ['blɛmɪʃ] n marca, mancha; (on reputation) tacha

blend [blɛnd] n mezcla ▷ vt mezclar ▷ vi (colours etc) combinarse, mezclarse; **blender** n (Culin) batidora

bless (pt, pp **blessed** or **blest**) [blɛs, blɛst] vt bendecir; **~ you!** (after sneeze) ¡Jesús!; **blessing** n bendición f; (advantage) beneficio, ventaja; **it was a blessing in disguise** no hay mal que por bien no venga

blew [blu:] pt of **blow**

blight [blaɪt] vt (hopes etc) frustrar, arruinar

blind [blaɪnd] adj ciego ▷ n (for window) persiana ▷ vt cegar; (dazzle) deslumbrar; **to ~ sb to ...** (deceive) cegar a algn a ...; **the blind** npl los ciegos; **blind alley** n callejón m sin salida; **blindfold** n venda ▷ adv con los ojos vendados ▷ vt vendar los ojos a

blink [blɪŋk] vi parpadear, pestañear; (light) oscilar

bliss [blɪs] n felicidad f

blister ['blɪstə'] n ampolla f ▷ vi ampollarse

blizzard ['blɪzəd] n ventisca

bloated ['bləʊtɪd] adj hinchado

blob [blɒb] n (drop) gota; (stain, spot) mancha

block [blɒk] n (also Comput) bloque m; (in pipes) obstáculo; (of buildings) manzana, cuadra (LAM) ▷ vt obstruir, cerrar; (progress) estorbar; **~ of flats** (BRIT) bloque m de pisos; **mental ~** bloqueo mental; **block up** vt tapar, obstruir; (pipe) atascar; **blockade** [blɔ'keɪd] n bloqueo ▷ vt bloquear; **blockage** n estorbo, obstrucción f; **blockbuster** n (book) best-seller m; (film) éxito de público; **block capitals** npl mayúsculas fpl; **block letters** npl mayúsculas fpl

blog [blɒg] n blog m ▷ vi bloguear; **he ~s about politics** tiene un blog sobre política

blogger ['blɒgə'] n (inf: person) bloguero/a

bloke [bləʊk] n (BRIT inf) tipo, tío

blond, blonde [blɒnd] adj, n rubio/a

blood [blʌd] n sangre f; **blood donor** n donante mf de sangre; **blood group** n grupo sanguíneo; **blood poisoning** n septicemia, envenenamiento de la sangre; **blood pressure** n tensión f, presión f sanguínea; **bloodshed** n baño de sangre; **bloodshot** adj inyectado en sangre; **bloodstream** n corriente f sanguínea; **blood test** n análisis m de sangre; **blood transfusion** n transfusión f de sangre; **blood type** n grupo sanguíneo; **blood vessel** n vaso sanguíneo; **bloody** adj sangriento; (BRIT inf!): **this bloody ...** este condenado or puñetero or fregado (LAM ... !) ▷ adv (BRIT inf!): **bloody strong/good** terriblemente fuerte/bueno

bloom [bluːm] n floración f ▷ vi florecer

blossom ['blɒsəm] n flor f ▷ vi florecer

blot [blɒt] n borrón m ▷ vt (stain) manchar

blouse [blauz] n blusa

blow [bləʊ] (pt **blew**, pp **blown**) n golpe m ▷ vi soplar; (fuse) fundirse ▷ vt (fuse) quemar; (instrument) tocar; **to ~ one's nose** sonarse; **blow away** vt llevarse, arrancar; **blow out** vt apagar ▷ vi apagarse; **blow up** vi estallar ▷ vt volar; (tyre) inflar; (Phot) ampliar; **blow-dry** n secado con secador de mano

blown [bləʊn] pp of **blow**

blue [bluː] adj azul; **~ film** película porno; **~ joke** chiste verde; **to come out of the ~** (fig) ser completamente inesperado; **bluebell** n campanilla, campánula azul; **blueberry** n arándano; **blue cheese** n queso azul; **blues** npl: **the blues** (Mus) el blues; **to have the blues** estar triste; **bluetit** n herrerillo m (común)

bluff [blʌf] vi tirarse un farol, farolear ▷ n farol m; **to call sb's ~** coger a algn en un renuncio

blunder ['blʌndə'] n patinazo, metedura de pata ▷ vi cometer un error, meter la pata

blunt [blʌnt] adj (knife) desafilado; (person) franco, directo

blur [bləː'] n aspecto borroso; **to become a ~** hacerse borroso ▷ vt (vision) enturbiar; **blurred** adj borroso

blush [blʌʃ] vi ruborizarse, ponerse colorado ▷ n rubor m; **blusher** n colorete m

board [bɔːd] n tabla, tablero; (on wall) tablón m; (for chess etc) tablero; (committee) junta, consejo; (in firm) mesa or junta directiva; (Naut, Aviat): **on ~** a bordo ▷ vt (ship) embarcar en; (train) subira; **full ~** (BRIT) pensión f completa; **half ~** (BRIT) media pensión; **to go by the ~** (fig) irse por la borda; **board game** n juego de tablero; **boarding card** n (BRIT Aviat, Naut) tarjeta de embarque; **boarding pass** n (US) = **boarding card**; **boarding school** n internado; **board room** n sala de juntas

boast [bəust] vi: **to ~ (about** or **of)** alardear (de)

boat [bəut] n barco, buque m; (small) barca, bote m

bob [bɔb] vi (also: **~ up and down**) menearse, balancearse

body ['bɔdɪ] n cuerpo; (corpse) cadáver m; (of car) caja, carrocería; (fig: public body) organismo; **body-building** n culturismo; **bodyguard** n guardaespaldas m inv; **bodywork** n carrocería

bog [bɔg] n pantano, ciénaga ▷vt: **to get ~ged down** (fig) empantanarse, atascarse

bogus ['bəugəs] adj falso, fraudulento

boil [bɔɪl] vt hervir; (eggs) pasar por agua ▷ vi hervir; (fig: with anger) estar furioso ▷ n (Med) furúnculo, divieso; **to come to the** (BRIT) or **a** (US) **~** comenzar a hervir; **~ed egg** huevo pasado por agua; **~ed potatoes** patatas fpl or papas fpl (LAM) cocidas; **boil over** vi (liquid) salirse; (anger, resentment) llegar al colmo; **boiler** n caldera; **boiling** adj: **I'm boiling (hot)** (inf) estoy asado; **boiling point** n punto de ebullición f

bold [bəuld] adj valiente, audaz; (pej) descarado; (colour) llamativo

Bolivia [bə'lɪvɪə] n Bolivia; **Bolivian** adj, n boliviano/a

bollard ['bɔləd] n (BRIT Aut) poste m

bolt [bəult] n (lock) cerrojo; (with nut) perno, tornillo ▷ adv: **~ upright** rígido, erguido ▷ vt (door) echar el cerrojo a; (food) engullir ▷ vi fugarse; (horse) desbocarse

bomb [bɔm] n bomba ▷ vt bombardear

bombard [bɔm'bɑːd] vt bombardear; (fig) asediar

bomb: bomber n (Aviat) bombardero; **bomb scare** n amenaza de bomba

bond [bɔnd] n (binding promise) fianza; (Finance) bono; (link) vínculo, lazo; **in ~** (Comm) en depósito bajo fianza

bone [bəun] n hueso; (of fish) espina ▷ vt deshuesar; quitar las espinas a

bonfire ['bɔnfaɪər] n hoguera, fogata

bonnet ['bɔnɪt] n gorra; (BRIT: of car) capó m

bonus ['bəunəs] n (payment) paga extraordinaria, plus m; (fig) bendición f

boo [buː] excl ¡uh! ▷ vt abuchear

book [buk] n libro; (of stamps etc) librillo; **~s** (Comm) cuentas fpl, contabilidad f ▷ vt (ticket, seat, room) reservar; **book in** vi (at hotel) registrarse; **book up** vt: **the hotel is ~ed up** el hotel está completo; **bookcase** n librería, estante m para libros; **booking** n reserva; **booking office** n (BRIT: Rail) despacho de billetes or boletos (LAM); (: Theat) taquilla, boletería (LAM); **bookkeeping** n contabilidad f; **booklet** n folleto; **bookmaker** n corredor m de apuestas; **bookmark** n (Comput) favorito, marcador m; **bookseller** n librero/a; **bookshelf** n estante m; **bookshop** n librería

book store n = **bookshop**

boom [buːm] n (noise) trueno, estampido; (in prices etc) alza rápida; (Econ) boom m ▷ vi (cannon) hacer gran estruendo, retumbar; (Econ) estar en alza

boost [buːst] n estímulo, empuje m ▷ vt estimular, empujar

boot [buːt] n bota; (BRIT: of car) maleta, maletero ▷ vt (Comput) arrancar; **to ~** (in addition) además, por añadidura

booth [buːð] n (telephone booth, voting booth) cabina

booze [buːz] (*inf*) *n* bebida

border ['bɔːdə^r] *n* borde *m*, margen *m*; (*of a country*) frontera *f*; (*for flowers*) arriate *m* ▷ *adj* fronterizo; **the B-s** región fronteriza entre Escocia e Inglaterra; **border on** *vt fus* lindar con; **borderline** *n* (*fig*) frontera; **on the borderline** en el límite

bore [bɔː^r] *pt of* **bear** ▷ *vt* (*hole*) hacer; (*person*) aburrir ▷ *n* (*person*) pelmazo, pesado; (*of gun*) calibre *m*; **bored** *adj* aburrido; **he's bored to tears** *or* **to death** *or* **stiff** está aburrido como una ostra, está muerto de aburrimiento; **boredom** *n* aburrimiento

boring ['bɔːrɪŋ] *adj* aburrido

born [bɔːn] *adj*: **to be ~** nacer; **I was ~ in 1960** nací en 1960

borne [bɔːn] *pp of* **bear**

borough ['bʌrə] *n* municipio

borrow ['bɔrəʊ] *vt*: **to ~ sth (from sb)** tomar algo prestado (a alguien)

Bosnia ['bɒznɪə] *n* Bosnia; **Bosnia-Herzegovina, Bosnia-Hercegovina** ['bɒznɪəhɜːrzə'ɡəʊviːnə] *n* Bosnia-Herzegovina; **Bosnian** *adj*, *n* bosnio/a

bosom ['bʊzəm] *n* pecho

boss [bɒs] *n* jefe/a *m/f* ▷ *vt* (*also*: **~ about** *or* **around**) mangonear; **bossy** *adj* mandón/ona

both [bəʊθ] *adj*, *pron* ambos/as, los/las dos; **~ of us went, we ~ went** fuimos los dos, ambos fuimos ▷ *adv*: **~ A and B** tanto A como B

bother ['bɒðə^r] *vt* (*worry*) preocupar; (*disturb*) molestar, fastidiar ▷ *vi*: **to o.s.** molestarse ▷ *n* (*trouble*) dificultad *f*; (*nuisance*) molestia, lata; **to ~ doing** tomarse la molestia de hacer

bottle ['bɒtl] *n* botella, (*small*) frasco; (*baby's*) biberón *m* ▷ *vt* embotellar; **bottle bank** *n* contenedor *m* de vidrio; **bottle-opener** *n* abrebotellas *m inv*

bottom ['bɒtəm] *n* (*of box, sea*) fondo; (*buttocks*) trasero, culo; (*of page, mountain, tree*) pie *m*; (*of list*) final *m* ▷ *adj* (*lowest*) más bajo; (*last*) último

bought [bɔːt] *pt*, *pp of* **buy**

boulder ['bəʊldə^r] *n* canto rodado

bounce [baʊns] *vi* (*ball*) (re)botar; (*cheque*) ser rechazado ▷ *vt* hacer (re)botar ▷ *n* (*rebound*) (re)bote *m*; **bouncer** *n* (*inf*) gorila *m*

bound [baʊnd] *pt*, *pp of* **bind** ▷ *n* (*leap*) salto; (*gen pl: limit*) límite *m* ▷ *vi* (*leap*) saltar ▷ *adj*: **~ by** rodeado de; **to be ~ to do sth** (*obliged*) tener el deber de hacer algo; **he's ~ to come** es seguro que vendrá; **"out of ~s to the public"** "prohibido el paso"; **~ for** con destino a

boundary ['baʊndrɪ] *n* límite *m*

bouquet [buːˈkeɪ] *n* (*of flowers*) ramo

bourbon ['bʊəbən] *n* (*us: also:* **~ whiskey**) whisky *m* americano, bourbon *m*

bout [baʊt] *n* (*of malaria etc*) ataque *m*; (*Boxing etc*) combate *m*, encuentro

boutique [buːˈtiːk] *n* boutique *f*, tienda de ropa

bow[1] [bəʊ] *n* (*knot*) lazo; (*weapon, Mus*) arco

bow[2] [baʊ] *n* (*of the head*) reverencia; (*Naut: also:* **~s**) proa ▷ *vi* inclinarse, hacer una reverencia

bowels ['baʊəlz] *npl* intestinos *mpl*, vientre *m*; (*fig*) entrañas *fpl*

bowl [bəʊl] *n* tazón *m*, cuenco; (*ball*) bola ▷ *vi* (*Cricket*) arrojar la pelota; *see also* **bowls**; **bowler** *n* (*Cricket*) lanzador *m* (de la pelota); (*BRIT: also:* **bowler hat**) hongo, bombín *m*; **bowling** *n* (*game*) bolos *mpl*; **bowling alley** *n* bolera; **bowling green** *n* pista para bochas; **bowls** *n* juego de los bolos, bochas *fpl*

bow tie [bəʊ-] *n* corbata de lazo, pajarita

box [bɒks] *n* (*also:* **cardboard ~**) caja, cajón *m*; (*Theat*) palco ▷ *vt* encajonar ▷ *vi* (*Sport*) boxear; **boxer** *n* (*person*) boxeador *m*; (*dog*) bóxer *m*; **boxer shorts** *npl* bóxers; **a pair of boxer shorts** unos bóxers; **boxing** *n* (*Sport*) boxeo; **Boxing Day** *n* (*BRIT*) día *m* de San Esteban; **boxing gloves** *npl* guantes *mpl* de boxeo; **boxing ring**

n ring *m*, cuadrilátero; **box office** *n* taquilla, boletería (*LAm*)

boy [bɔɪ] *n* (*young*) niño *m*; (*older*) muchacho, chico, (*son*) hijo *m*; **boy band** *n* boy band *m* (*grupo musical de chicos*)

boycott ['bɔɪkɔt] *n* boicot *m* ▷ *vt* boicotear

boyfriend [ˈbɔɪfrend] *n* novio

bra [bra:] *n* sostén *m*, sujetador *m*

brace [breɪs] *n* (*BRIT: on teeth*) corrector *m*, aparato; (*tool*) berbiquí *m* ▷ *vt* asegurar, reforzar; **to ~ o.s. (for)** (*fig*) prepararse (para); *see also* **braces**

bracelet [ˈbreɪslɪt] *n* pulsera, brazalete *m*

braces [ˈbreɪsɪz] *npl* (*on teeth*) corrector *m*; (*BRIT: for trousers*) tirantes *mpl*

bracket [ˈbrækɪt] *n* (*Tech*) soporte *m*, puntal *m*; (*group*) clase *f*, categoría; (*also:* **brace ~**) soporte *m*, abrazadera; (*also:* **round ~**) paréntesis *m inv*; **in ~s** entre paréntesis

brag [bræg] *vi* jactarse

braid [breɪd] *n* (*trimming*) galón *m*; (*of hair*) trenza

brain [breɪn] *n* cerebro; **brains** *npl* sesos *mpl*; **she's got ~s** es muy lista

braise [breɪz] *vt* cocer a fuego lento

brake [breɪk] *n* (*on vehicle*) freno ▷ *vi* frenar; **brake light** *n* luz *f* de frenado

bran [bræn] *n* salvado

branch [bra:ntʃ] *n* rama; (*Comm*) sucursal *f* ▷ *vi* ramificarse; (*fig*) extenderse; **branch off** *vi*: **a small road ~es off to the right** hay una carretera pequeña que sale hacia la derecha; **branch out** *vi* (*fig*) extenderse

brand [brænd] *n* marca; (*fig: type*) tipo ▷ *vt* (*cattle*) marcar con hierro candente; **brand name** *n* marca; **brand-new** *adj* flamante, completamente nuevo

brandy [ˈbrændɪ] *n* coñac *m*

brash [bræʃ] *adj* (*cheeky*) descarado

brass [bra:s] *n* latón *m*; **the ~** (*Mus*) los cobres; **brass band** *n* banda de metal

brat [bræt] *n* (*pej*) mocoso/a

brave [breɪv] *adj* valiente, valeroso ▷ *vt* (*challenge*) desafiar; (*resist*) aguantar; **bravery** *n* valor *m*, valentía

brawl [brɔ:l] *n* pelea, reyerta

Brazil [brəˈzɪl] *n* (el) Brasil; **Brazilian** *adj*, *n* brasileño/a

breach [bri:tʃ] *vt* abrir brecha en ▷ *n* (*gap*) brecha; (*breaking*): **~ of contract** infracción *f* de contrato; **~ of the peace** perturbación *f* del orden público

bread [bred] *n* pan *m*; **breadbin** *n* panera; **breadbox** *n* (*us*) panera; **breadcrumbs** *npl* migajas *fpl*; (*Culin*) pan *m* sg rallado

breadth [bretθ] *n* anchura; (*fig*) amplitud *f*

break [breɪk] (*pt* **broke**, *pp* **broken**) *vt* romper; (*promise*) faltar a; (*law*) violar, infringir; (*record*) batir ▷ *vi* romperse, quebrarse; (*storm*) estallar; (*weather*) cambiar; (*news etc*) darse a conocer ▷ *n* (*gap*) abertura; (*fracture*) fractura; (*time*) intervalo; (: *at school*) (período de) recreo; (*chance*) oportunidad *f*; **break down** *vt* (*figures*, *data*) analizar, descomponer ▷ *vi* estropearse; (*Aut*) averiarse; (*person*) romper a llorar; (*talks*) fracasar; **break in** *vt* (*horse etc*) domar ▷ *vi* (*burglar*) forzar una entrada; **break into** *vt fus* (*house*) forzar; **break off** *vi* (*speaker*) pararse, detenerse; (*branch*) partir; **break out** *vi* estallar; (*prisoner*) escaparse; **to ~ out in spots** salir a algn granos; **break up** *vi* (*marriage*) deshacerse; (*ship*) hacerse pedazos; (*crowd*, *meeting*) disolverse; (*Scol*) terminar (el curso); (*line*) cortarse ▷ *vt* (*rocks etc*) partir; (*journey*) partir; (*fight etc*) acabar con; **the line's** or **you're ~ing up** se corta; **breakdown** *n* (*Aut*) avería; (*in communications*) interrupción *f*; (*Med: also:* **nervous breakdown**) colapso, crisis *f* nerviosa; (*of marriage*, *talks*) fracaso; (*of figures*) desglose *m*;

breakdown truck, breakdown van n (camión m) grúa

breakfast ['brekfəst] n desayuno

break: break-in n robo con allanamiento de morada; **breakthrough** n (fig) avance m

breast [brest] n (of woman) pecho, seno; (chest) pecho; (of bird) pechuga; **breast-feed** vt, vi (irreg: like **feed**) amamantar, dar el pecho

breaststroke ['breststrəuk] n braza de pecho

breath [breθ] n aliento, respiración f; **to take a deep ~** respirar hondo; **out of ~** sin aliento, sofocado

Breathalyser® ['breθəlaɪzəʳ] n (BRIT) alcoholímetro m

breathe [bri:ð] vt, vi respirar; **breathe in** vt, vi aspirar; **breathe out** vt, vi espirar; **breathing** n respiración f

breath: breathless adj sin aliento, jadeante; **breathtaking** adj imponente, pasmoso; **breath test** n prueba de la alcoholemia

bred [bred] pt, pp of **breed**

breed [bri:d] (pt, pp **bred**) vt criar ⊳ vi reproducirse, procrear ⊳ n raza, casta

breeze [bri:z] n brisa

breezy ['bri:zɪ] adj de mucho viento, ventoso; (person) despreocupado

brew [bru:] vt (tea) hacer; (beer) elaborar ⊳ vi (fig: trouble) prepararse; (storm) amenazar; **brewery** n fábrica de cerveza

bribe [braɪb] n soborno ⊳ vt sobornar, cohechar; **bribery** n soborno, cohecho

bric-a-brac ['brɪkəbræk] n inv baratijas fpl

brick [brɪk] n ladrillo; **bricklayer** n albañil m

bride n novia; **bridegroom** n novio; **bridesmaid** n dama de honor

bridge [brɪdʒ] n puente m; (Naut) puente m de mando; (of nose) caballete m; (Cards) bridge m ⊳ vt (fig): **to ~ a gap** llenar un vacío

bridle ['braɪdl] n brida, freno

brief [bri:f] adj breve, corto ⊳ n (Law) escrito ⊳ vt informar; **briefcase** n cartera, portafolio(s) m inv (LAM); **briefing** n (Press) informe m; **briefly** adv (smile, glance) brevemente; (explain, say) en pocas palabras

briefs npl (for men) calzoncillos mpl; (for women) bragas fpl

brigadier [brɪgə'dɪəʳ] n general m de brigada

bright [braɪt] adj brillante; (room) luminoso; (day) de sol; (person: clever) listo, inteligente; (: lively) alegre; (colour) vivo; (future) prometedor(a)

brilliant ['brɪljənt] adj brillante; (clever) genial

brim [brɪm] n borde m; (of hat) ala

brine [braɪn] n (Culin) salmuera

bring [brɪŋ] (pt, pp **brought**) vt (thing) traer; (person) conducir; **bring about** vt ocasionar, producir; **bring back** vt volver a traer; (return) devolver; **bring down** vt (government, plane) derribar; (price) rebajar; **bring in** vt (harvest) recoger; (person) hacer entrar or pasar; (object) traer; (Pol: bill, law) presentar; (produce: income) producir, rendir; **bring on** vt (illness, attack) producir, causar; (player, substitute) sacar (de la reserva), hacer salir; **bring out** vt (object) sacar; (book) publicar; **bring round** vt (unconscious person) hacer volver en sí; (convince) convencer; **bring up** vt (person) educar, criar; (question) sacar a colación; (food: vomit) devolver, vomitar

brink [brɪŋk] n borde m

brisk [brɪsk] adj (walk) enérgico, vigoroso; (speedy) rápido; (wind) fresco; (trade) activo; (abrupt) brusco

bristle ['brɪsl] n cerda ⊳ vi (fur) erizarse; **to ~ in anger** temblar de rabia

Brit [brɪt] n abbr (inf: = British person) británico/a

Britain ['brɪtən] n (also: **Great ~**) Gran Bretaña

British ['brɪtɪʃ] *adj* británico; **the British** *npl* los británicos; **the British Isles** *npl* las Islas Británicas
Briton ['brɪtən] *n* británico/a
brittle ['brɪtl] *adj* quebradizo, frágil
broad [brɔːd] *adj* ancho; *(range)* amplio; *(accent)* cerrado; **in - daylight** en pleno día; **broadband** *n* banda ancha; **broad bean** *n* haba; **broadcast** *(pt, pp* **broadcast***) n* emisión ▷ *vt (Radio)* emitir; *(TV)* transmitir ▷ *vi* emitir; transmitir; **broaden** *vt* ampliar ▷ *vi* ensancharse; **to broaden one's mind** hacer más tolerante a algn; **broadly** *adv* en general; **broad-minded** *adj* tolerante, liberal
broccoli ['brɒkəlɪ] *n* brécol m
brochure ['brəʊʃjʊə'] *n* folleto
broil [brɔɪl] *vt (us)* asar a la parrilla
broiler ['brɔɪlə'] *n (grill)* parrilla
broke [brəʊk] *pt of* **break** ▷ *adj (inf)* pelado, sin blanca
broken ['brəʊkən] *pp of* **break** ▷ *adj* roto; **- leg** pierna rota; **in - English** en un inglés chapurreado
broken-down ['brəʊkn'daʊn] *adj (car)* averiado; *(machine)* estropeado
broker ['brəʊkə'] *n* corredor(a) m/f de bolsa
bronchitis [brɒŋ'kaɪtɪs] *n* bronquitis f
bronze [brɒnz] *n* bronce m
brooch [brəʊtʃ] *n* broche m
brood [bruːd] *n* camada, cría ▷ *vi (hen)* empollar; **to - over** dar vueltas a
broom [brum] *n* escoba; *(Bot)* retama
Bros. *abbr (Comm: = Brothers)* Hnos
broth [brɒθ] *n* caldo
brothel ['brɒθl] *n* burdel m
brother ['brʌðə'] *n* hermano; **brother-in-law** *n* cuñado
brought [brɔːt] *pt, pp of* **bring**
brow [braʊ] *n (forehead)* frente f; *(eyebrow)* ceja; *(of hill)* cumbre f
brown [braʊn] *adj* marrón; *(hair)* castaño; *(tanned)* moreno ▷ *n (colour)* marrón m ▷ *vt (Culin)* dorar; **brown bread** *n* pan m integral

Brownie ['braʊnɪ] *n* niña exploradora
brown rice *n* arroz m integral
brown sugar *n* azúcar m moreno
browse [braʊz] *vi (animal)* pacer; *(among books)* hojear libros; **to - through a book** hojear un libro; **browser** *n (Comput)* navegador m
bruise [bruːz] *n (on person)* cardenal m ▷ *vt* magullar
brunette [bruː'net] *n* morena
brush [brʌʃ] *n* cepillo; *(for painting, shaving etc)* brocha; *(artist's)* pincel m ▷ *vt (sweep)* barrer; *(groom)* cepillar; **to - past, - against** rozar al pasar
Brussels ['brʌslz] *n* Bruselas
Brussels sprout *n* col f de Bruselas
brutal ['bruːtl] *adj* brutal
BSc *abbr (= Bachelor of Science)* licenciado en Ciencias
BSE *n abbr (= bovine spongiform encephalopathy)* encefalopatía espongiforme bovina
bubble ['bʌbl] *n* burbuja ▷ *vi* burbujear, borbotar; **bubble bath** *n* espuma del baño; **bubble gum** *n* chicle m *(de globo)*; **bubblejet printer** ['bʌbldʒet-] *n* impresora de inyección por burbujas
buck [bʌk] *n (rabbit)* macho; *(deer)* gamo; *(us inf)* dólar m ▷ *vi* corcovear; **to pass the - (to sb)** echar la culpa a (algn)
bucket ['bʌkɪt] *n* cubo, balde m *(esp LAM)*
buckle ['bʌkl] *n* hebilla ▷ *vt* abrochar con hebilla ▷ *vi* combarse
bud [bʌd] *n (of plant)* brote m, yema; *(of flower)* capullo ▷ *vi* brotar, echar brotes
Buddhism ['bʊdɪzm] *n* Budismo
Buddhist ['bʊdɪst] *adj, n* budista mf
buddy ['bʌdɪ] *n (us)* compañero, compinche m
budge [bʌdʒ] *vt* mover; *(fig)* hacer ceder ▷ *vi* moverse
budgerigar ['bʌdʒərɪgɑː'] *n* periquito
budget ['bʌdʒɪt] *n* presupuesto ▷ *vi*: **to - for sth** presupuestar algo
budgie ['bʌdʒɪ] *n* = **budgerigar**

buff [bʌf] adj (colour) color de ante ▷ n (enthusiast) entusiasta mf

buffalo [ˈbʌfələʊ] n (pl **buffalo** or **buffaloes**) n (BRIT) búfalo; (US: bison) bisonte m

buffer [ˈbʌfəʳ] n (Rail) tope m; (Comput) memoria intermedia, buffer m

buffet [ˈbʊfeɪ] n (BRIT: bar) bar m, cafetería; (food) buffet m; **buffet car** n (BRIT Rail) coche-restaurante m

bug [bʌg] n (insect) bicho, sabandija; (germ) microbio, bacilo; (spy device) micrófono oculto; (Comput) error m ▷ vt (annoy) fastidiar; (room) poner un micrófono oculto en

build [bɪld] n (of person) tipo ▷ vt (pt, pp **built**) construir, edificar; **build up** vt (morale, forces, production) acrecentar; (stocks) acumular; **builder** n (contractor) contratista mf

building [ˈbɪldɪŋ] n construcción f; (habitation, offices) edificio m; **building site** n obra, solar m (SP); **building society** n (BRIT) sociedad f de préstamo inmobiliario

built [bɪlt] pt, pp of **build**; **built-in** adj (cupboard) empotrado; (device) interior, incorporado; **built-up** adj (area) urbanizado

bulb [bʌlb] n (of Bot) bulbo; (Elec) bombilla, bombillo (LAM), foco (LAM)

Bulgaria [bʌlˈgɛərɪə] n Bulgaria; **Bulgarian** adj búlgaro ▷ n búlgaro/a

bulge [bʌldʒ] n bulto ▷ vi bombearse, pandearse; **to ~ (with)** rebosar (de)

bulimia [bəˈlɪmɪə] n bulimia

bulimic adj, n bulímico/a

bulk [bʌlk] n (mass) bulto, volumen m; **in ~** (Comm) a granel; **the ~ of** la mayor parte de; **bulky** adj voluminoso, abultado

bull [bʊl] n toro

bulldozer [ˈbʊldəʊzəʳ] n buldózer m

bullet [ˈbʊlɪt] n bala; **~ wound** balazo

bulletin [ˈbʊlɪtɪn] n comunicado, parte m; (journal) boletín m; **bulletin board** n (US) tablón m de anuncios; (Comput) tablero de noticias

bullfight [ˈbʊlfaɪt] n corrida de toros; **bullfighter** n torero; **bullfighting** n los toros mpl, el toreo

bully [ˈbʊlɪ] n valentón m, matón m ▷ vt intimidar, tiranizar; **bullying** n (at school) acoso escolar

bum [bʌm] n (inf: BRIT: backside) culo; (esp US: tramp) vagabundo

bumblebee [ˈbʌmblbiː] n abejorro

bump [bʌmp] n (blow) tope m, choque m; (jolt) sacudida; (on road etc) bache m; (on head) chichón m ▷ vt (strike) chocar contra; **bump into** vt fus chocar contra, tropezar con; (person) topar con; **bumper** n (BRIT) parachoques m inv ▷ adj: **bumper crop/harvest** cosecha abundante; **bumpy** adj (road) lleno de baches

bun [bʌn] n (BRIT: cake) pastel m; (US: bread) bollo; (of hair) moño

bunch [bʌntʃ] n (of flowers) ramo; (of keys) manojo; (of bananas) piña; (of people) grupo; (pej) pandilla; **bunches** npl (in hair) coletas fpl

bundle [ˈbʌndl] n bulto, fardo; (of sticks) haz m; (of papers) legajo ▷ vt (also: **~ up**) atar, envolver; **to ~ sth/sb into** meter algo/a algn precipitadamente en

bungalow [ˈbʌŋgələʊ] n bungalow m, chalé m

bungee jumping [ˈbʌndʒiːˈdʒʌmpɪŋ] n puenting m, banyi m

bunion [ˈbʌnjən] n juanete m

bunk [bʌŋk] n litera; **~ beds** npl literas fpl

bunker [ˈbʌŋkəʳ] n (coal store) carbonera; (Mil) refugio; (Golf) bunker m

bunny [ˈbʌnɪ] n (also: **~ rabbit**) conejito

buoy [bɔɪ] n boya; **buoyant** adj (ship) capaz de flotar; (carefree) boyante, optimista; (Comm: market, prices etc) sostenido; (: economy) boyante

burden [ˈbəːdn] n carga ▷ vt cargar

bureau (pl **bureaux**) [ˈbjʊərəʊ, -z] n (BRIT: writing desk) escritorio, buró m;

(US: chest of drawers) cómoda; *(office)* oficina, agencia
bureaucracy [bjuəˈrɒkrəsɪ] *n* burocracia
bureaucrat [ˈbjuərəkræt] *n* burócrata *mf*
bureau de change [-dəˈʃɑ̃ʒ] *(pl* **bureaux de change)** *n* caja *f* de cambio
bureaux [ˈbjuərəuz] *npl of* **bureau**
burger [ˈbɜːɡəʳ] *n* hamburguesa
burglar [ˈbɜːɡləʳ] *n* ladrón/ona *m/f*; **burglar alarm** *n* alarma *f* contra robo; **burglary** *n* robo con allanamiento or fractura, robo de una casa
burial [ˈbɛrɪəl] *n* entierro
burn [bɜːn] *(pt, pp* **burned** or **burnt)** *vt* quemar; *(house)* incendiar ▷ *vi* quemarse, arder; incendiarse; *(sting)* escocer ▷ *n (Med)* quemadura; **burn down** *vt* incendiar; **burn out** *vt (writer etc)*: **to ~ o.s. out** agotarse; **burning** *adj (building, forest)* en llamas; *(hot: sand etc)* abrasador(a); *(ambition)* ardiente
Burns' Night [bɜːnz-] *n* ver nota "Burns' Night"

○ **BURNS' NIGHT**
○
○ Cada veinticinco de enero los
○ escoceses celebran la llamada *Burns'*
○ *Night* (noche de Burns), en honor
○ al poeta escocés Robert Burns
○ (1759-1796). Es tradición hacer una
○ cena en la que, al son de la música
○ de la gaita escocesa, se sirve *haggis*,
○ plato tradicional de asadura de
○ cordero cocida en el estómago del
○ animal, acompañado de nabos y
○ puré de patatas. Durante la misma
○ se recitan poemas del autor y varios
○ discursos conmemorativos de
○ carácter festivo.

burnt [bɜːnt] *pt, pp of* **burn**
burp [bɜːp] *(inf)* *n* eructo ▷ *vi* eructar
burrow [ˈbʌrəu] *n* madriguera ▷ *vt* hacer una madriguera

burst [bɜːst] *(pt, pp* **burst)** *vt (balloon, pipe)* reventar; *(banks etc)* romper ▷ *vi* reventarse; romperse; *(tyre)* pincharse ▷ *n (explosion)* estallido; *(also: ~ pipe)* reventón *m*; **to ~ out laughing** soltar la carcajada; **to ~ into tears** deshacerse en lágrimas; **to be ~ing with** reventar de; **a ~ of energy** una explosión de energía; **a ~ of speed** un acelerón; **to ~ open** abrirse de golpe; **burst into** *vt fus (room etc)* irrumpir en
bury [ˈbɛrɪ] *vt* enterrar; *(body)* enterrar, sepultar
bus [bʌs] *n* autobús *m*; **bus conductor** *n* cobrador(a) *m/f*
bush [buʃ] *n* arbusto; *(scrub land)* monte *m* bajo; **to beat about the ~** andar(se) con rodeos
business [ˈbɪznɪs] *n (matter, affair)* asunto; *(trading)* comercio, negocios *mpl*; *(firm)* empresa, casa; *(occupation)* oficio; **to be away on ~** estar en viaje de negocios; **it's my ~ to ...** me toca or corresponde ...; **it's none of my ~** no es asunto mío; **he means ~** habla en serio; **business class** *n (Aviat)* clase *f* preferente; **businesslike** *adj* eficiente; **businessman** *n* hombre *m* de negocios; **business trip** *n* viaje *m* de negocios; **businesswoman** *n* mujer *f* de negocios
busker [ˈbʌskəʳ] *n (BRIT)* músico/a ambulante
bus: bus pass *n* bonobús; **bus shelter** *n* parada cubierta; **bus station** *n* estación *f* or terminal *f* de autobuses; **bus-stop** *n* parada de autobús
bust [bʌst] *n (Anat)* pecho; *(sculpture)* busto ▷ *adj (inf: broken)* roto, estropeado; **to go ~** quebrar
bustling [ˈbʌslɪŋ] *adj (town)* animado, bullicioso
busy [ˈbɪzɪ] *adj* ocupado, atareado; *(shop, street)* concurrido, animado ▷ *vt*: **to ~ o.s. with** ocuparse en; **the line's ~** está comunicando; **busy signal** *n (US Tel)* señal *f* de comunicando

KEYWORD

but [bʌt] *conj* 1 pero; **he's not very bright, but he's hard-working** no es muy inteligente, pero es trabajador 2 (*in direct contradiction*) sino; **he's not English but French** no es inglés sino francés; **he didn't sing but he shouted** no cantó sino que gritó 3 (*showing disagreement, surprise etc*): **but that's far too expensive!** ¡pero eso es carísimo!; **but it does work!** ¡(pero) sí que funciona!
▸ *prep* (*apart from, except*) menos, salvo; **we've had nothing but trouble** no hemos tenido más que problemas; **no-one but him can do it** nadie más que él puede hacerlo; **who but a lunatic would do such a thing?** ¡sólo un loco haría una cosa así!; **but for you/your help** si no fuera por ti/tu ayuda; **anything but that** cualquier cosa menos eso
▸ *adv* (*just, only*): **she's but a child** no es más que una niña; **had I but known** si lo hubiera sabido; **I can but try** al menos lo puedo intentar; **it's all but finished** está casi acabado

butcher [ˈbʊtʃəʳ] *n* carnicero,a ▸ *vt* hacer una carnicería con; (*cattle etc for meat*) matar; **~'s (shop)** carnicería

butler [ˈbʌtləʳ] *n* mayordomo

butt [bʌt] *n* (*cask*) tonel m; (*of gun*) culata; (*of cigarette*) colilla; (BRIT fig: *target*) blanco ▸ *vt* dar cabezadas contra

butter [ˈbʌtəʳ] *n* mantequilla ▸ *vt* untar con mantequilla; **buttercup** *n* ranúnculo

butterfly [ˈbʌtəflaɪ] *n* mariposa; (*Swimming: also:* **~ stroke**) (braza de) mariposa

buttocks [ˈbʌtəks] *npl* nalgas *fpl*

button [ˈbʌtn] *n* botón m ▸ *vt* (*also:* **~ up**) abotonar, abrochar ▸ *vi* abrocharse

buy [baɪ] (*pt, pp* **bought**) *vt* comprar ▸ *n* compra; **to ~ sb sth/sth from sb**

comprarle algo a algn; **to ~ sb a drink** invitar a algn a tomar algo ▸ *vt* (*partner*) comprar la parte de; **buy up** *vt* (*property*) acaparar; (*stock*) comprar todas las existencias de; **buyer** *n* comprador(a) *m/f*; **buyer's market** mercado favorable al comprador

buzz [bʌz] *n* zumbido; (*inf: phone call*) llamada (telefónica) ▸ *vi* zumbar; **buzzer** *n* timbre m

KEYWORD

by [baɪ] *prep* 1 (*referring to cause, agent*) por; **abandoned by his mother** abandonado por su madre; **a painting by Picasso** un cuadro de Picasso
2 (*referring to method, manner, means*): **by bus/car/train** en autobús/coche/tren; **to pay by cheque** pagar con cheque; **by moonlight/candlelight** a la luz de la luna/una vela; **by saving hard, he ...** ahorrando, ...
3 (*via, through*) por; **we came by Dover** vinimos por Dover
4 (*close to, past*): **the house by the river** la casa junto al río; **she rushed by me** pasó a mi lado como una exhalación; **I go by the post office every day** paso por delante de Correos todos los días
5 (*time: not later than*) para; (*: during*): **by daylight** de día; **by 4 o'clock** para las cuatro; **by this time tomorrow** mañana a estas horas; **by the time I got here it was too late** cuando llegué ya era demasiado tarde
6 (*amount*): **by the metre/kilo** por metro/kilo; **paid by the hour** pagado por hora
7 (*in measurements, sums*): **to divide/multiply by 3** dividir/multiplicar por 3; **a room 3 metres by 4** una habitación de 3 metros por 4; **it's broader by a metre** es un metro más ancho
8 (*according to*) según, de acuerdo con; **it's 3 o'clock by my watch** según mi

reloj, son las tres; **it's all right by me** por mí, está bien

9: **(all) by oneself** *etc* todo solo; **he did it (all) by himself** lo hizo él solo; **he was standing (all) by himself in a corner** estaba de pie solo en un rincón

10: **by the way** a propósito, por cierto; **this wasn't my idea, by the way** pues, no fue idea mía

▶ *adv* 1 *see* **go, pass**

2: **by and by** finalmente; **they'll come back by and by** acabarán volviendo; **by and large** en líneas generales, en general

by-election *n* (BRIT) elección *f* parcial
bypass ['baɪpɑːs] *n* carretera de circunvalación; (*Med*) (operación *f* de) bypass *m* ▶ *vt* evitar
byte [baɪt] *n* (*Comput*) byte *m*, octeto

C

C, c [siː] *n* (*Mus*) do *m*
cab [kæb] *n* taxi *m*; (*of truck*) cabina *f*
cabaret ['kæbəreɪ] *n* cabaret *m*
cabbage ['kæbɪdʒ] *n* col *f*, berza *f*
cabin ['kæbɪn] *n* cabaña *f*; (*on ship*) camarote *m*; **cabin crew** *n* tripulación *f* de cabina
cabinet ['kæbɪnɪt] *n* (*Pol*) consejo de ministros; (*furniture*) armario *m*; (*also:* **display ~**) vitrina; **cabinet minister** *n* ministro/a (del gabinete)
cable ['keɪbl] *n* cable *m* ▶ *vt* cablegrafiar; **cable car** *n* teleférico; **cable television** *n* televisión *f* por cable
cactus (*pl* **cacti**) ['kæktəs, -taɪ] *n* cacto
café ['kæfeɪ] *n* café *m*
cafeteria [kæfɪ'tɪərɪə] *n* cafetería (*con autoservicio para comer*)
caffeine ['kæfiːn] *n* cafeína *f*
cage [keɪdʒ] *n* jaula *f*
cagoule [kə'guːl] *n* chubasquero

cake [keɪk] n (large) tarta; (small) pastel m; (of soap) pastilla
calcium ['kælsɪəm] n calcio
calculate ['kælkjʊleɪt] vt calcular; **calculation** n cálculo, cómputo; **calculator** n calculadora
calendar ['kæləndə'] n calendario
calf [kɑːf] (pl **calves**) n (of cow) ternero, becerro; (of other animals) cría; (also: **~skin**) piel f de becerro; (Anat) pantorrilla
calibre, (us) **caliber** ['kælɪbə'] n calibre m
call [kɔːl] vt llamar; (meeting, strike) convocar ▷ vi (shout) llamar; (telephone) llamar (por teléfono); (visit: also: **~ in, ~ round**) hacer una visita ▷ n llamada; (of bird) canto; **to be ~ed** llamarse; **on ~** (nurse, doctor etc) de guardia; **call back** vi (return) volver; (Tel) volver a llamar; **call for** vt fus (demand) pedir, exigir; (fetch) pasar a recoger; **call in** vt (doctor, expert, police) llamar; **call off** vt (cancel: meeting, race) cancelar; (: deal) anular; (: strike) desconvocar; **call on** vt fus (visit) visitar; (turn to) acudir a; **call out** vi gritar; **call up** vt (Mil) llamar a filas; **callbox** n (BRIT) cabina telefónica; **call centre** n (BRIT) centro de atención al cliente; **caller** n visita f; (Tel) usuario/a
callous ['kæləs] adj insensible, cruel
calm [kɑːm] adj tranquilo, (sea) tranquilo, en calma ▷ n calma, tranquilidad f ▷ vt calmar, tranquilizar; **calm down** vi calmarse, tranquilizarse ▷ vt calmar, tranquilizar; **calmly** adv tranquilamente, con calma
Calor gas® ['kælə'-] n butano
calorie ['kælərɪ] n caloría
calves [kɑːvz] npl of **calf**
camcorder ['kæmkɔːdə'] n videocámara
came [keɪm] pt of **come**
camel ['kæməl] n camello
camera ['kæmərə] n cámara or máquina fotográfica; (Cine, TV)

cámara; **in ~** (Law) a puerta cerrada; **cameraman** n cámara m; **camera phone** n teléfono m con cámara
camouflage ['kæməflɑːʒ] n camuflaje n ▷ vt camuflar
camp [kæmp] n campamento, camping m; (Mil) campamento; (for prisoners) campo; (fig: faction) bando ▷ vi acampar ▷ adj afectado, afeminado; **to go ~ing** ir de or hacer camping
campaign [kæm'peɪn] n (Mil, Pol etc) campaña ▷ vi: **to ~ (for/against)** hacer campaña (a favor de/en contra de); **campaigner** n: **campaigner for** defensor/a m/f de
camp: campbed n (BRIT) cama plegable; **camper** n campista mf; (vehicle) caravana; **campground** n (us) camping m, campamento; **camping** n camping m; **campsite** n camping m
campus ['kæmpəs] n campus m
can[1] [kæn] n (of oil, water) bidón m; (tin) lata, bote m ▷ vt enlatar

KEYWORD

can[2] [kæn] (negative **cannot, can't**, conditional, pt **could**) aux vb 1 (be able to) poder; **you can do it if you try** puedes hacerlo si lo intentas; **I can't see you** no te veo
2 (know how to) saber; **I can swim/play tennis/drive** sé nadar/jugar al tenis/conducir; **can you speak French?** ¿hablas or sabes hablar francés?
3 (may) poder; **can I use your phone?** ¿me dejas or puedo usar tu teléfono?
4 (expressing disbelief, puzzlement etc): **it can't be true!** ¡no puede ser (verdad)!; **what CAN he want?** ¿qué querrá?
5 (expressing possibility, suggestion etc): **he could be in the library** podría estar en la biblioteca; **she could have been delayed** puede que se haya retrasado

Canada ['kænədə] n Canadá m;
Canadian [kə'neɪdɪən] adj, n
canadiense mf

canal [kə'næl] n canal m

canary [kə'neərɪ] n canario

Canary Islands npl las (Islas) Canarias

cancel ['kænsəl] vt cancelar;
(train) suprimir; (cross out) tachar;
cancellation [kænsə'leɪʃən] n
cancelación f; supresión f

cancer ['kænsə⁺] n cáncer m; **C~**
(Astro) Cáncer m

candidate ['kændɪdeɪt] n
candidato/a

candle ['kændl] n vela; (in church)
cirio; **candlestick** n (single) candelero;
(: low) palmatoria; (bigger, ornate)
candelabro

candy ['kændɪ] n azúcar m cande; (us)
caramelo; **candy bar** (us) n barrita
(dulce); **candyfloss** n (BRIT) algodón
m (azucarado)

cane [keɪn] n (Bot) caña; (stick) vara,
palmeta ▷ vt (BRIT Scol) castigar (con
palmeta)

canister ['kænɪstə⁺] n bote m, lata

cannabis ['kænəbɪs] n canabis m

canned [kænd] adj en lata, de lata

cannon ['kænən] (pl **cannon** or
cannons) n cañón m

cannot ['kænɔt] = **can not**

canoe [kə'nu:] n canoa; (Sport)
piragua; **canoeing** n piragüismo

canon ['kænən] n (clergyman)
canónigo; (standard) canon m

can opener n abrelatas m inv

can't [kænt] = **can not**

canteen [kæn'ti:n] n (eating place)
comedor m; (BRIT: of cutlery) juego

canter ['kæntə⁺] vi ir a medio galope

canvas ['kænvəs] n (material) lona;
(painting) lienzo; (Naut) velamen m

canvass ['kænvəs] vi (Pol): **to ~
for** solicitar votos por ▷ vt (Comm)
sondear

canyon ['kænjən] n cañón m

cap [kæp] n (hat) gorra; (of pen)
capuchón m; (of bottle) tapón m, tapa;

(BRIT: contraceptive) diafragma m ▷ vt
(outdo) superar; (limit) recortar

capability [keɪpə'bɪlɪtɪ] n
capacidad f

capable ['keɪpəbl] adj capaz

capacity [kə'pæsɪtɪ] n capacidad f;
(position) calidad f

cape [keɪp] n capa; (Geo) cabo

caper ['keɪpə⁺] n (Culin: also: **~s**)
alcaparra; (prank) travesura

capital ['kæpɪtl] n (also: **~ city**) capital
f; (money) capital m; (also: **~ letter**)
mayúscula; **capitalism** n capitalismo;
capitalist adj, n capitalista mf;
capital punishment n pena de
muerte

Capitol ['kæpɪtl] n: **the ~** el
Capitolio

○ **CAPITOL**
○
○ El Capitolio (Capitol) es el edificio en
○ el que se reúne el Congreso de los
○ Estados Unidos (Congress), situado
○ en la ciudad de Washington. Por
○ extensión, también se suele llamar
○ así al edificio en el que tienen lugar
○ las sesiones parlamentarias de
○ la cámara de representantes de
○ muchos de los estados.

Capricorn ['kæprɪkɔ:n] n
Capricornio

capsize [kæp'saɪz] vt volcar, hacer
zozobrar ▷ vi volcarse, zozobrar

capsule ['kæpsju:l] n cápsula

captain ['kæptɪn] n capitán m

caption ['kæpʃən] n (heading) título;
(to picture) leyenda

captivity [kæp'tɪvɪtɪ] n cautiverio

capture ['kæptʃə⁺] vt capturar; (place)
tomar; (attention) captar, llamar ▷ n
captura; toma; (Comput: also: **data ~**)
formulación f de datos

car [kɑ:⁺] n coche m, carro (LAM),
automóvil m; (us Rail) vagón m

carafe [kə'ræf] n jarra

caramel ['kærəməl] n caramelo

carat ['kærət] n quilate m

caravan ['kærəvæn] n caravana, rulot m; (of camels) caravana; **caravan site** n (BRIT) camping m para caravanas

carbohydrates [ka:bəu'haɪdreɪts] npl (foods) hidratos mpl de carbono

carbon ['ka:bən] n carbono; **carbon dioxide** n dióxido de carbono, anhídrido carbónico; **carbon footprint** n huella de carbono; **carbon monoxide** n monóxido de carbono

car boot sale n mercadillo (de objetos usados expuestos en el maletero del coche)

carburettor, (US) **carburetor** [ka:bju'retə'] n carburador m

card [ka:d] n (thin cardboard) cartulina; (playing card) carta, naipe m; (visiting card, greetings card etc) tarjeta; (index card) ficha; **cardboard** n cartón m, cartulina; **card game** n juego de naipes or cartas

cardigan ['ka:dɪgən] n rebeca

cardinal ['ka:dɪnl] adj cardinal; (importance, principal) esencial ▷ n cardenal m

cardphone ['ka:dfəun] n cabina que funciona con tarjetas telefónicas

care [kɛə'] n cuidado; (worry) preocupación f; (charge) cargo, custodia ▷ vi: **to ~ about** preocuparse por; **~ of (c/o)** en casa de, al cuidado de; **in sb's ~** a cargo de algn; **to take ~** cuidarse de, tener cuidado de; **to take ~ of** vt cuidar; **I don't ~** no me importa; **I couldn't ~ less** me trae sin cuidado; **care for** vt fus cuidar; (like) querer

career [kə'rɪə'] n profesión f ▷ vi (also: **~ along**) correr a toda velocidad

care: **carefree** adj despreocupado; **careful** adj cuidadoso; (cautious) cauteloso; **(be) careful!** ¡(ten) cuidado!; **carefully** adv con cuidado, cuidadosamente; **caregiver** (US) n (professional) enfermero/a; (unpaid) persona que cuida a un pariente o vecino; **careless** adj descuidado; (heedless) poco atento; **carelessness** n descuido, falta de atención; **carer** n (professional) enfermero/a; (unpaid) persona que cuida a un pariente o vecino; **caretaker** n portero/a, conserje mf

car-ferry ['ka:fɛrɪ] n transbordador m para coches

cargo ['ka:gəu] (pl **cargoes**) n cargamento, carga

car hire n alquiler m de coches

Caribbean [kærɪ'bi:ən] adj caribe, caribeño; **the ~ (Sea)** el (Mar) Caribe

caring ['kɛərɪŋ] adj humanitario

carnation [ka:'neɪʃən] n clavel m

carnival ['ka:nɪvəl] n carnaval m; (US) parque m de atracciones

carol ['kærəl] n: **(Christmas) ~** villancico

carousel [kærə'sɛl] n (US) tiovivo, caballitos mpl

car park n (BRIT) aparcamiento, parking m

carpenter ['ka:pɪntə'] n carpintero/a

carpet ['ka:pɪt] n alfombra ▷ vt alfombrar; **fitted ~** moqueta

car rental n (US) alquiler m de coches

carriage ['kærɪdʒ] n (BRIT Rail) vagón m; (horse-drawn) coche m; (for goods) transporte m; **~ paid** porte pagado; **carriageway** n (BRIT: part of road) calzada

carrier ['kærɪə'] n transportista mf; (company) empresa de transportes; (Med) portador(a) m/f; **carrier bag** n (BRIT) bolsa de papel or plástico

carrot ['kærət] n zanahoria

carry ['kærɪ] vt (person) llevar; (transport) transportar; (involve: responsibilities etc) entrañar ▷ vi (sound) oírse; **to get carried away** (fig) entusiasmarse; **carry on** vi (continue) seguir (adelante), continuar ▷ vt seguir, continuar; **carry out** vt (orders) cumplir; (investigation) llevar a cabo, realizar

c

cart [kɑːt] n carro, carreta ▷ vt (inf: transport) cargar con

carton [ˈkɑːtən] n caja (de cartón); (of milk etc) bote m

cartoon [kɑːˈtuːn] n (Press) chiste m; (comic strip) tira cómica; (film) dibujos mpl animados

cartridge [ˈkɑːtrɪdʒ] n cartucho

carve [kɑːv] vt (meat) trinchar; (wood) tallar; (stone) cincelar, esculpir; (on tree) grabar; **carving** n (in wood etc) escultura; (design) talla

car wash n túnel m de lavado

case [keɪs] n (container) caja; (Med) caso; (for jewels etc) estuche m; (Law) causa, proceso; (BRIT: also: **suit~**) maleta; **in ~ of** en caso de; **in any ~** en todo caso; **just in ~** por si acaso

cash [kæʃ] n (dinero en) efectivo; (inf: money) dinero ▷ vt cobrar, hacer efectivo; **to pay (in) ~** pagar al contado; **~ on delivery (COD)** entrega contra reembolso; **cashback** n (discount) devolución f; (at supermarket etc) retirada de dinero en efectivo de un establecimiento donde se ha pagado con tarjeta; también dinero retirado; **cash card** n tarjeta f de(l) cajero (automático); **cash desk** n (BRIT) caja; **cash dispenser** n cajero automático

cashew [kæˈʃuː] n (also: **~ nut**) anacardo

cashier [kæˈʃɪəʳ] n cajero/a

cashmere [ˈkæʃmɪəʳ] n cachemira

cash point n cajero automático

cash register n caja

casino [kəˈsiːnəu] n casino

casket [ˈkɑːskɪt] n cofre m, estuche m; (us: coffin) ataúd m

casserole [ˈkæsərəul] n (food, pot) cazuela

cassette [kæˈset] n cas(s)et(t)e m or f; **cassette player, cassette recorder** n cas(s)et(t)e m

cast [kɑːst] (pt, pp **cast**) vt (throw) echar, arrojar, lanzar; (Theat): **to ~ sb as Othello** dar a algn el papel de Otelo ▷ n (Theat) reparto; (also: **plaster ~**) vaciado; **to ~ one's vote** votar; **cast off** vi (Naut) soltar amarras; (Knitting) cerrar los puntos

castanets [kæstəˈnets] npl castañuelas fpl

caster sugar [ˈkɑːstəʳ-] n (BRIT) azúcar m extrafino

Castile [kæsˈtiːl] n Castilla; **Castilian** adj, n castellano/a

cast-iron [ˈkɑːstaɪən] adj (lit) (hecho) de hierro fundido or colado; (fig: alibi) irrebatible; (will) férreo

castle [ˈkɑːsl] n castillo; (Chess) torre f

casual [ˈkæʒjul] adj fortuito; (irregular: work etc) eventual, temporero; (unconcerned) despreocupado; (clothes) de sport

> Be careful not to translate casual by the Spanish word casual.

casualty [ˈkæʒjultɪ] n víctima, herido; (dead) muerto; **casualty ward** n urgencias fpl

cat [kæt] n gato

Catalan [ˈkætələæn] adj, n catalán/ ana m/f

catalogue [ˈkætələg] (us **catalog**) n catálogo ▷ vt catalogar

Catalonia [kætəˈləuniə] n Cataluña

catalytic converter [kætəˈlɪtɪkkənˈvəːtəʳ] n catalizador m

cataract [ˈkætərækt] n (Med) cataratas fpl

catarrh [kəˈtɑːʳ] n catarro

catastrophe [kəˈtæstrəfɪ] n catástrofe f

catch [kætʃ] (pt, pp **caught**) vt coger (SP), agarrar (LAM); (arrest) atrapar; (grasp) asir; (breath) recobrar; (person: by surprise) pillar; (attract: attention) captar; (Med) pillar, coger; (also: **~ up**) alcanzar ▷ vi (fire) encenderse; (in branches etc) engancharse ▷ n (of fish etc) captura; (act of catching) cogida; (of lock) pestillo, cerradura; **to ~ fire** prenderse; (house) incendiarse; **to**

~ sight of divisar; **catch up** vi (fig) ponerse al día; **catching** adj (Med) contagioso

category ['kætɪɡərɪ] n categoría

cater ['keɪtəʳ] vi: **to ~ for** (BRIT) abastecer a; (needs) atender a; (consumers) proveer a

caterpillar ['kætəpɪləʳ] n oruga

cathedral [kə'θiːdrəl] n catedral f

cattle ['kætl] npl ganado sg

catwalk ['kætwɔːk] n pasarela

caught [kɔːt] pt, pp of **catch**

cauliflower ['kɒlɪflauəʳ] n coliflor f

cause [kɔːz] n causa; (reason) motivo, razón f ▷ vt causar

caution ['kɔːʃən] n cautela, prudencia; (warning) advertencia, amonestación f ▷ vt amonestar; **cautious** adj cauteloso, prudente, precavido

cave [keɪv] n cueva, caverna; **cave in** vi (roof etc) derrumbarse, hundirse

caviar(e) ['kævɪɑːʳ] n caviar m

cavity ['kævɪtɪ] n hueco, cavidad f

cc abbr (= cubic centimetres) cc, cm³; (on letter etc) = **carbon copy**

CCTV n abbr = **closed-circuit television**

CD n abbr (= compact disc) CD m; **CD player** n reproductor m de CD; **CD-ROM** n abbr (= compact disc read-only memory) CD-ROM m; **CD writer** n grabadora f de CDs

cease [siːs] vt cesar; **ceasefire** n alto m el fuego

cedar ['siːdəʳ] n cedro

ceilidh ['keɪlɪ] n baile con música y danzas tradicionales escocesas o irlandesas

ceiling ['siːlɪŋ] n techo; (fig) límite m

celebrate ['sɛlɪbreɪt] vt celebrar ▷ vi: **let's ~!** ¡vamos a celebrarlo!; **celebration** n celebración f

celebrity [sɪ'lɛbrɪtɪ] n (person) famoso/a

celery ['sɛlərɪ] n apio

cell [sɛl] n celda; (Biol) célula; (Elec) elemento

cellar ['sɛləʳ] n sótano; (for wine) bodega

cello ['tʃɛləu] n violoncelo

Cellophane® ['sɛləfeɪn] n celofán m

cellphone ['sɛlfəun] n móvil

Celsius ['sɛlsɪəs] adj centígrado

Celtic ['kɛltɪk, 'sɛltɪk] adj celta

cement [sə'mɛnt] n cemento

cemetery ['sɛmɪtrɪ] n cementerio

censor ['sɛnsəʳ] n censor(a) m/f ▷ vt (cut) censurar; **censorship** n censura

census ['sɛnsəs] n censo

cent [sɛnt] n (us: unit of dollar) centavo; (unit of euro) céntimo; see also **per**

centenary [sɛn'tiːnərɪ], (us) **centennial** [sɛn'tɛnɪəl] n centenario

center ['sɛntəʳ] n (us) = **centre**

centi...: **centigrade** ['sɛntɪɡreɪd] adj centígrado; **centimetre**, (us) **centimeter** ['sɛntɪmiːtəʳ] n centímetro; **centipede** ['sɛntɪpiːd] n ciempiés m inv

central ['sɛntrəl] adj central; (house etc) céntrico; **Central America** n Centroamérica; **central heating** n calefacción f central; **central reservation** n (BRIT Aut) mediana

centre, (us)**center** ['sɛntəʳ] n centro ▷ vt centrar; **centre-forward** n (Sport) delantero centro; **centre-half** n (Sport) medio centro

century ['sɛntjurɪ] n siglo; **20th ~** siglo veinte

CEO n abbr = **chief executive officer**

ceramic [sɪ'ræmɪk] adj de cerámica

cereal ['siːrɪəl] n cereal m

ceremony ['sɛrɪmənɪ] n ceremonia; **to stand on ~** hacer ceremonias, andarse con cumplidos

certain ['səːtən] adj seguro; (particular) cierto; **for ~** a ciencia cierta; **a ~ Mr Smith** un tal Sr. Smith; **certainly** adv desde luego, por supuesto; **certainty** n certeza, certidumbre f, seguridad f

certificate [sə'tɪfɪkɪt] n certificado

certify ['sɜːtɪfaɪ] vt certificar; (declare insane) declarar loco
cf. abbr (= compare) cfr
CFC n abbr (= chlorofluorocarbon) CFC m
chain [tʃeɪn] n cadena; (of mountains) cordillera; (of events) sucesión f ▷ vt (also: ~ **up**) encadenar; **chain-smoke** vi fumar un cigarrillo tras otro
chair [tʃɛəʳ] n silla; (armchair) sillón m; (of university) cátedra ▷ vt (meeting) presidir; **chairlift** n telesilla m; **chairman** n presidente m; **chairperson** n presidente m/f; **chairwoman** n presidenta
chalet ['ʃæleɪ] n chalet m (de madera)
chalk [tʃɔːk] n (Geo) creta; (for writing) tiza, gis m (LAM); **chalkboard** (US) n pizarrón (LAM), pizarra (SP)
challenge ['tʃælɪndʒ] n desafío, reto ▷ vt desafiar, retar; (statement, right) poner en duda; **to ~ sb to do sth** retar a algn a que haga algo; **challenging** adj supone un reto; (tone) de desafío
chamber ['tʃeɪmbəʳ] n cámara, sala; **chambermaid** n camarera
champagne [ʃæm'peɪn] n champaña m, champán m
champion ['tʃæmpɪən] n campeón/ona m/f; (of cause) defensor(a) m/f; **championship** n campeonato
chance [tʃɑːns] n (opportunity) ocasión f, oportunidad f; (likelihood) posibilidad f; (risk) riesgo ▷ vt arriesgar, probar ▷ adj fortuito, casual; **to ~ it** arriesgarse, intentarlo; **to take a ~** arriesgarse; **by ~** por casualidad
chancellor ['tʃɑːnsələʳ] n canciller m; **C~ of the Exchequer** (BRIT) Ministro de Economía y Hacienda; see also **Downing Street**
chandelier [ʃændə'lɪəʳ] n araña (de luces)
change [tʃeɪndʒ] vt cambiar; (clothes, house) cambiarse de, mudarse de; (transform) transformar ▷ vi

cambiar(se); (change trains) hacer transbordo; (be transformed): **to ~ into** transformarse en ▷ n cambio; (alteration) modificación f, transformación f; (coins) suelto; (money returned) vuelta, vuelto (LAM); **to ~ one's mind** cambiar de opinión o idea; **to ~ gear** (Aut) cambiar de marcha; **for a ~** para variar; **change over** vi (from sth to sth) cambiar; (players etc) cambiar(se) ▷ vt (meeting) presidir; **changeable** adj (weather) cambiable; **change machine** n máquina de cambio; **changing room** n (BRIT) vestuario
channel ['tʃænl] n (TV) canal m; (of river) cauce m; (fig: medium) medio ▷ vt (river etc) encauzar: **the (English) C~** el Canal (de la Mancha); **the C~ Islands** las Islas Anglonormandas; **the C~ Tunnel** el túnel del Canal de la Mancha, el Eurotúnel
chant [tʃɑːnt] n (also Rel) canto; (of crowd) gritos mpl ▷ vt (slogan, word) repetir a gritos
chaos ['keɪɔs] n caos m
chaotic [keɪ'ɔtɪk] adj caótico
chap [tʃæp] n (BRIT inf: man) tío, tipo
chapel ['tʃæpl] n capilla
chapped [tʃæpt] adj agrietado
chapter ['tʃæptəʳ] n capítulo
character ['kærɪktəʳ] n carácter m, naturaleza, índole f; (in novel, film) personaje m; (individuality) carácter m; **characteristic** [kærɪktə'rɪstɪk] adj característico ▷ n característica; **characterize** vt caracterizar
charcoal ['tʃɑːkəul] n carbón m vegetal; (Art) carboncillo
charge [tʃɑːdʒ] n (Law) cargo, acusación f; (cost) precio, coste m; (responsibility) cargo ▷ vt (Law): **to ~ (with)** acusar (de); (gun, battery) cargar; (Mil: enemy) cargar; (price) pedir; (customer) cobrar ▷ vi precipitarse; **charge card** n tarjeta de cuenta; **charger** n (also: **battery charger**) cargador m (de baterías)

charismatic [kærɪz'mætɪk] adj carismático

charity ['tʃærɪtɪ] n caridad f; (organization) organización f benéfica; (money, gifts) limosnas f pl; **charity shop** n (BRIT) tienda de artículos de segunda mano que dedica su recaudación a causas benéficas

charm [tʃɑːm] n (attraction) atractivo; (spell) hechizo; (object) amuleto; (on bracelet) dije m ▷ vt encantar; **charming** adj encantador(a)

chart [tʃɑːt] n (table) cuadro; (graph) gráfica; (map) carta de navegación ▷ vt (course) trazar; (progress) seguir; (sales) hacer una gráfica de; **to be in the ~s** (record, pop group) estar en la lista de éxitos

charter ['tʃɑːtər] vt (bus) alquilar; (plane, ship) fletar ▷ n (document) carta; **chartered accountant** n (BRIT) contable m/f diplomado/a; **charter flight** n vuelo chárter

chase [tʃeɪs] vt (pursue) perseguir; (hunt) cazar ▷ n persecución f

chat [tʃæt] vi (also: **have a ~**) charlar; (Internet) chatear ▷ n charla; (Internet) chat m; **chat up** vt (inf: girl) ligar con, enrollarse con; **chat room** n (Internet) chat m, canal m de charla; **chat show** n (BRIT) programa m de entrevistas

chatter ['tʃætər] vi (person) charlar; (teeth) castañetear ▷ n (of birds) parloteo; (of people) charla, cháchara

chauffeur ['ʃəʊfər] n chófer m

chauvinist ['ʃəʊvɪnɪst] n (also: **male ~**) machista m; (nationalist) chovinista m/f

cheap [tʃiːp] adj barato; (joke) de mal gusto; (poor quality) de mala calidad ▷ adv barato; **cheap day return** n billete de ida y vuelta el mismo día; **cheaply** adv barato, a bajo precio

cheat [tʃiːt] vi hacer trampa ▷ vt estafar ▷ n (person) tramposo/a; **to ~ sb (out of sth)** estafar (algo) a algn; **cheat on** vt fus engañar

check [tʃɛk] vt (examine) controlar; (facts) comprobar; (count) contar; (halt) frenar; (restrain) refrenar, restringir ▷ n (inspection) control m, inspección f; (curb) freno; (bill) nota, cuenta; (US) = **cheque**; (pattern: gen pl) cuadro; **check in** vi (in hotel) registrarse; (at airport) facturar ▷ vt (luggage) facturar; **check off** vt (esp US: check) comprobar; (cross off) tachar; **check out** vi (of hotel) desocupar la habitación; **check up** vi: **to ~ up on sth** comprobar algo; **to ~ up on sb** investigar a algn

checkbook n (US) = **chequebook**; **checked** adj a cuadros inv; **checkers** n (US) damas f pl; **check-in** n (also: **check-in desk**: at airport) mostrador m de facturación; **checking account** n (US) cuenta corriente; **checklist** n lista; **checkmate** n jaque m mate; **checkout** n caja; **checkpoint** n (punto de) control m; **checkroom** n (US) consigna; **checkup** n (Med) reconocimiento general

cheddar ['tʃedər] n (also: **~ cheese**) queso m cheddar

cheek [tʃiːk] n mejilla; (impudence) descaro; **what a ~!** ¡qué cara!; **cheekbone** n pómulo; **cheeky** adj fresco, descarado

cheer [tʃɪər] vt vitorear, ovacionar; (gladden) alegrar, animar ▷ vi dar vivas ▷ n viva m; **cheer up** vi animarse ▷ vt alegrar, animar; **cheerful** adj alegre

cheerio [tʃɪərɪ'əʊ] excl (BRIT) ¡hasta luego!

cheerleader ['tʃɪəliːdər] n animador(a) m/f

cheese [tʃiːz] n queso; **cheeseburger** n hamburguesa con queso; **cheesecake** n pastel m de queso

chef [ʃef] n jefe/a m/f de cocina

chemical ['kemɪkəl] adj químico ▷ n producto químico

chemist ['kemɪst] n (BRIT: pharmacist) farmacéutico/a; (scientist) químico/a;

~'s (shop) n (BRIT) farmacia; chemistry n química

cheque, (US) **check** [tʃek] n cheque m; **chequebook** n talonario (de cheques), chequera (LAM); **cheque card** n (BRIT) tarjeta de identificación bancaria

cherry [tʃerɪ] n cereza; (also: **~ tree**) cerezo

chess [tʃes] n ajedrez m

chest [tʃest] n (Anat) pecho; (box) cofre m; **~ of drawers** n cómoda

chestnut [tʃesnʌt] n castaña; (also: **~ tree**) castaño

chew [tʃuː] vt mascar, masticar; **chewing gum** n chicle m

chic [ʃiːk] adj elegante

chick [tʃɪk] n pollito, polluelo; (US inf) chica

chicken [tʃɪkɪn] n gallina, pollo; (food) pollo; (inf: coward) gallina mf; **chicken out** vi (inf) rajarse; **chickenpox** n varicela

chickpea [tʃɪkpiː] n garbanzo

chief [tʃiːf] n jefe a m/f ⊳ adj principal; **chief executive (officer)** n director m general; **chiefly** adv principalmente

child (pl **children**) [tʃaɪld, tʃɪldrən] n niño/a; (offspring) hijo/a; **child abuse** n (with violence) malos tratos mpl a niños; (sexual) abuso m sexual de niños; **child benefit** n (BRIT) subsidio por cada hijo pequeño; **childbirth** n parto; **childcare** n cuidado de los niños; **childhood** n niñez f, infancia; **childish** adj pueril, infantil; **child minder** n (BRIT) madre f de día; **children** [tʃɪldrən] npl of **child**

Chile [tʃɪlɪ] n Chile m; **Chilean** adj, n chileno/a

chill [tʃɪl] n frío; (Med) resfriado ⊳ vt enfriar; (Culin) refrigerar; **chill out** vi (esp US inf) tranquilizarse

chilly [tʃɪlɪ] adj frío

chimney [tʃɪmnɪ] n chimenea

chimpanzee [tʃɪmpænziː] n chimpancé m

chin [tʃɪn] n mentón m, barbilla

China [tʃaɪnə] n China

china [tʃaɪnə] n porcelana; (crockery) loza

Chinese [tʃaɪniːz] adj chino ⊳ n (pl inv) chino/a; (Ling) chino

chip [tʃɪp] n (gen pl: Culin: BRIT) patata or (LAM) papa frita; (: US: also: **potato ~**) patata or (LAM) papa frita; (of wood) astilla; (stone) lasca; (in gambling) ficha; (Comput) chip m ⊳ vt (cup, plate) desconchar; **chip shop** n ver nota "chip shop"

CHIP SHOP

- Se denomina **chip shop** o **fish-and-chip shop** a un tipo de tienda popular
- de comida rápida en la que se
- despachan platos tradicionales
- británicos, principalmente filetes
- de pescado rebozado frito y patatas
- fritas.

chiropodist [kɪrɔpədɪst] n (BRIT) podólogo/a

chisel [tʃɪzl] n (for wood) escoplo; (for stone) cincel m

chives [tʃaɪvz] npl cebollinos mpl

chlorine [klɔːriːn] n cloro

choc-ice [tʃɒkaɪs] n (BRIT) helado m cubierto de chocolate

chocolate [tʃɒklɪt] n chocolate m; (sweet) bombón m

choice [tʃɔɪs] n elección f; (preference) preferencia ⊳ adj escogido

choir [kwaɪər] n coro

choke [tʃəʊk] vi ahogarse; (on food) atragantarse ⊳ vt ahogar; (block) atascar ⊳ n (Aut) estárter m

cholesterol [kɔlestərɔl] n colesterol m

chook [tʃuk] (AUST, NZ inf) n gallina; (as food) pollo

choose (pt **chose**, pp **chosen**) [tʃuːz, tʃəʊz, tʃəʊzn] vt escoger, elegir; (team) seleccionar; **to ~ to do sth** optar por hacer algo

chop [tʃɔp] vt (wood) cortar, talar; (Culin: also: **~ up**) picar ▷ n (Culin) chuleta; **chop down** vt (tree) talar; **chop off** vt cortar (de un tajo); **chopsticks** npl palillos mpl

chord [kɔːd] n (Mus) acorde m

chore [tʃɔːʳ] n faena, tarea; (routine task) trabajo rutinario

chorus ['kɔːrəs] n coro; (repeated part of song) estribillo

chose [tʃəuz] pt of **choose**

chosen ['tʃəuzn] pp of **choose**

Christ [kraɪst] n Cristo

christen ['krɪsn] vt bautizar; **christening** n bautizo

Christian ['krɪstɪən] adj, n cristiano/a; **Christianity** [krɪstɪ'ænɪtɪ] n cristianismo; **Christian name** n nombre m de pila

Christmas ['krɪsməs] n Navidad f; **Merry ~!** ¡Felices Navidades!; **Christmas card** n tarjeta de Navidad; **Christmas carol** n villancico m; **Christmas Day** n día m de Navidad; **Christmas Eve** n Nochebuena; **Christmas pudding** n (esp BRIT) pudín m de Navidad; **Christmas tree** n árbol m de Navidad

chrome [krəum] n = **chromium**

chromium ['krəumɪəm] n cromo; (also: **~ plating**) cromado

chronic ['krɔnɪk] adj crónico

chrysanthemum [krɪ'sænθəməm] n crisantemo

chubby ['tʃʌbɪ] adj rechoncho

chuck [tʃʌk] (inf) vt lanzar, arrojar; (BRIT: also: **~ in, ~ up**) abandonar; **chuck out** vt (person) echar (fuera); (rubbish etc) tirar

chuckle ['tʃʌkl] vi reírse entre dientes

chum [tʃʌm] n amiguete m/f

chunk [tʃʌŋk] n pedazo, trozo

church [tʃəːtʃ] n iglesia; **churchyard** n cementerio

churn [tʃəːn] n (for butter) mantequera; (for milk) lechera

chute [ʃuːt] n (also: **rubbish ~**) vertedero

chutney ['tʃʌtnɪ] n salsa picante de frutas y especias

CIA n abbr (US: = Central Intelligence Agency) CIA f

CID n abbr (BRIT: = Criminal Investigation Department) ≈ B.I.C. f (SP)

cider ['saɪdəʳ] n sidra

cigar [sɪ'gɑːʳ] n puro

cigarette [sɪgə'rɛt] n cigarrillo; **cigarette lighter** n mechero

cinema ['sɪnəmə] n cine m

cinnamon ['sɪnəmən] n canela

circle ['səːkl] n círculo; (in theatre) anfiteatro ▷ vi dar vueltas ▷ vt (surround) rodear, cercar; (move round) dar la vuelta a

circuit ['səːkɪt] n circuito; (track) pista; (lap) vuelta

circular ['səːkjuləʳ] adj circular ▷ n circular f

circulate ['səːkjuleɪt] vi circular; (person: socially) alternar, circular ▷ vt poner en circulación; **circulation** [səːkju'leɪʃən] n circulación f; (of newspaper etc) tirada

circumstances ['səːkəmstənsɪz] npl circunstancias fpl; (financial condition) situación económica

circus ['səːkəs] n circo

cite [saɪt] vt citar

citizen ['sɪtɪzn] n (Pol) ciudadano/a; (of city) habitante m/f, vecino/a; **citizenship** n ciudadanía; (BRIT Scol) civismo

citrus fruits ['sɪtrəs-] npl cítricos mpl

city ['sɪtɪ] n ciudad f; **the C~** centro financiero de Londres; **city centre** n centro de la ciudad

City Technology College n (BRIT) ≈ Centro de formación profesional

civic ['sɪvɪk] adj cívico; (authorities) municipal

civil ['sɪvɪl] adj civil; (polite) atento, cortés; **civilian** [sɪ'vɪlɪən] adj, n civil m/f

civilization [sɪvɪlaɪ'zeɪʃən] n civilización f

civilized ['sɪvɪlaɪzd] *adj* civilizado
civil: civil law *n* derecho civil; **civil rights** *npl* derechos *mpl* civiles; **civil servant** *n* funcionario/a (del Estado); **Civil Service** *n* administración *f* pública; **civil war** *n* guerra civil
CJD *n abbr* (= *Creutzfeldt-Jakob disease*) enfermedad *f* de Creutzfeldt-Jakob
claim [kleɪm] *vt* exigir, reclamar; (*rights etc*) reivindicar; (*assert*) pretender ▷ *vi* (*for insurance*) reclamar ▷ *n* (*for expenses*) reclamación *f*; (*Law*) demanda; (*pretension*) pretensión *f*; **claim form** *n* solicitud *f*
clam [klæm] *n* almeja
clamp [klæmp] *n* abrazadera; (*laboratory clamp*) grapa ▷ *vt* afianzar (con abrazadera)
clan [klæn] *n* clan *m*
clap [klæp] *vi* aplaudir
claret ['klærət] *n* burdeos *m inv*
clarify ['klærɪfaɪ] *vt* aclarar
clarinet [klærɪ'net] *n* clarinete *m*
clarity ['klærɪtɪ] *n* claridad *f*
clash [klæʃ] *n* estruendo; (*fig*) choque *m* ▷ *vi* enfrentarse; (*beliefs*) chocar; (*disagree*) estar en desacuerdo; (*colours*) desentonar; (*two events*) coincidir
clasp [klɑːsp] *n* (*hold*) apretón *m*; (*of necklace, bag*) cierre *m* ▷ *vt* (*hand*) apretar; (*embrace*) abrazar
class [klɑːs] *n* clase *f* ▷ *vt* clasificar
classic ['klæsɪk] *n* clásico; **classical** *adj* clásico
classification [klæsɪfɪ'keɪʃən] *n* clasificación *f*
classify ['klæsɪfaɪ] *vt* clasificar
classmate ['klɑːsmeɪt] *n* compañero/a de clase
classroom ['klɑːsrʊm] *n* aula; **classroom assistant** *n* profesor(a) *m/f* de apoyo
classy [klɑːsɪ] *adj* (*inf*) elegante, con estilo
clatter ['klætə*ʳ*] *n* ruido, estruendo ▷ *vi* hacer ruido *or* estruendo

clause [klɔːz] *n* cláusula; (*Ling*) oración *f*
claustrophobic [klɔːstrə'fəʊbɪk] *adj* claustrofóbico; **I feel ~** me entra claustrofobia
claw [klɔː] *n* (*of cat*) uña; (*of bird of prey*) garra; (*of lobster*) pinza
clay [kleɪ] *n* arcilla
clean [kliːn] *adj* limpio; (*record, reputation*) bueno, intachable; (*joke*) decente ▷ *vt* limpiar; (*hands etc*) lavar; **clean up** *vt* limpiar, asear; **cleaner** *n* encargado/a de la limpieza; (*also:* **dry cleaner**) tintorero/a; (*substance*) producto para la limpieza; **cleaning** *n* limpieza
cleanser ['klenzə*ʳ*] *n* (*cosmetic*) loción *f* or crema limpiadora
clear [klɪə*ʳ*] *adj* claro; (*road, way*) libre ▷ *vt* (*space*) despejar, limpiar; (*Law: suspect*) absolver; (*obstacle*) salvar, saltar por encima de; (*cheque*) aceptar ▷ *vi* (*fog etc*) despejarse ▷ *adv*: **~ of** a distancia de; **to ~ the table** recoger *or* quitar la mesa; **clear away** *vt* (*things, clothes etc*) quitar (de en medio); (*dishes*) retirar; **clear up** *vt* limpiar; (*mystery*) aclarar, resolver; **clearance** *n* (*removal*) despeje *m*; (*permission*) acreditación *f*; **clear-cut** *adj* bien definido, claro; **clearing** *n* (*in wood*) claro; **clearly** *adv* claramente; (*evidently*) sin duda; **clearway** *n* (*BRIT*) carretera en la que no se puede estacionar
clench [klentʃ] *vt* apretar, cerrar
clergy ['klɜːdʒɪ] *n* clero
clerk [klɑːk, *us* klɜːk] *n* oficinista *mf*; (*us*) dependiente/a *m/f*
clever ['klevə*ʳ*] *adj* (*mentally*) inteligente, listo; (*skilful*) hábil; (*device, arrangement*) ingenioso
cliché ['kliːʃeɪ] *n* cliché *m*, frase *f* hecha
click [klɪk] *vt* (*tongue*) chasquear ▷ *vi* (*Comput*) hacer clic; **to ~ one's heels** taconear; **to ~ on an icon** hacer clic en un icono
client ['klaɪənt] *n* cliente *mf*
cliff [klɪf] *n* acantilado

climate ['klaɪmɪt] n clima m; **climate change** n cambio climático

climax ['klaɪmæks] n (of battle, career) apogeo; (of film, book) punto culminante, clímax; (sexual) orgasmo

climb [klaɪm] vi subir, trepar ▷ vt (stairs) subir; (tree) trepar a; (mountain) escalar ▷ n subida, ascenso; **to ~ over a wall** saltar una tapia; **climb down** vi (fig) volverse atrás; **climber** n escalador(a) m/f; **climbing** n escalada

clinch [klɪntʃ] vt (deal) cerrar; (argument) remachar

cling (pt, pp **clung**) [klɪŋ, klʌŋ] vi: **to ~ (to)** agarrarse (a); (clothes) pegarse (a)

clinic ['klɪnɪk] n clínica

clip [klɪp] n (for hair) horquilla; (also: **paper ~**) sujetapapeles m inv, clip m ▷ vt (cut) cortar; (also: **~ together**) unir; **clipping** n (from newspaper) recorte m

cloak [kləʊk] n capa, manto ▷ vt (fig) encubrir, disimular; **cloakroom** n guardarropa m; (BRIT: WC) lavabo, aseos mpl, baño (esp LAM)

clock [klɒk] n reloj m; **clock in, clock on** vi fichar, picar; **clock off, clock out** vi fichar or picar la salida; **clockwise** adv en el sentido de las agujas del reloj; **clockwork** n aparato de relojería ▷ adj (toy, train) de cuerda

clog [klɒg] n zueco, chanclo ▷ vt atascar ▷ vi (also: **~ up**) atascarse

clone [kləʊn] n clon m ▷ vt clonar

close [kləʊs, kləʊz] adj (near): **~ (to)** cerca (de); (friend) íntimo; (connection) estrecho; (examination) detallado, minucioso; (weather) bochornoso ▷ adv cerca; **to ~** prep cerca de ▷ vt cerrar; (end) concluir, terminar ▷ vi (shop etc) cerrar; (end) concluir(se), terminar(se) ▷ n (end) fin m, final m, conclusión f; **to ~** (end) escaparse por un pelo; **~ by, ~ at hand** muy cerca; **close down** vi cerrar definitivamente; **closed** [kləʊzd] adj (shop etc) cerrado

closed-circuit ['kləʊzd'sɜːkɪt] adj: **~ television** televisión f por circuito cerrado

closely ['kləʊslɪ] adv (study) con detalle; (watch) de cerca

closet ['klɒzɪt] n armario

close-up ['kləʊsʌp] n primer plano

closing time ['kləʊzɪŋ-] n hora de cierre

closure ['kləʊʒə'] n cierre m

clot [klɒt] n (also: **blood ~**) coágulo; (inf: idiot) imbécil m/f ▷ vi (blood) coagularse

cloth [klɒθ] n (material) tela, paño; (rag) trapo

clothes [kləʊðz] npl ropa sg; **clothes line** n cuerda (para tender la ropa); **clothes peg, (us) clothes pin** n pinza

clothing ['kləʊðɪŋ] n = **clothes**

cloud [klaʊd] n nube f; **cloud over** vi (also fig) nublarse; **cloudy** adj nublado; (liquid) turbio

clove [kləʊv] n clavo; **~ of garlic** diente m de ajo

clown [klaʊn] n payaso ▷ vi (also: **~ about, ~ around**) hacer el payaso

club [klʌb] n (society) club m; (weapon) porra, cachiporra; (also: **golf ~**) palo ▷ vt aporrear ▷ vi: **to ~ together** (join forces) unir fuerzas; **clubs** npl (Cards) tréboles mpl; **club class** n (Aviat) clase f preferente

clue [kluː] n pista; (in crosswords) indicación f; **I haven't a ~** no tengo ni idea

clump [klʌmp] n (of trees) grupo

clumsy ['klʌmzɪ] adj (person) torpe; (tool) difícil de manejar

clung [klʌŋ] pt, pp of **cling**

cluster ['klʌstə'] n grupo ▷ vi agruparse, apiñarse

clutch [klʌtʃ] n (Aut) embrague m; **to fall into sb's ~es** caer en las garras de algn ▷ vt agarrar

cm abbr (= centimetre) cm

Co. abbr = **county; company**

c/o abbr (= care of) c/a, a, c/a

coach [kəʊtʃ] n autocar m (SP), autobús m; (horse-drawn) coche m;

(of train) vagón *m*, coche *m*; *(Sport)* entrenador(a) *m/f*, instructor(a) *m/f* ▷ vt *(student)* preparar, enseñar; **coach station** *n* *(BRIT)* estación *f* de autobuses *etc*; **coach trip** *n* excursión *f* en autocar

coal [kəul] *n* carbón *m*

coalition [kəuə'lɪʃən] *n* coalición *f*

coarse [kɔ:s] *adj* basto, burdo; *(vulgar)* grosero, ordinario

coast [kəust] *n* costa, litoral *m* ▷ vi *(Aut)* ir en punto muerto; **coastal** *adj* costero; **coastguard** *n* guardacostas *m inv*; **coastline** *n* litoral *m*

coat [kəut] *n* abrigo; *(of animal)* pelo, pelaje, lana; *(of paint)* mano *f*, capa ▷ vt cubrir, revestir; **coat hanger** *n* percha, gancho *(LAM)*; **coating** *n* capa, baño

coax [kəuks] *vt* engatusar

cob [kɒb] *n* see **corn**

cobbled [kɒbld] *adj*: ~ **street** calle *f* empedrada, calle *f* adoquinada

cobweb [kɔbweb] *n* telaraña

cocaine [kə'keɪn] *n* cocaína

cock [kɒk] *n (rooster)* gallo; *(male bird)* macho ▷ vt *(gun)* amartillar; **cockerel** *n* gallito

cockney [kɒknɪ] *n* habitante de ciertos barrios de Londres

cockpit [kɔkpɪt] *n* cabina

cockroach [kɔkrəutʃ] *n* cucaracha

cocktail [kɔkteɪl] *n* cóctel *m*

cocoa [kəukəu] *n* cacao *m*; *(drink)* chocolate *m*

coconut [kəukənʌt] *n* coco

COD *abbr* = **cash on delivery**; *(US: = collect on delivery)* C.A.E.

cod [kɒd] *n* bacalao

code [kəud] *n* código; *(cipher)* clave *f*; *(Tel)* prefijo

coeducational [kəuedjuːˈkeɪʃənl] *adj* mixto

coffee [kɔfɪ] *n* café *m*; **coffee bar** *n* *(BRIT)* cafetería; **coffee bean** *n* grano de café; **coffee break** *n* descanso *(para tomar café)*; **coffee maker** *n* máquina de hacer café, cafetera;

coffeepot *n* cafetera; **coffee shop** *n* café *m*; **coffee table** *n* mesita baja

coffin [kɔfɪn] *n* ataúd *m*

cog [kɔg] *n* diente *m*

cognac [kɔnjæk] *n* coñac *m*

coherent [kəuˈhɪərənt] *adj* coherente

coil [kɔɪl] *n* rollo; *(Aut, Elec)* bobina, carrete *m*; *(contraceptive)* DIU *m* ▷ vt enrollar

coin [kɔɪn] *n* moneda ▷ vt *(word)* inventar, acuñar

coincide [kəuɪnˈsaɪd] *vi* coincidir; **coincidence** [kəuˈɪnsɪdəns] *n* casualidad *f*

Coke® [kəuk] *n* Coca Cola® *f*

coke [kəuk] *n (coal)* coque *m*

colander [kɔləndə²] *n* escurridor *m*

cold [kəuld] *adj* frío ▷ *n* frío; *(Med)* resfriado; **to be ~** hace frío; **to be ~** tener frío; **to catch a ~** resfriarse, acatarrarse; **in ~ blood** a sangre fría; **cold sore** *n* herpes *m* labial

coleslaw [kəulslɔ:] *n* ensalada de col con zanahoria

colic [kɔlɪk] *n* cólico

collaborate [kəˈlæbəreɪt] *vi* colaborar

collapse [kəˈlæps] *vi* hundirse, derrumbarse; *(Med)* sufrir un colapso ▷ *n* hundimiento, derrumbamiento; *(Med)* colapso

collar [kɔlə²] *n (of coat, shirt)* cuello; *(for dog)* collar *m*; **collarbone** *n* clavícula

colleague [kɔli:g] *n* colega *mf*; *(at work)* compañero/a *mf*

collect [kəˈlekt] *vt* reunir; *(as a hobby)* coleccionar; *(BRIT: call and pick up)* recoger; *(debts)* recaudar; *(donations, subscriptions)* colectar ▷ *vi (crowd)* reunirse ▷ *adv (US Tel)*: **to call ~** llamar a cobro revertido; **collection** *n* colección *f*; *(of post)* recogida; **collective** *adj* colectivo; **collector** *n* coleccionista *mf*

college [kɔlɪdʒ] *n* colegio; *(of technology, agriculture etc)* escuela

collide [kə'laɪd] vi chocar

collision [kə'lɪʒən] n choque m

cologne [kə'ləʊn] n (also: **eau de ~**) (agua de) colonia

Colombia [kə'lɒmbɪə] n Colombia; **Colombian** adj, n colombiano/a

colon ['kəʊlən] n (sign) dos puntos; (Med) colon m

colonel ['kɜːnl] n coronel m

colonial [kə'ləʊnɪəl] adj colonial

colony ['kɒlənɪ] n colonia

colour, (us) color ['kʌlə] n color m ▷ vt colorear; (dye) teñir; (fig: account) adornar; (: judgement) distorsionar ▷ vi (blush) sonrojarse; **colour in** vt colorear; **colour-blind** adj daltónico; **coloured** adj de color; (photo) en color; (of race) de color; **colour film** n película en color; **colourful** adj lleno de color; (person) pintoresco; **colouring** n colorido, color; (substance) colorante m; **colour television** n televisión f en color

column ['kɒləm] n columna

coma ['kəʊmə] n coma m

comb [kəʊm] n peine m; (ornamental) peineta ▷ vt (hair) peinar; (area) registrar a fondo

combat ['kɒmbæt] n combate m ▷ vt combatir

combination [kɒmbɪ'neɪʃən] n combinación f

combine [kəm'baɪn] vt combinar; (qualities) reunir ▷ vi combinarse ▷ n ['kɒmbaɪn] (Econ) cartel m

KEYWORD

come [kʌm] (pt came, pp come) vi 1 (movement towards) venir; **to come running** venir corriendo
2 (arrive) llegar; **he's come here to work** ha venido aquí para trabajar; **to come home** volver a casa
3 (reach): **to come to** llegar a; **the bill came to £40** la cuenta ascendía a cuarenta libras
4 (occur): **an idea came to me** se me

ocurrió una idea
5 (be, become): **to come loose/undone** etc aflojarse/desabrocharse, desatarse etc; **I've come to like him** por fin ha llegado a gustarme
come across vt fus (person) encontrarse con; (thing) encontrar
come along vi (progress) ir
come back vi (return) volver
come down vi (price) bajar; (building: be demolished) ser derribado
come from vt fus (place, source) ser de
come in vi (visitor) entrar; (train, report) llegar; (fashion) ponerse de moda; (on deal etc) entrar
come off vi (button) soltarse, desprenderse; (attempt) salir bien
come on vi (pupil, work, project) marchar; (lights) encenderse; (electricity) volver; **come on!** ¡vamos!
come out vi (fact) salir a la luz; (book, sun) salir; (stain) quitarse
come round vi (after faint, operation) volver en sí
come to vi (wake) volver en sí
come up vi (sun) salir; (problem) surgir; (event) aproximarse; (in conversation) mencionarse
come up with vt fus (idea) sugerir; (money) conseguir

comeback ['kʌmbæk] n: **to make a ~** (Theat) volver a las tablas

comedian [kə'miːdɪən] n humorista mf

comedy ['kɒmɪdɪ] n comedia

comet ['kɒmɪt] n cometa m

comfort ['kʌmfət] n bienestar m; (relief) alivio ▷ vt consolar; **comfortable** adj cómodo; (income) adecuado; **comfort station** n (us) servicios mpl

comic ['kɒmɪk] adj (also: **~al**) cómico ▷ n (comedian) cómico; (magazine) tebeo; (for adults) cómic m; **comic book** n (us) libro de cómics; **comic strip** n tira cómica

comma ['kɒmə] n coma

command [kə'mɑːnd] n orden f, mandato; (Mil: authority) mando; (mastery) dominio ▷ vt (troops) mandar; (give orders to) mandar, ordenar; **commander** n (Mil) comandante mf, jefe/a m/f

commemorate [kə'mɛmǝreɪt] vt conmemorar

commence [kə'mɛns] vt, vi comenzar; **commencement** n (US) (Univ) (ceremonia de) graduación f

commend [kə'mɛnd] vt elogiar, alabar; (recommend) recomendar

comment ['kɔmɛnt] n comentario ▷ vi: **to ~ (on)** hacer comentarios (sobre); **"no ~"** (written) "sin comentarios"; (spoken) "no tengo nada que decir"; **commentary** n comentario; **commentator** n comentarista m

commerce ['kɔmǝːs] n comercio

commercial [kə'mǝːʃəl] adj comercial ▷ n (TV) anuncio; **commercial break** n intermedio para publicidad

commission [kə'mɪʃən] n (committee, fee, order for work of art etc) comisión f ▷ vt (work of art) encargar; **out of ~** fuera de servicio; **commissioner** n (Police) comisario m de policía

commit [kə'mɪt] vt (act) cometer; (resources) dedicar; (to sb's care) entregar; **to ~ o.s. (to do)** comprometerse (a hacer); **to ~ suicide** suicidarse; **commitment** n compromiso

committee [kə'mɪtɪ] n comité m

commodity [kə'mɔdɪtɪ] n mercancía

common ['kɔmən] adj común; (pej) ordinario ▷ n campo común; **commonly** adv comúnmente; **commonplace** adj corriente; **Commons** npl (BRIT Pol): **the Commons** (la Cámara de) los Comunes; **common sense** n sentido común; **Commonwealth** n: **the Commonwealth** la Commonwealth

communal ['kɔmjuːnl] adj comunal; (kitchen) común

commune ['kɔmjuːn] n (group) comuna ▷ vi [kə'mjuːn]: **to ~ with** comunicarse con

communicate [kə'mjuːnɪkeɪt] vt comunicar ▷ vi: **to ~ (with)** comunicarse (con); (in writing) estar en contacto (con)

communication [kəmjuːnɪ'keɪʃən] n comunicación f

communion [kə'mjuːnɪən] n (also: **Holy C~**) comunión f

communism ['kɔmjunɪzəm] n comunismo; **communist** adj, n comunista mf

community [kə'mjuːnɪtɪ] n comunidad f; (large group) colectividad f; **community centre** n centro social; **community service** n trabajo m comunitario (prestado en lugar de cumplir una pena de prisión)

commute [kə'mjuːt] vi viajar a diario de casa al trabajo ▷ vt conmutar; **commuter** n persona que viaja a diario de casa al trabajo

compact [kəm'pækt] adj compacto ▷ n ['kɔmpækt] (also: **powder ~**) polvera; **compact disc** n compact disc m; **compact disc player** n lector m or reproductor m de discos compactos

companion [kəm'pænɪən] n compañero/a

company ['kʌmpənɪ] n compañía; (Comm) empresa, compañía; **to keep sb ~** acompañar a algn; **company car** n coche m de la empresa; **company director** n director(a) m/f de empresa

comparable ['kɔmpərǝbl] adj comparable

comparative [kəm'pærǝtɪv] adj relativo; (study, linguistics) comparado; **comparatively** adv (relatively) relativamente

compare [kəm'pɛǝʳ] vt comparar ▷ vi: **to ~ (with)** poder compararse con

(con); **~d with** or **to** comparado con or a; **comparison** [kəmˈpærɪsn] n comparación f

compartment [kəmˈpɑːtmənt] n compartim(i)ento

compass [ˈkʌmpəs] n brújula; **compasses** npl compás m

compassion [kəmˈpæʃən] n compasión f

compatible [kəmˈpætɪbl] adj compatible

compel [kəmˈpel] vt obligar; **compelling** adj (fig: argument) convincente

compensate [ˈkɒmpənseɪt] vt compensar ▷ vi: **to ~ for** compensar; **compensation** n (for loss) indemnización f

compete [kəmˈpiːt] vi (take part) competir; (vie with) competir, hacer la competencia

competent [ˈkɒmpɪtənt] adj competente, capaz

competition [kɒmpɪˈtɪʃən] n (contest) concurso; (rivalry) competencia

competitive [kəmˈpetɪtɪv] adj (Econ, Sport) competitivo

competitor [kəmˈpetɪtəʳ] n (rival) competidor(a) m/f; (participant) concursante mf

complacent [kəmˈpleɪsənt] adj autocomplaciente

complain [kəmˈpleɪn] vi quejarse; (Comm) reclamar; **complaint** n queja; (Comm) reclamación f; (Med) enfermedad f

complement [ˈkɒmplɪmənt] n complemento; (esp ship's crew) dotación f ▷ vt [ˈkɒmplɪment] (enhance) complementar; **complementary** [kɒmplɪˈmentərɪ] adj complementario

complete [kəmˈpliːt] adj (full) completo; (finished) acabado ▷ vt (fulfil) completar; (finish) acabar; (a form) rellenar; **completely** adv completamente; **completion** n

terminación f; **on completion of contract** cuando se realice el contrato

complex [ˈkɒmpleks] n complejo

complexion [kəmˈplekʃən] n (of face) tez f, cutis m

compliance [kəmˈplaɪəns] n (submission) sumisión f; (agreement) conformidad f, **in ~ with** de acuerdo con

complicate [ˈkɒmplɪkeɪt] vt complicar; **complicated** adj complicado; **complication** [kɒmplɪˈkeɪʃən] n complicación f

compliment [ˈkɒmplɪmənt] n (formal) cumplido ▷ vt felicitar; **complimentary** [kɒmplɪˈmentərɪ] adj elogioso; (copy) de regalo

comply [kəmˈplaɪ] vi: **to ~ with** acatar

component [kəmˈpəʊnənt] adj componente ▷ n (Tech) pieza

compose [kəmˈpəʊz] vt componer; **to be ~d of** componerse de; **to ~ o.s.** tranquilizarse; **composer** n (Mus) compositor(a) m/f; **composition** [kɒmpəˈzɪʃən] n composición f

composure [kəmˈpəʊʒəʳ] n serenidad f, calma

compound [ˈkɒmpaʊnd] n (Chem) compuesto; (Ling) término compuesto; (enclosure) recinto ▷ adj compuesto; (fracture) complicado

comprehension [kɒmprɪˈhenʃən] n comprensión f

comprehensive [kɒmprɪˈhensɪv] adj (broad) exhaustivo; **~ (school)** n centro estatal de enseñanza secundaria ≈ Instituto Nacional de Bachillerato (sp)

compress [kəmˈpres] vt comprimir; (Comput) comprimir ▷ n [ˈkɒmpres] (Med) compresa

comprise [kəmˈpraɪz] vt (also: **be ~d of**) comprender, constar de

compromise [ˈkɒmprəmaɪz] n (agreement) arreglo ▷ vt comprometer ▷ vi transigir

compulsive [kəmˈpʌlsɪv] adj compulsivo; (viewing, reading) obligado

compulsory [kəmˈpʌlsərɪ] *adj* obligatorio

computer [kəmˈpjuːtəʳ] *n* ordenador *m*, computador *m*, computadora; **computer game** *n* juego de ordenador; **computerize** *vt* (*data*) computerizar; (*system*) informatizar; **computer programmer** *n* programador(a) *m/f*; **computer programming** *n* programación *f*; **computer science** *n* informática *f*; **computer studies** *npl* informática *fsg*, computación *fsg* (LAM); **computing** [kəmˈpjuːtɪŋ] *n* (*activity*) informática

con [kɒn] *vt* estafar ▷ *n* estafa; **to ~ sb into doing sth** (*inf*) engañar a algn para que haga algo

conceal [kənˈsiːl] *vt* ocultar

concede [kənˈsiːd] *vt* (*point*, *argument*) reconocer; (*territory*) ceder; **to ~ (defeat)** darse por vencido; **to ~ that** admitir que

conceited [kənˈsiːtɪd] *adj* orgulloso

conceive [kənˈsiːv] *vt*, *vi* concebir; **to ~ of sth** concebir algo

concentrate [ˈkɒnsəntreɪt] *vi* concentrarse ▷ *vt* concentrar

concentration [kɒnsənˈtreɪʃən] *n* concentración *f*

concept [ˈkɒnsept] *n* concepto

concern [kənˈsəːn] *n* (*matter*) asunto; (*Comm*) empresa; (*anxiety*) preocupación *f* ▷ *vt* (*worry*) preocupar; (*involve*) afectar; (*relate to*) tener que ver con; **to be ~ed (about)** interesarse (por), preocuparse (por); **concerning** *prep* sobre, acerca de

concert [ˈkɒnsət] *n* concierto; **concert hall** *n* sala de conciertos

concerto [kənˈtʃəːtəu] *n* concierto

concession [kənˈseʃən] *n* concesión *f*; **tax ~** privilegio fiscal

concise [kənˈsaɪs] *adj* conciso

conclude [kənˈkluːd] *vt* concluir; (*treaty etc*) firmar; (*agreement*) llegar a; (*decide*): **to ~ that ...** llegar a la conclusión de que ...; **conclusion** [kənˈkluːʒən] *n* conclusión *f*

concrete [ˈkɒnkriːt] *n* hormigón *m* ▷ *adj* de hormigón; (*fig*) concreto

concussion [kənˈkʌʃən] *n* conmoción *f* cerebral

condemn [kənˈdem] *vt* condenar; (*building*) declarar en ruina

condensation [kɒndənˈseɪʃən] *n* condensación *f*

condense [kənˈdens] *vi* condensarse ▷ *vt* condensar; (*text*) abreviar

condition [kənˈdɪʃən] *n* condición *f*; (*of health*) estado; (*disease*) enfermedad *f* ▷ *vt* condicionar; **on ~ that** a condición (de) que; **conditional** *adj* condicional; **conditioner** *n* suavizante *m*

condo [ˈkɒndəu] *n abbr* (*us inf*) = **condominium**

condom [ˈkɒndəm] *n* condón *m*

condominium [kɒndəˈmɪnɪəm] *n* (*us: building*) bloque *m* de pisos or apartamentos (*propiedad de quienes lo habitan*), condominio (LAM); (: *apartment*) piso or apartamento (en propiedad), condominio (LAM)

condone [kənˈdəun] *vt* condonar

conduct [ˈkɒndʌkt] *n* conducta, comportamiento ▷ *vt* [kənˈdʌkt] (*lead*) conducir; (*manage*) llevar, dirigir; (*Mus*) dirigir; **to ~ o.s.** comportarse; **conducted tour** *n* (BRIT) visita con guía; **conductor** *n* (*of orchestra*) director(a) *m/f*; (*us: on train*) revisor(a) *m/f*; (*on bus*) cobrador *m*; (*Elec*) conductor *m*

cone [kəun] *n* cono; (*pine cone*) piña; (*for ice cream*) cucurucho

confectionery [kənˈfekʃənrɪ] *n* dulces *mpl*

confer [kənˈfəːʳ] *vt*: **to ~ (on)** otorgar (a) ▷ *vi* conferenciar

conference [ˈkɒnfərns] *n* (*meeting*) reunión *f*; (*convention*) congreso

confess [kənˈfes] *vt* confesar ▷ *vi* confesar; **confession** *n* confesión *f*

confide [kənˈfaɪd] *vi*: **to ~ in** confiar en

confidence ['kɒnfɪdns] n (also: **self-~**) confianza; (secret) confidencia; **in ~** (speak, write) en confianza; **confident** adj seguro de sí mismo; **confidential** [kɒnfɪ'denʃəl] adj confidencial

confine [kən'faɪn] vt (limit) limitar; (shut up) encerrar; **confined** adj (space) reducido

confirm [kən'fɜːm] vt confirmar; **confirmation** [kɒnfə'meɪʃən] n confirmación f

confiscate ['kɒnfɪskeɪt] vt confiscar

conflict ['kɒnflɪkt] n conflicto ▷ vi [kən'flɪkt] (opinions) estar reñido

conform [kən'fɔːm] vi: **to ~ to** ajustarse a

confront [kən'frʌnt] vt (problems) hacer frente a; (enemy, danger) enfrentarse con; **confrontation** [kɒnfrʌn'teɪʃən] n enfrentamiento

confuse [kən'fjuːz] vt (perplex) desconcertar; (mix up) confundir; (complicate) complicar; **confused** adj confuso; (person) desconcertado; **confusing** adj confuso; **confusion** n confusión f

congestion [kən'dʒestʃən] n congestión f

congratulate [kən'grætjuleɪt] vt felicitar; **congratulations** [kəngrætjʊ'leɪʃənz] npl: **congratulations (on)** felicitaciones fpl (por); **congratulations!** ¡enhorabuena!

congregation [kɒŋgrɪ'geɪʃən] n (in church) fieles mpl

congress ['kɒŋgres] n congreso; (us Pol): **C~** el Congreso (de los Estados Unidos); **congressman** n (us) miembro del Congreso; **congresswoman** n (us) diputada, miembro f del Congreso

conifer ['kɒnɪfəʳ] n conífera

conjugate ['kɒndʒugeɪt] vt conjugar

conjugation [kɒndʒə'geɪʃən] n conjugación f

conjunction [kən'dʒʌŋkʃən] n conjunción f; **in ~ with** junto con

conjure ['kʌndʒəʳ] vi hacer juegos de manos

connect [kə'nekt] vt juntar, unir; (Elec) conectar; (fig) relacionar, asociar ▷ vi: **to ~ with** (train) enlazar con; **to be ~ed with** (associated) estar relacionado con; **I am trying to ~ you** (Tel) estoy intentando ponerle al habla; **connecting flight** n vuelo m de enlace; **connection** n juntura, unión f; (Elec) conexión f; (Rail) enlace m; (Tel) comunicación f; (fig) relación f

conquer ['kɒŋkəʳ] vt (territory) conquistar; (enemy, feelings) vencer

conquest ['kɒŋkwest] n conquista

cons [kɒnz] npl see **mod cons; pro**

conscience ['kɒnʃəns] n conciencia

conscientious [kɒnʃɪ'enʃəs] adj concienzudo; (objection) de conciencia

conscious ['kɒnʃəs] adj consciente; (deliberate: insult, error) premeditado, intencionado; **consciousness** n conciencia; (Med) conocimiento

consecutive [kən'sekjutɪv] adj consecutivo; **on 3 ~ occasions** en 3 ocasiones consecutivas

consensus [kən'sensəs] n consenso

consent [kən'sent] n consentimiento ▷ vi: **to ~ to** consentir en

consequence ['kɒnsɪkwəns] n consecuencia

consequently ['kɒnsɪkwəntlɪ] adv por consiguiente

conservation [kɒnsə'veɪʃən] n conservación f

conservative [kən'sɜːvətɪv] adj, n conservador(a); (cautious) moderado; **C~** adj (BRIT Pol) conservador(a) m/f

conservatory [kən'sɜːvətrɪ] n (greenhouse) invernadero

consider [kən'sɪdəʳ] vt considerar; (take into account) tener en cuenta; (study) estudiar, examinar; **to ~ doing sth** pensar en (la posibilidad de) hacer algo; **considerable** adj considerable; **considerably** adv bastante,

considerablemente; **considerate**
adj considerado; **consideration**
[kənsıdə'reıʃən] *n* consideración *f*;
to be under consideration estar
estudiándose; **considering** *prep*:
considering (that) teniendo en
cuenta (que)

consignment [kən'saınmənt] *n*
envío

consist [kən'sıst] *vi*: **to ~ of**
consistir en

consistency [kən'sıstənsı] *n (of
person etc)* consecuencia, coherencia;
(thickness) consistencia

consistent [kən'sıstənt] *adj
(person, argument)* consecuente,
coherente

consolation [kɒnsə'leıʃən] *n*
consuelo

console [kən'səul] *vt* consolar ⊳ *n*
['kɒnsəul] consola

consonant ['kɒnsənənt] *n*
consonante *f*

conspicuous [kən'spıkjuəs] *adj
(visible)* visible

conspiracy [kən'spırəsı] *n* conjura,
complot *m*

constable ['kʌnstəbl] *n (BRIT)*
agente *mf* (de policía); **chief ~** jefe
mf de policía

constant ['kɒnstənt] *adj* constante;
constantly *adv* constantemente

constipated ['kɒnstıpeıtəd] *adj*
estreñido

> Be careful not to translate
> *constipated* by the Spanish word
> *constipado*.

constipation [kɒnstı'peıʃən] *n*
estreñimiento

constituency [kən'stıtjuənsı]
n (Pol) distrito electoral; *(people)*
electorado

constitute ['kɒnstıtjuːt] *vt*
constituir

constitution [kɒnstı'tjuːʃən] *n*
constitución *f*

constraint [kən'streınt] *n (force)*
fuerza; *(limit)* restricción *f*

construct [kən'strʌkt] *vt* construir;
construction *n* construcción *f*;
constructive *adj* constructivo

consul ['kɒnsl] *n* cónsul *mf*;
consulate ['kɒnsjulıt] *n* consulado

consult [kən'sʌlt] *vt* consultar;
consultant *n (BRIT Med)* especialista
mf; *(other specialist)* asesor(a) *m/f*;
consultation *n* consulta; **consulting
room** *n (BRIT)* consultorio

consume [kən'sjuːm] *vt (eat)*
comerse; *(drink)* beberse; *(fire
etc)* consumir; *(Comm)* consumir;
consumer *n* consumidor(a) *m/f*

consumption [kən'sʌmpʃən] *n*
consumo

cont. *abbr (= continued)* sigue

contact ['kɒntækt] *n* contacto;
(person: pej) enchufe *m* ⊳ *vt* ponerse en
contacto con; **~ lenses** *n pl* lentes *fpl*
de contacto

contagious [kən'teıdʒəs] *adj*
contagioso

contain [kən'teın] *vt* contener;
to ~ o.s. contenerse; **container**
n recipiente *m*; *(for shipping etc)*
contenedor *m*

contaminate [kən'tæmıneıt] *vt*
contaminar

cont'd *abbr (= continued)* sigue

contemplate ['kɒntəmpleıt] *vt*
contemplar; *(reflect upon)* considerar

contemporary [kən'tempərərı] *adj,
n* contemporáneo/a

contempt [kən'tempt] *n* desprecio;
~ of court *(Law)* desacato (a los
tribunales o a la justicia)

contend [kən'tend] *vt (argue)* afirmar
⊳ *vi*: **to ~ with/for** luchar contra/por

content [kən'tent] *adj (happy)*
contento; *(satisfied)* satisfecho ⊳ *vt*
contentar; satisfacer ⊳ *n* ['kɒntent]
contenido; **contents** *npl* contenido
msg; **(table of) ~s** índice *m* de
materias; **contented** *adj* contento;
satisfecho

contest ['kɒntest] *n* contienda;
(competition) concurso ⊳ *vt* [kən'test]

(*dispute*) impugnar; (*Pol: election, seat*) presentarse como candidato/a a a
 Be careful not to translate *contest* by the Spanish word *contestar*.

contestant [kənˈtestənt] *n* concursante *mf*; (*in fight*) contendiente *mf*

context [ˈkɒntekst] *n* contexto

continent [ˈkɒntɪnənt] *n* continente *m*; **the C~** (BRIT) el continente europeo; **continental** *adj* continental; **continental breakfast** *n* desayuno estilo europeo; **continental quilt** *n* (BRIT) edredón *m*

continual [kənˈtɪnjuəl] *adj* continuo; **continually** *adv* continuamente

continue [kənˈtɪnjuː] *vi, vt* seguir, continuar

continuity [kɒntɪˈnjuːɪtɪ] *n* (*also Cine*) continuidad *f*

continuous [kənˈtɪnjuəs] *adj* continuo; **continuous assessment** *n* (BRIT) evaluación *f* continua; **continuously** *adv* continuamente

contour [ˈkɒntuəʳ] *n* contorno *m*; (*also:* **~ line**) curva de nivel

contraception [kɒntrəˈsepʃən] *n* contracepción *f*

contraceptive [kɒntrəˈseptɪv] *adj, n* anticonceptivo

contract [*n* ˈkɒntrækt, *vi, vt* kənˈtrækt] *n* contrato ▷ *vi* (Comm): **to ~ to do sth** comprometerse por contrato a hacer algo; (*become smaller*) contraerse, encogerse ▷ *vt* contraer; **contractor** *n* contratista *mf*

contradict [kɒntrəˈdɪkt] *vt* contradecir; **contradiction** *n* contradicción *f*

contrary¹ [ˈkɒntrərɪ] *adj* contrario ▷ *n* lo contrario; **on the ~** al contrario; **unless you hear to the ~** a no ser que le digan lo contrario

contrary² [kənˈtreərɪ] *adj* (*perverse*) terco

contrast [ˈkɒntrɑːst] *n* contraste *m* ▷ *vt* [kənˈtrɑːst] contrastar; **in ~ to or with** a diferencia de

contribute [kənˈtrɪbjuːt] *vi* contribuir ▷ *vt*: **to ~ to** contribuir a; (*newspaper*) colaborar en; (*discussion*) intervenir en; **contribution** *n* (*money*) contribución *f*; (*to debate*) intervención *f*; (*to journal*) colaboración *f*; **contributor** *n* (*to newspaper*) colaborador/a *m/f*

control [kənˈtrəul] *vt* controlar; (*traffic etc*) dirigir; (*machinery*) manejar; (*temper*) dominar; (*disease, fire*) dominar, controlar ▷ *n* control *m*; (*of car*) conducción *f*; (*check*) freno; **controls** *npl* (*of vehicle*) instrumentos *mpl* de mando; (*of radio*) instrumentos *mpl*; (*governmental*) medidas *fpl* de control; **everything is under ~** todo está bajo control; **to be in ~ of** estar al mando de; **the car went out of ~** perdió el control del coche; **control tower** *n* (Aviat) torre *f* de control

controversial [kɒntrəˈvɜːʃl] *adj* polémico

controversy [ˈkɒntrəvɜːsɪ] *n* polémica

convenience [kənˈviːnɪəns] *n* (*comfort*) comodidad *f*; (*advantage*) ventaja; **at your earliest ~** (Comm) tan pronto como le sea posible; **all modern ~s** (BRIT) todo confort

convenient [kənˈviːnɪənt] *adj* (*useful*) útil; (*place*) conveniente; (*time*) oportuno

convent [ˈkɒnvənt] *n* convento

convention [kənˈvenʃən] *n* convención *f*; (*meeting*) asamblea; **conventional** *adj* convencional

conversation [kɒnvəˈseɪʃən] *n* conversación *f*

conversely [kɒnˈvɜːslɪ] *adv* a la inversa

conversion [kənˈvɜːʃən] *n* conversión *f*

convert [kənˈvɜːt] *vt* (Rel, Comm) convertir; (*alter*) transformar ▷ *n* [ˈkɒnvɜːt] converso/a; **convertible** *adj* convertible ▷ *n* descapotable *m*

convey [kən'veɪ] vt transportar; (thanks) comunicar; (idea) expresar; **conveyor belt** n cinta transportadora

convict [kən'vɪkt] vt (find guilty) declarar culpable a ▷ n ['kɒnvɪkt] presidiario/a; **conviction** [kən'vɪkʃən] n condena; (belief) convicción f

convince [kən'vɪns] vt convencer; **to ~ sb (of sth/that)** convencer a algn (de algo/de que); **convinced** adj: **convinced of/that** convencido de/de que; **convincing** adj convincente

convoy ['kɒnvɔɪ] n convoy m

cook [kuk] vt (stew etc) guisar; (meal) preparar ▷ vi hacerse; (person) cocinar ▷ n cocinero/a; **cookbook** n libro de cocina; **cooker** n cocina; **cookery** n cocina; **cookery book** n (BRIT) = cookbook

cookie ['kukɪ] n (US) galleta; (Comput) cookie f

cooking ['kukɪŋ] n cocina

cool [ku:l] adj fresco; (not afraid) tranquilo; (unfriendly) frío ▷ vt enfriar ▷ vi enfriarse; **cool down** vi enfriarse; (fig: person, situation) calmarse; **cool off** vi (become calmer) calmarse, apaciguarse; (lose enthusiasm) perder (el) interés, enfriarse

cop [kɒp] n (inf) poli m

cope [kəup] vi: **to ~ with** (problem) hacer frente a

copper ['kɒpə'] n (metal) cobre m; (inf) poli m

copy ['kɒpɪ] n copia; (of book) ejemplar m ▷ vt (also Comput) copiar; **copyright** n derechos mpl de autor

coral ['kɒrəl] n coral m

cord [kɔ:d] n cuerda; (Elec) cable m; (fabric) pana; **cords** npl (trousers) pantalones mpl de pana; **cordless** adj sin hilos

corduroy ['kɔ:dərɔɪ] n pana

core [kɔ:'] n centro, núcleo; (of fruit) corazón m; (of problem etc) meollo ▷ vt quitar el corazón de

coriander [kɒrɪ'ændə'] n culantro

cork [kɔ:k] n corcho; (tree) alcornoque m; **corkscrew** n sacacorchos m inv

corn [kɔ:n] n (BRIT: wheat) trigo; (US: maize) maíz m; (on foot) callo; **~ on the cob** (Culin) maíz en la mazorca

corned beef ['kɔ:nd-] n carne f de vaca acecinada

corner ['kɔ:nə'] n (outside) esquina; (inside) rincón m; (in road) curva; (Football) córner m ▷ vt (trap) arrinconar; (Comm) acaparar ▷ vi (in car) tomar las curvas; **corner shop** n (BRIT) tienda de la esquina

cornflakes ['kɔ:nfleɪks] npl copos mpl de maíz, cornflakes mpl

cornflour ['kɔ:nflauə'] n (BRIT) harina de maíz

cornstarch ['kɔ:nstɑ:tʃ] n (US) = cornflour

Cornwall ['kɔ:nwəl] n Cornualles m

coronary ['kɒrənərɪ] n: **~ (thrombosis)** infarto

coronation [kɒrə'neɪʃən] n coronación f

coroner ['kɒrənə'] n juez mf de instrucción

corporal ['kɔ:pərl] n cabo ▷ adj: **~ punishment** castigo corporal

corporate ['kɔ:pərɪt] adj (action, ownership) colectivo; (finance, image) corporativo

corporation [kɔ:pə'reɪʃən] n (of town) ayuntamiento; (Comm) corporación f

corps (pl **corps**) [kɔ:', kɔ:z] n cuerpo; **press ~** gabinete m de prensa

corpse [kɔ:ps] n cadáver m

correct [kə'rekt] adj correcto; (accurate) exacto ▷ vt corregir; **correction** n (act) corrección f; (instance) rectificación f

correspond [kɒrɪs'pɒnd] vi: **to ~ (with)** (write) escribirse (con); (be in accordance) corresponder (con); **to ~ (to)** (be equivalent to) corresponder (a); **correspondence** n correspondencia; **correspondent** n corresponsal mf; **corresponding** adj correspondiente

corridor [ˈkɒrɪdɔːʳ] n pasillo
corrode [kəˈrəud] vt corroer ▷ vi
corroerse
corrupt [kəˈrʌpt] adj corrompido;
(person) corrupto ▷ vt corromper;
(Comput) degradar; **corruption** n
corrupción f; (of data) alteración f
Corsica [ˈkɔːsɪkə] n Córcega
cosmetic [kɒzˈmetɪk] n b adj
cosmético; **cosmetic surgery** n
cirugía f estética
cosmopolitan [kɒzməˈpɒlɪtn] adj
cosmopolita
cost [kɒst] (pt, pp **cost**) n (price) precio
▷ vi costar, valer ▷ vt preparar el
presupuesto de; **costs** npl (Law) costas
fpl; **how much does it ~?** ¿cuánto
cuesta?; **to ~ sb time/effort** costarle
a algn tiempo/esfuerzo; **it ~ him his
life** le costó la vida; **at all ~s** cueste
lo que cueste
co-star [ˈkəustɑːʳ] n coprotagonista
mf
Costa Rica [ˈkɒstəˈriːkə] n
Costa Rica; **Costa Rican** adj, n
costarriqueño/a
costly [ˈkɒstlɪ] adj costoso
costume [ˈkɒstjuːm] n traje m; (BRIT:
also: **swimming ~**) traje de baño
cosy (US) **cozy** [ˈkəuzɪ] adj cómodo;
(room, atmosphere) acogedor(a)
cot [kɒt] n (BRIT: child's) cuna; (US:
folding bed) cama plegable
cottage [ˈkɒtɪdʒ] n casita de campo;
cottage cheese n requesón m
cotton [ˈkɒtn] n algodón m; (thread)
hilo; **cotton on** vi (inf): **to ~ on (to
sth)** caer en la cuenta (de algo);
cotton bud n (BRIT) bastoncillo m
de algodón; **cotton candy** n (US)
algodón m (azucarado); **cotton wool**
n (BRIT) algodón m (hidrófilo)
couch [kautʃ] n sofá m; (in doctor's
surgery) camilla; (psychiatrist's) diván m
cough [kɒf] vi toser ▷ n tos f; **cough
mixture** n jarabe m para la tos
could [kud] pt of **can²**; **couldn't
= could not**

council [ˈkaunsl] n consejo; **city
or town ~** ayuntamiento, consejo
municipal; **council estate** n (BRIT)
barriada de viviendas sociales de
alquiler; **council house** n (BRIT)
vivienda social de alquiler; **councillor**
n concejal mf; **council tax** n (BRIT)
contribución f municipal (dependiente
del valor de la vivienda)
counsel [ˈkaunsl] n (advice) consejo;
(lawyer) abogado/a n ▷ vt aconsejar;
counselling, (US) **counseling** n
(Psych) asistencia f psicológica;
counsellor, (US) **counselor** n
consejero/a; abogado/a
count [kaunt] vt contar; (include)
incluir ▷ vi contar ▷ n cuenta; (of votes)
escrutinio; (nobleman) conde m; **count
in** (inf) vt: **to ~ sb in on sth** contar con
algn para algo; **count on** vt fus contar
con; **countdown** n cuenta atrás
counter [ˈkauntəʳ] n (in shop)
mostrador m; (in games) ficha ▷ vt
contrarrestar ▷ adv: **~ to** contrario a
counter-clockwise
[ˈkauntəˈklɒkwaɪz] adv en sentido
contrario al de las agujas del reloj
counterfeit [ˈkauntəfɪt] n
falsificación f ▷ vt falsificar ▷ adj falso,
falsificado
counterpart [ˈkauntəpɑːt] n
homólogo/a
countess [ˈkauntɪs] n condesa
countless [ˈkauntlɪs] n
innumerable
country [ˈkʌntrɪ] n país m; (native
land) patria; (as opposed to town)
campo; (region) región f, tierra;
country and western (music) n
música country; **country house** n
casa de campo; **countryside** n campo
county [ˈkauntɪ] n condado
coup [kuː] (pl **coups**) n golpe m;
(triumph) éxito; (also: **~ d'état**) golpe
de estado
couple [ˈkʌpl] n (of things) par m;
(of people) pareja; (married couple)
matrimonio; **a ~ of** un par de

coupon ['kuːpɒn] n cupón m; (voucher) valé m

courage ['kʌrɪdʒ] n valor m, valentía f; **courageous** [kə'reɪdʒəs] adj valiente

courgette [kuə'ʒet] n (BRIT) calabacín m

courier ['kʊrɪə*] n mensajero/a; (for tourists) guía mf (de turismo)

course [kɔːs] n (direction) dirección f; (of river) curso; (Scol) curso; (of ship) rumbo; (Golf) campo; (part of meal) plato; **of ~** adv desde luego, naturalmente; **of ~I** ¡claro!; **~ of treatment** (Med) tratamiento

court [kɔːt] n (royal) corte f; (Law) tribunal m, juzgado; (Tennis) pista, cancha (LAM); vt (woman) cortejar; **to take to ~** demandar

courtesy ['kɜːtəsɪ] n cortesía; **by ~ of** (por) cortesía de; **courtesy bus, courtesy coach** n autobús m gratuito

court: **courthouse** n (us) palacio de justicia; **courtroom** n sala de justicia; **courtyard** n patio

cousin ['kʌzn] n primo/a; **first ~** primo/a carnal

cover ['kʌvə*] vt cubrir; (with lid) tapar; (distance) cubrir, recorrer; (include) abarcar; (protect) abrigar; (journalist) investigar; (issues) tratar ⊳ n cubierta; (lid) tapa; (for chair etc) funda; (envelope) sobre m; (of magazine) portada; (shelter) abrigo; (insurance) cobertura; **to take ~** (shelter) protegerse, resguardarse; **under ~** (indoors) bajo techo; **under ~ of darkness** al amparo de la oscuridad; **under separate ~** (Comm) por separado; **cover up** vi: **to ~ up for sb** encubrir a algn; **coverage** n (in media) cobertura informativa; **cover charge** n precio del cubierto; **cover-up** n encubrimiento

cow [kaʊ] n vaca ⊳ vt intimidar

coward ['kaʊəd] n cobarde mf; **cowardly** adj cobarde

cowboy ['kaʊbɔɪ] n vaquero

cozy ['kəʊzɪ] adj (US) = **cosy**

crab [kræb] n cangrejo

crack [kræk] n grieta; (noise) crujido; (drug) crack m ⊳ vt agrietar, romper; (nut) cascar; (whip etc) chasquear; (knuckles) crujir; (joke) contar ⊳ adj (athlete) de primera clase; **crack down on** vt fus adoptar medidas severas contra; **cracked** adj (cup, window) rajado; (wall) resquebrajado; **cracker** n (biscuit) cráquer m; (Christmas cracker) petardo sorpresa

crackle ['krækl] vi crepitar

cradle ['kreɪdl] n cuna

craft [krɑːft] n (skill) arte m; (trade) oficio; (cunning) astucia; (boat) embarcación f; **craftsman** n artesano; **craftsmanship** n destreza

cram [kræm] vt (fill): **to ~ sth with** llenar algo (a reventar) de; (put): **to ~ sth into** meter algo a la fuerza en ⊳ vi (for exams) empollar

cramp [kræmp] n (Med) calambre m; **cramped** adj apretado

cranberry ['krænbərɪ] n arándano agrio

crane [kreɪn] n (Tech) grúa; (bird) grulla

crap [kræp] n (infl) mierda (!)

crash [kræʃ] n (noise) estrépito; (of cars, plane) accidente m; (of business) quiebra ⊳ vt (plane) estrellar ⊳ vi (plane) estrellarse; (two cars) chocar; **crash course** n curso acelerado; **crash helmet** n casco (protector)

crate [kreɪt] n cajón m de embalaje; (for bottles) caja

crave [kreɪv] vt, vi: **to ~ (for)** ansiar, anhelar

crawl [krɔːl] vi (drag o.s.) arrastrarse; (child) andar a gatas, gatear; (vehicle) avanzar (lentamente) ⊳ n (Swimming) crol m

crayfish ['kreɪfɪʃ] n (pl inv: freshwater) cangrejo (de río); (: saltwater) cigala

crayon ['kreɪən] n lápiz m de color

craze [kreɪz] n (fashion) moda

crazy ['kreɪzɪ] adj (person) loco; (idea) disparatado; **to be ~ about sb/sth** (inf) estar loco por algn/algo

creak [kriːk] vi crujir; (hinge etc) chirriar, rechinar

cream [kriːm] n (of milk) nata, crema; (lotion) crema; (fig) flor f y nata ▷ adj (colour) color m crema; **cream cheese** n queso blanco cremoso; **creamy** adj cremoso

crease [kriːs] n (fold) pliegue m; (in trousers) raya f; (wrinkle) arruga f ▷ vt (wrinkle) arrugar ▷ vi (wrinkle up) arrugarse

create [kriːˈeɪt] vt crear; **creation** n creación f; **creative** adj creativo; **creator** n creador(a) m/f

creature [ˈkriːtʃəˈ] n (animal) animal m; (insect) bicho; (person) criatura

crèche, creche [krɛʃ] n (BRIT) guardería (infantil)

credentials [krɪˈdɛnʃlz] npl referencias fpl

credibility [ˈkrɛdɪˈbɪlɪti] n credibilidad f

credible [ˈkrɛdɪbl] adj creíble

credit [ˈkrɛdɪt] n crédito; (merit) honor m, mérito ▷ vt (Comm) abonar; (believe) creer, dar crédito a ▷ adj crediticio; **to be in ~** (person, bank account) tener saldo a favor; **to ~ sb with** (fig) reconocer a algn el mérito de; see also **credits**; **credit card** n tarjeta de crédito; **credit crunch** n crisis f crediticia

credits [ˈkrɛdɪts] npl (Cine) títulos mpl or rótulos mpl de crédito, ficha técnica

creek [kriːk] n cala, ensenada; (us) riachuelo

creep (pt, pp **crept**) [kriːp, krɛpt] vi (animal) deslizarse

cremate [krɪˈmeɪt] vt incinerar

crematorium [krɛməˈtɔːriəm] (pl **crematoria**) n crematorio

crept [krɛpt] pt, pp of **creep**

crescent [ˈkrɛsnt] n media luna; (street) calle f (en forma de semicírculo)

cress [krɛs] n berro

crest [krɛst] n (of bird) cresta; (of hill) cima, cumbre f; (of coat of arms) blasón m

crew [kruː] n (of ship etc) tripulación f; (Cine etc) equipo; **crew-neck** n cuello a la caja

crib [krɪb] n cuna ▷ vt (inf) plagiar

cricket [ˈkrɪkɪt] n (insect) grillo; (game) críquet m; **cricketer** n jugador(a) m/f de críquet

crime [kraɪm] n crimen m; (less serious) delito; **criminal** [ˈkrɪmɪnl] n criminal mf, delincuente mf ▷ adj criminal; (law) penal

crimson [ˈkrɪmzn] adj carmesí

cringe [krɪndʒ] vi encogerse

cripple [ˈkrɪpl] n lisiado/a, cojo/a ▷ vt lisiar, mutilar

crisis [ˈkraɪsɪs] (pl **crises**) n crisis f

crisp [krɪsp] adj fresco; (toast, snow) crujiente; (manner) seco; **crispy** adj crujiente

criterion [kraɪˈtɪəriən] (pl **criteria**) n criterio

critic [ˈkrɪtɪk] n crítico/a; **critical** adj crítico; (illness) grave; **criticism** [ˈkrɪtɪsɪzm] n crítica; **criticize** [ˈkrɪtɪsaɪz] vt criticar

Croat [ˈkrəuæt] adj, n = **Croatian**

Croatia [krəuˈeɪʃə] n Croacia; **Croatian** adj, n croata mf ▷ n (Ling) croata m

crockery [ˈkrɒkəri] n loza, vajilla

crocodile [ˈkrɒkədaɪl] n cocodrilo

crocus [ˈkrəukəs] n crocus m, croco

croissant [ˈkrwæsɒ̃] n croissant m, medialuna (esp LAM)

crook [kruk] n ladrón/ona m/f; (of shepherd) cayado; **crooked** [ˈkrukɪd] adj torcido; (fig) corrupto

crop [krɒp] n (produce) cultivo; (amount produced) cosecha; (riding crop) látigo de montar ▷ vt cortar, recortar; **crop up** vi surgir, presentarse

cross [krɒs] n cruz f ▷ vt (street etc) cruzar, atravesar ▷ adj de mal humor, enojado; **cross off** vt tachar; **cross out** vt tachar; **cross over** vi cruzar; **cross-Channel ferry** n transbordador m que cruza el Canal de la Mancha; **cross-country (race)**

n carrera a campo traviesa, cross *m*; **crossing** *n* (*sea passage*) travesía; (*also*: **pedestrian crossing**) paso de peatones; **crossing guard** *n* (*us*) persona encargada de ayudar a los niños a cruzar la calle; **crossroads** *nsg* cruce *m*; (*fig*) encrucijada; **crosswalk** *n* (*us*) paso de peatones; **crossword** *n* crucigrama *m*

crotch [krɒtʃ] *n* (*of garment*) entrepierna

crouch [krautʃ] *vi* agacharse, acurrucarse

crouton ['kru:tɒn] *n* cubito de pan frito

crow [krəu] *n* (*bird*) cuervo; (*of cock*) canto, cacareo ▷ *vi* (*cock*) cantar

crowd [kraud] *n* muchedumbre *f* ▷ *vt* (*gather*) amontonar; (*fill*) llenar ▷ *vi* (*gather*) reunirse; (*pile up*) amontonarse; **crowded** *adj* (*full*) atestado; (*densely populated*) superpoblado

crown [kraun] *n* corona; (*of head*) coronilla; (*of hill*) cumbre *f*; (*for tooth*) funda ▷ *vt* coronar; **and to ~ it all ...** (*fig*) y para colmo o remate ...; **crown jewels** *npl* joyas *fpl* reales

crucial ['kru:ʃl] *adj* decisivo

crucifix ['kru:sıfıks] *n* crucifijo

crude [kru:d] *adj* (*materials*) bruto; (*basic*) tosco; (*vulgar*) ordinario ▷ *n* (*also*: **~ oil**) (petróleo) crudo

cruel ['kruəl] *adj* cruel; **cruelty** *n* crueldad *f*

cruise [kru:z] *n* crucero ▷ *vi* (*ship*) navegar; (*car*) ir a velocidad constante

crumb [krʌm] *n* miga, migaja

crumble ['krʌmbl] *vt* desmenuzar ▷ *vi* (*building*) desmoronarse

crumpet ['krʌmpıt] *n* = bollo para tostar

crumple ['krʌmpl] *vt* (*paper*) estrujar; (*material*) arrugar

crunch [krʌntʃ] *vt* (*with teeth*) mascar; (*underfoot*) hacer crujir ▷ *n* (*fig*) hora de la verdad; **crunchy** *adj* crujiente

crush [krʌʃ] *n* (*crowd*) aglomeración *f* ▷ *vt* aplastar; (*paper*) estrujar; (*cloth*)

arrugar; (*fruit*) exprimir; (*opposition*) aplastar; (*hopes*) destruir; **to have a ~ on sb** estar enamorado de algn

crust [krʌst] *n* corteza; (*bread*) crujiente; (*person*) de mal carácter

crutch [krʌtʃ] *n* muleta

cry [kraı] *vi* llorar; (*shout: also*: **~ out**) gritar ▷ *n* grito; (*of animal*) aullido; **cry out** *vi* (*call out, shout*) lanzar un grito, echar un grito ▷ *vt* gritar

crystal ['krıstl] *n* cristal *m*

cub [kʌb] *n* cachorro; (*also*: **~ scout**) niño explorador

Cuba ['kju:bə] *n* Cuba; **Cuban** *adj, n* cubano/a

cube [kju:b] *n* cubo ▷ *vt* (*Math*) elevar al cubo

cubicle ['kju:bıkl] *n* (*at pool*) caseta; (*for bed*) cubículo

cuckoo ['kuku:] *n* cuco

cucumber ['kju:kʌmbə'] *n* pepino

cuddle ['kʌdl] *vt* abrazar ▷ *vi* abrazarse

cue [kju:] *n* (*snooker cue*) taco; (*Theat etc*) entrada

cuff [kʌf] *n* (*BRIT: of shirt, coat etc*) puño; (*us: of trousers*) vuelta; (*blow*) bofetada; **off the ~** *adv* improvisado; **cufflinks** *npl* gemelos *mpl*

cuisine [kwı'zi:n] *n* cocina

cul-de-sac ['kʌldəsæk] *n* callejón *m* sin salida

cull [kʌl] *vt* (*kill selectively: animals*) matar selectivamente ▷ *n* matanza selectiva

culminate ['kʌlmıneıt] *vi*: **to ~ in** culminar en

culprit ['kʌlprıt] *n* culpable *mf*

cult [kʌlt] *n* culto

cultivate ['kʌltıveıt] *vt* (*also fig*) cultivar

cultural ['kʌltʃərəl] *adj* cultural

culture ['kʌltʃə'] *n* (*also fig*) cultura; (*Biol*) cultivo

cumin ['kʌmın] *n* (*spice*) comino

cunning ['kʌnıŋ] *n* astucia ▷ *adj* astuto

cup [kʌp] n taza; (prize, event) copa
cupboard ['kʌbəd] n armario; (in kitchen) alacena
cup final n (Football) final f de copa
curator [kjuəˈreɪtər] n director/a m/f
curb [kɜːb] vt refrenar ▷ n freno; (us) bordillo
curdle ['kɜːdl] vi cuajarse
cure [kjuər] vt curar ▷ n cura, curación f; (fig: solution) remedio
curfew ['kɜːfjuː] n toque m de queda
curiosity [kjuərɪˈɒsɪtɪ] n curiosidad f
curious ['kjuərɪəs] adj curioso; **I'm ~ about him** me intriga
curl [kɜːl] n rizo ▷ vt (hair) rizar ▷ vi rizarse; **curl up** vi (person) hacerse un ovillo; **curler** n bigudí m, rulo; **curly** adj rizado
currant ['kʌrnt] n pasa; (black, red) grosella
currency ['kʌrnsɪ] n moneda; **to gain ~** (fig) difundirse
current ['kʌrnt] n corriente f ▷ adj actual; **in ~ use** de uso corriente; **current account** n (BRIT) cuenta corriente; **current affairs** npl (noticias fpl de) actualidad f; **currently** adv actualmente
curriculum [kəˈrɪkjuləm] (pl **curriculums** or **curricula**) n plan m de estudios, currículo; **curriculum vitae** [-ˈviːtaɪ] n currículum m (vitae)
curry ['kʌrɪ] n curry m ▷ vt: **to ~ favour with** buscar el favor de; **curry powder** n curry m en polvo
curse [kɜːs] vi echar pestes, soltar palabrotas ▷ vt maldecir ▷ n maldición f; (swearword) palabrota, taco
cursor ['kɜːsər] n (Comput) cursor m
curt [kɜːt] adj seco
curtain ['kɜːtn] n cortina; (Theat) telón m; **to draw the ~s** (together) cerrar las cortinas; (apart) abrir las cortinas
curve [kɜːv] n curva ▷ vi (road) hacer una curva; (line etc) curvarse; **curved** adj curvo

cushion ['kuʃən] n cojín m; (Snooker) banda ▷ vt (shock) amortiguar
custard ['kʌstəd] n natillas fpl
custody ['kʌstədɪ] n custodia; **to take sb into ~** detener a algn
custom ['kʌstəm] n costumbre f; (Comm) clientela
customer ['kʌstəmər] n cliente mf
customized ['kʌstəmaɪzd] adj (car etc) hecho a encargo
customs ['kʌstəmz] npl aduana sg; **customs officer** n aduanero/a
cut [kʌt] (pt, pp **cut**) vt cortar; (price) rebajar; (reduce) reducir ▷ vi cortar ▷ n corte m; (in skin) cortadura; (in salary etc) rebaja; (in spending) reducción f, recorte m; (slice of meat) tajada; **to ~ and paste** (Comput) cortar y pegar; **cut back** vt (plants) podar; (production, expenditure) reducir; **cut down** vt (tree) derribar; (consumption, expenses) reducir; **cut off** vt cortar; (fig) aislar; **we've been ~ off** (Tel) nos han cortado la comunicación; **cut out** vt (shape) recortar; (delete) suprimir; **cut up** vt cortar (en pedazos); **cutback** n reducción f
cute [kjuːt] adj mono
cutlery ['kʌtlərɪ] n cubiertos mpl
cutlet ['kʌtlɪt] n chuleta
cut-price ['kʌtˈpraɪs] adj a precio reducido
cutting ['kʌtɪŋ] adj (remark) mordaz ▷ n (BRIT: from newspaper) recorte m; (from plant) esqueje m
CV n abbr = **curriculum vitae**
cyber attack ['saɪbərətæk] n ciberataque m
cyberbullying ['saɪbəbuliɪŋ] n ciberacoso
cybercafé ['saɪbəˈkæfeɪ] n cibercafé m
cyberspace ['saɪbəspeɪs] n ciberespacio
cycle ['saɪkl] n ciclo; (bicycle) bicicleta ▷ vi ir en bicicleta; **cycle hire** n alquiler m de bicicletas; **cycle lane** n carril m bici; **cycle path** n

carril-bici m; **cycling** n ciclismo; **cyclist** n ciclista mf

cyclone ['saɪkləʊn] n ciclón m

cylinder ['sɪlɪndəʳ] n cilindro

cymbals ['sɪmblz] npl platillos mpl

cynical ['sɪnɪkl] adj cínico

Cypriot ['sɪprɪət] adj, n chipriota mf

Cyprus ['saɪprəs] n Chipre f

cyst [sɪst] n quiste m; **cystitis** [sɪs'taɪtɪs] n cistitis f

czar [zɑː'] n zar m

Czech [tʃɛk] adj checo ▷ n checo/a; **the ~ Republic** la República Checa

d

D, d [diː] n (Mus) re m

dab [dæb] vt: **to ~ ointment onto a wound** aplicar pomada sobre una herida; **to ~ with paint** dar unos toques de pintura

dad [dæd], **daddy** ['dædɪ] n papá m

daffodil ['dæfədɪl] n narciso

daft [dɑːft] adj tonto

dagger ['dægəʳ] n puñal m, daga; **to look ~s at sb** fulminar a algn con la mirada

daily ['deɪlɪ] adj diario, cotidiano ▷ adv todos los días, cada día

dairy ['dɛərɪ] n (shop) lechería; (on farm) vaquería; **dairy produce** n productos mpl lácteos

daisy ['deɪzɪ] n margarita

dam [dæm] n presa ▷ vt embalsar

damage ['dæmɪdʒ] n daño; (fig) perjuicio; (to machine) avería ▷ vt dañar; perjudicar; averiar; **~ to property** daños materiales; **damages** npl (Law) daños y perjuicios

damn [dæm] vt condenar; (curse) maldecir ▷ n (inf): **I don't give a ~** me importa un pito ▷ adj (inf: also: **~ed**) maldito; **~ (it)!** ¡maldito sea!

damp [dæmp] adj húmedo, mojado ▷ n humedad f ▷ vt (also: **~en**: cloth, rag) mojar; (: enthusiasm) enfriar

dance [dɑ:ns] n baile m ▷ vi bailar; **dance floor** n pista f de baile; **dancer** n bailador(a) m/f; (professional) bailarín/ina m/f; **dancing** n baile m

dandelion [ˈdændɪlaɪən] n diente m de león

dandruff [ˈdændrəf] n caspa

D & T (BRIT Scol) n abbr (= design and technology) diseño y pretecnología

Dane [deɪn] n danés/esa m/f

danger [ˈdeɪndʒə*] n peligro; (risk) riesgo; **~!** (on sign) ¡peligro!; **to be in ~ of** correr riesgo de; **dangerous** adj peligroso

dangle [ˈdæŋgl] vt colgar ▷ vi pender, estar colgado

Danish [ˈdeɪnɪʃ] adj danés/esa ▷ n (Ling) danés m

dare [dɛə*] vt: **to ~ sb to do** desafiar a algn a hacer algo ▷ vi: **to ~ (to) do sth** atreverse a hacer algo; **I ~ say** (I suppose) puede ser; **daring** adj (person) osado; (plan, escape) audaz ▷ n atrevimiento, osadía

dark [dɑ:k] adj oscuro; (hair, complexion) moreno ▷ n: **in the ~ a** oscuras; **in the ~ about** (fig) ignorante de; **after ~** después del anochecer; **darken** vt (colour) hacer más oscuro ▷ vi oscurecerse; **darkness** n oscuridad f; **darkroom** n cuarto oscuro

darling [ˈdɑ:lɪŋ] adj, n querido/a

dart [dɑ:t] n dardo; (in sewing) pinza ▷ vi precipitarse; **dartboard** n diana; **darts** n dardos mpl

dash [dæʃ] n (small quantity: of liquid) gota, chorrito; (sign) raya ▷ vt (hopes) defraudar ▷ vi precipitarse, ir de prisa

dashboard [ˈdæʃbɔ:d] n (Aut) salpicadero

data [ˈdeɪtə] npl datos mpl; **database** n base f de datos; **data processing** n proceso or procesamiento de datos

date [deɪt] n (day) fecha; (with friend) cita; (fruit) dátil m ▷ vt fechar; (inf: girl etc) salir con; **~ of birth** fecha de nacimiento; **to ~** adv hasta la fecha; **dated** adj anticuado

daughter [ˈdɔ:tə*] n hija; **daughter-in-law** n nuera, hija política

daunting [ˈdɔ:ntɪŋ] adj desalentador/a

dawn [dɔ:n] n alba, amanecer m; (fig) nacimiento ▷ vi amanecer; (fig): **it ~ed on him that ...** cayó en la cuenta de que ...

day [deɪ] n día m; (working day) jornada; **the ~ before** el día anterior; **the ~ after tomorrow** pasado mañana; **the ~ before yesterday** anteayer; **the following ~** el día siguiente; **by ~** de día; **day-care centre** n centro de día; (for children) guardería infantil; **daydream** vi soñar despierto; **daylight** n luz f (del día); **day return** n (BRIT) billete m de ida y vuelta (en un día); **daytime** n día m; **day-to-day** adj cotidiano; **day trip** n excursión f (de un día)

dazed [deɪzd] adj aturdido

dazzle [ˈdæzl] vt deslumbrar; **dazzling** adj (light, smile) deslumbrante; (colour) fuerte

DC abbr (Elec) = **direct current**

dead [ded] adj muerto; (limb) dormido; (battery) agotado ▷ adv (completely) totalmente; (exactly) justo; **to shoot sb ~** matar a algn a tiros; **~ tired** muerto (de cansancio); **to stop ~** parar en seco; **dead end** n callejón m sin salida; **deadline** n fecha tope; **deadly** adj mortal, fatal; **deadly dull** aburridísimo; **Dead Sea** n: **the Dead Sea** el Mar Muerto

deaf [def] adj sordo; **deafen** vt ensordecer; **deafening** adj ensordecedor/a

deal [di:l] n (agreement) pacto, convenio ▷ vt (pt, pp **dealt**) dar; (card) repartir; **a great ~ (of)** bastante, mucho; **deal with** vt fus (people) tratar con; (problem) ocuparse de; (subject) tratar de; **dealer** n comerciante mf; (Cards) mano f; **dealings** npl (Comm) transacciones fpl; (relations) relaciones fpl

dealt [delt] pt, pp of **deal**

dean [di:n] n (Rel) deán m; (Scol) decano/a

dear [dɪəʳ] adj querido; (expensive) caro ▷ n: **my ~** querido/a; **~ me!** ¡Dios mío!; **D~ Sir/Madam** (in letter) Muy señor mío, Estimado señor/Estimada señora, De mi/nuestra (mayor) consideración (esp LAm); **D~ Mr/Mrs X** Estimado/a señor(a) X; **dearly** adv (love) mucho; (pay) caro

death [deθ] n muerte f; **death penalty** n pena de muerte; **death sentence** n condena a muerte

debate [dɪ'beɪt] n debate m ▷ vt discutir

debit ['debɪt] n debe m ▷ vt: **to ~ a sum to sb** or **to sb's account** cargar una suma en cuenta a algn; **debit card** n tarjeta f de débito

debris ['debri:] n escombros mpl

debt [det] n deuda; **to be in ~** tener deudas

debug ['di:'bʌg] vt (Comput) depurar, limpiar

début ['deɪbju:] n presentación f

Dec. abbr (= December) dic

decade ['dekeɪd] n década, decenio

decaffeinated [dɪ'kæfɪneɪtɪd] adj descafeinado

decay [dɪ'keɪ] n (of building) desmoronamiento m; (of tooth) caries f inv ▷ vi (rot) pudrirse

deceased [dɪ'si:st] n: **the ~** el/la difunto/a

deceit [dɪ'si:t] n engaño

deceive [dɪ'si:v] vt engañar

December [dɪ'sembəʳ] n diciembre m

decency ['di:sənsɪ] n decencia

decent ['di:sənt] adj (proper) decente; (person) amable, bueno

deception [dɪ'sepʃən] n engaño
Be careful not to translate *deception* by the Spanish word *decepción*.

deceptive [dɪ'septɪv] adj engañoso

decide [dɪ'saɪd] vt (person) decidir; (question, argument) resolver ▷ vi decidir; **to ~ to do/that** decidir hacer/que; **to ~ on sth** tomar una decisión sobre algo

decimal ['desɪməl] adj decimal ▷ n decimal f

decision [dɪ'sɪʒən] n decisión f

decisive [dɪ'saɪsɪv] adj decisivo; (manner, person) decidido

deck [dek] n (Naut) cubierta; (of bus) piso; (of cards) baraja; **record ~** n platina; **deckchair** n tumbona

declaration [deklə'reɪʃən] n declaración f

declare [dɪ'kleəʳ] vt declarar

decline [dɪ'klaɪn] n disminución f ▷ vt rehusar ▷ vi (person, business) decaer; (strength) disminuir

decorate ['dekəreɪt] vt (paint) pintar; (paper) empapelar; (adorn) **to ~ (with)** adornar (de), decorar (de); **decoration** n adorno; (act) decoración f; (medal) condecoración f; **decorator** n (workman) pintor m decorador

decrease ['di:kri:s] n disminución f ▷ vt [di:'kri:s] disminuir, reducir ▷ vi reducirse

decree [dɪ'kri:] n decreto

dedicate ['dedɪkeɪt] vt dedicar; **dedicated** adj dedicado; (Comput) especializado; **dedicated word processor** procesador m de textos especializado or dedicado; **dedication** n (devotion) dedicación f; (in book) dedicatoria

deduce [dɪ'dju:s] vt deducir

deduct [dɪ'dʌkt] vt restar; (from wage etc) descontar; **deduction** n (amount deducted) descuento; (conclusion) deducción f, conclusión f

deed [di:d] n hecho, acto; (feat) hazaña; (Law) escritura

deem [di:m] vt (formal) juzgar, considerar

deep [di:p] adj profundo; (voice) bajo; (breath) profundo ▷ adv: **the spectators stood 20 ~** los espectadores se formaron de 20 en fondo; **to be four metres ~** tener cuatro metros de profundidad;

deep-fry vt freír en aceite abundante; **deeply** adv (breathe) a pleno pulmón; (interested, moved, grateful) profundamente, hondamente

deer (pl **deer**) [dɪə'] n ciervo

default [dɪ'fɔːlt] n (Comput) defecto; **by ~** por incomparecencia

defeat [dɪ'fi:t] n derrota ▷ vt derrotar, vencer

defect ['di:fekt] n defecto ▷ vi [dɪ'fekt]: **to ~ to the enemy** pasarse al enemigo; **defective** [dɪ'fektɪv] adj defectuoso

defence, (US) **defense** [dɪ'fɛns] n defensa

defend [dɪ'fɛnd] vt defender; **defendant** n acusado/a; (in civil case) demandado/a; **defender** n defensor(a) m/f; (Sport) defensa mf

defense [dɪ'fɛns] n (US) = **defence**

defensive [dɪ'fɛnsɪv] adj defensivo ▷ n: **on the ~** a la defensiva

defer [dɪ'fə:'] vt aplazar

defiance [dɪ'faɪəns] n desafío; **in ~ of** en contra de; **defiant** [dɪ'faɪənt] adj (challenge) retador(a), desafiante

deficiency [dɪ'fɪʃənsɪ] n (lack) falta; (defect) defecto; **deficient** [dɪ'fɪʃənt] adj (lacking) insuficiente; **deficient in** deficiente en

deficit ['dɛfɪsɪt] n déficit m

define [dɪ'faɪn] vt definir; (limits etc) determinar

definite ['dɛfɪnɪt] adj (fixed) determinado; (clear, obvious) claro; **he was ~ about it** no dejó lugar a dudas (sobre ello); **definitely** adv: **he's definitely mad** no cabe duda de que está loco

definition [dɛfɪ'nɪʃən] n definición f

deflate [di:'fleɪt] vt desinflar

deflect [dɪ'flekt] vt desviar

defraud [dɪ'frɔːd] vt: **to ~ sb of sth** estafar algo a algn

defriend [di:'frend] vt (Internet) quitar de amigo a; **he has ~ed me on Facebook** la ha quitado de amiga en Facebook

defrost [di:'frɔst] vt (frozen food, fridge) descongelar

defuse [di:'fju:z] vt desarmar; (situation) calmar

defy [dɪ'faɪ] vt (resist) oponerse a; (challenge) desafiar; **it defies description** resulta imposible describirlo

degree [dɪ'gri:] n grado; (Scol) título; **to have a ~ in maths** ser licenciado/a en matemáticas; **by ~s** (gradually) poco a poco, por etapas; **to some ~** hasta cierto punto

dehydrated [di:haɪ'dreɪtɪd] adj deshidratado; (milk) en polvo

de-icer [di:'aɪsə'] n descongelador m

delay [dɪ'leɪ] vt demorar, aplazar; (person) entretener; (train) retrasar ▷ vi tardar ▷ n demora, retraso; **without ~** en seguida, sin tardar

delegate ['dɛlɪgɪt] n delegado/a ▷ vt ['dɛlɪgeɪt] (person) delegar en; (task) delegar

delete [dɪ'li:t] vt suprimir, tachar

deli ['dɛlɪ] n = **delicatessen**

deliberate [dɪ'lɪbərɪt] adj (intentional) intencionado; (slow) pausado, lento ▷ vi [dɪ'lɪbəreɪt] deliberar; **deliberately** adv (on purpose) a propósito

delicacy ['dɛlɪkəsɪ] n delicadeza; (choice food) manjar m

delicate ['dɛlɪkɪt] adj delicado; (fragile) frágil

delicatessen [dɛlɪkə'tesn] n tienda especializada en alimentos de calidad

delicious [dɪ'lɪʃəs] adj delicioso

delight [dɪ'laɪt] n (feeling) placer m, deleite m; (object) encanto, delicia ▷ vt encantar, deleitar; **to**

take ~ **in** deleitarse en; **delighted** adj: **delighted (at** or **with/to do)** encantado (con/de hacer); **delightful** adj encantador(a), delicioso

delinquent [dɪ'lɪŋkwənt] adj, n delincuente mf

deliver [dɪ'lɪvə*] vt (distribute) repartir; (hand over) entregar; (message) comunicar; (speech) pronunciar; (Med) asistir al parto de; **delivery** n reparto; entrega; (of speaker) modo de expresarse; (Med) parto, alumbramiento; **to take delivery of** recibir

delusion [dɪ'lu:ʒən] n ilusión f, engaño

de luxe [də'lʌks] adj de lujo

delve [dɛlv] vi: **to ~ into** hurgar en

demand [dɪ'mɑ:nd] vt exigir; (rights) reclamar ▷ n exigencia; (claim) reclamación f; (Econ) demanda; **to be in ~** ser muy solicitado; **on ~** a solicitud; **demanding** adj (boss) exigente; (work) absorbente

demise [dɪ'maɪz] n (death) fallecimiento

demo ['dɛməʊ] n abbr (inf: = demonstration) manifestación f

democracy [dɪ'mɒkrəsɪ] n democracia

democrat ['dɛməkræt] n demócrata mf; **democratic** [dɛmə'krætɪk] adj democrático; **the Democratic Party** el partido demócrata (estadounidense)

demolish [dɪ'mɒlɪʃ] vt derribar, demoler; (fig: argument) destruir

demolition [dɛmə'lɪʃən] n derribo, demolición f

demon ['di:mən] n (evil spirit) demonio

demonstrate ['dɛmənstreɪt] vt demostrar ▷ vi manifestarse; **demonstration** [dɛmən'streɪʃən] n (Pol) manifestación f; (proof) prueba, demostración f; **demonstrator** n (Pol) manifestante mf

demote [dɪ'məʊt] vt degradar

den [dɛn] n (of animal) guarida

denial [dɪ'naɪəl] n (refusal) denegación f; (of report etc) desmentido

denim ['dɛnɪm] n tela vaquera; **denims** npl vaqueros mpl

Denmark ['dɛnmɑ:k] n Dinamarca

denomination [dɪnɒmɪ'neɪʃən] n valor m; (Rel) confesión f

denounce [dɪ'naʊns] vt denunciar

dense [dɛns] adj (thick) espeso; (foliage etc) tupido; (stupid) torpe

density ['dɛnsɪtɪ] n densidad f; **single/double-~ disk** n (Comput) disco de densidad sencilla/de doble densidad

dent [dɛnt] n abolladura ▷ vt (also: **make a ~ in**) abollar

dental ['dɛntl] adj dental; **dental floss** n seda dental; **dental surgery** n clínica dental, consultorio dental

dentist ['dɛntɪst] n dentista mf

dentures ['dɛntʃəz] npl dentadura sg (postiza)

deny [dɪ'naɪ] vt negar; (charge) rechazar

deodorant [di:'əʊdərənt] n desodorante m

depart [dɪ'pɑ:t] vi irse, marcharse; (train) salir; **to ~ from** (fig: differ from) apartarse de

department [dɪ'pɑ:tmənt] n (Comm) sección f; (Scol) departamento; (Pol) ministerio; **department store** n grandes almacenes mpl

departure [dɪ'pɑ:tʃə*] n partida, ida; (of train) salida; **a new ~** un nuevo rumbo; **departure lounge** n (at airport) sala de embarque

depend [dɪ'pɛnd] vi: **to ~ (up)on** depender de; (rely on) contar con; **it ~s** depende, según; **~ing on the result** según el resultado; **dependant** n dependiente mf; **dependent** adj: **to be dependent (on)** depender (de) ▷ n = **dependant**

depict [dɪ'pɪkt] vt (in picture) pintar; (describe) representar

deport [dɪ'pɔ:t] vt deportar

deposit [dɪ'pɔzɪt] n depósito; (Chem) sedimento; (of ore, oil) yacimiento ▷ vt depositar; **deposit account** n (BRIT) cuenta de ahorros

depot ['depəu] n (storehouse) depósito; (for vehicles) parque m

depreciate [dɪ'priːʃɪeɪt] vi depreciarse, perder valor

depress [dɪ'prɛs] vt deprimir; (press down) apretar; **depressed** adj deprimido; **depressing** adj deprimente; **depression** n depresión f

deprive [dɪ'praɪv] vt: **to ~ sb of** privar a algn de; **deprived** adj necesitado

dept. abbr (= department) dto

depth [dɛpθ] n profundidad f; **at a ~ of three metres** a tres metros de profundidad; **to be out of one's ~** (swimmer) perder pie; (fig) sentirse perdido

deputy ['dɛpjutɪ] adj: **~ head** subdirector(a) m/f ▷ n sustituto/a, suplente m/f; (Pol) diputado/a

derail [dɪ'reɪl] vt: **to be ~ed** descarrilarse

derelict ['dɛrɪlɪkt] adj abandonado

derive [dɪ'raɪv] vt derivar; (benefit etc) obtener ▷ vi: **to ~ from** derivarse de

descend [dɪ'sɛnd] vt, vi descender, bajar; **to ~ from** descender de; **descendant** n descendiente mf

descent [dɪ'sɛnt] n descenso; (origin) descendencia

describe [dɪs'kraɪb] vt describir; **description** [dɪs'krɪpʃən] n descripción f; (sort) clase f, género

desert [n 'dɛzət, vt, vi dɪ'zəːt] n desierto ▷ vt abandonar ▷ vi (Mil) desertar; **deserted** adj desierto

deserve [dɪ'zəːv] vt merecer, ser digno de

design [dɪ'zaɪn] n (sketch) bosquejo; (of dress, car) diseño; (pattern) dibujo ▷ vt diseñar; **design and technology** n (BRIT Scol) diseño y tecnología

designate ['dɛzɪgneɪt] vt (appoint) nombrar; (destine) designar ▷ adj ['dɛzɪgnɪt] designado

designer [dɪ'zaɪnəʳ] n diseñador/a (m/f)

desirable [dɪ'zaɪərəbl] adj (proper) deseable; (attractive) atractivo

desire [dɪ'zaɪəʳ] n deseo ▷ vt desear

desk [dɛsk] n (in office) escritorio; (for pupil) pupitre m; (in hotel, at airport) recepción f; (BRIT: in shop, restaurant) caja

desktop ['dɛsktɔp] n (Comput) escritorio; **desktop publishing** n autoedición f

despair [dɪs'pɛəʳ] n desesperación f ▷ vi: **to ~ of** desesperar de

despatch [dɪs'pætʃ] n, vt = **dispatch**

desperate ['dɛspərɪt] adj desesperado; (fugitive) peligroso; **to be ~ for sth/to do** necesitar urgentemente algo/hacer; **desperately** adv desesperadamente; (very) terriblemente, gravemente

desperation [dɛspə'reɪʃən] n desesperación f; **in ~** desesperado

despise [dɪs'paɪz] vt despreciar

despite [dɪs'paɪt] prep a pesar de, pese a

dessert [dɪ'zəːt] n postre m; **dessertspoon** n cuchara (de postre)

destination [dɛstɪ'neɪʃən] n destino

destined ['dɛstɪnd] adj: **~ for London** con destino a Londres

destiny ['dɛstɪnɪ] n destino

destroy [dɪs'trɔɪ] vt destruir; **destruction** [dɪs'trʌkʃən] n destrucción f

destructive [dɪs'trʌktɪv] adj destructivo, destructor(a)

detach [dɪ'tætʃ] vt separar; (unstick) despegar; **detached** adj (attitude) objetivo, imparcial; **detached house** n chalé m, chalet m

detail ['diːteɪl] n detalle m ▷ vt detallar; (Mil) destacar; **in ~** detalladamente; **to go into ~(s)** entrar en detalles; **detailed** adj detallado

detain [dɪ'teɪn] vt retener; (in captivity) detener

detect [dɪ'tɛkt] vt descubrir; (Med, Police) identificar; (Mil, Radar, Tech) detectar; **detection** n descubrimiento; identificación f; **detective** n detective m; **detective story** n novela policíaca

detention [dɪ'tɛnʃən] n detención f, arresto; (Scol) castigo

deter [dɪ'tɜː'] vt (dissuade) disuadir

detergent [dɪ'tɜːdʒənt] n detergente m

deteriorate [dɪ'tɪərɪəreɪt] vi deteriorarse

determination [dɪtəːmɪ'neɪʃən] n resolución f

determine [dɪ'tɜːmɪn] vt determinar; **determined** adj: **to be determined to do sth** estar decidido or resuelto a hacer algo

deterrent [dɪ'tɛrənt] n fuerza de disuasión

detest [dɪ'tɛst] vt aborrecer

detour ['diːtuə'] n (us Aut: diversion) desvío

detract [dɪ'trækt] vt: **to ~ from** quitar mérito a, restar valor a

detrimental [dɛtrɪ'mɛntl] adj: **~ (to)** perjudicial a

devastating ['dɛvəsteɪtɪŋ] adj devastador/a; (fig) arrollador/a

develop [dɪ'vɛləp] vt desarrollar; (Phot) revelar; (disease) contraer; (habit) adquirir ▷ vi desarrollarse; (advance) progresar; **developing country** n país m en (vías de) desarrollo; **development** n desarrollo; (advance) progreso; (of affair, case) desenvolvimiento; (of land) urbanización f

device [dɪ'vaɪs] n (apparatus) aparato, mecanismo

devil ['dɛvl] n diablo, demonio

devious ['diːvɪəs] adj taimado

devise [dɪ'vaɪz] vt idear, inventar

devote [dɪ'vəut] vt: **to ~ sth to** dedicar algo a; **devoted** adj (loyal) leal, fiel; **to be devoted to sb** querer con devoción a algn; **the book is**

devoted to politics el libro trata de política; **devotion** n dedicación f; (Rel) devoción f

devour [dɪ'vauə'] vt devorar

devout [dɪ'vaut] adj devoto

dew [djuː] n rocío

diabetes [daɪə'biːtiːz] n diabetes f

diabetic [daɪə'bɛtɪk] n diabético/a

diagnose ['daɪəgnəuz] vt diagnosticar

diagnosis (pl **diagnoses**) [daɪəg'nəusɪs, -siːz] n diagnóstico

diagonal [daɪ'ægənl] adj diagonal ▷ n diagonal f

diagram ['daɪəgræm] n diagrama m, esquema m

dial ['daɪəl] n esfera; (of radio) dial; (of phone) disco ▷ vt (number) marcar

dialect ['daɪəlɛkt] n dialecto

dialling code ['daɪəlɪŋ-] n prefijo

dialling tone n señal f or tono de marcar

dialogue, (us)**dialog** ['daɪəlɔg] n diálogo

diameter [daɪ'æmɪtə'] n diámetro

diamond ['daɪəmənd] n diamante m; **diamonds** npl (Cards) diamantes npl

diaper ['daɪəpə'] n (us) pañal m

diarrhoea, (us)**diarrhea** [daɪə'riːə] n diarrea

diary ['daɪərɪ] n (daily account) diario; (book) agenda

dice [daɪs] n (pl inv) dados mpl ▷ vt (Culin) cortar en cuadritos

dictate [dɪk'teɪt] vt dictar; **dictation** n dictado

dictator [dɪk'teɪtə'] n dictador m

dictionary ['dɪkʃənrɪ] n diccionario

did [dɪd] pt of **do**

didn't ['dɪdnt] = **did not**

die [daɪ] vi morir; **to be dying for sth/to do sth** morirse por algo/de ganas de hacer algo; **die down** vi apagarse; (wind) amainar; **die out** vi desaparecer

diesel ['diːzl] n diesel m

diet ['daɪət] n dieta; (restricted food) régimen m ▷ vi (also: **be on a ~**) estar a dieta, hacer régimen

differ ['dɪfə*] vi (be different) ser distinto, diferenciarse; (disagree) discrepar; **difference** n ['dɪfrəns] n diferencia; (quarrel) desacuerdo; **different** adj diferente, distinto; **differentiate** [dɪfə'rɛnʃɪeɪt] vi: **to ~ between** distinguir entre; **differently** adv de otro modo, en forma distinta

difficult ['dɪfɪkəlt] adj difícil; **difficulty** n dificultad f

dig [dɪg] vt (pt, pp **dug**) (hole) cavar; (ground) remover ⊳ n (prod) empujón m; (archaeological) excavación f; (remark) indirecta; **to ~ one's nails into** clavar las uñas en; see also **digs**; **dig up** vt desenterrar; (plant) desarraigar

digest [daɪ'dʒɛst] vt (food) digerir; (facts) asimilar ⊳ n ['daɪdʒɛst] resumen m; **digestion** n digestión f

digit ['dɪdʒɪt] n (number) dígito; (finger) dedo; **digital** adj digital; **digital camera** n cámara digital; **digital TV** n televisión f digital

dignified ['dɪgnɪfaɪd] adj grave, solemne

dignity ['dɪgnɪtɪ] n dignidad f

digs [dɪgz] npl (BRIT inf) pensión f, alojamiento

dilemma [daɪ'lɛmə] n dilema m

dill [dɪl] n eneldo

dilute [daɪ'luːt] vt diluir

dim [dɪm] adj (light) débil; (outline) borroso; (stupid) lerdo; (room) oscuro ⊳ vt (light) bajar

dime [daɪm] n (us) moneda de diez centavos

dimension [dɪ'mɛnʃən] n dimensión f

diminish [dɪ'mɪnɪʃ] vt, vi disminuir

din [dɪn] n estruendo, estrépito

dine [daɪn] vi cenar; **diner** n (person) comensal mf

dinghy ['dɪŋgɪ] n bote m; (also: **rubber ~**) lancha (neumática)

dingy ['dɪndʒɪ] adj (room) sombrío; (dirty) sucio

dining car ['daɪnɪŋ-] n (BRIT) coche-restaurante m

dining room n comedor m

dining table n mesa f de comedor

dinkum ['dɪŋkəm] adj (AUST, NZ inf: also: **fair ~**) de verdad, auténtico; **fair ~?** ¿de verdad?

dinner ['dɪnə*] n (evening meal) cena; (lunch) comida; (public) cena, banquete m; **dinner jacket** n smoking m; **dinner party** n cena; **dinner time** n (evening) hora de cenar; (midday) hora de comer

dinosaur ['daɪnəsɔː*] n dinosaurio

dip [dɪp] n (slope) pendiente f; (in sea) chapuzón m ⊳ vt (in water) mojar; (ladle etc) meter; (BRIT AUT): **to ~ one's lights** poner la luz de cruce ⊳ vi descender, bajar

diploma [dɪ'pləʊmə] n diploma m

diplomacy [dɪ'pləʊməsɪ] n diplomacia

diplomat ['dɪpləmæt] n diplomático/a; **diplomatic** [dɪplə'mætɪk] adj diplomático

dipstick ['dɪpstɪk] n (Aut) varilla de nivel (del aceite)

dire [daɪə*] adj calamitoso

direct [daɪ'rɛkt] adj directo; (manner, person) franco ⊳ vt dirigir; **can you ~ me to ...?** ¿puede indicarme dónde está ...?; **to ~ sb to do sth** mandar a algn hacer algo; **direct debit** n domiciliación f bancaria de recibos

direction [dɪ'rɛkʃən] n dirección f; **sense of ~** sentido de la orientación; **directions** npl instrucciones fpl; **~s for use** modo de empleo

directly [dɪ'rɛktlɪ] adv (in straight line) directamente; (at once) en seguida

director [dɪ'rɛktə*] n director(a) m/f

directory [dɪ'rɛktərɪ] n (Tel) guía (telefónica); (Comput) directorio; **directory enquiries**, (us) **directory assistance** n (service) (servicio m de) información

dirt [dɜːt] n suciedad f; **dirty** adj sucio; (joke) verde, colorado (LAM) ⊳ vt ensuciar; (stain) manchar

disability [dɪsə'bɪlɪtɪ] n incapacidad f

disabled [dɪsˈeɪbld] adj (physically) minusválido/a; (mentally) deficiente mental

disadvantage [dɪsədˈvɑːntɪdʒ] n desventaja, inconveniente m

disagree [dɪsəˈɡriː] vi (differ) discrepar; **to ~ (with)** no estar de acuerdo (con); **disagreeable** adj desagradable; **disagreement** n desacuerdo

disappear [dɪsəˈpɪəʳ] vi desaparecer; **disappearance** n desaparición f

disappoint [dɪsəˈpɔɪnt] vt decepcionar; defraudar; **disappointed** adj decepcionado; **disappointing** adj decepcionante; **disappointment** n decepción f

disapproval [dɪsəˈpruːvəl] n desaprobación f

disapprove [dɪsəˈpruːv] vi: **to ~ of** desaprobar

disarm [dɪsˈɑːm] vt desarmar; **disarmament** n desarme m

disaster [dɪˈzɑːstəʳ] n desastre m

disastrous [dɪˈzɑːstrəs] adj desastroso

disbelief [dɪsbəˈliːf] n incredulidad f

disc [dɪsk] n disco (Comput); = **disk**

discard [dɪsˈkɑːd] vt tirar; (fig) descartar

discharge vt [dɪsˈtʃɑːdʒ] (task, duty) cumplir; (patient) dar de alta; (employee) despedir; (soldier) licenciar; (defendant) poner en libertad ▷ n [ˈdɪstʃɑːdʒ] (Elec) descarga; (dismissal) despedida; (of duty) desempeño; (of debt) pago, descargo

discipline [ˈdɪsɪplɪn] n disciplina ▷ vt disciplinar

disc jockey n pinchadiscos m inv f inv

disclose [dɪsˈkləʊz] vt revelar

disco [ˈdɪskəʊ] n abbr = **discothèque**

discoloured, (us) **discolored** [dɪsˈkʌləd] adj descolorido

discomfort [dɪsˈkʌmfət] n incomodidad f; (unease) inquietud f; (physical) malestar m

disconnect [dɪskəˈnɛkt] vt separar; (Elec etc) desconectar

discontent [dɪskənˈtɛnt] n descontento

discontinue [dɪskənˈtɪnjuː] vt interrumpir; (payments) suspender

discothèque [ˈdɪskəʊtɛk] n discoteca

discount [ˈdɪskaʊnt] n descuento ▷ vt [dɪsˈkaʊnt] descontar

discourage [dɪsˈkʌrɪdʒ] vt desalentar; **to ~ sb from doing** disuadir a algn de hacer

discover [dɪsˈkʌvəʳ] vt descubrir; **discovery** n descubrimiento

discredit [dɪsˈkrɛdɪt] vt desacreditar

discreet [dɪˈskriːt] adj (tactful) discreto; (careful) circunspecto, prudente

discrepancy [dɪˈskrɛpənsɪ] n (difference) diferencia

discretion [dɪˈskrɛʃən] n (tact) discreción f; **at the ~ of** a criterio de

discriminate [dɪˈskrɪmɪneɪt] vi: **to ~ between** distinguir entre; **to ~ against** discriminar contra; **discrimination** [dɪskrɪmɪˈneɪʃən] n (discernment) perspicacia; (bias) discriminación f

discuss [dɪsˈkʌs] vt discutir; (a theme) tratar; **discussion** n discusión f

disease [dɪˈziːz] n enfermedad f

disembark [dɪsɪmˈbɑːk] vt, vi desembarcar

disgrace [dɪsˈɡreɪs] n ignominia; (shame) vergüenza, escándalo ▷ vt deshonrar; **disgraceful** adj vergonzoso

disgruntled [dɪsˈɡrʌntld] adj disgustado, descontento

disguise [dɪsˈɡaɪz] n disfraz m ▷ vt disfrazar; **in ~** disfrazado

disgust [dɪsˈɡʌst] n repugnancia ▷ vt repugnar, dar asco a

■ Be careful not to translate disgust by the Spanish word disgustar.

disgusted [dɪsˈɡʌstɪd] adj indignado

■ Be careful not to translate disgusted by the Spanish word disgustado.

disgusting [dɪs'ɡʌstɪŋ] *adj*
repugnante, asqueroso

dish [dɪʃ] *n* plato; **to do** *or* **wash the
~es** fregar los platos; **dishcloth** *n*
(for washing) bayeta; (for drying) paño
de cocina

dishonest [dɪs'ɒnɪst] *adj* (person)
poco honrado, tramposo; (means)
fraudulento

dishtowel ['dɪʃtaʊəl] *n* (US) bayeta

dishwasher ['dɪʃwɒʃər] *n* lavaplatos
m inv

disillusion [dɪsɪ'lu:ʒən] *vt*
desilusionar

disinfectant [dɪsɪn'fɛktənt] *n*
desinfectante *m*

disintegrate [dɪs'ɪntɪɡreɪt] *vi*
disgregarse, desintegrarse

disk [dɪsk] *n* (Comput) disco, disquete
m; **single-/double-sided ~** disco
de una cara/dos caras; **disk drive**
n unidad *f* (de disco); **diskette** *n*
disquete *m*

dislike [dɪs'laɪk] *n* antipatía, aversión
f ⊳ *vt* tener antipatía a

dislocate ['dɪsləkeɪt] *vt* dislocar

disloyal [dɪs'lɔɪəl] *adj* desleal

dismal ['dɪzml] *adj* (dark) sombrío;
(depressing) triste; (very bad) fatal

dismantle [dɪs'mæntl] *vt*
desmontar, desarmar

dismay [dɪs'meɪ] *n* consternación *f*
⊳ *vt* consternar

dismiss [dɪs'mɪs] *vt* (worker) despedir;
(idea) rechazar; (Law) rechazar;
(possibility) descartar; **dismissal** *n*
despido

disobedient [dɪsə'bi:dɪənt] *adj*
desobediente

disobey [dɪsə'beɪ] *vt* desobedecer

disorder [dɪs'ɔ:dər] *n* desorden *m*;
(rioting) disturbio; (Med) trastorno

disorganized [dɪs'ɔ:ɡənaɪzd] *adj*
desorganizado

disown [dɪs'əʊn] *vt* renegar de

dispatch [dɪs'pætʃ] *vt* enviar ⊳ *n*
(sending) envío; (Press) informe *m*;
(Mil) parte *m*

dispel [dɪs'pɛl] *vt* disipar

dispense [dɪs'pɛns] *vt* (medicine)
preparar; **dispense with** *vt fus*
prescindir de; **dispenser** *n* (container)
distribuidor *m* automático

disperse [dɪs'pɜ:s] *vt* dispersar ⊳ *vi*
dispersarse

display [dɪs'pleɪ] *n* (in shop window)
escaparate *m*; (exhibition) exposición
f; (Comput) visualización *f*; (of feeling)
manifestación *f* ⊳ *vt* exponer;
manifestar; (ostentatiously) lucir

displease [dɪs'pli:z] *vt* (offend)
ofender; (annoy) fastidiar

disposable [dɪs'pəʊzəbl] *adj*
desechable; **~ personal income**
ingresos *mpl* personales disponibles

disposal [dɪs'pəʊzl] *n* (of rubbish)
destrucción *f*; **at one's ~** a la
disposición de algn

dispose [dɪs'pəʊz] *vi*: **~ of** (unwanted
goods) deshacerse de; (Comm: sell)
traspasar, vender

disposition [dɪspə'zɪʃən] *n*
disposición *f*; (temperament)
carácter *m*

disproportionate [dɪsprə'pɔ:ʃənət]
adj desproporcionado

dispute [dɪs'pju:t] *n* disputa; (also:
industrial ~) conflicto (laboral) ⊳ *vt*
(argue) disputar; (question) cuestionar

disqualify [dɪs'kwɒlɪfaɪ] *vt* (Sport)
desclasificar; **to ~ sb for sth/from
doing sth** incapacitar a algn para
algo/para hacer algo

disregard [dɪsrɪ'ɡɑ:d] *vt* (ignore) no
hacer caso de

disrupt [dɪs'rʌpt] *vt* (plans)
desbaratar, trastornar; (meeting, public
transport, conversation) interrumpir;
disruption *n* desbaratamiento;
trastorno; interrupción *f*

dissatisfaction [dɪssætɪs'fækʃən] *n*
disgusto, descontento

dissatisfied [dɪs'sætɪsfaɪd] *adj*
insatisfecho

dissect [dɪ'sɛkt] *vt* disecar

dissent [dɪ'sɛnt] *n* disensión *f*

dissertation [dɪsə'teɪʃən] n tesina

dissolve [dɪ'zɒlv] vt disolver ▷ vi disolverse

distance ['dɪstns] n distancia; **in the ~** a lo lejos

distant ['dɪstnt] adj lejano; (manner) reservado, frío

distil, (us) **distill** [dɪs'tɪl] vt destilar; **distillery** n destilería

distinct [dɪs'tɪŋkt] adj (different) distinto; (clear) claro; (unmistakeable) inequívoco; **as ~ from** a diferencia de; **distinction** n distinción f; (in exam) sobresaliente m; **distinctive** adj distintivo

distinguish [dɪs'tɪŋgwɪʃ] vt distinguir; **distinguished** adj (eminent) distinguido

distort [dɪs'tɔːt] vt deformar; (sound) distorsionar

distract [dɪs'trækt] vt distraer; **distracted** adj distraído; **distraction** n distracción f; (confusion) aturdimiento

distraught [dɪs'trɔːt] adj turbado, enloquecido

distress [dɪs'tres] n (anguish) angustia ▷ vt afligir; **distressing** adj angustioso; doloroso

distribute [dɪs'trɪbjuːt] vt distribuir; (share out) repartir; **distribution** [dɪstrɪ'bjuːʃən] n distribución f; **distributor** n (Aut) distribuidor m; (Comm) distribuidora

district ['dɪstrɪkt] n (of country) zona, región f; (of town) barrio; (Admin) distrito; **district attorney** n (us) fiscal mf

distrust [dɪs'trʌst] n desconfianza ▷ vt desconfiar de

disturb [dɪs'tɜːb] vt (person: bother, interrupt) molestar; (disorganize) desordenar; **disturbance** n (political etc) disturbio; (of mind) trastorno; **disturbed** adj (worried, upset) preocupado, angustiado; **to be emotionally/mentally disturbed** tener problemas emocionales/ser un

trastornado mental; **disturbing** adj inquietante, perturbador(a)

ditch [dɪtʃ] n zanja; (irrigation ditch) acequia ▷ vt (inf: partner) deshacerse de; (: plan, car etc) abandonar

ditto ['dɪtəu] adv ídem, lo mismo

dive [daɪv] n (from board) salto; (underwater) buceo; (of submarine) inmersión f ▷ vi (swimmer: into water) saltar; (: under water) zambullirse, bucear; (fish, submarine) sumergirse; (bird) lanzarse en picado; **to ~ into** (bag etc) meter la mano en; (place) meterse de prisa en; **diver** n (underwater) buzo

diverse [daɪ'vəːs] adj diversos/as, varios/as

diversion [daɪ'vəːʃən] n (BRIT Aut) desviación f; (distraction) diversión f; (Mil) diversión f

diversity [daɪ'vəːsɪtɪ] n diversidad f

divert [daɪ'vəːt] vt (train, plane, traffic) desviar

divide [dɪ'vaɪd] vt dividir; (separate) separar ▷ vi dividirse; (road) bifurcarse; **divided highway** n (us) carretera de doble calzada

divine [dɪ'vaɪn] adj divino

diving ['daɪvɪŋ] n (Sport) salto; (underwater) buceo; **diving board** n trampolín m

division [dɪ'vɪʒən] n división f; (sharing out) reparto; (disagreement) diferencias fpl; (Comm) sección f

divorce [dɪ'vɔːs] n divorcio ▷ vt divorciarse de; **divorced** adj divorciado; **divorcee** [dɪvɔː'siː] n divorciado/a

DIY adj, n abbr = **do-it-yourself**

dizzy ['dɪzɪ] adj (person) mareado; **to feel ~** marearse

DJ n abbr (= disc jockey) DJ mf

DNA n abbr (= deoxyribonucleic acid) ADN m

 KEYWORD

do [duː] (pt did, pp done) n (inf: party etc): **we're having a little do on**

Saturday damos una fiestecita el sábado; **it was rather a grand do** fue un acontecimiento a lo grande
▷ aux vb **1** (in negative constructions, not translated): **I don't understand** no entiendo
2 (to form questions, not translated): **didn't you know?** ¿no lo sabías?; **what do you think?** ¿qué opinas?
3 (for emphasis, in polite expressions): **people do make mistakes sometimes** a veces sí se cometen errores; **she does seem rather late** a mí también me parece que se ha retrasado; **do sit down/help yourself** siéntate/sírvete por favor; **do take care!** ¡ten cuidado! ¿eh?
4 (used to avoid repeating vb): **she sings better than I do** canta mejor que yo; **do you agree?** — **yes, I do/no, I don't** ¿estás de acuerdo? — sí (lo estoy)/no (lo estoy); **she lives in Glasgow — so do I** vive en Glasgow — yo también; **he didn't like it and neither did we** no le gustó y a nosotros tampoco; **who made this mess?** — **I did** ¿quién hizo esta chapuza? — yo; **he asked me to help him and I did** me pidió que le ayudara y lo hice
5 (in question tags): **you like him, don't you?** te gusta, ¿verdad? or ¿no?; **I don't know him, do I?** creo que no le conozco
▷ vt **1**: **what are you doing tonight?** ¿qué haces esta noche?; **what can I do for you?** (in shop) ¿en qué puedo servirle?; **to do the washing-up/cooking** fregar los platos/cocinar; **to do one's teeth/hair/nails** lavarse los dientes/arreglarse el pelo/arreglarse las uñas
2 (Aut etc): **the car was doing 100** el coche iba a 100; **we've done 200 km already** ya hemos hecho 200 km; **can I do 100 in that car?** puede ir a 100 en ese coche
▷ vi **1** (act, behave) hacer; **do as I do** haz como yo

2 (get on, fare): **he's doing well/badly at school** le va bien/mal en la escuela; **the firm is doing well** la empresa anda or va bien; **how do you do?** mucho gusto; (less formal) ¿qué tal?
3 (suit): **will it do?** ¿sirve?, ¿está or va bien?
4 (be sufficient) bastar; **will £10 do?** ¿será bastante con £10?; **that'll do** así está bien; **that'll do!** (in annoyance) ¡ya está bien!, ¡basta ya!; **to make do (with)** arreglárselas (con)
do up vt (laces) atar; (zip, dress, shirt) abrochar; (renovate: room, house) renovar
do with vt fus (need): **I could do with a drink/some help** no me vendría mal un trago/un poco de ayuda; (be connected with) tener que ver con; **what has it got to do with you?** ¿qué tiene que ver contigo?
do without vi: **if you're late for dinner then you'll do without** si llegas tarde tendrás que quedarte sin cenar ▷ vt fus pasar sin; **I can do without a car** puedo pasar sin coche

dock [dɔk] n (Naut) muelle m; (Law) banquillo (de los acusados) ▷ vi (enter dock) atracar (en el muelle); **docks** npl muelles mpl, puerto sg

doctor [ˈdɔktəʳ] n médico, -a m/f ▷ vt (drink etc) adulterar; **Doctor of Philosophy** n Doctor m (en Filosofía y Letras)

document [ˈdɔkjumənt] n documento; **documentary** [dɔkjuˈmɛntəri] adj documental ▷ n documental m; **documentation** [dɔkjumenˈteɪʃən] n documentación f

dodge [dɔdʒ] n (fig) truco ▷ vt evadir; (blow) esquivar

dodgy [ˈdɔdʒi] adj (BRIT inf: uncertain) dudoso; (shady) sospechoso; (risky) arriesgado

does [dʌz] vb see **do**

doesn't [ˈdʌznt] = **does not**

dog [dɒg] n perro ▷ vt seguir (de cerca); (memory etc) perseguir; **doggy bag** n bolsa para llevarse las sobras de la comida

do-it-yourself [duːɪtjɔː'self] n bricolaje m

dole [dəul] n (BRIT: payment) subsidio de paro; **on the ~** parado; **dole out** vt repartir

doll [dɒl] n muñeca

dollar ['dɒləʳ] n dólar m

dolphin ['dɒlfin] n delfín m

dome [dəum] n (Arch) cúpula

domestic [də'mestɪk] adj (animal, duty) doméstico; (flight, news, policy) nacional; **domestic appliance** n aparato m doméstico, aparato m de uso doméstico

dominant ['dɒmɪnənt] adj dominante

dominate ['dɒmɪneɪt] vt dominar

domino ['dɒmɪnəu] (pl **dominoes**) n ficha de dominó; **dominoes** n (game) dominó

donate [də'neɪt] vt donar; **donation** n donativo

done [dʌn] pp of **do**

donkey ['dɒŋkɪ] n burro

donor ['dəunəʳ] n donante mf; **donor card** n carnet m de donante de órganos

don't [dəunt] = **do not**

doodle ['duːdl] vi pintar dibujitos o garabatos

doom [duːm] n (fate) suerte f ▷ vt: **to be ~ed to failure** estar condenado al fracaso

door [dɔːʳ] n puerta; **doorbell** n timbre m; **door handle** n tirador m; (of car) manija; **doorknob** n pomo m de la puerta, manilla f (LAM); **doorstep** n peldaño; **doorway** n entrada, puerta

dope [dəup] n (inf: illegal drug) droga; (: person) imbécil mf ▷ vt (horse etc) drogar

dormitory ['dɔːmɪtrɪ] n (BRIT) dormitorio; (US) colegio mayor

DOS [dɒs] n abbr = **disk operating system**

dosage ['dəusɪdʒ] n dosis f inv

dose [dəus] n dosis f inv

dot [dɒt] n punto ▷ vi: **-ted with** salpicado de; **on the ~** en punto; **dotcom** n puntocom f; **dotted line** n: **to sign on the dotted line** firmar

double ['dʌbl] adj ▷ adv (twice): **to cost ~** costar el doble ▷ n doble m ▷ vi doblar ▷ vi doblarse; **on the ~**, (BRIT) **at the ~** corriendo; **double back** vi (person) volver sobre sus pasos; **double bass** n contrabajo; **double bed** n cama de matrimonio; **double-check** vt volver a revisar ▷ vi: **I'll double-check** voy a revisarlo otra vez; **double-click** vi (Comput) hacer doble clic; **double-cross** vt (trick) engañar; (betray) traicionar; **doubledecker** n autobús m de dos pisos; **double glazing** n (BRIT) doble acristalamiento; **double room** n habitación f doble; **doubles** n (Tennis) juego de dobles; **double yellow lines** npl (BRIT Aut) línea doble amarilla de prohibido aparcar = línea fsg amarilla continua

doubt [daut] n duda ▷ vt dudar; (suspect) dudar de; **to ~ that** dudar que; **doubtful** adj dudoso; (unconvinced): **to be doubtful about sth** tener dudas sobre algo; **doubtless** adv sin duda

dough [dəu] n masa, pasta; **doughnut** n dónut m

dove [dʌv] n paloma

down [daun] n (feathers) plumón m, flojel m; (hill) loma ▷ adv (also: **-wards**) abajo, hacia abajo; (on the ground) por/en tierra ▷ prep abajo ▷ vt (inf: drink) beberse; **~ with X!** ¡abajo X!; **down-and-out** n (tramp) vagabundo/a; **downfall** n caída, ruina; **downhill** adv: **to go downhill** ir cuesta abajo

Downing Street ['daunɪŋ-] n (BRIT) Downing Street f

Downing Street es la calle de Londres en la que tienen su residencia oficial tanto el Primer Ministro (*Prime Minister*) como el Ministro de Economía (*Chancellor of the Exchequer*). El primero vive en el nº 10 y el segundo en el nº 11. Es una calle cerrada al público que se encuentra en el barrio de Westminster, en el centro de Londres. *Downing Street* se usa también en lenguaje periodístico para referirse al jefe del gobierno británico.

down: download vt (*Comput*) descargar; **downloadable** *adj* (*Comput*) descargable; **downright** *adj* (*nonsense, lie*) manifiesto; (*refusal*) terminante

Down's syndrome [daunz-] *n* síndrome *m* de Down

down: downstairs *adv* (*below*) (en el piso de) abajo; (*motion*) escaleras abajo; **down-to-earth** *adj* práctico; **downtown** *adv* en el centro de la ciudad; **down under** *adv* en Australia (*or* Nueva Zelanda); **downward** ['daunwəd] *adj* hacia abajo; **downwards** ['daunwədz] *adv* hacia abajo

doz. *abbr* = **dozen**

doze [dəuz] *vi* dormitar

dozen ['dʌzn] *n* docena; **a ~ books** una docena de libros; **~s of** cantidad de

Dr, Dr. *abbr* (= *doctor*) Dr; (*in street names*) = **drive**

drab [dræb] *adj* gris, monótono

draft [drɑːft] *n* (*first copy*) borrador *m*; (*us: call-up*) quinta *f* ⊳ vt (*write roughly*) hacer un borrador de; *see also* **draught**

drag [dræg] vt arrastrar; (*river*) dragar, rastrear ⊳ vi arrastrarse por el suelo ⊳ n (*inf*) lata; (*women's clothing*): **in ~** vestido de mujer; **to ~ and drop** (*Comput*) arrastrar y soltar

dragon ['drægən] *n* dragón *m*

dragonfly ['drægənflaɪ] *n* libélula

drain [dreɪn] *n* desaguadero; (*in street*) sumidero ⊳ vt (*land, marshes*) desecar; (*reservoir*) desecar; (*fig*) agotar ⊳ vi escurrirse; **to be a ~ on** consumir, agotar; **drainage** *n* (*act*) desagüe *m*; (*Med, Agr*) drenaje *m*; (*sewage*) alcantarillado; **drainpipe** *n* tubo de desagüe

drama ['drɑːmə] *n* (*art*) teatro; (*play*) drama *m*; **dramatic** [drə'mætɪk] *adj* dramático; (*sudden, marked*) espectacular

drank [dræŋk] *pt of* **drink**

drape [dreɪp] vt (*cloth*) colocar; (*flag*) colgar

drastic ['dræstɪk] *adj* (*measure, reduction*) severo; (*change*) radical

draught, (us) **draft** [drɑːft] *n* (*of air*) corriente *f* de aire; (*Naut*) calado; **on ~** (*beer*) de barril; **draught beer** *n* cerveza de barril; **draughts** *n* (*BRIT*) juego de damas

draw [drɔː] (*pt* **drew**, *pp* **drawn**) vt (*take out*) sacar; (*attract*) atraer; (*picture*) dibujar; (*money*) retirar ⊳ vi (*Sport*) empatar ⊳ n (*Sport*) empate *m*; (*lottery*) sorteo; **draw out** vi (*lengthen*) alargarse; **draw up** vi (*stop*) pararse ⊳ vt (*document*) redactar; **drawback** *n* inconveniente *m*, desventaja

drawer *n* cajón *m*

drawing *n* dibujo; **drawing pin** *n* (*BRIT*) chincheta *m*; **drawing room** *n* salón *m*

drawn [drɔːn] *pp of* **draw**

dread [dred] *n* pavor *m*, terror *m* ⊳ vt temer, tener miedo *or* pavor a; **dreadful** *adj* espantoso

dream [driːm] *n* sueño ⊳ vt, vi soñar; **dreamer** *n* soñador(a) *m/f*

dreamt [dremt] *pt, pp of* **dream**

dreary ['drɪərɪ] *adj* monótono

drench [drentʃ] vt empapar

dress [dres] *n* vestido; (*clothing*) ropa ⊳ vt vestir; (*wound*) vendar ⊳ vi vestirse; **to ~ o.s., get ~ed** vestirse;

dress up vi vestirse de etiqueta; (in fancy dress) disfrazarse; dress circle n (BRIT) principal m; dresser n (furniture) aparador m; (: US) tocador m; dressing n (Med) vendaje m; (Culin) aliño; dressing gown n (LAM); driving instructor bata; dressing room n (Theat) camarín m; (Sport) vestuario; dressing table n tocador m; dressmaker n modista, costurera

drew [druː] pt of draw

dribble ['drɪbl] vi (baby) babear ▷ vt (ball) regatear

dried [draɪd] adj seco; (milk) en polvo

drier ['draɪə*] n = dryer

drift [drɪft] n (of current etc) flujo; (of snow) ventisquero; (meaning) significado ▷ vi (boat) ir a la deriva; (sand, snow) amontonarse

drill [drɪl] n taladro; (bit) broca; (of dentist) fresa; (for mining etc) perforadora, barrena; (Mil) instrucción f ▷ vt perforar, taladrar; (soldiers) ejercitar ▷ vi (for oil) perforar

drink [drɪŋk] n bebida ▷ vt, vi beber; to have a ~ tomar algo; tomar una copa o un trago; a ~ of water un trago de agua; drink-driving n: to be charged with drink-driving ser acusado de conducir borracho en un estado de embriaguez; drinker n bebedor(a) m/f; drinking water n agua potable

drip [drɪp] n (act) goteo; (one drip) gota; (Med) gota a gota m ▷ vi gotear

drive [draɪv] n (journey) viaje m (en coche); (also: ~way) entrada; (energy) energía, vigor m; (Comput: also: disk ~) unidad f (de disco) ▷ vt (car) conducir; (nail) clavar; (push) empujar; (Tech: motor) impulsar ▷ vi (Aut: at controls) conducir, manejar (LAM); (: travel) pasearse en coche; left-/right-hand ~ conducción f a la izquierda/derecha; to ~ sb mad volverle loco a algn; drive out vt (force out) expulsar, echar; drive-in adj (esp US): drive-in cinema autocine m

driven ['drɪvn] pp of drive

driver ['draɪvə*] n conductor(a) m/f, chofer m (LAM); driver's license n (US) carnet m or permiso de conducir

driveway ['draɪvweɪ] n camino de entrada

driving ['draɪvɪŋ] n conducir m, manejar m (LAM); driving instructor n instructor(a) m/f de autoescuela; driving lesson n clase f de conducir; driving licence n (BRIT) carnet m or permiso de conducir; driving test n examen m de conducir

drizzle ['drɪzl] n llovizna

droop [druːp] vi (flower) marchitarse; (shoulders) encorvarse; (head) inclinarse

drop [drɒp] n (of water) gota; (fall: in price) bajada ▷ vt dejar caer; (voice, eyes, price) bajar; (set down from car) dejar ▷ vi (object) caer; (price, temperature) bajar; (wind) amainar; drop in vi (inf: visit): to ~ in (on) pasar por casa (de); drop off vi (sleep) dormirse ▷ vt (passenger) dejar; drop out vi (withdraw) retirarse

drought [draʊt] n sequía

drove [drəʊv] pt of drive

drown [draʊn] vt ahogar ▷ vi ahogarse

drowsy ['draʊzɪ] adj soñoliento; to be ~ tener sueño

drug [drʌg] n medicamento; (narcotic) droga ▷ vt drogar; to be on ~s drogarse; drug addict n drogadicto/a m/f; drug dealer n traficante m/f de drogas; druggist n (US) farmacéutico/a; drugstore n (US) tienda de comestibles, periódicos y medicamentos

drum [drʌm] n tambor m; (for oil, petrol) bidón m; drums npl batería sg; drummer n tambor m

drunk [drʌŋk] pp of drink ▷ adj borracho ▷ n (also: drunkard) borracho/a m/f; drunken adj borracho

dry [draɪ] adj seco; (day) sin lluvia; (climate) árido, seco ▷ vt secar; (tears)

enjugarse ▷ *vi* secarse; **dry up** *vi* (*river*)
secarse; **dry-cleaner's** *n* tintorería;
dry-cleaning *n* lavado en seco; **dryer**
n (*for hair*) secador *m*; (*for clothes*)
secadora

DSS *n abbr* (BRIT) = **Department of
Social Security**; *see* **social security**

DTP *n abbr* = **desktop publishing**

dual ['djuəl] *adj* doble; **dual
carriageway** *n* (BRIT) autovía

dubious ['dju:bɪəs] *adj* (*questionable:
reputation*) dudoso; (: *character*)
sospechoso; (*unsure*) indeciso

duck [dʌk] *n* pato ▷ *vi* agacharse

due [dju:] *adj* (*proper*) debido ▷ *adv*: ~
north derecho al norte; **in ~ course** a
su debido tiempo; ~ **to** debido a; **the
train is ~ to arrive at 8.00** el tren
tiene (prevista) la llegada a las ocho;
the rent's ~ on the 30th hay que
pagar el alquiler el día 30

duel ['djuəl] *n* duelo

duet [dju:'ɛt] *n* dúo

dug [dʌg] *pt, pp of* **dig**

duke [dju:k] *n* duque *m*

dull [dʌl] *adj* (*light*) apagado; (*stupid*)
torpe; (*boring*) pesado; (*sound, pain*)
sordo; (*weather, day*) gris ▷ *vt* (*pain,
grief*) aliviar; (*mind, senses*) entorpecer

dumb [dʌm] *adj* mudo; (*stupid*)
estúpido

dummy ['dʌmɪ] *n* (*tailor's model*)
maniquí *m*; (BRIT: *for baby*) chupete *m*
▷ *adj* falso, postizo

dump [dʌmp] *n* (*place*) basurero,
vertedero ▷ *vt* (*put down*) dejar; (*get
rid of*) deshacerse de; (*Comput*) tirar (*en*
la papelera); (*Comm: goods*) inundar el
mercado de

dumpling ['dʌmplɪŋ] *n* bola de masa
hervida

dune [dju:n] *n* duna

dungarees [dʌŋgə'ri:z] *npl* mono *sg*,
overol *msg* (LAM)

dungeon ['dʌndʒən] *n* calabozo

duplex ['dju:plɛks] *n* dúplex *m*

duplicate ['dju:plɪkət] *n* duplicado
▷ *vt* ['dju:plɪkeɪt] duplicar; (*photocopy*)

fotocopiar; (*repeat*) repetir; **in ~** por
duplicado

durable ['djuərəbl] *adj* duradero

duration [djuə'reɪʃən] *n* duración *f*

during ['djuərɪŋ] *prep* durante

dusk [dʌsk] *n* crepúsculo, anochecer *m*

dust [dʌst] *n* polvo ▷ *vt* (*furniture*)
desempolvar; (*cake etc*) espolvorear
~ with espolvorear de; **dustbin** *n* (BRIT) cubo
de la basura, balde *m* (LAM); **duster** *n*
paño, trapo; **dustman** *n* basurero;
dustpan *n* cogedor *m*, pala; **dusty**
adj polvoriento

Dutch [dʌtʃ] *adj* holandés/esa
▷ *n* (*Ling*) holandés *m* ▷ *adv*: **to
go ~** pagar a escote; **the Dutch**
npl los holandeses; **Dutchman,
Dutchwoman** *n* holandés/esa *m/f*

duty ['dju:tɪ] *n* deber *m*; (*tax*) derechos
mpl de aduana; **on ~** de servicio;
(*at night etc*) de guardia; **off ~** libre
(de servicio); **duty-free** *adj* libre de
impuestos

duvet ['du:veɪ] *n* (BRIT) edredón *m*
(nórdico)

DVD *n abbr* (= *digital versatile or video
disc*) DVD *m*; **DVD player** *n* lector *m* de
DVD; **DVD writer** *n* grabadora de DVD

dwarf (*pl* **dwarves**) [dwɔ:f, dwɔ:vz] *n*
enano/a ▷ *vt* empequeñecer

dwell (*pt, pp* **dwelt**) [dwel, dwelt] *vi*
morar; **dwell on** *vt fus* explayarse en

dwindle ['dwɪndl] *vi* disminuir

dye [daɪ] *n* tinte *m* ▷ *vt* teñir

dying ['daɪɪŋ] *adj* moribundo

dynamic [daɪ'næmɪk] *adj* dinámico

dynamite ['daɪnəmaɪt] *n* dinamita

dyslexia [dɪs'lɛksɪə] *n* dislexia

dyslexic [dɪs'lɛksɪk] *adj, n* disléxico/a

e

E [iː] n (Mus) mi m

each [iːtʃ] adj cada uno; ~ **other** el uno a otro; **they hate ~ other** se odian (entre ellos or mutuamente)

eager ['iːgəʳ] adj (keen) entusiasmado; **to be ~ to do sth** estar deseoso de hacer algo; **to be ~ for** tener muchas ganas de

eagle ['iːgl] n águila

ear [ɪəʳ] n oreja; (sense of hearing) oído; (of corn) espiga; **earache** n dolor m de oídos; **eardrum** n tímpano

earl [əːl] n conde m

earlier ['əːlɪəʳ] adj anterior ▷ adv antes

early ['əːlɪ] adv temprano; (ahead of time) con tiempo, con anticipación ▷ adj temprano; (reply) pronto; (man) primitivo; (first: Christians, settlers) primero; **to have an ~ night** acostarse temprano; **in the ~ or ~ in the spring/19th century** a principios de primavera/del siglo diecinueve; **early retirement** n jubilación f anticipada

earmark ['ɪəmaːk] vt: **to ~ for** reservar para, destinar a

earn [əːn] vt (salary) percibir; (interest) devengar; (praise) ganarse

earnest ['əːnɪst] adj (wish) fervoroso; (person) serio, formal ▷ n: **in ~** adv en serio

earnings ['əːnɪŋz] npl (personal) ingresos mpl; (of company etc) ganancias fpl

ear: earphones npl auriculares mpl; **earplugs** npl tapones mpl para los oídos; **earring** n pendiente m, arete m (LAM)

earth [əːθ] n tierra; (BRIT Elec) toma de tierra ▷ vt (BRIT Elec) conectar a tierra; **earthquake** n terremoto

ease [iːz] n facilidad f; (comfort) comodidad ▷ vt (problem) mitigar; (pain) aliviar; **to ~ sth in/out** meter/sacar algo con cuidado; **at ~!** (Mil) ¡descansen!

easily ['iːzɪlɪ] adv fácilmente

east [iːst] n este m ▷ adj del este, oriental ▷ adv al este, hacia el este; **the E~** el Oriente; (Pol) el Este; **eastbound** adj en dirección este

Easter ['iːstəʳ] n Pascua (de Resurrección); **Easter egg** n huevo de Pascua

eastern ['iːstən] adj del este, oriental

Easter Sunday n Domingo de Resurrección

easy ['iːzɪ] adj fácil; (life) holgado, cómodo; (relaxed) natural ▷ adv: **to take it** or **things ~** (not worry) no preocuparse; (rest) descansar; **easy-going** adj acomodadizo

eat (pt **ate**, pp **eaten**) [iːt, eɪt, 'iːtn] vt comer; **eat out** vi comer fuera

eavesdrop ['iːvzdrɔp] vi: **to ~ (on sb)** escuchar a escondidas or con disimulo (a algn)

e-book ['iːbuk] n libro electrónico

e-business ['i:bɪznɪs] n (commerce) comercio electrónico; (company) negocio electrónico

EC n abbr (= European Community) CE f

eccentric [ɪk'sentrɪk] adj, n excéntrico/a

echo ['ekəʊ] (pl **echoes**) n eco m ▷ vt (sound) repetir ▷ vi resonar, hacer eco

eclipse [ɪ'klɪps] n eclipse m

eco-friendly ['i:kəʊfrendlɪ] adj ecológico

ecological [i:kə'lɒdʒɪkl] adj ecológico

ecology [ɪ'kɒlədʒɪ] n ecología

e-commerce [i:kə'mɜːs] n comercio electrónico

economic [i:kə'nɒmɪk] adj económico; (business etc) rentable; **economical** adj económico; **economics** n (Scol) economía

economist [ɪ'kɒnəmɪst] n economista mf

economize [ɪ'kɒnəmaɪz] vi economizar, ahorrar

economy [ɪ'kɒnəmɪ] n economía; **economy class** n (Aviat etc) clase f turista; **economy class syndrome** n síndrome m de la clase turista

ecstasy ['ekstəsɪ] n éxtasis m inv; (drug) éxtasis m inv; **ecstatic** [eks'tætɪk] adj extático

eczema ['eksɪmə] n eczema m

edge [edʒ] n (of knife etc) filo m; (of object) borde m; (of lake etc) orilla ▷ vt (Sewing) ribetear; **on** ~ (fig) = **edgy**; **to ~ away from** alejarse poco a poco de

edgy ['edʒɪ] adj nervioso, inquieto

edible ['edɪbl] adj comestible

Edinburgh ['edɪnbərə] n Edimburgo

edit ['edɪt] vt (be editor of) dirigir; (re-write) redactar; (Comput) editar; **edition** [ɪ'dɪʃən] n edición f; **editor** n (of newspaper) director(a) m/f; (of book) redactor(a) m/f; **editorial** [edɪ'tɔːrɪəl] adj editorial ▷ n editorial

educate ['edjʊkeɪt] vt educar; (instruct) instruir; **educated** ['edjʊkeɪtɪd] adj culto

education [edjʊ'keɪʃən] n educación f; (schooling) enseñanza; (Scol) pedagogía; **educational** adj (policy etc) de educación, educativo; (teaching) docente; (instructive) educativo

eel [i:l] n anguila

eerie ['ɪərɪ] adj espeluznante

effect [ɪ'fekt] n efecto ▷ vt efectuar, llevar a cabo; **effects** npl (property) efectos mpl; **to take ~** (law) entrar en vigor or vigencia; (drug) surtir efecto; **in ~** en realidad; **effective** adj eficaz; (real) efectivo; **effectively** adv eficazmente; (in reality) de hecho

efficiency [ɪ'fɪʃənsɪ] n eficiencia; (of machine) rendimiento

efficient [ɪ'fɪʃənt] adj eficiente; (machine, car) de buen rendimiento; **efficiently** adv eficientemente, de manera eficiente

effort ['efət] n esfuerzo; **effortless** adj sin ningún esfuerzo

e.g. adv abbr (= exempli gratia) p.ej.

egg [eg] n huevo; **hard-boiled/ soft-boiled/poached** ~ huevo duro or (LAM) a la copa or (LAM) tibio/ pasado por agua/escalfado; **eggcup** n huevera; **eggplant** n (esp US) berenjena; **eggshell** n cáscara de huevo; **egg white** n clara de huevo; **egg yolk** n yema de huevo

ego ['i:gəʊ] n ego

Egypt ['i:dʒɪpt] n Egipto; **Egyptian** [ɪ'dʒɪpʃən] adj, n egipcio/a

eight [eɪt] num ocho; **eighteen** num dieciocho; **eighteenth** adj decimoctavo; **the eighteenth floor** la planta dieciocho; **the eighteenth of August** el dieciocho de agosto; **eighth** [eɪtθ] adj octavo; **eightieth** ['eɪtɪɪθ] adj octogésimo; **eighty** ['eɪtɪ] num ochenta

Eire ['eərə] n Eire m

either ['aɪðə] adj cualquiera de los dos ...; (both, each) cada ▷ pron: ~ **(of them)** cualquiera (de los dos) ▷ adv tampoco ▷ conj: ~ **yes or no** o sí o no;

on ~ side en ambos lados; **I don't like ~** no me gusta ninguno de los dos; **no, I don't ~** no, yo tampoco

eject [ɪˈdʒɛkt] vt echar; (*tenant*) desahuciar

elaborate adj [ɪˈlæbərɪt] (*design, pattern*) complejo ▷ vt [ɪˈlæbəreɪt] elaborar; (*expand*) ampliar; (*refine*) refinar ▷ vi explicar con muchos detalles

elastic [ɪˈlæstɪk] adj, n elástico; **elastic band** n (BRIT) gomita

elbow [ˈɛlbəʊ] n codo

elder [ˈɛldəʳ] adj mayor ▷ n (*tree*) saúco; (*person*) mayor; **elderly** adj de edad, mayor ▷ npl: **the elderly** los mayores, los ancianos

eldest [ˈɛldɪst] adj, n el/la mayor

elect [ɪˈlɛkt] vt elegir; **to ~ to do** optar por hacer ▷ adj: **the president ~** el presidente electo; **election** n elección f; **electoral** adj electoral; **electorate** n electorado

electric [ɪˈlɛktrɪk] adj eléctrico; **electrical** adj eléctrico; **electric blanket** n manta eléctrica; **electric fire** n estufa eléctrica; **electrician** [ɪlɛkˈtrɪʃən] n electricista mf; **electricity** [ɪlɛkˈtrɪsɪtɪ] n electricidad f; **electric shock** n electrochoque m; **electrify** [ɪˈlɛktrɪfaɪ] vt (Rail) electrificar; (fig: audience) electrizar

electronic [ɪlɛkˈtrɒnɪk] adj electrónico; **electronic mail** n correo electrónico; **electronics** n electrónica

elegance [ˈɛlɪgəns] n elegancia

elegant [ˈɛlɪgənt] adj elegante

element [ˈɛlɪmənt] n elemento; (of heater, kettle etc) resistencia

elementary [ɛlɪˈmɛntərɪ] adj elemental; (*primitive*) rudimentario; **elementary school** n (us) escuela de enseñanza primaria

elephant [ˈɛlɪfənt] n elefante m

elevate [ˈɛlɪveɪt] vt elevar; (in rank) ascender

elevator [ˈɛlɪveɪtəʳ] n (us) ascensor m

eleven [ɪˈlɛvn] num once; **eleventh** [ɪˈlɛvnθ] adj undécimo

eligible [ˈɛlɪdʒəbl] adj: **an ~ young man/woman** un buen partido; **to be ~ for sth** llenar los requisitos para algo

eliminate [ɪˈlɪmɪneɪt] vt (a suspect, possibility) descartar

elm [ɛlm] n olmo

eloquent [ˈɛləkwənt] adj elocuente

else [ɛls] adv: **something ~** otra cosa o algo más; **somewhere ~** en otra parte; **everywhere ~** en todas partes menos aquí; **where ~?** ¿dónde más?, ¿en qué otra parte?; **there was little ~ to do** apenas quedaba otra cosa que hacer; **nobody ~** nadie más; **elsewhere** adv (be) en otra parte; (go) a otra parte

elusive [ɪˈluːsɪv] adj esquivo; (answer) difícil de encontrar

email [ˈiːmeɪl] n abbr (= electronic mail) email m, correo electrónico; **email address** n dirección f electrónica, email m

embankment [ɪmˈbæŋkmənt] n terraplén m

embargo [ɪmˈbɑːgəʊ] (pl **embargoes**) n prohibición f; (Comm, Naut) embargo; **to put an ~ on sth** poner un embargo en algo

embark [ɪmˈbɑːk] vi embarcarse ▷ vt embarcar; **to ~ on** (journey) emprender, iniciar

embarrass [ɪmˈbærəs] vt avergonzar, dar vergüenza a; **embarrassed** adj azorado, violento; **to be embarrassed** sentirse azorado or violento; **embarrassing** adj (situation) violento; (question) embarazoso; **embarrassment** n vergüenza

> Be careful not to translate *embarrassed* by the Spanish word *embarazada*.

embassy [ˈɛmbəsɪ] n embajada

embrace [ɪmˈbreɪs] vt abrazar, dar un abrazo a; (include) abarcar ▷ vi abrazarse ▷ n abrazo

embroider [ɪmˈbrɔɪdəʳ] vt bordar; **embroidery** n bordado

embryo [ˈembrɪəʊ] n embrión m

emerald [ˈemərəld] n esmeralda

emerge [ɪˈmɜːdʒ] vi salir; (arise) surgir

emergency [ɪˈmɜːdʒənsɪ] n crisis f inv; **in an ~** en caso de urgencia; **(to declare a) state of ~** (declarar) estado de emergencia or de excepción; **emergency brake** n (US) freno de mano; **emergency exit** n salida de emergencia; **emergency landing** n aterrizaje m forzoso; **emergency room** (US Med) n sala f de urgencias; **emergency service** n servicio de urgencia

emigrate [ˈemɪɡreɪt] vi emigrar; **emigration** n emigración f

eminent [ˈemɪnənt] adj eminente

emission [ɪˈmɪʃən] n emisión f

emit [ɪˈmɪt] vt emitir; (smell, smoke) despedir

emoticon [ɪˈməʊtɪkɒn] n emoticón n

emotion [ɪˈməʊʃən] n emoción f; **emotional** adj (person) sentimental; (scene) conmovedor(a), emocionante

emperor [ˈempərəʳ] n emperador m

emphasis (pl **emphases**) [ˈemfəsɪs, -siːz] n énfasis m inv

emphasize [ˈemfəsaɪz] vt (word, point) subrayar, recalcar; (feature) hacer resaltar

empire [ˈempaɪəʳ] n imperio m

employ [ɪmˈplɔɪ] vt emplear; **employee** [ɪmplɔɪˈiː] n empleado/a; **employer** n patrón/ona m/f; (businessman) empresario/a; **employment** n empleo m; **to find employment** encontrar trabajo; **employment agency** n agencia de colocaciones or empleo

empower [ɪmˈpaʊəʳ] vt: **to ~ sb to do sth** autorizar a algn para hacer algo

empress [ˈempris] n emperatriz f

emptiness [ˈemptinɪs] n vacío

empty [ˈemptɪ] adj vacío; (street, area) desierto; (threat) vano ▷ vt vaciar;

(place) dejar vacío ▷ vi vaciarse; (house) quedar(se) vacío or desocupado; **empty-handed** adj con las manos vacías

EMU n abbr (= European Monetary Union) UME f

emulsion [ɪˈmʌlʃən] n emulsión f

enable [ɪˈneɪbl] vt: **to ~ sb to do sth** permitir a algn hacer algo

enamel [ɪˈnæməl] n esmalte m

enchanting [ɪnˈtʃɑːntɪŋ] adj encantador(a)

encl. abbr (= enclosed) adj

enclose [ɪnˈkləʊz] vt (land) cercar; (with letter etc) adjuntar; **please find ~d** le mandamos adjunto

enclosure [ɪnˈkləʊʒəʳ] n cercado, recinto

encore [ɒŋˈkɔːʳ] excl ¡otra!, ¡bis! ▷ n bis m

encounter [ɪnˈkaʊntəʳ] n encuentro ▷ vt encontrar, encontrarse con; (difficulty) tropezar con

encourage [ɪnˈkʌrɪdʒ] vt alentar, animar; (growth) estimular; **encouragement** n estímulo; (of industry) fomento

encouraging [ɪnˈkʌrɪdʒɪŋ] adj alentador(a)

encyclop(a)edia [ɛnsaɪkləʊˈpiːdɪə] n enciclopedia

end [end] n fin m; (of table) extremo; (of street) final m; (Sport) lado ▷ vt terminar, acabar ▷ vi terminar, acabar; **to bring to an ~, put an ~ to** acabar con ▷ vi terminar, acabar; **in the ~** al final; **on ~** (object) de punta, de cabeza; **to stand on ~** (hair) erizarse; **for hours on ~** hora tras hora; **end up** vi: **to ~ up in** terminar en; (place) ir a parar a

endanger [ɪnˈdeɪndʒəʳ] vt poner en peligro; **an ~ed species** una especie en peligro de extinción

endearing [ɪnˈdɪərɪŋ] adj entrañable

endeavour [ɪnˈdevəʳ] (US **endeavor**) n esfuerzo; (attempt) tentativa ▷ vi: **to ~ to do** esforzarse por hacer; (try) procurar hacer

ending ['ɛndɪŋ] n (of book) desenlace m; (Ling) terminación f

endless ['ɛndlɪs] adj interminable, inacabable

endorse [ɪn'dɔːs] vt (cheque) endosar; (approve) aprobar; **endorsement** n (on driving licence) nota de sanción

endurance [ɪn'djuərəns] n resistencia

endure [ɪn'djuə] vt (bear) aguantar, soportar ▷ vi (last) perdurar

enemy ['ɛnəmɪ] adj, n enemigo/a

energetic [ɛnə'dʒɛtɪk] adj enérgico

energy ['ɛnədʒɪ] n energía

enforce [ɪn'fɔːs] vt (law) hacer cumplir

engaged [ɪn'geɪdʒd] adj (BRIT: busy, in use) ocupado; (betrothed) prometido; **to get ~** prometerse; **engaged tone** n (BRIT Tel) señal f de comunicando

engagement [ɪn'geɪdʒmənt] n (appointment) compromiso, cita; (to marry) compromiso; (period) noviazgo; **engagement ring** n anillo de pedida

engaging [ɪn'geɪdʒɪŋ] adj atractivo

engine ['ɛndʒɪn] n (Aut) motor m; (Rail) locomotora

engineer [ɛndʒɪ'nɪə] n ingeniero/a; (BRIT: for repairs) técnico; (us Rail) maquinista mf; **engineering** n ingeniería

England ['ɪŋɡlənd] n Inglaterra

English ['ɪŋɡlɪʃ] adj inglés/esa ▷ n (Ling) el inglés; **the English** npl los ingleses; **English Channel** n: **the English Channel** el Canal de la Mancha; **Englishman, Englishwoman** n inglés/esa m/f

engrave [ɪn'greɪv] vt grabar

engraving [ɪn'greɪvɪŋ] n grabado

enhance [ɪn'hɑːns] vt aumentar; (beauty) realzar

enjoy [ɪn'dʒɔɪ] vt (health, fortune) disfrutar de, gozar de; **I ~ doing ...** me gusta hacer ...; **to ~ o.s.** divertirse; **enjoyable** adj agradable; (amusing) divertido; **enjoyment** n (joy) placer m

enlarge [ɪn'lɑːdʒ] vt aumentar; (broaden) extender; (Phot) ampliar ▷ vi: **to ~ on** (subject) tratar con más detalles; **enlargement** n (Phot) ampliación f

enlist [ɪn'lɪst] vt alistar; (support) conseguir ▷ vi alistarse

enormous [ɪ'nɔːməs] adj enorme

enough [ɪ'nʌf] adj: **~ time/books** bastante tiempo/bastantes libros ▷ n: **have you got ~?** ¿tiene usted bastante? ▷ adv: **big ~** bastante grande; **he has not worked ~** no ha trabajado bastante; **(that's) ~!** ¡basta ya!, ¡ya está bien!; **that's ~, thanks** con eso basta, gracias; **I've had ~** estoy harto; **... which, funnily ~ ...** lo que, por extraño que parezca ...

enquire [ɪn'kwaɪə] vt, vi = **inquire**

enrage [ɪn'reɪdʒ] vt enfurecer

enrich [ɪn'rɪtʃ] vt enriquecer

enrol, (us) enroll [ɪn'rəul] vt (member) inscribir; (Scol) matricular ▷ vi inscribirse; (Scol) matricularse; **enrolment, (us) enrollment** n inscripción f; matriculación f

en route [ɔn'ruːt] adv durante el viaje

en suite [ɔn'swiːt] adj: **with ~ bathroom** con baño

ensure [ɪn'ʃuə] vt asegurar

entail [ɪn'teɪl] vt suponer

enter ['ɛntə] vt (room, profession) entrar en; (club) hacerse socio de; (army) alistarse en; (sb for a competition) inscribir; (write down) anotar, apuntar; (Comput) introducir ▷ vi entrar

enterprise ['ɛntəpraɪz] n empresa; (spirit) iniciativa; **free ~** la libre empresa; **private ~** la iniciativa privada; **enterprising** adj emprendedor/a

entertain [ɛntə'teɪn] vt (amuse) divertir; (receive: guest) recibir (en casa); (idea) abrigar; **entertainer** n artista mf; **entertaining** adj divertido, entretenido; **entertainment** n (amusement) diversión f; (show) espectáculo

enthusiasm [ɪn'θuːzɪæzəm] n entusiasmo

enthusiast [ɪn'θuːzɪæst] n entusiasta mf; **enthusiastic** [ɪnθuːzɪ'æstɪk] adj entusiasta; **to be enthusiastic about sb/sth** estar entusiasmado con algn/algo

entire [ɪn'taɪə^r] adj entero; **entirely** adv totalmente

entitle [ɪn'taɪtl] vt: **to ~ sb to sth** dar a algn derecho a; **entitled** adj (book) titulado; **to be entitled to sth/to do sth** tener derecho a algo/a hacer algo

entrance ['entrəns] n entrada ▷ vt [ɪn'trɑːns] encantar, hechizar; **to gain ~ to** (university etc) ingresar en; **entrance examination** n examen m de ingreso; **entrance fee** n (to a show) entrada; (to a club) cuota; **entrance ramp** n (US Aut) rampa de acceso

entrant ['entrənt] n (in race, competition) participante mf; (in exam) candidato/a

entrepreneur [ɒntrəprə'nɜː^r] n empresario/a

entrust [ɪn'trʌst] vt: **to ~ sth to sb** confiar algo a algn

entry ['entrɪ] n entrada; (in register, diary, ship's log) apunte m; (in account book, ledger, list) partida; **no ~** prohibido el paso; (Aut) dirección prohibida; **entry phone** n portero automático

envelope ['envələup] n sobre m

envious ['envɪəs] adj envidioso; (look) de envidia

environment [ɪn'vaɪərnmənt] n (surroundings) entorno; **Department of the E~** ministerio del medio ambiente; **environmental** [ɪnvaɪərn'mentl] adj (medio)ambiental; **environmentally** [ɪnvaɪərn'mentlɪ] adv: **environmentally sound/friendly** ecológico

envisage [ɪn'vɪzɪdʒ] vt prever

envoy ['envɔɪ] n enviado/a

envy ['envɪ] n envidia ▷ vt tener envidia a; **to ~ sb sth** envidiar algo a algn

epic ['epɪk] n épica ▷ adj épico

epidemic [epɪ'demɪk] n epidemia

epilepsy ['epɪlepsɪ] n epilepsia

epileptic [epɪ'leptɪk] adj, n epiléptico/a; **epileptic fit** n ataque m de epilepsia, acceso m epiléptico

episode ['epɪsəud] n episodio

equal ['iːkwl] adj igual; (treatment) equitativo ▷ n igual mf ▷ vt ser igual a; (fig) igualar; **to be ~ to** (task) estar a la altura de; **equality** [iː'kwɔlɪtɪ] n igualdad f; **equalize** vi (Sport) empatar; **equally** adv igualmente; (share etc) a partes iguales

equation [ɪ'kweɪʒən] n (Math) ecuación f

equator [ɪ'kweɪtə^r] n ecuador m

equip [ɪ'kwɪp] vt equipar; (person) proveer; **to be well ~ped** estar bien equipado; equipment [ɪ'kwɪpmənt] n equipo

equivalent [ɪ'kwɪvəlnt] adj, n equivalente m; **to be ~ to** equivaler a

ER abbr (BRIT: = Elizabeth Regina) la reina Isabel; (US Med) = **emergency room**

era ['ɪərə] n era, época

erase [ɪ'reɪz] vt borrar; **eraser** n goma de borrar

erect [ɪ'rekt] adj erguido ▷ vt erigir, levantar; (assemble) montar; **erection** n (of building) construcción f; (of assembly) montaje m; (Med) erección f

ERM n abbr (= Exchange Rate Mechanism) (mecanismo de cambios del) SME m

erode [ɪ'rəud] vt (Geo) erosionar; (metal) corroer, desgastar

erosion [ɪ'rəuʒən] n erosión f; desgaste m

erotic [ɪ'rɒtɪk] adj erótico

errand ['ernd] n recado, mandado (LAM)

erratic [ɪ'rætɪk] adj desigual, poco uniforme

error ['erə^r] n error m, equivocación f

erupt [ɪ'rʌpt] vi entrar en erupción; (fig) estallar; **eruption** n erupción f; (of anger, violence) estallido

escalate [ˈeskəleɪt] *vi* extenderse, intensificarse

escalator [ˈeskəleɪtə] *n* escalera mecánica

escape [ɪˈskeɪp] *n* fuga ▷ *vi* escaparse; (*flee*) huir, evadirse ▷ *vt* evitar, eludir; (*consequences*) escapar a; **his name ~s me** no me sale su nombre; **to ~ from** (*place*) escaparse de; (*person*) huir de

escort *n* [ˈeskɔːt] acompañante *mf*; (*Mil*) escolta ▷ *vt* [ɪˈskɔːt] acompañar

especially [ɪˈspeʃlɪ] *adv* especialmente; (*above all*) sobre todo; (*particularly*) en especial

espionage [ˈespɪənɑːʒ] *n* espionaje *m*

essay [ˈeseɪ] *n* (*Scol*) redacción *f*; (: *longer*) trabajo

essence [ˈesns] *n* esencia

essential [ɪˈsenʃl] *adj* (*necessary*) imprescindible; (*basic*) esencial ▷ *n* (*often pl*) lo esencial; **essentially** *adv* esencialmente

establish [ɪˈstæblɪʃ] *vt* establecer; (*prove*) demostrar; (*relations*) entablar; **establishment** *n* establecimiento; **the Establishment** la clase dirigente

estate [ɪˈsteɪt] *n* (*land*) finca, hacienda; (*inheritance*) herencia; **housing ~** (*BRIT*) urbanización *f*; **estate agent** *n* (*BRIT*) agente *mf* inmobiliario/a; **estate car** *n* (*BRIT*) ranchera, coche *m* familiar

estimate *n* [ˈestɪmət] *n* estimación *f*; (*assessment*) tasa, cálculo; (*Comm*) presupuesto ▷ *vt* [ˈestɪmeɪt] estimar, tasar, calcular

etc *abbr* (= *et cetera*) etc

eternal [ɪˈtɜːnl] *adj* eterno

eternity [ɪˈtɜːnɪtɪ] *n* eternidad *f*

ethical [ˈeθɪkl] *adj* ético; **ethics** [ˈeθɪks] *n* ética ▷ *npl* moralidad *f*

Ethiopia [iːθɪˈəupɪə] *n* Etiopía

ethnic [ˈeθnɪk] *adj* étnico; **ethnic minority** *n* minoría étnica

e-ticket [ˈiːtɪkɪt] *n* billete electrónico, boleto electrónico (*LAM*)

etiquette [ˈetɪkɛt] *n* etiqueta

EU *n abbr* (= *European Union*) UE *f*

euro [ˈjuərəu] *n* euro

Europe [ˈjuərəp] *n* Europa; **European** [juərəˈpiːən] *adj*, *n* europeo/a; **European Community** *n* Comunidad *f* Europea; **European Union** *n* Unión *f* Europea

Eurostar® [ˈjuərəustɑː²] *n* Eurostar® *m*

evacuate [ɪˈvækjueɪt] *vt* evacuar; (*place*) desocupar

evade [ɪˈveɪd] *vt* evadir, eludir

evaluate [ɪˈvæljueɪt] *vt* evaluar; (*value*) tasar; (*evidence*) interpretar

evaporate [ɪˈvæpəreɪt] *vi* evaporarse; (*fig*) desvanecerse

eve [iːv] *n*: **on the ~ of** en vísperas de

even [ˈiːvn] *adj* (*level*) llano; (*smooth*) liso; (*speed*, *temperature*) uniforme; (*number*) par ▷ *adv* hasta, incluso; ~: **if**, **~ though** aunque + *subjun*, así + *subjun* (*LAM*); **~ more** aun más; **~ so** aun así; **not ~** ni siquiera; **~ he was there** hasta él estaba allí; **~ on Sundays** incluso los domingos; **to get ~ with sb** ajustar cuentas con algn

evening [ˈiːvnɪŋ] *n* tarde *f*; (*night*) noche *f*; **in the ~** por la tarde; **this ~** esta tarde or noche; **tomorrow/ yesterday ~** mañana/ayer por la tarde or noche; **evening class** *n* clase *f* nocturna; **evening dress** *n* (*man's*) traje *m* de etiqueta; (*woman's*) traje *m* de noche

event [ɪˈvent] *n* suceso, acontecimiento; (*Sport*) prueba; **in the ~ of** en caso de; **eventful** *adj* (*life*) azaroso; (*day*) ajetreado; (*game*) lleno de emoción; (*journey*) lleno de incidentes

eventual [ɪˈventʃuəl] *adj* final; **eventually** *adv* (*finally*) por fin; (*in time*) con el tiempo

> Be careful not to translate *eventual* by the Spanish word *eventual*.

ever [ˈevə²] *adv* nunca, jamás; (*at all times*) siempre ▷ *conj* después de que; **for ~** (para) siempre; **the best ~** lo nunca visto; **have you ~ seen it?** ¿lo has visto alguna vez?; **better than ~** mejor que nunca; **~ since** adv desde entonces; **evergreen** n árbol m de hoja perenne

O KEYWORD

every ['ɛvrɪ] adj 1 (each) cada; **every one of them** (persons) todos ellos/ as; (objects) cada uno de ellos/as; **every shop in the town was closed** todas las tiendas de la ciudad estaban cerradas

2 (all possible) todo/a; **I gave you every assistance** te di toda la ayuda posible; **I have every confidence in him** tiene toda mi confianza; **we wish you every success** te deseamos toda suerte de éxitos

3 (showing recurrence) todo/a; **every day/week** todos los días/todas las semanas; **every other car had been broken into** habían forzado uno de cada dos coches; **she visits me every other/third day** me visita cada dos/ tres días; **every now and then** de vez en cuando

everybody ['ɛvrɪbɔdɪ] pron todos pron pl, todo el mundo
everyday ['ɛvrɪdeɪ] adj (daily: use, occurrence, experience) cotidiano; (usual: expression) corriente
everyone ['ɛvrɪwʌn] pron = **everybody**
everything ['ɛvrɪθɪŋ] pron todo
everywhere ['ɛvrɪwɛə] adv (be) en todas partes; (go) a or por todas partes; **~ you go you meet ...** en todas partes encuentras ...

evict [ɪ'vɪkt] vt desahuciar
evidence ['ɛvɪdəns] n (proof) prueba; (of witness) testimonio; **to give ~** prestar declaración, dar testimonio
evident ['ɛvɪdənt] adj evidente, manifiesto; **evidently** adv por lo visto
evil ['iːvl] adj malo; (influence) funesto
▷ n mal m

evoke [ɪ'vəuk] vt evocar
evolution [iːvə'luːʃən] n evolución f
evolve [ɪ'vɔlv] vt desarrollar ▷ vi evolucionar, desarrollarse
ewe [juː] n oveja
ex [ɛks] (inf) n: **my ex** mi ex
ex- [ɛks] pref (husband, president etc) ex-
exact [ɪg'zækt] adj exacto ▷ vt: **to ~ sth (from)** exigir algo (de); **exactly** adv exactamente; **exactly!** ¡exacto!
exaggerate [ɪg'zædʒəreɪt] vt, vi exagerar; **exaggeration** [ɪgzædʒə'reɪʃən] n exageración f
exam [ɪg'zæm] n abbr (Scol); = **examination**
examination [ɪgzæmɪ'neɪʃən] n examen m; (Med) reconocimiento
examine [ɪg'zæmɪn] vt examinar; (inspect) inspeccionar; (Med) reconocer; **examiner** n examinador(a) m/f
example [ɪg'zɑːmpl] n ejemplo; **for ~ por** ejemplo
exasperate [ɪg'zɑːspəreɪt] vt exasperar; **~d by or at or with** exasperado por or con
excavate ['ɛkskəveɪt] vt excavar
exceed [ɪk'siːd] vt exceder; (number) pasar de; (speed limit) sobrepasar; (powers) excederse en; (hopes) superar; **exceedingly** adv sumamente, sobremanera
excel [ɪk'sɛl] vi sobresalir; **to ~ o.s.** lucirse
excellence ['ɛksələns] n excelencia
excellent ['ɛksələnt] adj excelente
except [ɪk'sɛpt] prep (also: **~ for, ~ing**) excepto, salvo ▷ vt exceptuar, excluir; **~ if/when** excepto si/cuando; **~ that** salvo que; **exception** n excepción f; **to take exception to** ofenderse por; **exceptional** adj excepcional; **exceptionally** adv excepcionalmente, extraordinariamente
excerpt ['ɛksəːpt] n extracto
excess [ɪk'sɛs] n exceso; **excess baggage** n exceso de equipaje; **excessive** adj excesivo

exchange [ɪks'tʃeɪndʒ] n intercambio, (also: **telephone ~**) central f (telefónica) ▷ vt: **to ~ (for)** cambiar (por); **exchange rate** n tipo de cambio

excite [ɪk'saɪt] vt (stimulate) estimular; **to get ~d** emocionarse; **excitement** n emoción f; **exciting** adj emocionante

exclaim [ɪk'skleɪm] vi exclamar

exclamation [ekskla'meɪʃən] n exclamación f; **exclamation mark**, (us) **exclamation point** n signo de admiración

exclude [ɪk'sklu:d] vt excluir; (except) exceptuar

excluding [ɪk'sklu:dɪŋ] prep: **~ VAT** IVA no incluido

exclusion [ɪks'klu:ʒən] n exclusión f; **to the ~ of** con exclusión de

exclusive [ɪks'klu:sɪv] adj exclusivo; (club, district) selecto; **~ of tax** excluyendo impuestos; **exclusively** adv únicamente

excruciating [ɪks'skru:ʃɪeɪtɪŋ] adj (pain) agudísimo, atroz

excursion [ɪks'skə:ʒən] n excursión f

excuse n [ɪk'skju:s] disculpa, excusa; (evasion) pretexto ▷ vt [ɪk'skju:z] disculpar, perdonar; (justify) justificar; **to ~ sb from doing sth** dispensar a algn de hacer algo; **~ me!** ¡perdone!; (attracting attention) ¡oiga (, por favor)!; **if you will ~ me** con su permiso

ex-directory ['eksdɪ'rektərɪ] adj (BRIT): **~ (phone) number** número que no figura en la guía telefónica

execute ['eksɪkju:t] vt (plan) realizar; (order) cumplir; (person) ajusticiar, ejecutar; **execution** n realización f; cumplimiento; ejecución f

executive [ɪg'zekjutɪv] n (Comm) ejecutivo/a; (Pol) poder m ejecutivo ▷ adj ejecutivo

exempt [ɪg'zempt] adj: **~ from** exento de ▷ vt: **to ~ sb from** eximir a algn de

exercise ['eksəsaɪz] n ejercicio ▷ vt ejercer; (patience etc) proceder con; (dog) sacar de paseo ▷ vi hacer ejercicio; **exercise book** n cuaderno de ejercicios

exert [ɪg'zə:t] vt ejercer; **to ~ o.s.** esforzarse; **exertion** [ɪg'zə:ʃən] n esfuerzo

exhale [eks'heɪl] vt despedir ▷ vi espirar

exhaust [ɪg'zɔ:st] n (pipe) (tubo de) escape m; (fumes) gases mpl de escape ▷ vt agotar; **exhausted** adj agotado; **exhaustion** [ɪg'zɔ:stʃən] n agotamiento; **nervous exhaustion** agotamiento nervioso

exhibit [ɪg'zɪbɪt] n (Art) obra expuesta; (Law) objeto expuesto ▷ vt (show: emotions) manifestar; (: courage, skill) demostrar; (paintings) exponer; **exhibition** [eksɪ'bɪʃən] n exposición f

exhilarating [ɪg'zɪləreɪtɪŋ] adj estimulante, tónico

exile ['eksaɪl] n exilio; (person) exiliado/a ▷ vt desterrar, exiliar

exist [ɪg'zɪst] vi existir; **existence** n existencia; **existing** adj existente, actual

exit ['eksɪt] n salida ▷ vi (Theat) hacer mutis; (Comput) salir (del sistema); **exit ramp** n (us Aut) vía de acceso

⬛ Be careful not to translate exit by the Spanish word éxito.

exotic [ɪg'zɔtɪk] adj exótico

expand [ɪk'spænd] vt ampliar, extender; (number) aumentar ▷ vi (trade etc) ampliarse, expandirse; (gas, metal) dilatarse; **to ~ on** (notes, story etc) ampliar

expansion [ɪk'spænʃən] n ampliación f; aumento; (of trade) expansión f

expect [ɪk'spekt] vt esperar; (count on) contar con; (suppose) suponer ▷ vi: **to be ~ing** estar encinta; **expectation** [ekspek'teɪʃən] n (hope) esperanza; (belief) expectativa

expedition [ɛkspə'dɪʃən] n
expedición f

expel [ɪk'spɛl] vt expulsar

expenditure [ɪk'spɛndɪtʃə'] n
gastos mpl, desembolso; (of time,
effort) gasto

expense [ɪk'spɛns] n gasto, gastos
mpl; (high cost) coste m; **expenses** npl
(Comm) gastos mpl; **at the ~ of** a costa
de; **expense account** n cuenta de
gastos (de representación)

expensive [ɪk'spɛnsɪv] adj caro,
costoso

experience [ɪk'spɪərɪəns] n
experiencia ▷ vt experimentar;
(suffer) sufrir; **experienced** adj
experimentado

experiment [ɪk'spɛrɪmənt] n
experimento ▷ vi hacer experimentos;
experimental [ɪkspɛrɪ'mɛntl] adj
experimental; **the process is still at
the experimental stage** el proceso
está todavía en prueba

expert ['ɛkspə:t] adj experto,
perito ▷ n experto/a, perito/a;
(specialist) especialista mf; **expertise**
[ɛkspə:'ti:z] n pericia

expire [ɪk'spaɪə'] vi caducar, vencerse;
expiry [ɪk'spaɪərɪ] n vencimiento;
expiry date n (of medicine, food item)
fecha de caducidad

explain [ɪk'spleɪn] vt explicar;
explanation [ɛksplə'neɪʃən] n
explicación f

explicit [ɪk'splɪsɪt] adj explícito

explode [ɪk'spləud] vi estallar,
explotar; (with anger) reventar

exploit ['ɛksplɔɪt] n hazaña f ▷ vt
[ɪk'splɔɪt] explotar; **exploitation**
[ɛksplɔɪ'teɪʃən] n explotación f

explore [ɪk'splɔ:'] vt explorar;
examinar, sondear; **explorer** n
explorador(a) m/f

explosion [ɪk'spləuʒən] n explosión
f; **explosive** [ɪk'spləusɪv] adj, n
explosivo

export vt [ɛk'spɔ:t] exportar ▷ n
['ɛkspɔ:t] exportación f ▷ cpd de

exportación; **exporter** [ɛk'spɔ:tə'] n
exportador(a) m/f

expose [ɪk'spəuz] vt exponer;
(unmask) desenmascarar; **exposed**
adj expuesto

exposure [ɪk'spəuʒə'] n exposición f;
(Phot: speed) (tiempo m de) exposición
f; (: shot) fotografía f; **to die from ~**
(Med) morir de frío

express [ɪk'sprɛs] adj (definite)
expreso, explícito; (BRIT: letter
etc) urgente ▷ n (train) rápido ▷ vt
expresar; **expression** [ɪk'sprɛʃən] n
expresión f; **expressway** n (us: urban
motorway) autopista f

exquisite [ɛk'skwɪzɪt] adj exquisito

extend [ɪk'stɛnd] vt (visit, street)
prolongar; (building) ampliar;
(invitation) ofrecer ▷ vi (land)
extenderse; **the contract ~s to/
for ...** el contrato se prolonga hasta/
por ...

extension [ɪk'stɛnʃən] n extensión
f; (building) ampliación f; (Tel: line)
extensión f; (: telephone) supletorio m;
(of deadline) prórroga

extensive [ɪk'stɛnsɪv] adj extenso;
(damage) importante; (knowledge)
amplio

extent [ɪk'stɛnt] n (breadth) extensión
f; (scope) alcance m; **to some ~** hasta
cierto punto; **to the ~ of ...** hasta el
punto de ...; **to such an ~ that ...**
hasta tal punto que ...; **to what ~?**
¿hasta qué punto?

exterior [ɛk'stɪərɪə'] adj exterior,
externo ▷ n exterior m

external [ɛk'stə:nl] adj externo

extinct [ɪk'stɪŋkt] adj (volcano)
extinguido; (race) extinguido;
extinction n extinción f

extinguish [ɪk'stɪŋgwɪʃ] vt extinguir,
apagar

extra ['ɛkstrə] adj adicional ▷ adv (in
addition) más ▷ n (addition) extra m;
(Theat) extra m, comparsa mf

extract vt [ɪk'strækt] sacar; (tooth)
extraer ▷ n ['ɛkstrækt] extracto

extradite ['ɛkstrədaɪt] *vt* extraditar
extraordinary [ɪk'strɔːdnrɪ] *adj* extraordinario; (*odd*) raro
extravagance [ɪk'strævəgəns] *n* derroche *m*; (*thing bought*) extravagancia
extravagant [ɪk'strævəgənt] *adj* (*wasteful*) derrochador(a); (*taste, gift*) excesivamente caro; (*price*) exorbitante
extreme [ɪk'striːm] *adj* extremo; extremado ▷ *n* extremo; **extremely** *adv* sumamente, extremadamente
extremist [ɪk'striːmɪst] *adj, n* extremista *mf*
extrovert ['ɛkstrəvəːt] *n* extrovertido/a
eye [aɪ] *n* ojo ▷ *vt* mirar; **to keep an ~ on** vigilar; **eyeball** *n* globo ocular; **eyebrow** *n* ceja; **eyedrops** *npl* gotas *fpl* para los ojos; **eyelash** *n* pestaña; **eyelid** *n* párpado; **eyeliner** *n* lápiz *m* de ojos; **eyeshadow** *n* sombra de ojos; **eyesight** *n* vista; **eye witness** *n* testigo *mf* ocular

f

F [ɛf] *n* (*Mus*) fa *m*
fabric ['fæbrɪk] *n* tejido, tela
> Be careful not to translate *fabric* by the Spanish word *fábrica*.
fabulous ['fæbjuləs] *adj* fabuloso
face [feɪs] *n* (*Anat*) cara, rostro; (*of clock*) esfera ▷ *vt* (*direction*) estar de cara a; (*situation*) hacer frente a; (*facts*) aceptar; **~ down** (*person, card*) boca abajo; **to lose ~** desprestigiarse; **to make** *or* **pull a ~** hacer muecas; **in the ~ of** (*difficulties etc*) ante; **on the ~ of it** a primera vista; **~ to ~** cara a cara; **face up to** *vt fus* hacer frente a, enfrentarse a; **face cloth** *n* (*BRIT*) toallita; **face pack** *n* (*BRIT*) mascarilla
facial ['feɪʃəl] *adj* de la cara ▷ *n* (*also:* **beauty ~**) tratamiento facial, limpieza
facilitate [fə'sɪlɪteɪt] *vt* facilitar
facility [fə'sɪlɪtɪ] *n* facilidad *f*; **facilities** *npl* instalaciones *fpl*; **credit ~** facilidades de crédito
fact [fækt] *n* hecho; **in ~** en realidad

faction ['fækʃən] n facción f
factor ['fæktə'] n factor m
factory ['fæktərɪ] n fábrica f
factual ['fæktjuəl] adj basado en los hechos
faculty ['fækəltɪ] n facultad f; (us: teaching staff) personal m docente
fad [fæd] n novedad f, moda
fade [feɪd] vi desteñirse; (sound, hope) desvanecerse; (light) apagarse; (flower) marchitarse vi (sound) apagarse; **fade away** vi (sound) apagarse
fag [fæg] n (BRIT inf: cigarette) pitillo (SP), cigarro
Fahrenheit ['fɑːrənhaɪt] n Fahrenheit m
fail [feɪl] vt suspender; (memory etc) fallar a ⊳ vi suspender; (be unsuccessful) fracasar; (strength, brakes, engine) fallar; **to ~ to do sth** (neglect) dejar de hacer algo; (be unable) no poder hacer algo; **without ~** sin falta; **failing** n falta, defecto ⊳ prep a falta de; **failure** ['feɪljə'] n fracaso; (person) fracasado/a; (mechanical etc) fallo
faint [feɪnt] adj débil; (recollection) vago; (mark) apenas visible ⊳ n desmayo ⊳ vi desmayarse; **to feel ~** estar mareado, marearse; **faintest** adj: **I haven't the faintest idea** no tengo la más remota idea; **faintly** adv (vaguely) vagamente
fair [feə'] adj justo; (hair, person) rubio; (weather) bueno; (good enough) suficiente; (sizeable) considerable ⊳ adv: **to play ~** jugar limpio ⊳ n feria; (BRIT: funfair) parque m de atracciones; **fairground** n recinto ferial; **fair-haired** adj (person) rubio; **fairly** adv (justly) con justicia; (quite) bastante; **fair trade** n comercio justo; **fairway** n (Golf) calle f
fairy ['feərɪ] n hada; **fairy tale** n cuento de hadas
faith [feɪθ] n fe f; (trust) confianza; (sect) religión f; **faithful** adj, adj (loyal: troops etc) leal; (spouse) fiel; (account) exacto; **faithfully** adv fielmente;

yours faithfully (BRIT: in letters) le saluda atentamente
fake [feɪk] n (painting etc) falsificación f; (person) impostor(a) m/f ⊳ adj falso ⊳ vt fingir; (painting etc) falsificar
falcon ['fɔːlkən] n halcón m
fall [fɔːl] n caída; (us) otoño ⊳ vi (pt **fell**, pp **fallen**) caer; (accidentally) caerse; (price) bajar; **falls** npl (waterfall) cataratas fpl, salto sg de agua; **to ~ flat** vi (on one's face) caerse de bruces; (joke, story) no hacer gracia; **fall apart** vi deshacerse; **fall down** vi (person) caerse; (building) derrumbarse; **fall for** vt fus (trick) tragar; (person) enamorarse de; **fall off** vi caerse; (diminish) disminuir; **fall out** vi (friends etc) reñir; (hair, teeth) caerse; **fall over** vi caer(se); **fall through** vi (plan, project) fracasar
fallen ['fɔːlən] pp of **fall**
fallout ['fɔːlaut] n lluvia radioactiva
false [fɔːls] adj falso; **under- pretences** con engaños; **false alarm** n falsa alarma; **false teeth** npl (BRIT) dentadura sg postiza
fame [feɪm] n fama
familiar [fə'mɪlɪə'] adj familiar; (well-known) conocido; (tone) de confianza; **to be ~ with** (subject) conocer (bien); **familiarize** [fə'mɪlɪəraɪz] vt: **to familiarize o.s. with** familiarizarse con
family ['fæmɪlɪ] n familia; **family doctor** n médico/a de cabecera; **family planning** n planificación f familiar
famine ['fæmɪn] n hambre f, hambruna
famous ['feɪməs] adj famoso, célebre
fan [fæn] n abanico; (Elec) ventilador m; (Sport) hincha mf; (of pop star) fan mf ⊳ vt abanicar; (fire, quarrel) atizar
fanatic [fə'nætɪk] n fanático/a
fan belt n correa del ventilador
fan club n club m de fans
fancy ['fænsɪ] n (whim) capricho, antojo; (imagination) imaginación f

▷ adj (luxury) de lujo ▷ vt (feel like, want) tener ganas de; (imagine) imaginarse; **to take a ~ to sb** tomar cariño a algn; **he fancies her** le gusta (ella) mucho; **fancy dress** n disfraz m

fan heater n calefactor m de aire

fantasize ['fæntəsaɪz] vi fantasear, hacerse ilusiones

fantastic [fæn'tæstɪk] adj fantástico

fantasy ['fæntəzɪ] n fantasía

fanzine ['fænziːn] n fanzine m

FAQs npl abbr (= frequently asked questions) preguntas fpl frecuentes

far [fɑːʳ] adj (distant) lejano ▷ adv lejos; **~ away, ~ off** (a lo) lejos; **~ better** mucho mejor; **~ from** lejos de; **by ~** con mucho; **go as ~ as the farm** vaya hasta la granja; **as ~ as I know** que yo sepa; **how ~?** ¿hasta dónde?; (fig) ¿hasta qué punto?

farce [fɑːs] n farsa

fare [fɛəʳ] n (on trains, buses) precio (del billete); (in taxi: cost) tarifa; (food) comida; **half/full ~** medio billete m/ billete m completo

Far East n: **the ~** el Extremo or Lejano Oriente

farewell [fɛəˈwel] excl, n adiós m

farm [fɑːm] n granja, finca, estancia (LAM), chacra (LAM) ▷ vt cultivar; **farmer** n granjero/a, estanciero/a (LAM); **farmhouse** n granja, casa de hacienda (LAM); **farming** n agricultura; (tilling) cultivo; **sheep farming** cría de ovejas; **farmyard** n corral m

far-reaching [fɑːˈriːtʃɪŋ] adj (reform, effect) de gran alcance

fart [fɑːt] (inf!) vi tirarse un pedo (!)

farther ['fɑːðəʳ] adv más lejos, más allá ▷ adj más lejano

farthest ['fɑːðɪst] superlative of **far**

fascinate ['fæsɪneɪt] vt fascinar; **fascinated** adj fascinado; **fascinating** adj fascinante; **fascination** [fæsɪ'neɪʃən] n fascinación f; **fascinator** n (hat) tocado (de plumas, flores o cintas)

fascist ['fæʃɪst] adj, n fascista mf

fashion ['fæʃən] n moda; (clothes industry) industria de la moda; (manner) manera ▷ vt formar; **in ~** a la moda; **out of ~** pasado de moda; **fashionable** adj de moda; **fashion show** n desfile m de modelos

fast [fɑːst] adj (also Phot: film) rápido; (dye, colour) sólido; (clock): **to be ~** estar adelantado ▷ adv rápidamente, de prisa; (stuck, held) firmemente ▷ n ayuno ▷ vi ayunar; **~ asleep** profundamente dormido

fasten ['fɑːsn] vt asegurar, sujetar; (coat, belt) abrochar ▷ vi cerrarse

fast food n comida rápida, platos mpl preparados

fat [fæt] adj (mistake) gordo; (book) grueso; (profit) grande, pingüe ▷ n grasa; (on person) carnes fpl; (lard) manteca

fatal ['feɪtl] adj (injury) mortal; **fatality** [fə'tælɪtɪ] n (road death etc) víctima f mortal; **fatally** adv: **fatally injured** herido de muerte

fate [feɪt] n destino

father ['fɑːðəʳ] n padre m; **Father Christmas** n Papá m Noel; **father-in-law** n suegro

fatigue [fə'tiːg] n fatiga, cansancio

fatten ['fætn] vt, vi engordar; **chocolate is ~ing** el chocolate engorda

fatty ['fætɪ] adj (food) graso ▷ n (inf) gordito/a, gordinflón/ona mf

faucet ['fɔːsɪt] n (us) grifo, llave f, canilla (LAM)

fault [fɔːlt] n (blame) culpa; (defect: in character) defecto; (Geo) falla ▷ vt criticar; **it's my ~** es culpa mía; **to find ~ with** criticar, poner peros a; **at ~** culpable; **faulty** adj defectuoso

fauna ['fɔːnə] n fauna

favour ['feɪvəʳ], (us) **favor** n favor m; (approval) aprobación f ▷ vt (proposition) estar a favor de, aprobar; (assist) favorecer; **to do sb a ~** hacer un favor a algn; **to find ~ with sb** (person) caer en gracia a algn; **in ~ of**

a favor de; **favourable** adj favorable; **favourite** ['feɪvərɪt] adj, n favorito/a, preferido/a

fawn [fɔːn] n cervato ▷ adj (also: **~-coloured**) de color cervato, leonado ▷ vi: **to ~ (up)on** adular

fax [fæks] n fax m ▷ vt mandar or enviar por fax

FBI n abbr (US: = Federal Bureau of Investigation) FBI m

fear [fɪə'] n miedo, temor m ▷ vt temer; **for ~ of** por temor a; **fearful** adj temeroso; (awful) espantoso; **fearless** adj audaz

feasible ['fiːzəbl] adj factible

feast [fiːst] n banquete m; (Rel: also: **~ day**) fiesta ▷ vi festejar

feat [fiːt] n hazaña

feather ['feðə'] n pluma

feature ['fiːtʃə'] n característica; (article) reportaje m ▷ vt (film) presentar ▷ vi figurar; **features** fpl (of face) facciones fpl; **feature film** n largometraje m

Feb. abbr (= February) feb

February ['febrʊərɪ] n febrero

fed [fed] pt, pp of **feed**

federal ['fedərəl] adj federal

federation [fedə'reɪʃən] n federación f

fee [fiː] n (professional) honorarios mpl; (of school) matrícula; (also: **membership ~**) cuota

feeble ['fiːbl] adj débil

feed [fiːd] n comida; (of animal) pienso; (on printer) dispositivo de alimentación ▷ vt (pt, pp **fed**) alimentar; (BRIT: breastfeed) dar el pecho a; (animal, baby) dar de comer a; **feed into** vt dar entrada a; **feedback** n reacción f; realimentación

feel [fiːl] n (sensation) sensación f; (sense of touch) tacto m ▷ vt (pt, pp **felt**) tocar; (cold, pain etc) sentir; (think, believe) creer; **to ~ hungry/cold** tener hambre/frío; **to ~ lonely/better** sentirse solo/mejor; **I don't ~ well** no me siento bien; **it ~s soft** es suave

al tacto; **to ~ like** (want) tener ganas de; **feeling** n (physical) sensación f; (foreboding) presentimiento; (emotion) sentimiento

feet [fiːt] npl of **foot**

fell [fel] pt of **fall** ▷ vt (tree) talar

fellow ['feləʊ] n tipo, tío (SP); (of learned society) socio m; (of university) **fellow citizen** n conciudadano/a; **fellow countryman** n compatriota m; **fellow men** npl semejantes mpl; **fellowship** n compañerismo; (grant) beca

felony ['felənɪ] n crimen m

felt [felt] pt, pp of **feel** ▷ n fieltro; **felt-tip pen** n rotulador m

female ['fiːmeɪl] n (woman) mujer f; (Zool) hembra ▷ adj femenino

feminine ['femɪnɪn] adj femenino

feminist ['femɪnɪst] n feminista mf

fence [fens] n valla, cerca ▷ vt (also: **~ in**) cercar ▷ vi hacer esgrima; **fencing** n esgrima

fend [fend] vi: **to ~ for o.s.** valerse por sí mismo; **fend off** vt (attack, attacker) rechazar; (awkward question) esquivar

fender ['fendə'] n (US Aut) parachoques m inv

fennel ['fenl] n hinojo

ferment vi [fə'ment] fermentar ▷ n ['fɜːment] (fig) agitación f

fern [fɜːn] n helecho

ferocious [fə'rəʊʃəs] adj feroz

ferret ['ferɪt] n hurón m

ferry ['ferɪ] n (small) barca de pasaje, balsa; (large: also: **~boat**) transbordador m, ferry m ▷ vt transportar

fertile ['fɜːtaɪl] adj fértil; (Biol) fecundo; **fertilize** ['fɜːtɪlaɪz] vt (Biol) fecundar; (Agr) abonar; **fertilizer** n abono

festival ['festɪvəl] n (Rel) fiesta; (Art, Mus) festival m

festive ['festɪv] adj festivo; **the ~ season** (BRIT: Christmas) las Navidades

fetch [fetʃ] vt ir a buscar; (sell for) venderse por

fête [feɪt] n fiesta

fetus [ˈfiːtəs] n (US) = **foetus**

feud [fjuːd] n (hostility) enemistad f; (quarrel) disputa

fever [ˈfiːvəʳ] n fiebre f; **feverish** adj febril

few [fjuː] adj (not many) pocos ▷ pron algunos; **a ~** adj unos pocos; **fewer** adj menos; **fewest** adj los/las menos

fiancé [fɪˈɑːnseɪ] n novio, prometido; **fiancée** n novia, prometida

fiasco [fɪˈæskəʊ] n fiasco

fib [fɪb] n mentirijilla

fibre, (US) **fiber** [ˈfaɪbəʳ] n fibra; **fibreglass**, (US) **fiberglass** n fibra de vidrio

fickle [ˈfɪkl] adj inconstante

fiction [ˈfɪkʃən] n ficción f; **fictional** adj novelesco

fiddle [ˈfɪdl] n (Mus) violín m; (cheating) trampa ▷ vt (BRIT: accounts) falsificar; **fiddle with** vt fus juguetear con

fidelity [fɪˈdelɪtɪ] n fidelidad f

field [fiːld] n campo; (fig) campo, esfera; (Sport) campo, cancha (LAM); **field marshal** n mariscal m

fierce [fɪəs] adj feroz; (wind, attack) violento; (heat) intenso; (fighting, enemy) encarnizado

fifteen [fɪfˈtiːn] num quince; **fifteenth** adj decimoquinto; **the fifteenth floor** la planta quince; **the fifteenth of August** el quince de agosto

fifth [fɪfθ] adj quinto

fiftieth [ˈfɪftɪɪθ] adj quincuagésimo

fifty [ˈfɪftɪ] num cincuenta; **fifty-fifty** adj (deal, split) a medias ▷ adv: **to go fifty-fifty with sb** ir a medias con algn

fig [fɪg] n higo

fight [faɪt] (pt, pp **fought**) n pelea; (Mil) combate m; (struggle) lucha ▷ vt luchar contra; (cancer, alcoholism) combatir ▷ vi pelear, luchar; **fight back** vi defenderse; (after illness) recuperarse ▷ vt (tears) contener; **fight off** vt (attack, attacker) rechazar;

(disease, sleep, urge) luchar contra; **fighting** n combate m, pelea

figure [ˈfɪgəʳ] n (Drawing, Geom) figura, dibujo; (number, cipher) cifra; (person, outline) figura ▷ vt (esp US: think, calculate) calcular, imaginarse ▷ vi (appear) figurar; **figure out** vt (work out) resolver

file [faɪl] n (tool) lima; (dossier) expediente m; (folder) carpeta; (Comput) fichero; (row) fila ▷ vt limar; (Law: claim) presentar; (store) archivar; **filing cabinet** n archivo

Filipino [fɪlɪˈpiːnəʊ] adj filipino ▷ n (person) filipino/a

fill [fɪl] vt llenar; (vacancy) cubrir ▷ n: **to eat one's ~** comer hasta hartarse; **fill in** vt rellenar; **fill out** vt (form, receipt) rellenar; **fill up** vt llenar (hasta el borde) ▷ vi (Aut) echar gasolina

fillet [ˈfɪlɪt] n filete m; **fillet steak** n filete m de ternera

filling [ˈfɪlɪŋ] n (Culin) relleno; (for tooth) empaste m; **filling station** n estación f de servicio

film [fɪlm] n película ▷ vt (scene) filmar ▷ vi rodar; **film star** n estrella de cine

filter [ˈfɪltəʳ] n filtro ▷ vt filtrar; **filter lane** n (BRIT) carril m de selección

filth [fɪlθ] n suciedad f; **filthy** adj sucio; (language) obsceno

fin [fɪn] n aleta

final [ˈfaɪnl] adj (last) final, último; (definitive) definitivo ▷ n (Sport) final f; **finals** npl (Scol) exámenes mpl finales

finale [fɪˈnɑːlɪ] n final m

finalist n (Sport) finalista mf; **finalize** vt ultimar; **finally** adv (lastly) por último, finalmente; (eventually) por fin

finance [faɪˈnæns] n (money, funds) fondos mpl ▷ vt financiar; **finances** npl finanzas fpl; **financial** [faɪˈnænʃəl] adj financiero; **financial year** n ejercicio (financiero)

find [faɪnd] (pt, pp **found**) vt encontrar, hallar; (come upon) descubrir ▷ n hallazgo;

descubrimiento; **to ~ sb guilty** (*Law*) declarar culpable a algn; **find out** *vt* averiguar; (*truth, secret*) descubrir ▷ *vi*: **to ~ out about** enterarse de; **findings** *npl* (*Law*) veredicto *sg*, fallo *sg*; (*of report*) recomendaciones *fpl*

fine [faɪn] *adj* (*delicate*) fino ▷ *adv* (*well*) bien ▷ *n* (*Law*) multa ▷ *vt* (*Law*) multar; **he's ~** está muy bien; **fine arts** *npl* bellas artes *fpl*

finger ['fɪŋɡəʳ] *n* dedo ▷ *vt* (*touch*) manosear; **little/index ~** (dedo) meñique *m*/índice *m*; **fingernail** *n* uña; **fingerprint** *n* huella dactilar; **fingertip** *n* yema del dedo

finish ['fɪnɪʃ] *n* (*end*) fin *m*; (*Sport*) meta; (*polish etc*) acabado ▷ *vt, vi* terminar; **to ~ doing sth** acabar de hacer algo; **to ~ first/second/third** llegar el primero/segundo/tercero; **finish off** *vt* acabar, terminar; (*kill*) rematar; **finish up** *vt* acabar, terminar ▷ *vi* ir a parar, terminar

Finland ['fɪnlənd] *n* Finlandia

Finn [fɪn] *n* finlandés/esa *m/f*; **Finnish** *adj* finlandés/esa *m* ▷ *n* (*Ling*) finlandés *m*

fir [fəːʳ] *n* abeto

fire ['faɪəʳ] *n* fuego; (*accidental, damaging*) incendio; (*heater*) estufa ▷ *vt* (*gun*) disparar; (*interest*) despertar; (*dismiss*) despedir ▷ *vi* encenderse; **on ~** ardiendo, en llamas; **fire alarm** *n* alarma de incendios; **firearm** *n* arma de fuego; **fire brigade**, (*us*) **fire department** *n* (cuerpo de) bomberos *mpl*; **fire engine** *n* coche *m* de bomberos; **fire escape** *n* escalera de incendios; **fire exit** *n* salida de incendios; **fire extinguisher** *n* extintor *m*; **fireman** *n* bombero; **fireplace** *n* chimenea; **fire station** *n* parque *m* de bomberos; **firetruck** *n* (*us*) = **fire engine**; **firewall** *n* (*Internet*) firewall *m*; **firewood** *n* leña; **fireworks** *npl* fuegos *mpl* artificiales

firm [fəːm] *adj* firme ▷ *n* empresa; **firmly** *adv* firmemente

first [fəːst] *adj* primero ▷ *adv* (*before others*) primero; (*when listing reasons etc*) en primer lugar, primeramente ▷ *n* (*person: in race*) primero/a; (*Aut*) primera; **at ~** al principio; **~ of all** ante todo; **first aid** *n* primeros auxilios *mpl*; **first aid kit** *n* botiquín *m*; **first-class** *adj* de primera clase; **first-hand** *adj* de primera mano; **first lady** *n* (*esp us*) primera dama; **firstly** *adv* en primer lugar; **first name** *n* nombre *m* de pila; **first-rate** *adj* de primera (clase)

fiscal ['fɪskəl] *adj* fiscal; **~ year** año fiscal, ejercicio

fish [fɪʃ] *n* (*pl inv*) pez *m*; (*food*) pescado ▷ *vt* pescar en ▷ *vi* pescar; **to go ~ing** ir de pesca; **~ and chips** pescado frito con patatas fritas; **fisherman** *n* pescador *m*; **fish fingers** *npl* (*BRIT*) palitos *mpl* de pescado (empanado); **fishing boat** *n* barca de pesca; **fishing line** *n* sedal *m*; **fishmonger** *n* (*BRIT*) pescadero/a; **fishmonger's (shop)** *n* (*BRIT*) pescadería; **fish sticks** *npl* (*us*) = **fish fingers**; **fishy** *adj* (*fig*) sospechoso

fist [fɪst] *n* puño

fit [fɪt] *adj* (*Med, Sport*) en (buena) forma; (*proper*) adecuado, apropiado ▷ *vt* (*clothes*) quedar bien a; (*instal*) poner; (*equip*) proveer; (*match: facts*) cuadrar or corresponder or coincidir con ▷ *vi* (*clothes*) quedar bien; (*in space, gap*) caber; (*facts*) coincidir ▷ *n* (*Med*) ataque *m*; **~ to** apto para; **~ for** apropiado para; **a ~ of anger/ enthusiasm** un arranque de cólera/ entusiasmo; **this dress is a good ~** este vestido me queda bien; **by ~s and starts** a rachas; **fit in** *vi* encajar; **fitness** *n* (*Med*) forma física; **fitted** *adj* (*jacket, shirt*) entallado; (*sheet*) de cuatro picos; **fitted carpet** *n* moqueta; **fitted kitchen** *n* cocina amueblada; **fitting** *adj* apropiado ▷ *n* (*of dress*) prueba; **fitting room** *n* (*in shop*) probador *m*; **fittings** *npl* instalaciones *fpl*

five [faɪv] num cinco; **fiver** n (inf: BRIT) billete m de cinco libras; (: US) billete m de cinco dólares

fix [fɪks] vt (secure) fijar, asegurar; (mend) arreglar; (meal, drink) preparar ▷ n: **to be in a ~** estar en un aprieto; **fix up** vt (date, meeting) arreglar; **to ~ sb up with sth** conseguirle algo a algn; **fixed** adj (prices etc) fijo; **fixture** n (Sport) encuentro

fizzy [fɪzɪ] adj (drink) gaseoso

flag [flæg] n bandera; (stone) losa ▷ vi decaer; **flag down** vt: **to ~ sb down** hacer señas a algn para que se pare; **flagpole** n asta de bandera

flair [flɛər] n aptitud f especial

flak [flæk] n (Mil) fuego antiaéreo; (inf: criticism) lluvia de críticas

flake [fleɪk] n (of rust, paint) desconchón m; (of snow) copo m; (of soap powder) escama ▷ vi (also: **~ off**) desconcharse

flamboyant [flæmˈbɔɪənt] adj (dress) vistoso; (person) extravagante

flame [fleɪm] n llama

flamingo [fləˈmɪŋgəʊ] n flamenco

flammable [ˈflæməbl] adj inflamable

flan [flæn] n (BRIT) tarta

> Be careful not to translate **flan** by the Spanish word **flan**.

flank [flæŋk] n flanco ▷ vt flanquear

flannel [ˈflænl] n (BRIT: also: **face ~**) toallita; (fabric) franela; **flannels** npl pantalones mpl de franela

flap [flæp] n (of pocket, envelope) solapa ▷ vt (wings) batir ▷ vi (sail, flag) ondear

flare [flɛər] n llamarada; (Mil) bengala; (in skirt etc) vuelo; **flares** npl (trousers) pantalones mpl de campana; **flare up** vi encenderse; (fig: person) encolerizarse; (: revolt) estallar

flash [flæʃ] n relámpago; (also: **news ~**) noticias fpl de última hora; (Phot) flash m ▷ vt (light, headlights) lanzar destellos con ▷ vi brillar; (hazard light etc) lanzar destellos; **in a ~** en un instante; **he ~ed by** or **past** pasó como un rayo; **flashback** n flashback

m; **flashbulb** n bombilla de flash; **flashlight** n linterna

flask [flɑːsk] n petaca; (also: **vacuum ~**) termo

flat [flæt] adj llano; (smooth) liso; (tyre) desinflado; (battery) descargado; (beer) sin gas; (Mus: instrument) desafinado ▷ n (BRIT: apartment) piso (SP), departamento (LAM), apartamento; (Aut) pinchazo; (Mus) bemol m; **(to work) ~ out** (trabajar) a tope; **flatten** vt (also: **flatten out**) allanar; (smooth out) alisar; (house, city) arrasar

flatter [ˈflætər] vt adular, halagar; **flattering** adj halagador(a); (clothes etc) que favorece

flaunt [flɔːnt] vt ostentar, lucir

flavour, (US) **flavor** [ˈfleɪvər] n sabor m, gusto ▷ vt sazonar, condimentar; **strawberry ~ed** con sabor a fresa; **flavouring**, (US) **flavoring** n (in product) aromatizante m

flaw [flɔː] n defecto; **flawless** adj impecable

flea [fliː] n pulga; **flea market** n rastro, mercadillo

flee (pt, pp **fled**) [fliː, flɛd] vt huir de ▷ vi huir

fleece [fliːs] n vellón m; (wool) lana; (top) forro polar ▷ vt (inf) desplumar

fleet [fliːt] n flota; (of cars, lorries etc) parque m

fleeting [ˈfliːtɪŋ] adj fugaz

Flemish [ˈflɛmɪʃ] adj flamenco

flesh [flɛʃ] n carne f; (skin) piel f; (of fruit) pulpa

flew [fluː] pt of **fly**

flex [flɛks] n cable m ▷ vt (muscles) tensar; **flexibility** n flexibilidad f; **flexible** adj flexible; **flexitime** n horario flexible

flick [flɪk] n capirotazo ▷ vt dar un golpecito a; **flick through** vt fus hojear

flicker [ˈflɪkər] vi (light) parpadear; (flame) vacilar

flies [flaɪz] npl of **fly**

flight [flaɪt] n vuelo; (escape) huida, fuga; (also: **~ of steps**) tramo (de escaleras); **flight attendant** n auxiliar mf de vuelo

flimsy ['flɪmzɪ] adj (thin) muy ligero; (excuse) flojo

flinch [flɪntʃ] vi encogerse; **to ~ from** retroceder ante

fling [flɪŋ] (pt, pp **flung**) vt arrojar

flint [flɪnt] n pedernal m; (in lighter) piedra

flip [flɪp] vt: **to ~ a coin** echar a cara o cruz

flip-flops ['flɪpflɒps] npl (esp BRIT) chancletas fpl

flipper ['flɪpə'] n aleta

flirt [flə:t] vi coquetear, flirtear ▷ n coqueta f

float [fləʊt] n flotador m; (in procession) carroza; (sum of money) reserva ▷ vi (currency) flotar; (swimmer) hacer la plancha

flock [flɒk] n (of sheep) rebaño; (of birds) bandada b vi: **to ~** acudir en tropel a

flood [flʌd] n inundación f; (of letters, imports etc) avalancha ▷ vt inundar ▷ vi (place) inundarse; (people): **to ~ into** inundar; **flooding** n inundaciones fpl; **floodlight** n foco

floor [flɔ:'] n suelo; (storey) piso; (of sea, valley) fondo ▷ vt (with blow) derribar; (fig: baffle) dejar anonadado; **ground ~**, (us) **first ~** planta baja; **first ~**, (us) **second ~** primer piso; **floorboard** n tabla; **flooring** n suelo; (material) solería; **floor show** n cabaret m

flop [flɒp] n fracaso ▷ vi (fail) fracasar; **floppy** adj flojo ▷ n (Comput: also: **floppy disk**) floppy m

flora ['flɔ:rə] n flora

floral ['flɔ:rl] adj (pattern) floreado

florist ['flɒrɪst] n florista mf; **~'s (shop)** n floristería

flotation [fləʊ'teɪʃən] n (of shares) emisión f; (of company) lanzamiento

flour ['flaʊə'] n harina

flourish ['flʌrɪʃ] vi florecer ▷ n ademán m, movimiento (ostentoso)

flow [fləʊ] n (movement) flujo; (of traffic) circulación f; (Elec) corriente f ▷ vi (river, blood) fluir; (traffic) circular

flower ['flaʊə'] n flor f ▷ vi florecer; **flower bed** n macizo; **flowerpot** n tiesto

flown [fləʊn] pp of **fly**

fl. oz. abbr = fluid ounce

flu [flu:] n: **to have ~** tener la gripe

fluctuate ['flʌktjʊeɪt] vi fluctuar

fluent ['flu:ənt] adj (speech) elocuente; **he speaks ~ French, he's ~ in French** domina el francés

fluff [flʌf] n pelusa; **fluffy** adj de pelo suave

fluid ['flu:ɪd] adj (movement) fluido, líquido; (situation) inestable ▷ n fluido, líquido; **fluid ounce** n onza f líquida

fluke [flu:k] (inf) n chiripa

flung [flʌŋ] pt, pp of **fling**

fluorescent [fluə'resnt] adj fluorescente

fluoride ['fluəraɪd] n fluoruro

flurry ['flʌrɪ] n (of snow) ventisca; **~ of activity** frenesí m de actividad

flush [flʌʃ] n rubor m; (fig: of youth, beauty) resplandor m ▷ vt limpiar con agua ▷ vi ruborizarse ▷ adj: **~ with** a ras de; **to ~ the toilet** tirar de la cadena (del wáter)

flute [flu:t] n flauta travesera

flutter ['flʌtə'] n (of wings) revoloteo, aleteo ▷ vi revolotear

fly [flaɪ] (pt **flew**, pp **flown**) n mosca; (on trousers: also: **flies**) bragueta ▷ vt (plane) pilotar; (cargo) transportar (en avión); (distance) recorrer en avión ▷ vi volar; (passenger) ir en avión; (escape) evadirse; (flag) ondear; **fly away** vi (bird, insect) irse volando; **fly off** vi irse volando; **fly-drive** n: **fly-drive holiday** vacaciones que incluyen vuelo y alquiler de coche; **flying** n (activity) (el) volar ▷ adj: **flying visit** visita relámpago; **with flying colours** con lucimiento;

flying saucer n platillo volante; **flyover** n (BRIT) paso elevado or (LAM) a desnivel

FM abbr (Radio: = frequency modulation) FM

foal [fəul] n potro

foam [fəum] n espuma ▷ vi hacer espuma

focus ['fəukəs] (pl **focuses**) n foco; (centre) centro ▷ vt (field glasses etc) enfocar ▷ vi: **to ~ (on)** enfocar (a); (issue etc) centrarse en; **in/out of ~** enfocado/desenfocado

foetus, (US)**fetus** ['fi:təs] n feto

fog [fɔg] n niebla; **foggy** adj: **it's foggy** hay niebla; **fog lamp**, (US)**fog light** n (Aut) faro antiniebla

foil [fɔil] vt frustrar ▷ n hoja; (also: **kitchen ~**) papel m (de) aluminio; (Fencing) florete m

fold [fəuld] n (bend, crease) pliegue m; (Agr) redil m ▷ vt doblar; **to ~ one's arms** cruzarse de brazos; **fold up** vi plegarse, doblarse; (business) quebrar ▷ vt (map etc) plegar; **folder** n (for papers) carpeta; (Comput) directorio; **folding** adj (chair, bed) plegable

foliage ['fəuliidʒ] n follaje m

folk [fəuk] npl gente f ▷ adj popular, folklórico; **folks** npl familia, parientes mpl; **folklore** ['fəukləː] n folklore m; **folk music** n música folk; **folk song** n canción f popular or folk

follow ['fɔləu] vt seguir ▷ vi seguir; (result) resultar; **he ~ed suit** hizo lo mismo; **follow up** vt (letter, offer) responder a; (case) investigar; **follower** n seguidor(a) m/f; (Pol) partidario/a; **following** adj siguiente ▷ n seguidores mpl, afición f; **follow-up** n continuación f

fond [fɔnd] adj (loving) cariñoso; **to be ~ of sb** tener cariño a algn; **she's ~ of swimming** tiene afición a la natación, le gusta nadar

food [fu:d] n comida; **food mixer** n batidora; **food poisoning** n intoxicación f alimenticia; **food**

processor n robot m de cocina; **food stamp** n (US) vale m para comida

fool [fu:l] n tonto/a; (Culin) puré m de frutas con nata ▷ vt engañar; **fool about, fool around** vi hacer el tonto; **foolish** adj tonto; (careless) imprudente; **foolproof** adj (plan etc) infalible

foot [fut] (pl **feet**) n (Anat) pie m; (measure) pie m (= 304 mm); (of animal, table) pata ▷ vt (bill) pagar; **on ~** a pie; **footage** n (Cine) imágenes fpl; **foot-and-mouth (disease)** n fiebre f aftosa; **football** n balón m; (game: BRIT) fútbol m; (: US) fútbol m americano; **footballer** n (BRIT) = **football player**; **football match** n partido de fútbol; **football player** n futbolista mf, jugador(a) m/f de fútbol; **footbridge** n puente m para peatones; **foothills** npl estribaciones fpl; **foothold** n pie m firme; **footing** n (fig) nivel m; **to lose one's footing** perder pie; **footnote** n nota (de pie de página); **footpath** n sendero; **footprint** n huella, pisada; **footstep** n paso; **footwear** n calzado

KEYWORD

for [fɔː] prep 1 (indicating destination, intention) para; **the train for London** el tren con destino a Londres; **he left for Rome** marchó para Roma; **he went for the paper** fue por el periódico; **is this for me?** ¿es esto para mí?; **it's time for lunch** es la hora de comer

2 (indicating purpose) para; **what's it) for?** ¿para qué (es)?; **to pray for peace** rezar por la paz

3 (on behalf of, representing): **the MP for Hove** el diputado por Hove; **he works for the government/a local firm** trabaja para el gobierno/en una empresa local; **I'll ask him for you** se lo pediré por ti; **G for George** G de Gerona

4 (because of) por esta razón; **for fear of being criticized** por temor a ser criticado
5 (with regard to) para; **it's cold for July** hace frío para julio; **he has a gift for languages** tiene don de lenguas
6 (in exchange for) por; **I sold it for £5** lo vendí por £5; **to pay 50 pence for a ticket** pagar 50 peniques por un billete
7 (in favour of): **are you for or against us?** ¿estás con nosotros o contra nosotros?; **I'm all for it** estoy totalmente a favor; **vote for X** vote (a) X
8 (referring to distance): **there are roadworks for 5 km** hay obras en 5 km; **we walked for miles** caminamos kilómetros y kilómetros
9 (referring to time): **he was away for two years** estuvo fuera (durante) dos años; **it hasn't rained for three weeks** no ha llovido durante or en tres semanas; **I have known her for years** la conozco desde hace años; **can you do it for tomorrow?** ¿lo podrás hacer para mañana?
10 (with infinitive clauses): **it is not for me to decide** la decisión no es cosa mía; **it would be best for you to leave** sería mejor que te fueras; **there is still time for you to do it** todavía te queda tiempo para hacerlo; **for this to be possible ...** para que esto sea posible ...
11 (in spite of) a pesar de; **for all his complaints** a pesar de sus quejas
▸ conj (since, as: formal) puesto que

forbid (pt **forbad(e)**, pp **forbidden**) [fə'bɪd, -'bæd, -'bɪdn] vt prohibir; **to ~ sb to do sth** prohibir a algn hacer algo; **forbidden** pt of **forbid** ▸ adj (food, area) prohibido; (word, subject) tabú
force [fɔːs] n fuerza ▸ vt forzar; **to ~ o.s. to do** hacer un esfuerzo por

hacer; **forced** adj forzado; **forceful** adj enérgico
ford [fɔːd] n vado
fore [fɔːʳ] n: **to come to the ~** empezar a destacar; **forearm** n antebrazo; **forecast** n pronóstico ▸ vt (irreg: like **cast**) pronosticar; **forecourt** n patio; (of garage) área de entrada; **forefinger** n (dedo) índice m; **forefront** n: **in the forefront of** en la vanguardia de; **foreground** n (also Comput) primer plano m; **forehead** ['fɔrɛd] n frente f
foreign ['fɔrɪn] adj extranjero; (trade) exterior; **foreign currency** n divisas fpl; **foreigner** n extranjero/a; **foreign exchange** n divisas fpl; **Foreign Office** n (BRIT) Ministerio de Asuntos Exteriores; **Foreign Secretary** n (BRIT) Ministro/a de Asuntos Exteriores
fore: foreman n capataz m; **foremost** adj principal ▸ adv: **first and foremost** ante todo; **forename** n nombre m (de pila)
forensic [fə'rɛnsɪk] adj forense
foresee (pt **foresaw**, pp **foreseen**) [fɔː'siː, -'sɔː, -'siːn] vt prever; **foreseeable** adj previsible
forest ['fɔrɪst] n bosque m; **forestry** n silvicultura
forever [fə'rɛvəʳ] adv para siempre; (endlessly) constantemente
foreword ['fɔːwəːd] n prefacio
forfeit ['fɔːfɪt] vt perder (derecho a)
forgave [fə'geɪv] pt of **forgive**
forge [fɔːdʒ] n herrería ▸ vt (signature, money) falsificar; (metal) forjar; **forger** n falsificador(a) m/f; **forgery** n falsificación f
forget (pt **forgot**, pp **forgotten**) [fə'get, -'got, -'gotn] vt olvidar ▸ vi olvidarse; **forgetful** adj olvidadizo, despistado
forgive (pt **forgave**, pp **forgiven**) [fə'gɪv, -'geɪv, -'gɪvn] vt perdonar; **to ~ sb for sth/for doing sth** perdonar algo a algn/a algn por haber hecho algo

forgot [fə'gɒt] pt of **forget**

forgotten [fə'gɒtn] pp of **forget**

fork [fɔːk] n (for eating) tenedor m; (for gardening) horca; (of roads) bifurcación f ▷ vi (road) bifurcarse

forlorn [fə'lɔːn] adj (person) triste, melancólico; (cottage) abandonado; (attempt) desesperado

form [fɔːm] n forma; (BRIT Scol) curso; (document) formulario, planilla (LAM) ▷ vt formar; **in top ~** en plena forma; **to ~ a circle/a queue** hacer una curva/una cola

formal ['fɔːməl] adj (offer, receipt) por escrito; (person etc) correcto; (occasion, dinner) ceremonioso; **~ dress** traje m de vestir; **formality** [fɔː'mælɪtɪ] n ceremonia

format ['fɔːmæt] n formato ▷ vt (Comput) formatear

formation [fɔː'meɪʃən] n formación f

former ['fɔːmə'] adj anterior; (earlier) antiguo; (ex) ex; **the ~ ... the latter ...** aquél ... éste ...; **formerly** adv antes

formidable ['fɔːmɪdəbl] adj formidable

formula ['fɔːmjulə] n fórmula

fort [fɔːt] n fuerte m

forthcoming [fɔːθ'kʌmɪŋ] adj próximo, venidero; (character) comunicativo

fortieth ['fɔːtɪɪθ] adj cuadragésimo

fortify ['fɔːtɪfaɪ] vt fortalecer

fortnight ['fɔːtnaɪt] n (BRIT) quincena; **it's a ~ since ...** hace quince días que ...; **fortnightly** adj quincenal ▷ adv quincenalmente

fortress ['fɔːtrɪs] n fortaleza

fortunate ['fɔːtʃənɪt] adj: **it is ~ that ...** (es una) suerte que ...; **fortunately** adv afortunadamente

fortune ['fɔːtʃən] n suerte f; (wealth) fortuna; **fortune-teller** n adivino/a

forty ['fɔːtɪ] num cuarenta

forum ['fɔːrəm] n foro

forward ['fɔːwəd] adj (position) avanzado; (movement) hacia delante; (front) delantero; (not shy) atrevido ▷ n

(Sport) delantero ▷ vt (letter) remitir; (career) promocionar; **to move ~** avanzar; **forwarding address** n destinatario; **forward slash** n barra diagonal

fossick ['fɒsɪk] vi (AUST, NZ inf) buscar; **to ~ for sth** buscar algo

fossil ['fɒsl] n fósil m

foster ['fɒstə'] vt (child) acoger en familia; (idea) fomentar; **foster child** n hijo/a adoptivo/a; **foster mother** n madre f adoptiva

fought [fɔːt] pt, pp of **fight**

foul [faul] adj sucio, puerco; (weather, smell etc) asqueroso; (language) grosero; (temper) malísimo ▷ n (Football) falta ▷ vt (dirty) ensuciar; **foul play** n (Law) muerte f violenta

found [faund] pt, pp of **find** ▷ vt fundar; **foundation** [faun'deɪʃən] n (act) fundación f; (basis) base f; (also: **foundation cream**) crema de base; **foundations** npl (of building) cimientos mpl

founder ['faundə'] n fundador(a) m/f ▷ vi irse a pique

fountain ['fauntɪn] n fuente f; **fountain pen** n (pluma) estilográfica, plumafuente f (LAM)

four [fɔː'] num cuatro; **on all ~s** a gatas; **four-letter word** n taco; **four-poster** n (also: **four-poster bed**) cama de columnas; **fourteen** num catorce; **fourteenth** adj decimocuarto; **fourth** adj cuarto; **four-wheel drive** n tracción f a las cuatro ruedas

fowl [faul] n ave f (de corral)

fox [fɒks] n zorro ▷ vt confundir

foyer ['fɔɪeɪ] n vestíbulo

fraction ['frækʃən] n fracción f

fracture ['fræktʃə'] n fractura

fragile ['frædʒaɪl] adj frágil

fragment ['frægmənt] n fragmento

fragrance ['freɪgrəns] n fragancia

frail [freɪl] adj frágil, quebradizo

frame [freɪm] n (Tech) armazón f; (of picture, door etc) marco; (of spectacles:

also: **~s**) montura ▷ *vt* enmarcar; **framework** *n* marco

France ['frɑːns] *n* Francia

franchise ['fræntʃaɪz] *n* (*Pol*) derecho al voto, sufragio; (*Comm*) licencia, concesión f

frank [fræŋk] *adj* franco ▷ *vt* (*letter*) franquear; **frankly** *adv* francamente

frantic ['fræntɪk] *adj* (*need, desire*) desesperado; (*search*) frenético

fraud [frɔːd] *n* fraude *m*; (*person*) impostor(a) *m/f*

fraught [frɔːt] *adj*: **~ with** cargado de

fray [freɪ] *vi* deshilacharse

freak [friːk] *n* (*person*) fenómeno; (*event*) suceso anormal

freckle ['frekl] *n* peca

free [friː] *adj* libre; (*gratis*) gratuito ▷ *vt* (*prisoner etc*) poner en libertad; (*jammed object*) soltar; **~ (of charge)**, **for ~** gratis; **freedom** *n* libertad f; **Freefone®** *n* número gratuito; **free gift** *n* regalo; **free kick** *n* tiro libre; **freelance** *adj* independiente ▷ *adv* por cuenta propia; **freely** *adv* libremente; (*liberally*) generosamente; **Freepost®** *n* porte *m* pagado; **free-range** *adj* (*hen, egg*) de granja; **freeway** *n* (*US*) autopista; **free will** *n* libre albedrío; **of one's own free will** por su propia voluntad

freeze [friːz] (*pt* **froze**, *pp* **frozen**) *vi* helarse, congelarse ▷ *vt* helar; (*prices, food, salaries*) congelar ▷ *n* helada; (*on arms, wages*) congelación f; **freezer** *n* congelador *m*

freezing ['friːzɪŋ] *adj* helado; **freezing point** *n* punto de congelación

freight [freɪt] *n* (*goods*) carga; (*money charged*) flete *m*; **freight train** *n* (*US*) tren *m* de mercancías

French [frentʃ] *adj* francés/esa ▷ *n* (*Ling*) francés *m*; **the French** *npl* los franceses; **French bean** *n* judía verde; **French bread** *n* pan *m* francés; **French dressing** *n* (*Culin*) vinagreta; **French fried potatoes**, (*US*) **French**

fries *npl* patatas *fpl or* (*LAM*) papas *fpl* fritas; **Frenchman** *n* francés *m*; **French stick** *n* barra de pan; **French window** *n* puerta ventana; **Frenchwoman** *n* francesa

frenzy ['frenzi] *n* frenesí *m*

frequency ['friːkwənsi] *n* frecuencia

frequent *adj* ['friːkwənt] frecuente ▷ *vt* [frɪ'kwɛnt] frecuentar; **frequently** *adv* frecuentemente, a menudo

fresh [freʃ] *adj* fresco; (*bread*) tierno; (*new*) nuevo; **freshen** *vi* (*wind*) arreciar; (*air*) refrescar; **freshen up** *vi* (*person*) arreglarse; **fresher** *n* (*BRIT Scol: inf*) estudiante *mf* de primer año; **freshly** *adv*: **freshly painted/ arrived** recién pintado/llegado; **freshman** *n* (*US Scol*): **= fresher**; **freshwater** *adj* (*fish*) de agua dulce

fret [frɛt] *vi* inquietarse

Fri. *abbr* (= *Friday*) vier

friction ['frɪkʃən] *n* fricción f

Friday ['fraɪdɪ] *n* viernes *m inv*

fridge [frɪdʒ] *n* (*BRIT*) nevera, frigo, refrigeradora (*LAM*), heladera (*LAM*)

fried [fraɪd] *adj*: **~ egg** huevo frito

friend [frend] *n* amigo/a ▷ *vt* (*Internet*) añadir como amigo a; **friendly** *adj* simpático; (*government*) amigo; (*place*) acogedor(a); (*match*) amistoso; **friendship** *n* amistad f

fries [fraɪz] *npl* (*esp US*) = **French fried potatoes**

frigate ['frɪgɪt] *n* fragata

fright [fraɪt] *n* susto; **to take ~** asustarse; **frighten** *vt* asustar; **frightened** *adj* asustado; **frightening** *adj*: **it's frightening** da miedo; **frightful** *adj* espantoso, horrible

frill [frɪl] *n* volante *m*

fringe [frɪndʒ] *n* (*BRIT: of hair*) flequillo; (*of forest etc*) borde *m*, margen *m*

Frisbee® ['frɪzbɪ] *n* frisbee®*m*

fritter ['frɪtə*] *n* buñuelo

frivolous ['frɪvələs] *adj* frívolo

fro [frəʊ] *see* **to**

frock [frɔk] n vestido

frog [frɔg] n rana; **frogman** n hombre-rana m

○ **KEYWORD**

from [frɔm] prep 1 (indicating starting place) de, desde; **where do you come from?** ¿de dónde eres?; **from London to Glasgow** de Londres a Glasgow; **to escape from sth/sb** escaparse de algo/algn

2 (indicating origin etc) de; **a letter/ telephone call from my sister** una carta/llamada de mi hermana; **tell him from me that …** dígale de mi parte que …

3 (indicating time): **from one o'clock to** or **until** or **till nine** de la una a las nueve, desde la una hasta las nueve; **from January (on)** a partir de enero

4 (indicating distance) de; **the hotel is 1 km from the beach** el hotel está a 1 km de la playa

5 (indicating price, number etc) de; **prices range from £10 to £50** los precios van desde £10 a or hasta £50; **the interest rate was increased from 9% to 10%** el tipo de interés fue incrementado de un 9% a un 10%

6 (indicating difference): **he can't tell red from green** no sabe distinguir el rojo del verde; **to be different from sb/sth** ser diferente a algn/algo

7 (because of, on the basis of): **from what he says** por lo que dice; **weak from hunger** debilitado por el hambre

front [frʌnt] n (foremost part) parte f delantera; (of house) fachada; (promenade: also: **sea ~**) paseo marítimo; (Mil, Pol, Meteorology) frente m; (fig: appearances) apariencia ▷ adj (wheel, leg) delantero; (row, line) primero; **in ~ (of)** delante del; **front door** n puerta principal; **frontier** ['frʌntɪə'] n frontera; **front page** n

primera plana; **front-wheel drive** n tracción f delantera

frost [frɔst] n helada; (also: **hoar~**) escarcha; **frostbite** n congelación f; **frosting** n (esp us: icing) glaseado; **frosty** adj (welcome etc) glacial; (weather) de helada; (welcome etc) glacial

froth [frɔθ] n espuma

frown [fraun] vi fruncir el ceño

froze [frəuz] pt of **freeze**

frozen ['frəuzn] pp of **freeze**

fruit [fruːt] n (pl inv) fruta; **fruit juice** n jugo or (sp) zumo de fruta; **fruit machine** n (BRIT) máquina tragaperras; **fruit salad** n macedonia or (LAM) ensalada de frutas

frustrate [frʌs'treɪt] vt frustrar; **frustrated** adj frustrado

fry [fraɪ] (pt, pp **fried**) vt freír ▷ n: **small ~** gente f menuda; **frying pan** n sartén f

ft. abbr = **foot; feet**

fudge [fʌdʒ] n (Culin) caramelo blando

fuel [fjuəl] n (for heating) combustible m; (coal) carbón m; (wood) leña; (for engine) carburante m; **fuel tank** n depósito de combustible

fulfil [ful'fɪl] vt (function) desempeñar; (condition) cumplir; (wish, desire) realizar

full [ful] adj lleno; (fig) pleno; (complete) completo; (maximum) máximo; (information) detallado; (price) íntegro ▷ adv: **~ well** perfectamente; **I'm ~ (up)** estoy lleno; **~ employment** pleno empleo; **a ~ two hours** dos horas enteras; **at ~ speed** a toda velocidad; **in ~** (reproduce, quote) íntegramente; **full-length** adj (portrait) de cuerpo entero; **full moon** n luna llena; **full-scale** adj (attack, war, search, retreat) en gran escala; (plan, model) de tamaño natural; **full stop** n punto; **full-time** adj (work) de tiempo completo ▷ adv: **to work full-time** trabajar a tiempo completo; **fully** adv completamente; (at least) al menos

fumble ['fʌmbl] *vi*: **to ~ with** manejar torpemente

fume [fjuːm] *vi* estar furioso, echar humo; **fumes** *npl* humo *sg*, gases *mpl*

fun [fʌn] *n* (amusement) diversión *f*; **to have ~** divertirse; **for ~** por gusto; **to make ~ of** reírse de

function ['fʌŋkʃən] *n* función *f* ▷ *vi* funcionar

fund [fʌnd] *n* (reserve) reserva; **funds** *npl* (money) fondos *mpl*

fundamental [fʌndə'mentl] *adj* fundamental

funeral ['fjuːnərəl] *n* (burial) entierro; (ceremony) funerales *mpl*; **funeral director** *n* director(a) *m/f* de pompas fúnebres; **funeral parlour** *n* (BRIT) funeraria

funfair ['fʌnfɛəʳ] *n* (BRIT) parque *m* de atracciones

fungus (*pl* **fungi**) ['fʌŋgəs, -gaɪ] *n* hongo; (mould) moho

funnel ['fʌnl] *n* embudo; (of ship) chimenea

funny ['fʌnɪ] *adj* gracioso, divertido; (strange) curioso, raro

fur [fəːʳ] *n* piel *f*; (BRIT: on tongue etc) sarro; **fur coat** *n* abrigo de pieles

furious ['fjʊərɪəs] *adj* furioso; (effort, argument) violento

furnish ['fəːnɪʃ] *vt* amueblar; (supply) proporcionar; (information) facilitar; **furnishings** *npl* mobiliario *sg*

furniture ['fəːnɪtʃəʳ] *n* muebles *mpl*; **piece of ~** mueble *m*

furry ['fəːrɪ] *adj* peludo

further ['fəːðəʳ] *adj* (new) nuevo ▷ *adv* más lejos; (more) más; (moreover) además ▷ *vt* hacer avanzar; **how much ~ is it?** ¿a qué distancia queda?; **~ to your letter of ...** (Comm) con referencia a su carta de ...; **to ~ one's interests** fomentar sus intereses; **further education** *n* educación *f* postescolar; **furthermore** *adv* además

furthest ['fəːðɪst] *superlative of* **far**

fury ['fjʊərɪ] *n* furia

fuse, (US) **fuze** [fjuːz] *n* fusible *m*; (for bomb etc) mecha ▷ *vt* (metal) fundir; (fig) fusionar ▷ *vi* fundirse; fusionarse; (BRIT Elec): **to ~ the lights** fundir los plomos; **fuse box** *n* caja de fusibles

fusion ['fjuːʒən] *n* fusión *f*

fuss [fʌs] *n* (excitement) conmoción *f*; (complaint) alboroto; **to make a ~** armar jaleo; **fussy** *adj* (person) quisquilloso

future ['fjuːtʃəʳ] *adj* futuro; (coming) venidero ▷ *n* futuro, porvenir; **in ~** de ahora en adelante; **futures** *npl* (Comm) operaciones *fpl* a término, futuros *mpl*

fuze [fjuːz] *n*, *vb* (US) = **fuse**

fuzzy ['fʌzɪ] *adj* (Phot) borroso; (hair) muy rizado

g

G [dʒiː] n (Mus) sol m

g. abbr (= gram(s), gravity) g

gadget ['gædʒɪt] n aparato

Gaelic ['geɪlɪk] adj, n (Ling) gaélico

gag [gæg] n (on mouth) mordaza; (joke) chiste m ▷ vt amordazar

gain [geɪn] n ganancia ▷ vt ganar ▷ vi (watch) adelantarse; **to ~ by sth** ganar con algo; **to ~ ground** ganar terreno; **to ~ 3 lbs (in weight)** engordar 3 libras; **gain (up)on** vt fus alcanzar

gal., gall. abbr = **gallon**

gala ['gɑːlə] n gala

galaxy ['gæləksɪ] n galaxia

gale [geɪl] n (wind) vendaval m; **~ force 10** vendaval de fuerza 10

gall bladder n vesícula biliar

gallery ['gælərɪ] n (also: **art ~**: state-owned) pinacoteca or museo de arte; (: private) galería de arte

gallon ['gæln] n galón m (= 8 pintas; Brit = 4,546 litros; US = 3,785 litros)

gallop ['gæləp] n galope m ▷ vi galopar

gallstone ['gɔːlstəun] n cálculo biliar

gamble ['gæmbl] n (risk) jugada arriesgada; (bet) apuesta ▷ vt: **to ~ on** apostar a; (fig) contar con ▷ vi jugar; (take a risk) jugárselas; (Comm) especular; **to ~ on the Stock Exchange** jugar a la bolsa; **gambler** n jugador(a) m/f; **gambling** n juego

game [geɪm] n juego; (match) partido; (of cards) partida; (Hunting) caza ▷ adj valiente; (ready): **to be ~ for anything** estar dispuesto a todo; **~s** (Scol) deportes mpl; **games console** n consola de juegos; **game show** n programa m concurso inv, concurso

gaming ['geɪmɪŋ] n (with video games) juegos mpl de ordenador or computadora

gammon ['gæmən] n (bacon) tocino ahumado; (ham) jamón m ahumado

gang [gæŋ] n (of criminals etc) banda; (of kids) pandilla; (of workmen) brigada

gangster ['gæŋstər] n gángster m

gap [gæp] n hueco; (in trees, traffic) claro; (in time) intervalo

gape [geɪp] vi mirar boquiabierto

gap year n año sabático (antes de empezar a estudiar en la universidad)

garage ['gærɑːʒ] n garaje m; (for repairs) taller m; **garage sale** n venta de objetos usados (en el jardín de una casa particular)

garbage ['gɑːbɪdʒ] n (us) basura; (nonsense) bobadas fpl; **garbage can** n (us) cubo or balde m (LAm) or bote m (LAm) de la basura; **garbage collector** n (us) basurero/a

garden ['gɑːdn] n jardín m; **gardens** npl (public) parque m; **garden centre** n (BRIT) centro de jardinería; **gardener** n jardinero/a; **gardening** n jardinería

garlic ['gɑːlɪk] n ajo

garment ['gɑːmənt] n prenda (de vestir)

garnish ['gɑːnɪʃ] vt (Culin) aderezar

garrison ['gærɪsn] n guarnición f

gas [gæs] n gas m; (us: gasoline) gasolina ▷ vt asfixiar con gas; **gas cooker** n (BRIT) cocina de gas; **gas cylinder** n bombona de gas; **gas fire** n estufa de gas

gasket ['gæskɪt] n (Aut) junta

gasoline ['gæsəliːn] n (us) gasolina

gasp [gɑːsp] n grito sofocado ▷ vi (pant) jadear

gas: gas pedal n (esp us) acelerador m; **gas station** n (us) gasolinera; **gas tank** n (us Aut) depósito (de gasolina)

gate [geɪt] n (also at airport) puerta; (metal) verja

gatecrash ['geɪtkræʃ] vt colarse en

gateway ['geɪtweɪ] n puerta

gather ['gæðəʳ] vt (flowers, fruit) coger (SP), recoger (LAM); (assemble) reunir; (pick up) recoger; (Sewing) fruncir; (understand) sacar en consecuencia ▷ vi (assemble) reunirse; **to ~ speed** ganar velocidad; **gathering** n reunión f, asamblea

gauge, (us) gage [geɪdʒ] n (instrument) indicador m ▷ vt medir; (fig) juzgar

gave [geɪv] pt of **give**

gay [geɪ] adj (homosexual) gay; (colour, person) alegre

gaze [geɪz] n mirada fija ▷ vi: **to ~ at sth** mirar algo fijamente

GB abbr (= Great Britain) GB

GCSE n abbr (BRIT: = General Certificate of Secondary Education) certificado del último ciclo de la enseñanza secundaria obligatoria

gear [gɪəʳ] n equipo; (Tech) engranaje m; (Aut) velocidad f, marcha ▷ vt (fig: adapt): **to ~ sth to** adaptar or ajustar algo a; **top** or (us) **high/low** ~ cuarta/primera; **in** ~ con la marcha metida; **gear up** vi prepararse; **gear box** n caja de cambios; **gear lever**, (us) **gear shift** n palanca de cambio; **gear stick** n (BRIT) = **gear lever**

geese [giːs] npl of **goose**

gel [dʒel] n gel m

gem [dʒem] n piedra preciosa

Gemini ['dʒemɪnaɪ] n Géminis m

gender ['dʒendəʳ] n género

gene [dʒiːn] n gen(e) m

general ['dʒenərl] n general m ▷ adj general; **in ~** en general; **general anaesthetic**, (us) **general anesthetic** n anestesia general; **general election** n elecciones fpl generales; **generalize** vi generalizar; **generally** adv generalmente, en general; **general practitioner** n médico/a de medicina general; **general store** n tienda (que vende de todo) (LAM, SP), almacén m (SC, SP)

generate ['dʒenəreɪt] vt generar

generation [dʒenə'reɪʃən] n generación f

generator ['dʒenəreɪtəʳ] n generador m

generosity [dʒenə'rɒsɪtɪ] n generosidad f

generous ['dʒenərəs] adj generoso

genetic [dʒɪ'netɪk] adj genético; **~ engineering** ingeniería genética; **~ fingerprinting** identificación f genética; **genetically modified organism** n organismo transgénico; **genetics** n genética

genitals ['dʒenɪtlz] npl (órganos mpl) genitales mpl

genius ['dʒiːnɪəs] n genio

genome ['giːnəum] n genoma m

gent [dʒent] n abbr (BRIT inf): **= gentleman**

gentle ['dʒentl] adj (sweet) dulce; (touch etc) ligero, suave

> Be careful not to translate gentle by the Spanish word gentil.

gentleman ['dʒentlmən] n señor m; (well-bred man) caballero

gently ['dʒentlɪ] adv suavemente

gents [dʒents] n servicios mpl (de caballeros)

genuine ['dʒenjuɪn] adj auténtico; (person) sincero; **genuinely** adv sinceramente

geographic(al) [dʒɪə'græfɪk(l)] adj geográfico

geography [dʒɪˈɔgrəfɪ] n geografía
geology [dʒɪˈɔlədʒɪ] n geología
geometry [dʒɪˈɔmɪtrɪ] n geometría
geranium [dʒɪˈreɪnɪəm] n geranio
gerbil [ˈdʒɜːbɪl] n gerbo
geriatric [dʒɛrɪˈætrɪk] adj, n
geriátrico/a
germ [dʒɜːm] n (microbe) microbio,
bacteria; (seed) germen m
German [ˈdʒɜːmən] adj alemán/ana
▷ n alemán/ana m/f; (Ling) alemán m;
German measles n rubeola, rubéola
Germany [ˈdʒɜːmənɪ] n Alemania
gesture [ˈdʒɛstʃəʳ] n gesto

⊘ **KEYWORD**

get [gɛt] (pt, pp **got**, pp **gotten** (US))
vi **1** (become, be) ponerse, volverse; **to
get old/tired** envejecer/cansarse;
to get drunk emborracharse; **to
get dirty** ensuciarse; **when do I
get paid?** ¿cuándo me pagan or se
me paga?; **it's getting late** se está
haciendo tarde
2 (go): **to get to/from** llegar a/de; **to
get home** llegar a casa
3 (begin) empezar a; **to get to
know sb** (llegar a) conocer a algn;
I'm getting to like him me está
empezando a gustar; **let's get going
or started** ¡vamos (a empezar)!
4 (modal aux vb): **you've got to do it**
tienes que hacerlo
▶ vt **1**: **to get sth done** (finish) hacer
algo; (have done) mandar hacer algo;
to get one's hair cut cortarse el
pelo; **to get the car going or to go**
arrancar el coche; **to get sb to do
sth** conseguir or hacer que algn haga
algo; **to get sth/sb ready** preparar
algo/a algn
2 (obtain: money, permission, results)
conseguir; (find: job, flat) encontrar;
(fetch: person, doctor) buscar; (: object)
ir a buscar, traer; **to get sth for sb**
conseguir algo para algn; **get me Mr
Jones, please** (Tel) póngame or (LAM)

comuníqueme con el Sr. Jones, por
favor; **can I get you a drink?** ¿quieres
algo de beber?
3 (receive: present, letter) recibir;
(acquire: reputation) alcanzar; (: prize)
ganar; **what did you get for your
birthday?** ¿qué te regalaron por
tu cumpleaños?; **how much did
you get for the painting?** ¿cuánto
sacaste por el cuadro?
4 (catch) coger (SP), agarrar (LAM);
(hit: target etc) dar en; **to get sb by
the arm/throat** coger or agarrar a
algn por el brazo/cuello; **get him!**
¡cógelo! (SP), ¡atrápalo! (LAM); **the
bullet got him in the leg** la bala le dio
en la pierna
5 (take, move) llevar; **to get sth to sb**
hacer llegar algo a algn; **do you think
we'll get it through the door?** ¿crees
que lo podremos meter por la puerta?
6 (catch, take: plane, bus etc) coger
(SP), tomar (LAM); **where do I get
the train for Birmingham?** ¿dónde
se coge or se toma el tren para
Birmingham?
7 (understand) entender; (hear) oír;
I've got it! ¡ya lo tengo!, ¡eureka!;
I don't get your meaning no te
entiendo; **I'm sorry, I didn't get your
name** lo siento, no me he enterado
de tu nombre
8 (have, possess): **to have got** tener
get away vi marcharse; (escape)
escaparse
get away with vt fus hacer
impunemente
get back vi (return) volver ▷ vt
recobrar
get in vi entrar; (train) llegar; (arrive
home) volver a casa, regresar
get into vt fus entrar en; (vehicle) subir
a; **to get into a rage** enfadarse
get off vi (from train etc) bajar(se);
(depart: person, car) marcharse ▷ vt
(remove) quitar ▷ vt fus (train, bus)
bajar(se) de
get on vi (at exam etc): **how are you**

getting on? ¿cómo te va?; **to get on (with)** (agree) llevarse bien (con) vt fus subir(se) a

get out vi salir; (of vehicle) bajar(se) ▷ vt sacar

get out of vt fus salir de; (duty etc) escaparse de

get over vt fus (illness) recobrarse de

get through vi (Tel) lograr comunicar

get up vi (rise) levantarse ▷ vt fus subir

getaway ['getəweɪ] n fuga

Ghana ['gɑ:nə] n Ghana

ghastly ['gɑ:stlɪ] adj horrible

ghetto ['getəʊ] n gueto

ghost [gəʊst] n fantasma m

giant ['dʒaɪənt] n gigante mf ▷ adj gigantesco, gigante

gift [gɪft] n regalo; (ability) don m; **gifted** adj dotado; **gift shop**, (us) **gift store** n tienda de regalos; **gift token**, **gift voucher** n vale-regalo m

gig [gɪg] n (inf: concert) actuación

gigabyte ['gɪgəbaɪt] n gigabyte m

gigantic [dʒaɪˈgæntɪk] adj gigantesco

giggle ['gɪgl] vi reírse tontamente

gills [gɪlz] npl (of fish) branquias fpl, agallas fpl

gilt [gɪlt] adj, n dorado

gimmick ['gɪmɪk] n reclamo

gin [dʒɪn] n ginebra

ginger ['dʒɪndʒə'] n jengibre m

gipsy ['dʒɪpsɪ] n gitano/a

giraffe [dʒɪˈrɑ:f] n jirafa

girl [gɜ:l] n (small) niña; (young woman) chica, joven f, muchacha; **an English ~** una (chica) inglesa; **girl band** n girl band m (grupo musical de chicas); **girlfriend** n (of girl) amiga; (of boy) novia

gist [dʒɪst] n lo esencial

give (pt **gave**, pp **given**) [gɪv, geɪv, 'gɪvn] vt dar; (deliver) entregar; (as gift) regalar ▷ vi (break) romperse; (stretch: fabric) dar de sí; **to ~ sb sth**, **~ sth to sb** dar algo a algn; **give**

away vt (give free) regalar; (betray) traicionar; (disclose) revelar; **give back** vt devolver; **give in** vi ceder ▷ vt entregar; **give out** vt distribuir; **give up** vi rendirse, darse por vencido ▷ vt renunciar a; **to ~ up smoking** dejar de fumar; **to ~ o.s. up** entregarse

given ['gɪvn] pp of **give** ▷ adj (fixed: time, amount) determinado ▷ conj: **~ (that) ...** dado (que) ...; **~ the circumstances ...** dadas las circunstancias ...

glacier ['glæsɪə'] n glaciar m

glad [glæd] adj contento; **gladly** adv con mucho gusto

glamorous ['glæmərəs] adj con glamour, glam(o)uroso

glamour, (us) **glamor** ['glæmə'] n encanto, atractivo

glance [glɑ:ns] n ojeada, mirada ▷ vi: **to ~ at** echar una ojeada a

gland [glænd] n glándula

glare [glɛə'] n deslumbramiento, brillo ▷ vi deslumbrar; **to ~ at** mirar con odio; **glaring** adj (mistake) manifiesto

glass [glɑ:s] n vidrio, cristal m; (for drinking) vaso; (with stem) copa; **glasses** [glɑ:sɪz] npl gafas fpl

glaze [gleɪz] vt (window) acristalar; (pottery) vidriar ▷ n barniz m

gleam [gli:m] vi relucir

glen [glɛn] n cañada

glide [glaɪd] vi deslizarse; (Aviat: bird) planear; **glider** n (Aviat) planeador m

glimmer ['glɪmə'] n luz f tenue; (of hope) rayo

glimpse [glɪmps] n vislumbre m ▷ vt vislumbrar, entrever

glint [glɪnt] vi centellear

glisten ['glɪsn] vi relucir, brillar

glitter ['glɪtə'] vi relucir, brillar

global ['gləʊbl] adj mundial; **globalization** ['gləʊbəlaɪzeɪʃən] n globalización f; **global warming** n (re) calentamiento global or de la tierra

globe [gləʊb] n globo; (model) globo terráqueo

gloom [glu:m] n penumbra; (sadness) desaliento, melancolía; (gloomy adj (dark) oscuro; (sad) triste; (pessimistic) pesimista

glorious ['glɔ:rɪəs] adj glorioso; (weather, sunshine) espléndido

glory ['glɔ:rɪ] n gloria

gloss [glɔs] n (shine) brillo; (also: ~ paint) (pintura) esmalte m

glossary ['glɔsərɪ] n glosario

glossy ['glɔsɪ] adj lustroso; (magazine) de papel satinado or couché

glove [glʌv] n guante m; **glove compartment** n (Aut) guantera f

glow [gləu] vi brillar

glucose ['glu:kəus] n glucosa

glue [glu:] n pegamento ▷ vt pegar

GM adj abbr (= genetically-modified) transgénico

gm abbr (= gram) g

GMT abbr (= Greenwich Mean Time) GMT

gnaw [nɔ:] vt roer

go [gəu] (pt went, pp gone) vi ir; (travel) viajar; (depart) irse, marcharse; (work) funcionar, marchar; (be sold) venderse; (time) pasar; (become) ponerse; (break etc) estropearse, romperse ▷ n: **to have a go (at)** probar suerte (con); **to be on the go** no parar; **whose go is it?** ¿a quién le toca?; **he's going to do it** va a hacerlo; **to go for a walk** ir a dar un paseo; **to go dancing** ir a bailar; **how did it go?** ¿qué tal salió or resultó?, ¿cómo ha ido?; **go ahead** vi seguir adelante; **go around** vi = **go round**; **go away** vi irse, marcharse; **go back** vi volver; **go by** vi (years, time) pasar ▷ vt fus guiarse por; **go down** vi bajar; (ship) hundirse; (sun) ponerse ▷ vt fus bajar por; **go for** vt fus (fetch) ir por; (like) gustar; (attack) atacar; **go in** vi entrar; **go into** vt fus entrar en; (investigate) investigar; (embark on) dedicarse a; **go off** vi irse, marcharse; (food) pasarse; (explode) estallar; (event) realizarse ▷ vt fus perder el interés por; **I'm going off him/the idea** ya

no me gusta tanto él/la idea; **go on** vi (continue) seguir, continuar; (happen) pasar, ocurrir; **to go on doing sth** seguir haciendo algo; **go out** vi salir; (fire, light) apagarse; **go over** vi (ship) zozobrar ▷ vt fus (check) revisar; **go past** vi, vt fus pasar; **go round** vi (circulate: news, rumour) correr; (suffice) alcanzar, bastar; (revolve) girar, dar vueltas; (make a detour): **to go round (by)** dar la vuelta (por); (visit): **to go round (to sb's)** pasar a ver (a algn) ▷ vt fus: **to go round the back** pasar por detrás; **go through** vt fus (town etc) atravesar; **go up** vi subir; **go with** vt fus (accompany) ir con; (fit, suit) hacer juego con, acompañar a; **go without** vt fus pasarse sin

go-ahead ['gəuəhed] adj emprendedor(a) ▷ n luz f verde

goal [gəul] n meta; (score) gol m; **goalkeeper** n portero; **goal post** n poste m (de la portería)

goat [gəut] n cabra f

gobble ['gɔbl] vt (also: ~ down, ~ up) engullir

god [gɔd] n dios m; **G~** Dios m; **godchild** n ahijado/a; **goddaughter** n ahijada; **goddess** n diosa; **godfather** n padrino; **godmother** n madrina; **godson** n ahijado

goggles ['gɔglz] npl gafas fpl

going ['gəuɪŋ] n (conditions) cosas fpl ▷ adj: **the ~ rate** la tarifa corriente or en vigor

gold [gəuld] n oro ▷ adj de oro; **golden** adj (made of gold) de oro; (colour) dorado; **goldfish** n pez m de colores; **goldmine** n mina de oro; **gold-plated** adj chapado en oro

golf [gɔlf] n golf m; **golf ball** n (for game) pelota de golf; (on typewriter) esfera impresora; **golf club** n club m de golf; (stick) palo de golf; **golf course** n campo de golf; **golfer** n golfista mf

gone [gɔn] pp of **go**

gong [gɔŋ] n gong m

good [gud] *adj* bueno; *(before m sg n)* buen; *(well-behaved)* educado ▷ n bien m; **~!** ¡qué bien!; **he's ~ at it** se le da bien; **to be ~ for** servir para; **it's ~ for you** te hace bien; **would you be ~ enough to ...?** ¿sería tan amable de ...?; **a ~ deal (of)** mucho; **a ~ many** muchos; **to make ~** reparar; **it's no ~ complaining** no sirve de nada quejarse; **for ~ (for ever)** para siempre, definitivamente; **~ morning/ afternoon!** ¡buenos días/buenas tardes!; **~ evening!** ¡buenas noches!; **~ night!** ¡buenas noches!

goodbye [gud'baɪ] *excl* ¡adiós!; **to say ~ (to)** *(person)* despedirse (de)

good: Good Friday *n* Viernes m Santo; **good-looking** *adj* guapo; **good-natured** *adj (person)* de buen carácter; **goodness** *n (of person)* bondad f; **for goodness sake!** ¡por Dios!; **goodness gracious!** ¡madre mía!; **goods** *npl (Comm etc)* mercancías fpl; **goods train** *n (BRIT)* tren m de mercancías; **goodwill** *n* buena voluntad f

google ['gu:gəl] *vt, vi* buscar en Google®

goose *(pl* **geese)** [gu:s, gi:s] *n* ganso, oca

gooseberry ['guzbərɪ] *n* grosella espinosa or silvestre; **to play ~** hacer de carabina

gorge [gɔ:dʒ] *n* garganta ▷ vr: **to ~ o.s. (on)** atracarse (de)

gorgeous ['gɔ:dʒəs] *adj* precioso; *(weather)* estupendo; *(person)* guapísimo

gorilla [gə'rɪlə] *n* gorila m

gosh [gɔʃ] *(inf)* *excl* ¡cielos!

gospel ['gɔspl] *n* evangelio

gossip ['gɔsɪp] *n* cotilleo; *(person)* cotilla mf ▷ vi cotillear; **gossip column** *n* ecos mpl de sociedad

got [gɔt] *pt, pp of* **get**

gotten ['gɔtn] *(us)* *pp of* **get**

gourmet ['guəmeɪ] *n* gastrónomo/a

govern ['gʌvən] *vt* gobernar; **government** *n* gobierno; **governor** *n* gobernador(a) m/f; *(of school etc)* miembro del consejo; *(of jail)* director(a) m/f

gown [gaun] *n* vestido; *(of teacher, judge)* toga

GP *n abbr (Med)* = **general practitioner**

GPS *n abbr (= global positioning system)* GPS m

grab [græb] *vt* agarrar, coger *(SP)*; **to ~ at** intentar agarrar

grace [greɪs] *n* gracia ▷ vt honrar; *(adorn)* adornar; **5 days' ~** un plazo de 5 días; **graceful** *adj* grácil, ágil; *(style, shape)* elegante, gracioso; **gracious** ['greɪʃəs] *adj* amable

grade [greɪd] *n (quality)* clase f, calidad f; *(in hierarchy)* grado; *(Scol: mark)* nota; *(us: Scol)* curso ▷ vt clasificar; **grade crossing** *n (us)* paso a nivel; **grade school** *n (us)* escuela primaria

gradient ['greɪdɪənt] *n* pendiente f

gradual ['grædjuəl] *adj* gradual; **gradually** *adv* gradualmente

graduate *n* ['grædjuɪt] licenciado/a, graduado/a ▷ vi ['grædjueɪt] licenciarse, graduarse; **graduation** [grædju'eɪʃən] *n* graduación f; *(us Scol)* entrega de los títulos de bachillerato

graffiti [grə'fi:tɪ] *npl* pintadas fpl

graft [grɑːft] *n (Agr, Med)* injerto; *(bribery)* corrupción f ▷ vt injertar; **hard ~** *(inf)* trabajo duro

grain [greɪn] *n (single particle)* grano; *(no pl: cereals)* cereales mpl; *(in wood)* veta

gram [græm] *n* gramo

grammar ['græmə*] *n* gramática; **grammar school** *n (BRIT)* = instituto (de segunda enseñanza)

gramme [græm] *n* = **gram**

gran [græn] *(BRIT inf)* abuelita

grand [grænd] *adj* magnífico, imponente; *(wonderful)* estupendo; *(gesture etc)* grandioso; **grandad** *(inf)* *n* = **granddad**; **grandchild** *(pl*

grandchildren n nieto/a; **granddad** n yayo, abuelito; **granddaughter** n nieta; **grandfather** n abuelo; **grandma** n yaya, abuelita; **grandmother** n abuela; **grandpa** n = **granddad**; **grandparents** npl abuelos mpl; **grand piano** n piano de cola; **Grand Prix** [ˌɡrɑ̃ˈpriː] n (Aut) gran premio, Grand Prix m; **grandson** n nieto

granite [ˈɡrænɪt] n granito

granny [ˈɡrænɪ] n abuelita, yaya

grant [ɡrɑːnt] vt (concede) conceder; (admit): **to ~ (that)** reconocer (que) ▷ n (Scol) beca; **to take sth for ~ed** dar algo por sentado

grape [ɡreɪp] n uva

grapefruit [ˈɡreɪpfruːt] n pomelo (sc, sp), toronja (LAM)

graph [ɡrɑːf] n gráfica; **graphic** [ˈɡræfɪk] adj gráfico; **graphics** n artes fpl gráficas ▷ npl (drawings, Comput) gráficos mpl

grasp [ɡrɑːsp] vt agarrar, asir; (understand) comprender ▷ n (grip) asimiento; (understanding) comprensión f

grass [ɡrɑːs] n hierba; (lawn) césped m; **grasshopper** n saltamontes m inv

grate [ɡreɪt] n parrilla ▷ vi chirriar ▷ vt (Culin) rallar

grateful [ˈɡreɪtful] adj agradecido

grater [ˈɡreɪtəʳ] n rallador m

gratitude [ˈɡrætɪtjuːd] n agradecimiento

grave [ɡreɪv] n tumba ▷ adj serio, grave

gravel [ˈɡrævl] n grava

gravestone [ˈɡreɪvstəun] n lápida

graveyard [ˈɡreɪvjɑːd] n cementerio

gravity [ˈɡrævɪtɪ] n gravedad f

gravy [ˈɡreɪvɪ] n salsa de carne

gray [ɡreɪ] adj (us) = **grey**

graze [ɡreɪz] vi pacer ▷ vt (touch lightly, scrape) rozar ▷ n (Med) rozadura

grease [ɡriːs] n (fat) grasa; (lubricant) lubricante m ▷ vt engrasar; **greasy** adj grasiento

great [ɡreɪt] adj grande; (inf) estupendo; **Great Britain** n Gran Bretaña; **great-grandfather** n bisabuelo; **great-grandmother** n bisabuela; **greatly** adv muy; (with verb) mucho

Greece [ɡriːs] n Grecia

greed [ɡriːd] n (also: **-iness**) codicia; (for food) gula; (for power etc) avidez f; **greedy** adj codicioso; (for food) glotón/ona

Greek [ɡriːk] adj griego ▷ n griego/a; (Ling) griego

green [ɡriːn] adj verde; (inexperienced) novato ▷ n verde m; (stretch of grass) césped m; (of golf course) green m; **the G- party** (Pol) el partido verde; **greens** npl verduras fpl; **green card** n (Aut) carta verde; (us: work permit) permiso de trabajo para los extranjeros en EE. UU.; **greengage** n (ciruela) claudia; **greengrocer** n (BRIT) verdulero/a; **greenhouse** n invernadero; **greenhouse effect** n efecto invernadero

Greenland [ˈɡriːnlənd] n Groenlandia

green salad n ensalada f (de lechuga, pepino, pimiento verde, etc)

greet [ɡriːt] vt saludar; (news) recibir; **greeting** n (welcome) bienvenida; **greeting(s) card** n tarjeta de felicitación

grew [ɡruː] pt of **grow**

grey [ɡreɪ] adj gris; **grey-haired** adj canoso; **greyhound** n galgo

grid [ɡrɪd] n rejilla; (Elec) red f; **gridlock** n retención f

grief [ɡriːf] n dolor m, pena

grievance [ˈɡriːvəns] n motivo de queja, agravio

grieve [ɡriːv] vi afligirse, acongojarse ▷ vt afligir, apenar; **to ~ for** llorar por

grill [ɡrɪl] n (on cooker) parrilla ▷ vt (BRIT) asar a la parrilla; (question) interrogar

grille [ɡrɪl] n rejilla

grim [grɪm] adj (place) lúgubre; (person) adusto

grime [graɪm] n mugre f

grin [grɪn] n sonrisa abierta ▷ vi: **to ~ (at)** sonreír abiertamente (a)

grind [graɪnd] (pt, pp **ground**) vt (coffee, pepper etc) moler; (us: meat) picar; (make sharp) afilar ▷ n: **the daily ~** (inf) la rutina diaria

grip [grɪp] n (hold) asimiento; (handle) asidero ▷ vt agarrar; **to get to ~s with** enfrentarse con; **to lose one's ~** (fig) perder el control; **gripping** adj absorbente

grit [grɪt] n gravilla; (courage) valor m ▷ vt (road) poner gravilla en; **to ~ one's teeth** apretar los dientes

grits [grɪts] npl (us) maíz msg a medio moler

groan [grəun] n gemido, quejido ▷ vi gemir, quejarse

grocer ['grəusə*] n tendero (de ultramarinos); **~'s (shop)** n tienda de ultramarinos or (LAM) de abarrotes, **groceries** npl comestibles mpl, **grocery** n (shop) tienda de ultramarinos

groin [grɔɪn] n ingle f

groom [gruːm] n mozo/a de cuadra; (also: **bride-**) novio ▷ vt (horse) almohazar; (fig): **to ~ sb for** preparar a algn para; **well-~ed** acicalado

groove [gruːv] n ranura; surco

grope [grəup] vi: **to ~ for** buscar a tientas

gross [grəus] adj (neglect, injustice) grave; (vulgar: behaviour) grosero; (: appearance) de mal gusto; (Comm) bruto; **grossly** adv (greatly) enormemente

grotesque [grə'tɛsk] adj grotesco

ground [graund] pt, pp of **grind** ▷ n suelo, tierra; (Sport) campo, terreno; (reason: gen pl) motivo, razón f; (us: also: **~ wire**) tierra ▷ vt (plane) mantener en tierra; (us Elec) conectar con tierra; **grounds** npl (of coffee etc) poso sg; (gardens etc) jardines mpl,

parque m; **on the ~** en el suelo; **to gain/lose ~** ganar/perder terreno; **to the ~** al suelo; **ground floor** n (BRIT) planta baja; **groundsheet** (BRIT) n tela impermeable; **groundwork** n trabajo preliminar

group [gruːp] n grupo; (Mus: pop group) conjunto, grupo ▷ vt (also: **~ together**) agrupar ▷ vi agruparse

grouse [graus] n (pl inv: bird) urogallo ▷ vi (complain) quejarse

grovel ['grɔvl] vi (fig) arrastrarse

grow (pt **grew**, pp **grown**) [grəu, gruː, grəun] vi crecer; (increase) aumentar; (expand) desarrollarse; (become) volverse ▷ vt cultivar; (hair, beard) dejar crecer; **to ~ rich/weak** enriquecerse/debilitarse; **grow on** vt fus: **that painting's ~ing on me** ese cuadro me gusta cada vez más; **grow up** vi crecer, hacerse hombre/mujer

growl [graul] vi gruñir

grown [graun] pp of **grow**; **grown-up** n adulto/a, mayor mf

growth [grəuθ] n crecimiento; desarrollo; (what has grown) brote m; (Med) tumor m

grub [grʌb] n gusano; (inf: food) comida

grubby ['grʌbɪ] adj sucio, mugriento

grudge [grʌdʒ] n rencor ▷ vt: **to ~ sb sth** dar algo a algn de mala gana; **to bear sb a ~** guardar rencor a algn

gruelling, (us) **grueling** ['grəuəl] adj agotador

gruesome ['gruːsəm] adj horrible

grumble ['grʌmbl] vi refunfuñar, quejarse

grumpy ['grʌmpɪ] adj gruñón/ona

grunt [grʌnt] vi gruñir

guarantee [gærən'tiː] n garantía ▷ vt garantizar

guard [gɑːd] n guardia; (person) guarda mf; (BRIT Rail) jefe m de tren; (on machine) cubierta de protección; (fireguard) pantalla ▷ vt guardar; **to be on one's ~** (fig) estar en guardia;

guardian n guardián/ana m/f; (of minor) tutor(a) m/f
guerrilla [gə'rɪlə] n guerrillero/a
guess [gɛs] vi, vt adivinar; (suppose) suponer ▷ n suposición f, conjetura; **to take** or **have a** ~ tratar de adivinar
guest [gɛst] n invitado/a; (in hotel) huésped(a) m/f; **guest room** n cuarto de huéspedes
guidance ['gaɪdəns] n (advice) consejos mpl
guide [gaɪd] n (person) guía m/f; (book, fig) guía f; (also: **girl** ~) exploradora ▷ vt guiar; **guidebook** n guía; **guide dog** n perro guía; **guided tour** n visita f con guía; **guidelines** npl (fig) directrices fpl
guild [gɪld] n gremio
guilt [gɪlt] n culpabilidad f; **guilty** adj culpable
guinea pig n cobaya; (fig) conejillo de Indias
guitar [gɪ'tɑːʳ] n guitarra; **guitarist** n guitarrista m/f
gulf [gʌlf] n golfo; (abyss) abismo
gull [gʌl] n gaviota
gulp [gʌlp] vi tragar saliva ▷ vt (also: ~ **down**) tragarse
gum [gʌm] n (Anat) encía; (glue) goma, cemento (LAm); (sweet) gominola; (also: **chewing-**) chicle m ▷ vt pegar con goma
gun [gʌn] n (small) pistola; (shotgun) escopeta; (rifle) fusil m; (cannon) cañón m; **gunfire** n disparos mpl; **gunman** n pistolero; **gunpoint** n: **at gunpoint** a mano armada; **gunpowder** n pólvora; **gunshot** n disparo
gush [gʌʃ] vi chorrear, salir a raudales; (fig) deshacerse en efusiones
gust [gʌst] n (of wind) ráfaga
gut [gʌt] n intestino; (Mus etc) cuerda de tripa; **guts** npl (courage) agallas fpl, valor m; (inf: innards: of people, animals) tripas fpl
gutter ['gʌtəʳ] n (of roof) canalón m; (in street) cuneta

guy [gaɪ] n (also: ~**rope**) viento, cuerda; (inf: man) tío (sp), tipo
Guy Fawkes' Night [gaɪ'fɔːks-] n ver nota **"Guy Fawkes' Night"**

- **GUY FAWKES' NIGHT**

  La noche del cinco de noviembre, Guy Fawkes' Night, se celebra el fracaso de la conspiración de la pólvora (Gunpowder Plot), el intento fallido de volar el parlamento de Jaime 1 en 1605. Esa noche se lanzan fuegos artificiales y se queman en muchas hogueras muñecos de trapo que representan a Guy Fawkes, uno de los cabecillas. Días antes los niños tienen por costumbre pedir a los viandantes "a penny for the guy", dinero para comprar los cohetes.

gym [dʒɪm] n (also: **gymnasium**) gimnasio; (also: **gymnastics**) gimnasia; **gymnasium** n gimnasio; **gymnast** n gimnasta m/f; **gymnastics** n gimnasia; **gym shoes** npl zapatillas fpl de gimnasia
gynaecologist, (us) **gynecologist** [gaɪnɪ'kɔlədʒɪst] n ginecólogo/a
gypsy ['dʒɪpsɪ] n = **gipsy**

h

haberdashery ['hæbə'dæʃərɪ] n (BRIT) mercería

habit ['hæbɪt] n hábito, costumbre f; (drug habit) adicción f

habitat ['hæbɪtæt] n hábitat m

hack [hæk] vt (cut) cortar; (slice) tajar ▷ n (pej: writer) escritor(a) m/f a sueldo; **hacker** n (Comput) pirata m informático

had [hæd] pt, pp of **have**

haddock ['hædək] (pl **haddock** or **haddocks**) n especie de merluza

hadn't ['hædnt] = **had not**

haemorrhage, (US) **hemorrhage** ['hɛmərɪdʒ] n hemorragia

haemorrhoids, (US) **hemorrhoids** ['hɛmərɔɪdz] npl hemorroides fpl

haggle ['hægl] vi regatear

Hague [heɪg] n: **The ~** La Haya

hail [heɪl] n (weather) granizo ▷ vt saludar; (call) llamar a ▷ vi granizar; **hailstone** n (piedra de) granizo

hair [hɛəʳ] n pelo, cabellos mpl; (one hair) pelo, cabello; (on legs etc) vello; **to do one's ~** arreglarse el pelo; **grey ~** canas fpl; **hairband** n cinta; **hairbrush** n cepillo (para el pelo); **haircut** n corte m de pelo; **hairdo** n peinado; **hairdresser** n peluquero/a; **hairdresser's** peluquería f; **hairdryer** n secador m (de pelo); **hair gel** n fijador; **hair spray** n laca; **hairstyle** n peinado; **hairy** adj peludo, velludo; (inf: frightening) espeluznante

haka ['hɑːkə] n (NZ) haka m or f

hake [heɪk] n merluza

half [hɑːf] (pl **halves**) n mitad f; (of beer) ~ caña (SP), media pinta; (Rail) billete m de niño ▷ adj medio ▷ adv medio, a medias; **two and a ~** dos y media; **~ a dozen** media docena; **~ a pound** media libra, ≈ 250 gr.; **to cut sth in ~** cortar algo por la mitad; **half board** n (BRIT: in hotel) media pensión; **half-brother** n hermanastro; **half day** n medio día m, media jornada; **half fare** n medio pasaje m; **half-hearted** adj indiferente, poco entusiasta; **half-hour** n media hora; **half-price** adj a mitad de precio; **half term** n (BRIT Scol) vacaciones de medio del trimestre; **half-time** n descanso; **halfway** adv a medio camino

hall [hɔːl] n (for concerts) sala; (entrance way) vestíbulo

hallmark ['hɔːlmɑːk] n sello

hallo [hə'ləu] excl = **hello**

hall of residence n (BRIT) residencia universitaria

Hallowe'en [hæləu'iːn] n víspera de Todos los Santos

- **HALLOWE'EN**
-
- La tradición anglosajona dice
- que en la noche del 31 de octubre,
- Hallowe'en, víspera de Todos los
- Santos, es fácil ver a brujas y
- fantasmas. Es una ocasión festiva

en la que los niños se disfrazan y van de puerta en puerta llevando un farol hecho con una calabaza en forma de cabeza humana. Cuando se les abre la puerta gritan *"trick or treat"* para indicar que gastarán una broma a quien no les dé un pequeño regalo (como golosinas o dinero).

hallucination [həluːsɪˈneɪʃən] *n* alucinación *f*

hallway [ˈhɔːlweɪ] *n* vestíbulo

halo [ˈheɪləʊ] *n* (*of saint*) aureola, halo

halt [hɔːlt] *n* (*stop*) alto, parada ▷ *vt* parar ▷ *vi* pararse

halve [hɑːv] *vt* partir por la mitad

halves [hɑːvz] *pl of* **half**

ham [hæm] *n* jamón *m* (cocido)

hamburger [ˈhæmbəːgəˈ] *n* hamburguesa

hamlet [ˈhæmlɪt] *n* aldea

hammer [ˈhæməˈ] *n* martillo ▷ *vt* (*nail*) clavar; **to ~ a point home to sb** remacharle un punto a algn

hammock [ˈhæmək] *n* hamaca

hamper [ˈhæmpəˈ] *vt* estorbar ▷ *n* cesto

hamster [ˈhæmstəˈ] *n* hámster *m*

hamstring [ˈhæmstrɪŋ] *n* (Anat) tendón *m* de la corva

hand [hænd] *n* mano *f*; (*of clock*) aguja; (*writing*) letra; (*worker*) obrero ▷ *vt* dar, pasar; **to give sb a ~** echar una mano a algn, ayudar a algn; **at ~** a mano; **in ~ entre manos; on ~** (*person, services*) a mano, al alcance; **to ~** (*information etc*) a mano; **on the one ~ ..., on the other ~ ...** por una parte ... por otra (parte) ...; **hand down** *vt* pasar, bajar; (*tradition*) transmitir; (*heirloom*) dejar en herencia; (*us: sentence, verdict*) imponer; **hand in** *vt* entregar; **hand out** *vt* distribuir; **hand over** *vt* (*deliver*) entregar; **handbag** *n* bolso, cartera (LAM); **hand baggage** *n* = **hand luggage**; **handbook** *n* manual *m*; **handbrake** *n* freno de mano;

handcuffs *npl* esposas *fpl*; **handful** *n* puñado

handicap [ˈhændɪkæp] *n* desventaja; (Sport) hándicap *m* ▷ *vt* estorbar; **handicapped** *adj*: **to be mentally handicapped** ser discapacitado/a mental; **to be physically handicapped** ser minusválido/a

handkerchief [ˈhæŋkətʃɪf] *n* pañuelo

handle [ˈhændl] *n* (*of door etc*) pomo, tirador *m*; (*of cup etc*) asa; (*of knife etc*) mango; (*for winding*) manivela ▷ *vt* (*touch*) tocar; (*deal with*) encargarse de; (*treat: people*) manejar; **"~ with care"** (*manéjese*) con cuidado"; **to fly off the ~** perder los estribos; **handlebar(s)** *n(pl)* manillar *msg*

hand: **hand luggage** *n* equipaje *m* de mano; **handmade** *adj* hecho a mano; **handout** *n* (*charity*) limosna; (*leaflet*) folleto

hands-free [ˈhændzfriː] *adj* (Tel: telephone) manos libres; **~ kit** manos libres *m inv*

handsome [ˈhænsəm] *adj* guapo

handwriting [ˈhændraɪtɪŋ] *n* letra

handy [ˈhændɪ] *adj* (*close at hand*) a mano; (*machine, tool etc*) práctico; (*skilful*) hábil, diestro

hang [hæŋ] (*pt, pp* hung) *vt* colgar; (*criminal*) ahorcar; **to get the ~ of sth** (*inf*) coger el tranquillo a algo; **hang about, hang around** *vi* haraganear; **hang down** *vi* colgar, pender; **hang on** *vi* (*wait*) esperar; **hang out** *vt* (*washing*) tender, colgar ▷ *vi* (*inf*: live) vivir; **to ~ out of sth** colgar fuera de algo; **hang round** *vi* = **hang about; hang up** *vt* colgar ▷ *vi* (Tel) colgar

hanger [ˈhæŋəˈ] *n* percha

hang-gliding [ˈhæŋglaɪdɪŋ] *n* vuelo con ala delta

hangover [ˈhæŋəʊvəˈ] *n* (*after drinking*) resaca

hankie, hanky [ˈhæŋkɪ] *n abbr* = **handkerchief**

happen ['hæpən] *vi* suceder, ocurrir; *(chance)*: **he ~ed to hear/see** dio la casualidad de que oyó/vio; **as it ~s da** la casualidad de que

happily ['hæpɪlɪ] *adv (luckily)* afortunadamente; *(cheerfully)* alegremente

happiness ['hæpɪnɪs] *n* felicidad *f*; *(joy)* alegría

happy ['hæpɪ] *adj* feliz; *(cheerful)* alegre; **to be ~ (with)** estar contento (con); **yes, I'd be ~ to** sí, con mucho gusto; **~ birthday!** ¡feliz cumpleaños!

harass ['hærəs] *vt* acosar, hostigar; **harassment** *n* persecución *f*

harbour, *(us)***harbor** ['hɑ:bə'] *n* puerto ▷ *vt (fugitive)* dar abrigo a; *(hope etc)* abrigar

hard ['hɑ:d] *adj* duro; *(difficult)* difícil; *(work)* arduo; *(person)* severo ▷ *adv (work)* mucho, duro; *(think)* profundamente; **to look ~ at sb/ sth** clavar los ojos en algn/algo; **to try ~** esforzarse; **no ~ feelings!** ¡sin rencor(es)!; **to be ~ of hearing** ser duro de oído; **to be ~ done by** ser tratado injustamente; **hardback** *n* libro de tapa dura; **hardboard** *n* aglomerado *m (de madera)*; **hard disk** *n (Comput)* disco duro; **harden** *vt* endurecer; *(fig)* curtir ▷ *vi* endurecerse; *(fig)* curtirse

hardly ['hɑ:dlɪ] *adv* apenas; **~ ever** casi nunca

hard: hardship *n (troubles)* penas *fpl*; *(financial)* apuro; **hard shoulder** *n (Aut)* arcén *m*; **hard-up** *adj (inf)* sin un duro *(sp)*, sin plata *(lam)*; **hardware** *n* ferretería; *(Comput)* hardware *m*; **hardware store** *n* ferretería; **hard-working** *adj* trabajador(a)

hardy ['hɑ:dɪ] *adj* fuerte; *(plant)* resistente

hare [hεə'] *n* liebre *f*

harm [hɑ:m] *n* daño, mal *m* ▷ *vt (person)* hacer daño a; *(health, interests)* perjudicar; *(thing)* dañar; **out of ~'s**

way a salvo; **harmful** *adj* dañino; **harmless** *adj (person)* inofensivo; *(joke etc)* inocente

harmony ['hɑ:mənɪ] *n* armonía

harness ['hɑ:nɪs] *n* arreos *mpl* ▷ *vt (horse)* enjaezar; *(resources)* aprovechar

harp [hɑ:p] *n* arpa *f* ▷ *vi*: **to ~ on (about)** machacar (con)

harsh [hɑ:ʃ] *adj (cruel)* duro, cruel; *(severe)* severo

harvest ['hɑ:vɪst] *n (harvest time)* siega; *(of cereals etc)* cosecha; *(of grapes)* vendimia ▷ *vt* cosechar

has [hæz] *vb see* **have**

hasn't ['hæznt] = **has not**

hassle ['hæsl] *n (inf)* lío, rollo ▷ *vt* incordiar

haste [heɪst] *n* prisa; **hasten** ['heɪsn] *vt* acelerar ▷ *vi* darse prisa; **hastily** *adv* de prisa; **hasty** *adj* apresurado

hat [hæt] *n* sombrero

hatch *n (Naut: also:* **~way***)* escotilla ▷ *vi* salir del cascarón ▷ *vt* incubar; *(scheme, plot)* tramar; **5 eggs have ~ed** han salido 5 pollos

hatchback ['hætʃbæk] *n (Aut)* tres o cinco puertas *m*

hate [heɪt] *vt* odiar, aborrecer ▷ *n* odio; **hatred** ['heɪtrɪd] *n* odio

haul [hɔ:l] *vt* tirar ▷ *n (of fish)* redada; *(of stolen goods etc)* botín *m*

haunt [hɔ:nt] *vt (ghost)* aparecer en; *(obsess)* obsesionar ▷ *n* guarida; **haunted** *adj (castle etc)* embrujado; *(look)* de angustia

KEYWORD

have [hæv] *(pt, pp* **had***) aux vb* **1** haber; **to have arrived/eaten** haber llegado/comido; **having finished** or **when he had finished, he left** cuando hubo acabado, se fue

2 *(in tag questions)*: **you've done it, haven't you?** lo has hecho, ¿verdad? or ¿no?

3 *(in short answers and questions)*: **I haven't no**; **so I have** pues, es

h

verdad; **we haven't paid — yes we have!** no hemos pagado — ¡sí que hemos pagado!; **I've been there before, have you?** he estado allí antes, ¿y tú?

▸ modal aux vb (be obliged): **to have (got) to do sth** tener que hacer algo; **you haven't to tell her** no hay que or no debes decírselo

▸ vt **1** (possess); **he has (got) blue eyes/dark hair** tiene los ojos azules/ el pelo negro

2 (referring to meals etc): **to have breakfast/lunch/dinner** desayunar/ comer/cenar; **to have a drink/a cigarette** tomar algo/fumar un cigarrillo

3 (receive) recibir; **may I have your address?** ¿puedes darme tu dirección?; **you can have it for £5** te lo puedes quedar por £5; **I must have it by tomorrow** lo necesito para mañana; **to have a baby** tener un niño or bebé

4 (maintain, allow): **I won't have it!** ¡no lo permitiré!; **I won't have this nonsense!** ¡no permitiré estas tonterías!; **we can't have that** no podemos permitir eso

5: **to have sth done** hacer or mandar hacer algo; **to have one's hair cut** cortarse el pelo; **to have sb do sth** hacer que algn haga algo

6 (experience, suffer): **to have a cold/ flu** tener un resfriado/la gripe; **she had her bag stolen/her arm broken** le robaron el bolso/se rompió un brazo; **to have an operation** operarse

7 (+ noun): **to have a swim/walk/ bath/rest** nadar/dar un paseo/darse un baño/descansar; **let's have a look** vamos a ver; **to have a meeting/ party** celebrar una reunión/una fiesta; **let me have a try** déjame intentarlo

haven ['heɪvn] n puerto m; (fig) refugio

haven't ['hævnt] = **have not**

havoc ['hævək] n estragos mpl

Hawaii [hə'waiːiː] n (Islas fpl) Hawai m

hawk [hɔːk] n halcón m

hawthorn ['hɔːθɔːn] n espino

hay [heɪ] n heno; **hay fever** n fiebre f del heno; **haystack** n almiar m

hazard ['hæzəd] n peligro ▸ vt aventurar; **hazardous** adj peligroso; **hazard warning lights** npl (Aut) señales fpl de emergencia

haze [heɪz] n neblina

hazel ['heɪzl] n (tree) avellano ▸ adj (eyes) color m de avellano; **hazelnut** n avellana

hazy ['heɪzɪ] adj brumoso; (idea) vago

he [hiː] pron él; **he who ...** aquél que ..., quien ...

head [hɛd] n cabeza; (leader) jefe/a m/f ▸ vt (list) encabezar; (group) capitanear; **~s (or tails)** cara (o cruz); **~ first** de cabeza; **~ over heels in love** perdidamente enamorado; **to ~ the ball** cabecear (el balón); **head for** vt fus dirigirse a; (disaster) ir camino de; **head off** vt (threat, danger) evitar; **headache** n dolor m de cabeza; **heading** n título; **headlamp** n (BRIT) = **headlight**; **headlight** n faro; **headline** n titular m; **head office** n oficina central, central f; **headphones** npl auriculares mpl; **headquarters** npl sede f central; (Mil) cuartel m general; **headroom** n (in car) altura interior; (under bridge) (límite m de) altura; **headscarf** n pañuelo; **headset** n cascos mpl; **head teacher** n director(a); **head waiter** n maître m

heal [hiːl] vt curar ▸ vi cicatrizar

health [hɛlθ] n salud f; **health care** n asistencia sanitaria; **health centre** n ambulatorio, centro médico; **health food** n alimentos mpl orgánicos; **Health Service** n (BRIT) servicio de salud pública, ≈ Insalud m (SP); **healthy** adj sano; saludable

heap [hiːp] n montón m ▸ vt amontonar; **~s of** (inf: lots) montones de; **to ~ favours/praise/gifts** etc **on sb** colmar a algn de favores/elogios/regalos etc

hear [hɪəʳ] (pt, pp **heard**) vt oír; (news) saber ▷ vi oír; **to ~ about** oír hablar de; **to ~ from sb** tener noticias de algn

heard [hɜːd] pt, pp of **hear**

hearing ['hɪərɪŋ] n (sense) oído; (Law) vista; **hearing aid** n audífono

hearse [hɜːs] n coche m fúnebre

heart [hɑːt] n corazón m; (fig) valor m; (of lettuce) cogollo; **hearts** npl (Cards) corazones mpl; **at ~** en el fondo; **by ~** (learn, know) de memoria; **to take ~** cobrar ánimos; **heart attack** n infarto (de miocardio); **heartbeat** n latido (del corazón); **heartbroken** adj: **she was heartbroken about it** eso le partió el corazón; **heartburn** n acedía; **heart disease** n enfermedad f cardíaca

hearth [hɑːθ] n (fireplace) chimenea

heartless ['hɑːtlɪs] adj despiadado

hearty ['hɑːtɪ] adj (person) campechano; (laugh) sano; (dislike, support) absoluto

heat [hiːt] n calor m; (Sport: also: **qualifying ~**) prueba eliminatoria ▷ vt calentar; **heat up** vi calentarse ▷ vt calentar; **heated** adj caliente; (fig) acalorado; **heater** n calentador m, estufa

heather ['heðəʳ] n brezo

heating ['hiːtɪŋ] n calefacción f

heatwave ['hiːtweɪv] n ola de calor

heaven ['hevn] n cielo; (Rel) paraíso; **heavenly** adj celestial

heavily ['hevɪlɪ] adv pesadamente; (drink, smoke) en exceso; (sleep, sigh) profundamente

heavy ['hevɪ] adj pesado; (work) duro; (sea, rain, meal) fuerte; (drinker, smoker) empedernido; (responsibility) grave; (schedule) ocupado; (weather) bochornoso; **~ goods vehicle** n vehículo pesado

Hebrew ['hiːbruː] adj, n (Ling) hebreo

hectare ['hektɑːʳ] n (BRIT) hectárea

hectic ['hektɪk] adj agitado

he'd [hiːd] = **he would; he had**

hedge [hedʒ] n seto ▷ vi contestar con evasivas; **to ~ one's bets** (fig) cubrirse

hedgehog ['hedʒhɒg] n erizo

heed [hiːd] vt (also: **take ~ of**) hacer caso de

heel [hiːl] n talón m; (of shoe) tacón m ▷ vt (shoe) poner tacón a

hefty ['heftɪ] adj (person) fornido; (price) alto

height [haɪt] n (of person) talla, estatura; (of building) altura; (high ground) cerro; (altitude) altitud f; **at the ~ of summer** en los días más calurosos del verano; **heighten** vt elevar; (fig) aumentar

heir [eəʳ] n heredero; **heiress** n heredera

held [held] pt, pp of **hold**

helicopter ['helɪkɒptəʳ] n helicóptero

hell [hel] n infierno; **oh ~!** (inf) ¡demonios!

he'll [hiːl] = **he will; he shall**

hello [hə'ləu] excl ¡hola!; (to attract attention) ¡oiga!; (surprise) ¡caramba!

helmet ['helmɪt] n casco

help [help] n ayuda; (charwoman etc) criada, asistenta ▷ vt ayudar; **~!** ¡socorro!; **~ yourself** sírvete; **he can't ~ it** no lo puede evitar; **help out** vi ayudar, echar una mano ▷ vt: **to ~ sb out** ayudar a algn, echar una mano a algn; **helper** n ayudante mf; **helpful** adj útil; (person) servicial; **helping** n ración f; **helpless** adj (incapable) incapaz; (defenceless) indefenso; **helpline** n teléfono de asistencia al público

hem [hem] n dobladillo ▷ vt poner or coser el dobladillo a

hemisphere ['hemɪsfɪəʳ] n hemisferio

hemorrhage ['hemərɪdʒ] n (US) = **haemorrhage**

hemorrhoids ['hemərɔɪdz] npl (US) = **haemorrhoids**

hen [hɛn] n gallina; (female bird) hembra

hence [hɛns] adv (therefore) por lo tanto; **two years ~** de aquí a dos años

hen night n (inf) despedida de soltera

hepatitis [hɛpəˈtaɪtɪs] n hepatitis f inv

her [həː] n (direct) la; (indirect) le; (stressed, after prep) ella ▷ adj su; see also **me; my**

herb [həːb] n hierba; **herbal** [ˈhəːbl] adj de hierbas; **herbal tea** n infusión f de hierbas

herd [həːd] n rebaño

here [hɪə] adv aquí; **~!** (present) ¡presente!; **~ is/are** aquí está/están; **~ she is** aquí está

hereditary [hɪˈrɛdɪtrɪ] adj hereditario

heritage [ˈhɛrɪtɪdʒ] n patrimonio

hernia [ˈhəːnɪə] n hernia

hero [ˈhɪərəʊ] n (pl **heroes**) n héroe m; (in book, film) protagonista m; **heroic** [hɪˈrəʊɪk] adj heroico

heroin [ˈhɛrəʊɪn] n heroína

heroine [ˈhɛrəʊɪn] n heroína; (in book, film) protagonista

heron [ˈhɛrən] n garza

herring [ˈhɛrɪŋ] n (pl inv) n arenque m

hers [həːz] pron (el) suyo/(la) suya etc; see also **mine**

herself [həːˈsɛlf] pron (reflexive) se; (emphatic) ella misma; (after prep) sí misma; see also **oneself**

he's [hiːz] = **he is; he has**

hesitant [ˈhɛzɪtənt] adj indeciso

hesitate [ˈhɛzɪteɪt] vi vacilar; (in speech) titubear; (be unwilling) resistirse a; **hesitation** [hɛzɪˈteɪʃən] n indecisión f

heterosexual [hɛtərəʊˈsɛksjuəl] adj, n heterosexual mf

hexagon [ˈhɛksəgən] n hexágono

hey [heɪ] excl ¡oye!, ¡oiga!

heyday [ˈheɪdeɪ] n: **the ~ of** el apogeo de

HGV n abbr = **heavy goods vehicle**

hi [haɪ] excl ¡hola!

hibernate [ˈhaɪbəneɪt] vi invernar

hiccough, hiccup [ˈhɪkʌp] vi hipar

hid [hɪd] pt of **hide**

hidden [ˈhɪdn] pp of **hide** ▷ adj: **~ agenda** plan m encubierto

hide [haɪd] (pt **hid**, pp **hidden**) n (skin) piel f ▷ vt esconder; ocultar ▷ vi: **to ~ (from sb)** esconderse or ocultarse (de algn)

hideous [ˈhɪdɪəs] adj horrible

hiding [ˈhaɪdɪŋ] n (beating) paliza; **to be in ~** (concealed) estar escondido

hi-fi [ˈhaɪfaɪ] n estéreo, hifi m ▷ adj de alta fidelidad

high [haɪ] adj (speed, number) grande; (price) elevado; (wind) fuerte; (voice) agudo ▷ adv alto, a gran altura; **it is 20 m ~** tiene 20 m de altura; **~ in the air** en lo alto; **highchair** n silla alta (para niños); **high-class** adj (hotel) de lujo; (person) distinguido, de categoría; (food) de alta categoría; **higher education** n educación f or enseñanza superior; **high heels** npl (heels) tacones mpl altos; (shoes) zapatos mpl de tacón; **high jump** n (Sport) salto de altura; **highlands** npl tierras fpl altas; **the Highlands** npl (in Scotland) las Tierras Altas de Escocia; **highlight** n (fig: of event) punto culminante ▷ vt subrayar; **highlights** npl (in hair) reflejos mpl; **highlighter** n rotulador; **highly** adv sumamente; **highly paid** muy bien pagado; **to speak highly of** hablar muy bien de; **highness** n altura; **Her** or **His Highness** Su Alteza; **high-rise** adj (also: **high-rise block, high-rise building**) torre f de pisos; **high school** n = Instituto Nacional de Bachillerato (SP); **high season** n (BRIT) temporada alta; **high street** n (BRIT) calle f mayor; **high-tech** (inf) adj de alta tecnología; **highway** n carretera; (US) autopista; **Highway Code** n (BRIT) código de la circulación

hijack [ˈhaɪdʒæk] vt secuestrar; **hijacker** n secuestrador(a) m/f

hike [haɪk] vi (go walking) ir de excursión (a pie) ▷ n caminata; **hiker** n excursionista mf; **hiking** n senderismo

hilarious [hɪˈlɛərɪəs] adj divertidísimo

hill [hɪl] n colina; (high) montaña; (slope) cuesta; **hillside** n ladera; **hill walking** n senderismo (de montaña); **hilly** adj montañoso

him [hɪm] pron (direct) le, lo; (indirect) le; (stressed, after prep) él; see also **me**; **himself** pron (reflexive) se; (emphatic) él mismo; (after prep) sí (mismo); see also **oneself**

hind [haɪnd] adj posterior

hinder [ˈhɪndəʳ] vt estorbar, impedir

hindsight [ˈhaɪndsaɪt] n: **with** ~ en retrospectiva

Hindu [ˈhɪnduː] n hindú mf; **Hinduism** [ˈhɪnduːɪzm] n (Rel) hinduismo

hinge [hɪndʒ] n bisagra, gozne m ▷ vi (fig): **to** ~ **on** depender de

hint [hɪnt] n indirecta; (advice) consejo ▷ vt: **to** ~ **that** insinuar que ▷ vi: **to** ~ **at** aludir a

hip [hɪp] n cadera

hippie [ˈhɪpɪ] n hippie mf, jipi mf

hippo [ˈhɪpəʊ] (pl **hippos**) n hipopótamo; **hippopotamus** (pl **hippopotamuses** or **hippopotami** [hɪpəˈpɒtəməs, -ˈpɒtəmaɪ]) n hipopótamo

hippy [ˈhɪpɪ] n = **hippie**

hire [haɪəʳ] vt (BRIT: car, equipment) alquilar; (worker) contratar ▷ n alquiler m; **for** ~ se alquila; (taxi) libre; **hire(d) car** n (BRIT) coche m de alquiler; **hire purchase** n (BRIT) compra a plazos; **to buy sth on hire purchase** comprar algo a plazos

his [hɪz] pron (el) suyo/(la) suya etc ▷ adj su; see also **my; mine**

Hispanic [hɪsˈpænɪk] adj hispánico

hiss [hɪs] vi silbar

historian [hɪˈstɔːrɪən] n historiador(a) m/f

historic(al) [hɪˈstɔːrɪk(l)] adj histórico

history [ˈhɪstərɪ] n historia

hit [hɪt] vt (strike) golpear, pegar; (reach: target) alcanzar; (collide with: car) chocar contra; (fig: affect) afectar ▷ n golpe m; (success) éxito; (on website) visita; (in web search) correspondencia; **to ~ it off with sb** llevarse bien con algn; **hit back** vi defenderse; (fig) devolver golpe por golpe

hitch [hɪtʃ] vt (fasten) atar, amarrar; (also: ~ **up**) arremangarse ▷ n (difficulty) problema, pega; **to ~ a lift** hacer autostop

hitch-hike [ˈhɪtʃhaɪk] vi hacer autostop; **hitch-hiker** n autostopista mf; **hitch-hiking** n autostop m

hi-tech [haɪˈtɛk] adj de alta tecnología

hitman [ˈhɪtmæn] n asesino a sueldo

HIV n abbr (= human immunodeficiency virus) VIH m; **~-negative** VIH negativo; **~-positive** VIH positivo, seropositivo

hive [haɪv] n colmena

hoard [hɔːd] n (treasure) tesoro; (stockpile) provisión f ▷ vt acumular

hoarse [hɔːs] adj ronco

hoax [həʊks] n engaño

hob [hɒb] n quemador m

hobble [ˈhɒbl] vi cojear

hobby [ˈhɒbɪ] n pasatiempo, afición f

hobo [ˈhəʊbəʊ] n (us) vagabundo

hockey [ˈhɒkɪ] n hockey m; **hockey stick** n palo m de hockey

hog [hɒg] n cerdo, puerco ▷ vt (fig) acaparar; **to go the whole** ~ echar el todo por el todo

Hogmanay [hɒgməˈneɪ] n Nochevieja

- **HOGMANAY**
-
- La Nochevieja o New Year's Eve se
- conoce como Hogmanay en Escocia,
- donde se festeje de forma especial.
- La familia y los amigos se suelen
- juntar para oír las campanadas del
- reloj y luego se hace el first-footing,

● costumbre que consiste en visitar a
los amigos y vecinos llevando algo
de beber (generalmente whisky) y
un trozo de carbón que se supone
que traerá buena suerte para el año
entrante.

hoist [hɔɪst] n (crane) grúa ▷ vt
levantar, alzar

hold [həʊld] (pt, pp **held**) vt sostener;
(contain) contener; (have: power,
qualification) tener; (keep back) retener;
(believe) sostener; (meeting) celebrar
▷ vi (withstand: pressure) resistir; (be
valid) ser válido; (stick) pegarse ▷ n
(grasp) asimiento; (fig) dominio; **~
the line!** (Tel) ¡no cuelgue!; **to ~ one's
own** (fig) defenderse; **to catch** or **get
(a) ~ of** agarrarse o asirse de; **hold
back** vt retener; (secret) ocultar; **hold
on** vi agarrarse bien; (wait) esperar; **~
on!** (Tel) ¡espere un momento!; **hold
out** vt ofrecer ▷ vi (resist) resistir; **hold
up** vt (raise) levantar; (support) apoyar;
(delay) retrasar; (rob) asaltar; **holdall** n
(BRIT) bolsa; **holder** n (of ticket, record)
poseedor/a m/f; (of passport, post,
office, title etc) titular mf

hole [həʊl] n agujero

holiday ['hɒlədɪ] n vacaciones fpl;
(day off) día m de) fiesta, día m festivo
or feriado (LAM); **on ~** de vacaciones;
holiday camp n (BRIT) colonia or
centro vacacional; **holiday job** n
(BRIT) trabajo para las vacaciones;
holidaymaker n (BRIT) turista mf;
holiday resort n centro turístico

Holland ['hɒlənd] n Holanda

hollow ['hɒləʊ] adj hueco; (fig) vacío;
(eyes) hundido; (sound) sordo ▷ n
hueco; (in ground) hoyo ▷ vt: **to ~ out**
ahuecar

holly ['hɒlɪ] n acebo

Hollywood ['hɒlɪwʊd] n Hollywood
m

holocaust ['hɒləkɔːst] n holocausto

holy ['həʊlɪ] adj santo, sagrado; (water) bendito

home [həʊm] n casa; (country) patria;
(institution) asilo ▷ adj (domestic)
casero, de casa; (Econ, Pol) nacional
▷ adv (direction) a casa; **at ~** en casa;
to go/come ~ ir/volver a casa; **make
yourself at ~** ¡estás en tu casa!; **home
address** n domicilio; **homeland** n
tierra natal; **homeless** adj sin hogar,
sin casa; **homely** adj (simple) sencillo;
home-made adj casero; **Home
match** n partido en casa; **Home
Office** n (BRIT) Ministerio del Interior;
home owner n propietario/a de una
casa; **home page** n (Comput) página
de inicio; **Home Secretary** n (BRIT)
Ministro del Interior; **homesick** adj:
to be homesick tener morriña or
nostalgia; **home town** n ciudad f
natal; **homework** n deberes mpl

homicide ['hɒmɪsaɪd] n (us)
homicidio

homoeopathic, (us)
homeopathic [həʊmɪəʊ'pæθɪk]
adj homeopático

homoeopathy, (us) **homeopathy**
[həʊmɪ'ɒpəθɪ] n homeopatía

homosexual [hɒməʊ'seksjʊəl] adj,
n homosexual mf

honest ['ɒnɪst] adj honrado;
(sincere) franco, sincero; **honestly**
adv honradamente; francamente;
honesty n honradez f

honey ['hʌnɪ] n miel f; **honeymoon**
n luna de miel; **honeysuckle** n
madreselva

Hong Kong ['hɒŋ'kɒŋ] n Hong-
Kong m

honorary ['ɒnərərɪ] adj no
remunerado; (duty, title) honorífico;
~ degree doctorado honoris causa

honour, (us) **honor** ['ɒnə] vt honrar;
(commitment, promise) cumplir con ▷ n
honor m, honra; **honourable**, (us)
honorable ['ɒnərəbl] adj honorable;
honours degree n (Univ) licenciatura
superior

hood [hʊd] n capucha; (BRIT Aut)
capota; (us Aut) capó m; (of cooker)

campana de humos; **hoodie** ['hʊdɪ] n (pullover) sudadera f con capucha; (young person) capuchero/a

hoof (pl **hoofs** or **hooves**) [huːf, huːvz] n pezuña

hook [hʊk] n gancho; (on dress) corchete m, broche m; (for fishing) anzuelo ▷ vt enganchar

hooligan ['huːlɪɡən] n gamberro

hoop [huːp] n aro

hooray [huːˈreɪ] excl = **hurrah**

hoot [huːt] vi (BRIT Aut) tocar la bocina; (siren) sonar; (owl) ulular

hooves [huːvz] pl of **hoof**

hop [hɒp] vi saltar, brincar; (on one foot) saltar con un pie

hope [həʊp] vt, vi esperar ▷ n esperanza; **I - so/not** espero que sí/no; (situation) prometedor adj (person) optimista; **hopefully** adv con esperanza; **hopefully he will recover** esperamos que se recupere; **hopeless** adj desesperado

hops [hɒps] npl lúpulo sg

horizon [həˈraɪzn] n horizonte m; **horizontal** [hɒrɪˈzɒntl] adj horizontal

hormone ['hɔːməʊn] n hormona

horn [hɔːn] n cuerno; (Mus: also: **French ~**) trompa; (Aut) bocina, claxon m

horoscope ['hɒrəskəʊp] n horóscopo

horrendous [həˈrendəs] adj horrendo

horrible ['hɒrɪbl] adj horrible

horrid ['hɒrɪd] adj horrible, horroroso

horrific [həˈrɪfɪk] adj (accident) horroroso; (film) horripilante

horrifying ['hɒrɪfaɪɪŋ] adj horroroso

horror ['hɒrə] n horror m; **horror film** n película de terror o miedo

hors d'oeuvre [ɔːˈdəːvrə] n entremeses mpl

horse [hɔːs] n caballo; **horseback** n: **on horseback** a caballo; **horse chestnut** n (tree) castaño de Indias; (nut) castaña de Indias; **horsepower** n caballo (de fuerza), potencia en caballos; **horse-racing** n carreras fpl

de caballos; **horseradish** n rábano picante; **horse riding** n (BRIT) equitación f

hose [həʊz] n (also: **~pipe**) manguera

hospital ['hɒspɪtl] n hospital m

hospitality [hɒspɪˈtælɪtɪ] n hospitalidad f

host [həʊst] n anfitrión m; (TV, Radio) presentador/a) m/f; (Rel) hostia; (large number): **a - of** multitud de

hostage ['hɒstɪdʒ] n rehén m

hostel ['hɒstl] n hostal m; (youth) ~ albergue m juvenil

hostess [ˈhəʊstɪs] n anfitriona; (BRIT: air hostess) azafata; (TV, Radio) presentadora

hostile ['hɒstaɪl] adj hostil

hostility [hɒˈstɪlɪtɪ] n hostilidad f

hot [hɒt] adj caliente; (weather) caluroso, de calor; (as opposed to only warm) muy caliente; (spicy) picante; **to be ~** (person) tener calor; (object) estar caliente; (weather) hacer calor; **hot dog** n perrito caliente

hotel [həʊˈtel] n hotel m

hotspot ['hɒtspɒt] n (Comput: also: **wireless ~**) punto de acceso inalámbrico

hot-water bottle [hɒtˈwɔːtə-] n bolsa de agua caliente

hound [haʊnd] vt acosar ▷ n perro de caza

hour ['aʊə] n hora; **hourly** adj (de) cada hora

house [haʊs] n casa; (Pol) cámara; (Theat) sala ▷ vt [haʊz] (person) alojar; **it's on the** ~ (fig) la casa invita; **household** n familia; **householder** n propietario/a; (head of house) cabeza de familia; **housekeeper** n ama de llaves; **housekeeping** n (work) trabajos mpl domésticos; **housewife** n ama de casa; **house wine** n vino m de la casa; **housework** n faenas fpl (de la casa)

housing ['haʊzɪŋ] n (act) alojamiento; (houses) viviendas *fpl*; **housing development,** (BRIT); **housing estate** *n* urbanización *f*

hover ['hɒvə'] *vi* flotar (en el aire); **hovercraft** *n* aerodeslizador *m*

how [hau] *adv* cómo; **~ are you?** ¿cómo estás?; **~ long have you been here?** ¿cuánto (tiempo) hace que estás aquí?, ¿cuánto (tiempo) llevas aquí?; **~ lovely!** ¡qué bonito!; **~ many/much?** ¿cuántos/cuánto?; **~ much does it cost?** ¿cuánto cuesta?; **~ old are you?** ¿cuántos años tienes?; **~ is school?** ¿qué tal la escuela?; **~ was the film?** ¿qué tal la película?

however [hau'ɛvə'] *adv* de cualquier manera; (+ *adjective*) por muy ... que; (*in questions*) cómo *▷ conj* sin embargo, no obstante; **~ I do it** lo haga como lo haga; **~ cold it is** por mucho frío que haga; **~ did you do it?** ¿cómo lo hiciste?

howl [haul] *n* aullido *▷ vi* aullar; (*person*) dar alaridos; (*wind*) ulular

HP *n abbr* (BRIT) = **hire purchase**

hp *abbr* = **horsepower**

HQ *n abbr* = **headquarters**

hr(s) *abbr* (= *hour(s)*) h

HTML *n abbr* (= *hypertext markup language*) HTML *m*

hubcap ['hʌbkæp] *n* tapacubos *m inv*

huddle ['hʌdl] *vi*: **to ~ together** amontonarse

huff [hʌf] *n*: **in a ~** enojado

hug [hʌg] *vt* abrazar *▷ n* abrazo

huge [hjuːdʒ] *adj* enorme

hull [hʌl] *n* (*of ship*) casco

hum [hʌm] *vt* tararear, canturrear *▷ vi* tararear, canturrear; (*insect*) zumbar

human ['hjuːmən] *adj* humano

humane [hjuː'meɪn] *adj* humano, humanitario

humanitarian [hjuːmænɪ'tɛərɪən] *adj* humanitario

humanity [hjuː'mænɪtɪ] *n* humanidad *f*

human rights *npl* derechos *mpl* humanos

humble ['hʌmbl] *adj* humilde

humid ['hjuːmɪd] *adj* húmedo; **humidity** [hjuː'mɪdɪtɪ] *n* humedad *f*

humiliate [hjuː'mɪlɪeɪt] *vt* humillar

humiliating [hjuː'mɪlɪeɪtɪŋ] *adj* humillante, vergonzoso

humiliation [hjuːmɪlɪ'eɪʃən] *n* humillación *f*

hummus ['huməs] *n* humus *m*

humorous ['hjuːmərəs] *adj* gracioso, divertido

humour, (US) **humor** ['hjuːmə'] *n* humorismo, sentido del humor; (*mood*) humor *m ▷ vt* (*person*) complacer

hump [hʌmp] *n* (*in ground*) montículo; (*camel's*) giba

hunch [hʌntʃ] *n* (*premonition*) presentimiento

hundred ['hʌndrəd] *num* ciento; (*before n*) cien; **~s of** centenares de; **hundredth** *adj* centésimo

hung [hʌŋ] *pt, pp of* **hang**

Hungarian [hʌŋ'gɛərɪən] *adj* húngaro *▷ n* húngaro/a

Hungary ['hʌŋgərɪ] *n* Hungría

hunger ['hʌŋgə'] *n* hambre *f ▷ vi*: **to ~ for** (*fig*) tener hambre de, anhelar

hungry ['hʌŋgrɪ] *adj* hambriento; **to be ~** tener hambre

hunt [hʌnt] *vt* (*seek*) buscar; (*Sport*) cazar *▷ vi* (*search*): **to ~ (for)** buscar; (*Sport*) cazar *▷ n* caza, cacería; **hunter** *n* cazador(a) *m/f*; **hunting** *n* caza

hurdle ['hɜːdl] *n* (*Sport*) valla; (*fig*) obstáculo

hurl [hɜːl] *vt* lanzar, arrojar

hurrah [hu'rɑː], **hurray** [hu'reɪ] *n* ¡viva!

hurricane ['hʌrɪkən] *n* huracán *m*

hurry ['hʌrɪ] *n* prisa *▷ vt* (*person*) dar prisa a; (*work*) apresurar, hacer de prisa; **to be in a ~** tener prisa; **hurry up** vi darse prisa, apurarse (LAM)

hurt [hɜːt] (*pt, pp* **hurt**) *vt* hacer daño a *▷ vi* doler *▷ adj* lastimado

husband ['hʌzbənd] *n* marido

hush [hʌʃ] *n* silencio *▷ vt* hacer callar; **~!** ¡chitón!, ¡cállate!

husky ['hʌskɪ] *adj* ronco ▷ *n* perro esquimal
hut [hʌt] *n* cabaña; (*shed*) cobertizo
hyacinth ['haɪəsɪnθ] *n* jacinto
hydrangea [haɪ'dreɪndʒə] *n* hortensia
hydrofoil ['haɪdrəfɔɪl] *n* aerodeslizador *m*
hydrogen ['haɪdrədʒən] *n* hidrógeno
hygiene ['haɪdʒiːn] *n* higiene *f*;
hygienic [haɪ'dʒiːnɪk] *adj* higiénico
hymn [hɪm] *n* himno
hype [haɪp] *n* (*inf*) bombo
hyperlink ['haɪpəlɪŋk] *n* hiperenlace *m*
hyphen ['haɪfn] *n* guión *m*
hypnotize ['hɪpnətaɪz] *vt* hipnotizar
hypocrite ['hɪpəkrɪt] *n* hipócrita *mf*
hypocritical [hɪpə'krɪtɪkl] *adj* hipócrita
hypothesis (*pl* **hypotheses**) [haɪ'pɒθɪsɪs, -siːz] *n* hipótesis *f inv*
hysterical [hɪ'sterɪkl] *adj* histérico
hysterics [hɪ'sterɪks] *npl* histeria *sg*, histerismo *sg*; **to be in ~** (*fig*) morirse de risa

◆

I

I [aɪ] *pron* yo
ice [aɪs] *n* hielo ▷ *vt* (*cake*) alcorzar ▷ *vi* (*also:* **~ over, ~ up**) helarse; **iceberg** *n* iceberg *m*; **ice cream** *n* helado; **ice cube** *n* cubito de hielo; **ice hockey** *n* hockey *m* sobre hielo
Iceland ['aɪslənd] *n* Islandia; **Icelander** *n* islandés/esa *m/f*; **Icelandic** [aɪs'lændɪk] *adj* islandés/esa ▷ *n* (*Ling*) islandés *m*
ice: ice lolly *n* (*BRIT*) polo; **ice rink** *n* pista de hielo; **ice-skating** *n* patinaje *m* sobre hielo
icing ['aɪsɪŋ] *n* (*Culin*) alcorza; **icing sugar** *n* (*BRIT*) azúcar *m* glas(eado)
icon ['aɪkɔn] *n* icono
ICT *n abbr* (= *Information and Communication(s) Technology*) TIC *f*; (*BRIT Scol*) informática
icy ['aɪsɪ] *adj* helado
I'd [aɪd] = **I would; I had**
ID card *n* (*identity card*) DNI *m*
idea [aɪ'dɪə] *n* idea

ideal [aɪˈdɪəl] n ideal m ⊳ adj ideal;
ideally [aɪˈdɪəlɪ] adv

identical [aɪˈdɛntɪkl] adj idéntico

identification [aɪdɛntɪfɪˈkeɪʃən]
n identificación f; **means of ~**
documentos mpl personales

identify [aɪˈdɛntɪfaɪ] vt identificar

identity [aɪˈdɛntɪtɪ] n identidad f;
identity card n carnet m de identidad;
identity theft n robo de identidad

ideology [aɪdɪˈɒlədʒɪ] n ideología f

idiom [ˈɪdɪəm] n modismo; (style of
speaking) lenguaje m

  Be careful not to translate idiom by
  the Spanish word idioma.

idiot [ˈɪdɪət] n idiota mf

idle [ˈaɪdl] adj (inactive) ocioso; (lazy)
holgazán/ana; (unemployed) parado,
desocupado; (talk) frívolo ⊳ vi (machine)
funcionar o marchar en vacío

idol [ˈaɪdl] n ídolo

idyllic [ɪˈdɪlɪk] adj idílico

i.e. abbr (= id est) es decir

if [ɪf] conj si; **if necessary** si resultase
necesario; **if I were you** yo en tu
lugar; **if only** si solamente; **as if**
como si

ignite [ɪgˈnaɪt] vt (set fire to) encender
⊳ vi encenderse

ignition [ɪgˈnɪʃən] n (Aut: process)
ignición f; (: mechanism) encendido; **to
switch on/off the ~** arrancar/apagar
el motor

ignorance [ˈɪgnərəns] n ignorancia

ignorant [ˈɪgnərənt] adj ignorante;
to be ~ of ignorar

ignore [ɪgˈnɔː] vt (person) no hacer
caso de; (fact) pasar por alto

ill [ɪl] adj enfermo, malo ⊳ n mal m
⊳ adv mal; **to take** or **be taken ~** caer
o ponerse enfermo

I'll [aɪl] = **I will; I shall**

illegal [ɪˈliːgl] adj ilegal

illegible [ɪˈlɛdʒɪbl] adj ilegible

illegitimate [ɪlɪˈdʒɪtɪmət] adj
ilegítimo

ill health n mala salud f; **to be in ~**
estar mal de salud

illiterate [ɪˈlɪtərət] adj analfabeto

illness [ˈɪlnɪs] n enfermedad f

illuminate [ɪˈluːmɪneɪt] vt (room,
street) iluminar, alumbrar

illusion [ɪˈluːʒən] n ilusión f

illustrate [ˈɪləstreɪt] vt ilustrar

illustration [ɪləˈstreɪʃən] n (example)
ejemplo, ilustración f; (in book) lámina

I'm [aɪm] = **I am**

image [ˈɪmɪdʒ] n imagen f

imaginary [ɪˈmædʒɪnərɪ] adj
imaginario

imagination [ɪmædʒɪˈneɪʃən] n
imaginación f; (inventiveness) inventiva

imaginative [ɪˈmædʒɪnətɪv] adj
imaginativo

imagine [ɪˈmædʒɪn] vt imaginarse

imbalance [ɪmˈbæləns] n
desequilibrio

imitate [ˈɪmɪteɪt] vt imitar; **imitation**
[ɪmɪˈteɪʃən] n imitación f; (copy) copia

immaculate [ɪˈmækjulət] adj
inmaculado

immature [ɪməˈtjuəʳ] adj (person)
inmaduro

immediate [ɪˈmiːdɪət] adj
inmediato; (pressing) urgente,
apremiante; (nearest: family)
próximo; (: neighbourhood) inmediato;
immediately adv (at once) en
seguida; (directly) inmediatamente;
immediately next to justo al lado de

immense [ɪˈmɛns] adj inmenso,
enorme; **immensely** adv
enormemente

immerse [ɪˈmɜːs] vt (submerge)
sumergir; **to be ~d in** (fig) estar
absorto en

immigrant [ˈɪmɪgrənt] n inmigrante
mf; **immigration** [ɪmɪˈgreɪʃən] n
inmigración f

imminent [ˈɪmɪnənt] adj inminente

immoral [ɪˈmɒrl] adj inmoral

immortal [ɪˈmɔːtl] adj inmortal

immune [ɪˈmjuːn] adj: **~ (to)** inmune
(a); **immune system** n sistema m
inmunitario

immunize [ˈɪmjunaɪz] vt inmunizar

impact ['ɪmpækt] n impacto

impair [ɪm'peəʳ] vt perjudicar

impartial [ɪm'pɑːʃl] adj imparcial

impatience [ɪm'peɪʃəns] n impaciencia

impatient [ɪm'peɪʃənt] adj impaciente; **to get** or **grow ~** impacientarse

impeccable [ɪm'pekəbl] adj impecable

impending [ɪm'pendɪŋ] adj inminente

imperative [ɪm'perətɪv] adj (tone) imperioso; (necessary) imprescindible

imperfect [ɪm'pɜːfɪkt] adj (goods etc) defectuoso ▷ n (Ling: also: **~ tense**) imperfecto

imperial [ɪm'pɪərɪəl] adj imperial

impersonal [ɪm'pɜːsənl] adj impersonal

impersonate [ɪm'pɜːsəneɪt] vt hacerse pasar por

impetus ['ɪmpətəs] n ímpetu m; (fig) impulso

implant [ɪm'plɑːnt] vt (Med) injertar, implantar; (fig: idea, principle) inculcar

implement n ['ɪmplɪmənt] herramienta ▷ vt ['ɪmplɪment] hacer efectivo; (carry out) realizar

implicate ['ɪmplɪkeɪt] vt (compromise) comprometer; **to ~ sb in sth** comprometer a algn en algo

implication [ɪmplɪ'keɪʃən] n consecuencia; **by ~** indirectamente

implicit [ɪm'plɪsɪt] adj implícito; (absolute) absoluto

imply [ɪm'plaɪ] vt (involve) suponer; (hint) insinuar

impolite [ɪmpə'laɪt] adj mal educado

import vt [ɪm'pɔːt] importar ▷ n ['ɪmpɔːt] (Comm) importación f; (: article) producto importado; (meaning) significado, sentido

importance [ɪm'pɔːtəns] n importancia

important [ɪm'pɔːtənt] adj importante; **it's not ~** no importa, no tiene importancia

importer [ɪm'pɔːtəʳ] n importador(a) m/f

impose [ɪm'pəuz] vt imponer ▷ vi: **to ~ on sb** abusar de algn; **imposing** adj imponente, impresionante

impossible [ɪm'pɒsɪbl] adj imposible; (person) insoportable

impotent ['ɪmpətənt] adj impotente

impoverished [ɪm'pɒvərɪʃt] adj necesitado

impractical [ɪm'præktɪkl] adj (person) poco práctico

impress [ɪm'pres] vt impresionar; (mark) estampar; **to ~ sth on sb** convencer a algn de la importancia de algo

impression [ɪm'preʃən] n impresión f; **to be under the ~ that** tener la impresión de que

impressive [ɪm'presɪv] adj impresionante

imprison [ɪm'prɪzn] vt encarcelar; **imprisonment** n encarcelamiento; (term of imprisonment) cárcel f

improbable [ɪm'prɒbəbl] adj improbable, inverosímil

improper [ɪm'prɒpəʳ] adj (incorrect) impropio; (unseemly) indecoroso; (indecent) indecente; (dishonest: activities) deshonesto

improve [ɪm'pruːv] vt mejorar; (foreign language) perfeccionar ▷ vi mejorar; **improvement** n mejora; perfeccionamiento

improvise ['ɪmprəvaɪz] vt, vi improvisar

impulse ['ɪmpʌls] n impulso; **to act on ~** actuar sin reflexionar; **impulsive** [ɪm'pʌlsɪv] adj irreflexivo

○ **KEYWORD**

in [ɪn] prep 1 (indicating place, position, with place names): **in the house/garden** en (la) casa/el jardín; **in here/there** aquí/ahí or allí dentro; **in London/England** en Londres/Inglaterra

2 (*indicating time*) en; **in spring** en (la) primavera; **in 1988/May** en 1988/ mayo; **in the afternoon** por la tarde; **at four o'clock in the afternoon** a las cuarto de la tarde; **I did it in three hours/days** lo hice en tres horas/ días; **I'll see you in two weeks** *or* **in two weeks' time** te veré dentro de dos semanas

3 (*indicating manner etc*) en; **in a loud/soft voice** en voz alta/baja; **in pencil/ink** a lápiz/bolígrafo; **the boy in the blue shirt** el chico de la camisa azul

4 (*indicating circumstances*): **in the sun/shade** al sol/a la sombra; **in the rain** bajo la lluvia; **a change in policy** un cambio de política

5 (*indicating mood, state*): **in tears** llorando; **in anger/despair** enfadado/desesperado; **to live in luxury** vivir lujosamente

6 (*with ratios, numbers*): **1 in 10 households, 1 household in 10** una de cada 10 familias; **20 pence in the pound** 20 peniques por libra; **they lined up in twos** se alinearon de dos en dos

7 (*referring to people, works*) en; entre; **the disease is common in children** la enfermedad es común entre los niños; **in (the works of) Dickens** en (las obras de) Dickens

8 (*indicating profession etc*): **to be in teaching** dedicarse a la enseñanza

9 (*after superlative*) de; **the best pupil in the class** el/la mejor alumno/a de la clase

10 (*with present participle*): **in saying this** al decir esto

▸ *adv*: **to be in** (*person: at home*) estar en casa; (: *at work*) estar; (*train, ship, plane*) haber llegado; (*in fashion*) estar de moda; **she'll be in later today** llegará más tarde hoy; **to ask sb in** hacer pasar a algn; **to run/limp** *etc* **in** entrar corriendo/ cojeando *etc*

▸ *n*: **the ins and outs** (*of proposal, situation etc*) los detalles

inability [ɪnəˈbɪlɪtɪ] *n*: **~ (to do)** incapacidad *f* (de hacer)

inaccurate [ɪnˈækjʊrət] *adj* inexacto, incorrecto

inadequate [ɪnˈædɪkwət] *adj* (*insufficient*) insuficiente; (*person*) incapaz

inadvertently [ɪnədˈvɜ:tntlɪ] *adv* por descuido

inappropriate [ɪnəˈprəʊprɪət] *adj* inadecuado

inaugurate [ɪˈnɔːgjʊreɪt] *vt* inaugurar; (*president, official*) investir

Inc. *abbr* = **incorporated**

incapable [ɪnˈkeɪpəbl] *adj*: **~ (of doing sth)** incapaz (de hacer algo)

incense *n* [ˈɪnsɛns] incienso ▸ *vt* [ɪnˈsɛns] (*anger*) indignar, encolerizar

incentive [ɪnˈsɛntɪv] *n* incentivo, estímulo

inch [ɪntʃ] *n* pulgada; **to be within an ~ of** estar a dos dedos de; **he didn't give an ~** no hizo la más mínima concesión

incidence [ˈɪnsɪdns] *n* (*of crime, disease*) incidencia

incident [ˈɪnsɪdnt] *n* incidente *m*

incidentally [ɪnsɪˈdɛntəlɪ] *adv* (*by the way*) por cierto

inclination [ɪnklɪˈneɪʃən] *n* (*tendency*) tendencia, inclinación *f*

incline *n* [ˈɪnklaɪn, *vt, vi* ɪnˈklaɪn] pendiente *f*, cuesta ▸ *vt* (*head*) poner de lado ▸ *vi* inclinarse; **to be ~d to** (*tend*) ser propenso a

include [ɪnˈkluːd] *vt* incluir; (*in letter*) adjuntar; **including** *prep* incluso, inclusive; **including tip** propina incluida

inclusion [ɪnˈkluːʒən] *n* inclusión *f*

inclusive [ɪnˈkluːsɪv] *adj* inclusivo; **~ of tax** incluidos los impuestos

income [ˈɪnkʌm] *n* (*personal*) ingresos *mpl*; (*from property etc*) renta; (*profit*) rédito; **income support** *n* (BRIT)

≈ ayuda familiar; **income tax** n impuesto sobre la renta

incoming ['ɪnkʌmɪŋ] adj (passengers, flight) de llegada; (government) entrante; (tenant) nuevo

incompatible [ɪnkəm'pætɪbl] adj incompatible

incompetence [ɪn'kɔmpɪtəns] n incompetencia

incompetent [ɪn'kɔmpɪtənt] adj incompetente

incomplete [ɪnkəm'pli:t] adj incompleto; (unfinished) sin terminar

inconsistent [ɪnkən'sɪstnt] adj inconsecuente; (contradictory) incongruente; **~ with** que no concuerda con

inconvenience [ɪnkən'vi:njəns] n inconvenientes mpl; (trouble) molestia ▷ vt incomodar

inconvenient [ɪnkən'vi:njənt] adj incómodo, poco práctico; (time, place) inoportuno

incorporate [ɪn'kɔːpəreɪt] vt incorporar; (contain) comprender; (add) agregar

incorporated [ɪn'kɔːpəreɪtɪd] adj: **~ company** (US) ≈ Sociedad f Anónima (S.A.)

incorrect [ɪnkə'rekt] adj incorrecto

increase [n 'ɪnkri:s, vi, vt ɪn'kri:s] n aumento ▷ vi aumentar; (grow) crecer; (price) subir ▷ vt aumentar; (price) subir; **increasingly** adv cada vez más

incredible adj increíble; **incredibly** adv increíblemente

incur [ɪn'kə:ʳ] vt (expenses) incurrir en; (loss) sufrir; (anger, disapproval) provocar

indecent [ɪn'di:snt] adj indecente

indeed [ɪn'di:d] adv efectivamente, en realidad; (in fact) en efecto; (furthermore) es más; **¡**claro que sí!

indefinitely [ɪn'defɪnɪtlɪ] adv (wait) indefinidamente

independence [ɪndɪ'pendns] n independencia; **Independence Day** n Día m de la Independencia

○ **INDEPENDENCE DAY**

○ El cuatro de julio es la fiesta nacional
○ de los Estados Unidos, *Independence*
○ *Day*, en conmemoración de la
○ Declaración de Independencia
○ escrita por Thomas Jefferson
○ y adoptada en 1776. En ella se
○ proclamaba la ruptura total con
○ Gran Bretaña de las trece colonias
○ americanas que fueron el origen de
○ los Estados Unidos de América.

independent [ɪndɪ'pendənt] adj independiente; **independent school** n (BRIT) escuela f privada, colegio m privado

index ['ɪndeks] n (pl **indexes**) (in book) índices m; (in library etc) catálogo; (pl **indexes**: ratio, sign) exponente m

India ['ɪndɪə] n la India; **Indian** adj, n india/o; (pej): **Red Indian** piel roja mf

indicate ['ɪndɪkeɪt] vt indicar; **indication** [ɪndɪ'keɪʃən] n indicio, señal f; **indicative** [ɪn'dɪkətɪv] adj: **to be indicative of sth** indicar algo; **indicator** n indicador m; (Aut) intermitente m

indices ['ɪndɪsiːz] npl of **index**

indict [ɪn'daɪt] vt acusar; **indictment** n acusación f

indifference [ɪn'dɪfrəns] n indiferencia

indifferent [ɪn'dɪfrənt] adj indiferente; (poor) regular

indigenous [ɪn'dɪdʒɪnəs] adj indígena

indigestion [ɪndɪ'dʒestʃən] n indigestión f

indignant [ɪn'dɪgnənt] adj: **to be ~ about sth** indignarse por algo

indirect [ɪndɪ'rekt] adj indirecto

indispensable [ɪndɪ'spensəbl] adj indispensable, imprescindible

individual [ɪndɪ'vɪdjuəl] n individuo ▷ adj individual; (personal) personal; (particular) particular; **individually** adv individualmente

Indonesia [ɪndəˈniːzɪə] n Indonesia

indoor [ˈɪndɔːʳ] adj (swimming pool)
cubierto; (plant) de interior; (sport)
bajo cubierta; **indoors** [ɪnˈdɔːz] adv
dentro

induce [ɪnˈdjuːs] vt inducir, persuadir;
(bring about) producir

indulge [ɪnˈdʌldʒ] vt (whim)
satisfacer; (person) complacer; (child)
mimar ⊳ vi: **to ~ in** darse el gusto de;
indulgent adj indulgente

industrial [ɪnˈdʌstrɪəl] adj industrial;
industrial estate n (BRIT) polígono or
(LAM) zona industrial; **industrialist**
n industrial mf; **industrial park** n (US)
= **industrial estate**

industry [ˈɪndəstrɪ] n industria;
(diligence) aplicación f

inefficient [ɪnɪˈfɪʃənt] adj ineficaz,
ineficiente

inequality [ɪnɪˈkwɔlɪtɪ] n
desigualdad f

inevitable [ɪnˈevɪtəbl] adj inevitable;
(necessary) forzoso; **inevitably** adv
inevitablemente

inexpensive [ɪnɪkˈspensɪv] adj
económico

inexperienced [ɪnɪkˈspɪərɪənst] adj
inexperto

inexplicable [ɪnɪkˈsplɪkəbl] adj
inexplicable

infamous [ˈɪnfəməs] adj infame

infant [ˈɪnfənt] n niño/a; (baby)
niño/a pequeño/a, bebé mf

infantry [ˈɪnfəntrɪ] n infantería

infant school n (BRIT) escuela
infantil

infect [ɪnˈfekt] vt (wound) infectar;
(food) contaminar; (person, animal)
contagiar; **infection** [ɪnˈfekʃən] n
infección f; (fig) contagio; **infectious**
[ɪnˈfekʃəs] adj contagioso

infer [ɪnˈfəːʳ] vt deducir, inferir

inferior [ɪnˈfɪərɪəʳ] adj, n inferior mf

infertile [ɪnˈfəːtaɪl] adj estéril;
(person) infecundo

infertility [ɪnfəˈtɪlɪtɪ] n esterilidad f;
infecundidad f

infested [ɪnˈfestɪd] adj: **~ (with)**
plagado (de)

infinite [ˈɪnfɪnɪt] adj infinito;
infinitely adv infinitamente

infirmary [ɪnˈfəːmərɪ] n hospital m

inflamed [ɪnˈfleɪmd] adj: **to become
~** inflamarse

inflammation [ɪnfləˈmeɪʃən] n
inflamación f

inflatable [ɪnˈfleɪtəbl] adj inflable

inflate [ɪnˈfleɪt] vt (tyre) inflar; (fig)
hinchar; **inflation** [ɪnˈfleɪʃən] n (Econ)
inflación f

inflexible [ɪnˈfleksɪbl] adj inflexible

inflict [ɪnˈflɪkt] vt: **to ~ on** infligir en

influence [ˈɪnfluəns] n influencia ⊳ vt
influir en, influenciar; **under the ~
of alcohol** en estado de embriaguez;
influential [ɪnfluˈenʃl] adj influyente

influx [ˈɪnflʌks] n afluencia

info [ˈɪnfəu] n (inf) = **information**

inform [ɪnˈfɔːm] vt: **to ~ sb of sth**
informar a algn sobre or de algo ⊳ vi:
to ~ on sb delatar a algn

informal [ɪnˈfɔːml] adj (manner,
tone) desenfadado; (dress, occasion)
informal; (visit, meeting) extraoficial

information [ɪnfəˈmeɪʃən]
n información f; (knowledge)
conocimientos; **a piece of
~** un dato; **information office**
n información f; **information
technology** n informática

informative [ɪnˈfɔːmətɪv] adj
informativo

infra-red [ˈɪnfrəˈred] adj infrarrojo

infrastructure [ˈɪnfrəstrʌktʃəʳ] n
infraestructura

infrequent [ɪnˈfriːkwənt] adj
infrecuente

infuriate [ɪnˈfjuərɪeɪt] vt: **to
become ~d** ponerse furioso

infuriating [ɪnˈfjuərɪeɪtɪŋ] adj (habit,
noise) enloquecedor(a)

ingenious [ɪnˈdʒiːnjəs] adj
ingenioso

ingredient [ɪnˈɡriːdɪənt] n
ingrediente m

inhabit [ɪnˈhæbɪt] vt vivir en;
inhabitant n habitante mf

inhale [ɪnˈheɪl] vt inhalar ▷ vi (breathe
in) aspirar; (in smoking) tragar; **inhaler**
n inhalador m

inherent [ɪnˈhɪərənt] adj: ~ **in** or **to** ~
inherente a

inherit [ɪnˈherɪt] vt heredar;
inheritance n herencia; (fig)
patrimonio

inhibit [ɪnˈhɪbɪt] vt inhibir, impedir;
inhibition n cohibición f

initial [ɪˈnɪʃl] adj primero ▷ n inicial
f ▷ vt firmar con las iniciales; **initials**
npl iniciales fpl; (abbreviation) siglas fpl;
initially adv en un principio

initiate [ɪˈnɪʃieɪt] vt iniciar; **to ~**
proceedings against sb (Law) poner
una demanda contra algn

initiative [ɪˈnɪʃətɪv] n iniciativa f; **to ~**
take the ~ tomar la iniciativa

inject [ɪnˈdʒekt] vt inyectar; **injection**
[ɪnˈdʒekʃən] n inyección f

injure [ˈɪndʒə*] vt herir; (hurt) lastimar;
(fig: reputation etc) perjudicar; **injured**
adj herido; **injury** n herida, lesión f;
(wrong) perjuicio, daño

> Be careful not to translate **injury**
> by the Spanish word **injuria**.

injustice [ɪnˈdʒʌstɪs] n injusticia

ink [ɪŋk] n tinta; **ink-jet printer**
[ˈɪŋkdʒet-] n impresora de chorro
de tinta

inland adj [ˈɪnlənd] interior ▷ adv
[ɪnˈlænd] tierra adentro; **Inland**
Revenue n (BRIT) ≈ Hacienda,
≈ Agencia Tributaria

in-laws [ˈɪnlɔːz] npl suegros mpl

inmate [ˈɪnmeɪt] n (in prison) preso/a,
presidiario/a; (in asylum) internado/a

inn [ɪn] n posada, mesón m

inner [ˈɪnə*] adj interior; (feelings)
íntimo; **inner-city** adj (schools,
problems) de las zonas céntricas
pobres, de los barrios céntricos pobres

inning [ˈɪnɪŋ] n (US Baseball) inning m,
entrada; **~s** (Cricket) entrada, turno

innocence [ˈɪnəsns] n inocencia

innocent [ˈɪnəsnt] adj inocente

innovation [ɪnəʊˈveɪʃən] n novedad f

innovative [ˈɪnəʊvətɪv] adj
innovador

in-patient [ˈɪnpeɪʃənt] n (paciente
mf) interno/a

input [ˈɪnput] n entrada; (of resources)
inversión f; (Comput) entrada de datos

inquest [ˈɪnkwest] n (coroner's)
investigación f post-mortem

inquire [ɪnˈkwaɪə*] vi preguntar
▷ vt: **to ~ when/where/whether**
preguntar cuándo/dónde/si; **to ~**
about (person) preguntar por; (fact)
informarse de; **inquiry** n pregunta;
(Law) investigación f, pesquisa;
"**Inquiries**" "Información"

insane [ɪnˈseɪn] adj loco; (Med)
demente

insanity [ɪnˈsænɪti] n demencia,
locura

insect [ˈɪnsekt] n insecto; **insect**
repellent n loción f contra los
insectos

insecure [ɪnsɪˈkjuə*] adj inseguro

insecurity [ɪnsɪˈkjuərɪti] n
inseguridad f

insensitive [ɪnˈsensɪtɪv] adj
insensible

insert vt [ɪnˈsəːt] (into sth) introducir;
(Comput) insertar ▷ n [ˈɪnsəːt]
encarte m

inside [ɪnˈsaɪd] n interior m ▷ adj
interior, interno ▷ adv (within) (por)
dentro; (with movement) hacia dentro
▷ prep dentro de; (of time): **~ 10**
minutes en menos de 10 minutos;
~ out adv (turn) al revés; (know) a
fondo; **inside lane** n (Aut: BRIT) carril
m izquierdo; (: in US, Europe etc) carril
m derecho

insight [ˈɪnsaɪt] n perspicacia

insignificant [ɪnsɪgˈnɪfɪkənt] adj
insignificante

insincere [ɪnsɪnˈsɪə*] adj poco sincero

insist [ɪnˈsɪst] vi insistir; **to ~ on**
doing empeñarse en hacer; **to ~**
that insistir en que; (claim) exigir que;

insistent adj insistente; (noise, action) persistente

insomnia [ɪnˈsɒmnɪə] n insomnio

inspect [ɪnˈspɛkt] vt inspeccionar, examinar; (troops) pasar revista a; **inspection** [ɪnˈspɛkʃən] n inspección f, examen m; (of troops) revista; **inspector** n inspector(a) m/f; (BRIT: on buses, trains) revisor(a) m/f

inspiration [ɪnspəˈreɪʃən] n inspiración f; **inspire** [ɪnˈspaɪər] vt inspirar; **inspiring** adj inspirador(a)

instability [ɪnstəˈbɪlɪtɪ] n inestabilidad f

install, (us) **instal** [ɪnˈstɔːl] vt instalar; **installation** [ɪnstəˈleɪʃən] n instalación f

instalment, (us) **installment** [ɪnˈstɔːlmənt] n plazo; (of story) entrega; (of TV serial etc) capítulo; **in ~s** (pay, receive) a plazos

instance [ˈɪnstəns] n ejemplo, caso; **for ~** por ejemplo; **in the first ~** en primer lugar

instant [ˈɪnstənt] n instante m, momento ▷ adj inmediato; (coffee) instantáneo; **instantly** adv en seguida, al instante; **instant messaging** n mensajería instantánea

instead [ɪnˈstɛd] adv en cambio; **~ of** en lugar de, en vez de

instinct [ˈɪnstɪŋkt] n instinto; **instinctive** adj instintivo

institute [ˈɪnstɪtjuːt] n instituto; (professional body) colegio ▷ vt (begin) iniciar, empezar; (proceedings) entablar

institution [ɪnstɪˈtjuːʃən] n institución f; (Med: home) asilo; (: asylum) manicomio

instruct [ɪnˈstrʌkt] vt: **to ~ sb in sth** instruir a algn en or sobre algo; **to ~ sb to do sth** dar instrucciones a algn de or mandar a algn hacer algo; **instruction** [ɪnˈstrʌkʃən] n (teaching) instrucción f; **instructions** npl órdenes fpl; **instructions (for use)** modo sg de empleo; **instructor** n instructor(a) m/f

instrument [ˈɪnstrəmənt] n instrumento; **instrumental** [ɪnstrəˈmɛntl] adj (Mus) instrumental; **to be instrumental in** ser el artífice de

insufficient [ɪnsəˈfɪʃənt] adj insuficiente

insulate [ˈɪnsjuleɪt] vt aislar; **insulation** [ɪnsjuˈleɪʃən] n aislamiento

insulin [ˈɪnsjulɪn] n insulina

insult n [ˈɪnsʌlt] insulto ▷ vt [ɪnˈsʌlt] insultar; **insulting** adj insultante

insurance [ɪnˈʃuərəns] n seguro; **fire/life ~** seguro contra incendios/ de vida; **insurance company** n compañía f de seguros; **insurance policy** n póliza (de seguros)

insure [ɪnˈʃuər] vt asegurar

intact [ɪnˈtækt] adj íntegro; (untouched) intacto

intake [ˈɪnteɪk] n (of food) ingestión f; (BRIT Scol): **an ~ of 200 a year** 200 matriculados al año

integral [ˈɪntɪɡrəl] adj (whole) íntegro; (part) integrante

integrate [ˈɪntɪɡreɪt] vt integrar ▷ vi integrarse

integrity [ɪnˈtɛɡrɪtɪ] n honradez f, rectitud f

intellect [ˈɪntəlɛkt] n intelecto; **intellectual** [ɪntəˈlɛktjuəl] adj, n intelectual mf

intelligence [ɪnˈtɛlɪdʒəns] n inteligencia

intelligent [ɪnˈtɛlɪdʒənt] adj inteligente

intend [ɪnˈtɛnd] vt (gift etc): **to ~ sth for** destinar algo a; **to ~ to do sth** tener intención de or pensar hacer algo

intense [ɪnˈtɛns] adj intenso

intensify [ɪnˈtɛnsɪfaɪ] vt intensificar; (increase) aumentar

intensity [ɪnˈtɛnsɪtɪ] n intensidad f

intensive [ɪnˈtɛnsɪv] adj intensivo; **intensive care** n: **to be in intensive care** estar bajo cuidados intensivos;

intensive care unit unidad f de vigilancia intensiva

intent [ɪn'tent] n propósito; (Law) premeditación f ⊳ adj (absorbed) absorto; (attentive) atento; **to all -s and purposes** a efectos prácticos; **to be - on doing sth** estar resuelto o decidido a hacer algo

intention [ɪn'tenʃən] n intención f, propósito; **intentional** adj deliberado

interact [ɪntər'ækt] vi influirse mutuamente; **interaction** [ɪntər'ækʃən] n interacción f, acción f recíproca; **interactive** adj (Comput) interactivo

intercept [ɪntə'sept] vt interceptar; (stop) detener

interchange [ɪntə'tʃeɪndʒ] n intercambio; (on motorway) intersección f

intercourse ['ɪntəkɔːs] n (also: sexual ~) relaciones fpl sexuales

interest ['ɪntrɪst] n (Comm) interés m ⊳ vt interesar; **interested** adj interesado; **to be interested in** interesarse por; **interesting** adj interesante; **interest rate** n tipo de interés

interface ['ɪntəfeɪs] n (Comput) junción f

interfere [ɪntə'fɪə*] vi: **to ~ in** entrometerse en; **to ~ with** (hinder) estorbar; (damage) estropear

interference [ɪntə'fɪərəns] n intromisión f; (Radio, TV) interferencia f

interim ['ɪntərɪm] adj provisional ⊳ n: **in the ~** en el ínterin

interior [ɪn'tɪərɪə*] n interior m ⊳ adj interior; **interior design** n interiorismo, decoración f de interiores

intermediate [ɪntə'miːdɪət] adj intermedio

intermission [ɪntə'mɪʃən] n (Theat) descanso

intern vt [ɪn'təːn] internar ⊳ n ['ɪntəːn] (esp us: doctor) médico/a

interno/a; (: on work placement) becario/a

internal [ɪn'təːnl] adj interior; (injury, structure, memo) internal; **~ injuries** heridas fpl or lesiones fpl internas; **Internal Revenue Service** n (us) = Hacienda, = Agencia Tributaria

international [ɪntə'næʃənl] adj internacional; **~ (game)** partido internacional

internet, Internet ['ɪntənet] n: **the ~** (el or la) Internet; **internet café** n cibercafé m; **Internet Service Provider** n proveedor m de (acceso a) Internet; **internet user** n internauta mf

interpret [ɪn'təːprɪt] vt interpretar; (translate) traducir; (understand) entender ⊳ vi hacer de intérprete; **interpretation** [ɪntəːprɪ'teɪʃən] n interpretación f; traducción f; **interpreter** n intérprete mf

interrogate [ɪn'terəʊgeɪt] vt interrogar; **interrogation** [ɪnterəʊ'geɪʃən] n interrogatorio; **interrogative** [ɪntə'rɒgətɪv] adj interrogativo

interrupt [ɪntə'rʌpt] vt, vi interrumpir; **interruption** [ɪntə'rʌpʃən] n interrupción f

intersection [ɪntə'sekʃən] n (of roads) cruce m

interstate ['ɪntəsteɪt] n (us) carretera interestatal

interval ['ɪntəvl] n intervalo; (BRIT Theat, Sport) descanso; (Scol) recreo; **at -s** a ratos, de vez en cuando

intervene [ɪntə'viːn] vi intervenir; (take part) participar; (occur) sobrevenir

interview ['ɪntəvjuː] n entrevista ⊳ vt entrevistar a; **interviewer** n entrevistador(a) m/f

intimate adj ['ɪntɪmət] íntimo; (friendship) estrecho; (knowledge) profundo ⊳ vt ['ɪntɪmeɪt] dar a entender

intimidate [ɪnˈtɪmɪdeɪt] vt intimidar, amedrentar; **intimidating** adj amedrentador, intimidante

into [ˈɪntu:] prep en; (towards) a; (inside) hacia el interior de; **~ three pieces/French** en tres pedazos/al francés

intolerant [ɪnˈtɒlərənt] adj: **~ (of)** intolerante (con)

intranet [ˈɪntrənet] n intranet f

intransitive [ɪnˈtrænsɪtɪv] adj intransitivo

intricate [ˈɪntrɪkət] adj (design, pattern) intrincado

intrigue [ɪnˈtri:g] n intriga ▷ vt fascinar; **intriguing** adj fascinante

introduce [ɪntrəˈdju:s] vt introducir, meter; (speaker, TV show etc) presentar; **to ~ sb (to sb)** presentar a algn (a algn); **to ~ sb to** (pastime, technique) introducir a algn a; **introduction** [ɪntrəˈdʌkʃən] n introducción f; (of person) presentación f; **introductory** [ɪntrəˈdʌktərɪ] adj introductorio; **an introductory offer** una oferta introductoria

intrude [ɪnˈtru:d] vi (person) entrometerse; **to ~ on** estorbar; **intruder** n intruso/a

intuition [ɪntju:ˈɪʃən] n intuición f

inundate [ˈɪnʌndeɪt] vt: **to ~ with** inundar de

invade [ɪnˈveɪd] vt invadir

invalid n [ˈɪnvəlɪd] minusválido/a ▷ adj [ɪnˈvælɪd] (not valid) inválido, nulo

invaluable [ɪnˈvæljuəbl] adj inestimable

invariably [ɪnˈvɛərɪəblɪ] adv sin excepción, siempre; **she is ~ late** siempre llega tarde

invasion [ɪnˈveɪʒən] n invasión f

invent [ɪnˈvent] vt inventar; **invention** [ɪnˈvenʃən] n invento; (lie) invención f; **inventor** [ɪnˈventəʳ] n inventor(a) m/f

inventory [ˈɪnvəntrɪ] n inventario

inverted commas [ɪnˈvɜ:tɪd-] npl (BRIT) comillas fpl

invest [ɪnˈvest] vt invertir ▷ vi: **to ~ in** (company etc) invertir dinero en; (fig: sth useful) comprar; **to ~ sb with sth** conferir algo a algn

investigate [ɪnˈvestɪgeɪt] vt investigar; **investigation** [ɪnvestɪˈgeɪʃən] n investigación f, pesquisa

investigator [ɪnˈvestɪgeɪtəʳ] n investigador(a) m/f; **private ~** investigador(a) m/f privado/a

investment [ɪnˈvestmənt] n inversión f

investor [ɪnˈvestəʳ] n inversor(a) m/f

invisible [ɪnˈvɪzɪbl] adj invisible

invitation [ɪnvɪˈteɪʃən] n invitación f

invite [ɪnˈvaɪt] vt invitar; (opinions etc) solicitar, pedir; **inviting** adj atractivo; (food) apetitoso

invoice [ˈɪnvɔɪs] n factura ▷ vt facturar

involve [ɪnˈvɒlv] vt suponer, implicar, tener que ver con; (concern, affect) corresponder a; **to ~ sb (in sth)** involucrar a algn (en algo), comprometer a algn (con algo); **involved** adj complicado; **to be involved in sth** (take part) estar involucrado en algo; (engrossed in) estar muy metido; **involvement** [ɪnˈvɒlvmənt] n participación f, dedicación f; (obligation) compromiso; (difficulty) apuro

inward [ˈɪnwəd] adj (movement) interior, interno; (thought, feeling) íntimo; **inwards** adv hacia dentro

iPod® [ˈaɪpɒd] n iPod® m

IQ n abbr (= intelligence quotient) C.I. m

IRA n abbr (= Irish Republican Army) IRA m

Iran [ɪˈrɑːn] n Irán m; **Iranian** [ɪˈreɪnɪən] adj iraní ▷ n iraní mf

Iraq [ɪˈrɑːk] n Irak m; **Iraqi** [ɪˈrɑːkɪ] adj, n iraquí mf

Ireland [ˈaɪələnd] n Irlanda

iris (pl **irises**) [ˈaɪrɪs, -ɪz] n (Anat) iris m; (Bot) lirio

Irish [ˈaɪrɪʃ] adj irlandés/esa ▷ npl: **the ~** los irlandeses; **Irishman** n irlandés m; **Irishwoman** n irlandesa

iron [ˈaɪən] n hierro; (for clothes) plancha ▷ adj de hierro ▷ vt (clothes) planchar

ironic(al) [aɪˈrɒnɪk(l)] adj irónico

ironic: ironically adv irónicamente

ironing [ˈaɪənɪŋ] n (act) planchado; (ironed clothes) ropa planchada; (clothes to be ironed) ropa por planchar; **ironing board** n tabla de planchar

irony [ˈaɪrənɪ] n ironía

irrational [ɪˈræʃənl] adj irracional

irregular [ɪˈreɡjʊləˈ] adj irregular; (surface) desigual; (action, event) anómalo; (behaviour) poco ortodoxo

irrelevant [ɪˈrɛləvənt] adj: **to be ~** estar fuera de lugar

irresistible [ɪrɪˈzɪstɪbl] adj irresistible

irresponsible [ɪrɪˈspɒnsɪbl] adj (act) irresponsable; (person) poco serio

irrigation [ɪrɪˈɡeɪʃən] n riego

irritable [ˈɪrɪtəbl] adj (person) de mal humor

irritate [ˈɪrɪteɪt] vt fastidiar; (Med) picar; **irritating** adj fastidioso; **irritation** [ɪrɪˈteɪʃən] n fastidio; picazón f

IRS n abbr (us) = **Internal Revenue Service**

is [ɪz] vb see **be**

ISDN n abbr (= Integrated Services Digital Network) RDSI f

Islam [ˈɪzlɑːm] n Islam m; **Islamic** [ɪzˈlæmɪk] adj islámico

island [ˈaɪlənd] n isla; **islander** n isleño/a

isle [aɪl] n isla

isn't [ˈɪznt] = **is not**

isolated [ˈaɪsəleɪtɪd] adj aislado

isolation [aɪsəˈleɪʃən] n aislamiento

ISP n abbr = **Internet Service Provider**

Israel [ˈɪzreɪl] n Israel m; **Israeli** [ɪzˈreɪlɪ] adj, n israelí mf

issue [ˈɪsjuː] n cuestión f; (outcome) resultado; (of banknotes etc) emisión f; (of newspaper etc) número ▷ vt (rations, equipment) distribuir, repartir; (orders) dar; (certificate, passport) expedir; (decree) promulgar; (magazine) publicar; (cheque) extender; (banknotes, stamp) emitir; **at ~** en cuestión; **to take ~ with sb (over)** disentir con algn (en); **to make an ~ of sth** dar a algo más importancia de lo necesario

IT n abbr = **information technology**

KEYWORD

it [ɪt] pron 1 (specific subject: not generally translated) él/ella; (direct object) lo/la; (indirect object) le; (after prep) (abstract concept) ello; **it's on the table** está en la mesa; **I can't find it** no lo (or la) encuentro; **give it to me** dámelo (or dámela); **I spoke to him about it** le hablé del asunto; **what did you learn from it?** ¿qué aprendiste de él (or ella)?; **did you go to it?** (party, concert etc) ¿fuiste?

2 (impersonal): **it's raining** llueve, está lloviendo; **it's 6 o'clock/the 10th of August** son las 6/es el 10 de agosto; **how far is it? — it's 10 miles/2 hours on the train** ¿a qué distancia está? — a 10 millas/2 horas en el tren; **who is it? — it's me** ¿quién es? — soy yo

Italian [ɪˈtæljən] adj italiano ▷ n italiano/a; (Ling) italiano

italic [ɪˈtælɪk] adj cursivo; **italics** npl cursiva sg

Italy [ˈɪtəlɪ] n Italia

itch [ɪtʃ] n picazón f ▷ vi (part of body) picar; **to be ~ing to do sth** rabiar por or morirse de ganas de hacer algo; **itchy** adj: **to be itchy** picar; **my hand is itchy** me pica la mano

it'd [ˈɪtd] = **it would**; **it had**

item [ˈaɪtəm] n artículo; (on agenda) asunto (a tratar); (also: **news ~**) noticia

itinerary [aɪˈtɪnərərɪ] n itinerario

it'll [ˈɪtl] = **it will; it shall**

its [ɪts] *adj* su

it's [ɪts] = **it is; it has**

itself [ɪt'sɛlf] *pron* (*reflexive*) sí mismo/a; (*emphatic*) él mismo/a

ITV *n abbr* (BRIT: = *Independent Television*) cadena de televisión comercial

I've [aɪv] = **I have**

ivory ['aɪvərɪ] *n* marfil *m*

ivy ['aɪvɪ] *n* hiedra

jab [dʒæb] *n* (*Med: inf*) pinchazo ▷ *vt*: **to ~ sth into sth** clavar algo en algo

jack [dʒæk] *n* (*Aut*) gato; (*Cards*) sota

jacket ['dʒækɪt] *n* chaqueta, americana, saco (LAM); (*of book*) sobrecubierta; **jacket potato** *n* patata asada (con piel)

jackpot ['dʒækpɔt] *n* premio gordo

Jacuzzi® [dʒə'ku:zɪ] *n* jacuzzi® *m*

jagged ['dʒægɪd] *adj* dentado

jail [dʒeɪl] *n* cárcel *f* ▷ *vt* encarcelar; **jail sentence** *n* pena *f* de cárcel

jam [dʒæm] *n* mermelada; (*also:* **traffic ~**) embotellamiento; (*difficulty*) apuro ▷ *vt* (*passage etc*) obstruir; (*mechanism, drawer etc*) atascar; (*Radio*) interferir ▷ *vi* atascarse, trabarse; **to ~ sth into sth** meter algo a la fuerza en algo

Jamaica [dʒə'meɪkə] *n* Jamaica

jammed [dʒæmd] *adj* atascado

Jan. *abbr* (= *January*) ene

janitor ['dʒænɪtə'] *n* (*caretaker*) portero, conserje *m*

January ['dʒænjuərɪ] *n* enero

Japan [dʒə'pæn] *n* (el) Japón;
Japanese [dʒæpə'niːz] *adj* japonés/
esa ▷ *n* (*pl inv*) japonés/esa *m/f*; (*Ling*)
japonés *m*

jar *n* (*glass: large*) jarra; (: *small*)
tarro ▷ *vi* (*sound*) chirriar; (*colours*)
desentonar

jargon ['dʒɑːgən] *n* jerga

javelin ['dʒævlɪn] *n* jabalina

jaw [dʒɔː] *n* mandíbula

jazz [dʒæz] *n* jazz *m*

jealous ['dʒeləs] *adj* celoso; (*envious*)
envidioso; **jealousy** *n* celos *mpl*;
envidia

jeans [dʒiːnz] *npl* (pantalones *mpl*)
vaqueros *mpl* o tejanos *mpl*, bluejean
m inv (LAM)

Jello® ['dʒeləu] *n* (US) gelatina

jelly ['dʒelɪ] *n* (*jam*) jalea; (*dessert etc*)
gelatina; **jellyfish** *n* medusa

jeopardize ['dʒepədaɪz] *vt* arriesgar,
poner en peligro

jerk [dʒɜːk] *n* (*jolt*) sacudida; (*wrench*)
tirón *m*; (*us inf*) imbécil *mf* ▷ *vt* tirar
bruscamente de ▷ *vi* (*vehicle*) dar una
sacudida

Jersey ['dʒɜːzɪ] *n* Jersey *m*

jersey ['dʒɜːzɪ] *n* jersey *m*; (*fabric*)
tejido de punto

Jesus ['dʒiːzəs] *n* Jesús *m*

jet [dʒet] *n* (*of gas, liquid*) chorro;
(*Aviat*) avión *m* a reacción; **jet lag** *n*
desorientación *f* por desfase horario;
jet-ski *vi* practicar el motociclismo
acuático

jetty ['dʒetɪ] *n* muelle *m*, embarcadero

Jew [dʒuː] *n* judío/a

jewel ['dʒuːəl] *n* joya; (*in watch*) rubí
m; **jeweller**, (*us*) **jeweler** *n* joyero/a;
jeweller's (shop) joyería; **jewellery**,
(*us*) **jewelry** *n* joyas *fpl*, alhajas *fpl*

Jewish ['dʒuːɪʃ] *adj* judío

jigsaw ['dʒɪgsɔː] *n* (*also:* **~ puzzle**)
rompecabezas *m inv*, puzle *m*

job [dʒɒb] *n* (*task*) tarea; (*post*) empleo;
it's a good ~ that ... menos mal que
...; **just the ~!** ¡justo lo que necesito!;

that's not my ~ eso no me incumbe *or*
toca a mí; **job centre** *n* (BRIT) oficina
de empleo; **jobless** *adj* sin trabajo

jockey ['dʒɔkɪ] *n* jockey *mf* ▷ *vi*: **to ~
for position** maniobrar para sacar
delantera

jog [dʒɔg] *vt* empujar (ligeramente)
▷ *vi* (*run*) hacer footing; **to ~ sb's
memory** refrescar la memoria a algn;
jogging *n* footing *m*

join [dʒɔɪn] *vt* (*things*) unir, juntar;
(*club*) hacerse socio de; (*Pol: party*)
afiliarse a; (*meet: people*) reunirse con;
(*fig*) unirse a ▷ *vi* (*roads*) empalmar;
(*rivers*) confluir ▷ *n* juntura; **join in** *vi*
tomar parte, participar ▷ *vt fus* tomar
parte *or* participar en; **join up** *vi*
unirse; (*Mil*) alistarse

joiner ['dʒɔɪnə^r] *n* carpintero/a

joint [dʒɔɪnt] *n* (*Tech*) juntura, unión *f*;
(*Anat*) articulación *f*; (BRIT *Culin*) pieza
de carne (para asar); (*inf: place*) garito;
(*of cannabis*) porro ▷ *adj* (*common*)
común; (*combined*) conjunto; **joint
account** *n* (*with bank etc*) cuenta
común; **jointly** *adv* en común;
(*together*) conjuntamente

joke [dʒəuk] *n* chiste *m*; (*also:*
practical ~) broma ▷ *vi* bromear; **to
play a ~ on** gastar una broma a algn;
joker *n* (*Cards*) comodín *m*

jolly ['dʒɒlɪ] *adj* (*merry*) alegre;
(*enjoyable*) divertido ▷ *adv* (*inf*) muy

jolt [dʒəult] *n* (*shake*) sacudida;
(*shock*) susto ▷ *vt* (*physically*) sacudir;
(*emotionally*) asustar

Jordan ['dʒɔːdən] *n* (*country*) Jordania;
(*river*) Jordán *m*

journal ['dʒɜːnl] *n* (*magazine*)
revista; (*diary*) diario; **journalism** *n*
periodismo; **journalist** *n* periodista *mf*

journey ['dʒɜːnɪ] *n* viaje *m*; (*distance
covered*) trayecto

joy [dʒɔɪ] *n* alegría; **joyrider** *n* persona
que se da una vuelta en un coche robado

joystick ['dʒɔɪstɪk] *n* (*Aviat*) palanca
de mando; (*Comput*) palanca de
control

Jr abbr = **junior**

judge ['dʒʌdʒ] n juez mf ▷ vt juzgar; (estimate) considerar; **judg(e)ment** n juicio

judo ['dʒu:dəu] n judo

jug [dʒʌg] n jarra

juggle ['dʒʌgl] vi hacer juegos malabares; **juggler** n malabarista mf

juice [dʒu:s] n jugo, zumo (SP); **juicy** adj jugoso

Jul. abbr (= July) jul

July [dʒu:'laɪ] n julio

jumble ['dʒʌmbl] n revoltijo ▷ vt (also: ~ up) revolver; **jumble sale** n (BRIT) mercadillo

jumbo ['dʒʌmbəu], **jumbo jet** n jumbo

jump [dʒʌmp] vi saltar, dar saltos; (increase) aumentar ▷ vt saltar ▷ n salto; (increase) aumento; **to ~ the queue** (BRIT) colarse

jumper ['dʒʌmpə'] n (BRIT: pullover) jersey m, suéter m; (US: dress) pichi m

jump leads, (US) **jumper cables** npl cables mpl puente de batería

Jun. abbr = **junior**

junction ['dʒʌŋkʃən] n (BRIT: of roads) cruce m; (Rail) empalme m

June [dʒu:n] n junio

jungle ['dʒʌŋgl] n selva, jungla

junior ['dʒu:nɪə'] adj (in age) menor, más joven; (position) subalterno ▷ n

menor mf, joven mf; **junior high school** n (US) centro de educación secundaria; **junior school** n (BRIT) escuela primaria

junk [dʒʌŋk] n (cheap goods) baratijas fpl; (rubbish) basura; **junk food** n comida basura or de plástico

junkie ['dʒʌŋkɪ] n (inf) yonqui mf

junk mail n propaganda (buzoneada)

Jupiter ['dʒu:pɪtə'] n (Mythology, Astro) Júpiter m

jurisdiction [dʒuərɪs'dɪkʃən] n jurisdicción f; **it falls/comes within/outside our ~** es/no es de nuestra competencia

jury ['dʒuərɪ] n jurado

just [dʒʌst] adj justo ▷ adv (exactly) exactamente; (only) sólo, solamente; **he's ~ done it/left** acaba de hacerlo/irse; **~ right** perfecto; **~ two o'clock** las dos en punto; **she's ~ as clever as you** es tan lista como tú; **~ as well that ...** menos mal que ...; **~ as he was leaving** en el momento en que se marchaba; **~ before/enough** justo antes/lo suficiente; **~ here** aquí mismo; **he ~ missed** falló por poco; **~ listen to this** escucha esto un momento

justice ['dʒʌstɪs] n justicia; (US: judge) juez mf; **to do ~ to** (fig) hacer justicia a

justification [dʒʌstɪfɪ'keɪʃən] n justificación f

justify ['dʒʌstɪfaɪ] vt justificar; (text) alinear

jut [dʒʌt] vi (also: ~ out) sobresalir

juvenile ['dʒu:vənaɪl] adj (humour, mentality) infantil ▷ n menor mf de edad

K

K *abbr* (= *one thousand*) mil; (= *kilobyte*) K
kangaroo [kæŋgə'ruː] *n* canguro
karaoke [kɑːrə'əʊki] *n* karaoke
karate [kə'rɑːtɪ] *n* karate *m*
kebab [kə'bæb] *n* pincho moruno
keel [kiːl] *n* quilla; **on an even ~** (*fig*)
en equilibrio
keen [kiːn] *adj* (*interest, desire*)
grande, vivo; (*eye, intelligence*) agudo;
(*competition*) reñido; (*edge*) afilado;
(*BRIT: eager*) entusiasta; **to be ~ to do**
or on doing sth tener muchas ganas
de hacer algo; **to be ~ on sth/sb**
interesarse por algo/algn
keep [kiːp] (*pt, pp* **kept**) *vt* (*retain,*
preserve) guardar; (*hold back*) quedarse
con; (*shop*) ser propietario de; (*feed:*
family etc) mantener; (*promise*)
cumplir; (*chickens, bees etc*) criar ▷ *vi*
(*food*) conservarse; (*remain*) seguir,
continuar ▷ *n* (*of castle*) torreón *m*;
(*food etc*) comida, sustento; **to ~**
doing sth seguir haciendo algo; **to**
~ sb from doing sth impedir a algn
hacer algo; **to ~ sb happy** tener a
algn contento; **to ~ a place tidy**
mantener un lugar limpio; **to ~ sth to**
o.s. no decirle algo a nadie; **to ~ time**
(*clock*) mantener la hora exacta; **keep**
away *vt*: **to ~ sth/sb away from**
sb mantener algo/a algn apartado
de algn ▷ *vi*: **to ~ away (from)**
mantenerse apartado (de); **keep back**
vt (*crowd, tears*) contener; (*money*)
quedarse con; (*conceal: information*):
to ~ sth back from sb ocultar algo a
algn ▷ *vi* hacerse a un lado; **keep off**
vt (*dog, person*) mantener a distancia
▷ *vi* evitar; **~ your hands off!** ¡no
toques!; **"~ off the grass"** "prohibido
pisar el césped"; **keep on** *vi*: **to ~ on**
doing seguir *or* continuar haciendo;
to ~ on (about sth) no parar de
hablar (de algo); **keep out** *vi*
permanecer fuera; **"~ out"** "prohibida
la entrada"; **keep up** *vt* mantener,
conservar ▷ *vi* no rezagarse; **to ~**
up with (*pace*) ir al paso de; (*level*)
mantenerse a la altura de; **keeper** *n*
guarda *mf*; **keeping** *n* (*care*) cuidado;
in keeping with de acuerdo con
kennel ['kɛnl] *n* perrera; **kennels** *npl*
residencia canina
Kenya ['kɛnjə] *n* Kenia
kept [kɛpt] *pt, pp of* **keep**
kerb [kɜːb] *n* (*BRIT*) bordillo
kerosene ['kɛrəsiːn] *n* keroseno
ketchup ['kɛtʃəp] *n* salsa de tomate,
ketchup *m*
kettle ['kɛtl] *n* hervidor *m*
key [kiː] *n* llave *f*; (*Mus*) tono; (*of piano,*
typewriter) tecla; (*on map*) clave *f* ▷ *cpd*
(*vital: position, issue, industry etc*) clave
▷ *vt* (*also:* **~ in**) teclear; **keyboard**
n teclado; **keyhole** *n* ojo (de la
cerradura); **keyring** *n* llavero
kg *abbr* (= *kilogram*) kg
khaki ['kɑːki] *n* caqui
kick [kɪk] *vt* (*person*) dar una patada a;
(*inf: habit*) quitarse de ▷ *vi* (*horse*) dar
coces ▷ *n* patada; puntapié *m*; (*thrill*):

he does it for ~s lo hace por pura diversión; **kick off** vi (Sport) hacer el saque inicial; **kick-off** n saque inicial; **the kick-off is at 10 o'clock** el partido empieza a las diez

kid [kɪd] n (inf: child) chiquillo/a; (animal) cabrito; (leather) cabritilla ▷ vi (inf) bromear

kidnap ['kɪdnæp] vt secuestrar; **kidnapping** n secuestro

kidney ['kɪdnɪ] n riñón m; **kidney bean** n judía, alubia

kill [kɪl] vt matar; (murder) asesinar ▷ n matanza; **to ~ time** matar el tiempo; **killer** n asesino/a; **killing** n (one) asesinato; (several) matanza; **to make a killing** hacer su agosto

kiln [kɪln] n horno

kilo ['kiːləʊ] n abbr (= kilogram(me)) kilo; **kilobyte** ['kɪləʊbaɪt] n (Comput) kilobyte m; **kilogram(me)** ['kɪləʊɡræm] n kilogramo; **kilometre**, (us) **kilometer** ['kɪləmiːtə] n kilómetro; **kilowatt** ['kɪləʊwɔt] n kilovatio

kilt [kɪlt] n falda escocesa

kin [kɪn] n parientes mpl

kind [kaɪnd] adj amable, atento ▷ n clase f, especie f; (species) género; **in ~** (Comm) en especie; **a ~ of** una especie de; **to be two of a ~** ser tal para cual

kindergarten ['kɪndəɡɑːtn] n jardín m de infancia

kindly ['kaɪndlɪ] adj bondadoso; (gentle) cariñoso ▷ adv bondadosamente, amablemente; **will you ~ ...** sería usted tan amable de ...

kindness ['kaɪndnɪs] n bondad f, amabilidad f; (act) favor m

king [kɪŋ] n rey m; **kingdom** n reino; **kingfisher** n martín m pescador; **king-size(d)** adj de tamaño gigante; **king-size bed** cama de matrimonio extragrande

kiosk ['kiːɔsk] n quiosco; (BRIT Tel) cabina

kipper ['kɪpə'] n arenque m ahumado

kiss [kɪs] n beso ▷ vt besar; **~ of life** (artificial respiration) respiración f boca a boca; **to ~ (each other)** besarse

kit [kɪt] n equipo; (set of tools etc) (caja de) herramientas fpl; (assembly kit) juego de armar

kitchen ['kɪtʃɪn] n cocina

kite [kaɪt] n (toy) cometa

kitten ['kɪtn] n gatito/a

kiwi ['kiːwiː] n (also: ~ fruit) kiwi m

km abbr (= kilometre) km

km/h abbr (= kilometres per hour) km/h

knack [næk] n: **to have the ~ of doing sth** tener facilidad para hacer algo

knee [niː] n rodilla; **kneecap** n rótula

kneel (pt, pp **knelt**) [niːl, nɛlt] vi (also: ~ **down**) arrodillarse

knelt [nɛlt] pt, pp of **kneel**

knew [njuː] pt of **know**

knickers ['nɪkəz] npl (BRIT) bragas fpl

knife [naɪf] (pl **knives**) n cuchillo ▷ vt acuchillar

knight [naɪt] n caballero; (Chess) caballo

knit [nɪt] vt tejer, tricotar ▷ vi hacer punto, tricotar; (bones) soldarse; **knitting** n labor f de punto; **knitting needle**, (us) **knit pin** n aguja de hacer punto or tejer; **knitwear** n prendas fpl de punto

knives [naɪvz] pl of **knife**

knob [nɔb] n (of door) pomo; (of stick) puño; (on radio, TV) botón m

knock [nɔk] vt (strike) golpear; (bump into) chocar contra; (inf) criticar ▷ vi (at door etc): **to ~ at/ on** llamar a ▷ n golpe m; (on door) llamada; **knock down** vt atropellar; **knock off** vi (inf: finish) salir del trabajo ▷ vt (inf: steal) birlar; **knock out** vt dejar sin sentido; (Boxing) poner fuera de combate, dejar K.O.; (in competition) eliminar; **knock over** vt (object) tirar; (pedestrian) atropellar; **knockout** n (Boxing) K.O. m, knockout m

knot [nɔt] n nudo ▷ vt anudar

know (pt **knew**, pp **known**) [nəu, njuː, nəun] vt saber; (person, author, place) conocer; (recognize) reconocer ▷ vi: **to ~ how to swim** saber nadar; **to ~ about** or **of sb/sth** saber de algn/algo; **know-all** n sabelotodo m inv/f inv; **know-how** n conocimientos mpl; **knowing** adj (look etc) de complicidad; **knowingly** adv (purposely) a sabiendas; (smile, look) con complicidad; **know-it-all** n (US) = **know-all**

knowledge ['nɒlɪdʒ] n conocimiento; (learning) saber m, conocimientos mpl; **knowledgeable** adj entendido

known [nəun] pp of **know** ▷ adj (thief, facts) conocido; (expert) reconocido

knuckle ['nʌkl] n nudillo

koala [kəu'ɑːlə] n (also: ~ **bear**) koala m

Koran [kɔ'rɑːn] n Corán m

Korea [kə'rɪə] n Corea; **Korean** adj, n coreano/a

kosher ['kəuʃəʳ] adj autorizado por la ley judía

Kosovar (kɒsəvɑːʳ], **Kosovan** ['kɒsəvən] adj kosovar; **Kosovo** ['kɒsəvəu] n Kosovo m

Kremlin ['kremlɪn] n: **the ~** el Kremlin

Kuwait [ku'weɪt] n Kuwait m

L abbr (BRIT Aut = learner) L

lab [læb] n abbr = **laboratory**

label ['leɪbl] n etiqueta ▷ vt poner una etiqueta a

labor ['leɪbəʳ] n, vb (US) = **labour**

laboratory [lə'bɒrətərɪ] n laboratorio

Labor Day n (US) día m de los trabajadores (primer lunes de septiembre)

labor union n (US) sindicato

labour, (US) **labor** ['leɪbəʳ] n (task) trabajo; (also: ~ **force**) mano f de obra; (Med) (dolores mpl de) parto ▷ vi: **to ~ (at)** trabajar (en) ▷ vt: **to ~ a point** insistir en un punto; **to be in ~** (Med) estar de parto; **the L~ party** (BRIT) el partido laborista, los laboristas mpl; **labourer** n peón m; (on farm) peón m; (day labourer) jornalero

lace [leɪs] n encaje m; (of shoe etc) cordón m ▷ vt (shoes: also: ~ **up**) atarse

lack [læk] n (absence) falta ▷ vt faltarle a algn, carecer de; **through** or **for**

~ of por falta de; **to be ~ing**: faltar, no haber; **to be ~ing in sth** faltarle a algn algo

lacquer [ˈlækəʳ] n laca

lacy [ˈleɪsɪ] adj (like lace) como de encaje

lad [læd] n muchacho, chico

ladder [ˈlædəʳ] n escalera (de mano); (BRIT: in tights) carrera

ladle [ˈleɪdl] n cucharón m

lady [ˈleɪdɪ] n señora; (distinguished, noble) dama; **young ~** señorita; **the ladies' (room)** los servicios de señoras; **"ladies and gentlemen ..."** "señoras y caballeros..."; **ladybird**, (US)**ladybug** n mariquita

lag [læg] vi (also: **~ behind**) retrasarse, quedarse atrás ▷ vt (pipes) revestir

lager [ˈlɑːɡəʳ] n cerveza (rubia)

lagoon [ləˈɡuːn] n laguna

laid [leɪd] pt, pp of **lay**

laid-back [leɪdˈbæk] adj (inf) relajado

lain [leɪn] pp of **lie**

lake [leɪk] n lago

lamb [læm] n cordero; (meat) carne f de cordero

lame [leɪm] adj cojo; (excuse) poco convincente

lament [ləˈmɛnt] n lamento ▷ vt lamentarse de

lamp [læmp] n lámpara; **lamppost** n (BRIT) farola; **lampshade** n pantalla

land [lænd] n tierra; (country) país m; (piece of land) terreno; (estate) finca fpl, finca ▷ vi (from ship) desembarcar; (Aviat) aterrizar; (fig: fall) caer ▷ vt (passengers, goods) desembarcar; **to ~ sb with sth** (inf) hacer cargar a algn con algo; **landing** n aterrizaje m; (of staircase) rellano; **landing card** n tarjeta de desembarque; **landlady** n (owner) dueña; (of boarding house) patrona; **landline** n (teléfono) fijo; **landlord** n propietario; (of pub etc) patrón m; **landmark** n lugar m conocido; **to be a landmark** (fig) hacer época; **landowner** n terrateniente mf; **landscape** n paisaje

m; **landslide** n (Geo) corrimiento de tierras; (fig: Pol) victoria arrolladora

lane [leɪn] n (in country) camino; (Aut) carril m; (in race) calle f

language [ˈlæŋɡwɪdʒ] n lenguaje m; (national tongue) idioma m, lengua; **bad ~** palabrotas fpl; **language laboratory** n laboratorio de idiomas; **language school** n academia de idiomas

lantern [ˈlæntn] n linterna, farol m

lap [læp] n (of track) vuelta; (of body) regazo ▷ vi (waves) chapotear; **to sit on sb's ~** sentarse en las rodillas de algn; **lap up** vt beber a lengüetadas o con la lengua

lapel [ləˈpɛl] n solapa

lapse [læps] n fallo; (moral) desliz m ▷ vi (expire) caducar; (time) pasar, transcurrir; **to ~ into bad habits** volver a las andadas; **~ of time** lapso, intervalo

lard [lɑːd] n manteca (de cerdo)

larder [ˈlɑːdəʳ] n despensa

large [lɑːdʒ] adj grande; **at ~** (free) en libertad; (generally) en general; **largely** adv (mostly) en su mayor parte; (introducing reason) en gran parte; **large-scale** adj (map, drawing) a gran escala; (reforms, business activities) importante

▌ Be careful not to translate *large* by the Spanish word *largo*.

lark [lɑːk] n (bird) alondra; (joke) broma

larrikin [ˈlærɪkɪn] n (AUST, NZ inf) gamberro/a

laryngitis [lærɪnˈdʒaɪtɪs] n laringitis f

lasagne [ləˈzænjə] n lasaña

laser [ˈleɪzəʳ] n láser m; **laser printer** n impresora láser

lash [læʃ] n latigazo; (also: eyelash) pestaña, vi azotar; (tie) atar; **lash out** vi: **to ~ out (at sb)** (hit) arremeter (contra algn); **to ~ out against sb** lanzar invectivas contra algn

lass [læs] n chica

last [lɑːst] adj último; (final) final ▷ adv (finally) por último ▷ vi durar (*continue*) continuar, seguir; **~ night** anoche; **~ week** la semana pasada; **at ~** por fin; **~ but one** penúltimo

lastly *adv* por último, finalmente

last-minute *adj* de última hora

latch [lætʃ] *n* pestillo; **latch on to** *vt fus* (*person*) pegarse a; (*idea*) aferrarse a

late [leɪt] *adj* (*not on time*) tarde, atrasado; (*deceased*) fallecido ▷ *adv* tarde; (*behind time, schedule*) con retraso; **of ~** últimamente; **~ at night** a última hora de la noche; **in ~ May** hacia fines de mayo; **the ~ Mr X** el difunto Sr. X; **latecomer** *n* recién llegado/a; **lately** *adv* últimamente; **later** *adj* (*date etc*) posterior; (*version etc*) más reciente ▷ *adv* más tarde, después; **latest** ['leɪtɪst] *adj* último; **at the latest** a más tardar

lather ['lɑːðə*r*] *n* espuma (de jabón) ▷ *vt* enjabonar

Latin ['lætɪn] *n* latín *m* ▷ *adj* latino; **Latin America** *n* América Latina; **Latin American** *adj*, *n* latinoamericano/a

latitude ['lætɪtjuːd] *n* latitud *f*; (*fig*) libertad *f*

latter ['lætə*r*] *adj* último; (*of two*) segundo ▷ *n*: **the ~** el último, éste

laugh [lɑːf] *n* risa ▷ *vi* reírse, reír; (**to do sth**) **for a ~** (hacer algo) en broma; **laugh at** *vt fus* reírse de; **laughter** *n* risa

launch [lɔːntʃ] *n* (*boat*) lancha ▷ *vt* (*ship*) botar; (*rocket, plan*) lanzar; (*fig*) comenzar; **launch into** *vt fus* lanzarse a

launder ['lɔːndə*r*] *vt* lavar

Launderette® [lɔːn'drɛt], (*US*) **Laundromat®** ['lɔːndrəmæt] *n* lavandería (automática)

laundry ['lɔːndrɪ] *n* lavandería; (*clothes: dirty*) ropa sucia; (*: clean*) colada

lava ['lɑːvə] *n* lava

lavatory ['lævətərɪ] *n* wáter *m*

lavender ['lævəndə*r*] *n* lavanda

lavish ['lævɪʃ] *adj* abundante; pródigo en; **to ~ sth on sb** colmar a algn de algo

law [lɔː] *n* ley *f*; (*study*) derecho; (*of game*) regla; **lawful** *adj* legítimo, lícito; **lawless** *adj* (*act*) ilegal

lawn [lɔːn] *n* césped *m*; **lawnmower** *n* cortacésped *m*

lawsuit ['lɔːsuːt] *n* pleito

lawyer ['lɔːjə*r*] *n* abogado/a; (*for sales, wills etc*) notario/a

lax [læks] *adj* (*discipline*) relajado; (*person*) negligente

laxative ['læksətɪv] *n* laxante *m*

lay [leɪ] *pt* of **lie** ▷ *adj* (*not expert*) lego ▷ *vt* (*pt, pp* **laid**) (*place*) colocar; (*eggs, table*) poner; (*trap*) tender; (*carpet*) extender; **lay down** *vt* (*pen etc*) dejar; (*rules etc*) establecer; **to ~ down the law** imponer las normas; **lay off** *vt* (*workers*) despedir; **lay on** *vt* (*meal, facilities*) proveer; **lay out** *vt* (*display*) exponer; **lay-by** *n* (*BRIT Aut*) área de descanso

layer ['leɪə*r*] *n* capa

layman ['leɪmən] *n* lego

layout ['leɪaʊt] *n* (*design*) plan *m*, trazado; (*Press*) composición *f*

lazy ['leɪzɪ] *adj* perezoso, vago

lb. *abbr* (*weight*) = **pound**

lead¹ [liːd] (*pt, pp* **led**) *n* (*front position*) delantera; (*clue*) pista; (*Elec*) cable *m*; (*for dog*) correa; (*Theat*) papel *m* principal ▷ *vt* conducir; (*be the leader of*) dirigir; (*Sport*) ir en cabeza de ▷ *vi* primero; **to be in the ~** (*Sport*) llevar la delantera; (*fig*) ir a la cabeza; **lead up to** *vt fus* (*events*) conducir a; (*in conversation*) preparar el terreno para

lead² [lɛd] *n* (*metal*) plomo; (*in pencil*) mina

leader ['liːdə*r*] *n* jefe/a *m/f*, líder *m*; **leadership** *n* dirección *f*; **qualities of leadership** iniciativa *sg*

lead-free ['lɛdfriː] *adj* sin plomo

leading ['liːdɪŋ] *adj* (*main*) principal; (*first*) primero; (*front*) delantero

lead singer [liːd-] *n* cantante *mf*

leaf [liːf] (*pl* **leaves**) *n* hoja; **to turn over a new ~** hacer borrón y cuenta nueva; **leaf through** *vt fus* (*book*) hojear

leaflet ['liːflɪt] *n* folleto

league [liːg] *n* sociedad *f*; (*Football*) liga; **to be in ~ with** estar confabulado con

leak [liːk] *n* (*of liquid, gas*) escape *m*, fuga; (*in pipe*) agujero; (*in roof*) gotera; (*fig: of information, in security*) filtración *f* ▷ *vi* (*ship*) hacer agua; (*pipe*) tener un escape; (*roof*) tener goteras; (*also: ~ out: liquid, gas*) escaparse ▷ *vt* (*fig*) filtrar

lean [liːn] (*pt, pp* **leaned** *or* **leant**) *adj* (*thin*) flaco; (*meat*) magro ▷ *vt*: **to ~ sth on sth** apoyar algo en algo ▷ *vi* (*slope*) inclinarse; **to ~ against** apoyarse contra; **to ~ on** apoyarse en; **lean forward** *vi* inclinarse hacia adelante; **lean over** *vi* inclinarse; **leaning** *n*: **leaning (towards)** inclinación *f* (hacia)

leant [lɛnt] *pt, pp of* **lean**

leap [liːp] *n* salto ▷ *vi* (*pt, pp* **leaped** *or* **leapt**) saltar

leapt [lɛpt] *pt, pp of* **leap**

leap year *n* año bisiesto

learn (*pt, pp* **learned** *or* **learnt**) [lɜːn, -t] *vt* aprender; (*come to know of*) enterarse de ▷ *vi* aprender; **to ~ how to do sth** aprender a hacer algo; **learner** *n* (*BRIT: also:* **learner driver**) conductor(a) *m/f* en prácticas; *see also* **L-plates**; **learning** *n* saber *m*, conocimientos *mpl*

learnt [lɜːnt] *pp of* **learn**

lease [liːs] *n* arriendo ▷ *vt* arrendar

leash [liːʃ] *n* correa

least [liːst] *adj* (*slightest*) menor, más pequeño; (*smallest amount of*) mínimo ▷ *adv* menos; **the ~ expensive car** el coche menos caro; **at ~** por lo menos; **al menos; not in the ~** en absoluto

leather ['lɛðə'] *n* cuero

leave [liːv] (*pt, pp* **left**) *vt* dejar; (*go away from*) abandonar ▷ *vi* irse; (*train*)

salir ▷ *n* permiso; **to be left** quedar, sobrar; **there's some milk left over** sobra *or* queda algo de leche; **on ~** de permiso; **leave behind** *vt* (*on purpose*) dejar (atrás); (*accidentally*) olvidar; **leave out** *vt* omitir

leaves [liːvz] *pl of* **leaf**

Lebanon ['lɛbənən] *n*: **the ~** el Líbano

lecture ['lɛktʃə'] *n* conferencia; (*Scol*) clase *f* ▷ *vi* dar clase(s) ▷ *vt* (*reprove*) echar una reprimenda a; **to give a ~ on** dar una conferencia sobre; **lecture hall** *n* sala de conferencias; (*Univ*) aula; **lecturer** *n* conferenciante *mf*; (*BRIT: at university*) profesor(a) *m/f*; **lecture theatre** *n* = **lecture hall**

led [lɛd] *pt, pp of* **lead**

ledge [lɛdʒ] *n* (*on wall*) repisa; (*of window*) alféizar *m*; (*of mountain*) saliente *m*

leek [liːk] *n* puerro

left [lɛft] *pt, pp of* **leave** ▷ *adj* izquierdo; (*remaining*): **there are two ~** quedan dos ▷ *n* izquierda ▷ *adv* a la izquierda; **on** *or* **to the ~** a la izquierda; **the L~** (*Pol*) la izquierda; **left-hand** *adj*: **the left-hand side** la izquierda; **left-hand drive** *n* conducción *f* por la izquierda; **left-handed** *adj* zurdo; **left-luggage locker** *n* (*BRIT*) consigna *f* automática; **left-luggage (office)** *n* (*BRIT*) consigna; **left-overs** *npl* sobras *fpl*; **left-wing** *adj* (*Pol*) de izquierda(s), izquierdista

leg [lɛg] *n* pierna; (*of animal, chair*) pata; (*Culin: of meat*) pierna; (*: of chicken*) pata; (*of journey*) etapa

legacy ['lɛgəsɪ] *n* herencia

legal ['liːgl] *adj* (*permitted by law*) lícito; (*of law*) legal; **legal holiday** *n* (*US*) fiesta oficial; **legalize** *vt* legalizar; **legally** *adv* legalmente

legend ['lɛdʒənd] *n* leyenda; **legendary** *adj* legendario

leggings ['lɛgɪŋz] *npl* mallas *fpl*, leggins *mpl*

legible ['lɛdʒəbl] *adj* legible

legislation [ˌlɛdʒɪs'leɪʃən] n
legislación f

legislative [ˈlɛdʒɪslətɪv] adj
legislativo

legitimate [lɪ'dʒɪtɪmət] adj legítimo

leisure [ˈlɛʒəʳ] n ocio, tiempo libre;
at ~ con tranquilidad; **leisure centre**
n polideportivo m; **leisurely** adj sin
prisa; lento

lemon [ˈlɛmən] n limón m; **lemonade**
n (fizzy) gaseosa f; **lemon tea** n té m
con limón

lend [lɛnd] (pt, pp **lent**) vt: **to ~ sth to
sb** prestar algo a algn

length [lɛŋθ] n (size) largo, longitud
f; (of rope etc) largo; (of wood, string)
trozo; (amount of time) duración f; **at ~**
(at last) por fin, finalmente; (lengthily)
largamente; **lengthen** vt alargar ▷ vi
alargarse; **lengthways** adv a lo largo;
lengthy adj largo, extenso

lens [lɛnz] n (of spectacles) lente f; (of
camera) objetivo

Lent [lɛnt] n Cuaresma

lent [lɛnt] pt, pp of **lend**

lentil [ˈlɛntl] n lenteja

Leo [ˈliːəʊ] n Leo

leopard [ˈlɛpəd] n leopardo

leotard [ˈliːətɑːd] n malla

leprosy [ˈlɛprəsɪ] n lepra

lesbian [ˈlɛzbɪən] n lesbiana f

less [lɛs] adj (in size, degree etc) menor;
(in quantity) menos ▷ pron, adv menos;
~ than half menos de la mitad; **~
than ever** menos que nunca; **~ 5%**
menos el cinco por ciento; **~ and ~**
cada vez menos; **the ~ he works ...**
cuanto menos trabaja ...; **lessen** vi
disminuir, reducirse ▷ vt disminuir,
reducir; **lesser** [ˈlɛsəʳ] adj menor; **to
a lesser extent o degree** en menor
grado

lesson [ˈlɛsn] n clase f; **it taught him
a ~** (fig) le sirvió de lección

let (pt, pp **let**) [lɛt] vt (allow) dejar,
permitir; (BRIT: lease) alquilar; **to ~
sb do sth** dejar que algn haga algo;
to ~ sb know sth comunicar algo a

algn; **~'s go** ¡vamos!; **~ him come** que
venga; **"to ~"** se alquila"; **let down** vt
(tyre) desinflar; (disappoint) defraudar;
let in vt dejar entrar; (visitor etc)
hacer pasar; **let off** vt dejar escapar;
(firework etc) disparar; (bomb) accionar;
let out vt dejar salir

lethal [ˈliːθl] adj (weapon) mortífero;
(poison, wound) mortal

letter [ˈlɛtəʳ] n (of alphabet) letra;
(correspondence) carta; **letterbox** n
(BRIT) buzón m

lettuce [ˈlɛtɪs] n lechuga

leukaemia, (US) **leukemia**
[luːˈkiːmɪə] n leucemia

level [ˈlɛvl] adj (flat) llano ▷ adv a nivel
▷ n nivel m; (height) altura ▷ vt nivelar,
allanar; (destroy: building) derribar;
to be ~ with estar a nivel de; **A ~s**
(BRIT) = exámenes mpl de bachillerato
superior; **on the ~** (fig: honest) en
serio; **level crossing** n (BRIT) paso
a nivel

lever [ˈliːvəʳ] n palanca ▷ vt: **to ~ up**
levantar con palanca; **leverage** n (fig:
influence) influencia

levy [ˈlɛvɪ] n impuesto ▷ vt exigir,
recaudar

liability [laɪəˈbɪlətɪ] n (pej: person,
thing) estorbo, lastre m; (Law:
responsibility) responsabilidad f;
(handicap) desventaja

liable [ˈlaɪəbl] adj (subject): **~ to** sujeto
a; (responsible): **~ for** responsable de;
(likely): **~ to do** propenso a hacer

liaise [liːˈeɪz] vi: **to ~ (with)** colaborar
(con)

liar [ˈlaɪəʳ] n mentiroso/a

liberal [ˈlɪbərl] adj liberal; (generous):
~ with generoso con; **Liberal
Democrat** n (BRIT) demócrata mf
liberal

liberate [ˈlɪbəreɪt] vt (people: from
poverty etc) librar; (prisoner) libertar;
(country) liberar

liberation [lɪbəˈreɪʃən] n liberación f

liberty [ˈlɪbətɪ] n libertad f; **to be at ~**
(criminal) estar en libertad; **to be at ~**

to do estar libre para hacer; **to take the ~ of do** tomarse la libertad de hacer algo

Libra ['liːbrə] n Libra

librarian [laɪˈbreəriən] n bibliotecario/a

library ['laɪbrərɪ] n biblioteca

> Be careful not to translate *library* by the Spanish word *librería*.

Libya ['lɪbɪə] n Libia

lice [laɪs] pl of **louse**

licence, (us) **license** ['laɪsns] n licencia; (permit) permiso; (also: **driving ~**, (us) **driver's license**) carnet de conducir, permiso de manejar (LAM)

license ['laɪsns] n (us) = **licence** ▷ vt autorizar, dar permiso a; **licensed** adj (for alcohol) autorizado para vender bebidas alcohólicas; **license plate** n (us) placa (de matrícula); **licensing hours** npl (BRIT) horas durante las cuales se permite la venta y consumo de alcohol (en un bar etc)

lick [lɪk] vt lamer; (inf: defeat) dar una paliza a; **to ~ one's lips** relamerse

lid [lɪd] n (of box, case, pan) tapa, tapadera

lie [laɪ] n mentira ▷ vi (pt **lay**, pp **lain**) mentir; (rest) estar echado, estar acostado; (of object: be situated) estar, encontrarse; **to tell ~s** mentir; **to ~ low** (fig) mantenerse a escondidas; **lie about, lie around** vi (things) estar tirado; (BRIT: people) estar acostado or tumbado; **lie down** vi echarse, tumbarse

Liechtenstein ['lɪktənstaɪn] n Liechtenstein m

lie-in ['laɪɪn] n (BRIT): **to have a ~** quedarse en la cama

lieutenant [lef'tenənt] [(us) luː'tenənt] n (Mil) teniente m

life (pl **lives**) [laɪf, laɪvz] n vida; **life assurance** n (BRIT) seguro de vida; **lifebelt** n (BRIT) cinturón m salvavidas; **lifeboat** n lancha de socorro; **lifeguard** n vigilante mf, socorrista

mf; **life insurance** n = **life assurance**; **life jacket** n chaleco salvavidas; **lifelike** adj natural; **life preserver** n (us) = **lifebelt**; **life sentence** n cadena perpetua; **lifestyle** n estilo de vida; **lifetime** n: **in his lifetime** durante su vida

lift [lɪft] vt levantar; (copy) plagiar ▷ vi (fog) disiparse ▷ n (BRIT: elevator) ascensor m; **to give sb a ~** (BRIT) llevar a algn en coche; **lift up** vt levantar; **lift-off** n despegue m

light [laɪt] n luz f; (lamp) luz f, lámpara; (headlight) faro; (for cigarette etc): **have you got a ~?** ¿tienes fuego? ▷ vt (pt, pp **lit**) (candle, cigarette, fire) encender; (room) alumbrar ▷ adj (colour) claro; (room) con mucha luz; **lights** npl (traffic lights) semáforos mpl; **in the ~ of** a la luz de; **to come to ~** salir a la luz; **light up** vi (smoke) encender un cigarrillo; (face) iluminarse ▷ vt (illuminate) iluminar, alumbrar; (set fire to) encender; **light bulb** n bombilla, bombillo (LAM), foco (LAM); **lighten** vt (make less heavy) aligerar; **lighter** n (also: **cigarette lighter**) encendedor m, mechero; **light-hearted** adj (person) alegre; (remark etc) divertido; **lighthouse** n faro; **lighting** n (system) alumbrado; **lightly** adv ligeramente; (not seriously) con poca seriedad; **to get off lightly** ser castigado con poca severidad

lightning ['laɪtnɪŋ] n relámpago, rayo

lightweight adj (suit) ligero ▷ n (Boxing) peso ligero

like [laɪk] vt (person) querer a ▷ prep como ▷ adj parecido, semejante ▷ n: **his ~s and dislikes** sus gustos y aversiones; **the ~s of him** personas como él; **I would ~**, **I'd ~** me gustaría; (for purchase) quisiera; **would you ~ a coffee?** ¿te apetece un café?; **I ~ swimming** me gusta nadar; **to be or look ~ sb/sth** parecerse a algn/algo; **that's just ~ him** es muy de él, es

típico de él; **do it ~ this** hazlo así; **it is nothing ~ ...** no tiene parecido alguno con ...; **what's he ~?** ¿cómo es (él)?;
likeable *adj* simpático, agradable
likelihood ['laɪklɪhud] *n* probabilidad *f*
likely ['laɪklɪ] *adj* probable; **he's ~ to leave** es probable or (LAM) capaz que se vaya; **not ~!** ¡ni hablar!
likewise ['laɪkwaɪz] *adv* igualmente;
to do ~ hacer lo mismo
liking ['laɪkɪŋ] *n*: **~ (for)** (person) cariño (a); (thing) afición (a); **to be to sb's ~** ser del gusto de algn
lilac ['laɪlək] *n* (tree) lilo; (flower) lila
Lilo® ['laɪləʊ] *n* colchoneta inflable
lily ['lɪlɪ] *n* lirio, azucena; **~ of the valley** *n* lirio de los valles
limb [lɪm] *n* miembro
limbo ['lɪmbəʊ] *n*: **to be in ~** (fig) quedar a la expectativa
lime [laɪm] *n* (tree) limero; (fruit) lima; (Geo) cal *f*
limelight ['laɪmlaɪt] *n*: **to be in the ~** (fig) ser el centro de atención
limestone ['laɪmstəʊn] *n* piedra caliza
limit ['lɪmɪt] *n* límite *m* ▷ *vt* limitar;
limited *adj* limitado; **to be limited to** limitarse a
limousine ['lɪməziːn] *n* limusina
limp [lɪmp] *n*: **to have a ~** tener cojera ▷ *vi* cojear ▷ *adj* flojo
line [laɪn] *n* línea; (rope) cuerda; (for fishing) sedal *m*; (wire) hilo; (row, series) fila, hilera; (of writing) renglón *m*; (on face) arruga; (Rail) vía *f* ▷ *vt* (Sewing):
to ~ (with) forrar (de); **to ~ the streets** ocupar las aceras; **in ~ with** de acuerdo con; **line up** *vi* hacer cola ▷ *vt* alinear; **to have sth ~d up** tener algo arreglado
linear ['lɪnɪə'] *adj* lineal
linen ['lɪnɪn] *n* ropa blanca; (cloth) lino
liner ['laɪnə'] *n* vapor *m* de línea transatlántico; **dustbin ~** bolsa de la basura

line-up ['laɪnʌp] *n* (us: queue) cola; (Sport) alineación *f*
linger ['lɪŋgə'] *vi* retrasarse, tardar en marcharse; (smell, tradition) persistir
lingerie ['lænʒəriː] *n* ropa interior (de mujer), lencería
linguist ['lɪŋgwɪst] *n* lingüista *mf*;
linguistic *adj* lingüístico
lining ['laɪnɪŋ] *n* forro
link [lɪŋk] *n* (of chain) eslabón *m*; (relationship) relación *f*; (bond) vínculo, lazo; (Internet) enlace *m* ▷ *vt* vincular, unir; (associate): **to ~ with** or **to** relacionar con; **links** *npl* (Golf); **link up** *vt* acoplar ▷ *vi* unirse
lion ['laɪən] *n* león *m*; **lioness** *n* leona
lip [lɪp] *n* labio; **lip-read** *vi* leer los labios; **lip salve** *n* crema protectora para labios; **lipstick** *n* lápiz *m* or barra de labios, carmín *m*
liqueur [lɪ'kjuə'] *n* licor *m*
liquid ['lɪkwɪd] *adj*, *n* líquido;
liquidizer ['lɪkwɪdaɪzə'] *n* (Culin) licuadora
liquor ['lɪkə'] *n* licor *m*, bebidas *fpl* alcohólicas; **liquor store** *n* (us) bodega, tienda de vinos y bebidas alcohólicas
Lisbon ['lɪzbən] *n* Lisboa
lisp [lɪsp] *n* ceceo ▷ *vi* cecear
list [lɪst] *n* lista ▷ *vt* (write down) hacer una lista de; (mention) enumerar
listen ['lɪsn] *vi* escuchar, oír; **listener** *n* oyente *mf*
lit [lɪt] *pt*, *pp* of **light**
liter ['liːtə'] *n* (us) = **litre**
literacy ['lɪtərəsɪ] *n* capacidad *f* de leer y escribir
literal ['lɪtərl] *adj* literal; **literally** *adv* literalmente
literary ['lɪtərərɪ] *adj* literario
literate ['lɪtərət] *adj* que sabe leer y escribir; (educated) culto
literature ['lɪtərɪtʃə'] *n* literatura; (brochures etc) folletos *mpl*
litre, (us) **liter** ['liːtə'] *n* litro
litter ['lɪtə'] *n* (rubbish) basura; (young animals) camada, cría; **litter bin** *n*

(BRIT) papelera; **littered** adj: **littered with** lleno de

little ['lɪtl] adj (small) pequeño; (not much) poco; (diminutive): **~ house** casita ▷ adv poco; **a ~** un poco (de); **a ~ bit** un poquito; **~ by ~** poco a poco; **little finger** n dedo meñique

live¹ [laɪv] adj (animal) vivo; (wire) conectado; (broadcast) en directo; (unexploded) sin explotar

live² [lɪv] vi vivir; **to ~ together** vivir juntos; **live up to** vt fus (fulfil) cumplir con

livelihood ['laɪvlɪhud] n sustento

lively ['laɪvlɪ] adj vivo; (place, book etc) animado

liven up ['laɪvn-] vt animar ▷ vi animarse

liver ['lɪvəʳ] n hígado

lives [laɪvz] npl of **life**

livestock ['laɪvstɔk] n ganado

living ['lɪvɪŋ] adj (alive) vivo ▷ n: **to earn** or **make a ~** ganarse la vida; **living room** n sala (de estar)

lizard ['lɪzəd] n lagartija

load [ləud] n carga; (weight) peso ▷ vt (also Comput) cargar; **a ~ of, ~s of** (fig) (gran) cantidad de, montones de; **to ~ (up) with** cargar con or de; **loaded** adj cargado

loaf (pl **loaves**) [ləuf, 'ləuvz] n (barra de) pan m

loan [ləun] n préstamo ▷ vt prestar; **on ~** prestado

loathe [ləuð] vt aborrecer; (person) odiar

loaves [ləuvz] pl of **loaf**

lobby ['lɔbɪ] n vestíbulo, sala de espera; (Pol: pressure group) grupo de presión ▷ vt presionar

lobster ['lɔbstəʳ] n langosta

local ['ləukl] adj local ▷ n (pub) bar m; **the locals** npl los vecinos, los del lugar; **local anaesthetic**, (US) **local anesthetic** n (Med) anestesia local; **local authority** n municipio, ayuntamiento (sp); **local government** n gobierno municipal; **locally** ['ləukəlɪ] adv en la vecindad

locate [ləu'keɪt] vt (find) localizar; (situate): **to be ~d in** estar situado en

location [ləu'keɪʃən] n situación f; **on ~** (Cine) en exteriores

loch [lɔx] n lago

lock [lɔk] n (of door, box) cerradura; (of canal) esclusa; (of hair) mechón m ▷ vt (with key) cerrar con llave a ▷ vi (door etc) cerrarse con llave; (wheels) trabarse; **lock in** vt encerrar; **lock out** vt (person) cerrar la puerta a; **lock up** vt (criminal) meter en la cárcel; (mental patient) encerrar; (house) cerrar (con llave) ▷ vi echar la llave

locker ['lɔkəʳ] n casillero; **locker-room** n (US Sport) vestuario

locksmith ['lɔksmɪθ] n cerrajero/a

locomotive [ləukə'məutɪv] n locomotora

lodge [lɔdʒ] n casa del guarda ▷ vi (person): **to ~ (with)** alojarse (en casa de) ▷ vt presentar; **lodger** ['lɔdʒəʳ] n huésped mf

lodging ['lɔdʒɪŋ] n alojamiento, hospedaje m

loft [lɔft] n desván m

log [lɔg] n (of wood) leño, tronco; (written account) diario ▷ vt anotar; **log in, log on** vi (Comput) iniciar la sesión; **log off, log out** vi (Comput) finalizar la sesión

logic ['lɔdʒɪk] n lógica; **logical** adj lógico

login ['lɔgɪn] n (Comput) login m

lollipop ['lɔlɪpɔp] n pirulí m; **lollipop man, lollipop lady** n (BRIT) persona encargada de ayudar a los niños a cruzar la calle

lolly ['lɔlɪ] n (inf: ice cream) polo; (: lollipop) piruleta; (: money) guita

London ['lʌndən] n Londres m; **Londoner** n londinense mf

lone [ləun] adj solitario

loneliness ['ləunlɪnɪs] n soledad f, aislamiento

lonely ['ləunlɪ] adj (situation) solitario; (person) solo; (place) aislado

long [lɔŋ] adj largo ▷ adv mucho tiempo, largamente ▷ vi: **to ~ for sth**

anhelar algo; **so** or **as ~ as** mientras, con tal de que; **don't be ~!** ¡no tardes!, ¡vuelve pronto!; **how ~ is the street?** ¿cuánto tiene la calle de largo?; **how ~ is the lesson?** ¿cuánto dura la clase?; **six metres** ~ que mide seis metros, de seis metros de largo; **six months** ~ que dura seis meses, de seis meses de duración; **all night** ~ toda la noche; **he no ~er comes** ya no viene; ~ **before** mucho antes; **before ~** (+ *future*) dentro de poco; (+ *past*) poco tiempo después; **at ~ last** al fin, por fin; **long-distance** *adj* (*race*) de larga distancia; (*call*) interurbano; **long-haul** *adj* (*flight*) de larga distancia; **longing** *n* anhelo, ansia; (*nostalgia*) nostalgia ▷ *adj* anhelante

longitude ['lɔŋgɪtjuːd] *n* longitud *f*

long: **long jump** *n* salto de longitud; **long-life** *adj* (*batteries*) de larga duración; (*milk*) uperizado; **long-sighted** *adj* (BRIT) présbita; **long-standing** *adj* de mucho tiempo; **long-term** *adj* a largo plazo

loo [luː] *n* (BRIT *inf*) váter *m*

look [lʊk] *vi* mirar; (*seem*) parecer; (*building etc*): **to ~ south/on to the sea** dar al sur/al mar ▷ *n* mirada; (*glance*) vistazo; (*appearance*) aire *m*, aspecto; **looks** *npl* belleza *sg*; ~ **(here)!** (*expressing annoyance etc*) ¡oye!; ~**!** (*expressing surprise*) ¡mira!; **look after** *vt fus* (*care for*) cuidar a; (*deal with*) encargarse de; **look around** *vi* echar una mirada alrededor; **look at** *vt fus* mirar; (*consider*) considerar; **look back** *vi* mirar hacia atrás; **look down on** *vt fus* (*fig*) despreciar, mirar con desprecio; **look for** *vt fus* buscar; **look forward to** *vt fus* esperar con ilusión; (*in letters*): **we ~ forward to hearing from you** quedamos a la espera de su respuesta or contestación; **look into** *vt fus* investigar; **look out** *vi* (*beware*): **look out (for)** tener cuidado de; **look out for** *vt fus* (*seek*) buscar; (*await*) esperar; **look round** *vi* volver la cabeza; **look

through** *vt fus* (*papers, book*) hojear; **look to** *vt fus* ocuparse de; (*rely on*) contar con; **look up** *vi* mirar hacia arriba; (*improve*) mejorar ▷ *vt* (*word*) buscar; **look up to** *vt fus* admirar

look-out *n* (*tower etc*) puesto de observación; (*person*) vigía *mf*; **to be on the ~ for sth** estar al acecho de algo

loom [luːm] *vi* ~ **(up)** (*threaten*) surgir, amenazar; (*event: approach*) aproximarse

loony ['luːnɪ] *adj*, *n* (*inf*) loco/a

loop [luːp] *n* lazo; **loophole** *n* laguna

loose [luːs] *adj* suelto; (*clothes*) ancho; (*morals, discipline*) relajado; **to be at a ~ end** o (*us*) **at ~ ends** no saber qué hacer; **loosely** *adv* libremente, aproximadamente; **loosen** *vt* aflojar

loot [luːt] *n* botín *m* ▷ *vt* saquear

lop-sided ['lɔp'saɪdɪd] *adj* torcido; (*fig*) desequilibrado

lord [lɔːd] *n* señor *m*; **L~ Smith** Lord Smith; **the L~** el Señor; **the (House of) L~s** (BRIT) la Cámara de los Lores

lorry ['lɔrɪ] *n* (BRIT) camión *m*; **lorry driver** *n* camionero/a

lose (*pt, pp* **lost**) [luːz, lɔst] *vt* perder ▷ *vi* perder, ser vencido; **to ~ (time)** (*clock*) atrasarse; **lose out** *vi* salir perdiendo; **loser** *n* perdedor(a) *m/f*

loss [lɔs] *n* pérdida; **heavy ~es** (Mil) grandes pérdidas *fpl*; **to be at a ~** no saber qué hacer; **to make a ~** sufrir pérdidas

lost [lɔst] *pt, pp* of **lose** ▷ *adj* perdido; **lost property**, (US) **lost and found** *n* objetos *mpl* perdidos

lot [lɔt] *n* (*at auction*) lote *m*; **the ~** el todo, todos, todas *mpl*, todas *fpl*; **a ~** mucho, bastante; **a ~ of**, **~s of** muchos/as; (*with singular noun*) mucho/a; **I read a ~** leo bastante; **to draw ~s (for sth)** echar suertes (para decidir algo)

lotion ['ləʊʃən] *n* loción *f*

lottery ['lɔtərɪ] *n* lotería

loud [laʊd] *adj* (*voice, sound*) fuerte; (*laugh, shout*) estrepitoso; (*gaudy*) chillón/ona ▷ *adv* (*speak etc*) fuerte;

out ~ en voz alta; **loudly** adv (noisily) fuerte; (in a loud voice) en voz alta; **loudspeaker** n altavoz m

lounge [laundʒ] n salón m, sala de estar; (of hotel) salón m; (of airport) sala de embarque m ▷ vi (also: ~ **about**, ~ **around**) holgazanear

louse (pl **lice**) [laus, laɪs] n piojo

lousy ['lauzɪ] adj (fig) vil, asqueroso; (ill) fatal

love [lʌv] n (romantic, sexual) amor m; (kind, caring) cariño ▷ vt amar, querer; ~ **from Anne** (in letter) con cariño de Anne; **I ~ to read** me encanta leer; **to be in ~ with** estar enamorado de; **to make ~** hacer el amor; **I ~ you** te quiero; **for the ~ of** por amor a; **"15 ~"** (Tennis) "15 a cero"; **I ~ paella** me encanta la paella; **love affair** n aventura sentimental o amorosa; **love life** n vida sentimental

lovely ['lʌvlɪ] adj (delightful) encantador(a); (beautiful) precioso

lover ['lʌvə*] n amante mf; (amateur): **a ~ of** un(a) aficionado a o un(a) amante de

loving ['lʌvɪŋ] adj amoroso, cariñoso

low [ləu] adj, adv bajo ▷ n (Meteorology) área de baja presión; **to feel ~** sentirse deprimido; **to turn (down)** ~ bajar; **low-alcohol** adj bajo en alcohol; **low-calorie** adj bajo en calorías

lower ['ləuə*] adj más bajo; (less important) menos importante ▷ vt bajar; (reduce) reducir; **to ~ o.s. to** (fig) rebajarse a

low-fat adj (milk, yoghurt) desnatado; (diet) bajo en calorías

loyal ['lɔɪəl] adj leal; **loyalty** n lealtad f; **loyalty card** n tarjeta cliente

LP n abbr (= long-playing record) elepé m

L-plates ['elpleɪts] npl (BRIT) (placas fpl de) la L

● **L-PLATES**

● En el Reino Unido las personas
● que están aprendiendo a conducir

● han de llevar indicativos blancos
● con una L en rojo llamados
● normalmente L-plates (de learner)
● en la parte delantera y trasera de
● los automóviles que conducen. No
● tienen que ir a clases teóricas, sino
● que desde el principio se les entrega
● un carnet de conducir provisional
● (provisional driving licence) para
● que realicen sus prácticas, que
● han de estar supervisadas por un
● conductor con carnet definitivo
● (full driving licence). Tampoco
● se les permite hacer prácticas
● en autopistas aunque vayan
● acompañados.

Lt. abbr (= lieutenant) Tte.

Ltd abbr (Comm: = limited company) S.A.

luck [lʌk] n suerte f; **good/bad ~** buena/mala suerte; **good ~!** ¡que tengas! suerte!; **bad** or **hard** or **tough ~!** ¡qué pena!; **luckily** adv afortunadamente; **lucky** adj afortunado; (at cards etc) con suerte; (object) que trae suerte

lucrative ['lu:krətɪv] adj lucrativo

ludicrous ['lu:dɪkrəs] adj absurdo

luggage ['lʌgɪdʒ] n equipaje m; **luggage rack** n (on car) baca, portaequipajes m inv

lukewarm ['lu:kwɔ:m] adj tibio

lull [lʌl] n tregua ▷ vt (child) acunar; (person, fear) calmar; **to ~ sb to sleep** arrullar a algn; **to ~ sb into a false sense of security** dar a algn una falsa sensación de seguridad

lullaby ['lʌləbaɪ] n nana

lumber ['lʌmbə*] n (junk) trastos mpl viejos; (wood) maderos mpl

luminous ['lu:mɪnəs] adj luminoso

lump [lʌmp] n terrón m; (fragment) trozo; (swelling) bulto ▷ vt (also: ~ **together**) juntar; **lump sum** n suma global; **lumpy** adj (sauce) lleno de grumos

lunatic ['lu:nətɪk] adj, n loco/a

lunch [lʌntʃ] n almuerzo, comida ▷ vi almorzar; **lunch break, lunch hour** n hora del almuerzo

lunchtime ['lʌntʃtaɪm] n hora del almuerzo or de comer

lung [lʌŋ] n pulmón m

lure [luə²] n (bait) cebo; (decoy) señuelo; (attraction) atracción f ▷ vt convencer con engaños

lurk [lə:k] vi (wait) estar al acecho; (fig) acechar

lush [lʌʃ] adj exuberante

lust [lʌst] n lujuria; (greed) codicia

Luxembourg ['lʌksəmbə:g] n Luxemburgo

luxurious [lʌg'zjuərɪəs] adj lujoso

luxury ['lʌkʃərɪ] n lujo ▷ cpd de lujo

Lycra® ['laɪkrə] n licra®

lying ['laɪɪŋ] n mentiras fpl ▷ adj mentiroso

lyric ['lɪrɪk] adj lírico; **lyrics** npl (of song) letra sg

m abbr (= metre) m.; **= mile**; **million**

MA n abbr (Scol) **= Master of Arts**

ma [mɑ:] n (inf) mamá

mac [mæk] n (BRIT) impermeable m

macaroni [mækə'rəʊnɪ] n macarrones mpl

Macedonia [mæsɪ'dəʊnɪə] n Macedonia; **Macedonian** [mæsɪ'dəʊnɪən] adj macedonio ▷ n macedonio/a; (Ling) macedonio

machine [mə'ʃi:n] n máquina ▷ vt (dress etc) coser a máquina; (Tech) trabajar a máquina; **machine gun** n ametralladora; **machinery** n maquinaria; (fig) mecanismo; **machine washable** adj lavable a máquina

macho ['mætʃəʊ] adj macho

mackerel ['mækrl] n (pl inv) caballa

mackintosh ['mækɪntɒʃ] n (BRIT) impermeable m

mad [mæd] adj loco; (idea) disparatado; (angry) furioso; **to be ~ (keen) about** or **on sth** estar loco por algo

madam ['mædəm] n señora

mad cow disease n encefalopatía espongiforme bovina

made [meɪd] pt, pp of **make**; **made-to-measure** adj (BRIT) hecho a la medida; **made-up** adj (story) ficticio

madly ['mædlɪ] adv locamente

madman ['mædmən] n loco

madness ['mædnɪs] n locura

Madrid [mə'drɪd] n Madrid m

Mafia ['mæfɪə] n Mafia

mag [mæg] n abbr (BRIT inf); = **magazine**

magazine [mægə'ziːn] n revista

maggot ['mægət] n gusano

magic ['mædʒɪk] n magia ▷ adj mágico; **magical** adj mágico; **magician** [mə'dʒɪʃən] n mago/a

magistrate ['mædʒɪstreɪt] n juez mf (municipal)

magnet ['mægnɪt] n imán m; **magnetic** [mæg'netɪk] adj magnético

magnificent [mæg'nɪfɪsnt] adj magnífico

magnify ['mægnɪfaɪ] vt (object) ampliar; (sound) aumentar; **magnifying glass** n lupa

magpie ['mægpaɪ] n urraca

mahogany [mə'hɔgənɪ] n caoba

maid [meɪd] n criada; **old ~** (pej) solterona

maiden name n apellido de soltera

mail [meɪl] n correo; (letters) cartas fpl ▷ vt echar al correo; **mailbox** n (US) buzón m; **mailing list** n lista de direcciones; **mailman** n (US) cartero; **mail-order** n pedido postal

main [meɪn] adj principal, mayor ▷ n (pipe) cañería principal or maestra; (US) red f eléctrica; **the ~s** (BRIT Elec) la red eléctrica; **in the ~** en general; **main course** n (Culin) plato principal; **mainland** n continente m; **mainly** adv principalmente; **main road** n carretera principal; **mainstream** n corriente f principal; **main street** n calle f mayor

maintain [meɪn'teɪn] vt mantener

maintenance ['meɪntənəns] n mantenimiento; (alimony) pensión f alimenticia

maisonette [meɪzə'net] n dúplex m

maize [meɪz] n (BRIT) maíz m, choclo (LAM)

majesty ['mædʒɪstɪ] n majestad f; **Your M~** Su Majestad

major ['meɪdʒə*] n (Mil) comandante m ▷ adj principal; (Mus) mayor

Majorca [mə'jɔːkə] n Mallorca

majority [mə'dʒɔrɪtɪ] n mayoría

make [meɪk] (pt, pp **made**) vt (manufacture) hacer, fabricar; (mistake) cometer; (speech) pronunciar; (cause to be): **to ~ sb sad** poner triste or entristecer a algn; (force): **to ~ sb do sth** obligar a algn a hacer algo; (equal): **2 and 2 ~ 4** 2 y 2 son 4 ▷ n marca; **to ~ a fool of sb** poner a algn en ridículo; **to ~ a profit/loss** obtener ganancias/sufrir pérdidas; **to ~ it** (arrive) llegar; (achieve sth) tener éxito; **what time do you ~ it?** ¿qué hora tienes?; **to ~ do with** contentarse con; **make off** vi largarse; **make out** vt (decipher) descifrar; (understand) entender; (see) distinguir; (cheque) extender; **make up** vt (invent) inventar; (parcel) hacer ▷ vi reconciliarse; (with cosmetics) maquillarse; **make up for** vt fus compensar; **makeover** n cambio de imagen; **to give sb a makeover** hacerle a algn un cambio de imagen; **maker** n fabricante m/f; (of film, programme) autor(a) m/f; **makeshift** adj improvisado; **make-up** n maquillaje m

making ['meɪkɪŋ] n (fig): **in the ~** en vías de formación; **to have the ~s of** (person) tener madera de

malaria [mə'lɛərɪə] n malaria

Malaysia [mə'leɪzɪə] n Malaisia, Malaysia

male [meɪl] n (Biol, Elec) macho ▷ adj (sex, attitude) masculino; (child etc) varón

malicious [məˈlɪʃəs] *adj* malicioso; rencoroso

malignant [məˈlɪɡnənt] *adj* (Med) maligno

mall [mɔːl] *n* (US: also: **shopping ~**) centro comercial

mallet [ˈmælɪt] *n* mazo

malnutrition [mælnjuːˈtrɪʃən] *n* desnutrición *f*

malpractice [mælˈpræktɪs] *n* negligencia profesional

malt [mɔːlt] *n* malta; (whisky) whisky *m* de malta

Malta [ˈmɔːltə] *n* Malta; **Maltese** [mɔːlˈtiːz] *adj* maltés/esa ⊳ *n* (*pl inv*) maltés/esa *m/f*

mammal [ˈmæml] *n* mamífero

mammoth [ˈmæməθ] *n* mamut *m* ⊳ *adj* gigantesco

man (*pl* **men**) [mæn, mɛn] *n* hombre *m*; (*mankind*) el hombre ⊳ *vt* (*Naut*) tripular; (*Mil*) defender; (*operate: machine*) manejar; **an old ~** un viejo; **~ and wife** marido y mujer

manage [ˈmænɪdʒ] *vi* arreglárselas ⊳ *vt* (*be in charge of*) dirigir; (*person etc*) manejar; **manageable** *adj* manejable; **management** *n* dirección *f*; **manager** *n* director(a) *m/f*; (*of pop star*) mánager *mf*; (*Sport*) entrenador *m/f*; **manageress** *n* directora; (*Sport*) entrenadora; **managerial** [mænəˈdʒɪərɪəl] *adj* directivo; **managing director** *n* director(a) *m/f* general

mandarin [ˈmændərɪn] *n* (also: **~ orange**) mandarina; (*person*) mandarín *m*

mandate [ˈmændeɪt] *n* mandato

mandatory [ˈmændətərɪ] *adj* obligatorio

mane [meɪn] *n* (*of horse*) crin *f*; (*of lion*) melena

maneuver [məˈnuːvər] *vb, n* (US) = **manoeuvre**

mangetout [mɒnʒˈtuː] *n* tirabeque *m*

mango [ˈmæŋɡəʊ] (*pl* **mangoes**) *n* mango

man: manhole *n* boca de alcantarilla; **manhood** *n* edad *f* viril; (*manliness*) virilidad *f*

mania [ˈmeɪnɪə] *n* manía; **maniac** [ˈmeɪnɪæk] *n* maníaco/a; (*fig*) maníatico

manic [ˈmænɪk] *adj* frenético

manicure [ˈmænɪkjʊər] *n* manicura

manifest [ˈmænɪfɛst] *vt* manifestar, mostrar ⊳ *adj* manifiesto

manifesto [mænɪˈfɛstəʊ] *n* manifiesto

manipulate [məˈnɪpjʊleɪt] *vt* manipular

man: mankind [mænˈkaɪnd] *n* humanidad *f*, género humano; **manly** *adj* varonil; **man-made** *adj* artificial

manner [ˈmænər] *n* manera, modo; (*behaviour*) conducta, manera de ser; (*type*) clase *f*; **manners** *npl* modales *mpl*; **bad ~s** falta *sg* de educación

manoeuvre, (US) **maneuver** [məˈnuːvər] *vt, vi* maniobrar ⊳ *n* maniobra

manpower [ˈmænpaʊər] *n* mano *f* de obra

mansion [ˈmænʃən] *n* mansión *f*

manslaughter [ˈmænslɔːtər] *n* homicidio involuntario

mantelpiece [ˈmæntlpiːs] *n* repisa de la chimenea

manual [ˈmænjuəl] *adj* manual ⊳ *n* manual *m*

manufacture [mænjuˈfæktʃər] *vt* fabricar ⊳ *n* fabricación *f*; **manufacturer** *n* fabricante *mf*

manure [məˈnjuər] *n* estiércol *m*

manuscript [ˈmænjuskrɪpt] *n* manuscrito

many [ˈmɛnɪ] *adj* muchos/as ⊳ *pron* muchos/as; **a great ~** muchísimos, un buen número de; **~ a time** muchas veces

map [mæp] *n* mapa *m*; **map out** *vt* proyectar

maple [ˈmeɪpl] *n* arce *m*, maple *m* (LAM)

mar [mɑːr] *vt* estropear

Mar. abbr (= March) mar

marathon ['mærəθən] n maratón m

marble ['mɑːbl] n mármol m; (toy) canica

March [mɑːtʃ] n marzo

march [mɑːtʃ] vi (Mil) marchar; (demonstrators) manifestarse ▷ n marcha; (demonstration) manifestación f

mare [mɛəʳ] n yegua

margarine [mɑːdʒəˈriːn] n margarina

margin ['mɑːdʒɪn] n margen m; (Comm: profit margin) margen m de beneficios; **marginal** adj marginal; **marginally** adv ligeramente

marigold ['mærɪɡəʊld] n caléndula

marijuana [mærɪˈwɑːnə] n marihuana

marina [məˈriːnə] n puerto deportivo

marinade [mærɪˈneɪd] n adobo

marinate ['mærɪneɪt] vt adobar

marine [məˈriːn] adj marino ▷ n soldado de infantería de marina

marital ['mærɪtl] adj matrimonial; **~ status** estado civil

maritime ['mærɪtaɪm] adj marítimo

marjoram ['mɑːdʒərəm] n mejorana

mark [mɑːk] n marca, señal f; (in snow, mud etc) huella; (stain) mancha; (BRIT Scol) nota ▷ vt (Sport: player) marcar; (stain) manchar; (BRIT Scol) calificar, corregir; **to ~ time** marcar el paso; (fig) marcar(se) un ritmo; **marked** adj marcado, acusado; **marker** n (sign) marcador m; (bookmark) registro

market ['mɑːkɪt] n mercado ▷ vt (Comm) comercializar; **marketing** n marketing m; **marketplace** n mercado; **market research** n (Comm) estudios mpl de mercado

marmalade ['mɑːməleɪd] n mermelada de naranja

maroon [məˈruːn] vt: **to be ~ed** (shipwrecked) quedar aislado; (fig) quedar abandonado ▷ n (colour) granate m

marquee [mɑːˈkiː] n entoldado

marriage ['mærɪdʒ] n (state) matrimonio; (wedding) boda; (act) casamiento; **marriage certificate** n partida de casamiento

married ['mærɪd] adj casado; (life, love) conyugal

marrow ['mærəʊ] n médula; (vegetable) calabacín m

marry ['mærɪ] vt casarse con; (father, priest etc) casar ▷ vi (also: **get married**) casarse

Mars [mɑːz] n Marte m

marsh [mɑːʃ] n pantano; (salt marsh) marisma

marshal ['mɑːʃl] n (Mil) mariscal m; (at sports meeting, demonstration etc) oficial m; (us: of police, fire department) jefe/a m/f ▷ vt (facts) ordenar; (soldiers) formar

martyr ['mɑːtəʳ] n mártir mf

marvel ['mɑːvl] n maravilla, prodigio ▷ vi: **to ~ (at)** maravillarse (de); **marvellous**, (us) **marvelous** ['mɑːvləs] adj maravilloso

Marxism ['mɑːksɪzəm] n marxismo

Marxist ['mɑːksɪst] adj, n marxista mf

marzipan ['mɑːzɪpæn] n mazapán m

mascara [mæsˈkɑːrə] n rímel m

mascot ['mæskət] n mascota

masculine ['mæskjʊlɪn] adj masculino

mash [mæʃ] vt machacar; **mashed potatoes** npl puré m de patatas or (LAM) papas

mask [mɑːsk] n máscara ▷ vt (hide: feelings) esconder; **to ~ one's face** (cover) ocultarse la cara

mason ['meɪsn] n (also: **stone~**) albañil m; (also: **free~**) masón m; **masonry** n (in building) mampostería

mass [mæs] n (people) muchedumbre f; (Physics) masa; (Rel) misa; (great quantity) montón m ▷ vi reunirse; (Mil) concentrarse; **the ~es** las masas

massacre ['mæsəkəʳ] n masacre f

massage ['mæsɑːʒ] n masaje m ▷ vt dar masajes or un masaje a

massive ['mæsɪv] adj enorme; (support, intervention) masivo

mass media npl medios mpl de comunicación de masas

mass-produce ['mæsprə'dju:s] vt fabricar en serie

mast [mɑ:st] n (Naut) mástil m; (Radio etc) torre f

master ['mɑ:stə'] n (of servant, animal) amo; (of situation) dueño; (Art, Mus) maestro; (in secondary school) profesor m; (title for boys): **M~ X** Señorito X ▷ vt dominar; **mastermind** n inteligencia superior ▷ vt dirigir, planear; **Master of Arts** n licenciatura superior en Letras; see also **master's degree**; **Master of Science** n licenciatura superior en Ciencias; see also **master's degree**; **masterpiece** n obra maestra; **master's degree** n máster m

- **MASTER'S DEGREE**

- Los estudios de postgrado
- británicos que llevan a la obtención
- de un master's degree consisten
- generalmente en una combinación
- de curso(s) académico(s) y tesina
- (dissertation) sobre un tema original,
- o bien únicamente en la redacción
- de una tesina. El primer caso es el
- más frecuente para los títulos de
- MA (Master of Arts) y MSc (Master
- of Science), mientras que los de
- MLitt (Master of Letters) o MPhil
- (Master of Philosophy) se obtienen
- normalmente mediante tesina.
- En algunas universidades, como
- las escocesas, el título de master's
- degree no es de postgrado, sino que
- corresponde a la licenciatura.

masturbate ['mæstəbeɪt] vi masturbarse

mat [mæt] n alfombrilla; (also: **door~**) felpudo ▷ adj = **matt**

match [mætʃ] n cerilla, fósforo; (game) partido; (fig) igual mf ◇ vt emparejar; (go well with) hacer juego con; (equal)

igualar; (correspond to) corresponderse con; (pair: also: **~ up**) casar con ▷ vi hacer juego; **to be a good ~** hacer buena pareja; **matchbox** n caja de cerillas; **matching** adj que hace juego

mate [meɪt] n (workmate) colega mf; (inf: friend) amigo/a; (animal) macho/ hembra; (in merchant navy) primer oficial m, segundo de a bordo ▷ vi acoplarse, aparearse ▷ vt acoplar, aparear

material [mə'tɪərɪəl] n (substance) materia; (equipment) material m; (cloth) tela, tejido ▷ adj material; (important) esencial; **materials** npl materiales mpl

materialize [mə'tɪərɪəlaɪz] vi materializarse

maternal [mə'tə:nl] adj maternal

maternity [mə'tə:nɪtɪ] n maternidad f; **maternity hospital** n hospital m de maternidad; **maternity leave** n baja por maternidad

math [mæθ] n abbr (US: = mathematics) matemáticas fpl

mathematical [mæθə'mætɪkl] adj matemático

mathematician [mæθəmə'tɪʃən] n matemático/a

mathematics [mæθə'mætɪks] n matemáticas fpl

maths [mæθs] n abbr (BRIT: = mathematics) matemáticas fpl

matinée ['mætɪneɪ] n sesión f de tarde

matron ['meɪtrən] n (in hospital) enfermera jefe; (in school) ama de llaves

matt [mæt] adj mate

matter ['mætə'] n cuestión f, asunto; (Physics) sustancia, materia; (Med: pus) pus m ▷ vi importar; **it doesn't ~** no importa; **what's the ~?** ¿qué pasa?; **no ~ what** pase lo que pase; **as a ~ of course** por rutina; **as a ~ of fact** en realidad; **printed ~** impresos mpl; **reading ~** material m de lectura

mattress ['mætrɪs] n colchón m

mature [mə'tjuəʳ] *adj* maduro
▷ *vi* madurar; **mature student** *n*
estudiante de más de 21 años; **maturity**
n madurez *f*

maul [mɔːl] *vt* magullar

mauve [məuv] *adj* de color malva

max *abbr* = **maximum**

maximize ['mæksɪmaɪz] *vt* (*profits etc*)
llevar al máximo; (*chances*) maximizar

maximum ['mæksɪməm] *adj*
máximo ▷ *n* máximo

May [meɪ] *n* mayo

may [meɪ] *vi* (*indicating possibility*):
he ~ come puede que venga; (*be
allowed to*): **~ I smoke?** ¿puedo fumar?;
(*wishes*): **~ God bless you!** ¡que Dios
le bendiga!

maybe ['meɪbiː] *adv* quizá(s)

May Day *n* el primero de Mayo

mayhem ['meɪhɛm] *n* caos *m* total

mayonnaise [meɪə'neɪz] *n*
mayonesa

mayor [mɛəʳ] *n* alcalde *m*; **mayoress**
n alcaldesa

maze [meɪz] *n* laberinto

MD *n abbr* (*Comm*) = **managing
director**

me [miː] *pron* (*direct*) me; (*stressed,
after pronoun*) mí; **can you hear me?**
¿me oyes?; **he heard ME!** me oyó
a mí; **it's me** soy yo; **give them to
me** dámelos; **with/without me**
conmigo/sin mí

meadow ['mɛdəu] *n* prado, pradera

meagre, (*us*) **meager** ['miːgəʳ] *adj*
escaso, pobre

meal [miːl] *n* comida; (*flour*) harina;
mealtime *n* hora de comer

mean [miːn] *adj* (*with money*) tacaño;
(*unkind*) mezquino, malo; (*average*)
medio ▷ *vt* (*signify*) querer decir,
significar; (*intend*): **to ~ to do sth**
tener la intención de *or* pensar hacer
algo ▷ *n* medio, término medio; **do
you ~ it?** ¿lo dices en serio?; **what
do you ~?** ¿qué quiere decir?; **to be
meant for sb/sth** ser para algn/algo;
see also **means**

meaning ['miːnɪŋ] *n* significado,
sentido; **meaningful** *adj* significativo;
meaningless *adj* sin sentido

means *npl* medio *sg*, manera *sg*;
(*resource*) recursos *mpl*, medios *mpl*; **by
~ of** mediante, por medio de; **by all ~!**
¡naturalmente!, ¡claro que sí!

meant [mɛnt] *pt, pp of* **mean**

meantime ['miːntaɪm],
meanwhile ['miːnwaɪl] *adv* (*also*:
in the ~) mientras tanto

measles ['miːzlz] *n* sarampión *m*

measure ['mɛʒəʳ] *vt* medir ▷ *vi* medir
▷ *n* medida; (*ruler*) cinta métrica,
metro; **measurement** *n* (*measure*)
medida; (*act*) medición *f*; **to take sb's
measurements** tomar las medidas
a algn

meat [miːt] *n* carne *f*; **cold ~s**
fiambres *mpl*; **meatball** *n* albóndiga

Mecca ['mɛkə] *n* la Meca

mechanic [mɪ'kænɪk] *n* mecánico/a;
mechanical *adj* mecánico;
mechanism ['mɛkənɪzəm] *n*
mecanismo

medal ['mɛdl] *n* medalla; **medallist**,
(*us*) **medalist** ['mɛdlɪst] *n* (*Sport*)
medallista *mf*

meddle ['mɛdl] *vi*: **to ~ in**
entrometerse en; **to ~ with sth**
manosear algo

media ['miːdɪə] *npl* medios *mpl* de
comunicación

mediaeval [mɛdɪ'iːvl] *adj*
= **medieval**

mediate ['miːdɪeɪt] *vi* mediar

medical ['mɛdɪkl] *adj* médico ▷ *n*
reconocimiento médico; **medical
certificate** *n* certificado *m* médico

medicated ['mɛdɪkeɪtɪd] *adj*
medicinal

medication [mɛdɪ'keɪʃən] *n*
medicación *f*

medicine ['mɛdsɪn] *n* medicina;
(*drug*) medicamento

medieval [mɛdɪ'iːvl] *adj* medieval

mediocre [miːdɪ'əukəʳ] *adj* mediocre

meditate ['mɛdɪteɪt] *vi* meditar

meditation [mɛdɪˈteɪʃən] n
meditación f

Mediterranean [mɛdɪtəˈreɪnɪən]
adj mediterráneo; **the ~ (Sea)** el (mar
m) Mediterráneo

medium [ˈmiːdɪəm] adj mediano
▷ n (means) medio; (person) médium
mf; **medium-sized** adj de tamaño
mediano; (clothes) de (la) talla
mediana; **medium wave** n onda
media

meek [miːk] adj manso, sumiso

meet [miːt] (pt, pp **met**) vt encontrar;
(accidentally) encontrarse con; (by
arrangement) reunirse con; (for the
first time) conocer; (go and fetch) ir a
buscar; (opponent) enfrentarse con;
(obligations) cumplir ▷ vi encontrarse;
(in session) reunirse; (join: objects)
unirse; (get to know) conocerse; **meet
up** vi: **to ~ up with sb** reunirse con
algn; **meet with** vt fus (difficulty)
tropezar con; **meeting** n encuentro;
(arranged) cita, compromiso (LAM);
(formal session, business meeting)
reunión f; (Pol) mitin m; **meeting
place** n lugar m de reunión or
encuentro

megabyte [ˈmɛgəbaɪt] n (Comput)
megabyte m, megaocteto

megaphone [ˈmɛgəfəʊn] n
megáfono

megapixel [ˈmɛgəpɪksl] n megapixel
m

melancholy [ˈmɛlənkəlɪ] n
melancolía ▷ adj melancólico

melody [ˈmɛlədɪ] n melodía

melon [ˈmɛlən] n melón m

melt [mɛlt] vi (metal) fundirse; (snow)
derretirse ▷ vt fundir

member [ˈmɛmbəʳ] n miembro; (of
club) socio/a; **M~ of Parliament**
(BRIT) diputado/a; **M~ of the
European Parliament** (BRIT)
eurodiputado/a; **M~ of the Scottish
Parliament** (BRIT) diputado/a del
Parlamento escocés; **membership** n
(members) miembros mpl; (numbers)

número de miembros or socios;
membership card n carnet m de
socio

memento [məˈmɛntəʊ] n recuerdo

memo [ˈmɛməʊ] n apunte m, nota

memorable [ˈmɛmərəbl] adj
memorable

memorandum (pl **memoranda**)
[mɛməˈrændəm, -də] n nota (de
servicio); (Pol) memorándum m

memorial [mɪˈmɔːrɪəl] n
monumento conmemorativo ▷ adj
conmemorativo

memorize [ˈmɛməraɪz] vt aprender
de memoria

memory [ˈmɛmərɪ] n recuerdo;
(Comput) memoria; **memory card** n
tarjeta de memoria; **memory stick** n
(Comput) llave f de memoria

men [mɛn] pl of **man**

menace [ˈmɛnəs] n amenaza ▷ vt
amenazar

mend [mɛnd] vt reparar, arreglar;
(darn) zurcir ▷ vi reponerse ▷ n
remiendo; (darn) zurcido; **to be on
the ~** ir mejorando; **to ~ one's ways**
enmendarse

meningitis [mɛnɪnˈdʒaɪtɪs] n
meningitis f

menopause [ˈmɛnəʊpɔːz] n
menopausia

men's room n (US): **the ~** el servicio
de caballeros

menstruation [mɛnstruˈeɪʃən] n
menstruación f

menswear [ˈmɛnzwɛəʳ] n confección
f de caballero

mental [ˈmɛntl] adj mental; **mental
hospital** n (hospital m) psiquiátrico;
mentality [mɛnˈtælɪtɪ] n mentalidad
f; **mentally** adv: **to be mentally ill**
tener una enfermedad mental

menthol [ˈmɛnθɒl] n mentol m

mention [ˈmɛnʃən] n mención f ▷ vt
mencionar; (speak of) hablar de; **don't
~ it!** ¡de nada!

menu [ˈmɛnjuː] n (set menu) menú m;
(printed) carta; (Comput) menú m

m

MEP n abbr = **Member of the European Parliament**

mercenary ['mɜːsɪnərɪ] adj, n mercenario/a

merchandise ['mɜːtʃəndaɪz] n mercancías fpl

merchant ['mɜːtʃənt] n comerciante mf; **merchant navy**, (US) **merchant marine** n marina mercante

merciless ['mɜːsɪlɪs] adj despiadado

mercury ['mɜːkjʊrɪ] n mercurio

mercy ['mɜːsɪ] n compasión f; (Rel) misericordia f; **at the ~ of** a la merced de

mere [mɪə'] adj simple, mero; **merely** adv simplemente, sólo

merge [mɜːdʒ] vt (join) unir ⊳ vi unirse; (Comm) fusionarse; **merger** n (Comm) fusión f

meringue [mə'ræŋ] n merengue m

merit ['merɪt] n mérito ⊳ vt merecer

mermaid ['mɜːmeɪd] n sirena

merry ['merɪ] adj alegre; **M~ Christmas!** ¡Felices Pascuas!; **merry-go-round** n tiovivo

mesh [meʃ] n malla

mess [mes] n confusión f; (of objects) revoltijo m; (dirt) porquería f; (Mil) comedor m; **mess about, mess around** vi (inf) perder el tiempo; (pass the time) pasar el rato; **mess up** vt (inf: spoil) estropear; (dirty) ensuciar; **mess with** vt fus (inf: challenge, confront) meterse con (inf); (interfere with) interferir con

message ['mesɪdʒ] n mensaje m, recado ⊳ vt (inf: person) mandar un mensaje a; (: comment) mandar

messenger ['mesɪndʒə'] n mensajero/a

Messrs abbr (on letters: = Messieurs) Sres.

messy ['mesɪ] adj (dirty) sucio; (untidy) desordenado

met [met] pt, pp of **meet**

metabolism [me'tæbəlɪzəm] n metabolismo

metal ['metl] n metal m; **metallic** [me'tælɪk] adj metálico

metaphor ['metəfə'] n metáfora

meteor ['miːtɪə'] n meteoro; **meteorite** ['miːtɪəraɪt] n meteorito

meteorology [miːtɪə'rɒlədʒɪ] n meteorología

meter ['miːtə'] n (instrument) contador m; (us: unit); = **metre** ⊳ vt (us Post) franquear

method ['meθəd] n método; **methodical** adj metódico

meths [meθs], n (BRIT) = **methylated spirit**

methylated spirit ['meθɪleɪtɪd-] n (BRIT) alcohol m metilado or desnaturalizado

meticulous [me'tɪkjʊləs] adj meticuloso

metre, (US) **meter** ['miːtə'] n metro

metric ['metrɪk] adj métrico

metropolitan [metrə'pɒlɪtən] adj metropolitano

Metropolitan Police n (BRIT): **the ~** la policía londinense

Mexican ['meksɪkən] adj, n mexicano/a, mejicano/a

Mexico ['meksɪkəʊ] n México, Méjico

mg abbr (= milligram) mg

mice [maɪs] pl of **mouse**

micro... ['maɪkrəʊ] pref micro...;
microchip n microplaqueta;
microphone n micrófono;
microscope n microscopio;
microwave n (also: **microwave oven**) horno microondas

mid [mɪd] adj: **in ~ May** a mediados de mayo; **in ~ afternoon** a media tarde; **in ~ air** en el aire; **midday** n mediodía m

middle ['mɪdl] n centro; (half-way point) medio; (waist) cintura ⊳ adj de en medio; **in the ~ of the night** en plena noche; **middle-aged** adj de mediana edad; **Middle Ages** npl: **the Middle Ages** la Edad Media; **middle class** n: **the middle class(es)** la clase media ⊳ adj: **middle-class** de clase media; **Middle East** n Oriente m Medio; **middle name** n segundo nombre m; **middle school** n (US) colegio para niños de doce a catorce años; (BRIT) colegio para niños de ocho o nueve a doce o trece años

midge [mɪdʒ] n mosquito

midget ['mɪdʒɪt] n enano/a

midnight ['mɪdnaɪt] n medianoche f

midst [mɪdst] n: **in the ~ of** en medio de; (situation, action) en mitad de

midsummer [mɪd'sʌmə*] n: **a ~ day** un día de pleno verano

midway [mɪd'weɪ] adj, adv: **~ (between)** a medio camino (entre); **~ through** a la mitad (de)

midweek [mɪd'wiːk] adv entre semana

midwife (pl **midwives**) ['mɪdwaɪf, -waɪvz] n matrona, comadrona

midwinter [mɪd'wɪntə*] n: **in ~** en pleno invierno

might [maɪt] vb see **may** ▷ n fuerza, poder m; **mighty** adj fuerte, poderoso

migraine ['miːɡreɪn] n jaqueca

migrant ['maɪɡrənt] adj migratorio; (worker) emigrante

migrate [maɪ'ɡreɪt] vi emigrar

migration [maɪ'ɡreɪʃən] n emigración f

mike [maɪk] n abbr (= microphone) micro

mild [maɪld] adj (person) apacible; (climate) templado; (slight) ligero; (taste) suave; (illness) leve; **mildly** adv ligeramente; suavemente; **to put it mildly** por no decir algo peor

mile [maɪl] n milla; **mileage** n número de millas; (Aut) kilometraje m; **mileometer** [maɪ'lɒmɪtə*] n (BRIT) = **milometer**; **milestone** n mojón m

military ['mɪlɪtərɪ] adj militar

militia [mɪ'lɪʃə] n milicia

milk [mɪlk] n leche f ▷ vt (cow) ordeñar; (fig) chupar; **milk chocolate** n chocolate m con leche; **milkman** n lechero; **milky** adj lechoso

mill [mɪl] n (windmill etc) molino; (coffee mill) molinillo; (factory)

fábrica ▷ vt moler ▷ vi (also: **~ about**) arremolinarse

millennium (pl **millenniums** or **millennia**) [mɪ'lɛniəm, -'lɛniə] n milenio, milenario

milli... ['mɪlɪ] pref mili...;
milligram(me) ['mɪlɪɡræm] n miligramo; **millilitre**, (US) **milliliter** ['mɪlɪliːtə*] n mililitro; **millimetre**, (US) **millimeter** ['mɪlɪmiːtə*] n milímetro

million ['mɪljən] n millón m; **a ~ times** un millón de veces; **millionaire** [mɪljə'nɛə*] n millonario/a; **millionth** adj millonésimo

milometer [maɪ'lɒmɪtə*] n (BRIT) cuentakilómetros m inv

mime [maɪm] n mímica; (actor) mimo/a ▷ vt remedar ▷ vi actuar de mimo

mimic ['mɪmɪk] n imitador(a) m/f ▷ adj mímico ▷ vt remedar, imitar

min. abbr (= minute(s)) m.; = **minimum**

mince [mɪns] vt picar ▷ n (BRIT Culin) carne f picada; **mincemeat** n conserva de fruta picada; (US: meat) carne f picada; **mince pie** n pastelillo relleno de fruta picada

mind [maɪnd] n mente f; (contrasted with matter) espíritu m ▷ vt (attend to, look after) ocuparse de, cuidar; (be careful of) tener cuidado con; (object to): **I don't ~ the noise** no me molesta el ruido; **it is on my ~** me preocupa; **to bear sth in ~** tomar or tener algo en cuenta; **to make up one's ~** decidirse; **I don't ~** me es igual; **~ you, ...** te advierto que ...; **never ~!** ¡es igual!, ¡no importa!; (don't worry) ¡no te preocupes!; **"~ the step"** "cuidado con el escalón"; **mindless** adj (violence, crime) sin sentido; (work) de autómata

mine [maɪn] pron (el) mío/(la) mía etc ▷ adj: **this book is ~** este libro es mío ▷ n mina ▷ vt (coal) extraer; (ship, beach) minar; **minefield** n campo de minas; **miner** n minero/a

m

mineral ['mɪnərəl] adj mineral ▷ n mineral m; **mineral water** n agua mineral

mingle ['mɪŋgl] vi: **to ~ with** mezclarse con

miniature ['mɪnətʃə] adj (en) miniatura ▷ n miniatura

minibar ['mɪnɪbɑː] n minibar m

minibus ['mɪnɪbʌs] n microbús m

minicab ['mɪnɪkæb] n taxi m (que sólo puede pedirse por teléfono)

minimal ['mɪnɪml] adj mínimo

minimize ['mɪnɪmaɪz] vt minimizar; (play down) empequeñecer

minimum ['mɪnɪməm] n mínimo ▷ adj mínimo

mining ['maɪnɪŋ] n minería

miniskirt ['mɪnɪskɜːt] n minifalda

minister ['mɪnɪstə] n (BRIT Pol) ministro/a; (: junior) secretario/a de Estado; (Rel) pastor m ▷ vi: **to ~ to** atender a

ministry ['mɪnɪstrɪ] n (BRIT Pol) ministerio; (Rel) sacerdocio

minor ['maɪnə] adj (repairs, injuries) leve; (poet, planet) menor; (Mus) menor ▷ n (Law) menor mf de edad

Minorca [mɪ'nɔːkə] n Menorca

minority [maɪ'nɒrɪtɪ] n minoría

mint [mɪnt] n (plant) menta, hierbabuena; (sweet) caramelo de menta ▷ vt (coins) acuñar; **the (Royal) M~,** (us): **the (US) M~** la Casa de la Moneda; **in perfect state** en perfecto estado

minus ['maɪnəs] n (also: **~ sign**) signo menos ▷ prep menos; **12 - 6 equals 6** 12 menos 6 son 6; **-24°C** menos 24 grados

minute[1] ['mɪnɪt] n minuto; (fig) momento; **minutes** npl (of meeting) actas fpl; **at the last ~** a última hora

minute[2] [maɪ'njuːt] adj diminuto; (search) minucioso

miracle ['mɪrəkl] n milagro

miraculous [mɪ'rækjuləs] adj milagroso

mirage ['mɪrɑːʒ] n espejismo

mirror ['mɪrə] n espejo; (in car) retrovisor m

misbehave [mɪsbɪ'heɪv] vi portarse mal

misc. abbr = **miscellaneous**

miscarriage ['mɪskærɪdʒ] n (Med) aborto (no provocado); **~ of justice** error m judicial

miscellaneous [mɪsɪ'leɪnɪəs] adj varios/as, diversos/as

mischief ['mɪstʃɪf] n travesura; (maliciousness) malicia; **mischievous** ['mɪstʃɪvəs] adj travieso

misconception ['mɪskən'sepʃən] n idea equivocada; equivocación f

misconduct [mɪs'kɒndʌkt] n mala conducta; **professional ~** falta profesional

miser ['maɪzə] n avaro/a

miserable ['mɪzərəbl] adj (unhappy) triste, desgraciado; (wretched) miserable

misery ['mɪzərɪ] n tristeza; (wretchedness) miseria, desdicha

misfortune [mɪs'fɔːtʃən] n desgracia

misgiving [mɪs'gɪvɪŋ] n (apprehension) presentimiento; **to have ~s about sth** tener dudas sobre algo

misguided [mɪs'gaɪdɪd] adj equivocado

mishap ['mɪshæp] n desgracia, contratiempo

misinterpret [mɪsɪn'tɜːprɪt] vt interpretar mal

misjudge [mɪs'dʒʌdʒ] vt juzgar mal

mislay [mɪs'leɪ] vt extraviar, perder

mislead [mɪs'liːd] vt llevar a conclusiones erróneas; **misleading** adj engañoso

misplace [mɪs'pleɪs] vt extraviar

misprint ['mɪsprɪnt] n errata, error m de imprenta

misrepresent [mɪsreprɪ'zent] vt falsificar

Miss [mɪs] n Señorita

miss [mɪs] vt (train etc) perder; (target) errar; (regret the absence of): **I ~ him** le echo de menos ▷ vi fallar ▷ n (shot) tiro fallido; **miss out** (BRIT) omitir; **miss out** vt fus (fun, party, opportunity) perderse

missile ['mɪsaɪl] n (Aviat) misil m; (object thrown) proyectil m

missing ['mɪsɪŋ] adj (pupil) ausente; (thing) perdido; **~ in action** desaparecido en combate

mission ['mɪʃən] n misión f; **missionary** n misionero/a

misspell [mɪs'spel] vt (irreg: like spell) escribir mal

mist [mɪst] n (light) neblina; (heavy) niebla; (at sea) bruma ▷ vi (also: **~ over, ~ up**: BRIT: windows) empañarse

mistake [mɪs'teɪk] n error m ▷ vt (irreg: like take) entender mal; **by ~** por equivocación; **to make a ~** equivocarse; **to ~ A for B** confundir A con B; **mistaken** pp of **mistake** ▷ adj equivocado; **to be mistaken** equivocarse, engañarse

mister ['mɪstə*] n (inf) señor m; see also **Mr**

mistletoe ['mɪsltəu] n muérdago

mistook [mɪs'tuk] pt of **mistake**

mistress ['mɪstrɪs] n (lover) amante f; (of house) señora (de la casa); (BRIT: in primary school) maestra; (: in secondary school) profesora

mistrust [mɪs'trʌst] vt desconfiar de

misty ['mɪstɪ] adj (day) de niebla; (glasses) empañado

misunderstand [mɪsʌndə'stænd] vt, vi (irreg: like understand) entender mal; **misunderstanding** n malentendido

misunderstood [mɪsʌndə'stud] pt, pp of **misunderstand** ▷ adj (person) incomprendido

misuse n [mɪs'juːs] mal uso; (of power) abuso; (of funds) malversación f ▷ vt [mɪs'juːz] abusar de; (funds) malversar

mix [mɪks] vt mezclar; (combine) unir ▷ vi mezclarse; (people) llevarse bien ▷ n mezcla; **mix up** vt mezclar; (confuse) confundir; **mixed** adj mixto;

(feelings etc) encontrado; **mixed grill** n (BRIT) parrillada mixta; **mixed salad** n ensalada mixta; **mixed-up** adj (confused) confuso, revuelto; **mixer** n (for food) batidora; (person): **he's a good mixer** tiene don de gentes; **mixture** n mezcla; **mix-up** n confusión f

ml abbr (= millilitre(s)) ml

mm abbr (= millimetre) mm

moan [məun] n gemido ▷ vi gemir; (inf: complain): **to ~ (about)** quejarse (de)

moat [məut] n foso

mob [mɔb] n multitud f ▷ vt acosar

mobile ['məubaɪl] adj móvil ▷ n móvil m; **mobile home** n caravana; **mobile phone** n teléfono móvil

mobility [məu'bɪlɪtɪ] n movilidad f

mobilize ['məubɪlaɪz] vt movilizar

mock [mɔk] vt (make ridiculous) ridiculizar; (laugh at) burlarse de ▷ adj fingido; **~ exams** (BRIT: Scol) exámenes mpl de prueba; **mockery** n burla

mod cons ['mɔd'kɔnz] npl abbr = **modern conveniences**; see **convenience**

mode [məud] n modo

model ['mɔdl] n modelo; (for fashion, art) modelo mf ▷ adj modelo inv ▷ vt modelar; **to ~ o.s. on** tomar como modelo a ▷ vi ser modelo; **to ~ clothes** pasar modelos, ser modelo

modem ['məudəm] n módem m

moderate adj n ['mɔdərət] moderado/a ▷ vi ['mɔdəreɪt] moderarse, calmarse ▷ vt ['mɔdəreɪt] moderar

moderation [mɔdə'reɪʃən] n moderación f; **in ~** con moderación

modern ['mɔdən] adj moderno; **modernize** vt modernizar

modest ['mɔdɪst] adj modesto; (small) módico; **modesty** ['mɔdɪstɪ] n modestia

modification [mɔdɪfɪ'keɪʃən] n modificación f

modify ['mɒdɪfaɪ] vt modificar
module ['mɒdjuːl] n módulo
mohair ['məuheə'] n mohair m
Mohammed [mə'hæmed] n
Mahoma m
moist [mɔɪst] adj húmedo; **moisture**
['mɔɪstʃə'] n humedad f; **moisturizer**
['mɔɪstʃəraɪzə'] n crema hidratante
mold [məuld] n, vt (US) = **mould**
mole [məul] n (animal) topo; (spot)
lunar m
molecule ['mɒlɪkjuːl] n molécula
molest [mə'lest] vt importunar;
(sexually) abusar sexualmente de
⊠ Be careful not to translate molest
by the Spanish word molestar.
molten ['məultən] adj fundido;
(lava) líquido
mom [mɒm] n (US) = **mum**
moment ['məumənt] n momento;
at or **for the** ~ de momento, por
ahora; **momentarily**
['məuməntrɪlɪ]
adv momentáneamente; (US:
very soon) de un momento a otro;
momentary adj momentáneo;
momentous [məu'mentəs] adj
trascendental, importante
momentum [məu'mentəm] n
momento; (fig) ímpetu m; **to gather** ~
cobrar velocidad; (fig) cobrar fuerza
mommy ['mɒmɪ] n (US) = **mummy**
Mon. abbr (= Monday) lun.
Monaco ['mɒnəkəu] n Mónaco
monarch ['mɒnək] n monarca mf;
monarchy n monarquía
monastery ['mɒnəstərɪ] n
monasterio
Monday ['mʌndɪ] n lunes m inv
monetary ['mʌnɪtərɪ] adj monetario
money ['mʌnɪ] n dinero; **to make** ~
ganar dinero; **money belt** n riñonera;
money order n giro
mongrel ['mʌŋgrəl] n (dog) perro
cruzado
monitor ['mɒnɪtə'] n (Scol) monitor
m; (also: **television** ~) receptor m de
control; (of computer) monitor m ▷ vt
controlar

monk [mʌŋk] n monje m
monkey ['mʌŋkɪ] n mono
monologue ['mɒnəlɒg] n monólogo
monopoly [mə'nɒpəlɪ] n monopolio
monotonous [mə'nɒtənəs] adj
monótono
monsoon [mɒn'suːn] n monzón m
monster ['mɒnstə'] n monstruo
month [mʌnθ] n mes m; **300 dollars**
a ~ 300 dólares al mes; **every** ~ cada
mes; **monthly** adj mensual ▷ adv
mensualmente
monument ['mɒnjumənt] n
monumento
mood [muːd] n humor m; **to be in**
a good/bad ~ estar de buen/mal
humor; **moody** adj (changeable) de
humor variable; (sullen) malhumorado
moon [muːn] n luna; **moonlight** n
luz f de la luna
moor [muə'] n páramo ▷ vt (ship)
amarrar ▷ vi echar las amarras
moose [muːs] n (pl inv) alce m
mop [mɒp] n fregona; (of hair) melena
▷ vt fregar; **mop up** vt limpiar
mope [məup] vi estar deprimido
moped ['məuped] n ciclomotor m
moral ['mɒrl] adj moral ▷ n moraleja;
morals npl moralidad f, moral f
morale [mɒ'rɑːl] n moral f
morality [mə'rælɪtɪ] n moralidad f
morbid ['mɔːbɪd] adj (interest)
morboso; (Med) mórbido

KEYWORD

more [mɔː'] adj 1 (greater in number
etc) más; **more people/work than**
before más gente/trabajo que antes
2 (additional) más; **do you want**
(some) more tea? ¿quieres más té?;
is there any more wine? ¿queda
vino?; **it'll take a few more weeks**
tardará unas semanas más; **it's 2 kms**
more to the house faltan 2 kms para
la casa; **more time/letters than we**
expected más tiempo del que/más
cartas de las que esperábamos

▶ pron (greater amount, additional amount) más; **more than 10** más de 10; **it cost more than the other one/than we expected** costó más que el otro/más de lo que esperábamos; **is there any more?** ¿hay más?; **many/much more** muchos/as más, mucho/a más ▶ adv más; **more dangerous/easily (than)** más peligroso/fácilmente (que); **more and more expensive** cada vez más caro; **more or less** más o menos; **more than ever** más que nunca

moreover [mɔːˈrəʊvəʳ] adv además, por otra parte

morgue [mɔːg] n depósito de cadáveres

morning ['mɔːnɪŋ] n mañana; (early morning) madrugada; **in the** ~ por la mañana; **7 o'clock in the** ~ las 7 de la mañana; **morning sickness** n náuseas fpl del embarazo

Moroccan [məˈrɒkən] adj, n marroquí mf

Morocco [məˈrɒkəʊ] n Marruecos m

moron ['mɔːrɒn] n imbécil mf

morphine ['mɔːfiːn] n morfina

Morse [mɔːs] n (also: ~ **code**) (código) morse m

mortal ['mɔːtl] adj, n mortal m

mortar ['mɔːtəʳ] n argamasa

mortgage ['mɔːgɪdʒ] n hipoteca ▶ vt hipotecar

mortician [mɔːˈtɪʃən] n (us) director(a) m/f de pompas fúnebres

mortified ['mɔːtɪfaɪd] adj: **I was** ~ me dio muchísima vergüenza

mortuary ['mɔːtjuərɪ] n depósito de cadáveres

mosaic [məʊˈzeɪɪk] n mosaico

Moslem ['mɒzləm] adj, n = **Muslim**

mosque [mɒsk] n mezquita

mosquito [mɒsˈkiːtəʊ] n (pl **mosquitoes**) n mosquito, zancudo (LAM)

moss [mɒs] n musgo

most [məʊst] adj la mayor parte de, la mayoría de ▶ pron la mayor parte, la mayoría ▶ adv el más; (very) muy; **the** ~ (also: + adjective) el más; ~ **of them** la mayor parte de ellos; **I saw the** ~ yo fui el que más vi; **at the (very)** ~ a lo sumo, todo lo más; **to make the ~ of** aprovechar (al máximo); **a ~ interesting book** un libro interesantísimo; **mostly** adv en su mayor parte, principalmente

MOT n abbr (BRIT) = **Ministry of Transport; the ~ (test)** = la ITV

motel [məʊˈtɛl] n motel m

moth [mɒθ] n mariposa nocturna; (clothes moth) polilla

mother ['mʌðəʳ] n madre f ▶ adj materno ▶ vt (care for) cuidar (como una madre); **motherhood** n maternidad f; **mother-in-law** n suegra; **mother-of-pearl** n nácar m; **Mother's Day** n Día m de la Madre; **mother-to-be** n futura madre; **mother tongue** n lengua materna

motif [məʊˈtiːf] n motivo

motion ['məʊʃən] n movimiento; (gesture) ademán m, señal f; (at meeting) moción f ▶ vt, vi: **to ~ (to) sb to do sth** hacer señas a algn para que haga algo; **motionless** adj inmóvil; **motion picture** n película

motivate ['məʊtɪveɪt] vt motivar

motivation [məʊtɪˈveɪʃən] n motivación f

motive ['məʊtɪv] n motivo

motor ['məʊtəʳ] n motor m; (BRIT inf: vehicle) coche m, carro (LAM), automóvil m, auto m (LAM) ▶ adj motor (f: motora o motriz); **motorbike** n moto f; **motorboat** n lancha motora; **motorcar** n (BRIT) coche m, carro (LAM), automóvil m, auto m (LAM); **motorcycle** n motocicleta; **motorcyclist** n motociclista mf; **motoring** n (BRIT) automovilismo; **motorist** n conductor(a) m/f, automovilista mf; **motor racing** n (BRIT) carreras fpl de coches, automovilismo; **motorway** n (BRIT) autopista

motto ['mɒtəʊ] (pl **mottoes**) n lema m; (watchword) consigna

mould, (US) **mold** [məʊld] n molde m; (mildew) moho ▷ vt moldear; (fig) formar; **mouldy** adj enmohecido

mound [maʊnd] n montón m, montículo

mount [maʊnt] n monte m ▷ vt montar en, subir a; (picture) enmarcar ▷ vi (also: ~ **up**: increase) aumentar; (on horse) montar

mountain ['maʊntɪn] n montaña ▷ cpd de montaña; **mountain bike** n bicicleta de montaña; **mountaineer** n alpinista mf, andinista mf (LAM); **mountaineering** n montañismo, alpinismo, andinismo (LAM); **mountainous** adj montañoso; **mountain range** n sierra

mourn [mɔːn] vt llorar, lamentar ▷ vi: **to ~ for** llorar la muerte de; **mourner** n doliente mf; **mourning** n luto; **in mourning** de luto

mouse (pl **mice**) [maʊs, maɪs] n (also Comput) ratón m; **mouse mat** n (Comput) alfombrilla, almohadilla

mousse [muːs] n (Culin) mousse f; (for hair) espuma (moldeadora)

moustache [məs'tɑːʃ], (US) **mustache** ['mʌstæʃ] n bigote m

mouth (pl **mouths**) [maʊθ, -ðz] n boca; (of river) desembocadura; **mouthful** n bocado; **mouth organ** n armónica; **mouthpiece** n (of musical instrument) boquilla; (spokesman) portavoz mf; **mouthwash** n enjuague m bucal

move [muːv] n (movement) movimiento; (in game) jugada; (: turn to play) turno; (change of house) mudanza ▷ vt mover; (emotionally) conmover; (Pol: resolution etc) proponer ▷ vi moverse; (traffic) circular; (also: ~ **house**) trasladarse, mudarse; **to get a ~ on** darse prisa; **to ~ sb to do sth** mover a algn a hacer

algo; **move back** vi volver; **move in** vi (to a house) instalarse; **move off** vi ponerse en camino; **move on** vi seguir viaje; **move out** vi (of house) mudarse; **move over** vi hacerse a un lado, correrse; **move up** vi (employee) ascender; **movement** n movimiento

movie ['muːvɪ] n película; **to go to the ~s** ir al cine; **movie theater** n (US) cine m

moving ['muːvɪŋ] adj (emotional) conmovedor(a); (that moves) móvil

mow (pt **mowed**, pp **mowed** or **mown**) [məʊ, -n] vt (grass) cortar; (corn) segar; **mower** n (also: **lawnmower**) cortacésped m

Mozambique [məʊzæm'biːk] n Mozambique m

MP n abbr (BRIT) = **Member of Parliament**

mpg n abbr (= miles per gallon) 30 mpg = 9.4 l. per 100 km

mph abbr (= miles per hour) 60 mph = 96 km/h

MP3 ['empiː'θriː] n MP3 m; **MP3 player** n reproductor m MP3

Mr, Mr. ['mɪstəʳ] n: **Mr Smith** (el) Sr. Smith

Mrs, Mrs. ['mɪsɪz] n: ~ **Smith** (la) Sra. de Smith

Ms, Ms. [mɪz] n (Miss or Mrs) abreviatura con la que se evita hacer expreso el estado civil de una mujer; **Ms Smith** (la) Sra. Smith

MSP n abbr (BRIT) = **Member of the Scottish Parliament**

Mt abbr (Geo: = mount) m.

much [mʌtʃ] adj mucho ▷ adv, n, pron mucho; (before pp) muy; **how ~ is it?** ¿cuánto es?, ¿cuánto cuesta?; **too ~** demasiado; **it's not ~** no es mucho; **as ~ as** tanto como; **however ~ he tries** por mucho que se esfuerce

muck [mʌk] n suciedad f; **muck up** vt (inf) estropear; **mucky** adj (dirty) sucio

mucus ['mjuːkəs] n mucosidad f, moco

mud [mʌd] n barro, lodo

muddle ['mʌdl] n desorden m, confusión f; (mix-up) embrollo, lío ▷ vt (also: ~ up) embrollar, confundir

muddy ['mʌdɪ] adj fangoso, cubierto de lodo

mudguard ['mʌdgɑːd] n guardabarros m inv

muesli ['mjuːzlɪ] n muesli m

muffin ['mʌfɪn] n bollo, ≈ magdalena

muffled ['mʌfld] adj apagado; (noise etc) amortiguado

muffler ['mʌflə*] n (scarf) bufanda; (us: Aut) silenciador m

mug [mʌg] n (cup) taza alta; (for beer) jarra; (inf: face) jeta ▷ vt (assault) atracar; **mugger** n atracador(a) m/f; **mugging** n atraco callejero

muggy ['mʌgɪ] adj bochornoso

mule [mjuːl] n mula

multicoloured, (us) **multicolored** ['mʌltɪkʌləd] adj multicolor

multimedia [mʌltɪ'miːdɪə] adj multimedia inv

multinational [mʌltɪ'næʃənl] n multinacional f ▷ adj multinacional

multiple ['mʌltɪpl] adj múltiple ▷ n múltiplo; **multiple choice** n (also: **multiple choice test**) examen m de tipo test; **multiple sclerosis** n esclerosis f múltiple

multiplex ['mʌltɪpleks] n (also: ~ **cinema**) multicines m inv

multiplication [mʌltɪplɪ'keɪʃən] n multiplicación f

multiply ['mʌltɪplaɪ] vt multiplicar ▷ vi multiplicarse

multistorey [mʌltɪ'stɔːrɪ] adj (BRIT) de muchos pisos

mum [mʌm] n (BRIT) mamá f ▷ adj: **to keep ~ (about sth)** no decir ni mu (de algo)

mumble ['mʌmbl] vt decir entre dientes ▷ vi hablar entre dientes, musitar

mummy ['mʌmɪ] n (BRIT: mother) mamá f; (embalmed) momia

mumps [mʌmps] n paperas fpl

munch [mʌntʃ] vt, vi mascar

municipal [mjuːˈnɪsɪpl] adj municipal

mural ['mjuərl] n (pintura) mural m

murder ['məːdə*] n asesinato; (in law) homicidio ▷ vt asesinar, matar; **murderer** n asesino

murky ['məːkɪ] adj (water, past) turbio; (room) sombrío

murmur ['məːmə*] n murmullo ▷ vt, vi murmurar

muscle ['mʌsl] n músculo; (fig: strength) garra, fuerza; **muscular** ['mʌskjulə*] adj muscular; (person) musculoso

museum [mjuːˈzɪəm] n museo

mushroom ['mʌʃrum] n seta, hongo; (small) champiñón m ▷ vi crecer de la noche a la mañana

music ['mjuːzɪk] n música; **musical** adj musical; (sound) melodioso; (person) con talento musical ▷ n (show) (comedia) musical m; **musical instrument** n instrumento musical; **musician** [mjuːˈzɪʃən] n músico/a

Muslim ['mʌzlɪm] adj, n musulmán/ ana m/f

muslin ['mʌzlɪn] n muselina

mussel ['mʌsl] n mejillón m

must [mʌst] aux vb (obligation): **I ~ do it** debo hacerlo, tengo que hacerlo; (probability): **he ~ be there by now** ya debe (de) estar allí ▷ n: **it's a ~** es imprescindible

mustache ['mʌstæʃ] n (us) = **moustache**

mustard ['mʌstəd] n mostaza

mustn't ['mʌsnt] = **must not**

mute [mjuːt] adj, n mudo/a

mutilate ['mjuːtɪleɪt] vt mutilar

mutiny ['mjuːtɪnɪ] n motín m ▷ vi amotinarse

mutter ['mʌtə*] vt, vi murmurar

mutton ['mʌtn] n (carne f de) cordero

mutual ['mjuːtʃuəl] adj mutuo; (friend) común

m

muzzle ['mʌzl] n hocico; (*protective device*) bozal m; (*of gun*) boca ▷ vt (*dog*) poner un bozal a

my [maɪ] adj mi(s); **my house/ brother/sisters** mi casa/hermano/ mis hermanas; **I've washed my hair/ cut my finger** me he lavado el pelo/ cortado un dedo; **is this my pen or yours?** ¿este bolígrafo es mío o tuyo?

myself [maɪ'sɛlf] pron (*reflexive*) me; (*emphatic*) yo mismo; (*after prep*) mí (mismo); *see also* **oneself**

mysterious [mɪs'tɪərɪəs] adj misterioso

mystery ['mɪstərɪ] n misterio

mystical ['mɪstɪkl] adj místico

mystify ['mɪstɪfaɪ] vt (*perplex*) dejar perplejo

myth [mɪθ] n mito; **mythology** [mɪ'θɒlədʒɪ] n mitología

n/a abbr (= not applicable) no interesa

nag [næg] vt (*scold*) regañar

nail [neɪl] n (*human*) uña; (*metal*) clavo ▷ vt clavar; **to ~ sb down to a date/price** hacer que algn se comprometa a una fecha/un precio; **nailbrush** n cepillo para las uñas; **nailfile** n lima para las uñas; **nail polish** n esmalte m or laca para las uñas; **nail polish remover** n quitaesmalte m; **nail scissors** npl tijeras fpl para las uñas; **nail varnish** n (BRIT) = **nail polish**

naïve [naɪ'iːv] adj ingenuo

naked ['neɪkɪd] adj (*nude*) desnudo; (*flame*) expuesto al aire

name [neɪm] n nombre m; (*surname*) apellido; (*reputation*) fama, renombre m ▷ vt (*child*) poner nombre a; (*criminal*) identificar; (*price, date etc*) fijar; **by ~** de nombre; **in the ~ of** en nombre de; **what's your ~?** ¿cómo se llama usted?; **to give one's ~ and**

address dar sus señas; **namely** adv a saber

nanny ['nænɪ] n niñera

nap [næp] n (sleep) sueñecito, siesta

napkin ['næpkɪn] n (also: **table ~**) servilleta

nappy ['næpɪ] n (BRIT) pañal m

narcotic [naː'kɒtɪk] adj, n narcótico; **narcotics** npl estupefacientes mpl, narcóticos mpl

narrative ['nærətɪv] n narrativa ▷ adj narrativo

narrator [nə'reɪtə] n narrador(a) m/f

narrow ['nærəu] adj estrecho ▷ vi estrecharse; (diminish) reducirse; **to have a ~ escape** escaparse por los pelos; **narrow down** vt (search, investigation, possibilities) restringir, limitar; (list) reducir; **narrowly** adv (miss) por poco; **narrow-minded** adj de miras estrechas

nasal ['neɪzl] adj nasal

nasty ['naːstɪ] adj (remark) feo; (person) antipático; (revolting: taste, smell) asqueroso; (wound, disease etc) peligroso, grave

nation ['neɪʃən] n nación f

national ['næʃənl] adj nacional ▷ n súbdito/a; **national anthem** n himno nacional; **national dress** n traje m típico del país; **National Health Service** n (BRIT) servicio nacional de salud, ≈ INSALUD m (SP); **National Insurance** n (BRIT) seguro social nacional; **nationalist** adj, n nacionalista mf; **nationality** n nacionalidad f; **nationalize** vt nacionalizar; **National Trust** n (BRIT) organización encargada de preservar el patrimonio histórico británico

nationwide ['neɪʃənwaɪd] adj a escala nacional

native ['neɪtɪv] n (local inhabitant) natural mf ▷ adj (indigenous) indígena; (country) natal; (innate) natural, innato; **a ~ of Russia** un(a) natural de Rusia; **Native American** adj, n americano/a indígena, amerindio/a

native speaker n hablante mf nativo/a

NATO ['neɪtəu] n abbr (= North Atlantic Treaty Organization) OTAN f

natural ['nætʃrəl] adj natural; **natural gas** n gas m natural; **natural history** n historia natural; **naturally** adv (speak etc) naturalmente; (of course) desde luego, por supuesto; **natural resources** npl recursos mpl naturales

nature ['neɪtʃə] n naturaleza; (group, sort) género, clase f; (character) modo de ser, carácter m; **by ~** por naturaleza; **nature reserve** n reserva natural

naughty ['nɔːtɪ] adj (child) travieso

nausea ['nɔːsɪə] n náusea

naval ['neɪvl] adj naval, de marina

navel ['neɪvl] n ombligo

navigate ['nævɪgeɪt] vt gobernar ▷ vi navegar; (Aut) ir de copiloto; **navigation** [nævɪ'geɪʃən] n (action) navegación f; (science) náutica

navy ['neɪvɪ] n marina de guerra; (ships) armada, flota

Nazi ['naːtsɪ] n nazi mf

NB abbr (= nota bene) nótese

near [nɪə] adj (place, relation) cercano; (time) próximo ▷ adv cerca ▷ prep (also: **~ to**: space) cerca de, junto a; (time) cerca de ▷ vt acercarse a, aproximarse a; **nearby** [nɪə'baɪ] adj cercano, próximo ▷ adv cerca; **nearly** adv casi, por poco; **I nearly fell** por poco me caigo; **near-sighted** adj miope, corto de vista

neat [niːt] adj (place) ordenado, bien cuidado; (person) pulcro; (plan) ingenioso; (spirits) solo; **neatly** adv (tidily) con esmero; (skilfully) ingeniosamente

necessarily ['nesɪsrɪlɪ] adv necesariamente

necessary ['nesɪsrɪ] adj necesario, preciso

necessity [nɪ'sesɪtɪ] n necesidad f

neck [nek] n (Anat) cuello; (of animal) pescuezo ▷ vi besuquearse; **~ and ~**

parejos; **necklace** ['nɛklɪs] n collar m;
necktie n (us) corbata

nectarine ['nɛktərɪn] n nectarina

need [niːd] n (lack) escasez f, falta;
(necessity) necesidad f ▷ vt (require)
necesitar; **I ~ to do it** tengo que
hacerlo; **you don't ~ to go** no hace
falta que vayas

needle ['niːdl] n aguja ▷ vt (fig: inf)
picar, fastidiar

needless ['niːdlɪs] adj innecesario;
~ to say huelga decir que

needlework ['niːdlwɜːk] n (activity)
costura, labor f de aguja

needn't ['niːdnt] = **need not**

needy ['niːdɪ] adj necesitado

negative ['nɛgətɪv] n (Phot)
negativo; (Ling) negación f ▷ adj
negativo

neglect [nɪ'glɛkt] vt (one's duty)
faltar a, no cumplir con; (child)
descuidar, desatender ▷ n (state)
abandono; (personal) dejadez f;
(of child) desatención f; (of duty)
incumplimiento

negotiate [nɪ'gəʊʃɪeɪt] vt (treaty,
loan) negociar; (obstacle) franquear;
(bend in road) tomar ▷ vi: **to ~ (with)**
negociar (con)

negotiation [nɪgəʊʃɪ'eɪʃən] n
negociación f; **negotiations** npl
negociaciones

negotiator [nɪ'gəʊʃɪeɪtəʳ] n
negociador(a) m/f

neighbour, (us)**neighbor** ['neɪbəʳ]
n vecino/a; **neighbourhood,** (us)
neighborhood n (place) vecindad
f, barrio; (people) vecindario;
neighbouring, (us)**neighboring**
['neɪbərɪŋ] adj vecino

neither ['naɪðəʳ] adj vi ▷ conj: **I
didn't move and ~ did John** no me
he movido, ni Juan tampoco ▷ pron
ninguno ▷ adv: **~ good nor bad** ni
bueno ni malo

neon ['niːɔn] n neón m

Nepal [nɪ'pɔːl] n Nepal m

nephew ['nɛvjuː] n sobrino

nerve [nɜːv] n (Anat) nervio; (courage)
valor m; (impudence) descaro, frescura;
nerves (nervousness) nerviosismo
msg, nervios mpl; adj: **a fit of ~s** un ataque
de nervios

nervous ['nɜːvəs] adj (anxious)
nervioso; (Anat) nervioso; (timid)
tímido, miedoso; **nervous
breakdown** n crisis f nerviosa

nest [nɛst] n (of bird) nido ▷ vi anidar

net [nɛt] n red f; (fabric) tul m ▷ adj
(Comm) neto, líquido ▷ vt coger (sp) or
agarrar (LAM) con red; (Sport) marcar;
netball n balonred m

Netherlands ['nɛðələndz] npl: **the ~**
los Países Bajos

nett [nɛt] adj = **net**

nettle ['nɛtl] n ortiga

network ['nɛtwɜːk] n red f

neurotic [njuə'rɔtɪk] adj, n
neurótico/a

neuter ['njuːtəʳ] adj (Ling) neutro ▷ vt
castrar, capar

neutral ['njuːtrəl] adj (person) neutral;
(colour etc) neutro; (Elec) neutro ▷ n
(Aut) punto muerto

never ['nɛvəʳ] adv nunca, jamás; **I
~ went** no fui nunca; **~ in my life**
jamás en la vida; see also **mind**;
never-ending adj interminable, sin
fin; **nevertheless** [nɛvəðə'lɛs] adv sin
embargo, no obstante

new [njuː] adj nuevo; (recent) reciente;
New Age n Nueva era; **newborn**
adj recién nacido; **newcomer**
['njuːkʌməʳ] n recién venido or
llegado; **newly** adv recién

news [njuːz] n noticias fpl; **a piece
of ~** una noticia; **the ~** (Radio, TV)
las noticias fpl; **news agency** n
agencia de noticias; **newsagent** n
(BRIT) vendedor(a) m/f de periódicos;
newscaster n presentador(a) m/f,
locutor(a) m/f; **news dealer** n (us)
= **newsagent**; **newsletter** n hoja
informativa, boletín m; **newspaper**
n periódico, diario; **newsreader**
n = **newscaster**

newt [nju:t] n tritón m

New Year n Año Nuevo; **New Year's Day** n Día m de Año Nuevo; **New Year's Eve** n Nochevieja

New Zealand [-'zi:lənd] n Nueva Zelanda (sp), Nueva Zelandia (Lam); **New Zealander** n neozelandés/esa m/f

next [nɛkst] adj (house, room) vecino, de al lado; (meeting) próximo; (page) siguiente ▷ adv después; **the ~ day** el día siguiente; **~ time** la próxima vez; **~ year** el año próximo o que viene; **~ to** junto a, al lado de; **~ to nothing** casi nada; **next door** adv en la casa de al lado ▷ adj vecino, de al lado; **next-of-kin** n pariente(s) m(pl) más cercano(s)

NHS n abbr (brit) = **National Health Service**

nibble ['nɪbl] vt mordisquear

nice [naɪs] adj (likeable) simpático; (kind) amable; (pleasant) agradable; (attractive) bonito; **nicely** adv amablemente (of health etc) bien

niche [ni:ʃ] n (Arch) nicho, hornacina

nick [nɪk] n (wound) rasguño; (cut, indentation) mella, muesca ▷ vt (inf) birlar; **in the ~ of time** justo a tiempo

nickel ['nɪkl] n níquel m; (us) moneda de 5 centavos

nickname ['nɪkneɪm] n apodo, mote m ▷ vt apodar

nicotine ['nɪkəti:n] n nicotina

niece [ni:s] n sobrina

Nigeria [naɪ'dʒɪərɪə] n Nigeria

night [naɪt] n noche f; (evening) tarde f; **the ~ before last** anteanoche; **at ~, by ~** de noche, por la noche; **night club** n club nocturno, discoteca; **nightdress** n (brit) camisón m

nightgown ['naɪtgaʊn], **nightie** ['naɪtɪ] (brit) n = **nightdress**

night: night life n vida nocturna; **nightly** adj de todas las noches ▷ adv todas las noches, cada noche; **nightmare** n pesadilla; **night school** n clase(s) f(pl) nocturna(s); **night shift** n turno nocturno or de noche; **nighttime** n noche f

nil [nɪl] n (brit Sport) cero, nada

nine [naɪn] num nueve; **nineteen** ['naɪn'ti:n] num diecinueve; **nineteenth** [naɪn'ti:nθ] adj decimonoveno, decimonono; **ninetieth** ['naɪntɪɪθ] adj nonagésimo; **ninety** num noventa

ninth [naɪnθ] adj noveno

nip [nɪp] vt (pinch) pellizcar; (bite) morder

nipple ['nɪpl] n (Anat) pezón m

nitrogen ['naɪtrədʒən] n nitrógeno

KEYWORD

no [nəʊ] adv (opposite of "yes") no; **are you coming? — no (I'm not)** ¿vienes? — no; **would you like some more? — no thank you** ¿quieres más? — no gracias

▷ adj 1 (not any): **I have no money/time/books** no tengo dinero/tiempo/libros; **no other man would have done it** ningún otro lo hubiera hecho

2: **"no entry"** "prohibido el paso"; **"no smoking"** "prohibido fumar"

▷ n (pl **noes**) no m

nobility [nəʊ'bɪlɪtɪ] n nobleza

noble ['nəʊbl] adj noble

nobody ['nəʊbədɪ] pron nadie

nod [nɔd] vi saludar con la cabeza; (in agreement) asentir con la cabeza ▷ vt: **to ~ one's head** inclinar la cabeza ▷ n inclinación f de cabeza; **nod off** vi cabecear

noise [nɔɪz] n ruido; (din) escándalo, estrépito; **noisy** adj ruidoso; (child) escandaloso

nominal ['nɔmɪnl] adj nominal

nominate ['nɔmɪneɪt] vt (propose) proponer; (appoint) nombrar; **nomination** [nɔmɪ'neɪʃən] n propuesta; nombramiento; **nominee** [nɔmɪ'ni:] n candidato/a

none [nʌn] *pron* ninguno/a ▷ *adv* de
ninguna manera; **~ of you** ninguno
de vosotros; **I've ~ left** no me queda
ninguno/a; **he's ~ the worse for it** no
le ha perjudicado; **I have ~** no tengo
ninguno; **~ at all** (*not one*) ni uno

nonetheless [nʌnðəˈles] *adv* sin
embargo, no obstante

non-fiction *n* no ficción *f*

nonsense [ˈnɒnsəns] *n* tonterías *fpl*,
disparates *fpl*; **~!** ¡qué tonterías!

non-: non-smoker [ˈnɒnˈsməukəʳ]
n no fumador *m/f*; **non-smoking**
adj (*de*) no fumador; **non-stick**
[ˈnɒnˈstɪk] *adj* (*pan, surface*)
antiadherente

noodles [ˈnuːdlz] *npl* tallarines *mpl*

noon [nuːn] *n* mediodía *m*

no-one [ˈnəuwʌn] *pron* =**nobody**

nor [nɔːʳ] *conj* =**neither** ▷ *adv* *see*
neither

norm [nɔːm] *n* norma

normal [ˈnɔːml] *adj* normal;
normally *adv* normalmente

north [nɔːθ] *n* norte *m* ▷ *adj* (*del*)
norte ▷ *adv* al o hacia el norte; **North
America** *n* América del Norte; **North
American** *n*, *a* norteamericano/a;
northbound [ˈnɔːθbaund] *adj* (*traffic*)
que se dirige al norte; (*carriageway*) de
dirección norte; **north-east** *n* nor(d)
este *m*; **northeastern** *adj* nor(d)este,
del nor(d)este; **northern** [ˈnɔːðən]
adj norteño, del norte; **Northern
Ireland** *n* Irlanda del Norte; **North
Korea** *n* Corea del Norte; **North Pole**
n: **the North Pole** el Polo Norte;
North Sea *n*: **the North Sea** el mar
del Norte; **north-west** *n* noroeste *m*;
northwestern [ˌnɔːθˈwestən] *adj*
noroeste, del noroeste

Norway [ˈnɔːweɪ] *n* Noruega

Norwegian [nɔːˈwiːdʒən] *adj*
noruego/a ▷ *n* noruego/a; (*Ling*)
noruego

nose [nəuz] *n* (*Anat*) nariz *f*; (*Zool*)
hocico; (*sense of smell*) olfato; **nose
about, nose around** *vi* curiosear;

nosebleed *n* hemorragia nasal;
nosey *adj* curioso, fisgón/ona

nostalgia [nɒsˈtældʒɪə] *n* nostalgia

nostalgic [nɒsˈtældʒɪk] *adj*
nostálgico

nostril [ˈnɒstrɪl] *n* ventana *or* orificio
de la nariz

nosy [ˈnəuzɪ] *adj* =**nosey**

not [nɒt] *adv* no; **~ that ...** no es
que ...; **it's too late, isn't it?** es
demasiado tarde, ¿verdad?; **why ~?**
¿por qué no?

notable [ˈnəutəbl] *adj* notable;
notably *adv* especialmente

notch [nɒtʃ] *n* muesca, corte *m*

note [nəut] *n* (*Mus, record, letter*)
nota; (*banknote*) billete *m*; (*tone*) tono
▷ *vt* (*observe*) notar, observar; (*write
down*) apuntar, anotar; **notebook**
n libreta, cuaderno; **noted** *adj*
célebre, conocido; **notepad** *n* bloc *m*;
notepaper *n* papel *m* para cartas

nothing [ˈnʌθɪŋ] *n* nada; (*zero*) cero;
he does ~ no hace nada; **~ new** nada
nuevo; **~ much** no mucho; **for ~** (*free*)
gratis; (*in vain*) en balde

notice [ˈnəutɪs] *n* (*announcement*)
anuncio; (*warning*) aviso; (*dismissal*)
despido; (*resignation*) dimisión *f* ▷ *vt*
(*observe*) notar, observar; **to bring
sth to sb's** (*attention*) llamar la
atención de algo sobre algo; **to take
~ of** hacer caso de, prestar atención
a; **at short ~** con poca antelación;
until further ~ hasta nuevo aviso; **to
hand in one's ~** dimitir, renunciar;
noticeable *adj* evidente, obvio

> Be careful not to translate *notice*
> by the Spanish word *noticia*.

notify [ˈnəutɪfaɪ] *vt*: **to ~ sb (of sth)**
comunicar (algo) a algn

notion [ˈnəuʃən] *n* noción *f*, idea;
(*opinion*) opinión *f*

notions [ˈnəuʃənz] *npl* (*us*) mercería

notorious [nəuˈtɔːrɪəs] *adj* notorio

notwithstanding
[ˌnɒtwɪθˈstændɪŋ] *adv* no obstante,
sin embargo; **~ this** a pesar de esto

nought [nɔːt] n cero

noun [naun] n nombre m, sustantivo

nourish ['nʌrɪʃ] vt nutrir; (fig)
alimentar; **nourishment** n alimento,
sustento

Nov. abbr (= November) nov.

novel ['nɒvl] n novela ▷ adj (new)
nuevo, original; (unexpected) insólito;
novelist n novelista mf; **novelty** n
novedad f

November [nəu'vembə^r] n
noviembre m

novice ['nɒvɪs] n (Rel) novicio/a

now [nau] adv (at the present time)
ahora; (these days) actualmente, hoy
día ▷ conj: ~ (that) ya que, ahora que;
right ~ ahora mismo; **by ~** ya; **I'll do
it just ~** ahora mismo lo hago; ~ **and
then**, ~ **and again** de vez en cuando;
from ~ on de ahora en adelante;
nowadays ['nauədeɪz] adv hoy (en)
día, actualmente

nowhere ['nəuweə^r] adv (direction) a
ninguna parte; (location) en ninguna
parte

nozzle ['nɒzl] n boquilla

nr abbr (BRIT) = **near**

nuclear ['njuːklɪə^r] adj nuclear

nucleus (pl **nuclei**) ['njuːklɪəs,
'njuːklɪaɪ] n núcleo

nude [njuːd] adj, n desnudo m; **in the
~** desnudo

nudge [nʌdʒ] vt dar un codazo a

nudist ['njuːdɪst] n nudista mf

nudity ['njuːdɪtɪ] n desnudez f

nuisance ['njuːsns] n molestia,
fastidio; (person) pesado, latoso;
what a ~! ¡qué lata!

numb [nʌm] adj: **to be ~ with cold**
estar entumecido de frío; ~ **with fear/
grief** paralizado de miedo/dolor

number ['nʌmbə^r] n número;
(quantity) cantidad f ▷ vt (pages etc)
numerar, poner número a; (amount to)
sumar, ascender a; **to be ~ed among**
figurar entre; **a ~ of** varios, algunos;
they were ten in ~ eran diez; **number
plate** n (BRIT) matrícula, placa;

Number Ten n (BRIT: 10 Downing
Street) residencia del primer ministro

numerical [njuː'merɪkl] adj
numérico

numerous ['njuːmərəs] adj
numeroso

nun [nʌn] n monja, religiosa

nurse [nɜːs] n enfermero/a; (nanny)
niñera ▷ vt (patient) cuidar, atender

nursery ['nɜːsərɪ] n (institution)
guardería infantil; (room) cuarto de los
niños; (for plants) criadero, semillero;
nursery rhyme n canción f infantil;
nursery school n escuela infantil;
nursery slope n (BRIT Ski) cuesta para
principiantes

nursing ['nɜːsɪŋ] n (profession)
profesión f de enfermera; (care)
asistencia, cuidado; **nursing home** n
clínica de reposo

nurture ['nɜːtʃə^r] vt (child, plant)
alimentar, nutrir

nut [nʌt] n (Tech) tuerca; (Bot) nuez f

nutmeg ['nʌtmeg] n nuez f moscada

nutrient ['njuːtrɪənt] adj nutritivo
▷ n elemento nutritivo

nutrition [njuː'trɪʃən] n nutrición f,
alimentación f

nutritious [njuː'trɪʃəs] adj nutritivo

nuts [nʌts] adj (inf) chiflado

NVQ n abbr (BRIT) = **national vocational
qualification**) título de formación
profesional

nylon ['naɪlɒn] n nilón m ▷ adj de nilón

n

O

importa lo que cueste; **I ~!** ¡protesto!; **objection** [əbˈdʒɛkʃən] n objeción f; **I have no objection to ...** no tengo inconveniente en que ...; **objective** adj, n objetivo

obligation [ɒblɪˈɡeɪʃən] n obligación f; (debt) deber m; **"without ~"** "sin compromiso"

obligatory [əˈblɪɡətərɪ] adj obligatorio

oblige [əˈblaɪdʒ] vt (do a favour for) complacer, hacer un favor a; **to ~ sb to do sth** obligar a algn a hacer algo; **to be ~d to sb for sth** estarle agradecido a algn por algo

oblique [əˈbliːk] adj oblicuo; (allusion) indirecto

obliterate [əˈblɪtəreɪt] vt borrar

oblivious [əˈblɪvɪəs] adj: **~ of** inconsciente de

oblong [ˈɒblɒŋ] adj rectangular ▷ n rectángulo

obnoxious [əbˈnɒkʃəs] adj odioso, detestable; (smell) nauseabundo

oboe [ˈəʊbəʊ] n oboe m

obscene [əbˈsiːn] adj obsceno

obscure [əbˈskjʊər] adj oscuro ▷ vt oscurecer; (hide: sun) ocultar

observant [əbˈzɜːvnt] adj observador(a)

observation [ɒbzəˈveɪʃən] n (Med) observación f

observatory [əbˈzɜːvətrɪ] n observatorio

observe [əbˈzɜːv] vt observar; (rule) cumplir; **observer** n observador(a) m/f

obsess [əbˈsɛs] vt obsesionar; **obsession** [əbˈsɛʃən] n obsesión f; **obsessive** adj obsesivo

obsolete [ˈɒbsəliːt] adj obsoleto

obstacle [ˈɒbstəkl] n obstáculo; (nuisance) estorbo

obstinate [ˈɒbstɪnɪt] adj terco, obstinado

obstruct [əbˈstrʌkt] vt obstruir; (hinder) estorbar, obstaculizar; **obstruction** [əbˈstrʌkʃən] n

oak [əʊk] n roble m ▷ adj de roble

OAP n abbr (BRIT) = **old-age pensioner**

oar [ɔːr] n remo

oasis (pl **oases**) [əʊˈeɪsɪs, əʊˈeɪsiːz] n oasis m inv

oath [əʊθ] n juramento; (swear word) palabrota; **on** (BRIT) or **under ~** bajo juramento

oatmeal [ˈəʊtmiːl] n harina de avena

oats [əʊts] npl avena

obedience [əˈbiːdɪəns] n obediencia

obedient [əˈbiːdɪənt] adj obediente

obese [əʊˈbiːs] adj obeso

obesity [əʊˈbiːsɪtɪ] n obesidad f

obey [əˈbeɪ] vt obedecer; (instructions) cumplir

obituary [əˈbɪtjʊərɪ] n necrología

object n [ˈɒbdʒɪkt] objeto; (purpose) objeto, propósito; (Ling) complemento ▷ vi [əbˈdʒɛkt]: **to ~ to** (attitude) estar en contra de; (proposal) oponerse a; **to ~ that** objetar que; **expense is no ~** no

obstrucción f; (object) estorbo, obstáculo

obtain [əb'teɪn] vt obtener; (achieve) conseguir

obvious ['ɒbvɪəs] adj obvio, evidente; **obviously** adv evidentemente; **obviously not!** ¡por supuesto que no!

occasion [ə'keɪʒən] n oportunidad f, ocasión f; (event) acontecimiento; **occasional** adj poco frecuente, ocasional; **occasionally** adv de vez en cuando

occult [ɒ'kʌlt] adj oculto

occupant ['ɒkjupənt] n (of house) inquilino/a; (of boat, car) ocupante mf

occupation [ɒkju'peɪʃən] n (job) trabajo; (pastime) ocupaciones fpl

occupy ['ɒkjupaɪ] vt (seat, post, time) ocupar; (house) habitar; **to ~ o.s. with** or **by doing** (as job) dedicarse a hacer; (to pass time) entretenerse haciendo

occur [ə'kɜː] vi ocurrir, suceder; **to ~ to sb** ocurrírsele a algn; **occurrence** [ə'kʌrəns] n suceso

ocean ['əʊʃən] n océano

o'clock [ə'klɒk] adv: **it is five ~** son las cinco

Oct. abbr (= October) oct.

October [ɒk'təʊbə] n octubre m

octopus ['ɒktəpəs] n pulpo

odd [ɒd] adj (strange) extraño, raro; (number) impar; (sock, shoe etc) suelto; **60–~** 60 y pico; **at ~ times** de vez en cuando; **to be the ~ one out** estar de más; **oddly** adv extrañamente; **odds** npl (in betting) puntos mpl de ventaja; **it makes no odds** da lo mismo; **at odds** reñidos/as; **odds and ends** cachivaches mpl

odometer [ɒ'dɒmɪtə] n (us) cuentakilómetros m inv

odour, (us) **odor** ['əʊdə] n olor m; (unpleasant) hedor m

KEYWORD

of [ɒv, əv] prep 1 de; **a friend of ours** un amigo nuestro; **a boy of 10** un

chico de 10 años; **that was kind of you** eso fue muy amable de tu parte 2 (expressing quantity, amount, dates etc) de; **a kilo of flour** un kilo de harina; **there were three of them** había tres; **three of us went** tres de nosotros fuimos; **the 5th of July** el 5 de julio 3 (from, out of) de; **made of wood** (hecho) de madera

off [ɒf] adj, adv (engine, light) apagado; (tap) cerrado; (BRIT: food: bad) malo; (: milk) cortado; (cancelled) suspendido ▷ prep de; **to be ~** (leave) irse, marcharse; **to be ~ sick** estar enfermo or de baja; **a day ~** un día libre; **to have an ~ day** tener un mal día; **he had his coat ~** se había quitado el abrigo; **10% ~** (Comm) (con el) 10% de descuento; **5 km ~ (the road)** a 5 km (de la carretera); **~ the coast** frente a la costa; **I'm ~ meat** (no longer eat/like it) paso de la carne; **on the ~ chance** por si acaso; **on and ~** de vez en cuando

offence, (us) **offense** [ə'fɛns] n (crime) delito; **to take ~ at** ofenderse por

offend [ə'fɛnd] vt (person) ofender; **offender** n delincuente mf

offense [ə'fɛns] n (us) = **offence**

offensive [ə'fɛnsɪv] adj ofensivo; (smell etc) repugnante ▷ n (Mil) ofensiva

offer ['ɒfə] n oferta, ofrecimiento; (proposal) propuesta ▷ vt ofrecer; **"on ~"** (Comm) "en oferta"

offhand [ɒf'hænd] adj informal ▷ adv de improviso

office ['ɒfɪs] n (place) oficina; (room) despacho; (position) cargo, oficio; **doctor's ~** (us) consultorio; **to take ~** entrar en funciones; **office block**, (us) **office building** n bloque m de oficinas; **office hours** npl horas fpl de oficina; (us Med) horas fpl de consulta

officer ['ɒfɪsə] n (Mil etc) oficial mf; (of organization) director(a) m/f; (also: **police ~**) agente m/f de policía

office worker n oficinista mf

official [əˈfɪʃl] adj oficial, autorizado
▷ n funcionario/a

off-licence n (BRIT: shop) tienda de bebidas alcohólicas

> **OFF-LICENCE**
>
> En el Reino Unido una *off-licence* es una tienda especializada en la venta de bebidas alcohólicas para el consumo fuera del establecimiento. De ahí su nombre, pues se necesita un permiso especial para tal venta, que está estrictamente regulada. Suelen vender además bebidas sin alcohol, tabaco, chocolate, patatas fritas etc y a menudo son parte de grandes cadenas nacionales.

off: off-peak adj (electricity) de banda económica; (ticket) billete de precio reducido por viajar fuera de las horas punta; **off-putting** adj (BRIT: person) poco amable, difícil; (remark) desalentador(a); **off-season** [ˈɔfˈsiːzn] adj, adv fuera de temporada; **offset** [ˈɔfset] vt (irreg: like **set**) contrarrestar, compensar; **offshore** [ɔfˈʃɔː*] adj (breeze, island) costero; (fishing) de bajura; **offside** [ˈɔfsaɪd] adj (Sport) fuera de juego; (Aut: in UK) del lado derecho; (: in US, Europe etc) del lado izquierdo

offspring [ˈɔfsprɪŋ] n descendencia

often [ˈɔfn] adv a menudo, con frecuencia; **how ~ do you go?** ¿cada cuánto vas?

oh [əu] excl ¡ah!

oil [ɔɪl] n aceite m; (petroleum) petróleo ▷ vt engrasar; **oil filter** n (Aut) filtro de aceite; **oil painting** n pintura al óleo; **oil refinery** n refinería de petróleo; **oil rig** n torre f (de perforación); (truck) camión m cisterna; **oil well** n pozo (de petróleo); **oily** adj aceitoso; (food) grasiento

ointment [ˈɔɪntmənt] n ungüento

O.K., okay [ˈauˈkeɪ] excl O.K., ¡está bien!, ¡vale! ▷ adj bien ▷ vt dar el visto bueno a

old [əuld] adj viejo; (former) antiguo; **how ~ are you?** ¿cuántos años tienes?, ¿qué edad tienes?; **he's 10 years ~** tiene 10 años; **~er brother** hermano mayor; **old age** n vejez f; **old-age pension** n (BRIT) jubilación f, pensión f; **old-age pensioner** n (BRIT) jubilado/a; **old-fashioned** adj anticuado, pasado de moda; **old people's home** n (esp BRIT) residencia f de ancianos

olive [ˈɔlɪv] n (fruit) aceituna; (tree) olivo ▷ adj (also: **~-green**) verde oliva inv; **olive oil** n aceite m de oliva

Olympic [əuˈlɪmpɪk] adj olímpico; **the ~ Games, the ~s** n pl las Olimpiadas

omelet(te) [ˈɔmlɪt] n tortilla, tortilla de huevo (LAM)

omen [ˈəumən] n presagio

ominous [ˈɔmɪnəs] adj de mal agüero, amenazador(a)

omit [əuˈmɪt] vt omitir

O

KEYWORD

on [ɔn] prep 1 (indicating position) en; sobre; **on the wall** en la pared; **it's on the table** está sobre la mesa; **on the left** a la izquierda
2 (indicating means, method, condition etc): **on foot** a pie; **on the train/plane** (go) en tren/avión; (be) en el tren/el avión; **on the radio/television** por o en la radio/televisión; **on the telephone** al teléfono; **to be on drugs** drogarse; (Med) estar a tratamiento; **to be on holiday/business** estar de vacaciones/en viaje de negocios
3 (referring to time): **on Friday** el viernes; **on Fridays** los viernes; **on June 20th** el 20 de junio; **a week on Friday** del viernes en una semana;

on arrival al llegar; **on seeing this** al ver esto

4 (about, concerning) sobre, acerca de; **a book on physics** un libro de or sobre física

▸ adv 1 (referring to dress): **to have one's coat on** tener or llevar el abrigo puesto; **she put her gloves on** se puso los guantes

2 (referring to covering): **"screw the lid on tightly"** "cerrar bien la tapa"

3 (further, continuously): **to walk/run etc on** seguir caminando/corriendo etc

▸ adj 1 (functioning, in operation): machine, radio, TV, light) encendido (SP), prendido (LAM), (: tap) abierto, (: brakes) echado, puesto; **is the meeting still on?** (in progress) ¿todavía continúa la reunión?; (not cancelled) ¿va a haber reunión al fin?; **there's a good film on at the cinema** ponen una buena película en el cine

2: **that's not on!** (inf: not possible) ¡eso ni hablar!; (: not acceptable) ¡eso no se hace!

once [wʌns] adv una vez; (formerly) antiguamente ▸ conj una vez que; **~ he had left/it was done** una vez que se había marchado/se hizo; **at ~** en seguida, inmediatamente; (simultaneously) a la vez; **~ a week** una vez a la semana; **~ more** otra vez; **~ and for all** de una vez por todas; **~ upon a time** érase una vez

oncoming ['ɒnkʌmɪŋ] adj (traffic) que viene de frente

KEYWORD

one [wʌn] num un/una; **one hundred and fifty** ciento cincuenta; **one by one** uno a uno

▸ adj 1 (sole) único; **the one book which** el único libro que; **the one man who** el único que

2 (same) mismo/a; **they came in the one car** vinieron en un solo coche

▸ pron 1: **this one** este, éste; **that one** ese, ése; (more remote) aquel, aquél; **I've already got a (red) one** ya tengo uno/a (rojo/a); **one by one** uno/a por uno/a

2: **one another** (us) nos; (you) (sP): (you: formal, them) se; **do you two ever see one another?** ¿os veis alguna vez? (sP), ¿se ven alguna vez?; **the two boys didn't dare look at one another** los dos chicos no se atrevieron a mirarse (el uno al otro); **they all kissed one another** se besaron unos a otros

3 (impers) **one never knows** nunca se sabe; **to cut one's finger** cortarse el dedo; **one needs to eat** hay que comer

one: **one-off** n (BRIT inf: event) caso especial; **oneself** pron (reflexive) se; (after prep) sí; (emphatic) uno/a mismo/a; **to hurt oneself** hacerse daño; **to keep sth for oneself** guardarse algo; **to talk to oneself** hablar solo; **one-shot** ['wʌnʃɒt] n (US) = **one-off**; **one-sided** adj (argument) parcial; (decision, view) unilateral; (game, contest) desigual; **one-to-one** (relationship) individualizado/a; **one-way** adj (street, traffic) de dirección única

ongoing ['ɒngəʊɪŋ] adj continuo

onion ['ʌnjən] n cebolla

online [ɒn'laɪn] adj, adv (Comput) en línea

onlooker ['ɒnlʊkəʳ] n espectador(a) m/f

only ['əʊnlɪ] adv solamente, solo, sólo (to avoid confusion with adj) ▸ adj único, solo ▸ conj solamente que, pero; **an ~ child** un hijo único; **not ~ ... but also ...** no sólo ... sino también ...

on-screen [ɒn'skriːn] adj (Comput etc) en pantalla; (romance, kiss) cinematográfico

onset ['ɒnset] n comienzo

onto ['ɒntu] prep = **on to**

onward(s) ['ɒnwəd(z)] adv (move) (hacia) adelante; **from that time onward** desde entonces en adelante

oops [ups] excl (also: **~-a-daisy!**) ¡huy!

ooze [u:z] vi rezumar

opaque [əu'peɪk] adj opaco

open ['əupn] adj abierto; (car) descubierto; (road, view) despejado; (meeting) público; (admiration) manifiesto ▷ vt abrir ▷ vi abrirse; (book etc: commence) comenzar; **in the ~ (air)** al aire libre; **open up** vt abrir; (blocked road) despejar ▷ vi abrirse; **opening** n abertura f; (beginning) comienzo; (opportunity) oportunidad f; **opening hours** npl horario de apertura; **open learning** n enseñanza flexible a tiempo parcial; **openly** adv abiertamente; **open-minded** adj de amplias miras, sin prejuicios; **open-necked** adj sin corbata; **open-plan** adj diáfano, sin tabiques; **Open University** n (BRIT) ≈ Universidad f Nacional de Enseñanza a Distancia, UNED f

- **OPEN UNIVERSITY**
- La Open University, fundada en 1969, está especializada en impartir cursos a distancia y a tiempo parcial con sus propios materiales de apoyo diseñados para tal fin, entre ellos programas de radio y televisión emitidos por la BBC. Los trabajos se envían por correo y se complementan con la asistencia obligatoria a cursos de verano. Para obtener la licenciatura es necesario estudiar un mínimo de módulos y alcanzar un determinado número de créditos.

opera ['ɒpərə] n ópera; **opera house** n teatro de la ópera; **opera singer** n cantante mf de ópera

operate ['ɒpəreɪt] vt (machine) hacer funcionar; (company) dirigir ▷ vi funcionar; **to ~ on sb** (Med) operar a algn; **operating theatre**, (US) **operating room** n quirófano, sala de operaciones

operation [ɒpə'reɪʃən] n operación f; (of machine) funcionamiento; **to be in ~** estar funcionando o en funcionamiento; **to have an ~** (Med) ser operado; **operational** adj operacional, en buen estado

operative ['ɒpərətɪv] adj en vigor

operator ['ɒpəreɪtə] n (of machine) operario/a, maquinista mf; (Tel) operador(a) mf, telefonista mf

opinion [ə'pɪnjən] n opinión f; **in my ~** en mi opinión, a mi juicio; **opinion poll** n encuesta, sondeo

opponent [ə'pəunənt] n adversario/a, contrincante mf

opportunity [ɒpə'tju:nɪtɪ] n oportunidad f; **to take the ~ to do** or **of doing** aprovechar la ocasión para hacer

oppose [ə'pəuz] vt oponerse a; **to be ~d to sth** oponerse a algo; **as ~d to** a diferencia de

opposite ['ɒpəzɪt] adj opuesto, contrario; (house etc) de enfrente ▷ adv en frente ▷ prep en frente de, frente a ▷ n lo contrario

opposition [ɒpə'zɪʃən] n oposición f

oppress [ə'pres] vt oprimir

opt [ɒpt] vi: **to ~ for** optar por; **to ~ to do** optar por hacer; **opt out** vi: **to ~ out of** optar por no hacer

optician [ɒp'tɪʃən] n óptico/a

optimism ['ɒptɪmɪzəm] n optimismo

optimist ['ɒptɪmɪst] n optimista mf; **optimistic** [ɒptɪ'mɪstɪk] adj optimista

optimum ['ɒptɪməm] adj óptimo

option ['ɒpʃən] n opción f; **optional** adj opcional

or [ɔ:'] conj o; (before o, ho) u; (with negative): **he hasn't seen or heard anything** no ha visto ni oído nada; **or else** si no

oral ['ɔːrəl] adj oral ▷ n examen m oral

orange ['ɒrɪndʒ] n (fruit) naranja f ▷ adj (de color) naranja inv; **orange juice** n jugo m de naranja, zumo m de naranja (SP); **orange squash** n bebida de naranja

orbit ['ɔːbɪt] n órbita ▷ vt, vi orbitar

orchard ['ɔːtʃəd] n huerto

orchestra ['ɔːkɪstrə] n orquesta; (US: seating) platea

orchid ['ɔːkɪd] n orquídea

ordeal [ɔːˈdiːl] n experiencia terrible

order ['ɔːdəʳ] n orden m; (command) orden f; (state) estado; (Comm) pedido ▷ vt (also: **put in ~**) ordenar, poner en orden; (Comm) pedir; (command) mandar, ordenar; **in ~** en orden; (of document) en regla; **in (working) ~** en funcionamiento; **to be out of ~** estar desordenado; (not working) no funcionar; **in ~ to do** para hacer; **on ~** (Comm) pedido; **to ~ sb to do sth** mandar a algn hacer algo; **order form** n hoja de pedido; **orderly** n (Mil) ordenanza m; (Med) auxiliar mf (de hospital) ▷ adj ordenado

ordinary ['ɔːdnrɪ] adj corriente, normal; (pej) común y corriente; **out of the ~** fuera de lo común

ore [ɔːʳ] n mineral m

oregano [ɒrɪˈɡɑːnəu] n orégano

organ ['ɔːɡən] n órgano

organic [ɔːˈɡænɪk] adj orgánico

organism n organismo

organization [ɔːɡənaɪˈzeɪʃən] n organización f

organize ['ɔːɡənaɪz] vt organizar; **organized** ['ɔːɡənaɪzd] adj organizado; **to get organized** organizarse; **organizer** n organizador(a) m/f

orgasm ['ɔːɡæzəm] n orgasmo

orgy ['ɔːdʒɪ] n orgía

oriental [ɔːrɪˈɛntl] adj oriental

orientation [ɔːrɪɛnˈteɪʃən] n orientación f

origin ['ɒrɪdʒɪn] n origen m

original [əˈrɪdʒɪnl] adj original; (first) primero; (earlier) primitivo ▷ n original m; **originally** adv al principio

originate [əˈrɪdʒɪneɪt] vi: **to ~ from**, **to ~ in** surgir de, tener su origen en

Orkneys ['ɔːknɪz] npl: **the ~** (also: **the Orkney Islands**) las Orcadas

ornament ['ɔːnəmənt] n adorno; (trinket) chuchería; **ornamental** [ɔːnəˈmɛntl] adj decorativo, de adorno

ornate [ɔːˈneɪt] adj recargado

orphan ['ɔːfn] n huérfano/a

orthodox ['ɔːθədɒks] adj ortodoxo

orthopaedic, (US) **orthopedic** [ɔːθəˈpiːdɪk] adj ortopédico

osteopath ['ɔstɪəpæθ] n osteópata mf

ostrich ['ɒstrɪtʃ] n avestruz m

other ['ʌðəʳ] adj otro ▷ pron: **the ~ one** el/la otro/a; **~ than** aparte de; **otherwise** adv, conj de otra manera; (if not) si no

otter ['ɒtəʳ] n nutria

ouch [autʃ] excl ¡ay!

ought [ɔːt] aux vb: **I ~ to do it** debería hacerlo; **this ~ to have been corrected** esto debiera de haberse corregido; **he ~ to win** (probability) debiera ganar

ounce [auns] n onza (=28.35g: 16oz = lb)

our ['auəʳ] adj nuestro; see also **my**; **ours** pron (el) nuestro/(la) nuestra etc; see also **mine**; **ourselves** pron pl (reflexive, after prep) nosotros/as; (emphatic) nosotros mismos/as; see also **oneself**

oust [aust] vt desalojar

out [aut] adv fuera, afuera; (not at home) fuera (de casa); (light, fire) apagado; **~ there** allí (fuera); **he's ~** (absent) no está, ha salido; **to be ~ in one's calculations** equivocarse (en sus cálculos); **to run ~** salir corriendo; **~ loud** en alta voz; **~ of** (outside) fuera de; (because of: anger etc) por; **~ of petrol** sin gasolina;

O

"~ of order" "no funciona"; **outback** n interior m; **outbound** adj (flight) de salida; (flight: not return) de ida; **outbound from/for** con salida de/hacia; **outbreak** n (of war) comienzo; (of disease) epidemia; (of violence etc) ola; **outburst** n explosión f, arranque m; **outcast** n paria mf; **outcome** n resultado; **outcry** n protestas fpl; **outdated** adj anticuado; **outdoor** adj al aire libre; (clothes) de calle; **outdoors** adv al aire libre

outer ['autə'] adj exterior, externo; **outer space** n espacio exterior

outfit n (clothes) traje m

out: outgoing adj (president, tenant) saliente; (character) extrovertido; **outgoings** npl (BRIT) gastos mpl; **outhouse** n excusado; **outing** n excursión f, paseo; **outlaw** n proscrito/a ▷ vt (practice) declarar ilegal; **outlay** n inversión f; **outlet** n salida; (of pipe) desagüe m; (US Elec) toma de corriente; (also: **retail outlet**) punto de venta; **outline** n (shape) contorno, perfil m; (sketch, plan) esbozo ▷ vt (plan etc) esbozar; **in outline** adj a grandes rasgos; **outlook** n (fig: prospects) perspectivas fpl; (: for weather) pronóstico; (: opinion) punto de vista; **outnumber** vt exceder o superar en número; **out-of-date** adj (passport) caducado, (clothes, customs) pasado de moda; **out-of-doors** adv al aire libre; **out-of-the-way** adj apartado; **outpatient** n paciente mf externo/a; **outpost** n puesto avanzado; **output** n (volumen m de) producción f, rendimiento; (Comput) salida

outrage ['autreidʒ] n escándalo; (atrocity) atrocidad f ▷ vt ultrajar; **outrageous** [aut'reidʒəs] adj (clothes) extravagante; (behaviour) escandaloso

outright adv [aut'rait] (ask, deny) francamente; (refuse) rotundamente;

(win) de manera absoluta; (be killed) en el acto ▷ adj ['autrait] complete, (refusal) rotundo

outset ['autset] n principio

outside [aut'said] n exterior m ▷ adj exterior, externo ▷ adv fuera ▷ prep fuera de; (beyond) más allá de; **at the** ~ (fig) a lo sumo; **outside lane** n (Aut: in Britain) carril m de la derecha; (: in US, Europe etc) carril m de la izquierda; **outside line** n (Tel) línea (exterior); **outsider** n (stranger) forastero/a

out: outsize adj (clothes) de talla grande; **outskirts** npl alrededores mpl, afueras fpl; **outspoken** adj muy franco; **outstanding** adj excepcional, destacado; (unfinished) pendiente

outward ['autwəd] adj externo; (journey) de ida

outweigh [aut'wei] vt pesar más que

oval ['əuvl] adj ovalado ▷ n óvalo

ovary ['əuvəri] n ovario

oven ['ʌvn] n horno; **oven glove** n guante m para el horno, manopla para el horno; **ovenproof** adj resistente al horno; **oven-ready** adj listo para el horno

over ['əuvə'] adv encima, por encima ▷ adj (finished) terminado; (surplus) de sobra ▷ prep por encima de; (above) sobre; (on the other side of) al otro lado de; (more than) más de; (during) durante; ~ **here** (por) aquí; ~ **there** (por) allí o allá; **~ and ~** (everywhere) por todas partes; **~ and ~ (again)** una y otra vez; **~ and above** además de; **to ask sb ~** invitar a algn a casa; **to bend ~** inclinarse

overall ['əuvərɔ:l] adj (length) total; (study) de conjunto ▷ adv [əuvər'ɔ:l] en conjunto ▷ n (BRIT) guardapolvo; **overalls** npl mono sg, overol msg (LAM)

over: overboard adv (Naut) por la borda; **overcame** pt of **overcome**; **overcast** adj encapotado; **overcharge** vt: **to overcharge sb** cobrar un precio excesivo a algn; **overcoat** n abrigo; **overcome** vt (irreg: like **come**) vencer; (difficulty) superar; **overcrowded** adj atestado de gente; (city, country) superpoblado; **overdo** vt (irreg: like **do**) exagerar; (overcook) cocer demasiado hecho; **to overdo it** (work etc) pasarse; **overdone** adj (vegetables) recocido; (steak) demasiado hecho; **overdose** n sobredosis f inv; **overdraft** n saldo deudor; **overdrawn** adj (account) en descubierto; **overdue** adj retrasado; **overestimate** vt sobreestimar

overflow [əuvə'fləu] vi desbordarse ▷ n ['əuvəfləu] (also: ~ **pipe**) (cañería de) desagüe m

over: overgrown [əuvə'grəun] adj (garden) cubierto de hierba; **overhaul** vt [əuvə'hɔːl] revisar, repasar ▷ n ['əuvəhɔːl] revisión f

overhead adv [əuvə'hɛd] por arriba or encima ▷ adj ['əuvəhɛd] (cable) aéreo ▷ n ['əuvəhɛd] (us) = **overheads**; **overhead projector** n retroproyector; **overheads** npl gastos mpl generales

over: overhear vt (irreg: like **hear**) oír por casualidad; **overheat** vi (engine) recalentarse; **overland** adj, adv por tierra; **overlap** vi [əuvə'læp] superponerse; **overleaf** adv al dorso; **overload** vt sobrecargar; **overlook** vt (have view of) dar a, tener vistas a; (miss) pasar por alto; (excuse) perdonar

overnight [əuvə'naɪt] adv durante la noche; (fig) de la noche a la mañana ▷ adj de noche; **to stay ~** pasar la noche; **overnight bag** n fin m de semana, neceser m de viaje

overpass n (us) paso elevado or a desnivel

overpower [əuvə'pauə'] vt dominar; (fig) embargar; **overpowering** adj (heat) agobiante; (smell) penetrante

over: overreact vi [əuvərɪ'ækt] vi reaccionar de manera exagerada; **overrule** vt (decision) anular; (claim) denegar; **overrun** vt (irreg: like **run**: country) invadir; (: time limit) rebasar,

exceder; **overseas** [əuvə'siːz] adv (abroad) en el extranjero ▷ adj (trade) exterior; (visitor) extranjero; **oversee** (irreg: like **see**) vt supervisar; **overshadow** vt (fig) eclipsar; **to be overshadowed by** estar a la sombra de; **oversight** n descuido; **oversleep** vi (irreg: like **sleep**) dormir más de la cuenta, no despertarse a tiempo; **overspend** vi (irreg: like **spend**) gastar más de la cuenta; **we have overspent by five dollars** hemos excedido el presupuesto en cinco dólares

overt [əu'vəːt] adj abierto

over: overtake vt (irreg: like **take**) sobrepasar; (BRIT Aut) adelantar; **overthrow** vt (irreg: like **throw**: government) derrocar; **overtime** n horas fpl extraordinarias; **overtook** [əuvə'tuk] pt of **overtake**; **overturn** vt volcar; (fig: plan) desbaratar; (: government) derrocar ▷ vi volcar; **overweight** adj demasiado gordo or pesado; **overwhelm** vt aplastar; **overwhelming** adj (victory, defeat) arrollador(a); (desire) irresistible

owe [əu] vt deber; **to ~ sb sth, to ~ sth to sb** deber algo a algn; **owing to** prep debido a, por causa de

owl [aul] n búho; (also: **barn ~**) lechuza

own [əun] vt tener, poseer ▷ adj propio; **a room of my ~** mi propia habitación; **to get one's ~ back** tomarse la revancha; **on one's ~** solo, a solas; **own up** vi confesar; **owner** n dueño/a; **ownership** n posesión f

ox (pl **oxen**) [ɔks, 'ɔksn] n buey m

Oxbridge ['ɔksbrɪdʒ] n universidades de Oxford y Cambridge

oxen ['ɔksən] npl of **ox**

oxygen ['ɔksɪdʒən] n oxígeno

oyster ['ɔɪstə'] n ostra

oz. abbr = **ounce**

ozone ['əuzəun] n ozono; **ozone-friendly** adj que no daña la capa de ozono; **ozone layer** n capa de ozono

P

p _abbr_ (BRIT) = **penny**; **pence**
PA _n abbr_ = **personal assistant**; **public address system**
p.a. _abbr_ = **per annum**
pace [peɪs] _n_ paso ▷ _vi_: **to ~ up and down** pasearse de un lado a otro; **to keep ~ with** llevar el mismo paso que; **pacemaker** _n_ (Med) marcapasos _m inv_; (Sport: also: **pacesetter**) liebre _f_
pacific [pə'sɪfɪk] _adj_ pacífico ▷ _n_: **the P~ (Ocean)** el (océano) Pacífico
pacifier ['pæsɪfaɪə'] _n_ (US: dummy) chupete _m_
pack [pæk] _n_ (packet) paquete _m_; (of hounds) jauría; (of people) manada; (of thieves etc) banda; (of cards) baraja; (bundle) fardo; (US: of cigarettes) paquete _m_ ▷ _vt_ (fill) llenar; (in suitcase etc) meter, poner; (cram) llenar, atestar; **to ~ (one's bags)** hacer las maletas; **to ~ sb off** (inf) despachar a algn; **pack in** _vi_ (inf: break down) estropearse ▷ _vt_ (inf) dejar; **~ it in!**

¡para!, ¡basta ya!; **pack up** _vi_ (inf: machine) estropearse; (person) irse ▷ _vt_ (belongings, clothes) recoger; (goods, presents) empaquetar, envolver
package ['pækɪdʒ] _n_ paquete _m_; (bulky) bulto; (also: **~ deal**) acuerdo global ▷ _vt_ (Comm: goods) envasar, embalar; **package holiday** _n_ viaje _m_ organizado (con todo incluido); **package tour** _n_ viaje _m_ organizado
packaging ['pækɪdʒɪŋ] _n_ envase _m_
packed [pækt] _adj_ abarrotado; **packed lunch** _n_ almuerzo frío
packet ['pækɪt] _n_ paquete _m_
packing ['pækɪŋ] _n_ embalaje _m_
pact [pækt] _n_ pacto
pad [pæd] _n_ (of paper) bloc _m_; (cushion) cojinete _m_; (inf: flat) casa ▷ _vt_ rellenar; **padded** _adj_ (jacket) acolchado; (bra) reforzado
paddle ['pædl] _n_ (oar) canalete _m_, pala; (us: for table tennis) pala ▷ _vt_ remar ▷ _vi_ (with feet) chapotear; **paddling pool** _n_ (BRIT) piscina para niños
paddock ['pædək] _n_ (field) potrero
padlock ['pædlɔk] _n_ candado
paedophile, (US) **pedophile** ['piːdəfaɪl] _adj_ de pedófilos ▷ _n_ pedófilo/a
page [peɪdʒ] _n_ página; (of newspaper) plana; (also: **~ boy**) paje _m_ ▷ _vt_ (in hotel etc) llamar por altavoz a
pager ['peɪdʒə'] _n_ busca _m_
paid [peɪd] _pt, pp of_ **pay** ▷ _adj_ (work) remunerado; (holiday) pagado; (official) a sueldo; **to put ~ to** (BRIT) acabar con
pain [peɪn] _n_ dolor _m_; **to be in ~** sufrir; _see also_ **pains**; **painful** _adj_ doloroso; (difficult) penoso; (disagreeable) desagradable; **painkiller** _n_ analgésico; **pains** _npl_: **to take pains to do sth** tomarse el trabajo de hacer algo; **painstaking** ['peɪnzteɪkɪŋ] _adj_ (person) concienzudo, esmerado
paint [peɪnt] _n_ pintura ▷ _vt_ pintar; **to ~ the door blue** pintar la puerta

de azul; **paintbrush** n (artist's) pincel m; (decorator's) brocha; **painter** n pintor(a) m/f; **painting** n pintura

pair [peəʳ] n (of shoes, gloves etc) par m; (of people) pareja; **a ~ of scissors** unas tijeras; **a ~ of trousers** unos pantalones, un pantalón

pajamas [pɪˈdʒɑːməz] npl (us) pijama msg

Pakistan [pɑːkɪˈstɑːn] n Paquistán m; **Pakistani** adj, n paquistaní mf

pal [pæl] n (inf) amiguete a m/f, colega mf

palace [ˈpæləs] n palacio

pale [peɪl] adj pálido; (colour) claro ▷ n: **to be beyond the ~** pasarse de la raya

Palestine [ˈpælɪstaɪn] n Palestina; **Palestinian** [pælɪsˈtɪnɪən] adj, n palestino/a

palm [pɑːm] n (Anat) palma; (also: **~ tree**) palmera, palma ▷ vt: **to ~ sth off on sb** (BRIT inf) endosarle algo a algn

pamper [ˈpæmpəʳ] vt mimar

pamphlet [ˈpæmflət] n folleto

pan [pæn] n (also: **sauce~**) cacerola, cazuela, olla; (also: **frying ~**) sartén f

pancake [ˈpænkeɪk] n crepe f

panda [ˈpændə] n panda m

pandemic [pænˈdemɪk] n pandemia; **flu ~** pandemia de gripe

pane [peɪn] n cristal m

panel [ˈpænl] n (of wood) panel m; (Radio, TV) panel m de invitados

panhandler [ˈpænhændləʳ] n (us inf) mendigo/a

panic [ˈpænɪk] n pánico ▷ vi dejarse llevar por el pánico

panorama [pænəˈrɑːmə] n panorama m

pansy [ˈpænzɪ] n (Bot) pensamiento; (inf, pej) maricón m

pant [pænt] vi jadear

panther [ˈpænθəʳ] n pantera

panties [ˈpæntɪz] npl bragas fpl

pantomime [ˈpæntəmaɪm] n (BRIT) representación f musical navideña

• **PANTOMIME**

• En época navideña los teatros
• británicos ponen en escena
• representaciones llamadas
• pantomimes, versiones libres
• de cuentos tradicionales como
• Aladino o El gato con botas. En ella
• nunca faltan personajes como la
• dama (dame), papel que siempre
• interpreta un actor; el protagonista
• joven (principal boy), normalmente
• interpretado por una actriz, y el
• malvado (villain). Es un espectáculo
• familiar dirigido a los niños pero
• con grandes dosis de humor para
• adultos en el que se alienta la
• participación del público.

pants [pænts] npl (BRIT: underwear: woman's) bragas fpl; (: man's) calzoncillos mpl; (us: trousers) pantalones mpl

paper [ˈpeɪpəʳ] n papel m; (also: **news~**) periódico, diario; (study, article) artículo; (exam) examen m ▷ adj de papel o El empapelar; **(identity) ~s** npl papeles mpl, documentos mpl; **paperback** n libro de bolsillo; **paper bag** n bolsa de papel; **paper clip** n clip m; **paper shop** n (BRIT) tienda de periódicos; **paperwork** n trabajo administrativo

paprika [ˈpæprɪkə] n pimentón m

par [pɑːʳ] n par f; (Golf) par m; **to be on a ~ with** estar a la par con

paracetamol [pærəˈsiːtəmɔl] n (BRIT) paracetamol m

parachute [ˈpærəʃuːt] n paracaídas m inv

parade [pəˈreɪd] n desfile m ▷ vt (show off) hacer alarde de ▷ vi desfilar; (Mil) pasar revista

paradise [ˈpærədaɪs] n paraíso

paradox [ˈpærədɔks] n paradoja

paraffin [ˈpærəfɪn] n (BRIT): **~ (oil)** parafina

paragraph [ˈpærəɡrɑːf] n párrafo

parallel ['pærəlel] *adj:* ~ **(with/to)** en paralelo (con/a); *(fig)* semejante (a) ▷ *n (line)* paralela; *(fig)* paralelo; *(Geo)* paralelo

paralysis [pə'rælɪsɪs] *n* parálisis *f inv;* **paralyze** *vt* paralizar; **paralyzed** *adj* paralizado

paramedic [pærə'medɪk] *n* auxiliar *mf* sanitario/a

paranoid ['pærənɔɪd] *adj (person, feeling)* paranoico

parasite ['pærəsaɪt] *n* parásito/a

parcel ['pɑːsl] *n* paquete *m* ▷ *vt (also:* ~ up) empaquetar, embalar

pardon ['pɑːdn] *n (Law)* indulto ▷ *vt* perdonar; ~ **me!, I beg your ~!** ¡perdone usted!; **(I beg your) ~?,** *(us:* ~ **me?** ¿cómo (dice)?

parent ['peərənt] *n (mother)* madre *f;* *(father)* padre *m;* **parents** *npl* padres *mpl;* **parental** [pə'rentl] *adj* paternal/maternal

> Be careful not to translate *parent* by the Spanish word *pariente*.

Paris ['pærɪs] *n* París *m*

parish ['pærɪʃ] *n* parroquia

Parisian [pə'rɪzɪən] *adj, n* parisiense *mf*

park [pɑːk] *n* parque *m* ▷ *vt, vi* aparcar, estacionar

parking ['pɑːkɪŋ] *n* aparcamiento, estacionamiento; **"no ~"** "prohibido aparcar or estacionarse"; **parking lot** *n (us)* parking *m;* **parking meter** *n* parquímetro; **parking ticket** *n* multa de aparcamiento

parkway ['pɑːkweɪ] *n (us)* alameda

parliament ['pɑːləmənt] *n* parlamento, *(Spanish)* las Cortes *fpl; ver nota* **"parliament"**; **parliamentary** *adj* parlamentario

El Parlamento británico *(Parliament)* tiene como sede el palacio de Westminster, también llamado *Houses of Parliament*. Consta de

dos cámaras; la Cámara de los Comunes *(House of Commons)* está formada por 650 diputados *(Members of Parliament)* que acceden a ella tras ser elegidos por sufragio universal en su respectiva área o circunscripción electoral *(constituency)*. Se reúne 175 días al año y sus sesiones son presididas y moderadas por el Presidente de la Cámara *(Speaker)*. La cámara alta es la Cámara de los Lores *(House of Lords)* y sus miembros son nombrados por el monarca o bien han heredado su escaño. Su poder es limitado, aunque actúa como tribunal supremo de apelación, excepto en Escocia.

Parmesan [pɑːmɪ'zæn] *n (also:* ~ **cheese)** queso parmesano

parole [pə'rəʊl] *n:* **on** ~ en libertad condicional

parrot ['pærət] *n* loro, papagayo

parsley ['pɑːslɪ] *n* perejil *m*

parsnip ['pɑːsnɪp] *n* chirivía

parson ['pɑːsn] *n* cura *m*

part [pɑːt] *n* parte *f;* *(Mus)* parte *f;* *(bit)* trozo; *(of machine)* pieza; *(Theat etc)* papel *m;* *(of serial)* entrega; *(us: in hair)* raya ▷ *adv* = **partly** ▷ *vt* separar ▷ *vi (people)* separarse; *(crowd)* apartarse; **to take** ~ **in** participar or tomar parte en; **to take sb's** ~ tomar partido por algn; **for my** ~ por mi parte; **for the most** ~ en su mayor parte; ~ **of speech** *(Ling)* categoría gramatical; **part with** *vt fus* ceder, entregar; *(money)* pagar; *(get rid of)* deshacerse de

partial ['pɑːʃl] *adj* parcial; **to be** ~ **to** *(like)* ser aficionado a

participant [pɑː'tɪsɪpənt] *n (in competition)* concursante *mf*

participate [pɑː'tɪsɪpeɪt] *vi:* **to** ~ **in** participar en

particle ['pɑːtɪkl] *n* partícula; *(of dust)* mota

particular [pəˈtɪkjuləʳ] adj (special) particular; (concrete) concreto; (given) determinado; (fussy) quisquilloso; (demanding) exigente; **particulars** npl (information) datos mpl; (details) pormenores mpl; **in ~** en particular; **particularly** adv (in particular) sobre todo; (difficult, good etc) especialmente

parting [ˈpɑːtɪŋ] n (act of) separación f; (farewell) despedida; (BRIT: in hair) raya ▷ adj de despedida

partition [pɑːˈtɪʃən] n (Pol) división f; (wall) tabique m

partly [ˈpɑːtlɪ] adv en parte

partner [ˈpɑːtnəʳ] n (Comm) socio/a; (Sport) pareja; (at dance) pareja; (spouse) cónyuge mf; (friend etc) compañero/a; **partnership** n asociación f, sociedad f

partridge [ˈpɑːtrɪdʒ] n perdiz f

part-time [ˈpɑːtˈtaɪm] adj, adv a tiempo parcial

party [ˈpɑːtɪ] n (Pol) partido; (celebration) fiesta; (group) grupo; (Law) parte f ▷ adj (Pol) de partido

pass [pɑːs] vt (time, object) pasar; (place) pasar por; (exam, law) aprobar; (overtake, surpass) rebasar; (approve) aprobar ▷ vi pasar; (Scol) aprobar ▷ n (permit) permiso; (membership card) carnet m; (in mountains) puerto; (Sport) pase m; (Scol: also: ~ **mark**) aprobado; **to ~ sth through sth** pasar algo por algo; **to make a ~ at sb** (inf) insinuársele a algn; **pass away** vi fallecer; **pass by** vi pasar ▷ vt (ignore) pasar por alto; **pass on** vt: **to ~ on (to)** transmitir (a); **pass out** vi desmayarse; **pass over** vt omitir, pasar por alto; **pass up** vt (opportunity) dejar pasar, no aprovechar; **passable** adj (road) transitable; (tolerable) pasable

passage [ˈpæsɪdʒ] n pasillo; (act of passing) tránsito; (fare, in book) pasaje m; (by boat) travesía

passenger [ˈpæsɪndʒəʳ] n pasajero/a, viajero/a

passer-by [pɑːsəˈbaɪ] n transeúnte mf

passing place n (Aut) apartadero

passion [ˈpæʃən] n pasión f; **passionate** adj apasionado; **passion fruit** n fruta de la pasión, granadilla

passive [ˈpæsɪv] adj (also Ling) pasivo

passport [ˈpɑːspɔːt] n pasaporte m; **passport control** n control m de pasaporte; **passport office** n oficina de pasaportes

password [ˈpɑːswəːd] n contraseña

past [pɑːst] prep (further than) más allá de; (later than) después de ▷ adj pasado; (president etc) antiguo ▷ n (time) pasado; (of person) antecedentes mpl; **quarter/half ~ four** las cuatro y cuarto/media; **he's ~ forty** tiene más de cuarenta años; **for the ~ few/three days** durante los últimos días/últimos tres días; **to run ~** pasar corriendo

pasta [ˈpæstə] n pasta

paste [peɪst] n pasta; (glue) engrudo ▷ vt pegar

pastel [ˈpæstl] adj pastel; (painting) al pastel

pasteurized [ˈpæstəraɪzd] adj pasteurizado

pastime [ˈpɑːstaɪm] n pasatiempo

pastor [ˈpɑːstəʳ] n pastor m

past participle n (Ling) participio m (de) pasado or (de) pretérito, or pasivo

pastry [ˈpeɪstrɪ] n (dough) pasta; (cake) pastel m

pasture [ˈpɑːstʃəʳ] n pasto

pasty n [ˈpæstɪ] empanada ▷ adj [ˈpeɪstɪ] (complexion) pálido

pat [pæt] vt dar una palmadita a; (dog etc) acariciar

patch [pætʃ] n (of material) parche m; (mended part) remiendo; (of land) terreno ▷ vt remendar; **(to go through) a bad ~** (pasar por) una mala racha; **patchy** adj desigual

pâté [ˈpæteɪ] n paté m

patent [ˈpeɪtnt] n patente f ▷ vt patentar ▷ adj patente, evidente

paternal [pə'tɜːnl] adj paternal; (relation) paterno

paternity [pə'tɜːnɪtɪ] n paternidad f; **paternity leave** n permiso m por paternidad, licencia por paternidad

path [pɑːθ] n camino, sendero; (trail, track) pista; (of missile) trayectoria

pathetic [pə'θetɪk] adj patético; (very bad) malísimo

pathway ['pɑːθweɪ] n sendero, vereda

patience ['peɪʃns] n paciencia; (BRIT Cards) solitario

patient ['peɪʃnt] n paciente mf ▷ adj paciente, sufrido

patio ['pætɪəʊ] n patio

patriotic [pætrɪ'ɒtɪk] adj patriótico

patrol [pə'trəʊl] n patrulla ▷ vt patrullar por; **patrol car** n coche m patrulla

patron ['peɪtrən] n (in shop) cliente mf; (of charity) patrocinador(a) m/f; **~ of the arts** mecenas m

patronizing ['pætrənaɪzɪŋ] adj condescendiente

pattern ['pætən] n (Sewing) patrón m; (design) dibujo; **patterned** adj (material) estampado

pause [pɔːz] n pausa ▷ vi hacer una pausa

pave [peɪv] vt pavimentar; **to ~ the way for** preparar el terreno para

pavement ['peɪvmənt] n (BRIT) acera, vereda (LAM), andén m (LAM), banqueta (LAM)

pavilion [pə'vɪlɪən] n (Sport) vestuarios mpl

paving ['peɪvɪŋ] n pavimento, enlosado

paw [pɔː] n pata

pawn [pɔːn] n (Chess) peón m; (fig) instrumento ▷ vt empeñar; **pawnbroker** ['pɔːnbrəʊkə'] n prestamista mf

pay [peɪ] (pt, pp **paid**) (wage etc) sueldo, salario ▷ vt pagar ▷ vi (be profitable) rendir; **to ~ attention (to)** prestar atención (a); **pay back**

vt (money) reembolsar; (person) pagar; **pay for** vt fus pagar; **pay in** vt ingresar; **pay off** vt saldar ▷ vi (scheme, decision) dar resultado; **pay out** vt (money) gastar, desembolsar; **pay up** vt pagar; **payable** adj pagadero; **to make a cheque payable to sb** extender un cheque a favor de algn; **pay day** n día m de paga; **pay envelope** n (US) = **pay packet; payment** n pago; **monthly payment** mensualidad f; **payout** n pago; (in competition) premio en metálico; **pay packet** n (BRIT) sobre m (de la paga); **pay-phone** n teléfono público; **payroll** n plantilla, nómina; **pay slip** n nómina, hoja del sueldo; **pay television** n televisión f de pago

PC n abbr (= personal computer) PC m, OP m; (BRIT) = **police constable** ▷ adj abbr = **politically correct**

pc abbr = **per cent**

PDA n abbr (= personal digital assistant) agenda electrónica

PE n abbr (= physical education) ed. física

pea [piː] n guisante m, chícharo (LAM), arveja (LAM)

peace [piːs] n paz f; (calm) paz f, tranquilidad f; **peaceful** adj (gentle) pacífico; (calm) tranquilo, sosegado

peach [piːtʃ] n melocotón m, durazno (LAM)

peacock ['piːkɒk] n pavo real

peak [piːk] n (of mountain) cumbre f, cima; (of cap) visera; (fig) cumbre f; **peak hours** npl horas fpl punta

peanut ['piːnʌt] n cacahuete m, maní m (LAM); **peanut butter** n mantequilla de cacahuete

pear [peə'] n pera

pearl [pɜːl] n perla

peasant ['peznt] n campesino/a

peat [piːt] n turba

pebble ['pebl] n guijarro

peck [pek] vt (also: **~ at**) picotear ▷ n picotazo; (kiss) besito; **peckish** adj (BRIT inf): **I feel peckish** tengo ganas de picar algo

peculiar [pɪˈkjuːlɪə^r] adj (odd) extraño, raro; (typical) propio, característico; **~ to** propio de

pedal [ˈpɛdl] n pedal m ▷ vi pedalear

pedalo [ˈpɛdələu] n patín m a pedal

pedestal [ˈpɛdəstl] n pedestal m

pedestrian [pɪˈdɛstrɪən] n peatón m ▷ adj pedestre; **pedestrian crossing** n (BRIT) paso de peatones; **pedestrianized** adj: **a pedestrianized street** una calle peatonal; **pedestrian precinct,** (US) **pedestrian zone** n zona reservada para peatones

pedigree [ˈpɛdɪgriː] n genealogía; (of animal) pedigrí m ▷ cpd (animal) de raza, de casta

pedophile [ˈpiːdəufaɪl] n (US) = **paedophile**

pee [piː] vi (inf) mear

peek [piːk] vi mirar a hurtadillas

peel [piːl] n piel f; (of orange, lemon) cáscara; (: removed) peladuras fpl ▷ vt pelar ▷ vi (paint etc) descancharse; (wallpaper) despegarse, desprenderse; (skin) pelar

peep [piːp] n (look) mirada furtiva; (sound) pío ▷ vi (look) mirar furtivamente

peer [pɪə^r] vi: **to ~ at** escudriñar ▷ n (noble) par m; (equal) igual m; (contemporary) contemporáneo/a

peg [pɛg] n (for coat etc) gancho, colgador m; (BRIT: also: **clothes ~**) pinza

pelican [ˈpɛlɪkən] n pelícano; **pelican crossing** n (BRIT Aut) paso de peatones señalizado

pelt [pɛlt] vt: **to ~ sb with sth** arrojarle algo a algn ▷ vi (rain: also: **~ down**) llover a cántaros; (inf: run) correr ▷ n pellejo

pelvis [ˈpɛlvɪs] n pelvis f

pen [pɛn] n (also: **ballpoint ~**) bolígrafo; (also: **fountain ~**) pluma; (for sheep) redil m

penalty [ˈpɛnltɪ] n pena; (fine) multa

pence [pɛns] pl of **penny**

pencil [ˈpɛnsl] n lápiz m ▷ vt (also: **~ in**) escribir con lápiz; (fig) apuntar con carácter provisional; **pencil case** n estuche m; **pencil sharpener** n sacapuntas m inv

pendant [ˈpɛndnt] n pendiente m

pending [ˈpɛndɪŋ] prep antes de ▷ adj pendiente

penetrate [ˈpɛnɪtreɪt] vt penetrar

penfriend [ˈpɛnfrɛnd] n (BRIT) amigo/a por correspondencia

penguin [ˈpɛŋgwɪn] n pingüino

penicillin [pɛnɪˈsɪlɪn] n penicilina

peninsula [pəˈnɪnsjulə] n península

penis [ˈpiːnɪs] n pene m

penitentiary [pɛnɪˈtɛnʃərɪ] n (US) cárcel f, presidio

penknife [ˈpɛnnaɪf] n navaja

penniless [ˈpɛnɪlɪs] adj sin dinero

penny (pl **pennies** or (Brit) **pence**) [ˈpɛnɪ, ˈpɛnɪz, pɛns] n (BRIT) penique m; (US) centavo

penpal [ˈpɛnpæl] n amigo/a por correspondencia

pension [ˈpɛnʃən] n (allowance, state payment) pensión f; (old-age) jubilación f; **pensioner** n (BRIT) jubilado/a

pentagon [ˈpɛntəgən] n pentágono; **the P~** (US Pol) el Pentágono

> **PENTAGON**
>
> • Se conoce como el Pentágono
> • (the Pentagon) al edificio de
> • planta pentagonal que acoge
> • las dependencias del Ministerio
> • de Defensa estadounidense
> • (Department of Defense) en Arlington,
> • Virginia. En lenguaje periodístico se
> • aplica también a la dirección militar
> • del país.

penthouse [ˈpɛnthaus] n ático (de lujo)

penultimate [pɛˈnʌltɪmət] adj penúltimo

people [ˈpiːpl] npl gente f; (citizens) pueblo sg, ciudadanos mpl; (Pol): **the**

~ el pueblo ▷ el pueblo ▷ (nation, race) pueblo, nación f; **several ~ came** vinieron varias personas; **~ say that ...** dice la gente que ...

pepper ['pepə'] n (spice) pimienta; (vegetable) pimiento ▷ vt: **to ~ with** (fig) salpicar de; **peppermint** n (sweet) pastilla de menta

per [pə:'] prep por; **~ day/person** por día/persona; **~ annum** al año

perceive [pə'si:v] vt percibir; (realize) darse cuenta de

per cent, (us) **percent** n por ciento

percentage [pə'sεntidʒ] n porcentaje m

perception [pə'sεpʃən] n percepción f; (insight) perspicacia

perch [pə:tʃ] n (fish) perca; (for bird) percha ▷ vi: **to ~ (on)** (bird) posarse (en); (person) encaramarse (en)

percussion [pə'kʌʃən] n percusión f

perfect adj ['pə:fıkt] perfecto ▷ n (also: **~ tense**) perfecto ▷ vt [pə'fεkt] perfeccionar; **perfection** n perfección f; **perfectly** adv perfectamente

perform [pə'fɔ:m] vt (carry out) realizar, llevar a cabo; (Theat) representar; (piece of music) interpretar ▷ vi (Tech) funcionar; **performance** n (of a play) representación f; (of player etc) actuación f; (of engine) rendimiento f; **performer** n (actor) actor m, actriz f

perfume ['pə:fju:m] n perfume m

perhaps [pə'hæps] adv quizá(s), tal vez

perimeter [pə'rımıtə'] n perímetro

period ['pıərıəd] n período; (Scol) clase f; (full stop) punto; (Med) regla ▷ adj (costume, furniture) de época; **periodical** [pıərı'ɔdıkl] adj periódico; **periodically** adv de vez en cuando, cada cierto tiempo

perish ['pεrıʃ] vi perecer; (decay) echarse a perder

perjury ['pə:dʒərı] n (Law) perjurio

perk [pə:k] n extra m

perm [pə:m] n permanente f

permanent ['pə:mənənt] adj permanente; **permanently** adv (lastingly) para siempre, de modo definitivo; (all the time) permanentemente

permission [pə'mıʃən] n permiso

permit n ['pə:mıt] permiso, licencia ▷ vt [pə'mıt] permitir

perplex [pə'plεks] vt dejar perplejo

persecute ['pə:sıkju:t] vt perseguir

persecution [pə:sı'kju:ʃən] n persecución f

persevere [pə:sı'vıə'] vi perseverar

Persian ['pə:ʃən] adj, n persa mf; **the ~ Gulf** el Golfo Pérsico

persist [pə'sıst] vi persistir; **to ~ in doing sth** empeñarse en hacer algo; **persistent** adj persistente; (determined) porfiado

person ['pə:sn] n persona; **in ~** en persona; **personal** adj personal, individual; (visit) en persona; **personal assistant** n ayudante mf personal; **personal computer** n ordenador m personal; **personality** [pə:sə'nælıtı] n personalidad f; **personally** adv personalmente; (in person) en persona; **to take sth personally** tomarse algo a mal; **personal organizer** n agenda; **personal stereo** n walkman® m

personnel [pə:sə'nεl] n personal m

perspective [pə'spεktıv] n perspectiva

perspiration [pə:spı'reıʃən] n transpiración f

persuade [pə'sweıd] vt: **to ~ sb to do sth** persuadir a algn para que haga algo

persuasion [pə'sweıʒən] n persuasión f; (persuasiveness) persuasiva

persuasive [pə'sweısıv] adj persuasivo

perverse [pə'və:s] adj perverso; (wayward) travieso

pervert n ['pə:və:t] pervertido/a ▷ vt [pə'və:t] pervertir

pessimism ['pesɪmɪzəm] n pesimismo

pessimist ['pesɪmɪst] n pesimista mf; **pessimistic** [pesɪ'mɪstɪk] adj pesimista

pest [pest] n (insect) insecto nocivo; (fig) lata, molestia

pester ['pestə'] vt molestar, acosar

pesticide ['pestɪsaɪd] n pesticida m

pet [pet] n animal m doméstico; (favourite) favorito/a ▷ vt acariciar ▷ cpd: **teacher's ~** favorito/a (del profesor); **~ hate** manía

petal ['petl] n pétalo

petite [pə'tiːt] adj chiquita

petition [pə'tɪʃən] n petición f

petrified ['petrɪfaɪd] adj horrorizado

petrol ['petrəl] (BRIT) n gasolina

petroleum [pə'trəʊlɪəm] n petróleo

petrol: petrol pump n (BRIT: in garage) surtidor m de gasolina; **petrol station** n (BRIT) gasolinera; **petrol tank** n (BRIT) depósito (de gasolina)

petticoat ['petɪkəʊt] n combinación f, enagua(s) f(pl) (LAM)

petty ['petɪ] adj (mean) mezquino; (unimportant) insignificante

pew [pjuː] n banco

pewter ['pjuːtə'] n peltre m

phantom ['fæntəm] n fantasma m

pharmacist ['fɑːməsɪst] n farmacéutico/a

pharmacy ['fɑːməsɪ] n (US) farmacia

phase [feɪz] n fase f; **phase in** vt introducir progresivamente; **phase out** vt (machinery, process) retirar progresivamente; (job, subsidy) eliminar por etapas

pheasant ['feznt] n faisán m

phenomena [fɪ'nɒmɪnə] npl of **phenomenon**

phenomenal [fɪ'nɒmɪnl] adj fenomenal, extraordinario

phenomenon (pl **phenomena**) [fə'nɒmɪnən, -nə] n fenómeno

Philippines ['fɪlɪpiːnz] npl: **the ~** (las Islas) Filipinas

philosopher [fɪ'lɒsəfə'] n filósofo/a

philosophical [fɪlə'sɒfɪkl] adj filosófico

philosophy [fɪ'lɒsəfɪ] n filosofía

phlegm [flem] n flema

phobia ['fəʊbjə] n fobia

phone [fəʊn] n teléfono ▷ vi telefonear, llamar por teléfono; **on the ~** tener teléfono; (be calling) estar hablando por teléfono; **phone back** vt, vi volver a llamar; **phone up** vt, vi llamar por teléfono; **phone book** n guía telefónica; **phone box, phone booth** n cabina telefónica; **phone call** n llamada (telefónica); **phonecard** n tarjeta telefónica; **phone number** n número de teléfono

phonetics [fə'netɪks] n fonética

phoney ['fəʊnɪ] adj = **phony**

phony ['fəʊnɪ] adj falso

photo ['fəʊtəʊ] n foto f; **photo album** n álbum m de fotos; **photocopier** n fotocopiadora; **photocopy** n fotocopia ▷ vt fotocopiar

photograph ['fəʊtəgrɑːf] n fotografía ▷ vt fotografiar; **photographer** n fotógrafo/a; **photography** [fə'tɒgrəfɪ] n fotografía

phrase [freɪz] n frase f ▷ vt expresar; **phrase book** n libro de frases

physical ['fɪzɪkl] adj físico; **physical education** n educación f física; **physically** adv físicamente

physician [fɪ'zɪʃən] n médico/a

physicist ['fɪzɪsɪst] n físico/a

physics ['fɪzɪks] n física

physiotherapist [fɪzɪəʊ'θerəpɪst] n fisioterapeuta mf; **physiotherapy** n fisioterapia

physique [fɪ'ziːk] n físico

pianist ['pɪənɪst] n pianista mf

piano [pɪ'ænəʊ] n piano

pick [pɪk] n (tool: also: **-axe**) pico, piqueta f ▷ vt (select) elegir, escoger; (gather) coger (SP), recoger (LAM); (lock) abrir con ganzúa; **take your ~** escoja lo que quiera; **the ~ of** lo mejor de; **to ~ one's nose/teeth** hurgarse

la nariz/escarp... ...stinguish)
pick on vt fu... ...erse con; (improve: sales) ir
pick out vt reponerse; (: Finance)
identificar recoger; (learn)
mejor; (Police: arrest) detener;
reco... (TV, Tel) captar; (understand)
...erarse; **to ~ o.s. up** levantarse

pickle ['pɪkl] n (also: **~s**: as condiment)
escabeche m; (fig: mess) apuro ▷ vt
conservar en escabeche; (in vinegar)
conservar en vinagre

pickpocket ['pɪkpɔkɪt] n carterista
mf

pickup ['pɪkʌp] n (also: **~ truck, ~ van**)
furgoneta, camioneta

picnic ['pɪknɪk] n merienda ▷ vi hacer
un picnic; **picnic area** n zona de
picnic; (Aut) área de descanso

picture ['pɪktʃə*] n cuadro; (painting)
pintura; (photograph) fotografía; (film)
película; (TV) imagen f; (fig: description)
descripción f; (: situation) situación f
▷ vt (imagine) imaginar; **the ~s** (BRIT)
el cine; **picture frame** n marco;
picture messaging n (envío de)
mensajes mpl con imágenes

picturesque [pɪktʃə'rɛsk] adj
pintoresco

pie [paɪ] n (of meat etc: large) pastel m;
(: small) empanada; (sweet) tarta

piece [piːs] n pedazo, trozo; (of cake)
trozo; (item:) ~ **of furniture/advice**
un mueble/un consejo ▷ vt: **to ~
together** juntar; (Tech) armar; **to
take to ~s** desmontar

pie chart n gráfico de sectores or
de tarta

pier [pɪə*] n muelle m, embarcadero

pierce [pɪəs] vt perforar; **to have
one's ears ~d** hacerse los agujeros
de las orejas

pig [pɪg] n cerdo, chancho (LAM);
(person: greedy) tragón/ona m/f,
comilón/ona m/f; (: nasty) cerdo/a

pigeon ['pɪdʒən] n paloma; (as food)
pichón m

piggy bank ['pɪgɪbæŋk] n hucha (en
forma de cerdito)

pigsty ['pɪgstaɪ] n pocilga

pigtail ['pɪgteɪl] n (girl's) trenza

pike [paɪk] n (fish) lucio

pilchard ['pɪltʃəd] n sardina

pile [paɪl] n montón m; (of carpet)
pelo; **pile up** vi (accumulate: work)
amontonarse, acumularse ▷ vt
(put in a heap: books, clothes) apilar,
amontonar; (accumulate) acumular;
piles npl (Med) almorranas fpl,
hemorroides mpl; **pile-up** n (Aut)
accidente m múltiple

pilgrimage ['pɪlgrɪmɪdʒ] n
peregrinación f, romería

pill [pɪl] n píldora; **the ~** la píldora

pillar ['pɪlə*] n pilar m

pillow ['pɪləʊ] n almohada;
pillowcase ['pɪləʊkeɪs] n funda (de
almohada)

pilot ['paɪlət] n piloto mf ▷ adj (scheme
etc) piloto inv ▷ vt pilotar; **pilot light**
n piloto

pimple ['pɪmpl] n grano

PIN n abbr (= personal identification
number) PIN m

pin [pɪn] n alfiler m ▷ vt prender con
(alfiler); **~s and needles** hormigueo
sg; **to ~ sth on sb** (fig) cargar a algn
con la culpa de algo; **pin down** vt (fig):
to ~ sb down hacer que algn concrete

pinafore ['pɪnəfɔː*] n delantal m

pinch [pɪntʃ] n (of salt etc) pizca ▷ vt
pellizcar; (inf: steal) birlar; **at a ~** en
caso de apuro

pine [paɪn] n (also: **~ tree**) pino ▷ vi: **to
~ for** suspirar por

pineapple ['paɪnæpl] n piña,
ananá(s) m (LAM)

ping [pɪŋ] n (noise) sonido agudo;
Ping-Pong® n pingpong m

pink [pɪŋk] adj (de color) rosa inv f
(colour) rosa m; (Bot) clavel m

pinpoint ['pɪnpɔɪnt] vt precisar

pint [paɪnt] n pinta (Brit = 0,57 l, US
= 0,47 l); (BRIT inf: of beer) pinta de
cerveza, ≈ jarra (SP)

pioneer [paɪəˈnɪəʳ] n pionero/a
pious [ˈpaɪəs] adj piadoso, devoto
pip [pɪp] n (seed) pepita; **the ~s** (BRIT) la señal
pipe [paɪp] n tubería, cañería; (for smoking) pipa ▷ vt conducir en cañerías; **pipeline** n (for oil) oleoducto; (for natural gas) gaseoducto; **piper** n gaitero/a
pirate [ˈpaɪərət] n pirata mf ▷ vt (record, video, book) hacer una copia pirata de, piratear
Pisces [ˈpaɪsiːz] n Piscis m
piss [pɪs] vi (inf!) mear; **pissed** adj (inf!: drunk) mamado, pedo
pistol [ˈpɪstl] n pistola
piston [ˈpɪstən] n pistón m, émbolo
pit [pɪt] n hoyo; (also: **coal ~**) mina; (in garage) foso de inspección; (also: **orchestra ~**) foso de la orquesta ▷ vt: **to ~ one's wits against sb** medir fuerzas con algn
pitch [pɪtʃ] n (Mus) tono; (BRIT Sport) campo, terreno; (tar) brea ▷ vt (throw) arrojar, lanzar ▷ vi (fall) caer(se); **to ~ a tent** montar una tienda de campaña; **pitch-black** adj negro como boca de lobo
pitfall [ˈpɪtfɔːl] n riesgo
pith [pɪθ] n (of orange) piel f blanca
pitiful [ˈpɪtɪful] adj (touching) lastimoso, conmovedor/a
pity [ˈpɪtɪ] n compasión f, piedad f ▷ vt compadecer(se de); **what a ~!** ¡qué pena!
pizza [ˈpiːtsə] n pizza
placard [ˈplækɑːd] n (in march etc) pancarta
place [pleɪs] n lugar m, sitio; (seat) plaza, asiento; (post) puesto; (home): **at/to his ~** en/a su casa ▷ vt (object) poner, colocar; (identify) reconocer; **to take ~** tener lugar; **to be ~d** (in race, exam) colocarse; **out of ~** (not suitable) fuera de lugar; **in the first ~** en primer lugar; **to change ~s with sb** cambiarse de sitio con algn; **~ of birth** lugar m de nacimiento; **place**

mat n (wooden etc) salvamanteles m inv; (in linen etc) mantel m individual; **placement** n colocación f; (at work) emplazamiento
placid [ˈplæsɪd] adj apacible
plague [pleɪg] n plaga; (Med) peste f ▷ vt (fig) acosar, atormentar
plaice [pleɪs] n (pl inv) platija
plain [pleɪn] adj (clear) claro, evidente; (simple) sencillo; (not handsome) poco atractivo ▷ adv claramente ▷ n llano, llanura; **plain chocolate** n chocolate m oscuro or amargo; **plainly** adv claramente
plaintiff [ˈpleɪntɪf] n demandante mf
plait [plæt] n trenza
plan [plæn] n (drawing) plano; (scheme) plan m, proyecto ▷ vt proyectar ▷ vi hacer proyectos; **to ~ to do** pensar hacer
plane [pleɪn] n (Aviat) avión m; (tree) plátano; (tool) cepillo; (Math) plano
planet [ˈplænɪt] n planeta m
plank [plæŋk] n tabla
planning [ˈplænɪŋ] n planificación f; **family ~** n planificación familiar
plant [plɑːnt] n planta; (machinery) maquinaria; (factory) fábrica ▷ vt plantar; (field) sembrar; (bomb) colocar
plantation [plænˈteɪʃən] n plantación f; (estate) hacienda
plaque [plæk] n placa
plaster [ˈplɑːstəʳ] n (for walls) yeso; (also: **~ of Paris**) yeso mate; (BRIT: also: **sticking ~**) tirita ▷ vt enyesar; (cover) llenar o cubrir de; **plaster cast** n (Med) escayola; (Med, statue) vaciado de yeso
plastic [ˈplæstɪk] n plástico ▷ adj de plástico; **plastic bag** n bolsa de plástico; **plastic surgery** n cirugía plástica
plate [pleɪt] n (dish) plato; (metal, in book) lámina; (dental plate) placa de dentadura postiza
plateau (pl **plateaus** or **plateaux**) [ˈplætəu, -z] n meseta, altiplanicie f

p

platform ['plætfɔːm] n (Rail) andén m; (stage) plataforma; (at meeting) tribuna; (Pol) programa m (electoral)
platinum ['plætinəm] n platino
platoon [plə'tuːn] n pelotón m
platter ['plætə'] n fuente f
plausible ['plɔːzɪbl] adj verosímil; (person) convincente
play [pleɪ] n juego; (Theat) obra ▷ vt (game) jugar; (football, tennis, cards) jugar a; (compete against) jugar contra; (instrument) tocar; (Theat: part) hacer el papel de ▷ vi jugar; (band) tocar; (tape, record) sonar; **to ~ safe** ir a lo seguro; **play back** vt (tape) poner; **play up** vi (cause trouble) dar guerra; **player** n jugador(a) m/f; (Theat) actor m, actriz f; (Mus) músico/a; **playful** adj juguetón/ona; **playground** n (in school) patio de recreo; (in park) parque m infantil; **playgroup** n jardín m de infancia; **playing card** n naipe m, carta; **playing field** n campo de deportes; **playschool** n = **playgroup**; **playtime** n (Scol) (hora de) recreo; **playwright** n dramaturgo/a
plc abbr (BRIT: = public limited company) S.A.
plea [pliː] n súplica, petición f; (Law) alegato, defensa
plead [pliːd] vt (give as excuse) poner como pretexto; (Law): **to ~ sb's case** defender a algn ▷ vi (Law) declararse; (beg): **to ~ with sb** suplicar or rogar a algn
pleasant ['plɛznt] adj agradable
please [pliːz] excl ¡por favor! ▷ vt (give pleasure to) dar gusto a, agradar ▷ vi (think fit): **do as you ~** haz lo que quieras or lo que te dé la gana; **~ yourself!** ¡haz lo que quieras!, ¡como quieras!; **pleased** adj (happy) alegre, contento; **pleased (with)** satisfecho (de); **pleased to meet you** ¡encantado!, ¡tanto or mucho gusto!
pleasure ['plɛʒə'] n placer m, gusto; **"it's a ~"** "el gusto es mío"
pleat [pliːt] n pliegue m

pledge [plɛdʒ] n (promise) promesa, voto ▷ vt prometer
plentiful ['plɛntɪful] adj copioso, abundante
plenty ['plɛntɪ] n: **~ of** mucho(s)/a(s)
pliers ['plaɪəz] npl alicates mpl, tenazas fpl
plight [plaɪt] n condición f or situación f difícil
plod [plɔd] vi caminar con paso pesado; (fig) trabajar laboriosamente
plonk [plɔŋk] (inf) n (BRIT: wine) vino peleón ▷ vt: **to ~ sth down** dejar caer algo
plot [plɔt] n (scheme) complot m, conjura; (of story, play) argumento; (of land) terreno ▷ vt (mark out) trazar; (conspire) tramar, urdir ▷ vi conspirar
plough, (US) **plow** [plau] n arado ▷ vt (earth) arar
plow [plau] n, vb (US) = **plough**
ploy [plɔɪ] n truco, estratagema
pluck [plʌk] vt (fruit) coger (SP), recoger (LAM); (musical instrument) puntear; (bird) desplumar; **to ~ up courage** hacer de tripas corazón; **to ~ one's eyebrows** depilarse las cejas
plug [plʌg] n tapón m; (Elec) enchufe m, clavija f; (Aut: also: **spark(ing) ~**) bujía f ▷ vt (hole) tapar; (inf: advertise) dar publicidad a; **plug in** vt (Elec) enchufar; **plughole** n desagüe m
plum [plʌm] n (fruit) ciruela
plumber ['plʌmə'] n fontanero/a, plomero/a (LAM)
plumbing ['plʌmɪŋ] n (trade) fontanería, plomería (LAM); (piping) cañerías
plummet ['plʌmɪt] vi: **to ~ (down)** caer a plomo
plump [plʌmp] adj rechoncho, rollizo; **plump for** vt fus (inf: choose) optar por
plunge [plʌndʒ] n zambullida ▷ vt sumergir, hundir ▷ vi (fall) caer; (dive) saltar; (person) arrojarse; **to take the ~** lanzarse
plural ['pluərl] adj plural ▷ n plural m

plus [plʌs] n (also: **~ sign**) signo más ▷ prep más, y, además de; **ten/twenty ~** más de diez/veinte

ply [plaɪ] vt (a trade) ejercer ▷ vi (ship) ir y venir; **to ~ sb with drink** no dejar de ofrecer copas a algn; **plywood** n madera contrachapada

PM n abbr (BRIT) = **Prime Minister**

p.m. adv abbr (= post meridiem) de la tarde or noche

PMS n abbr (= premenstrual syndrome) SPM m

PMT n abbr (= premenstrual tension) SPM m

pneumatic drill n taladradora neumática

pneumonia [njuːˈməʊnɪə] n pulmonía

poach [pəʊtʃ] vt (cook) escalfar; (steal) cazar/pescar en vedado ▷ vi cazar/pescar en vedado; **poached** adj (egg) escalfado

PO Box n abbr (= Post Office Box) apdo., aptdo.

pocket [ˈpɒkɪt] n bolsillo; (fig) bolsa ▷ vt meter en el bolsillo; (steal) embolsarse; **to be out of ~** salir perdiendo; **pocketbook** n (us) cartera; **pocket money** n asignación f

pod [pɒd] n vaina

podcast [ˈpɒdkɑːst] n podcast m ▷ vi podcastear

podiatrist [pɒˈdiːətrɪst] n (us) podólogo,a

podium [ˈpəʊdɪəm] n podio

poem [ˈpəʊɪm] n poema m

poet [ˈpəʊɪt] n poeta mf; **poetic** [pəʊˈetɪk] adj poético; **poetry** n poesía

poignant [ˈpɔɪnjənt] adj conmovedor(a)

point [pɔɪnt] n punto; (tip) punta; (purpose) fin m, propósito; (use) utilidad f; (significant part) lo esencial; (also: **decimal ~**): **2 ~ 3 (2.3)** dos coma tres (2,3) ▷ vt (gun etc): **to ~ sth at sb** apuntar con algo a algn ▷ vi: **to ~ at** señalar; **points** npl (Aut) contactos

mpl; (Rail) agujas fpl; **to be on the ~ of doing sth** estar a punto de hacer algo; **to make a ~ of doing sth** poner empeño en hacer algo; **to get the ~** comprender; **to come to the ~** ir al meollo; **there's no ~ (in doing)** no tiene sentido (hacer); **point out** vt señalar; **point-blank** adv (say, refuse) sin más hablar; (also: **at point-blank range**) a quemarropa; **pointed** adj (shape) puntiagudo, afilado; (remark) intencionado; **pointer** n (needle) aguja, indicador m; **pointless** adj sin sentido; **point of view** n punto de vista

poison [ˈpɔɪzn] n veneno ▷ vt envenenar; **poisonous** adj venenoso; (fumes etc) tóxico

poke [pəʊk] vt (jab with finger, stick etc) empujar; (put): **to ~ sth in(to)** introducir algo en; **poke about** vi fisgonear; **poke out** vi (stick out) salir

poker [ˈpəʊkər] n atizador m; (Cards) póker m

Poland [ˈpəʊlənd] n Polonia

polar [ˈpəʊlər] adj polar; **polar bear** n oso polar

Pole [pəʊl] n polaco/a

pole [pəʊl] n palo; (Geo) polo; (Tel) poste m; **pole bean** n (us) judía trepadora; **pole vault** n salto con pértiga

police [pəˈliːs] n policía ▷ vt vigilar; **police car** n coche-patrulla m; **police constable** n (BRIT) guardia m, policía m; **police force** n cuerpo de policía; **policeman** n guardia m, policía m; **police officer** n guardia mf, policía mf; **police station** n comisaría; **policewoman** n (mujer f) policía

policy [ˈpɒlɪsɪ] n política; (also: **insurance ~**) póliza

polio [ˈpəʊlɪəʊ] n polio f

Polish [ˈpəʊlɪʃ] adj polaco ▷ n (Ling) polaco

polish [ˈpɒlɪʃ] n (for shoes) betún m; (for floor) cera (de lustrar); (shine) brillo, lustre m; (fig: refinement) refinamiento ▷ vt (shoes) limpiar; (make shiny) pulir, sacar brillo a; **polish off** vt (food) despachar; **polished** adj (fig: person) refinado

polite [pə'laɪt] adj cortés, atento; **politeness** n cortesía

political [pə'lɪtɪkl] adj político; **politically** adv políticamente; **politically correct** adj políticamente correcto

politician [pɒlɪ'tɪʃən] n político/a

politics ['pɒlɪtɪks] n política

poll [pəʊl] n (votes) votación f; (also: **opinion** ~) sondeo, encuesta ▷ vt (votes) obtener

pollen ['pɒlən] n polen m

polling station n centro electoral

pollute [pə'luːt] vt contaminar

pollution [pə'luːʃən] n contaminación f

polo ['pəʊləʊ] n (sport) polo; **poloneck** adj de cuello vuelto ▷ n (sweater) suéter m de cuello vuelto; **polo shirt** n polo, niqui m

polyester [pɒlɪ'estəʳ] n poliéster m

polystyrene [pɒlɪ'staɪriːn] n poliestireno

polythene ['pɒlɪθiːn] n (Brit) polietileno; **polythene bag** n bolsa de plástico

pomegranate ['pɒmɪɡrænɪt] n granada

pompous ['pɒmpəs] adj pomposo

pond [pɒnd] n (natural) charca; (artificial) estanque m

ponder ['pɒndəʳ] vt meditar

pony ['pəʊnɪ] n poney m; **ponytail** n coleta; **pony trekking** n (Brit) excursión f a caballo

poodle ['puːdl] n caniche m

pool [puːl] n (natural) charca; (also: **swimming** ~) piscina, alberca (LAM) ▷ vt juntar; (**football**) ~s npl quinielas fpl

poor [pʊəʳ] adj pobre; (bad) malo ▷ npl: **the** ~ los pobres; **poorly** adj mal, enfermo ▷ adv mal

pop [pɒp] n (sound) ruido seco; (Mus) (música) pop m; (inf: father) papá m; (drink) gaseosa ▷ vt (burst) hacer reventar ▷ vi reventar; (cork) saltar; **pop in** vi entrar un momento; **pop out** vi salir un momento; **popcorn** n palomitas fpl (de maíz)

poplar ['pɒpləʳ] n álamo

popper ['pɒpəʳ] n corchete m, botón m automático

poppy ['pɒpɪ] n amapola; see also **Remembrance Day**

Popsicle® ['pɒpsɪkl] n (US) polo

pop star n estrella del pop

popular ['pɒpjʊləʳ] adj popular; **popularity** [pɒpjʊ'lærɪtɪ] n popularidad f

population [pɒpjʊ'leɪʃən] n población f

porcelain ['pɔːslɪn] n porcelana

porch [pɔːtʃ] n pórtico, entrada; (US) veranda

pore [pɔːʳ] n poro ▷ vi: **to ~ over** enfrascarse en

pork [pɔːk] n (carne f de) cerdo or chancho (LAM); **pork chop** n chuleta de cerdo; **pork pie** n (Brit Culin) empanada de carne de cerdo

porn [pɔːn] adj (inf) porno inv ▷ n porno; **pornographic** [pɔːnə'ɡræfɪk] adj pornográfico; **pornography** [pɔː'nɒɡrəfɪ] n pornografía

porridge ['pɒrɪdʒ] n gachas fpl de avena

port [pɔːt] n puerto; (Naut: left side) babor m; (wine) oporto; **~ of call** n puerto de escala

portable ['pɔːtəbl] adj portátil

porter ['pɔːtəʳ] n (for luggage) maletero; (doorkeeper) portero/a, conserje mf

portfolio [pɔːt'fəʊlɪəʊ] n (case, of artist) cartera, carpeta; (Pol, Finance) cartera

portion ['pɔːʃən] n porción f; (helping) ración f

portrait ['pɔːtreɪt] n retrato

portray [pɔːˈtreɪ] vt retratar; (in writing) representar

Portugal [ˈpɔːtjʊgl] n Portugal m

Portuguese [ˌpɔːtjʊˈgiːz] adj portugués/esa ▷ n (pl inv) portugués/esa m/f; (Ling) portugués m

pose [pəʊz] n postura, actitud f ▷ vi (pretend): **to ~ as** hacerse pasar por ▷ vt (question) plantear; **to ~ for** posar para

posh [pɒʃ] adj (inf) elegante, de lujo

position [pəˈzɪʃən] n posición f; (job) puesto ▷ vt colocar

positive [ˈpɒzɪtɪv] adj positivo; (certain) seguro; (definite) definitivo; **positively** adv (affirmatively, enthusiastically) de forma positiva; (inf: really) absolutamente

possess [pəˈzɛs] vt poseer; **possession** [pəˈzɛʃən] n posesión f; **possessions** npl (belongings) pertenencias fpl; **possessive** adj posesivo

possibility [ˌpɒsɪˈbɪlɪtɪ] n posibilidad f

possible [ˈpɒsɪbl] adj posible; **as big as ~** lo más grande posible; **possibly** adv posiblemente; **I cannot possibly come** me es imposible venir

post [pəʊst] n (BRIT: system) correos mpl; (: letters, delivery) correo m; (job, situation) puesto; (pole) poste m; (on blog, social network) post m ▷ vt (BRIT: appoint): **to ~ to** destinar a; **postage** n porte m, franqueo; **postal** adj postal, de correos; **postal order** n giro postal; **postbox** n buzón m; **postcard** n (tarjeta) postal f; **postcode** n (BRIT) código postal

poster [ˈpəʊstəʳ] n cartel m

postgraduate [ˈpəʊstˈɡrædjuːt] n posgraduado/a

postman [ˈpəʊstmən] (irreg: like **man**) n (BRIT) cartero

postmark [ˈpəʊstmɑːk] n matasellos m inv

post-mortem [pəʊstˈmɔːtəm] n autopsia

post office n (building) (oficina de) correos m; (organization): **the Post Office** Dirección f General de Correos

postpone [pəsˈpəʊn] vt aplazar

posture [ˈpɒstʃəʳ] n postura, actitud f

postwoman [ˈpəʊstwʊmən] (irreg: like **woman**) n (BRIT) cartera

pot [pɒt] n (for cooking) olla; (teapot) tetera; (coffeepot) cafetera; (for flowers) maceta; (for jam) tarro, bote m (LAM); (inf: marijuana) costo, chocolate m ▷ vt (plant) poner en tiesto; **to go to ~** (inf) irse al traste

potato [pəˈteɪtəʊ] (pl **potatoes**) n patata, papa (LAM); **potato peeler** n pelapatatas m inv

potent [ˈpəʊtnt] adj potente, poderoso; (drink) fuerte

potential [pəˈtɛnʃl] adj potencial, posible ▷ n potencial m

pothole [ˈpɒthəʊl] n (in road) bache m; (BRIT: underground) gruta

pot plant n planta de interior

potter [ˈpɒtəʳ] n alfarero/a ▷ vi: **to ~ around, ~ about** entretenerse haciendo cosillas; **pottery** [ˈpɒtərɪ] n cerámica; (factory) alfarería

potty [ˈpɒtɪ] n orinal m de niño

pouch [paʊtʃ] n (Zool) bolsa; (for tobacco) petaca

poultry [ˈpəʊltrɪ] n aves fpl de corral; (meat) pollo

pounce [paʊns] vi: **to ~ on** precipitarse sobre

pound [paʊnd] n libra ▷ vt (beat) golpear; (crush) machacar ▷ vi (beat) dar golpes; **pound sterling** n libra esterlina

pour [pɔːʳ] vt echar; (tea) servir ▷ vi correr, fluir; **to ~ sb a drink** servirle a algn una copa; **pour in** vi (people) entrar en tropel; **pour out** vi salir en tropel ▷ vt (drink) echar, servir; (fig): **to ~ out one's feelings** desahogarse; **pouring** adj: **pouring rain** lluvia torrencial

pout [paut] *vi* hacer pucheros

poverty ['pɒvətɪ] *n* pobreza, miseria

powder ['paudə'] *n* polvo; *(also:* **face ~)** polvos *mpl* ▷ *vt* empolvar; **to ~ one's face** empolvarse la cara; **powdered milk** *n* leche *f* en polvo

power ['pauə'] *n* poder *m*; *(strength)* fuerza; *(nation)* potencia; *(drive)* empuje *m*; *(Tech)* potencia; *(Elec)* energía ▷ *vt* impulsar; **to be in ~** *(Pol)* estar en el poder; **power cut** *n* (BRIT) apagón *m*; **power failure** *n* **power cut**; **powerful** *adj* poderoso; *(engine)* potente; *(play, speech)* convincente; **powerless** *adj* impotente; **power point** *n* (BRIT) enchufe *m*; **power station** *n* central f eléctrica

pp *abbr* (= *per procurationem; by proxy*) p.p.; = **pages**

PR *n abbr* (= *public relations*) relaciones *fpl* públicas

practical ['præktɪkl] *adj* práctico; **practical joke** *n* broma pesada; **practically** *adv* (*almost*) casi, prácticamente

practice ['præktɪs] *n* (*habit*) costumbre f; (*exercise*) práctica; (*training*) adiestramiento; (*Med: of profession*) práctica, ejercicio; (*Med, Law: business*) consulta ▷ *vt, vi* (US) = **practise**; **in ~** (*in reality*) en la práctica; **out of ~** desentrenado

practise, (US) **practice** ['præktɪs] *vt* (*carry out*) practicar; (*profession*) ejercer; (*train at*) practicar ▷ *vi* ejercer; (*train*) practicar; **practising**, (US) **practicing** *adj* (*Christian etc*) practicante; (*lawyer*) en ejercicio

practitioner [præk'tɪʃənə'] *n* (*Med*) médico/a

pragmatic [præg'mætɪk] *adj* pragmático

prairie ['prɛərɪ] *n* pampa

praise [preɪz] *n* alabanza(s) *f(pl)*, elogio(s) *m(pl)* ▷ *vt* alabar, elogiar

pram [præm] *n* (BRIT) cochecito de niño

prank [præŋk] *n* travesura

prawn [prɔːn] *n* gamba; **prawn cocktail** *n* cóctel *m* de gambas

pray [preɪ] *vi* rezar; **prayer** [prɛə'] *n* oración f, rezo; (*entreaty*) ruego, súplica

preach [priːtʃ] *vi* predicar; **preacher** *n* predicador(a) *m/f*

precarious [prɪ'kɛərɪəs] *adj* precario

precaution [prɪ'kɔːʃən] *n* precaución f

precede [prɪ'siːd] *vt, vi* preceder; **precedent** ['presɪdənt] *n* precedente *m*; **preceding** [prɪ'siːdɪŋ] *adj* precedente

precinct ['priːsɪŋkt] *n* recinto

precious ['preʃəs] *adj* precioso

precise [prɪ'saɪs] *adj* preciso, exacto; **precisely** *adv* exactamente, precisamente

precision [prɪ'sɪʒən] *n* precisión f

predator ['predətə'] *n* depredador *m*

predecessor ['priːdɪsesə'] *n* antecesor(a) *m/f*

predicament [prɪ'dɪkəmənt] *n* apuro

predict [prɪ'dɪkt] *vt* pronosticar; **predictable** *adj* previsible; **prediction** [prɪ'dɪkʃən] *n* predicción f

predominantly [prɪ'dɒmɪnəntlɪ] *adv* en su mayoría

preface ['prefəs] *n* prefacio

prefect ['priːfekt] *n* (BRIT: *in school*) monitor(a) *m/f*

prefer [prɪ'fəː'] *vt* preferir; **to ~ coffee to tea** preferir el café al té; **preferable** ['prefrəbl] *adj* preferible; **preferably** ['prefrəbli] *adv* preferentemente, más bien; **preference** ['prefrəns] *n* preferencia; (*priority*) prioridad f

prefix ['priːfɪks] *n* prefijo

pregnancy ['pregnənsɪ] *n* (*of woman*) embarazo; (*of animal*) preñez f

pregnant ['pregnənt] *adj* (*woman*) embarazada; (*animal*) preñada

prehistoric ['priːhɪs'tɔrɪk] *adj* prehistórico

prejudice ['predʒudɪs] *n* prejuicio; **prejudiced** *adj* (*person*) predispuesto

preliminary [prɪˈlɪmɪnərɪ] *adj* preliminar

prelude [ˈprɛljuːd] *n* preludio

premature [ˈprɛmətʃuər] *adj* prematuro

premier [ˈprɛmɪər] *adj* primero, principal ▷ *n* (Pol) primer(a) ministro/a

première [ˈprɛmɪɛər] *n* estreno

Premier League [prɛmɪəˈliːg] *n* primera división

premises [ˈprɛmɪsɪz] *npl* local *msg*; **on the ~** en el lugar mismo

premium [ˈpriːmɪəm] *n* premio; (insurance) prima; **to be at a ~** estar muy solicitado

premonition [prɛməˈnɪʃən] *n* presentimiento

preoccupied [priːˈɒkjupaɪd] *adj* ensimismado

prepaid [priːˈpeɪd] *adj* porte pagado

preparation [prɛpəˈreɪʃən] *n* preparación *f*; **preparations** *npl* preparativos *mpl*

preparatory school *n* (BRIT) colegio privado de enseñanza primaria; (US) colegio privado de enseñanza secundaria

prepare [prɪˈpɛər] *vt* preparar, disponer; (Culin) preparar ▷ *vi*: **to ~ for** (action) prepararse or disponerse para; (event) hacer preparativos para; **prepared adj** (willing): **to be prepared to help sb** estar dispuesto a ayudar a algn; **prepared for** listo para

preposition [prɛpəˈzɪʃən] *n* preposición *f*

prep school [prɛp-] *n* = **preparatory school**

prerequisite [priːˈrɛkwɪzɪt] *n* requisito previo

preschool [ˈpriːskuːl] *adj* preescolar

prescribe [prɪˈskraɪb] *vt* (Med) recetar

prescription [prɪˈskrɪpʃən] *n* (Med) receta

presence [ˈprɛzns] *n* presencia; **in sb's ~** en presencia de algn; **~ of mind** aplomo

present *adj* [ˈprɛznt] (in attendance) presente; (current) actual ▷ *n* [ˈprɛznt]

(gift) regalo; (actuality): **the ~** la actualidad, el presente ▷ *vt* [prɪˈzɛnt] (introduce) presentar; (expound) exponer; (give) presentar, dar, ofrecer; (Theat) representar; **to give sb a ~** regalar algo a algn; **at ~** actualmente; **presentable** [prɪˈzɛntəbl] *adj*: **to make o.s. presentable** arreglarse; **presentation** [prɛznˈteɪʃən] *n* presentación *f*; (of case) exposición *f*; **present-day** *adj* actual; **presenter** [prɪˈzɛntər] *n* (Radio, TV) locutor(a) *m/f*; **presently** *adv* (soon) dentro de poco; (now) ahora; **present participle** *n* participio (de) presente

preservation [prɛzəˈveɪʃən] *n* conservación *f*

preservative [prɪˈzəːvətɪv] *n* conservante *m*

preserve [prɪˈzəːv] *vt* (keep safe) preservar, proteger; (maintain) mantener; (food) conservar ▷ *n* (for game) coto, vedado; (often pl: jam) confitura

preside [prɪˈzaɪd] *vi* presidir

president [ˈprɛzɪdənt] *n* presidente *mf*; (US: of company) director(a) *m/f*; **presidential** [prɛzɪˈdɛnʃl] *adj* presidencial

press [prɛs] *n* (tool, machine, newspapers) prensa; (printer's) imprenta; (of hand) apretón *m* ▷ *vt* (push) empujar; (squeeze: button) apretar; (iron: clothes) planchar; (pressure) presionar; (insist): **to ~ sth on sb** insistir en que algn acepte algo ▷ *vi* (squeeze) apretar; **we are ~ed for time** tenemos poco tiempo; **to ~ sb to do or into doing sth** (urge, entreat) presionar a algn para que haga algo; **press conference** *n* rueda de prensa; **pressing** *adj* apremiante; **press stud** *n* (BRIT) botón *m* de presión; **press-up** *n* (BRIT) flexión *f*

pressure [ˈprɛʃər] *n* presión *f*; **to put ~ on sb** presionar a algn; **pressure cooker** *n* olla a presión; **pressure group** *n* grupo de presión

prestige [presˈtiːʒ] n prestigio

prestigious [presˈtɪdʒəs] adj prestigioso

presumably [prɪˈzjuːməblɪ] adv es de suponer que, cabe presumir que

presume [prɪˈzjuːm] vt: **to ~ (that)** presumir (que), suponer (que)

pretence, (us) **pretense** [prɪˈtens] n fingimiento; **under false ~s** con engaños

pretend [prɪˈtend] vt, vi fingir
▌ Be careful not to translate pretend by the Spanish word pretender.

pretense [prɪˈtens] n (us) = **pretence**

pretentious [prɪˈtenʃəs] adj pretencioso; (ostentatious) ostentoso, aparatoso

pretext [ˈpriːtekst] n pretexto

pretty [ˈprɪtɪ] adj bonito, lindo (LAM)
▷ adv bastante

prevail [prɪˈveɪl] vi (gain mastery) prevalecer; (be current) predominar; **prevailing** adj (dominant) predominante

prevalent [ˈprevələnt] adj (widespread) extendido

prevent [prɪˈvent] vt: **to ~ (sb) from doing sth** impedir (a algn) hacer algo; **to ~ sth from happening** evitar que ocurra algo; **prevention** [prɪˈvenʃən] n prevención f; **preventive** adj preventivo

preview [ˈpriːvjuː] n (of film) preestreno

previous [ˈpriːvɪəs] adj previo, anterior; **previously** adv antes

prey [preɪ] n presa f ▷ vi: **to ~ on** (feed on) alimentarse de; **it was ~ing on his mind** le obsesionaba

price [praɪs] n precio ▷ vt (goods) fijar el precio de; **priceless** adj que no tiene precio; **price list** n tarifa

prick [prɪk] n (sting) picadura ▷ vt pinchar; (hurt) picar; **to ~ up one's ears** aguzar el oído

prickly [ˈprɪklɪ] adj espinoso; (fig: person) enojadizo

pride [praɪd] n orgullo; (pej) soberbia
▷ vt: **to ~ o.s. on** enorgullecerse de

priest [priːst] n sacerdote m

primarily [ˈpraɪmərɪlɪ] adv ante todo

primary [ˈpraɪmərɪ] adj (first in importance) principal ▷ n (us: also: **~ election**) (elección f) primaria; **primary school** n (BRIT) escuela primaria

prime [praɪm] adj primero, principal; (excellent) selecto, de primera clase ▷ n: **in the ~ of life** en la flor de la vida ▷ vt (wood, also fig) preparar; **~ example** ejemplo típico; **Prime Minister** n primer(a) ministro/a; ver nota **"Downing Street"**

primitive [ˈprɪmɪtɪv] adj primitivo; (crude) rudimentario

primrose [ˈprɪmrəuz] n primavera, prímula

prince [prɪns] n príncipe m

princess [prɪnˈses] n princesa

principal [ˈprɪnsɪpl] adj principal ▷ n director(a) m/f; **principally** adv principalmente

principle [ˈprɪnsɪpl] n principio; **in ~** en principio; **on ~** por principio

print [prɪnt] n (impression) marca, impresión f; (footprint) huella; (fingerprint) huella dactilar; (letters) letra de molde; (fabric) estampado; (Art) grabado; (Phot) impresión f ▷ vt imprimir; (write in capitals) escribir en letras de molde; **out of ~** agotado; **print out** n (Comput) imprimir; **printer** n (person) impresor(a) m/f; (machine) impresora; **printout** n (Comput) copia impresa

prior [ˈpraɪər] adj anterior, previo; (more important) más importante; **~ to doing** antes de o hasta hacer

priority [praɪˈɔrɪtɪ] n prioridad f; **to have** o **take ~ over sth** tener prioridad sobre algo

prison [ˈprɪzn] n cárcel f, prisión f ▷ cpd carcelario; **prisoner** n (in prison) preso/a; (captured person) prisionero/a

pristine [ˈprɪstiːn] adj prístino

privacy ['prɪvəsɪ] n intimidad f
private ['praɪvɪt] adj (personal)
particular; (property, industry, discussion
etc) privado; (person) reservado; (place)
tranquilo ▷ n soldado raso; "~" (on
envelope) "confidencial"; (on door)
"privado"; **in ~** en privado; **privately**
adv en privado; (in o.s.) en secreto;
private property n propiedad f
privada; **private school** n colegio
privado
privatize ['praɪvətaɪz] vt privatizar
privilege ['prɪvɪlɪdʒ] n privilegio;
(prerogative) prerrogativa
prize [praɪz] n premio ▷ adj de primera
clase ▷ vt apreciar, estimar; **prize-
giving** n distribución f de premios;
prizewinner n premiado/a
pro [prəʊ] n (Sport) profesional mf; **the
~s and cons** los pros y los contras
probability [prɔbə'bɪlɪtɪ] n
probabilidad f; **in all ~** lo más probable
probable ['prɔbəbl] adj probable
probably ['prɔbəblɪ] adv
probablemente
probation [prə'beɪʃən] n: **on ~**
(employee) a prueba; (Law) en libertad
condicional
probe [prəʊb] n (Med, Space) sonda;
(enquiry) investigación f ▷ vt sondar;
(investigate) investigar
problem ['prɔbləm] n problema m
procedure [prə'si:dʒər] n
procedimiento; (bureaucratic)
trámites mpl
proceed [prə'si:d] vi proceder;
(continue) **to ~ (with)** continuar (con);
proceedings npl acto(s) m(pl); (Law)
proceso sg; **proceeds** ['prəʊsi:dz] npl
ganancias fpl, ingresos mpl
process ['prəʊses] n proceso ▷ vt
tratar, elaborar
procession [prə'seʃən] n desfile m;
funeral ~ cortejo fúnebre
proclaim [prə'kleɪm] vt (announce)
anunciar
prod [prɔd] vt empujar ▷ n
empujoncito; codazo

produce n ['prɔdju:s] (Agr) productos
mpl agrícolas ▷ vt [prə'dju:s] producir;
(Theat) presentar; **producer** n
(Theat) director(a) m/f; (Agr, Cine)
productor(a) m/f
product ['prɔdʌkt] n producto;
production [prə'dʌkʃən] n (act)
producción f; (Theat) representación
f; **productive** [prə'dʌktɪv] adj
productivo; **productivity**
[prɔdʌk'tɪvɪtɪ] n productividad f
Prof. [prɔf] abbr (= professor) Prof
profession [prə'feʃən] n profesión f;
professional n profesional mf; (skilled
person) perito
professor [prə'fesər] n (BRIT)
catedrático/a; (us: teacher) profesor(a)
m/f
profile ['prəʊfaɪl] n perfil m
profit ['prɔfɪt] n (Comm) ganancia ▷ vi:
to ~ by or **from** aprovechar or sacar
provecho de; **profitable** adj (Econ)
rentable
profound [prə'faʊnd] adj profundo
programme (us or Comput)
program ['prəʊgræm] n programa
m ▷ vt programar; **programmer**,
(us) **programer** ['prəʊgræmər] n
programador(a) m/f; **programming**,
(us) **programing** ['prəʊgræmɪŋ] n
programación f
progress n ['prəʊgres] progreso;
(development) desarrollo ▷ vi [prə'gres]
progresar, avanzar; **in ~** en curso;
progressive [prə'gresɪv] adj
progresivo; (person) progresista
prohibit [prə'hɪbɪt] vt prohibir; **to
~ sb from doing sth** prohibir a algn
hacer algo
project n ['prɔdʒekt] proyecto ▷ vt
[prə'dʒekt] proyectar ▷ vi (stick
out) salir, sobresalir; **projection**
[prə'dʒekʃən] n proyección f;
(overhang) saliente m; **projector**
[prə'dʒektər] n proyector m
prolific [prə'lɪfɪk] adj prolífico
prolong [prə'lɔŋ] vt prolongar,
extender

... h abbr (BRIT)
...e; = promenade
...s: ball) baile m de gala; ver
...**"**

...conciertos de música clásica
...s conocidos en Inglaterra son
...s llamados Proms (o promenade
...oncerts), que tienen lugar en el
...Royal Albert Hall de Londres, aunque
... también se llama así a cualquier
... concierto de esas características.
... Su nombre se debe al hecho de que
... en un principio el público paseaba
... durante las actuaciones; en la
... actualidad parte de la gente que
... acude a ellos permanece de pie.
... En Estados Unidos se llama prom
... a un baile de gala en un colegio o
... universidad.

promenade [prɔməˈnɑːd] n (by sea) paseo marítimo
prominent [ˈprɔminənt] adj (standing out) saliente; (important) eminente, importante
promiscuous [prəˈmɪskjuəs] adj (sexually) promiscuo
promise [ˈprɔmɪs] n promesa ▷ vt, vi prometer; **promising** adj prometedor(a)
promote [prəˈməut] vt (Mil) ascender; (employee) ascender; (ideas) fomentar; **promotion** [prəˈməuʃən] n promoción f; (Mil) ascenso
prompt [prɔmpt] adj pronto ▷ adv: **at six o'clock** = a las seis en punto ▷ n (Comput) aviso, guía ▷ vt (urge) mover, incitar; (when talking) instar; (Theat) apuntar; **to ~ sb to do sth** instar a algn a hacer algo; **promptly** adv (punctually) puntualmente; (rapidly) rápidamente
prone [prəun] adj (lying) postrado; **~ to** propenso a
prong [prɔŋ] n diente m, punta

pronoun [ˈprəunaun] n pronombre m
pronounce [prəˈnauns] vt pronunciar
pronunciation [prənʌnsɪˈeɪʃən] n pronunciación f
proof [pruːf] n prueba f ▷ adj: **~ against** a prueba de
prop [prɔp] n apoyo; (fig) sostén m; **props** npl accesorios mpl, at(t)rezzo msg; **prop up** vt (roof, structure) apuntalar; (economy) respaldar
propaganda [prɔpəˈgændə] n propaganda
propeller [prəˈpelə] n hélice f
proper [ˈprɔpə] adj (suited, right) propio; (exact) justo; (seemly) correcto, decente; (authentic) verdadero; **properly** adv (adequately) correctamente; (decently) decentemente; **proper noun** n nombre m propio
property [ˈprɔpətɪ] n propiedad f; **personal ~** bienes mpl muebles
prophecy [ˈprɔfɪsɪ] n profecía
prophet [ˈprɔfɪt] n profeta mf
proportion [prəˈpɔːʃən] n proporción f; (share) parte f; **proportions** npl (size) dimensiones fpl; **proportional** adj: **proportional (to)** en proporción (con)
proposal [prəˈpəuzl] n (offer of marriage) oferta de matrimonio; (plan) proyecto
propose [prəˈpəuz] vt proponer ▷ vi declararse; **to ~ to do** tener intención de hacer
proposition [prɔpəˈzɪʃən] n propuesta
proprietor [prəˈpraɪətə] n propietario/a, dueño/a
prose [prəuz] n prosa
prosecute [ˈprɔsɪkjuːt] vt (Law) procesar; **prosecution** [prɔsɪˈkjuːʃən] n proceso, causa; (accusing side) acusación f; **prosecutor** n acusador(a) m/f; (also: **public prosecutor**) fiscal mf

prospect n ['prɒspɛkt] (chance) posibilidad f; (outlook) perspectiva ▷ vi [prə'spɛkt] buscar; **prospects** npl (for work etc) perspectivas fpl; **prospective** [prə'spɛktɪv] adj futuro

prospectus [prə'spɛktəs] n prospecto

prosper ['prɒspə] vi prosperar; **prosperity** [prɒ'spɛrɪtɪ] n prosperidad f; **prosperous** adj próspero

prostitute ['prɒstɪtjuːt] n prostituta; **male ~** prostituto

protect [prə'tɛkt] vt proteger; **protection** [prə'tɛkʃən] n protección f; **protective** adj protector(a)

protein ['prəʊtiːn] n proteína

protest n ['prəʊtɛst] protesta ▷ vi [prə'tɛst]: **to ~ about** or **at/against** protestar de/contra ▷ vt (insist): **to ~ (that)** insistir en (que)

Protestant ['prɒtɪstənt] adj, n protestante mf

protester, protestor n manifestante mf

protractor [prə'træktə] n (Geom) transportador m

proud [praud] adj orgulloso; (pej) soberbio, altanero

prove [pruːv] vt probar; (show) demostrar ▷ vi: **to ~ correct** resultar correcto; **to ~ o.s.** ponerse a prueba

proverb ['prɒvɜːb] n refrán m

provide [prə'vaɪd] vt proporcionar, dar; **to ~ sb with sth** proveer a algn de algo; **provide for** vt fus (person) mantener a; (problem etc) tener en cuenta; **provided (that)** conj a condición de que; **providing** [prə'vaɪdɪŋ] conj: **providing (that)** a condición de que, con tal de que

province ['prɒvɪns] n provincia; (fig) esfera; **provincial** [prə'vɪnʃəl] adj provincial; (pej) provinciano

provision [prə'vɪʒən] n (supply) suministro, abastecimiento;

provisions npl provisiones fpl, víveres mpl; **provisional** adj provisional

provocative [prə'vɒkətɪv] adj provocativo

provoke [prə'vəuk] vt (arouse) provocar, incitar; (anger) enojar

prowl [praul] vi (also: **~ about, ~ around**) merodear ▷ n: **on the ~** de merodeo

proximity [prɒk'sɪmɪtɪ] n proximidad f

proxy ['prɒksɪ] n: **by ~** por poderes

prudent ['pruːdnt] adj prudente

prune [pruːn] n ciruela pasa ▷ vt podar

pry [praɪ] vi: **to ~ into** entrometerse en

PS abbr (= postscript) P.D.

pseudonym ['sjuːdənɪm] n seudónimo

PSHE n abbr (BRIT Scol: = personal, social, and health education) formación social y sanitaria para la vida adulta

psychiatric [saɪkɪ'ætrɪk] adj psiquiátrico

psychiatrist [saɪ'kaɪətrɪst] n psiquiatra mf

psychic ['saɪkɪk] adj (also: **~al**) psíquico

psychoanalysis (pl **psychoanalyses**) [saɪkəuə'næləsɪs, -siːz] n psicoanálisis m inv

psychological [saɪkə'lɒdʒɪkl] adj psicológico

psychologist [saɪ'kɒlədʒɪst] n psicólogo/a

psychology [saɪ'kɒlədʒɪ] n psicología

psychotherapy [saɪkəu'θɛrəpɪ] n psicoterapia

pt abbr = **pint; point**

PTO abbr (= please turn over) sigue

pub [pʌb] n abbr (= public house) pub m, bar m

puberty ['pjuːbətɪ] n pubertad f

public ['pʌblɪk] adj público ▷ n: **the ~** el público; **in ~** en público; **to make sth ~** revelar or hacer público algo

publication [pʌblɪˈkeɪʃən] n
publicación f

public: **public company** n sociedad
f anónima; **public convenience** n
(BRIT) aseos mpl públicos, sanitarios
mpl (LAM); **public holiday** n día m
de fiesta, (día) feriado (LAM); **public
house** n (BRIT) pub m, bar m

publicity [pʌbˈlɪsɪtɪ] n publicidad f
publicize [ˈpʌblɪsaɪz] vt publicitar
public: **public limited company** n
sociedad f anónima (S.A.); **publicly**
adv públicamente, en público;
public opinion n opinión f pública;
public relations fpl relaciones fpl
públicas; **public school** n (BRIT)
colegio privado; (US) instituto; **public
transport** n transporte m público

publish [ˈpʌblɪʃ] vt publicar;
publisher n (person) editor(a) m/f;
(firm) editorial f; **publishing** n
(industry) industria del libro

pub lunch n almuerzo que se sirve en un
pub; **to go for a ~** almorzar o comer
en un pub

pudding [ˈpʊdɪŋ] n pudín m; (BRIT:
sweet) postre m; **black ~** morcilla
puddle [ˈpʌdl] n charco
Puerto Rico [-ˈriːkəʊ] n Puerto Rico
puff [pʌf] n soplo; (of smoke) bocanada;
(of breathing, engine) resoplido ▷ vt:
to ~ one's pipe dar chupadas a la
pipa ▷ vi (pant) jadear; **puff pastry** n
hojaldre m

pull [pʊl] n ▷ vt tirar de; (haul) tirar,
arrastrar ▷ vi tirar, jalar (LAM); **to
give sth a ~** (tug) dar un tirón a algo;
to ~ to pieces hacer pedazos; **to ~
one's punches** andarse con bromas;
to ~ one's weight hacer su parte;
to ~ o.s. together tranquilizarse,
sobreponerse; **to ~ sb's leg** tomar
el pelo a algn; **pull apart** vt (break)
romper; **pull away** vi (vehicle: move off)
salir, arrancar; (draw back) apartarse
bruscamente; **pull back** vt (lever etc)
tirar hacia sí; (curtains) descorrer ▷ vi
(refrain) contenerse; (Mil: withdraw)

retirarse; **pull down** vt (house)
derribar; **pull in** vi (Aut: at the kerb)
parar (junto a la acera); (Rail) llegar;
pull off vt (deal etc) cerrar; **pull out** vi
(car, train etc) salir ▷ vt sacar, arrancar;
pull over vi (Aut) hacerse a un lado;
pull up vi (stop) parar ▷ vt (uproot)
arrancar, desarraigar
pulley [ˈpʊlɪ] n polea
pullover [ˈpʊləʊvəʳ] n jersey m,
suéter m
pulp [pʌlp] n (of fruit) pulpa
pulpit [ˈpʊlpɪt] n púlpito
pulse [pʌls] n (Anat) pulso; (of music,
engine) pulsación f; (Bot) legumbre f;
pulses npl legumbres
puma [ˈpjuːmə] n puma m
pump [pʌmp] n bomba; (shoe)
zapatilla de tenis ▷ vt sacar con una
bomba; **pump up** vt inflar
pumpkin [ˈpʌmpkɪn] n calabaza
pun [pʌn] n juego de palabras
punch [pʌntʃ] n (blow) golpe m,
puñetazo; (tool) punzón m; (drink)
ponche m ▷ vt: **to ~ sb/sth** (hit) dar
un puñetazo or golpear a algn/algo;
punch-up n (BRIT inf) riña
punctual [ˈpʌŋktjʊəl] adj puntual
punctuation [pʌŋktjuˈeɪʃən] n
puntuación f
puncture [ˈpʌŋktʃəʳ] (BRIT) n
pinchazo ▷ vt pinchar
punish [ˈpʌnɪʃ] vt castigar;
punishment n castigo
punk [pʌŋk] n (also: **~ rocker**) punki
mf; (also: **~ rock**) música punk; (US inf:
hoodlum) matón m
pup [pʌp] n cachorro
pupil [ˈpjuːpl] n alumno/a; (of eye)
pupila
puppet [ˈpʌpɪt] n títere m
puppy [ˈpʌpɪ] n cachorro, perrito
purchase [ˈpɜːtʃɪs] n compra ▷ vt
comprar
pure [pjʊəʳ] adj puro; **purely** adv
puramente
purify [ˈpjʊərɪfaɪ] vt purificar, depurar
purity [ˈpjʊərɪtɪ] n pureza

purple ['pə:pl] *adj* morado

purpose ['pə:pəs] *n* propósito; **on ~a** propósito, adrede

purr [pə:ʴ] *vi* ronronear

purse [pə:s] *n* monedero; (*US: handbag*) bolso, cartera (LAM) ▷ *vt* fruncir

pursue [pə'sju:] *vt* seguir

pursuit [pə'sju:t] *n* (*chase*) caza; (*occupation*) actividad *f*

pus [pʌs] *n* pus *m*

push [puʃ] *n* empujón *m*; (*drive*) empuje *m* ▷ *vt* empujar; (*button*) apretar; (*promote*) promover ▷ *vi* empujar; **to ~ for** (*better pay, conditions*) reivindicar; **push in** *vi* colarse; **push off** *vi* (*inf*) largarse; **push on** *vi* seguir adelante; **push over** *vt* (*cause to fall*) hacer caer, derribar; (*knock over*) volcar; **push through** *vi* (*crowd*) abrirse paso a empujones ▷ *vt* (*measure*) despachar; **pushchair** *n* (BRIT) silla de niño; **pusher** *n* (*also*: **drug pusher**) traficante *mf* de drogas; **push-up** *n* (US) flexión *f*

puss [pus], **pussy(-cat)** ['pusi-] *n* minino

put (*pt, pp* **put**) [put] *vt* (*place*) poner, colocar; (*put into*) meter; (*express, say*) expresar; (*a question*) hacer; (*estimate*) calcular; **put aside** *vt* (*lay down: book etc*) dejar o poner a un lado; (*save*) ahorrar; (*in shop*) guardar; **put away** *vt* (*store*) guardar; **put back** *vt* (*replace*) devolver a su lugar; (*postpone*) aplazar; **put by** *vt* (*money*) guardar; **put down** *vt* (*on ground*) poner en el suelo; (*animal*) sacrificar; (*in writing*) apuntar; (*revolt etc*) sofocar; (*attribute*) atribuir; **put forward** *vt* (*ideas*) presentar, proponer; **put in** *vt* (*application, complaint*) presentar; (*time*) dedicar; **put off** *vt* (*postpone*) aplazar; (*discourage*) desanimar; **put on** *vt* ponerse; (*light etc*) encender; (*play etc*) presentar; (*brake*) echar; (*record, kettle etc*) poner; (*assume*) adoptar; **put out** *vt* (*fire, light*) apagar; (*rubbish etc*) sacar; (*cat etc*) echar; (*one's hand*) alargar; **put through** *vt* (*call*) poner; (*plan etc*) hacer aprobar; **put together** *vt* unir, reunir; (*assemble: furniture etc*) armar, montar; (*meal*) preparar; **put up** *vt* (*raise*) levantar, alzar; (*hang*) colgar; (*build*) construir; (*increase*) aumentar; (*accommodate*) alojar; **put up with** *vt fus* aguantar

putt [pʌt] *n* putt *m*; **putting green** *n* green *m*, minigolf *m*

puzzle ['pʌzl] *n* rompecabezas *m inv*; (*also*: **crossword ~**) crucigrama *m*; (*mystery*) misterio ▷ *vt* dejar perplejo, confundir ▷ *vi*: **to ~ over** devanarse los sesos sobre; **puzzling** *adj* misterioso, extraño

pyjamas, (US) **pajamas** [pɪ'dʒɑ:məz] *npl* pijama *msg*

pylon ['paɪlən] *n* torre *f* de conducción eléctrica

pyramid ['pɪrəmɪd] *n* pirámide *f*

p

q

quack [kwæk] n graznido; (*pej: doctor*) curandero/a
quadruple [kwɒˈdruːpl] vt, vi cuadruplicar
quail [kweɪl] n codorniz f ▷ vi amedrentarse
quaint [kweɪnt] adj extraño; (*picturesque*) pintoresco
quake [kweɪk] vi temblar ▷ n abbr = **earthquake**
qualification [kwɒlɪfɪˈkeɪʃən] n (*ability*) capacidad f; (*often pl: diploma etc*) título; (*reservation*) salvedad f
qualified [ˈkwɒlɪfaɪd] adj capacitado; (*limited*) limitado; (*professionally*) titulado
qualify [ˈkwɒlɪfaɪ] vt (*capacitate*) capacitar; (*modify*) matizar ▷ vi: **to ~ (for)** (*in competition*) calificarse (para); (*be eligible*) reunir los requisitos (para); **to ~ (as)** (*pass examination*) calificarse (de), graduarse (en)

quality [ˈkwɒlɪtɪ] n calidad f; (*moral*) cualidad f
qualm [kwɑːm] n escrúpulo
quantify [ˈkwɒntɪfaɪ] vt cuantificar
quantity [ˈkwɒntɪtɪ] n cantidad f; **in ~** en grandes cantidades
quarantine [ˈkwɒrntiːn] n cuarentena
quarrel [ˈkwɒrl] n riña, pelea ▷ vi reñir, pelearse
quarry [ˈkwɒrɪ] n cantera
quart [kwɔːt] n cuarto de galón = 1.136 l
quarter [ˈkwɔːtər] n cuarto, cuarta parte f; (*us: coin*) moneda de 25 centavos; (*of year*) trimestre m; (*district*) barrio ▷ vt dividir en cuartos; (*Mil: lodge*) alojar; **quarters** npl (*barracks*) cuartel msg; (*living quarters*) alojamiento sg; **a ~ of an hour** un cuarto de hora; **quarter final** n cuarto de final; **quarterly** adj trimestral ▷ adv cada 3 meses, trimestralmente
quartet(te) [kwɔːˈtet] n cuarteto
quartz [kwɔːts] n cuarzo
quay [kiː] n (*also:* **~side**) muelle m
queasy [ˈkwiːzɪ] adj: **to feel ~** tener náuseas
queen [kwiːn] n reina; (*Cards etc*) dama
queer [kwɪər] adj raro, extraño ▷ n (*pej, infl*) marica (!) m
quench [kwentʃ] vt: **to ~ one's thirst** apagar la sed
query [ˈkwɪərɪ] n (*question*) pregunta ▷ vt dudar de
quest [kwest] n busca, búsqueda
question [ˈkwestʃən] n pregunta; (*matter*) asunto, cuestión f ▷ vt (*doubt*) dudar de; (*interrogate*) interrogar, hacer preguntas a; **beyond ~** fuera de toda duda; **out of the ~** imposible, ni hablar; **questionable** adj dudoso; **question mark** n signo de interrogación; **questionnaire** [kwestʃəˈnɛər] n cuestionario
queue [kjuː] (*BRIT*) n cola ▷ vi hacer cola
quiche [kiːʃ] n quiche m

quick [kwɪk] *adj* rápido; (*agile*) ágil; (*mind*) listo ▷ *n*: **cut to the ~** (*fig*) herido en lo más vivo; **be ~!** ¡date prisa!; **quickly** *adv* rápidamente, de prisa

quid [kwɪd] *n* (*pl inv*: BRIT *inf*) libra

quiet [ˈkwaɪət] *adj* (*voice, music etc*) bajo; (*person, place*) tranquilo ▷ *n* silencio; (*calm*) tranquilidad *f*; **quietly** *adv* tranquilamente; (*silently*) silenciosamente

⬛ Be careful not to translate *quiet* by the Spanish word *quieto*.

quilt [kwɪlt] *n* edredón *m*

quirky [ˈkwɜːkɪ] *adj* raro, estrafalario

quit [kwɪt] (*pt, pp* **quit** *or* **quitted**) *vt* dejar, abandonar; (*premises*) desocupar ▷ *vi* (*give up*) renunciar; (*resign*) dimitir

quite [kwaɪt] *adv* (*rather*) bastante; (*entirely*) completamente; **~ a few of them** un buen número de ellos; **~ (so)!** ¡así es!, ¡exactamente!; **that's not ~ right** eso no está del todo bien

quits [kwɪts] *adj*: **~ (with)** en paz (con); **let's call it ~** quedamos en paz

quiver [ˈkwɪvəʳ] *vi* estremecerse

quiz [kwɪz] *n* concurso

quota [ˈkwəʊtə] *n* cuota

quotation [kwəʊˈteɪʃən] *n* cita; (*estimate*) presupuesto; **quotation marks** *npl* comillas *fpl*

quote [kwəʊt] *n* cita ▷ *vt* (*sentence*) citar; (*Comm: sum, figure*) cotizar ▷ *vi*: **to ~ from** citar de; **quotes** *npl* (*inverted commas*) comillas *fpl*

r

rabbi [ˈræbaɪ] *n* rabino

rabbit [ˈræbɪt] *n* conejo

rabies [ˈreɪbiːz] *n* rabia

RAC *n abbr* (BRIT: = *Royal Automobile Club*) ≈ RACE *m* (SP)

raccoon [rəˈkuːn] *n* mapache *m*

race [reɪs] *n* carrera; (*species*) raza ▷ *vt* (*horse*) hacer correr; (*engine*) acelerar ▷ *vi* (*compete*) competir; (*run*) correr; (*pulse*) latir a ritmo acelerado; **race car** *n* (US) = **racing car**; **racecourse** *n* hipódromo; **racehorse** *n* caballo de carreras; **racetrack** *n* hipódromo; (*for cars*) circuito de carreras

racial [ˈreɪʃl] *adj* racial

racing [ˈreɪsɪŋ] *n* carreras *fpl*; **racing car** *n* (BRIT) coche *m* de carreras; **racing driver** *n* (BRIT) piloto *mf* de carreras

racism [ˈreɪsɪzəm] *n* racismo

racist [ˈreɪsɪst] *adj, n* racista *mf*

rack [ræk] *n* (*also*: **luggage ~**) rejilla (portaequipajes); (*shelf*) estante *m*;

(also: **roof ~**) baca; (also: **clothes ~**) perchero ▷ vt atormentar; **to ~ one's brains** devanarse los sesos

racket ['rækɪt] n (for tennis) raqueta; (inf: noise) ruido, estrépito; (: swindle) estafa, timo

racquet ['rækɪt] n raqueta

radar ['reɪdɑ:ᵊ] n radar m

radiation [reɪdɪ'eɪʃən] n radiación f

radiator ['reɪdɪeɪtəᵊ] n radiador m

radical ['rædɪkl] adj radical

radio ['reɪdɪəu] n radio f; **on the ~** en or por la radio; **radioactive** adj radi(o)activo; **radio station** n emisora

radish ['rædɪʃ] n rábano

RAF n abbr (BRIT) = **Royal Air Force**

raffle ['ræfl] n rifa, sorteo

raft [rɑ:ft] n balsa; (also: **life ~**) balsa salvavidas

rag [ræg] n (piece of cloth) trapo; (torn cloth) harapo; (pej: newspaper) periodicucho; (for charity) actividades estudiantiles benéficas; **rags** npl harapos mpl

rage [reɪdʒ] n rabia, furor m ▷ vi (person) rabiar, estar furioso; (storm) bramar; **it's all the ~** es lo último; (very fashionable) está muy de moda

ragged ['rægɪd] adj (edge) desigual, mellado; (cuff) roto; (appearance) andrajoso, harapiento

raid [reɪd] n (Mil) incursión f; (criminal) asalto; (by police) redada ▷ vt invadir, atacar; asaltar

rail [reɪl] n (on stair) barandilla, pasamanos m inv; (on bridge) pretil m; (of balcony, ship) barandilla; **railcard** n (BRIT) tarjeta para obtener descuentos en el tren; **railing(s)** n(pl) verja sg; **railway**, (US) **railroad** n ferrocarril m, vía férrea; **railway line** n (BRIT) línea (de ferrocarril); **railway station** n (BRIT) estación f de ferrocarril

rain [reɪn] n lluvia ▷ vi llover; **in the ~** bajo la lluvia; **it's ~ing** llueve, está lloviendo; **rainbow** n arco iris; **raincoat** n impermeable m; **raindrop** n gota de lluvia; **rainfall** n lluvia;

rainforest n selva tropical; **rainy** adj lluvioso

raise [reɪz] n aumento ▷ vt levantar; (increase) aumentar; (improve: morale) subir; (: standards) mejorar; (doubts) suscitar; (a question) plantear; (cattle, family) criar; (crop) cultivar; (army) reclutar; (loan) obtener; **to ~ one's voice** alzar la voz

raisin ['reɪzn] n pasa de Corinto

rake [reɪk] n (tool) rastrillo; (person) libertino ▷ vt (garden) rastrillar

rally ['rælɪ] n reunión f; (Pol) mitin m; (Aut) rallye m; (Tennis) peloteo ▷ vt reunir ▷ vi recuperarse

RAM [ræm] n abbr (= random access memory) RAM f

ram [ræm] n carnero; (Tech) pisón m; (also: **battering ~**) ariete m ▷ vt (crash into) dar contra, chocar con; (push: fist etc) empujar con fuerza

Ramadan ['ræmædæn] n Ramadán m

ramble ['ræmbl] n caminata, excursión f en el campo ▷ vi (pej: also: **~ on**) divagar; **rambler** n excursionista mf; (Bot) trepadera; **rambling** adj (speech) inconexo; (Bot) trepador(a); (house) laberíntico

ramp [ræmp] n rampa; **on/off ~** n (US Aut) vía de acceso/salida

rampage [ræm'peɪdʒ] n: **to be on the ~** desmandarse ▷ vi: **they went rampaging through the town** recorrieron la ciudad armando alboroto

ran [ræn] pt of **run**

ranch [rɑ:ntʃ] n hacienda, estancia

random ['rændəm] adj fortuito, sin orden; (Comput, Math) aleatorio ▷ n: **at ~** al azar

rang [ræŋ] pt of **ring**

range [reɪndʒ] n (of mountains) cadena de montañas, cordillera; (of missile) alcance m; (of voice) registro; (series) serie f; (of products) surtido; (Mil: also: **shooting ~**) campo de tiro; (also: **kitchen ~**) fogón m ▷ vt (place) colocar; (arrange) arreglar ▷ vi: **to ~**

over (*extend*) extenderse por; **to ~ from ... to ...** oscilar entre ... y ...

ranger ['reɪndʒəʳ] n guardabosques m inv

rank [ræŋk] n (*row*) fila; (*Mil*) rango; (*status*) categoría; (BRIT: *also*: **taxi ~**) parada ▷ vi: **to ~ among** figurar entre ▷ adj fétido, rancio; **the ~ and file** (*fig*) las bases

ransom ['rænsəm] n rescate m; **to hold sb to ~** (*fig*) poner a algn entre la espada y la pared

rant [rænt] vi despotricar

rap [ræp] vt golpear, dar un golpecito en ▷ n (*music*) rap m

rape [reɪp] n violación f; (*Bot*) colza ▷ vt violar

rapid ['ræpɪd] adj rápido; **rapidly** adv rápidamente; **rapids** npl (*Geo*) rápidos mpl

rapist ['reɪpɪst] n violador m

rapport [ræ'pɔːʳ] n entendimiento

rare [rɛəʳ] adj raro, poco común; (*Culin*: *steak*) poco hecho; **rarely** adv pocas veces

rash [ræʃ] adj imprudente, precipitado ▷ n (*Med*) sarpullido, erupción f (cutánea)

rasher ['ræʃəʳ] n loncha

raspberry ['rɑːzbərɪ] n frambuesa

rat [ræt] n rata

rate [reɪt] n (*ratio*) razón f; (*price*) precio; (*of hotel*) tarifa; (*of interest*) tipo; (*speed*) velocidad f ▷ vt (*value*) tasar; (*estimate*) estimar; **rates** npl (BRIT) impuesto sg municipal; (*fees*) tarifa sg; **to ~ sb/sth highly** tener a algn/algo en alta estima

rather ['rɑːðəʳ] adv: **it's ~ expensive** es algo caro; (*too much*) es demasiado caro; **there's ~ a lot** hay bastante; **I would** *or* **I'd ~ go** preferiría ir; **or ~** o mejor dicho

rating ['reɪtɪŋ] n tasación f; **ratings** npl (*Radio*, TV) niveles mpl de audiencia

ratio ['reɪʃɪəu] n razón f; **in the ~ of 100 to 1** a razón de or en la proporción de 100 a 1

ration ['ræʃən] n ración f ▷ vt racionar; **rations** npl víveres mpl

rational ['ræʃənl] adj (*solution*, *reasoning*) lógico, razonable; (*person*) cuerdo, sensato

rattle ['rætl] n golpeteo; (*of train etc*) traqueteo; (*object*: *of baby*) sonaja, sonajero ▷ vi (*small objects*) castañetear; (*car*, *bus*): **to ~ along** traquetear ▷ vt hacer sonar agitando

rave [reɪv] vi (*in anger*) encolerizarse; (*with enthusiasm*) entusiasmarse; (*Med*) delirar, desvariar ▷ n (*inf*: *party*) rave m

raven ['reɪvən] n cuervo

ravine [rə'viːn] n barranco

raw [rɔː] adj crudo; (*not processed*) bruto; (*sore*) vivo; (*inexperienced*) novato, inexperto; **~ materials** materias primas

ray [reɪ] n rayo; **~ of hope** (rayo de) esperanza

razor ['reɪzəʳ] n (*open*) navaja; (*safety razor*) máquina de afeitar; (*electric razor*) máquina (eléctrica) de afeitar; **razor blade** n hoja de afeitar

Rd abbr = **road**

RE n abbr (BRIT: *Scol*) = **religious education**; (: *Mil*) = **Royal Engineers**

re [riː] prep con referencia a

reach [riːtʃ] n alcance m; (*of river etc*) extensión f entre dos recodos ▷ vt alcanzar, llegar a; (*achieve*) lograr ▷ vi extenderse; **within ~** al alcance (de la mano); **out of ~** fuera del alcance; **reach out** vt (*hand*) tender ▷ vi: **to ~ out for sth** alargar or tender la mano para tomar algo

react [riː'ækt] vi reaccionar; **reaction** [riː'ækʃən] n reacción f; **reactor** [riː'æktəʳ] n (*also*: **nuclear reactor**) reactor m (nuclear)

read (*pt*, *pp* **read**) [riːd, rɛd] vi leer ▷ vt leer; (*understand*) entender; (*study*) estudiar; **read out** vt leer en alta voz; **reader** n lector(a) m/f; (BRIT: *at university*) profesor(a) m/f

readily ['rɛdɪlɪ] *adv* (willingly) de buena gana; (easily) fácilmente; (quickly) en seguida

reading ['riːdɪŋ] *n* lectura; (on instrument) indicación *f*

ready ['rɛdɪ] *adj* listo, preparado; (willing) dispuesto; (available) disponible ▷ *adv*: **~-cooked** listo para comer ▷ *n*: **at the ~** (Mil) listo para tirar ▷ *vt* preparar; **to get ~** *vi* prepararse; **ready-made** *adj* confeccionado

real [rɪəl] *adj* verdadero, auténtico; **in ~ terms** en términos reales; **real ale** *n* cerveza elaborada tradicionalmente; **real estate** *n* bienes *mpl* raíces; **realistic** [rɪə'lɪstɪk] *adj* realista

reality [riː'ælɪti] *n* realidad *f*; **reality TV** *n* telerrealidad *f*

realization [rɪəlar'zeɪʃən] *n* comprensión *f*; (of a project) realización *f*; (Comm) realización *f*

realize ['rɪəlaɪz] *vt* (understand) darse cuenta de

really ['rɪəlɪ] *adv* realmente; (for emphasis) verdaderamente; **what happened** (actually) lo que pasó en realidad; **~?** ¿de veras?; **~!** (annoyance) ¡vamos!, ¡por favor!

realm [rɛlm] *n* reino; (fig) esfera

reappear [riːə'pɪəʳ] *vi* reaparecer

rear [rɪəʳ] *adj* trasero ▷ *n* parte *f* trasera ▷ *vt* (cattle, family) criar ▷ *vi* (also: **~ up**) (animal) encabritarse

rearrange [riːə'reɪndʒ] *vt* ordenar or arreglar de nuevo

rear: **rear-view mirror** *n* (Aut) espejo retrovisor; **rear-wheel drive** *n* tracción *f* trasera

reason ['riːzn] *n* razón *f* ▷ *vi*: **to ~ with sb** tratar de que algn entre en razón; **it stands to ~ that ...** es lógico que ...; **reasonable** *adj* razonable; (sensible) sensato; **reasonably** *adv* razonablemente; **reasoning** *n* razonamiento, argumentos *mpl*

reassurance [riːə'ʃuərəns] *n* consuelo

reassure [riːə'ʃuəʳ] *vt* tranquilizar; **to ~ sb that** tranquilizar a algn asegurándole que

rebate ['riːbeɪt] *n* (on tax etc) desgravación *f*

rebel *n* ['rɛbl] rebelde *mf* ▷ *vi* [rɪ'bɛl] rebelarse, sublevarse; **rebellion** *n* rebelión *f*, sublevación *f*; **rebellious** *adj* rebelde; (child) revoltoso

rebuild [riː'bɪld] *vt* reconstruir

recall [rɪ'kɔːl] *vt* (remember) recordar; (ambassador etc) retirar ▷ *n* recuerdo

recd., rec'd *abbr* (= received) recibido

receipt [rɪ'siːt] *n* (document) recibo; (act of receiving) recepción *f*; **receipts** *npl* (Comm) ingresos *mpl*

> Be careful not to translate *receipt* by the Spanish word *receta*.

receive [rɪ'siːv] *vt* recibir; (guest) acoger; (wound) sufrir; **receiver** *n* (Tel) auricular *m*; (Radio) receptor *m*; (of stolen goods) perista *mf*; (Law) administrador *m* jurídico

recent ['riːsnt] *adj* reciente; **recently** *adv* recientemente; **recently arrived** recién llegado

reception [rɪ'sɛpʃən] *n* recepción *f*; (welcome) acogida *f*; **reception desk** *n* recepción *f*; **receptionist** *n* recepcionista *mf*

recession [rɪ'sɛʃən] *n* recesión *f*

recharge [riː'tʃɑːdʒ] *vt* (battery) recargar

recipe ['rɛsɪpɪ] *n* receta; (for disaster, success) fórmula

recipient [rɪ'sɪpɪənt] *n* recibidor(a) *m/f*; (of letter) destinatario/a

recital [rɪ'saɪtl] *n* recital *m*

recite [rɪ'saɪt] *vt* (poem) recitar

reckless ['rɛkləs] *adj* temerario, imprudente; (speed) peligroso

reckon ['rɛkən] *vt* calcular; (consider) considerar ▷ *vi*: **I ... that ...** me parece que ...

reclaim [rɪ'kleɪm] *vt* (land) recuperar; (: from sea) rescatar; (demand back) reclamar

recline [rɪ'klaɪn] *vi* reclinarse

recognition [rɛkəɡˈnɪʃən] n reconocimiento; **transformed beyond ~** irreconocible

recognize [ˈrɛkəɡnaɪz] vt: **to ~ (by/as)** reconocer (por/como)

recollection [rɛkəˈlɛkʃən] n recuerdo

recommend [rɛkəˈmɛnd] vt recomendar; **recommendation** [rɛkəmɛnˈdeɪʃən] n recomendación f

reconcile [ˈrɛkənsaɪl] vt (two people) reconciliar; (two facts) conciliar; **to ~ o.s. to sth** resignarse or conformarse a algo

reconsider [riːkənˈsɪdəʳ] vt repensar

reconstruct [riːkənˈstrʌkt] vt reconstruir

record n [ˈrɛkɔːd] (Mus) disco; (of meeting etc) acta; (register) registro, partida; (file) archivo; (also: **police** or **criminal ~**) antecedentes mpl penales; (written) expediente m; (Sport) récord m; (Comput) registro ▷ vt [rɪˈkɔːd] registrar; (Mus: song etc) grabar; **in ~ time** en un tiempo récord; **off the ~** adj no oficial; adv confidencialmente; **recorded delivery** n (BRIT Post) entrega con acuse de recibo; **recorder** n (Mus) flauta de pico; **recording** n (Mus) grabación f; **record player** n tocadiscos m inv

recount vt [rɪˈkaʊnt] contar

recover [rɪˈkʌvəʳ] vt recuperar ▷ vi recuperarse; **recovery** n recuperación f

recreate [riːkrɪˈeɪt] vt recrear

recreation [rɛkrɪˈeɪʃən] n recreo; **recreational** adj de, recreo; **recreational drug** n droga recreativa; **recreational vehicle** n (US) caravana or roulotte f pequeña

recruit [rɪˈkruːt] n recluta mf ▷ vt reclutar; (staff) contratar; **recruitment** n reclutamiento

rectangle [ˈrɛktæŋgl] n rectángulo; **rectangular** [rɛkˈtæŋɡjʊləʳ] adj rectangular

rectify [ˈrɛktɪfaɪ] vt rectificar

rector [ˈrɛktəʳ] n (Rel) párroco

recur [rɪˈkəːʳ] vi repetirse; (pain, illness) producirse de nuevo; **recurring** adj (problem) repetido, constante

recyclable [riːˈsaɪkləbl] adj reciclable

recycle [riːˈsaɪkl] vt reciclar

recycling [riːˈsaɪklɪŋ] n reciclaje m

red [rɛd] n rojo ▷ adj rojo; (hair) pelirrojo; (wine) tinto; **to be in the ~** (account) estar en números rojos; (business) tener un saldo negativo; **to give sb the ~ carpet treatment** recibir a algn con todos los honores; **Red Cross** n Cruz f Roja; **redcurrant** n grosella roja

redeem [rɪˈdiːm] vt redimir; (promises) cumplir; (sth in pawn) desempeñar; (Rel: fig) rescatar

red: redhead n pelirrojo/a; **red-hot** adj candente; **red light** n: **to go through** or **jump a red light** (Aut) saltarse un semáforo; **red-light district** n barrio chino; **red meat** n carne f roja

reduce [rɪˈdjuːs] vt reducir; **to ~ sb to silence/despair/tears** hacer callar/desesperarse/llorar a algn; **reduced** adj (decreased) reducido, rebajado; **at a reduced price** con rebaja or descuento; **"greatly reduced prices"** "grandes rebajas"; **reduction** [rɪˈdʌkʃən] n reducción f; (of price) rebaja; (discount) descuento

redundancy [rɪˈdʌndənsɪ] n despido; (unemployment) desempleo

redundant [rɪˈdʌndənt] adj (BRIT: worker) parado, sin trabajo; (detail, object) superfluo; **to be made ~** (BRIT) quedar(se) sin trabajo

reed [riːd] n (Bot) junco, caña; (Mus) lengüeta

reef [riːf] n (at sea) arrecife m

reel [riːl] n carrete m, bobina; (of film) rollo ▷ vt (Tech) devanar; (also: **~ in**) sacar ▷ vi (sway) tambalear(se)

ref [rɛf] n abbr (inf); = **referee**

refectory [rɪˈfɛktərɪ] n comedor m

refer [rɪˈfəːʳ] vt (send: patient) referir; (: matter) remitir ▷ vi: **to ~ to** (allude *to)* referirse a, aludir a; *(apply to)* relacionarse con; *(consult)* remitirse a

referee [rɛfə'riː] *n* árbitro; (BRIT: *for job application)*: **to be a ~ for sb** proporcionar referencias a algn ▷ *vt* *(match)* arbitrar en

reference ['refrəns] *n* referencia; *(for job application: letter)* carta de recomendación; **with ~ to** (Comm: *in letter)* me remito a; **reference number** *n* número de referencia

refill *vt* [riː'fɪl] rellenar ▷ *n* ['riːfɪl] repuesto, recambio

refine [rɪ'faɪn] *vt* refinar; **refined** *adj* *(person, taste)* refinado; **refinery** *n* refinería

reflect [rɪ'flɛkt] *vt* reflejar ▷ *vi* *(think)* reflexionar, pensar; **it ~s badly/well on him** le perjudica/le hace honor; **reflection** [rɪ'flɛkʃən] *n* *(act)* reflexión *f*; *(image)* reflejo; *(discredit)* crítica; **on reflection** pensándolo bien

reflex ['riːflɛks] *adj*, *n* reflejo

reform [rɪ'fɔːm] *n* reforma ▷ *vt* reformar

refrain [rɪ'freɪn] *vi*: **to ~ from doing** abstenerse de hacer ▷ *n* estribillo

refresh [rɪ'frɛʃ] *vt* refrescar; **refreshing** *adj* refrescante; **refreshments** *npl* refrescos *mpl*

refrigerator [rɪ'frɪdʒəreɪtəʳ] *n* frigorífico, refrigeradora (LAM), heladera (LAM)

refuel [riː'fjual] *vi* repostar (combustible)

refuge ['refjuːdʒ] *n* refugio, asilo; **to take ~ in** refugiarse en; **refugee** [refju'dʒiː] *n* refugiado/a

refund *n* ['riːfʌnd] reembolso ▷ *vt* [rɪ'fʌnd] devolver, reembolsar

refurbish [riː'fəːbɪʃ] *vt* restaurar, renovar

refusal [rɪ'fjuːzəl] *n* negativa; **to have first ~ on sth** tener la primera opción a algo

refuse[1] ['refjuːs] *n* basura

refuse[2] [rɪ'fjuːz] *vt* *(reject)* rechazar; *(invitation)* declinar; *(permission)*

denegar; *(say no to)* negarse a ▷ *vi* negarse; *(horse)* rehusar; **to ~ to do sth** negarse a o rehusar hacer algo

regain [rɪ'geɪn] *vt* recobrar, recuperar

regard [rɪ'gɑːd] *n* mirada; *(esteem)* respeto; *(attention)* consideración *f* ▷ *vt* *(consider)* considerar; **to give one's ~s to** saludar de su parte a; **"with kindest ~s"** "con muchos recuerdos"; **as ~s, with ~ to** con respecto a, en cuanto a; **regarding** *prep* con respecto a, en cuanto a; **regardless** *adv* a pesar de todo; **regardless of** sin reparar en

regenerate [rɪ'dʒɛnəreɪt] *vt* regenerar

reggae ['regeɪ] *n* reggae *m*

regiment ['redʒɪmənt] *n* regimiento

region ['riːdʒən] *n* región *f*; **in the ~ of** *(fig)* alrededor de; **regional** *adj* regional

register ['redʒɪstəʳ] *n* registro ▷ *vt* registrar; *(birth)* declarar; *(car)* matricular; *(letter)* certificar; *(instrument)* marcar, indicar ▷ *vi* *(at hotel)* registrarse; *(as student)* matricularse; *(make impression)* producir impresión; **registered** *adj* *(letter)* certificado

registrar ['redʒɪstrɑːʳ] *n* secretario/a (del registro civil)

registration [redʒɪs'treɪʃən] *n* *(act)* declaración *f*; *(Aut: also: ~ number)* matrícula

registry office *n* (BRIT) registro civil; **to get married in a ~** casarse por lo civil

regret [rɪ'gret] *n* sentimiento, pesar *m* ▷ *vt* sentir, lamentar; **regrettable** *adj* lamentable

regular ['regjuləʳ] *adj* regular; *(soldier)* profesional; *(usual)* habitual ▷ *n* *(client etc)* cliente/a *m* f/habitual; **regularly** *adv* con regularidad

regulate ['regjuleɪt] *vt* controlar; **regulation** [regju'leɪʃən] *n* *(rule)* regla, reglamento

rehabilitation [ˈriːəbɪlɪˈteɪʃən] n rehabilitación f

rehearsal [rɪˈhɜːsəl] n ensayo

rehearse [rɪˈhɜːs] vt ensayar

reign [reɪn] n reinado; (fig) predominio ▷ vi reinar; (fig) imperar

reimburse [ˈriːɪmˈbɜːs] vt reembolsar

rein [reɪn] n (for horse) rienda

reincarnation [ˈriːɪnkɑːˈneɪʃən] n reencarnación f

reindeer [ˈreɪndɪəʳ] n (pl inv) reno

reinforce [riːɪnˈfɔːs] vt reforzar

reinforcement [riːɪnˈfɔːsmənt] n refuerzo; **reinforcements** npl (Mil) refuerzos mpl

reinstate [riːɪnˈsteɪt] vt (worker) reintegrar (a su puesto); (tax, law) reinstaurar

reject n [ˈriːdʒekt] (thing) desecho ▷ vt [rɪˈdʒekt] rechazar; (proposition, offer etc) descartar; **rejection** [rɪˈdʒekʃən] n rechazo

rejoice [rɪˈdʒɔɪs] vi: **to ~ at** or **over** regocijarse or alegrarse de

relate [rɪˈleɪt] vt (tell) contar, relatar; (connect) relacionar ▷ vi relacionarse; **related** adj afín; (person) emparentado; **to be related to** (connected) guardar relación con; (by family) ser pariente de; **relating: relating to** prep referente a

relation [rɪˈleɪʃən] n (person) pariente mf; (link) relación f; **relations** npl (relatives) familiares mpl; **relationship** n relación f; (personal) relaciones fpl; (also: **family relationship**) parentesco

relative [ˈrelətɪv] n pariente mf, familiar mf ▷ adj relativo; **relatively** adv (fairly, rather) relativamente

relax [rɪˈlæks] vi descansar; (quieten down) relajarse ▷ vt relajar; (grip) aflojar; **relaxation** [riːlækˈseɪʃən] n descanso; (easing) relajamiento m; (entertainment) diversión f; **relaxed** adj relajado; (tranquil) tranquilo; **relaxing** adj relajante

relay n [ˈriːleɪ] (race) carrera de relevos ▷ vt [rɪˈleɪ] (Radio, TV) retransmitir

release [rɪˈliːs] n (liberation) liberación f; (discharge) puesta en libertad; (of gas etc) escape m; (of film etc) estreno; (of record) lanzamiento ▷ vt (prisoner) poner en libertad; (film) estrenar; (book) lanzar; (piece of news) difundir; (gas etc) despedir, arrojar; (free: from wreckage etc) liberar; (Tech: catch, spring etc) desenganchar

relegate [ˈrelɪgeɪt] vt relegar; (Sport): **to be ~d** to bajar a

relent [rɪˈlent] vi ablandarse; **relentless** adj implacable

relevant [ˈreləvənt] adj (fact) pertinente; **~ to** relacionado con

reliable [rɪˈlaɪəbl] adj (person, firm) de confianza, de fiar; (method, machine) seguro; (source) fidedigno

relic [ˈrelɪk] n (Rel) reliquia; (of the past) vestigio

relief [rɪˈliːf] n (from pain, anxiety) alivio; (help, supplies) socorro, ayuda; (Art, Geo) relieve m

relieve [rɪˈliːv] vt (pain, patient) aliviar; (bring help to) ayudar, socorrer; (take over from) sustituir a; (: guard) relevar; **to ~ sb of sth** quitar algo a algn; **to ~ o.s.** hacer sus necesidades; **relieved** adj: **to be relieved** sentir un gran alivio

religion [rɪˈlɪdʒən] n religión f

religious [rɪˈlɪdʒəs] adj religioso; **religious education** n educación f religiosa

relish [ˈrelɪʃ] n (Culin) salsa; (enjoyment) entusiasmo ▷ vt (food, challenge etc) saborear; **to ~ doing** gozar haciendo

relocate [riːləʊˈkeɪt] vt trasladar ▷ vi trasladarse

reluctance [rɪˈlʌktəns] n renuencia

reluctant [rɪˈlʌktənt] adj reacio; **to be ~ to do sth** resistirse a hacer algo; **reluctantly** adv de mala gana

rely [rɪˈlaɪ]: **to ~ on** vt fus depender de; **you can ~ on my discretion** puedes contar con mi discreción

remain [rɪˈmeɪn] vi (survive) quedar; (be left) sobrar; (continue) quedar(se), permanecer; **remainder** n resto; **remaining** adj restante, que queda(n); **remains** npl restos mpl

remand [rɪˈmɑːnd] n: **on ~** detenido (bajo custodia) ▷ vt: **to ~ in custody** mantener bajo custodia

remark [rɪˈmɑːk] n comentario ▷ vt comentar; **remarkable** adj (outstanding) extraordinario

remarry [riːˈmærɪ] vi volver a casarse

remedy [ˈremədɪ] n remedio ▷ vt remediar, curar

remember [rɪˈmembəʳ] vt recordar, acordarse de; (bear in mind) tener presente; **~ me to your wife and children** ¡déle recuerdos a su familia!

Remembrance Day, Remembrance Sunday n (BRIT) ver nota **"Remembrance Day"**

● REMEMBRANCE DAY
●
● En el Reino Unido el domingo
● más cercano al 11 de noviembre es
● Remembrance Day o Remembrance
● Sunday, aniversario de la firma
● del armisticio de 1918 que puso
● fin a la Primera Guerra Mundial.
● Tal día se recuerda a todos
● aquellos que murieron en las
● dos guerras mundiales con dos
● minutos de silencio a las once de
● la mañana (hora en que se firmó el
● armisticio), durante los actos de
● conmemoración celebrados en los
● monumentos a los caídos. Allí se
● colocan coronas de amapolas, flor
● que también se suele llevar prendida
● en el pecho tras pagar un donativo
● para los inválidos de guerra.

remind [rɪˈmaɪnd] vt: **to ~ sb to do sth** recordar a algn que haga algo; **to ~ sb of sth** recordar algo a algn; **she ~s me of her mother** me recuerda a

su madre; **reminder** n notificación f; (memento) recuerdo

reminiscent [remɪˈnɪsnt] adj: **to be ~ of sth** recordar algo

remnant [ˈremnənt] n resto; (of cloth) retal m

remorse [rɪˈmɔːs] n remordimientos mpl

remote [rɪˈməut] adj (distant) lejano; (person) distante; **remote control** n mando a distancia; **remotely** adv remotamente; (slightly) levemente

removal [rɪˈmuːvəl] n (taking away) (el) quitar; (BRIT: from house) mudanza; (from office: dismissal) destitución f; (Med) extirpación f; **removal man** n (BRIT) mozo de mudanzas; **removal van** n (BRIT) camión m de mudanzas

remove [rɪˈmuːv] vt quitar; (employee) destituir; (name from list) tachar, borrar; (doubt) disipar; (Med) extirpar

Renaissance [rɪˈneɪsɔ̃s] n: **the ~** el Renacimiento

rename [riːˈneɪm] vt poner nuevo nombre a

render [ˈrendəʳ] vt (thanks) dar; (aid) proporcionar; prestar; **to ~ sth useless** hacer algo inútil

renew [rɪˈnjuː] vt renovar; (resume) reanudar; (extend date) prorrogar; **renewable** adj renovable; **renewable energy, renewables** energías renovables

renovate [ˈrenəveɪt] vt renovar

renowned [rɪˈnaund] adj renombrado

rent [rent] n (for house) arriendo, renta ▷ vt alquilar; **rental** n (for television, car) alquiler m

reorganize [riːˈɔːɡənaɪz] vt reorganizar

rep [rep] n abbr (Comm); = **representative**

repair [rɪˈpeəʳ] n reparación f ▷ vt reparar; **in good/bad ~** en buen/mal estado; **repair kit** n caja de herramientas

repay [ri:'peɪ] vt (money) devolver, reembolsar; (person) pagar; (debt) liquidar; (sb's efforts) devolver, corresponder a; **repayment** n reembolso, devolución f; (sum of money) recompensa

repeat [ri'pi:t] n (Radio, TV) reposición f ▷ vt repetir ▷ vi repetirse; **repeatedly** adv repetidas veces; **repeat prescription** n (BRIT) receta renovada

repellent [ri'pɛlənt] adj repugnante ▷ n: **insect ~** crema/loción f antiinsectos

repercussion [ri:pə'kʌʃən] n (consequence) repercusión f; **to have ~s** repercutir

repetition [rɛpɪ'tɪʃən] n repetición f

repetitive [ri'pɛtitɪv] adj repetitivo

replace [ri'pleɪs] vt (put back) devolver a su sitio; (take the place of) reemplazar, sustituir; **replacement** n (act) reposición f; (thing) recambio; (person) suplente mf

replay [ri:'pleɪ] n (Sport) partido de desempate; (TV) repetición f

replica ['rɛplɪkə] n réplica, reproducción f

reply [ri'plaɪ] n respuesta, contestación f ▷ vi contestar, responder

report [ri'pɔ:t] n informe m; (Press etc) reportaje m; (BRIT: also: **school ~**) informe m escolar; (of gun) detonación f ▷ vt informar sobre; (Press etc) hacer un reportaje sobre; (notify: accident, culprit) denunciar ▷ vi (make a report) presentar un informe; (present o.s.): **to ~ (to sb)** presentarse (ante algn); **report card** n (US, SCOTTISH) cartilla escolar; **reportedly** adv según se dice; **reporter** n periodista mf

represent [rɛpri'zɛnt] vt representar; (Comm) ser agente de; **representation** [rɛprɪzɛn'teɪʃən] n representación f; **representative** n (US Pol) representante mf, diputado/a; (Comm) representante m ▷ adj:

representative (of) representativo (de)

repress [ri'prɛs] vt reprimir; **repression** [ri'prɛʃən] n represión f

reprimand ['rɛprimɑːnd] n reprimenda ▷ vt reprender

reproduce [ri:prə'dju:s] vt reproducir ▷ vi reproducirse; **reproduction** [ri:prə'dʌkʃən] n reproducción f

reptile ['rɛptaɪl] n reptil m

republic [ri'pʌblɪk] n república; **republican** adj, n republicano/a

reputable ['rɛpjʊtəbl] adj (make etc) de renombre

reputation [rɛpjʊ'teɪʃən] n reputación f

request [ri'kwɛst] n solicitud f, petición f ▷ vt: **to ~ sth of** or **from sb** solicitar algo a algn; **request stop** n (BRIT) parada discrecional

require [ri'kwaɪə'] vt (need: person) necesitar, tener necesidad de; (: thing, situation) exigir; (want) pedir; **to ~ sb to do sth/sth of sb** exigir que algn haga algo; **requirement** n requisito; (need) necesidad f

resat [ri:'sæt] pt, pp of **resit**

rescue ['rɛskju:] n rescate m ▷ vt rescatar

research [ri'sə:tʃ] n investigaciones fpl ▷ vt investigar

resemblance [ri'zɛmbləns] n parecido

resemble [ri'zɛmbl] vt parecerse a

resent [ri'zɛnt] vt resentirse por, ofenderse por; **resentful** adj resentido; **resentment** n resentimiento

reservation [rɛzə'veɪʃən] n reserva; **reservation desk** n (US: in hotel) recepción f

reserve [ri'zə:v] n reserva; (Sport) suplente mf ▷ vt (seats etc) reservar; **reserved** adj reservado

reservoir ['rɛzəvwɑː'] n (artificial lake) embalse m, represa; (tank) depósito m

residence ['rɛzɪdəns] n (formal: home) domicilio; (length of stay)

r

permanencia; **residence permit** n (BRIT)

resident ['rezɪdənt] n vecino/a f; (in hotel) huésped(a) m/f ▷ adj residente; (population) permanente; **residential** [rezɪ'denʃəl] adj residencial

residue ['rezɪdjuː] n resto

resign [rɪ'zaɪn] vt renunciar a ▷ vi: **to ~ (from)** dimitir (de); **to ~ o.s. to** resignarse a; **resignation** [rezɪg'neɪʃən] n dimisión f; (state of mind) resignación f

resin ['rezɪn] n resina

resist [rɪ'zɪst] vt (temptation, damage) resistir; **resistance** n resistencia

resit ['riːsɪt] (pt, pp **resat**) vt (BRIT: exam) volver a presentarse a; (: subject) recuperar, volver a examinarse de (SP)

resolution [rezə'luːʃən] n resolución f

resolve [rɪ'zɔlv] n resolución f ▷ vt resolver ▷ vi: **to ~ to do** resolver hacer

resort [rɪ'zɔːt] n (town) centro turístico; (recourse) recurso ▷ vi: **to ~** recurrir a; **in the last ~** como último recurso

resource [rɪ'sɔːs] n recurso; **resourceful** adj ingenioso

respect [rɪs'pekt] n respeto ▷ vt respetar; **respectable** adj respetable; (amount etc) apreciable; (passable) tolerable; **respectful** adj respetuoso

respective adj respectivo; **respectively** adv respectivamente

respond [rɪs'pɔnd] vi responder; (react) reaccionar; **response** [rɪs'pɔns] n respuesta; (reaction) reacción f

responsibility [rɪspɔnsɪ'bɪlɪtɪ] n responsabilidad f

responsible [rɪs'pɔnsɪbl] adj (liable): **~ (for)** responsable (de); (character) serio, formal; (job) de responsabilidad; **responsibly** adv con seriedad

responsive [rɪs'pɔnsɪv] adj sensible

rest [rest] n descanso, reposo; (Mus) pausa, silencio; (support) apoyo; (remainder) resto ▷ vi descansar; (be

supported): **to ~ on** apoyarse en ▷ vt: **to ~ sth on/against** apoyar algo en or sobre/contra; **the ~ of them** (people, objects) los demás; **it ~s with him** depende de él

restaurant ['rɛstərɒŋ] n restaurante m; **restaurant car** n (BRIT) coche-comedor m

restless ['restlɪs] adj inquieto

restoration [restə'reɪʃən] n restauración f; (giving back) devolución f

restore [rɪ'stɔː'] vt (building) restaurar; (sth stolen) devolver; (health) restablecer

restrain [rɪs'treɪn] vt (feeling) contener, refrenar; (person): **to ~ (from doing)** disuadir (de hacer); **restraint** n (moderation) moderación f; (of style) reserva

restrict [rɪs'trɪkt] vt restringir, limitar; **restriction** [rɪs'trɪkʃən] n restricción f, limitación f

rest room n (US) aseos mpl

restructure [riː'strʌktʃə'] vt reestructurar

result [rɪ'zʌlt] n resultado ▷ vi: **to ~ in** terminar en, tener por resultado; **as a ~ of** a or como consecuencia de

resume [rɪ'zjuːm] vt reanudar ▷ vi (meeting) continuar

⬛ Be careful not to translate resume by the Spanish word resumir.

résumé ['reɪzjuːmeɪ] n resumen m

resuscitate [rɪ'sʌsɪteɪt] vt (Med) resucitar

retail ['riːteɪl] cpd al por menor; **retailer** n detallista mf

retain [rɪ'teɪn] vt (keep) retener, conservar

retaliation [rɪtælɪ'eɪʃən] n represalias fpl

retarded [rɪ'tɑːdɪd] adj retrasado

retire [rɪ'taɪə'] vi (give up work) jubilarse; (withdraw) retirarse; (go to bed) acostarse; **retired** adj (person) jubilado; **retirement** n jubilación f

retort [rɪ'tɔːt] vi replicar

retreat [rɪ'triːt] n (place) retiro; (Mil) retirada ▷ vi retirarse

retrieve [rɪ'triːv] vt recobrar; (situation, honour) salvar; (Comput) recuperar; (error) reparar

retrospect ['rɛtrəspɛkt] n: **in ~** retrospectivamente; **retrospective** [rɛtrə'spɛktɪv] adj retrospectivo; (law) retroactivo

return [rɪ'təːn] n (going or coming back) vuelta, regreso; (of sth stolen etc) devolución f; (Finance: from land, shares) ganancia, ingresos mpl ▷ cpd (journey) de regreso; (BRIT: ticket) de ida y vuelta; (match) de vuelta ▷ vi (person etc: come or go back) volver, regresar; (symptoms etc) reaparecer ▷ vt devolver; (favour, love etc) corresponder a; (verdict) pronunciar; (Pol: candidate) elegir; **returns** npl (Comm) ingresos mpl; **in ~ (for)** a cambio (de); **by ~ of post** a vuelta de correo; **many happy ~s (of the day)!** ¡feliz cumpleaños!; **return ticket** n (esp BRIT) billete m (SP) or boleto m (LAM) de ida y vuelta, billete m redondo (MEX)

reunion [riː'juːnɪən] n (of family) reunión f; (of two people, school) reencuentro

reunite [riːjuː'naɪt] vt reunir; (reconcile) reconciliar

revamp [riː'væmp] vt renovar

reveal [rɪ'viːl] vt revelar; **revealing** adj revelador(a)

revel ['rɛvl] vi: **to ~ in sth/in doing sth** gozar de algo/haciendo algo

revelation [rɛvə'leɪʃən] n revelación f

revenge [rɪ'vɛndʒ] n venganza; **to take ~ on** vengarse de

revenue ['rɛvənjuː] n ingresos mpl, rentas fpl

Reverend ['rɛvərənd] adj (in titles): **the ~ John Smith** (Anglican) el Reverendo John Smith; (Catholic) el Padre John Smith; (Protestant) el Pastor John Smith

reversal [rɪ'vəːsl] n (of order) inversión f; (of policy) cambio de rumbo; (of decision) revocación f

reverse [rɪ'vəːs] n (opposite) contrario; (back: of cloth) revés m; (: of coin) reverso; (: of paper) dorso; (Aut: also: **~ gear**) marcha atrás ▷ adj (order) inverso; (direction) contrario ▷ vt (decision) dar marcha atrás a; (Aut) dar marcha atrás a; (position, function) invertir ▷ vi (BRIT Aut) poner en marcha atrás; **reverse-charge call** n (BRIT) llamada a cobro revertido; **reversing lights** npl (BRIT Aut) luces fpl de marcha atrás

revert [rɪ'vəːt] vi: **to ~ to** volver or revertir a

review [rɪ'vjuː] n (magazine, also Mil) revista; (of book, film) reseña; (: examination) repaso, examen m ▷ vt repasar, examinar; (Mil) pasar revista a; (book, film) reseñar

revise [rɪ'vaɪz] vt (manuscript) corregir; (opinion) modificar; (price, procedure) revisar; (BRIT: study: subject) repasar; **revision** [rɪ'vɪʒən] n corrección f; modificación f; (of subject) repaso

revival [rɪ'vaɪvl] n (recovery) reanimación f; (of interest) renacimiento; (Theat) reestreno; (of faith) despertar m

revive [rɪ'vaɪv] vt resucitar; (custom) restablecer; (hope, courage) reanimar; (play) reestrenar ▷ vi (person) volver en sí; (business) reactivarse

revolt [rɪ'vəult] n rebelión f ▷ vi rebelarse, sublevarse ▷ vt dar asco a, repugnar; **revolting** adj asqueroso, repugnante

revolution [rɛvə'luːʃən] n revolución f; **revolutionary** adj, n revolucionario/a

revolve [rɪ'vɔlv] vi dar vueltas, girar; **to ~ (a)round** girar en torno a

revolver [rɪ'vɔlvə*] n revólver m

reward [rɪ'wɔːd] n premio, recompensa ▷ vt **to ~ (for)**

r

recompensar or premiar (por); **rewarding** adj (fig) gratificante
rewind [riːˈwaɪnd] vt rebobinar
rewritable [riːˈraɪtəbl] adj reescribible
rewrite [riːˈraɪt] vt (irreg: like **write**) reescribir
rheumatism [ˈruːmətɪzəm] n reumatismo, reúma
rhinoceros [raɪˈnɔsərəs] n rinoceronte m
rhubarb [ˈruːbɑːb] n ruibarbo
rhyme [raɪm] n rima; (verse) poesía
rhythm [ˈrɪðm] n ritmo
rib [rɪb] n (Anat) costilla ▷ vt (mock) tomar el pelo a
ribbon [ˈrɪbən] n cinta; **in ~s** (torn) hecho trizas
rice [raɪs] n arroz m; **rice pudding** n arroz m con leche
rich [rɪtʃ] adj rico; (soil) fértil; (food) pesado; (: sweet) empalagoso; **to be ~ in sth** abundar en algo
rid (pt, pp **rid**) [rɪd] vt: **to ~ sb of sth** librar a algn de algo; **to get ~ of** deshacerse or desembarazarse de
riddle [ˈrɪdl] n (conundrum) acertijo; (mystery) enigma m, misterio ▷ vt: **to be ~d with** ser lleno o plagado de
ride [raɪd] (pt **rode**, pp **ridden**) n paseo; (distance covered) viaje m, recorrido ▷ vi (on horse, as rider) montar; (go somewhere: on horse, bicycle) dar un paseo, pasearse; (journey: on bicycle, motor cycle, bus) viajar ▷ vt (a horse) montar a; (distance) recorrer; **to ~ a bicycle** andar en bicicleta; **to take sb for a ~** (fig) tomar el pelo a algn; **rider** n (on horse) jinete m; (on bicycle) ciclista mf; (on motorcycle) motociclista mf
ridge [rɪdʒ] n (of hill) cresta; (of roof) caballete m; (wrinkle) arruga
ridicule [ˈrɪdɪkjuːl] n irrisión f, burla ▷ vt poner en ridículo a, burlarse de; **ridiculous** [rɪˈdɪkjuləs] adj ridículo
riding [ˈraɪdɪŋ] n equitación f; **I like ~** me gusta montar a caballo; **riding school** n escuela de equitación

rife [raɪf] adj: **to be ~** ser muy común; **to be ~ with** abundar en
rifle [ˈraɪfl] n rifle m, fusil m ▷ vt saquear
rift [rɪft] n (fig: between friends) desavenencia
rig [rɪg] n (also: **oil ~**: at sea) plataforma petrolera ▷ vt (election etc) amañar los resultados de
right [raɪt] adj (true, correct) correcto, exacto; (suitable) indicado, debido; (proper) apropiado; (just) justo; (morally good) bueno; (not left) derecho ▷ n (title, claim) derecho; (not left) derecha ▷ adv bien, correctamente; (not on the left) a la derecha ▷ vt (put straight) enderezar; (correct) corregir ▷ excl ¡bueno!, ¡está bien!; **to be ~** (person) tener razón; (answer) ser correcto; by **~s** en justicia; **on the ~** a la derecha; **to be in the ~** tener razón; **~ now** ahora mismo; **~ in the middle** exactamente en el centro; **~ away** en seguida; **right angle** n ángulo recto; **rightful** adj legítimo; **right-hand** adj: **right-hand drive** conducción f por la derecha; **the right-hand side** derecha; **right-handed** adj (person) que usa la mano derecha, diestro; **rightly** adv correctamente, debidamente; (with reason) con razón; **right of way** n (on path etc) derecho de paso; (Aut) prioridad f de paso; **right-wing** adj (Pol) derechista
rigid [ˈrɪdʒɪd] adj rígido; (person, ideas) inflexible
rigorous [ˈrɪgərəs] adj riguroso
rim [rɪm] n borde m; (of spectacles) aro; (of wheel) llanta
rind [raɪnd] n (of bacon, cheese) corteza; (of lemon etc) cáscara
ring [rɪŋ] (pt **rang**, pp **rung**) n (of metal) aro; (on finger) anillo; (of people) corro; (of objects) círculo; (gang) banda; (for boxing) cuadrilátero; (of circus) pista; (bull ring) ruedo, plaza; (sound of bell) toque m ▷ vi (on telephone) llamar por teléfono; (large bell) repicar; (doorbell,

phone) sonar; (*also:* ~ **out**) sonar; (*ears*) zumbar ▷ vt (*BRIT Tel*) llamar; (*bell etc*) hacer sonar; (*doorbell*) tocar; **to give sb a** ~ (*BRIT Tel*) llamar a algn, dar un telefonazo a algn; **ring back** vt, vi (*Tel*) devolver la llamada; **ring off** vi (*BRIT Tel*) colgar, cortar la comunicación; **ring up** vt (*BRIT Tel*) llamar, telefonear; **ringing tone** n (*BRIT Tel*) tono de llamada; **ringleader** n cabecilla mf; **ring road** n (*BRIT*) carretera periférica or de circunvalación; **ringtone** n tono de llamada

rink [rɪŋk] n (*also:* **ice ~**) pista de hielo

rinse [rɪns] n (*of dishes*) enjuague m; (*of clothes*) aclarado m; (*hair colouring*) reflejo m ▷ vt enjuagar, aclarar; (*hair*) dar reflejos a

riot ['raɪət] n motín m, disturbio m ▷ vi amotinarse; **to run** ~ desmandarse

rip [rɪp] n rasgón m ▷ vt rasgar, desgarrar ▷ vi rasgarse; **rip off** vt (*inf: cheat*) estafar; **rip up** vt hacer pedazos

ripe [raɪp] adj maduro

rip-off ['rɪpɔf] n (*inf*): **it's a ~!** ¡es una estafa!, ¡es un timo!

ripple ['rɪpl] n onda, rizo; (*sound*) murmullo ▷ vi rizarse

rise (*pt* **rose**, *pp* **risen**) [raɪz, rəuz, 'rɪzn] n (*slope*) cuesta, pendiente f; (*hill*) altura; (*in wages*) aumento; (*in prices, temperature*) subida; (*fig: to power etc*) ascenso ▷ vi subir; (*waters*) crecer; (*sun*) salir; (*person: from bed etc*) levantarse; (*also:* ~ **up**: *rebel*) sublevarse; (*in rank*) ascender; **to give** ~ **to** dar lugar or origen a; **to** ~ **to the occasion** ponerse a la altura de las circunstancias; **risen** ['rɪzn] pp of **rise**; **rising** adj (*increasing: number*) creciente; (: *prices*) en aumento or alza; (*tide*) creciente; (*sun, moon*) naciente

risk [rɪsk] n riesgo, peligro ▷ vt arriesgar; **to take** or **run the ~ of doing** correr el riesgo de hacer; **at** ~ en peligro; **at one's own** ~ bajo su propia responsabilidad; **risky** adj arriesgado, peligroso

rite [raɪt] n rito; **last ~s** últimos sacramentos mpl

ritual ['rɪtjuəl] adj ritual ▷ n ritual m, rito

rival ['raɪvl] n rival mf; (*in business*) competidor(a) m/f ▷ adj rival, opuesto ▷ vt competir con; **rivalry** n competencia

river ['rɪvər] n río ▷ cpd (*port, traffic*) de río; **up/down** ~ río arriba/abajo; **riverbank** n orilla del río

rivet ['rɪvɪt] n roblón m, remache m ▷ vt (*fig*) fascinar

road [rəud] n camino; (*motorway etc*) carretera; (*in town*) calle f; **major/minor** ~ carretera general/ secundaria; **roadblock** n barricada; **road map** n mapa m de carreteras; **road rage** n conducta agresiva de los conductores; **road safety** n seguridad f vial; **roadside** n borde m (del camino); **roadsign** n señal f de tráfico; **road tax** n (*BRIT*) impuesto de rodaje; **roadworks** npl obras fpl

roam [rəum] vi vagar

roar [rɔːr] n rugido; (*of vehicle, storm*) estruendo; (*of laughter*) carcajada ▷ vi rugir; hacer estruendo; **to** ~ **with laughter** reírse a carcajadas; **roaring** adj: **to do a roaring trade** hacer buen negocio

roast [rəust] n carne f asada, asado ▷ vt asar; (*coffee*) tostar; **roast beef** n rosbif m

rob [rɔb] vt robar; **to** ~ **sb of sth** robar algo a algn; (*fig: deprive*) quitar algo a algn; **robber** n ladrón/ona m/f; **robbery** n robo

robe [rəub] n (*for ceremony etc*) toga; (*also:* **bath ~**) bata, albornoz m

robin ['rɔbɪn] n petirrojo

robot ['rəubɔt] n robot m

robust [rəu'bʌst] adj robusto, fuerte

rock [rɔk] n roca; (*boulder*) peña, peñasco; (*BRIT: sweet*) = pirulí m ▷ vt (*swing gently*) mecer; (*shake*) sacudir; ▷ vi mecerse, balancearse; sacudirse; **on the ~s** (*drink*) con hielo; **their**

marriage is on the ~s su matrimonio se está yendo a pique; **rock and roll** n rocanrol m; **rock climbing** n (Sport) escalada

rocket ['rɒkɪt] n cohete m

rocking chair ['rɒkɪŋ-] n mecedora

rocky ['rɒkɪ] adj rocoso

rod [rɒd] n vara, varilla; (also: **fishing ~**) caña

rode [rəʊd] pt of **ride**

rodent ['rəʊdnt] n roedor m

rogue [rəʊg] n pícaro, pillo

role [rəʊl] n papel m; **role-model** n modelo a imitar

roll [rəʊl] n rollo; (of bank notes) fajo; (also: **bread ~**) panecillo; (register) lista, nómina; (sound: of drums etc) redoble m ▷ vt hacer rodar; (also: **~ up**: string) enrollar; (: cigarettes) liar; (also: **~ out**: pastry) aplanar ▷ vi rodar; (drum) redoblar; (ship) balancearse; **roll over** vi dar una vuelta; **roll up** vi (inf: arrive) aparecer ▷ vt (carpet, cloth, map) arrollar; (sleeves) arremangar

roller n rodillo; (wheel) rueda; (for road) apisonadora; (for hair) rulo; **Rollerblades** npl patines mpl en línea; **roller coaster** n montaña rusa; **roller skates** npl patines mpl de rueda; **roller-skating** n patinaje sobre ruedas; **to go roller-skating** ir a patinar (sobre ruedas)

rolling pin n rodillo (de cocina)

ROM [rɒm] n abbr (Comput: = read-only memory) (memoria) ROM f

Roman ['rəʊmən] adj, n romano/a; **Roman Catholic** adj, n católico/a (romano/a)

romance [rə'mæns] n (love affair) amor m; (charm) lo romántico; (novel) novela de amor

Romania [ruː'meɪnɪə] n = **Rumania**

Roman numeral n número romano

romantic [rə'mæntɪk] adj romántico

Rome [rəʊm] n Roma

roof [ruːf] n techo; (of house) tejado ▷ vt techar, poner techo a; **~ of the**

mouth paladar m; **roof rack** n (Aut) baca, portaequipajes msg

rook [rʊk] n (bird) graja; (Chess) torre f

room [ruːm] n cuarto, habitación f, pieza (esp LAM); (also: **bed~**) dormitorio; (in school etc) sala; (space) sitio; **roommate** n compañero/a de cuarto; **room service** n servicio de habitaciones; **roomy** adj espacioso

rooster ['ruːstə] n gallo

root [ruːt] n raíz f ▷ vi arraigar(se)

rope [rəʊp] n cuerda; (Naut) cable m ▷ vt (box) atar o o amarrar (con una) cuerda; (climbers: also: **~ together**) encordarse; **to know the ~s** (fig) conocer los trucos (del oficio)

rort [rɔːt] (AUST, NZ inf) n estafa f ▷ vt estafar

rose [rəʊz] pt of **rise** ▷ n rosa; (also: **~bush**) rosal m; (on watering can) roseta

rosé ['rəʊzeɪ] n vino rosado

rosemary ['rəʊzmərɪ] n romero

rosy ['rəʊzɪ] adj rosado, sonrosado; **the future looks ~** el futuro parece prometedor

rot [rɒt] n podredumbre f; (fig: pej) tonterías fpl ▷ vt pudrir ▷ vi pudrirse

rota ['rəʊtə] n lista (de tareas)

rotate [rəʊ'teɪt] vt (revolve) hacer girar, dar vueltas a; (jobs) alternar ▷ vi girar, dar vueltas

rotten ['rɒtn] adj podrido, (fig) corrompido; (inf: bad) pésimo; **to feel ~** (ill) sentirse mal

rough [rʌf] adj (skin, surface) áspero; (terrain) accidentado; (road) desigual; (voice) bronco; (person, manner) tosco, grosero; (weather) borrascoso; (treatment) brutal; (sea) embravecido; (town, area) peligroso; (cloth) basto; (plan) preliminar; (guess) aproximado ▷ n (Golf): **in the ~** en las hierbas altas; **to ~ it** vivir sin comodidades; **to sleep ~** (BRIT) pasar la noche al raso; **roughly** adv (handle) torpemente; (make) toscamente; (approximately) aproximadamente; **roughly speaking** más o menos

roulette [ruː'let] n ruleta

round [raund] adj redondo ▷ n círculo; (of policeman) ronda; (of milkman) recorrido; (of doctor) visitas fpl; (game: in competition, cards) partida; (of ammunition) cartucho; (Boxing) asalto; (of talks) ronda ▷ vt (corner) doblar ▷ prep alrededor de; (surrounding): **~ his neck/the table** en su cuello/alrededor de la mesa; (in a circular movement): **to move ~ the room/sail ~ the world** dar una vuelta a la habitación/circunnavegar el mundo; (in various directions): **to move ~ a room/house** moverse por toda la habitación/casa ▷ adv: **all ~** por todos lados; **all the year ~** durante todo el año; **the long way ~** por el camino menos directo; **it's just ~ the corner** (fig) está a la vuelta de la esquina; **~ the clock** adv las 24 horas; **to go ~ to sb's (house)** ir a casa de algn; **to go ~ the back** pasar por atrás; **enough to go ~** bastante (para todos); **a ~ of applause** una salva de aplausos; **a ~ of drinks/sandwiches** una ronda de bebidas/bocadillos; **a ~ of toast** (BRIT) una tostada; **round off** vt (speech etc) acabar, poner término a; **round up** vt (cattle) acorralar; (people) reunir; (prices) redondear; **roundabout** n (BRIT: Aut) glorieta, rotonda; (: at fair) tiovivo ▷ adj (route, means) indirecto; **round trip** n viaje m de ida y vuelta, viaje m redondo; (of criminals) redada; **a roundup of the latest news** un resumen de las últimas noticias

rouse [rauz] vt (wake up) despertar; (stir up) suscitar

route [ruːt] n ruta, camino; (of bus) recorrido; (of shipping) derrota

routine [ruː'tiːn] adj rutinario ▷ n rutina; (Theat) número

row¹ [rəu] n (line) fila, hilera; (Knitting) vuelta ▷ vi (in boat) remar ▷ vt (boat)

conducir remando; **four days in a ~** cuatro días seguidos

row² [rau] n (noise) escándalo; (dispute) bronca, pelea; (scolding) reprimenda ▷ vi reñir(se)

rowboat ['rəubəut] n (US) bote m de remos

rowing ['rəuɪŋ] n remo; **rowing boat** n (BRIT) bote m o barco de remos

royal ['rɔɪəl] adj real; **Royal Air Force** n Fuerzas Aéreas Británicas fpl; **royalty** n (royal persons) (miembros mpl de la) familia real; (payment to author) derechos mpl de autor

rpm abbr (= revolutions per minute) r.p.m.

RSVP abbr (= répondez s'il vous plaît) SRC

Rt. Hon. abbr (BRIT: = Right Honourable) tratamiento honorífico de diputado

rub [rʌb] vt frotar; (hard) restregar ▷ n: **to give sth a ~** frotar algo; **to rub sb up** or (US)**~ sb the wrong way** sacar de quicio a algn; **rub in** vt (ointment) frotar; **rub off** vt borrarse; **rub out** vt borrar

rubber ['rʌbəʳ] n caucho, goma; (BRIT: eraser) goma de borrar; **rubber band** n goma, gomita; **rubber gloves** npl guantes mpl de goma

rubbish ['rʌbɪʃ] (BRIT) n (from household) basura; (waste) desperdicios mpl; (fig: pej) tonterías fpl; (trash) basura, porquería; **rubbish bin** n cubo or bote m (LAM) de la basura; **rubbish dump** n vertedero, basurero

rubble ['rʌbl] n escombros mpl

ruby ['ruːbɪ] n rubí m

rucksack ['rʌksæk] n mochila

rudder ['rʌdəʳ] n timón m

rude [ruːd] adj (impolite: person) maleducado; (: word, manners) grosero; (indecent) indecente

ruffle ['rʌfl] vt (hair) despeinar; (clothes) arrugar; (fig: person) agitar

rug [rʌg] n alfombra; (BRIT: for knees) manta

rugby ['rʌgbɪ] n rugby m

rugged ['rʌgɪd] *adj* (landscape) accidentado; (features) robusto

ruin ['ruːɪn] *n* ruina ▷ *vt* arruinar; (spoil) estropear; **ruins** *npl* ruinas *fpl*, restos *mpl*

rule [ruːl] *n* (norm) norma, costumbre *f*; (regulation, ruler) regla; (government) dominio ▷ *vt* (country, person) gobernar ▷ *vi* gobernar; (Law) fallar; **as a ~** por regla general; **rule out** *vt* excluir; **ruler** *n* (sovereign) soberano; (for measuring) regla; **ruling** *adj* (party) gobernante; (class) dirigente ▷ *n* (Law) fallo, decisión *f*

rum [rʌm] *n* ron *m*

Rumania [ruːˈmeɪnɪə] *n* Rumanía; **Rumanian** *adj*, *n* rumano/a

rumble ['rʌmbl] *n* ruido sordo ▷ *vi* retumbar, hacer un ruido sordo; (stomach, pipe) sonar

rumour, (us) **rumor** ['ruːmə*r*] *n* rumor *m* ▷ *vt*: **it is ~ed that ...** se rumorea que ...; **~ has it that ...** corre la voz de que ...

rump steak *n* filete *m* de lomo

run [rʌn] (*pt* **ran**, *pp* **run**) *n* (Sport) carrera; (outing) paseo, excursión *f*; (distance travelled) trayecto; (series) serie *f*; (Theat) temporada; (Ski) pista; (in tights, stockings) carrera ▷ *vt* (operate: business) dirigir; (: competition, course) organizar; (: hotel, house) administrar, llevar; (Comput) ejecutar; (to pass: hand) pasar; (Press: feature) publicar ▷ *vi* correr; (work: machine) funcionar, marchar; (bus, train: operate) circular, ir; (: travel) ir; (continue: play) seguir en cartel; (: contract) ser válido; (flow: river, bath) fluir; (colours, washing) desteñirse; (in election) ser candidato; **there was a ~ on** (meat, tickets) hubo mucha demanda de; **in the long ~** a la larga; **on the ~** en fuga; **I'll ~ you to the station** te llevaré a la estación en coche; **to ~ a risk** correr un riesgo; **to ~ a bath** llenar la bañera; **run after** *vt fus* (to catch up) correr tras; (chase) perseguir; **run away** *vi* huir;

run down *vt* (reduce: production) ir reduciendo; (factory) restringir la producción de; (Aut) atropellar; (criticize) criticar; **to be ~ down** (person: tired) encontrarse agotado; **run into** *vt fus* (meet: person, trouble) tropezar con; (collide with) chocar con; **run off** *vt* (water) dejar correr ▷ *vi* huir corriendo; **run out** *vi* (person) salir corriendo; (liquid) irse; (lease) caducar, vencer; (money) acabarse; **run out of** *vt fus* quedar sin; **run over** *vt* (Aut) atropellar ▷ *vt fus* (revise) repasar; **run through** *vt fus* (instructions) repasar; **run up** *vt* (debt) incurrir en; **to ~ up against** (difficulties) tropezar con;

runaway *adj* (horse) desbocado; (truck) sin frenos; (person) fugitivo

rung [rʌŋ] *pp of* **ring** ▷ *n* (of ladder) escalón *m*, peldaño

runner ['rʌnə*r*] *n* (in race: person) corredor(a) *m/f*; (: horse) caballo; (on sledge) patín *m*; **runner bean** *n* (BRIT) judía verde; **runner-up** *n* subcampeón/ona *m/f*

running ['rʌnɪŋ] *n* (sport) atletismo; (race) carrera ▷ *adj* (costs, water) corriente; (commentary) en directo; **to be in/out of the ~ for sth** tener/no tener posibilidades de ganar algo; **6 days ~** 6 días seguidos

runny ['rʌnɪ] *adj* líquido; (eyes) lloroso; **to have a ~ nose** tener mocos

run-up ['rʌnʌp] *n*: **~ to** (election etc) período previo a

runway ['rʌnweɪ] *n* (Aviat) pista (de aterrizaje)

rupture ['rʌptʃə*r*] *n* (Med) hernia ▷ *vt*: **to ~ o.s.** causarse una hernia

rural ['ruərl] *adj* rural

rush [rʌʃ] *n* ímpetu *m*; (hurry) prisa; (Comm) demanda repentina; (Bot) junco; (current) corriente *f* fuerte; (of feeling) torrente *m* ▷ *vt* apresurar; (work) hacer de prisa ▷ *vi* correr, precipitarse; **rush hour** *n* horas *fpl* punta

Russia ['rʌʃə] *n* Rusia; **Russian** *adj* ruso ▷ *n* ruso/a; (Ling) ruso

rust [rʌst] n herrumbre f, moho ▷ vi
oxidarse
rusty ['rʌstɪ] adj oxidado
ruthless ['ruːθlɪs] adj despiadado
RV n abbr (us) = **recreational vehicle**
rye [raɪ] n centeno

S

Sabbath ['sæbəθ] n domingo; (Jewish)
sábado
sabotage ['sæbətɑːʒ] n sabotaje m
▷ vt sabotear
saccharin(e) ['sækərɪn] n sacarina
sachet ['sæʃeɪ] n sobrecito
sack [sæk] n (bag) saco, costal m ▷ vt
(dismiss) despedir; (plunder) saquear;
to get the ~ ser despedido
sacred ['seɪkrɪd] adj sagrado, santo
sacrifice ['sækrɪfaɪs] n sacrificio ▷ vt
sacrificar
sad [sæd] adj (unhappy) triste;
(deplorable) lamentable
saddle ['sædl] n silla (de montar); (of
cycle) sillín m ▷ vt (horse) ensillar; **to
be ~d with sth** (inf) quedar cargado
con algo
sadistic [sə'dɪstɪk] adj sádico
sadly ['sædlɪ] adv tristemente; **~
lacking (in)** muy deficiente (en)
sadness ['sædnɪs] n tristeza
safari [sə'fɑːrɪ] n safari m

safe [seɪf] *adj* (*out of danger*) fuera de peligro; (*not dangerous, sure*) seguro; (*unharmed*) ileso ▷ *n* caja de caudales, caja fuerte; **~ and sound** sano y salvo; **(just) to be on the ~ side** para mayor seguridad; **safely** *adv* seguramente, con seguridad; **to arrive safely** llegar bien; **safe sex** *n* sexo seguro or sin riesgo

safety ['seɪftɪ] *n* seguridad *f*; **safety belt** *n* cinturón *m* (de seguridad); **safety pin** *n* imperdible *m*, seguro (LAM)

saffron ['sæfrən] *n* azafrán *m*

sag [sæg] *vi* aflojarse

sage [seɪdʒ] *n* (*herb*) salvia; (*man*) sabio

Sagittarius [sædʒɪ'tɛərɪəs] *n* Sagitario

Sahara [sə'hɑːrə] *n*: **the ~ (Desert)** el Sáhara

said [sed] *pt, pp of* **say**

sail [seɪl] *n* (*on boat*) vela ▷ *vt* (*boat*) gobernar ▷ *vi* (*travel: ship*) navegar; (*Sport*) hacer vela; **they ~ed into Copenhagen** arribaron a Copenhague; **sailboat** *n* (US) velero, barco de vela; **sailing** *n* (*Sport*) vela; **to go sailing** hacer vela; **sailing boat** *n* velero, barco de vela; **sailor** *n* marinero, marino

saint [seɪnt] *n* santo

sake [seɪk] *n*: **for the ~ of** por

salad ['sæləd] *n* ensalada; **salad cream** *n* (BRIT) mayonesa; **salad dressing** *n* aliño

salami [sə'lɑːmɪ] *n* salami *m*, salchichón *m*

salary ['sælərɪ] *n* sueldo

sale [seɪl] *n* venta; (*at reduced prices*) liquidación *f*, saldo; (*auction*) subasta; **sales** *npl* (*total amount sold*) ventas *fpl*, facturación *f*; **"for ~"** "se vende"; **on ~** en venta; **on ~ or return** (*goods*) venta por reposición; **sales assistant** *n* (BRIT) dependiente/a *m/f*; **sales clerk** *n* (US) dependiente/a *m/f*; **salesman** *n* vendedor *m*; (*in shop*) dependiente *m*; **salesperson** (*irreg*) *n* vendedor(a)

m/f, dependiente/a *m/f*; **sales rep** *n* representante *mf*, agente *mf* comercial

saline ['seɪlaɪn] *adj* salino

saliva [sə'laɪvə] *n* saliva

salmon ['sæmən] *n* (*pl inv*) salmón *m*

salon ['sælɒn] *n* (*hairdressing salon, beauty salon*) salón *m*

saloon [sə'luːn] *n* (US) bar *m*, taberna; (BRIT Aut) (coche *m* de) turismo; (*ship's lounge*) cámara, salón *m*

salt [sɔːlt] *n* sal *f* ▷ *vt* salar; (*put salt on*) poner sal en; **saltwater** *adj* de agua salada; **salty** *adj* salado

salute [sə'luːt] *n* saludo; (*of guns*) salva ▷ *vt* saludar

salvage ['sælvɪdʒ] *n* (*saving*) salvamento, recuperación *f*; (*things saved*) objetos *mpl* salvados ▷ *vt* salvar

Salvation Army *n* Ejército de Salvación

same [seɪm] *adj* mismo ▷ *pron*: **the ~ el mismo/la misma**; **the ~ book as** el mismo libro que; **at the ~ time** (*at the same moment*) al mismo tiempo; (*yet*) sin embargo; **all** *or* **just the ~** sin embargo, aun así; **to do the ~ (as sb)** hacer lo mismo (que otro); **and the ~ to you!** ¡igualmente!

sample ['sɑːmpl] *n* muestra ▷ *vt* (*food, wine*) probar

sanction ['sæŋkʃən] *n* sanción *f* ▷ *vt* sancionar; **sanctions** *npl* (Pol) sanciones *fpl*

sanctuary ['sæŋktjuərɪ] *n* santuario; (*refuge*) asilo, refugio; (*for wildlife*) reserva

sand [sænd] *n* arena; (*beach*) playa; **sands** *npl* playa *sg* de arena ▷ *vt* (*also:* **~ down**: *wood etc*) lijar

sandal ['sændl] *n* sandalia

sand: sandbox *n* (US) = **sandpit**; **sandcastle** *n* castillo de arena; **sand dune** *n* duna; **sandpaper** *n* papel *m* de lija; **sandpit** *n* (*for children*) cajón *m* de arena; **sandstone** *n* piedra arenisca

sandwich ['sændwɪtʃ] *n* bocadillo (SP), sándwich *m* (LAM) ▷ *vt* (*also:* **~ in**) intercalar; **to be ~ed between** estar apretujado entre; **cheese/ham ~** sandwich de queso/jamón

sandy ['sændɪ] *adj* arenoso; *(colour)* rojizo

sane [seɪn] *adj* cuerdo, sensato
⚠ Be careful not to translate *sane* by the Spanish word *sano*.

sang [sæŋ] *pt of* **sing**

sanitary towel *n*, *(us)* **sanitary napkin** *n* paño higiénico, compresa

sanity ['sænɪtɪ] *n* cordura; *(of judgment)* sensatez *f*

sank [sæŋk] *pt of* **sink**

Santa Claus [sæntə'klɔːz] *n* San Nicolás *m*, Papá Noel *m*

sap [sæp] *n (of plants)* savia ▷ *vt (strength)* minar, agotar

sapphire ['sæfaɪə'] *n* zafiro

sarcasm ['sɑːkæzm] *n* sarcasmo

sarcastic [sɑː'kæstɪk] *adj* sarcástico

sardine [sɑː'diːn] *n* sardina

SASE *n abbr* (us: = *self-addressed stamped envelope*) *sobre con las propias señas de uno y con sello*

sat [sæt] *pt, pp of* **sit**

Sat. *abbr* (= *Saturday*) sáb.

satchel ['sætʃl] *n (child's)* cartera, mochila (LAM)

satellite ['sætəlaɪt] *n* satélite *m*; **satellite dish** *n (antena)* parabólica, f; **satellite television** *n* televisión *f* por satélite

satin ['sætɪn] *n* raso ▷ *adj* de raso

satire ['sætaɪə'] *n* sátira

satisfaction [sætɪs'fækʃən] *n* satisfacción *f*

satisfactory [sætɪs'fæktərɪ] *adj* satisfactorio

satisfied ['sætɪsfaɪd] *adj* satisfecho; **to be ~ (with sth)** estar satisfecho (de algo)

satisfy ['sætɪsfaɪ] *vt* satisfacer; *(convince)* convencer

satnav ['sætnæv] *n abbr* (= *satellite navigation*) navegador *m* (GPS)

Saturday ['sætədɪ] *n* sábado

sauce [sɔːs] *n* salsa; *(sweet)* crema; **saucepan** *n* cacerola, olla

saucer ['sɔːsə'] *n* platillo

Saudi Arabia *n* Arabia Saudí *or* Saudita

sauna ['sɔːnə] *n* sauna

sausage ['sɒsɪdʒ] *n* salchicha; **sausage roll** *n* empanadilla de salchicha

sautéed ['səuteɪd] *adj* salteado

savage ['sævɪdʒ] *adj (cruel, fierce)* feroz, furioso; *(primitive)* salvaje ▷ *n* salvaje *mf* ▷ *vt (attack)* embestir

save [seɪv] *vt (rescue)* salvar, rescatar; *(money, time)* ahorrar; *(put by)* guardar; *(Comput)* salvar (y guardar); *(avoid: trouble)* evitar; *(Sport)* parar ▷ *vi (also:* **~ up**) ahorrar ▷ *n (Sport)* parada ▷ *prep* salvo, excepto

saving ['seɪvɪŋ] *n (on price etc)* economía; **savings** *npl* ahorros *mpl*; **savings account** *n* cuenta de ahorros; **savings and loan association** *n* (us) sociedad *f* de ahorro y préstamo

savoury, *(us)* **savory** ['seɪvərɪ] *adj* sabroso; *(dish: not sweet)* salado

saw [sɔː] *pt of* **see** ▷ *n (tool)* sierra ▷ *vt* serrar; **sawdust** *n* (a)serrín *m*

sawn [sɔːn] *pp of* **saw**

saxophone ['sæksəfəun] *n* saxófono

say *(pt, pp* **said)** [seɪ, sed] *n*: **to have one's ~** expresar su opinión ▷ *vt, vi* decir; **to have a** *or* **some ~ in sth** tener voz y voto en algo; **to ~ yes/no** decir que sí/no; **that is to ~** es decir; **that goes without ~ing** ni que decir tiene; **saying** *n* dicho, refrán *m*

scab [skæb] *n* costra; *(pej)* esquirol(a) *m/f*

scaffolding ['skæfəldɪŋ] *n* andamio, andamiaje *m*

scald [skɔːld] *n* escaldadura ▷ *vt* escaldar

scale [skeɪl] *n* (Mus) escala; *(of fish)* escama; *(of salaries, fees etc)* escalafón *m* ▷ *vt (mountain)* escalar; *(tree)* trepar; **scales** *npl (small)* balanza

scallion ['skæljən] n (us) cebolleta

scallop ['skɔləp] n (Zool) venera; (Sewing) festón m

scalp [skælp] n cabellera ▷ vt escalpar

scalpel ['skælpl] n bisturí m

scam [skæm] n (inf) estafa, timo

scampi ['skæmpı] npl gambas fpl

scan [skæn] vt (examine) escudriñar; (glance at quickly) dar un vistazo a; (TV, Radar) explorar, registrar ▷ n (Med) examen m ultrasónico; **to have a ~** pasar por el escáner

scandal ['skændl] n escándalo; (gossip) chismes mpl

Scandinavia [skændı'neıvıə] n Escandinavia; **Scandinavian** adj, n escandinavo/a

scanner ['skænə'] n (Radar, Med, Comput) escáner m

scapegoat ['skeıpgəut] n cabeza de turco, chivo expiatorio

scar [skɑ:] n cicatriz f ▷ vt marcar con una cicatriz

scarce [skɛəs] adj escaso; **to make o.s. ~** (inf) esfumarse; **scarcely** adv apenas

scare [skɛə'] n susto, sobresalto; (panic) pánico ▷ vt asustar, espantar; **to ~ sb stiff** dar a algn un susto de muerte; **bomb ~** amenaza de bomba; **scarecrow** n espantapájaros m inv; **scared** adj: **to be scared** estar asustado

scarf (pl **scarves**) [skɑ:f, skɑ:vz] n (long) bufanda; (square) pañuelo

scarlet ['skɑ:lıt] adj escarlata

scarves [skɑ:vz] npl of **scarf**

scary ['skɛərı] adj (inf) de miedo

scatter ['skætə'] vt (spread) esparcir, desparramar; (put to flight) dispersar ▷ vi desparramarse; dispersarse

scenario [sı'nɑ:rıəu] n (Theat) argumento; (Cine) guión m; (fig) escenario

sg; (large) báscula sg; **on a large ~** a gran escala; **~ of charges** tarifa, lista de precios

scene [si:n] n (Theat) escena; (of crime, accident) escenario; (sight, view) vista, panorama; (fuss) escándalo; **scenery** n (Theat) decorado; (landscape) paisaje m; **scenic** adj pintoresco

> Be careful not to translate scenery by the Spanish word escenario.

scent [sɛnt] n perfume m, olor m; (fig: track) rastro, pista

sceptical, (us) **skeptical** ['skɛptıkl] adj escéptico

schedule ['ʃɛdju:l, us 'skɛdju:l] n (of trains) horario; (of events) programa m; (list) lista ▷ vt (visit) fijar la hora de; **on ~** a la hora, sin retraso; **to be ahead of/behind ~** ir adelantado/retrasado

scheduled ['ʃɛdju:ld, us 'skɛdju:ld] adj (date, time) fijado; **~ flight** vuelo regular

scheme [ski:m] n (plan) plan m, proyecto; (plot) intriga; (arrangement) disposición f; (pension scheme etc) sistema m ▷ vi (intrigue) intrigar

schizophrenic [skɪtsə'frɛnɪk] adj esquizofrénico

scholar ['skɔlə'] n (pupil) alumno/a; (learned person) sabio/a, erudito/a; **scholarship** n erudición f; (grant) beca

school [sku:l] n escuela, colegio; (in university) facultad f; **schoolbook** n libro de texto; **schoolboy** n alumno; **schoolchild** schoolchildren n alumno/a; **schoolgirl** n alumna; **schooling** n enseñanza; **schoolteacher** n (primary) maestro/a; (secondary) profesor/a m/f

science ['saıəns] n ciencia; **science fiction** n ciencia-ficción f; **scientific** [saıən'tıfık] adj científico; **scientist** n científico/a

sci-fi ['saıfaı] n abbr (inf) = **science fiction**

scissors ['sızəz] npl tijeras fpl; **a pair of ~** unas tijeras

scold [skəuld] vt regañar

scone [skɔn] n pastel de pan

scoop [sku:p] n (for flour etc) pala; (Press) exclusiva

scooter ['sku:tə'] n (motor cycle) Vespa®; (toy) patinete m

scope [skəup] n (of plan, undertaking) ámbito; (of person) competencia; (opportunity) libertad f (de acción)

scorching ['skɔ:tʃɪŋ] adj abrasador(a)

score [skɔ:'] n (points etc) puntuación f; (Mus) partitura; (twenty) veintena ▷ vt (goal, point) ganar; (mark, cut) rayar ▷ vi marcar un tanto; (Football) marcar un gol; (keep score) llevar el tanteo; **on that ~** en lo que se refiere a eso; **~ 6 out of 10** obtener una puntuación de 6 sobre 10; **score out** vt tachar; **scoreboard** n marcador m; **scorer** n marcador(a) m/f; (keep score) encargado/a del marcador

scorn [skɔ:n] n desprecio

Scorpio ['skɔ:pɪəu] n Escorpión m

scorpion ['skɔ:pɪən] n alacrán m

Scot [skɒt] n escocés/esa m/f

Scotch tape® n (us) cinta adhesiva, celo, scotch®m

Scotland ['skɒtlənd] n Escocia

Scots [skɒts] adj escocés/esa; **Scotsman** n escocés m; **Scotswoman** n escocesa

Scottish ['skɒtɪʃ] adj escocés/esa; **the ~ Parliament** el Parlamento escocés

scout [skaut] n explorador m; **girl ~** (us) niña exploradora

scowl [skaul] vi fruncir el ceño; **to ~ at sb** mirar con ceño a algn

scramble ['skræmbl] n (climb) subida (difícil); (struggle) pelea ▷ vi: **to ~ out/through** salir/abrirse paso con dificultad; **to ~ for** pelear por; **scrambled eggs** npl huevos mpl revueltos

scrap [skræp] n (bit) pedacito; (fig) pizca; (fight) riña, bronca; (also: **~ iron**) chatarra, hierro viejo ▷ vt (discard) desechar, descartar ▷ vi reñir, armar (una) bronca; **scraps** npl (waste) sobras fpl, desperdicios mpl; **scrapbook** n álbum m de recortes

scrape [skreɪp] n (fig) lío, apuro ▷ vt raspar; (skin etc) rasguñar; (also: **~ against**) rozar; **to get into a ~** meterse en un lío; **scrape through** vi (in exam) aprobar por los pelos

scrap paper n pedazos mpl de papel

scratch [skrætʃ] n rasguño; (from claw) arañazo ▷ vt (paint, car) rayar; (with claw, nail) rasguñar, arañar ▷ vi rascarse; **to start from ~** partir de cero; **to be up to ~** cumplir con los requisitos; **scratch card** n (BRIT) tarjeta f de "rasque y gane"

scream [skri:m] n chillido ▷ vi chillar

screen [skri:n] n (Cine, TV) pantalla; (movable) biombo ▷ vt (conceal) tapar; (from the wind etc) proteger; (film) proyectar; (fig: person: for security) investigar; **screening** n (Med) exploración f; **screenplay** n guión m; **screen saver** n (Comput) salvapantallas m inv

screw [skru:] n tornillo; (propeller) hélice f ▷ vt atornillar; **screw up** vt (paper, material etc) arrugar; **to ~ up one's eyes** arrugar el entrecejo; **screwdriver** n destornillador m

scribble ['skrɪbl] n garabatos mpl ▷ vi garabatear ▷ vt: **to ~ sth down** garabatear algo

script [skrɪpt] n (Cine etc) guión m; (writing) escritura, letra

scroll [skrəul] n rollo

scrub [skrʌb] n (land) maleza ▷ vt fregar, restregar; (reject) cancelar, anular

scruffy ['skrʌfɪ] adj desaliñado

scrum(mage) ['skrʌm(ɪdʒ)] n (Rugby) melée f

scrutiny ['skru:tɪnɪ] n escrutinio, examen m

scuba diving ['sku:bə'daɪvɪŋ] n submarinismo

sculptor ['skʌlptə'] n escultor(a) m/f

sculpture ['skʌlptʃə'] n escultura

scum [skʌm] n (on liquid) espuma; (pej: people) escoria

scurry ['skʌrɪ] vi: **to ~ off** escabullirse

sea [siː] n mar m (or also f); **by ~** (travel) en barco; **on the ~** (boat) en el mar; (town) junto al mar; **to be all at ~** (fig) estar despistado; **out to** or **at ~** en alta mar; **seafood** n mariscos mpl; **sea front** n paseo marítimo; **seagull** n gaviota

seal [siːl] n (animal) foca; (stamp) sello ▷ vt (close) cerrar; **seal off** vt obturar

sea level n nivel m del mar

seam [siːm] n (in costura; (of metal) juntura; (of coal) veta, filón m

search [sɜːtʃ] n (for person, thing) busca, búsqueda; (of drawer, pockets) registro ▷ vt (look in) buscar en; (examine) examinar; (person, place) registrar ▷ vi: **to ~ for** buscar; **in ~ of** en busca de; **search engine** n (Internet) buscador m; **search party** n equipo de salvamento

sea: seashore n playa, orilla del mar; **seasick** adj mareado; **seaside** n playa, orilla del mar; **seaside resort** n centro turístico costero

season [siːzn] n (of year) estación f; (sporting etc) temporada ▷ vt (food) sazonar; **to be in/out of ~** estar en sazón/fuera de temporada; **seasonal** adj estacional; **seasoning** n condimento; **season ticket** n abono

seat [siːt] n (in bus, train) asiento; (chair) silla; (Parliament) escaño; (buttocks) trasero ▷ vt sentar; (have room for) tener cabida para; **to be ~ed** sentarse; **seat belt** n cinturón m de seguridad; **seats** n asientos mpl

sea: sea water n agua m del mar; **seaweed** n alga marina

sec. abbr = **second**

secluded [sɪˈkluːdɪd] adj retirado

second [ˈsɛkənd] adj segundo ▷ adv en segundo lugar ▷ n segundo; (Aut: also: ~ **gear**) segunda; (Comm) artículo con algún desperfecto; (Brit Scol: degree) título universitario de segunda clase ▷ vt (motion) apoyar; **to have ~ thoughts** cambiar de opinión;

on ~ thoughts or (US) **thought** pensándolo bien; **secondary** adj secundario; **secondary school** n escuela secundaria; **second-class** adj de segunda clase ▷ vt: **to travel second-class** viajar en segunda; **secondhand** adj de segunda mano, usado; **secondly** adv en segundo lugar; **second-rate** adj de segunda categoría

secrecy [ˈsiːkrəsɪ] n secreto

secret [ˈsiːkrɪt] adj, n secreto; **in ~** en secreto

secretary [ˈsɛkrətərɪ] n secretario/a; **S~ of State** (Brit Pol) Ministro (con cartera)

secretive [ˈsiːkrətɪv] adj reservado, sigiloso

secret service n servicio secreto

sect [sɛkt] n secta

section [ˈsɛkʃən] n sección f; (part) parte f; (of document) artículo; (of opinion) sector m

sector [ˈsɛktə] n sector m

secular [ˈsɛkjulə] adj secular, seglar

secure [sɪˈkjuə] adj seguro; (firmly fixed) firme, fijo ▷ vt (fix) asegurar, afianzar; (get) conseguir

security [sɪˈkjuərɪtɪ] n seguridad f; (for loan) fianza; (: object) prenda; **securities** npl (Comm) valores mpl, títulos mpl; **security guard** n guardia m/f de seguridad

sedan [sɪˈdæn] n (US Aut) sedán m

sedate [sɪˈdeɪt] adj tranquilo ▷ vt administrar sedantes a, sedar

sedative [ˈsɛdɪtɪv] n sedante m

seduce [sɪˈdjuːs] vt seducir; **seductive** [sɪˈdʌktɪv] adj seductor/a

see [siː] (pt **saw**, pp **seen**) vt ver; (understand) ver, comprender ▷ vi ver ▷ n sede f; **to ~ sb to the door** acompañar a algn a la puerta; **to ~ that** (ensure) asegurarse de que; **~ you soon/later/tomorrow!** ¡hasta pronto/luego/mañana!; **see off** vt despedir; **see out** vt (take to the door) acompañar hasta la puerta; **see**

through vt fus calar ▷ vt llevar a cabo; **see to** vt fus ocuparse de, encargarse de

seed [siːd] n semilla; (in fruit) pepita; (fig) germen m; (Tennis) preseleccionado/a; **to go to ~** (plant) granar; (fig) descuidarse

seeing ['siːɪŋ] conj: **~ (that)** visto que, en vista de que

seek (pt, pp **sought**) [siːk, sɔːt] vt buscar; (post) solicitar

seem [siːm] vi parecer; **there ~s to be ...** parece que hay ...; **seemingly** adv aparentemente, según parece

seen [siːn] pp of **see**

seesaw ['siːsɔː] n subibaja m

segment ['sɛgmənt] n segmento m; (of citrus fruit) gajo

segregate ['sɛgrɪgeɪt] vt segregar

seize [siːz] vt (grasp) agarrar, asir; (take possession of) secuestrar; (: territory) apoderarse de; (opportunity) aprovecharse de

seizure ['siːʒəʳ] n (Med) ataque m; (Law) incautación f

seldom ['sɛldəm] adv rara vez

select [sɪ'lɛkt] adj selecto, escogido ▷ vt escoger, elegir; (Sport) seleccionar; **selection** n selección f, elección f; (Comm) surtido m; **selective** adj selectivo

self [sɛlf] n uno mismo ▷ pref auto...; **the ~** el yo; **self-assured** adj seguro de sí mismo; **self-catering** adj (BRIT): **self-catering apartment** apartamento con cocina propia; **self-centred**, (US) **self-centered** adj egocéntrico; **self-confidence** n confianza en sí mismo; **self-confident** adj seguro de sí (mismo), lleno de confianza en sí mismo; **self-conscious** adj cohibido; **self-contained** adj (BRIT: flat) con entrada particular; **self-control** n autodominio; **self-defence**, (US) **self-defense** n defensa propia; **self-employed** adj que trabaja por cuenta propia; **self-esteem** n amor propio; **self-indulgent** adj indulgente consigo mismo; **self-interest** n

egoísmo; **selfish** adj egoísta; **self-pity** n lástima de sí mismo; **self-raising**, (US) **self-rising** adj: **self-raising flour** harina con levadura; **self-respect** n amor propio; **self-service** adj de autoservicio

sell (pt, pp **sold**) [sɛl, səʊld] vt vender ▷ vi venderse; **to ~ at** or for **£10** venderse a 10 libras; **sell off** vt liquidar; **sell out** vi: **the tickets are all sold out** las entradas están agotadas; **sell-by date** n fecha de caducidad; **seller** n vendedor(a) m/f

Sellotape® ['sɛləʊteɪp] n (BRIT) celo, scotch®m

selves [sɛlvz] npl of **self**

semester [sɪ'mɛstəʳ] n (US) semestre m

semi... pref semi..., medio...; **semicircle** n semicírculo; **semidetached (house)** n casa adosada; **semi-final** n semifinal f

seminar ['sɛmɪnɑːʳ] n seminario

semi-skimmed ['sɛmɪ'skɪmd] adj semidesnatado; **semi-skimmed (milk)** n leche semidesnatada

senate ['sɛnɪt] n senado; see also **Congress**; **senator** n senador(a) m/f

send (pt, pp **sent**) [sɛnd, sɛnt] vt mandar, enviar; **send back** vt devolver; **send for** vt fus mandar traer; (summon) hacer venir; **send in** vt (report, application, resignation) mandar; **send off** vt (goods) despachar; (BRIT Sport: player) expulsar; **send on** vt (letter, luggage) remitir; **send out** vt (invitation) mandar; (signal) emitir; **send up** vt (person, price) hacer subir; (BRIT: parody) parodiar; **sender** n remitente mf; **send-off** n: **a good send-off** una buena despedida

senile ['siːnaɪl] adj senil

senior ['siːnɪəʳ] adj (older) mayor, más viejo; (: on staff) de más antigüedad; (of higher rank) superior; **senior citizen** n persona de la tercera edad; **senior high school** n (US) ≈ instituto de enseñanza media

sensation [sɛnˈseɪʃən] n sensación f;
sensational adj sensacional
sense [sɛns] n (faculty, meaning)
sentido; (feeling) sensación f; (good
sense) sentido común, juicio ▷ vt
sentir, percibir; **it makes ~** tiene
sentido; **senseless** adj estúpido,
insensato; (unconscious) sin
conocimiento; **sense of humour** n
(BRIT) sentido del humor
sensible [ˈsɛnsɪbl] adj sensato;
(reasonable) razonable, lógico
▮ Be careful not to translate **sensible**
by the Spanish word **sensible**.
sensitive [ˈsɛnsɪtɪv] adj sensible;
(touchy) susceptible
sensual [ˈsɛnsjuəl] adj sensual
sensuous [ˈsɛnsjuəs] adj sensual
sent [sɛnt] pt, pp of **send**
sentence [ˈsɛntəns] n (Ling) oración
f; (Law) sentencia, fallo ▷ vt: **to ~ sb to
death/to five years** condenar a algn
a muerte/a cinco años de cárcel
sentiment [ˈsɛntɪmənt] n
sentimiento; (opinion) opinión f;
sentimental [sɛntɪˈmɛntl] adj
sentimental
Sep. abbr (= September) sep., set.
separate [ˈsɛprɪt] adj separado;
(distinct) distinto; **~s** npl (clothes)
coordinados mpl ▷ vt [ˈsɛpəreɪt]
separar; (part) dividir ▷ vi [ˈsɛpəreɪt]
separarse; **separately** adv por
separado; **separation** [sɛpəˈreɪʃən] n
separación f
September [sɛpˈtɛmbəʳ] n se(p)
tiembre m
septic [ˈsɛptɪk] adj séptico; **septic
tank** n fosa séptica
sequel [ˈsiːkwl] n consecuencia,
resultado; (of story) continuación f
sequence [ˈsiːkwəns] n sucesión f,
serie f; (Cine) secuencia
sequin [ˈsiːkwɪn] n lentejuela
Serb [səːb] adj, n = **Serbian**
Serbian [ˈsəːbiən] adj serbio ▷ n
serbio/a; (Ling) serbio
sergeant [ˈsɑːdʒənt] n sargento

serial [ˈsɪəriəl] n (TV) serie f; **serial
killer** n asesino/a múltiple; **serial
number** n número de serie
series [ˈsɪəriːz] n (pl inv) serie f
serious [ˈsɪəriəs] adj serio; (grave)
grave; **seriously** adv en serio; (ill,
wounded etc) gravemente
sermon [ˈsəːmən] n sermón m
servant [ˈsəːvənt] n servidor(a) m/f; (also:
house ~) criado/a
serve [səːv] vt servir; (customer)
atender; (train) tener parada en;
(apprenticeship) hacer; (prison term)
cumplir ▷ vi (servant, soldier etc) servir;
(Tennis) sacar ▷ n (Tennis) saque m; **it
~s him right** se lo tiene merecido;
server n (Comput) servidor m
service [ˈsəːvɪs] n servicio; (Rel) misa;
(Aut) mantenimiento; (of dishes) juego
▷ vt (car, washing machine) revisar;
(: repair) reparar; **services** npl (Econ:
tertiary sector) sector m terciario or
(de) servicios; (BRIT: on motorway)
área de servicio; **the S~s** las fuerzas
armadas; **to be of ~ to sb** ser útil
a algn; **~ included/not included**
servicio incluido/no incluido; **service
area** n (on motorway) área de servicios;
service charge n (BRIT) servicio;
serviceman n militar m; **service
station** n estación f de servicio
serviette [səːvɪˈɛt] n (BRIT) servilleta
session [ˈsɛʃən] n sesión f; **to be in ~**
estar en sesión
set [sɛt] (pt, pp **set**) n juego; (Radio)
aparato; (TV) televisor m; (of utensils)
batería; (of cutlery) cubierto m; (of books)
colección f; (Tennis) set m; (group of
people) grupo; (Cine) plató m; (Theat)
decorado; (Hairdressing) marcado
▷ adj (fixed) fijo; (ready) listo ▷ vt (place)
poner, colocar; (fix) fijar; (adjust)
ajustar, arreglar; (decide: rules etc)
establecer, decidir ▷ vi (sun) ponerse;
(jam, jelly) cuajarse; (concrete) fraguar;
to be ~ on doing sth estar empeñado
en hacer algo; **to ~ to music** poner
música a; **to ~ on fire** incendiar,

prender fuego a; **to ~ free** poner en libertad; **to ~ sth going** poner algo en marcha; **to ~ sail** zarpar, hacerse a la mar; **set aside** vt poner aparte, dejar de lado; **set down** vt (bus, train) dejar; **set in** vi (infection) declararse; (complications) comenzar; **the rain has ~ in for the day** parece que va a llover todo el día; **set off** vi partir ▷ vt (bomb) hacer estallar; (cause to start) poner en marcha; (show up well) hacer resaltar; **set out** vi partir ▷ vt (arrange) disponer; (state) exponer; **~ out to do sth** proponerse hacer algo; **set up** vt establecer; **setback** n revés m, contratiempo; **set menu** n menú m

settee [sɛ'tiː] n sofá m

setting ['sɛtɪŋ] n (scenery) marco; (of jewel) engaste m, montadura

settle ['sɛtl] vt (argument, matter) resolver; (pay: bill, accounts) pagar, liquidar; (Med: calm) calmar, sosegar ▷ vi (dust etc) depositarse; (weather) estabilizarse; **to ~ for sth** convenir en aceptar algo; **to ~ on sth** decidirse por algo; **settle down** vi (get comfortable) ponerse cómodo, acomodarse; (calm down) calmarse, tranquilizarse; (live quietly) echar raíces; **settle in** vi instalarse; **settle up** vi: **to ~ up with sb** ajustar cuentas con algn; **settlement** n (payment) liquidación f; (agreement) acuerdo, convenio; (village etc) poblado

setup ['sɛtʌp] n sistema m

seven ['sɛvn] num siete; **seventeen** num diecisiete; **seventeenth** adj decimoséptimo; **seventh** adj séptimo; **seventieth** adj septuagésimo; **seventy** num setenta

sever ['sɛvə'] vt cortar; (relations) romper

several ['sɛvərl] adj, pron varios/ as m/f pl, algunos/as m/f pl; **~ of us** varios de nosotros

severe [sɪ'vɪə'] adj severo; (serious) grave; (hard) duro; (pain) intenso

sew (pt **sewed**, pp **sewn**) [səu, səud, səun] vt, vi coser

sewage ['suːɪdʒ] n aguas fpl residuales

sewer ['suːə'] n alcantarilla, cloaca

sewing ['səuɪŋ] n costura; **sewing machine** n máquina de coser

sewn [səun] pp of **sew**

sex [sɛks] n sexo; **to have ~** hacer el amor; **sexism** n sexismo; **sexist** adj, n sexista mf; **sexual** ['sɛksjuəl] adj sexual; **sexual intercourse** n relaciones fpl sexuales; **sexuality** [sɛksjuˈælɪtɪ] n sexualidad f; **sexy** adj sexy

shabby ['ʃæbɪ] adj (person) desharrapado; (clothes) raído, gastado

shack [ʃæk] n choza, chabola

shade [ʃeɪd] n (shadow) sombra; (for lamp) pantalla; (for eyes) visera; (of colour) tono m, tonalidad f ▷ vt dar sombra a; **shades** npl (US: sunglasses) gafas fpl de sol; **in the ~** a la sombra; **a ~ more** (small quantity) un poquito más

shadow ['ʃædəu] n sombra ▷ vt (follow) seguir y vigilar; **shadow cabinet** n (BRIT Pol) gobierno en la oposición

shady ['ʃeɪdɪ] adj sombreado; (fig: dishonest) sospechoso; (deal) turbio

shaft [ʃɑːft] n (of arrow, spear) astil m; (Aut, Tech) eje m, árbol m; (of mine) pozo; (of lift) hueco, caja; (of light) rayo

shake [ʃeɪk] (pt **shook**, pp **shaken**) vt sacudir; (building) hacer temblar ▷ vi (tremble) temblar; **to ~ one's head** (in refusal) negar con la cabeza; (in dismay) mover o menear la cabeza, incrédulo; **to ~ hands with sb** estrechar la mano a algn; **shake off** vt sacudirse; (fig) deshacerse de; **shake up** vt agitar; **shaky** adj (unstable) inestable, poco firme; (trembling) tembloroso

shall [ʃæl] aux vb: **I ~ go** iré; **~ I help you?** ¿quieres que te ayude?; **I'll buy three, ~ I?** compro tres, ¿no te parece?

shallow ['ʃæləu] adj poco profundo; (fig) superficial

S

sham [ʃæm] n fraude m, engaño

shambles [ˈʃæmblz] n confusión f

shame [ʃeɪm] n vergüenza f ▷ vt avergonzar; **it is a ~ that/to do es** una lástima or pena que/hacer; **what a ~!** ¡qué lástima or pena!; **shameful** adj vergonzoso; **shameless** adj descarado

shampoo [ʃæmˈpuː] n champú m ▷ vt lavar con champú

shandy [ˈʃændɪ] n clara, cerveza con gaseosa

shan't [ʃɑːnt] = **shall not**

shape [ʃeɪp] n forma ▷ vt formar, dar forma a; (sb's ideas) formar; (sb's life) determinar; **to take ~** tomar forma

share [ʃeəˈ] n (part) parte f, porción f; (contribution) cuota; (Comm) acción f ▷ vt dividir; (have in common) compartir; **to ~ out (among** or **between)** repartir (entre); **shareholder** n (BRIT) accionista mf

shark [ʃɑːk] n tiburón m

sharp [ʃɑːp] adj (razor, knife) afilado; (point) puntiagudo; (outline) definido; (pain) intenso; (Mus) desafinado; (contrast) marcado; (voice) agudo; (person: quick-witted) avispado; (: dishonest) poco escrupuloso ▷ n (Mus) sostenido ▷ adv: **at two o'clock ~** a las dos en punto; **sharpen** vt afilar; (pencil) sacar punta a; (fig) agudizar; **sharpener** n (also: **pencil sharpener**) sacapuntas m inv; **sharply** adv (abruptly) bruscamente; (clearly) claramente; (harshly) severamente

shatter [ˈʃætəˈ] vt hacer añicos or pedazos; (fig: ruin) destruir, acabar con ▷ vi hacerse añicos; **shattered** adj (grief-stricken) destrozado, deshecho; (exhausted) agotado, hecho polvo

shave [ʃeɪv] vt afeitar, rasurar ▷ vi afeitarse ▷ n: **to have a ~** afeitarse; **shaver** n (also: **electric shaver**) máquina de afeitar (eléctrica)

shaving [ˈʃeɪvɪŋ] n (action) afeitado; **shavings** npl (of wood etc) virutas fpl;

shaving cream n crema (de afeitar); **shaving foam** n espuma de afeitar

shawl [ʃɔːl] n chal m

she [ʃiː] pron ella

sheath [ʃiːθ] n vaina f; (contraceptive) preservativo

shed [ʃed] (pt, pp **shed**) [ʃed] n cobertizo ▷ vt (skin) mudar; (tears) derramar; (workers) despedir

she'd [ʃiːd] = **she had; she would**

sheep [ʃiːp] n (pl inv) oveja; **sheepdog** n perro pastor; **sheepskin** n piel f de carnero

sheer [ʃɪəˈ] adj (utter) puro, completo; (steep) escarpado; (material) diáfano ▷ adv verticalmente

sheet [ʃiːt] n (on bed) sábana; (of paper) hoja; (of glass, metal) lámina

sheik(h) [ʃeɪk] n jeque m

shelf (pl **shelves**) [ʃelf, ʃelvz] n estante m

shell [ʃel] n (on beach) concha; (of egg, nut etc) cáscara; (explosive) proyectil m, obús m; (of building) armazón m ▷ vt (peas) desenvainar; (Mil) bombardear

she'll [ʃiːl] = **she will; she shall**

shellfish [ˈʃelfɪʃ] n (pl inv) crustáceo; (pl: as food) mariscos mpl

shelter [ˈʃeltəˈ] n abrigo, refugio ▷ vt (aid) amparar, proteger; (give lodging to) abrigar ▷ vi abrigarse, refugiarse; **sheltered** adj (life) protegido; (spot) abrigado

shelves [ʃelvz] npl of **shelf**

shelving [ˈʃelvɪŋ] n estantería

shepherd [ˈʃepəd] n pastor m ▷ vt (guide) guiar, conducir; **shepherd's pie** n pastel de carne y puré de patatas

sheriff [ˈʃerɪf] n (US) sheriff m

sherry [ˈʃerɪ] n jerez m

she's [ʃiːz] = **she is; she has**

Shetland [ˈʃetlənd] n (also: **the ~s, the ~ Isles**) las Islas fpl Shetland

shield [ʃiːld] n escudo; (Tech) blindaje m ▷ vt: **to ~ (from)** proteger (de)

shift [ʃɪft] n (change) cambio; (at work) turno ▷ vt trasladar; (remove) quitar ▷ vi moverse

shin [ʃɪn] n espinilla
shine [ʃaɪn] (pt, pp **shone**) n brillo,
lustre m ▷ vi brillar, relucir ▷ vt (shoes)
lustrar, sacar brillo a; **to ~ a torch on
sth** dirigir una linterna hacia algo
shingles ['ʃɪŋglz] n (Med) herpes msg
shiny ['ʃaɪnɪ] adj brillante, lustroso
ship [ʃɪp] n buque m, barco ▷ vt (goods)
embarcar; (send) transportar or enviar
por vía marítima; **shipment** n (goods)
envío; **shipping** n (act) embarque
m; (traffic) buques mpl; **shipwreck** n
naufragio ▷ vt: **to be shipwrecked**
naufragar; **shipyard** n astillero
shirt [ʃəːt] n camisa; **in ~ sleeves** en
mangas de camisa
shit [ʃɪt] (infl) excl ¡mierda! (!)
shiver ['ʃɪvə*] n escalofrío ▷ vi temblar,
estremecerse; (with cold) tiritar
shock [ʃɔk] n (impact) choque m;
(Elec) descarga (eléctrica); (emotional)
conmoción f; (start) sobresalto, susto;
(Med) postración f nerviosa ▷ vt dar
un susto a; (offend) escandalizar;
shocking adj (awful) espantoso;
(improper) escandaloso
shoe [ʃuː] (pt, pp **shod**) n zapato;
(for horse) herradura ▷ vt (horse) herrar;
shoelace n cordón m; **shoe polish** n
betún m; **shoeshop** n zapatería
shone [ʃɔn] pt, pp of **shine**
shonky ['ʃɔŋkɪ] adj (AUST, NZ inf)
chapucero
shook [ʃuk] pt of **shake**
shoot [ʃuːt] (pt, pp **shot**) n (on branch,
seedling) retoño, vástago ▷ vt disparar;
(kill) matar a tiros; (execute) fusilar;
(Cine: film, scene) rodar, filmar ▷ vi
(Football) chutar; **shoot down** vt
(plane) derribar; **shoot up** vi (prices)
dispararse; **shooting** n (shots) tiros
mpl; (Hunting) caza con escopeta
shop [ʃɔp] n tienda; (workshop)
taller m ▷ vi (also: **go ~ping**) ir de
compras; **shop assistant** n (BRIT)
dependiente/a m/f; **shopkeeper** n
tendero/a; **shoplifting** n ratería, robo
(en las tiendas); **shopping** n (goods)

compras fpl; **shopping bag** n bolsa
(de compras); **shopping centre, (us)
shopping center** n centro comercial;
shopping mall n centro comercial;
shopping trolley n (BRIT) carrito de la
compra; **shop window** n escaparate
m, vidriera (LAM)
shore [ʃɔː*] n orilla ▷ vt: **to ~ (up)**
reforzar; **on ~** en tierra
short [ʃɔːt] adj corto; (in time) breve,
de corta duración; (person) bajo; (curt)
brusco, seco; **(a pair of) ~s** (unos)
pantalones mpl cortos; **to be ~ of
sth** estar falto de algo; **in ~** en pocas
palabras; **~ of doing ...** a menos
que hagamos etc ...; **everything
~ of ...** todo menos ...; **it is ~ for**
es la forma abreviada de; **to cut ~**
(speech, visit) interrumpir, terminar
inesperadamente; **to fall ~ of** no
alcanzar; **to run ~ of sth** acabársele
algo; **to stop ~** parar en seco; **to stop
~ of** detenerse antes de; **shortage**
['ʃɔːtɪdʒ] n falta; **shortbread** n galleta
de mantequilla especie de mantecada;
shortcoming n defecto, deficiencia;
short(crust) pastry n (BRIT) pasta
quebradiza; **shortcut** n atajo;
shorten vt acortar; (visit) interrumpir;
shortfall n déficit m; **shorthand** n
(BRIT) taquigrafía; **short-lived** adj
efímero; **shortly** adv en breve, dentro
de poco; **short-sighted** adj (BRIT)
miope; (fig) imprudente; **short-
sleeved** adj de manga corta; **short
story** n cuento; **short-tempered** adj
enojadizo; **short-term** adj (effect) a
corto plazo
shot [ʃɔt] pt, pp of **shoot** ▷ n (sound)
tiro, disparo; (try) tentativa; (injection)
inyección f; (Phot) toma, fotografía;
like a ~ (without any delay) como un
rayo; **shotgun** n escopeta
should [ʃud] aux vb: **I ~ go now** debo
irme ahora; **he ~ be there now** debe
de haber llegado (ya); **I ~ go if I were
you** yo en tu lugar me iría; **I ~ like to**
me gustaría

shoulder ['ʃəʊldəʳ] n hombro ▷ vt
(fig) cargar con; **shoulder blade** n
omóplato

shouldn't ['ʃʊdnt] = **should not**

shout [ʃaʊt] n grito ▷ vt gritar ▷ vi
gritar, dar voces

shove [ʃʌv] n empujón m ▷ vt empujar;
(inf: put): **to ~ sth in** meter algo a
empellones

shovel ['ʃʌvl] n pala; (mechanical)
excavadora ▷ vt mover con pala

show [ʃəʊ] (pt **showed**, pp **shown**)
n (of emotion) demostración f;
(semblance) apariencia; (exhibition)
exposición f; (Theat) función f,
espectáculo ▷ vt mostrar, enseñar;
(courage etc) manifestar;
(exhibit) exponer; (film) proyectar ▷ vi
mostrarse; (appear) aparecer ▷ on ~
(exhibits etc) expuesto; **it's just for ~**
es sólo para impresionar; **show in** vt
(person) hacer pasar; **show off** vi (pej)
presumir ▷ vt (display) lucir; **show
out**: **to ~ sb out** acompañar a algn
a la puerta; **show up** vi (stand out)
destacar; (inf: turn up) presentarse
▷ vt (unmask) desenmascarar; **show
business** n el mundo del espectáculo

shower ['ʃaʊəʳ] n (rain) chaparrón m,
chubasco; (of stones etc) lluvia; (also:
~ **bath**) ducha ▷ vi llover ▷ vt: **to ~
sb with** colmar a algn de algo; **to
have** or **take a ~** ducharse; **shower
cap** n gorro de baño; **shower gel** n
gel de ducha

showing ['ʃəʊɪŋ] n (of film)
proyección f

shown [ʃəʊn] pp of **show**

show: show-off ['ʃəʊɔf] n (inf: person)
fanfarrón/ona m/f; **showroom** n sala
de muestras

shrank [ʃræŋk] pt of **shrink**

shred [ʃrɛd] n (gen pl) triza, jirón m ▷ vt
hacer trizas; (Culin) desmenuzar

shrewd [ʃruːd] adj astuto

shriek [ʃriːk] n chillido ▷ vi chillar

shrimp [ʃrɪmp] n camarón m

shrine [ʃraɪn] n santuario, sepulcro

shrink [ʃrɪŋk] (pt **shrank**, pp **shrunk**) [ʃrɪŋk,
ʃræŋk, ʃrʌŋk] vi encogerse; (be
reduced) reducirse ▷ vt encoger ▷ n (inf,
pej) loquero/a; **to ~ from (doing) sth**
no atreverse a hacer algo

shrivel ['ʃrɪvl], **shrivel up** vt (dry)
secar ▷ vi secarse

shroud [ʃraʊd] n sudario ▷ vt: **~ed in
mystery** envuelto en el misterio

Shrove Tuesday ['ʃrəʊv-] n martes
m de carnaval

shrub [ʃrʌb] n arbusto

shrug [ʃrʌg] n encogimiento de
hombros ▷ vt, vi: **to ~ (one's
shoulders)** encogerse de hombros;
shrug off vt negar importancia a

shrunk [ʃrʌŋk] pp of **shrink**

shudder ['ʃʌdəʳ] n estremecimiento,
escalofrío ▷ vi estremecerse

shuffle ['ʃʌfl] vt (cards) barajar; **to ~
(one's feet)** arrastrar los pies

shun [ʃʌn] vt rehuir, esquivar

shut [ʃʌt] (pt, pp **shut**) vt cerrar ▷ vi
cerrarse; **shut down** vt, vi cerrar;
shut up vi (inf: keep quiet) callarse ▷ vt
(close) cerrar; (silence) callar; **shutter**
n contraventana; (Phot) obturador m

shuttle ['ʃʌtl] n lanzadera; (also:
~ **service**: Aviat) puente m aéreo;
shuttlecock n volante m

shy [ʃaɪ] adj tímido

sibling ['sɪblɪŋ] n (formal) hermano/a

sick [sɪk] adj (ill) enfermo; (nauseated)
mareado; (humour) morboso; **to
be ~** (BRIT) vomitar; **to feel ~** tener
náuseas; **to be ~ of** (fig) estar harto
de; **sickening** adj (fig) asqueroso; **sick
leave** n baja por enfermedad; **sickly**
adj enfermizo; (taste) empalagoso;
sickness n enfermedad f, mal m;
(vomiting) náuseas fpl

side [saɪd] n (gen; of body) costado,
lado; (of lake) orilla; (team) equipo; (of hill)
ladera ▷ adj (door, entrance) lateral ▷ n:
to ~ with sb tomar partido por algn;
by the ~ of al lado de; **~ by ~** juntos;
as; **from all ~s** de todos lados; **to**

take ~s (with) tomar partido (por);

sideboard n aparador m; **sideboards**, (BRIT) **sideburns** npl patillas fpl;

sidelight n (Aut) luz f lateral; **sideline** n (Sport) línea de banda; (fig) empleo suplementario; **side road** n (BRIT) calle f lateral; **side street** n calle f lateral; **sidetrack** vt (fig) desviar (de su propósito); **sidewalk** ['saɪdwɔːk] n (US) acera; **sideways** adv de lado

siege [siːdʒ] n cerco, sitio

sieve [sɪv] n colador m ▷ vt cribar

sift [sɪft] vt cribar ▷ vi: **to ~ through** (information) examinar cuidadosamente

sigh [saɪ] n suspiro ▷ vi suspirar

sight [saɪt] n (faculty) vista; (spectacle) espectáculo; (on gun) mira, alza ▷ vt divisar; **in ~** a la vista; **out of ~** fuera de (la) vista; **sightseeing** n turismo; **to go sightseeing** hacer turismo

sign [saɪn] n (with hand) señal f, seña; (trace) huella, rastro; (notice) letrero; (written) signo ▷ vt firmar; (Sport) fichar; **sign in** vi firmar el registro (al entrar); **sign on** vi (Mil) alistarse; (as unemployed) apuntarse al paro ▷ vt (Mil) alistar; (employee) contratar; **to ~ on for a course** inscribirse en un curso; **sign over** vt: **to ~ sth over to sb** traspasar algo a algn; **sign up** vi (Mil) alistarse; (for course) inscribirse ▷ vt (player) fichar

signal ['sɪɡnl] n señal f ▷ vi señalizar ▷ vt (person) hacer señas a; (message) transmitir

signature ['sɪɡnətʃəʳ] n firma

significance [sɪɡ'nɪfɪkəns] n (importance) trascendencia

significant [sɪɡ'nɪfɪkənt] adj significativo; (important) trascendente

signify ['sɪɡnɪfaɪ] vt significar

sign language n mímica, lenguaje m por or de señas

signpost ['saɪnpəust] n indicador m

Sikh [siːk] adj, n sij mf

silence ['saɪləns] n silencio ▷ vt hacer callar, acallar; (guns) reducir al silencio

silent ['saɪlənt] adj silencioso; (not speaking) callado; (film) mudo; **to keep or remain ~** guardar silencio

silhouette [sɪluːˈɛt] n silueta

silicon chip n chip m, plaqueta de silicio

silk [sɪlk] n seda ▷ cpd de seda

silly ['sɪlɪ] adj (person) tonto; (idea) absurdo

silver ['sɪlvəʳ] n plata; (money) moneda suelta ▷ adj de plata; **silver-plated** adj plateado

SIM card ['sɪm-] n (Tel) SIM card m or f, tarjeta SIM

similar ['sɪmɪləʳ] adj: **~ to** parecido or semejante a; **similarity** [sɪmɪ'lærɪtɪ] n semejanza; **similarly** adv del mismo modo

simmer ['sɪməʳ] vi hervir a fuego lento

simple ['sɪmpl] adj (easy) sencillo; (foolish) simple; (Comm) simple; **simplicity** [sɪm'plɪsɪtɪ] n sencillez f; **simplify** ['sɪmplɪfaɪ] vt simplificar; **simply** adv (live, talk) sencillamente; (just, merely) sólo

simulate ['sɪmjuleɪt] vt simular

simultaneous [sɪməl'teɪnɪəs] adj simultáneo; **simultaneously** adv simultáneamente

sin [sɪn] n pecado ▷ vi pecar

since [sɪns] adv desde entonces ▷ prep desde ▷ conj (time) desde que; (because) ya que, puesto que; **~ then, ever ~** desde entonces

sincere [sɪn'sɪəʳ] adj sincero; **sincerely** adv: **yours sincerely** (in letters) le saluda atentamente

sing (pt **sang**, pp **sung**) [sɪŋ, sæŋ, sʌŋ] vt cantar ▷ vi cantar

Singapore [sɪŋə'pɔːʳ] n Singapur m

singer ['sɪŋəʳ] n cantante mf

singing ['sɪŋɪŋ] n canto

single ['sɪŋɡl] adj único, solo; (unmarried) soltero; (not double) individual, sencillo ▷ n (BRIT: also: **~ ticket**) billete m sencillo; (record) sencillo, single m; **singles** npl (Tennis) individual msg; **single out** vt (*choose*) escoger; **single bed** n cama individual; **single file** n: **in single file** en fila de uno; **single-handed** adv sin ayuda; **single-minded** adj resuelto, firme; **single parent** n (*mother*) madre f soltera; (*father*) padre m soltero; **single-parent family** familia monoparental; **single room** n habitación f individual

singular ['sɪŋɡjʊlə'] adj raro, extraño; (*outstanding*) excepcional ▷ n (*Ling*) singular m

sinister ['sɪnɪstə'] adj siniestro

sink [sɪŋk] (*pt* **sank**, *pp* **sunk**) n fregadero ▷ vt (*ship*) hundir, echar a pique; (*foundations*) excavar; (*piles etc*): **to ~ sth into** hundir algo en ▷ vi hundirse; **sink in** vi (*fig*) penetrar, calar

sinus ['saɪnəs] n (*Anat*) seno

sip [sɪp] n sorbo ▷ vt sorber, beber a sorbitos

sir [sə:'] n señor m; **S~ John Smith** Sir John Smith; **yes ~** sí, señor

siren ['saɪərn] n sirena

sirloin ['sə:lɔɪn] n solomillo

sirloin steak n filete m de solomillo

sister ['sɪstə'] n hermana; (BRIT: *nurse*) enfermera jefe; **sister-in-law** n cuñada

sit (*pt*, *pp* **sat**) [sɪt, sæt] vi sentarse; (*be sitting*) estar sentado; (*assembly*) reunirse; (*for painter*) posar ▷ vt (*exam*) presentarse a; **sit back** vi (*in seat*) recostarse; **sit down** vi sentarse; **sit on** vt fus (*jury, committee*) ser miembro de, formar parte de; **sit up** vi incorporarse; (*not go to bed*) no acostarse

sitcom ['sɪtkɔm] n abbr (TV: = *situation comedy*) telecomedia

site [saɪt] n sitio; (*also*: **building ~**) solar m ▷ vt situar

sitting ['sɪtɪŋ] n (*of assembly etc*) sesión f; (*in canteen*) turno; **sitting room** n sala de estar

situated ['sɪtjʊeɪtd] adj situado

situation [sɪtjʊ'eɪʃən] n situación f; **"~s vacant"** (BRIT) "ofertas de trabajo"

six [sɪks] num seis; **sixteen** num dieciséis; **sixteenth** adj decimosexto; **sixth** [sɪksθ] adj sexto; **sixth form** n (BRIT) clase f de alumnos del sexto año (*de 16 a 18 años de edad*); **sixth-form college** n instituto m para alumnos de 16 a 18 años; **sixtieth** adj sexagésimo; **sixty** num sesenta

size [saɪz] n tamaño; (*extent*) extensión f; (*of clothing*) talla; (*of shoes*) número; **sizeable** adj importante, considerable

sizzle ['sɪzl] vi crepitar

skate [skeɪt] n patín m; (*fish*: pl inv) raya ▷ vi patinar; **skateboard** n monopatín m; **skateboarding** n monopatín m; **skater** n patinador(a) m/f; **skating** n patinaje m; **skating rink** n pista de patinaje

skeleton ['skelɪtn] n esqueleto; (*Tech*) armazón m; (*outline*) esquema m

sketch [sketʃ] n (*drawing*) dibujo; (*outline*) esbozo, bosquejo; (*Theat*) pieza corta, sketch m ▷ vt dibujar; (*plan etc*: *also*: **~ out**) esbozar

skewer ['skju:ə'] n broqueta

ski [ski:] n esquí m ▷ vi esquiar; **ski boot** n bota de esquí

skid [skɪd] n patinazo ▷ vi patinar

ski: **skier** n esquiador(a) m/f; **skiing** n esquí m

skilful, (US)**skillful** ['skɪlful] adj diestro, experto

ski lift n telesilla m, telesquí m

skill [skɪl] n destreza, pericia; (*technique*) técnica; **skilled** adj hábil, diestro; (*worker*) cualificado

skim [skɪm] vt (*milk*) desnatar; (*glide over*) rozar, rasar ▷ vi: **to ~ through** (*book*) hojear; **skimmed milk** n leche f desnatada or descremada

skin [skɪn] n piel f; (*complexion*) cutis m ▷ vt (*fruit etc*) pelar; (*animal*) despellejar; **skinhead** n cabeza m/f rapada, skin(head) m/f; **skinny** adj flaco

skip [skɪp] n brinco, salto; (*container*) contenedor m ▷ vi brincar; (*with* rope) saltar a la comba ▷ vt (pass over) omitir, saltarse

ski: ski pass n forfait m (de esquí); **ski pole** n bastón m de esquiar

skipper ['skɪpə'] n (Naut, Sport) capitán m

skipping rope ['skɪpɪŋ-] n (BRIT) comba

skirt [skə:t] n falda, pollera (LAM) ▷ vt (go round) ladear

skirting board ['skə:tɪŋ-] n (BRIT) rodapié m

ski slope n pista de esquí

ski suit n traje m de esquiar

skull [skʌl] n calavera; (Anat) cráneo

skunk [skʌŋk] n mofeta

sky [skaɪ] n cielo; **skyscraper** n rascacielos m inv

slab [slæb] n (stone) bloque m; (flat) losa; (of cake) trozo

slack [slæk] adj (loose) flojo; (slow) de poca actividad; (careless) descuidado; **slacks** npl pantalones mpl

slain [sleɪn] pp of **slay**

slam [slæm] vt (throw) arrojar (violentamente); (criticize) vapulear, vituperar ▷ vi cerrarse de golpe; **to ~ the door** dar un portazo

slander ['slɑ:ndə'] n calumnia, difamación f

slang [slæŋ] n argot m; (jargon) jerga

slant [slɑ:nt] n sesgo, inclinación f; (fig) punto de vista, interpretación f

slap [slæp] n palmada; (in face) bofetada ▷ vt dar una palmada/bofetada a; (paint etc) **to ~ sth on sth** embadurnar algo con algo ▷ adv (directly) de lleno

slash [slæʃ] vt acuchillar; (fig: prices) fulminar

slate [sleɪt] n pizarra ▷ vt (BRIT fig: criticize) vapulear

slaughter ['slɔ:tə'] n (of animals) matanza; (of people) carnicería ▷ vt matar; **slaughterhouse** n matadero

Slav [slɑ:v] adj eslavo

slave [sleɪv] n esclavo/a ▷ vi (also: ~ **away**) trabajar como un negro; **slavery** n esclavitud f

slay (pt **slew**, pp **slain**) [sleɪ, slu:, sleɪn] vt matar

sleazy ['sli:zɪ] adj (fig: place) sórdido

sledge [slɛdʒ], (US) **sled** [slɛd] n trineo

sleek [sli:k] adj (shiny) lustroso

sleep [sli:p] (pt, pp **slept**) n sueño ▷ vi dormir; **to go to ~** dormirse; **sleep in** vi (oversleep) quedarse dormido; **sleeper** n (person) durmiente m/f; (BRIT: Rail: on track) traviesa; (: train) coche-cama m; **sleeping bag** n saco de dormir; **sleeping car** n coche-cama m; **sleeping pill** n somnífero; **sleepover** n: **we're having a sleepover at Fiona's** nos quedamos a dormir en casa de Fiona; **sleepwalk** vi caminar dormido; (habitually) ser sonámbulo; **sleepy** adj soñoliento; (place) soporífero

sleet [sli:t] n aguanieve f

sleeve [sli:v] n manga; (Tech) manguito; (of record) funda; **sleeveless** adj sin mangas

sleigh [sleɪ] n trineo

slender ['slɛndə'] adj delgado; (means) escaso

slept [slɛpt] pt, pp of **sleep**

slew [slu:] vi (veer) torcerse ▷ pt of **slay**

slice [slaɪs] n (of meat) tajada; (of bread) rebanada; (of lemon) rodaja; (utensil) paleta ▷ vt cortar; rebanar

slick [slɪk] adj (skilful) hábil, diestro; (clever) astuto ▷ n (also: **oil ~**) marea negra

slide [slaɪd] (pt, pp **slid**) n (in playground) tobogán m; (Phot) diapositiva; (BRIT: also: **hair ~**) pasador m ▷ vt correr, deslizar ▷ vi (slip) resbalarse; (glide) deslizarse; **sliding** adj (door) corredizo

slight [slaɪt] adj (slim) delgado; (frail) delicado; (pain etc) leve; (trifling) insignificante; (small) pequeño ▷ n desaire m ▷ vt (offend) ofender, desairar; **not in the ~est** en absoluto; **slightly** adv ligeramente, un poco

s

slim [slɪm] adj delgado, esbelto ▷ vi adelgazar; **slimming** n adelgazamiento

slimy ['slaɪmɪ] adj cenagoso

sling [pt, pp **slung**] [slɪŋ, slʌŋ] n (Med) cabestrillo; (weapon) honda ▷ vt tirar, arrojar

slip [slɪp] n (slide) resbalón m; (mistake) descuido; (underskirt) combinación f; (of paper) papelito n ▷ vt (slide) deslizar ▷ vi deslizarse; (stumble) resbalar(se); (decline) decaer; (move smoothly): **to ~ into/out of** (room etc) colarse en/salirse de; **to give sb the ~** dar esquinazo a algn; **a ~ of the tongue** un lapsus; **slip up** vi (make mistake) equivocarse; meter la pata

slipper ['slɪpəʳ] n zapatilla, pantufla

slippery ['slɪpərɪ] adj resbaladizo

slip road n (BRIT) carretera de acceso

slit [slɪt] (pt, pp **slit**) n raja; (cut) corte m ▷ vt rajar, cortar

slog [slɔg] (BRIT) vi sudar tinta ▷ n: **it was a ~** costó trabajo (hacerlo)

slogan ['sləʊgən] n eslogan m, lema m

slope [sləʊp] n (up) cuesta, pendiente f; (down) declive m; (side of mountain) falda, vertiente f ▷ vi: **to ~ down** estar en declive; **to ~ up** subir (en pendiente); **sloping** adj en pendiente; en declive

sloppy ['slɔpɪ] adj (work) descuidado; (appearance) desaliñado

slot [slɔt] n ranura ▷ vt: **to ~ into** encajar en; **slot machine** n (BRIT: vending machine) máquina expendedora; (for gambling) máquina tragaperras

Slovakia [sləʊ'vækɪə] n Eslovaquia

Slovene [sləʊ'viːn] adj esloveno ▷ n esloveno/a; (Ling) esloveno

Slovenia [sləʊ'viːnɪə] n Eslovenia; **Slovenian** adj, n = **Slovene**

slow [sləʊ] adj lento; (watch): **to be ~** ir atrasado ▷ adv lentamente, despacio ▷ vt (also: **~ down, ~ up**: engine, machine) reducir la marcha de ▷ vi (also: **~ down, ~ up**) ir más despacio;

"**~**" (road sign) "disminuir la velocidad"; **slowly** adv lentamente, despacio; **slow motion** n: **in slow motion** a cámara lenta

slug [slʌg] n babosa; (bullet) posta; **sluggish** adj lento; (lazy) perezoso

slum [slʌm] n casucha

slump [slʌmp] n (economic) depresión f ▷ vi hundirse; (prices) caer en picado

slung [slʌŋ] pt, pp of **sling**

slur [slɜːʳ] n calumnia ▷ vt (word) pronunciar mal; **to cast a ~ on sb** manchar la reputación de algn, difamar a algn

sly [slaɪ] adj astuto; (nasty) malicioso

smack [smæk] n (slap) bofetada ▷ vt dar una manotada a ▷ vi: **to ~ of** saber a, oler a

small [smɔːl] adj pequeño; **small ads** npl (BRIT) anuncios mpl por palabras; **small change** n suelto, cambio

smart [smɑːt] adj elegante; (clever) listo, inteligente; (quick) vivo ▷ vi escocer, picar; **smartcard** n tarjeta inteligente; **smart phone** n smartphone m

smash [smæʃ] n (also: **~-up**) choque m; (sound) estrépito ▷ vt (break) hacer pedazos; (car etc) estrellar; (Sport: record) batir ▷ vi hacerse pedazos; (against wall etc) estrellarse; **smashing** adj (inf) estupendo

smear [smɪəʳ] n mancha; (Med) frotis m inv (cervical) ▷ vt untar; **smear test** n (Med) citología, frotis m inv (cervical)

smell [smel] (pt, pp **smelt** or **smelled**) n olor m; (sense) olfato ▷ vt, vi oler; **smelly** adj maloliente

smelt [smelt] pt, pp of **smell**

smile [smaɪl] n sonrisa ▷ vi sonreír

smirk [smɜːk] n sonrisa falsa or afectada

smog [smɔg] n smog m

smoke [sməʊk] n humo ▷ vi fumar; (chimney) echar humo ▷ vt (cigarettes) fumar; **smoke alarm** n detector m de humo, alarma contra incendios; **smoked** adj (bacon, glass) ahumado;

smoker n fumador(a) m/f; **smoking** n; **"no smoking"** "prohibido fumar";
smoky adj (room) lleno de humo
🔲 Be careful not to translate smoking by the Spanish word smoking.

smooth [smu:ð] adj liso; (sea) tranquilo; (flavour, movement) suave; (person: pej) meloso ▷ vt alisar; (also: ~ out: creases) alisar; (difficulties) allanar

smother ['smʌðə'] vt sofocar; (repress) contener

SMS n abbr (= short message service) SMS m; **SMS message** n (mensaje m) SMS m

smudge [smʌdʒ] n mancha ▷ vt manchar

smug [smʌg] adj engreído

smuggle ['smʌgl] vt pasar de contrabando; **smuggling** n contrabando

snack [snæk] n bocado; **snack bar** n cafetería

snag [snæg] n problema m

snail [sneɪl] n caracol m

snake [sneɪk] n serpiente f

snap [snæp] n (sound) chasquido; (photograph) foto f ▷ adj (decision) instantáneo ▷ vt (break) quebrar ▷ vi quebrarse; (fig: person) contestar bruscamente; **to ~ shut** cerrarse de golpe; **snap at** vt fus: **to ~ (at sb)** (dog) intentar morder (a algn); **snap up** vt agarrar; **snapshot** n foto f (instantánea)

snarl [snɑ:l] vi gruñir

snatch [snætʃ] n (small piece) fragmento ▷ vt (snatch away) arrebatar; (grasp) agarrar; **to ~ some sleep** buscar tiempo para dormir

sneak [sni:k] vi: **to ~ in/out** entrar/ salir a hurtadillas ▷ n (inf) soplón/ona m/f; **to ~ up on sb** aparecérsele de improviso a algn; **sneakers** npl (us) zapatos mpl de lona

sneer [snɪə'] vi sonreír con desprecio; **to ~ at sth/sb** burlarse o mofarse de algo/algn

sneeze [sni:z] vi estornudar

sniff [snɪf] vi sorber (por la nariz) ▷ vt husmear, oler; (glue, drug) esnifar

snigger ['snɪgə'] vi reírse con disimulo

snip [snɪp] n (piece) recorte m; (bargain) ganga ▷ vt tijeretear

sniper ['snaɪpə'] n francotirador(a) m/f

snob [snɔb] n (e)snob mf

snooker ['snu:kə'] n snooker m, billar inglés

snoop [snu:p] vi: **to ~ about** fisgonear

snooze [snu:z] n siesta ▷ vi echar una siesta

snore [snɔ:'] vi roncar ▷ n ronquido

snorkel ['snɔ:kl] n tubo de respiración

snort [snɔ:t] n bufido ▷ vi bufar

snow [snəu] n nieve f ▷ vi nevar; **snowball** n bola de nieve ▷ vi ir aumentando; **snowstorm** n tormenta de nieve, nevasca

snub [snʌb] vt: **to ~ sb** desairar a algn ▷ n desaire m, repulsa

snug [snʌg] adj (cosy) cómodo; (fitted) ajustado

🔵 **KEYWORD**

so [səu] adv 1 (thus, likewise) así, de este modo; **if so** de ser así; **I like swimming — so do I** a mí me gusta nadar — a mí también; **I've got work to do — so has Paul** tengo trabajo que hacer — Paul también; **it's five o'clock — so it is!** son las cinco — ¡pues es verdad!; **I hope/think so** espero/creo que sí; **so far** hasta ahora; (in past) hasta este momento
2 (in comparisons etc: to such a degree) tan; **so quickly (that)** tan rápido (que); **she's not so clever as her brother** no es tan lista como su hermano; **we were so worried** estábamos preocupadísimos
3: **so much** adj, adv tanto; **so many** tantos/as
4 (phrases): **10 or so** unos 10, 10 o así; **so long!** (inf: goodbye) ¡hasta luego!

▶ conj 1 (expressing purpose): **so as to do** para hacer; **so (that)** para que + subjun

2 (expressing result) así que; **so you see, I could have gone** así que ya ves, (yo) podría haber ido

soak [səuk] vt (drench) empapar; (put in water) remojar ▷ vi remojarse, estar a remojo; **soak up** vt absorber; **soaking** adj (also: **soaking wet**) calado or empapado (hasta los huesos or el tuétano)

so-and-so ['səuənsəu] n (somebody) fulano/a de tal

soap [səup] n jabón m; **soap opera** n telenovela; **soap powder** n jabón m en polvo

soar [sɔːʳ] vi (on wings) remontarse; (building etc) elevarse; (price) dispararse

sob [sɔb] n sollozo ▷ vi sollozar

sober ['səubəʳ] adj (serious) serio; (not drunk) sobrio; (colour, style) discreto; **sober up** vi pasársele a algn la borrachera

so-called ['səu'kɔːld] adj llamado

soccer ['sɔkəʳ] n fútbol m

sociable ['səuʃəbl] adj sociable

social ['səuʃl] adj ▷ n velada, fiesta; **socialism** n socialismo; **socialist** adj, n socialista m/f; **socialize** vi hacer vida social; **social life** n vida social; **socially** adv socialmente; **social media** npl medios sociales; **social networking** n interacción f social a través de la red; **social networking site** n red f social; **social security** n seguridad f social; **social services** npl servicios mpl sociales; **social work** n asistencia social; **social worker** n asistente/a m/f social

society [sə'saɪətɪ] n sociedad f; (club) asociación f; (also: **high ~**) alta sociedad

sociology [səusɪ'ɔlədʒɪ] n sociología

sock [sɔk] n calcetín m

socket ['sɔkɪt] n (Elec) enchufe m

soda ['səudə] n (Chem) sosa; (also: **~ water**) soda; (US: also: **~ pop**) gaseosa

sodium ['səudɪəm] n sodio

sofa ['səufə] n sofá m; **sofa bed** n sofá-cama m

soft [sɔft] adj (teacher, parent) blando; (gentle, not loud) suave; **soft drink** n bebida no alcohólica; **soft drugs** npl drogas fpl blandas; **soften** ['sɔfn] vt ablandar; suavizar ▷ vi ablandarse; suavizarse; **softly** adv suavemente; (gently) delicadamente, con delicadeza; **software** n (Comput) software m

soggy ['sɔgɪ] adj empapado

soil [sɔɪl] n (earth) tierra, suelo ▷ vt ensuciar

solar ['səuləʳ] adj solar; **solar power** n energía solar; **solar system** n sistema m solar

sold [səuld] pt, pp of **sell**

soldier ['səuldʒəʳ] n soldado; (army man) militar m

sold out adj (Comm) agotado

sole [səul] n (of foot) planta; (of shoe) suela; (fish: pl inv) lenguado ▷ adj único; **solely** adv únicamente, sólo, solamente; **I will hold you solely responsible** le consideraré el único responsable

solemn ['sɔləm] adj solemne

solicitor [sə'lɪsɪtəʳ] n (BRIT: for wills etc) ≈ notario/a; (in court) ≈ abogado/a

solid ['sɔlɪd] adj sólido; (gold etc) macizo ▷ n sólido

solitary ['sɔlɪtərɪ] adj solitario, solo

solitude ['sɔlɪtjuːd] n soledad f

solo ['səuləu] n solo ▷ adv (fly) en solitario; **soloist** n solista m/f

soluble ['sɔljubl] adj soluble

solution [sə'luːʃən] n solución f

solve [sɔlv] vt resolver, solucionar

solvent ['sɔlvənt] adj (Comm) solvente ▷ n (Chem) solvente m

sombre, (US) **somber** ['sɔmbəʳ] adj sombrío

KEYWORD

some [sʌm] adj 1 (a certain amount or number of): **some tea/water/biscuits** té/agua/(unas) galletas; **there's some milk in the fridge** hay leche en el frigo; **there were some people outside** había algunas personas fuera; **I've got some money, but not much** tengo algo de dinero, pero no mucho 2 (certain: in contrasts) algunos/as; **some people say that ...** hay quien dice que ...; **some films were excellent, but most were mediocre** hubo películas algunas excelentes, pero la mayoría fueron mediocres 3 (unspecified): **some woman was asking for you** una mujer estuvo preguntando por ti; **some day** algún día; **some day next week** un día de la semana que viene; **he was asking for some book (or other)** pedía no se qué libro
▶ pron 1 (a certain number): **I've got some** (books etc) tengo algunos/as 2 (a certain amount) algo; **I've got some** (money, milk) tengo algo; **could I have some of that cheese?** ¿me puede dar un poco de ese queso?; **I've read some of the book** he leído parte del libro
▶ adv: **some 10 people** unas 10 personas, una decena de personas; **somebody** pron alguien; **somehow** adv de alguna manera; (for some reason) por una u otra razón; **someone** pron = **somebody**; **someplace** adv (US) = **somewhere**; **something** pron algo; **would you like something to eat/drink?** ¿te gustaría algo de comer/tomar algo?; **sometime** adv (in future) algún día, en algún momento; **sometime last month** durante el mes pasado; **sometimes** adv a veces; **somewhat** adv algo; **somewhere** adv (be) en alguna parte; (go) a alguna parte; **somewhere else** (be) en otra parte; (go) a otra parte

son [sʌn] n hijo
song [sɒŋ] n canción f
son-in-law [ˈsʌnɪnlɔː] n yerno
soon [suːn] adv pronto, dentro de poco; **~ afterwards** poco después; see also **as**; **sooner** adv (time) antes, más temprano; **I would sooner do that** preferiría hacer eso; **sooner or later** tarde o temprano
soothe [suːð] vt tranquilizar; (pain) aliviar
sophisticated [səˈfɪstɪkeɪtɪd] adj sofisticado
sophomore [ˈsɒfəmɔː] n (US) estudiante mf de segundo año
soprano [səˈprɑːnəʊ] n soprano f
sorbet [ˈsɔːbeɪ] n sorbete m
sordid [ˈsɔːdɪd] adj (place etc) sórdido; (motive etc) mezquino
sore [sɔː] adj (painful) doloroso, que duele ▷ n llaga
sorrow [ˈsɒrəʊ] n pena, dolor m
sorry [ˈsɒrɪ] adj (regretful) arrepentido; (condition, excuse) lastimoso; **~!** ¡perdón!, ¡perdone!; **~?** ¿cómo?; **I feel ~ for him** me da lástima or pena
sort [sɔːt] n clase f, género, tipo ▷ vt (also: **~ out**: papers) clasificar; (organize) ordenar, organizar; (resolve: problem, situation etc) arreglar, solucionar
SOS n SOS m
so-so [ˈsəʊsəʊ] adv regular, así así
sought [sɔːt] pt, pp of **seek**
soul [səʊl] n alma f
sound [saʊnd] adj (healthy) sano; (safe, not damaged) en buen estado; (dependable: person) de fiar; (sensible) sensato, razonable ▷ adj **~ asleep** profundamente dormido ▷ n (noise) sonido, ruido; (volume: on TV etc) volumen m; (Geo) estrecho ▷ vt (alarm) sonar ▷ vi sonar, resonar; (fig: seem) parecer; **to ~ like** sonar a; **soundtrack** n (of film) banda sonora
soup [suːp] n (thick) sopa; (thin) caldo
sour [ˈsaʊə] adj agrio; (milk) cortado; **it's sour ~ grapes!** (fig) ¡están verdes!

source [sɔːs] n fuente f

south [sauθ] n sur m ▷ adj del sur
▷ adv al sur, hacia el sur; **South Africa**
n Sudáfrica f; **South African** adj, n
sudafricano/a; **South America** n
América del Sur, Sudamérica f; **South
American** adj, n sudamericano/a;
southbound adj (con) rumbo al sur;
south-east n sudeste m, sureste
m ▷ adj (counties etc) (del) sudeste,
(del) sureste; **southeastern** adj (del)
sudeste, (del) sureste; **southern** adj
del sur, meridional; **South Korea** n
Corea del Sur; **South Pole** n Polo
Sur; **southward(s)** adv hacia el
sur; **south-west** n suroeste m;
southwestern adj suroeste

souvenir [suːvəˈnɪəʳ] n recuerdo

sovereign [ˈsɒvrɪn] adj, n soberano/a

sow¹ [sau] n cerda, puerca

sow² [səu] (pt **sowed**, pp **sown**) [səu, səun]
vt sembrar

soya [ˈsɔɪə], (US) **soy** [sɔɪ] n soja

spa [spɑː] n balneario

space [speɪs] n espacio; (room) sitio
▷ vt (also: ~ **out**) espaciar; **spacecraft**
n nave f espacial; **spaceship** n
= **spacecraft**

spacious [ˈspeɪʃəs] adj amplio

spade [speɪd] n pala; (child's) palas;
spades npl (Cards: British) picas fpl; (: Spanish)
espadas fpl

spaghetti [spəˈgɛtɪ] n espaguetis mpl

Spain [speɪn] n España

spam n (junk email) correo basura

span [spæn] n (of bird, plane)
envergadura; (of arch) luz f; (in time)
lapso ▷ vt extenderse sobre, cruzar;
(fig) abarcar

Spaniard [ˈspænjəd] n español(a) m/f

Spanish [ˈspænɪʃ] adj español/a
▷ n (Ling) español m, castellano; **the
Spanish** npl los españoles

spank [spæŋk] vt zurrar

spanner [ˈspænəʳ] n (BRIT) llave f
inglesa

spare [spɛəʳ] adj de reserva; (surplus)
sobrante, de más ▷ n (part) pieza de

repuesto ▷ vt (do without) pasarse sin;
(refrain from hurting) perdonar; **to ~**
(surplus) sobrante, de sobra; **spare
part** n pieza de repuesto; **spare room**
n cuarto de los invitados; **spare time**
n tiempo libre; **spare tyre**, (US) **spare
tire** n (Aut) neumático o llanta (LAM)
de recambio; **spare wheel** n (Aut)
rueda de recambio

spark [spɑːk] n chispa; (fig) chispazo

sparking plug [ˈspɑːkɪŋ-] n
= **spark plug**

sparkle [ˈspɑːkl] n centelleo, destello
▷ vi (shine) relucir, brillar

spark plug n bujía

sparrow [ˈspærəu] n gorrión m

sparse [spɑːs] adj esparcido, escaso

spasm [ˈspæzəm] n (Med) espasmo

spat [spæt] pt, pp of **spit**

spate [speɪt] n (fig): **~ of** torrente m de

spatula [ˈspætjulə] n espátula

speak [pt **spoke**, pp **spoken**] [spiːk,
spəuk, ˈspəukn] vt (language) hablar;
(truth) decir ▷ vi hablar; (make a speech)
intervenir; **to ~ to sb/of** or **about
sth** hablar con algn/de o sobre algo;
~ **up!** ¡habla más alto!; **speaker**
n (in public) orador(a) m/f; (also:
loudspeaker) altavoz m; (for stereo
etc) bafle m; **the Speaker** (Pol: BRIT) el
Presidente de la Cámara de los Comunes;
(: US) el Presidente del Congreso

spear [spɪəʳ] n lanza ▷ vt alancear

special [ˈspɛʃl] adj especial; (edition
etc) extraordinario; (delivery)
urgente; **by special delivery** n (Post)
por entrega urgente; **special delivery** n
entrega urgente; **special effects** npl (Cine)
efectos mpl especiales; **specialist**
n especialista mf; **speciality** n
especialidad f; **specialize** vi: **to
specialize (in)** especializarse (en);
specially adv especialmente; **special
offer** n (Comm) oferta especial;
special school n (BRIT) colegio m de
educación especial; **specialty** n (US)
= **speciality**

species [ˈspiːʃiːz] n especie f

specific [spə'sɪfɪk] adj específico; **specifically** adv específicamente

specify ['spesɪfaɪ] vt, vi especificar, precisar

specimen ['spesɪmən] n ejemplar m; (Med: of urine) espécimen m; (: of blood) muestra

speck [spek] n grano, mota

spectacle ['spektəkl] n espectáculo; **spectacles** npl (BRIT: glasses) gafas fpl (SP), anteojos mpl; **spectacular** [spek'tækjulə²] adj espectacular; (success) impresionante

spectator [spek'teɪtə²] n espectador(a) m/f

spectrum (pl **spectra**) ['spektrəm, -trə] n espectro

speculate ['spekjuleɪt] vi especular; **to ~ about** especular sobre

sped [sped] pt, pp of **speed**

speech [spiːtʃ] n (faculty) habla; (formal talk) discurso; (language) lenguaje m; **speechless** adj mudo, estupefacto

speed [spiːd] n velocidad f; (haste) prisa; (promptness) rapidez f; **at full** or **top ~** a máxima velocidad; **speed up** vi acelerarse ▷ vt acelerar; **speedboat** n lancha motora; **speeding** n (Aut) exceso de velocidad; **speed limit** n límite m de velocidad, velocidad f máxima; **speedometer** n velocímetro; **speedy** adj (fast) veloz, rápido; (prompt) pronto

spell [spel] n (also: **magic ~**) encanto, hechizo; (period of time) rato, período ▷ vt deletrear; (fig) anunciar, presagiar; **to cast a ~ on sb** hechizar a algn; **he can't ~** comete faltas de ortografía; **spell out** vt (explain): **to ~ sth out for sb** explicar algo a algn en detalle; **spellchecker** n (Comput) corrector m (ortográfico); **spelling** n ortografía

spelt [spelt] pt, pp of **spell**

spend (pt, pp **spent**) [spend, spent] vt (money) gastar; (time) pasar; (life) dedicar; **spending** n: **government spending** gastos mpl del gobierno

spent [spent] pt, pp of **spend** ▷ adj (cartridge, bullets, match) usado

sperm [spəːm] n esperma

sphere [sfɪə²] n esfera

spice [spaɪs] n especia ▷ vt especiar

spicy ['spaɪsɪ] adj picante

spider ['spaɪdə²] n araña

spike [spaɪk] n (point) punta; (Bot) espiga

spill (pt, pp **spilt** or **spilled**) [spɪl, spɪlt, spɪld] vt derramar, verter ▷ vi derramarse; **spill over** vi desbordarse

spin [spɪn] (pt, pp **spun**) n (Aviat) barrena; (trip in car) paseo (en coche) ▷ vt (wool etc) hilar; (wheel) girar ▷ vi girar, dar vueltas

spinach ['spɪnɪtʃ] n espinacas fpl

spinal ['spaɪnl] adj espinal

spin doctor n (inf) informador(a) parcial al servicio de un partido político

spin-dryer n (BRIT) secadora centrífuga

spine [spaɪn] n espinazo, columna vertebral; (thorn) espina

spiral ['spaɪərəl] n espiral f ▷ vi (prices) dispararse

spire ['spaɪə²] n aguja, chapitel m

spirit ['spɪrɪt] n (soul) alma f; (ghost) fantasma m; (attitude) espíritu m; (courage) valor m, ánimo; **spirits** npl (drink) alcohol msg, bebidas fpl alcohólicas; **in good ~s** alegre, de buen ánimo

spiritual ['spɪrɪtjuəl] adj espiritual ▷ n espiritual m

spit (pt, pp **spat**) [spɪt, spæt] n (for roasting) asador m, espetón m; (saliva) saliva ▷ vi escupir; (sound) chisporrotear

spite [spaɪt] n rencor m, ojeriza ▷ vt fastidiar; **in ~ of** a pesar de, pese a; **spiteful** adj rencoroso, malévolo

splash [splæʃ] n (sound) chapoteo; (of colour) mancha ▷ vt salpicar ▷ vi (also: **~ about**) chapotear; **splash out** vi (BRIT inf) derrochar dinero

splendid ['splendɪd] adj espléndido

splinter ['splɪntə'] n astilla; (in finger) espigón m ▷ vi astillarse, hacer astillas

split [splɪt] (pt, pp split) n hendedura, raja; (fig) división f; (Pol) escisión f ▷ vt partir, rajar; (party) dividir; (work, profits) repartir ▷ vi dividirse, escindirse; **split up** vi (couple) separarse; (meeting) acabarse

spoil (pt, pp **spoiled** or **spoiled**) [spɔɪl, spɔɪlt, spɔɪld] vt (damage) dañar; (ruin) estropear, echar a perder; (child) mimar, consentir

spoilt [spɔɪlt] pt, pp of **spoil** ▷ adj (child) mimado, consentido; (ballot paper) invalidado

spoke [spəʊk] pt of **speak** ▷ n rayo, radio

spoken ['spəʊkn] pp of **speak**

spokesman ['spəʊksmən] n portavoz m

spokesperson ['spəʊkspə:sn] n portavoz m/f, vocero/a (Lam)

spokeswoman ['spəʊkswʊmən] n portavoz f

sponge [spʌndʒ] n esponja; (also: ~ cake) bizcocho ▷ vt (wash) lavar con esponja ▷ vi: **to ~ on** or (us) **off sb** vivir a costa de algn; **sponge bag** n (BRIT) neceser m

sponsor ['spɒnsə'] n patrocinador(a) m/f ▷ vt patrocinar; apadrinar; **sponsorship** n patrocinio

spontaneous [spɒn'teɪnɪəs] adj espontáneo

spooky ['spu:kɪ] adj (inf) espeluznante, horripilante

spoon [spu:n] n cuchara; **spoonful** n cucharada

sport [spɔ:t] n deporte m; **to be a good ~** (person) ser muy majo; **sport jacket** n (us) = **sports jacket**; **sports car** n coche m sport; **sports centre** n (BRIT) polideportivo; **sports jacket**, (us) **sport jacket** n chaqueta deportiva; **sportsman** n deportista m; **sports utility vehicle** n todoterreno m inv; **sportswear** n

ropa de deporte; **sportswoman** n deportista f; **sporty** adj deportivo

spot [spɒt] n sitio, lugar m; (dot: on pattern) punto, mancha; (pimple) grano ▷ vt (notice) notar, observar; **on the ~** en el acto; (immediately) en el acto; **spotless** adj (clean) inmaculado; (reputation) intachable; **spotlight** n foco, reflector m; (Aut) faro auxiliar

spouse [spaʊz] n cónyuge mf

sprain [spreɪn] n torcedura ▷ vt: **to ~ one's ankle** torcerse el tobillo

sprang [spræŋ] pt of **spring**

sprawl [sprɔ:l] vi tumbarse

spray [spreɪ] n rociada; (of sea) espuma; (container) atomizador m; (of paint) pistola rociadora; (of flowers) ramita ▷ vt rociar; (crops) regar

spread [spred] (pt, pp **spread**) n extensión f; (inf: food) comilona ▷ vt extender; (butter) untar; (wings, sails) desplegar; (scatter) esparcir ▷ vi (also: ~ **out**: stain) extenderse; (news) diseminarse; **middle-age** ~ gordura de la mediana edad; **repayments will be ~ over 18 months** los pagos se harán a lo largo de 18 meses; **spread out** vi (move apart) separarse; **spreadsheet** n (Comput) hoja de cálculo

spree [spri:] n: **to go on a ~** ir de juerga or farra (Lam)

spring [sprɪŋ] (pt **sprang**, pp **sprung**) n (season) primavera; (leap) salto, brinco; (coiled metal) resorte m; (of water) fuente f, manantial m ▷ vi saltar, brincar; **spring up** vi (thing: appear) aparecer; (problem) surgir; **spring onion** n cebolleta

sprinkle ['sprɪŋkl] vt (pour: liquid) rociar; (: salt, sugar) espolvorear; **to ~ water etc on**, **~ with water etc** rociar or salpicar de agua etc

sprint [sprɪnt] n (e)sprint m ▷ vi esprintar

sprung [sprʌŋ] pp of **spring**

spun [spʌn] pt, pp of **spin**

spur [spə:'] n espuela; (fig) estímulo, aguijón m ▷ vt (also: ~ **on**) estimular, incitar; **on the ~ of the moment** de improviso

spurt [spə:t] n chorro; (of energy) arrebato ▷ vi chorrear

spy [spaɪ] n espía mf ▷ vi: **to ~ on** espiar a ▷ vt (see) divisar, lograr ver

sq. abbr (Math etc): = **square**

squabble ['skwɔbl] vi reñir, pelear

squad [skwɔd] n (Mil) pelotón m; (Police) brigada f; (Sport) equipo

squadron ['skwɔdrn] n (Mil) escuadrón m; (Aviat, Naut) escuadra

squander ['skwɔndər] vt (money) derrochar, despilfarrar; (chances) desperdiciar

square [skweər] n cuadro; (in town) plaza f; (inf: person) carca mf ▷ adj cuadrado; (inf: ideas, tastes) trasnochado ▷ vt (arrange) arreglar; (Math) cuadrar; (reconcile) compaginar; **all ~** igual(es); **a ~ meal** una comida decente; **two metres ~** dos metros por dos; **one ~ metre** un metro cuadrado; **square root** n raíz f cuadrada

squash [skwɔʃ] n (vegetable) calabaza; (Sport) squash m; (BRIT: drink): **lemon/orange ~** zumo (SP) or jugo (LAM) de limón/naranja ▷ vt aplastar

squat [skwɔt] adj achaparrado ▷ vi agacharse, sentarse en cuclillas; **squatter** n okupa mf

squeak [skwi:k] vi (hinge, wheel) chirriar, rechinar; (mouse) chillar

squeal [skwi:l] vi chillar, dar gritos agudos

squeeze [skwi:z] n presión f; (of hand) apretón m; (Comm) restricción f ▷ vt (hand, arm) apretar

squid [skwɪd] n (inv) calamar m

squint [skwɪnt] vi bizquear, ser bizco ▷ n (Med) estrabismo

squirm [skwə:m] vi retorcerse, revolverse

squirrel ['skwɪrəl] n ardilla

squirt [skwə:t] vi salir a chorros ▷ vt chiscar

Sr abbr = **senior**

Sri Lanka [srɪ'læŋkə] n Sri Lanka m

St abbr (= saint) Sto./a.; (= street) c/

stab [stæb] n (with knife etc) puñalada; (of pain) pinchazo; **to have a ~ at (doing) sth** (inf) probar (a hacer) algo ▷ vt apuñalar

stability [stə'bɪlɪtɪ] n estabilidad f

stable ['steɪbl] adj estable ▷ n cuadra, caballeriza

stack [stæk] n montón m, pila f ▷ vt amontonar, apilar

stadium ['steɪdɪəm] n estadio

staff [stɑːf] n (work force) personal m, plantilla f; (BRIT Scol) cuerpo docente ▷ vt proveer de personal

stag [stæg] n ciervo, venado

stage [steɪdʒ] n escena; (point) etapa; (platform) plataforma; **the ~** el teatro ▷ vt (play) poner en escena, representar; (organize) montar, organizar; **in ~s** por etapas

stagger ['stægər] vi tambalear ▷ vt (amaze) asombrar; (hours, holidays) escalonar; **staggering** adj asombroso

stagnant ['stægnənt] adj estancado

stag night, stag party n despedida de soltero

stain [steɪn] n mancha; (colouring) tintura ▷ vt manchar; (wood) teñir; **stained glass** n vidrio m de color; **stainless steel** n acero inoxidable

stair [steər] n (step) peldaño; **stairs** npl escaleras fpl

staircase ['steəkeɪs], **stairway** ['steəweɪ] n escalera

stake [steɪk] n estaca, poste m; (Comm) interés m; (Betting) apuesta ▷ vt (bet) apostar; **to be at ~** estar en juego; **to ~ a claim to (sth)** presentar reclamación por o reclamar (algo)

stale [steɪl] adj (bread) duro; (food) pasado; (smell) rancio; (beer) agrio

stalk [stɔ:k] n tallo, caña ▷ vt acechar, cazar al acecho

stall n (in market) puesto; (in stable) casilla (de establo) ▷ vt (Aut) calar; (fig) dar largas a ▷ vi (Aut) pararse, calarse; (fig) buscar evasivas

stamina ['stæmɪnə] n resistencia

stammer ['stæmə*'] n tartamudeo
▷ vi tartamudear

stamp [stæmp] n sello, estampilla
(LAM); (mark) marca, huella; (on
document) timbre m ▷ vi (also: **~ one's
foot**) patear ▷ vt (letter) poner sellos
en, franquear; (with rubber stamp)
marcar con sello; **~ed addressed
envelope (sae)** sobre m franqueado
con la dirección propia; **stamp out**
vt (fire) apagar con el pie; (crime,
opposition) acabar con

stampede [stæm'piːd] n estampida

stance [stæns] n postura

stand [stænd] (pt, pp **stood**) n
(attitude) posición f, postura; (for
taxis) parada; (also: **music ~**) atril m;
(Sport) tribuna; (at exhibition) stand
m ▷ vi (be) estar, encontrarse; (be on
foot) estar de pie; (rise) levantarse;
(remain) quedar en pie ▷ vt (place)
poner, colocar; (tolerate, withstand)
aguantar, soportar; **to make a ~** (fig)
mantener una postura firme; **to ~ for
parliament** (BRIT) presentarse (como
candidato) a las elecciones; **stand
back** vi retirarse; **stand by** vi (be ready)
estar listo ▷ vt fus (opinion) mantener;
stand down vi (withdraw) ceder el
puesto; (Mil, Law) retirarse; **stand
for** vt fus (signify) significar; (tolerate)
aguantar, permitir; **stand in for** vt
fus suplir a; **stand out** vi destacarse;
stand up vi levantarse, ponerse de
pie; **stand up for** vt fus defender;
stand up to vt fus hacer frente a

standard ['stændəd] n patrón m,
norma; (flag) estandarte m ▷ adj (size
etc) normal, corriente, estándar;
standards npl (morals) valores mpl
morales; **standard of living** n nivel
m de vida

standing ['stændɪŋ] adj (on foot) de
pie, en pie; (permanent) permanente
▷ n reputación f; **of many years' ~**
que lleva muchos años; **standing
order** n (BRIT: at bank) giro bancario

stand: standpoint n punto de vista;
standstill n: **at a standstill** (industry,
traffic) paralizado; **to come to a
standstill** pararse, quedar paralizado

stank [stæŋk] pt of **stink**

staple ['steɪpl] n (for papers) grapa
▷ adj (crop, industry, food etc) básico
▷ vt grapar

star [stɑː*] n estrella; (celebrity)
estrella, astro ▷ vi: **to ~ in** ser la
estrella de; **the stars** npl (Astrology)
el horóscopo

starboard ['stɑːbəd] n estribor m

starch [stɑːtʃ] n almidón m

stardom ['stɑːdəm] n estrellato

stare [stɛə*] n mirada fija ▷ vi: **to ~
at** mirar fijo

stark [stɑːk] adj (bleak) severo,
escueto ▷ adv: **~ naked** en cueros

start [stɑːt] n principio, comienzo;
(departure) salida; (sudden movement)
sobresalto; (advantage) ventaja ▷ vt
empezar, comenzar; (cause) causar;
(found) fundar; (engine) poner en
marcha ▷ vi comenzar, empezar;
(with fright) asustarse, sobresaltarse;
(train etc) salir; **to ~ doing** or **to do
sth** empezar a hacer algo; **start off**
vi empezar, comenzar; (leave) salir,
ponerse en camino; **start out** vi
(begin) empezar; (set out) partir, salir;
start up vi comenzar; (car) poner
en marcha ▷ vt comenzar; (car) poner
en marcha; **starter** n (Aut) botón m
de arranque; (Sport: official) juez mf de
salida; (: runner) corredor(a) m/f; (BRIT
Culin) entrada, entrante m; **starting
point** n punto de partida

startle ['stɑːtl] vt sobresaltar;
startling adj alarmante

starvation [stɑːˈveɪʃən] n hambre f

starve [stɑːv] vi pasar hambre; (to
death) morir de hambre ▷ vt hacer
pasar hambre

state [steɪt] n estado ▷ vt (say,
declare) afirmar; **to be in a ~** estar
agitado; **the S~s** los Estados Unidos;
statement n afirmación f; **state**

school n escuela or colegio estatal;
statesman n estadista m

static ['stætɪk] n (Radio) parásitos mpl
▷ adj estático

station ['steɪʃən] n estación f; (Radio)
emisora; (rank) posición f social ▷ vt
colocar, situar; (Mil) apostar

stationary ['steɪʃnərɪ] adj
estacionario, fijo

stationer's (shop) n (BRIT) papelería

stationery ['steɪʃənərɪ] n papel m de
escribir; (writing materials) artículos
mpl de escritorio

station wagon n (US) coche m
familiar con ranchera

statistic [stə'tɪstɪk] n estadística;
statistics n (science) estadística

statue ['stætjuː] n estatua

stature ['stætʃəʳ] n estatura; (fig) talla

status ['steɪtəs] n estado; (reputation)
estatus m; **status quo** n (e)statu
quo m

statutory ['stætjutrɪ] adj estatutario

staunch [stɔːntʃ] adj leal,
incondicional

stay [steɪ] n estancia ▷ vi quedar(se);
(as guest) hospedarse; **to ~ put** seguir
en el mismo sitio; **to ~ the night/5
days** pasar la noche/estar o quedarse
5 días; **stay away** vi (from person,
building) no acercarse; (from event) no
acudir; **stay behind** vi quedar atrás;
stay in vi quedarse en casa; **stay on**
vi quedarse; **stay out** vi (of house) no
volver a casa; (strikers) no volver al
trabajo; **stay up** vi (at night) velar, no
acostarse

steadily ['stedɪlɪ] adv (firmly)
firmemente; (unceasingly) sin parar;
(fixedly) fijamente

steady ['stedɪ] adj (fixed) firme;
(regular) regular; (boyfriend etc) formal,
fijo; (person, character) sensato,
juicioso ▷ vt (stabilize) estabilizar;
(nerves) calmar

steak [steɪk] n filete m; (beef) bistec m

steal (pt **stole**, pp **stolen**) [stiːl, stəul,
'stəuln] vt, vi robar

steam [stiːm] n vapor m; (mist) vaho,
humo ▷ vt (Culin) cocer al vapor ▷ vi
echar vapor; **steam up** vi (window)
empañarse; **to get ~ed up** about sth
(fig) ponerse negro por algo; **steamy**
adj (room) lleno de vapor; (window)
empañado; (heat, atmosphere)
bochornoso

steel [stiːl] n acero ▷ adj de acero

steep [stiːp] adj escarpado, abrupto;
(stair) empinado; (price) exorbitante,
excesivo ▷ vt empapar, remojar

steeple ['stiːpl] n aguja

steer [stɪəʳ] vt (car) conducir (SP),
manejar (LAM); (person) dirigir ▷ vi
conducir (SP), manejar (LAM);
steering n (Aut) dirección f; **steering
wheel** n volante m

stem [stem] n (of plant) tallo; (of glass)
pie m ▷ vt detener; (blood) restañar

step [step] n paso; (stair) peldaño,
escalón m ▷ vi: **to ~ forward** dar
un paso adelante; **steps** npl (BRIT)
= stepladder; **to be in/out of ~ with**
estar acorde con/estar en disonancia
con; **step down** vi (fig) retirarse;
step in vi entrar; (fig) intervenir;
step up vt (increase) aumentar;
stepbrother n hermanastro;
stepchild (pl **stepchildren**) n
hijastro/a; **stepdaughter** n
hijastra; **stepfather** n padrastro;
stepladder n escalera doble or de
tijera; **stepmother** n madrastra;
stepsister n hermanastra; **stepson**
n hijastro

stereo ['stɪərɪəu] n estéreo ▷ adj (also:
~phonic) estéreo, estereofónico

stereotype ['stɪərɪətaɪp] n
estereotipo ▷ vt estereotipar

sterile ['steraɪl] adj estéril; **sterilize**
['sterɪlaɪz] vt esterilizar

sterling ['stɜːlɪŋ] adj (silver) de ley ▷ n
(Econ) libras fpl esterlinas; **a pound ~**
una libra esterlina

stern [stɜːn] adj severo, austero ▷ n
(Naut) popa

steroid ['stɪərɔɪd] n esteroide m

stew [stjuː] n estofado ▷ vt, vi estofar, guisar; (fruit) cocer

steward ['stjuəd] n camarero; **stewardess** n azafata

stick [stɪk] (pt, pp **stuck**) n palo; (as weapon) porra; (also: **walking ~**) bastón m ▷ vt (glue) pegar; (inf: put) meter; (: tolerate) aguantar, soportar ▷ vi pegarse; (come to a stop) quedarse parado; **it stuck in my mind** se me quedó grabado; **stick out** vi sobresalir; **stick up** vi sobresalir; **stick up for** vt fus defender; **sticker** n (label) etiqueta adhesiva; (with slogan) pegatina; **sticking plaster** n (BRIT) esparadrapo; **stick insect** n insecto palo; **stick shift** n (US AUT) palanca de cambios

sticky ['stɪkɪ] adj pegajoso; (label) adhesivo; (fig) difícil

stiff [stɪf] adj rígido, tieso; (hard) duro; (difficult) difícil; (person) inflexible; (price) exorbitante ▷ adv: **scared/bored ~** muerto de miedo/aburrimiento

stifling ['staɪflɪŋ] adj (heat) sofocante, bochornoso

stigma ['stɪgmə] n estigma m

stiletto [stɪ'letəu] n (BRIT: also: **~ heel**) tacón m de aguja

still [stɪl] adj inmóvil, quieto ▷ adv todavía; (even) aún; (nonetheless) sin embargo, aun así

stimulate ['stɪmjuleɪt] vt estimular

stimulus (pl **stimuli**) ['stɪmjuləs, -laɪ] n estímulo, incentivo

sting [stɪŋ] (pt, pp **stung**) n (wound) picadura; (pain) escozor m, picazón m; (organ) aguijón m ▷ vt picar ▷ vi picar

stink (pt **stank**, pp **stunk**) [stɪŋk, stæŋk, stʌŋk] n hedor m, tufo ▷ vi heder, apestar

stir [stəːr] n (fig: agitation) conmoción f ▷ vt (tea etc) remover; (fig: emotions) provocar ▷ vi moverse; **stir up** vt (trouble) fomentar; **stir-fry** vt sofreír removiendo ▷ n plato preparado sofriendo y removiendo los ingredientes

stitch [stɪtʃ] n (Sewing) puntada; (Knitting) punto; (Med) punto de sutura; (pain) punzada ▷ vt coser; (Med) suturar

stock [stɒk] n (Comm: reserves) existencias fpl, stock m; (: selection) surtido; (Agr) ganado, ganadería; (Culin) caldo; (fig: lineage) estirpe f; (Finance) capital m ▷ adj (reply etc) clásico ▷ vt (have in stock) tener existencias de; **stocks** npl: **~s and shares** acciones y valores; **in ~** en existencia or almacén; **out of ~** agotado; **to take ~ of** (fig) considerar, examinar; **stockbroker** ['stɒkbrəukər] n agente m/or corredor(a) m/f de bolsa; **stock cube** n pastilla or cubito de caldo; **stock exchange** n bolsa; **stockholder** ['stɒkhəuldər] n (us) accionista m/f

stocking ['stɒkɪŋ] n media

stock market n bolsa (de valores)

stole [stəul] pt of **steal** ▷ n estola

stolen ['stəuln] pp of **steal**

stomach ['stʌmək] n (Anat) estómago; (belly) vientre m ▷ vt tragar, aguantar; **stomachache** n dolor m de estómago

stone [stəun] n piedra; (in fruit) hueso; (BRIT: weight) = 6.348 kg; 14lb ▷ adj de piedra ▷ vt apedrear; (fruit) deshuesar

stood [stud] pt, pp of **stand**

stool [stuːl] n taburete m

stoop [stuːp] vi (also: **~ down**) doblarse, agacharse; (also: **have a ~**) ser cargado de espaldas; (bend) inclinarse

stop [stɒp] n parada; (in punctuation) punto ▷ vt parar, detener; (break off) suspender; (block: pay) suspender; (: cheque) invalidar; (also: **put a ~ to**) poner término a ▷ vi pararse, detenerse; (end) acabarse; **to ~ doing sth** dejar de hacer algo; **stop by** vi pasar por; **stop off** vi interrumpir el viaje; **stopover** n parada intermedia; (Aviat) escala; **stoppage** n (strike) paro; (blockage) obstrucción f

storage ['stɔːrɪdʒ] n almacenaje m

store [stɔː'] n (stock) provisión f; (depot) almacén m; (BRIT: large shop) almacén m; (US) tienda; (reserve) reserva, repuesto ▷ vt almacenar; **stores** npl víveres mpl; **who knows what is in - for us** quién sabe lo que nos espera; **storekeeper** n (us) tendero/a

storey, (us) **story** ['stɔːrɪ] n piso

storm [stɔːm] n tormenta; (fig: of applause) salva; (: of criticism) nube f ▷ vi (fig) rabiar ▷ vt tomar por asalto; **stormy** adj tempestuoso

story ['stɔːrɪ] n historia; (lie) cuento; (US) = **storey**

stout [staut] adj (strong) sólido; (fat) gordo, corpulento ▷ n cerveza negra

stove [stəuv] n (for cooking) cocina; (for heating) estufa

straight [streɪt] adj recto, derecho; (frank) franco, directo ▷ adv derecho, directamente; (drink) solo; **to put or get sth -** dejar algo en claro; **- away, - off** en seguida; **straighten** vt (also: **straighten out**) enderezar, poner derecho ▷ vi (also: **straighten up**) enderezarse, ponerse derecho; **straightforward** [streɪt'fɔːwəd] adj (simple) sencillo; (honest) sincero

strain [streɪn] n tensión f; (Tech) presión f; (Med) torcedura; (of virus) variedad f ▷ vt (back etc) torcerse; (resources) agotar; (stretch) estirar; (filter) filtrar; **strained** adj (muscle) torcido; (laugh) forzado; (relations) tenso; **strainer** n colador m

strait [streɪt] n (Geo) estrecho; **to be in dire -s** (fig) estar en un gran aprieto

strand [strænd] n (of thread) hebra; (of rope) ramal m; **- of hair** un pelo; **stranded** adj (person: without money) desamparado; (: without transport) colgado

strange [streɪndʒ] adj (not known) desconocido; (odd) extraño, raro; **strangely** adv de un modo raro; see also **enough**; **stranger** n

desconocido/a; (from another area) forastero/a

> Be careful not to translate stranger by the Spanish word extranjero.

strangle ['stræŋgl] vt estrangular

strap [stræp] n correa; (of slip, dress) tirante m

strategic [strə'tiːdʒɪk] adj estratégico

strategy ['strætɪdʒɪ] n estrategia

straw [strɔː] n paja; (also: drinking ~) caña, pajita; **that's the last ~!** ¡eso es el colmo!

strawberry ['strɔːbərɪ] n fresa, frutilla (LAM)

stray [streɪ] adj (animal) extraviado; (bullet) perdido; (scattered) disperso ▷ vi extraviarse, perderse

streak [striːk] n raya ▷ vt rayar ▷ vi: **to - past** pasar como un rayo

stream [striːm] n riachuelo, arroyo; (jet) chorro; (flow) corriente f; (of people) oleada ▷ vt (Scol) dividir en grupos por habilidad ▷ vi correr, fluir; **to - in/out** (people) entrar/salir en tropel

street [striːt] n calle f; **streetcar** n (us) tranvía m; **street light** n farol m (LAM), farola (SP); **street map** n plano (de la ciudad); **street plan** n plano callejero

strength [streŋθ] n fuerza; (of girder, knot etc) resistencia; (fig: power) poder m; **strengthen** vt fortalecer, reforzar

strenuous ['strenjuəs] adj (energetic) enérgico

stress [stres] n presión f; (mental strain) estrés m; (Ling, Poetry) acento ▷ vt subrayar, recalcar; **stressed** adj (tense) estresado, agobiado; (syllable) acentuado; **stressful** adj (job) estresante

stretch [stretʃ] n (of sand etc) trecho ▷ vi estirarse; (extend): **to - to or as far as** extenderse hasta ▷ vt extender, estirar; (make demands of) exigir el máximo esfuerzo a; **stretch out** vi tenderse ▷ vt (arm etc) extender; (spread) estirar

stretcher ['strɛtʃəʳ] n camilla

strict [strɪkt] adj estricto; (discipline, ban) severo; **strictly** adv estrictamente; (totally) terminantemente

stride (pt **strode**, pp **stridden**) [straɪd, strəud, 'strɪdn] n zancada, tranco ▷ vi dar zancadas, andar a trancos

strike [straɪk] (pt, pp **struck**) n huelga; (of oil etc) descubrimiento; (attack) ataque m ▷ vt golpear, pegar; (oil etc) descubrir; (agreement, deal) alcanzar ▷ vi declarar la huelga; (attack) atacar; (clock) dar la hora; **on ~** (workers) en huelga; **to ~ a match** encender una cerilla; **striker** n huelguista mf; (Sport) delantero; **striking** ['straɪkɪŋ] adj (colour) llamativo; (obvious) notorio

string (pt, pp **strung**) [strɪŋ, strʌŋ] n cuerda; (row) hilera ▷ vt: **to ~ together** ensartar; **to ~** extenderse; **the strings** npl (Mus) los instrumentos de cuerda; **to pull ~s** (fig) mover palancas

strip [strɪp] n tira; (of land) franja; (of metal) cinta, lámina ▷ vt desnudar; (also: **~ down**: machine) desmontar ▷ vi desnudarse; **strip off** vt (paint etc) quitar ▷ vi (person) desnudarse

stripe [straɪp] n raya; (Mil) galón m; **striped** adj a rayas, rayado

stripper ['strɪpəʳ] n artista mf de striptease

strip-search ['strɪpsəːtʃ] vt: **to ~ sb** desnudar y registrar a algn

strive (pt **strove**, pp **striven**) [straɪv, strəuv, 'strɪvn] vi: **to ~ to do sth** esforzarse or luchar por hacer algo

strode [strəud] pt of **stride**

stroke [strəuk] n (blow) golpe m; (Swimming) brazada; (Med) apoplejía ▷ vt acariciar; **at a ~** de un solo golpe

stroll [strəul] n paseo, vuelta ▷ vi dar un paseo or una vuelta; **stroller** n (us: pushchair) cochecito

strong [strɔŋ] adj fuerte; **they are 50 ~** son 50; **stronghold** n fortaleza; (fig) baluarte m; **strongly** adv

fuertemente, con fuerza; (believe) firmemente

strove [strəuv] pt of **strive**

struck [strʌk] pt, pp of **strike**

structure ['strʌktʃəʳ] n estructura; (building) construcción f

struggle ['strʌgl] n lucha ▷ vi luchar

strung [strʌŋ] pt, pp of **string**

stub [stʌb] n (of ticket etc) matriz f; (of cigarette) colilla ▷ vt: **to ~ one's toe on sth** dar con el dedo del pie contra algo; **stub out** vt apagar

stubble ['stʌbl] n rastrojo; (on chin) barba (incipiente)

stubborn ['stʌbən] adj terco, testarudo

stuck [stʌk] pt, pp of **stick** ▷ adj (jammed) atascado

stud [stʌd] n (shirt stud) corchete m; (of boot) taco; (earring) pendiente m (de bolita); (also: **~ farm**) caballeriza; (also: **~ horse**) caballo semental m ▷ vt (fig): **~ded with** salpicado de

student ['stjuːdənt] n estudiante mf ▷ adj estudiantil; **student driver** n (us Aut) aprendiz(a) m/f de conductor; **students' union** n (BRIT: association) sindicato de estudiantes; (: building) centro de estudiantes

studio ['stjuːdɪəu] n estudio; (artist's) taller m; **studio flat** n estudio

study ['stʌdɪ] n estudio ▷ vt estudiar; (examine) examinar, investigar ▷ vi estudiar

stuff [stʌf] n materia; (substance) material m, sustancia; (things, belongings) cosas fpl ▷ vt llenar; (Culin) rellenar; (animal) disecar; **stuffing** n relleno; **stuffy** adj (room) mal ventilado; (person) de miras estrechas

stumble ['stʌmbl] vi tropezar, dar un traspié; **stumble across** vt fus (fig) tropezar con

stump [stʌmp] n (of tree) tocón m; (of limb) muñón m ▷ vt: **to be ~ed for an answer** quedarse sin saber qué contestar

stun [stʌn] vt aturdir

stung [stʌŋ] *pt, pp of* **sting**

stunk [stʌŋk] *pp of* **stink**

stunned [stʌnd] *adj* (dazed) aturdido, atontado; (amazed) pasmado; (shocked) anonadado

stunning ['stʌnɪŋ] *adj* (fig: news) pasmoso; (: outfit etc) sensacional

stunt [stʌnt] *n* (in film) escena peligrosa; (also: **publicity ~**) truco publicitario

stupid ['stjuːpɪd] *adj* estúpido, tonto; **stupidity** [stjuːˈpɪdɪtɪ] *n* estupidez *f*

sturdy ['stɜːdɪ] *adj* robusto, fuerte

stutter ['stʌtə^r] *n* tartamudeo ▷ *vi* tartamudear

style [staɪl] *n* estilo; **stylish** *adj* elegante, a la moda; **stylist** *n* (hair stylist) peluquero/a

sub... [sʌb] *pref* sub...; **subconscious** *adj* subconsciente

subdued [səbˈdjuːd] *adj* (light) tenue; (person) sumiso, manso

subject *n* ['sʌbdʒɪkt] súbdito; (Scol) tema m, materia; (Grammar) sujeto ▷ *vt* [səbˈdʒɛkt]: **to ~ sb to sth** someter a algn a algo ▷ *adj* ['sʌbdʒɪkt]: **to be ~ to** (law) estar sujeto a; (person) ser propenso a; **subjective** [səbˈdʒɛktɪv] *adj* subjetivo; **subject matter** *n* (content) contenido

subjunctive [səbˈdʒʌŋktɪv] *adj, n* subjuntivo

submarine [sʌbməˈriːn] *n* submarino

submission [səbˈmɪʃən] *n* sumisión *f*

submit [səbˈmɪt] *vt* someter ▷ *vi* someterse

subordinate [səˈbɔːdɪnət] *adj, n* subordinado/a

subscribe [səbˈskraɪb] *vi* suscribir; **to ~ to** (fund, opinion) suscribir, aprobar; (newspaper) suscribirse a

subscription [səbˈskrɪpʃən] *n* abono; (to magazine) suscripción *f*

subsequent ['sʌbsɪkwənt] *adj* subsiguiente, posterior;

subsequently *adv* posteriormente, más tarde

subside [səbˈsaɪd] *vi* hundirse; (flood) bajar; (wind) amainar

subsidiary [səbˈsɪdɪərɪ] *n* sucursal *f*, filial *f*

subsidize ['sʌbsɪdaɪz] *vt* subvencionar

subsidy ['sʌbsɪdɪ] *n* subvención *f*

substance ['sʌbstəns] *n* sustancia

substantial [səbˈstænʃl] *adj* sustancial, sustancioso; (fig) importante

substitute ['sʌbstɪtjuːt] *n* (person) suplente *mf*; (thing) sustituto ▷ *vt*: **to ~ A for B** sustituir B por A, reemplazar A por B; **substitution** *n* sustitución *f*

subtle ['sʌtl] *adj* sutil

subtract [səbˈtrækt] *vt* restar; sustraer

suburb ['sʌbəːb] *n* barrio residencial; **the ~s** las afueras (de la ciudad); **suburban** [səˈbəːbən] *adj* suburbano; (train etc) de cercanías

subway ['sʌbweɪ] *n* (BRIT) paso subterráneo o inferior; (US) metro

succeed [səkˈsiːd] *vi* (person) tener éxito; (plan) salir bien ▷ *vt* suceder a; **to ~ in doing** lograr hacer

success [səkˈsɛs] *n* éxito; **successful** *adj* (venture) de éxito, exitoso (esp LAM); **successfully** *adv* con éxito

> ⬛ Be careful not to translate success by the Spanish word suceso.

succession [səkˈseʃən] *n* sucesión *f*, serie *f*

successive [səkˈsesɪv] *adj* sucesivo

successor [səkˈsesə^r] *n* sucesor(a) *m/f*

succumb [səˈkʌm] *vi* sucumbir

such [sʌtʃ] *adj* tal, semejante; (of that kind): **~ a book** tal libro; (so much): **~ courage** tanto valor ▷ *adv* tan; **~ a long trip** un viaje tan largo; **~ a lot of** tanto; **~ as** (like) tal como; **as ~** como tal; **such-and-such** *adj* tal o cual

suck [sʌk] *vt* chupar; (bottle) sorber; (breast) mamar

Sudan [suˈdæn] *n* Sudán *m*

sudden ['sʌdn] adj (rapid) repentino, súbito; (unexpected) imprevisto; **all of a ~** de repente; **suddenly** adv de repente

sudoku [su'dəʊku:] n sudoku m

sue [su:] vt demandar

suede [sweɪd] n ante m, gamuza (LAM)

suffer ['sʌfəʳ] vt sufrir, padecer; (tolerate) aguantar, soportar ▷ vi sufrir, padecer; **to ~ from** padecer, sufrir; **suffering** n sufrimiento

suffice [sə'faɪs] vi bastar, ser suficiente

sufficient [sə'fɪʃənt] adj suficiente, bastante

suffocate ['sʌfəkeɪt] vi ahogarse, asfixiarse

sugar ['ʃʊgəʳ] n azúcar m ▷ vt echar azúcar a, azucarar

suggest [sə'dʒest] vt sugerir; **suggestion** [sə'dʒestʃən] n sugerencia

suicide ['suɪsaɪd] n suicidio; (person) suicida mf; **to commit ~** suicidarse; **suicide attack** n atentado suicida; **suicide bomber** n terrorista mf suicida; **suicide bombing** n atentado m suicida

suit [su:t] n traje m; (Law) pleito; (Cards) palo ▷ vt convenir; (clothes) sentar bien a, ir bien a; (adapt): **to ~ sth to** adaptar o ajustar algo a; **well ~ed** (couple) hechos el uno para el otro; **suitable** adj conveniente; (apt) indicado; **suitcase** n maleta, valija (LAM)

suite [swi:t] n (of rooms) suite f; (Mus) suite f; (furniture): **bedroom/dining room ~** (juego de) dormitorio/comedor m; **a three-piece ~** un tresillo

sulfur ['sʌlfəʳ] n (us) = **sulphur**

sulk [sʌlk] vi estar de mal humor

sulphur, (us)**sulfur** ['sʌlfəʳ] n azufre m

sultana [sʌl'tɑ:nə] n (fruit) pasa de Esmirna

sum [sʌm] n suma; (total) total m; **sum up** vt resumir ▷ vi hacer un resumen

summarize ['sʌməraɪz] vt resumir

summary ['sʌmərɪ] n resumen m ▷ adj (justice) sumario

summer ['sʌməʳ] n verano ▷ adj de verano; **in (the) ~** en (el) verano; **summer holidays** npl vacaciones fpl de verano; **summertime** n (season) verano

summit ['sʌmɪt] n cima, cumbre f; (also: ~ **conference**) (conferencia) cumbre f

summon ['sʌmən] vt (person) llamar; (meeting) convocar

sun [sʌn] n sol m

Sun. abbr (= Sunday) dom.

sun: **sunbathe** vi tomar el sol; **sunbed** n cama solar; **sunblock** n filtro solar; **sunburn** n (painful) quemadura del sol; (tan) bronceado; **sunburnt**, **sunburned** adj (tanned) bronceado; (painfully) quemado por el sol

Sunday ['sʌndɪ] n domingo

sunflower ['sʌnflaʊəʳ] n girasol m

sung [sʌŋ] pp of **sing**

sunglasses ['sʌnglɑ:sɪz] npl gafas fpl de sol

sunk [sʌŋk] pp of **sink**

sun: **sunlight** n luz f del sol; **sun lounger** n tumbona, perezosa (LAM); **sunny** ['sʌnɪ] adj soleado; (day) de sol; (fig) alegre; **sunrise** n salida del sol; **sun roof** n (Aut) techo corredizo o solar; **sunscreen** n filtro solar; **sunset** n puesta del sol; **sunshade** n (over table) sombrilla; **sunshine** ['sʌnʃaɪn] n sol m; **sunstroke** n insolación f; **suntan** n bronceado; **suntan lotion** n bronceador m; **suntan oil** n aceite m bronceador

super ['su:pəʳ] adj (inf) genial

superb [su:'pə:b] adj magnífico, espléndido

superficial [su:pə'fɪʃəl] adj superficial

superintendent [su:pərɪn'tendənt] n director(a) m/f; (also: **police ~**) subjefe/a m/f

superior [su'pɪərɪəˏ] adj superior; (smug) desdeñoso ⊳ n superior m

superlative [su'pə:lətɪv] n superlativo

supermarket ['su:pəma:kɪt] n supermercado

supernatural [su:pə'nætʃərəl] adj sobrenatural ⊳ n: **the ~** lo sobrenatural

superpower ['su:pəpauəˏ] n (Pol) superpotencia

superstition [su:pə'stɪʃən] n superstición f

superstitious [su:pə'stɪʃəs] adj supersticioso

superstore ['su:pəstɔ:ˏ] n (BRIT) hipermercado

supervise ['su:pəvaɪz] vt supervisar; **supervision** [su:pə'vɪʒən] n supervisión f; **supervisor** n supervisor(a) m/f

supper ['sʌpəˏ] n cena

supple ['sʌpl] adj flexible

supplement n ['sʌplɪmənt] suplemento ⊳ vt [sʌplɪˈment] suplir

supplier [sə'plaɪəˏ] n (Comm) distribuidor(a) m/f

supply [sə'plaɪ] vt (provide) suministrar; (equip): **to ~ (with)** proveer (de) ⊳ n provisión f; (of gas, water etc) suministro; **supplies** (food) víveres mpl; (Mil) pertrechos mpl

support [sə'pɔ:t] n apoyo; (Tech) soporte m ⊳ vt apoyar; (financially) mantener; (uphold) sostener; **supporter** n (Pol etc) partidario/a; (Sport) aficionado/a

> Be careful not to translate support by the Spanish word soportar.

suppose [sə'pəuz] vt suponer; (imagine) imaginarse; **to be ~d to do sth** deber hacer algo; **supposedly** [sə'pəuzɪdlɪ] adv según cabe suponer; **supposing** conj en caso de que

suppress [sə'pres] vt suprimir; (yawn) ahogar

supreme [su'pri:m] adj supremo

surcharge ['sə:tʃa:dʒ] n sobretasa, recargo

sure [ʃuəˏ] adj seguro; (definite, convinced) cierto; **to make ~ of sth/ that** asegurarse de algo/asegurar que; **~! (of course)** ¡claro!, ¡por supuesto!; **~ enough** efectivamente; **surely** adv (certainly) seguramente

surf [sə:f] n olas fpl ⊳ vt: **to ~ the Net** navegar por Internet

surface ['sə:fɪs] n superficie f; (road) revestir ⊳ vi salir a la superficie; **surface mail** n vía terrestre

surfboard ['sə:fbɔ:d] n tabla (de surf)

surfer ['sə:fəˏ] n surfista mf; **web** or **net ~** internauta mf

surfing ['sə:fɪŋ] n surf m

surge [sə:dʒ] n oleada, oleaje m ⊳ vi (wave) romper; (people) avanzar a tropel

surgeon ['sə:dʒən] n cirujano/a

surgery ['sə:dʒərɪ] n cirugía; (BRIT: room) consultorio

surname ['sə:neɪm] n apellido

surpass [sə:'pɑ:s] vt superar, exceder

surplus ['sə:pləs] n excedente m; (Comm) superávit m ⊳ adj excedente, sobrante

surprise [sə'praɪz] n sorpresa ⊳ vt sorprender; **surprised** adj (look, smile) de sorpresa; **to be surprised** sorprenderse; **surprising** adj sorprendente; **surprisingly** adv (easy, helpful) de modo sorprendente

surrender [sə'rendəˏ] n rendición f, entrega ⊳ vi rendirse, entregarse

surround [sə'raund] vt rodear, circundar; (Mil etc) cercar; **surrounding** adj circundante; **surroundings** npl alrededores mpl, cercanías fpl

surveillance [sə:'veɪləns] n vigilancia

survey n ['sə:veɪ] inspección f reconocimiento; (inquiry) encuesta

▷ vt examinar, inspeccionar; (look at) mirar, contemplar; **surveyor** n agrimensor(a) m/f

survival [sə'vaɪvl] n supervivencia

survive [sə'vaɪv] vi sobrevivir; (custom etc) perdurar ▷ vt sobrevivir a; **survivor** n superviviente mf

suspect adj, n ['sʌspekt] sospechoso/a ▷ vt [sas'pekt] sospechar

suspend [səs'pend] vt suspender; **suspended sentence** n (Law) libertad f condicional; **suspenders** npl (BRIT) ligas fpl; (US) tirantes mpl

suspense [səs'pens] n incertidumbre f, duda; (in film etc) suspense m; **to keep sb in ~** mantener a algn en suspense

suspension [səs'penʃən] n suspensión f; (of driving licence) privación f; **suspension bridge** n puente m colgante

suspicion [səs'pɪʃən] n sospecha; (distrust) recelo; **suspicious** adj receloso; (causing suspicion) sospechoso

sustain [səs'teɪn] vt sostener, apoyar; (suffer) sufrir, padecer

SUV ['es'juː'viː] n abbr (= sports utility vehicle) todoterreno m inv, cuatro por cuatro m inv

swallow ['swɒləʊ] n (bird) golondrina ▷ vt tragar

swam [swæm] pt of swim

swamp [swɒmp] n pantano, ciénaga ▷ vt abrumar, agobiar

swan [swɒn] n cisne m

swap [swɒp] n canje m ▷ vt: **to ~ (for)** canjear (por), cambiar (por)

swarm [swɔːm] n (of bees) enjambre m; (fig) multitud f ▷ vi (bees) formar un enjambre; (fig) pulular

sway [sweɪ] vi mecerse, balancearse ▷ vt (influence) mover, influir en

swear [pt swore, pp sworn] [sweəʳ, swɔːʳ, swɔːn] vi, vt: jurar; **swear in** vt: **to be sworn in** prestar juramento; **swearword** n taco, palabrota

sweat [swet] n sudor m ▷ vi sudar

sweater ['swetəʳ] n suéter m

sweatshirt ['swetʃə:t] n sudadera

sweaty ['sweti] adj sudoroso

Swede [swiːd] n sueco/a

swede [swiːd] n (BRIT) nabo

Sweden ['swiːdn] n Suecia

Swedish ['swiːdɪʃ] adj, n (Ling) sueco

sweep [swiːp] (pt, pp swept) n (act) barrida; (also: **chimney ~**) deshollinador(a) m/f ▷ vt barrer; (with arm) empujar; (current) arrastrar ▷ vi barrer

sweet [swiːt] n (BRIT: candy) dulce m, caramelo; (: pudding) postre m ▷ adj dulce; (charming: smile, character) dulce, amable; **sweetcorn** n maíz m (dulce); **sweetener** ['swiːtnəʳ] n (Culin) edulcorante m; **sweetheart** n novio/a; **sweetshop** n (BRIT) confitería, bombonería

swell [swel] (pt swelled, pp swollen or swelled) n (of sea) marejada, oleaje m ▷ adj (us inf: excellent) estupendo, fenomenal ▷ vt hinchar, inflar ▷ vi (also: **~ up**) hincharse; (numbers) aumentar; (sound, feeling) ir aumentando; **swelling** n (Med) hinchazón f

swept [swept] pt, pp of sweep

swerve [swɜːv] vi desviarse bruscamente

swift [swift] n (bird) vencejo ▷ adj rápido, veloz

swim [swim] (pt swam, pp swum) n: **to go for a ~** ir a nadar o a bañarse ▷ vi nadar; (head, room) dar vueltas ▷ vt pasar a nado; **to go ~ming** ir a nadar; **swimmer** n nadador(a) m/f; **swimming** n natación f; **swimming costume** n bañador m, traje m de baño; **swimming pool** n piscina, alberca (LAM); **swimming trunks** npl bañador msg; **swimsuit** n = **swimming costume**

swing [swiŋ] (pt, pp swung) n (in playground) columpio; (movement) balanceo, vaivén m; (change of *direction*) viraje m; (*rhythm*) ritmo ▷ vt balancear; (*also*: **~ round**) voltear, girar ▷ vi balancearse, columpiarse; (*also*: **~ round**) dar media vuelta; **to be in full ~** estar en plena marcha

swipe card [swaɪp-] n tarjeta magnética deslizante, tarjeta swipe

swirl [swəːl] vi arremolinarse

Swiss [swɪs] adj, n (pl inv) suizo/a

switch [swɪtʃ] n (for light, radio etc) interruptor m; (*change*) cambio ▷ vt (*change*) cambiar de; **switch off** vt apagar; (*engine*) parar; **switch on** vt encender, prender (LAM); (*engine*, *machine*) arrancar; **switchboard** n (Tel) centralita (de teléfonos), conmutador m (LAM)

Switzerland ['swɪtsələnd] n Suiza

swivel ['swɪvl] vi (*also*: **~ round**) girar

swollen ['swəulən] pp of **swell**

swoop [swuːp] n (*by police etc*) redada ▷ vi (*also*: **~ down**) caer en picado

swop [swɔp] n, vb = **swap**

sword [sɔːd] n espada; **swordfish** n pez m espada

swore [swɔːʳ] pt of **swear**

sworn [swɔːn] pp of **swear** ▷ adj (*statement*) bajo juramento; (*enemy*) implacable

swum [swʌm] pp of **swim**

swung [swʌŋ] pt, pp of **swing**

syllable ['sɪləbl] n sílaba

syllabus ['sɪləbəs] n programa m de estudios

symbol ['sɪmbl] n símbolo

symbolic(al) [sɪm'bɔlɪk(l)] adj simbólico; **to be symbolic of sth** simbolizar algo

symmetrical [sɪ'mɛtrɪkl] adj simétrico

symmetry ['sɪmɪtrɪ] n simetría

sympathetic [sɪmpə'θɛtɪk] adj (*understanding*) comprensivo; **to be ~ towards** (*person*) ser comprensivo con

> Be careful not to translate *sympathetic* by the Spanish word *simpático*.

sympathize ['sɪmpəθaɪz] vi: **to ~ with** (*person*) compadecerse de; (*feelings*) comprender; (*cause*) apoyar

sympathy ['sɪmpəθɪ] n (*pity*) compasión f

symphony ['sɪmfənɪ] n sinfonía

symptom ['sɪmptəm] n síntoma m, indicio

synagogue ['sɪnəgɔg] n sinagoga

syndicate ['sɪndɪkɪt] n sindicato; (*Press*) agencia (de noticias)

syndrome ['sɪndrəum] n síndrome m

synonym ['sɪnənɪm] n sinónimo

synthetic [sɪn'θɛtɪk] adj sintético

Syria ['sɪrɪə] n Siria

syringe [sɪ'rɪndʒ] n jeringa

syrup ['sɪrəp] n jarabe m, almíbar m

system ['sɪstəm] n sistema m; (*Anat*) organismo; **systematic** [sɪstə'mætɪk] adj sistemático; metódico; **systems analyst** n analista mf de sistemas

S

t

ta [tɑː] excl (BRIT inf) ¡gracias!
tab [tæb] n lengüeta; (label) etiqueta; **to keep ~s on** (fig) vigilar
table ['teɪbl] n mesa; (of statistics etc) cuadro, tabla ▷ vt (BRIT: motion etc) presentar; **to lay** o **set the ~** poner la mesa; **tablecloth** n mantel m; **table d'hôte** [tɑːbl'dəʊt] n menú m; **table lamp** n lámpara de mesa; **tablemat** n (for plate) posaplatos m inv; (for hot dish) salvamanteles m inv; **tablespoon** n cuchara grande; (also: **tablespoonful**: as measurement) cucharada grande
tablet ['tæblɪt] n (Med) pastilla, comprimido; (of stone) lápida
table tennis n ping-pong m, tenis m de mesa
tabloid ['tæblɔɪd] n periódico popular sensacionalista
taboo [tə'buː] adj, n tabú m
tack [tæk] n (nail) tachuela ▷ vt (nail) clavar con tachuelas; (stitch) hilvanar ▷ vi virar

tackle ['tækl] n (gear) equipo; (fishing tackle, for lifting) aparejo ▷ vt (difficulty) enfrentarse a; (challenge: person) hacer frente a; (grapple with) agarrar; (Football) entrar a; (Rugby) placar
tacky ['tækɪ] adj pegajoso; (inf) hortera inv, de mal gusto
tact [tækt] n tacto, discreción f; **tactful** adj discreto, diplomático
tactics ['tæktɪks] npl táctica sg
tactless ['tæktlɪs] adj indiscreto
tadpole ['tædpəʊl] n renacuajo
taffy ['tæfɪ] n (US) melcocha
tag [tæg] n (label) etiqueta
tail [teɪl] n cola; (of shirt, coat) faldón m ▷ vt (follow) vigilar a; **tails** npl (formal suit) levita
tailor ['teɪlə'] n sastre m
Taiwan [taɪ'wɑːn] n Taiwán m; **Taiwanese** adj, n taiwanés/esa
take [teɪk] (pt **took**, pp **taken**) vt tomar; (grab) coger (SP), agarrar (LAM); (gain: prize) ganar; (require: effort, courage) exigir; (support weight of) aguantar; (hold: passengers etc) tener cabida para; (accompany, bring, carry) llevar; (exam) presentarse a; **to ~ sth from** (drawer etc) sacar algo de; (person) quitar algo a, coger algo a (SP); **I ~ it that ...** supongo que ...; **take after** vt fus parecerse a; **take apart** vt desmontar; **take away** vt (remove) quitar; (carry off) llevar; **take back** vt (return) devolver; (one's words) retractar; **take down** vt (building) derribar; (message etc) apuntar; **take in** vt (deceive) engañar; (understand) entender; (include) abarcar; (lodger) acoger, recibir; **take off** vi (Aviat) despegar ▷ vt (remove) quitar; **take on** vt (work) emprender; (employee) contratar; (opponent) desafiar; **take out** vt sacar; **take over** vt (business) tomar posesión de ▷ vi: **to ~ over from sb** reemplazar a algn; **take up** vt (a dress) acortar; (occupy: time, space) ocupar; (engage in: hobby etc) dedicarse a; (accept) aceptar; **to ~ sb up on**

aceptar algo de algn; **takeaway** adj (BRIT: food) para llevar ▷ n tienda or restaurante m de comida para llevar; **taken** pp of **take**; **takeoff** n (Aviat) despegue m; **takeover** n (Comm) absorción f; **takings** npl (Comm) ingresos mpl

talc [tælk] n (also: **~um powder**) talco

tale [teɪl] n (story) cuento; (account) relación f; **to tell ~s** (fig) contar chismes

talent ['tælnt] n talento; **talented** adj de talento

talk [tɔ:k] n charla; (gossip) habladurías fpl, chismes mpl; (conversation) conversación f ▷ vi hablar; **talks** fpl (Pol etc) conversaciones fpl; **to ~ about** hablar de; **to ~ sb into doing sth** convencer a algn para que haga algo; **to ~ sb out of doing sth** disuadir a algn de que haga algo; **to ~ shop** hablar del trabajo; **talk over** vt discutir; **talk show** n programa m magazine

tall [tɔ:l] adj alto; (tree) grande; **to be 6 feet ~** ≈ medir 1 metro 80, tener 1 metro 80 de alto

tambourine [tæmbə'ri:n] n pandereta

tame [teɪm] adj domesticado; (fig: story, style, person) soso, anodino

tamper ['tæmpə*] vi: **to ~ with** (lock etc) intentar forzar

tampon ['tæmpɒn] n tampón m

tan [tæn] n (also: **sun~**) bronceado ▷ vi ponerse moreno ▷ adj (colour) marrón

tandem ['tændəm] n tándem m

tangerine [tændʒə'ri:n] n mandarina

tangle ['tæŋgl] n enredo; **to get in(to) a ~** enredarse

tank [tæŋk] n (also: **water ~**) depósito, tanque m; (for fish) acuario; (Mil) tanque m

tanker ['tæŋkə*] n (ship) petrolero; (truck) camión m cisterna

tanned [tænd] adj (skin) moreno

tantrum ['tæntrəm] n rabieta

Tanzania [tænzə'nɪə] n Tanzania

tap [tæp] n (BRIT: on sink etc) grifo, canilla (LAM); (gentle blow) golpecito; (gas tap) llave f ▷ vt (shoulder etc) dar palmaditas en; (resources) utilizar, explotar; (telephone conversation) intervenir; **on ~** (fig: resources) a mano; **beer on ~** cerveza de barril; **tap dancing** n claqué m

tape [teɪp] n cinta; (also: **magnetic ~**) cinta magnética; (sticky tape) cinta adhesiva ▷ vt (record) grabar (en cinta); **on ~** (song etc) grabado (en cinta); **tape measure** n cinta métrica, metro; **tape recorder** n grabadora

tapestry ['tæpɪstrɪ] n (object) tapiz m; (art) tapicería

tar [ta:*] n alquitrán m, brea

target ['ta:gɪt] n blanco

tariff ['tærɪf] n (on goods) arancel m; (BRIT: in hotels etc) tarifa

tarmac ['ta:mæk] n (BRIT: on road) asfalto; (Aviat) pista (de aterrizaje)

tarpaulin [ta:'pɔ:lɪn] n lona (impermeabilizada)

tarragon ['tærəgən] n estragón m

tart [ta:t] n (Culin) tarta; (BRIT inf, pej: woman) fulana ▷ adj agrio, ácido

tartan ['ta:tn] n tartán m, tela escocesa

task [ta:sk] n tarea; **to take to ~** reprender

taste [teɪst] n sabor m, gusto; (fig) muestra, idea ▷ vt probar ▷ vi: **to ~ of or like** (fish etc) saber a; **you can ~ the garlic (in it)** se nota el sabor a ajo; **in good/bad ~** de buen/mal gusto; **tasteful** adj de buen gusto; **tasteless** adj (food) soso; (remark) de mal gusto; **tasty** adj sabroso, rico

tatters ['tætəz] npl: **in ~** hecho jirones

tattoo [tə'tu:] n tatuaje m; (spectacle) espectáculo militar ▷ vt tatuar

taught [tɔ:t] pt, pp of **teach**

taunt [tɔ:nt] n pulla ▷ vt lanzar pullas a

Taurus ['tɔ:rəs] n Tauro

taut [tɔ:t] adj tirante, tenso

tax [tæks] *n* impuesto ▷ *vt* gravar
(con un impuesto); *(fig: test)* poner a
prueba; (: *patience*) agotar; **tax-free**
adj libre de impuestos

taxi ['tæksɪ] *n* taxi *m* ▷ *vi (Aviat)* rodar
por la pista; **taxi driver** *n* taxista *m/f*;
taxi rank, *(BRIT)* **taxi stand** *n* parada
de taxis

tax payer *n* contribuyente *mf*

TB *n abbr* = **tuberculosis**

tea [ti:] *n* té *m*; *(BRIT: snack)* ≈
merienda; **high ~** *(BRIT)* = merienda-
cena; **tea bag** *n* bolsita de té; **tea
break** *n (BRIT)* descanso para el té

teach *(pt, pp* **taught**) [ti:tʃ, tɔ:t] *vt*:
to ~ sb sth, ~ sth to sb enseñar algo
a algn ▷ *vi* enseñar; *(be a teacher)* ser
profesor(a); **teacher** *n (in secondary
school)* profesor(a) *m/f*; *(in primary
school)* maestro/a; **teaching** *n*
enseñanza

tea: tea cloth *n (BRIT)* paño de cocina,
trapo de cocina *(LAM)*; **teacup** *n* taza
de té; **tea leaves** *npl* hojas *fpl* de té

team [ti:m] *n* equipo; *(of animals)*
pareja; **team up** *vi* asociarse

teapot ['ti:pɒt] *n* tetera

tear¹ [tɪə*] *n* lágrima; **in ~s** llorando

tear² [tɛə*] *(pt* **tore***, pp* **torn**) *n* rasgón
m, desgarrón *m* ▷ *vt* romper, rasgar
▷ *vi* rasgarse; **tear apart** *vt (also
fig)* hacer pedazos; **tear down** *vt
(building, statue)* derribar; *(poster, flag)*
arrancar; **tear off** *vt (sheet of paper
etc)* arrancar; *(one's clothes)* quitarse
a tirones; **tear up** *vt (sheet of paper
etc)* romper

tearful ['tɪəful] *adj* lloroso

tear gas *n* gas *m* lacrimógeno

tearoom ['ti:ru:m] *n* salón *m* de té

tease [ti:z] *vt* tomar el pelo a

tea: teaspoon *n* cucharita; (*also*:
teaspoonful: *as measurement*)
cucharadita; **teatime** *n* hora del té;
tea towel *n (BRIT)* paño de cocina

technical ['tɛknɪkl] *adj* técnico

technician [tɛk'nɪʃn] *n* técnico/a

technique [tɛk'ni:k] *n* técnica

technology [tɛk'nɒlədʒɪ] *n*
tecnología

teddy (bear) ['tɛdɪ-] *n* osito de
peluche

tedious ['ti:dɪəs] *adj* pesado, aburrido

tee [ti:] *n (Golf)* tee *m*

teen [ti:n] *adj* = **teenage** ▷ *n (US)*
= **teenager**

teenage ['ti:neɪdʒ] *adj (fashions etc)*
juvenil; **teenager** ['ti:neɪdʒə*] *n*
adolescente *mf*

teens [ti:nz] *npl*: **to be in one's ~** ser
adolescente

teeth [ti:θ] *npl of* **tooth**

teetotal ['ti:'təutl] *adj* abstemio

telecommunications
['tɛlɪkəmjuːnɪ'keɪʃənz] *n*
telecomunicaciones *fpl*

telegram ['tɛlɪɡræm] *n* telegrama *m*

telegraph pole *n* poste *m*
telegráfico

telephone ['tɛlɪfəun] *n* teléfono
▷ *vt* llamar por teléfono, telefonear;
to be on the ~ *(subscriber)* tener
teléfono; *(be speaking)* estar hablando
por teléfono; **telephone book** *n*
guía *f* telefónica; **telephone booth**,
(BRIT) **telephone box** *n* cabina
telefónica; **telephone call** *n* llamada
telefónica; **telephone directory** *n*
guía telefónica; **telephone number** *n*
número de teléfono

telesales ['tɛlɪseɪlz] *npl* televentas *fpl*

telescope ['tɛlɪskəup] *n* telescopio

televise ['tɛlɪvaɪz] *vt* televisar

television ['tɛlɪvɪʒən] *n* televisión *f*;
to watch ~ mirar o ver la televisión;
television programme *n* programa
m de televisión

tell *(pt, pp* **told**) [tɛl, təuld] *vt* decir;
(relate: story) contar; *(distinguish)*:
to ~ sth from distinguir algo de ▷ *vi
(talk)*: **to ~ (of)** contar; *(have effect)*
tener efecto; **to ~ sb to do sth** decir
a algn que haga algo; **tell off** *vt*: **to
~ sb off** regañar a algn; **teller** *n (in
bank)* cajero/a

telly ['tɛlɪ] *n (BRIT inf)* tele *f*

temp [temp] n abbr (BRIT: = temporary office worker) empleado/a eventual

temper ['tempə'] n (mood) humor m; (bad temper) (mal) genio; (fit of anger) ira ▷ vt (moderate) moderar; **to be in a ~** estar furioso; **to lose one's ~** enfadarse, enojarse (LAM)

temperament ['tempərəmənt] n (nature) temperamento; **temperamental** [temprə'mɛntl] adj temperamental

temperature ['temprətfə'] n temperatura; **to have** or **run a ~** tener fiebre

temple ['templ] n (building) templo; (Anat) sien f

temporary ['tempərəri] adj provisional; (passing) transitorio; (worker) eventual; (job) temporal

tempt [tempt] vt tentar; **to ~ sb into doing sth** tentar or inducir a algn a hacer algo; **temptation** n tentación f; **tempting** adj tentador(a); (food) apetitoso

ten [ten] num diez

tenant ['tenənt] n inquilino/a

tend [tend] vt cuidar ▷ vi: **to ~ to do sth** tener tendencia a hacer algo; **tendency** ['tendənsi] n tendencia

tender ['tendə'] adj tierno, blando; (delicate) delicado; (meat) tierno; (sore) sensible ▷ n (Comm: offer) oferta; (money): **legal ~** moneda de curso legal ▷ vt ofrecer

tendon ['tendən] n tendón m

tenner ['tenə'] n (billete m de) diez libras f

tennis ['tenis] n tenis m; **tennis ball** n pelota de tenis; **tennis court** n cancha de tenis; **tennis match** n partido de tenis; **tennis player** n tenista mf; **tennis racket** n raqueta de tenis

tenor ['tenə'] n (Mus) tenor m

tenpin bowling ['tenpin-] n bolos mpl

tense [tens] adj tenso; (person) nervioso ▷ n (Ling) tiempo

tension ['tenfən] n tensión f

tent [tent] n tienda (de campaña), carpa (LAM)

tentative ['tentətiv] adj (person) indeciso; (provisional) provisional

tenth [tenθ] adj décimo

tent: tent peg n clavija, estaca; **tent pole** n mástil m

tepid ['tepid] adj tibio

term [tə:m] n (word) término; (period) período; (Scol) trimestre m ▷ vt llamar; **terms** npl (conditions) condiciones fpl; **in the short/long ~** a corto/largo plazo; **to be on good ~s with sb** llevarse bien con algn; **to come to ~s with** (problem) aceptar

terminal ['tə:minl] adj (disease) mortal; (patient) terminal ▷ n (Elec) borne m; (Comput) terminal m; (also: **air ~**) terminal f; (BRIT: also: **coach ~**) (estación f) terminal f

terminate ['tə:mineit] vt poner término a

termini ['tə:minai] npl of **terminus**

terminology [tə:mi'nɔlədʒi] n terminología

terminus (pl **termini**) ['tə:minəs, 'tə:minai] n término, (estación f) terminal f

terrace ['terəs] n terraza; (BRIT: row of houses) hilera de casas adosadas; **the ~s** (BRIT Sport) las gradas fpl; **terraced** adj (garden) escalonado; (house) adosado

terrain [te'rein] n terreno

terrestrial [ti'restriəl] adj (life) terrestre; (BRIT: channel) de transmisión (por) vía terrestre

terrible ['teribl] adj terrible, horrible; (inf) malísimo; **terribly** adv terriblemente; (very badly) malísimamente

terrier ['teriə'] n terrier m

terrific [tə'rifik] adj fantástico, fenomenal

terrify ['terifai] vt aterrorizar; **to be terrified** estar aterrado

t

or aterrorizado; **terrifying** adj aterrador(a)

territorial [tɛrɪˈtɔːrɪəl] adj territorial

territory [ˈtɛrɪtərɪ] n territorio

terror [ˈtɛrəʳ] n terror m; **terrorism** n terrorismo; **terrorist** n terrorista mf; **terrorist attack** n atentado (terrorista)

test [tɛst] n (trial, check) prueba; (Chem, Med) prueba; (exam) examen m, test m; (also: **driving ~**) examen m de conducir ▷ vt probar, poner a prueba; (Med) examinar

testicle [ˈtɛstɪkl] n testículo

testify [ˈtɛstɪfaɪ] vi (Law) prestar declaración; **to ~ to sth** atestiguar algo

testimony [ˈtɛstɪmənɪ] n (Law) testimonio

test: **test match** n partido internacional; **test tube** n probeta

tetanus [ˈtɛtənəs] n tétano

text [tɛkst] n texto; (on mobile) mensaje m de texto ▷ vt: **to ~ sb** enviar un mensaje (de texto) a algn; **textbook** n libro de texto

textiles [ˈtɛkstaɪlz] npl tejidos mpl

text message n mensaje m de texto

text messaging [-ˈmɛsɪdʒɪŋ] n (envío de) mensajes mpl de texto

texture [ˈtɛkstʃəʳ] n textura

Thai [taɪ] adj, n tailandés/esa m/f

Thailand [ˈtaɪlænd] n Tailandia

than [ðæn, ðən] conj que; (with numerals): **more ~ 10/once** más de 10/una vez; **I have more/less ~ you** tengo más/menos que tú; **it is better to phone ~ to write** es mejor llamar por teléfono que escribir

thank [θæŋk] vt dar las gracias a, agradecer; **~ you (very much)** (muchas) gracias; **~ God!** ¡gracias a Dios!; see also **thanks**; **thankfully** adv; **thankfully there were few victims** afortunadamente hubo pocas víctimas

thanks [θæŋks] npl gracias fpl ▷ excl ¡gracias!; **many ~, a lot** ¡muchas gracias!; **~ to** prep gracias a

Thanksgiving (Day) [ˈθæŋksɡɪvɪŋ-] n día m de Acción de Gracias

● **THANKSGIVING DAY**

● En Estados Unidos el cuarto jueves
● de noviembre es *Thanksgiving*
● *Day*, fiesta oficial en la que se
● conmemora la celebración que
● tuvieron los primeros colonos
● norteamericanos (*Pilgrims* o *Pilgrim*
● *Fathers*) tras la estupenda cosecha
● de 1621, por la que se dan gracias
● a Dios. En Canadá se celebra
● una fiesta semejante el segundo
● lunes de octubre, aunque no
● está relacionada con dicha fecha
● histórica.

 KEYWORD

that [ðæt] (pl **those**) adj (demonstrative) ese/a; (: more remote) aquel/aquella; **leave that book on the table** deja ese libro sobre la mesa; **that one** ese/esa, ése/ésa (to avoid confusion with adj); (more remote) aquel/aquella, aquél/aquélla (to avoid confusion with adj); **that one over there** ese/esa de ahí, ése/ésa de ahí; aquel/aquella de allá, aquél/aquélla de allá; see also **those**

▶ pron 1 (demonstrative) ese/a, ése/a (to avoid confusion with adj), eso (neuter); (: more remote) aquel/aquella, aquél/aquélla (to avoid confusion with adj), aquello (neuter); **what's that?** ¿qué es eso (or aquello)?; **who's that?** ¿quién es ese/a?; (pointing etc) ¿quién es ese/a?; **is that you?** ¿eres tú?; **will you eat all that?** ¿vas a comer todo eso?; **that's my house** esa es mi casa; **that's what he said** eso es lo que dijo; **that is (to say)** es decir; see also **those**

2 (relative, subject, object) que; (: with

preposition) (ella) que, ella cual; **the book (that) I read** el libro que leí; **the books that are in the library** los libros que están en la biblioteca; **all (that) I have** todo lo que tengo; **the box (that) I put it in** la caja en la que or donde lo puse; **the people (that) I spoke to** la gente con la que hablé
3 *(relative, of time)* que; **the day (that) he came** el día (en) que vino
▸ *conj* que; **he thought that I was ill** creyó que yo estaba enfermo
▸ *adv (demonstrative)*: **I can't work that much** no puedo trabajar tanto; **I didn't realize it was that bad** no creí que fuera tan malo; **that high** así de alto

thatched [θætʃt] *adj (roof)* de paja; **~ cottage** casita con tejado de paja

thaw [θɔː] *n* deshielo ▸ *vi (ice)* derretirse; *(food)* descongelarse ▸ *vt* descongelar

KEYWORD

the [ðiː, ðə] *def art* 1 el *m*, la *f*, los *mpl*, las *fpl* (NB = el used immediately before feminine noun beginning with stressed (h) *a*; *a + el = al*; *de + el = del*); **the boy/girl** el chico/la chica; **the books/flowers** los libros/las flores; **to the postman/from the drawer** al cartero/del cajón; **I haven't the time/money** no tengo tiempo/dinero
2 *(+ adj to form noun)*: lo; **the rich and the poor** los ricos y los pobres; **to attempt the impossible** intentar lo imposible
3 *(in titles, surnames)*: **Elizabeth the First** Isabel Primera; **Peter the Great** Pedro el Grande
4 *(in comparisons)*: **the more he works the more he earns** cuanto más trabaja más gana

theatre, *(us)* **theater** ['θɪətər] *n* teatro; *(also:* **lecture ~**) aula; *(Med: also:* **operating ~**) quirófano

theft [θeft] *n* robo

their [ðɛər] *adj* su; **theirs** *pron* (el) suyo/(la) suya *etc; see also* **my; mine**

them [ðɛm, ðəm] *pron (direct)* los/las; *(indirect)* les; *(stressed, after prep)* ellos/ellas; *see also* **me**

theme [θiːm] *n* tema *m*; **theme park** *n* parque *m* temático

themselves [ðəm'sɛlvz] *pron pl (subject)* ellos mismos/ellas mismas; *(complement)* se; *(after prep)* sí (mismos/as); *see also* **oneself**

then [ðɛn] *adv (at that time)* entonces; *(next)* pues; *(later)* luego, después; *(and also)* además ▸ *conj (therefore)* en ese caso, entonces ▸ *adj*: **the ~ president** el entonces presidente; **from ~ on** desde entonces

theology [θɪ'ɔlədʒɪ] *n* teología

theory ['θɪərɪ] *n* teoría

therapist ['θɛrəpɪst] *n* terapeuta *mf*

therapy ['θɛrəpɪ] *n* terapia

KEYWORD

there [ðɛər] *adv* 1: **there is, there are** hay; **there is no-one here** no hay nadie aquí; **there is no bread left** no queda pan; **there has been an accident** ha habido un accidente
2 *(referring to place)* ahí; *(: distant)* allí; **it's there** está ahí; **put it in/up/down there** ponlo ahí dentro/encima/arriba/abajo; **I want that book there** quiero ese libro de ahí; **there he is!** ¡ahí está!
3: **there, there** *(esp to child)* venga, venga, bueno; **thereabouts** *adv* por ahí; **thereafter** *adv* después; **thereby** *adv* así, de ese modo

therefore ['ðɛəfɔːʳ] *adv* por lo tanto

there's = **there is; there has**

thermal ['θɜːml] *adj* termal; *(paper)* térmico

thermometer [θə'mɔmɪtəʳ] *n* termómetro

thermostat ['θəːməustæt] n termostato

these [ðiːz] adj pl estos/as ▷ pron pl estos/as, éstos/as (to avoid confusion with adj); **~ children/flowers** estos chicos/estas flores; see also **this**

thesis (pl **theses**) ['θiːsɪs, -siːz] n tesis f inv

they [ðeɪ] pron pl ellos/ellas; **~ say that ...** (it is said that) se dice que ...; **they'd** [ðeɪd] = **they had; they would; they'll** = **they shall; they will; they're** = **they are; they've** = **they have**

thick [θɪk] adj (dense) espeso; (: vegetation, beard) tupido; (stupid) torpe ▷ n: **in the ~ of the battle** en lo más reñido de la batalla; **it's 20 cm ~** tiene 20 cm de espesor; **thicken** vi espesarse ▷ vt (sauce etc) espesar; **thickness** n espesor m, grueso

thief (pl **thieves**) [θiːf, θiːvz] n ladrón/ona m/f

thigh [θaɪ] n muslo

thin [θɪn] adj delgado; (hair) escaso; (crowd) disperso ▷ vt: **to ~ (down)** diluir

thing [θɪŋ] n cosa; (object) objeto, artículo; (contraption) chisme m; (mania) manía; **things** npl (belongings) cosas fpl; **the best ~ would be to ...** lo mejor sería ...; **how are ~s?** ¿qué tal van las cosas?

think (pl **thought**) [θɪŋk, θɔːt] vi pensar ▷ vt pensar, creer; **what did you ~ of them?** ¿qué te parecieron?; **to ~ about sth/sb** pensar en algo/algn; **I'll ~ about it** lo pensaré; **to ~ of doing sth** pensar en hacer algo; **I ~ so/not** creo que sí/no; **to ~ well of sb** tener buen concepto de algn; **think over** vt reflexionar sobre, meditar; **think up** vt imaginar

third [θəːd] adj (before n) tercer(a); (following n) tercero/a ▷ n tercero/a; (fraction) tercio; (Brit: degree) título universitario de tercera clase; **thirdly** adv en tercer lugar; **third party**

insurance n (Brit) seguro a terceros; **Third World** n: **the Third World** el Tercer Mundo

thirst [θəːst] n sed f; **thirsty** adj (person) sediento; **to be thirsty** tener sed

thirteen [θəːˈtiːn] num trece; **thirteenth** [θəːˈtiːnθ] adj decimotercero

thirtieth ['θəːtɪəθ] adj trigésimo

thirty ['θəːtɪ] num treinta

KEYWORD

this [ðɪs] (pl **these**) adj (demonstrative) este/a; **this man/woman** este hombre/esta mujer; **this one** (here) este/a, éste/a (to avoid confusion with adj), esto (de aquí); see also **these**
▷ pron (demonstrative) este/a, éste/a (to avoid confusion with adj), esto neuter; **who is this?** ¿quién es esteesta?; **what is this?** ¿qué es esto?; **this is where I live** aquí vivo; **this is what he said** esto es lo que dijo; **this is Mr Brown** (in introductions) le presento al Sr. Brown; (photo) este es el Sr. Brown; (on telephone) habla el Sr. Brown; see also **these**
▷ adv (demonstrative): **this high/long** así de alto/largo; **this far** hasta aquí

thistle ['θɪsl] n cardo

thorn [θɔːn] n espina

thorough ['θʌrə] adj (search) minucioso; (knowledge) profundo; (research) a fondo; **thoroughly** adv (search) minuciosamente; (study) profundamente; (wash) a fondo; (utterly: bad, wet etc) completamente, totalmente

those [ðəuz] adj pl esos/esas; aquellos/as ▷ pron pl esos/esas, ésos/ésas (to avoid confusion with adj); (more remote) aquellos/as, aquéllos/as (to avoid confusion with adj); **leave ~ books on the table** deja esos libros sobre la mesa

though [ðəu] *conj* aunque ▷ *adv* sin embargo, aún así; **even ~** aunque; **it's not so easy, ~** sin embargo no es tan fácil

thought [θɔ:t] *pt, pp of* **think** ▷ *n* pensamiento; (*opinion*) opinión f; **thoughtful** *adj* pensativo; (*considerate*) atento; **thoughtless** *adj* desconsiderado

thousand ['θauzənd] *num* mil; **two ~** dos mil; **~s of** miles de; **thousandth** *num* milésimo

thrash [θræʃ] *vt* dar una paliza a

thread [θred] *n* hilo; (*of screw*) rosca ▷ *vt* (*needle*) enhebrar

threat [θret] *n* amenaza; **threaten** ▷ *vt*: **to threaten sb with sth/to do** amenazar a algn con algo/con hacer; **threatening** ['θretnɪŋ] *adj* amenazador(a), amenazante

three [θri:] *num* tres; **three-dimensional** *adj* tridimensional; **three-piece** ['θri:pi:s] *cpd*: **three-piece suite** tresillo; **three-quarters** *npl* tres cuartas partes; **three-quarters full** tres cuartas partes lleno

threshold ['θreʃhəuld] *n* umbral m

threw [θru:] *pt of* **throw**

thrill [θrɪl] *n* (*excitement*) emoción f ▷ *vt* emocionar; **to be ~ed** (*with gift etc*) estar encantado; **thriller** *n* película/novela de suspense; **thrilling** *adj* emocionante

thriving ['θraɪvɪŋ] *adj* próspero

throat [θrəut] *n* garganta; **I have a sore ~** me duele la garganta

throb [θrɔb] *vi* latir; (*with pain*) dar punzadas

throne [θrəun] *n* trono

through [θru:] *prep* por, a través de; (*time*) durante; (*by means of*) por medio de, mediante; (*owing to*) gracias a ▷ *adj* (*ticket, train*) directo ▷ *adv* completamente, de parte a parte; de principio a fin; **to put sb ~ to** (*Tel*) poner or pasar a algn con; **to be ~** (*Tel*) tener comunicación;

(*have finished*) haber terminado; **"no ~ road"** (*BRIT*) "calle sin salida"; **throughout** *prep* (*place*) por todas partes de, por todo; (*time*) durante todo ▷ *adv* por or en todas partes

throw (*pt* **threw**, *pp* **thrown**) [θrəu, θru:, θrəun] *n* tiro; (*Sport*) lanzamiento ▷ *vt* tirar, echar; (*Sport*) lanzar; (*rider*) derribar; (*fig*) desconcertar; **to ~ a party** dar una fiesta; **throw away** *vt* tirar; **throw in** *vt* (*Sport: ball*) sacar; (*include*) incluir; **throw off** *vt* deshacerse de; **throw out** *vt* tirar; **throw up** *vi* vomitar

thru [θru:] *prep, adj, adv* (*us*) = **through**

thrush [θrʌʃ] *n* zorzal m, tordo

thrust [θrʌst] (*pt, pp* **thrust**) *vt* empujar

thud [θʌd] *n* golpe m sordo

thug [θʌg] *n* gamberro/a

thumb [θʌm] *n* (*Anat*) pulgar m ▷ *vt*: **to ~ a lift** hacer dedo; **thumbtack** *n* (*us*) chincheta

thump [θʌmp] *n* golpe m; (*sound*) ruido seco or sordo ▷ *vt, vi* golpear

thunder ['θʌndə'] *n* trueno ▷ *vi* tronar; (*train etc*): **to ~ past** pasar como un trueno; **thunderstorm** ['θʌndəstɔ:m] *n* tormenta

Thur(s). *abbr* (= *Thursday*) juev.

Thursday ['θɜ:zdɪ] *n* jueves m inv

thus [ðʌs] *adv* así, de este modo

thwart [θwɔ:t] *vt* frustrar

thyme [taɪm] *n* tomillo

Tibet [tɪ'bet] *n* el Tibet

tick [tɪk] *n* (*of clock*) tictac m; (*mark*) señal f (de visto bueno), palomita (*LAM*); (*Zool*) garrapata; (*BRIT inf*): **in a ~** en un instante ▷ *vi* hacer tictac ▷ *vt* marcar; **tick off** *vt* marcar; (*person*) reñir

ticket ['tɪkɪt] *n* billete m, boleto (*LAM*); (*for cinema etc*) entrada, boleto (*LAM*); (*in shop, on goods*) etiqueta; (*for library*) tarjeta; **to get a parking ~** (*Aut*) ser multado por estacionamiento ilegal; **ticket barrier** *n* (*BRIT Rail*) barrera más allá de la cual se necesita billete/ boleto; **ticket collector** n revisor(a) m/f; **ticket inspector** n revisor(a) m/f, inspector(a) m/f de boletos (LAM); **ticket machine** n máquina de billetes (SP) or boletos (LAM); **ticket office** n (Theat) taquilla, boletería (SP) or (Rail) despacho de billetes or boletos (LAM)

tickle ['tɪkl] vt hacer cosquillas a ▷ vi hacer cosquillas; **ticklish** adj (which tickles: blanket) que pica; (: cough) irritante; (fig: problem) delicado; **to be ticklish** tener cosquillas

tide [taɪd] n marea; (fig: of events) curso, marcha

tidy ['taɪdɪ] adj (room) ordenado; (drawing, work) limpio; (person) (bien) arreglado ▷ vt (also: **~ up**) poner en orden

tie [taɪ] n (string etc) atadura; (BRIT: necktie) corbata; (fig: link) vínculo, lazo; (Sport: draw) empate m ▷ vt atar ▷ vi (Sport) empatar; **to ~ in a bow** hacer un lazo; **to ~ a knot in sth** hacer un nudo en algo; **tie down** vt atar; (fig): **to ~ sb down to** obligar a algn a; **tie up** vt (dog) atar; (arrangements) concluir; **to be ~d up** (busy) estar ocupado

tier [tɪə^r] n grada; (of cake) piso

tiger ['taɪgə^r] n tigre m

tight [taɪt] adj (rope) tirante; (money) escaso; (clothes, shoe) ajustado; (programme) apretado; (budget) ajustado; (security) estricto; (inf: drunk) borracho ▷ adv (squeeze) muy fuerte; (shut) herméticamente; **tighten** vt (rope) estirar; (screw) apretar ▷ vi estirarse; apretarse; **tightly** adv (grasp) muy fuerte; **tights** npl (BRIT) medias fpl, panties npl

tile [taɪl] n (on roof) teja; (on floor) baldosa; (on wall) azulejo

till [tɪl] n caja (registradora) ▷ vt (land) cultivar ▷ prep, conj = **until**

tilt [tɪlt] vt inclinar ▷ vi inclinarse

timber ['tɪmbə^r] n (material) madera

time [taɪm] n tiempo; (epoch: often pl) época; (by clock) hora; (moment) momento; (occasion) vez f; (Mus) compás m ▷ vt calcular o medir el tiempo de; (race) cronometrar; (remark etc) elegir el momento para; **a long ~** mucho tiempo; **four at a ~** cuarto a la vez; **for the ~ being** de momento, por ahora; **at ~s** a veces; **from ~ to ~** de vez en cuando; **in ~** (soon enough) a tiempo; (after some time) con el tiempo; (Mus) al compás; **in a week's ~** dentro de una semana; **in no ~** en un abrir y cerrar de ojos; **any ~** cuando sea; **on ~** a la hora; **5 ~s 5** 5 por 5; **what ~ is it?** ¿qué hora es?; **to have a good ~** pasarlo bien, divertirse; **time limit** n plazo; **timely** adj oportuno; **timer** n (in kitchen) temporizador m; **timetable** n horario; **time zone** n huso horario

timid ['tɪmɪd] adj tímido

timing ['taɪmɪŋ] n (Sport) cronometraje m; **the ~ of his resignation** el momento que eligió para dimitir

tin [tɪn] n estaño; (also: **~ plate**) hojalata; (BRIT: can) lata; **tinfoil** n papel m de estaño

tingle ['tɪŋgl] vi (cheeks, skin: from cold) sentir comezón; (: from bad circulation) sentir hormigueo; **to ~ with** estremecerse de

tinker ['tɪŋkə^r]: **~ with** vt fus jugar con, tocar

tinned [tɪnd] adj (BRIT: food) en lata, en conserva

tin opener [-əupnə^r] n (BRIT) abrelatas m inv

tint [tɪnt] n matiz m; (for hair) tinte m; **tinted** adj (hair) teñido; (glass, spectacles) ahumado

tiny ['taɪnɪ] adj minúsculo, pequeñito

tip [tɪp] n (end) punta; (gratuity) propina; (BRIT: for rubbish) vertedero; (advice) consejo ▷ vt (waiter) dar una propina a; (tilt) inclinar; (empty: also:

~ **out**) vaciar, echar; **tip off** vt avisar, poner sobre aviso a

tiptoe ['tɪptəʊ] n: **on ~** de puntillas

tire ['taɪə'] n (us) = **tyre** ▷ vt cansar ▷ vi cansarse; (become bored) aburrirse; **tired** adj cansado; **to be tired of sth** estar harto de algo; **tire pressure** n (us) = **tyre pressure**; **tiring** adj cansado

tissue ['tɪʃuː] n tejido; (paper handkerchief) pañuelo de papel, kleenex®; **tissue paper** n papel m de seda

tit [tɪt] n (bird) herrerillo común; **to give ~ for tat** dar ojo por ojo

title ['taɪtl] n título

T-junction ['tiː'dʒʌŋkʃən] n cruce m en T

TM abbr (= trademark) marca de fábrica; = **transcendental meditation**

KEYWORD

to [tuː, tə] prep 1 (direction) a; **to go to France/London/school/ the station** ir a Francia/Londres/al colegio/a la estación; **to go to Claude's/the doctor's** ir a casa de Claude/al médico; **the road to Edinburgh** la carretera de Edimburgo

2 (as far as) hasta, a; **from here to London** de aquí a ahora Londres; **to count to 10** contar hasta 10; **from 40 to 50 people** entre 40 y 50 personas

3 (with expressions of time): **a quarter/ twenty to five** las cinco menos cuarto/veinte

4 (for, of): **the key to the front door** la llave de la puerta principal; **she is secretary to the director** es la secretaria del director; **a letter to his wife** una carta a o para su mujer

5 (expressing indirect object): **to give sth to sb** darle algo a algn; **to talk to sb** hablar con algn; **to be a danger to sb** ser un peligro para algn; **to carry out repairs to sth** hacer reparaciones en algo

6 (in relation to): **3 goals to 2** 3 goles a 2; **30 miles to the gallon** ≈ 9,4 litros a los cien (kilómetros)

7 (purpose, result): **to come to sb's aid** venir en auxilio or ayuda de algn; **to sentence sb to death** condenar a algn a muerte; **to my great surprise** con gran sorpresa mía

▶ infin particle 1 (simple infin): **to go/ eat** ir/comer

2 (following another vb; see also relevant vb): **to want/try/start to do** querer/intentar/empezar a hacer

3 (with vb omitted): **I don't want to** no quiero

4 (purpose, result): **I did it to help you** lo hice para ayudarte; **he came to see you** vino a verte

5 (equivalent to relative clause): **I have things to do** tengo cosas que hacer; **the main thing is to try** lo principal es intentarlo

6 (after adj etc): **ready to go** listo para irse; **too old to ...** demasiado viejo (como) para ...

▶ adv: **pull/push the door to** tirar de/empujar la puerta

toad [təʊd] n sapo; **toadstool** n seta venenosa

toast [təʊst] n (Culin) tostada; (drink, speech) brindis m inv ▷ vt (Culin) tostar; (drink to) brindar por; **toaster** n tostador m

tobacco [tə'bækəʊ] n tabaco

toboggan [tə'bɒgən] n tobogán m

today [tə'deɪ] adv, n (also fig) hoy m

toddler ['tɒdlə'] n niño/a (que empieza a andar)

toe [təʊ] n dedo (del pie); (of shoe) punta ▷ vt: **to ~ the line** (fig) acatar las normas; **toenail** n uña del pie

toffee ['tɒfɪ] n caramelo

together [tə'gɛðə'] adv juntos; (at same time) al mismo tiempo, a la vez; **~ with** junto con

toilet ['tɔɪlət] n (BRIT: lavatory) servicios mpl, baño ▷ cpd (bag, soap *etc)* de aseo; **toilet bag** n neceser m, bolsa de aseo; **toilet paper** n papel m higiénico; **toiletries** npl artículos mpl de tocador; **toilet roll** n rollo de papel higiénico

token ['təukən] n (sign) señal f, muestra; (souvenir) recuerdo; (disc) ficha ⊳ cpd (fee, strike) simbólico; **book/record ~** (BRIT) vale m para comprar libros/discos

Tokyo ['təukjəu] n Tokio, Tokío

told [təuld] pt, pp of **tell**

tolerant ['tɔlərnt] adj: **~ of** tolerante con

tolerate ['tɔləreɪt] vt tolerar

toll [təul] n (of casualties) número de víctimas; (tax, charge) peaje m ⊳ vi (bell) doblar; **toll call** n (US Tel) conferencia, llamada interurbana; **toll-free** adj, adv (US) gratis

tomato [tə'mɑːtəu] (pl **tomatoes**) n tomate m; **tomato sauce** n salsa de tomate

tomb [tuːm] n tumba; **tombstone** n lápida

tomorrow [tə'mɔrəu] adv, n (also fig) mañana; **the day after ~** pasado mañana; **~ morning** mañana por la mañana

ton [tʌn] n tonelada; **~s** of (inf) montones de

tone [təun] n tono ⊳ vi armonizar; **tone down** vt (criticism) suavizar; (colour) atenuar

tongs [tɔŋz] npl (for coal) tenazas fpl; (for hair) tenacillas fpl

tongue [tʌŋ] n lengua; **~ in cheek** en broma

tonic ['tɔnɪk] n (Med) tónico; (also: **~ water**) (agua) tónica

tonight [tə'naɪt] adv, n esta noche

tonsil ['tɔnsl] n amígdala; **tonsillitis** [tɔnsɪ'laɪtɪs] n amigdalitis f

too [tuː] adv (excessively) demasiado; (also) también; **~ much** demasiado; **~ many** demasiados/as

took [tuk] pt of **take**

tool [tuːl] n herramienta; **tool box** n caja de herramientas; **tool kit** n juego de herramientas

tooth (pl **teeth**) [tuːθ, tiːθ] n (Anat, Tech) diente m; (molar) muela; **toothache** n dolor m de muelas; **toothbrush** n cepillo de dientes; **toothpaste** n pasta de dientes; **toothpick** n palillo

top [tɔp] n (of mountain) cumbre f, cima; (of head) coronilla; (of ladder) (lo) alto; (of cupboard, table) superficie f; (lid: of box, jar) tapa; (: of bottle) tapón m; (of list, table, queue, page) cabeza; (toy) peonza; (Dress: blouse) blusa; (: T-shirt) camiseta ⊳ adj de arriba; (in rank) principal, primero; (best) mejor ⊳ vt (exceed) exceder; (be first in) encabezar; **on ~** sobre, encima de; **from ~ to bottom** de pies a cabeza; **top up** vt volver a llenar; (mobile phone) recargar el saldo de; **top floor** n último piso; **top hat** n sombrero de copa

topic ['tɔpɪk] n tema m; **topical** adj actual

topless ['tɔplɪs] adj (bather etc) topless inv

topping ['tɔpɪŋ] n (Culin): **with a ~ of cream** con nata por encima

topple ['tɔpl] vt derribar ⊳ vi caerse

top-up card n (for mobile phone) tarjeta prepago

torch [tɔːtʃ] n antorcha; (BRIT: electric) linterna

tore [tɔː²] pt of **tear¹**

torment n ['tɔːmɛnt] tormento ⊳ vt [tɔː'mɛnt] atormentar; (fig: annoy) fastidiar

torn [tɔːn] pp of **tear¹**

tornado [tɔː'neɪdəu] (pl **tornadoes**) n tornado

torpedo [tɔː'piːdəu] (pl **torpedoes**) n torpedo

torrent ['tɔrnt] n torrente m; **torrential** [tɔ'rɛnʃl] adj torrencial

tortoise ['tɔːtəs] n tortuga

torture ['tɔːtʃə²] n tortura ⊳ vt torturar; (fig) atormentar

Tory ['tɔːrɪ] *adj*, *n* (BRIT Pol) conservador(a) *m/f*

toss [tɔs] *vt* tirar, echar; (head) sacudir; **to ~ a coin** echar a cara o cruz; **to ~ up for sth** jugar algo a cara o cruz; **to ~ and turn** (in bed) dar vueltas (en la cama)

total ['təʊtl] *adj* total, entero; (emphatic: failure etc) completo, total ▷ *n* total *m*, suma *f* ▷ *vt* (add up) sumar; (amount to) ascender a

totalitarian [təʊtælɪ'tɛərɪən] *adj* totalitario

totally ['təʊtəlɪ] *adv* totalmente

touch [tʌtʃ] *n* tacto; (contact) contacto ▷ *vt* tocar; (emotionally) conmover; **a ~ of** (fig) una pizca or un poquito de; **to get in ~ with sb** ponerse en contacto con algn; **to lose ~** (friends) perder contacto; **touch down** *vi* (on land) aterrizar; **touchdown** *n* aterrizaje *m*; (us Football) ensayo *m*; **touched** *adj* conmovido; **touching** *adj* conmovedor(a); **touchline** *n* (Sport) línea de banda; **touch-sensitive** *adj* sensible al tacto

tough [tʌf] *adj* (meat) duro; (task, problem, situation) difícil; (person) fuerte

tour ['tʊəʳ] *n* viaje *m*; (also: **package ~**) viaje *m* con todo incluido; (of town, museum) visita ▷ *vt* viajar por; **to go on a ~ of** (region, country) ir de viaje por; (museum, castle) visitar; **to go on ~** partir or ir de gira; **tour guide** *n* guía *mf* turístico/a

tourism ['tʊərɪzm] *n* turismo

tourist ['tʊərɪst] *n* turista *mf* ▷ *cpd* turístico/a; **tourist office** *n* oficina de turismo

tournament ['tʊənəmənt] *n* torneo

tour operator *n* touroperador(a) *m/f*, operador(a) *m/f* turístico/a

tow [təʊ] *n* ▷ *vt* remolcar; **"on** (us) **in ~"** (Aut) "a remolque"; **tow away** *vt* llevarse a remolque

toward(s) [tə'wɔːd(z)] *prep* hacia; (of attitude) respecto a, con; (of purpose) para

towel ['taʊəl] *n* toalla; **towelling** *n* (fabric) felpa

tower ['taʊəʳ] *n* torre *f*; **tower block** *n* (BRIT) bloque *m* de pisos

town [taʊn] *n* ciudad *f*; **to go to ~** ir a la ciudad; (fig) tirar la casa por la ventana; **town centre** *n* centro de la ciudad; **town hall** *n* ayuntamiento

tow truck *n* (us) camión *m* grúa

toxic ['tɒksɪk] *adj* tóxico

toy [tɔɪ] *n* juguete *m*; **toy with** *vt fus* jugar con; (idea) acariciar; **toyshop** *n* juguetería

trace [treɪs] *n* rastro ▷ *vt* (draw) trazar, delinear; (locate) encontrar

track [træk] *n* (mark) huella, pista; (path) camino, senda; (: of bullet etc) trayectoria; (: of suspect, animal) pista, rastro; (Rail) vía; (Comput, Sport) pista; (on album) canción *f* ▷ *vt* seguir la pista de; **to keep ~ of** mantenerse al tanto de, seguir; **track down** *vt* (person) localizar; (sth lost) encontrar; **tracksuit** *n* chandal *m*

tractor ['træktəʳ] *n* tractor *m*

trade [treɪd] *n* comercio; (skill, job) oficio ▷ *vi* negociar, comerciar ▷ *vt* (exchange): **to ~ sth (for sth)** cambiar algo (por algo); **trade in** *vt* (old car etc) ofrecer como parte del pago; **trademark** *n* marca de fábrica; **trader** *n* comerciante *mf*; **tradesman** *n* (shopkeeper) comerciante *mf*; **trade union** *n* sindicato

trading ['treɪdɪŋ] *n* comercio

tradition [trə'dɪʃən] *n* tradición *f*; **traditional** *adj* tradicional

traffic ['træfɪk] *n* tráfico, circulación *f* ▷ *vi*: **to ~ in** (pej: liquor, drugs) traficar en; **air ~** tráfico aéreo; **traffic circle** *n* (us) rotonda, glorieta; **traffic island** *n* refugio, isleta; **traffic jam** *n* embotellamiento; **traffic lights** *npl* semáforo *sg*; **traffic warden** *n* guardia *mf* de tráfico

tragedy ['trædʒədɪ] *n* tragedia

tragic ['trædʒɪk] *adj* trágico

trail [treɪl] n (tracks) rastro, pista; (path) camino, sendero; (dust, smoke) estela ▷ vt arrastrar; (follow) seguir la pista de ▷ vi arrastrarse; (in contest etc) ir perdiendo; **trailer** n (Aut) remolque m; (caravan) caravana f; (Cine) trailer m, avance m

train [treɪn] n tren m; (of dress) cola ▷ vt (educate) formar; (sportsman) entrenar; (dog) amaestrar; (point: gun etc): **to ~ on** apuntar a ▷ vi (Sport) entrenarse; (be educated, learn a skill) formarse; **to ~ as a teacher** etc estudiar para profesor etc; **one's ~ of thought** el razonamiento de algn; **trainee** [treɪ'niː] n trabajador(a) m/f en prácticas; **trainer** n (Sport) entrenador(a) m/f; (of animals) domador(a) m/f; **trainers** npl (shoes) zapatillas fpl (de deporte); **training** n formación f, entrenamiento m; **to be in training** (Sport) estar entrenando; **training course** n curso de formación; **training shoes** npl zapatillas fpl (de deporte)

trait [treɪt] n rasgo

traitor ['treɪtə'] n traidor(a) m/f

tram [træm] n (BRIT: also: ~**car**) tranvía m

tramp [træmp] n (person) vagabundo/a; (inf, pej: woman) puta

trample ['træmpl] vt: **to ~ (underfoot)** pisotear

trampoline ['træmpəliːn] n trampolín m

tranquil ['træŋkwɪl] adj tranquilo; **tranquilizer**, (us) **tranquilizer** n (Med) tranquilizante m

transaction [træn'zækʃən] n transacción f, operación f

transatlantic [trænzət'læntɪk] adj transatlántico

transcript ['trænskrɪpt] n copia

transfer n ['trænsfə'] transferencia f; (Sport) traspaso m; (picture, design) calcomanía f ▷ vt [træns'fə:] trasladar; **to ~ the charges** (BRIT Tel) llamar a cobro revertido

transform [træns'fɔːm] vt transformar; **transformation** n transformación f

transfusion [træns'fjuːʒən] n transfusión f

transit ['trænzɪt] n: **in ~** en tránsito

transition [træn'zɪʃən] n transición f

transitive ['trænzɪtɪv] adj (Ling) transitivo

translate [trænz'leɪt] vt: **to ~ (from/into)** traducir (de/a); **translation** [trænz'leɪʃən] n traducción f; **translator** n traductor(a) m/f

transmission [trænz'mɪʃən] n transmisión f

transmit [trænz'mɪt] vt transmitir; **transmitter** n transmisor m

transparent [træns'pærnt] adj transparente

transplant n ['trænsplɑːnt] (Med) transplante m

transport n ['trænspɔːt] transporte m ▷ vt [træns'pɔːt] transportar; **transportation** [trænspɔː'teɪʃən] n transporte m

transvestite [trænz'vestaɪt] n travestí mf

trap [træp] n (snare, trick) trampa ▷ vt coger (sp) or agarrar (LAM) en una trampa; (trick) engañar; (confine) atrapar

trash [træʃ] n basura; (inf: nonsense) tonterías fpl; **the book/film is ~** el libro/la película no vale nada; **trash can** n (us) cubo, balde m (LAM) or bote m (LAM) de la basura

trauma ['trɔːmə] n trauma m; **traumatic** [trɔː'mætɪk] adj traumático

travel ['trævl] n viaje m ▷ vi viajar ▷ vt (distance) recorrer; **travel agency** n agencia de viajes; **travel agent** n agente mf de viajes; **travel insurance** n seguro de viaje; **traveler**, (us) **traveler** ['trævlə'] n viajero/a; **traveller's cheque**, (us) **traveler's check** n cheque m de viaje; **travelling**, (us) **traveling** ['trævlɪŋ] *n* los viajes, el viajar; **travel-sick** *adj*: **to get travel-sick** marearse al viajar; **travel sickness** *n* mareo

tray [treɪ] *n* bandeja; (*on desk*) cajón *m*

treacherous ['tretʃərəs] *adj* traidor/a; (*BRIT*) **road conditions are ~** el estado de las carreteras es peligroso

treacle ['triːkl] *n* (*BRIT*) melaza

tread (*pt* trod, *pp* trodden) [tred, trɒd, 'trɒdn] *n* paso, pisada; (*of tyre*) banda de rodadura ▷ *vi* pisar; **tread on** *vt fus* pisar

treasure ['treʒər] *n* tesoro ▷ *vt* (*value*) apreciar, valorar; **treasurer** *n* tesorero/a

treasury ['treʒərɪ] *n*: **the T~** ≈ el Ministerio de Economía y de Hacienda

treat [triːt] *n* (*present*) regalo ▷ *vt* tratar; **to ~ sb to sth** invitar a algn a algo; **treatment** *n* tratamiento

treaty ['triːtɪ] *n* tratado

treble ['trebl] *adj* triple ▷ *vt* triplicar ▷ *vi* triplicarse

tree [triː] *n* árbol *m*; **tree trunk** *n* tronco de árbol

trek [trek] *n* (*long journey*) expedición *f*; (*tiring walk*) caminata

tremble ['trembl] *vi* temblar

tremendous [trɪ'mendəs] *adj* tremendo; enorme; (*excellent*) estupendo

trench [trentʃ] *n* zanja

trend [trend] *n* (*tendency*) tendencia; (*of events*) curso; (*fashion*) moda; **trendy** *adj* de moda

trespass ['trespəs] *vi*: **to ~ on** entrar sin permiso en; **"no ~ing"** "prohibido el paso"

trial ['traɪəl] *n* (*Law*) juicio, proceso; (*test: of machine etc*) prueba; **trial period** *n* periodo de prueba

triangle ['traɪæŋgl] *n* (*Math, Mus*) triángulo

triangular [traɪ'æŋgjələr] *adj* triangular

tribe [traɪb] *n* tribu *f*

tribunal [traɪ'bjuːnl] *n* tribunal *m*

tribute ['trɪbjuːt] *n* homenaje *m*, tributo; **to pay ~ to** rendir homenaje a

trick [trɪk] *n* trampa; (*conjuring trick, deceit*) truco; (*joke*) broma; (*Cards*) baza ▷ *vt* engañar; **to play a ~ on sb** gastar una broma a algn; **that should do the ~** eso servirá

trickle ['trɪkl] *n* (*of water etc*) hilo ▷ *vi* gotear

tricky ['trɪkɪ] *adj* difícil; (*problem*) delicado

tricycle ['traɪsɪkl] *n* triciclo

trifle ['traɪfl] *n* bagatela; (*Culin*) dulce de bizcocho, gelatina, fruta y natillas ▷ *adv*: **a ~ long** un pelín largo

trigger ['trɪgər] *n* (*of gun*) gatillo

trim [trɪm] *adj* (*house, garden*) en buen estado; (*figure*): **to be ~** tener buen talle ▷ *vt* (*neaten*) arreglar; (*cut*) recortar; (*decorate*) adornar; (*Naut: a sail*) orientar

trio ['triːəʊ] *n* trío

trip [trɪp] *n* viaje *m*; (*excursion*) excursión *f*; (*stumble*) traspié *m* ▷ *vi* (*stumble*) tropezar; (*go lightly*) andar a paso ligero; **on a ~** de viaje; **trip up** *vi* tropezar, caerse ▷ *vt* hacer tropezar or caer

triple ['trɪpl] *adj* triple

triplets ['trɪplɪts] *npl* trillizos/as *m/f*

tripod ['traɪpɒd] *n* trípode *m*

triumph ['traɪʌmf] *n* triunfo ▷ *vi*: **to ~ (over)** vencer; **triumphant** [traɪ'ʌmfənt] *adj* triunfante

trivial ['trɪvɪəl] *adj* insignificante

trod [trɒd] *pt of* **tread**

trodden ['trɒdn] *pp of* **tread**

trolley ['trɒlɪ] *n* carrito

trolley bus *n* trolebús *m*

trombone [trɒm'bəʊn] *n* trombón *m*

troop [truːp] *n* grupo, banda; **troops** *npl* (*Mil*) tropas *fpl*

trophy ['trəʊfɪ] *n* trofeo

tropical ['trɒpɪkl] *adj* tropical

trot [trɒt] *n* trote *m* ▷ *vi* trotar; **on the ~** (*BRIT fig*) seguidos/as

t

trouble ['trʌbl] n problema m, dificultad f; (worry) preocupación f; (bother, effort) molestia, esfuerzo; (unrest) inquietud f ▷ vt molestar; (worry) preocupar, inquietar ▷ vi: **to do to sth** molestarse en hacer algo; **troubles** npl (Pol etc) conflictos mpl; **to be in ~** estar en un apuro; **it's no ~!** no es molestia (ninguna)!; **what's the ~?** ¿qué pasa?; **troubled** adj (person) preocupado; (epoch, life) agitado; **troublemaker** n agitador(a) m/f; **troublesome** adj molesto

trough [trɔf] n (also: **drinking ~**) abrevadero m; (also: **feeding ~**) comedero

trousers ['trauzəz] npl pantalones mpl; **short ~** pantalones mpl cortos

trout [traut] n (pl inv) trucha

trowel ['trauəl] n paleta

truant ['truənt] n: **to play ~**(BRIT) hacer novillos

truce [tru:s] n tregua

truck [trʌk] n (US) camión m; (Rail) vagón m; **truck driver** n camionero/a m/f; **true** [tru:] adj verdadero; (accurate) exacto; (genuine) auténtico; (faithful) fiel; **to come ~** realizarse

truly ['tru:lɪ] adv realmente; **yours ~** (in letter-writing) atentamente

trumpet ['trʌmpɪt] n trompeta

trunk [trʌŋk] n (of tree, person) tronco; (of elephant) trompa; (case) baúl m; (US Aut) maletero

trunks [trʌŋks] npl (also: **swimming ~**) bañador m

trust [trʌst] n confianza f; (Law) fideicomiso m ▷ vt (rely on) tener confianza en; **to ~ sth to sb** (entrust) confiar algo a algn; **to ~ (that)** (hope) esperar (que); **you'll have to take it on ~** tienes que aceptarlo a ojos cerrados; **trusted** adj de confianza; **trustworthy** adj digno de confianza

truth (pl **truths**) [tru:θ, tru:ðz] n verdad f; **truthful** adj (person) sincero; (account) fidedigno

try [traɪ] n tentativa, intento; (Rugby) ensayo ▷ vt (Law) juzgar, procesar; (test: sth new) probar, someter a prueba; (attempt) intentar; (strain: patience) hacer perder ▷ vi probar; **to give sth a ~** intentar hacer algo; **to ~ to do sth** intentar hacer algo; **~ again!** ¡vuelve a probar!; **~ harder!** ¡esfuérzate más!; **well, I tried** al menos lo intenté; **try on** vt (clothes) probarse; **trying** adj (annoying) pesado

T-shirt ['ti:ʃə:t] n camiseta

tub [tʌb] n cubo (SP), balde m (LAM); (bath) bañera, tina (LAM)

tube [tju:b] n tubo; (BRIT: underground) metro

tuberculosis [tjubə:kju'ləusɪs] n tuberculosis f inv

tube station n (BRIT) estación f de metro

tuck [tʌk] vt (put) poner; **tuck away** vt esconder; **tuck in** vt meter; (child) arropar ▷ vi (eat) comer con apetito

tucker ['tʌkə⁽] n (AUST, NZ inf) papeo

tuck shop n (Scol) tienda de golosinas

Tue(s). abbr (= Tuesday) mart.

Tuesday ['tju:zdɪ] n martes m inv

tug [tʌg] n (ship) remolcador m ▷ vt remolcar

tuition [tju:'ɪʃən] n (BRIT) enseñanza; (: private tuition) clases fpl particulares; (US: school fees) matrícula

tulip ['tju:lɪp] n tulipán m

tumble ['tʌmbl] n (fall) caída ▷ vi caerse; **to ~ to sth** (inf) caer en la cuenta de algo; **tumble dryer** n (BRIT) secadora

tumbler ['tʌmblə⁽] n vaso

tummy ['tʌmɪ] n (inf) barriga

tumour, (US) **tumor** ['tju:mə⁽] n tumor m

tuna ['tju:nə] n (pl inv also: **~ fish**) atún m

tune [tju:n] n melodía ▷ vt (Mus) afinar; (Radio, TV, Aut) sintonizar; **to be in/out of ~** (instrument) estar

afinado/desafinado; (singer) afinar/
desafinar; **to be in/out of ~ with** (fig)
armonizar/desentonar con; **tune in**
vi (Radio, TV): **to ~ in (to)** sintonizar
(con); **tune up** vi (musician) afinar (su
instrumento)

tunic ['tju:nɪk] n túnica

Tunisia [tju:'nɪzɪə] n Túnez m

tunnel ['tʌnl] n túnel m; (in mine)
galería ▷ vi construir un túnel/una
galería

turbulence [tə:'bjuləns] n (Aviat)
turbulencia

turf [tə:f] n césped m; (clod) tepe m ▷ vt
cubrir con césped

Turk [tə:k] n turco/a

Turkey ['tə:kɪ] n Turquía

turkey ['tə:kɪ] n pavo

Turkish ['tə:kɪʃ] adj turco ▷ n (Ling)
turco

turmoil ['tə:mɔɪl] n: **in ~** revuelto

turn [tə:n] n turno; (in road) curva;
(Theat) número; (Med) ataque m ▷ vt
girar, volver; (collar, steak) dar la vuelta
a; (change): **to ~ sth into** convertir
algo en ▷ vi volver; (person: look back)
volverse; (reverse direction) dar la
vuelta; (milk) cortarse; **a good ~** un
favor; **it gave me quite a ~** me dio
un susto; **"no left ~"** (Aut) "prohibido
girar a la izquierda"; **it's your ~** te
toca a ti; **in ~** por turnos; **to take ~s**
turnarse; **turn around** vi (person)
volverse, darse la vuelta ▷ vt (object)
dar la vuelta a, voltear (LAM); **turn
away** vi apartar la vista ▷ vt rechazar;
turn back vi volverse atrás ▷ vt hacer
retroceder; (clock) retrasar; **turn
down** vt (refuse) rechazar; (reduce)
bajar; (fold) doblar; **turn in** vi (inf: go
to bed) acostarse ▷ vt (fold) doblar
hacia dentro; **turn off** vi (from road)
desviarse ▷ vt (light, radio etc) apagar;
(engine) parar; **turn on** vt (light, radio
etc) encender, prender (LAM); (engine)
poner en marcha; **turn out** vt (light,
gas) apagar; (produce) producir ▷ vi:
to ~ out to be ... resultar ser ...; **turn**

over vi (person) volverse ▷ vt (mattress,
card) dar la vuelta a; (page) volver;
turn round vi volverse; (rotate) girar;
turn to vt fus: **to ~ to sb** acudir a algn;
turn up vi (person) llegar, presentarse;
(lost object) aparecer ▷ vt (collar) subir;
turning n (bend) curva; **turning
point** n (fig) momento decisivo

turnip ['tə:nɪp] n nabo

turnout ['tə:naut] n (attendance)
asistencia; (number of people attending)
número de asistentes; (spectators)
público; **turnover** n (Comm: amount
of money) facturación f; (: of goods)
movimiento; **turnstile** n torniquete
m; **turn-up** n (BRIT: on trousers) vuelta

turquoise ['tə:kwɔɪz] n (stone)
turquesa ▷ adj color turquesa inv

turtle ['tə:tl] n tortuga (marina);
turtleneck (sweater) ['tə:tlnɛk-] n
(jersey m de) cuello cisne

tusk [tʌsk] n colmillo

tutor ['tju:tə'] n profesor(a) m/f;
tutorial [tju:'tɔ:rɪəl] n (Scol) seminario

tuxedo [tʌk'si:dəu] n (US) smóking m,
esmoquin m

TV [ti:'vi:] n abbr (= television)
televisión f

tweed [twi:d] n tweed m

tweet [twi:t] n (on Twitter) tweet m
▷ vt, vi (on Twitter) tuitear

tweezers ['twi:zəz] npl pinzas fpl
(de depilar)

twelfth [twelfθ] num duodécimo

twelve [twelv] num doce; **at
~ o'clock** (midday) a mediodía; (:
midnight) a medianoche

twentieth ['twɛntɪɪθ] num vigésimo

twenty ['twɛntɪ] num veinte; **in ~
fourteen** en dos mil catorce

twice [twaɪs] adv dos veces; **~ as
much** dos veces más

twig [twɪg] n ramita

twilight ['twaɪlaɪt] n crepúsculo

twin [twɪn] adj, n gemelo/a ▷ vt
hermanar; **twin-bedded room** n
= **twin room**; **twin beds** npl camas
fpl gemelas

twinkle ['twɪŋkl] vi centellear; (*eyes*) parpadear

twin room n habitación f con dos camas

twist [twɪst] n (*action*) torsión f; (*in road, coil*) vuelta; (*in wire, flex*) doblez f; (*in story*) giro ▷ vt torcer; (*roll around*) enrollar; (*fig*) deformar ▷ vi serpentear

twit [twɪt] n (*inf*) tonto

twitch [twɪtʃ] n sacudida; (*nervous*) tic m nervioso ▷ vi moverse nerviosamente

two [tuː] num dos; **to put ~ and ~ together** atar cabos

type [taɪp] n (*category*) tipo, género; (*model*) modelo; (*Typ*) tipo, letra ▷ vt (*letter etc*) escribir a máquina; **typewriter** n máquina de escribir

typhoid ['taɪfɔɪd] n (*fiebre* f) tifoidea

typhoon [taɪˈfuːn] n tifón m

typical ['tɪpɪkl] adj típico; **typically** adv típicamente

typing ['taɪpɪŋ] n mecanografía

typist ['taɪpɪst] n mecanógrafo/a

tyre, (*US*) **tire** ['taɪə'] n neumático, llanta (*LAM*); **tyre pressure** n presión f de los neumáticos

U

UFO ['juːfəu] n abbr (= *unidentified flying object*) OVNI m

Uganda [juːˈɡændə] n Uganda

ugly ['ʌɡlɪ] adj feo; (*dangerous*) peligroso

UHT adj abbr = **ultra heat treated**; **~ milk** leche f uperizada

UK n abbr (= *United Kingdom*) R.U.

ulcer ['ʌlsə'] n úlcera; **mouth ~** llaga bucal

ultimate ['ʌltɪmət] adj último, final; (*greatest*) mayor; **ultimately** adv (*in the end*) por último, al final; (*fundamentally*) a fin de cuentas

ultimatum (*pl* **ultimatums** or **ultimata**) [ʌltɪˈmeɪtəm, -tə] n ultimátum m

ultrasound ['ʌltrəsaund] n (*Med*) ultrasonido

ultraviolet ['ʌltrəˈvaɪəlɪt] adj ultravioleta

umbrella [ʌmˈbrelə] n paraguas m inv

umpire ['ʌmpaɪə'] n árbitro

UN n abbr (= United Nations) ONU f

unable [ʌnˈeɪbl] adj: **to be ~ to do sth** no poder hacer algo

unacceptable [ʌnəkˈsɛptəbl] adj (proposal, behaviour, price) inaceptable; **it's ~ that** no se puede aceptar que

unanimous [juːˈnænɪməs] adj unánime

unarmed [ʌnˈɑːmd] adj (person) desarmado

unattended [ʌnəˈtɛndɪd] adj desatendido

unattractive [ʌnəˈtræktɪv] adj poco atractivo

unavailable [ʌnəˈveɪləbl] adj (article, room, book) no disponible; (person) ocupado

unavoidable [ʌnəˈvɔɪdəbl] adj inevitable

unaware [ʌnəˈwɛəʳ] adj: **to be ~ of** ignorar; **unawares** adv: **to catch sb unawares** pillar a algn desprevenido

unbearable [ʌnˈbɛərəbl] adj insoportable

unbeatable [ʌnˈbiːtəbl] adj invencible; (price) inmejorable

unbelievable [ʌnbɪˈliːvəbl] adj increíble

unborn [ʌnˈbɔːn] adj que va a nacer

unbutton [ʌnˈbʌtn] vt desabrochar

uncalled-for [ʌnˈkɔːldfɔːʳ] adj gratuito, inmerecido

uncanny [ʌnˈkænɪ] adj extraño

uncertain [ʌnˈsɜːtn] adj incierto; (indecisive) indeciso; **uncertainty** n incertidumbre f

unchanged [ʌnˈtʃeɪndʒd] adj sin cambiar or alterar

uncle [ˈʌŋkl] n tío

unclear [ʌnˈklɪəʳ] adj poco claro; **I'm still ~ about what I'm supposed to do** todavía no tengo muy claro lo que tengo que hacer

uncomfortable [ʌnˈkʌmfətəbl] adj incómodo; (uneasy) inquieto

uncommon [ʌnˈkɔmən] adj poco común, raro

unconditional [ʌnkənˈdɪʃənl] adj incondicional

unconscious [ʌnˈkɔnʃəs] adj sin sentido; (unaware) inconsciente ▷ n: **the ~** el inconsciente

uncontrollable [ʌnkənˈtrəuləbl] adj (temper) indomable; (laughter) incontenible

unconventional [ʌnkənˈvɛnʃənl] adj poco convencional

uncover [ʌnˈkʌvəʳ] vt descubrir; (take lid off) destapar

undecided [ʌndɪˈsaɪdɪd] adj (person) indeciso; (question) no resuelto

undeniable [ʌndɪˈnaɪəbl] adj innegable

under [ˈʌndəʳ] prep debajo de; (less than) menos de; (according to) según, de acuerdo con ▷ adv debajo, abajo; **~ there** ahí debajo; **~ construction** en construcción; **undercover** adj clandestino; **underdone** adj (Culin) poco hecho; **underestimate** vt subestimar; **undergo** vt (irreg: like **go**) sufrir; (treatment) recibir; **undergraduate** n estudiante mf; **underground** n (BRIT: railway) metro; (Pol) movimiento clandestino ▷ adj subterráneo ▷ adv (work) en la clandestinidad; **undergrowth** n maleza; **underline** vt subrayar; **undermine** vt socavar, minar; **underneath** [ʌndəˈniːθ] adv debajo ▷ prep debajo de, bajo; **underpants** npl calzoncillos mpl; **underpass** n (BRIT) paso subterráneo; **underprivileged** adj desposeído; **underscore** vt subrayar, sostener; **undershirt** n (US) camiseta; **underskirt** n (BRIT) enaguas fpl

understand [ʌndəˈstænd] vt, vi entender, comprender; (assume) tener entendido; **understandable** adj comprensible; **understanding** adj comprensivo ▷ n comprensión f, entendimiento ▷ n (agreement) acuerdo

understatement [ʌndəˈsteɪtmənt] n modestia (excesiva); **to say it was**

good is quite an ~ decir que estuvo bien es quedarse corto
understood [ʌndəˈstʊd] *pt, pp of* **understand** ▷ *adj* entendido; *(implied):* **it is ~ that** se sobreentiende que
undertake [ʌndəˈteɪk] *vt (irreg: like take)* emprender; **to ~ to do sth** comprometerse a hacer algo
undertaker [ˈʌndəteɪkəʳ] *n* director(a) *m/f* de pompas fúnebres
undertaking [ˈʌndəteɪkɪŋ] *n* empresa; *(promise)* promesa
under: **underwater** *adv* bajo el agua ▷ *adj* submarino; **underway** *adj:* **to be underway** *(meeting)* estar en marcha; *(investigation)* estar llevándose a cabo; **underwear** *n* ropa interior o íntima (LAM); **underwent** *vb see* **undergo**; **underworld** *n (of crime)* hampa, inframundo
undesirable [ʌndɪˈzaɪərəbl] *adj* indeseable
undisputed [ʌndɪˈspjuːtɪd] *adj* incontestable
undo [ʌnˈduː] *vt (irreg: like do: laces)* desatar; *(button etc)* desabrochar; *(spoil)* deshacer
undone [ʌnˈdʌn] *pp of* **undo** ▷ *adj:* **to come ~** *(clothes)* desabrocharse; *(parcel)* desatarse
undoubtedly [ʌnˈdautɪdlɪ] *adv* indudablemente, sin duda
undress [ʌnˈdrɛs] *vi* desnudarse
unearth [ʌnˈəːθ] *vt* desenterrar
uneasy [ʌnˈiːzɪ] *adj* intranquilo; *(worried)* preocupado; **to feel ~ about doing sth** sentirse incómodo con la idea de hacer algo
unemployed [ʌnɪmˈplɔɪd] *adj* parado, sin trabajo ▷ *n:* **the ~ los** parados
unemployment [ʌnɪmˈplɔɪmənt] *n* paro, desempleo; **unemployment benefit** *n (BRIT)* subsidio de desempleo o paro
unequal [ʌnˈiːkwəl] *adj (length, objects etc)* desigual; *(amounts)* distinto

uneven [ʌnˈiːvn] *adj* desigual; *(road etc)* con baches
unexpected [ʌnɪkˈspɛktɪd] *adj* inesperado; **unexpectedly** *adv* inesperadamente
unfair [ʌnˈfɛəʳ] *adj:* **~ (to sb)** injusto (con algn)
unfaithful [ʌnˈfeɪθful] *adj* infiel
unfamiliar [ʌnfəˈmɪlɪəʳ] *adj* extraño, desconocido; **to be ~ with sth** desconocer o ignorar algo
unfashionable [ʌnˈfæʃnəbl] *adj* pasado o fuera de moda
unfasten [ʌnˈfɑːsn] *vt* desatar
unfavourable, (US) **unfavorable** [ʌnˈfeɪvərəbl] *adj* desfavorable
unfinished [ʌnˈfɪnɪʃt] *adj* inacabado, sin terminar
unfit [ʌnˈfɪt] *adj* en baja forma; *(incompetent)* incapaz; **~ for work** no apto para trabajar
unfold [ʌnˈfəuld] *vt* desdoblar ▷ *vi* abrirse
unforgettable [ʌnfəˈgɛtəbl] *adj* inolvidable
unfortunate [ʌnˈfɔːtʃnət] *adj* desgraciado; *(event, remark)* inoportuno; **unfortunately** *adv* desgraciadamente
unfriend [ʌnˈfrɛnd] *vt (Internet)* quitar de amigo a; **he has ~ed her on Facebook** la ha quitado de amiga en Facebook
unfriendly [ʌnˈfrɛndlɪ] *adj* antipático; *(behaviour, remark)* hostil, poco amigable
unfurnished [ʌnˈfəːnɪʃt] *adj* sin amueblar
unhappiness [ʌnˈhæpɪnɪs] *n* tristeza
unhappy [ʌnˈhæpɪ] *adj (sad)* triste; *(unfortunate)* desgraciado; *(childhood)* infeliz; **~ with** *(arrangements etc)* poco contento con, descontento de
unhealthy [ʌnˈhɛlθɪ] *adj* malsano; *(person)* enfermizo; *(interest)* morboso
unheard-of [ʌnˈhəːdɔv] *adj* inaudito, sin precedente

unhelpful [ʌnˈhɛlpful] adj (person) poco servicial; (advice) inútil

unhurt [ʌnˈhəːt] adj ileso

unidentified [ʌnaɪˈdɛntɪfaɪd] adj no identificado; **~ flying object (UFO)** objeto volante no identificado

uniform [ˈjuːnɪfɔːm] n uniforme m ▷ adj uniforme

unify [ˈjuːnɪfaɪ] vt unificar, unir

unimportant [ʌnɪmˈpɔːtənt] adj sin importancia

uninhabited [ʌnɪnˈhæbɪtɪd] adj desierto

unintentional [ʌnɪnˈtɛnʃənəl] adj involuntario

union [ˈjuːnjən] n unión f; (also: **trade ~**) sindicato ▷ cpd sindical; **Union Jack** n bandera del Reino Unido

unique [juːˈniːk] adj único

unisex [ˈjuːnɪsɛks] adj unisex

unit [ˈjuːnɪt] n unidad f; (team, squad) grupo; **kitchen ~** módulo de cocina

unite [juːˈnaɪt] vt unir ▷ vi unirse; **united** adj unido; **United Kingdom** n Reino Unido

United Nations (Organization) n Naciones Unidas fpl

United States (of America) n Estados Unidos mpl (de América)

unity [ˈjuːnɪtɪ] n unidad f

universal [juːnɪˈvəːsl] adj universal

universe [ˈjuːnɪvəːs] n universo m

university [juːnɪˈvəːsɪtɪ] n universidad f

unjust [ʌnˈdʒʌst] adj injusto

unkind [ʌnˈkaɪnd] adj poco amable; (comment etc) cruel

unknown [ʌnˈnəun] adj desconocido

unlawful [ʌnˈlɔːful] adj ilegal, ilícito

unleaded [ʌnˈlɛdɪd] n (also: **~ petrol**) gasolina sin plomo

unleash [ʌnˈliːʃ] vt desatar

unless [ʌnˈlɛs] conj a menos que; **~ he comes** a menos que venga; **~ otherwise stated** salvo indicación contraria

unlike [ʌnˈlaɪk] adj distinto ▷ prep a diferencia de

unlikely [ʌnˈlaɪklɪ] adj improbable

unlimited [ʌnˈlɪmɪtɪd] adj ilimitado

unlisted [ʌnˈlɪstɪd] adj (us Tel) que no figura en la guía

unload [ʌnˈləud] vt descargar

unlock [ʌnˈlɔk] vt abrir (con llave)

unlucky [ʌnˈlʌkɪ] adj desgraciado; (object, number) que da mala suerte; **to be ~** tener mala suerte

unmarried [ʌnˈmærɪd] adj soltero

unmistakable [ʌnmɪsˈteɪkəbl] adj inconfundible

unnatural [ʌnˈnætʃrəl] adj antinatural; (manner) afectado; (habit) perverso

unnecessary [ʌnˈnɛsəsərɪ] adj innecesario, inútil

UNO [ˈjuːnəu] n abbr (= United Nations Organization) ONU f

unofficial [ʌnəˈfɪʃl] adj no oficial

unpack [ʌnˈpæk] vi deshacer las maletas ▷ vt deshacer

unpaid [ʌnˈpeɪd] adj (bill, debt) sin pagar, impagado; (Comm) pendiente; (holiday) sin sueldo; (work) sin pago, voluntario

unpleasant [ʌnˈplɛznt] adj (disagreeable) desagradable; (person, manner) antipático

unplug [ʌnˈplʌg] vt desenchufar, desconectar

unpopular [ʌnˈpɔpjulə] adj poco popular

unprecedented [ʌnˈprɛsɪdəntɪd] adj sin precedentes

unpredictable [ʌnprɪˈdɪktəbl] adj imprevisible

unprotected [ʌnprəˈtɛktɪd] adj (sex) sin protección

unqualified [ʌnˈkwɔlɪfaɪd] adj sin título, no cualificado; (success) total

unravel [ʌnˈrævl] vt desenmarañar

unreal [ʌnˈrɪəl] adj irreal

unrealistic [ʌnrɪəˈlɪstɪk] adj poco realista

unreasonable [ʌnˈriːznəbl] adj irrazonable; **to make ~ demands on sb** hacer demandas excesivas a algn

unrelated [ʌnrɪˈleɪtɪd] *adj* sin relación; (*family*) no emparentado

unreliable [ʌnrɪˈlaɪəbl] *adj* (*person*) informal; (*machine*) poco fiable

unrest [ʌnˈrɛst] *n* inquietud f, malestar m; (*Pol*) disturbios *mpl*

unroll [ʌnˈrəʊl] *vt* desenrollar

unruly [ʌnˈruːlɪ] *adj* indisciplinado

unsafe [ʌnˈseɪf] *adj* peligroso

unsatisfactory [ˈʌnsætɪsˈfæktərɪ] *adj* poco satisfactorio

unscrew [ʌnˈskruː] *vt* destornillar

unsettled [ʌnˈsɛtld] *adj* inquieto; (*weather*) variable

unsettling [ʌnˈsɛtlɪŋ] *adj* perturbador(a), inquietante

unsightly [ʌnˈsaɪtlɪ] *adj* desagradable

unskilled [ʌnˈskɪld] *adj*: **~ workers** mano f de obra no cualificada

unspoiled [ʌnˈspɔɪld], **unspoilt** [ʌnˈspɔɪlt] *adj* (*place*) que no ha perdido su belleza natural

unstable [ʌnˈsteɪbl] *adj* inestable

unsteady [ʌnˈstɛdɪ] *adj* inestable

unsuccessful [ʌnsəkˈsɛsful] *adj* (*attempt*) infructuoso; (*writer, proposal*) sin éxito; **to be ~** (*in attempting sth*) no tener éxito, fracasar

unsuitable [ʌnˈsuːtəbl] *adj* inapropiado; (*time*) inoportuno

unsure [ʌnˈʃuəʳ] *adj* inseguro, poco seguro

untidy [ʌnˈtaɪdɪ] *adj* (*room*) desordenado; (*appearance*) desaliñado

untie [ʌnˈtaɪ] *vt* desatar

until [ʌnˈtɪl] *prep* hasta ▷ *conj* hasta que; **~ he comes** hasta que venga; **~ now** hasta ahora; **~ then** hasta entonces

untrue [ʌnˈtruː] *adj* (*statement*) falso

unused [ʌnˈjuːzd] *adj* sin usar

unusual [ʌnˈjuːʒuəl] *adj* insólito, poco común; **unusually** *adv*: **he arrived unusually early** llegó más temprano de costumbre

unveil [ʌnˈveɪl] *vt* (*statue*) descubrir

unwanted [ʌnˈwɒntɪd] *adj* (*person, effect*) no deseado

unwell [ʌnˈwɛl] *adj*: **to feel ~** estar indispuesto, sentirse mal

unwilling [ʌnˈwɪlɪŋ] *adj*: **to be ~ to do sth** estar poco dispuesto a hacer algo

unwind [ʌnˈwaɪnd] (*irreg: like* **wind²**) *vt* desenvolver ▷ *vi* (*relax*) relajarse

unwise [ʌnˈwaɪz] *adj* imprudente

unwittingly [ʌnˈwɪtɪŋlɪ] *adv* inconscientemente, sin darse cuenta

unwrap [ʌnˈræp] *vt* desenvolver

unzip [ʌnˈzɪp] *vt* abrir la cremallera de; (*Comput*) descomprimir

---

KEYWORD

up [ʌp] *prep*: **to go/be up sth** subir/ estar subido en algo; **he went up the stairs/the hill** subió las escaleras/ la colina; **we walked/climbed up the hill** subimos la colina; **they live further up the street** viven más arriba en la calle; **go up that road and turn left** sigue por esa calle y gira a la izquierda

▷ *adv* 1 (*upwards, higher*) más arriba; **up in the mountains** en lo alto (de la montaña); **put it a bit higher up** ponlo un poco más arriba o alto; **up there** ahí o allí arriba; **up above** en lo alto, por encima, arriba

2: **to be up** (*out of bed*) estar levantado; (*prices, level*) haber subido

3: **up to** (*as far as*) hasta; **up to now** hasta ahora o la fecha

4: **to be up to** (*depending on*): **it's up to you** depende de ti; **he's not up to it** (*job, task etc*) no es capaz de hacerlo; **his work is not up to the required standard** su trabajo no da la talla; **what is he up to?** (*inf: doing*) ¿qué estará tramando?

▷ *n*: **ups and downs** altibajos *mpl*

up-and-coming [ʌpəndˈkʌmɪŋ] *adj* prometedor(a)

upbringing [ˈʌpbrɪŋɪŋ] n educación f
update [ʌpˈdeɪt] vt poner al día
upfront [ʌpˈfrʌnt] adj claro, directo ⊳ adv a las claras; (pay) por adelantado; **to be ~ about sth** admitir algo claramente
upgrade [ʌpˈgreɪd] vt ascender; (Comput) modernizar
upheaval [ʌpˈhiːvl] n trastornos mpl; (Pol) agitación f
uphill [ʌpˈhɪl] adj cuesta arriba; (fig: task) penoso, difícil ⊳ adv: **to go ~** ir cuesta arriba
upholstery [ʌpˈhəʊlstəri] n tapicería f
upload [ˈʌpləʊd] vt (Comput) subir
upmarket [ʌpˈmɑːkɪt] adj (product) de categoría
upon [əˈpɒn] prep sobre
upper [ˈʌpə] adj superior, de arriba ⊳ n (of shoe: also: **~s**) pala; **upper-class** adj de clase alta
upright [ˈʌpraɪt] adj vertical; (fig) honrado
uprising [ˈʌpraɪzɪŋ] n sublevación f
uproar [ˈʌprɔː] n escándalo
upset n [ˈʌpset] (to plan etc) revés m, contratiempo; (Med) trastorno ⊳ vt [ʌpˈset] (irreg: like set: glass etc) volcar; (plan) alterar; (person) molestar ⊳ adj [ʌpˈset] preocupado, perturbado; (stomach) revuelto
upside-down [ˈʌpsaɪdˈdaʊn] adv al revés; **to turn a place ~** (fig) revolverlo todo
upstairs [ʌpˈsteəz] adv arriba ⊳ adj (room) de arriba ⊳ n el piso superior
up-to-date [ˈʌptəˈdeɪt] adj actual, moderno
uptown [ˈʌptaʊn] adv (us) hacia las afueras ⊳ adj exterior, de las afueras
upward(s) [ˈʌpwəd(z)] adv hacia arriba; (more than): **~ of** más de
uranium [jʊəˈreɪnɪəm] n uranio
Uranus [ˈjʊərəɪnəs] n Urano
urban [ˈɜːbən] adj urbano
urge [ɜːdʒ] n (desire) deseo ⊳ vt: **to ~ sb to do sth** animar a algn a hacer algo

urgency [ˈɜːdʒənsɪ] n urgencia
urgent [ˈɜːdʒənt] adj urgente
urinal [ˈjʊərɪnl] n (building) urinario; (vessel) orinal m
urinate [ˈjʊərɪneɪt] vi orinar
urine [ˈjʊərɪn] n orina
US n abbr (= United States) EE.UU.
us [ʌs] pron nos; (after prep) nosotros/as; see also **me**
USA n abbr = **United States of America**; (Mil) = **United States Army**
USB abbr (= universal serial bus) USB m; **USB stick** n memoria USB, llave f de memoria
use n [juːs] uso, empleo; (usefulness) utilidad f ⊳ vt [juːz] usar, emplear; **in ~** en uso; **out of ~** en desuso; **to be of ~** servir; **it's no ~** (pointless) es inútil; (not useful) no sirve; **to be ~d to** estar acostumbrado a (SP), acostumbrar; **she ~d to do it** (ella) solía or acostumbraba hacerlo; **use up** vt (food) consumir; (money) gastar; **used** [juːzd] adj (car) usado; **useful** [juːsfʊl] adj útil; **useless** adj (unusable) inservible; **user** n usuario/a; **user-friendly** adj (Comput) fácil de utilizar
usual [ˈjuːʒuəl] adj normal, corriente; **as ~** como de costumbre; **usually** adv normalmente
ute [juːt] n abbr (AUST, NZ inf: = utility truck) camioneta
utensil [juːˈtensl] n utensilio; **kitchen ~s** batería f de cocina
utility [juːˈtɪlɪtɪ] n utilidad f; (public utility) empresa de servicio público
utilize [ˈjuːtɪlaɪz] vt utilizar
utmost [ˈʌtməʊst] adj mayor ⊳ n: **to do one's ~** hacer todo lo posible
utter [ˈʌtə] adj total, completo ⊳ vt pronunciar, proferir; **utterly** adv completamente, totalmente
U-turn [ˈjuːtɜːn] n cambio de sentido

u

V

v. *abbr* (= *verse*) vers.°; (= *see*) V, vid., vide; (= *versus*) vs.; = **volt**

vacancy ['veɪkənsɪ] *n* (*job*) vacante *f*; (*room*) cuarto libro; **"no vacancies"** "completo"

vacant ['veɪkənt] *adj* desocupado, libre; (*expression*) distraído

vacate [və'keɪt] *vt* (*house*) desocupar; (*job*) dejar (vacante)

vacation [və'keɪʃən] *n* vacaciones *fpl*; **vacationer** [və'keɪʃənə*], **vacationist** [və'keɪʃənɪst] *n* (*us*) turista *mf*

vaccination [væksɪ'neɪʃən] *n* vacunación *f*

vaccine ['væksiːn] *n* vacuna

vacuum ['vækjʊm] *n* vacío; **vacuum cleaner** *n* aspiradora

vagina [və'dʒaɪnə] *n* vagina

vague [veɪg] *adj* vago; (*memory*) borroso; (*ambiguous*) impreciso; (*person: absent-minded*) distraído; (: *evasive*): **to be ~** no decir las cosas claramente

vain [veɪn] *adj* (*conceited*) presumido; (*useless*) vano, inútil; **in ~** en vano

Valentine's Day *n* día de los enamorados (*el 14 de febrero, día de San Valentín*)

valid ['vælɪd] *adj* válido; (*ticket*) valedero; (*law*) vigente

valley ['vælɪ] *n* valle *m*

valuable ['væljʊəbl] *adj* (*jewel*) de valor; (*time*) valioso; **valuables** *npl* objetos *mpl* de valor

value ['væljuː] *n* valor *m*; (*importance*) importancia ▷ *vt* (*fix price of*) tasar, valorar; (*esteem*) apreciar; **values** *npl* (*moral*) valores *mpl* morales

valve [vælv] *n* válvula

vampire ['væmpaɪə*] *n* vampiro

van [væn] *n* (*Aut*) furgoneta, camioneta (*LAM*)

vandal ['vændl] *n* vándalo/a; **vandalism** *n* vandalismo; **vandalize** *vt* dañar, destruir

vanilla [və'nɪlə] *n* vainilla

vanish ['vænɪʃ] *vi* desaparecer

vanity ['vænɪtɪ] *n* vanidad *f*

vapour, (*us*) **vapor** ['veɪpə*] *n* vapor *m*; (*on breath, window*) vaho

variable ['vɛərɪəbl] *adj* variable

variant ['vɛərɪənt] *n* variante *f*

variation [vɛərɪ'eɪʃən] *n* variación *f*

varied ['vɛərɪd] *adj* variado

variety [və'raɪətɪ] *n* variedad *f*, diversidad *f*

various ['vɛərɪəs] *adj* varios/as, diversos/as

varnish ['vɑːnɪʃ] *n* barniz *m*; (*also*: **nail ~**) esmalte *m* ▷ *vt* barnizar; (*nails*) pintar (con esmalte)

vary ['vɛərɪ] *vt* variar; (*change*) cambiar ▷ *vi* variar

vase [vɑːz] *n* florero, jarrón *m*
  ■ Be careful not to translate *vase* by the Spanish word *vaso*.

Vaseline® ['væsɪliːn] *n* vaselina®

vast [vɑːst] *adj* enorme

VAT [væt] *n abbr* (BRIT: = *value added tax*) IVA *m*

vault [vɔ:lt] n (of roof) bóveda; (tomb) panteón m; (in bank) cámara acorazada ▷ vt (also: **~ over**) saltar (por encima de)

VCR n abbr = **video cassette recorder**

VDU n abbr (= visual display unit) UPVf

veal [vi:l] n ternera

veer [vɪə*] vi (vehicle) virar; (wind) girar

vegan ['vi:gən] n vegetariano/a estricto/a

vegetable ['vedʒtəbl] n (Bot) vegetal m; (edible plant) legumbre f, hortaliza f ▷ adj vegetal

vegetarian [vedʒɪ'tɛərɪən] adj, n vegetariano/a

vegetation [vedʒɪ'teɪʃən] n vegetación f

vehicle ['vi:ɪkl] n vehículo m; (fig) medio

veil [veɪl] n velo ▷ vt velar

vein [veɪn] n vena; (of ore etc) veta

Velcro® ['vɛlkrəʊ] n velcro®m

velvet ['vɛlvɪt] n terciopelo

vending machine ['vɛndɪŋ-] n máquina expendedora, expendedor m

vendor ['vɛndə*] n vendedor(a) m/f; **street ~** vendedor(a) m/f callejero/a

vengeance ['vɛndʒəns] n venganza; **with a ~** (fig) con creces

venison ['vɛnɪsn] n carne f de venado

venom ['vɛnəm] n veneno

vent [vɛnt] n (opening) abertura; (air-hole) respiradero; (in wall) rejilla de ventilación ▷ vt (fig: feelings) desahogar

ventilation [vɛntɪ'leɪʃən] n ventilación f

venture ['vɛntʃə*] n empresa ▷ vt (opinion) ofrecer ▷ vi arriesgarse, lanzarse; **a business ~** una empresa comercial

venue ['vɛnju:] n (meeting place) lugar m de reunión

Venus ['vi:nəs] n Venus m

verb [və:b] n verbo; **verbal** adj verbal

verdict ['və:dɪkt] n veredicto, fallo; (fig) opinión f, juicio

verge [və:dʒ] n (BRIT) borde m; **to be on the ~ of doing sth** estar a punto de hacer algo

verify ['vɛrɪfaɪ] vt comprobar, verificar

versatile ['və:sətaɪl] adj (person) polifacético; (machine, tool etc) versátil

verse [və:s] n poesía; (stanza) estrofa; (in bible) versículo

version ['və:ʃən] n versión f

versus ['və:səs] prep contra

vertical ['və:tɪkl] adj vertical

very ['vɛrɪ] adv muy ▷ adj: **the ~ book which** el mismo libro que; **the ~ last** el último (de todos); **at the ~ least** al menos; **~ much** muchísimo

vessel ['vɛsl] n (Anat) vaso; (ship) barco; (container) vasija

vest [vɛst] n (BRIT) camiseta; (US: waistcoat) chaleco

vet [vɛt] n abbr = **veterinary surgeon** ▷ vt revisar; **to ~ sb for a job** someter a investigación de algn para un trabajo

veteran ['vɛtərn] n veterano/a

veterinary surgeon (BRIT) veterinario/a

veto ['vi:təʊ] n veto ▷ vt prohibir

via ['vaɪə] prep por, por vía de

viable ['vaɪəbl] adj viable

vibrate [vaɪ'breɪt] vi vibrar

vibration [vaɪ'breɪʃən] n vibración f

vicar ['vɪkə*] n párroco

vice [vaɪs] n (evil) vicio; (Tech) torno de banco; **vice-chairman** n vicepresidente m

vice versa ['vaɪsɪ'və:sə] adv viceversa

vicinity [vɪ'sɪnɪtɪ] n: **in the ~ (of)** cercano/a

vicious ['vɪʃəs] adj (remark) malicioso; (blow) brutal; (dog, horse) resabido; **a ~ circle** un círculo vicioso

victim ['vɪktɪm] n víctima

victor ['vɪktə*] n vencedor(a) m/f

Victorian [vɪk'tɔ:rɪən] adj victoriano

victorious [vɪk'tɔ:rɪəs] adj vencedor(a)

victory ['vɪktərɪ] n victoria

video ['vɪdɪəʊ] n vídeo ▷ vt grabar (en vídeo); **video call** n videollamada; **video camera** n videocámara, cámara de vídeo; **video cassette recorder** n = **video recorder**; **video**

V

game n videojuego; **videophone** n videoteléfono, videófono; **video recorder** n vídeo; **video tape** n cinta de vídeo

vie [vaɪ] vi: **to ~ with** competir con

Vienna [vɪ'enə] n Viena

Vietnam [vjet'næm] n Vietnam m; **Vietnamese** [vjetnə'miːz] adj vietnamita ▷ n (pl inv) vietnamita mf

view [vjuː] n vista; (opinion) opinión f, criterio ▷ vt (look at) mirar; **on ~** (in museum etc) expuesto; **in full ~ of sb** a la vista de algn; **in ~ of the fact that** en vista de que; **viewer** n (TV) telespectador(a) m/f; **viewpoint** n punto de vista

vigilant ['vɪdʒɪlənt] adj vigilante

vigorous ['vɪɡərəs] adj enérgico, vigoroso

vile [vaɪl] adj (action) vil, infame; (smell) repugnante; (temper) endemoniado

villa ['vɪlə] n (country house) casa de campo; (suburban house) chalet m

village ['vɪlɪdʒ] n aldea; **villager** n aldeano/a

villain ['vɪlən] n (scoundrel) malvado/a; (criminal) maleante mf

vinaigrette [vɪneɪ'ɡret] n vinagreta

vine [vaɪn] n vid f

vinegar ['vɪnɪɡə'] n vinagre m

vineyard ['vɪnjɑːd] n viña, viñedo

vintage ['vɪntɪdʒ] n (year) vendimia, cosecha

vinyl ['vaɪnl] n vinilo

viola [vɪ'əʊlə] n (Mus) viola

violate ['vaɪəleɪt] vt violar

violation [vaɪə'leɪʃən] n violación f; **in ~ of sth** en violación de algo

violence ['vaɪələns] n violencia

violent ['vaɪələnt] adj violento; (pain) intenso

violet ['vaɪələt] adj violado, violeta inv ▷ n (plant) violeta

violin [vaɪə'lɪn] n violín m

VIP n abbr (= very important person) VIP m

viral adj (Med) vírico; (Comput) viral

virgin ['vɜːdʒɪn] n virgen mf

Virgo ['vɜːɡəʊ] n Virgo

virtual ['vɜːtjuəl] adj virtual; **virtually** adv prácticamente, virtualmente; **virtual reality** n (Comput) realidad f virtual

virtue ['vɜːtjuː] n virtud f; **by ~ of** en virtud de

virus ['vaɪərəs] n virus m inv

visa ['viːzə] n visado, visa (LAM)

vise [vaɪs] n (us Tech); = **vice**

visibility [vɪzɪ'bɪlɪtɪ] n visibilidad f

visible ['vɪzəbl] adj visible

vision ['vɪʒən] n (sight) vista; (foresight, in dream) visión f

visit ['vɪzɪt] n visita ▷ vt (person) visitar, hacer una visita a; (place) ir a, (ir a) conocer; **visiting hours** npl (in hospital etc) horas fpl de visita; **visitor** n visitante mf; (to one's house) visita; (tourist) turista mf; **visitor centre**, (us) **visitor center** n centro m de información

visual ['vɪzjuəl] adj visual; **visualize** vt imaginarse

vital ['vaɪtl] adj (essential) esencial, imprescindible; (organ) vital

vitality [vaɪ'tælɪtɪ] n energía, vitalidad f

vitamin ['vɪtəmɪn] n vitamina

vivid ['vɪvɪd] adj (account) gráfico; (light) intenso; (imagination) vivo

V-neck ['viːnɛk] n cuello de pico

vocabulary [vəʊ'kæbjʊlərɪ] n vocabulario

vocal ['vəʊkl] adj vocal; (articulate) elocuente

vocational [vəʊ'keɪʃənl] adj profesional

vodka ['vɒdkə] n vodka m

vogue [vəʊɡ] n: **to be in ~** estar de moda o en boga

voice [vɔɪs] n voz f; **voice mail** n fonobuzón m

void [vɔɪd] n vacío; (hole) hueco ▷ adj (invalid) nulo, inválido; (empty): **~ of** carente o desprovisto de

volatile ['vɒlətaɪl] adj (situation) inestable; (person) voluble; (liquid) volátil

volcano [vɔl'keɪnəu] (pl **volcanoes**) n volcán m

volleyball ['vɔlɪbɔːl] n voleibol m

volt [vəult] n voltio m; **voltage** n voltaje m

volume ['vɔljuːm] n (of tank) volumen m; (book) tomo

voluntarily ['vɔləntrɪlɪ] adv libremente, voluntariamente

voluntary ['vɔləntərɪ] adj voluntario

volunteer [vɔlən'tɪə*] n voluntario/a ⊳ vt (information) ofrecer ⊳ vi ofrecerse (de voluntario); **to ~ to do** ofrecerse a hacer

vomit ['vɔmɪt] n vómito ⊳ vt, vi vomitar

vote [vəut] n voto; (votes cast) votación f; (right to vote) derecho a votar; (franchise) sufragio ⊳ vt (chairman) elegir ⊳ vi votar, ir a votar; **~ of thanks** voto de gracias; **voter** n votante mf; **voting** n votación f

voucher ['vautʃə*] n (for meal, petrol) vale m

vow [vau] n voto ⊳ vi hacer voto ⊳ vt: **to ~ to do/that** jurar hacer/que

vowel ['vauəl] n vocal f

voyage ['vɔɪɪdʒ] n viaje m

vulgar ['vʌlgə*] adj (rude) ordinario, grosero; (in bad taste) de mal gusto

vulnerable ['vʌlnərəbl] adj vulnerable

vulture ['vʌltʃə*] n buitre m

W

waddle ['wɔdl] vi andar como un pato

wade [weɪd] vi (fig: a book) leer con dificultad; **to ~ through the water** caminar por el agua

wafer ['weɪfə*] n (biscuit) barquillo

waffle ['wɔfl] n (Culin) gofre m ⊳ vi meter el rollo

wag [wæg] vt menear, agitar ⊳ vi moverse, menearse

wage [weɪdʒ] n (also: **~s**) sueldo, salario ⊳ vt: **to ~ war** hacer la guerra

wag(g)on ['wægən] n (horse-drawn) carro; (BRIT Rail) vagón m

wail [weɪl] n gemido ⊳ vi gemir

waist [weɪst] n cintura, talle m; **waistcoat** n (BRIT) chaleco

wait [weɪt] n (interval) pausa ⊳ vi esperar; **to lie in ~ for** acechar a; **I can't ~ to** (fig) estoy deseando; **to ~ for** esperar (a); **wait on** vt fus servir a; **waiter** n camarero; **waiting list** n lista de espera; **waiting room** n

W

sala de espera; **waitress** ['weɪtrɪs] n camarera

waive [weɪv] vt suspender

wake [weɪk] (pt **woke** or **waked**, pp **woken** or **waked**) vt (also: **~ up**) despertar ▷ vi (also: **~ up**) despertarse ▷ n (for dead person) velatorio; (Naut) estela

Wales [weɪlz] n País de Gales

walk [wɔːk] n (stroll) paseo; (hike) excursión f a pie, caminata; (gait) paso, andar m; (in park etc) paseo ▷ vi andar, caminar; (for pleasure, exercise) pasearse ▷ vt (distance) recorrer a pie, andar; (dog) (sacar a) pasear; **10 minutes' ~ from here** a 10 minutos de aquí andando; **people from all ~s of life** gente de todas las esferas; **walk out** vi (go out) salir; (as protest) salirse; (strike) declararse en huelga; **walker** n (person) paseante mf, caminante mf; **walkie-talkie** ['wɔːkɪ'tɔːkɪ] n walkie-talkie m; **walking** n (el) andar; **walking shoes** npl zapatos mpl para andar; **walking stick** n bastón m; **Walkman®** n walkman®m; **walkway** n paseo

wall [wɔːl] n pared f; (exterior) muro; (city wall etc) muralla

wallet ['wɔlɪt] n cartera

wallpaper ['wɔːlpeɪpəʳ] n papel m pintado ▷ vt empapelar

walnut ['wɔːlnʌt] n nuez f; (tree) nogal m

walrus ['wɔːlrəs] (pl **walrus** or **walruses**) n morsa

waltz [wɔːlts] n vals m ▷ vi bailar el vals

wand [wɒnd] n (also: **magic ~**) varita (mágica)

wander ['wɒndəʳ] vi (person) vagar; deambular; (thoughts) divagar ▷ vt recorrer, vagar por

want [wɒnt] vt querer, desear; (need) necesitar ▷ n: **for ~ of** por falta de; **wanted** adj (criminal) buscado; **"wanted"** (in advertisements) "se busca"

war [wɔːʳ] n guerra; **to make ~** hacer la guerra

ward [wɔːd] n (in hospital) sala; (Pol) distrito electoral; (Law: child: also: **~ of court**) pupilo/a

warden ['wɔːdn] n (BRIT: of institution) director(a) m/f; (of park, game reserve) guardián/ana m/f; (BRIT: also: **traffic ~**) guardia mf

wardrobe ['wɔːdrəub] n armario, ropero

warehouse ['weəhaus] n almacén m, depósito

warfare ['wɔːfeəʳ] n guerra

warhead ['wɔːhed] n cabeza armada

warm [wɔːm] adj caliente; (thanks, congratulations, apologies) efusivo; (clothes etc) que abriga; (welcome, day) caluroso; **it's ~** hace calor; **I'm ~** tengo calor; **warm up** vi (room) calentarse; (person) entrar en calor; (athlete) hacer ejercicios de calentamiento ▷ vt calentar; **warmly** adv afectuosamente; **warmth** n calor m

warn [wɔːn] vt avisar, advertir; **warning** n aviso, advertencia; **warning light** n luz f de advertencia

warrant ['wɔrnt] n (Law: to arrest) orden f de detención; (: to search) mandamiento de registro

warranty ['wɔrntɪ] n garantía

warrior ['wɔrɪəʳ] n guerrero/a

Warsaw ['wɔːsɔː] n Varsovia

warship ['wɔːʃɪp] n buque m or barco de guerra

wart [wɔːt] n verruga

wartime ['wɔːtaɪm] n: **in ~** en tiempos de guerra, en la guerra

wary ['weərɪ] adj cauteloso

was [wɒz] pt of **be**

wash [wɒʃ] vt lavar; (sweep, carry: sea etc) llevar ▷ vi lavarse ▷ n (clothes etc) lavado; (of ship) estela; **to have a ~** lavarse; **wash up** vi (BRIT) fregar los platos; (US) lavarse; **washbasin** n lavabo; **washcloth** n (US) manopla; **washer** n (Tech) arandela; **washing**

n (dirty) ropa sucia; (clean) colada; **washing line** n cuerda de (colgar) la ropa; **washing machine** n lavadora; **washing powder** n (BRIT) detergente m (en polvo)

Washington ['wɔʃɪŋtən] n Washington m

wash: washing-up n fregado m; (dishes) platos mpl (para fregar); **washing-up liquid** n lavavajillas m inv; **washroom** n servicios mpl

wasn't ['wɔznt] = **was not**

wasp [wɔsp] n avispa

waste [weɪst] n derroche m, despilfarro; (of time) pérdida; (food) sobras fpl; (rubbish) basura, desperdicios mpl ▷ adj (material) de desecho; (left over) sobrante; (land, ground) baldío ▷ vt malgastar, derrochar; (time) perder; (opportunity) desperdiciar; **waste ground** n (BRIT) terreno baldío; **wastepaper basket** n papelera

watch [wɔtʃ] n reloj m; (vigilance) vigilancia; (Mil: guard) centinela m; (Naut: spell of duty) guardia ▷ vt (look at) mirar, observar; (: match, programme) ver; (spy on, guard) vigilar; (be careful of) cuidar, tener cuidado de ▷ vi ver, mirar; (keep guard) montar guardia; **watch out** vi cuidarse, tener cuidado; **watchdog** n perro guardián; (fig) organismo de control; **watch strap** n pulsera (de reloj)

water ['wɔːtər] n agua ▷ vt (plant) regar ▷ vi (eyes) llorar; **his mouth ~ed** se le hizo la boca agua; **water down** vt (milk etc) aguar; (fig: story) dulcificar, diluir; **watercolour**, (US) **watercolor** n acuarela; **watercress** n berro; **waterfall** n cascada, salto de agua; **watering can** n regadera; **watermelon** n sandía; **waterproof** adj impermeable; **water-skiing** n esquí m acuático

watt [wɔt] n vatio

wave [weɪv] n ola; (of hand) señal f con la mano; (Radio) onda; (in hair) onda;

(fig) oleada ▷ vi agitar la mano; (flag) ondear ▷ vt (handkerchief, gun) agitar; **wavelength** n longitud f de onda

waver ['weɪvər] vi (faith) flaquear

wavy ['weɪvɪ] adj ondulado

wax [wæks] n cera ▷ vt encerar ▷ vi (moon) crecer

way [weɪ] n camino; (distance) trayecto, recorrido; (direction) dirección f, sentido; (manner) modo, manera; (habit) costumbre f; **which ~? — this ~** ¿por dónde? or ¿en qué dirección? — por aquí; **on the ~** (en route) en (el) camino; **to be on one's ~** estar en camino; **to be in the ~** bloquear el camino; (fig) estorbar; **to go out of one's ~ to do sth** desvivirse por hacer algo; **to lose one's ~** extraviarse; **in a ~** en cierto modo or sentido; **by the ~** a propósito; **"~ in"** (BRIT) "entrada"; **"~ out"** (BRIT) "salida"; **the ~ back** el camino de vuelta; **"give ~"** (BRIT Aut) "ceda el paso"; **no ~!** (inf) ¡ni pensarlo!

WC ['dʌblju:'si:] n abbr (BRIT: = water closet) wáter m

we [wi:] pron pl nosotros/as

weak [wi:k] adj débil, flojo; (tea, coffee) flojo, aguado; (give way) ceder ▷ vt debilitar; **weakness** n debilidad f; (fault) punto débil; **to have a weakness for** tener debilidad por

wealth [welθ] n riqueza; (of details) abundancia; **wealthy** adj rico

weapon ['wepən] n arma; **~s of mass destruction** armas de destrucción masiva

wear [weər] (pt **wore**, pp **worn**) n (use) uso; (deterioration through use) desgaste m ▷ vt (clothes, beard) llevar; (shoes) calzar; (damage: through use) gastar ▷ vi (last) durar; (rub through etc) desgastarse; **evening ~** (man's) traje m de etiqueta; (woman's) traje m de noche; **wear off** vi (pain, excitement etc) pasar, desaparecer;

w

wear out vt desgastar; (person, strength) agotar

weary ['wɪərɪ] adj cansado; (dispirited) abatido ▷ vi: **to ~ of** cansarse de

weasel ['wiːzl] n (Zool) comadreja

weather ['weðəʳ] n tiempo ▷ vt (storm, crisis) hacer frente a; **under the ~** (fig: ill) mal, pachucho; **weather forecast** n boletín m meteorológico

weave (pt **wove**, pp **woven**) ['wiːv, wəuv, 'wəuvn] vt (cloth) tejer; (fig) entretejer

web [web] n (of spider) telaraña; (on foot) membrana; (network) red f; **the W~** la Red; **web address** n dirección f de página web; **webcam** n webcam f; **web page** n página f web; **website** n sitio web

wed [wed] (pt, pp **wedded**) vt casar ▷ vi casarse

Wed. abbr (= Wednesday) miérc.

we'd [wiːd] = **we had**; **we would**

wedding ['wedɪŋ] n boda, casamiento; **wedding anniversary** n aniversario de boda; **silver/golden wedding anniversary** bodas fpl de plata/de oro; **wedding day** n día m de la boda; **wedding dress** n traje m de novia; **wedding ring** n alianza

wedge [wedʒ] n (of wood etc) cuña; (of cake) trozo ▷ vt acuñar; (push) apretar

Wednesday ['wednzdɪ] n miércoles m inv

wee [wiː] adj (SCOTTISH) pequeñito

weed [wiːd] n mala hierba, maleza ▷ vt escardar, desherbar; **weedkiller** n herbicida m

week [wiːk] n semana; **a ~ today** de hoy en ocho días; **a ~ on Tuesday** del martes en una semana; **weekday** n día m laborable; **weekend** n fin m de semana; **weekly** adv semanalmente, cada semana ▷ adj semanal ▷ n semanario

weep (pt, pp **wept**) [wiːp, wept] vi, vt llorar

weigh [weɪ] vt, vi pesar; **to ~ anchor** levar anclas; **weigh up** vt sopesar

weight [weɪt] n peso; (on scale) pesa; **to lose/put on ~** adelgazar/engordar; **weightlifting** n levantamiento de pesas

weir [wɪəʳ] n presa

weird [wɪəd] adj raro, extraño

welcome ['welkəm] adj bienvenido ▷ n bienvenida ▷ vt dar la bienvenida a; (be glad of) alegrarse de; **thank you — you're —** gracias — de nada

weld [weld] n soldadura ▷ vt soldar

welfare ['welfeəʳ] n bienestar m; (social aid) asistencia social; **welfare state** n estado del bienestar

well [wel] n pozo ▷ adv bien ▷ adj: **to be ~** estar bien (de salud) ▷ excl ¡vaya!, ¡bueno!; **as ~** también; **as ~ as** además de; **~ done!** ¡bien hecho!; **get ~ soon!** ¡que te mejores pronto!; **to do ~** (business) ir bien; **I did ~ in my exams** me han salido bien los exámenes

we'll [wiːl] = **we will**; **we shall**

well: well-behaved adj: **to be well-behaved** portarse bien; **well-built** adj (person) fornido; **well-dressed** adj bien vestido

wellies ['welɪz] npl (BRIT inf) botas de goma

well: well-known adj (person) conocido; **well-off** adj acomodado; **well-paid** [wel'peɪd] adj bien pagado, bien retribuido

Welsh [welʃ] adj galés/esa ▷ n (Ling) galés m; **Welshman** n galés m; **Welshwoman** n galesa

went [went] pt of **go**

wept [wept] pt, pp of **weep**

were [wəːʳ] pt of **be**

we're [wɪəʳ] = **we are**

weren't [wəːnt] = **were not**

west [west] n oeste m ▷ adj occidental, del oeste ▷ adv al o hacia el oeste; **the W~** Occidente m; **westbound** ['westbaund] adj (traffic, carriageway) con rumbo al oeste; **western** adj occidental ▷ n (Cine) película del oeste; **West Indian** adj, n antillano/a

wet [wɛt] *adj* (*damp*) húmedo; (*wet through*) mojado; (*rainy*) lluvioso; **to get ~** mojarse; **"~ paint"** "recién pintado"; **wetsuit** *n* traje *m* de buzo

we've [wiːv] = **we have**

whack [wæk] *vt* dar un buen golpe a

whale [weɪl] *n* (*Zool*) ballena

wharf (*pl* **wharves**) [wɔːf, wɔːvz] *n* muelle *m*

KEYWORD

what [wɒt] *adj* **1** (*in direct/indirect questions*) qué; **what size is he?** ¿qué talla usa?; **what colour/shape is it?** ¿de qué color/forma es?
2 (*in exclamations*): **what a mess!** ¡qué desastre!; **what a fool I am!** ¡qué tonto soy!
▶ *pron* **1** (*interrogative*) qué; **what are you doing?** ¿qué haces or estás haciendo?; **what's happening?** ¿qué pasa or está pasando?; **what is it called?** ¿cómo se llama?; **what about me?** ¿y yo qué?; **what about doing ...?** ¿qué tal si hacemos ...?
2 (*relative*) lo que; **I saw what you did/was on the table** vi lo que hiciste/había en la mesa
▶ *excl* (*disbelieving*) ¡cómo!; **what, no coffee!** ¡que no hay café!

whatever [wɒtˈɛvəʳ] *adj*: **~ book you choose** cualquier libro que elijas
▶ *pron*: **do ~ is necessary** haga lo que sea necesario; **no reason** – ninguna razón en absoluto; **nothing** – nada en absoluto; **~ it costs** cueste lo que cueste

whatsoever [wɒtsəuˈɛvəʳ] *adj see* **whatever**

wheat [wiːt] *n* trigo

wheel [wiːl] *n* rueda; (*Aut: also:* **steering ~**) volante *m*; (*Naut*) timón *m* ▶ *vt* (*pram etc*) empujar ▶ *vi* (*also:* **~ round**) dar la vuelta, girar; **wheelbarrow** *n* carretilla; **wheelchair** *n* silla de ruedas; **wheel clamp** *n* (*Aut*) cepo

wheeze [wiːz] *vi* resollar

KEYWORD

when [wɛn] *adv* cuando; **when did it happen?** ¿cuándo ocurrió?; **I know when it happened** sé cuándo ocurrió
▶ *conj* **1** (*at, during, after the time that*) cuando; **be careful when you cross the road** ten cuidado al cruzar la calle; **that was when I needed you** entonces era cuando te necesitaba
2 (*on, at which*): **on the day when I met him** el día en qué le conocí
3 (*whereas*) cuando

whenever [wɛnˈɛvəʳ] *conj* cuando; (*every time*) cada vez que

where [wɛəʳ] *adv* dónde ▶ *conj* donde; **this is ~** aquí es donde; **whereabouts** *adv* dónde ▶ *n*: **nobody knows his whereabouts** nadie conoce su paradero; **whereas** *conj* mientras; **whereby** *adv* mediante el/la cual etc, por lo/la cual etc; **wherever** [wɛəʳˈɛvəʳ] *adv* dondequiera que; (*interrogative*) dónde

whether [ˈwɛðəʳ] *conj* si; **I don't know ~ to accept or not** no sé si aceptar o no; **~ you go or not** vayas o no vayas

KEYWORD

which [wɪtʃ] *adj* **1** (*interrogative, direct, indirect*) qué; **which picture(s) do you want?** ¿qué cuadro(s) quieres?; **which one?** ¿cuál?
2: **in which case** en cuyo caso; **we got there at eight pm, by which time the cinema was full** llegamos allí a las ocho, cuando el cine estaba lleno
▶ *pron* **1** (*interrogative*) cuál; **I don't mind which** el/la que sea
2 (*relative, replacing noun*) que; (: *replacing clause*) lo que; (: *after preposition*) (el/la) que, el/la cual; **the**

apple which you ate/which is on the table la manzana que comiste/que está en la mesa; **the chair on which you are sitting** la silla en la que estás sentado; **he didn't believe it, which upset me** no se lo creyó, lo cual *or* lo que me disgustó

whichever [wɪtʃ'ɛvəʳ] *adj*: **take ~ book you prefer** coja el libro que prefiera; **~ book you take** cualquier libro que coja

while [waɪl] *n* rato, momento ▷ *conj* mientras; *(although)* aunque; **for a ~** durante algún tiempo

whilst [waɪlst] *conj* = **while**

whim [wɪm] *n* capricho

whine [waɪn] *n (of pain)* gemido; *(of engine)* zumbido ▷ *vi* gemir; zumbar; *(fig: complain)* gimotear

whip [wɪp] *n* látigo; *(BRIT Pol)* diputado encargado de la disciplina del partido en el parlamento ▷ *vt* azotar; *(Culin)* batir; **whipped cream** *n* nata montada

whirl [wə:l] *vt* hacer girar, dar vueltas a ▷ *vi* girar, dar vueltas; *(leaves, dust, water etc)* arremolinarse

whisk [wɪsk] *n (BRIT Culin)* batidor *m* ▷ *vt (BRIT Culin)* batir; **to ~ sb away** *or* **off** llevarse volando a algn

whiskers [wɪskəz] *npl (of animal)* bigotes *mpl*; *(of man)* patillas *fpl*

whisky, *(US, IRELAND)* **whiskey** [wɪskɪ] *n* whisky *m*

whisper [wɪspəʳ] *n* susurro ▷ *vi* susurrar ▷ *vt* susurrar

whistle [wɪsl] *n (sound)* silbido; *(object)* silbato ▷ *vi* silbar

white [waɪt] *adj* blanco; *(pale)* pálido ▷ *n* blanco; *(of egg)* clara; **whiteboard** *n* pizarra blanca; **interactive whiteboard** pizarra interactiva; **White House** *n (US)* Casa Blanca; **whitewash** *n (paint)* cal *f*, jalbegue *m* ▷ *vt* blanquear

whiting [waɪtɪŋ] *n (pl inv: fish)* pescadilla

Whitsun [wɪtsn] *n (BRIT)* Pentecostés *m*

whittle [wɪtl] *vt*: **to ~ away**, **~ down** ir reduciendo

whizz [wɪz] *vi*: **to ~ past** *or* **by** pasar a toda velocidad

KEYWORD

who [hu:] *pron* **1** *(interrogative)* quién; **who is it?**, **who's there?** ¿quién es?; **who are you looking for?** ¿a quién buscas?; **I told her who I was** le dije quién era yo

2 *(relative)* que; **the man/woman who spoke to me** el hombre/la mujer que habló conmigo; **those who can swim** los que saben *or* sepan nadar

whoever [hu:'ɛvəʳ] *pron*: **~ finds it** cualquiera *or* quienquiera que lo encuentre; **ask ~ you like** pregunta a quien quieras; **~ he marries** se case con quien se case

whole [həul] *adj (complete)* todo, entero; *(not broken)* intacto ▷ *n (total)* total *m*; *(sum)* conjunto; **the ~ of the town** toda la ciudad, la ciudad entera; **on the ~**, **as a ~** en general; **wholefood(s)** *n(pl)* alimento(s) *m(pl)* integral(es); **wholeheartedly** [həul'hɑ:tɪdlɪ] *adv* con entusiasmo; **wholemeal** *adj (BRIT: flour, bread)* integral; **wholesale** *n* venta al por mayor ▷ *adj* al por mayor; *(destruction)* sistemático; **wholewheat** *adj* = **wholemeal**; **wholly** *adv* totalmente, enteramente

KEYWORD

whom [hu:m] *pron* **1** *(interrogative)*: **whom did you see?** ¿a quién viste?; **to whom did you give it?** ¿a quién se lo diste?; **tell me from whom you received it** dígame de quién lo recibiste

2 *(relative)* que; **to whom** a quien(es);

of whom de quien(es), del/de la que; **the man whom I saw** el hombre que vi; **the lady about whom I was talking** la señora de (la) que hablaba; **the lady with whom I was talking** la señora con quien o (la) que hablaba

whore [hɔːʳ] n (inf, pej) puta

KEYWORD

whose [huːz] adj 1 (possessive, interrogative): **whose book is this?, whose is this book?** ¿de quién es este libro?; **whose pencil have you taken?** ¿de quién es el lápiz que has cogido?; **whose daughter are you?** ¿de quién eres hija?
2 (possessive, relative) cuyo/a, cuyos/as m/f pl; **the man whose son they rescued** el hombre cuyo hijo rescataron; **those whose passports I have** aquellas personas cuyos pasaportes tengo; **the woman whose car was stolen** la mujer a quien le robaron el coche
▸ pron de quién; **whose is this?** ¿de quién es esto?; **I know whose it is** sé de quién es

---

KEYWORD

why [waɪ] adv por qué; **why not?** ¿por qué no?; **why not do it now?** ¿por qué no lo haces or hacemos ahora?
▸ conj: **I wonder why he said that** me pregunto por qué dijo eso; **that's not why I'm here** no es por eso (por lo) que estoy aquí; **the reason why** la razón por la que
▸ excl (expressing surprise, shock, annoyance) ¡hombre!, ¡vaya!; (explaining): **why, it's you!** ¡hombre, eres tú!; **why, that's impossible** ¡pero si eso es imposible!

wicked ['wɪkɪd] adj malvado, cruel

wicket ['wɪkɪt] n (Cricket) palos mpl

wide [waɪd] adj ancho; (area, knowledge) vasto, grande; (choice) amplio ▸ adv: **to open ~** abrir de par en par; **to shoot ~** errar el tiro; **widely** adv (differing) muy; **it is widely believed that ...** existe la creencia generalizada de que ...; **widen** vt ensanchar; (experience) ampliar ▸ vi ensancharse; **wide open** adj abierto de par en par; **widespread** adj extendido, general

widow ['wɪdəʊ] n viuda; **widower** n viudo

width [wɪdθ] n anchura; (of cloth) ancho

wield [wiːld] vt (sword) blandir; (power) ejercer

wife (pl **wives**) [waɪf, waɪvz] n mujer f, esposa

Wi-Fi ['waɪfaɪ] n abbr (= wireless fidelity) wi-fi m

wig [wɪg] n peluca

wild [waɪld] adj (animal) salvaje; (plant) silvestre; (idea) descabellado; (rough: sea) bravo; (: land) agreste; (: weather) muy revuelto; (inf: angry) furioso; **wilderness** ['wɪldənɪs] n desierto; **wildlife** n fauna; **wildly** adv (roughly) violentamente; (foolishly) locamente; (rashly) descabelladamente; (lash out) a diestro y siniestro; (guess) a lo loco; (happy) a más no poder

---

KEYWORD

will [wɪl] aux vb 1 (forming future tense): **I will finish it tomorrow** lo terminaré or voy a terminar mañana; **I will have finished it by tomorrow** lo habré terminado para mañana; **will you do it? — yes I will/no I won't** ¿lo harás? — sí/no
2 (in conjectures, predictions): **he will** or **he'll be there by now** ya habrá llegado, ya debe (de) haber llegado; **that will be the postman** será el cartero, debe ser el cartero

3 (in commands, requests, offers): **will you be quiet?** ¿quieres callarte?; **will you help me?** ¿quieres ayudarme?; **will you have a cup of tea?** ¿te apetece un té?; **I won't put up with it!** ¡no lo soporto!
▸ vt: **to will sb to do sth** desear que algn haga algo; **he willed himself to go on** con gran fuerza de voluntad, continuó
▸ n **1** voluntad f
2 (Law) testamento

willing ['wɪlɪŋ] adj (with goodwill) de buena voluntad; (enthusiastic) entusiasta; **he's ~ to do it** está dispuesto a hacerlo; **willingly** adv con mucho gusto

willow ['wɪləu] n sauce m

willpower ['wɪlpauə'] n fuerza de voluntad

wilt [wɪlt] vi marchitarse

win [wɪn] (pt, pp **won**) n victoria, triunfo ▸ vt ganar; (obtain) conseguir, lograr ▸ vi ganar; **win over** vt convencer a

wince [wɪns] vi encogerse

wind¹ [wɪnd] n viento; (Med) gases mpl ▸ vt (take breath away from) dejar sin aliento a; **into** or **against the ~** contra el viento; **to get ~ of sth** enterarse de algo; **to break ~** ventosear

wind² [waɪnd] (pt, pp **wound**) vt enrollar; (wrap) envolver; (clock, toy) dar cuerda a ▸ vi (road, river) serpentear; **wind down** vt (car window) bajar; (fig: production, business) disminuir; **wind up** vt (clock) dar cuerda a; (debate) concluir, terminar

windfall ['wɪndfɔːl] n golpe m de suerte

wind farm n parque m eólico

winding ['waɪndɪŋ] adj (road) tortuoso

windmill ['wɪndmɪl] n molino de viento

window ['wɪndəu] n ventana; (in car, train) ventana; (in shop etc) escaparate m, vidriera (LAM); **window box** n jardinera (de ventana); **window cleaner** n (person) limpiacristales m inv; **window pane** n cristal m; **window seat** n asiento junto a la ventana; **windowsill** n alféizar m, repisa

wind: **windscreen** n parabrisas m inv; (US) **windshield** n windscreen wiper, (US) windshield wiper n limpiaparabrisas m inv; **windsurfing** n windsurf m; **wind turbine** n m aerogenerador m; **windy** adj de mucho viento; **it's windy** hace viento

wine [waɪn] n vino; **wine bar** n bar especializado en vinos; **wine glass** n copa (de or para vino); **wine list** n lista de vinos; **wine tasting** n degustación f de vinos

wing [wɪŋ] n ala; (Aut) aleta; **wing mirror** n (espejo) retrovisor m

wink [wɪŋk] n guiño; (blink) pestañeo ▸ vi guiñar; (blink) pestañear

winner ['wɪnə'] n ganador(a) m/f

winning ['wɪnɪŋ] adj (team) ganador(a); (goal) decisivo; (charming) encantador(a)

winter ['wɪntə'] n invierno ▸ vi invernar; **winter sports** npl deportes mpl de invierno; **wintertime** n invierno

wipe [waɪp] n: **to give sth a ~** pasar un trapo sobre algo ▸ vt limpiar; (tape) borrar; **wipe out** vt (debt) liquidar; (memory) borrar; (destroy) destruir; **wipe up** vt limpiar

wire [waɪə'] n alambre m; (Elec) cable m (eléctrico); (Tel) telegrama m ▸ vt (house) poner la instalación eléctrica en; (also: ~ **up**) conectar

wireless ['waɪəlɪs] adj inalámbrico; **wireless technology** n tecnología inalámbrica

wiring ['waɪərɪŋ] n instalación f eléctrica

wisdom ['wɪzdəm] n sabiduría, saber m; (good sense) cordura; **wisdom tooth** n muela del juicio

wise [waɪz] adj sabio; (sensible) juicioso

wish [wɪʃ] n deseo ▷ vt querer; **best ~es** (on birthday etc) felicidades fpl; **with best ~es** (in letter) saludos mpl, recuerdos mpl; **he ~ed me well** me deseó mucha suerte; **to ~ to do/sb to do sth** querer hacer/que algn haga algo; **to ~ for** desear

wistful ['wɪstfʊl] adj pensativo

wit [wɪt] n ingenio, gracia; (also: **~s**) inteligencia; (person) chistoso/a

witch [wɪtʃ] n bruja

○ **KEYWORD**

with [wɪð, wɪθ] prep **1** (accompanying, in the company of) con (con +mí, ti, sí = conmigo, contigo, consigo); **I was with him** estaba con él; **we stayed with friends** nos quedamos en casa de unos amigos

2 (descriptive, indicating manner etc) con; de; **a room with a view** una habitación con vistas; **the man with the grey hat/blue eyes** el hombre del sombrero gris/de los ojos azules; **red with anger** rojo de ira; **to shake with fear** temblar de miedo; **to fill sth with water** llenar algo de agua

3: **I'm with you** (understand) ya te entiendo/no te entiendo; **to be with it** (inf: person: up-to-date) estar al tanto; (alert) ser despabilado

withdraw [wɪθ'drɔː] vt (irreg: like **draw**) retirar ▷ vi retirarse; **to ~ money (from the bank)** retirar fondos (del banco); **withdrawal** n retirada; (of money) reintegro; **withdrawn** adj (person) reservado, introvertido ▷ pp of **withdraw**

withdrew [wɪθ'druː] pt of **withdraw**

wither ['wɪðəʳ] vi marchitarse

withhold [wɪθ'həʊld] vt (irreg: like **hold**: money) retener; (decision) aplazar; (permission) negar; (information) ocultar

within [wɪð'ɪn] prep dentro de ▷ adv dentro; **~ reach** al alcance de la mano; **~ sight of** a la vista de; **~ the week** antes de que acabe la semana; **~ a mile (of)** a menos de una milla (de)

without [wɪð'aʊt] prep sin; **to go or do ~ sth** prescindir de algo

withstand [wɪθ'stænd] vt (irreg: like **stand**) resistir a

witness ['wɪtnɪs] n testigo mf ▷ vt (event) presenciar; (document) atestiguar la veracidad de; **to bear ~ to** (fig) ser testimonio de

witty ['wɪtɪ] adj ingenioso

wives [waɪvz] npl of **wife**

wizard ['wɪzəd] n hechicero

wk abbr = **week**

wobble ['wɒbl] vi tambalearse

woe [wəʊ] n desgracia

woke [wəʊk] pt of **wake**

woken ['wəʊkən] pp of **wake**

wolf (pl **wolves**) [wʊlf, wʊlvz] n lobo

woman (pl **women**) ['wʊmən, 'wɪmɪn] n mujer f

womb [wuːm] n matriz f, útero

women ['wɪmɪn] npl of **woman**

won [wʌn] pt, pp of **win**

wonder ['wʌndəʳ] n maravilla, prodigio; (feeling) asombro ▷ vi: **to ~ whether** preguntarse si; **to ~ at** asombrarse de; **to ~ about** pensar sobre or en; **it's no ~ that** no es de extrañar que; **wonderful** adj maravilloso

won't [wəʊnt] = **will not**

wood [wʊd] n (timber) madera; (forest) bosque m; **wooden** adj de madera; (fig) inexpresivo; **woodwind** n (Mus) instrumentos mpl de viento de madera; **woodwork** n carpintería

wool [wʊl] n lana; **to pull the ~ over sb's eyes** (fig) dar a algn gato por liebre; **woollen**, (US) **woolen** adj de lana; **woolly**, (us) **wooly** adj de lana; (fig: ideas) confuso

word [wəːd] n palabra; (news) noticia; (promise) palabra de honor) ▷ vt redactar; **in other ~s** en otras palabras; **to break/keep one's ~** faltar a la palabra/cumplir la promesa; **to have ~s with sb** discutir or reñir con algn; **wording** n redacción f; **word processing** n procesamiento or tratamiento de textos; **word processor** [-'prəusesəʳ] n procesador m de textos

wore [wɔːʳ] pt of **wear**

work [wəːk] n trabajo; (job) empleo, trabajo; (Art, Lit) obra ▷ vi trabajar; (mechanism) funcionar, marchar; (medicine) ser eficaz, surtir efecto ▷ vt (shape) trabajar; (stone etc) tallar; (mine etc) explotar; (machine) manejar, hacer funcionar; **to be out of ~** estar parado, no tener trabajo; **to ~ loose** (part) desprenderse; (knot) aflojarse; see also **works**; **work out** vi (plans etc) salir bien, funcionar ▷ vt (problem) resolver; (plan) elaborar; **it ~s out at £100** asciende a 100 libras; **worker** n trabajador(a) m/f, obrero/a; **work experience** n: **I'm going to do my work experience in a factory** voy a hacer las prácticas en una fábrica; **work force** n mano f de obra; **working class** n clase f obrera ▷ adj; **working-class** adj obrero; **working week** n semana laboral; **workman** (irreg) n obrero; **work of art** n obra de arte; **workout** n (Sport) sesión f de ejercicios; **work permit** n permiso de trabajo; **workplace** n lugar m de trabajo; **works** nsg (BRIT: factory) fábrica ▷ npl (of clock, machine) mecanismo; **worksheet** n hoja de ejercicios; **workshop** n taller m; **work station** n estación f de trabajo; **work surface** n encimera; **worktop** n encimera

world [wəːld] n mundo ▷ cpd (champion) del mundo; (power, war) mundial; **to think the ~ of sb** (fig) tener un concepto muy alto de algn; **World Cup** n (Football): **the World Cup** (los) Mundiales m; **world-wide** adj mundial, universal; **World Wide Web** n: **the World-Wide Web** el World Wide Web

worm [wəːm] n (earthworm) lombriz f

worn [wɔːn] pp of **wear** ▷ adj usado; **worn-out** adj (object) gastado; (person) rendido, agotado

worried [ˈwʌrɪd] adj preocupado

worry [ˈwʌrɪ] n preocupación f ▷ vt preocupar, inquietar ▷ vi preocuparse; **to ~ about** or **over sth/sb** preocuparse por algo/algn; **worrying** adj inquietante

worse [wəːs] adj, adv peor ▷ n lo peor; **a change for the ~** un empeoramiento; **worsen** vt, vi empeorar; **worse off** adj (financially): **to be worse off** tener menos dinero; (fig): **you'll be worse off this way** de esta forma estarás peor que antes

worship [ˈwəːʃɪp] n adoración f ▷ vt adorar; **Your W~** (BRIT: to mayor) Ilustrísima; (: to judge) su señoría

worst [wəːst] adj (el/la) peor ▷ adv peor ▷ n lo peor; **at ~** en el peor de los casos

worth [wəːθ] n valor m ▷ adj: **to be ~** valer; **it's ~ it** vale or merece la pena; **to be ~ one's while (to do)** merecer la pena (hacer); **worthless** adj sin valor; (useless) inútil; **worthwhile** adj (activity) que merece la pena; (cause) loable

worthy [ˈwəːðɪ] adj (person) respetable; (motive) honesto; **~ of** digno de

KEYWORD

would [wud] aux vb 1 (conditional tense): **if you asked him he would do it** si se lo pidieras, lo haría; **if you had asked him he would have done it** si se lo hubieras pedido, lo habría or hubiera hecho

2 (in offers, invitations, requests): **would you like a biscuit?** ¿quieres una galleta?; (formal) ¿querría una galleta?; **would you ask him to come in?** ¿quiere hacerle pasar?; **would you open the window please?** ¿quiere o podría abrir la ventana, por favor?
3 (in indirect speech): **I said I would do it** dije que lo haría
4 (emphatic): **it WOULD have to snow today!** ¡tenía que nevar precisamente hoy!
5 (insistence): **she wouldn't behave** no quiso comportarse bien
6 (conjecture): **it would have been midnight** sería medianoche; **it would seem so** parece ser que sí
7 (indicating habit): **he would go there on Mondays** iba allí los lunes

wouldn't ['wudnt] = **would not**
wound¹ [wu:nd] n herida ▷ vt herir
wound² [waund] pt, pp of **wind²**
wove [wauv] pt of **weave**
woven ['wauvan] pp of **weave**
wrap [ræp] (also: ~ **up**) vt envolver; (gift) envolver, abrigar ▷ vi (dress warmly) abrigarse; **wrapper** n (BRIT: of book) sobrecubierta; (on chocolate etc) envoltura; **wrapping paper** n papel m de envolver
wreath (pl **wreaths**) [ri:θ, ri:ðz] n (also: funeral ~) corona
wreck [rɛk] n (ship: destruction) naufragio; (: remains) restos mpl del barco; (pej: person) ruina ▷ vt destrozar; (chances) arruinar; **wreckage** n restos mpl; (of building) escombros mpl
wren [rɛn] n (Zool) reyezuelo
wrench [rɛntʃ] n (Tech) llave f inglesa; (tug) tirón m ▷ vt arrancar; **to ~ sth from sb** arrebatar algo violentamente a algn
wrestle ['rɛsl] vi: **to ~ (with sb)** luchar (con o contra algn); **wrestler** ['rɛslə'] n luchador(a) m/f (de lucha libre); **wrestling** n lucha libre

wretched ['rɛtʃɪd] adj miserable
wriggle ['rɪgl] vi serpentear; (also: ~ **about**) menearse, retorcerse
wring (pt, pp **wrung**) [rɪŋ, rʌŋ] vt torcer, retorcer; (wet clothes) escurrir; (fig): **to ~ sth out of sb** sacar algo por la fuerza a algn
wrinkle ['rɪŋkl] n arruga ▷ vt arrugar ▷ vi arrugarse
wrist [rɪst] n muñeca
writable ['raɪtəbl] adj (CD, DVD) escribible
write (pt **wrote**, pp **written**) [raɪt, rəut, 'rɪtn] vt escribir; (cheque) extender ▷ vi escribir; **write down** vt apuntar; (note) apuntar; **write off** vt (debt) borrar (como incobrable); (fig) desechar por inútil; **write out** vt escribir; **write up** vt redactar; **write-off** n siniestro total; **writer** n escritor(a) m/f
writing ['raɪtɪŋ] n escritura; (handwriting) letra; (of author) obras fpl; **in ~** por escrito; **writing paper** n papel m de escribir
written ['rɪtn] pp of **write**
wrong [rɔŋ] adj (wicked) malo; (unfair) injusto; (incorrect) equivocado, incorrecto; (not suitable) inoportuno, inconveniente ▷ adv mal ▷ n injusticia ▷ vt ser injusto con; **you are ~ to do it** haces mal en hacerlo; **you are ~ about that, you've got it** = en eso estás equivocado; **to be in the ~** no tener razón; tener la culpa; **what's ~?** ¿qué pasa?; **to go ~** (person) equivocarse; (plan) salir mal; (machine) estropearse; **wrongly** adv incorrectamente; **wrong number** n (Tel): **you've got the wrong number** se ha equivocado de número
wrote [rəut] pt of **write**
wrung [rʌŋ] pt, pp of **wring**
WWW n abbr (= World Wide Web) WWW m o f

W

XL *abbr* = **extra large**
Xmas ['ɛksməs] *n abbr* = **Christmas**
X-ray [eks'reɪ] *n* radiografía ▷ *vt* radiografiar
xylophone ['zaɪləfəun] *n* xilófono

yacht [jɔt] *n* yate m; **yachting** *n* (*sport*) balandrismo
yakka ['jækə] *n* (AUST, NZ: *inf*) curro
yard [jɑːd] *n* patio; (*measure*) yarda; **yard sale** *n* (US) venta de objetos usados (*en el jardín de una casa particular*)
yarn [jɑːn] *n* hilo; (*tale*) cuento (chino), historia
yawn [jɔːn] *n* bostezo ▷ *vi* bostezar
yd. *abbr* (= *yard*) yda
yeah [jɛə] *adv* (*inf*) sí
year [jɪə'] *n* año; **to be eight ~s old** tener ocho años; **an eight-~-old child** un niño de ocho años (de edad); **yearly** *adj* anual ▷ *adv* anualmente, cada año
yearn [jəːn] *vi*: **to ~ for sth** añorar algo, suspirar por algo
yeast [jiːst] *n* levadura
yell [jel] *n* grito, alarido ▷ *vi* gritar
yellow ['jɛləu] *adj* amarillo; **Yellow Pages**® *npl* páginas *fpl* amarillas

yes [jɛs] *adv, n* sí *m*; **to say/answer ~** decir/contestar que sí

yesterday ['jɛstədɪ] *adv, n* ayer *m*; **~ morning/evening** ayer por la mañana/tarde; **all day ~** todo el día de ayer

yet [jɛt] *adv* todavía ▷ *conj* sin embargo, a pesar de todo; **it is not finished ~** todavía no está acabado; **the best ~** el/la mejor hasta ahora; **as ~** hasta ahora, todavía

yew [ju:] *n* tejo

Yiddish ['jɪdɪʃ] *n* yiddish *m*

yield [ji:ld] *n* (*Agr*) cosecha; (*Comm*) rendimiento ▷ *vt* producir, dar; (*profit*) rendir ▷ *vi* rendirse, ceder; (*us Aut*) ceder el paso

yob(bo) ['jɔb(bəu)] *n* (*BRIT inf*) gamberro

yoga ['jəugə] *n* yoga *m*

yog(h)urt ['jəugət] *n* yogur *m*

yolk [jəuk] *n* yema (de huevo)

KEYWORD

you [ju:] *pron* **1** (*subject, familiar, singular*) tú; (: *plural*) vosotros/as (*SP*), ustedes (*LAM*); (: *polite*) usted, ustedes *pl*; **you are very kind** eres/es *etc* muy amable; **you French enjoy your food** a vosotros (*or* ustedes) los franceses os (*or* les) gusta la comida; **you and I will go** iremos tú y yo

2 (*object, direct, familiar, singular*) te; (: *plural*) os (*SP*), les (*LAM*); (: *polite, singular masc*) lo *or* le; (: *plural masc*) los *or* les; (: *singular fem*) la; (: *plural fem*) las; **I know you** te/le *etc* conozco

3 (*object, indirect, familiar, singular*) te; (: *plural*) os (*SP*), les (*LAM*); (: *polite*) le, les; **I gave the letter to you yesterday** te/os *etc* di la carta ayer

4 (*stressed*): **I told YOU to do it** a ti te dije que lo hicieras, es a ti a quien dije que lo hicieras; *see also* **you**

5 (*after prep, NB:* con + ti = contigo, *familiar, singular*) ti; (: *plural*) vosotros/as (*SP*), ustedes (*LAM*); (: *polite*) usted,

ustedes *pl*; **it's for you** es para ti/vosotros *etc*

6 (*comparisons, familiar, singular*) tú; (: *plural*) vosotros/as (*SP*), ustedes (*LAM*); (: *polite*) usted, ustedes *pl*; **she's younger than you** es más joven que tú/vosotros *etc*

7 (*impersonal: one*): **fresh air does you good** el aire puro (te) hace bien; **you never know** nunca se sabe; **you can't do that!** ¡eso no se hace!

you'd [ju:d] = **you had; you would**

you'll [ju:l] = **you will; you shall**

young [jʌŋ] *adj* joven ▷ *npl* (*of animal*) cría; (*people*): **the ~ los** jóvenes, la juventud; **youngster** *n* joven *mf*

your [jɔ:ʳ] *adj* tu, vuestro *pl*; (*formal*) su; *see also* **my**

you're [juəʳ] = **you are**

yours [jɔ:z] *pron* tuyo, vuestro *pl*; (*formal*) suyo; *see also* **faithfully; mine; sincerely**

yourself [jɔ:'sɛlf] *pron* tú mismo; (*complement*) te; (*after prep*) ti (mismo); (*formal*) usted mismo; (: *complement*) se; (: *after prep*) sí (mismo); **yourselves** *pron pl* vosotros mismos; (*after prep*) vosotros (mismos); (*formal*) ustedes (mismos); (: *complement*) se; (: *after prep*) sí mismos

youth [ju:θ] *n* juventud *f*; (*young man*) joven *m*; **youth club** *n* club *m* juvenil; **youthful** *adj* juvenil; **youth hostel** *n* albergue *m* juvenil

you've [ju:v] = **you have**

Z

zoom [zuːm] *vi*: **to ~ past** pasar zumbando; **zoom lens** *n* zoom *m*

zucchini [zuːˈkiːnɪ] *n(pl)* (us) calabacín(ines) *m(pl)*

zeal [ziːl] *n* celo, entusiasmo

zebra [ˈziːbrə] *n* cebra; **zebra crossing** *n* (BRIT) paso de peatones

zero [ˈzɪərəu] *n* cero

zest [zɛst] *n* ánimo, vivacidad *f*; (*of orange*) piel *f*

zigzag [ˈzɪgzæg] *n* zigzag *m* ▷ *vi* zigzaguear

Zimbabwe [zɪmˈbɑːbwɪ] *n* Zimbabwe *m*

zinc [zɪŋk] *n* cinc *m*, zinc *m*

zip [zɪp] *n* (*also*: **~ fastener**, (us) **zipper**) cremallera, cierre *m* relámpago (LAM) ▷ *vt* (Comput) comprimir; (*also*: **~ up**) cerrar la cremallera de; **zip code** *n* (us) código postal; **zip file** *n* (Comput) archivo *m* comprimido; **zipper** *n* (us) cremallera

zit [zɪt] *n* grano

zodiac [ˈzəudɪæk] *n* zodíaco

zone [zəun] *n* zona

zoo [zuː] *n* zoo, (parque *m*) zoológico

zoology [zuːˈɔlədʒɪ] *n* zoología

I have - Yo tengo
I go - Yo voy
I eat - Yo como
I am - Yo soy / Yo estoy (temp)
I

I have – Yo tengo
I go – Yo voy
I eat – Yo como
I am – Yo soy / Yo estoy (temp)
I